C# 6.0

IN A NUTSHELL

Joseph Albahari & Ben Albahari

Beijing · Boston · Farnham · Sebastopol · Tokyo

C# 6.0 in a Nutshell

by Joseph Albahari and Ben Albahari

Printed in the United States of America.

Published by O'Reilly Media, Inc., 1005 Gravenstein Highway North, Sebastopol, CA 95472.

O'Reilly books may be purchased for educational, business, or sales promotional use. Online editions are also available for most titles (*http://safaribooksonline.com*). For more information, contact our corporate/institutional sales department: 800-998-9938 or *corporate@oreilly.com*.

Editor: Brian MacDonald
Production Editor: Kristen Brown
Proofreader: Amanda Kersey
Indexer: Angela Howard

Interior Designer: David Futato
Cover Designer: Karen Montgomery
Illustrator: Rebecca Demarest

December 2015:   Sixth Edition

Revision History for the Sixth Edition
2015-11-03:   First Release

See *http://oreilly.com/catalog/errata.csp?isbn=9781491927069* for release details.

978-1-491-92706-9

[M]

Table of Contents

Preface

C# 6.0 represents the fifth major update to Microsoft's flagship programming language, positioning C# as a language with unusual flexibility and breadth. At one end, it offers high-level abstractions such as query expressions and asynchronous continuations; while at the other end, it allows low-level efficiency through constructs such as custom value types and the optional use of pointers.

The price of this growth is that there's more than ever to learn. Although tools such as Microsoft's IntelliSense—and online references—are excellent in helping you on the job, they presume an existing map of conceptual knowledge. This book provides exactly that map of knowledge in a concise and unified style—free of clutter and long introductions.

Like the past three editions, *C# 6.0 in a Nutshell* is organized around concepts and use cases, making it friendly both to sequential reading and to random browsing. It also plumbs significant depths while assuming only basic background knowledge—making it accessible to intermediate as well as advanced readers.

This book covers C#, the CLR, and the core Framework assemblies. We've chosen this focus to allow space for difficult topics such as concurrency, security, and application domains—without compromising depth or readability. Features new to C# 6.0 and the associated Framework are flagged so that you can also use this book as a C# 5.0 reference.

Intended Audience

This book targets intermediate to advanced audiences. No prior knowledge of C# is required, but some general programming experience is necessary. For the beginner, this book complements, rather than replaces, a tutorial-style introduction to programming.

If you're already familiar with C# 5.0, you'll find updated language sections, and a new chapter on "Roslyn," the compiler-as-a-service.

This book is an ideal companion to any of the vast array of books that focus on an applied technology such as WPF, ASP.NET, or WCF. The areas of the language and .NET Framework that such books omit, *C# 6.0 in a Nutshell* covers in detail—and vice versa.

If you're looking for a book that skims every .NET Framework technology, this is not for you. This book is also unsuitable if you want to learn about APIs specific to tablet or Windows Phone development.

How This Book Is Organized

The first three chapters after the introduction concentrate purely on C#, starting with the basics of syntax, types, and variables, and finishing with advanced topics such as unsafe code and preprocessor directives. If you're new to the language, you should read these chapters sequentially.

The remaining chapters cover the core .NET Framework, including such topics as LINQ, XML, collections, code contracts, concurrency, I/O and networking, memory management, reflection, dynamic programming, attributes, security, application domains, and native interoperability. You can read most of these chapters randomly, except for Chapters 6 and 7, which lay a foundation for subsequent topics. The three chapters on LINQ are also best read in sequence, and some chapters assume some knowledge of concurrency, which we cover in Chapter 14.

What You Need to Use This Book

The examples in this book require a C# 6.0 compiler and Microsoft .NET Framework 4.6. You will also find Microsoft's .NET documentation useful to look up individual types and members (which is available online).

While it's possible to write source code in Notepad and invoke the compiler from the command line, you'll be much more productive with a *code scratchpad* for instantly testing code snippets, plus an *integrated development environment* (IDE) for producing executables and libraries.

For a code scratchpad, download LINQPad 5 or later from *http://www.linqpad.net* (free). LINQPad fully supports C# 6.0 and is maintained by one of the authors.

For an IDE, download Microsoft Visual Studio 2015: any edition, except the free express edition, is suitable for what's taught in this book.

 All code listings for Chapters 2 through 10, plus the chapters on concurrency, parallel programming, and dynamic programming are available as interactive (editable) LINQPad samples. You can download the whole lot in a single click: go to LINQPad's Sample Libraries page (*http://www.linqpad.net/ RichClient/SampleLibraries.aspx*) and choose "C# 6.0 in a Nutshell."

Conventions Used in This Book

The book uses basic UML notation to illustrate relationships between types, as shown in Figure P-1. A slanted rectangle means an abstract class; a circle means an interface. A line with a hollow triangle denotes inheritance, with the triangle pointing to the base type. A line with an arrow denotes a one-way association; a line without an arrow denotes a two-way association.

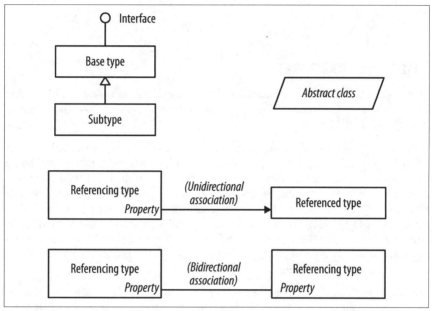

Figure P-1. Sample diagram

The following typographical conventions are used in this book:

Italic
> Indicates new terms, URIs, filenames, and directories

`Constant width`
> Indicates C# code, keywords and identifiers, and program output

`Constant width bold`
> Shows a highlighted section of code

`Constant width italic`
> Shows text that should be replaced with user-supplied values

This element signifies a tip or suggestion.

 This element signifies a general note.

 This element indicates a warning or caution.

Using Code Examples

Supplemental material (code examples, exercises, etc.) is available for download at LINQPad's Sample Libraries page (*http://www.linqpad.net/RichClient/SampleLibra ries.aspx*): choose "C# 6.0 in a Nutshell."

This book is here to help you get your job done. In general, if example code is offered with this book, you may use it in your programs and documentation. You do not need to contact us for permission unless you're reproducing a significant portion of the code. For example, writing a program that uses several chunks of code from this book does not require permission. Selling or distributing a CD-ROM of examples from O'Reilly books does require permission. Answering a question by citing this book and quoting example code does not require permission. Incorporating a significant amount of example code from this book into your product's documentation does require permission.

We appreciate, but do not require, attribution. An attribution usually includes the title, author, publisher, and ISBN. For example: "*C# 6.0 in a Nutshell* by Joseph Albahari and Ben Albahari (O'Reilly). Copyright 2016 Joseph Albahari and Ben Albahari, 978-1-491-92706-9."

If you feel your use of code examples falls outside fair use or the permission given above, feel free to contact us at *permissions@oreilly.com*.

Safari® Books Online

 *Safari Books Online* is an on-demand digital library that delivers expert content in both book and video form from the world's leading authors in technology and business.

Technology professionals, software developers, web designers, and business and creative professionals use Safari Books Online as their primary resource for research, problem solving, learning, and certification training.

Safari Books Online offers a range of plans and pricing for enterprise, government, education, and individuals.

Members have access to thousands of books, training videos, and prepublication manuscripts in one fully searchable database from publishers like O'Reilly Media, Prentice Hall Professional, Addison-Wesley Professional, Microsoft Press, Sams, Que, Peachpit Press, Focal Press, Cisco Press, John Wiley & Sons, Syngress, Morgan Kaufmann, IBM Redbooks, Packt, Adobe Press, FT Press, Apress, Manning, New Riders, McGraw-Hill, Jones & Bartlett, Course Technology, and hundreds more. For more information about Safari Books Online, please visit us online.

How to Contact Us

Please address comments and questions concerning this book to the publisher:

O'Reilly Media, Inc.
1005 Gravenstein Highway North
Sebastopol, CA 95472
800-998-9938 (in the United States or Canada)
707-829-0515 (international or local)
707-829-0104 (fax)

We have a web page for this book, where we list errata, examples, and any additional information. You can access this page at *http://bit.ly/c-sharp6_nutshell*.

To comment or ask technical questions about this book, send email to *bookquestions@oreilly.com*.

For more information about our books, courses, conferences, and news, see our website at *http://www.oreilly.com*.

Find us on Facebook: *http://facebook.com/oreilly*

Follow us on Twitter: *http://twitter.com/oreillymedia*

Watch us on YouTube: *http://www.youtube.com/oreillymedia*

Acknowledgments

Joseph Albahari

First, I want to thank my brother, Ben Albahari, for persuading me to take on *C# 3.0 in a Nutshell*, whose success has spawned three subsequent editions. Ben shares my willingness to question conventional wisdom and tenacity to pull things apart until it becomes clear how they *really* work.

It's been an honor to have superb technical reviewers on the team. In this edition, we had invaluable and extensive feedback from Jared Parsons, Stephen Toub, Matthew Groves, Dixin Yan, Lee Coward, Bonnie DeWitt, Wonseok Chae, Lori Lalonde and James Montemagno.

The book was built on previous editions, whose technical reviewers I owe a similar honor: Eric Lippert, Jon Skeet, Stephen Toub, Nicholas Paldino, Chris Burrows, Shawn Farkas, Brian Grunkemeyer, Maoni Stephens, David DeWinter, Mike Barnett, Melitta Andersen, Mitch Wheat, Brian Peek, Krzysztof Cwalina, Matt Warren, Joel Pobar, Glyn Griffiths, Ion Vasilian, Brad Abrams, Sam Gentile, and Adam Nathan.

I appreciate that many of the technical reviewers are accomplished individuals at Microsoft, and I particularly thank you for taking out time to raise this book to the next quality bar.

Finally, I want to thank the O'Reilly team, including my best ever editor, Brian MacDonald, and extend personal thanks to Miri and Sonia.

Ben Albahari

Because my brother wrote his acknowledgments first, you can infer most of what I want to say. :) We've actually both been programming since we were kids (we shared an Apple IIe; he was writing his own operating system while I was writing Hangman), so it's cool that we're now writing books together. I hope the enriching experience we had writing the book will translate into an enriching experience for you reading the book.

I'd also like to thank my former colleagues at Microsoft. Many smart people work there, not just in terms of intellect but also in a broader emotional sense, and I miss working with them. In particular, I learned a lot from Brian Beckman, to whom I am indebted.

Introducing C# and the .NET Framework

C# is a general-purpose, type-safe, object-oriented programming language. The goal of the language is programmer productivity. To this end, the language balances simplicity, expressiveness, and performance. The chief architect of the language since its first version is Anders Hejlsberg (creator of Turbo Pascal and architect of Delphi). The C# language is platform-neutral, but it was written to work well with the Microsoft .NET Framework.

Object Orientation

C# is a rich implementation of the object-orientation paradigm, which includes *encapsulation, inheritance*, and *polymorphism*. Encapsulation means creating a boundary around an *object*, to separate its external (public) behavior from its internal (private) implementation details. The distinctive features of C# from an object-oriented perspective are:

Unified type system
> The fundamental building block in C# is an encapsulated unit of data and functions called a *type*. C# has a *unified type system*, where all types ultimately share a common base type. This means that all types, whether they represent business objects or are primitive types such as numbers, share the same basic set of functionality. For example, an instance of any type can be converted to a string by calling its `ToString` method.

Classes and interfaces
> In a traditional object-oriented paradigm, the only kind of type is a class. In C#, there are several other kinds of types, one of which is an *interface*. An interface is like a class, except that it only *describes* members. The implementation for those members comes from types that *implement* the interface. Interfaces are particularly useful in scenarios where multiple inheri-

tance is required (unlike languages such as C++ and Eiffel, C# does not support multiple inheritance of classes).

Properties, methods, and events
In the pure object-oriented paradigm, all functions are *methods* (this is the case in Smalltalk). In C#, methods are only one kind of *function member*, which also includes *properties* and *events* (there are others, too). Properties are function members that encapsulate a piece of an object's state, such as a button's color or a label's text. Events are function members that simplify acting on object state changes.

While C# is primarily an object-oriented language, it also borrows from the *functional programming* paradigm. Specifically:

Functions can be treated as values
Through the use of *delegates*, C# allows functions to be passed as values to and from other functions.

C# supports patterns for purity
Core to functional programming is avoiding the use of variables whose values change, in favor of declarative patterns. C# has key features to help with those patterns, including the ability to write unnamed functions on the fly that "capture" variables (*lambda expressions*) and the ability to perform list or reactive programming via *query expressions*. C# 6.0 also includes read-only auto-properties to help with writing *immutable* (read-only) types.

Type Safety

C# is primarily a *type-safe* language, meaning that instances of types can interact only through protocols they define, thereby ensuring each type's internal consistency. For instance, C# prevents you from interacting with a *string* type as though it were an *integer* type.

More specifically, C# supports *static typing*, meaning that the language enforces type safety at *compile time*. This is in addition to type safety being enforced at *runtime*.

Static typing eliminates a large class of errors before a program is even run. It shifts the burden away from runtime unit tests onto the compiler to verify that all the types in a program fit together correctly. This makes large programs much easier to manage, more predictable, and more robust. Furthermore, static typing allows tools such as IntelliSense in Visual Studio to help you write a program, since it knows for a given variable what type it is, and hence what methods you can call on that variable.

 C# also allows parts of your code to be dynamically typed via the dynamic keyword (introduced in C# 4.0). However, C# remains a predominantly statically typed language.

C# is also called a *strongly typed language* because its type rules (whether enforced statically or at runtime) are very strict. For instance, you cannot call a function that's designed to accept an integer with a floating-point number, unless you first *explicitly* convert the floating-point number to an integer. This helps prevent mistakes.

Strong typing also plays a role in enabling C# code to run in a sandbox—an environment where every aspect of security is controlled by the host. In a sandbox, it is important that you cannot arbitrarily corrupt the state of an object by bypassing its type rules.

Memory Management

C# relies on the runtime to perform automatic memory management. The Common Language Runtime has a garbage collector that executes as part of your program, reclaiming memory for objects that are no longer referenced. This frees programmers from explicitly deallocating the memory for an object, eliminating the problem of incorrect pointers encountered in languages such as C++.

C# does not eliminate pointers: it merely makes them unnecessary for most programming tasks. For performance-critical hotspots and interoperability, pointers may be used, but they are permitted only in blocks that are explicitly marked unsafe.

Platform Support

Historically, C# was used almost entirely for writing code to run on Windows platforms. Recently, however, Microsoft and other companies have invested in other platforms, including Mac OS X and iOS, and Android. Xamarin™ allows cross-platform C# development for mobile applications, and Portable Class Libraries are becoming increasingly widespread. Microsoft's ASP.NET 5 is a new web hosting framework that can run either on the .NET Framework or on .NET Core, a new small, fast, open source, cross-platform runtime.

C#'s Relationship with the CLR

C# depends on a runtime equipped with a host of features such as automatic memory management and exception handling. The design of C# closely maps to the design of Microsoft's *Common Language Runtime* (CLR), which provides these runtime features (although C# is technically independent of the CLR). Furthermore, the C# type system maps closely to the CLR type system (e.g., both share the same definitions for predefined types).

The CLR and .NET Framework

The .NET Framework consists of the CLR plus a vast set of libraries. The libraries consist of core libraries (which this book is concerned with) and applied libraries, which depend on the core libraries. Figure 1-1 is a visual overview of those libraries (and also serves as a navigational aid to the book).

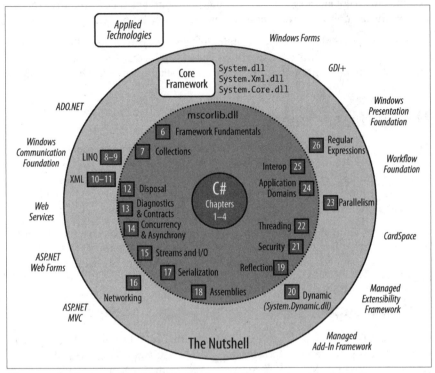

Figure 1-1. Topics covered in this book and the chapters in which they are found. Topics not covered are shown outside the large circle.

The CLR is the runtime for executing *managed code*. C# is one of several *managed languages* that get compiled into managed code. Managed code is packaged into an *assembly*, in the form of either an executable file (an *.exe*) or a library (a *.dll*), along with type information, or *metadata*.

Managed code is represented in *intermediate language* or *IL*. When the CLR loads an assembly, it converts the IL into the native code of the machine, such as x86. This conversion is done by the CLR's JIT (just-in-time) compiler. An assembly retains almost all of the original source language constructs, which makes it easy to inspect and even generate code dynamically.

 You can examine and decompile the contents of an IL assembly with tools such as ILSpy, dotPeek (JetBrains) or Reflector (Red Gate).

When writing Windows Store apps, you also now have the option of generating native code directly (".NET Native"). This improves startup performance and memory usage (which is particularly beneficial on mobile devices) and also runtime performance through static linking and other optimizations.

The CLR performs as a host for numerous runtime services. Examples of these services include memory management, the loading of libraries, and security services. The CLR is language-neutral, allowing developers to build applications in multiple languages (e.g., C#, F#, Visual Basic .NET and Managed C++).

The .NET Framework contains libraries for writing just about any Windows- or web-based application. Chapter 5 gives an overview of the .NET Framework libraries.

C# and Windows Runtime

C# also interoperates with *Windows Runtime* (WinRT) libraries. WinRT is an execution interface and runtime environment for accessing libraries in a language-neutral and object-oriented fashion. It ships with Windows 8 and newer and is (in part) an enhanced version of Microsoft's *Component Object Model* or COM (see Chapter 25).

Windows 8 and newer ship with a set of unmanaged WinRT libraries that serve as a framework for touch-enabled applications delivered through Microsoft's application store. (The term *WinRT* also refers to these libraries.) Being WinRT, the libraries can easily be consumed not only from C# and VB, but C++ and JavaScript.

 Some WinRT libraries can also be consumed in normal non-tablet applications. However, taking a dependency on WinRT gives your application a *minimum* OS requirement of Windows 8.

The WinRT libraries support the new "modern" user interface (for writing immersive touch-first applications), mobile device-specific features (sensors, text messaging and so on), and a range of core functionality that overlaps with parts of the .NET Framework. Because of this overlap, Visual Studio includes a *reference profile* (a set of .NET *reference assemblies*) for Windows Store projects that hides the portions of the .NET Framework that overlap with WinRT. This profile also hides large portions of the .NET Framework considered unnecessary for tablet apps (such as accessing a database). Microsoft's application store, which controls the distribution of software to consumer devices, rejects any program that attempts to access a hidden type.

 A *reference assembly* exists purely to compile against and may have a restricted set of types and members. This allows developers to install the full .NET Framework on their machines while coding certain projects as though they had only a subset. The actual functionality comes at runtime from assemblies in the *global assembly cache* (see Chapter 18) that may superset the reference assemblies.

Hiding most of the .NET Framework eases the learning curve for developers new to the Microsoft platform, although there are two more important goals:

- It *sandboxes* applications (restricts functionality to reduce the impact of malware). For instance, arbitrary file access is forbidden, and there the ability to start or communicate with other programs on the computer is extremely restricted.

- It allows low-powered Windows RT-only tablets to ship with a reduced .NET Framework, lowering the OS footprint.

What distinguishes WinRT from ordinary COM is that WinRT *projects* its libraries into a multitude of languages, namely C#, VB, C++ and JavaScript, so that each language sees WinRT types (almost) as though they were written especially for it. For example, WinRT will adapt capitalization rules to suit the standards of the target language, and will even remap some functions and interfaces. WinRT assemblies also ship with rich *metadata* in *.winmd* files, which have the same format as .NET assembly files, allowing transparent consumption without special ritual. In fact, you might even be unaware that you're using WinRT rather than .NET types, aside of namespace differences. Another clue is that WinRT types are subject to COM-style restrictions; for instance, they offer limited support for inheritance and generics.

 WinRT does not supersede the full .NET Framework. The latter is still recommended (and necessary) for standard desktop and server-side development, and has the following advantages:

- Programs are not restricted to running in a sandbox.

- Programs can use the entire .NET Framework and any third-party library.

- Application distribution does not rely on the Windows Store.

- Applications can target the latest Framework version without requiring users to have the latest OS version.

What's New in C# 6.0

C# 6.0's biggest new feature is that the compiler has been completely rewritten in C#. Known as project "Roslyn," the new compiler exposes the entire compilation pipeline via libraries, allowing you to perform code analysis on arbitrary source code (see Chapter 27). The compiler itself is open source, and the source code is available at *github.com/dotnet/roslyn*.

In addition, C# 6.0 features a number of minor but significant enhancements, aimed primarily at reducing code clutter.

The *null-conditional* ("Elvis") operator (see "Null Operators" on page 55, Chapter 2) avoids having to explicitly check for null before calling a method or accessing a type member. In the following example, `result` evaluates to null instead of throwing a `NullReferenceException`:

```
System.Text.StringBuilder sb = null;
string result = sb?.ToString();      // result is null
```

Expression-bodied functions (see "Methods" on page 74, Chapter 3) allow methods, properties, operators, and indexers that comprise a single expression to be written more tersely, in the style of a lambda expression:

```
public int TimesTwo (int x) => x * 2;
public string SomeProperty => "Property value";
```

Property initializers (Chapter 3) let you assign an initial value to an automatic property:

```
public DateTime Created { get; set; } = DateTime.Now;
```

Initialized properties can also be read-only:

```
public DateTime Created { get; } = DateTime.Now;
```

Read-only properties can also be set in the constructor, making it easier to create immutable (read-only) types.

Index initializers (Chapter 4) allow single-step initialization of any type that exposes an indexer:

```
new Dictionary<int,string>()
{
  [3] = "three",
  [10] = "ten"
}
```

String interpolation (see "String Type" on page 36, Chapter 2) offers a succinct alternative to string.Format:

```
string s = $"It is {DateTime.Now.DayOfWeek} today";
```

Exception filters (see "try Statements and Exceptions" on page 148, Chapter 4) let you apply a condition to a catch block:

```
try
{
  new WebClient().DownloadString("http://asef");
}
catch (WebException ex) when (ex.Status == WebExceptionStatus.Timeout)
{
  ...
}
```

The using static (see "Namespaces" on page 65, Chapter 2) directive lets you import all the static members of a type, so that you can use those members unqualified:

```
using static System.Console;
...
WriteLine ("Hello, world");  // WriteLine instead of Console.WriteLine
```

The `nameof` (Chapter 3) operator returns the name of a variable, type or other symbol as a string. This avoids breaking code when you rename a symbol in Visual Studio:

```
int capacity = 123;
string x = nameof (capacity);   // x is "capacity"
string y = nameof (Uri.Host);   // y is "Host"
```

And finally, you're now allowed to `await` inside `catch` and `finally` blocks.

What Was New in C# 5.0

C# 5.0's big new feature was support for *asynchronous functions* via two new keywords, `async` and `await`. Asynchronous functions enable *asynchronous continuations*, which make it easier to write responsive and thread-safe, rich-client applications. They also make it easy to write highly concurrent and efficient I/O-bound applications that don't tie up a thread resource per operation.

We cover asynchronous functions in detail in Chapter 14.

What Was New in C# 4.0

The features new to C# 4.0 were:

- Dynamic binding
- Optional parameters and named arguments
- Type variance with generic interfaces and delegates
- COM interoperability improvements

Dynamic binding (Chapters 4 and 20) defers *binding*—the process of resolving types and members—from compile time to runtime and is useful in scenarios that would otherwise require complicated reflection code. Dynamic binding is also useful when interoperating with dynamic languages and COM components.

Optional parameters (Chapter 2) allow functions to specify default parameter values so that callers can omit arguments, and *named arguments* allow a function caller to identify an argument by name rather than position.

Type variance rules were relaxed in C# 4.0 (Chapters 3 and 4), such that type parameters in generic interfaces and generic delegates can be marked as *covariant* or *contravariant*, allowing more natural type conversions.

COM interoperability (Chapter 25) was enhanced in C# 4.0 in three ways. First, arguments can be passed by reference without the `ref` keyword (particularly useful in conjunction with optional parameters). Second, assemblies that contain COM interop types can be *linked* rather than *referenced*. Linked interop types support type equivalence, avoiding the need for *Primary Interop Assemblies* and putting an end to versioning and deployment headaches. Third, functions that return COM-Variant types from linked interop types are mapped to `dynamic` rather than `object`, eliminating the need for casting.

What Was New in C# 3.0

The features added to C# 3.0 were mostly centered on *Language Integrated Query* capabilities, or *LINQ* for short. LINQ enables queries to be written directly within a C# program and checked *statically* for correctness, and to query both local collections (such as lists or XML documents) or remote data sources (such as a database). The C# 3.0 features added to support LINQ comprised implicitly typed local variables, anonymous types, object initializers, lambda expressions, extension methods, query expressions, and expression trees.

Implicitly typed local variables (`var` keyword, Chapter 2) let you omit the variable type in a declaration statement, allowing the compiler to infer it. This reduces clutter as well as allowing *anonymous types* (Chapter 4), which are simple classes created on the fly that are commonly used in the final output of LINQ queries. Arrays can also be implicitly typed (Chapter 2).

Object initializers (Chapter 3) simplify object construction by allowing properties to be set inline after the constructor call. Object initializers work with both named and anonymous types.

Lambda expressions (Chapter 4) are miniature functions created by the compiler on the fly and are particularly useful in "fluent" LINQ queries (Chapter 8).

Extension methods (Chapter 4) extend an existing type with new methods (without altering the type's definition), making static methods feel like instance methods. LINQ's query operators are implemented as extension methods.

Query expressions (Chapter 8) provide a higher-level syntax for writing LINQ queries that can be substantially simpler when working with multiple sequences or range variables.

Expression trees (Chapter 8) are miniature code DOMs (Document Object Models) that describe lambda expressions assigned to the special type `Expression<TDelegate>`. Expression trees make it possible for LINQ queries to execute remotely (e.g., on a database server) because they can be introspected and translated at runtime (e.g., into a SQL statement).

C# 3.0 also added automatic properties and partial methods.

Automatic properties (Chapter 3) cut the work in writing properties that simply `get`/`set` a private backing field by having the compiler do that work automatically. *Partial methods* (Chapter 3) let an auto-generated partial class provide customizable hooks for manual authoring which "melt away" if unused.

2

C# Language Basics

In this chapter, we introduce the basics of the C# language.

All programs and code snippets in this and the following two chapters are available as interactive samples in LINQPad. Working through these samples in conjunction with the book accelerates learning in that you can edit the samples and instantly see the results without needing to set up projects and solutions in Visual Studio.

To download the samples, go to LINQPad's Sample Libraries page (*http://www.linqpad.net/RichClient/SampleLibraries.aspx*) and choose "C# 6.0 in a Nutshell." LINQPad is free—go to *http://www.linqpad.net.*

A First C# Program

Here is a program that multiplies 12 by 30 and prints the result, 360, to the screen. The double forward slash indicates that the remainder of a line is a *comment*:

```
using System;              // Importing namespace

class Test                 // Class declaration
{
  static void Main()       // Method declaration
  {
    int x = 12 * 30;       // Statement 1
    Console.WriteLine (x); // Statement 2
  }                        // End of method
}                          // End of class
```

At the heart of this program lie two *statements*:

```
int x = 12 * 30;
Console.WriteLine (x);
```

Statements in C# execute sequentially and are terminated by a semicolon (or a *code block*, as we'll see later). The first statement computes the *expression* 12 * 30 and stores the result in a *local variable*, named x, which is an integer type. The second statement calls the Console class's WriteLine *method*, to print the variable x to a text window on the screen.

A *method* performs an action in a series of statements, called a *statement block*—a pair of braces containing zero or more statements. We defined a single method named Main:

```
static void Main()
{
    ...
}
```

Writing higher-level functions that call upon lower-level functions simplifies a program. We can *refactor* our program with a reusable method that multiplies an integer by 12 as follows:

```
using System;

class Test
{
  static void Main()
  {
    Console.WriteLine (FeetToInches (30));     // 360
    Console.WriteLine (FeetToInches (100));    // 1200
  }

  static int FeetToInches (int feet)
  {
    int inches = feet * 12;
    return inches;
  }
}
```

A method can receive *input* data from the caller by specifying *parameters* and *output* data back to the caller by specifying a *return type*. We defined a method called Feet ToInches that has a parameter for inputting feet, and a return type for outputting inches:

```
static int FeetToInches (int feet ) {...}
```

The *literals* 30 and 100 are the *arguments* passed to the FeetToInches method. The Main method in our example has empty parentheses because it has no parameters, and is void because it doesn't return any value to its caller:

```
static void Main()
```

C# recognizes a method called Main as signaling the default entry point of execution. The Main method may optionally return an integer (rather than void) in order to return a value to the execution environment (where a nonzero value typically indicates an error). The Main method can also optionally accept an array of strings

---

as a parameter (that will be populated with any arguments passed to the executable). For example:

```
static int Main (string[] args) {...}
```

 An array (such as string[]) represents a fixed number of elements of a particular type. Arrays are specified by placing square brackets after the element type and are described in "Arrays" on page 38.

Methods are one of several kinds of functions in C#. Another kind of function we used in our example program was the * *operator*, which performs multiplication. There are also *constructors*, *properties*, *events*, *indexers*, and *finalizers*.

In our example, the two methods are grouped into a class. A *class* groups function members and data members to form an object-oriented building block. The Console class groups members that handle command-line input/output functionality, such as the WriteLine method. Our Test class groups two methods—the Main method and the FeetToInches method. A class is a kind of *type*, which we will examine in "Type Basics" on page 17.

At the outermost level of a program, types are organized into *namespaces*. The using directive was used to make the System namespace available to our application, to use the Console class. We could define all our classes within the TestPrograms namespace, as follows:

```
using System;

namespace TestPrograms
{
  class Test  {...}
  class Test2 {...}
}
```

The .NET Framework is organized into nested namespaces. For example, this is the namespace that contains types for handling text:

```
using System.Text;
```

The using directive is there for convenience; you can also refer to a type by its fully qualified name, which is the type name prefixed with its namespace, such as System.Text.StringBuilder.

Compilation

The C# compiler compiles source code, specified as a set of files with the *.cs* extension, into an *assembly*. An assembly is the unit of packaging and deployment in .NET. An assembly can be either an *application* or a *library*. A normal console or Windows application has a Main method and is an *.exe* file. A library is a *.dll* and is equivalent to an *.exe* without an entry point. Its purpose is to be called upon (*refer-*

enced) by an application or by other libraries. The .NET Framework is a set of libraries.

The name of the C# compiler is *csc.exe*. You can either use an IDE such as Visual Studio to compile, or call `csc` manually from the command line. (The compiler is also available as a library; see Chapter 27.) To compile manually, first save a program to a file such as *MyFirstProgram.cs*, and then go to the command line and invoke `csc` (located in *%ProgramFiles(X86)%\msbuild\14.0\bin*) as follows:

```
csc MyFirstProgram.cs
```

This produces an application named *MyFirstProgram.exe*.

 Peculiarly, .NET Framework 4.6 ships with the C# 5 compiler. To obtain the C# 6 command-line compiler, you must install Visual Studio or MSBuild 14.

To produce a library (*.dll*), do the following:

```
csc /target:library MyFirstProgram.cs
```

We explain assemblies in detail in Chapter 18.

Syntax

C# syntax is inspired by C and C++ syntax. In this section, we will describe C#'s elements of syntax, using the following program:

```
using System;

class Test
{
  static void Main()
  {
    int x = 12 * 30;
    Console.WriteLine (x);
  }
}
```

Identifiers and Keywords

Identifiers are names that programmers choose for their classes, methods, variables, and so on. These are the identifiers in our example program, in the order they appear:

```
System   Test   Main   x   Console   WriteLine
```

An identifier must be a whole word, essentially made up of Unicode characters starting with a letter or underscore. C# identifiers are case-sensitive. By convention, parameters, local variables, and private fields should be in camel case (e.g., `myVaria ble`), and all other identifiers should be in Pascal case (e.g., `MyMethod`).

Keywords are names that mean something special to the compiler. These are the keywords in our example program:

```
using   class   static   void   int
```

Most keywords are *reserved*, which means that you can't use them as identifiers. Here is the full list of C# reserved keywords:

abstract	do	in	public	try
as	double	int	readonly	typeof
base	else	interface	ref	uint
bool	enum	internal	return	ulong
break	event	is	sbyte	unchecked
byte	explicit	lock	sealed	unsafe
case	extern	longnamespace	short	ushort
catch	false	new	sizeof	using
char	finally	null	stackalloc	virtual
checked	fixed	object	static	void
class	float	operator	string	volatile
const	for	out	struct	while
continue	foreach	override	switch	
decimal	goto	params	this	
default	if	private	throw	
delegate	implicit	protected	true	

Avoiding conflicts

If you really want to use an identifier that clashes with a reserved keyword, you can do so by qualifying it with the @ prefix. For instance:

```
class class  {...}      // Illegal
class @class {...}      // Legal
```

The @ symbol doesn't form part of the identifier itself. So @myVariable is the same as myVariable.

> The @ prefix can be useful when consuming libraries written in other .NET languages that have different keywords.

Contextual keywords

Some keywords are *contextual*, meaning they can also be used as identifiers—without an @ symbol. These are:

add	dynamic	in	orderby	var
ascending	equals	into	partial	when
async	from	join	remove	where
await	get	let	select	yield
by	global	nameof	set	
descending	group	on	value	

With contextual keywords, ambiguity cannot arise within the context in which they are used.

Literals, Punctuators, and Operators

Literals are primitive pieces of data lexically embedded into the program. The literals we used in our example program are 12 and 30.

Punctuators help demarcate the structure of the program. These are the punctuators we used in our example program:

```
{   }   ;
```

The braces group multiple statements into a *statement block*.

The semicolon terminates a statement. (Statement blocks, however, do not require a semicolon.) Statements can wrap multiple lines:

```
Console.WriteLine
   (1 + 2 + 3 + 4 + 5 + 6 + 7 + 8 + 9 + 10);
```

An *operator* transforms and combines expressions. Most operators in C# are denoted with a symbol, such as the multiplication operator, *. We will discuss operators in more detail later in this chapter. These are the operators we used in our example program:

```
.   ()   *   =
```

A period denotes a member of something (or a decimal point with numeric literals). Parentheses are used when declaring or calling a method; empty parentheses are used when the method accepts no arguments. (Parentheses also have other purposes that we'll see later in this chapter.) An equals sign performs *assignment*. (The double equals sign, ==, performs equality comparison, as we'll see later.)

Comments

C# offers two different styles of source-code documentation: *single-line comments* and *multiline comments*. A single-line comment begins with a double forward slash and continues until the end of the line. For example:

```
int x = 3;   // Comment about assigning 3 to x
```

A multiline comment begins with /* and ends with */. For example:

```
int x = 3;    /* This is a comment that
                 spans two lines */
```

Comments may embed XML documentation tags, explained in "XML Documentation" on page 193 in Chapter 4.

Type Basics

A *type* defines the blueprint for a value. In our example, we used two literals of type int with values 12 and 30. We also declared a *variable* of type int whose name was x:

```
static void Main()
{
  int x = 12 * 30;
  Console.WriteLine (x);
}
```

A *variable* denotes a storage location that can contain different values over time. In contrast, a *constant* always represents the same value (more on this later):

```
const int y = 360;
```

All values in C# are *instances* of a type. The meaning of a value, and the set of possible values a variable can have, is determined by its type.

Predefined Type Examples

Predefined types are types that are specially supported by the compiler. The int type is a predefined type for representing the set of integers that fit into 32 bits of memory, from -2^{31} to $2^{31}-1$, and is the default type for numeric literals within this range. We can perform functions such as arithmetic with instances of the int type as follows:

```
int x = 12 * 30;
```

Another predefined C# type is string. The string type represents a sequence of characters, such as ".NET" or "*http://oreilly.com*." We can work with strings by calling functions on them as follows:

```
string message = "Hello world";
string upperMessage = message.ToUpper();
Console.WriteLine (upperMessage);          // HELLO WORLD

int x = 2015;
message = message + x.ToString();
Console.WriteLine (message);               // Hello world2015
```

The predefined bool type has exactly two possible values: true and false. The bool type is commonly used to conditionally branch execution flow based with an if statement. For example:

```
bool simpleVar = false;
if (simpleVar)
```

```
Console.WriteLine ("This will not print");

int x = 5000;
bool lessThanAMile = x < 5280;
if (lessThanAMile)
  Console.WriteLine ("This will print");
```

 In C#, predefined types (also referred to as built-in types) are recognized with a C# keyword. The System namespace in the .NET Framework contains many important types that are not predefined by C# (e.g., DateTime).

Custom Type Examples

Just as we can build complex functions from simple functions, we can build complex types from primitive types. In this example, we will define a custom type named UnitConverter—a class that serves as a blueprint for unit conversions:

```
using System;

public class UnitConverter
{
  int ratio;                                              // Field
  public UnitConverter (int unitRatio) {ratio = unitRatio; } // Constructor
  public int Convert   (int unit)    {return unit * ratio; } // Method
}

class Test
{
  static void Main()
  {
    UnitConverter feetToInchesConverter = new UnitConverter (12);
    UnitConverter milesToFeetConverter  = new UnitConverter (5280);

    Console.WriteLine (feetToInchesConverter.Convert(30));   // 360
    Console.WriteLine (feetToInchesConverter.Convert(100));  // 1200
    Console.WriteLine (feetToInchesConverter.Convert(
                        milesToFeetConverter.Convert(1)));   // 63360
  }
}
```

Members of a type

A type contains *data members* and *function members*. The data member of UnitConverter is the *field* called ratio. The function members of UnitConverter are the Convert method and the UnitConverter's *constructor*.

Symmetry of predefined types and custom types

A beautiful aspect of C# is that predefined types and custom types have few differences. The predefined int type serves as a blueprint for integers. It holds data—32 bits—and provides function members that use that data, such as ToString. Similarly, our custom UnitConverter type acts as a blueprint for unit conversions. It holds data—the ratio—and provides function members to use that data.

Constructors and instantiation

Data is created by *instantiating* a type. Predefined types can be instantiated simply by using a literal such as 12 or "Hello world". The new operator creates instances of a custom type. We created and declared an instance of the UnitConverter type with this statement:

```
UnitConverter feetToInchesConverter = new UnitConverter (12);
```

Immediately after the new operator instantiates an object, the object's *constructor* is called to perform initialization. A constructor is defined like a method, except that the method name and return type are reduced to the name of the enclosing type:

```
public class UnitConverter
{
  ...
  public UnitConverter (int unitRatio) { ratio = unitRatio; }
  ...
}
```

Instance versus static members

The data members and function members that operate on the *instance* of the type are called instance members. The UnitConverter's Convert method and the int's ToString method are examples of instance members. By default, members are instance members.

Data members and function members that don't operate on the instance of the type, but rather on the type itself, must be marked as static. The Test.Main and Console.WriteLine methods are static methods. The Console class is actually a *static class*, which means *all* its members are static. You never actually create instances of a Console—one console is shared across the whole application.

Let's contrast instance from static members. In the following code, the instance field Name pertains to an instance of a particular Panda, whereas Population pertains to the set of all Panda instances:

```
public class Panda
{
  public string Name;              // Instance field
  public static int Population;     // Static field

  public Panda (string n)           // Constructor
  {
    Name = n;                       // Assign the instance field
    Population = Population + 1;     // Increment the static Population field
  }
}
```

The following code creates two instances of the Panda, prints their names, and then prints the total population:

```
using System;

class Test
{
  static void Main()
  {
    Panda p1 = new Panda ("Pan Dee");
    Panda p2 = new Panda ("Pan Dah");

    Console.WriteLine (p1.Name);       // Pan Dee
    Console.WriteLine (p2.Name);       // Pan Dah

    Console.WriteLine (Panda.Population);   // 2
  }
}
```

Attempting to evaluate p1.Population or Panda.Name will generate a compile-time error.

The public keyword

The public keyword exposes members to other classes. In this example, if the Name field in Panda was not marked as public, it would be private, and the Test class could not access it. Marking a member public is how a type communicates: "Here is what I want other types to see—everything else is my own private implementation details." In object-oriented terms, we say that the public members *encapsulate* the private members of the class.

Conversions

C# can convert between instances of compatible types. A conversion always creates a new value from an existing one. Conversions can be either *implicit* or *explicit*: implicit conversions happen automatically, and explicit conversions require a *cast*. In the following example, we *implicitly* convert an int to a long type (which has twice the bitwise capacity of an int) and *explicitly* cast an int to a short type (which has half the capacity of an int):

```
int x = 12345;        // int is a 32-bit integer
long y = x;           // Implicit conversion to 64-bit integer
short z = (short)x;   // Explicit conversion to 16-bit integer
```

Implicit conversions are allowed when both of the following are true:

- The compiler can guarantee they will always succeed.
- No information is lost in conversion.[1]

Conversely, *explicit* conversions are required when one of the following is true:

- The compiler cannot guarantee they will always succeed.
- Information may be lost during conversion.

(If the compiler can determine that a conversion will *always* fail, both kinds of conversion are prohibited. Conversions that involve generics can also fail in certain conditions—see "Type Parameters and Conversions" on page 121 in Chapter 3.)

The *numeric conversions* that we just saw are built into the language. C# also supports *reference conversions* and *boxing conversions* (see Chapter 3) as well as *custom conversions* (see "Operator Overloading" on page 168 in Chapter 4). The compiler doesn't enforce the aforementioned rules with custom conversions, so it's possible for badly designed types to behave otherwise.

Value Types Versus Reference Types

All C# types fall into the following categories:

- Value types
- Reference types
- Generic type parameters
- Pointer types

In this section, we'll describe value types and reference types. We'll cover generic type parameters in "Generics" on page 114 in Chapter 3, and pointer types in "Unsafe Code and Pointers" on page 187 in Chapter 4.

Value types comprise most built-in types (specifically, all numeric types, the `char` type, and the `bool` type), as well as custom `struct` and `enum` types.

Reference types comprise all class, array, delegate, and interface types. (This includes the predefined `string` type.)

The fundamental difference between value types and reference types is how they are handled in memory.

---

1 A minor caveat is that very large `long` values lose some precision when converted to `double`.

Value types

The content of a *value type* variable or constant is simply a value. For example, the content of the built-in value type, int, is 32 bits of data.

You can define a custom value type with the struct keyword (see Figure 2-1):

```
public struct Point { public int X; public int Y; }
```

or more tersely:

```
public struct Point { public int X, Y; }
```

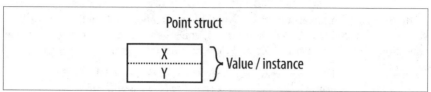

Figure 2-1. A value-type instance in memory

The assignment of a value-type instance always *copies* the instance. For example:

```
static void Main()
{
  Point p1 = new Point();
  p1.X = 7;

  Point p2 = p1;             // Assignment causes copy

  Console.WriteLine (p1.X);  // 7
  Console.WriteLine (p2.X);  // 7

  p1.X = 9;                  // Change p1.X

  Console.WriteLine (p1.X);  // 9
  Console.WriteLine (p2.X);  // 7
}
```

Figure 2-2 shows that p1 and p2 have independent storage.

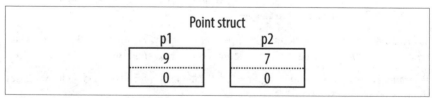

Figure 2-2. Assignment copies a value-type instance

Reference types

A reference type is more complex than a value type, having two parts: an *object* and the *reference* to that object. The content of a reference-type variable or constant is a reference to an object that contains the value. Here is the Point type from our previous example rewritten as a class, rather than a struct (shown in Figure 2-3):

```
public class Point { public int X, Y; }
```

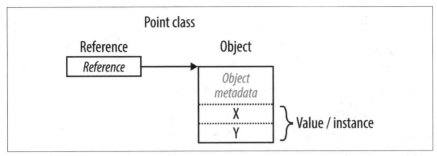

Figure 2-3. A reference-type instance in memory

Assigning a reference-type variable copies the reference, not the object instance. This allows multiple variables to refer to the same object—something not ordinarily possible with value types. If we repeat the previous example, but with Point now a class, an operation to p1 affects p2:

```
static void Main()
{
  Point p1 = new Point();
  p1.X = 7;

  Point p2 = p1;            // Copies p1 reference

  Console.WriteLine (p1.X); // 7
  Console.WriteLine (p2.X); // 7

  p1.X = 9;                 // Change p1.X

  Console.WriteLine (p1.X); // 9
  Console.WriteLine (p2.X); // 9
}
```

Figure 2-4 shows that p1 and p2 are two references that point to the same object.

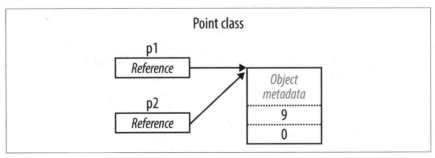

Figure 2-4. Assignment copies a reference

Null

A reference can be assigned the literal null, indicating that the reference points to no object:

```
class Point {...}
...

Point p = null;
Console.WriteLine (p == null);   // True

// The following line generates a runtime error
// (a NullReferenceException is thrown):
Console.WriteLine (p.X);
```

In contrast, a value type cannot ordinarily have a null value:

```
struct Point {...}
...

Point p = null;  // Compile-time error
int x = null;    // Compile-time error
```

C# also has a construct called *nullable types* for representing value-type nulls (see "Nullable Types" on page 162 in Chapter 4).

Storage overhead

Value-type instances occupy precisely the memory required to store their fields. In this example, Point takes eight bytes of memory:

```
struct Point
{
  int x;  // 4 bytes
  int y;  // 4 bytes
}
```

Technically, the CLR positions fields within the type at an address that's a multiple of the fields' size (up to a maximum of eight bytes). Thus, the following actually consumes 16 bytes of memory (with the seven bytes following the first field "wasted"):

```
struct A { byte b; long l; }
```

You can override this behavior with the StructLayout attribute (see "Mapping a Struct to Unmanaged Memory" on page 1011 in Chapter 25).

Reference types require separate allocations of memory for the reference and object. The object consumes as many bytes as its fields, plus additional administrative overhead. The precise overhead is intrinsically private to the implementation of the .NET runtime, but at minimum, the overhead is eight bytes, used to store a key to the object's type, as well as temporary information such as its lock state for multithreading and a flag to indicate whether it has been fixed from movement by the garbage collector. Each reference to an object requires an extra four or eight bytes, depending on whether the .NET runtime is running on a 32- or 64-bit platform.

Predefined Type Taxonomy

The predefined types in C# are:

Value types
- Numeric

    —Signed integer (sbyte, short, int, long)

    —Unsigned integer (byte, ushort, uint, ulong)

    —Real number (float, double, decimal)
- Logical (bool)
- Character (char)

Reference types
- String (string)
- Object (object)

Predefined types in C# alias Framework types in the System namespace. There is only a syntactic difference between these two statements:

```
int i = 5;
System.Int32 i = 5;
```

The set of predefined *value* types, excluding decimal, are known as *primitive types* in the CLR. Primitive types are so called because they are supported directly via instructions in compiled code, and this usually translates to direct support on the underlying processor. For example:

```
                   // Underlying hexadecimal representation
int i = 7;         // 0x7
bool b = true;     // 0x1
char c = 'A';      // 0x41
float f = 0.5f;    // uses IEEE floating-point encoding
```

The System.IntPtr and System.UIntPtr types are also primitive (see Chapter 25).

Numeric Types

C# has the predefined numeric types shown in Table 2-1.

Table 2-1. Predefined numeric types in C#

C# type	System type	Suffix	Size	Range
Integral—signed				
sbyte	SByte		8 bits	-2^7 to 2^7-1
short	Int16		16 bits	-2^{15} to $2^{15}-1$
int	Int32		32 bits	-2^{31} to $2^{31}-1$
long	Int64	L	64 bits	-2^{63} to $2^{63}-1$
Integral—unsigned				
byte	Byte		8 bits	0 to 2^8-1
ushort	UInt16		16 bits	0 to $2^{16}-1$
uint	UInt32	U	32 bits	0 to $2^{32}-1$
ulong	UInt64	UL	64 bits	0 to $2^{64}-1$
Real				
float	Single	F	32 bits	$\pm$ (~10^{-45} to 10^{38})
double	Double	D	64 bits	$\pm$ (~10^{-324} to 10^{308})
decimal	Decimal	M	128 bits	$\pm$ (~10^{-28} to 10^{28})

Of the *integral* types, int and long are first-class citizens and are favored by both C# and the runtime. The other integral types are typically used for interoperability or when space efficiency is paramount.

Of the *real* number types, float and double are called *floating-point types*[2] and are typically used for scientific and graphical calculations. The decimal type is typically used for financial calculations, where base-10-accurate arithmetic and high precision are required.

Numeric Literals

Integral literals can use decimal or hexadecimal notation; hexadecimal is denoted with the 0x prefix. For example:

```
int x = 127;
long y = 0x7F;
```

Real literals can use decimal and/or exponential notation. For example:

---

2 Technically, decimal is a floating-point type too, although it's not referred to as such in the C# language specification.

```
double d = 1.5;
double million = 1E06;
```

Numeric literal type inference

By default, the compiler *infers* a numeric literal to be either `double` or an integral type:

- If the literal contains a decimal point or the exponential symbol (E), it is a `double`.
- Otherwise, the literal's type is the first type in this list that can fit the literal's value: `int`, `uint`, `long`, and `ulong`.

For example:

```
Console.WriteLine (        1.0.GetType());  // Double   (double)
Console.WriteLine (       1E06.GetType());  // Double   (double)
Console.WriteLine (          1.GetType());  // Int32    (int)
Console.WriteLine ( 0xF0000000.GetType());  // UInt32   (uint)
Console.WriteLine (0x100000000.GetType());  // Int64    (long)
```

Numeric suffixes

Numeric suffixes explicitly define the type of a literal. Suffixes can be either lower- or uppercase, and are as follows:

Category	C# type	Example
F	float	float f = 1.0F;
D	double	double d = 1D;
M	decimal	decimal d = 1.0M;
U	uint	uint i = 1U;
L	long	long i = 1L;
UL	ulong	ulong i = 1UL;

The suffixes U and L are rarely necessary, because the `uint`, `long`, and `ulong` types can nearly always be either *inferred* or *implicitly converted* from `int`:

```
long i = 5;    // Implicit lossless conversion from int literal to long
```

The D suffix is technically redundant, in that all literals with a decimal point are inferred to be `double`. And you can always add a decimal point to a numeric literal:

```
double x = 4.0;
```

The F and M suffixes are the most useful and should always be applied when specifying `float` or `decimal` literals. Without the F suffix, the following line would not compile, because 4.5 would be inferred to be of type `double`, which has no implicit conversion to `float`:

```
float f = 4.5F;
```

The same principle is true for a decimal literal:

```
decimal d = -1.23M;      // Will not compile without the M suffix.
```

We describe the semantics of numeric conversions in detail in the following section.

Numeric Conversions

Integral to integral conversions

Integral conversions are *implicit* when the destination type can represent every possible value of the source type. Otherwise, an *explicit* conversion is required. For example:

```
int x = 12345;          // int is a 32-bit integral
long y = x;             // Implicit conversion to 64-bit integral
short z = (short)x;     // Explicit conversion to 16-bit integral
```

Floating-point to floating-point conversions

A float can be implicitly converted to a double, since a double can represent every possible value of a float. The reverse conversion must be explicit.

Floating-point to integral conversions

All integral types may be implicitly converted to all floating-point types:

```
int i = 1;
float f = i;
```

The reverse conversion must be explicit:

```
int i2 = (int)f;
```

 When you cast from a floating-point number to an integral, any fractional portion is truncated; no rounding is performed. The static class System.Convert provides methods that round while converting between various numeric types (see Chapter 6).

Implicitly converting a large integral type to a floating-point type preserves *magnitude* but may occasionally lose *precision*. This is because floating-point types always have more magnitude than integral types, but may have less precision. Rewriting our example with a larger number demonstrates this:

```
int i1 = 100000001;
float f = i1;           // Magnitude preserved, precision lost
int i2 = (int)f;        // 100000000
```

Decimal conversions

All integral types can be implicitly converted to the decimal type, since a decimal can represent every possible C# integral value. All other numeric conversions to and from a decimal type must be explicit.

Arithmetic Operators

The arithmetic operators (+, -, *, /, %) are defined for all numeric types except the 8- and 16-bit integral types:

```
+    Addition
-    Subtraction
*    Multiplication
/    Division
%    Remainder after division
```

Increment and Decrement Operators

The increment and decrement operators (++, --) increment and decrement numeric types by 1. The operator can either follow or precede the variable, depending on whether you want its value *before* or *after* the increment/decrement. For example:

```
int x = 0, y = 0;
Console.WriteLine (x++);   // Outputs 0; x is now 1
Console.WriteLine (++y);   // Outputs 1; y is now 1
```

Specialized Integral Operations

Integral division

Division operations on integral types always truncate remainders (round toward zero). Dividing by a variable whose value is zero generates a runtime error (a Divid eByZeroException):

```
int a = 2 / 3;      // 0

int b = 0;
int c = 5 / b;      // throws DivideByZeroException
```

Dividing by the *literal* or *constant* 0 generates a compile-time error.

Integral overflow

At runtime, arithmetic operations on integral types can overflow. By default, this happens silently—no exception is thrown, and the result exhibits "wraparound" behavior, as though the computation was done on a larger integer type and the extra significant bits discarded. For example, decrementing the minimum possible int value results in the maximum possible int value:

```
int a = int.MinValue;
a--;
Console.WriteLine (a == int.MaxValue); // True
```

Integral arithmetic overflow check operators

The checked operator tells the runtime to generate an `OverflowException` rather than overflowing silently when an integral expression or statement exceeds the arithmetic limits of that type. The checked operator affects expressions with the ++, --, +, - (binary and unary), *, /, and explicit conversion operators between integral types.

 The checked operator has no effect on the `double` and `float` types (which overflow to special "infinite" values, as we'll see soon) and no effect on the `decimal` type (which is always checked).

checked can be used around either an expression or a statement block. For example:

```csharp
int a = 1000000;
int b = 1000000;

int c = checked (a * b);    // Checks just the expression.

checked                     // Checks all expressions
{                           // in statement block.
    ...
    c = a * b;
    ...
}
```

You can make arithmetic overflow checking the default for all expressions in a program by compiling with the /checked+ command-line switch (in Visual Studio, go to Advanced Build Settings). If you then need to disable overflow checking just for specific expressions or statements, you can do so with the unchecked operator. For example, the following code will not throw exceptions—even if compiled with /checked+:

```csharp
int x = int.MaxValue;
int y = unchecked (x + 1);
unchecked { int z = x + 1; }
```

Overflow checking for constant expressions

Regardless of the /checked compiler switch, expressions evaluated at compile time are always overflow-checked—unless you apply the unchecked operator:

```csharp
int x = int.MaxValue + 1;               // Compile-time error
int y = unchecked (int.MaxValue + 1);   // No errors
```

Bitwise operators

C# supports the following bitwise operators:

Operator	Meaning	Sample expression	Result
~	Complement	~0xfU	0xfffffff0U
&	And	0xf0 & 0x33	0x30
|	Or	0xf0 | 0x33	0xf3
^	Exclusive Or	0xff00 ^ 0x0ff0	0xf0f0
<<	Shift left	0x20 << 2	0x80
>>	Shift right	0x20 >> 1	0x10

8- and 16-Bit Integrals

The 8- and 16-bit integral types are byte, sbyte, short, and ushort. These types lack their own arithmetic operators, so C# implicitly converts them to larger types as required. This can cause a compile-time error when trying to assign the result back to a small integral type:

```
short x = 1, y = 1;
short z = x + y;          // Compile-time error
```

In this case, x and y are implicitly converted to int so that the addition can be performed. This means the result is also an int, which cannot be implicitly cast back to a short (because it could cause loss of data). To make this compile, we must add an explicit cast:

```
short z = (short) (x + y);   // OK
```

Special Float and Double Values

Unlike integral types, floating-point types have values that certain operations treat specially. These special values are NaN (not a number), +∞, −∞, and −0. The float and double classes have constants for NaN, +∞, and −∞, as well as other values (Max Value, MinValue, and Epsilon). For example:

```
Console.WriteLine (double.NegativeInfinity);   // -Infinity
```

The constants that represent special values for double and float are as follows:

Special value	Double constant	Float constant
NaN	double.NaN	float.NaN
+∞	double.PositiveInfinity	float.PositiveInfinity
−∞	double.NegativeInfinity	float.NegativeInfinity
−0	−0.0	−0.0f

Dividing a nonzero number by zero results in an infinite value. For example:

```
Console.WriteLine ( 1.0 /  0.0);             //  Infinity
Console.WriteLine (−1.0 /  0.0);             // -Infinity
```

```
Console.WriteLine ( 1.0 / -0.0);                    // -Infinity
Console.WriteLine (-1.0 / -0.0);                    //  Infinity
```

Dividing zero by zero, or subtracting infinity from infinity, results in a NaN. For example:

```
Console.WriteLine ( 0.0 /  0.0);                    //  NaN
Console.WriteLine ((1.0 /  0.0) - (1.0 / 0.0));    //  NaN
```

When using ==, a NaN value is never equal to another value, even another NaN value:

```
Console.WriteLine (0.0 / 0.0 == double.NaN);       // False
```

To test whether a value is NaN, you must use the float.IsNaN or double.IsNaN method:

```
Console.WriteLine (double.IsNaN (0.0 / 0.0));      // True
```

When using object.Equals, however, two NaN values are equal:

```
Console.WriteLine (object.Equals (0.0 / 0.0, double.NaN));  // True
```

> NaNs are sometimes useful in representing special values. In WPF, double.NaN represents a measurement whose value is "Automatic". Another way to represent such a value is with a nullable type (Chapter 4); another is with a custom struct that wraps a numeric type and adds an additional field (Chapter 3).

float and double follow the specification of the IEEE 754 format types, supported natively by almost all processors. You can find detailed information on the behavior of these types at *http://www.ieee.org*.

double Versus decimal

double is useful for scientific computations (such as computing spatial coordinates). decimal is useful for financial computations and values that are "man-made" rather than the result of real-world measurements. Here's a summary of the differences:

Category	double	decimal
Internal representation	Base 2	Base 10
Decimal precision	15–16 significant figures	28–29 significant figures
Range	$\pm(\sim10^{-324}$ to $\sim10^{308})$	$\pm(\sim10^{-28}$ to $\sim10^{28})$
Special values	+0, −0, +∞, −∞, and NaN	None
Speed	Native to processor	Non-native to processor (about 10 times slower than double)

Real-Number Rounding Errors

float and double internally represent numbers in base 2. For this reason, only numbers expressible in base 2 are represented precisely. Practically, this means most literals with a fractional component (which are in base 10) will not be represented precisely. For example:

```
float tenth = 0.1f;                        // Not quite 0.1
float one   = 1f;
Console.WriteLine (one - tenth * 10f);     // -1.490116E-08
```

This is why `float` and `double` are bad for financial calculations. In contrast, `decimal` works in base 10 and so can precisely represent numbers expressible in base 10 (as well as its factors, base 2 and base 5). Since real literals are in base 10, `decimal` can precisely represent numbers such as 0.1. However, neither `double` nor `decimal` can precisely represent a fractional number whose base 10 representation is recurring:

```
decimal m = 1M / 6M;       // 0.1666666666666666666666666667M
double  d = 1.0 / 6.0;     // 0.16666666666666666
```

This leads to accumulated rounding errors:

```
decimal notQuiteWholeM = m+m+m+m+m+m;   // 1.0000000000000000000000000002M
double  notQuiteWholeD = d+d+d+d+d+d;   // 0.99999999999999989
```

which breaks equality and comparison operations:

```
Console.WriteLine (notQuiteWholeM == 1M);    // False
Console.WriteLine (notQuiteWholeD < 1.0);    // True
```

Boolean Type and Operators

C#'s `bool` type (aliasing the `System.Boolean` type) is a logical value that can be assigned the literal `true` or `false`.

Although a Boolean value requires only one bit of storage, the runtime will use one byte of memory, since this is the minimum chunk that the runtime and processor can efficiently work with. To avoid space inefficiency in the case of arrays, the Framework provides a `BitArray` class in the `System.Collections` namespace that is designed to use just one bit per Boolean value.

Bool Conversions

No casting conversions can be made from the `bool` type to numeric types or vice versa.

Equality and Comparison Operators

`==` and `!=` test for equality and inequality of any type, but always return a `bool` value.[3] Value types typically have a very simple notion of equality:

---

3 It's possible to *overload* these operators (Chapter 4) such that they return a non-`bool` type, but this is almost never done in practice.

```
int x = 1;
int y = 2;
int z = 1;
Console.WriteLine (x == y);        // False
Console.WriteLine (x == z);        // True
```

For reference types, equality, by default, is based on *reference*, as opposed to the actual *value* of the underlying object (more on this in Chapter 6):

```
public class Dude
{
  public string Name;
  public Dude (string n) { Name = n; }
}
...
Dude d1 = new Dude ("John");
Dude d2 = new Dude ("John");
Console.WriteLine (d1 == d2);      // False
Dude d3 = d1;
Console.WriteLine (d1 == d3);      // True
```

The equality and comparison operators, ==, !=, <, >, >=, and <=, work for all numeric types, but should be used with caution with real numbers (as we saw in "Real-Number Rounding Errors" on page 32). The comparison operators also work on enum type members, by comparing their underlying integral values. We describe this in "Enums" on page 109 in Chapter 3.

We explain the equality and comparison operators in greater detail in "Operator Overloading" on page 168 in Chapter 4, and in "Equality Comparison" on page 267 and "Order Comparison" on page 278 in Chapter 6.

Conditional Operators

The && and || operators test for *and* and *or* conditions. They are frequently used in conjunction with the ! operator, which expresses *not*. In this example, the UseUm brella method returns true if it's rainy or sunny (to protect us from the rain or the sun), as long as it's not also windy (since umbrellas are useless in the wind):

```
static bool UseUmbrella (bool rainy, bool sunny, bool windy)
{
  return !windy && (rainy || sunny);
}
```

The && and || operators *short-circuit* evaluation when possible. In the preceding example, if it is windy, the expression (rainy || sunny) is not even evaluated. Short-circuiting is essential in allowing expressions such as the following to run without throwing a NullReferenceException:

```
if (sb != null && sb.Length > 0) ...
```

The & and | operators also test for *and* and *or* conditions:

```
return !windy & (rainy | sunny);
```

The difference is that they *do not short-circuit*. For this reason, they are rarely used in place of conditional operators.

 Unlike in C and C++, the & and | operators perform (non-short-circuiting) *Boolean* comparisons when applied to bool expressions. The & and | operators perform *bitwise* operations only when applied to numbers.

Conditional operator (ternary operator)

The *conditional operator* (more commonly called the *ternary operator*, as it's the only operator that takes three operands) has the form q ? a : b, where if condition q is true, a is evaluated, else b is evaluated. For example:

```
static int Max (int a, int b)
{
  return (a > b) ? a : b;
}
```

The conditional operator is particularly useful in LINQ queries (Chapter 8).

Strings and Characters

C#'s char type (aliasing the System.Char type) represents a Unicode character and occupies 2 bytes. A char literal is specified inside single quotes:

```
char c = 'A';       // Simple character
```

Escape sequences express characters that cannot be expressed or interpreted literally. An escape sequence is a backslash followed by a character with a special meaning. For example:

```
char newLine = '\n';
char backSlash = '\\';
```

The escape sequence characters are shown in Table 2-2.

Table 2-2. Escape sequence characters

Char	Meaning	Value
\'	Single quote	0x0027
\"	Double quote	0x0022
\\	Backslash	0x005C
\0	Null	0x0000
\a	Alert	0x0007
\b	Backspace	0x0008
\f	Form feed	0x000C

Char	Meaning	Value
\n	New line	0x000A
\r	Carriage return	0x000D
\t	Horizontal tab	0x0009
\v	Vertical tab	0x000B

The \u (or \x) escape sequence lets you specify any Unicode character via its four-digit hexadecimal code:

```
char copyrightSymbol = '\u00A9';
char omegaSymbol     = '\u03A9';
char newLine         = '\u000A';
```

Char Conversions

An implicit conversion from a char to a numeric type works for the numeric types that can accommodate an unsigned short. For other numeric types, an explicit conversion is required.

String Type

C#'s string type (aliasing the System.String type, covered in depth in Chapter 6) represents an immutable sequence of Unicode characters. A string literal is specified inside double quotes:

```
string a = "Heat";
```

> string is a reference type, rather than a value type. Its equality operators, however, follow value-type semantics:
>
> ```
> string a = "test";
> string b = "test";
> Console.Write (a == b);  // True
> ```

The escape sequences that are valid for char literals also work inside strings:

```
string a = "Here's a tab:\t";
```

The cost of this is that whenever you need a literal backslash, you must write it twice:

```
string a1 = "\\\\server\\fileshare\\helloworld.cs";
```

To avoid this problem, C# allows *verbatim* string literals. A verbatim string literal is prefixed with @ and does not support escape sequences. The following verbatim string is identical to the preceding one:

```
string a2 = @ "\\server\fileshare\helloworld.cs";
```

A verbatim string literal can also span multiple lines:

```
string escaped  = "First Line\r\nSecond Line";
string verbatim = @"First Line
```

```
Second Line";

// True if your IDE uses CR-LF line separators:
Console.WriteLine (escaped == verbatim);
```

You can include the double-quote character in a verbatim literal by writing it twice:

```
string xml = @"<customer id=""123""></customer>";
```

String concatenation

The + operator concatenates two strings:

```
string s = "a" + "b";  .
```

One of the operands may be a nonstring value, in which case ToString is called on that value. For example:

```
string s = "a" + 5;   // a5
```

Using the + operator repeatedly to build up a string is inefficient: a better solution is to use the System.Text.StringBuilder type (described in Chapter 6).

String interpolation (C# 6)

A string preceded with the $ character is called an *interpolated string*. Interpolated strings can include expressions inside braces:

```
int x = 4;
Console.Write ($"A square has {x} sides");  // Prints: A square has 4 sides
```

Any valid C# expression of any type can appear within the braces, and C# will convert the expression to a string by calling its ToString method or equivalent. You can change the formatting by appending the expression with a colon and a *format string* (format strings are described in "Formatting and parsing" on page 233 in Chapter 6):

```
string s = $"255 in hex is {byte.MaxValue:X2}";   // X2 = 2-digit Hexadecimal
// Evaluates to "255 in hex is FF"
```

Interpolated strings must complete on a single line, unless you also specify the verbatim string operator. Note that the $ operator must come before @:

```
int x = 2;
string s = $@"this spans {
x} lines";
```

To include a brace literal in an interpolated string, repeat the desired brace character.

String comparisons

string does not support < and > operators for comparisons. You must use the string's CompareTo method, described in Chapter 6.

Arrays

An array represents a fixed number of variables (called *elements*) of a particular type. The elements in an array are always stored in a contiguous block of memory, providing highly efficient access.

An array is denoted with square brackets after the element type. For example:

```
char[] vowels = new char[5];    // Declare an array of 5 characters
```

Square brackets also *index* the array, accessing a particular element by position:

```
vowels[0] = 'a';
vowels[1] = 'e';
vowels[2] = 'i';
vowels[3] = 'o';
vowels[4] = 'u';
Console.WriteLine (vowels[1]);    // e
```

This prints "e" because array indexes start at 0. We can use a for loop statement to iterate through each element in the array. The for loop in this example cycles the integer i from 0 to 4:

```
for (int i = 0; i < vowels.Length; i++)
  Console.Write (vowels[i]);        // aeiou
```

The Length property of an array returns the number of elements in the array. Once an array has been created, its length cannot be changed. The System.Collection namespace and subnamespaces provide higher-level data structures, such as dynamically sized arrays and dictionaries.

An *array initialization expression* lets you declare and populate an array in a single step:

```
char[] vowels = new char[] {'a','e','i','o','u'};
```

or simply:

```
char[] vowels = {'a','e','i','o','u'};
```

All arrays inherit from the System.Array class, providing common services for all arrays. These members include methods to get and set elements regardless of the array type, and are described in "The Array Class" on page 297 in Chapter 7.

Default Element Initialization

Creating an array always preinitializes the elements with default values. The default value for a type is the result of a bitwise zeroing of memory. For example, consider creating an array of integers. Since int is a value type, this allocates 1,000 integers in one contiguous block of memory. The default value for each element will be 0:

```
int[] a = new int[1000];
Console.Write (a[123]);        // 0
```

Value types versus reference types

Whether an array element type is a value type or a reference type has important performance implications. When the element type is a value type, each element value is allocated as part of the array. For example:

```
public struct Point { public int X, Y; }
...

Point[] a = new Point[1000];
int x = a[500].X;                      // 0
```

Had `Point` been a class, creating the array would have merely allocated 1,000 null references:

```
public class Point { public int X, Y; }


...
Point[] a = new Point[1000];
int x = a[500].X;                      // Runtime error, NullReferenceException
```

To avoid this error, we must explicitly instantiate 1,000 `Points` after instantiating the array:

```
Point[] a = new Point[1000];
for (int i = 0; i < a.Length; i++) // Iterate i from 0 to 999
    a[i] = new Point();                // Set array element i with new point
```

An array *itself* is always a reference type object, regardless of the element type. For instance, the following is legal:

```
int[] a = null;
```

Multidimensional Arrays

Multidimensional arrays come in two varieties: *rectangular* and *jagged*. Rectangular arrays represent an *n*-dimensional block of memory, and jagged arrays are arrays of arrays.

Rectangular arrays

Rectangular arrays are declared using commas to separate each dimension. The following declares a rectangular two-dimensional array, where the dimensions are 3 x 3:

```
int[,] matrix = new int[3,3];
```

The `GetLength` method of an array returns the length for a given dimension (starting at 0):

```
for (int i = 0; i < matrix.GetLength(0); i++)
  for (int j = 0; j < matrix.GetLength(1); j++)
    matrix[i,j] = i * 3 + j;
```

A rectangular array can be initialized as follows (to create an array identical to the previous example):

```
int[,] matrix = new int[,]
{
  {0,1,2},
  {3,4,5},
  {6,7,8}
};
```

Jagged arrays

Jagged arrays are declared using successive square brackets to represent each dimension. Here is an example of declaring a jagged two-dimensional array, where the outermost dimension is 3:

```
int[][] matrix = new int[3][];
```

 Interestingly, this is `new int[3][]` and not `new int[][3]`. Eric Lippert has written an excellent article on why this is so: see *http://albahari.com/jagged*.

The inner dimensions aren't specified in the declaration because, unlike a rectangular array, each inner array can be an arbitrary length. Each inner array is implicitly initialized to null rather than an empty array. Each inner array must be created manually:

```
for (int i = 0; i < matrix.Length; i++)
{
  matrix[i] = new int[3];                      // Create inner array
  for (int j = 0; j < matrix[i].Length; j++)
    matrix[i][j] = i * 3 + j;
}
```

A jagged array can be initialized as follows (to create an array identical to the previous example with an additional element at the end):

```
int[][] matrix = new int[][]
{
  new int[] {0,1,2},
  new int[] {3,4,5},
  new int[] {6,7,8,9}
};
```

Simplified Array Initialization Expressions

There are two ways to shorten array initialization expressions. The first is to omit the new operator and type qualifications:

```
char[] vowels = {'a','e','i','o','u'};

int[,] rectangularMatrix =
{
  {0,1,2},
  {3,4,5},
```

```
    {6,7,8}
  };

  int[][] jaggedMatrix =
  {
    new int[] {0,1,2},
    new int[] {3,4,5},
    new int[] {6,7,8}
  };
```

The second approach is to use the `var` keyword, which tells the compiler to implicitly type a local variable:

```
  var i = 3;              // i is implicitly of type int
  var s = "sausage";      // s is implicitly of type string

  // Therefore:

  var rectMatrix = new int[,]     // rectMatrix is implicitly of type int[,]
  {
    {0,1,2},
    {3,4,5},
    {6,7,8}
  };

  var jaggedMat = new int[][]     // jaggedMat is implicitly of type int[][]
  {
    new int[] {0,1,2},
    new int[] {3,4,5},
    new int[] {6,7,8}
  };
```

Implicit typing can be taken one stage further with arrays: you can omit the type qualifier after the `new` keyword and have the compiler *infer* the array type:

```
  var vowels = new[] {'a','e','i','o','u'};   // Compiler infers char[]
```

For this to work, the elements must all be implicitly convertible to a single type (and at least one of the elements must be of that type, and there must be exactly one best type). For example:

```
  var x = new[] {1,10000000000};   // all convertible to long
```

Bounds Checking

All array indexing is bounds-checked by the runtime. An `IndexOutOfRangeException` is thrown if you use an invalid index:

```
  int[] arr = new int[3];
  arr[3] = 1;                      // IndexOutOfRangeException thrown
```

As with Java, array bounds checking is necessary for type safety and simplifies debugging.

Generally, the performance hit from bounds checking is minor, and the JIT (just-in-time) compiler can perform optimizations, such as determining in advance whether all indexes will be safe before entering a loop, thus avoiding a check on each iteration. In addition, C# provides "unsafe" code that can explicitly bypass bounds checking (see "Unsafe Code and Pointers" on page 187 in Chapter 4).

Variables and Parameters

A variable represents a storage location that has a modifiable value. A variable can be a *local variable*, *parameter* (*value*, *ref*, or *out*), *field* (*instance* or *static*), or *array element*.

The Stack and the Heap

The stack and the heap are the places where variables and constants reside. Each has very different lifetime semantics.

Stack

The stack is a block of memory for storing local variables and parameters. The stack logically grows and shrinks as a function is entered and exited. Consider the following method (to avoid distraction, input argument checking is ignored):

```
static int Factorial (int x)
{
  if (x == 0) return 1;
  return x * Factorial (x-1);
}
```

This method is recursive, meaning that it calls itself. Each time the method is entered, a new `int` is allocated on the stack, and each time the method exits, the `int` is deallocated.

Heap

The heap is a block of memory in which *objects* (i.e., reference-type instances) reside. Whenever a new object is created, it is allocated on the heap, and a reference to that object is returned. During a program's execution, the heap starts filling up as new objects are created. The runtime has a garbage collector that periodically deallocates objects from the heap, so your program does not run out of memory. An object is eligible for deallocation as soon as it's not referenced by anything that's itself "alive."

In the following example, we start by creating a `StringBuilder` object referenced by the variable `ref1`, and then write out its content. That `StringBuilder` object is then immediately eligible for garbage collection, because nothing subsequently uses it.

Then, we create another StringBuilder referenced by variable ref2, and copy that reference to ref3. Even though ref2 is not used after that point, ref3 keeps the same StringBuilder object alive—ensuring that it doesn't become eligible for collection until we've finished using ref3:

```
using System;
using System.Text;

class Test
{
  static void Main()
  {
    StringBuilder ref1 = new StringBuilder ("object1");
    Console.WriteLine (ref1);
    // The StringBuilder referenced by ref1 is now eligible for GC.

    StringBuilder ref2 = new StringBuilder ("object2");
    StringBuilder ref3 = ref2;
    // The StringBuilder referenced by ref2 is NOT yet eligible for GC.

    Console.WriteLine (ref3);                     // object2
  }
}
```

Value-type instances (and object references) live wherever the variable was declared. If the instance was declared as a field within a class type, or as an array element, that instance lives on the heap.

You can't explicitly delete objects in C#, as you can in C++. An unreferenced object is eventually collected by the garbage collector.

The heap also stores static fields. Unlike objects allocated on the heap (which can get garbage-collected), these live until the application domain is torn down.

Definite Assignment

C# enforces a definite assignment policy. In practice, this means that outside of an unsafe context, it's impossible to access uninitialized memory. Definite assignment has three implications:

- Local variables must be assigned a value before they can be read.
- Function arguments must be supplied when a method is called (unless marked as optional—see "Optional parameters" on page 48).
- All other variables (such as fields and array elements) are automatically initialized by the runtime.

For example, the following code results in a compile-time error:

```
static void Main()
{
  int x;
  Console.WriteLine (x);        // Compile-time error
}
```

Fields and array elements are automatically initialized with the default values for their type. The following code outputs 0, because array elements are implicitly assigned to their default values:

```
static void Main()
{
  int[] ints = new int[2];
  Console.WriteLine (ints[0]);    // 0
}
```

The following code outputs 0, because fields are implicitly assigned a default value:

```
class Test
{
  static int x;
  static void Main() { Console.WriteLine (x); }   // 0
}
```

Default Values

All type instances have a default value. The default value for the predefined types is the result of a bitwise zeroing of memory:

Type	Default value
All reference types	null
All numeric and enum types	0
char type	'\0'
bool type	false

You can obtain the default value for any type with the default keyword (in practice, this is useful with generics which we'll cover in Chapter 3):

```
decimal d = default (decimal);
```

The default value in a custom value type (i.e., struct) is the same as the default value for each field defined by the custom type.

Parameters

A method has a sequence of parameters. Parameters define the set of arguments that must be provided for that method. In this example, the method Foo has a single parameter named p, of type int:

```
static void Foo (int p)
{
  p = p + 1;                  // Increment p by 1
```

```
    Console.WriteLine (p);      // Write p to screen
}

static void Main()
{
  Foo (8);                      // Call Foo with an argument of 8
}
```

You can control how parameters are passed with the `ref` and `out` modifiers:

Parameter modifier	Passed by	Variable must be definitely assigned
(None)	Value	Going *in*
ref	Reference	Going *in*
out	Reference	Going *out*

Passing arguments by value

By default, arguments in C# are *passed by value*, which is by far the most common case. This means a copy of the value is created when passed to the method:

```
class Test
{
  static void Foo (int p)
  {
    p = p + 1;                 // Increment p by 1
    Console.WriteLine (p);     // Write p to screen
  }

  static void Main()
  {
    int x = 8;
    Foo (x);                   // Make a copy of x
    Console.WriteLine (x);     // x will still be 8
  }
}
```

Assigning p a new value does not change the contents of x, since p and x reside in different memory locations.

Passing a reference-type argument by value copies the *reference*, but not the object. In the following example, Foo sees the same `StringBuilder` object that Main instantiated, but has an independent *reference* to it. In other words, sb and fooSB are separate variables that reference the same `StringBuilder` object:

```
class Test
{
  static void Foo (StringBuilder fooSB)
  {
    fooSB.Append ("test");
    fooSB = null;
  }
```

```
static void Main()
{
  StringBuilder sb = new StringBuilder();
  Foo (sb);
  Console.WriteLine (sb.ToString());     // test
}
}
```

Because fooSB is a *copy* of a reference, setting it to null doesn't make sb null. (If, however, fooSB was declared and called with the ref modifier, sb *would* become null.)

The ref modifier

To *pass by reference*, C# provides the ref parameter modifier. In the following example, p and x refer to the same memory locations:

```
class Test
{
  static void Foo (ref int p)
  {
    p = p + 1;                 // Increment p by 1
    Console.WriteLine (p);     // Write p to screen
  }

  static void Main()
  {
    int x = 8;
    Foo (ref  x);             // Ask Foo to deal directly with x
    Console.WriteLine (x);    // x is now 9
  }
}
```

Now assigning p a new value changes the contents of x. Notice how the ref modifier is required both when writing and when calling the method.[4] This makes it very clear what's going on.

The ref modifier is essential in implementing a swap method (later, in "Generics" on page 114 in Chapter 3, we will show how to write a swap method that works with any type):

```
class Test
{
  static void Swap (ref string a, ref string b)
  {
    string temp = a;
    a = b;
    b = temp;
  }
```

---

4 An exception to this rule is when calling COM methods. We discuss this in Chapter 25.

```
static void Main()
{
  string x = "Penn";
  string y = "Teller";
  Swap (ref x, ref y);
  Console.WriteLine (x);    // Teller
  Console.WriteLine (y);    // Penn
}
}
```

A parameter can be passed by reference or by value, regardless
of whether the parameter type is a reference type or a value
type.

The out modifier

An out argument is like a ref argument, except it:

- Need not be assigned before going into the function
- Must be assigned before it comes *out* of the function

The out modifier is most commonly used to get multiple return values back from a
method. For example:

```
class Test
{
  static void Split (string name, out string firstNames,
                     out string lastName)
  {
    int i = name.LastIndexOf (' ');
    firstNames = name.Substring (0, i);
    lastName    = name.Substring (i + 1);
  }

  static void Main()
  {
    string a, b;
    Split ("Stevie Ray Vaughan", out a, out b);
    Console.WriteLine (a);                      // Stevie Ray
    Console.WriteLine (b);                      // Vaughan
  }
}
```

Like a ref parameter, an out parameter is passed by reference.

Implications of passing by reference

When you pass an argument by reference, you alias the storage location of an existing variable rather than create a new storage location. In the following example, the
variables x and y represent the same instance:

```
class Test
{
```

```
static int x;

static void Main() { Foo (out x); }

static void Foo (out int y)
{
  Console.WriteLine (x);          // x is 0
  y = 1;                          // Mutate y
  Console.WriteLine (x);          // x is 1
  }
}
```

The params modifier

The `params` parameter modifier may be specified on the last parameter of a method
so that the method accepts any number of arguments of a particular type. The
parameter type must be declared as an array. For example:

```
class Test
{
  static int Sum (params int[] ints)
  {
    int sum = 0;
    for (int i = 0; i < ints.Length; i++)
      sum += ints[i];              // Increase sum by ints[i]
    return sum;
  }

  static void Main()
  {
    int total = Sum (1, 2, 3, 4);
    Console.WriteLine (total);     // 10
  }
}
```

You can also supply a `params` argument as an ordinary array. The first line in `Main` is
semantically equivalent to this:

```
int total = Sum (new int[] { 1, 2, 3, 4 } );
```

Optional parameters

From C# 4.0, methods, constructors, and indexers (Chapter 3) can declare *optional
parameters*. A parameter is optional if it specifies a *default value* in its declaration:

```
void Foo (int x = 23) { Console.WriteLine (x); }
```

Optional parameters may be omitted when calling the method:

```
Foo();     // 23
```

The *default argument* of 23 is actually *passed* to the optional parameter x—the compiler bakes the value 23 into the compiled code at the *calling* side. The preceding call
to `Foo` is semantically identical to:

```
Foo (23);
```

because the compiler simply substitutes the default value of an optional parameter wherever it is used.

 Adding an optional parameter to a public method that's called from another assembly requires recompilation of both assemblies—just as though the parameter were mandatory.

The default value of an optional parameter must be specified by a constant expression, or a parameterless constructor of a value type. Optional parameters cannot be marked with ref or out.

Mandatory parameters must occur *before* optional parameters in both the method declaration and the method call (the exception is with params arguments, which still always come last). In the following example, the explicit value of 1 is passed to x, and the default value of 0 is passed to y:

```
void Foo (int x = 0, int y = 0) { Console.WriteLine (x + ", " + y); }

void Test()
{
  Foo(1);    // 1, 0
}
```

To do the converse (pass a default value to x and an explicit value to y), you must combine optional parameters with *named arguments*.

Named arguments

Rather than identifying an argument by position, you can identify an argument by name. For example:

```
void Foo (int x, int y) { Console.WriteLine (x + ", " + y); }

void Test()
{
  Foo (x:1, y:2);  // 1, 2
}
```

Named arguments can occur in any order. The following calls to Foo are semantically identical:

```
Foo (x:1, y:2);
Foo (y:2, x:1);
```

 A subtle difference is that argument expressions are evaluated in the order in which they appear at the *calling* site. In general, this makes a difference only with interdependent side-effecting expressions such as the following, which writes 0, 1:

```
int a = 0;
Foo (y: ++a, x: --a);  // ++a is evaluated first
```

Of course, you would almost certainly avoid writing such code in practice!

You can mix named and positional arguments:

```
Foo (1, y:2);
```

However, there is a restriction: positional arguments must come before named arguments. So we couldn't call Foo like this:

```
Foo (x:1, 2);          // Compile-time error
```

Named arguments are particularly useful in conjunction with optional parameters. For instance, consider the following method:

```
void Bar (int a = 0, int b = 0, int c = 0, int d = 0) { ... }
```

We can call this supplying only a value for d as follows:

```
Bar (d:3);
```

This is particularly useful when calling COM APIs, and is discussed in detail in Chapter 25.

var—Implicitly Typed Local Variables

It is often the case that you declare and initialize a variable in one step. If the compiler is able to infer the type from the initialization expression, you can use the keyword var (introduced in C# 3.0) in place of the type declaration. For example:

```
var x = "hello";
var y = new System.Text.StringBuilder();
var z = (float)Math.PI;
```

This is precisely equivalent to:

```
string x = "hello";
System.Text.StringBuilder y = new System.Text.StringBuilder();
float z = (float)Math.PI;
```

Because of this direct equivalence, implicitly typed variables are statically typed. For example, the following generates a compile-time error:

```
var x = 5;
x = "hello";       // Compile-time error; x is of type int
```

 var can decrease code readability in the case when *you can't deduce the type purely by looking at the variable declaration*. For example:

```
Random r = new Random();
var x = r.Next();
```

What type is x?

In "Anonymous Types" on page 174 in Chapter 4, we will describe a scenario where the use of var is mandatory.

Expressions and Operators

An *expression* essentially denotes a value. The simplest kinds of expressions are constants and variables. Expressions can be transformed and combined using operators. An *operator* takes one or more input *operands* to output a new expression.

Here is an example of a *constant expression*:

```
12
```

We can use the * operator to combine two operands (the literal expressions 12 and 30), as follows:

```
12 * 30
```

Complex expressions can be built because an operand may itself be an expression, such as the operand (12 * 30) in the following example:

```
1 + (12 * 30)
```

Operators in C# can be classed as *unary, binary,* or *ternary*—depending on the number of operands they work on (one, two, or three). The binary operators always use *infix* notation, where the operator is placed *between* the two operands.

Primary Expressions

Primary expressions include expressions composed of operators that are intrinsic to the basic plumbing of the language. Here is an example:

```
Math.Log (1)
```

This expression is composed of two primary expressions. The first expression performs a member-lookup (with the . operator), and the second expression performs a method call (with the () operator).

Void Expressions

A void expression is an expression that has no value. For example:

```
Console.WriteLine (1)
```

A void expression, since it has no value, cannot be used as an operand to build more complex expressions:

```
1 + Console.WriteLine (1)      // Compile-time error
```

Assignment Expressions

An assignment expression uses the = operator to assign the result of another expression to a variable. For example:

```
x = x * 5
```

An assignment expression is not a void expression—it has a value of whatever was assigned, and so can be incorporated into another expression. In the following example, the expression assigns 2 to x and 10 to y:

```
y = 5 * (x = 2)
```

This style of expression can be used to initialize multiple values:

```
a = b = c = d = 0
```

The *compound assignment operators* are syntactic shortcuts that combine assignment with another operator. For example:

```
x *= 2     // equivalent to x = x * 2
x <<= 1    // equivalent to x = x << 1
```

(A subtle exception to this rule is with *events*, which we describe in Chapter 4: the += and -= operators here are treated specially and map to the event's add and remove accessors.)

Operator Precedence and Associativity

When an expression contains multiple operators, *precedence* and *associativity* determine the order of their evaluation. Operators with higher precedence execute before operators of lower precedence. If the operators have the same precedence, the operator's associativity determines the order of evaluation.

Precedence

The following expression:

```
1 + 2 * 3
```

is evaluated as follows because * has a higher precedence than +:

```
1 + (2 * 3)
```

Left-associative operators

Binary operators (except for assignment, lambda, and null-coalescing operators) are *left-associative*; in other words, they are evaluated from left to right. For example, the following expression:

```
8 / 4 / 2
```

is evaluated as follows due to left associativity:

```
( 8 / 4 ) / 2    // 1
```

You can insert parentheses to change the actual order of evaluation:

```
8 / ( 4 / 2 )    // 4
```

Right-associative operators

The *assignment operators*, lambda, null-coalescing, and conditional operator are *right-associative*; in other words, they are evaluated from right to left. Right associativity allows multiple assignments such as the following to compile:

```
x = y = 3;
```

This first assigns 3 to y, and then assigns the result of that expression (3) to x.

Operator Table

Table 2-3 lists C#'s operators in order of precedence. Operators in the same category have the same precedence. We explain user-overloadable operators in "Operator Overloading" on page 168 in Chapter 4.

Table 2-3. C# operators (categories in order of precedence)

Category	Operator symbol	Operator name	Example	User-overloadable
Primary	.	Member access	x.y	No
	-> (unsafe)	Pointer to struct	x->y	No
	()	Function call	x()	No
	[]	Array/index	a[x]	Via indexer
	++	Post-increment	x++	Yes
	--	Post-decrement	x--	Yes
	new	Create instance	new Foo()	No
	stackalloc	Unsafe stack allocation	stackalloc(10)	No
	typeof	Get type from identifier	typeof(int)	No
	nameof	Get name of identifier	nameof(x)	No
	checked	Integral overflow check on	checked(x)	No
	unchecked	Integral overflow check off	unchecked(x)	No
	default	Default value	default(char)	No
Unary	await	Await	await myTask	No
	sizeof	Get size of struct	sizeof(int)	No
	?.	Null-conditional	x?.y	No
	+	Positive value of	+x	Yes
	−	Negative value of	−x	Yes
	!	Not	!x	Yes

Category	Operator symbol	Operator name	Example	User-overloadable
	~	Bitwise complement	~x	Yes
	++	Pre-increment	++x	Yes
	--	Pre-decrement	--x	Yes
	( )	Cast	(int)x	No
	* (unsafe)	Value at address	*x	No
	& (unsafe)	Address of value	&x	No
Multiplicative	*	Multiply	x * y	Yes
	/	Divide	x / y	Yes
	%	Remainder	x % y	Yes
Additive	+	Add	x + y	Yes
	-	Subtract	x - y	Yes
Shift	<<	Shift left	x << 1	Yes
	>>	Shift right	x >> 1	Yes
Relational	<	Less than	x < y	Yes
	>	Greater than	x > y	Yes
	<=	Less than or equal to	x <= y	Yes
	>=	Greater than or equal to	x >= y	Yes
	is	Type is or is subclass of	x is y	No
	as	Type conversion	x as y	No
Equality	==	Equals	x == y	Yes
	!=	Not equals	x != y	Yes
Logical And	&	And	x & y	Yes
Logical Xor	^	Exclusive Or	x ^ y	Yes
Logical Or	|	Or	x | y	Yes
Conditional And	&&	Conditional And	x && y	Via &
Conditional Or	||	Conditional Or	x || y	Via |
Null-coalescing	??	Null-coalescing	x ?? y	No
Conditional	?:	Conditional	isTrue ? thenThis Value : elseThis Value	No
Assignment & Lambda	=	Assign	x = y	No
	*=	Multiply self by	x *= 2	Via *

Category	Operator symbol	Operator name	Example	User-overloadable
	/=	Divide self by	x /= 2	Via /
	+=	Add to self	x += 2	Via +
	-=	Subtract from self	x -= 2	Via -
	<<=	Shift self left by	x <<= 2	Via <<
	>>=	Shift self right by	x >>= 2	Via >>
	&=	And self by	x &= 2	Via &
	^=	Exclusive-Or self by	x ^= 2	Via ^
	|=	Or self by	x |= 2	Via |
	=>	Lambda	x => x + 1	No

Null Operators

C# provides two operators to make it easier to work with nulls: the *null-coalescing operator* and the *null-conditional operator*.

Null-Coalescing Operator

The ?? operator is the *null-coalescing operator*. It says "If the operand is non-null, give it to me; otherwise, give me a default value." For example:

```
string s1 = null;
string s2 = s1 ?? "nothing";   // s2 evaluates to "nothing"
```

If the left-hand expression is non-null, the right-hand expression is never evaluated. The null-coalescing operator also works with nullable value types (see "Nullable Types" on page 162 in Chapter 4).

Null-conditional operator (C# 6)

The ?. operator is the *null-conditional* or "Elvis" operator, and is new to C# 6. It allows you to call methods and access members just like the standard dot operator, except that if the operand on the left is null, the expression evaluates to null instead of throwing a NullReferenceException:

```
System.Text.StringBuilder sb = null;
string s = sb?.ToString();  // No error; s instead evaluates to null
```

The last line is equivalent to:

```
string s = (sb == null ? null : sb.ToString());
```

Upon encountering a null, the Elvis operator short-circuits the remainder of the expression. In the following example, s evaluates to null, even with a standard dot operator between ToString() and ToUpper():

```
System.Text.StringBuilder sb = null;
string s = sb?.ToString().ToUpper();   // s evaluates to null without error
```

Repeated use of Elvis is necessary only if the operand immediately to its left may be null. The following expression is robust to both x being null and x.y being null:

```
x?.y?.z
```

and is equivalent to the following (except that x.y is evaluated only once):

```
x == null ? null
        : (x.y == null ? null : x.y.z)
```

The final expression must be capable of accepting a null. The following is illegal:

```
System.Text.StringBuilder sb = null;
int length = sb?.ToString().Length;    // Illegal : int cannot be null
```

We can fix this with the use of nullable value types (see "Nullable Types" on page 162 in Chapter 4): If you're already familiar with nullable types, here's a preview:

```
int? length = sb?.ToString().Length;   // OK : int? can be null
```

You can also use the null-conditional operator to call a void method:

```
someObject?.SomeVoidMethod();
```

If someObject is null, this becomes a "no-operation" rather than throwing a NullRe
ferenceException.

The null-conditional operator can be used with the commonly used type members that we describe in Chapter 3, including *methods*, *fields*, *properties* and *indexers*. It also combines well with the *null-coalescing operator*:

```
System.Text.StringBuilder sb = null;
string s = sb?.ToString() ?? "nothing";   // s evaluates to "nothing"
```

The last line is equivalent to:

```
string s = (sb == null ? "nothing" : sb.ToString());
```

Statements

Functions comprise statements that execute sequentially in the textual order in which they appear. A *statement block* is a series of statements appearing between braces (the {} tokens).

Declaration Statements

A declaration statement declares a new variable, optionally initializing the variable with an expression. A declaration statement ends in a semicolon. You may declare multiple variables of the same type in a comma-separated list. For example:

```
string someWord = "rosebud";
int someNumber = 42;
bool rich = true, famous = false;
```

A constant declaration is like a variable declaration, except that it cannot be changed after it has been declared, and the initialization must occur with the declaration (see "Constants" on page 83 in Chapter 3):

```
const double c = 2.99792458E08;
c += 10;                          // Compile-time Error
```

Local variables

The scope of a local variable or local constant extends throughout the current block. You cannot declare another local variable with the same name in the current block or in any nested blocks. For example:

```
static void Main()
{
  int x;
  {
    int y;
    int x;          // Error - x already defined
  }
  {
    int y;          // OK - y not in scope
  }
  Console.Write (y);  // Error - y is out of scope
}
```

 A variable's scope extends in *both directions* throughout its code block. This means that if we moved the initial declaration of x in this example to the bottom of the method, we'd get the same error. This is in contrast to C++ and is somewhat peculiar, given that it's not legal to refer to a variable or constant before it's declared.

Expression Statements

Expression statements are expressions that are also valid statements. An expression statement must either change state or call something that might change state. Changing state essentially means changing a variable. The possible expression statements are:

- Assignment expressions (including increment and decrement expressions)
- Method call expressions (both void and nonvoid)
- Object instantiation expressions

Here are some examples:

```
// Declare variables with declaration statements:
string s;
int x, y;
System.Text.StringBuilder sb;

// Expression statements
```

```
x = 1 + 2;                 // Assignment expression
x++;                       // Increment expression
y = Math.Max (x, 5);       // Assignment expression
Console.WriteLine (y);     // Method call expression
sb = new StringBuilder();  // Assignment expression
new StringBuilder();       // Object instantiation expression
```

When you call a constructor or a method that returns a value, you're not obliged to use the result. However, unless the constructor or method changes state, the statement is completely useless:

```
new StringBuilder();       // Legal, but useless
new string ('c', 3);       // Legal, but useless
x.Equals (y);              // Legal, but useless
```

Selection Statements

C# has the following mechanisms to conditionally control the flow of program execution:

- Selection statements (if, switch)
- Conditional operator (?:)
- Loop statements (while, do..while, for, foreach)

This section covers the simplest two constructs: the if-else statement and the switch statement.

The if statement

An if statement executes a statement if a bool expression is true. For example:

```
if (5 < 2 * 3)
    Console.WriteLine ("true");        // true
```

The statement can be a code block:

```
if (5 < 2 * 3)
{
  Console.WriteLine ("true");
  Console.WriteLine ("Let's move on!");
}
```

The else clause

An if statement can optionally feature an else clause:

```
if (2 + 2 == 5)
  Console.WriteLine ("Does not compute");
else
  Console.WriteLine ("False");         // False
```

Within an else clause, you can nest another if statement:

```
if (2 + 2 == 5)
  Console.WriteLine ("Does not compute");
else
  if (2 + 2 == 4)
    Console.WriteLine ("Computes");    // Computes
```

Changing the flow of execution with braces

An else clause always applies to the immediately preceding if statement in the statement block. For example:

```
if (true)
  if (false)
    Console.WriteLine();
  else
    Console.WriteLine ("executes");
```

This is semantically identical to:

```
if (true)
{
  if (false)
    Console.WriteLine();
  else
    Console.WriteLine ("executes");
}
```

We can change the execution flow by moving the braces:

```
if (true)
{
  if (false)
    Console.WriteLine();
}
else
  Console.WriteLine ("does not execute");
```

With braces, you explicitly state your intention. This can improve the readability of nested if statements—even when not required by the compiler. A notable exception is with the following pattern:

```
static void TellMeWhatICanDo (int age)
{
  if (age >= 35)
    Console.WriteLine ("You can be president!");
  else if (age >= 21)
    Console.WriteLine ("You can drink!");
  else if (age >= 18)
    Console.WriteLine ("You can vote!");
  else
    Console.WriteLine ("You can wait!");
}
```

Here, we've arranged the if and else statements to mimic the "elseif" construct of other languages (and C#'s #elif preprocessor directive). Visual Studio's auto-formatting recognizes this pattern and preserves the indentation. Semantically, though, each if statement following an else statement is functionally nested within the else clause.

The switch statement

switch statements let you branch program execution based on a selection of possible values that a variable may have. switch statements may result in cleaner code than multiple if statements, since switch statements require an expression to be evaluated only once. For instance:

```
static void ShowCard(int cardNumber)
{
  switch (cardNumber)
  {
    case 13:
      Console.WriteLine ("King");
      break;
    case 12:
      Console.WriteLine ("Queen");
      break;
    case 11:
      Console.WriteLine ("Jack");
      break;
    case -1:                          // Joker is -1
      goto case 12;                   // In this game joker counts as queen
    default:                          // Executes for any other cardNumber
      Console.WriteLine (cardNumber);
      break;
  }
}
```

You can only switch on an expression of a type that can be statically evaluated, which restricts it to the built-in integral types, bool, and enum types (and nullable versions of these—see Chapter 4), and string type.

At the end of each case clause, you must say explicitly where execution is to go next, with some kind of jump statement. Here are the options:

- break (jumps to the end of the switch statement)
- goto case *x* (jumps to another case clause)
- goto default (jumps to the default clause)
- Any other jump statement—namely, return, throw, continue, or goto *label*

When more than one value should execute the same code, you can list the common cases sequentially:

```
switch (cardNumber)
{
  case 13:
  case 12:
  case 11:
```

```
      Console.WriteLine ("Face card");
      break;
    default:
      Console.WriteLine ("Plain card");
      break;
  }
```

This feature of a switch statement can be pivotal in terms of producing cleaner code than multiple if-else statements.

Iteration Statements

C# enables a sequence of statements to execute repeatedly with the while, do-while, for, and foreach statements.

while and do-while loops

while loops repeatedly execute a body of code while a bool expression is true. The expression is tested *before* the body of the loop is executed. For example:

```
int i = 0;
while (i < 3)
{
  Console.WriteLine (i);
  i++;
}

OUTPUT:
0
1
2
```

do-while loops differ in functionality from while loops only in that they test the expression *after* the statement block has executed (ensuring that the block is always executed at least once). Here's the preceding example rewritten with a do-while loop:

```
int i = 0;
do
{
  Console.WriteLine (i);
  i++;
}
while (i < 3);
```

for loops

for loops are like while loops with special clauses for *initialization* and *iteration* of a loop variable. A for loop contains three clauses as follows:

```
for (initialization-clause; condition-clause; iteration-clause)
  statement-or-statement-block
```

Initialization clause

> Executed before the loop begins; used to initialize one or more *iteration variables*

Condition clause

> The `bool` expression that, while true, will execute the body

Iteration clause

> Executed *after* each iteration of the statement block; used typically to update the iteration variable

For example, the following prints the numbers 0 through 2:

```
for (int i = 0; i < 3; i++)
    Console.WriteLine (i);
```

The following prints the first 10 Fibonacci numbers (where each number is the sum of the previous two):

```
for (int i = 0, prevFib = 1, curFib = 1; i < 10; i++)
{
    Console.WriteLine (prevFib);
    int newFib = prevFib + curFib;
    prevFib = curFib; curFib = newFib;
}
```

Any of the three parts of the `for` statement may be omitted. One can implement an infinite loop such as the following (though `while(true)` may be used instead):

```
for (;;)
    Console.WriteLine ("interrupt me");
```

foreach loops

The `foreach` statement iterates over each element in an enumerable object. Most of the types in C# and the .NET Framework that represent a set or list of elements are enumerable. For example, both an array and a string are enumerable. Here is an example of enumerating over the characters in a string, from the first character through to the last:

```
foreach (char c in "beer")   // c is the iteration variable
    Console.WriteLine (c);

OUTPUT:
b
e
e
r
```

We define enumerable objects in "Enumeration and Iterators" on page 156 in Chapter 4.

Jump Statements

The C# jump statements are break, continue, goto, return, and throw.

 Jump statements obey the reliability rules of try statements (see "try Statements and Exceptions" on page 148 in Chapter 4). This means that:

- A jump out of a try block always executes the try's finally block before reaching the target of the jump.
- A jump cannot be made from the inside to the outside of a finally block (except via throw).

The break statement

The break statement ends the execution of the body of an iteration or switch statement:

```
int x = 0;
while (true)
{
  if (x++ > 5)
    break ;      // break from the loop
}
// execution continues here after break
...
```

The continue statement

The continue statement forgoes the remaining statements in a loop and makes an early start on the next iteration. The following loop skips even numbers:

```
for (int i = 0; i < 10; i++)
{
  if ((i % 2) == 0)      // If i is even,
    continue;            // continue with next iteration

  Console.Write (i + " ");
}
OUTPUT: 1 3 5 7 9
```

The goto statement

The goto statement transfers execution to another label within a statement block. The form is as follows:

```
goto statement-label;
```

Or, when used within a switch statement:

```
goto case case-constant;
```

A label is a placeholder in a code block that precedes a statement, denoted with a colon suffix. The following iterates the numbers 1 through 5, mimicking a `for` loop:

```
int i = 1;
startLoop:
if (i <= 5)
{
  Console.Write (i + " ");
  i++;
  goto startLoop;
}

OUTPUT: 1 2 3 4 5
```

The `goto case` *case-constant* transfers execution to another case in a `switch` block (see "The switch statement" on page 60).

The return statement

The `return` statement exits the method and must return an expression of the method's return type if the method is nonvoid:

```
static decimal AsPercentage (decimal d)
{
  decimal p = d * 100m;
  return p;                 // Return to the calling method with value
}
```

A `return` statement can appear anywhere in a method (except in a `finally` block).

The throw statement

The `throw` statement throws an exception to indicate an error has occurred (see "try Statements and Exceptions" on page 148 in Chapter 4):

```
if (w == null)
  throw new ArgumentNullException (...);
```

Miscellaneous Statements

The `using` statement provides an elegant syntax for calling `Dispose` on objects that implement `IDisposable`, within a `finally` block (see "try Statements and Exceptions" on page 148 in Chapter 4 and "IDisposable, Dispose, and Close" on page 499 in Chapter 12).

> C# overloads the `using` keyword to have independent meanings in different contexts. Specifically, the `using` *directive* is different from the `using` *statement*.

The `lock` statement is a shortcut for calling the `Enter` and `Exit` methods of the `Moni` `tor` class (see Chapter 14 and Chapter 23).

Namespaces

A namespace is a domain for type names. Types are typically organized into hierarchical namespaces, making them easier to find and avoiding conflicts. For example, the RSA type that handles public key encryption is defined within the following namespace:

```
System.Security.Cryptography
```

A namespace forms an integral part of a type's name. The following code calls RSA's Create method:

```
System.Security.Cryptography.RSA rsa =
    System.Security.Cryptography.RSA.Create();
```

 Namespaces are independent of assemblies, which are units of deployment such as an *.exe* or *.dll* (described in Chapter 18).

Namespaces also have no impact on member visibility—`public`, `internal`, `private`, and so on.

The `namespace` keyword defines a namespace for types within that block. For example:

```
namespace Outer.Middle.Inner
{
  class Class1 {}
  class Class2 {}
}
```

The dots in the namespace indicate a hierarchy of nested namespaces. The code that follows is semantically identical to the preceding example:

```
namespace Outer
{
  namespace Middle
  {
    namespace Inner
    {
      class Class1 {}
      class Class2 {}
    }
  }
}
```

You can refer to a type with its *fully qualified name*, which includes all namespaces from the outermost to the innermost. For example, we could refer to `Class1` in the preceding example as `Outer.Middle.Inner.Class1`.

Types not defined in any namespace are said to reside in the *global namespace*. The global namespace also includes top-level namespaces, such as `Outer` in our example.

The using Directive

The using directive *imports* a namespace, allowing you to refer to types without their fully qualified names. The following imports the previous example's Outer.Mid dle.Inner namespace:

```
using Outer.Middle.Inner;

class Test
{
  static void Main()
  {
    Class1 c;     // Don't need fully qualified name
  }
}
```

 It's legal (and often desirable) to define the same type name in different namespaces. However, you'd typically do so only if it was unlikely for a consumer to want to import both namespaces at once. A good example, from the .NET Framework, is the TextBox class which is defined both in System.Win dows.Controls (WPF) and System.Web.UI.WebControls (ASP.NET).

using static (C# 6)

From C# 6, you can import not just a namespace, but a specific type, with the using static directive. All static members of that type can then be used without being qualified with the type name. In the following example, we call the Console class's static WriteLine method:

```
using static System.Console;

class Test
{
  static void Main() { WriteLine ("Hello"); }
}
```

The using static directive imports all accessible static members of the type, including fields, properties and nested types (Chapter 3). You can also apply this directive to enum types (Chapter 3), in which case their members are imported. So, if we import the following enum type:

```
using static System.Windows.Visibility;
```

we can specify Hidden instead of Visibility.Hidden:

```
var textBox = new TextBox { Visibility = Hidden };    // XAML-style
```

Should an ambiguity arise between multiple static imports, the C# compiler is not smart enough to infer the correct type from the context, and will generate an error.

Rules Within a Namespace

Name scoping

Names declared in outer namespaces can be used unqualified within inner namespaces. In this example, Class1 does not need qualification within Inner:

```
namespace Outer
{
  class Class1 {}

  namespace Inner
  {
    class Class2 : Class1 {}
  }
}
```

If you want to refer to a type in a different branch of your namespace hierarchy, you can use a partially qualified name. In the following example, we base SalesReport on Common.ReportBase:

```
namespace MyTradingCompany
{
  namespace Common
  {
    class ReportBase {}
  }
  namespace ManagementReporting
  {
    class SalesReport : Common.ReportBase {}
  }
}
```

Name hiding

If the same type name appears in both an inner and an outer namespace, the inner name wins. To refer to the type in the outer namespace, you must qualify its name. For example:

```
namespace Outer
{
  class Foo { }

  namespace Inner
  {
    class Foo { }

    class Test
    {
      Foo f1;          // = Outer.Inner.Foo
      Outer.Foo f2;    // = Outer.Foo
    }
```

```
      }
    }
```

 All type names are converted to fully qualified names at compile time. Intermediate language (IL) code contains no unqualified or partially qualified names.

Repeated namespaces

You can repeat a namespace declaration, as long as the type names within the namespaces don't conflict:

```
namespace Outer.Middle.Inner
{
  class Class1 {}
}

namespace Outer.Middle.Inner
{
  class Class2 {}
}
```

We can even break the example into two source files such that we could compile
each class into a different assembly.

Source file 1:

```
namespace Outer.Middle.Inner
{
  class Class1 {}
}
```

Source file 2:

```
namespace Outer.Middle.Inner
{
  class Class2 {}
}
```

Nested using directive

You can nest a using directive within a namespace. This allows you to scope the
using directive within a namespace declaration. In the following example, Class1 is
visible in one scope, but not in another:

```
namespace N1
{
  class Class1 {}
}

namespace N2
{
  using N1;

  class Class2 : Class1 {}
```

```
}

namespace N2
{
  class Class3 : Class1 {}    // Compile-time error
}
```

Aliasing Types and Namespaces

Importing a namespace can result in type-name collision. Rather than importing the whole namespace, you can import just the specific types you need, giving each type an alias. For example:

```
using PropertyInfo2 = System.Reflection.PropertyInfo;
class Program { PropertyInfo2 p; }
```

An entire namespace can be aliased, as follows:

```
using R = System.Reflection;
class Program { R.PropertyInfo p; }
```

Advanced Namespace Features

Extern

Extern aliases allow your program to reference two types with the same fully qualified name (i.e., the namespace and type name are identical). This is an unusual scenario and can occur only when the two types come from different assemblies. Consider the following example.

Library 1:

```
// csc target:library /out:Widgets1.dll widgetsv1.cs

namespace Widgets
{
  public class Widget {}
}
```

Library 2:

```
// csc target:library /out:Widgets2.dll widgetsv2.cs

namespace Widgets
{
  public class Widget {}
}
```

Application:

```
// csc /r:Widgets1.dll /r:Widgets2.dll application.cs

using Widgets;

class Test
{
```

```
  static void Main()
  {
    Widget w = new Widget();
  }
}
```

The application cannot compile, because Widget is ambiguous. Extern aliases can resolve the ambiguity in our application:

```
// csc /r:W1=Widgets1.dll /r:W2=Widgets2.dll application.cs

extern alias W1;
extern alias W2;

class Test
{
  static void Main()
  {
    W1.Widgets.Widget w1 = new W1.Widgets.Widget();
    W2.Widgets.Widget w2 = new W2.Widgets.Widget();
  }
}
```

Namespace alias qualifiers

As we mentioned earlier, names in inner namespaces hide names in outer namespaces. However, sometimes even the use of a fully qualified type name does not resolve the conflict. Consider the following example:

```
namespace N
{
  class A
  {
    public class B {}                  // Nested type
    static void Main() { new A.B(); }   // Instantiate class B
  }
}

namespace A
{
  class B {}
}
```

The Main method could be instantiating either the nested class B, or the class B within the namespace A. The compiler always gives higher precedence to identifiers in the current namespace; in this case, the nested B class.

To resolve such conflicts, a namespace name can be qualified, relative to one of the following:

- The global namespace—the root of all namespaces (identified with the contextual keyword global)
- The set of extern aliases

The :: token is used for namespace alias qualification. In this example, we qualify using the global namespace (this is most commonly seen in auto-generated code to avoid name conflicts):

```
namespace N
{
  class A
  {
    static void Main()
    {
      System.Console.WriteLine (new A.B());
      System.Console.WriteLine (new global::A.B());
    }

    public class B {}
  }
}

namespace A
{
  class B {}
}
```

Here is an example of qualifying with an alias (adapted from the example in "Extern" on page 69):

```
extern alias W1;
extern alias W2;
class Test
{
  static void Main()
  {
    W1::Widgets.Widget w1 = new W1::Widgets.Widget();
    W2::Widgets.Widget w2 = new W2::Widgets.Widget();
  }
}
```

3

Creating Types in C#

In this chapter, we will delve into types and type members.

Classes

A class is the most common kind of reference type. The simplest possible class declaration is as follows:

```
class YourClassName
{
}
```

A more complex class optionally has the following:

Preceding the keyword `class`	*Attributes* and *class modifiers*. The non-nested class modifiers are `public`, `internal`, `abstract`, `sealed`, `static`, `unsafe`, and `partial`
Following `YourClassName`	*Generic type parameters*, a *base class*, and *interfaces*
Within the braces	*Class members* (these are *methods, properties, indexers, events, fields, constructors, overloaded operators, nested types*, and a *finalizer*)

This chapter covers all of these constructs except attributes, operator functions, and the `unsafe` keyword, which are covered in Chapter 4. The following sections enumerate each of the class members.

Fields

A *field* is a variable that is a member of a class or struct. For example:

```
class Octopus
{
  string name;
  public int Age = 10;
}
```

Fields allow the following modifiers:

Static modifier	`static`
Access modifiers	`public internal private protected`
Inheritance modifier	`new`
Unsafe code modifier	`unsafe`
Read-only modifier	`readonly`
Threading modifier	`volatile`

The readonly modifier

The `readonly` modifier prevents a field from being modified after construction. A read-only field can be assigned only in its declaration or within the enclosing type's constructor.

Field initialization

Field initialization is optional. An uninitialized field has a default value (0, \0, null, false). Field initializers run before constructors:

```
public int Age = 10;
```

Declaring multiple fields together

For convenience, you may declare multiple fields of the same type in a comma-separated list. This is a convenient way for all the fields to share the same attributes and field modifiers. For example:

```
static readonly int legs = 8,
                    eyes = 2;
```

Methods

A method performs an action in a series of statements. A method can receive *input* data from the caller by specifying *parameters* and *output* data back to the caller by specifying a *return type*. A method can specify a void return type, indicating that it doesn't return any value to its caller. A method can also output data back to the caller via ref/out parameters.

A method's *signature* must be unique within the type. A method's signature comprises its name and parameter types (but not the parameter *names*, nor the return type).

Methods allow the following modifiers:

Static modifier	static
Access modifiers	public internal private protected
Inheritance modifiers	new virtual abstract override sealed
Partial method modifier	partial
Unmanaged code modifiers	unsafe extern
Asynchronous code modifier	async

Expression-bodied methods (C# 6)

A method that comprises a single expression, such as the following:

```
int Foo (int x) { return x * 2; }
```

can be written more tersely as an *expression-bodied method*. A fat arrow replaces the braces and return keyword:

```
int Foo (int x) => x * 2;
```

Expression-bodied functions can also have a void return type:

```
void Foo (int x) => Console.WriteLine (x);
```

Overloading methods

A type may overload methods (have multiple methods with the same name), as long as the signatures are different. For example, the following methods can all coexist in the same type:

```
void Foo (int x) {...}
void Foo (double x) {...}
void Foo (int x, float y) {...}
void Foo (float x, int y) {...}
```

However, the following pairs of methods cannot coexist in the same type, since the return type and the params modifier are not part of a method's signature:

```
void  Foo (int x) {...}
float Foo (int x) {...}             // Compile-time error

void  Goo (int[] x) {...}
void  Goo (params int[] x) {...}  // Compile-time error
```

Pass-by-value versus pass-by-reference

Whether a parameter is pass-by-value or pass-by-reference is also part of the signature. For example, Foo(int) can coexist with either Foo(ref int) or Foo(out int). However, Foo(ref int) and Foo(out int) cannot coexist:

```
void Foo (int x) {...}
void Foo (ref int x) {...}      // OK so far
void Foo (out int x) {...}      // Compile-time error
```

Instance Constructors

Constructors run initialization code on a class or struct. A constructor is defined like a method, except that the method name and return type are reduced to the name of the enclosing type:

```
public class Panda
{
  string name;                  // Define field
  public Panda (string n)       // Define constructor
  {
    name = n;                   // Initialization code (set up field)
  }
}
...

    Panda p = new Panda ("Petey");   // Call constructor
```

Instance constructors allow the following modifiers:

Access modifiers	public internal private protected
Unmanaged code modifiers	unsafe extern

Overloading constructors

A class or struct may overload constructors. To avoid code duplication, one constructor may call another, using the this keyword:

```
using System;

public class Wine
{
  public decimal Price;
  public int Year;
  public Wine (decimal price) { Price = price; }
  public Wine (decimal price, int year) : this (price) { Year = year; }
}
```

When one constructor calls another, the *called constructor* executes first.

You can pass an *expression* into another constructor as follows:

```
public Wine (decimal price, DateTime year) : this (price, year.Year) { }
```

The expression itself cannot make use of the `this` reference, for example, to call an instance method. (This is enforced because the object has not been initialized by the constructor at this stage, so any methods that you call on it are likely to fail.) It can, however, call static methods.

Implicit parameterless constructors

For classes, the C# compiler automatically generates a parameterless public constructor if and only if you do not define any constructors. However, as soon as you define at least one constructor, the parameterless constructor is no longer automatically generated.

Constructor and field initialization order

We saw previously that fields can be initialized with default values in their declaration:

```
class Player
{
  int shields = 50;    // Initialized first
  int health = 100;    // Initialized second
}
```

Field initializations occur *before* the constructor is executed and in the declaration order of the fields.

Nonpublic constructors

Constructors do not need to be public. A common reason to have a nonpublic constructor is to control instance creation via a static method call. The static method could be used to return an object from a pool rather than necessarily creating a new object, or return various subclasses based on input arguments:

```
public class Class1
{
  Class1() {}                              // Private constructor
  public static Class1 Create (...)
  {
    // Perform custom logic here to return an instance of Class1
    ...
  }
}
```

Object Initializers

To simplify object initialization, any accessible fields or properties of an object can be set via an *object initializer* directly after construction. For example, consider the following class:

```
public class Bunny
{
  public string Name;
  public bool LikesCarrots;
```

```
    public bool LikesHumans;

    public Bunny () {}
    public Bunny (string n) { Name = n; }
}
```

Using object initializers, you can instantiate Bunny objects as follows:

```
// Note parameterless constructors can omit empty parentheses
Bunny b1 = new Bunny { Name="Bo", LikesCarrots=true, LikesHumans=false };
Bunny b2 = new Bunny ("Bo")    { LikesCarrots=true, LikesHumans=false };
```

The code to construct b1 and b2 is precisely equivalent to:

```
Bunny temp1 = new Bunny();    // temp1 is a compiler-generated name
temp1.Name = "Bo";
temp1.LikesCarrots = true;
temp1.LikesHumans = false;
Bunny b1 = temp1;

Bunny temp2 = new Bunny ("Bo");
temp2.LikesCarrots = true;
temp2.LikesHumans = false;
Bunny b2 = temp2;
```

The temporary variables are to ensure that if an exception is thrown during initialization, you can't end up with a half-initialized object.

Object initializers were introduced in C# 3.0.

Object Initializers Versus Optional Parameters

Instead of using object initializers, we could make Bunny's constructor accept optional parameters:

```
public Bunny (string name,
              bool likesCarrots = false,
              bool likesHumans = false)
{
  Name = name;
  LikesCarrots = likesCarrots;
  LikesHumans = likesHumans;
}
```

This would allow us to construct a Bunny as follows:

```
Bunny b1 = new Bunny (name: "Bo",
                      likesCarrots: true);
```

An advantage of this approach is that we could make Bunny's fields (or *properties*, as we'll explain shortly) read-only if we choose. Making fields or properties read-only is good practice when there's no valid reason for them to change throughout the life of the object.

The disadvantage in this approach is that each optional parameter value is baked into the *calling site*. In other words, C# translates our constructor call into this:

```
Bunny b1 = new Bunny ("Bo", true, false);
```

This can be problematic if we instantiate the Bunny class from another assembly and later modify Bunny by adding another optional parameter—such as likesCats. Unless the referencing assembly is also recompiled, it will continue to call the (now nonexistent) constructor with three parameters and fail at runtime. (A subtler problem is that if we changed the value of one of the optional parameters, callers in other assemblies would continue to use the old optional value until they were recompiled.)

Hence, you should exercise caution with optional parameters in public functions if you want to offer binary compatibility between assembly versions.

The this Reference

The this reference refers to the instance itself. In the following example, the Marry method uses this to set the partner's mate field:

```
public class Panda
{
  public Panda Mate;

  public void Marry (Panda partner)
  {
    Mate = partner;
    partner.Mate = this;
  }
}
```

The this reference also disambiguates a local variable or parameter from a field. For example:

```
public class Test
{
  string name;
  public Test (string name) { this.name = name; }
}
```

The this reference is valid only within nonstatic members of a class or struct.

Properties

Properties look like fields from the outside, but internally they contain logic, like methods do. For example, you can't tell by looking at the following code whether CurrentPrice is a field or a property:

```
Stock msft = new Stock();
msft.CurrentPrice = 30;
msft.CurrentPrice -= 3;
Console.WriteLine (msft.CurrentPrice);
```

A property is declared like a field, but with a get/set block added. Here's how to implement CurrentPrice as a property:

```
public class Stock
{
  decimal currentPrice;          // The private "backing" field

  public decimal CurrentPrice    // The public property
  {
    get { return currentPrice; }
    set { currentPrice = value; }
  }
}
```

get and set denote property *accessors*. The get accessor runs when the property is read. It must return a value of the property's type. The set accessor runs when the property is assigned. It has an implicit parameter named value of the property's type that you typically assign to a private field (in this case, currentPrice).

Although properties are accessed in the same way as fields, they differ in that they give the implementer complete control over getting and setting its value. This control enables the implementer to choose whatever internal representation is needed, without exposing the internal details to the user of the property. In this example, the set method could throw an exception if value was outside a valid range of values.

 Throughout this book, we use public fields extensively to keep the examples free of distraction. In a real application, you would typically favor public properties over public fields, in order to promote encapsulation.

Properties allow the following modifiers:

Static modifier	static
Access modifiers	public internal private protected
Inheritance modifiers	new virtual abstract override sealed
Unmanaged code modifiers	unsafe extern

Read-only and calculated properties

A property is read-only if it specifies only a get accessor, and it is write-only if it specifies only a set accessor. Write-only properties are rarely used.

A property typically has a dedicated backing field to store the underlying data. However, a property can also be computed from other data. For example:

```
decimal currentPrice, sharesOwned;

public decimal Worth
{
  get { return currentPrice * sharesOwned; }
}
```

Expression-bodied properties (C# 6)

From C# 6, you can declare a read-only property, such as the preceding one, more tersely as an *expression-bodied property*. A fat arrow replaces all the braces and the get and return keywords:

```
public decimal Worth => currentPrice * sharesOwned;
```

Automatic properties

The most common implementation for a property is a getter and/or setter that simply reads and writes to a private field of the same type as the property. An *automatic property* declaration instructs the compiler to provide this implementation. We can improve the first example in this section by declaring CurrentPrice as an automatic property:

```
public class Stock
{
  ...
  public decimal CurrentPrice { get; set; }
}
```

The compiler automatically generates a private backing field of a compiler-generated name that cannot be referred to. The set accessor can be marked private or protected if you want to expose the property as read-only to other types. Automatic properties were introduced in C# 3.0.

Property initializers (C# 6)

From C# 6, you can add a *property initializer* to automatic properties, just as with fields:

```
public decimal CurrentPrice { get; set; } = 123;
```

This gives CurrentPrice an initial value of 123. Properties with an initializer can be read-only:

```
public int Maximum { get; } = 999;
```

Just as with read-only fields, read-only automatic properties can also be assigned in the type's constructor. This is useful in creating *immutable* (read-only) types.

get and set accessibility

The `get` and `set` accessors can have different access levels. The typical use case for this is to have a `public` property with an `internal` or `private` access modifier on the setter:

```
public class Foo
{
  private decimal x;
  public decimal X
  {
    get           { return x;  }
    private set { x = Math.Round (value, 2); }
  }
}
```

Notice that you declare the property itself with the more permissive access level (`public`, in this case) and add the modifier to the accessor you want to be *less* accessible.

CLR property implementation

C# property accessors internally compile to methods called get_*XXX* and set_*XXX*:

```
public decimal get_CurrentPrice {...}
public void set_CurrentPrice (decimal value) {...}
```

Simple nonvirtual property accessors are *inlined* by the JIT (just-in-time) compiler, eliminating any performance difference between accessing a property and a field. Inlining is an optimization in which a method call is replaced with the body of that method.

With WinRT properties, the compiler assumes the put_*XXX* naming convention rather than set_*XXX*.

Indexers

Indexers provide a natural syntax for accessing elements in a class or struct that encapsulate a list or dictionary of values. Indexers are similar to properties but are accessed via an index argument rather than a property name. The `string` class has an indexer that lets you access each of its `char` values via an `int` index:

```
string s = "hello";
Console.WriteLine (s[0]); // 'h'
Console.WriteLine (s[3]); // 'l'
```

The syntax for using indexers is like that for using arrays, except that the index argument(s) can be of any type(s).

Indexers have the same modifiers as properties (see "Properties" on page 79) and can be called null-conditionally by inserting a question mark before the square bracket (see "Null Operators" on page 55 in Chapter 2):

```
string s = null;
Console.WriteLine (s?[0]);  // Writes nothing; no error.
```

Implementing an indexer

To write an indexer, define a property called this, specifying the arguments in square brackets. For instance:

```
class Sentence
{
  string[] words = "The quick brown fox".Split();

  public string this [int wordNum]      // indexer
  {
    get { return words [wordNum];  }
    set { words [wordNum] = value; }
  }
}
```

Here's how we could use this indexer:

```
Sentence s = new Sentence();
Console.WriteLine (s[3]);       // fox
s[3] = "kangaroo";
Console.WriteLine (s[3]);       // kangaroo
```

A type may declare multiple indexers, each with parameters of different types. An indexer can also take more than one parameter:

```
public string this [int arg1, string arg2]
{
  get { ... }  set { ... }
}
```

If you omit the set accessor, an indexer becomes read-only, and expression-bodied syntax may be used in C# 6 to shorten its definition:

```
public string this [int wordNum] => words [wordNum];
```

CLR indexer implementation

Indexers internally compile to methods called get_Item and set_Item, as follows:

```
public string get_Item (int wordNum) {...}
public void set_Item (int wordNum, string value) {...}
```

Constants

A *constant* is a static field whose value can never change. A constant is evaluated statically at compile time, and the compiler literally substitutes its value whenever used (rather like a macro in C++). A constant can be any of the built-in numeric types, bool, char, string, or an enum type.

A constant is declared with the `const` keyword and must be initialized with a value. For example:

```
public class Test
{
  public const string Message = "Hello World";
}
```

A constant is much more restrictive than a `static readonly` field—both in the types you can use and in field initialization semantics. A constant also differs from a `static readonly` field in that the evaluation of the constant occurs at compile time. For example:

```
public static double Circumference (double radius)
{
  return 2 * System.Math.PI * radius;
}
```

is compiled to:

```
public static double Circumference (double radius)
{
  return 6.2831853071795862 * radius;
}
```

It makes sense for `PI` to be a constant, since it can never change. In contrast, a `static readonly` field can have a different value per application.

A `static readonly` field is also advantageous when exposing to other assemblies a value that might change in a later version. For instance, suppose assembly X exposes a constant as follows:

```
public const decimal ProgramVersion = 2.3;
```

If assembly Y references X and uses this constant, the value 2.3 will be baked into assembly Y when compiled. This means that if X is later recompiled with the constant set to 2.4, Y will still use the old value of 2.3 *until* Y *is recompiled*. A `static readonly` field avoids this problem.

Another way of looking at this is that any that value that might change in the future is not constant by definition, and so should not be represented as one.

Constants can also be declared local to a method. For example:

```
static void Main()
{
  const double twoPI  = 2 * System.Math.PI;
  ...
}
```

Non-local constants allow the following modifiers:

Access modifiers	`public internal private protected`
Inheritance modifier	`new`

Static Constructors

A static constructor executes once per *type*, rather than once per *instance*. A type can define only one static constructor, and it must be parameterless and have the same name as the type:

```
class Test
{
    static Test() { Console.WriteLine ("Type Initialized"); }
}
```

The runtime automatically invokes a static constructor just prior to the type being used. Two things trigger this:

- Instantiating the type
- Accessing a static member in the type

The only modifiers allowed by static constructors are `unsafe` and `extern`.

 If a static constructor throws an unhandled exception (Chapter 4), that type becomes *unusable* for the life of the application.

Static constructors and field initialization order

Static field initializers run just *before* the static constructor is called. If a type has no static constructor, field initializers will execute just prior to the type being used—or *anytime earlier* at the whim of the runtime.

Static field initializers run in the order in which the fields are declared. The following example illustrates this—X is initialized to 0 and Y is initialized to 3:

```
class Foo
{
    public static int X = Y;    // 0
    public static int Y = 3;    // 3
}
```

If we swap the two field initializers around, both fields are initialized to 3. The next example prints 0 followed by 3 because the field initializer that instantiates a Foo executes before X is initialized to 3:

```
class Program
{
    static void Main() { Console.WriteLine (Foo.X); }    // 3
}
```

```
class Foo
{
  public static Foo Instance = new Foo();
  public static int X = 3;

  Foo() { Console.WriteLine (X); }    // 0
}
```

If we swap the two lines in boldface, the example prints 3 followed by 3.

Static Classes

A class can be marked `static`, indicating that it must be composed solely of static members and cannot be subclassed. The `System.Console` and `System.Math` classes are good examples of static classes.

Finalizers

Finalizers are class-only methods that execute before the garbage collector reclaims the memory for an unreferenced object. The syntax for a finalizer is the name of the class prefixed with the ~ symbol:

```
class Class1
{
  ~Class1()
  {
    ...
  }
}
```

This is actually C# syntax for overriding `Object`'s `Finalize` method, and the compiler expands it into the following method declaration:

```
protected override void Finalize()
{
  ...
  base.Finalize();
}
```

We discuss garbage collection and finalizers fully in Chapter 12.

Finalizers allow the following modifier:

Unmanaged code modifier `unsafe`

Partial Types and Methods

Partial types allow a type definition to be split—typically across multiple files. A common scenario is for a partial class to be auto-generated from some other source (such as a Visual Studio template or designer) and for that class to be augmented with additional hand-authored methods. For example:

```
// PaymentFormGen.cs - auto-generated
partial class PaymentForm { ... }

// PaymentForm.cs - hand-authored
partial class PaymentForm { ... }
```

Each participant must have the `partial` declaration; the following is illegal:

```
partial class PaymentForm {}
class PaymentForm {}
```

Participants cannot have conflicting members. A constructor with the same parameters, for instance, cannot be repeated. Partial types are resolved entirely by the compiler, which means that each participant must be available at compile time and must reside in the same assembly.

You can specify a base class on one or more partial class declarations, as long as the base class, if specified, is the same. In addition, each participant can independently specify interfaces to implement. We cover base classes and interfaces in "Inheritance" on page 88 and "Interfaces" on page 104.

The compiler makes no guarantees with regard field initialization order between partial type declarations.

Partial methods

A partial type may contain *partial methods*. These let an auto-generated partial type provide customizable hooks for manual authoring. For example:

```
partial class PaymentForm     // In auto-generated file
{
  ...
  partial void ValidatePayment (decimal amount);
}

partial class PaymentForm     // In hand-authored file
{
  ...
  partial void ValidatePayment (decimal amount)
  {
    if (amount > 100)
      ...
  }
}
```

A partial method consists of two parts: a *definition* and an *implementation*. The definition is typically written by a code generator, and the implementation is typically manually authored. If an implementation is not provided, the definition of the partial method is compiled away (as is the code that calls it). This allows auto-generated code to be liberal in providing hooks, without having to worry about bloat. Partial methods must be `void` and are implicitly `private`.

Partial methods were introduced in C# 3.0.

The nameof operator (C# 6)

The `nameof` operator returns the name of any symbol (type, member, variable, and so on) as a string:

```
int count = 123;
string name = nameof (count);        // name is "count"
```

Its advantage over simply specifying a string is that of static type checking. Tools such as Visual Studio can understand the symbol reference, so if you rename the symbol in question, all its references will be renamed, too.

To specify the name of a type member such as a field or property, include the type as well. This works with both static and instance members:

```
string name = nameof (StringBuilder.Length);
```

This evaluates to "Length". To return "StringBuilder.Length", you would do this:

```
nameof (StringBuilder) + "." + nameof (StringBuilder.Length);
```

Inheritance

A class can *inherit* from another class to extend or customize the original class. Inheriting from a class lets you reuse the functionality in that class instead of building it from scratch. A class can inherit from only a single class but can itself be inherited by many classes, thus forming a class hierarchy. In this example, we start by defining a class called `Asset`:

```
public class Asset
{
  public string Name;
}
```

Next, we define classes called `Stock` and `House`, which will inherit from `Asset`. `Stock` and `House` get everything an `Asset` has, plus any additional members that they define:

```
public class Stock : Asset   // inherits from Asset
{
  public long SharesOwned;
}

public class House : Asset   // inherits from Asset
{
  public decimal Mortgage;
}
```

Here's how we can use these classes:

```
Stock msft = new Stock { Name="MSFT",
                         SharesOwned=1000 };

Console.WriteLine (msft.Name);        // MSFT
Console.WriteLine (msft.SharesOwned); // 1000
```

```
House mansion = new House { Name="Mansion",
                            Mortgage=250000 };

Console.WriteLine (mansion.Name);      // Mansion
Console.WriteLine (mansion.Mortgage);  // 250000
```

The *derived classes*, Stock and House, inherit the Name property from the *base class*, Asset.

A derived class is also called a *subclass*.

A base class is also called a *superclass*.

Polymorphism

References are polymorphic. This means a variable of type *x* can refer to an object that subclasses *x*. For instance, consider the following method:

```
public static void Display (Asset asset)
{
    System.Console.WriteLine (asset.Name);
}
```

This method can display both a Stock and a House, since they are both Assets:

```
Stock msft   = new Stock ... ;
House mansion = new House ... ;

Display (msft);
Display (mansion);
```

Polymorphism works on the basis that subclasses (Stock and House) have all the features of their base class (Asset). The converse, however, is not true. If Display was modified to accept a House, you could not pass in an Asset:

```
static void Main() { Display (new Asset()); }   // Compile-time error
public static void Display (House house)        // Will not accept Asset
{
    System.Console.WriteLine (house.Mortgage);
}
```

Casting and Reference Conversions

An object reference can be:

- Implicitly *upcast* to a base class reference
- Explicitly *downcast* to a subclass reference

Upcasting and downcasting between compatible reference types performs *reference conversions*: a new reference is (logically) created that points to the *same* object. An upcast always succeeds; a downcast succeeds only if the object is suitably typed.

Upcasting

An upcast operation creates a base class reference from a subclass reference. For example:

```
Stock msft = new Stock();
Asset a = msft;                    // Upcast
```

After the upcast, variable a still references the same Stock object as variable msft. The object being referenced is not itself altered or converted:

```
Console.WriteLine (a == msft);     // True
```

Although a and msft refer to the identical object, a has a more restrictive view on that object:

```
Console.WriteLine (a.Name);        // OK
Console.WriteLine (a.SharesOwned); // Error: SharesOwned undefined
```

The last line generates a compile-time error because the variable a is of type Asset, even though it refers to an object of type Stock. To get to its SharesOwned field, you must *downcast* the Asset to a Stock.

Downcasting

A downcast operation creates a subclass reference from a base class reference. For example:

```
Stock msft = new Stock();
Asset a = msft;                     // Upcast
Stock s = (Stock)a;                 // Downcast
Console.WriteLine (s.SharesOwned);  // <No error>
Console.WriteLine (s == a);         // True
Console.WriteLine (s == msft);      // True
```

As with an upcast, only references are affected—not the underlying object. A downcast requires an explicit cast because it can potentially fail at runtime:

```
House h = new House();
Asset a = h;            // Upcast always succeeds
Stock s = (Stock)a;     // Downcast fails: a is not a Stock
```

If a downcast fails, an InvalidCastException is thrown. This is an example of *runtime type checking* (we will elaborate on this concept in "Static and Runtime Type Checking" on page 99).

The as operator

The as operator performs a downcast that evaluates to null (rather than throwing an exception) if the downcast fails:

```
Asset a = new Asset();
Stock s = a as Stock;       // s is null; no exception thrown
```

This is useful when you're going to subsequently test whether the result is null:

```
if (s != null) Console.WriteLine (s.SharesOwned);
```

 Without such a test, a cast is advantageous, because if it fails, a more helpful exception is thrown. We can illustrate by comparing the following two lines of code:

```
int shares = ((Stock)a).SharesOwned;    // Approach #1
int shares = (a as Stock).SharesOwned;   // Approach #2
```

If a is not a Stock, the first line throws an InvalidCastException, which is an accurate description of what went wrong. The second line throws a NullReferenceException, which is ambiguous. Was a not a Stock or was a null?

Another way of looking at it is that with the cast operator, you're saying to the compiler: "I'm *certain* of a value's type; if I'm wrong, there's a bug in my code, so throw an exception!" Whereas with the as operator, you're uncertain of its type and want to branch according to the outcome at runtime.

The as operator cannot perform *custom conversions* (see "Operator Overloading" on page 168 in Chapter 4) and it cannot do numeric conversions:

```
long x = 3 as long;    // Compile-time error
```

 The as and cast operators will also perform upcasts, although this is not terribly useful because an implicit conversion will do the job.

The is operator

The is operator tests whether a reference conversion would succeed; in other words, whether an object derives from a specified class (or implements an interface). It is often used to test before downcasting:

```
if (a is Stock)
    Console.WriteLine (((Stock)a).SharesOwned);
```

The is operator also evaluates to true if an *unboxing conversion* would succeed (see "The object Type" on page 97). However, it does not consider custom or numeric conversions.

Virtual Function Members

A function marked as virtual can be *overridden* by subclasses wanting to provide a specialized implementation. Methods, properties, indexers, and events can all be declared virtual:

```
public class Asset
{
  public string Name;
```

```
    public virtual decimal Liability => 0;    // Expression-bodied property
}
```

(Liability => 0 is a shortcut for { get { return 0; } }. See "Expression-bodied properties (C# 6)" on page 81 for more details on this syntax.)

A subclass overrides a virtual method by applying the override modifier:

```
public class Stock : Asset
{
  public long SharesOwned;
}

public class House : Asset
{
  public decimal Mortgage;
  public override decimal Liability => Mortgage;
}
```

By default, the Liability of an Asset is 0. A Stock does not need to specialize this behavior. However, the House specializes the Liability property to return the value of the Mortgage:

```
House mansion = new House { Name="McMansion", Mortgage=250000 };
Asset a = mansion;
Console.WriteLine (mansion.Liability);    // 250000
Console.WriteLine (a.Liability);          // 250000
```

The signatures, return types, and accessibility of the virtual and overridden methods must be identical. An overridden method can call its base class implementation via the base keyword (we will cover this in "The base Keyword" on page 94).

 Calling virtual methods from a constructor is potentially dangerous because authors of subclasses are unlikely to know, when overriding the method, that they are working with a partially initialized object. In other words, the overriding method may end up accessing methods or properties which rely on fields not yet initialized by the constructor.

Abstract Classes and Abstract Members

A class declared as *abstract* can never be instantiated. Instead, only its concrete *subclasses* can be instantiated.

Abstract classes are able to define *abstract members*. Abstract members are like virtual members, except they don't provide a default implementation. That implementation must be provided by the subclass, unless that subclass is also declared abstract:

```
public abstract class Asset
{
  // Note empty implementation
  public abstract decimal NetValue { get; }
}
```

```
public class Stock : Asset
{
  public long SharesOwned;
  public decimal CurrentPrice;

  // Override like a virtual method.
  public override decimal NetValue => CurrentPrice * SharesOwned;
}
```

Hiding Inherited Members

A base class and a subclass may define identical members. For example:

```
public class A      { public int Counter = 1; }
public class B : A  { public int Counter = 2; }
```

The Counter field in class B is said to *hide* the Counter field in class A. Usually, this happens by accident, when a member is added to the base type *after* an identical member was added to the subtype. For this reason, the compiler generates a warning, and then resolves the ambiguity as follows:

- References to A (at compile time) bind to A.Counter.
- References to B (at compile time) bind to B.Counter.

Occasionally, you want to hide a member deliberately, in which case you can apply the new modifier to the member in the subclass. The new modifier *does nothing more than suppress the compiler warning that would otherwise result*:

```
public class A      { public     int Counter = 1; }
public class B : A { public new int Counter = 2; }
```

The new modifier communicates your intent to the compiler—and other programmers—that the duplicate member is not an accident.

> C# overloads the new keyword to have independent meanings in different contexts. Specifically, the new *operator* is different from the new *member modifier*.

new versus override

Consider the following class hierarchy:

```
public class BaseClass
{
  public virtual void Foo()  { Console.WriteLine ("BaseClass.Foo"); }
}

public class Overrider : BaseClass
{
  public override void Foo() { Console.WriteLine ("Overrider.Foo"); }
}

public class Hider : BaseClass
```

```
    {
        public new void Foo()       { Console.WriteLine ("Hider.Foo"); }
    }
```

The differences in behavior between Overrider and Hider are demonstrated in the following code:

```
    Overrider over = new Overrider();
    BaseClass b1 = over;
    over.Foo();                         // Overrider.Foo
    b1.Foo();                           // Overrider.Foo

    Hider h = new Hider();
    BaseClass b2 = h;
    h.Foo();                            // Hider.Foo
    b2.Foo();                           // BaseClass.Foo
```

Sealing Functions and Classes

An overridden function member may *seal* its implementation with the sealed keyword to prevent it from being overridden by further subclasses. In our earlier virtual function member example, we could have sealed House's implementation of Lia bility, preventing a class that derives from House from overriding Liability, as follows:

```
    public sealed override decimal Liability { get { return Mortgage; } }
```

You can also seal the class itself, implicitly sealing all the virtual functions, by applying the sealed modifier to the class itself. Sealing a class is more common than sealing a function member.

Although you can seal against overriding, you can't seal a member against being *hidden*.

The base Keyword

The base keyword is similar to the this keyword. It serves two essential purposes:

- Accessing an overridden function member from the subclass
- Calling a base-class constructor (see the next section)

In this example, House uses the base keyword to access Asset's implementation of Liability:

```
    public class House : Asset
    {
        ...
        public override decimal Liability => base.Liability + Mortgage;
    }
```

With the base keyword, we access Asset's Liability property *nonvirtually*. This means we will always access Asset's version of this property—regardless of the instance's actual runtime type.

The same approach works if Liability is *hidden* rather than *overridden*. (You can also access hidden members by casting to the base class before invoking the function.)

Constructors and Inheritance

A subclass must declare its own constructors. The base class's constructors are *accessible* to the derived class but are never automatically *inherited*. For example, if we define Baseclass and Subclass as follows:

```
public class Baseclass
{
  public int X;
  public Baseclass () { }
  public Baseclass (int x) { this.X = x; }
}

public class Subclass : Baseclass { }
```

the following is illegal:

```
Subclass s = new Subclass (123);
```

Subclass must hence "redefine" any constructors it wants to expose. In doing so, however, it can call any of the base class's constructors with the base keyword:

```
public class Subclass : Baseclass
{
  public Subclass (int x) : base (x) { }
}
```

The base keyword works rather like the this keyword, except that it calls a constructor in the base class.

Base-class constructors always execute first; this ensures that *base* initialization occurs before *specialized* initialization.

Implicit calling of the parameterless base-class constructor

If a constructor in a subclass omits the base keyword, the base type's *parameterless* constructor is implicitly called:

```
public class BaseClass
{
  public int X;
  public BaseClass() { X = 1; }
}

public class Subclass : BaseClass
{
```

```
      public Subclass() { Console.WriteLine (X); }  // 1
    }
```

If the base class has no accessible parameterless constructor, subclasses are forced to use the base keyword in their constructors.

Constructor and field initialization order

When an object is instantiated, initialization takes place in the following order:

1. From subclass to base class:

    a. Fields are initialized.

    b. Arguments to base-class constructor calls are evaluated.

2. From base class to subclass:

    a. Constructor bodies execute.

The following code demonstrates:

```
public class B
{
  int x = 1;          // Executes 3rd
  public B (int x)
  {
    ...               // Executes 4th
  }
}
public class D : B
{
  int y = 1;          // Executes 1st
  public D (int x)
    : base (x + 1)    // Executes 2nd
  {
    ...               // Executes 5th
  }
}
```

Overloading and Resolution

Inheritance has an interesting impact on method overloading. Consider the following two overloads:

```
static void Foo (Asset a) { }
static void Foo (House h) { }
```

When an overload is called, the most specific type has precedence:

```
House h = new House (...);
Foo(h);                     // Calls Foo(House)
```

The particular overload to call is determined statically (at compile time) rather than at runtime. The following code calls `Foo(Asset)`, even though the runtime type of a is `House`:

```
Asset a = new House (...);
Foo(a);                    // Calls Foo(Asset)
```

 If you cast `Asset` to `dynamic` (Chapter 4), the decision as to which overload to call is deferred until runtime and is then based on the object's actual type:

```
Asset a = new House (...);
Foo ((dynamic)a);   // Calls Foo(House)
```

The object Type

`object` (`System.Object`) is the ultimate base class for all types. Any type can be upcast to `object`.

To illustrate how this is useful, consider a general-purpose *stack*. A stack is a data structure based on the principle of LIFO—"last in, first out." A stack has two operations: *push* an object on the stack, and *pop* an object off the stack. Here is a simple implementation that can hold up to 10 objects:

```
public class Stack
{
  int position;
  object[] data = new object[10];
  public void Push (object obj)   { data[position++] = obj;  }
  public object Pop()             { return data[--position]; }
}
```

Because `Stack` works with the object type, we can `Push` and `Pop` instances of *any type* to and from the `Stack`:

```
Stack stack = new Stack();
stack.Push ("sausage");
string s = (string) stack.Pop();   // Downcast, so explicit cast is needed

Console.WriteLine (s);             // sausage
```

`object` is a reference type, by virtue of being a class. Despite this, value types, such as `int`, can also be cast to and from `object`, and so be added to our stack. This feature of C# is called *type unification* and is demonstrated here:

```
stack.Push (3);
int three = (int) stack.Pop();
```

When you cast between a value type and `object`, the CLR must perform some special work to bridge the difference in semantics between value and reference types. This process is called *boxing* and *unboxing*.

In "Generics" on page 114, we'll describe how to improve our Stack class to better handle stacks with same-typed elements.

Boxing and Unboxing

Boxing is the act of converting a value-type instance to a reference-type instance. The reference type may be either the object class or an interface (which we will visit later in the chapter).[1] In this example, we box an int into an object:

```
int x = 9;
object obj = x;            // Box the int
```

Unboxing reverses the operation by casting the object back to the original value type:

```
int y = (int)obj;          // Unbox the int
```

Unboxing requires an explicit cast. The runtime checks that the stated value type matches the actual object type and throws an InvalidCastException if the check fails. For instance, the following throws an exception, because long does not exactly match int:

```
object obj = 9;            // 9 is inferred to be of type int
long x = (long) obj;       // InvalidCastException
```

The following succeeds, however:

```
object obj = 9;
long x = (int) obj;
```

As does this:

```
object obj = 3.5;          // 3.5 is inferred to be of type double
int x = (int) (double) obj;  // x is now 3
```

In the last example, (double) performs an *unboxing*, and then (int) performs a *numeric conversion*.

Boxing conversions are crucial in providing a unified type system. The system is not perfect, however: we'll see in "Generics" on page 114 that variance with arrays and generics supports only *reference conversions* and not *boxing conversions*:

```
object[] a1 = new string[3];   // Legal
object[] a2 = new int[3];      // Error
```

---

1 The reference type may also be System.ValueType or System.Enum (Chapter 6).

Copying semantics of boxing and unboxing

Boxing *copies* the value-type instance into the new object, and unboxing *copies* the contents of the object back into a value-type instance. In the following example, changing the value of i doesn't change its previously boxed copy:

```
int i = 3;
object boxed = i;
i = 5;
Console.WriteLine (boxed);    // 3
```

Static and Runtime Type Checking

C# programs are type-checked both statically (at compile time) and at runtime (by the CLR).

Static type checking enables the compiler to verify the correctness of your program without running it. The following code will fail because the compiler enforces static typing:

```
int x = "5";
```

Runtime type checking is performed by the CLR when you downcast via a reference conversion or unboxing. For example:

```
object y = "5";
int z = (int) y;           // Runtime error, downcast failed
```

Runtime type checking is possible because each object on the heap internally stores a little type token. This token can be retrieved by calling the GetType method of object.

The GetType Method and typeof Operator

All types in C# are represented at runtime with an instance of System.Type. There are two basic ways to get a System.Type object:

- Call GetType on the instance.
- Use the typeof operator on a type name.

GetType is evaluated at runtime; typeof is evaluated statically at compile time (when generic type parameters are involved, it's resolved by the just-in-time compiler).

System.Type has properties for such things as the type's name, assembly, base type, and so on. For example:

```
using System;

public class Point { public int X, Y; }

class Test
{
```

```
static void Main()
{
  Point p = new Point();
  Console.WriteLine (p.GetType().Name);              // Point
  Console.WriteLine (typeof (Point).Name);           // Point
  Console.WriteLine (p.GetType() == typeof(Point));  // True
  Console.WriteLine (p.X.GetType().Name);            // Int32
  Console.WriteLine (p.Y.GetType().FullName);        // System.Int32
}
}
```

System.Type also has methods that act as a gateway to the runtime's reflection model, described in Chapter 19.

The ToString Method

The ToString method returns the default textual representation of a type instance. This method is overridden by all built-in types. Here is an example of using the int type's ToString method:

```
int x = 1;
string s = x.ToString();    // s is "1"
```

You can override the ToString method on custom types as follows:

```
public class Panda
{
  public string Name;
  public override string ToString() => Name;
}
...

Panda p = new Panda { Name = "Petey" };
Console.WriteLine (p);   // Petey
```

If you don't override ToString, the method returns the type name.

When you call an *overridden* object member such as ToString directly on a value type, boxing doesn't occur. Boxing then occurs only if you cast:

```
int x = 1;
string s1 = x.ToString();    // Calling on nonboxed value
object box = x;
string s2 = box.ToString();  // Calling on boxed value
```

Object Member Listing

Here are all the members of object:

```
public class Object
{
  public Object();

  public extern Type GetType();
```

```
    public virtual bool Equals (object obj);
    public static bool Equals  (object objA, object objB);
    public static bool ReferenceEquals (object objA, object objB);

    public virtual int GetHashCode();

    public virtual string ToString();

    protected virtual void Finalize();
    protected extern object MemberwiseClone();
}
```

We describe the `Equals`, `ReferenceEquals`, and `GetHashCode` methods in "Equality Comparison" on page 267 in Chapter 6.

Structs

A *struct* is similar to a class, with the following key differences:

- A struct is a value type, whereas a class is a reference type.
- A struct does not support inheritance (other than implicitly deriving from `object`, or more precisely, `System.ValueType`).

A struct can have all the members a class can, except the following:

- A parameterless constructor
- Field initializers
- A finalizer
- Virtual or protected members

A struct is appropriate when value-type semantics are desirable. Good examples of structs are numeric types, where it is more natural for assignment to copy a value rather than a reference. Because a struct is a value type, each instance does not require instantiation of an object on the heap; this incurs a useful savings when creating many instances of a type. For instance, creating an array of value type requires only a single heap allocation.

Struct Construction Semantics

The construction semantics of a struct are as follows:

- A parameterless constructor that you can't override implicitly exists. This performs a bitwise-zeroing of its fields.
- When you define a struct constructor, you must explicitly assign every field.

(And you can't have field initializers.) Here is an example of declaring and calling struct constructors:

```
public struct Point
{
  int x, y;
  public Point (int x, int y) { this.x = x; this.y = y; }
}


...
Point p1 = new Point ();        // p1.x and p1.y will be 0
Point p2 = new Point (1, 1);    // p1.x and p1.y will be 1
```

The next example generates three compile-time errors:

```
public struct Point
{
  int x = 1;                         // Illegal: field initializer
  int y;
  public Point() {}                  // Illegal: parameterless constructor
  public Point (int x) {this.x = x;} // Illegal: must assign field y
}
```

Changing struct to class makes this example legal.

Access Modifiers

To promote encapsulation, a type or type member may limit its *accessibility* to other types and other assemblies by adding one of five *access modifiers* to the declaration:

public

> Fully accessible. This is the implicit accessibility for members of an enum or interface.

internal

> Accessible only within the containing assembly or friend assemblies. This is the default accessibility for non-nested types.

private

> Accessible only within the containing type. This is the default accessibility for members of a class or struct.

protected

> Accessible only within the containing type or subclasses.

protected internal

> The *union* of protected and internal accessibility. Eric Lippert explains it as follows: Everything is as private as possible by default, and each modifier makes the thing *more accessible*. So something that is protected internal is made more accessible in two ways.

> The CLR has the concept of the *intersection* of protected and internal accessibility, but C# does not support this.

Examples

Class2 is accessible from outside its assembly; Class1 is not:

```
class Class1 {}                   // Class1 is internal (default)
public class Class2 {}
```

ClassB exposes field x to other types in the same assembly; ClassA does not:

```
class ClassA { int x;        } // x is private (default)
class ClassB { internal int x; }
```

Functions within Subclass can call Bar but not Foo:

```
class BaseClass
{
  void Foo()              {}       // Foo is private (default)
  protected void Bar() {}
}

class Subclass : BaseClass
{
  void Test1() { Foo(); }    // Error - cannot access Foo
  void Test2() { Bar(); }    // OK
}
```

Creating
Types in C#

Friend Assemblies

In advanced scenarios, you can expose internal members to other *friend* assemblies by adding the System.Runtime.CompilerServices.InternalsVisibleTo assembly attribute, specifying the name of the friend assembly as follows:

```
[assembly: InternalsVisibleTo ("Friend")]
```

If the friend assembly has a strong name (see Chapter 18), you must specify its *full* 160-byte public key:

```
[assembly: InternalsVisibleTo ("StrongFriend, PublicKey=0024f000048c...")]
```

You can extract the full public key from a strongly named assembly with a LINQ query (we explain LINQ in detail in Chapter 8):

```
string key = string.Join ("",
  Assembly.GetExecutingAssembly().GetName().GetPublicKey()
    .Select (b => b.ToString ("x2")));
```

> The companion sample in LINQPad invites you to browse to an assembly and then copies the assembly's full public key to the clipboard.

Accessibility Capping

A type caps the accessibility of its declared members. The most common example of capping is when you have an internal type with public members. For example:

```
class C { public void Foo() {} }
```

C's (default) `internal` accessibility caps Foo's accessibility, effectively making Foo `internal`. A common reason Foo would be marked `public` is to make for easier refactoring, should C later be changed to `public`.

Restrictions on Access Modifiers

When overriding a base class function, accessibility must be identical on the overridden function. For example:

```
class BaseClass              { protected virtual  void Foo() {} }
class Subclass1 : BaseClass { protected override void Foo() {} }  // OK
class Subclass2 : BaseClass { public    override void Foo() {} }  // Error
```

(An exception is when overriding a `protected internal` method in another assembly, in which case the override must simply be `protected`.)

The compiler prevents any inconsistent use of access modifiers. For example, a subclass itself can be less accessible than a base class, but not more:

```
internal class A {}
public class B : A {}        // Error
```

Interfaces

An interface is similar to a class, but it provides a specification rather than an implementation for its members. An interface is special in the following ways:

- Interface members are *all implicitly abstract*. In contrast, a class can provide both abstract members and concrete members with implementations.

- A class (or struct) can implement *multiple* interfaces. In contrast, a class can inherit from only a *single* class, and a struct cannot inherit at all (aside from deriving from `System.ValueType`).

An interface declaration is like a class declaration, but it provides no implementation for its members, since all its members are implicitly abstract. These members will be implemented by the classes and structs that implement the interface. An interface can contain only methods, properties, events, and indexers, which noncoincidentally are precisely the members of a class that can be abstract.

Here is the definition of the `IEnumerator` interface, defined in `System.Collec tions`:

```
public interface IEnumerator
{
  bool MoveNext();
  object Current { get; }
  void Reset();
}
```

Interface members are always implicitly public and cannot declare an access modifier. Implementing an interface means providing a `public` implementation for all its members:

```
internal class Countdown : IEnumerator
{
  int count = 11;
  public bool MoveNext() => count-- > 0;
  public object Current => count;
  public void Reset() { throw new NotSupportedException(); }
}
```

You can implicitly cast an object to any interface that it implements. For example:

```
IEnumerator e = new Countdown();
while (e.MoveNext())
  Console.Write (e.Current);      // 109876543210
```

Even though `Countdown` is an internal class, its members that implement `IEnumerator` can be called publicly by casting an instance of `Countdown` to `IEnumerator`. For instance, if a public type in the same assembly defined a method as follows:

```
public static class Util
{
  public static object GetCountDown() => new CountDown();
}
```

a caller from another assembly could do this:

```
IEnumerator e = (IEnumerator) Util.GetCountDown();
e.MoveNext();
```

If `IEnumerator` was itself defined as `internal`, this wouldn't be possible.

Extending an Interface

Interfaces may derive from other interfaces. For instance:

```
public interface IUndoable              { void Undo(); }
public interface IRedoable : IUndoable { void Redo(); }
```

`IRedoable` "inherits" all the members of `IUndoable`. In other words, types that implement `IRedoable` must also implement the members of `IUndoable`.

Explicit Interface Implementation

Implementing multiple interfaces can sometimes result in a collision between member signatures. You can resolve such collisions by *explicitly implementing* an interface member. Consider the following example:

```
interface I1 { void Foo(); }
interface I2 { int Foo(); }

public class Widget : I1, I2
{
  public void Foo()
```

```
  {
    Console.WriteLine ("Widget's implementation of I1.Foo");
  }

  int I2.Foo()
  {
    Console.WriteLine ("Widget's implementation of I2.Foo");
    return 42;
  }
}
```

Because both I1 and I2 have conflicting Foo signatures, Widget explicitly implements I2's Foo method. This lets the two methods coexist in one class. The only way
to call an explicitly implemented member is to cast to its interface:

```
Widget w = new Widget();
w.Foo();                    // Widget's implementation of I1.Foo
((I1)w).Foo();              // Widget's implementation of I1.Foo
((I2)w).Foo();              // Widget's implementation of I2.Foo
```

Another reason to explicitly implement interface members is to hide members that
are highly specialized and distracting to a type's normal use case. For example, a
type that implements ISerializable would typically want to avoid flaunting its
ISerializable members unless explicitly cast to that interface.

Implementing Interface Members Virtually

An implicitly implemented interface member is, by default, sealed. It must be
marked virtual or abstract in the base class in order to be overridden. For example:

```
public interface IUndoable { void Undo(); }

public class TextBox : IUndoable
{
  public virtual void Undo() => Console.WriteLine ("TextBox.Undo");
}

public class RichTextBox : TextBox
{
  public override void Undo() => Console.WriteLine ("RichTextBox.Undo");
}
```

Calling the interface member through either the base class or the interface calls the
subclass's implementation:

```
RichTextBox r = new RichTextBox();
r.Undo();                    // RichTextBox.Undo
((IUndoable)r).Undo();       // RichTextBox.Undo
((TextBox)r).Undo();         // RichTextBox.Undo
```

An explicitly implemented interface member cannot be marked virtual, nor can it
be overridden in the usual manner. It can, however, be *reimplemented*.

Reimplementing an Interface in a Subclass

A subclass can reimplement any interface member already implemented by a base class. Reimplementation *hijacks* a member implementation (when called through the interface) and works whether or not the member is virtual in the base class. It also works whether a member is implemented implicitly or explicitly—although it works best in the latter case, as we will demonstrate.

In the following example, TextBox implements IUndoable.Undo explicitly, and so it cannot be marked as virtual. In order to "override" it, RichTextBox must re-implement IUndoable's Undo method:

```
public interface IUndoable { void Undo(); }

public class TextBox : IUndoable
{
    void IUndoable.Undo() => Console.WriteLine ("TextBox.Undo");
}

public class RichTextBox : TextBox, IUndoable
{
    public void Undo() => Console.WriteLine ("RichTextBox.Undo");
}
```

Calling the reimplemented member through the interface calls the subclass's implementation:

```
RichTextBox r = new RichTextBox();
r.Undo();                  // RichTextBox.Undo      Case 1
((IUndoable)r).Undo();     // RichTextBox.Undo      Case 2
```

Assuming the same RichTextBox definition, suppose that TextBox implemented Undo *implicitly*:

```
public class TextBox : IUndoable
{
    public void Undo() => Console.WriteLine ("TextBox.Undo");
}
```

This would give us another way to call Undo, which would "break" the system, as shown in Case 3:

```
RichTextBox r = new RichTextBox();
r.Undo();                  // RichTextBox.Undo      Case 1
((IUndoable)r).Undo();     // RichTextBox.Undo      Case 2
((TextBox)r).Undo();       // TextBox.Undo          Case 3
```

Case 3 demonstrates that reimplementation hijacking is effective only when a member is called through the interface and not through the base class. This is usually undesirable as it can mean inconsistent semantics. This makes reimplementation most appropriate as a strategy for overriding *explicitly* implemented interface members.

Creating
Types in C#

Alternatives to interface reimplementation

Even with explicit member implementation, interface reimplementation is problematic for a couple of reasons:

- The subclass has no way to call the base class method.
- The base class author may not anticipate that a method be reimplemented and may not allow for the potential consequences.

Reimplementation can be a good last resort when subclassing hasn't been anticipated. A better option, however, is to design a base class such that reimplementation will never be required. There are two ways to achieve this:

- When implicitly implementing a member, mark it `virtual` if appropriate.
- When explicitly implementing a member, use the following pattern if you anticipate that subclasses might need to override any logic:

```
public class TextBox : IUndoable
{
  void IUndoable.Undo()          => Undo();     // Calls method below
  protected virtual void Undo() => Console.WriteLine ("TextBox.Undo");
}

public class RichTextBox : TextBox
{
  protected override void Undo() => Console.WriteLine("RichTextBox.Undo");
}
```

If you don't anticipate any subclassing, you can mark the class as `sealed` to preempt interface reimplementation.

Interfaces and Boxing

Converting a struct to an interface causes boxing. Calling an implicitly implemented member on a struct does not cause boxing:

```
interface  I { void Foo();            }
struct S : I { public void Foo() {} }

...
S s = new S();
s.Foo();        // No boxing.

I i = s;        // Box occurs when casting to interface.
i.Foo();
```

Writing a Class Versus an Interface

As a guideline:

- Use classes and subclasses for types that naturally share an implementation.
- Use interfaces for types that have independent implementations.

Consider the following classes:

```
abstract class Animal {}
abstract class Bird         : Animal {}
abstract class Insect       : Animal {}
abstract class FlyingCreature : Animal {}
abstract class Carnivore    : Animal {}

// Concrete classes:

class Ostrich : Bird {}
class Eagle   : Bird, FlyingCreature, Carnivore {}  // Illegal
class Bee     : Insect, FlyingCreature {}           // Illegal
class Flea    : Insect, Carnivore {}                // Illegal
```

The Eagle, Bee, and Flea classes do not compile because inheriting from multiple classes is prohibited. To resolve this, we must convert some of the types to interfaces. The question then arises, which types? Following our general rule, we could say that insects share an implementation, and birds share an implementation, so they remain classes. In contrast, flying creatures have independent mechanisms for flying, and carnivores have independent strategies for eating animals, so we would convert FlyingCreature and Carnivore to interfaces:

```
interface IFlyingCreature {}
interface ICarnivore      {}
```

In a typical scenario, Bird and Insect might correspond to a Windows control and a web control; FlyingCreature and Carnivore might correspond to IPrintable and IUndoable.

Enums

An enum is a special value type that lets you specify a group of named numeric constants. For example:

```
public enum BorderSide { Left, Right, Top, Bottom }
```

We can use this enum type as follows:

```
BorderSide topSide = BorderSide.Top;
bool isTop = (topSide == BorderSide.Top);    // true
```

Each enum member has an underlying integral value. By default:

- Underlying values are of type `int`.
- The constants 0, 1, 2... are automatically assigned, in the declaration order of the enum members.

You may specify an alternative integral type, as follows:

```
public enum BorderSide : byte { Left, Right, Top, Bottom }
```

You may also specify an explicit underlying value for each enum member:

```
public enum BorderSide : byte { Left=1, Right=2, Top=10, Bottom=11 }
```

The compiler also lets you explicitly assign *some* of the enum members. The unassigned enum members keep incrementing from the last explicit value. The preceding example is equivalent to the following:

```
public enum BorderSide : byte
    { Left=1, Right, Top=10, Bottom }
```

Enum Conversions

You can convert an `enum` instance to and from its underlying integral value with an explicit cast:

```
int i = (int) BorderSide.Left;
BorderSide side = (BorderSide) i;
bool leftOrRight = (int) side <= 2;
```

You can also explicitly cast one enum type to another. Suppose `HorizontalAlign ment` is defined as follows:

```
public enum HorizontalAlignment
{
  Left = BorderSide.Left,
  Right = BorderSide.Right,
  Center
}
```

A translation between the enum types uses the underlying integral values:

```
HorizontalAlignment h = (HorizontalAlignment) BorderSide.Right;
// same as:
HorizontalAlignment h = (HorizontalAlignment) (int) BorderSide.Right;
```

The numeric literal 0 is treated specially by the compiler in an enum expression and does not require an explicit cast:

```
BorderSide b = 0;    // No cast required
if (b == 0) ...
```

There are two reasons for the special treatment of 0:

- The first member of an enum is often used as the "default" value.

- For *combined enum* types, 0 means "no flags."

Flags Enums

You can combine enum members. To prevent ambiguities, members of a combinable enum require explicitly assigned values, typically in powers of two. For example:

```
[Flags]
public enum BorderSides { None=0, Left=1, Right=2, Top=4, Bottom=8 }
```

To work with combined enum values, you use bitwise operators, such as | and &. These operate on the underlying integral values:

```
BorderSides leftRight = BorderSides.Left | BorderSides.Right;

if ((leftRight & BorderSides.Left) != 0)
  Console.WriteLine ("Includes Left");      // Includes Left

string formatted = leftRight.ToString();   // "Left, Right"

BorderSides s = BorderSides.Left;
s |= BorderSides.Right;
Console.WriteLine (s == leftRight);   // True

s ^= BorderSides.Right;               // Toggles BorderSides.Right
Console.WriteLine (s);                // Left
```

By convention, the `Flags` attribute should always be applied to an enum type when its members are combinable. If you declare such an enum without the `Flags` attribute, you can still combine members, but calling `ToString` on an enum instance will emit a number rather than a series of names.

By convention, a combinable enum type is given a plural rather than singular name.

For convenience, you can include combination members within an enum declaration itself:

```
[Flags]
public enum BorderSides
{
  None=0,
  Left=1, Right=2, Top=4, Bottom=8,
  LeftRight = Left | Right,
  TopBottom = Top  | Bottom,
  All       = LeftRight | TopBottom
}
```

Enum Operators

The operators that work with enums are:

```
=    ==   !=   <   >   <=   >=   +   -   ^   &   |   ~
+=   -=   ++   --    sizeof
```

The bitwise, arithmetic, and comparison operators return the result of processing the underlying integral values. Addition is permitted between an enum and an integral type, but not between two enums.

Type-Safety Issues

Consider the following enum:

```
public enum BorderSide { Left, Right, Top, Bottom }
```

Since an enum can be cast to and from its underlying integral type, the actual value it may have may fall outside the bounds of a legal enum member. For example:

```
BorderSide b = (BorderSide) 12345;
Console.WriteLine (b);              // 12345
```

The bitwise and arithmetic operators can produce similarly invalid values:

```
BorderSide b = BorderSide.Bottom;
b++;                               // No errors
```

An invalid `BorderSide` would break the following code:

```
void Draw (BorderSide side)
{
    if      (side == BorderSide.Left)  {...}
    else if (side == BorderSide.Right) {...}
    else if (side == BorderSide.Top)   {...}
    else                               {...} // Assume BorderSide.Bottom
}
```

One solution is to add another `else` clause:

```
...
else if (side == BorderSide.Bottom) ...
else throw new ArgumentException ("Invalid BorderSide: " + side, "side");
```

Another workaround is to explicitly check an enum value for validity. The static `Enum.IsDefined` method does this job:

```
BorderSide side = (BorderSide) 12345;
Console.WriteLine (Enum.IsDefined (typeof (BorderSide), side));   // False
```

Unfortunately, `Enum.IsDefined` does not work for flagged enums. However, the following helper method (a trick dependent on the behavior of `Enum.ToString()`) returns `true` if a given flagged enum is valid:

```
static bool IsFlagDefined (Enum e)
{
  decimal d;
  return !decimal.TryParse(e.ToString(), out d);
}

[Flags]
public enum BorderSides { Left=1, Right=2, Top=4, Bottom=8 }
static void Main()
{
  for (int i = 0; i <= 16; i++)
  {
    BorderSides side = (BorderSides)i;
    Console.WriteLine (IsFlagDefined (side) + " " + side);
  }
}
```

Nested Types

A *nested type* is declared within the scope of another type. For example:

```
public class TopLevel
{
  public class Nested { }                  // Nested class
  public enum Color { Red, Blue, Tan }  // Nested enum
}
```

A nested type has the following features:

- It can access the enclosing type's private members and everything else the enclosing type can access.
- It can be declared with the full range of access modifiers, rather than just pub lic and internal.
- The default accessibility for a nested type is private rather than internal.
- Accessing a nested type from outside the enclosing type requires qualification with the enclosing type's name (like when accessing static members).

For example, to access Color.Red from outside our TopLevel class, we'd have to do this:

```
TopLevel.Color color = TopLevel.Color.Red;
```

All types (classes, structs, interfaces, delegates and enums) can be nested inside either a class or a struct.

Here is an example of accessing a private member of a type from a nested type:

```
public class TopLevel
{
  static int x;
  class Nested
  {
```

```
   static void Foo() { Console.WriteLine (TopLevel.x); }
  }
}
```

Here is an example of applying the `protected` access modifier to a nested type:

```
public class TopLevel
{
  protected class Nested { }
}

public class SubTopLevel : TopLevel
{
  static void Foo() { new TopLevel.Nested(); }
}
```

Here is an example of referring to a nested type from outside the enclosing type:

```
public class TopLevel
{
  public class Nested { }
}

class Test
{
  TopLevel.Nested n;
}
```

Nested types are used heavily by the compiler itself when it generates private classes that capture state for constructs such as iterators and anonymous methods.

If the sole reason for using a nested type is to avoid cluttering a namespace with too many types, consider using a nested namespace instead. A nested type should be used because of its stronger access control restrictions, or when the nested class must access private members of the containing class.

Generics

C# has two separate mechanisms for writing code that is reusable across different types: *inheritance* and *generics*. Whereas inheritance expresses reusability with a base type, generics express reusability with a "template" that contains "placeholder" types. Generics, when compared to inheritance, can *increase type safety* and *reduce casting and boxing*.

C# generics and C++ templates are similar concepts, but they work differently. We explain this difference in "C# Generics Versus C++ Templates" on page 126.

Generic Types

A generic type declares *type parameters*—placeholder types to be filled in by the consumer of the generic type, which supplies the *type arguments*. Here is a generic

---

type Stack<T>, designed to stack instances of type T. Stack<T> declares a single type parameter T:

```
public class Stack<T>
{
  int position;
  T[] data = new T[100];
  public void Push (T obj)  => data[position++] = obj;
  public T Pop()            => data[--position];
}
```

We can use Stack<T> as follows:

```
var stack = new Stack<int>();
stack.Push (5);
stack.Push (10);
int x = stack.Pop();    // x is 10
int y = stack.Pop();    // y is 5
```

Stack<int> fills in the type parameter T with the type argument int, implicitly creating a type on the fly (the synthesis occurs at runtime). Attempting to push a string onto our Stack<int> would, however, produce a compile-time error. Stack<int> effectively has the following definition (substitutions appear in bold, with the class name hashed out to avoid confusion):

```
public class ###
{
  int position;
  int[] data;
  public void Push (int obj)  => data[position++] = obj;
  public int Pop()            => data[--position];
}
```

Technically, we say that Stack<T> is an *open type*, whereas Stack<int> is a *closed type*. At runtime, all generic type instances are closed—with the placeholder types filled in. This means that the following statement is illegal:

```
var stack = new Stack<T>();   // Illegal: What is T?
```

unless inside a class or method which itself defines T as a type parameter:

```
public class Stack<T>
{
  ...
  public Stack<T> Clone()
  {
    Stack<T> clone = new Stack<T>();   // Legal
    ...
  }
}
```

Why Generics Exist

Generics exist to write code that is reusable across different types. Suppose we needed a stack of integers, but we didn't have generic types. One solution would be to hardcode a separate version of the class for every required element type (e.g., IntStack, StringStack, etc.). Clearly, this would cause considerable code duplication. Another solution would be to write a stack that is generalized by using object as the element type:

```
public class ObjectStack
{
  int position;
  object[] data = new object[10];
  public void Push (object obj) => data[position++] = obj;
  public object Pop()          => data[--position];
}
```

An ObjectStack, however, wouldn't work as well as a hardcoded IntStack for specifically stacking integers. Specifically, an ObjectStack would require boxing and downcasting that could not be checked at compile time:

```
// Suppose we just want to store integers here:
ObjectStack stack = new ObjectStack();

stack.Push ("s");          // Wrong type, but no error!
int i = (int)stack.Pop();  // Downcast - runtime error
```

What we need is both a general implementation of a stack that works for all element types, and a way to easily specialize that stack to a specific element type for increased type safety and reduced casting and boxing. Generics give us precisely this, by allowing us to parameterize the element type. Stack<T> has the benefits of both ObjectStack and IntStack. Like ObjectStack, Stack<T> is written once to work *generally* across all types. Like IntStack, Stack<T> is *specialized* for a particular type—the beauty is that this type is T, which we substitute on the fly.

 ObjectStack is functionally equivalent to Stack<object>.

Generic Methods

A generic method declares type parameters within the signature of a method.

With generic methods, many fundamental algorithms can be implemented in a general-purpose way only. Here is a generic method that swaps the contents of two variables of any type T:

```
static void Swap<T> (ref T a, ref T b)
{
  T temp = a;
  a = b;
  b = temp;
}
```

Swap<T> can be used as follows:

```
int x = 5;
int y = 10;
Swap (ref x, ref y);
```

Generally, there is no need to supply type arguments to a generic method, because the compiler can implicitly infer the type. If there is ambiguity, generic methods can be called with the type arguments as follows:

```
Swap<int> (ref x, ref y);
```

Within a generic *type*, a method is not classed as generic unless it *introduces* type parameters (with the angle bracket syntax). The Pop method in our generic stack merely uses the type's existing type parameter, T, and is not classed as a generic method.

Methods and types are the only constructs that can introduce type parameters. Properties, indexers, events, fields, constructors, operators, and so on cannot declare type parameters, although they can partake in any type parameters already declared by their enclosing type. In our generic stack example, for instance, we could write an indexer that returns a generic item:

```
public T this [int index] => data [index];
```

Similarly, constructors can partake in existing type parameters, but not *introduce* them:

```
public Stack<T>() { }   // Illegal
```

Declaring Type Parameters

Type parameters can be introduced in the declaration of classes, structs, interfaces, delegates (covered in Chapter 4), and methods. Other constructs, such as properties, cannot *introduce* a type parameter, but can *use* one. For example, the property Value uses T:

```
public struct Nullable<T>
{
  public T Value { get; }
}
```

A generic type or method can have multiple parameters. For example:

```
class Dictionary<TKey, TValue> {...}
```

To instantiate:

```
Dictionary<int,string> myDic = new Dictionary<int,string>();
```

Or:

```
var myDic = new Dictionary<int,string>();
```

Generic type names and method names can be overloaded as long as the number of type parameters is different. For example, the following three type names do not conflict:

```
class A        {}
class A<T>     {}
class A<T1,T2> {}
```

 By convention, generic types and methods with a *single* type parameter typically name their parameter T, as long as the intent of the parameter is clear. When using *multiple* type parameters, each parameter is prefixed with T, but has a more descriptive name.

typeof and Unbound Generic Types

Open generic types do not exist at runtime: open generic types are closed as part of compilation. However, it is possible for an *unbound* generic type to exist at runtime —purely as a Type object. The only way to specify an unbound generic type in C# is with the typeof operator:

```
class A<T> {}
class A<T1,T2> {}
...

Type a1 = typeof (A<>);    // Unbound type (notice no type arguments).
Type a2 = typeof (A<,>);   // Use commas to indicate multiple type args.
```

Open generic types are used in conjunction with the Reflection API (Chapter 19).

You can also use the typeof operator to specify a closed type:

```
Type a3 = typeof (A<int,int>);
```

or an open type (which is closed at runtime):

```
class B<T> { void X() { Type t = typeof (T); } }
```

The default Generic Value

The default keyword can be used to get the default value for a generic type parameter. The default value for a reference type is null, and the default value for a value type is the result of bitwise-zeroing the value type's fields:

```
static void Zap<T> (T[] array)
{
  for (int i = 0; i < array.Length; i++)
    array[i] = default(T);
}
```

Generic Constraints

By default, a type parameter can be substituted with any type whatsoever. *Constraints* can be applied to a type parameter to require more specific type arguments. These are the possible constraints:

```
where T : base-class   // Base-class constraint
where T : interface    // Interface constraint
where T : class        // Reference-type constraint
```

```
where T : struct        // Value-type constraint (excludes Nullable types)
where T : new()         // Parameterless constructor constraint
where U : T             // Naked type constraint
```

In the following example, GenericClass<T,U> requires T to derive from (or be identical to) SomeClass and implement Interface1, and requires U to provide a parameterless constructor:

```
class    SomeClass {}
interface Interface1 {}

class GenericClass<T,U> where T : SomeClass, Interface1
                        where U : new()
{...}
```

Constraints can be applied wherever type parameters are defined, in both methods and type definitions.

A *base-class constraint* specifies that the type parameter must subclass (or match) a particular class; an *interface constraint* specifies that the type parameter must implement that interface. These constraints allow instances of the type parameter to be implicitly converted to that class or interface. For example, suppose we want to write a generic Max method, which returns the maximum of two values. We can take advantage of the generic interface defined in the framework called IComparable<T>:

```
public interface IComparable<T>   // Simplified version of interface
{
  int CompareTo (T other);
}
```

CompareTo returns a positive number if this is greater than other. Using this interface as a constraint, we can write a Max method as follows (to avoid distraction, null checking is omitted):

```
static T Max <T> (T a, T b) where T : IComparable<T>
{
  return a.CompareTo (b) > 0 ? a : b;
}
```

The Max method can accept arguments of any type implementing IComparable<T> (which includes most built-in types such as int and string):

```
int z = Max (5, 10);          // 10
string last = Max ("ant", "zoo");  // zoo
```

The *class constraint* and *struct constraint* specify that T must be a reference type or (non-nullable) value type. A great example of the struct constraint is the System.Nullable<T> struct (we will discuss this class in depth in "Nullable Types" on page 162 in Chapter 4):

```
struct Nullable<T> where T : struct {...}
```

The *parameterless constructor constraint* requires T to have a public parameterless constructor. If this constraint is defined, you can call new() on T:

```
static void Initialize<T> (T[] array) where T : new()
{
  for (int i = 0; i < array.Length; i++)
    array[i] = new T();
}
```

The *naked type constraint* requires one type parameter to derive from (or match) another type parameter. In this example, the method `FilteredStack` returns another `Stack`, containing only the subset of elements where the type parameter `U` is of the type parameter `T`:

```
class Stack<T>
{
  Stack<U> FilteredStack<U>() where U : T {...}
}
```

Subclassing Generic Types

A generic class can be subclassed just like a nongeneric class. The subclass can leave the base class's type parameters open, as in the following example:

```
class Stack<T>                     {...}
class SpecialStack<T> : Stack<T> {...}
```

Or the subclass can close the generic type parameters with a concrete type:

```
class IntStack : Stack<int>  {...}
```

A subtype can also introduce fresh type arguments:

```
class List<T>                     {...}
class KeyedList<T,TKey> : List<T> {...}
```

Technically, *all* type arguments on a subtype are fresh: you could say that a subtype closes and then reopens the base type arguments. This means that a subclass can give new (and potentially more meaningful) names to the type arguments it reopens:

```
class List<T> {...}
class KeyedList<TElement,TKey> : List<TElement> {...}
```

Self-Referencing Generic Declarations

A type can name *itself* as the concrete type when closing a type argument:

```
public interface IEquatable<T> { bool Equals (T obj); }

public class Balloon : IEquatable<Balloon>
{
  public string Color { get; set; }
  public int CC { get; set; }

  public bool Equals (Balloon b)
  {
    if (b == null) return false;
    return b.Color == Color && b.CC == CC;
```

```
    }
  }
```

The following are also legal:

```
class Foo<T> where T : IComparable<T> { ... }
class Bar<T> where T : Bar<T> { ... }
```

Static Data

Static data is unique for each closed type:

```
class Bob<T> { public static int Count; }

class Test
{
  static void Main()
  {
    Console.WriteLine (++Bob<int>.Count);     // 1
    Console.WriteLine (++Bob<int>.Count);     // 2
    Console.WriteLine (++Bob<string>.Count);  // 1
    Console.WriteLine (++Bob<object>.Count);  // 1
  }
}
```

Type Parameters and Conversions

C#'s cast operator can perform several kinds of conversion, including:

- Numeric conversion

- Reference conversion

- Boxing/unboxing conversion

- Custom conversion (via operator overloading; see Chapter 4)

The decision as to which kind of conversion will take place happens at *compile time*, based on the known types of the operands. This creates an interesting scenario with generic type parameters, because the precise operand types are unknown at compile time. If this leads to ambiguity, the compiler generates an error.

The most common scenario is when you want to perform a reference conversion:

```
StringBuilder Foo<T> (T arg)
{
  if (arg is StringBuilder)
    return (StringBuilder) arg;    // Will not compile
  ...
}
```

Without knowledge of T's actual type, the compiler is concerned that you might have intended this to be a *custom conversion*. The simplest solution is to instead use the as operator, which is unambiguous because it cannot perform custom conversions:

```
StringBuilder Foo<T> (T arg)
{
  StringBuilder sb = arg as StringBuilder;
  if (sb != null) return sb;
  ...
}
```

A more general solution is to first cast to object. This works because conversions to/from object are assumed not to be custom conversions, but reference or boxing/unboxing conversions. In this case, StringBuilder is a reference type, so it has to be a reference conversion:

```
return (StringBuilder) (object) arg;
```

Unboxing conversions can also introduce ambiguities. The following could be an unboxing, numeric, or custom conversion:

```
int Foo<T> (T x) => (int) x;      // Compile-time error
```

The solution, again, is to first cast to object and then to int (which then unambiguously signals an unboxing conversion in this case):

```
int Foo<T> (T x) => (int) (object) x;
```

Covariance

Assuming A is convertible to B, X has a covariant type parameter if X<A> is convertible to X<B>.

With C#'s notion of covariance (and contravariance), "convertible" means convertible via an *implicit reference conversion*— such as A *subclassing* B, or A *implementing* B. Numeric conversions, boxing conversions and custom conversions are not included.

For instance, type IFoo<T> has a covariant T if the following is legal:

```
IFoo<string> s = ...;
IFoo<object> b = s;
```

From C# 4.0, interfaces permit covariant type parameters (as do delegates—see Chapter 4), but classes do not. Arrays also allow covariance (A[] can be converted to B[] if A has an implicit reference conversion to B), and are discussed here for comparison.

Covariance and contravariance (or simply "variance") are advanced concepts. The motivation behind introducing and enhancing variance in C# was to allow generic interface and generic types (in particular, those defined in the Framework, such as IEnumerable<T>) to work *more as you'd expect*. You can benefit from this without understanding the details behind covariance and contravariance.

Variance is not automatic

To ensure static type safety, type parameters are not automatically variant. Consider the following:

```
class Animal {}
class Bear : Animal {}
class Camel : Animal {}

public class Stack<T>    // A simple Stack implementation
{
  int position;
  T[] data = new T[100];
  public void Push (T obj)  => data[position++] = obj;
  public T Pop()            => data[--position];
}
```

The following fails to compile:

```
Stack<Bear> bears = new Stack<Bear>();
Stack<Animal> animals = bears;              // Compile-time error
```

That restriction prevents the possibility of runtime failure with the following code:

```
animals.Push (new Camel());      // Trying to add Camel to bears
```

Lack of covariance, however, can hinder reusability. Suppose, for instance, we wanted to write a method to Wash a stack of animals:

```
public class ZooCleaner
{
  public static void Wash (Stack<Animal> animals) {...}
}
```

Calling Wash with a stack of bears would generate a compile-time error. One workaround is to redefine the Wash method with a constraint:

```
class ZooCleaner
{
  public static void Wash<T> (Stack<T> animals) where T : Animal { ... }
}
```

We can now call Wash as follows:

```
Stack<Bear> bears = new Stack<Bear>();
ZooCleaner.Wash (bears);
```

Another solution is to have Stack<T> implement an interface with a covariant type parameter, as we'll see shortly.

Arrays

For historical reasons, array types support covariance. This means that B[] can be cast to A[] if B subclasses A (and both are reference types). For example:

```
Bear[] bears = new Bear[3];
Animal[] animals = bears;     // OK
```

The downside of this reusability is that element assignments can fail at runtime:

```
animals[0] = new Camel();      // Runtime error
```

Declaring a covariant type parameter

As of C# 4.0, type parameters on interfaces and delegates can be declared covariant by marking them with the out modifier. This modifier ensures that, unlike with arrays, covariant type parameters are fully type-safe.

We can illustrate this with our Stack<T> class by having it implement the following interface:

```
public interface IPoppable<out T> { T Pop(); }
```

The out modifier on T indicates that T is used only in *output positions* (e.g., return types for methods). The out modifier flags the type parameter as *covariant* and allows us to do this:

```
var bears = new Stack<Bear>();
bears.Push (new Bear());
// Bears implements IPoppable<Bear>. We can convert to IPoppable<Animal>:
IPoppable<Animal> animals = bears;    // Legal
Animal a = animals.Pop();
```

The conversion from bears to animals is permitted by the compiler—by virtue of the type parameter being covariant. This is type-safe because the case the compiler is trying to avoid—pushing a Camel onto the stack—can't occur as there's no way to feed a Camel *in*to an interface where T can appear only in *out*put positions.

 Covariance (and contravariance) in interfaces is something that you typically *consume*: it's less common that you need to *write* variant interfaces.

 Curiously, method parameters marked as out are not eligible for covariance, due to a limitation in the CLR.

We can leverage the ability to cast covariantly to solve the reusability problem described earlier:

```
public class ZooCleaner
{
  public static void Wash (IPoppable<Animal> animals) { ... }
}
```

 The IEnumerator<T> and IEnumerable<T> interfaces described in Chapter 7 have a covariant T. This allows you to cast IEnumerable<string> to IEnumerable<object>, for instance.

The compiler will generate an error if you use a covariant type parameter in an *input* position (e.g., a parameter to a method or a writable property).

Covariance (and contravariance) works only for elements with *reference conversions*—not *boxing conversions*. (This applies both to type parameter variance and array variance.) So, if you wrote a method that accepted a parameter of type IPoppable<object>, you could call it with IPoppable<string>, but not IPoppable<int>.

Contravariance

We previously saw that, assuming that A allows an implicit reference conversion to B, a type X has a covariant type parameter if X<A> allows a reference conversion to X<B>. *Contravariance* is when you can convert in the reverse direction—from X<B> to X<A>. This is supported if the type parameter appears only in *input* positions, and is designated with the in modifier. Extending our previous example, if the Stack<T> class implements the following interface:

```
public interface IPushable<in T> { void Push (T obj); }
```

we can legally do this:

```
IPushable<Animal> animals = new Stack<Animal>();
IPushable<Bear> bears = animals;    // Legal
bears.Push (new Bear());
```

No member in IPushable *outputs* a T, so we can't get into trouble by casting animals to bears (there's no way to Pop, for instance, through that interface).

Our Stack<T> class can implement both IPushable<T> and IPoppable<T>—despite T having opposing variance annotations in the two interfaces! This works because you must exercise variance through the interface and not the class; therefore, you must commit to the lens of either IPoppable or IPushable before performing a variant conversion. This lens then restricts you to the operations that are legal under the appropriate variance rules.

This also illustrates why *classes* do not allow variant type parameters: concrete implementations typically require data to flow in both directions.

To give another example, consider the following interface, defined as part of the .NET Framework:

```
public interface IComparer<in T>
{
  // Returns a value indicating the relative ordering of a and b
  int Compare (T a, T b);
}
```

Because the interface has a contravariant T, we can use an IComparer<**object**> to compare two *strings*:

```
var objectComparer = Comparer<object>.Default;
// objectComparer implements IComparer<object>
IComparer<string> stringComparer = objectComparer;
int result = stringComparer.Compare ("Brett", "Jemaine");
```

Mirroring covariance, the compiler will report an error if you try to use a contravariant type parameter in an output position (e.g., as a return value, or in a readable property).

C# Generics Versus C++ Templates

C# generics are similar in application to C++ templates, but they work very differently. In both cases, a synthesis between the producer and consumer must take place, where the placeholder types of the producer are filled in by the consumer. However, with C# generics, producer types (i.e., open types such as List<T>) can be compiled into a library (such as *mscorlib.dll*). This works because the synthesis between the producer and the consumer that produces closed types doesn't actually happen until runtime. With C++ templates, this synthesis is performed at compile time. This means that in C++ you don't deploy template libraries as *.dlls*—they exist only as source code. It also makes it difficult to dynamically inspect, let alone create, parameterized types on the fly.

To dig deeper into why this is the case, consider the Max method in C#, once more:

```
static T Max <T> (T a, T b) where T : IComparable<T>
    => a.CompareTo (b) > 0 ? a : b;
```

Why couldn't we have implemented it like this?

```
static T Max <T> (T a, T b)
    => (a > b ? a : b);                 // Compile error
```

The reason is that Max needs to be compiled once and work for all possible values of T. Compilation cannot succeed, because there is no single meaning for > across all values of T—in fact, not every T even has a > operator. In contrast, the following code shows the same Max method written with C++ templates. This code will be compiled separately for each value of T, taking on whatever semantics > has for a particular T, failing to compile if a particular T does not support the > operator:

```
template <class T> T Max (T a, T b)
{
  return a > b ? a : b;
}
```

4

Advanced C#

In this chapter, we cover advanced C# topics that build on concepts explored in Chapters 2 and 3. You should read the first four sections sequentially; you can read the remaining sections in any order.

Delegates

A delegate is an object that knows how to call a method.

A *delegate type* defines the kind of method that *delegate instances* can call. Specifically, it defines the method's *return type* and its *parameter types*. The following defines a delegate type called `Transformer`:

```
delegate int Transformer (int x);
```

`Transformer` is compatible with any method with an `int` return type and a single `int` parameter, such as this:

```
static int Square (int x) { return x * x; }
```

or more tersely:

```
static int Square (int x) => x * x;
```

Assigning a method to a delegate variable creates a delegate *instance*:

```
Transformer t = Square;
```

which can be invoked in the same way as a method:

```
int answer = t(3);    // answer is 9
```

Here's a complete example:

```
delegate int Transformer (int x);

class Test
{
  static void Main()
```

```
  {
    Transformer t = Square;        // Create delegate instance
    int result = t(3);             // Invoke delegate
    Console.WriteLine (result);    // 9
  }
  static int Square (int x) => x * x;
}
```

A delegate instance literally acts as a delegate for the caller: the caller invokes the delegate, and then the delegate calls the target method. This indirection decouples the caller from the target method.

The statement:

```
Transformer t = Square;
```

is shorthand for:

```
Transformer t = new Transformer (Square);
```

Technically, we are specifying a *method group* when we refer to Square without brackets or arguments. If the method is overloaded, C# will pick the correct overload based on the signature of the delegate to which it's being assigned.

The expression:

```
t(3)
```

is shorthand for:

```
t.Invoke(3)
```

A delegate is similar to a *callback*, a general term that captures constructs such as C function pointers.

Writing Plug-in Methods with Delegates

A delegate variable is assigned a method at runtime. This is useful for writing plug-in methods. In this example, we have a utility method named Transform that applies a transform to each element in an integer array. The Transform method has a delegate parameter, for specifying a plug-in transform.

```
public delegate int Transformer (int x);

class Util
{
  public static void Transform (int[] values, Transformer t)
  {
    for (int i = 0; i < values.Length; i++)
      values[i] = t (values[i]);
  }
}

class Test
```

```
{
  static void Main()
  {
    int[] values = { 1, 2, 3 };
    Util.Transform (values, Square);      // Hook in the Square method
    foreach (int i in values)
      Console.Write (i + "  ");            // 1   4   9
  }

  static int Square (int x) => x * x;
}
```

Multicast Delegates

All delegate instances have *multicast* capability. This means that a delegate instance can reference not just a single target method, but also a list of target methods. The + and += operators combine delegate instances. For example:

```
SomeDelegate d = SomeMethod1;
d += SomeMethod2;
```

The last line is functionally the same as:

```
d = d + SomeMethod2;
```

Invoking d will now call both SomeMethod1 and SomeMethod2. Delegates are invoked in the order they are added.

The - and -= operators remove the right delegate operand from the left delegate operand. For example:

```
d -= SomeMethod1;
```

Invoking d will now cause only SomeMethod2 to be invoked.

Calling + or += on a delegate variable with a null value works, and it is equivalent to assigning the variable to a new value:

```
SomeDelegate d = null;
d += SomeMethod1;          // Equivalent (when d is null) to d = SomeMethod1;
```

Similarly, calling -= on a delegate variable with a single target is equivalent to assigning null to that variable.

 Delegates are *immutable*, so when you call += or -=, you're in fact creating a *new* delegate instance and assigning it to the existing variable.

If a multicast delegate has a nonvoid return type, the caller receives the return value from the last method to be invoked. The preceding methods are still called, but their return values are discarded. In most scenarios in which multicast delegates are used, they have void return types, so this subtlety does not arise.

All delegate types implicitly derive from System.MulticastDe
legate, which inherits from System.Delegate. C# compiles +,
-, +=, and -= operations made on a delegate to the static Com
bine and Remove methods of the System.Delegate class.

Multicast delegate example

Suppose you wrote a method that took a long time to execute. That method could
regularly report progress to its caller by invoking a delegate. In this example, the
HardWork method has a ProgressReporter delegate parameter, which it invokes to
indicate progress:

```
public delegate void ProgressReporter (int percentComplete);

public class Util
{
  public static void HardWork (ProgressReporter p)
  {
    for (int i = 0; i < 10; i++)
    {
      p (i * 10);                              // Invoke delegate
      System.Threading.Thread.Sleep (100);  // Simulate hard work
    }
  }
}
```

To monitor progress, the Main method creates a multicast delegate instance p, such
that progress is monitored by two independent methods:

```
class Test
{
  static void Main()
  {
    ProgressReporter p = WriteProgressToConsole;
    p += WriteProgressToFile;
    Util.HardWork (p);
  }

  static void WriteProgressToConsole (int percentComplete)
    => Console.WriteLine (percentComplete);

  static void WriteProgressToFile (int percentComplete)
    => System.IO.File.WriteAllText ("progress.txt",
                                    percentComplete.ToString());
}
```

Instance Versus Static Method Targets

When an *instance* method is assigned to a delegate object, the latter must maintain a
reference not only to the method, but also to the *instance* to which the method
belongs. The System.Delegate class's Target property represents this instance (and
will be null for a delegate referencing a static method). For example:

```
public delegate void ProgressReporter (int percentComplete);

class Test
{
  static void Main()
  {
    X x = new X();
    ProgressReporter p = x.InstanceProgress;
    p(99);                                    // 99
    Console.WriteLine (p.Target == x);        // True
    Console.WriteLine (p.Method);             // Void InstanceProgress(Int32)
  }
}

class X
{
  public void InstanceProgress (int percentComplete)
    => Console.WriteLine (percentComplete);
}
```

Generic Delegate Types

A delegate type may contain generic type parameters. For example:

```
public delegate T Transformer<T> (T arg);
```

With this definition, we can write a generalized Transform utility method that works on any type:

```
public class Util
{
  public static void Transform<T> (T[] values, Transformer<T> t)
  {
    for (int i = 0; i < values.Length; i++)
      values[i] = t (values[i]);
  }
}

class Test
{
  static void Main()
  {
    int[] values = { 1, 2, 3 };
    Util.Transform (values, Square);      // Hook in Square
    foreach (int i in values)
      Console.Write (i + "  ");           // 1   4   9
  }
  static int Square (int x) => x * x;
}
```

The Func and Action Delegates

With generic delegates, it becomes possible to write a small set of delegate types that are so general they can work for methods of any return type and any (reasonable) number of arguments. These delegates are the Func and Action delegates, defined in the System namespace (the in and out annotations indicate *variance*, which we will cover shortly):

```
delegate TResult Func <out TResult>                 ();
delegate TResult Func <in T, out TResult>           (T arg);
delegate TResult Func <in T1, in T2, out TResult>   (T1 arg1, T2 arg2);
... and so on, up to T16
delegate void Action                     ();
delegate void Action <in T>              (T arg);
delegate void Action <in T1, in T2>      (T1 arg1, T2 arg2);
... and so on, up to T16
```

These delegates are extremely general. The Transformer delegate in our previous example can be replaced with a Func delegate that takes a single argument of type T and returns a same-typed value:

```
public static void Transform<T> (T[] values, Func<T,T> transformer)
{
  for (int i = 0; i < values.Length; i++)
    values[i] = transformer (values[i]);
}
```

The only practical scenarios not covered by these delegates are ref/out and pointer parameters.

 Prior to Framework 2.0, the Func and Action delegates did not exist (because generics did not exist). It's for this historical reason that much of the Framework uses custom delegate types rather than Func and Action.

Delegates Versus Interfaces

A problem that can be solved with a delegate can also be solved with an interface. For instance, we can rewrite our original example with an interface called ITransformer instead of a delegate:

```
public interface ITransformer
{
  int Transform (int x);
}

public class Util
{
 public static void TransformAll (int[] values, ITransformer t)
 {
   for (int i = 0; i < values.Length; i++)
     values[i] = t.Transform (values[i]);
 }
}

class Squarer : ITransformer
{
  public int Transform (int x) => x * x;
}
```

```
  ...
  static void Main()
  {
    int[] values = { 1, 2, 3 };
    Util.TransformAll (values, new Squarer());
    foreach (int i in values)
      Console.WriteLine (i);
  }
```

A delegate design may be a better choice than an interface design if one or more of these conditions are true:

- The interface defines only a single method.

- Multicast capability is needed.

- The subscriber needs to implement the interface multiple times.

In the ITransformer example, we don't need to multicast. However, the interface defines only a single method. Furthermore, our subscriber may need to implement ITransformer multiple times, to support different transforms, such as square or cube. With interfaces, we're forced into writing a separate type per transform, since Test can implement ITransformer only once. This is quite cumbersome:

```
  class Squarer : ITransformer
  {
    public int Transform (int x) => x * x;
  }

  class Cuber : ITransformer
  {
    public int Transform (int x) => x * x * x;
  }
  ...

  static void Main()
  {
    int[] values = { 1, 2, 3 };
    Util.TransformAll (values, new Cuber());
    foreach (int i in values)
      Console.WriteLine (i);
  }
```

Delegate Compatibility

Type compatibility

Delegate types are all incompatible with one another, even if their signatures are the same:

```
  delegate void D1();
  delegate void D2();
  ...
```

```
D1 d1 = Method1;
D2 d2 = d1;                              // Compile-time error
```

The following, however, is permitted:

```
D2 d2 = new D2 (d1);
```

Delegate instances are considered equal if they have the same method targets:

```
delegate void D();
...

D d1 = Method1;
D d2 = Method1;
Console.WriteLine (d1 == d2);        // True
```

Multicast delegates are considered equal if they reference the same methods *in the same order*.

Parameter compatibility

When you call a method, you can supply arguments that have more specific types than the parameters of that method. This is ordinary polymorphic behavior. For exactly the same reason, a delegate can have more specific parameter types than its method target. This is called *contravariance*.

Here's an example:

```
delegate void StringAction (string s);

class Test
{
  static void Main()
  {
    StringAction sa = new StringAction (ActOnObject);
    sa ("hello");
  }

  static void ActOnObject (object o) => Console.WriteLine (o);   // hello
}
```

(As with type parameter variance, delegates are variant only for *reference conversions*.)

A delegate merely calls a method on someone else's behalf. In this case, the String Action is invoked with an argument of type string. When the argument is then relayed to the target method, the argument gets implicitly upcast to an object.

The standard event pattern is designed to help you leverage contravariance through its use of the common EventArgs base class. For example, you can have a single method invoked by two different delegates, one passing a MouseEventArgs and the other passing a KeyEventArgs.

Return type compatibility

If you call a method, you may get back a type that is more specific than what you asked for. This is ordinary polymorphic behavior. For exactly the same reason, a delegate's target method may return a more specific type than described by the delegate. This is called *covariance*. For example:

```
delegate object ObjectRetriever();

class Test
{
  static void Main()
  {
    ObjectRetriever o = new ObjectRetriever (RetrieveString);
    object result = o();
    Console.WriteLine (result);      // hello
  }
  static string RetrieveString() => "hello";
}
```

`ObjectRetriever` expects to get back an `object`, but an `object` *subclass* will also do: delegate return types are *covariant*.

Generic delegate type parameter variance

In Chapter 3, we saw how generic interfaces support covariant and contravariant type parameters. The same capability exists for delegates too (from C# 4.0 onward).

If you're defining a generic delegate type, it's good practice to:

- Mark a type parameter used only on the return value as covariant (`out`).

- Mark any type parameters used only on parameters as contravariant (`in`).

Doing so allows conversions to work naturally by respecting inheritance relationships between types.

The following delegate (defined in the `System` namespace) has a covariant `TResult`:

```
delegate TResult Func<out TResult>();
```

allowing:

```
Func<string> x = ...;
Func<object> y = x;
```

The following delegate (defined in the `System` namespace) has a contravariant `T`:

```
delegate void Action<in T> (T arg);
```

allowing:

```
Action<object> x = ...;
Action<string> y = x;
```

Events

When using delegates, two emergent roles commonly appear: *broadcaster* and *subscriber*.

The *broadcaster* is a type that contains a delegate field. The broadcaster decides when to broadcast by invoking the delegate.

The *subscribers* are the method target recipients. A subscriber decides when to start and stop listening by calling += and -= on the broadcaster's delegate. A subscriber does not know about, or interfere with, other subscribers.

Events are a language feature that formalizes this pattern. An `event` is a construct that exposes just the subset of delegate features required for the broadcaster/subscriber model. The main purpose of events is to *prevent subscribers from interfering with one another*.

The easiest way to declare an event is to put the `event` keyword in front of a delegate member:

```
// Delegate definition
public delegate void PriceChangedHandler (decimal oldPrice,
                                           decimal newPrice);

public class Broadcaster
{
  // Event declaration
  public event PriceChangedHandler PriceChanged;
}
```

Code within the `Broadcaster` type has full access to `PriceChanged` and can treat it as a delegate. Code outside of `Broadcaster` can only perform += and -= operations on the `PriceChanged` event.

How Do Events Work on the Inside?

Three things happen under the covers when you declare an event as follows:

```
public class Broadcaster
{
  public event PriceChangedHandler PriceChanged;
}
```

First, the compiler translates the event declaration into something close to the following:

```
PriceChangedHandler priceChanged;   // private delegate
public event PriceChangedHandler PriceChanged
{
  add    { priceChanged += value; }
  remove { priceChanged -= value; }
}
```

The add and remove keywords denote explicit *event accessors*—which act rather like property accessors. We'll describe how to write these later.

Second, the compiler looks *within* the Broadcaster class for references to Price Changed that perform operations other than += or -= and redirects them to the underlying priceChanged delegate field.

Third, the compiler translates += and -= operations on the event to calls to the event's add and remove accessors. Interestingly, this makes the behavior of += and -= unique when applied to events: unlike in other scenarios, it's not simply a shortcut for + and - followed by an assignment.

Consider the following example. The Stock class fires its PriceChanged event every time the Price of the Stock changes:

```
public delegate void PriceChangedHandler (decimal oldPrice,
                                           decimal newPrice);
public class Stock
{
  string symbol;
  decimal price;

  public Stock (string symbol) { this.symbol = symbol; }

  public event PriceChangedHandler PriceChanged;

  public decimal Price
  {
    get { return price; }
    set
    {
      if (price == value) return;      // Exit if nothing has changed
      decimal oldPrice = price;
      price = value;
      if (PriceChanged != null)        // If invocation list not
        PriceChanged (oldPrice, price);  // empty, fire event.
    }
  }
}
```

If we remove the event keyword from our example so that PriceChanged becomes an ordinary delegate field, our example would give the same results. However, Stock would be less robust, in that subscribers could do the following things to interfere with each other:

- Replace other subscribers by reassigning PriceChanged (instead of using the += operator).
- Clear all subscribers (by setting PriceChanged to null).
- Broadcast to other subscribers by invoking the delegate.

WinRT events have slightly different semantics in that attaching to an event returns a token which is required to detach from the event. The compiler transparently bridges this gap (by maintaining an internal dictionary of tokens) so that you can consume WinRT events as though they were ordinary CLR events.

Standard Event Pattern

The .NET Framework defines a standard pattern for writing events. Its purpose is to provide consistency across both Framework and user code. At the core of the standard event pattern is System.EventArgs, a predefined Framework class with no members (other than the static Empty property). EventArgs is a base class for conveying information for an event. In our Stock example, we would subclass EventArgs to convey the old and new prices when a PriceChanged event is fired:

```
public class PriceChangedEventArgs : System.EventArgs
{
  public readonly decimal LastPrice;
  public readonly decimal NewPrice;

  public PriceChangedEventArgs (decimal lastPrice, decimal newPrice)
  {
    LastPrice = lastPrice;
    NewPrice = newPrice;
  }
}
```

For reusability, the EventArgs subclass is named according to the information it contains (rather than the event for which it will be used). It typically exposes data as properties or as read-only fields.

With an EventArgs subclass in place, the next step is to choose or define a delegate for the event. There are three rules:

- It must have a void return type.
- It must accept two arguments: the first of type object, and the second a subclass of EventArgs. The first argument indicates the event broadcaster, and the second argument contains the extra information to convey.
- Its name must end with *EventHandler*.

The Framework defines a generic delegate called System.EventHandler<> that satisfies these rules:

```
public delegate void EventHandler<TEventArgs>
  (object source, TEventArgs e) where TEventArgs : EventArgs;
```

Before generics existed in the language (prior to C# 2.0), we would have had to instead write a custom delegate as follows:

```
public delegate void PriceChangedHandler
    (object sender, PriceChangedEventArgs e);
```

For historical reasons, most events within the Framework use delegates defined in this way.

The next step is to define an event of the chosen delegate type. Here, we use the generic `EventHandler` delegate:

```
public class Stock
{
    ...
    public event EventHandler<PriceChangedEventArgs> PriceChanged;
}
```

Finally, the pattern requires that you write a protected virtual method that fires the event. The name must match the name of the event, prefixed with the word *On*, and then accept a single `EventArgs` argument:

```
public class Stock
{
    ...

    public event EventHandler<PriceChangedEventArgs> PriceChanged;

    protected virtual void OnPriceChanged (PriceChangedEventArgs e)
    {
        if (PriceChanged != null) PriceChanged (this, e);
    }
}
```

In multithreaded scenarios (Chapter 14), you need to assign the delegate to a temporary variable before testing and invoking it to avoid a thread-safety error:

```
var temp = PriceChanged;
if (temp != null) temp (this, e);
```

We can achieve the same functionality without the `temp` variable from C# 6 with the null-conditional operator:

```
PriceChanged?.Invoke (this, e);
```

Being both thread-safe and succinct, this is now the best general way to invoke events.

This provides a central point from which subclasses can invoke or override the event (assuming the class is not sealed).

Here's the complete example:

```
using System;

public class PriceChangedEventArgs : EventArgs
{
    public readonly decimal LastPrice;
```

```csharp
  public readonly decimal NewPrice;

  public PriceChangedEventArgs (decimal lastPrice, decimal newPrice)
  {
    LastPrice = lastPrice; NewPrice = newPrice;
  }
}

public class Stock
{
  string symbol;
  decimal price;

  public Stock (string symbol) {this.symbol = symbol;}

  public event EventHandler<PriceChangedEventArgs> PriceChanged;

  protected virtual void OnPriceChanged (PriceChangedEventArgs e)
  {
    PriceChanged?.Invoke (this, e);
  }

  public decimal Price
  {
    get { return price; }
    set
    {
      if (price == value) return;
      decimal oldPrice = price;
      price = value;
      OnPriceChanged (new PriceChangedEventArgs (oldPrice, price));
    }
  }
}

class Test
{
  static void Main()
  {
    Stock stock = new Stock ("THPW");
    stock.Price = 27.10M;
    // Register with the PriceChanged event
    stock.PriceChanged += stock_PriceChanged;
    stock.Price = 31.59M;
  }

  static void stock_PriceChanged (object sender, PriceChangedEventArgs e)
  {
    if ((e.NewPrice - e.LastPrice) / e.LastPrice > 0.1M)
      Console.WriteLine ("Alert, 10% stock price increase!");
  }
}
```

The predefined nongeneric `EventHandler` delegate can be used when an event doesn't carry extra information. In this example, we rewrite `Stock` such that the `PriceChanged` event is fired after the price changes, and no information about the event is necessary, other than it happened. We also make use of the `EventArgs.Empty` property in order to avoid unnecessarily instantiating an instance of `EventArgs`.

```
public class Stock
{
  string symbol;
  decimal price;

  public Stock (string symbol) { this.symbol = symbol; }

  public event EventHandler PriceChanged;

  protected virtual void OnPriceChanged (EventArgs e)
  {
    PriceChanged?.Invoke (this, e);
  }

  public decimal Price
  {
    get { return price; }
    set
    {
      if (price == value) return;
      price = value;
      OnPriceChanged (EventArgs.Empty);
    }
  }
}
```

Event Accessors

An event's *accessors* are the implementations of its += and -= functions. By default, accessors are implemented implicitly by the compiler. Consider this event declaration:

```
public event EventHandler PriceChanged;
```

The compiler converts this to the following:

- A private delegate field
- A public pair of event accessor functions (add_PriceChanged and remove_PriceChanged), whose implementations forward the += and -= operations to the private delegate field

You can take over this process by defining *explicit* event accessors. Here's a manual implementation of the `PriceChanged` event from our previous example:

```
private EventHandler priceChanged;        // Declare a private delegate

public event EventHandler PriceChanged
```

```
   {
     add    { priceChanged += value; }
     remove { priceChanged -= value; }
   }
```

This example is functionally identical to C#'s default accessor implementation (except that C# also ensures thread safety around updating the delegate via a lock-free compare-and-swap algorithm—see *http://albahari.com/threading*). By defining event accessors ourselves, we instruct C# not to generate default field and accessor logic.

With explicit event accessors, you can apply more complex strategies to the storage and access of the underlying delegate. There are three scenarios where this is useful:

- When the event accessors are merely relays for another class that is broadcasting the event.

- When the class exposes a large number of events, where most of the time very few subscribers exist, such as a Windows control. In such cases, it is better to store the subscriber's delegate instances in a dictionary, since a dictionary will contain less storage overhead than dozens of null delegate field references.

- When explicitly implementing an interface that declares an event.

Here is an example that illustrates the last point:

```
public interface IFoo { event EventHandler Ev; }

class Foo : IFoo
{
  private EventHandler ev;

  event EventHandler IFoo.Ev
  {
    add    { ev += value; }
    remove { ev -= value; }
  }
}
```

 The add and remove parts of an event are compiled to add_*XXX* and remove_*XXX* methods.

Event Modifiers

Like methods, events can be virtual, overridden, abstract, or sealed. Events can also be static:

```
public class Foo
{
  public static event EventHandler<EventArgs> StaticEvent;
  public virtual event EventHandler<EventArgs> VirtualEvent;
}
```

Lambda Expressions

A lambda expression is an unnamed method written in place of a delegate instance. The compiler immediately converts the lambda expression to either:

- A delegate instance.

- An *expression tree*, of type Expression<TDelegate>, representing the code inside the lambda expression in a traversable object model. This allows the lambda expression to be interpreted later at runtime (see "Building Query Expressions" on page 385 in Chapter 8).

Given the following delegate type:

```
delegate int Transformer (int i);
```

we could assign and invoke the lambda expression x => x * x as follows:

```
Transformer sqr = x => x * x;
Console.WriteLine (sqr(3));    // 9
```

 Internally, the compiler resolves lambda expressions of this type by writing a private method, and moving the expression's code into that method.

A lambda expression has the following form:

```
(parameters) => expression-or-statement-block
```

For convenience, you can omit the parentheses if and only if there is exactly one parameter of an inferable type.

In our example, there is a single parameter, x, and the expression is x * x:

```
x => x * x;
```

Each parameter of the lambda expression corresponds to a delegate parameter, and the type of the expression (which may be void) corresponds to the return type of the delegate.

In our example, x corresponds to parameter i, and the expression x * x corresponds to the return type int, therefore being compatible with the Transformer delegate:

```
delegate int Transformer (int i);
```

A lambda expression's code can be a *statement block* instead of an expression. We can rewrite our example as follows:

```
x => { return x * x; };
```

Lambda expressions are used most commonly with the Func and Action delegates, so you will most often see our earlier expression written as follows:

```
Func<int,int> sqr = x => x * x;
```

Here's an example of an expression that accepts two parameters:

```
Func<string,string,int> totalLength = (s1, s2) => s1.Length + s2.Length;
int total = totalLength ("hello", "world");   // total is 10;
```

Lambda expressions were introduced in C# 3.0.

Explicitly Specifying Lambda Parameter Types

The compiler can usually *infer* the type of lambda parameters. When this is not the case, you must specify the type of each parameter explicitly. Consider the following two methods:

```
void Foo<T> (T x)        {}
void Bar<T> (Action<T> a) {}
```

The following code will fail to compile because the compiler cannot infer the type of x:

```
Bar (x => Foo (x));     // What type is x?
```

We can fix this by explicitly specify x's type as follows:

```
Bar ((int x) => Foo (x));
```

This particular example is simple enough that it can be fixed in two other ways:

```
Bar<int> (x => Foo (x));   // Specify type parameter for Bar
Bar<int> (Foo);            // As above, but with method group
```

Capturing Outer Variables

A lambda expression can reference the local variables and parameters of the method in which it's defined (*outer variables*). For example:

```
static void Main()
{
  int factor = 2;
  Func<int, int> multiplier = n => n * factor;
  Console.WriteLine (multiplier (3));          // 6
}
```

Outer variables referenced by a lambda expression are called *captured variables*. A lambda expression that captures variables is called a *closure*.

Captured variables are evaluated when the delegate is actually *invoked*, not when the variables were *captured*:

```
int factor = 2;
Func<int, int> multiplier = n => n * factor;
factor = 10;
Console.WriteLine (multiplier (3));          // 30
```

Lambda expressions can themselves update captured variables:

```
int seed = 0;
Func<int> natural = () => seed++;
Console.WriteLine (natural());       // 0
Console.WriteLine (natural());       // 1
Console.WriteLine (seed);            // 2
```

Captured variables have their lifetimes extended to that of the delegate. In the following example, the local variable seed would ordinarily disappear from scope when Natural finished executing. But because seed has been *captured*, its lifetime is extended to that of the capturing delegate, natural:

```
static Func<int> Natural()
{
  int seed = 0;
  return () => seed++;     // Returns a closure
}

static void Main()
{
  Func<int> natural = Natural();
  Console.WriteLine (natural());     // 0
  Console.WriteLine (natural());     // 1
}
```

A local variable *instantiated* within a lambda expression is unique per invocation of the delegate instance. If we refactor our previous example to instantiate seed *within* the lambda expression, we get a different (in this case, undesirable) result:

```
static Func<int> Natural()
{
  return() => { int seed = 0; return seed++; };
}

static void Main()
{
  Func<int> natural = Natural();
  Console.WriteLine (natural());     // 0
  Console.WriteLine (natural());     // 0
}
```

Capturing is internally implemented by "hoisting" the captured variables into fields of a private class. When the method is called, the class is instantiated and lifetime-bound to the delegate instance.

Capturing iteration variables

When you capture the iteration variable of a for loop, C# treats that variable as though it was declared *outside* the loop. This means that the *same* variable is captured in each iteration. The following program writes 333 instead of writing 012:

```
Action[] actions = new Action[3];

for (int i = 0; i < 3; i++)
  actions [i] = () => Console.Write (i);

foreach (Action a in actions) a();      // 333
```

Each closure (shown in boldface) captures the same variable, i. (This actually makes sense when you consider that i is a variable whose value persists between loop iterations; you can even explicitly change i within the loop body if you want.) The consequence is that when the delegates are later invoked, each delegate sees i's value at the time of *invocation*—which is 3. We can illustrate this better by expanding the for loop as follows:

```
Action[] actions = new Action[3];
int i = 0;
actions[0] = () => Console.Write (i);
i = 1;
actions[1] = () => Console.Write (i);
i = 2;
actions[2] = () => Console.Write (i);
i = 3;
foreach (Action a in actions) a();      // 333
```

The solution, if we want to write 012, is to assign the iteration variable to a local variable that's scoped *inside* the loop:

```
Action[] actions = new Action[3];
for (int i = 0; i < 3; i++)
{
  int loopScopedi = i;
  actions [i] = () => Console.Write (loopScopedi);
}
foreach (Action a in actions) a();      // 012
```

Because loopScopedi is freshly created on every iteration, each closure captures a *different* variable.

Prior to C# 5.0, foreach loops worked in the same way:

```
Action[] actions = new Action[3];
int i = 0;

foreach (char c in "abc")
  actions [i++] = () => Console.Write (c);

foreach (Action a in actions) a();   // ccc in C# 4.0
```

This caused considerable confusion: unlike with a for loop, the iteration variable in a foreach loop is immutable, and so one would expect it to be treated as local to the loop body. The good news is that it's been fixed since C# 5.0, and the example above now writes "abc."

Technically, this is a breaking change because recompiling a C# 4.0 program in C# 5.0 could create a different result. In general, the C# team tries to avoid breaking changes; however in this case, a "break" would almost certainly indicate an undetected bug in the C# 4.0 program rather than intentional reliance on the old behavior.

Anonymous Methods

Anonymous methods are a C# 2.0 feature that has been mostly subsumed by C# 3.0 lambda expressions. An anonymous method is like a lambda expression, but it lacks the following features:

- Implicitly typed parameters.
- Expression syntax (an anonymous method must always be a statement block).
- The ability to compile to an expression tree by assigning to `Expression<T>`.

To write an anonymous method, you include the `delegate` keyword followed (optionally) by a parameter declaration and then a method body. For example, given this delegate:

```
delegate int Transformer (int i);
```

we could write and call an anonymous method as follows:

```
Transformer sqr = delegate (int x) {return x * x;};
Console.WriteLine (sqr(3));                              // 9
```

The first line is semantically equivalent to the following lambda expression:

```
Transformer sqr =       (int x) => {return x * x;};
```

or simply:

```
Transformer sqr =       x  => x * x;
```

Anonymous methods capture outer variables in the same way lambda expressions do.

A unique feature of anonymous methods is that you can omit the parameter declaration entirely—even if the delegate expects it. This can be useful in declaring events with a default empty handler:

```
public event EventHandler Clicked = delegate { };
```

This avoids the need for a null check before firing the event. The following is also legal:

```
// Notice that we omit the parameters:
Clicked += delegate { Console.WriteLine ("clicked"); };
```

try Statements and Exceptions

A `try` statement specifies a code block subject to error-handling or cleanup code. The `try` *block* must be followed by a `catch` *block*, a `finally` *block*, or both. The `catch` block executes when an error occurs in the `try` block. The `finally` block executes after execution leaves the `try` block (or if present, the `catch` block) to perform cleanup code, whether or not an error occurred.

A `catch` block has access to an `Exception` object that contains information about the error. You use a `catch` block to either compensate for the error or *rethrow* the exception. You rethrow an exception if you merely want to log the problem or if you want to rethrow a new, higher-level exception type.

A `finally` block adds determinism to your program: the CLR endeavors to always execute it. It's useful for cleanup tasks such as closing network connections.

A `try` statement looks like this:

```
try
{
    ... // exception may get thrown within execution of this block
}
catch (ExceptionA ex)
{
    ... // handle exception of type ExceptionA
}
catch (ExceptionB ex)
{
    ... // handle exception of type ExceptionB
}
finally
{
    ... // cleanup code
}
```

Consider the following program:

```
class Test
{
    static int Calc (int x) => 10 / x;

    static void Main()
    {
        int y = Calc (0);
        Console.WriteLine (y);
    }
}
```

Because x is zero, the runtime throws a `DivideByZeroException`, and our program terminates. We can prevent this by catching the exception as follows:

```
class Test
{
  static int Calc (int x) => 10 / x;

  static void Main()
  {
    try
    {
      int y = Calc (0);
      Console.WriteLine (y);
    }
    catch (DivideByZeroException ex)
    {
      Console.WriteLine ("x cannot be zero");
    }
    Console.WriteLine ("program completed");
  }
}
```

```
OUTPUT:
x cannot be zero
program completed
```

This is a simple example to illustrate exception handling. We could deal with this particular scenario better in practice by checking explicitly for the divisor being zero before calling Calc.

Checking for preventable errors is preferable to relying on try/catch blocks because exceptions are relatively expensive to handle, taking hundreds of clock cycles or more.

When an exception is thrown, the CLR performs a test: *Is execution currently within a* try *statement that can catch the exception?*

- If so, execution is passed to the compatible catch block. If the catch block successfully finishes executing, execution moves to the next statement after the try statement (if present, executing the finally block first).

- If not, execution jumps back to the caller of the function, and the test is repeated (after executing any finally blocks that wrap the statement).

If no function takes responsibility for the exception, an error dialog box is displayed to the user, and the program terminates.

The catch Clause

A catch clause specifies what type of exception to catch. This must either be System.Exception or a subclass of System.Exception.

Catching System.Exception catches all possible errors. This is useful when:

- Your program can potentially recover regardless of the specific exception type.

- You plan to rethrow the exception (perhaps after logging it).

- Your error handler is the last resort, prior to termination of the program.

More typically, though, you catch *specific exception types*, in order to avoid having to deal with circumstances for which your handler wasn't designed (e.g., an OutOfMe moryException).

You can handle multiple exception types with multiple catch clauses (again, this example could be written with explicit argument checking rather than exception handling):

```
class Test
{
  static void Main (string[] args)
  {
    try
    {
      byte b = byte.Parse (args[0]);
      Console.WriteLine (b);
    }
    catch (IndexOutOfRangeException ex)
    {
      Console.WriteLine ("Please provide at least one argument");
    }
    catch (FormatException ex)
    {
      Console.WriteLine ("That's not a number!");
    }
    catch (OverflowException ex)
    {
      Console.WriteLine ("You've given me more than a byte!");
    }
  }
}
```

Only one catch clause executes for a given exception. If you want to include a safety net to catch more general exceptions (such as System.Exception), you must put the more specific handlers *first*.

An exception can be caught without specifying a variable if you don't need to access its properties:

```
catch (OverflowException)   // no variable
{
  ...
}
```

Furthermore, you can omit both the variable and the type (meaning that all exceptions will be caught):

```
catch { ... }
```

Exception filters (C# 6)

From C# 6.0, you can specify an *exception filter* in a catch clause by adding a when clause:

```
catch (WebException ex) when (ex.Status == WebExceptionStatus.Timeout)
{
  ...
}
```

If a WebException is thrown in this example, the Boolean expression following the when keyword is then evaluated. If the result is false, the catch block in question is ignored, and any subsequent catch clauses are considered. With exception filters, it can be meaningful to catch the same exception type again:

```
catch (WebException ex) when (ex.Status == WebExceptionStatus.Timeout)
{ ... }
catch (WebException ex) when (ex.Status == WebExceptionStatus.SendFailure)
{ ... }
```

The Boolean expression in the when clause can be side-effecting, such as a method that logs the exception for diagnostic purposes.

The finally Block

A finally block always executes—whether or not an exception is thrown and whether or not the try block runs to completion. finally blocks are typically used for cleanup code.

A finally block executes either:

- After a catch block finishes
- After control leaves the try block because of a jump statement (e.g., return or goto)
- After the try block ends

The only things that can defeat a finally block are an infinite loop or the process ending abruptly.

A finally block helps add determinism to a program. In the following example, the file that we open *always* gets closed, regardless of whether:

- The try block finishes normally
- Execution returns early because the file is empty (EndOfStream)
- An IOException is thrown while reading the file

```
static void ReadFile()
{
  StreamReader reader = null;    // In System.IO namespace
  try
```

```
  {
    reader = File.OpenText ("file.txt");
    if (reader.EndOfStream) return;
    Console.WriteLine (reader.ReadToEnd());
  }
  finally
  {
    if (reader != null) reader.Dispose();
  }
}
```

In this example, we closed the file by calling `Dispose` on the `StreamReader`. Calling `Dispose` on an object within a `finally` block is a standard convention throughout the .NET Framework and is supported explicitly in C# through the `using` statement.

The using statement

Many classes encapsulate unmanaged resources, such as file handles, graphics handles, or database connections. These classes implement `System.IDisposable`, which defines a single parameterless method named `Dispose` to clean up these resources. The `using` statement provides an elegant syntax for calling `Dispose` on an `IDisposable` object within a `finally` block.

The following:

```
using (StreamReader reader = File.OpenText ("file.txt"))
{
  ...
}
```

is precisely equivalent to:

```
{
  StreamReader reader = File.OpenText ("file.txt");
  try
  {
    ...
  }
  finally
  {
    if (reader != null)
      ((IDisposable)reader).Dispose();
  }
}
```

We cover the disposal pattern in more detail in Chapter 12.

Throwing Exceptions

Exceptions can be thrown either by the runtime or in user code. In this example, `Display` throws a `System.ArgumentNullException`:

```
class Test
{
  static void Display (string name)
```

```
  {
    if (name == null)
      throw new ArgumentNullException (nameof (name));

    Console.WriteLine (name);
  }

  static void Main()
  {
    try { Display (null); }
    catch (ArgumentNullException ex)
    {
      Console.WriteLine ("Caught the exception");
    }
  }
}
```

Rethrowing an exception

You can capture and rethrow an exception as follows:

```
try {  ...  }
catch (Exception ex)
{
  // Log error
  ...
  throw;          // Rethrow same exception
}
```

If we replaced throw with throw ex, the example would still work, but the StackTrace property of the newly propagated exception would no longer reflect the original error.

Rethrowing in this manner lets you log an error without *swallowing* it. It also lets you back out of handling an exception should circumstances turn out to be outside what you expected:

```
using System.Net;        // (See Chapter 16)
...

string s = null;
using (WebClient wc = new WebClient())
  try { s = wc.DownloadString ("http://www.albahari.com/nutshell/");  }
  catch (WebException ex)
  {
    if (ex.Status == WebExceptionStatus.Timeout)
      Console.WriteLine ("Timeout");
    else
      throw;        // Can't handle other sorts of WebException, so rethrow
  }
```

From C# 6.0, this can be written more tersely with an exception filter:

```
catch (WebException ex) when (ex.Status == WebExceptionStatus.Timeout)
{
```

```
    Console.WriteLine ("Timeout");
}
```

The other common scenario is to rethrow a more specific exception type. For example:

```
try
{
    ... // Parse a DateTime from XML element data
}
catch (FormatException ex)
{
    throw new XmlException ("Invalid DateTime", ex);
}
```

Notice that when we constructed XmlException, we passed in the original exception, ex, as the second argument. This argument populates the InnerException property of the new exception and aids debugging. Nearly all types of exception offer a similar constructor.

Rethrowing a *less* specific exception is something you might do when crossing a trust boundary so as not to leak technical information to potential hackers.

Key Properties of System.Exception

The most important properties of System.Exception are the following:

StackTrace
    A string representing all the methods that are called from the origin of the exception to the catch block.

Message
    A string with a description of the error.

InnerException
    The inner exception (if any) that caused the outer exception. This, itself, may have another InnerException.

> All exceptions in C# are runtime exceptions—there is no equivalent to Java's compile-time checked exceptions.

Common Exception Types

The following exception types are used widely throughout the CLR and .NET Framework. You can throw these yourself or use them as base classes for deriving custom exception types.

System.ArgumentException
    Thrown when a function is called with a bogus argument. This generally indicates a program bug.

`System.ArgumentNullException`

Subclass of `ArgumentException` that's thrown when a function argument is (unexpectedly) `null`.

`System.ArgumentOutOfRangeException`

Subclass of `ArgumentException` that's thrown when a (usually numeric) argument is too big or too small. For example, this is thrown when passing a negative number into a function that accepts only positive values.

`System.InvalidOperationException`

Thrown when the state of an object is unsuitable for a method to successfully execute, regardless of any particular argument values. Examples include reading an unopened file or getting the next element from an enumerator where the underlying list has been modified partway through the iteration.

`System.NotSupportedException`

Thrown to indicate that a particular functionality is not supported. A good example is calling the `Add` method on a collection for which `IsReadOnly` returns `true`.

`System.NotImplementedException`

Thrown to indicate that a function has not yet been implemented.

`System.ObjectDisposedException`

Thrown when the object upon which the function is called has been disposed.

Another commonly encountered exception type is `NullReferenceException`. The CLR throws this exception when you attempt to access a member of an object whose value is `null` (indicating a bug in your code). You can throw a `NullReferenceException` directly (for testing purposes) as follows:

```
throw null;
```

The TryXXX Method Pattern

When writing a method, you have a choice, when something goes wrong, to return some kind of failure code or throw an exception. In general, you throw an exception when the error is outside the normal workflow—or if you expect that the immediate caller won't be able to cope with it. Occasionally, though, it can be best to offer both choices to the consumer. An example of this is the `int` type, which defines two versions of its `Parse` method:

```
public int Parse     (string input);
public bool TryParse (string input, out int returnValue);
```

If parsing fails, `Parse` throws an exception; `TryParse` returns `false`.

You can implement this pattern by having the *XXX* method call the `Try`*XXX* method as follows:

```
public return-type XXX (input-type input)
{
  return-type returnValue;
  if (!TryXXX (input, out returnValue))
    throw new YYYException (...)
  return returnValue;
}
```

Alternatives to Exceptions

As with `int.TryParse`, a function can communicate failure by sending an error code back to the calling function via a return type or parameter. Although this can work with simple and predictable failures, it becomes clumsy when extended to all errors, polluting method signatures and creating unnecessary complexity and clutter. It also cannot generalize to functions that are not methods, such as operators (e.g., the division operator) or properties. An alternative is to place the error in a common place where all functions in the call stack can see it (e.g., a static method that stores the current error per thread). This, though, requires each function to participate in an error-propagation pattern that is cumbersome and, ironically, itself error-prone.

Enumeration and Iterators

Enumeration

An *enumerator* is a read-only, forward-only cursor over a *sequence of values*. An enumerator is an object that implements either of the following interfaces:

- `System.Collections.IEnumerator`
- `System.Collections.Generic.IEnumerator<T>`

Technically, any object that has a method named `MoveNext` and a property called `Current` is treated as an enumerator. This relaxation was introduced in C# 1.0 to avoid the boxing/unboxing overhead when enumerating value type elements but was made redundant when generics were introduced in C# 2.

The `foreach` statement iterates over an *enumerable* object. An enumerable object is the logical representation of a sequence. It is not itself a cursor, but an object that produces cursors over itself. An enumerable object either:

- Implements `IEnumerable` or `IEnumerable<T>`
- Has a method named `GetEnumerator` that returns an *enumerator*

IEnumerator and IEnumerable are defined in System.Collec
tions. IEnumerator<T> and IEnumerable<T> are defined in
System.Collections.Generic.

The enumeration pattern is as follows:

```
class Enumerator     // Typically implements IEnumerator or IEnumerator<T>
{
  public IteratorVariableType Current { get {...} }
  public bool MoveNext() {...}
}

class Enumerable     // Typically implements IEnumerable or IEnumerable<T>
{
  public Enumerator GetEnumerator() {...}
}
```

Here is the high-level way of iterating through the characters in the word *beer* using
a foreach statement:

```
foreach (char c in "beer")
  Console.WriteLine (c);
```

Here is the low-level way of iterating through the characters in *beer* without using a
foreach statement:

```
using (var enumerator = "beer".GetEnumerator())
  while (enumerator.MoveNext())
  {
    var element = enumerator.Current;
    Console.WriteLine (element);
  }
```

If the enumerator implements IDisposable, the foreach statement also acts as a
using statement, implicitly disposing the enumerator object.

Chapter 7 explains the enumeration interfaces in further detail.

Collection Initializers

You can instantiate and populate an enumerable object in a single step. For example:

```
using System.Collections.Generic;
...

List<int> list = new List<int> {1, 2, 3};
```

The compiler translates this to the following:

```
using System.Collections.Generic;
...

List<int> list = new List<int>();
list.Add (1);
list.Add (2);
list.Add (3);
```

This requires that the enumerable object implements the System.Collections.IEnumerable interface and that it has an Add method that has the appropriate number of parameters for the call. You can similarly initialize dictionaries (see "Dictionaries" on page 314 in Chapter 4) as follows:

```
var dict = new Dictionary<int, string>()
{
  { 5, "five" },
  { 10, "ten" }
};
```

Or, as of C# 6:

```
var dict = new Dictionary<int, string>()
{
  [3] = "three",
  [10] = "ten"
};
```

The latter is valid not only with dictionaries, but with any type for which an indexer exists.

Iterators

Whereas a foreach statement is a *consumer* of an enumerator, an iterator is a *producer* of an enumerator. In this example, we use an iterator to return a sequence of Fibonacci numbers (where each number is the sum of the previous two):

```
using System;
using System.Collections.Generic;

class Test
{
  static void Main()
  {
    foreach (int fib in Fibs(6))
      Console.Write (fib + "  ");
  }

  static IEnumerable<int> Fibs (int fibCount)
  {
    for (int i = 0, prevFib = 1, curFib = 1; i < fibCount; i++)
    {
      yield return prevFib;
      int newFib = prevFib+curFib;
      prevFib = curFib;
      curFib = newFib;
    }
  }
}
```

```
OUTPUT: 1  1  2  3  5  8
```

Whereas a return statement expresses "Here's the value you asked me to return from this method," a yield return statement expresses "Here's the next element you asked me to yield from this enumerator." On each yield statement, control is returned to the caller, but the callee's state is maintained so that the method can continue executing as soon as the caller enumerates the next element. The lifetime of this state is bound to the enumerator such that the state can be released when the caller has finished enumerating.

 The compiler converts iterator methods into private classes that implement IEnumerable<T> and/or IEnumerator<T>. The logic within the iterator block is "inverted" and spliced into the MoveNext method and Current property on the compiler-written enumerator class. This means that when you call an iterator method, all you're doing is instantiating the compiler-written class; none of your code actually runs! Your code runs only when you start enumerating over the resultant sequence, typically with a foreach statement.

Iterator Semantics

An iterator is a method, property, or indexer that contains one or more yield statements. An iterator must return one of the following four interfaces (otherwise, the compiler will generate an error):

```
// Enumerable interfaces
System.Collections.IEnumerable
System.Collections.Generic.IEnumerable<T>

// Enumerator interfaces
System.Collections.IEnumerator
System.Collections.Generic.IEnumerator<T>
```

An iterator has different semantics, depending on whether it returns an *enumerable* interface or an *enumerator* interface. We describe this in Chapter 7.

Multiple yield statements are permitted. For example:

```
class Test
{
  static void Main()
  {
    foreach (string s in Foo())
      Console.WriteLine(s);        // Prints "One","Two","Three"
  }

  static IEnumerable<string> Foo()
  {
    yield return "One";
    yield return "Two";
    yield return "Three";
  }
}
```

yield break

The `yield break` statement indicates that the iterator block should exit early without returning more elements. We can modify `Foo` as follows to demonstrate:

```
static IEnumerable<string> Foo (bool breakEarly)
{
  yield return "One";
  yield return "Two";

  if (breakEarly)
    yield break;

  yield return "Three";
}
```

 A `return` statement is illegal in an iterator block—you must use a `yield break` instead.

Iterators and try/catch/finally blocks

A `yield return` statement cannot appear in a `try` block that has a `catch` clause:

```
IEnumerable<string> Foo()
{
  try { yield return "One"; }    // Illegal
  catch { ... }
}
```

Nor can `yield return` appear in a `catch` or `finally` block. These restrictions are due to the fact that the compiler must translate iterators into ordinary classes with `MoveNext`, `Current`, and `Dispose` members, and translating exception handling blocks would create excessive complexity.

You can, however, yield within a `try` block that has (only) a `finally` block:

```
IEnumerable<string> Foo()
{
  try { yield return "One"; }    // OK
  finally { ... }
}
```

The code in the `finally` block executes when the consuming enumerator reaches the end of the sequence or is disposed. A `foreach` statement implicitly disposes the enumerator if you break early, making this a safe way to consume enumerators. When working with enumerators explicitly, a trap is to abandon enumeration early without disposing it, circumventing the `finally` block. You can avoid this risk by wrapping explicit use of enumerators in a `using` statement:

```
string firstElement = null;
var sequence = Foo();
using (var enumerator = sequence.GetEnumerator())
  if (enumerator.MoveNext())
    firstElement = enumerator.Current;
```

Composing Sequences

Iterators are highly composable. We can extend our example, this time to output
even Fibonacci numbers only:

```
using System;
using System.Collections.Generic;

class Test
{
  static void Main()
  {
    foreach (int fib in EvenNumbersOnly (Fibs(6)))
      Console.WriteLine (fib);
  }

  static IEnumerable<int> Fibs (int fibCount)
  {
    for (int i = 0, prevFib = 1, curFib = 1; i < fibCount; i++)
    {
      yield return prevFib;
      int newFib = prevFib+curFib;
      prevFib = curFib;
      curFib = newFib;
    }
  }

  static IEnumerable<int> EvenNumbersOnly (IEnumerable<int> sequence)
  {
    foreach (int x in sequence)
      if ((x % 2) == 0)
        yield return x;
  }
}
```

Each element is not calculated until the last moment—when requested by a Move
Next() operation. Figure 4-1 shows the data requests and data output over time.

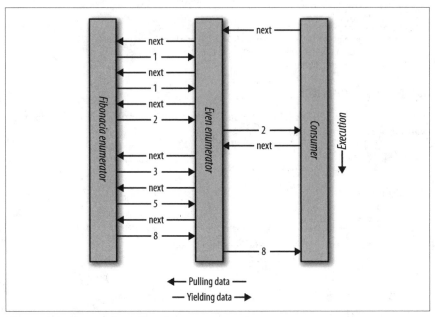

Figure 4-1. Composing sequences

The composability of the iterator pattern is extremely useful in LINQ; we discuss the subject again in Chapter 8.

Nullable Types

Reference types can represent a nonexistent value with a null reference. Value types, however, cannot ordinarily represent null values. For example:

```
string s = null;      // OK, Reference Type
int i = null;         // Compile Error, Value Type cannot be null
```

To represent null in a value type, you must use a special construct called a *nullable type*. A nullable type is denoted with a value type followed by the ? symbol:

```
int? i = null;                      // OK, Nullable Type
Console.WriteLine (i == null);      // True
```

Nullable<T> struct

T? translates into System.Nullable<T>, which is a lightweight immutable structure, having only two fields, to represent Value and HasValue. The essence of System.Nullable<T> is very simple:

```
public struct Nullable<T> where T : struct
{
  public T Value {get;}
  public bool HasValue {get;}
```

```
    public T GetValueOrDefault();
    public T GetValueOrDefault (T defaultValue);
    ...
}
```

The code:

```
int? i = null;
Console.WriteLine (i == null);              // True
```

translates to:

```
Nullable<int> i = new Nullable<int>();
Console.WriteLine (! i.HasValue);           // True
```

Attempting to retrieve Value when HasValue is false throws an InvalidOperatio
nException. GetValueOrDefault() returns Value if HasValue is true; otherwise, it
returns new T() or a specified custom default value.

The default value of T? is null.

Implicit and explicit nullable conversions

The conversion from T to T? is implicit, and from T? to T is explicit. For example:

```
int? x = 5;        // implicit
int y = (int)x;    // explicit
```

The explicit cast is directly equivalent to calling the nullable object's Value property.
Hence, an InvalidOperationException is thrown if HasValue is false.

Boxing and unboxing nullable values

When T? is boxed, the boxed value on the heap contains T, not T?. This optimization is possible because a boxed value is a reference type that can already express
null.

C# also permits the unboxing of nullable types with the as operator. The result will
be null if the cast fails:

```
object o = "string";
int? x = o as int?;
Console.WriteLine (x.HasValue);   // False
```

Operator Lifting

The Nullable<T> struct does not define operators such as <, >, or even ==. Despite
this, the following code compiles and executes correctly:

```
int? x = 5;
int? y = 10;
bool b = x < y;       // true
```

This works because the compiler borrows, or "lifts," the less-than operator from the underlying value type. Semantically, it translates the preceding comparison expression into this:

```
bool b = (x.HasValue && y.HasValue) ? (x.Value < y.Value) : false;
```

In other words, if both x and y have values, it compares via int's less-than operator; otherwise, it returns false.

Operator lifting means you can implicitly use T's operators on T?. You can define operators for T? in order to provide special-purpose null behavior, but in the vast majority of cases, it's best to rely on the compiler automatically applying systematic nullable logic for you. Here are some examples:

```
int? x = 5;
int? y = null;

// Equality operator examples
Console.WriteLine (x == y);    // False
Console.WriteLine (x == null); // False
Console.WriteLine (x == 5);    // True
Console.WriteLine (y == null); // True
Console.WriteLine (y == 5);    // False
Console.WriteLine (y != 5);    // True

// Relational operator examples
Console.WriteLine (x < 6);     // True
Console.WriteLine (y < 6);     // False
Console.WriteLine (y > 6);     // False

// All other operator examples
Console.WriteLine (x + 5);     // 10
Console.WriteLine (x + y);     // null (prints empty line)
```

The compiler performs null logic differently depending on the category of operator. The following sections explain these different rules.

Equality operators (== and !=)

Lifted equality operators handle nulls just like reference types do. This means two null values are equal:

```
Console.WriteLine (       null ==        null);   // True
Console.WriteLine ((bool?)null == (bool?)null);   // True
```

Further:

- If exactly one operand is null, the operands are unequal.
- If both operands are non-null, their Values are compared.

Relational operators (<, <=, >=, >)

The relational operators work on the principle that it is meaningless to compare null operands. This means comparing a null value to either a null or a non-null value returns false:

```
bool b = x < y;    // Translation:

bool b = (x.HasValue && y.HasValue)
            ? (x.Value < y.Value)
            : false;

// b is false (assuming x is 5 and y is null)
```

All other operators (+, −, *, /, %, &, |, ^, <<, >>, +, ++, --, !, ~)

These operators return null when any of the operands are null. This pattern should be familiar to SQL users:

```
int? c = x + y;    // Translation:

int? c = (x.HasValue && y.HasValue)
            ? (int?) (x.Value + y.Value)
            : null;

// c is null (assuming x is 5 and y is null)
```

An exception is when the & and | operators are applied to bool?, which we will discuss shortly.

Mixing nullable and non-nullable operators

You can mix and match nullable and non-nullable types (this works because there is an implicit conversion from T to T?):

```
int? a = null;
int b = 2;
int? c = a + b;    // c is null - equivalent to a + (int?)b
```

bool? with & and | Operators

When supplied operands of type bool? the & and | operators treat null as an *unknown value*. So, null | true is true, because:

- If the unknown value is false, the result would be true.
- If the unknown value is true, the result would be true.

Similarly, null & false is false. This behavior would be familiar to SQL users. The following example enumerates other combinations:

```
bool? n = null;
bool? f = false;
bool? t = true;
```

```
Console.WriteLine (n | n);    // (null)
Console.WriteLine (n | f);    // (null)
Console.WriteLine (n | t);    // True
Console.WriteLine (n & n);    // (null)
Console.WriteLine (n & f);    // False
Console.WriteLine (n & t);    // (null)
```

Nullable Types & Null Operators

Nullable types work particularly well with the ?? operator (see "Null-Coalescing Operator" on page 55) in Chapter 2. For example:

```
int? x = null;
int y = x ?? 5;        // y is 5

int? a = null, b = 1, c = 2;
Console.WriteLine (a ?? b ?? c);  // 1 (first non-null value)
```

Using ?? on a nullable value type is equivalent to calling GetValueOrDefault with an explicit default value, except that the expression for the default value is never evaluated if the variable is not null.

Nullable types also work well with the null-conditional operator (see "Null-conditional operator (C# 6)" on page 55 in Chapter 2). In the following example, length evaluates to null:

```
System.Text.StringBuilder sb = null;
int? length = sb?.ToString().Length;
```

We can combine this with the null-coalescing operator to evaluate to zero instead of null:

```
int length = sb?.ToString().Length ?? 0;   // Evaluates to 0 if sb is null
```

Scenarios for Nullable Types

One of the most common scenarios for nullable types is to represent unknown values. This frequently occurs in database programming, where a class is mapped to a table with nullable columns. If these columns are strings (e.g., an EmailAddress column on a Customer table), there is no problem, as string is a reference type in the CLR, which can be null. However, most other SQL column types map to CLR struct types, making nullable types very useful when mapping SQL to the CLR. For example:

```
// Maps to a Customer table in a database
public class Customer
{
  ...
  public decimal? AccountBalance;
}
```

A nullable type can also be used to represent the backing field of what's sometimes called an *ambient property*. An ambient property, if null, returns the value of its parent. For example:

```
public class Row
{
  ...
  Grid parent;
  Color? color;

  public Color Color
  {
    get { return color ?? parent.Color; }
    set { color = value == parent.Color ? (Color?)null : value; }
  }
}
```

Alternatives to Nullable Types

Before nullable types were part of the C# language (i.e., before C# 2.0), there were many strategies to deal with nullable value types, examples of which still appear in the .NET Framework for historical reasons. One of these strategies is to designate a particular non-null value as the "null value"; an example is in the string and array classes. `String.IndexOf` returns the magic value of –1 when the character is not found:

```
int i = "Pink".IndexOf ('b');
Console.WriteLine (i);          // –1
```

However, `Array.IndexOf` returns –1 only if the index is 0-bounded. The more general formula is that `IndexOf` returns 1 less than the lower bound of the array. In the next example, `IndexOf` returns 0 when an element is not found:

```
// Create an array whose lower bound is 1 instead of 0:

Array a = Array.CreateInstance (typeof (string),
                                new int[] {2}, new int[] {1});
a.SetValue ("a", 1);
a.SetValue ("b", 2);
Console.WriteLine (Array.IndexOf (a, "c"));  // 0
```

Nominating a "magic value" is problematic for several reasons:

- It means that each value type has a different representation of null. In contrast, nullable types provide one common pattern that works for all value types.

- There may be no reasonable designated value. In the previous example, –1 could not always be used. The same is true for our earlier example representing an unknown account balance.

- Forgetting to test for the magic value results in an incorrect value that may go unnoticed until later in execution—when it pulls an unintended magic trick. Forgetting to test `HasValue` on a null value, however, throws an `InvalidOpera tionException` on the spot.

- The ability for a value to be null is not captured in the *type*. Types communicate the intention of a program, allow the compiler to check for correctness, and enable a consistent set of rules enforced by the compiler.

Operator Overloading

Operators can be overloaded to provide more natural syntax for custom types. Operator overloading is most appropriately used for implementing custom structs that represent fairly primitive data types. For example, a custom numeric type is an excellent candidate for operator overloading.

The following symbolic operators can be overloaded:

+ (unary)	- (unary)	!	~	++
- -	+	-	*	/
%	&	|	^	<<
>>	==	!=	>	<
>=	<=			

The following operators are also overloadable:

- Implicit and explicit conversions (with the `implicit` and `explicit` keywords)
- The `true` and `false` *operators* (not *literals*).

The following operators are indirectly overloaded:

- The compound assignment operators (e.g., +=, /=) are implicitly overridden by overriding the noncompound operators (e.g., +, /).

- The conditional operators && and || are implicitly overridden by overriding the bitwise operators & and |.

Operator Functions

An operator is overloaded by declaring an *operator function*. An operator function has the following rules:

- The name of the function is specified with the `operator` keyword followed by an operator symbol.

- The operator function must be marked `static` and `public`.

- The parameters of the operator function represent the operands.

- The return type of an operator function represents the result of an expression.

- At least one of the operands must be the type in which the operator function is declared.

In the following example, we define a struct called `Note` representing a musical note and then overload the + operator:

```
public struct Note
{
  int value;
  public Note (int semitonesFromA) { value = semitonesFromA; }
  public static Note operator + (Note x, int semitones)
  {
    return new Note (x.value + semitones);
  }
}
```

This overload allows us to add an `int` to a `Note`:

```
Note B = new Note (2);
Note CSharp = B + 2;
```

Overloading an operator automatically overloads the corresponding compound assignment operator. In our example, since we overrode +, we can use += too:

```
CSharp += 2;
```

Just as with methods and properties, C# 6 allows operator functions comprising a single expression to be written more tersely with expression-bodied syntax:

```
public static Note operator + (Note x, int semitones)
                        => new Note (x.value + semitones);
```

Overloading Equality and Comparison Operators

Equality and comparison operators are sometimes overridden when writing structs and in rare cases, when writing classes. Special rules and obligations come with overloading the equality and comparison operators, which we explain in Chapter 6. A summary of these rules is as follows:

Pairing

> The C# compiler enforces operators that are logical pairs to both be defined. These operators are (== !=), (< >), and (<= >=).

`Equals` *and* `GetHashCode`

> In most cases, if you overload (==) and (!=), you will usually need to override the `Equals` and `GetHashCode` methods defined on `object` in order to get meaningful behavior. The C# compiler will give a warning if you do not

do this. (See "Equality Comparison" on page 267 in Chapter 6 for more details.)

`IComparable` *and* `IComparable<T>`

If you overload (< >) and (<= >=), you should implement `IComparable` and `IComparable<T>`.

Custom Implicit and Explicit Conversions

Implicit and explicit conversions are overloadable operators. These conversions are typically overloaded to make converting between strongly related types (such as numeric types) concise and natural.

To convert between weakly related types, the following strategies are more suitable:

- Write a constructor that has a parameter of the type to convert from.
- Write To*XXX* and (static) From*XXX* methods to convert between types.

As explained in the discussion on types, the rationale behind implicit conversions is that they are guaranteed to succeed and not lose information during the conversion. Conversely, an explicit conversion should be required either when runtime circumstances will determine whether the conversion will succeed or if information may be lost during the conversion.

In this example, we define conversions between our musical `Note` type and a double (which represents the frequency in hertz of that note):

```
...
// Convert to hertz
public static implicit operator double (Note x)
  => 440 * Math.Pow (2, (double) x.value / 12 );

// Convert from hertz (accurate to the nearest semitone)
public static explicit operator Note (double x)
  => new Note ((int) (0.5 + 12 * (Math.Log (x/440) / Math.Log(2) ) ));
...

Note n = (Note)554.37;  // explicit conversion
double x = n;           // implicit conversion
```

Following our own guidelines, this example might be better implemented with a `ToFrequency` method (and a static `From Frequency` method) instead of implicit and explicit operators.

Custom conversions are ignored by the `as` and `is` operators:

```
Console.WriteLine (554.37 is Note);  // False
Note n = 554.37 as Note;             // Error
```

Overloading true and false

The `true` and `false` operators are overloaded in the extremely rare case of types that are Boolean "in spirit" but do not have a conversion to `bool`. An example is a type that implements three-state logic: by overloading `true` and `false`, such a type can work seamlessly with conditional statements and operators—namely, `if`, `do`, `while`, `for`, `&&`, `||`, and `?:`. The `System.Data.SqlTypes.SqlBoolean` struct provides this functionality. For example:

```
SqlBoolean a = SqlBoolean.Null;
if (a)
  Console.WriteLine ("True");
else if (!a)
  Console.WriteLine ("False");
else
  Console.WriteLine ("Null");

OUTPUT:
Null
```

The following code is a reimplementation of the parts of `SqlBoolean` necessary to demonstrate the `true` and `false` operators:

```
public struct SqlBoolean
{
  public static bool operator true (SqlBoolean x)
    => x.m_value == True.m_value;

  public static bool operator false (SqlBoolean x)
    => x.m_value == False.m_value;

  public static SqlBoolean operator ! (SqlBoolean x)
  {
    if (x.m_value == Null.m_value)  return Null;
    if (x.m_value == False.m_value) return True;
    return False;
  }

  public static readonly SqlBoolean Null =  new SqlBoolean(0);
  public static readonly SqlBoolean False = new SqlBoolean(1);
  public static readonly SqlBoolean True =  new SqlBoolean(2);

  private SqlBoolean (byte value) { m_value = value; }
  private byte m_value;
}
```

Extension Methods

Extension methods allow an existing type to be extended with new methods without altering the definition of the original type. An extension method is a static method of a static class, where the `this` modifier is applied to the first parameter. The type of the first parameter will be the type that is extended. For example:

```
public static class StringHelper
{
  public static bool IsCapitalized (this string s)
  {
    if (string.IsNullOrEmpty(s)) return false;
    return char.IsUpper (s[0]);
  }
}
```

The IsCapitalized extension method can be called as though it were an instance method on a string, as follows:

```
Console.WriteLine ("Perth".IsCapitalized());
```

An extension method call, when compiled, is translated back into an ordinary static method call:

```
Console.WriteLine (StringHelper.IsCapitalized ("Perth"));
```

The translation works as follows:

```
arg0.Method (arg1, arg2, ...);              // Extension method call
StaticClass.Method (arg0, arg1, arg2, ...); // Static method call
```

Interfaces can be extended, too:

```
public static T First<T> (this IEnumerable<T> sequence)
{
  foreach (T element in sequence)
    return element;

  throw new InvalidOperationException ("No elements!");
}
...
Console.WriteLine ("Seattle".First());   // S
```

Extension methods were added in C# 3.0.

Extension Method Chaining

Extension methods, like instance methods, provide a tidy way to chain functions. Consider the following two functions:

```
public static class StringHelper
{
  public static string Pluralize (this string s) {...}
  public static string Capitalize (this string s) {...}
}
```

x and y are equivalent and both evaluate to "Sausages", but x uses extension methods, whereas y uses static methods:

```
string x = "sausage".Pluralize().Capitalize();
string y = StringHelper.Capitalize (StringHelper.Pluralize ("sausage"));
```

Ambiguity and Resolution

Namespaces

An extension method cannot be accessed unless its class is in scope, typically by its namespace being imported. Consider the extension method IsCapitalized in the following example:

```
using System;

namespace Utils
{
  public static class StringHelper
  {
    public static bool IsCapitalized (this string s)
    {
      if (string.IsNullOrEmpty(s)) return false;
      return char.IsUpper (s[0]);
    }
  }
}
```

To use IsCapitalized, the following application must import Utils in order to avoid a compile-time error:

```
namespace MyApp
{
  using Utils;

  class Test
  {
    static void Main() => Console.WriteLine ("Perth".IsCapitalized());
  }
}
```

Extension methods versus instance methods

Any compatible instance method will always take precedence over an extension method. In the following example, Test's Foo method will always take precedence—even when called with an argument x of type int:

```
class Test
{
  public void Foo (object x) { }    // This method always wins
}

static class Extensions
{
  public static void Foo (this Test t, int x) { }
}
```

The only way to call the extension method in this case is via normal static syntax; in other words, Extensions.Foo(...).

Extension methods versus extension methods

If two extension methods have the same signature, the extension method must be called as an ordinary static method to disambiguate the method to call. If one extension method has more specific arguments, however, the more specific method takes precedence.

To illustrate, consider the following two classes:

```
static class StringHelper
{
  public static bool IsCapitalized (this string s) {...}
}
static class ObjectHelper
{
  public static bool IsCapitalized (this object s) {...}
}
```

The following code calls StringHelper's IsCapitalized method:

```
bool test1 = "Perth".IsCapitalized();
```

Classes and structs are considered more specific than interfaces.

Anonymous Types

An anonymous type is a simple class created by the compiler on the fly to store a set of values. To create an anonymous type, use the new keyword followed by an object initializer, specifying the properties and values the type will contain. For example:

```
var dude = new { Name = "Bob", Age = 23 };
```

The compiler translates this to (approximately) the following:

```
internal class AnonymousGeneratedTypeName
{
  private string name;  // Actual field name is irrelevant
  private int    age;   // Actual field name is irrelevant

  public AnonymousGeneratedTypeName (string name, int age)
  {
    this.name = name; this.age = age;
  }

  public string Name { get { return name; } }
  public int    Age  { get { return age;  } }

  // The Equals and GetHashCode methods are overridden (see Chapter 6).
  // The ToString method is also overridden.
}
...

var dude = new AnonymousGeneratedTypeName ("Bob", 23);
```

You must use the `var` keyword to reference an anonymous type because it doesn't have a name.

The property name of an anonymous type can be inferred from an expression that is itself an identifier (or ends with one). For example:

```
int Age = 23;
var dude = new { Name = "Bob", Age, Age.ToString().Length };
```

is equivalent to:

```
var dude = new { Name = "Bob", Age = Age, Length = Age.ToString().Length };
```

Two anonymous type instances declared within the same assembly will have the same underlying type if their elements are named and typed identically:

```
var a1 = new { X = 2, Y = 4 };
var a2 = new { X = 2, Y = 4 };
Console.WriteLine (a1.GetType() == a2.GetType());   // True
```

Additionally, the `Equals` method is overridden to perform equality comparisons:

```
Console.WriteLine (a1 == a2);        // False
Console.WriteLine (a1.Equals (a2));  // True
```

You can create arrays of anonymous types as follows:

```
var dudes = new[]
{
  new { Name = "Bob", Age = 30 },
  new { Name = "Tom", Age = 40 }
};
```

Anonymous types are used primarily when writing LINQ queries (see Chapter 8), and were added in C# 3.0.

Dynamic Binding

Dynamic binding defers *binding*—the process of resolving types, members, and operations—from compile time to runtime. Dynamic binding is useful when at compile time *you* know that a certain function, member, or operation exists, but the *compiler* does not. This commonly occurs when you are interoperating with dynamic languages (such as IronPython) and COM and in scenarios when you might otherwise use reflection.

A dynamic type is declared with the contextual keyword `dynamic`:

```
dynamic d = GetSomeObject();
d.Quack();
```

A dynamic type tells the compiler to relax. We expect the runtime type of d to have a Quack method. We just can't prove it statically. Since d is dynamic, the compiler defers binding Quack to d until runtime. To understand what this means requires distinguishing between *static binding* and *dynamic binding*.

Static Binding Versus Dynamic Binding

The canonical binding example is mapping a name to a specific function when compiling an expression. To compile the following expression, the compiler needs to find the implementation of the method named Quack:

```
d.Quack();
```

Let's suppose the static type of d is Duck:

```
Duck d = ...
d.Quack();
```

In the simplest case, the compiler does the binding by looking for a parameterless method named Quack on Duck. Failing that, the compiler extends its search to methods taking optional parameters, methods on base classes of Duck, and extension methods that take Duck as its first parameter. If no match is found, you'll get a compilation error. Regardless of what method gets bound, the bottom line is that the binding is done by the compiler, and the binding utterly depends on statically knowing the types of the operands (in this case, d). This makes it *static binding*.

Now let's change the static type of d to object:

```
object d = ...
d.Quack();
```

Calling Quack gives us a compilation error, because although the value stored in d can contain a method called Quack, the compiler cannot know it since the only information it has is the type of the variable, which in this case is object. But let's now change the static type of d to dynamic:

```
dynamic d = ...
d.Quack();
```

A dynamic type is like object—it's equally nondescriptive about a type. The difference is that it lets you use it in ways that aren't known at compile time. A dynamic object binds at runtime based on its runtime type, not its compile-time type. When the compiler sees a dynamically bound expression (which in general is an expression that contains any value of type dynamic), it merely packages up the expression such that the binding can be done later at runtime.

At runtime, if a dynamic object implements IDynamicMetaObjectProvider, that interface is used to perform the binding. If not, binding occurs in almost the same way as it would have had the compiler known the dynamic object's runtime type. These two alternatives are called *custom binding* and *language binding*.

 COM interop can be considered to use a third kind of dynamic binding (see Chapter 25).

Custom Binding

Custom binding occurs when a dynamic object implements `IDynamicMetaObject Provider` (IDMOP). Although you can implement IDMOP on types that you write in C#, and that is useful to do, the more common case is that you have acquired an IDMOP object from a dynamic language that is implemented in .NET on the DLR, such as IronPython or IronRuby. Objects from those languages implicitly implement IDMOP as a means by which to directly control the meanings of operations performed on them.

We will discuss custom binders in greater detail in Chapter 20, but we will write a simple one now to demonstrate the feature:

```
using System;
using System.Dynamic;

public class Test
{
  static void Main()
  {
    dynamic d = new Duck();
    d.Quack();                // Quack method was called
    d.Waddle();               // Waddle method was called
  }
}

public class Duck : DynamicObject
{
  public override bool TryInvokeMember (
    InvokeMemberBinder binder, object[] args, out object result)
  {
    Console.WriteLine (binder.Name + " method was called");
    result = null;
    return true;
  }
}
```

The `Duck` class doesn't actually have a `Quack` method. Instead, it uses custom binding to intercept and interpret all method calls.

Language Binding

Language binding occurs when a dynamic object does not implement `IDynamicMe taObjectProvider`. Language binding is useful when working around imperfectly designed types or inherent limitations in the .NET type system (we'll explore more scenarios in Chapter 20). A typical problem when using numeric types is that they have no common interface. We have seen that methods can be bound dynamically; the same is true for operators:

```csharp
static dynamic Mean (dynamic x, dynamic y) => (x + y) / 2;

static void Main()
{
  int x = 3, y = 4;
  Console.WriteLine (Mean (x, y));
}
```

The benefit is obvious—you don't have to duplicate code for each numeric type. However, you lose static type safety, risking runtime exceptions rather than compile-time errors.

 Dynamic binding circumvents static type safety, but not runtime type safety. Unlike with reflection (Chapter 19), you can't circumvent member accessibility rules with dynamic binding.

By design, language runtime binding behaves as similarly as possible to static binding, had the runtime types of the dynamic objects been known at compile time. In our previous example, the behavior of our program would be identical if we hardcoded Mean to work with the int type. The most notable exception in parity between static and dynamic binding is for extension methods, which we discuss in "Uncallable Functions" on page 182.

 Dynamic binding also incurs a performance hit. Because of the DLR's caching mechanisms, however, repeated calls to the same dynamic expression are optimized—allowing you to efficiently call dynamic expressions in a loop. This optimization brings the typical overhead for a simple dynamic expression on today's hardware down to less than 100 ns.

RuntimeBinderException

If a member fails to bind, a RuntimeBinderException is thrown. You can think of this like a compile-time error at runtime:

```csharp
dynamic d = 5;
d.Hello();                 // throws RuntimeBinderException
```

The exception is thrown because the int type has no Hello method.

Runtime Representation of Dynamic

There is a deep equivalence between the dynamic and object types. The runtime treats the following expression as true:

```csharp
typeof (dynamic) == typeof (object)
```

This principle extends to constructed types and array types:

```csharp
typeof (List<dynamic>) == typeof (List<object>)
typeof (dynamic[]) == typeof (object[])
```

Like an object reference, a dynamic reference can point to an object of any type (except pointer types):

```
dynamic x = "hello";
Console.WriteLine (x.GetType().Name);  // String
x = 123;  // No error (despite same variable)
Console.WriteLine (x.GetType().Name);  // Int32
```

Structurally, there is no difference between an object reference and a dynamic reference. A dynamic reference simply enables dynamic operations on the object it
points to. You can convert from object to dynamic to perform any dynamic operation you want on an object:

```
object o = new System.Text.StringBuilder();
dynamic d = o;
d.Append ("hello");
Console.WriteLine (o);  // hello
```

> Reflecting on a type exposing (public) dynamic members
> reveals that those members are represented as annotated
> objects. For example:
>
> ```
> public class Test
> {
>   public dynamic Foo;
> }
> ```
>
> is equivalent to:
>
> ```
> public class Test
> {
>   [System.Runtime.CompilerServices.DynamicAttribute]
>   public object Foo;
> }
> ```
>
> This allows consumers of that type to know that Foo should be
> treated as dynamic, while allowing languages that don't sup-
> port dynamic binding to fall back to object.

Dynamic Conversions

The dynamic type has implicit conversions to and from all other types:

```
int i = 7;
dynamic d = i;
long j = d;        // No cast required (implicit conversion)
```

For the conversion to succeed, the runtime type of the dynamic object must be
implicitly convertible to the target static type. The preceding example worked
because an int is implicitly convertible to a long.

The following example throws a RuntimeBinderException because an int is not
implicitly convertible to a short:

```
int i = 7;
dynamic d = i;
short j = d;       // throws RuntimeBinderException
```

var Versus dynamic

The var and dynamic types bear a superficial resemblance, but the difference is deep:

- var says, "Let the *compiler* figure out the type."
- dynamic says, "Let the *runtime* figure out the type."

To illustrate:

```
dynamic x = "hello";   // Static type is dynamic, runtime type is string
var y = "hello";       // Static type is string, runtime type is string
int i = x;             // Runtime error      (cannot convert string to int)
int j = y;             // Compile-time error (cannot convert string to int)
```

The static type of a variable declared with var can be dynamic:

```
dynamic x = "hello";
var y = x;             // Static type of y is dynamic
int z = y;             // Runtime error (cannot convert string to int)
```

Dynamic Expressions

Fields, properties, methods, events, constructors, indexers, operators, and conversions can all be called dynamically.

Trying to consume the result of a dynamic expression with a void return type is prohibited—just as with a statically typed expression. The difference is that the error occurs at runtime:

```
dynamic list = new List<int>();
var result = list.Add (5);        // RuntimeBinderException thrown
```

Expressions involving dynamic operands are typically themselves dynamic, since the effect of absent type information is cascading:

```
dynamic x = 2;
var y = x * 3;       // Static type of y is dynamic
```

There are a couple of obvious exceptions to this rule. First, casting a dynamic expression to a static type yields a static expression:

```
dynamic x = 2;
var y = (int)x;      // Static type of y is int
```

Second, constructor invocations always yield static expressions—even when called with dynamic arguments. In this example, x is statically typed to a StringBuilder:

```
dynamic capacity = 10;
var x = new System.Text.StringBuilder (capacity);
```

In addition, there are a few edge cases where an expression containing a dynamic argument is static, including passing an index to an array and delegate creation expressions.

Dynamic Calls Without Dynamic Receivers

The canonical use case for dynamic involves a dynamic *receiver*. This means that a dynamic object is the receiver of a dynamic function call:

```
dynamic x = ...;
x.Foo();          // x is the receiver
```

However, you can also call statically known functions with dynamic arguments. Such calls are subject to dynamic overload resolution and can include:

- Static methods

- Instance constructors

- Instance methods on receivers with a statically known type

In the following example, the particular Foo that gets dynamically bound is dependent on the runtime type of the dynamic argument:

```
class Program
{
  static void Foo (int x)    { Console.WriteLine ("1"); }
  static void Foo (string x) { Console.WriteLine ("2"); }

  static void Main()
  {
    dynamic x = 5;
    dynamic y = "watermelon";

    Foo (x);                 // 1
    Foo (y);                 // 2
  }
}
```

Because a dynamic receiver is not involved, the compiler can statically perform a basic check to see whether the dynamic call will succeed. It checks that a function with the right name and number of parameters exists. If no candidate is found, you get a compile-time error. For example:

```
class Program
{
  static void Foo (int x)    { Console.WriteLine ("1"); }
  static void Foo (string x) { Console.WriteLine ("2"); }

  static void Main()
  {
    dynamic x = 5;
    Foo (x, x);              // Compiler error - wrong number of parameters
    Fook (x);                // Compiler error - no such method name
  }
}
```

Static Types in Dynamic Expressions

It's obvious that dynamic types are used in dynamic binding. It's not so obvious that static types are also used—wherever possible—in dynamic binding. Consider the following:

```
class Program
{
  static void Foo (object x, object y) { Console.WriteLine ("oo"); }
  static void Foo (object x, string y) { Console.WriteLine ("os"); }
  static void Foo (string x, object y) { Console.WriteLine ("so"); }
  static void Foo (string x, string y) { Console.WriteLine ("ss"); }

  static void Main()
  {
    object o = "hello";
    dynamic d = "goodbye";
    Foo (o, d);                  // os
  }
}
```

The call to Foo(o,d) is dynamically bound because one of its arguments, d, is dynamic. But since o is statically known, the binding—even though it occurs dynamically—will make use of that. In this case, overload resolution will pick the second implementation of Foo due to the static type of o and the runtime type of d. In other words, the compiler is "as static as it can possibly be."

Uncallable Functions

Some functions cannot be called dynamically. You cannot call:

- Extension methods (via extension method syntax)
- Members of an interface, if you need to cast to that interface to do so
- Base members hidden by a subclass

Understanding why this is so is useful in understanding dynamic binding.

Dynamic binding requires two pieces of information: the name of the function to call, and the object upon which to call the function. However, in each of the three uncallable scenarios, an *additional type* is involved, which is known only at compile time. As of C# 6, there's no way to specify these additional types dynamically.

When calling extension methods, that additional type is implicit. It's the static class on which the extension method is defined. The compiler searches for it given the using directives in your source code. This makes extension methods compile-time-only concepts, since using directives melt away upon compilation (after they've done their job in the binding process in mapping simple names to namespace-qualified names).

When calling members via an interface, you specify that additional type via an implicit or explicit cast. There are two scenarios where you might want to do this: when calling explicitly implemented interface members and when calling interface members implemented in a type internal to another assembly. We can illustrate the former with the following two types:

```
interface IFoo   { void Test();         }
class Foo : IFoo { void IFoo.Test() {} }
```

To call the Test method, we must cast to the IFoo interface. This is easy with static typing:

```
IFoo f = new Foo();   // Implicit cast to interface
f.Test();
```

Now consider the situation with dynamic typing:

```
IFoo f = new Foo();
dynamic d = f;
d.Test();             // Exception thrown
```

The implicit cast shown in bold tells the *compiler* to bind subsequent member calls on f to IFoo rather than Foo—in other words, to view that object through the lens of the IFoo interface. However, that lens is lost at runtime, so the DLR cannot complete the binding. The loss is illustrated as follows:

```
Console.WriteLine (f.GetType().Name);    // Foo
```

A similar situation arises when calling a hidden base member: you must specify an additional type via either a cast or the base keyword—and that additional type is lost at runtime.

Attributes

You're already familiar with the notion of attributing code elements of a program with modifiers, such as virtual or ref. These constructs are built into the language. *Attributes* are an extensible mechanism for adding custom information to code elements (assemblies, types, members, return values, parameters, and generic type parameters). This extensibility is useful for services that integrate deeply into the type system, without requiring special keywords or constructs in the C# language.

A good scenario for attributes is serialization—the process of converting arbitrary objects to and from a particular format. In this scenario, an attribute on a field can specify the translation between C#'s representation of the field and the format's representation of the field.

Attribute Classes

An attribute is defined by a class that inherits (directly or indirectly) from the abstract class System.Attribute. To attach an attribute to a code element, specify the attribute's type name in square brackets, before the code element. For example, the following attaches the ObsoleteAttribute to the Foo class:

```
[ObsoleteAttribute]
public class Foo {...}
```

This attribute is recognized by the compiler and will cause compiler warnings if a type or member marked obsolete is referenced. By convention, all attribute types end in the word *Attribute*. C# recognizes this and allows you to omit the suffix when attaching an attribute:

```
[Obsolete]
public class Foo {...}
```

ObsoleteAttribute is a type declared in the System namespace as follows (simplified for brevity):

```
public sealed class ObsoleteAttribute : Attribute {...}
```

The C# language and the .NET Framework include a number of predefined attributes. We describe how to write your own attributes in Chapter 19.

Named and Positional Attribute Parameters

Attributes may have parameters. In the following example, we apply XmlElementAttribute to a class. This attribute tells XML serializer (in System.Xml.Serialization) how an object is represented in XML and accepts several *attribute parameters*. The following attribute maps the CustomerEntity class to an XML element named Customer, belonging to the http://oreilly.com namespace:

```
[XmlElement ("Customer", Namespace="http://oreilly.com")]
public class CustomerEntity { ... }
```

Attribute parameters fall into one of two categories: positional or named. In the preceding example, the first argument is a *positional parameter*; the second is a *named parameter*. Positional parameters correspond to parameters of the attribute type's public constructors. Named parameters correspond to public fields or public properties on the attribute type.

When specifying an attribute, you must include positional parameters that correspond to one of the attribute's constructors. Named parameters are optional.

In Chapter 19, we describe the valid parameter types and rules for their evaluation.

Attribute Targets

Implicitly, the target of an attribute is the code element it immediately precedes, which is typically a type or type member. You can also attach attributes, however, to an assembly. This requires that you explicitly specify the attribute's target.

Here is an example of using the CLSCompliant attribute to specify CLS compliance for an entire assembly:

```
[assembly:CLSCompliant(true)]
```

Specifying Multiple Attributes

Multiple attributes can be specified for a single code element. Each attribute can be listed either within the same pair of square brackets (separated by a comma) or in separate pairs of square brackets (or a combination of the two). The following three examples are semantically identical:

```
[Serializable, Obsolete, CLSCompliant(false)]
public class Bar {...}

[Serializable] [Obsolete] [CLSCompliant(false)]
public class Bar {...}

[Serializable, Obsolete]
[CLSCompliant(false)]
public class Bar {...}
```

Caller Info Attributes (C# 5)

From C# 5, you can tag optional parameters with one of three *caller info attributes*, which instruct the compiler to feed information obtained from the caller's source code into the parameter's default value:

- `[CallerMemberName]` applies the caller's member name
- `[CallerFilePath]` applies the path to caller's source code file
- `[CallerLineNumber]` applies the line number in caller's source code file

The Foo method in the following program demonstrates all three:

```
using System;
using System.Runtime.CompilerServices;

class Program
{
  static void Main() => Foo();

  static void Foo (
    [CallerMemberName] string memberName = null,
    [CallerFilePath] string filePath = null,
    [CallerLineNumber] int lineNumber = 0)
  {
    Console.WriteLine (memberName);
    Console.WriteLine (filePath);
    Console.WriteLine (lineNumber);
  }
}
```

Assuming our program resides in c:\source\test\Program.cs, the output would be:

```
Main
c:\source\test\Program.cs
6
```

As with standard optional parameters, the substitution is done at the *calling site*. Hence, our Main method is syntactic sugar for this:

```
static void Main() => Foo ("Main", @"c:\source\test\Program.cs", 6);
```

Caller info attributes are useful for logging—and for implementing patterns such as firing a single change notification event whenever any property on an object changes. In fact, there's a standard interface in the .NET Framework for this called INotifyPropertyChanged (in System.ComponentModel):

```
public interface INotifyPropertyChanged
{
  event PropertyChangedEventHandler PropertyChanged;
}

public delegate void PropertyChangedEventHandler
  (object sender, PropertyChangedEventArgs e);

public class PropertyChangedEventArgs : EventArgs
{
  public PropertyChangedEventArgs (string propertyName);
  public virtual string PropertyName { get; }
}
```

Notice that PropertyChangedEventArgs requires the name of the property that changed. By applying the [CallerMemberName] attribute, however, we can implement this interface and invoke the event without ever specifying property names:

```
public class Foo : INotifyPropertyChanged
{
  public event PropertyChangedEventHandler PropertyChanged = delegate { };

  void RaisePropertyChanged ([CallerMemberName] string propertyName = null)
  {
    PropertyChanged (this, new PropertyChangedEventArgs (propertyName));
  }

  string customerName;
  public string CustomerName
  {
    get { return customerName; }
    set
    {
      if (value == customerName) return;
      customerName = value;
      RaisePropertyChanged();
      // The compiler converts the above line to:
      // RaisePropertyChanged ("CustomerName");
    }
  }
}
```

Unsafe Code and Pointers

C# supports direct memory manipulation via pointers within blocks of code marked unsafe and compiled with the /unsafe compiler option. Pointer types are primarily useful for interoperability with C APIs but may also be used for accessing memory outside the managed heap or for performance-critical hotspots.

Pointer Basics

For every value type or pointer type *V*, there is a corresponding pointer type *V**. A pointer instance holds the address of a variable. Pointer types can be (unsafely) cast to any other pointer type. The main pointer operators are:

Operator	Meaning
&	The *address-of* operator returns a pointer to the address of a variable
*	The *dereference* operator returns the variable at the address of a pointer
->	The *pointer-to-member* operator is a syntactic shortcut, in which x->y is equivalent to (*x).y

Unsafe Code

By marking a type, type member, or statement block with the unsafe keyword, you're permitted to use pointer types and perform C++ style pointer operations on memory within that scope. Here is an example of using pointers to quickly process a bitmap:

```
unsafe void BlueFilter (int[,] bitmap)
{
  int length = bitmap.Length;
  fixed (int* b = bitmap)
  {
    int* p = b;
    for (int i = 0; i < length; i++)
      *p++ &= 0xFF;
  }
}
```

Unsafe code can run faster than a corresponding safe implementation. In this case, the code would have required a nested loop with array indexing and bounds checking. An unsafe C# method may also be faster than calling an external C function, since there is no overhead associated with leaving the managed execution environment.

The fixed Statement

The fixed statement is required to pin a managed object, such as the bitmap in the previous example. During the execution of a program, many objects are allocated and deallocated from the heap. In order to avoid unnecessary waste or fragmentation of memory, the garbage collector moves objects around. Pointing to an object is

---

futile if its address could change while referencing it, so the fixed statement tells the garbage collector to "pin" the object and not move it around. This may have an impact on the efficiency of the runtime, so fixed blocks should be used only briefly, and heap allocation should be avoided within the fixed block.

Within a fixed statement, you can get a pointer to any value type, an array of value types, or a string. In the case of arrays and strings, the pointer will actually point to the first element, which is a value type.

Value types declared inline within reference types require the reference type to be pinned, as follows:

```
class Test
{
  int x;
  static void Main()
  {
    Test test = new Test();
    unsafe
    {
      fixed (int* p = &test.x)    // Pins test
      {
        *p = 9;
      }
      System.Console.WriteLine (test.x);
    }
  }
}
```

We describe the fixed statement further in "Mapping a Struct to Unmanaged Memory" on page 1011 in Chapter 25.

The Pointer-to-Member Operator

In addition to the & and * operators, C# also provides the C++ style -> operator, which can be used on structs:

```
struct Test
{
  int x;
  unsafe static void Main()
  {
    Test test = new Test();
    Test* p = &test;
    p->x = 9;
    System.Console.WriteLine (test.x);
  }
}
```

Arrays

The stackalloc keyword

Memory can be allocated in a block on the stack explicitly using the `stackalloc` keyword. Since it is allocated on the stack, its lifetime is limited to the execution of the method, just as with any other local variable (whose life hasn't been extended by virtue of being captured by a lambda expression, iterator block, or asynchronous function). The block may use the [ ] operator to index into memory:

```
int* a = stackalloc int [10];
for (int i = 0; i < 10; ++i)
    Console.WriteLine (a[i]);    // Print raw memory
```

Fixed-size buffers

The `fixed` keyword has another use, which is to create fixed-size buffers within structs:

```
unsafe struct UnsafeUnicodeString
{
  public short Length;
  public fixed byte Buffer[30];    // Allocate block of 30 bytes
}

unsafe class UnsafeClass
{
  UnsafeUnicodeString uus;

  public UnsafeClass (string s)
  {
    uus.Length = (short)s.Length;
    fixed (byte* p = uus.Buffer)
      for (int i = 0; i < s.Length; i++)
        p[i] = (byte) s[i];
  }
}
class Test
{
  static void Main() { new UnsafeClass ("Christian Troy"); }
}
```

The `fixed` keyword is also used in this example to pin the object on the heap that contains the buffer (which will be the instance of `UnsafeClass`). Hence, `fixed` means two different things: fixed in *size* and fixed in *place*. The two are often used together, in that a fixed-size buffer must be fixed in place to be used.

void*

A *void pointer* (void*) makes no assumptions about the type of the underlying data and is useful for functions that deal with raw memory. An implicit conversion exists from any pointer type to void*. A void* cannot be dereferenced, and arithmetic operations cannot be performed on void pointers. For example:

```
class Test
{
  unsafe static void Main()
  {
    short[ ] a = {1,1,2,3,5,8,13,21,34,55};
    fixed (short* p = a)
    {
      //sizeof returns size of value-type in bytes
      Zap (p, a.Length * sizeof (short));
    }
    foreach (short x in a)
      System.Console.WriteLine (x);    // Prints all zeros
  }

  unsafe static void Zap (void* memory, int byteCount)
  {
    byte* b = (byte*) memory;
      for (int i = 0; i < byteCount; i++)
        *b++ = 0;
  }
}
```

Pointers to Unmanaged Code

Pointers are also useful for accessing data outside the managed heap (such as when interacting with C DLLs or COM) or when dealing with data not in the main memory (such as graphics memory or a storage medium on an embedded device).

Preprocessor Directives

Preprocessor directives supply the compiler with additional information about regions of code. The most common preprocessor directives are the conditional directives, which provide a way to include or exclude regions of code from compilation. For example:

```
#define DEBUG
class MyClass
{
  int x;
  void Foo()
  {
    #if DEBUG
    Console.WriteLine ("Testing: x = {0}", x);
    #endif
  }
  ...
}
```

In this class, the statement in Foo is compiled as conditionally dependent upon the presence of the DEBUG symbol. If we remove the DEBUG symbol, the statement is not compiled. Preprocessor symbols can be defined within a source file (as we have done), and they can be passed to the compiler with the /define:*symbol* command-line option.

With the #if and #elif directives, you can use the ||, &&, and ! operators to perform *or*, *and*, and *not* operations on multiple symbols. The following directive instructs the compiler to include the code that follows if the TESTMODE symbol is defined and the DEBUG symbol is not defined:

```
#if TESTMODE && !DEBUG
    ...
```

Bear in mind, however, that you're not building an ordinary C# expression, and the symbols upon which you operate have absolutely no connection to *variables*—static or otherwise.

The #error and #warning symbols prevent accidental misuse of conditional directives by making the compiler generate a warning or error given an undesirable set of compilation symbols. Table 4-1 lists the preprocessor directives.

Table 4-1. Preprocessor directives

Preprocessor directive	Action
#define *symbol*	Defines *symbol*
#undef *symbol*	Undefines *symbol*
#if *symbol* [*operator symbol2*]...	*symbol* to test
	operators are ==, !=, &&, and || followed by #else, #elif, and #endif
#else	Executes code to subsequent #endif
#elif *symbol* [*operator symbol2*]	Combines #else branch and #if test
#endif	Ends conditional directives
#warning *text*	*text* of the warning to appear in compiler output
#error *text*	*text* of the error to appear in compiler output
#pragma warning [disable | restore]	Disables/restores compiler warning(s)
#line [*number* ["*file*"] | hidden]	*number* specifies the line in source code; *file* is the filename to appear in computer output; hidden instructs debuggers to skip over code from this point until the next #line directive
#region *name*	Marks the beginning of an outline
#endregion	Ends an outline region

Conditional Attributes

An attribute decorated with the Conditional attribute will be compiled only if a given preprocessor symbol is present. For example:

```
// file1.cs
#define DEBUG
using System;
using System.Diagnostics;
[Conditional("DEBUG")]
public class TestAttribute : Attribute {}

// file2.cs
#define DEBUG
[Test]
class Foo
{
  [Test]
  string s;
}
```

The compiler will only incorporate the [Test] attributes if the DEBUG symbol is in scope for *file2.cs*.

Pragma Warning

The compiler generates a warning when it spots something in your code that seems unintentional. Unlike errors, warnings don't ordinarily prevent your application from compiling.

Compiler warnings can be extremely valuable in spotting bugs. Their usefulness, however, is undermined when you get *false* warnings. In a large application, maintaining a good signal-to-noise ratio is essential if the "real" warnings are to get noticed.

To this effect, the compiler allows you to selectively suppress warnings with the #pragma warning directive. In this example, we instruct the compiler not to warn us about the field Message not being used:

```
public class Foo
{
  static void Main() { }

  #pragma warning disable 414
  static string Message = "Hello";
  #pragma warning restore 414
}
```

Omitting the number in the #pragma warning directive disables or restores all warning codes.

If you are thorough in applying this directive, you can compile with the /warnaserror switch—this tells the compiler to treat any residual warnings as errors.

XML Documentation

A *documentation comment* is a piece of embedded XML that documents a type or member. A documentation comment comes immediately before a type or member declaration and starts with three slashes:

```
/// <summary>Cancels a running query.</summary>
public void Cancel() { ... }
```

Multiline comments can be done either like this:

```
/// <summary>
/// Cancels a running query
/// </summary>
public void Cancel() { ... }
```

or like this (notice the extra star at the start):

```
/**
    <summary> Cancels a running query. </summary>
*/
public void Cancel() { ... }
```

If you compile with the /doc directive (in Visual Studio, go to the *Build* tab of *Project Properties*), the compiler extracts and collates documentation comments into a single XML file. This has two main uses:

- If placed in the same folder as the compiled assembly, Visual Studio (and LINQPad) automatically read the XML file and use the information to provide IntelliSense member listings to consumers of the assembly of the same name.
- Third-party tools (such as Sandcastle and NDoc) can transform the XML file into an HTML help file.

Standard XML Documentation Tags

Here are the standard XML tags that Visual Studio and documentation generators recognize:

`<summary>`
```
<summary>...</summary>
```

Indicates the tool tip that IntelliSense should display for the type or member; typically a single phrase or sentence.

`<remarks>`
```
<remarks>...</remarks>
```

Additional text that describes the type or member. Documentation generators pick this up and merge it into the bulk of a type or member's description.

<param>

```
<param name="name">...</param>
```

Explains a parameter on a method.

<returns>

```
<returns>...</returns>
```

Explains the return value for a method.

<exception>

```
<exception [cref="type"]>...</exception>
```

Lists an exception that a method may throw (`cref` refers to the exception type).

<permission>

```
<permission [cref="type"]>...</permission>
```

Indicates an `IPermission` type required by the documented type or member.

<example>

```
<example>...</example>
```

Denotes an example (used by documentation generators). This usually contains both description text and source code (source code is typically within a <c> or <code> tag).

<c>

```
<c>...</c>
```

Indicates an inline code snippet. This tag is usually used inside an <example> block.

<code>

```
<code>...</code>
```

Indicates a multiline code sample. This tag is usually used inside an <example> block.

<see>

```
<see cref="member">...</see>
```

Inserts an inline cross-reference to another type or member. HTML documentation generators typically convert this to a hyperlink. The compiler emits a warning if the type or member name is invalid. To refer to generic types, use curly braces; for example, `cref="Foo{T,U}"`.

`<seealso>`

```
<seealso cref="member">...</seealso>
```

Cross-references another type or member. Documentation generators typically write this into a separate "See Also" section at the bottom of the page.

`<paramref>`

```
<paramref name="name"/>
```

References a parameter from within a `<summary>` or `<remarks>` tag.

`<list>`

```
<list type=[ bullet | number | table ]>
  <listheader>
    <term>...</term>
    <description>...</description>
  </listheader>
  <item>
    <term>...</term>
    <description>...</description>
  </item>
</list>
```

Instructs documentation generators to emit a bulleted, numbered, or table-style list.

`<para>`

```
<para>...</para>
```

Instructs documentation generators to format the contents into a separate paragraph.

`<include>`

```
<include file='filename' path='tagpath[@name="id"]'>...</include>
```

Merges an external XML file that contains documentation. The path attribute denotes an XPath query to a specific element in that file.

User-Defined Tags

Little is special about the predefined XML tags recognized by the C# compiler, and you are free to define your own. The only special processing done by the compiler is on the `<param>` tag (in which it verifies the parameter name and that all the parameters on the method are documented) and the `cref` attribute (in which it verifies that the attribute refers to a real type or member and expands it to a fully qualified type or member ID). The `cref` attribute can also be used in your own tags and is verified and expanded just as it is in the predefined `<exception>`, `<permission>`, `<see>`, and `<seealso>` tags.

Type or Member Cross-References

Type names and type or member cross-references are translated into IDs that uniquely define the type or member. These names are composed of a prefix that defines what the ID represents and a signature of the type or member. The member prefixes are:

XML type prefix	ID prefixes applied to...
N	Namespace
T	Type (class, struct, enum, interface, delegate)
F	Field
P	Property (includes indexers)
M	Method (includes special methods)
E	Event
!	Error

The rules describing how the signatures are generated are well documented, although fairly complex.

Here is an example of a type and the IDs that are generated:

```
// Namespaces do not have independent signatures
namespace NS
{
  /// T:NS.MyClass
  class MyClass
  {
    /// F:NS.MyClass.aField
    string aField;

    /// P:NS.MyClass.aProperty
    short aProperty {get {...} set {...}}

    /// T:NS.MyClass.NestedType
    class NestedType {...};

    /// M:NS.MyClass.X()
    void X() {...}

    /// M:NS.MyClass.Y(System.Int32,System.Double@,System.Decimal@)
    void Y(int p1, ref double p2, out decimal p3) {...}

    /// M:NS.MyClass.Z(System.Char[ ],System.Single[0:,0:])
    void Z(char[ ] 1, float[,] p2) {...}

    /// M:NS.MyClass.op_Addition(NS.MyClass,NS.MyClass)
    public static MyClass operator+(MyClass c1, MyClass c2) {...}

    /// M:NS.MyClass.op_Implicit(NS.MyClass)~System.Int32
    public static implicit operator int(MyClass c) {...}
```

```
    /// M:NS.MyClass.#ctor
    MyClass() {...}

    /// M:NS.MyClass.Finalize
    ~MyClass() {...}

    /// M:NS.MyClass.#cctor
    static MyClass() {...}
  }
}
```

5

Framework Overview

Almost all the capabilities of the .NET Framework are exposed via a vast set of managed types. These types are organized into hierarchical namespaces and packaged into a set of assemblies, which together with the CLR comprise the .NET platform.

Some of the .NET types are used directly by the CLR and are essential for the managed hosting environment. These types reside in an assembly called *mscorlib.dll* and include C#'s built-in types, as well as the basic collection classes, types for stream processing, serialization, reflection, threading, and native interoperability ("mscorlib" is an abbreviation for Multi-language Standard Common Object Runtime Library).

At a level above this are additional types that "flesh out" the CLR-level functionality, providing features such as XML, networking, and LINQ. These reside in *System.dll*, *System.Xml.dll*, and *System.Core.dll*, and together with *mscorlib*, they provide a rich programming environment upon which the rest of the Framework is built. This "core framework" largely defines the scope of the rest of this book.

The remainder of the .NET Framework consists of applied APIs, most of which cover three areas of functionality:

- User interface technologies
- Backend technologies
- Distributed system technologies

Table 5-1 shows the history of compatibility between each version of C#, the CLR, and the .NET Framework. C# 6.0 targets CLR 4.6, which is a "patched" version of CLR 4.0 (an in-place update). This means that applications targeting CLR 4.0 will actually run on CLR 4.6 after you install the latter; hence Microsoft has taken extreme care to ensure backward compatibility.

Table 5-1. C#, CLR, and .NET Framework versions

C# version	CLR version	Framework versions
1.0	1.0	1.0
1.2	1.1	1.1
2.0	2.0	2.0, 3.0
3.0	2.0 (SP2)	3.5
4.0	4.0	4.0
5.0	4.5 (Patched CLR 4.0)	4.5
6.0	4.6 (Patched CLR 4.0)	4.6

This chapter skims all key areas of the .NET Framework—starting with the core types covered in this book and finishing with an overview of the applied technologies.

What's New in .NET Framework 4.6

- The Garbage Collector offers more control over when (not) to collect via new methods on the GC class. There are also more fine-tuning options when calling GC.Collect.

- There's a brand-new faster 64-bit JIT compiler.

- The System.Numerics namespace now includes hardware-accelerated matrix and vector types.

- There's a new System.AppContext class, designed to give library authors a consistent mechanism for letting consumers switch new API features in or out.

- Tasks now pick up the current thread's culture and UI culture when created.

- More collection types now implement IReadOnlyCollection<T>.

- WPF has further improvements, including better touch and high-DPI handling.

- ASP.NET now supports HTTP/2 and the Token Binding Protocol in Windows 10.

The release of Framework 4.6 is also timed with ASP.NET 5 and MVC 6, available on NuGet. ASP.NET 5 features a lighter-weight modular architecture, with the ability to self-host in a custom process, cross-platform interoperability, and an open-source license. Unlike its predecessors, ASP.NET 5 is not dependent on System.Web and its historical baggage.

Assemblies and namespaces in the .NET Framework *cross-cut*. The most extreme examples are *mscorlib.dll* and *System.Core.dll*, both defining types in dozens of namespaces, none of which is prefixed with *mscorlib* or *System.Core*. The less obvious cases are the more confusing ones, however, such as the types in System.Security.Cryptography. Most types in this namespace reside in *System.dll*, except for a handful, which reside in *System.Security.dll*. The book's companion website contains a complete mapping of Framework namespaces to assemblies (*http://www.albahari.com/nutshell/Namespa ceReference.aspx*).

Many of the core types are defined in the following assemblies: *mscorlib.dll*, *System.dll*, and *System.Core.dll*. The first of these, *mscorlib.dll*, comprises the types required by the runtime environment itself; *System.dll* and *System.Core.dll* contain additional core types required by you as a programmer. The reason the latter two are separate is historical: when Microsoft introduced Framework 3.5, they made it *additive* insofar as it ran as a layer over the existing CLR 2.0. Therefore, almost all new core types (such as the classes supporting LINQ) went into a new assembly that Microsoft called *System.Core.dll*.

What's New in .NET Framework 4.5

New features of Framework 4.5 included:

- Extensive support for asynchrony through Task-returning methods
- Support for the ZIP compression protocol (Chapter 15)
- Improved HTTP support through the new HttpClient class (Chapter 16)
- Performance improvements to the garbage collector and assembly resource retrieval
- Support for WinRT interoperability and APIs for building Windows Store mobile apps

They also added a new TypeInfo class (Chapter 19) and the ability to specify timeouts when matching regular expression timeouts (Chapter 26).

In the Parallel Computing space, a specialized new library was added called Dataflow for building producer/consumer-style networks.

There were also improvements to the WPF, WCF, and WF (Workflow Foundation) libraries.

The CLR and Core Framework

System Types

The most fundamental types live directly in the System namespace. These include C#'s built-in types, the Exception base class, the Enum, Array, and Delegate base classes, and Nullable, Type, DateTime, TimeSpan, and Guid. The System namespace also includes types for performing mathematical functions (Math), generating random numbers (Random), and converting between various types (Convert and Bit Converter).

Chapter 6 describes these types—as well as the interfaces that define standard protocols used across the .NET Framework for such tasks as formatting (IFormatta ble) and order comparison (IComparable).

The System namespace also defines the IDisposable interface and the GC class for interacting with the garbage collector. These topics are saved for Chapter 12.

Text Processing

The System.Text namespace contains the StringBuilder class (the editable or *mutable* cousin of string) and the types for working with text encodings, such as UTF-8 (Encoding and its subtypes). We cover this in Chapter 6.

The System.Text.RegularExpressions namespace contains types that perform advanced pattern-based search-and-replace operations; these are described in Chapter 26.

Collections

The .NET Framework offers a variety of classes for managing collections of items. These include both list- and dictionary-based structures, and work in conjunction with a set of standard interfaces that unify their common characteristics. All collection types are defined in the following namespaces, covered in Chapter 7:

```
System.Collections             // Nongeneric collections
System.Collections.Generic     // Generic collections
System.Collections.Specialized // Strongly typed collections
System.Collections.ObjectModel // Bases for your own collections
System.Collections.Concurrent  // Thread-safe collection (Chapter 23)
```

Queries

Language Integrated Query (LINQ) was added in Framework 3.5. LINQ allows you to perform type-safe queries over local and remote collections (e.g., SQL Server tables) and is described in Chapters 8 through 10. A big advantage of LINQ is that it presents a consistent querying API across a variety of domains. The types for resolving LINQ queries reside in these namespaces:

```
System.Linq                  // LINQ to Objects and PLINQ
System.Linq.Expressions      // For building expressions manually
System.Xml.Linq              // LINQ to XML
```

The full .NET profile also includes the following:

```
System.Data.Linq             // LINQ to SQL
System.Data.Entity           // LINQ to Entities (Entity Framework)
```

(The Windows Store profile excludes the entire System.Data.* namespace.)

The LINQ to SQL and Entity Framework APIs leverage lower-level ADO.NET types in the System.Data namespace.

XML

XML is used widely within the .NET Framework and so is supported extensively. Chapter 10 focuses entirely on LINQ to XML—a lightweight XML document object model that can be constructed and queried through LINQ. Chapter 11 describes the older W3C DOM, as well as the performant low-level reader/writer classes and the Framework's support for XML schemas, stylesheets, and XPath. The XML namespaces are:

```
System.Xml                   // XmlReader, XmlWriter + the old W3C DOM
System.Xml.Linq              // The LINQ to XML DOM
System.Xml.Schema            // Support for XSD
System.Xml.Serialization     // Declarative XML serialization for .NET types
```

The following namespaces are available in the desktop .NET profiles (not Windows Store):

```
System.Xml.XPath             // XPath query language
System.Xml.Xsl               // Stylesheet support
```

Diagnostics and Code Contracts

In Chapter 13, we cover .NET's logging and assertion facilities and the code contracts system that was introduced in Framework 4.0. We also describe how to interact with other processes, write to the Windows event log, and use performance counters for monitoring. The types for this are defined in and under System.Diag nostics.

Concurrency and Asynchrony

Most modern applications need to deal with more than one thing happening at a time. Since C# 5.0, this has become easier through asynchronous functions and high-level constructs such as tasks and task combinators. Chapter 14 explains all of this in detail, after starting with the basics of multithreading. Types for working with threads and asynchronous operations are in the System.Threading and Sys tem.Threading.Tasks namespaces.

Streams and I/O

The Framework provides a stream-based model for low-level input/output. Streams are typically used to read and write directly to files and network connections, and can be chained or wrapped in decorator streams to add compression or encryption functionality. Chapter 15 describes .NET's stream architecture, as well as the specific support for working with files and directories, compression, isolated storage, pipes, and memory-mapped files. The .NET Stream and I/O types are defined in and under the System.IO namespace, and the WinRT types for file I/O are in and under Windows.Storage.

Networking

You can directly access standard network protocols such as HTTP, FTP, TCP/IP, and SMTP via the types in System.Net. In Chapter 16, we demonstrate how to communicate using each of these protocols, starting with simple tasks such as downloading from a web page, and finishing with using TCP/IP directly to retrieve POP3 email. Here are the namespaces we cover:

```
System.Net
System.Net.Http         // HttpClient
System.Net.Mail         // For sending mail via SMTP
System.Net.Sockets      // TCP, UDP, and IP
```

The latter two namespaces are not available to Windows Store applications, which must instead use third-party libraries for sending mail, and the WinRT types in Windows.Networking.Sockets for working with sockets.

Serialization

The Framework provides several systems for saving and restoring objects to a binary or text representation. Such systems are required for distributed application technologies, such as WCF, Web Services, and Remoting, and also to save and restore objects to a file. In Chapter 17, we cover all three serialization engines: the data contract serializer, the binary serializer, and the XML serializer. The types for serialization reside in the following namespaces:

```
System.Runtime.Serialization
System.Xml.Serialization
```

The Windows Store profile excludes the binary serialization engine.

Assemblies, Reflection, and Attributes

The assemblies into which C# programs compile comprise executable instructions (stored as intermediate language or IL) and metadata, which describes the program's types, members, and attributes. Through reflection, you can inspect this metadata at runtime and do such things as dynamically invoke methods. With Reflection.Emit, you can construct new code on the fly.

In Chapter 18, we describe the makeup of assemblies and how to sign them, use the global assembly cache and resources, and resolve file references. In Chapter 19, we cover reflection and attributes—describing how to inspect metadata, dynamically invoke functions, write custom attributes, emit new types, and parse raw IL. The types for using reflection and working with assemblies reside in the following namespaces:

```
System
System.Reflection
System.Reflection.Emit  (Desktop only)
```

Dynamic Programming

In Chapter 20, we look at some of the patterns for dynamic programming and leveraging the Dynamic Language Runtime, which has been a part of the CLR since Framework 4.0. We describe how to implement the Visitor pattern, write custom dynamic objects, and interoperate with IronPython. The types for dynamic programming are in System.Dynamic.

Security

The .NET Framework provides its own security layer, allowing you to both sandbox other assemblies and be sandboxed yourself. In Chapter 21, we cover code access, role, and identity security, and the transparency model introduced in CLR 4.0. We then describe cryptography in the Framework, covering encryption, hashing, and data protection. The types for this are defined in:

```
System.Security
System.Security.Permissions
System.Security.Policy
System.Security.Cryptography
```

Only System.Security is available to Windows Store apps; cryptography is handled instead in the WinRT types in Windows.Security.Cryptography.

Advanced Threading

C#'s asynchronous functions make concurrent programming significantly easier because they lessen the need for lower-level techniques. However, there are still times when you need signaling constructs, thread-local storage, reader/writer locks, and so on. Chapter 22 explains this in depth. Threading types are in the System.Threading namespace.

Parallel Programming

In Chapter 23, we cover in detail the libraries and types for leveraging multicore processors, including APIs for task parallelism, imperative data parallelism, and functional parallelism (PLINQ).

Application Domains

The CLR provides an additional level of isolation within a process, called an *application domain*. In Chapter 24, we examine the properties of an application domain with which you can interact, and demonstrate how to create and use additional application domains within the same process for such purposes as unit testing. We also describe how to use *Remoting* to communicate with these application domains. The AppDomain type defined in the System namespace is not applicable to Windows Store apps.

Native and COM Interoperability

You can interoperate with both native and COM code. Native interoperability allows you to call functions in unmanaged DLLs, register callbacks, map data structures, and interoperate with native data types. COM interoperability allows you to call COM types and expose .NET types to COM. The types that support these functions are in System.Runtime.InteropServices, and we cover them in Chapter 25.

Applied Technologies

User Interface Technologies

User-interface-based applications can be divided into two categories: *thin client*, which amounts to a website, and *rich client*, which is a program the end user must download and install on a computer or mobile device.

For thin-client applications, .NET provides the ASP.NET library.

For rich-client applications that target Windows desktop, .NET provides the WPF and Windows Forms APIs. For rich-client apps that target mobile devices, you have the option of Windows RT (Windows Store apps only), or Xamarin™ for cross-platform apps.

Finally, there's a hybrid technology called Silverlight, which has been largely abandoned since the rise of HTML5.

ASP.NET

Applications written using ASP.NET host under Windows IIS (or a custom process with ASP.NET 5) and can be accessed from any web browser. Here are the advantages of ASP.NET over rich-client technologies:

- There is zero deployment at the client end.
- Clients can run a non-Windows platform.
- Updates are easily deployed.

Further, because most of what you write in an ASP.NET application runs on the server, you design your data access layer to run in the same application domain—

without limiting security or scalability. In contrast, a rich client that does the same is not generally as secure or scalable. (The solution, with the rich client, is to insert a *middle tier* between the client and database. The middle tier runs on a remote application server [often alongside the database server] and communicates with the rich clients via WCF, Web Services, or Remoting.)

In writing your web pages, you can choose between the traditional Web Forms and the newer MVC (Model-View-Controller) API. Both build on the ASP.NET infrastructure. Web Forms has been part of the Framework since its inception; MVC was written much later in response to the success of Ruby on Rails and MonoRail. It provides, in general, a better programming abstraction than Web Forms; it also allows more control over the generated HTML. What you lose over Web Forms is a designer. This makes Web Forms still a good choice for web pages with predominately static content.

The limitations of ASP.NET are largely a reflection of the limitations of thin-client systems in general:

- While a web browser can offer a rich compelling interface with HTML5 and AJAX, it's still inferior to a native rich-client API such as WPF in capability and performance.
- Maintaining state on the client—or on behalf of the client—can be cumbersome.

The types for writing ASP.NET applications are in the System.Web.UI namespace and its subnamespaces and are in the *System.Web.dll* assembly. ASP.NET 5 is available on NuGet.

Windows Presentation Foundation (WPF)

WPF was introduced in Framework 3.0 for writing rich-client applications. The benefits of WPF over its predecessor, Windows Forms, are as follows:

- It supports sophisticated graphics, such as arbitrary transformations, 3D rendering, and true transparency.
- Its primary measurement unit is not pixel-based, so applications display correctly at any DPI (dots per inch) setting.
- It has extensive dynamic layout support, which means you can localize an application without danger of elements overlapping.
- Rendering uses DirectX and is fast, taking good advantage of graphics hardware acceleration.
- User interfaces can be described declaratively in XAML files that can be maintained independently of the "code-behind" files—this helps to separate appearance from functionality.

WPF's size and complexity, however, make for a steep learning curve.

The types for writing WPF applications are in the System.Windows namespace and all subnamespaces except for System.Windows.Forms.

Windows Forms

Windows Forms is a rich-client API that's as old as the .NET Framework. Compared to WPF, Windows Forms is a relatively simple technology that provides most of the features you need in writing a typical Windows application. It also has significant relevancy in maintaining legacy applications. It has a number of drawbacks, though, compared to WPF:

- Controls are positioned and sized in pixels, making it easy to write applications that break on clients whose DPI settings differ from the developer's.

- The API for drawing nonstandard controls is GDI+, which, although reasonably flexible, is slow in rendering large areas (and without double buffering, may flicker).

- Controls lack true transparency.

- Dynamic layout is difficult to get right reliably.

The last point is an excellent reason to favor WPF over Windows Forms—even if you're writing a business application that needs just a user interface and not a "user experience." The layout elements in WPF, such as Grid, make it easy to assemble labels and text boxes such that they always align—even after language-changing localization—without messy logic and without any flickering. Further, you don't have to bow to the lowest common denominator in screen resolution—WPF layout elements have been designed from the outset to adapt properly to resizing.

On the positive side, Windows Forms is relatively simple to learn and still has a wealth of support in third-party controls.

The Windows Forms types are in the System.Windows.Forms (in *System.Windows.Forms.dll*) and System.Drawing (in *System.Drawing.dll*) namespaces. The latter also contains the GDI+ types for drawing custom controls.

Windows RT and Xamarin

Also not technically part of the .NET Framework, Windows 8 and higher includes Windows Runtime for writing touch-first user interfaces aimed at mobile devices (see "C# and Windows Runtime" on page 5 in Chapter 1). Its rich-client API was inspired by WPF and uses XAML for layout, and applications that you write with this API are deployed via the Window Store (hence "Windows Store" apps). The namespaces are Windows.UI and Windows.UI.Xaml.

Another popular solution for mobile application development is Xamarin™. With this third-party product, you can write mobile apps in C# that target iOS and Android, as well as Windows Phone.

Silverlight

Silverlight is not part of the main .NET Framework: it's a separate Framework that includes a subset of the Framework's core features—plus the ability to run as a web browser plug-in. Its graphics model is essentially a subset of WPF, and this allows you to leverage existing knowledge in developing Silverlight applications. Silverlight is available as a small cross-platform download for web browsers—much like Macromedia's Flash.

With the rise of HTML 5, Microsoft's focus has shifted away from Silverlight.

Backend Technologies

ADO.NET

ADO.NET is the managed data access API. Although the name is derived from the 1990s-era ADO (ActiveX Data Objects), the technology is completely different. ADO.NET contains two major low-level components:

Provider layer
> The provider model defines common classes and interfaces for low-level access to database providers. These interfaces comprise connections, commands, adapters, and readers (forward-only, read-only cursors over a database). The Framework ships with native support for Microsoft SQL Server, and numerous third-party drivers are available for other databases.

DataSet model
> A DataSet is a structured cache of data. It resembles a primitive in-memory database, which defines SQL constructs such as tables, rows, columns, relationships, constraints, and views. By programming against a cache of data, you can reduce the number of trips to the server, increasing server scalability and the responsiveness of a rich-client user interface. DataSets are serializable and are designed to be sent across the wire between client and server applications.

Sitting above the provider layer are two APIs that offer the ability to query databases via LINQ:

- Entity Framework (introduced in Framework 3.5 SP1)

- LINQ to SQL (introduced in Framework 3.5)

Both technologies include *object/relational mappers* (ORMs), meaning they automatically map objects (based on classes that you define) to rows in the database. This allows you to query those objects via LINQ (instead of writing SQL `select` statements)—and update them without manually writing SQL `insert/delete/update` statements. This cuts the volume of code in an application's data access layer (particularly the "plumbing" code) and provides strong static type safety. These technologies also avoid the need for DataSets as receptacles of data—although Data-

Sets still provide the unique ability to store and serialize state changes (something particularly useful in multitier applications). You can use Entity Framework or LINQ to SQL in conjunction with DataSets, although the process is somewhat clumsy and DataSets are inherently ungainly. In other words, there's no straightforward out-of-the-box solution for writing *n*-tier applications with Microsoft's ORMs as yet.

LINQ to SQL is simpler and faster than Entity Framework, and has historically produced better SQL (although Entity Framework has benefited from numerous updates). Entity Framework is more flexible in that you can create elaborate mappings between the database and the classes that you query, and offers a model that allows third-party support for databases other than SQL Server.

Windows Workflow

Windows Workflow is a framework for modeling and managing potentially long-running business processes. Workflow targets a standard runtime library, providing consistency and interoperability. Workflow also helps reduce coding for dynamically controlled decision-making trees.

Windows Workflow is not strictly a backend technology—you can use it anywhere (an example is page flow, in the UI).

Workflow came originally with .NET Framework 3.0, with its types defined in the System.WorkFlow namespace. Workflow was substantially revised in Framework 4.0; the new types live in and under the System.Activities namespace.

COM+ and MSMQ

The Framework allows you to interoperate with COM+ for services such as distributed transactions, via types in the System.EnterpriseServices namespace. It also supports MSMQ (Microsoft Message Queuing) for asynchronous, one-way messaging through types in System.Messaging.

Distributed System Technologies

Windows Communication Foundation (WCF)

WCF is a sophisticated communications infrastructure introduced in Framework 3.0. WCF is flexible and configurable enough to make both of its predecessors—Remoting and (.ASMX) Web Services—*mostly* redundant.

WCF, Remoting, and Web Services are all alike in that they implement the following basic model in allowing a client and server application to communicate:

- On the server, you indicate what methods you'd like remote client applications to be able to call.

- On the client, you specify or infer the *signatures* of the server methods you'd like to call.

- On both the server and the client, you choose a transport and communication protocol (in WCF, this is done through a *binding*).

- The client establishes a connection to the server.

- The client calls a remote method, which executes transparently on the server.

WCF further decouples the client and server through service contracts and data contracts. Conceptually, the client sends an (XML or binary) message to an endpoint on a remote *service*, rather than directly invoking a remote *method*. One of the benefits of this decoupling is that clients have no dependency on the .NET platform or on any proprietary communication protocols.

WCF is highly configurable and provides the most extensive support for standardized messaging protocols, including WS-*. This lets you communicate with parties running different software—possibly on different platforms—while still supporting advanced features such as encryption. In practice however, the complexity of these protocols has limited their adoption across other platforms, and the best option right now for interoperable messaging is REST over HTTP, which Microsoft supports through the Web API layer over ASP.NET.

For .NET-to-.NET communication, however, WCF offers richer serialization and better tooling than with REST APIs. It's also potentially faster as it's not tied to HTTP and can use binary serialization.

The types for communicating with WCF are in, and below, the `System.ServiceMo del` namespace.

Web API

Web API runs over ASP.NET and is architecturally similar to Microsoft's MVC API, except that it's designed to expose services and data instead of web pages. Its advantage over WCF is in allowing you to follow popular REST-over-HTTP conventions, offering easy interoperability with the widest range of platforms.

REST implementations are internally simpler than the SOAP and WS- protocols that WCF relies on for interoperability. REST APIs are also architecturally more elegant for loosely-coupled systems, building on de-facto standards and making excellent use of what HTTP already provides.

Remoting and .ASMX Web Services

Remoting and .ASMX Web Services are WCF's predecessors. Remoting is almost redundant in WCF's wake, and .ASMX Web Services has become entirely redundant.

Remoting's remaining niche is in communicating between application domains within the same process (see Chapter 24). Remoting is geared toward tightly coupled applications. A typical example is when the client and server are both .NET applications written by the same company (or companies sharing common assemblies). Communication typically involves exchanging potentially complex custom .NET objects that the Remoting infrastructure serializes and deserializes without needing intervention.

The types for Remoting are in or under `System.Runtime.Remoting`; the types for Web Services are under `System.Web.Services`.

6

Framework Fundamentals

Many of the core facilities that you need when programming are provided not by the C# language, but by types in the .NET Framework. In this chapter, we cover the Framework's role in fundamental programming tasks, such as virtual equality comparison, order comparison, and type conversion. We also cover the basic Framework types, such as String, DateTime, and Enum.

The types in this section reside in the System namespace, with the following exceptions:

- StringBuilder is defined in System.Text, as are the types for *text encodings*.

- CultureInfo and associated types are defined in System.Globalization.

- XmlConvert is defined in System.Xml.

String and Text Handling

Char

A C# char represents a single Unicode character and aliases the System.Char struct. In Chapter 2, we described how to express char literals. For example:

```
char c = 'A';
char newLine = '\n';
```

System.Char defines a range of static methods for working with characters, such as ToUpper, ToLower, and IsWhiteSpace. You can call these through either the System.Char type or its char alias:

```
Console.WriteLine (System.Char.ToUpper ('c'));    // C
Console.WriteLine (char.IsWhiteSpace ('\t'));     // True
```

ToUpper and ToLower honor the end user's locale, which can lead to subtle bugs. The following expression evaluates to false in Turkey:

```
char.ToUpper ('i') == 'I'
```

because in Turkey, char.ToUpper ('i') is 'İ' (notice the dot on top!). To avoid this problem, System.Char (and System.String) also provides culture-invariant versions of ToUpper and ToLower ending with the word *Invariant*. These always apply English culture rules:

```
Console.WriteLine (char.ToUpperInvariant ('i'));    // I
```

This is a shortcut for:

```
Console.WriteLine (char.ToUpper ('i', CultureInfo.InvariantCulture))
```

For more on locales and culture, see "Formatting and parsing" on page 233.

Most of char's remaining static methods are related to categorizing characters and are listed in Table 6-1.

Table 6-1. Static methods for categorizing characters

Static method	Characters included	Unicode categories included
IsLetter	A–Z, a–z, and letters of other alphabets	UpperCaseLetter LowerCaseLetter TitleCaseLetter ModifierLetter OtherLetter
IsUpper	Uppercase letters	UpperCaseLetter
IsLower	Lowercase letters	LowerCaseLetter
IsDigit	0–9 plus digits of other alphabets	DecimalDigitNumber
IsLetterOrDigit	Letters plus digits	(IsLetter, IsDigit)
IsNumber	All digits plus Unicode fractions and Roman numeral symbols	DecimalDigitNumber LetterNumber OtherNumber
IsSeparator	Space plus all Unicode separator characters	LineSeparator ParagraphSeparator
IsWhiteSpace	All separators plus \n, \r, \t, \f, and \v	LineSeparator ParagraphSeparator
IsPunctuation	Symbols used for punctuation in Western and other alphabets	DashPunctuation ConnectorPunctuation InitialQuotePunctuation FinalQuotePunctuation
IsSymbol	Most other printable symbols	MathSymbol ModifierSymbol OtherSymbol

Static method	Characters included	Unicode categories included
IsControl	Nonprintable "control" characters below 0x20, such as \r, \n, \t, \0, and characters between 0x7F and 0x9A	(None)

For more granular categorization, char provides a static method called GetUnicode Category; this returns a UnicodeCategory enumeration whose members are shown in the rightmost column of Table 6-1.

> By explicitly casting from an integer, it's possible to produce a char outside the allocated Unicode set. To test a character's validity, call char.GetUnicodeCategory: if the result is Unico deCategory.OtherNotAssigned, the character is invalid.

A char is 16 bits wide—enough to represent any Unicode character in the *Basic Multilingual Plane*. To go outside this, you must use surrogate pairs: we describe the methods for doing this in "Text Encodings and Unicode" on page 223.

String

A C# string (== System.String) is an immutable (unchangeable) sequence of characters. In Chapter 2, we described how to express string literals, perform equality comparisons, and concatenate two strings. This section covers the remaining functions for working with strings, exposed through the static and instance members of the System.String class.

Constructing strings

The simplest way to construct a string is to assign a literal, as we saw in Chapter 2:

```
string s1 = "Hello";
string s2 = "First Line\r\nSecond Line";
string s3 = @"\\server\fileshare\helloworld.cs";
```

To create a repeating sequence of characters, you can use string's constructor:

```
Console.Write (new string ('*', 10));     // **********
```

You can also construct a string from a char array. The ToCharArray method does the reverse:

```
char[] ca = "Hello".ToCharArray();
string s = new string (ca);               // s = "Hello"
```

string's constructor is also overloaded to accept various (unsafe) pointer types, in order to create strings from types such as char*.

Null and empty strings

An empty string has a length of zero. To create an empty string, you can use either a literal or the static `string.Empty` field; to test for an empty string, you can either perform an equality comparison or test its `Length` property:

```
string empty = "";
Console.WriteLine (empty == "");              // True
Console.WriteLine (empty == string.Empty);    // True
Console.WriteLine (empty.Length == 0);         // True
```

Because strings are reference types, they can also be `null`:

```
string nullString = null;
Console.WriteLine (nullString == null);        // True
Console.WriteLine (nullString == "");          // False
Console.WriteLine (nullString.Length == 0);    // NullReferenceException
```

The static `string.IsNullOrEmpty` method is a useful shortcut for testing whether a given string is either null or empty.

Accessing characters within a string

A string's indexer returns a single character at the given index. As with all functions that operate on strings, this is zero-indexed:

```
string str  = "abcde";
char letter = str[1];       // letter == 'b'
```

`string` also implements `IEnumerable<char>`, so you can `foreach` over its characters:

```
foreach (char c in "123") Console.Write (c + ",");    // 1,2,3,
```

Searching within strings

The simplest methods for searching within strings are `StartsWith`, `EndsWith` and `Contains`. These all return `true` or `false`:

```
Console.WriteLine ("quick brown fox".EndsWith ("fox"));      // True
Console.WriteLine ("quick brown fox".Contains ("brown"));    // True
```

`StartsWith` and `EndsWith` are overloaded to let you specify a `StringComparison` enum or a `CultureInfo` object to control case and culture sensitivity (see "Ordinal versus culture comparison" on page 220). The default is to perform a case-sensitive match using rules applicable to the current (localized) culture. The following instead performs a case-insensitive search using the *invariant* culture's rules:

```
"abcdef".StartsWith ("abc", StringComparison.InvariantCultureIgnoreCase)
```

The `Contains` method doesn't offer the convenience of this overload, although you can achieve the same result with the `IndexOf` method.

`IndexOf` is more powerful: it returns the first position of a given character or substring (or –1 if the substring isn't found):

```
Console.WriteLine ("abcde".IndexOf ("cd"));    // 2
```

IndexOf is also overloaded to accept a startPosition (an index from which to begin searching), as well as a StringComparison enum:

```
Console.WriteLine ("abcde abcde".IndexOf ("CD", 6,
                    StringComparison.CurrentCultureIgnoreCase));    // 8
```

LastIndexOf is like IndexOf but works backward through the string.

IndexOfAny returns the first matching position of any one of a set of characters:

```
Console.Write ("ab,cd ef".IndexOfAny (new char[] {' ', ','} ));    // 2
Console.Write ("pas5w0rd".IndexOfAny ("0123456789".ToCharArray() ));  // 3
```

LastIndexOfAny does the same in the reverse direction.

Manipulating strings

Because String is immutable, all the methods that "manipulate" a string return a new one, leaving the original untouched (the same goes for when you reassign a string variable).

Substring extracts a portion of a string:

```
string left3 = "12345".Substring (0, 3);    // left3 = "123";
string mid3  = "12345".Substring (1, 3);    // mid3 = "234";
```

If you omit the length, you get the remainder of the string:

```
string end3  = "12345".Substring (2);       // end3 = "345";
```

Insert and Remove insert or remove characters at a specified position:

```
string s1 = "helloworld".Insert (5, ", ");  // s1 = "hello, world"
string s2 = s1.Remove (5, 2);               // s2 = "helloworld";
```

PadLeft and PadRight pad a string to a given length with a specified character (or a space if unspecified):

```
Console.WriteLine ("12345".PadLeft (9, '*'));  // ****12345
Console.WriteLine ("12345".PadLeft (9));       //     12345
```

If the input string is longer than the padding length, the original string is returned unchanged.

TrimStart and TrimEnd remove specified characters from the beginning or end of a string; Trim does both. By default, these functions remove whitespace characters (including spaces, tabs, new lines, and Unicode variations of these):

```
Console.WriteLine ("  abc \t\r\n ".Trim().Length);    // 3
```

Replace replaces all (nonoverlapping) occurrences of a particular character or sub-string:

```
Console.WriteLine ("to be done".Replace (" ", " | ") );  // to | be | done
Console.WriteLine ("to be done".Replace (" ", "")    );  // tobedone
```

ToUpper and ToLower return upper- and lowercase versions of the input string. By default, they honor the user's current language settings; ToUpperInvariant and ToLowerInvariant always apply English alphabet rules.

Splitting and joining strings

Split divides a string up into pieces:

```
string[] words = "The quick brown fox".Split();

foreach (string word in words)
  Console.Write (word + "|");     // The|quick|brown|fox|
```

By default, Split uses whitespace characters as delimiters; it's also overloaded to accept a params array of char or string delimiters. Split also optionally accepts a StringSplitOptions enum, which has an option to remove empty entries: this is useful when words are separated by several delimiters in a row.

The static Join method does the reverse of Split. It requires a delimiter and string array:

```
string[] words = "The quick brown fox".Split();
string together = string.Join (" ", words);       // The quick brown fox
```

The static Concat method is similar to Join but accepts only a params string array and applies no separator. Concat is exactly equivalent to the + operator (the compiler, in fact, translates + to Concat):

```
string sentence     = string.Concat ("The", " quick", " brown", " fox");
string sameSentence = "The" + " quick" + " brown" + " fox";
```

String.Format and composite format strings

The static Format method provides a convenient way to build strings that embed variables. The embedded variables (or values) can be of any type; the Format simply calls ToString on them.

The master string that includes the embedded variables is called a *composite format string*. When calling String.Format, you provide a composite format string followed by each of the embedded variables. For example:

```
string composite = "It's {0} degrees in {1} on this {2} morning";
string s = string.Format (composite, 35, "Perth", DateTime.Now.DayOfWeek);

// s == "It's 35 degrees in Perth on this Friday morning"
```

(And that's Celsius!)

From C# 6, we can use interpolated string literals to the same effect (see "String Type" on page 36 in Chapter 2). Just precede the string with the $ symbol and put the expressions in braces:

```
string s = $"It's hot this {DateTime.Now.DayOfWeek} morning";
```

Each number in curly braces is called a *format item*. The number corresponds to the argument position and is optionally followed by:

- A comma and a *minimum width* to apply
- A colon and a *format string*

The minimum width is useful for aligning columns. If the value is negative, the data is left-aligned; otherwise, it's right-aligned. For example:

```
string composite = "Name={0,-20} Credit Limit={1,15:C}";

Console.WriteLine (string.Format (composite, "Mary", 500));
Console.WriteLine (string.Format (composite, "Elizabeth", 20000));
```

Here's the result:

```
Name=Mary              Credit Limit=      $500.00
Name=Elizabeth         Credit Limit=   $20,000.00
```

The equivalent without using `string.Format` is this:

```
string s = "Name=" + "Mary".PadRight (20) +
           " Credit Limit=" + 500.ToString ("C").PadLeft (15);
```

The credit limit is formatted as currency by virtue of the "C" format string. We describe format strings in detail in "Formatting and parsing" on page 233.

Comparing Strings

In comparing two values, the .NET Framework differentiates the concepts of *equality comparison* and *order comparison*. Equality comparison tests whether two instances are semantically the same; order comparison tests which of two (if any) instances comes first when arranging them in ascending or descending sequence.

Equality comparison is not a *subset* of order comparison; the two systems have different purposes. It's legal, for instance, to have two unequal values in the same ordering position. We resume this topic in "Equality Comparison" on page 267.

For string-equality comparison, you can use the == operator or one of `string`'s `Equals` methods. The latter are more versatile because they allow you to specify options such as case insensitivity.

Another difference is that == does not work reliably on strings if the variables are cast to the `object` type. We explain why this is so in "Equality Comparison" on page 267.

For string order comparison, you can use either the `CompareTo` instance method or the static `Compare` and `CompareOrdinal` methods: these return a positive or negative number—or zero—depending on whether the first value comes before, after, or alongside the second.

Before going into the details of each, we need to examine .NET's underlying string-comparison algorithms.

Ordinal versus culture comparison

There are two basic algorithms for string comparison: *ordinal* and *culture-sensitive.* Ordinal comparisons interpret characters simply as numbers (according to their numeric Unicode value); culture-sensitive comparisons interpret characters with reference to a particular alphabet. There are two special cultures: the "current culture," which is based on settings picked up from the computer's control panel; and the "invariant culture," which is the same on every computer (and closely matches American culture).

For equality comparison, both ordinal and culture-specific algorithms are useful. For ordering, however, culture-specific comparison is nearly always preferable: to order strings alphabetically, you need an alphabet. Ordinal relies on the numeric Unicode point values, which happen to put English characters in alphabetical order —but even then not exactly as you might expect. For example, assuming case sensitivity, consider the strings "Atom", "atom", and "Zamia". The invariant culture puts them in the following order:

```
"Atom", "atom", "Zamia"
```

Ordinal arranges them instead as follows:

```
"Atom", "Zamia", "atom"
```

This is because the invariant culture encapsulates an alphabet, which considers uppercase characters adjacent to their lowercase counterparts (aAbBcCdD...). The ordinal algorithm, however, puts all the uppercase characters first, and then all lowercase characters (A...Z, a...z). This is essentially a throwback to the ASCII character set invented in the 1960s.

String equality comparison

Despite ordinal's limitations, string's == operator always performs *ordinal case-sensitive* comparison. The same goes for the instance version of string.Equals when called without arguments; this defines the "default" equality-comparison behavior for the string type.

> The ordinal algorithm was chosen for string's == and Equals functions because it's both highly efficient and *deterministic.* String-equality comparison is considered fundamental and is performed far more frequently than order comparison.
>
> A "strict" notion of equality is also consistent with the general use of the == operator.

The following methods allow culture-aware or case-insensitive comparisons:

```
public bool Equals(string value, StringComparison comparisonType);
```

```
public static bool Equals (string a, string b,
                           StringComparison comparisonType);
```

The static version is advantageous in that it still works if one or both of the strings are null. StringComparison is an enum defined as follows:

```
public enum StringComparison
{
  CurrentCulture,                  // Case-sensitive
  CurrentCultureIgnoreCase,
  InvariantCulture,                // Case-sensitive
  InvariantCultureIgnoreCase,
  Ordinal,                         // Case-sensitive
  OrdinalIgnoreCase
}
```

For example:

```
Console.WriteLine (string.Equals ("foo", "FOO",
                   StringComparison.OrdinalIgnoreCase));   // True

Console.WriteLine ("ü" == "ü");                            // False

Console.WriteLine (string.Equals ("ü", "ü",
                   StringComparison.CurrentCulture));      // ?
```

(The result of the third example is determined by the computer's current language settings.)

String-order comparison

String's CompareTo instance method performs *culture-sensitive, case-sensitive* order comparison. Unlike the == operator, CompareTo does not use ordinal comparison: for ordering, a culture-sensitive algorithm is much more useful.

Here's the method's definition:

```
public int CompareTo (string strB);
```

 The CompareTo instance method implements the generic ICom parable interface, a standard comparison protocol used across the .NET Framework. This means string's CompareTo defines the default ordering behavior of strings, in such applications as sorted collections, for instance. For more information on IComparable, see "Order Comparison" on page 278.

For other kinds of comparison, you can call the static Compare and CompareOrdinal methods:

```
public static int Compare (string strA, string strB,
                           StringComparison comparisonType);

public static int Compare (string strA, string strB, bool ignoreCase,
                           CultureInfo culture);
```

```
public static int Compare (string strA, string strB, bool ignoreCase);

public static int CompareOrdinal (string strA, string strB);
```

The last two methods are simply shortcuts for calling the first two methods.

All of the order-comparison methods return a positive number, a negative number, or zero, depending on whether the first value comes after, before, or alongside the second value:

```
Console.WriteLine ("Boston".CompareTo ("Austin"));    // 1
Console.WriteLine ("Boston".CompareTo ("Boston"));    // 0
Console.WriteLine ("Boston".CompareTo ("Chicago"));   // -1
Console.WriteLine ("ü".CompareTo ("ü"));              // 0
Console.WriteLine ("foo".CompareTo ("FOO"));          // -1
```

The following performs a case-insensitive comparison using the current culture:

```
Console.WriteLine (string.Compare ("foo", "FOO", true));   // 0
```

By supplying a CultureInfo object, you can plug in any alphabet:

```
// CultureInfo is defined in the System.Globalization namespace

CultureInfo german = CultureInfo.GetCultureInfo ("de-DE");
int i = string.Compare ("Müller", "Muller", false, german);
```

StringBuilder

The StringBuilder class (System.Text namespace) represents a mutable (editable) string. With a StringBuilder, you can Append, Insert, Remove, and Replace substrings without replacing the whole StringBuilder.

StringBuilder's constructor optionally accepts an initial string value, as well as a starting size for its internal capacity (default is 16 characters). If you go above this, StringBuilder automatically resizes its internal structures to accommodate (at a slight performance cost) up to its maximum capacity (default is int.MaxValue).

A popular use of StringBuilder is to build up a long string by repeatedly calling Append. This approach is much more efficient than repeatedly concatenating ordinary string types:

```
StringBuilder sb = new StringBuilder();
for (int i = 0; i < 50; i++) sb.Append (i + ",");
```

To get the final result, call ToString():

```
Console.WriteLine (sb.ToString());

0,1,2,3,4,5,6,7,8,9,10,11,12,13,14,15,16,17,18,19,20,21,22,23,24,25,26,
27,28,29,30,31,32,33,34,35,36,37,38,39,40,41,42,43,44,45,46,47,48,49,
```

In our example, the expression i + "," means that we're still repeatedly concatenating strings. However, this incurs only a small performance cost in that the strings in question are small and don't grow with each loop iteration. For maximum performance, however, we could change the loop body to this:

```
{ sb.Append (i); sb.Append (","); }
```

AppendLine performs an Append that adds a new line sequence ("\r\n" in Windows). AppendFormat accepts a composite format string, just like String.Format.

As well as the Insert, Remove, and Replace methods (Replace works like string's Replace), StringBuilder defines a Length property and a writable indexer for getting/setting individual characters.

To clear the contents of a StringBuilder, either instantiate a new one or set its Length to zero.

Setting a StringBuilder's Length to zero doesn't shrink its *internal* capacity. So, if the StringBuilder previously contained one million characters, it will continue to occupy around 2 MB of memory after zeroing its Length. If you want to release the memory, you must create a new StringBuilder and allow the old one to drop out of scope (and be garbage-collected).

Text Encodings and Unicode

A *character set* is an allocation of characters, each with a numeric code or *code point*. There are two character sets in common use: Unicode and ASCII. Unicode has an address space of approximately one million characters, of which about 100,000 are currently allocated. Unicode covers most spoken world languages, as well as some historical languages and special symbols. The ASCII set is simply the first 128 characters of the Unicode set, which covers most of what you see on a US-style keyboard. ASCII predates Unicode by 30 years and is still sometimes used for its simplicity and efficiency: each character is represented by one byte.

The .NET type system is designed to work with the Unicode character set. ASCII is implicitly supported, though, by virtue of being a subset of Unicode.

A *text encoding* maps characters from their numeric code point to a binary representation. In .NET, text encodings come into play primarily when dealing with text files or streams. When you read a text file into a string, a *text encoder* translates the file data from binary into the internal Unicode representation that the char and string types expect. A text encoding can restrict what characters can be represented, as well as impacting storage efficiency.

There are two categories of text encoding in .NET:

- Those that map Unicode characters to another character set
- Those that use standard Unicode encoding schemes

The first category contains legacy encodings such as IBM's EBCDIC and 8-bit character sets with extended characters in the upper-128 region that were popular prior to Unicode (identified by a code page). The ASCII encoding is also in this category: it encodes the first 128 characters and drops everything else. This category contains the *nonlegacy* GB18030 as well, which is the mandatory standard for applications written in China—or sold to China—since 2000.

In the second category are UTF-8, UTF-16, and UTF-32 (and the obsolete UTF-7). Each differs in space efficiency. UTF-8 is the most space-efficient for most kinds of text: it uses *between 1 and 4 bytes* to represent each character. The first 128 characters require only a single byte, making it compatible with ASCII. UTF-8 is the most popular encoding for text files and streams (particularly on the Internet), and it is the default for stream I/O in .NET (in fact, it's the default for almost everything that implicitly uses an encoding).

UTF-16 uses one or two 16-bit words to represent each character and is what .NET uses internally to represent characters and strings. Some programs also write files in UTF-16.

UTF-32 is the least space-efficient: it maps each code point directly to 32 bits, so every character consumes 4 bytes. UTF-32 is rarely used for this reason. It does, however, make random access very easy because every character takes an equal number of bytes.

Obtaining an Encoding object

The Encoding class in System.Text is the common base type for classes that encapsulate text encodings. There are several subclasses—their purpose is to encapsulate families of encodings with similar features. The easiest way to instantiate a correctly configured class is to call Encoding.GetEncoding with a standard IANA (Internet Assigned Numbers Authority) Character Set name:

```
Encoding utf8 = Encoding.GetEncoding ("utf-8");
Encoding chinese = Encoding.GetEncoding ("GB18030");
```

The most common encodings can also be obtained through dedicated static properties on Encoding:

Encoding name	Static property on Encoding
UTF-8	Encoding.UTF8
UTF-16	Encoding.Unicode (*not* UTF16)
UTF-32	Encoding.UTF32
ASCII	Encoding.ASCII

The static `GetEncodings` method returns a list of all supported encodings, with their standard IANA names:

```
foreach (EncodingInfo info in Encoding.GetEncodings())
  Console.WriteLine (info.Name);
```

The other way to obtain an encoding is to directly instantiate an encoding class. Doing so allows you to set various options via constructor arguments, including:

- Whether to throw an exception if an invalid byte sequence is encountered when decoding. The default is false.

- Whether to encode/decode UTF-16/UTF-32 with the most significant bytes first (*big endian*) or the least significant bytes first (*little endian*). The default is *little endian*, the standard on the Windows operating system.

- Whether to emit a byte-order mark (a prefix that indicates *endianness*).

Encoding for file and stream I/O

The most common application for an `Encoding` object is to control how text is read and written to a file or stream. For example, the following writes "Testing..." to a file called *data.txt* in UTF-16 encoding:

```
System.IO.File.WriteAllText ("data.txt", "Testing...", Encoding.Unicode);
```

If you omit the final argument, `WriteAllText` applies the ubiquitous UTF-8 encoding.

 UTF-8 is the default text encoding for all file and stream I/O.

We resume this subject in Chapter 15, in "Stream Adapters" on page 639.

Encoding to byte arrays

You can also use an `Encoding` object to go to and from a byte array. The `GetBytes` method converts from `string` to `byte[]` with the given encoding; `GetString` converts from `byte[]` to `string`:

```
byte[] utf8Bytes  = System.Text.Encoding.UTF8.GetBytes    ("0123456789");
byte[] utf16Bytes = System.Text.Encoding.Unicode.GetBytes ("0123456789");
byte[] utf32Bytes = System.Text.Encoding.UTF32.GetBytes   ("0123456789");

Console.WriteLine (utf8Bytes.Length);    // 10
Console.WriteLine (utf16Bytes.Length);   // 20
Console.WriteLine (utf32Bytes.Length);   // 40

string original1 = System.Text.Encoding.UTF8.GetString    (utf8Bytes);
string original2 = System.Text.Encoding.Unicode.GetString (utf16Bytes);
string original3 = System.Text.Encoding.UTF32.GetString   (utf32Bytes);
```

```
Console.WriteLine (original1);      // 0123456789
Console.WriteLine (original2);      // 0123456789
Console.WriteLine (original3);      // 0123456789
```

UTF-16 and surrogate pairs

Recall that .NET stores characters and strings in UTF-16. Because UTF-16 requires one or two 16-bit words per character, and a char is only 16 bits in length, some Unicode characters require two chars to represent. This has a couple of consequences:

- A string's Length property may be greater than its real character count.
- A single char is not always enough to fully represent a Unicode character.

Most applications ignore this, because nearly all commonly used characters fit into a section of Unicode called the *Basic Multilingual Plane* (BMP) which requires only one 16-bit word in UTF-16. The BMP covers several dozen world languages and includes more than 30,000 Chinese characters. Excluded are characters of some ancient languages, symbols for musical notation, and some less common Chinese characters.

If you need to support two-word characters, the following static methods in char convert a 32-bit code point to a string of two chars, and back again:

```
string ConvertFromUtf32 (int utf32)
int    ConvertToUtf32   (char highSurrogate, char lowSurrogate)
```

Two-word characters are called *surrogates*. They are easy to spot because each word is in the range 0xD800 to 0xDFFF. You can use the following static methods in char to assist:

```
bool IsSurrogate     (char c)
bool IsHighSurrogate (char c)
bool IsLowSurrogate  (char c)
bool IsSurrogatePair (char highSurrogate, char lowSurrogate)
```

The StringInfo class in the System.Globalization namespace also provides a range of methods and properties for working with two-word characters.

Characters outside the BMP typically require special fonts and have limited operating system support.

Dates and Times

Three immutable structs in the System namespace do the job of representing dates and times: DateTime, DateTimeOffset, and TimeSpan. C# doesn't define any special keywords that map to these types.

TimeSpan

A `TimeSpan` represents an interval of time—or a time of the day. In the latter role, it's simply the "clock" time (without the date), which is equivalent to the time since midnight, assuming no daylight saving transition. A `TimeSpan` has a resolution of 100 ns, has a maximum value of about 10 million days, and can be positive or negative.

There are three ways to construct a `TimeSpan`:

- Through one of the constructors
- By calling one of the static `From...` methods
- By subtracting one `DateTime` from another

Here are the constructors:

```
public TimeSpan (int hours, int minutes, int seconds);
public TimeSpan (int days, int hours, int minutes, int seconds);
public TimeSpan (int days, int hours, int minutes, int seconds,
                                                int milliseconds);
public TimeSpan (long ticks);    // Each tick = 100ns
```

The static `From...` methods are more convenient when you want to specify an interval in just a single unit, such as minutes, hours, and so on:

```
public static TimeSpan FromDays (double value);
public static TimeSpan FromHours (double value);
public static TimeSpan FromMinutes (double value);
public static TimeSpan FromSeconds (double value);
public static TimeSpan FromMilliseconds (double value);
```

For example:

```
Console.WriteLine (new TimeSpan (2, 30, 0));    // 02:30:00
Console.WriteLine (TimeSpan.FromHours (2.5));    // 02:30:00
Console.WriteLine (TimeSpan.FromHours (-2.5));   // -02:30:00
```

`TimeSpan` overloads the < and > operators, as well as the + and - operators. The following expression evaluates to a `TimeSpan` of 2.5 hours:

```
TimeSpan.FromHours(2) + TimeSpan.FromMinutes(30);
```

The next expression evaluates to one second short of 10 days:

```
TimeSpan.FromDays(10) - TimeSpan.FromSeconds(1);    // 9.23:59:59
```

Using this expression, we can illustrate the integer properties `Days`, `Hours`, `Minutes`, `Seconds`, and `Milliseconds`:

```
TimeSpan nearlyTenDays = TimeSpan.FromDays(10) - TimeSpan.FromSeconds(1);

Console.WriteLine (nearlyTenDays.Days);       // 9
Console.WriteLine (nearlyTenDays.Hours);      // 23
Console.WriteLine (nearlyTenDays.Minutes);    // 59
```

Framework
Fundamentals

```
Console.WriteLine (nearlyTenDays.Seconds);        // 59
Console.WriteLine (nearlyTenDays.Milliseconds);   // 0
```

In contrast, the Total... properties return values of type double describing the entire time span:

```
Console.WriteLine (nearlyTenDays.TotalDays);         // 9.99998842592593
Console.WriteLine (nearlyTenDays.TotalHours);        // 239.999722222222
Console.WriteLine (nearlyTenDays.TotalMinutes);      // 14399.9833333333
Console.WriteLine (nearlyTenDays.TotalSeconds);      // 863999
Console.WriteLine (nearlyTenDays.TotalMilliseconds); // 863999000
```

The static Parse method does the opposite of ToString, converting a string to a TimeSpan. TryParse does the same but returns false rather than throwing an exception if the conversion fails. The XmlConvert class also provides TimeSpan/string-conversion methods that follow standard XML formatting protocols.

The default value for a TimeSpan is TimeSpan.Zero.

TimeSpan can also be used to represent the time of the day (the elapsed time since midnight). To obtain the current time of day, call DateTime.Now.TimeOfDay.

DateTime and DateTimeOffset

DateTime and DateTimeOffset are immutable structs for representing a date, and optionally, a time. They have a resolution of 100 ns and a range covering the years 0001 through 9999.

DateTimeOffset was added in Framework 3.5 and is functionally similar to Date Time. Its distinguishing feature is that it also stores a UTC offset; this allows more meaningful results when comparing values across different time zones.

 An excellent article on the rationale behind the introduction of DateTimeOffset is available on the MSDN BCL blogs. The title is "A Brief History of DateTime," by Anthony Moore.

Choosing between DateTime and DateTimeOffset

DateTime and DateTimeOffset differ in how they handle time zones. A DateTime incorporates a three-state flag indicating whether the DateTime is relative to:

- The local time on the current computer
- UTC (the modern equivalent of Greenwich Mean Time)
- Unspecified

A DateTimeOffset is more specific—it stores the offset from UTC as a TimeSpan:

```
July 01 2007 03:00:00 -06:00
```

This influences equality comparisons, which is the main factor in choosing between DateTime and DateTimeOffset. Specifically:

- `DateTime` ignores the three-state flag in comparisons and considers two values equal if they have the same year, month, day, hour, minute, and so on.

- `DateTimeOffset` considers two values equal if they refer to the *same point in time*.

> Daylight saving time can make this distinction important even if your application doesn't need to handle multiple geographic time zones.

So, `DateTime` considers the following two values different, whereas `DateTimeOffset` considers them equal:

```
July 01 2007 09:00:00 +00:00 (GMT)
July 01 2007 03:00:00 -06:00 (local time, Central America)
```

In most cases, `DateTimeOffset`'s equality logic is preferable. For example, in calculating which of two international events is more recent, a `DateTimeOffset` implicitly gives the right answer. Similarly, a hacker plotting a distributed denial of service attack would reach for a `DateTimeOffset`! To do the same with `DateTime` requires standardizing on a single time zone (typically UTC) throughout your application. This is problematic for two reasons:

- To be friendly to the end user, UTC `DateTime`s require explicit conversion to local time prior to formatting.

- It's easy to forget and incorporate a local `DateTime`.

`DateTime` is better, though, at specifying a value relative to the local computer at runtime—for example, if you want to schedule an archive at each of your international offices for next Sunday, at 3 A.M. local time (when there's least activity). Here, `DateTime` would be more suitable because it would respect each site's local time.

> Internally, `DateTimeOffset` uses a short integer to store the UTC offset in minutes. It doesn't store any regional information, so there's nothing present to indicate whether an offset of +08:00, for instance, refers to Singapore time or Perth time.

We revisit time zones and equality comparison in more depth in "Dates and Time Zones" on page 234.

> SQL Server 2008 introduced direct support for `DateTimeOff` set through a new data type of the same name.

Constructing a DateTime

`DateTime` defines constructors that accept integers for the year, month, and day— and optionally, the hour, minute, second, and millisecond:

```
public DateTime (int year, int month, int day);

public DateTime (int year, int month, int day,
                 int hour, int minute, int second, int millisecond);
```

If you specify only a date, the time is implicitly set to midnight (0:00).

The DateTime constructors also allow you to specify a DateTimeKind—an enum with the following values:

```
Unspecified, Local, Utc
```

This corresponds to the three-state flag described in the preceding section. Unspecified is the default, and it means that the DateTime is time-zone-agnostic. Local means relative to the local time zone on the current computer. A local DateTime does not include information about *which particular time zone* it refers to, nor, unlike DateTimeOffset, the numeric offset from UTC.

A DateTime's Kind property returns its DateTimeKind.

DateTime's constructors are also overloaded to accept a Calendar object as well— this allows you to specify a date using any of the Calendar subclasses defined in System.Globalization. For example:

```
DateTime d = new DateTime (5767, 1, 1,
                 new System.Globalization.HebrewCalendar());

Console.WriteLine (d);   // 12/12/2006 12:00:00 AM
```

(The formatting of the date in this example depends on your computer's control panel settings.) A DateTime always uses the default Gregorian calendar—this example, a one-time conversion, takes place during construction. To perform computations using another calendar, you must use the methods on the Calendar subclass itself.

You can also construct a DateTime with a single *ticks* value of type long, where *ticks* is the number of 100 ns intervals from midnight 01/01/0001.

For interoperability, DateTime provides the static FromFileTime and FromFileTimeUtc methods for converting from a Windows file time (specified as a long) and FromOADate for converting from an OLE automation date/time (specified as a double).

To construct a DateTime from a string, call the static Parse or ParseExact method. Both methods accept optional flags and format providers; ParseExact also accepts a format string. We discuss parsing in greater detail in "Formatting and parsing" on page 233.

Constructing a DateTimeOffset

DateTimeOffset has a similar set of constructors. The difference is that you also specify a UTC offset as a TimeSpan:

```
public DateTimeOffset (int year, int month, int day,
                       int hour, int minute, int second,
                       TimeSpan offset);

public DateTimeOffset (int year, int month, int day,
                       int hour, int minute, int second, int millisecond,
                       TimeSpan offset);
```

The `TimeSpan` must amount to a whole number of minutes, or an exception is thrown.

`DateTimeOffset` also has constructors that accept a `Calendar` object, a `long` *ticks* value, and static `Parse` and `ParseExact` methods that accept a string.

You can construct a `DateTimeOffset` from an existing `DateTime` either by using these constructors:

```
public DateTimeOffset (DateTime dateTime);
public DateTimeOffset (DateTime dateTime, TimeSpan offset);
```

or with an implicit cast:

```
DateTimeOffset dt = new DateTime (2000, 2, 3);
```

> The implicit cast from `DateTime` to `DateTimeOffset` is handy because most of the .NET Framework supports `DateTime`— not `DateTimeOffset`.

If you don't specify an offset, it's inferred from the `DateTime` value using these rules:

- If the `DateTime` has a `DateTimeKind` of `Utc`, the offset is zero.

- If the `DateTime` has a `DateTimeKind` of `Local` or `Unspecified` (the default), the offset is taken from the current local time zone.

To convert in the other direction, `DateTimeOffset` provides three properties that return values of type `DateTime`:

- The `UtcDateTime` property returns a `DateTime` in UTC time.

- The `LocalDateTime` property returns a `DateTime` in the current local time zone (converting it if necessary).

- The `DateTime` property returns a `DateTime` in whatever zone it was specified, with a `Kind` of `Unspecified` (i.e., it returns the UTC time plus the offset).

The current DateTime/DateTimeOffset

Both `DateTime` and `DateTimeOffset` have a static `Now` property that returns the current date and time:

```
Console.WriteLine (DateTime.Now);          // 11/11/2015 1:23:45 PM
Console.WriteLine (DateTimeOffset.Now);    // 11/11/2015 1:23:45 PM -06:00
```

DateTime also provides a Today property that returns just the date portion:

```
Console.WriteLine (DateTime.Today);        // 11/11/2015 12:00:00 AM
```

The static UtcNow property returns the current date and time in UTC:

```
Console.WriteLine (DateTime.UtcNow);       // 11/11/2015 7:23:45 AM
Console.WriteLine (DateTimeOffset.UtcNow); // 11/11/2015 7:23:45 AM +00:00
```

The precision of all these methods depends on the operating system and is typically in the 10–20 ms region.

Working with dates and times

DateTime and DateTimeOffset provide a similar set of instance properties that return various date/time elements:

```
DateTime dt = new DateTime (2000, 2, 3,
                            10, 20, 30);

Console.WriteLine (dt.Year);         // 2000
Console.WriteLine (dt.Month);        // 2
Console.WriteLine (dt.Day);          // 3
Console.WriteLine (dt.DayOfWeek);    // Thursday
Console.WriteLine (dt.DayOfYear);    // 34

Console.WriteLine (dt.Hour);         // 10
Console.WriteLine (dt.Minute);       // 20
Console.WriteLine (dt.Second);       // 30
Console.WriteLine (dt.Millisecond);  // 0
Console.WriteLine (dt.Ticks);        // 630851700300000000
Console.WriteLine (dt.TimeOfDay);    // 10:20:30  (returns a TimeSpan)
```

DateTimeOffset also has an Offset property of type TimeSpan.

Both types provide the following instance methods to perform computations (most accept an argument of type double or int):

```
AddYears  AddMonths   AddDays
AddHours  AddMinutes  AddSeconds  AddMilliseconds  AddTicks
```

These all return a new DateTime or DateTimeOffset, and they take into account such things as leap years. You can pass in a negative value to subtract.

The Add method adds a TimeSpan to a DateTime or DateTimeOffset. The + operator is overloaded to do the same job:

```
TimeSpan ts = TimeSpan.FromMinutes (90);
Console.WriteLine (dt.Add (ts));
Console.WriteLine (dt + ts);            // same as above
```

You can also subtract a TimeSpan from a DateTime/DateTimeOffset and subtract one DateTime/DateTimeOffset from another. The latter gives you a TimeSpan:

```
DateTime thisYear = new DateTime (2015, 1, 1);
DateTime nextYear = thisYear.AddYears (1);
TimeSpan oneYear = nextYear - thisYear;
```

Formatting and parsing

Calling ToString on a DateTime formats the result as a *short date* (all numbers) followed by a *long time* (including seconds). For example:

```
11/11/2015 11:50:30 AM
```

The operating system's control panel, by default, determines such things as whether the day, month, or year comes first, the use of leading zeros, and whether 12- or 24-hour time is used.

Calling ToString on a DateTimeOffset is the same, except that the offset is returned also:

```
11/11/2015 11:50:30 AM -06:00
```

The ToShortDateString and ToLongDateString methods return just the date portion. The long date format is also determined by the control panel; an example is "Wednesday, 11 November 2015". ToShortTimeString and ToLongTimeString return just the time portion, such as 17:10:10 (the former excludes seconds).

These four methods just described are actually shortcuts to four different *format strings*. ToString is overloaded to accept a format string and provider, allowing you to specify a wide range of options and control how regional settings are applied. We describe this in "Formatting and parsing" on page 233.

 DateTimes and DateTimeOffsets can be misparsed if the culture settings differ from those in force when formatting takes place. You can avoid this problem by using ToString in conjunction with a format string that ignores culture settings (such as "o"):

```
DateTime dt1 = DateTime.Now;
string cannotBeMisparsed = dt1.ToString ("o");
DateTime dt2 = DateTime.Parse (cannotBeMisparsed);
```

The static Parse/TryParse and ParseExact/TryParseExact methods do the reverse of ToString, converting a string to a DateTime or DateTimeOffset. These methods are also overloaded to accept a format provider. The Try* methods return false instead of throwing a FormatException.

Null DateTime and DateTimeOffset values

Because DateTime and DateTimeOffset are structs, they are not intrinsically nullable. When you need nullability, there are two ways around this:

- Use a Nullable type (i.e., DateTime? or DateTimeOffset?).

- Use the static field `DateTime.MinValue` or `DateTimeOffset.MinValue` (the *default values* for these types).

A nullable type is usually the best approach because the compiler helps to prevent mistakes. `DateTime.MinValue` is useful for backward compatibility with code written prior to C# 2.0 (when nullable types were introduced).

Calling `ToUniversalTime` or `ToLocalTime` on a `DateTime.Min Value` can result in it no longer being `DateTime.MinValue` (depending on which side of GMT you are on). If you're right on GMT (England, outside daylight saving), the problem won't arise at all because local and UTC times are the same. This is your compensation for the English winter!

Dates and Time Zones

In this section, we examine in more detail how time zones influence `DateTime` and `DateTimeOffset`. We also look at the `TimeZone` and `TimeZoneInfo` types, which provide information on time zone offsets and daylight saving time.

DateTime and Time Zones

`DateTime` is simplistic in its handling of time zones. Internally, it stores a `DateTime` using two pieces of information:

- A 62-bit number, indicating the number of ticks since 1/1/0001
- A 2-bit enum, indicating the `DateTimeKind` (`Unspecified`, `Local`, or `Utc`)

When you compare two `DateTime` instances, only their *ticks* values are compared; their `DateTimeKinds` are ignored:

```
DateTime dt1 = new DateTime (2015, 1, 1, 10, 20, 30, DateTimeKind.Local);
DateTime dt2 = new DateTime (2015, 1, 1, 10, 20, 30, DateTimeKind.Utc);
Console.WriteLine (dt1 == dt2);        // True
DateTime local = DateTime.Now;
DateTime utc = local.ToUniversalTime();
Console.WriteLine (local == utc);      // False
```

The instance methods `ToUniversalTime`/`ToLocalTime` convert to universal/local time. These apply the computer's current time zone settings and return a new `Date Time` with a `DateTimeKind` of `Utc` or `Local`. No conversion happens if you call `ToUni versalTime` on a `DateTime` that's already `Utc`, or `ToLocalTime` on a `DateTime` that's already `Local`. You will get a conversion, however, if you call `ToUniversalTime` or `ToLocalTime` on a `DateTime` that's `Unspecified`.

You can construct a `DateTime` that differs from another only in `Kind` with the static `DateTime.SpecifyKind` method:

```
DateTime d = new DateTime (2015, 12, 12);  // Unspecified
DateTime utc = DateTime.SpecifyKind (d, DateTimeKind.Utc);
Console.WriteLine (utc);                    // 12/12/2015 12:00:00 AM
```

DateTimeOffset and Time Zones

Internally, DateTimeOffset comprises a DateTime field whose value is always in UTC and a 16-bit integer field for the UTC offset in minutes. Comparisons look only at the (UTC) DateTime; the Offset is used primarily for formatting.

The ToUniversalTime/ToLocalTime methods return a DateTimeOffset representing the same point in time, but with a UTC or local offset. Unlike with DateTime, these methods don't affect the underlying date/time value, only the offset:

```
DateTimeOffset local = DateTimeOffset.Now;
DateTimeOffset utc   = local.ToUniversalTime();

Console.WriteLine (local.Offset);    // -06:00:00 (in Central America)
Console.WriteLine (utc.Offset);      // 00:00:00

Console.WriteLine (local == utc);               // True
```

To include the Offset in the comparison, you must use the EqualsExact method:

```
Console.WriteLine (local.EqualsExact (utc));    // False
```

TimeZone and TimeZoneInfo

The TimeZone and TimeZoneInfo classes provide information on time zone names, UTC offsets, and daylight saving time rules. TimeZoneInfo is the more powerful of the two and was introduced in Framework 3.5.

The biggest difference between the two types is that TimeZone lets you access only the current local time zone, whereas TimeZoneInfo provides access to all the world's time zones. Further, TimeZoneInfo exposes a richer (although at times, more awkward) rules-based model for describing daylight saving time.

TimeZone

The static TimeZone.CurrentTimeZone method returns a TimeZone object based on the current local settings. The following demonstrates the result if run in California:

```
TimeZone zone = TimeZone.CurrentTimeZone;
Console.WriteLine (zone.StandardName);    // Pacific Standard Time
Console.WriteLine (zone.DaylightName);    // Pacific Daylight Time
```

The IsDaylightSavingTime and GetUtcOffset methods work as follows:

```
DateTime dt1 = new DateTime (2015, 1, 1);
DateTime dt2 = new DateTime (2015, 6, 1);
Console.WriteLine (zone.IsDaylightSavingTime (dt1));    // True
Console.WriteLine (zone.IsDaylightSavingTime (dt2));    // False
Console.WriteLine (zone.GetUtcOffset (dt1));            // 08:00:00
Console.WriteLine (zone.GetUtcOffset (dt2));            // 09:00:00
```

The GetDaylightChanges method returns specific daylight saving time information for a given year:

```
DaylightTime day = zone.GetDaylightChanges (2015);
Console.WriteLine (day.Start.ToString ("M"));    // 08 March
Console.WriteLine (day.End.ToString ("M"));      // 01 November
Console.WriteLine (day.Delta);                   // 01:00:00
```

TimeZoneInfo

The TimeZoneInfo class works in a similar manner. TimeZoneInfo.Local returns the current local time zone:

```
TimeZoneInfo zone = TimeZoneInfo.Local;
Console.WriteLine (zone.StandardName);    // Pacific Standard Time
Console.WriteLine (zone.DaylightName);    // Pacific Daylight Time
```

TimeZoneInfo also provides IsDaylightSavingTime and GetUtcOffset methods—the difference is that they accept either a DateTime or a DateTimeOffset.

You can obtain a TimeZoneInfo for any of the world's time zones by calling FindSystemTimeZoneById with the zone ID. This feature is unique to TimeZoneInfo, as is everything else that we demonstrate from this point on. We'll switch to Western Australia for reasons that will soon become clear:

```
TimeZoneInfo wa = TimeZoneInfo.FindSystemTimeZoneById
                  ("W. Australia Standard Time");

Console.WriteLine (wa.Id);                          // W. Australia Standard Time
Console.WriteLine (wa.DisplayName);                 // (GMT+08:00) Perth
Console.WriteLine (wa.BaseUtcOffset);               // 08:00:00
Console.WriteLine (wa.SupportsDaylightSavingTime);  // True
```

The Id property corresponds to the value passed to FindSystemTimeZoneById. The static GetSystemTimeZones method returns all world time zones; hence, you can list all valid zone ID strings as follows:

```
foreach (TimeZoneInfo z in TimeZoneInfo.GetSystemTimeZones())
  Console.WriteLine (z.Id);
```

You can also create a custom time zone by calling TimeZoneInfo.CreateCustomTimeZone. Because TimeZoneInfo is immutable, you must pass in all the relevant data as method arguments.

You can serialize a predefined or custom time zone to a (semi) human-readable string by calling ToSerializedString—and deserialize it by calling TimeZoneInfo.FromSerializedString.

The static ConvertTime method converts a DateTime or DateTimeOffset from one time zone to another. You can include either just a destination TimeZoneInfo, or both source and destination TimeZoneInfo objects. You can also convert directly from or to UTC with the methods ConvertTimeFromUtc and ConvertTimeToUtc.

For working with daylight saving time, TimeZoneInfo provides the following additional methods:

- IsInvalidTime returns true if a DateTime is within the hour (or delta) that's skipped when the clocks move forward.

- IsAmbiguousTime returns true if a DateTime or DateTimeOffset is within the hour (or delta) that's repeated when the clocks move back.

- GetAmbiguousTimeOffsets returns an array of TimeSpans representing the valid offset choices for an ambiguous DateTime or DateTimeOffset.

Unlike with TimeZone, you can't obtain simple dates from a TimeZoneInfo indicating the start and end of daylight saving time. Instead, you must call GetAdjustmentRules, which returns a declarative summary of all daylight saving rules that apply to all years. Each rule has a DateStart and DateEnd indicating the date range within which the rule is valid:

```
foreach (TimeZoneInfo.AdjustmentRule rule in wa.GetAdjustmentRules())
  Console.WriteLine ("Rule: applies from " + rule.DateStart +
                                " to " + rule.DateEnd);
```

Western Australia first introduced daylight saving time in 2006, *midseason* (and then rescinded it in 2009). This required a special rule for the first year; hence, there are two rules:

```
Rule: applies from 1/01/2006 12:00:00 AM to 31/12/2006 12:00:00 AM
Rule: applies from 1/01/2007 12:00:00 AM to 31/12/2009 12:00:00 AM
```

Each AdjustmentRule has a DaylightDelta property of type TimeSpan (this is one hour in almost every case) and properties called DaylightTransitionStart and DaylightTransitionEnd. The latter two are of type TimeZoneInfo.Transition Time, which has the following properties:

```
public bool IsFixedDateRule { get; }
public DayOfWeek DayOfWeek { get; }
public int Week { get; }
public int Day { get; }
public int Month { get; }
public DateTime TimeOfDay { get; }
```

A transition time is somewhat complicated in that it needs to represent both fixed and floating dates. An example of a floating date is "the last Sunday in March." Here are the rules for interpreting a transition time:

1. If, for an end transition, IsFixedDateRule is true, Day is 1, Month is 1, and TimeOfDay is DateTime.MinValue, there is no end to daylight saving time in that year (this can happen only in the southern hemisphere, upon the initial introduction of daylight saving time to a region).

2. Otherwise, if IsFixedDateRule is true, the Month, Day, and TimeOfDay properties determine the start or end of the adjustment rule.

3. Otherwise, if IsFixedDateRule is false, the Month, DayOfWeek, Week, and Time OfDay properties determine the start or end of the adjustment rule.

In the last case, Week refers to the week of the month, with "5" meaning the last week. We can demonstrate this by enumerating the adjustment rules for our wa time zone:

```
foreach (TimeZoneInfo.AdjustmentRule rule in wa.GetAdjustmentRules())
{
  Console.WriteLine ("Rule: applies from " + rule.DateStart +
                                " to " + rule.DateEnd);

  Console.WriteLine ("   Delta: " + rule.DaylightDelta);

  Console.WriteLine ("   Start: " + FormatTransitionTime
                        (rule.DaylightTransitionStart, false));

  Console.WriteLine ("   End:   " + FormatTransitionTime
                        (rule.DaylightTransitionEnd, true));
  Console.WriteLine();
}
```

In FormatTransitionTime, we honor the rules just described:

```
static string FormatTransitionTime (TimeZoneInfo.TransitionTime tt,
                                    bool endTime)
{
  if (endTime && tt.IsFixedDateRule
          && tt.Day == 1 && tt.Month == 1
          && tt.TimeOfDay == DateTime.MinValue)
    return "-";

  string s;
  if (tt.IsFixedDateRule)
    s = tt.Day.ToString();
  else
    s = "The " +
        "first second third fourth last".Split() [tt.Week - 1] +
        " " + tt.DayOfWeek + " in";

  return s + " " + DateTimeFormatInfo.CurrentInfo.MonthNames [tt.Month-1]
        + " at " + tt.TimeOfDay.TimeOfDay;
}
```

The result with Western Australia is interesting in that it demonstrates both fixed and floating date rules—as well as an absent end date:

```
Rule: applies from 1/01/2006 12:00:00 AM to 31/12/2006 12:00:00 AM
   Delta: 01:00:00
   Start: 3 December at 02:00:00
   End:   -

Rule: applies from 1/01/2007 12:00:00 AM to 31/12/2009 12:00:00 AM
   Delta: 01:00:00
```

```
Start: The last Sunday in October at 02:00:00
End:   The last Sunday in March at 03:00:00
```

Western Australia is actually unique in this regard. Here's how
we found it:

```
from zone in TimeZoneInfo.GetSystemTimeZones()
let rules = zone.GetAdjustmentRules()
where
  rules.Any
   (r => r.DaylightTransitionEnd.IsFixedDateRule) &&
  rules.Any
   (r => !r.DaylightTransitionEnd.IsFixedDateRule)
select zone
```

Daylight Saving Time and DateTime

If you use a DateTimeOffset or a UTC DateTime, equality comparisons are unimpe-
ded by the effects of daylight saving time. But with local DateTimes, daylight saving
can be problematic.

The rules can be summarized as follows:

- Daylight saving impacts local time but not UTC time.

- When the clocks turn back, comparisons that rely on time moving forward will
  break if (and only if) they use local DateTimes.

- You can always reliably round-trip between UTC and local times (on the same
  computer)—even as the clocks turn back.

The IsDaylightSavingTime tells you whether a given local DateTime is subject to
daylight saving time. UTC times always return false:

```
Console.Write (DateTime.Now.IsDaylightSavingTime());    // True or False
Console.Write (DateTime.UtcNow.IsDaylightSavingTime()); // Always False
```

Assuming dto is a DateTimeOffset, the following expression does the same:

```
dto.LocalDateTime.IsDaylightSavingTime
```

The end of daylight saving time presents a particular complication for algorithms
that use local time. When the clocks go back, the same hour (or more precisely,
Delta) repeats itself. We can demonstrate this by instantiating a DateTime right in
the "twilight zone" on your computer, and then subtracting Delta (this example
requires that you practice daylight saving time to be interesting!):

```
DaylightTime changes = TimeZone.CurrentTimeZone.GetDaylightChanges (2010);
TimeSpan halfDelta = new TimeSpan (changes.Delta.Ticks / 2);
DateTime utc1 = changes.End.ToUniversalTime() - halfDelta;
DateTime utc2 = utc1 - changes.Delta;
```

Converting these variables to local times demonstrates why you should use UTC
and not local time if your code relies on time moving forward:

```
DateTime loc1 = utc1.ToLocalTime();  // (Pacific Standard Time)
DateTime loc2 = utc2.ToLocalTime();
```

```
Console.WriteLine (loc1);         // 2/11/2010 1:30:00 AM
Console.WriteLine (loc2);         // 2/11/2010 1:30:00 AM
Console.WriteLine (loc1 == loc2); // True
```

Despite loc1 and loc2 reporting as equal, they are different inside. DateTime reserves a special bit for indicating on which side of the twilight zone an ambiguous local date lies! This bit is ignored in comparison—as we just saw—but comes into play when you format the DateTime unambiguously:

```
Console.Write (loc1.ToString ("o"));  // 2010-11-02T02:30:00.0000000-08:00
Console.Write (loc2.ToString ("o"));  // 2010-11-02T02:30:00.0000000-07:00
```

This bit also is read when you convert back to UTC, ensuring perfect round-tripping between local and UTC times:

```
Console.WriteLine (loc1.ToUniversalTime() == utc1);  // True
Console.WriteLine (loc2.ToUniversalTime() == utc2);  // True
```

 You can reliably compare any two DateTimes by first calling ToUniversalTime on each. This strategy fails if (and only if) exactly one of them has a DateTimeKind of Unspecified. This potential for failure is another reason for favoring DateTimeOffset.

Formatting and Parsing

Formatting means converting *to* a string; parsing means converting *from* a string. The need to format or parse arises frequently in programming, in a variety of situations. Hence, the .NET Framework provides a variety of mechanisms:

ToString *and* Parse
> These methods provide default functionality for many types.

Format providers
> These manifest as additional ToString (and Parse) methods that accept a *format string* and/or a *format provider*. Format providers are highly flexible and culture-aware. The .NET Framework includes format providers for the numeric types and DateTime/DateTimeOffset.

XmlConvert
> This is a static class with methods that format and parse while honoring XML standards. XmlConvert is also useful for general-purpose conversion when you need culture independence or you want to preempt misparsing. XmlConvert supports the numeric types, bool, DateTime, DateTimeOffset, TimeSpan, and Guid.

Type converters
> These target designers and XAML parsers.

In this section, we discuss the first two mechanisms, focusing particularly on format providers. In the section following, we describe XmlConvert and type converters, as well as other conversion mechanisms.

ToString and Parse

The simplest formatting mechanism is the ToString method. It gives meaningful output on all simple value types (bool, DateTime, DateTimeOffset, TimeSpan, Guid, and all the numeric types). For the reverse operation, each of these types defines a static Parse method. For example:

```
string s = true.ToString();    // s = "True"
bool b = bool.Parse (s);       // b = true
```

If the parsing fails, a FormatException is thrown. Many types also define a Try Parse method, which returns false if the conversion fails, rather than throwing an exception:

```
int i;
bool failure = int.TryParse ("qwerty", out i);
bool success = int.TryParse ("123", out i);
```

If you anticipate an error, calling TryParse is faster and more elegant than calling Parse in an exception handling block.

The Parse and TryParse methods on DateTime(Offset) and the numeric types respect local culture settings; you can change this by specifying a CultureInfo object. Specifying invariant culture is often a good idea. For instance, parsing "1.234" into a double gives us 1234 in Germany:

```
Console.WriteLine (double.Parse ("1.234"));    // 1234  (In Germany)
```

This is because in Germany, the period indicates a thousands separator rather than a decimal point. Specifying *invariant culture* fixes this:

```
double x = double.Parse ("1.234", CultureInfo.InvariantCulture);
```

The same applies when calling ToString():

```
string x = 1.234.ToString (CultureInfo.InvariantCulture);
```

Format Providers

Sometimes you need more control over how formatting and parsing take place. There are dozens of ways to format a DateTime(Offset), for instance. Format providers allow extensive control over formatting and parsing, and are supported for numeric types and date/times. Format providers are also used by user interface controls for formatting and parsing.

The gateway to using a format provider is IFormattable. All numeric types—and DateTime(Offset)—implement this interface:

```
public interface IFormattable
{
   string ToString (string format, IFormatProvider formatProvider);
}
```

The first argument is the *format string*; the second is the *format provider*. The format string provides instructions; the format provider determines how the instructions are translated. For example:

```
NumberFormatInfo f = new NumberFormatInfo();
f.CurrencySymbol = "$$";
Console.WriteLine (3.ToString ("C", f));        // $$ 3.00
```

Here, `"C"` is a format string that indicates *currency*, and the `NumberFormatInfo` object is a format provider that determines how currency—and other numeric representations—are rendered. This mechanism allows for globalization.

All format strings for numbers and dates are listed in "Standard Format Strings and Parsing Flags" on page 246.

If you specify a `null` format string or provider, a default is applied. The default format provider is `CultureInfo.CurrentCulture`, which, unless reassigned, reflects the computer's runtime control panel settings. For example, on this computer:

```
Console.WriteLine (10.3.ToString ("C", null));  // $10.30
```

For convenience, most types overload `ToString` such that you can omit a `null` provider:

```
Console.WriteLine (10.3.ToString ("C"));    // $10.30
Console.WriteLine (10.3.ToString ("F4"));   // 10.3000 (Fix to 4 D.P.)
```

Calling `ToString` on a `DateTime(Offset)` or a numeric type with no arguments is equivalent to using a default format provider, with an empty format string.

The .NET Framework defines three format providers (all of which implement `IFormatProvider`):

```
NumberFormatInfo
DateTimeFormatInfo
CultureInfo
```

All enum types are also formattable, though there's no special `IFormatProvider` class.

Format providers and CultureInfo

Within the context of format providers, `CultureInfo` acts as an indirection mechanism for the other two format providers, returning a `NumberFormatInfo` or `DateTimeFormatInfo` object applicable to the culture's regional settings.

In the following example, we request a specific culture (*en*glish language in *Great Britain*):

```
CultureInfo uk = CultureInfo.GetCultureInfo ("en-GB");
Console.WriteLine (3.ToString ("C", uk));      // £3.00
```

This executes using the default `NumberFormatInfo` object applicable to the en-GB culture.

The next example formats a `DateTime` with invariant culture. Invariant culture is always the same, regardless of the computer's settings:

```
DateTime dt = new DateTime (2000, 1, 2);
CultureInfo iv = CultureInfo.InvariantCulture;
Console.WriteLine (dt.ToString (iv));      // 01/02/2000 00:00:00
Console.WriteLine (dt.ToString ("d", iv));      // 01/02/2000
```

 Invariant culture is based on American culture, with the following differences:

- The currency symbol is ¤ instead of $.
- Dates and times are formatted with leading zeros (though still with the month first).
- Time uses the 24-hour format rather than an AM/PM designator.

Using NumberFormatInfo or DateTimeFormatInfo

In the next example, we instantiate a `NumberFormatInfo` and change the group separator from a comma to a space. We then use it to format a number to three decimal places:

```
NumberFormatInfo f = new NumberFormatInfo ();
f.NumberGroupSeparator = " ";
Console.WriteLine (12345.6789.ToString ("N3", f));    // 12 345.679
```

The initial settings for a `NumberFormatInfo` or `DateTimeFormatInfo` are based on the invariant culture. Sometimes, however, it's more useful to choose a different starting point. To do this, you can `Clone` an existing format provider:

```
NumberFormatInfo f = (NumberFormatInfo)
                CultureInfo.CurrentCulture.NumberFormat.Clone();
```

A cloned format provider is always writable—even if the original was read-only.

Composite formatting

Composite format strings allow you to combine variable substitution with format strings. The static `string.Format` method accepts a composite format string—we illustrated this in "String.Format and composite format strings" on page 218:

```
string composite = "Credit={0:C}";
Console.WriteLine (string.Format (composite, 500));    // Credit=$500.00
```

The Console class itself overloads its Write and WriteLine methods to accept composite format strings, allowing us to shorten this example slightly:

```
Console.WriteLine ("Credit={0:C}", 500);    // Credit=$500.00
```

You can also append a composite format string to a StringBuilder (via AppendFormat), and to a TextWriter for I/O (see Chapter 15).

string.Format accepts an optional format provider. A simple application for this is to call ToString on an arbitrary object while passing in a format provider. For example:

```
string s = string.Format (CultureInfo.InvariantCulture, "{0}", someObject);
```

This is equivalent to:

```
string s;
if (someObject is IFormattable)
  s = ((IFormattable)someObject).ToString (null,
                                           CultureInfo.InvariantCulture);
else if (someObject == null)
  s = "";
else
  s = someObject.ToString();
```

Parsing with format providers

There's no standard interface for parsing through a format provider. Instead, each participating type overloads its static Parse (and TryParse) method to accept a format provider, and optionally, a NumberStyles or DateTimeStyles enum.

NumberStyles and DateTimeStyles control how parsing work: they let you specify such things as whether parentheses or a currency symbol can appear in the input string. (By default, the answer to both of these questions is *no*.) For example:

```
int error = int.Parse ("(2)");    // Exception thrown

int minusTwo = int.Parse ("(2)", NumberStyles.Integer |
                          NumberStyles.AllowParentheses);    // OK

decimal fivePointTwo = decimal.Parse ("£5.20", NumberStyles.Currency,
                       CultureInfo.GetCultureInfo ("en-GB"));
```

The next section lists all NumberStyles and DateTimeStyles members—as well as the default parsing rules for each type.

IFormatProvider and ICustomFormatter

All format providers implement IFormatProvider:

```
public interface IFormatProvider { object GetFormat (Type formatType); }
```

The purpose of this method is to provide indirection—this is what allows CultureInfo to defer to an appropriate NumberFormatInfo or DateTimeInfo object to do the work.

By implementing IFormatProvider—along with ICustomFormatter—you can also write your own format provider that works in conjunction with existing types. ICustomFormatter defines a single method as follows:

```
string Format (string format, object arg, IFormatProvider formatProvider);
```

The following custom format provider writes numbers as words:

```
// Program can be downloaded from http://www.albahari.com/nutshell/

public class WordyFormatProvider : IFormatProvider, ICustomFormatter
{
  static readonly string[] _numberWords =
  "zero one two three four five six seven eight nine minus point".Split();

  IFormatProvider _parent;   // Allows consumers to chain format providers

  public WordyFormatProvider () : this (CultureInfo.CurrentCulture) { }
  public WordyFormatProvider (IFormatProvider parent)
  {
    _parent = parent;
  }

  public object GetFormat (Type formatType)
  {
    if (formatType == typeof (ICustomFormatter)) return this;
    return null;
  }

  public string Format (string format, object arg, IFormatProvider prov)
  {
    // If it's not our format string, defer to the parent provider:
    if (arg == null || format != "W")
      return string.Format (_parent, "{0:" + format + "}", arg);

    StringBuilder result = new StringBuilder();
    string digitList = string.Format (CultureInfo.InvariantCulture,
                                      "{0}", arg);
    foreach (char digit in digitList)
    {
      int i = "0123456789-.".IndexOf (digit);
      if (i == -1) continue;
      if (result.Length > 0) result.Append (' ');
      result.Append (_numberWords[i]);
    }
    return result.ToString();
  }
}
```

Notice that in the Format method, we used string.Format to convert the input number to a string—with InvariantCulture. It would have been much simpler just to call ToString() on arg, but then CurrentCulture would have been used instead. The reason for needing the invariant culture is evident a few lines later:

```
int i = "0123456789-.".IndexOf (digit);
```

It's critical here that the number string comprises only the characters 0123456789-.
and not any internationalized versions of these.

Here's an example of using WordyFormatProvider:

```
double n = -123.45;
IFormatProvider fp = new WordyFormatProvider();
Console.WriteLine (string.Format (fp, "{0:C} in words is {0:W}", n));

// -$123.45 in words is minus one two three point four five
```

Custom format providers can be used only in composite format strings.

Standard Format Strings and Parsing Flags

The standard format strings control how a numeric type or DateTime/DateTimeOff
set is converted to a string. There are two kinds of format strings:

Standard format strings
> With these, you provide general guidance. A standard format string con-
> sists of a single letter, followed, optionally, by a digit (whose meaning
> depends on the letter). An example is "C" or "F2".

Custom format strings
> With these, you micromanage every character with a template. An example
> is "0:#.000E+00".

Custom format strings are unrelated to custom format providers.

Numeric Format Strings

Table 6-2 lists all standard numeric format strings.

Table 6-2. Standard numeric format strings

Letter	Meaning	Sample input	Result	Notes
G or g	"General"	1.2345, "G"	1.2345	Switches to exponential notation for
		0.00001, "G"	1E-05	small or large numbers
		0.00001, "g"	1e-05	G3 limits precision to three digits in
		1.2345, "G3"	1.23	*total* (before + after point)
		12345, "G3"	1.23E04	
F	Fixed point	2345.678, "F2"	2345.68	F2 rounds to two decimal places
		2345.6, "F2"	2345.60	
N	Fixed point with *group separator* ("Numeric")	2345.678, "N2"	2,345.68	As above, with group (1,000s) separator (details from format provider)
		2345.6, "N2"	2,345.60	
D	Pad with leading zeros	123, "D5"	00123	For integral types only
		123, "D1"	123	D5 pads left to five digits; does not truncate

Letter	Meaning	Sample input	Result	Notes
E or e	Force exponential notation	56789, "E" 56789, "e" 56789, "E2"	5.678900E+004 5.678900e+004 5.68E+004	Six-digit default precision
C	Currency	1.2, "C" 1.2, "C4"	$1.20 $1.2000	C with no digit uses default number of D.P. from format provider
P	Percent	.503, "P" .503, "P0"	50.30 % 50 %	Uses symbol and layout from format provider Decimal places can optionally be overridden
X or x	Hexadecimal	47, "X" 47, "x" 47, "X4"	2F 2f 002F	X for uppercase hex digits; x for lowercase hex digits Integrals only
R	Round-trip	1f / 3f, "R"	0.333333**43**	For the float and double types, R or G17 squeeze out all digits to ensure exact round-tripping

Supplying no numeric format string (or a null or blank string) is equivalent to using the "G" standard format string followed by no digit. This exhibits the following behavior:

- Numbers smaller than 10^{-4} or larger than the type's precision are expressed in exponential (scientific) notation.

- The two decimal places at the limit of float or double's precision are rounded away to mask the inaccuracies inherent in conversion to decimal from their underlying binary form.

> The automatic rounding just described is usually beneficial and goes unnoticed. However, it can cause trouble if you need to round-trip a number; in other words, convert it to a string and back again (maybe repeatedly) while preserving value equality. For this reason, the "R" and "G17" format strings exist to circumvent this implicit rounding.
>
> In Framework 4.6, "R" and "G17" do the same thing; in prior Frameworks, "R" is essentially a buggy version of "G17" and should not be used.

Table 6-3 lists custom numeric format strings.

Table 6-3. Custom numeric format strings

Specifier	Meaning	Sample input	Result	Notes
#	Digit placeholder	12.345, ".##" 12.345, ".####"	12.35 12.345	Limits digits after D.P.
0	Zero placeholder	12.345, ".00" 12.345, ".0000" 99, "000.00"	12.35 12.3450 099.00	As above, but also pads with zeros before and after D.P.
.	Decimal point			Indicates D.P. Actual symbol comes from NumberFormatInfo
,	Group separator	1234, "#,###,###" 1234, "0,000,000"	1,234 0,001,234	Symbol comes from Number FormatInfo
, (as above)	Multiplier	1000000, "#," 1000000, "#,,	1000 1	If comma is at end or before D.P., it acts as a multiplier— dividing result by 1,000, 1,000,000, etc.
%	Percent notation	0.6, "00%"	60%	First multiplies by 100 and then substitutes percent symbol obtained from Num berFormatInfo
E0, e0, E+0, e+0 E-0, e-0	Exponent notation	1234, "0E0" 1234, "0E+0" 1234, "0.00E00" 1234, "0.00e00"	1E3 1E+3 1.23E03 1.23e03	
\	Literal character quote	50, @"\#0"	#50	Use in conjunction with an @ prefix on the string—or use \\
'xx''xx'	Literal string quote	50, "0 '...'"	50 ...	
;	Section separator	15, "#;(#);zero"	15	(If positive)
		-5, "#;(#);zero"	(5)	(If negative)
		0, "#;(#);zero"	zero	(If zero)
Any other char	Literal	35.2, "$0 . 00c"	$35 . 20c	

NumberStyles

Each numeric type defines a static Parse method that accepts a NumberStyles argument. NumberStyles is a flags enum that lets you determine how the string is read as it's converted to a numeric type. It has the following combinable members:

```
AllowLeadingWhite      AllowTrailingWhite
AllowLeadingSign       AllowTrailingSign
AllowParentheses       AllowDecimalPoint
AllowThousands         AllowExponent
AllowCurrencySymbol    AllowHexSpecifier
```

NumberStyles also defines these composite members:

```
None  Integer  Float  Number  HexNumber  Currency  Any
```

Except for None, all composite values include AllowLeadingWhite and AllowTrai
lingWhite. Their remaining makeup is shown in Figure 6-1, with the most useful
three emphasized.

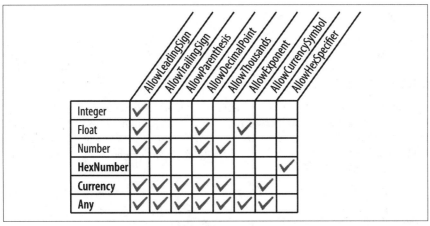

Figure 6-1. Composite NumberStyles

When you call Parse without specifying any flags, the defaults in Figure 6-2 are
applied.

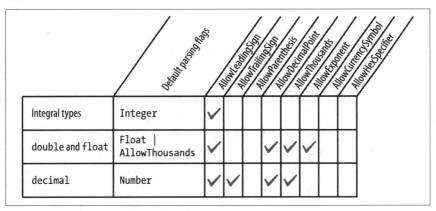

Figure 6-2. Default parsing flags for numeric types

If you don't want the defaults shown in Figure 6-2, you must explicitly specify Num berStyles:

```
int thousand = int.Parse ("3E8", NumberStyles.HexNumber);
int minusTwo = int.Parse ("(2)", NumberStyles.Integer |
                                  NumberStyles.AllowParentheses);
double aMillion = double.Parse ("1,000,000", NumberStyles.Any);
decimal threeMillion = decimal.Parse ("3e6", NumberStyles.Any);
decimal fivePointTwo = decimal.Parse ("$5.20", NumberStyles.Currency);
```

Because we didn't specify a format provider, this example works with your local currency symbol, group separator, decimal point, and so on. The next example is hard-coded to work with the euro sign and a blank group separator for currencies:

```
NumberFormatInfo ni = new NumberFormatInfo();
ni.CurrencySymbol = "€";
ni.CurrencyGroupSeparator = " ";
double million = double.Parse ("€1 000 000", NumberStyles.Currency, ni);
```

Date/Time Format Strings

Format strings for DateTime/DateTimeOffset can be divided into two groups, based on whether they honor culture and format provider settings. Those that do are listed in Table 6-4; those that don't are listed in Table 6-5. The sample output comes from formatting the following DateTime (with *invariant culture*, in the case of Table 6-4):

```
new DateTime (2000, 1, 2,  17, 18, 19);
```

Table 6-4. Culture-sensitive date/time format strings

Format string	Meaning	Sample output
d	Short date	01/02/2000
D	Long date	Sunday, 02 January 2000
t	Short time	17:18
T	Long time	17:18:19
f	Long date + short time	Sunday, 02 January 2000 17:18
F	Long date + long time	Sunday, 02 January 2000 17:18:19
g	Short date + short time	01/02/2000 17:18
G (default)	Short date + long time	01/02/2000 17:18:19
m, M	Month and day	02 January
y, Y	Year and month	January 2000

Table 6-5. Culture-insensitive date/time format strings

Format string	Meaning	Sample output	Notes
o	Round-trippable	`2000-01-02T17:18:19.0000000`	Will append time zone information unless `DateTimeKind` is `Unspecified`
r, R	RFC 1123 standard	`Sun, 02 Jan 2000 17:18:19 GMT`	You must explicitly convert to UTC with `DateTime.ToUniversalTime`
s	Sortable; ISO 8601	`2000-01-02T17:18:19`	Compatible with text-based sorting
u	"Universal" sortable	`2000-01-02 17:18:19Z`	Similar to above; must explicitly convert to UTC
U	UTC	`Sunday, 02 January 2000 17:18:19`	Long date + short time, converted to UTC

The format strings `"r"`, `"R"`, and `"u"` emit a suffix that implies UTC; yet they don't automatically convert a local to a UTC `DateTime` (so you must do the conversion yourself). Ironically, `"U"` automatically converts to UTC but doesn't write a time zone suffix! In fact, `"o"` is the only format specifier in the group that can write an unambiguous `DateTime` without intervention.

`DateTimeFormatInfo` also supports custom format strings: these are analogous to numeric custom format strings. The list is fairly exhaustive, and you can find it in the MSDN. An example of a custom format string is:

```
yyyy-MM-dd HH:mm:ss
```

Parsing and misparsing DateTimes

Strings that put the month or day first are ambiguous and can easily be misparsed—particularly if you or any of your customers live outside the United States. This is not a problem in user-interface controls because the same settings are in force when parsing as when formatting. But when writing to a file, for instance, day/month misparsing can be a real problem. There are two solutions:

- Always state the same explicit culture when formatting and parsing (e.g., invariant culture).

- Format `DateTime` and `DateTimeOffsets` in a manner *independent* of culture.

The second approach is more robust—particularly if you choose a format that puts the four-digit year first: such strings are much harder to misparse by another party. Further, strings formatted with a *standards-compliant* year-first format (such as `"o"`) can parse correctly alongside locally formatted strings—rather like a "universal donor." (Dates formatted with `"s"` or `"u"` have the further benefit of being sortable.)

To illustrate, suppose we generate a culture-insensitive `DateTime` string s as follows:

```
string s = DateTime.Now.ToString ("o");
```

 The "o" format string includes milliseconds in the output. The following custom format string gives the same result as "o", but without milliseconds:

```
yyyy-MM-ddTHH:mm:ss K
```

We can reparse this in two ways. ParseExact demands strict compliance with the specified format string:

```
DateTime dt1 = DateTime.ParseExact (s, "o", null);
```

(You can achieve a similar result with XmlConvert's ToString and ToDateTime methods.)

Parse, however, implicitly accepts both the "o" format and the CurrentCulture format:

```
DateTime dt2 = DateTime.Parse (s);
```

This works with both DateTime and DateTimeOffset.

 ParseExact is usually preferable if you know the format of the string that you're parsing. It means that if the string is incorrectly formatted, an exception will be thrown—which is usually better than risking a misparsed date.

DateTimeStyles

DateTimeStyles is a flags enum that provides additional instructions when calling Parse on a DateTime(Offset). Here are its members:

```
None,
AllowLeadingWhite, AllowTrailingWhite, AllowInnerWhite,
AssumeLocal, AssumeUniversal, AdjustToUniversal,
NoCurrentDateDefault, RoundTripKind
```

There is also a composite member, AllowWhiteSpaces:

```
AllowWhiteSpaces = AllowLeadingWhite | AllowTrailingWhite | AllowInnerWhite
```

The default is None. This means that extra whitespace is normally prohibited (whitespace that's part of a standard DateTime pattern is exempt).

AssumeLocal and AssumeUniversal apply if the string doesn't have a time zone suffix (such as Z or +9:00). AdjustToUniversal still honors time zone suffixes but then converts to UTC using the current regional settings.

If you parse a string comprising a time but no date, today's date is applied by default. If you apply the NoCurrentDateDefault flag, however, it instead uses 1st January 0001.

Enum Format Strings

In "Enums" in Chapter 3, we describe formatting and parsing enum values. Table 6-6 lists each format string and the result of applying it to the following expression:

```
Console.WriteLine (System.ConsoleColor.Red.ToString (formatString));
```

Table 6-6. Enum format strings

Format string	Meaning	Sample output	Notes
G or g	"General"	Red	Default
F or f	Treat as though Flags attribute were present	Red	Works on combined members even if enum has no Flags attribute
D or d	Decimal value	12	Retrieves underlying integral value
X or x	Hexadecimal value	0000000C	Retrieves underlying integral value

Other Conversion Mechanisms

In the previous two sections, we covered format providers—.NET's primary mechanism for formatting and parsing. Other important conversion mechanisms are scattered through various types and namespaces. Some convert to and from string, and some do other kinds of conversions. In this section, we discuss the following topics:

- The Convert class and its functions:
  - Real to integral conversions that round rather than truncate
  - Parsing numbers in base 2, 8, and 16
  - Dynamic conversions
  - Base 64 translations
- XmlConvert and its role in formatting and parsing for XML
- Type converters and their role in formatting and parsing for designers and XAML
- BitConverter, for binary conversions

Convert

The .NET Framework calls the following types *base types*:

- bool, char, string, System.DateTime, and System.DateTimeOffset
- All of the C# numeric types

The static `Convert` class defines methods for converting every base type to every other base type. Unfortunately, most of these methods are useless: either they throw exceptions or they are redundant alongside implicit casts. Among the clutter, however, are some useful methods, listed in the following sections.

 All base types (explicitly) implement `IConvertible`, which defines methods for converting to every other base type. In most cases, the implementation of each of these methods simply calls a method in `Convert`. On rare occasions, it can be useful to write a method that accepts an argument of type `IConvertible`.

Rounding real-to-integral conversions

In Chapter 2, we saw how implicit and explicit casts allow you to convert between numeric types. In summary:

- Implicit casts work for nonlossy conversions (e.g., `int` to `double`).

- Explicit casts are required for lossy conversions (e.g., `double` to `int`).

Casts are optimized for efficiency; hence, they *truncate* data that won't fit. This can be a problem when converting from a real number to an integer, because often you want to *round* rather than truncate. `Convert`'s numerical conversion methods address just this issue; they always *round*:

```
double d = 3.9;
int i = Convert.ToInt32 (d);    // i == 4
```

`Convert` uses banker's rounding, which snaps midpoint values to even integers (this avoids positive or negative bias). If banker's rounding is a problem, first call `Math.Round` on the real number: this accepts an additional argument that allows you to control midpoint rounding.

Parsing numbers in base 2, 8, and 16

Hidden among the `To(integral-type)` methods are overloads that parse numbers in another base:

```
int thirty = Convert.ToInt32 ("1E", 16);   // Parse in hexadecimal
uint five  = Convert.ToUInt32 ("101", 2);  // Parse in binary
```

The second argument specifies the base. It can be any base you like—as long as it's 2, 8, 10, or 16!

Dynamic conversions

Occasionally, you need to convert from one type to another—but you don't know what the types are until runtime. For this, the `Convert` class provides a `ChangeType` method:

```
public static object ChangeType (object value, Type conversionType);
```

The source and target types must be one of the "base" types. ChangeType also accepts an optional IFormatProvider argument. Here's an example:

```
Type targetType = typeof (int);
object source = "42";

object result = Convert.ChangeType (source, targetType);

Console.WriteLine (result);            // 42
Console.WriteLine (result.GetType());  // System.Int32
```

An example of when this might be useful is in writing a deserializer that can work with multiple types. It can also convert any enum to its integral type (see "Enums" on page 109 in Chapter 3).

A limitation of ChangeType is that you cannot specify a format string or parsing flag.

Base 64 conversions

Sometimes you need to include binary data such as a bitmap within a text document such as an XML file or email message. Base 64 is a ubiquitous means of encoding binary data as readable characters, using 64 characters from the ASCII set.

Convert's ToBase64String method converts from a byte array to base 64; From Base64String does the reverse.

XmlConvert

If you're dealing with data that's originated from or destined for an XML file, XmlConvert (in the System.Xml namespace) provides the most suitable methods for formatting and parsing. The methods in XmlConvert handle the nuances of XML formatting without needing special format strings. For instance, true in XML is "true" and not "True". The .NET Framework internally uses XmlConvert extensively. XmlConvert is also good for general-purpose, culture-independent serialization.

The formatting methods in XmlConvert are all provided as overloaded ToString methods; the parsing methods are called ToBoolean, ToDateTime, and so on. For example:

```
string s = XmlConvert.ToString (true);    // s = "true"
bool isTrue = XmlConvert.ToBoolean (s);
```

The methods that convert to and from DateTime accept an XmlDateTimeSerializationMode argument. This is an enum with the following values:

```
Unspecified, Local, Utc, RoundtripKind
```

Local and Utc cause a conversion to take place when formatting (if the DateTime is not already in that time zone). The time zone is then appended to the string:

```
2010-02-22T14:08:30.9375            // Unspecified
2010-02-22T14:07:30.9375+09:00      // Local
2010-02-22T05:08:30.9375Z           // Utc
```

Unspecified strips away any time zone information embedded in the DateTime (i.e., DateTimeKind) before formatting. RoundtripKind honors the DateTime's Date TimeKind—so when it's reparsed, the resultant DateTime struct will be exactly as it was originally.

Type Converters

Type converters are designed to format and parse in design-time environments. They also parse values in XAML (Extensible Application Markup Language) documents—as used in Windows Presentation Foundation and Workflow Foundation.

In the .NET Framework, there are more than 100 type converters—covering such things as colors, images, and URIs. In contrast, format providers are implemented for only a handful of simple value types.

Type converters typically parse strings in a variety of ways—without needing hints. For instance, in an ASP.NET application in Visual Studio, if you assign a control a BackColor by typing **"Beige"** into the property window, Color's type converter figures out that you're referring to a color name and not an RGB string or system color. This flexibility can sometimes make type converters useful in contexts outside of designers and XAML documents.

All type converters subclass TypeConverter in System.ComponentModel. To obtain a TypeConverter, call TypeDescriptor.GetConverter. The following obtains a Type Converter for the Color type (in the System.Drawing namespace, *System.Drawing.dll*):

```
TypeConverter cc = TypeDescriptor.GetConverter (typeof (Color));
```

Among many other methods, TypeConverter defines methods to ConvertToString and ConvertFromString. We can call these as follows:

```
Color beige  = (Color) cc.ConvertFromString ("Beige");
Color purple = (Color) cc.ConvertFromString ("#800080");
Color window = (Color) cc.ConvertFromString ("Window");
```

By convention, type converters have names ending in *Converter* and are usually in the same namespace as the type they're converting. A type links to its converter via a TypeConverterAttribute, allowing designers to pick up converters automatically.

Type converters can also provide design-time services such as generating standard value lists for populating a drop-down list in a designer or assisting with code serialization.

BitConverter

Most base types can be converted to a byte array by calling BitConverter.GetBytes:

```
foreach (byte b in BitConverter.GetBytes (3.5))
  Console.Write (b + " ");                        // 0 0 0 0 0 0 12 64
```

`BitConverter` also provides methods, such as `ToDouble`, for converting in the other direction.

The `decimal` and `DateTime(Offset)` types are not supported by `BitConverter`. You can, however, convert a `decimal` to an `int` array by calling `decimal.GetBits`. To go the other way around, `decimal` provides a constructor that accepts an `int` array.

In the case of `DateTime`, you can call `ToBinary` on an instance—this returns a `long` (upon which you can then use `BitConverter`). The static `DateTime.FromBinary` method does the reverse.

Globalization

There are two aspects to *internationalizing* an application: *globalization* and *localization*.

Globalization is concerned with three tasks (in decreasing order of importance):

1. Making sure that your program doesn't *break* when run in another culture

2. Respecting a local culture's formatting rules—for instance, when displaying dates

3. Designing your program so that it picks up culture-specific data and strings from satellite assemblies that you can later write and deploy

Localization means concluding that last task by writing satellite assemblies for specific cultures. This can be done *after* writing your program—we cover the details in "Resources and Satellite Assemblies" on page 770 in Chapter 18.

The .NET Framework helps you with the second task by applying culture-specific rules by default. We've already seen how calling `ToString` on a `DateTime` or number respects local formatting rules. Unfortunately, this makes it easy to fail the first task and have your program break because you're expecting dates or numbers to be formatted according to an assumed culture. The solution, as we've seen, is either to specify a culture (such as the invariant culture) when formatting and parsing, or to use culture-independent methods such as those in `XmlConvert`.

Globalization Checklist

We've already covered the important points in this chapter. Here's a summary of the essential work required:

- Understand Unicode and text encodings (see "Text Encodings and Unicode" on page 223).

- Be mindful that methods such as `ToUpper` and `ToLower` on `char` and `string` are culture-sensitive: use `ToUpperInvariant`/`ToLowerInvariant` unless you want culture sensitivity.

- Favor culture-independent formatting and parsing mechanisms for `DateTime` and `DateTimeOffsets` such as `ToString("o")` and `XmlConvert`.

- Otherwise, specify a culture when formatting/parsing numbers or date/times (unless you *want* local-culture behavior).

Testing

You can test against different cultures by reassigning `Thread`'s `CurrentCulture` property (in `System.Threading`). The following changes the current culture to Turkey:

```
Thread.CurrentThread.CurrentCulture = CultureInfo.GetCultureInfo ("tr-TR");
```

Turkey is a particularly good test case because:

- `"i".ToUpper() != "I"` and `"I".ToLower() != "i"`.

- Dates are formatted as day.month.year (note the period separator).

- The decimal-point indicator is a comma instead of a period.

You can also experiment by changing the number and date formatting settings in the Windows Control Panel: these are reflected in the default culture (`CulturyeInfo.CurrentCulture`).

`CultureInfo.GetCultures()` returns an array of all available cultures.

> `Thread` and `CultureInfo` also support a `CurrentUICulture` property. This is concerned more with localization: we cover this in Chapter 18.

Working with Numbers

Conversions

We covered numeric conversions in previous chapters and sections; Table 6-7 summarizes all the options.

Table 6-7. Summary of numeric conversions

Task	Functions	Examples

Parsing base 10 numbers	Parse
	TryParse
		`double d = double.Parse ("3.5");`
		`int i;`
		`bool ok = int.TryParse ("3", out i);`

Parsing from base 2, 8, or 16	Convert.To*Integral*	`int i = Convert.ToInt32 ("1E", 16);`
Formatting to hexadecimal	ToString ("X")	`string hex = 45.ToString ("X");`

Task	Functions	Examples
Lossless numeric conversion	Implicit cast	`int i = 23;` `double d = i;`
Truncating numeric conversion	Explicit cast	`double d = 23.5;` `int i = (int) d;`
Rounding numeric conversion (real to integral)	`Convert.ToIntegral`	`double d = 23.5;` `int i = Convert.ToInt32 (d);`

Math

Table 6-8 lists the members of the static `Math` class. The trigonometric functions accept arguments of type `double`; other methods such as `Max` are overloaded to operate on all numeric types. The `Math` class also defines the mathematical constants `E` (*e*) and `PI`.

Table 6-8. Methods in the static Math class

Category	Methods
Rounding	`Round, Truncate, Floor, Ceiling`
Maximum/minimum	`Max, Min`
Absolute value and sign	`Abs, Sign`
Square root	`Sqrt`
Raising to a power	`Pow, Exp`
Logarithm	`Log, Log10`

Trigonometric	`Sin, Cos, Tan`
	`Sinh, Cosh, Tanh`
	`Asin, Acos, Atan`

The `Round` method lets you specify the number of decimal places with which to round, as well as how to handle midpoints (away from zero, or with banker's rounding). `Floor` and `Ceiling` round to the nearest integer: `Floor` always rounds down, and `Ceiling` always rounds up—even with negative numbers.

`Max` and `Min` accept only two arguments. If you have an array or sequence of numbers, use the `Max` and `Min` extension methods in `System.Linq.Enumerable`.

BigInteger

The `BigInteger` struct is a specialized numeric type introduced in .NET Framework 4.0. It lives in the new `System.Numerics` namespace in *System.Numerics.dll* and allows you to represent an arbitrarily large integer without any loss of precision.

C# doesn't provide native support for `BigInteger`, so there's no way to represent `BigInteger` literals. You can, however, implicitly convert from any other integral type to a `BigInteger`. For instance:

```
BigInteger twentyFive = 25;     // implicit conversion from integer
```

To represent a bigger number, such as one googol (10^{100}), you can use one of `BigInteger`'s static methods, such as `Pow` (raise to the power):

```
BigInteger googol = BigInteger.Pow (10, 100);
```

Alternatively, you can `Parse` a string:

```
BigInteger googol = BigInteger.Parse ("1".PadRight (100, '0'));
```

Calling `ToString()` on this prints every digit:

```
Console.WriteLine (googol.ToString()); // 100000000000000000000000000000
00000000000000000000000000000000000000000000000000000000000000000000000
```

You can perform potentially lossy conversions between `BigInteger` and the standard numeric types with the explicit cast operator:

```
double g2 = (double) googol;        // Explicit cast
BigInteger g3 = (BigInteger) g2;    // Explicit cast
Console.WriteLine (g3);
```

The output from this demonstrates the loss of precision:

```
99999999999999997733361688041166912...
```

`BigInteger` overloads all the arithmetic operators including remainder (%), as well as the comparison and equality operators.

You can also construct a `BigInteger` from a byte array. The following code generates a 32-byte random number suitable for cryptography and then assigns it to a `BigInteger`:

```
// This uses the System.Security.Cryptography namespace:
RandomNumberGenerator rand = RandomNumberGenerator.Create();
byte[] bytes = new byte [32];
rand.GetBytes (bytes);
var bigRandomNumber = new BigInteger (bytes);    // Convert to BigInteger
```

The advantage of storing such a number in a `BigInteger` over a byte array is that you get value-type semantics. Calling `ToByteArray` converts a `BigInteger` back to a byte array.

Complex

The `Complex` struct is another specialized numeric type new to Framework 4.0 and is for representing complex numbers with real and imaginary components of type double. `Complex` resides in the *System.Numerics.dll* assembly (along with `BigInteger`).

To use `Complex`, instantiate the struct, specifying the real and imaginary values:

```
var c1 = new Complex (2, 3.5);
var c2 = new Complex (3, 0);
```

There are also implicit conversions from the standard numeric types.

The `Complex` struct exposes properties for the real and imaginary values, as well as the phase and magnitude:

```
Console.WriteLine (c1.Real);       // 2
Console.WriteLine (c1.Imaginary);  // 3.5
Console.WriteLine (c1.Phase);      // 1.05165021254837
Console.WriteLine (c1.Magnitude);  // 4.03112887414927
```

You can also construct a `Complex` number by specifying magnitude and phase:

```
Complex c3 = Complex.FromPolarCoordinates (1.3, 5);
```

The standard arithmetic operators are overloaded to work on `Complex` numbers:

```
Console.WriteLine (c1 + c2);    // (5, 3.5)
Console.WriteLine (c1 * c2);    // (6, 10.5)
```

The `Complex` struct exposes static methods for more advanced functions, including:

- Trigonometric (`Sin`, `Asin`, `Sinh`, `Tan`, etc.)

- Logarithms and exponentiations

- `Conjugate`

Random

The `Random` class generates a pseudorandom sequence of random `bytes`, `integers`, or `doubles`.

To use `Random`, you first instantiate it, optionally providing a seed to initiate the random number series. Using the same seed guarantees the same series of numbers (if run under the same CLR version), which is sometimes useful when you want reproducibility:

```
Random r1 = new Random (1);
Random r2 = new Random (1);
Console.WriteLine (r1.Next (100) + ", " + r1.Next (100));    // 24, 11
Console.WriteLine (r2.Next (100) + ", " + r2.Next (100));    // 24, 11
```

If you don't want reproducibility, you can construct `Random` with no seed—then it uses the current system time to make one up.

Because the system clock has limited granularity, two `Random` instances created close together (typically within 10 ms) will yield the same sequence of values. A common trap is to instantiate a new `Random` object every time you need a random number, rather than reusing the *same* object.

A good pattern is to declare a single static `Random` instance. In multithreaded scenarios, however, this can cause trouble because `Random` objects are not thread-safe. We describe a workaround in "Thread-Local Storage" on page 936 in Chapter 22.

Calling `Next(n)` generates a random integer between 0 and *n*–1. `NextDouble` generates a random `double` between 0 and 1. `NextBytes` fills a byte array with random values.

`Random` is not considered random enough for high-security applications, such as cryptography. For this, the .NET Framework provides a *cryptographically strong* random number generator, in the `System.Security.Cryptography` namespace. Here's how it's used:

```
var rand = System.Security.Cryptography.RandomNumberGenerator.Create();
byte[] bytes = new byte [32];
rand.GetBytes (bytes);        // Fill the byte array with random numbers.
```

The downside is that it's less flexible: filling a byte array is the only means of obtaining random numbers. To obtain an integer, you must use `BitConverter`:

```
byte[] bytes = new byte [4];
rand.GetBytes (bytes);
int i = BitConverter.ToInt32 (bytes, 0);
```

Enums

In Chapter 3, we described C#'s enum type, and showed how to combine members, test equality, use logical operators, and perform conversions. The Framework extends C#'s support for enums through the `System.Enum` type. This type has two roles:

- Providing type unification for all `enum` types
- Defining static utility methods

Type unification means you can implicitly cast any enum member to a `System.Enum` instance:

```
enum Nut  { Walnut, Hazelnut, Macadamia }
enum Size { Small, Medium, Large }

static void Main()
{
  Display (Nut.Macadamia);   // Nut.Macadamia
  Display (Size.Large);      // Size.Large
```

```
}
static void Display (Enum value)
{
  Console.WriteLine (value.GetType().Name + "." + value.ToString());
}
```

The static utility methods on System.Enum are primarily related to performing conversions and obtaining lists of members.

Enum Conversions

There are three ways to represent an enum value:

- As an enum member
- As its underlying integral value
- As a string

In this section, we describe how to convert between each.

Enum to integral conversions

Recall that an explicit cast converts between an enum member and its integral value. An explicit cast is the correct approach if you know the enum type at compile time:

```
[Flags] public enum BorderSides { Left=1, Right=2, Top=4, Bottom=8 }
...
int i = (int) BorderSides.Top;        // i == 4
BorderSides side = (BorderSides) i;   // side == BorderSides.Top
```

You can cast a System.Enum instance to its integral type in the same way. The trick is to first cast to an object, and then the integral type:

```
static int GetIntegralValue (Enum anyEnum)
{
  return (int) (object) anyEnum;
}
```

This relies on you knowing the integral type: the method we just wrote would crash if passed an enum whose integral type was long. To write a method that works with an enum of any integral type, you can take one of three approaches. The first is to call Convert.ToDecimal:

```
static decimal GetAnyIntegralValue (Enum anyEnum)
{
  return Convert.ToDecimal (anyEnum);
}
```

This works because every integral type (including ulong) can be converted to decimal without loss of information. The second approach is to call Enum.GetUnderlyingType in order to obtain the enum's integral type, and then call Convert.Change Type:

```
static object GetBoxedIntegralValue (Enum anyEnum)
{
  Type integralType = Enum.GetUnderlyingType (anyEnum.GetType());
  return Convert.ChangeType (anyEnum, integralType);
}
```

This preserves the original integral type, as the following example shows:

```
object result = GetBoxedIntegralValue (BorderSides.Top);
Console.WriteLine (result);                          // 4
Console.WriteLine (result.GetType());                // System.Int32
```

 Our GetBoxedIntegralType method in fact performs no value conversion; rather, it *reboxes* the same value in another type. It translates an integral value in *enum-type* clothing to an integral value in *integral-type* clothing. We describe this further in "How Enums Work" on page 265.

The third approach is to call Format or ToString specifying the "d" or "D" format string. This gives you the enum's integral value as a string, and it is useful when writing custom serialization formatters:

```
static string GetIntegralValueAsString (Enum anyEnum)
{
  return anyEnum.ToString ("D");        // returns something like "4"
}
```

Integral-to-enum conversions

Enum.ToObject converts an integral value to an enum instance of the given type:

```
object bs = Enum.ToObject (typeof (BorderSides), 3);
Console.WriteLine (bs);                              // Left, Right
```

This is the dynamic equivalent of this:

```
BorderSides bs = (BorderSides) 3;
```

ToObject is overloaded to accept all integral types, as well as object. (The latter works with any boxed integral type.)

String conversions

To convert an enum to a string, you can either call the static Enum.Format method or call ToString on the instance. Each method accepts a format string, which can be "G" for default formatting behavior, "D" to emit the underlying integral value as a string, "X" for the same in hexadecimal, or "F" to format combined members of an enum without the Flags attribute. We listed examples of these in "Standard Format Strings and Parsing Flags" on page 246.

Enum.Parse converts a string to an enum. It accepts the enum type and a string that can include multiple members:

```
BorderSides leftRight = (BorderSides) Enum.Parse (typeof (BorderSides),
                                                  "Left, Right");
```

An optional third argument lets you perform case-insensitive parsing. An `Argumen` `tException` is thrown if the member is not found.

Enumerating Enum Values

`Enum.GetValues` returns an array comprising all members of a particular enum type:

```
foreach (Enum value in Enum.GetValues (typeof (BorderSides)))
   Console.WriteLine (value);
```

Composite members such as `LeftRight = Left | Right` are included, too.

`Enum.GetNames` performs the same function but returns an array of *strings*.

 Internally, the CLR implements `GetValues` and `GetNames` by reflecting over the fields in the enum's type. The results are cached for efficiency.

How Enums Work

The semantics of enums are enforced largely by the compiler. In the CLR, there's no runtime difference between an enum instance (when unboxed) and its underlying integral value. Further, an enum definition in the CLR is merely a subtype of `Sys` `tem.Enum` with static integral-type fields for each member. This makes the ordinary use of an enum highly efficient, with a runtime cost matching that of integral constants.

The downside of this strategy is that enums can provide *static* but not *strong* type safety. We saw an example of this in Chapter 3:

```
public enum BorderSides { Left=1, Right=2, Top=4, Bottom=8 }
...
BorderSides b = BorderSides.Left;
b += 1234;                         // No error!
```

When the compiler is unable to perform validation (as in this example), there's no backup from the runtime to throw an exception.

What we said about there being no runtime difference between an enum instance and its integral value might seem at odds with the following:

```
[Flags] public enum BorderSides { Left=1, Right=2, Top=4, Bottom=8 }
...
Console.WriteLine (BorderSides.Right.ToString());        // Right
Console.WriteLine (BorderSides.Right.GetType().Name);    // BorderSides
```

Given the nature of an enum instance at runtime, you'd expect this to print 2 and `Int32`! The reason for its behavior is down to some more compile-time trickery. C# explicitly *boxes* an enum instance before calling its virtual methods—such as `ToString` or `GetType`. And when an enum instance is boxed, it gains a runtime wrapping that references its enum type.

Tuples

Framework 4.0 introduced a new set of generic classes for holding a set of differently typed elements. These are called *tuples*:

```
public class Tuple <T1>
public class Tuple <T1, T2>
public class Tuple <T1, T2, T3>
public class Tuple <T1, T2, T3, T4>
public class Tuple <T1, T2, T3, T4, T5>
public class Tuple <T1, T2, T3, T4, T5, T6>
public class Tuple <T1, T2, T3, T4, T5, T6, T7>
public class Tuple <T1, T2, T3, T4, T5, T6, T7, TRest>
```

Each has read-only properties called Item1, Item2, and so on (one for each type parameter).

You can instantiate a tuple either via its constructor:

```
var t = new Tuple<int,string> (123, "Hello");
```

or via the static helper method Tuple.Create:

```
Tuple<int,string> t = Tuple.Create (123, "Hello");
```

The latter leverages generic type inference. You can combine this with implicit typing:

```
var t = Tuple.Create (123, "Hello");
```

You can then access the properties as follows (notice that each is statically typed):

```
Console.WriteLine (t.Item1 * 2);          // 246
Console.WriteLine (t.Item2.ToUpper());    // HELLO
```

Tuples are convenient in returning more than one value from a method—or creating collections of value *pairs* (we'll cover collections in the following chapter).

An alternative to tuples is to use an object array. However, you then lose static type safety, incur the cost of boxing/unboxing for value types, and require clumsy casts that cannot be validated by the compiler:

```
object[] items = { 123, "Hello" };
Console.WriteLine ( ((int)    items[0]) * 2          );   // 246
Console.WriteLine ( ((string) items[1]).ToUpper() );     // HELLO
```

Comparing Tuples

Tuples are classes (and therefore reference types). In keeping with this, comparing two distinct instances with the equality operator returns false. However, the Equals method is overridden to compare each individual element instead:

```
var t1 = Tuple.Create (123, "Hello");
var t2 = Tuple.Create (123, "Hello");
Console.WriteLine (t1 == t2);           // False
Console.WriteLine (t1.Equals (t2));     // True
```

You can also pass in a custom equality comparer (by virtue of tuples implementing IStructuralEquatable). We cover equality and order comparison later in this chapter.

The Guid Struct

The Guid struct represents a globally unique identifier: a 16-byte value that, when generated, is almost certainly unique in the world. Guids are often used for keys of various sorts—in applications and databases. There are 2^{128} or 3.4×10^{38} unique Guids.

The static Guid.NewGuid method generates a unique Guid:

```
Guid g = Guid.NewGuid ();
Console.WriteLine (g.ToString()); // 0d57629c-7d6e-4847-97cb-9e2fc25083fe
```

To instantiate an existing value, you use one of the constructors. The two most useful constructors are:

```
public Guid (byte[] b);    // Accepts a 16-byte array
public Guid (string g);    // Accepts a formatted string
```

When represented as a string, a Guid is formatted as a 32-digit hexadecimal number, with optional hyphens after the 8th, 12th, 16th, and 20th digits. The whole string can also be optionally wrapped in brackets or braces:

```
Guid g1 = new Guid ("{0d57629c-7d6e-4847-97cb-9e2fc25083fe}");
Guid g2 = new Guid ("0d57629c7d6e484797cb9e2fc25083fe");
Console.WriteLine (g1 == g2);  // True
```

Being a struct, a Guid honors value-type semantics; hence, the equality operator works in the preceding example.

The ToByteArray method converts a Guid to a byte array.

The static Guid.Empty property returns an empty Guid (all zeros). This is often used in place of null.

Equality Comparison

Until now, we've assumed that the == and != operators are all there is to equality comparison. The issue of equality, however, is more complex and subtler, sometimes requiring the use of additional methods and interfaces. This section explores the standard C# and .NET protocols for equality, focusing particularly on two questions:

- When are == and != adequate—and inadequate—for equality comparison, and what are the alternatives?
- How and when should you customize a type's equality logic?

But before exploring the details of equality protocols and how to customize them, we must first look at the preliminary concept of value versus referential equality.

Value Versus Referential Equality

There are two kinds of equality:

Value equality
    Two values are *equivalent* in some sense.

Referential equality
    Two references refer to *exactly the same object.*

By default:

- Value types use *value equality.*
- Reference types use *referential equality.*

Value types, in fact, can *only* use value equality (unless boxed). A simple demonstration of value equality is to compare two numbers:

```
int x = 5, y = 5;
Console.WriteLine (x == y);   // True (by virtue of value equality)
```

A more elaborate demonstration is to compare two DateTimeOffset structs. The following prints True because the two DateTimeOffsets refer to the *same point in time* and so are considered equivalent:

```
var dt1 = new DateTimeOffset (2010, 1, 1, 1, 1, 1, TimeSpan.FromHours(8));
var dt2 = new DateTimeOffset (2010, 1, 1, 2, 1, 1, TimeSpan.FromHours(9));
Console.WriteLine (dt1 == dt2);   // True
```

 DateTimeOffset is a struct whose equality semantics have been tweaked. By default, structs exhibit a special kind of value equality called *structural equality*, where two values are considered equal if all of their members are equal. (You can see this by creating a struct and calling its Equals method; more on this later.)

Reference types exhibit referential equality by default. In the following example, f1 and f2 are not equal—despite their objects having identical content:

```
class Foo { public int X; }
...
Foo f1 = new Foo { X = 5 };
Foo f2 = new Foo { X = 5 };
Console.WriteLine (f1 == f2);   // False
```

In contrast, f3 and f1 are equal because they reference the same object:

```
Foo f3 = f1;
Console.WriteLine (f1 == f3);   // True
```

We'll explain later in this section how reference types can be *customized* to exhibit value equality. An example of this is the Uri class in the System namespace:

```
Uri uri1 = new Uri ("http://www.linqpad.net");
Uri uri2 = new Uri ("http://www.linqpad.net");
Console.WriteLine (uri1 == uri2);          // True
```

Standard Equality Protocols

There are three standard protocols that types can implement for equality comparison:

- The == and != operators
- The virtual Equals method in object
- The IEquatable<T> interface

In addition, there are the *pluggable* protocols and the IStructuralEquatable interface that we describe in Chapter 7.

== and !=

We've already seen in many examples how the standard == and != operators perform equality/inequality comparisons. The subtleties with == and != arise because they are *operators* and so are statically resolved (in fact, they are implemented as static functions). So, when you use == or !=, C# makes a *compile-time* decision as to which type will perform the comparison, and no virtual behavior comes into play. This is normally desirable. In the following example, the compiler hard-wires == to the int type because x and y are both int:

```
int x = 5;
int y = 5;
Console.WriteLine (x == y);      // True
```

But in the next example, the compiler wires the == operator to the object type:

```
object x = 5;
object y = 5;
Console.WriteLine (x == y);      // False
```

Because object is a class (and so a reference type), object's == operator uses *referential equality* to compare x and y. The result is false, because x and y each refer to different boxed objects on the heap.

The virtual Object.Equals method

To correctly equate x and y in the preceding example, we can use the virtual Equals method. Equals is defined in System.Object and so is available to all types:

```
object x = 5;
object y = 5;
Console.WriteLine (x.Equals (y));      // True
```

Equals is resolved at runtime—according to the object's actual type. In this case, it calls Int32's Equals method, which applies *value equality* to the operands, returning true. With reference types, Equals performs referential equality comparison by default; with structs, Equals performs structural comparison by calling Equals on each of its fields.

Why the Complexity?

You might wonder why the designers of C# didn't avoid the problem by making == virtual, and so functionally identical to Equals. There are three reasons for this:

- If the first operand is null, Equals fails with a NullReferenceException; a static operator does not.

- Because the == operator is statically resolved, it executes extremely quickly. This means that you can write computationally intensive code without penalty —and without needing to learn another language such as C++.

- Sometimes it can be useful to have == and Equals apply different definitions of equality. We describe this scenario later in this section.

Essentially, the complexity of the design reflects the complexity of the situation: the concept of equality covers a multitude of scenarios.

Hence, Equals is suitable for equating two objects in a type-agnostic fashion. The following method equates two objects of any type:

```
public static bool AreEqual (object obj1, object obj2)
  => obj1.Equals (obj2);
```

There is one case, however, in which this fails. If the first argument is null, you get a NullReferenceException. Here's the fix:

```
public static bool AreEqual (object obj1, object obj2)
{
  if (obj1 == null) return obj2 == null;
  return obj1.Equals (obj2);
}
```

Or more succinctly:

```
public static bool AreEqual (object obj1, object obj2)
  => obj1 == null ? obj2 == null : obj1.Equals (obj2);
```

The static object.Equals method

The object class provides a static helper method that does the work of AreEqual in the preceding example. Its name is Equals—just like the virtual method—but there's no conflict because it accepts *two* arguments:

```
public static bool Equals (object objA, object objB)
```

This provides a null-safe equality comparison algorithm for when the types are unknown at compile time. For example:

```
object x = 3, y = 3;
Console.WriteLine (object.Equals (x, y));   // True
x = null;
Console.WriteLine (object.Equals (x, y));   // False
y = null;
Console.WriteLine (object.Equals (x, y));   // True
```

A useful application is when writing generic types. The following code will not compile if object.Equals is replaced with the == or != operator:

```
class Test <T>
{
  T _value;
  public void SetValue (T newValue)
  {
    if (!object.Equals (newValue, _value))
    {
      _value = newValue;
      OnValueChanged();
    }
  }
  protected virtual void OnValueChanged() { ... }
}
```

Operators are prohibited here because the compiler cannot bind to the static method of an unknown type.

A more elaborate way to implement this comparison is with the EqualityComparer<T> class. This has the advantage of avoiding boxing:

```
if (!EqualityComparer<T>.Default.Equals (newValue, _value))
```

We discuss EqualityComparer<T> in more detail in Chapter 7 (see "Plugging in Equality and Order" on page 327).

The static object.ReferenceEquals method

Occasionally, you need to force referential equality comparison. The static object.ReferenceEquals method does just this:

```
class Widget { ... }

class Test
{
  static void Main()
  {
    Widget w1 = new Widget();
    Widget w2 = new Widget();
    Console.WriteLine (object.ReferenceEquals (w1, w2));   // False
  }
}
```

You might want to do this because it's possible for `Widget` to override the virtual `Equals` method, such that `w1.Equals(w2)` would return `true`. Further, it's possible for `Widget` to overload the `==` operator so that `w1==w2` would also return `true`. In such cases, calling `object.ReferenceEquals` guarantees normal referential equality semantics.

 Another way to force referential equality comparison is to cast the values to `object` and then apply the `==` operator.

The IEquatable<T> interface

A consequence of calling `object.Equals` is that it forces boxing on value types. This is undesirable in highly performance-sensitive scenarios because boxing is relatively expensive compared to the actual comparison. A solution was introduced in C# 2.0, with the `IEquatable<T>` interface:

```
public interface IEquatable<T>
{
  bool Equals (T other);
}
```

The idea is that `IEquatable<T>`, when implemented, gives the same result as calling `object`'s virtual `Equals` method—but more quickly. Most basic .NET types implement `IEquatable<T>`. You can use `IEquatable<T>` as a constraint in a generic type:

```
class Test<T> where T : IEquatable<T>
{
  public bool IsEqual (T a, T b)
  {
    return a.Equals (b);     // No boxing with generic T
  }
}
```

If we remove the generic constraint, the class would still compile, but `a.Equals(b)` would instead bind to the slower `object.Equals` (slower assuming T was a value type).

When Equals and == are not equal

We said earlier that it's sometimes useful for `==` and `Equals` to apply different definitions of equality. For example:

```
double x = double.NaN;
Console.WriteLine (x == x);          // False
Console.WriteLine (x.Equals (x));    // True
```

The `double` type's `==` operator enforces that one NaN can never equal anything else —even another NaN. This is most natural from a mathematical perspective, and it reflects the underlying CPU behavior. The `Equals` method, however, is obliged to apply *reflexive* equality; in other words:

`x.Equals (x)` must *always* return true.

Collections and dictionaries rely on `Equals` behaving this way; otherwise, they could not find an item they previously stored.

Having `Equals` and `==` apply different definitions of equality is actually quite rare with value types. A more common scenario is with reference types and happens when the author customizes `Equals` so that it performs value equality while leaving `==` to perform (default) referential equality. The `StringBuilder` class does exactly this:

```
var sb1 = new StringBuilder ("foo");
var sb2 = new StringBuilder ("foo");
Console.WriteLine (sb1 == sb2);        // False (referential equality)
Console.WriteLine (sb1.Equals (sb2));  // True  (value equality)
```

Let's now look at how to customize equality.

Equality and Custom Types

Recall default equality comparison behavior:

- Value types use *value equality*.
- Reference types use *referential equality*.

Further:

- A struct's `Equals` method applies *structural value equality* by default (i.e., it compares each field in the struct).

Sometimes it makes sense to override this behavior when writing a type. There are two cases for doing so:

- To change the meaning of equality
- To speed up equality comparisons for structs

Changing the meaning of equality

Changing the meaning of equality makes sense when the default behavior of `==` and `Equals` is unnatural for your type and is *not what a consumer would expect*. An example is `DateTimeOffset`, a struct with two private fields: a UTC `DateTime` and a numeric integer offset. If you were writing this type, you'd probably want to ensure that equality comparisons considered only the UTC `DateTime` field and not the off-set field. Another example is numeric types that support `NaN` values such as `float` and `double`. If you were implementing such types yourself, you'd want to ensure that `NaN`-comparison logic was supported in equality comparisons.

With classes, it's sometimes more natural to offer *value equality* as the default instead of *referential equality*. This is often the case with small classes that hold a simple piece of data—such as System.Uri (or System.String).

Speeding up equality comparisons with structs

The default *structural equality* comparison algorithm for structs is relatively slow. Taking over this process by overriding Equals can improve performance by a factor of five. Overloading the == operator and implementing IEquatable<T> allows unboxed equality comparisons, and this can speed things up by a factor of five again.

 Overriding equality semantics for reference types doesn't benefit performance. The default algorithm for referential equality comparison is already very fast because it simply compares two 32- or 64-bit references.

There's actually another, rather peculiar case for customizing equality, and that's to improve a struct's hashing algorithm for better performance in a hashtable. This comes of the fact that equality comparison and hashing are joined at the hip. We'll examine hashing in a moment.

How to override equality semantics

Here is a summary of the steps:

1. Override GetHashCode() and Equals().
2. (Optionally) overload != and ==.
3. (Optionally) implement IEquatable<T>.

Overriding GetHashCode

It might seem odd that System.Object—with its small footprint of members—defines a method with a specialized and narrow purpose. GetHashCode is a virtual method in Object that fits this description—it exists primarily for the benefit of just the following two types:

```
System.Collections.Hashtable
System.Collections.Generic.Dictionary<TKey,TValue>
```

These are *hashtables*—collections where each element has a key used for storage and retrieval. A hashtable applies a very specific strategy for efficiently allocating elements based on their key. This requires that each key have an Int32 number, or *hash code*. The hash code need not be unique for each key but should be as varied as possible for good hashtable performance. Hashtables are considered important enough that GetHashCode is defined in System.Object—so that every type can emit a hash code.

We describe hashtables in detail in "Dictionaries" on page 314 in Chapter 7.

Both reference and value types have default implementations of GetHashCode, meaning you don't need to override this method—*unless you override* Equals. (And if you override GetHashCode, you will almost certainly want to also override Equals.)

Here are the other rules for overriding object.GetHashCode:

- It must return the same value on two objects for which Equals returns true (hence, GetHashCode and Equals are overridden together).
- It must not throw exceptions.
- It must return the same value if called repeatedly on the same object (unless the object has *changed*).

For maximum performance in hashtables, GetHashCode should be written so as to minimize the likelihood of two different values returning the same hashcode. This gives rise to the third reason for overriding Equals and GetHashCode on structs, which is to provide a more efficient hashing algorithm than the default. The default implementation for structs is at the discretion of the runtime and may be based on every field in the struct.

In contrast, the default GetHashCode implementation for *classes* is based on an internal object token, which is unique for each instance in the CLR's current implementation.

If an object's hashcode changes after it's been added as a key to a dictionary, the object will no longer be accessible in the dictionary. You can preempt this by basing hashcode calculations on immutable fields.

A complete example illustrating how to override GetHashCode is listed shortly.

Overriding Equals

The axioms for object.Equals are as follows:

- An object cannot equal null (unless it's a nullable type).
- Equality is *reflexive* (an object equals itself).
- Equality is *commutative* (if a.Equals(b), then b.Equals(a)).
- Equality is *transitive* (if a.Equals(b) and b.Equals(c), then a.Equals(c)).
- Equality operations are repeatable and reliable (they don't throw exceptions).

Overloading == and !=

In addition to overriding `Equals`, you can optionally overload the equality and inequality operators. This is nearly always done with structs, because the consequence of not doing so is that the == and != operators will simply not work on your type.

With classes, there are two ways to proceed:

- Leave == and != alone—so that they apply referential equality.
- Overload == and != in line with `Equals`.

The first approach is most common with custom types—especially *mutable* types. It ensures that your type follows the expectation that == and != should exhibit referential equality with reference types and this avoids confusing consumers. We saw an example earlier:

```
var sb1 = new StringBuilder ("foo");
var sb2 = new StringBuilder ("foo");
Console.WriteLine (sb1 == sb2);          // False (referential equality)
Console.WriteLine (sb1.Equals (sb2));    // True  (value equality)
```

The second approach makes sense with types for which a consumer would never want referential equality. These are typically immutable—such as the `string` and `System.Uri` classes—and are sometimes good candidates for `structs`.

 Although it's possible to overload != such that it means something other than !(==), this is almost never done in practice, except in cases such as comparing `float.NaN`.

Implementing IEquatable<T>

For completeness, it's also good to implement `IEquatable<T>` when overriding `Equals`. Its results should always match those of the overridden object's `Equals` method. Implementing `IEquatable<T>` comes at no programming cost if you structure your `Equals` method implementation, as in the following example.

An example: The Area struct

Imagine we need a struct to represent an area whose width and height are interchangeable. In other words, 5 × 10 is equal to 10 × 5. (Such a type would be suitable in an algorithm that arranges rectangular shapes.)

Here's the complete code:

```
public struct Area : IEquatable <Area>
{
  public readonly int Measure1;
  public readonly int Measure2;

  public Area (int m1, int m2)
```

```
    {
      Measure1 = Math.Min (m1, m2);
      Measure2 = Math.Max (m1, m2);
    }

    public override bool Equals (object other)
    {
      if (!(other is Area)) return false;
      return Equals ((Area) other);        // Calls method below
    }

    public bool Equals (Area other)        // Implements IEquatable<Area>
      => Measure1 == other.Measure1 && Measure2 == other.Measure2;

    public override int GetHashCode()
      => Measure2 * 31 + Measure1;     // 31 = some prime number

    public static bool operator == (Area a1, Area a2) => a1.Equals (a2);

    public static bool operator != (Area a1, Area a2) => !a1.Equals (a2);
}
```

 Here's another way to implement the Equals method, leveraging nullable types:

```
Area? otherArea = other as Area?;
return otherArea.HasValue && Equals (otherArea.Value);
```

In implementing GetHashCode, we've helped to improve the likelihood of uniqueness by multiplying the larger measure by some prime number (ignoring any overflow) before adding the two together. When there are more than two fields, the following pattern, suggested by Josh Bloch, gives good results while being performant:

```
int hash = 17;                          // 17 = some prime number
hash = hash * 31 + field1.GetHashCode();  // 31 = another prime number
hash = hash * 31 + field2.GetHashCode();
hash = hash * 31 + field3.GetHashCode();
...
return hash;
```

(See *http://albahari.com/hashprimes* for a link to a discussion on primes and hashcodes.)

Here's a demo of the Area struct:

```
Area a1 = new Area (5, 10);
Area a2 = new Area (10, 5);
Console.WriteLine (a1.Equals (a2));    // True
Console.WriteLine (a1 == a2);          // True
```

Pluggable equality comparers

If you want a type to take on different equality semantics just for a particular scenario, you can use a pluggable IEqualityComparer. This is particularly useful in conjunction with the standard collection classes, and we describe it in the following chapter, in "Plugging in Equality and Order" on page 327.

Order Comparison

As well as defining standard protocols for equality, C# and .NET define standard protocols for determining the order of one object relative to another. The basic protocols are:

- The IComparable interfaces (IComparable and IComparable<T>)
- The > and < operators

The IComparable interfaces are used by general-purpose sorting algorithms. In the following example, the static Array.Sort method works because System.String implements the IComparable interfaces:

```
string[] colors = { "Green", "Red", "Blue" };
Array.Sort (colors);
foreach (string c in colors) Console.Write (c + " ");   // Blue Green Red
```

The < and > operators are more specialized, and they are intended mostly for numeric types. Because they are statically resolved, they can translate to highly efficient bytecode, suitable for computationally intensive algorithms.

The .NET Framework also provides pluggable ordering protocols, via the IComparer interfaces. We describe these in the final section of Chapter 7.

IComparable

The IComparable interfaces are defined as follows:

```
public interface IComparable      { int CompareTo (object other); }
public interface IComparable<in T> { int CompareTo (T other);      }
```

The two interfaces represent the same functionality. With value types, the generic type-safe interface is faster than the nongeneric interface. In both cases, the CompareTo method works as follows:

- If a comes after b, a.CompareTo(b) returns a positive number.
- If a is the same as b, a.CompareTo(b) returns 0.
- If a comes before b, a.CompareTo(b) returns a negative number.

For example:

```
Console.WriteLine ("Beck".CompareTo ("Anne"));     // 1
Console.WriteLine ("Beck".CompareTo ("Beck"));     // 0
Console.WriteLine ("Beck".CompareTo ("Chris"));    // -1
```

Most of the base types implement both IComparable interfaces. These interfaces are also sometimes implemented when writing custom types. An example is given shortly.

IComparable versus Equals

Consider a type that both overrides Equals and implements the IComparable interfaces. You'd expect that when Equals returns true, CompareTo should return 0. And you'd be right. But here's the catch:

- When Equals returns false, CompareTo can return what it likes (as long as it's internally consistent)!

In other words, equality can be "fussier" than comparison, but not vice versa (violate this and sorting algorithms will break). So, CompareTo can say "All objects are equal" while Equals says "But some are more equal than others!"

A great example of this is System.String. String's Equals method and == operator use *ordinal* comparison, which compares the Unicode point values of each character. Its CompareTo method, however, uses a less fussy *culture-dependent* comparison. On most computers, for instance, the strings "ü" and "ü" are different according to Equals, but the same according to CompareTo.

In Chapter 7, we discuss the pluggable ordering protocol, IComparer, which allows you to specify an alternative ordering algorithm when sorting or instantiating a sorted collection. A custom IComparer can further extend the gap between CompareTo and Equals—a case-insensitive string comparer, for instance, will return 0 when comparing "A" and "a". The reverse rule still applies, however: CompareTo can never be fussier than Equals.

When implementing the IComparable interfaces in a custom type, you can avoid running afoul of this rule by writing the first line of CompareTo as follows:

```
if (Equals (other)) return 0;
```

After that, it can return what it likes, as long as it's consistent!

< and >

Some types define < and > operators. For instance:

```
bool after2010 = DateTime.Now > new DateTime (2010, 1, 1);
```

You can expect the < and > operators, when implemented, to be functionally consistent with the IComparable interfaces. This is standard practice across the .NET Framework.

It's also standard practice to implement the IComparable interfaces whenever < and > are overloaded, although the reverse is not true. In fact, most .NET types that implement IComparable *do not* overload < and >. This differs from the situation with equality, where it's normal to overload == when overriding Equals.

Typically, > and < are overloaded only when:

- A type has a strong intrinsic concept of "greater than" and "less than" (versus IComparable's broader concepts of "comes before" and "comes after").
- There is only one way *or context* in which to perform the comparison.
- The result is invariant across cultures.

System.String doesn't satisfy the last point: the results of string comparisons can vary according to language. Hence, string doesn't support the > and < operators:

```
bool error = "Beck" > "Anne";        // Compile-time error
```

Implementing the IComparable Interfaces

In the following struct, representing a musical note, we implement the IComparable interfaces, as well as overloading the < and > operators. For completeness, we also override Equals/GetHashCode and overload == and !=:

```
public struct Note : IComparable<Note>, IEquatable<Note>, IComparable
{
  int _semitonesFromA;
  public int SemitonesFromA { get { return _semitonesFromA; } }

  public Note (int semitonesFromA)
  {
    _semitonesFromA = semitonesFromA;
  }

  public int CompareTo (Note other)             // Generic IComparable<T>
  {
    if (Equals (other)) return 0;    // Fail-safe check
    return _semitonesFromA.CompareTo (other._semitonesFromA);
  }

  int IComparable.CompareTo (object other)      // Nongeneric IComparable
  {
    if (!(other is Note))
      throw new InvalidOperationException ("CompareTo: Not a note");
    return CompareTo ((Note) other);
  }

  public static bool operator < (Note n1, Note n2)
    => n1.CompareTo (n2) < 0;

  public static bool operator > (Note n1, Note n2)
    => n1.CompareTo (n2) > 0;

  public bool Equals (Note other)     // for IEquatable<Note>
    => _semitonesFromA == other._semitonesFromA;
```

```csharp
  public override bool Equals (object other)
  {
    if (!(other is Note)) return false;
    return Equals ((Note) other);
  }

  public override int GetHashCode() => _semitonesFromA.GetHashCode();

  public static bool operator == (Note n1, Note n2) => n1.Equals (n2);

  public static bool operator != (Note n1, Note n2) => !(n1 == n2);
}
```

Utility Classes

Console

The static Console class handles standard input/output for console-based applications. In a command-line (console) application, the input comes from the keyboard via Read, ReadKey, and ReadLine, and the output goes to the text window via Write and WriteLine. You can control the window's position and dimensions with the properties WindowLeft, WindowTop, WindowHeight, and WindowWidth. You can also change the BackgroundColor and ForegroundColor properties and manipulate the cursor with the CursorLeft, CursorTop, and CursorSize properties:

```csharp
Console.WindowWidth = Console.LargestWindowWidth;
Console.ForegroundColor = ConsoleColor.Green;
Console.Write ("test... 50%");
Console.CursorLeft -= 3;
Console.Write ("90%");      // test... 90%
```

The Write and WriteLine methods are overloaded to accept a composite format string (see String.Format in "String and Text Handling" on page 213). However, neither method accepts a format provider, so you're stuck with CultureInfo.CurrentCulture. (The workaround, of course, is to explicitly call string.Format.)

The Console.Out property returns a TextWriter. Passing Console.Out to a method that expects a TextWriter is a useful way to get that method to write to the Console for diagnostic purposes.

You can also redirect the Console's input and output streams via the SetIn and SetOut methods:

```csharp
// First save existing output writer:
System.IO.TextWriter oldOut = Console.Out;

// Redirect the console's output to a file:
using (System.IO.TextWriter w = System.IO.File.CreateText
                                  ("e:\\output.txt"))
{
  Console.SetOut (w);
```

```
    Console.WriteLine ("Hello world");
}

// Restore standard console output
Console.SetOut (oldOut);

// Open the output.txt file in Notepad:
System.Diagnostics.Process.Start ("e:\\output.txt");
```

In Chapter 15, we describe how streams and text writers work.

 When running WPF or Windows Forms applications under Visual Studio, the Console's output is automatically redirected to Visual Studio's output window (in debug mode). This can make Console.Write useful for diagnostic purposes; although in most cases, the Debug and Trace classes in the System.Diag nostics namespace are more appropriate (see Chapter 13).

Environment

The static System.Environment class provides a range of useful properties:

Files and folders
    CurrentDirectory, SystemDirectory, CommandLine

Computer and operating system
    MachineName, ProcessorCount, OSVersion, NewLine

User logon
    UserName, UserInteractive, UserDomainName

Diagnostics
    TickCount, StackTrace, WorkingSet, Version

You can obtain additional folders by calling GetFolderPath; we describe this in "File and Directory Operations" on page 650 in Chapter 15.

You can access OS environment variables (what you see when you type "set" at the command prompt) with the following three methods: GetEnvironmentVariable, GetEnvironmentVariables, and SetEnvironmentVariable.

The ExitCode property lets you set the return code, for when your program is called from a command or batch file, and the FailFast method terminates a program immediately, without performing cleanup.

The Environment class available to Windows Store apps offers just a limited number of members (ProcessorCount, NewLine, and FailFast).

Process

The Process class in System.Diagnostics allows you to launch a new process.

The static `Process.Start` method has a number of overloads; the simplest accepts a simple filename with optional arguments:

```
Process.Start ("notepad.exe");
Process.Start ("notepad.exe", "e:\\file.txt");
```

You can also specify just a filename, and the registered program for its extension will be launched:

```
Process.Start ("e:\\file.txt");
```

The most flexible overload accepts a `ProcessStartInfo` instance. With this, you can capture and redirect the launched process's input, output, and error output (if you set `UseShellExecute` to `false`). The following captures the output of calling `ipcon fig`:

```
ProcessStartInfo psi = new ProcessStartInfo
{
  FileName = "cmd.exe",
  Arguments = "/c ipconfig /all",
  RedirectStandardOutput = true,
  UseShellExecute = false
};
Process p = Process.Start (psi);
string result = p.StandardOutput.ReadToEnd();
Console.WriteLine (result);
```

You can do the same to invoke the `csc` compiler, if you set `FileName` to the following:

```
psi.FileName = System.IO.Path.Combine (
  System.Runtime.InteropServices.RuntimeEnvironment.GetRuntimeDirectory(),
  "csc.exe");
```

If you don't redirect output, `Process.Start` executes the program in parallel to the caller. If you want to wait for the new process to complete, you can call `WaitForExit` on the `Process` object, with an optional timeout.

The `Process` class also allows you to query and interact with other processes running on the computer (see Chapter 13).

 For security reasons, the `Process` class is not available to Windows Store apps, and you cannot start arbitrary processes. Instead, you must use the `Windows.System.Launcher` class to "launch" a URI or file to which you have access, e.g.:

```
Launcher.LaunchUriAsync (new Uri ("http://albahari.com"));
```

```
var file = await KnownFolders.DocumentsLibrary
                        .GetFileAsync ("foo.txt");
Launcher.LaunchFileAsync (file);
```

This opens the URI or file, using whatever program is associated with the URI scheme or file extension. Your program must be in the foreground for this to work.

AppContext

The `System.AppContext` class is new to Framework 4.6. It provides a global string-keyed dictionary of Boolean values and is intended to offer library writers a standard mechanism for allowing consumers to switch new features on or off. This untyped approach makes sense with experimental features that you want to keep undocumented to the majority of users.

The consumer of a library requests that a feature be enabled as follows:

```
AppContext.SetSwitch ("MyLibrary.SomeBreakingChange", true);
```

Code inside that library can then check for that switch as follows:

```
bool isDefined, switchValue;
isDefined = AppContext.TryGetSwitch ("MyLibrary.SomeBreakingChange",
                                     out switchValue);
```

`TryGetSwitch` returns `false` if the switch is undefined; this lets you distinguish an undefined switch from one whose value is set to `false`, should this be necessary.

> Ironically, the design of `TryGetSwitch` illustrates how not to write APIs. The out parameter is unnecessary, and the method should instead return a nullable `bool` whose value is `true`, `false`, or `null` for undefined. This would then enable the following use:
>
> ```
> bool switchValue = AppContext.GetSwitch ("...") ?? false;
> ```

7

Collections

The .NET Framework provides a standard set of types for storing and managing collections of objects. These include resizable lists, linked lists, sorted and unsorted dictionaries as well as arrays. Of these, only arrays form part of the C# language; the remaining collections are just classes you instantiate like any other.

The types in the Framework for collections can be divided into the following categories:

- Interfaces that define standard collection protocols
- Ready-to-use collection classes (lists, dictionaries, etc.)
- Base classes for writing application-specific collections

This chapter covers each of these categories, with an additional section on the types used in determining element equality and order.

The collection namespaces are as follows:

Namespace	Contains
`System.Collections`	Nongeneric collection classes and interfaces
`System.Collections.Specialized`	Strongly typed nongeneric collection classes
`System.Collections.Generic`	Generic collection classes and interfaces
`System.Collections.ObjectModel`	Proxies and bases for custom collections
`System.Collections.Concurrent`	Thread-safe collections (see Chapter 23)

Enumeration

In computing, there are many different kinds of collections, ranging from simple data structures, such as arrays or linked lists, to more complex ones, such as red/black trees and hashtables. Although the internal implementation and external characteristics of these data structures vary widely, the ability to traverse the contents of the collection is an almost universal need. The Framework supports this need via a pair of interfaces (IEnumerable, IEnumerator, and their generic counterparts) that allow different data structures to expose a common traversal API. These are part of a larger set of collection interfaces, illustrated in Figure 7-1.

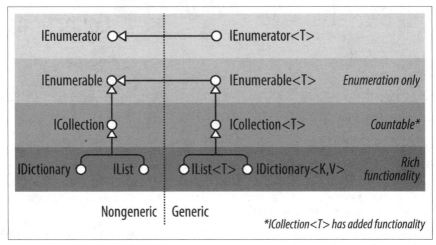

Figure 7-1. Collection interfaces

IEnumerable and IEnumerator

The IEnumerator interface defines the basic low-level protocol by which elements in a collection are traversed—or enumerated—in a forward-only manner. Its declaration is as follows:

```
public interface IEnumerator
{
  bool MoveNext();
  object Current { get; }
  void Reset();
}
```

MoveNext advances the current element or "cursor" to the next position, returning false if there are no more elements in the collection. Current returns the element at the current position (usually cast from object to a more specific type). MoveNext must be called before retrieving the first element—this is to allow for an empty collection. The Reset method, if implemented, moves back to the start, allowing the collection to be enumerated again. Reset exists mainly for COM interop; calling it directly is generally avoided because it's not universally supported (and is unnecessary in that it's usually just as easy to instantiate a new enumerator.)

Collections do not usually *implement* enumerators; instead, they *provide* enumerators, via the interface IEnumerable:

```
public interface IEnumerable
{
  IEnumerator GetEnumerator();
}
```

By defining a single method retuning an enumerator, IEnumerable provides flexibility in that the iteration logic can be farmed off to another class. Moreover, it means that several consumers can enumerate the collection at once without interfering with each other. IEnumerable can be thought of as "IEnumeratorProvider," and it is the most basic interface that collection classes implement.

The following example illustrates low-level use of IEnumerable and IEnumerator:

```
string s = "Hello";

// Because string implements IEnumerable, we can call GetEnumerator():
IEnumerator rator = s.GetEnumerator();

while (rator.MoveNext())
{
  char c = (char) rator.Current;
  Console.Write (c + ".");
}

// Output:  H.e.l.l.o.
```

However, it's rare to call methods on enumerators directly in this manner, because C# provides a syntactic shortcut: the foreach statement. Here's the same example rewritten using foreach:

```
string s = "Hello";        // The String class implements IEnumerable

foreach (char c in s)
  Console.Write (c + ".");
```

IEnumerable<T> and IEnumerator<T>

IEnumerator and IEnumerable are nearly always implemented in conjunction with their extended generic versions:

```
public interface IEnumerator<T> : IEnumerator, IDisposable
{
  T Current { get; }
}

public interface IEnumerable<T> : IEnumerable
{
  IEnumerator<T> GetEnumerator();
}
```

By defining a typed version of Current and GetEnumerator, these interfaces strengthen static type safety, avoid the overhead of boxing with value-type elements, and are more convenient to the consumer. Arrays automatically implement IEnumerable<T> (where T is the member type of the array).

Thanks to the improved static type safety, calling the following method with an array of characters will generate a compile-time error:

```
void Test (IEnumerable<int> numbers) { ... }
```

It's a standard practice for collection classes to publicly expose IEnumerable<T> while "hiding" the nongeneric IEnumerable through explicit interface implementation. This is so that if you directly call GetEnumerator(), you get back the type-safe generic IEnumerator<T>. There are times, though, when this rule is broken for reasons of backward compatibility (generics did not exist prior to C# 2.0). A good example is arrays—these must return the nongeneric (the nice way of putting it is "classic") IEnumerator to avoid breaking earlier code. In order to get a generic IEnumerator<T>, you must cast to expose the explicit interface:

```
int[] data = { 1, 2, 3 };
var rator = ((IEnumerable <int>)data).GetEnumerator();
```

Fortunately, you rarely need to write this sort of code, thanks to the foreach statement.

IEnumerable<T> and IDisposable

IEnumerator<T> inherits from IDisposable. This allows enumerators to hold references to resources such as database connections—and ensure that those resources are released when enumeration is complete (or abandoned partway through). The foreach statement recognizes this detail and translates this:

```
foreach (var element in somethingEnumerable) { ... }
```

into the logical equivalent of this:

```
using (var rator = somethingEnumerable.GetEnumerator())
  while (rator.MoveNext())
  {
    var element = rator.Current;
    ...
  }
```

The using block ensures disposal—more on IDisposable in Chapter 12.

When to Use the Nongeneric Interfaces

Given the extra type safety of the generic collection interfaces such as IEnumerable<T>, the question arises: do you ever need to use the nongeneric IEnumerable (or ICollection or IList)?

In the case of IEnumerable, you must implement this interface in conjunction with IEnumerable<T>—because the latter derives from the former. However, it's very rare that you actually implement these interfaces from scratch: in nearly all cases, you can take the higher-level approach of using iterator methods, Collection<T>, and LINQ.

So, what about as a consumer? In nearly all cases, you can manage entirely with the generic interfaces. The nongeneric interfaces are still occasionally useful, though, in their ability to provide type unification for collections across all element types. The following method, for instance, counts elements in any collection *recursively*:

```
public static int Count (IEnumerable e)
{
  int count = 0;
  foreach (object element in e)
  {
    var subCollection = element as IEnumerable;
    if (subCollection != null)
      count += Count (subCollection);
    else
      count++;
  }
  return count;
}
```

Because C# offers covariance with generic interfaces, it might seem valid to have this method instead accept IEnumerable<object>. This, however, would fail with value-type elements and with legacy collections that don't implement IEnumerable<T>— an example is ControlCollection in Windows Forms.

(On a slight tangent, you might have noticed a potential bug in our example: *cyclic* references will cause infinite recursion and crash the method. We could fix this most easily with the use of a HashSet (see "HashSet<T> and SortedSet<T>" on page 312.)

Implementing the Enumeration Interfaces

You might want to implement IEnumerable or IEnumerable<T> for one or more of the following reasons:

- To support the foreach statement
- To interoperate with anything expecting a standard collection
- To meet the requirements of a more sophisticated collection interface
- To support collection initializers

To implement IEnumerable/IEnumerable<T>, you must provide an enumerator. You can do this in one of three ways:

- If the class is "wrapping" another collection, by returning the wrapped collection's enumerator
- Via an iterator using yield return
- By instantiating your own IEnumerator/IEnumerator<T> implementation

Collections

You can also subclass an existing collection: Collection<T> is designed just for this purpose (see "Customizable Collections and Proxies" on page 321). Yet another approach is to use the LINQ query operators that we'll cover in the next chapter.

Returning another collection's enumerator is just a matter of calling GetEnumerator on the inner collection. However, this is viable only in the simplest scenarios, where the items in the inner collection are exactly what are required. A more flexible approach is to write an iterator, using C#'s yield return statement. An *iterator* is a C# language feature that assists in writing collections, in the same way the foreach statement assists in consuming collections. An iterator automatically handles the implementation of IEnumerable and IEnumerator—or their generic versions. Here's a simple example:

```
public class MyCollection : IEnumerable
{
  int[] data = { 1, 2, 3 };

  public IEnumerator GetEnumerator()
  {
    foreach (int i in data)
      yield return i;
  }
}
```

Notice the "black magic": GetEnumerator doesn't appear to return an enumerator at all! Upon parsing the yield return statement, the compiler writes a hidden nested enumerator class behind the scenes and then refactors GetEnumerator to instantiate and return that class. Iterators are powerful and simple (and are used extensively in the implementation of LINQ-to-Object's standard query operators).

Keeping with this approach, we can also implement the generic interface IEnumerable<T>:

```
public class MyGenCollection : IEnumerable<int>
{
  int[] data = { 1, 2, 3 };

  public IEnumerator<int> GetEnumerator()
  {
    foreach (int i in data)
      yield return i;
  }

  IEnumerator IEnumerable.GetEnumerator()      // Explicit implementation
  {                                            // keeps it hidden.
    return GetEnumerator();
  }
}
```

Because IEnumerable<T> inherits from IEnumerable, we must implement both the generic and the nongeneric versions of GetEnumerator. In accordance with standard practice, we've implemented the nongeneric version explicitly. It can simply

call the generic GetEnumerator because IEnumerator<T> inherits from IEnumera
tor.

The class we've just written would be suitable as a basis from which to write a more sophisticated collection. However, if we need nothing above a simple IEnumera ble<T> implementation, the yield return statement allows for an easier variation. Rather than writing a class, you can move the iteration logic into a method returning a generic IEnumerable<T> and let the compiler take care of the rest. Here's an example:

```
public class Test
{
  public static IEnumerable <int> GetSomeIntegers()
  {
    yield return 1;
    yield return 2;
    yield return 3;
  }
}
```

Here's our method in use:

```
foreach (int i in Test.GetSomeIntegers())
  Console.WriteLine (i);

// Output
1
2
3
```

The final approach in writing GetEnumerator is to write a class that implements IEnumerator directly. This is exactly what the compiler does behind the scenes, in resolving iterators. (Fortunately, it's rare that you'll need to go this far yourself.) The following example defines a collection that's hardcoded to contain the integers 1, 2, and 3:

```
public class MyIntList : IEnumerable
{
  int[] data = { 1, 2, 3 };

  public IEnumerator GetEnumerator()
  {
    return new Enumerator (this);
  }

  class Enumerator : IEnumerator      // Define an inner class
  {                                   // for the enumerator.
    MyIntList collection;
    int currentIndex = -1;

    public Enumerator (MyIntList collection)
    {
      this.collection = collection;
    }
```

```
    public object Current
    {
      get
      {
        if (currentIndex == -1)
          throw new InvalidOperationException ("Enumeration not started!");
        if (currentIndex == collection.data.Length)
          throw new InvalidOperationException ("Past end of list!");
        return collection.data [currentIndex];
      }
    }

    public bool MoveNext()
    {
      if (currentIndex >= collection.data.Length - 1) return false;
      return ++currentIndex < collection.data.Length;
    }

    public void Reset() { currentIndex = -1; }
  }
}
```

Implementing Reset is optional—you can instead throw a Not
SupportedException.

Note that the first call to MoveNext should move to the first (and not the second) item in the list.

To get on par with an iterator in functionality, we must also implement IEnumerator<T>. Here's an example with bounds checking omitted for brevity:

```
class MyIntList : IEnumerable<int>
{
  int[] data = { 1, 2, 3 };

  // The generic enumerator is compatible with both IEnumerable and
  // IEnumerable<T>. We implement the nongeneric GetEnumerator method
  // explicitly to avoid a naming conflict.

  public IEnumerator<int> GetEnumerator() { return new Enumerator(this); }
  IEnumerator IEnumerable.GetEnumerator() { return new Enumerator(this); }

  class Enumerator : IEnumerator<int>
  {
    int currentIndex = -1;
    MyIntList collection;

    public Enumerator (MyIntList collection)
    {
      this.collection = collection;
    }

    public int Current => collection.data [currentIndex];
```

```
    object IEnumerator.Current => Current;

    public bool MoveNext() => ++currentIndex < collection.data.Length;

    public void Reset() => currentIndex = -1;

    // Given we don't need a Dispose method, it's good practice to
    // implement it explicitly, so it's hidden from the public interface.
    void IDisposable.Dispose() {}
  }
}
```

The example with generics is faster because IEnumerator<int>.Current doesn't require casting from int to object, and so avoids the overhead of boxing.

The ICollection and IList Interfaces

Although the enumeration interfaces provide a protocol for forward-only iteration over a collection, they don't provide a mechanism to determine the size of the collection, access a member by index, search, or modify the collection. For such functionality, the .NET Framework defines the ICollection, IList, and IDictionary interfaces. Each comes in both generic and nongeneric versions; however, the nongeneric versions exist mostly for legacy support.

The inheritance hierarchy for these interfaces was shown in Figure 7-1. The easiest way to summarize them is as follows:

IEnumerable<T> *(and* IEnumerable*)*
    Provides minimum functionality (enumeration only)

ICollection<T> *(and* ICollection*)*
    Provides medium functionality (e.g., the Count property)

IList <T>/IDictionary <K,V> *and their nongeneric versions*
    Provide maximum functionality (including "random" access by index/key)

 It's rare that you'll need to *implement* any of these interfaces. In nearly all cases when you need to write a collection class, you can instead subclass Collection<T> (see "Customizable Collections and Proxies" on page 321). LINQ provides yet another option that covers many scenarios.

The generic and nongeneric versions differ in ways over and above what you might expect, particularly in the case of ICollection. The reasons for this are mostly historical: because generics came later, the generic interfaces were developed with the benefit of hindsight, leading to a different (and better) choice of members. For this reason, ICollection<T> does not extend ICollection, IList<T> does not extend IList, and IDictionary<TKey, TValue> does not extend IDictionary. Of course, a collection class itself is free to implement both versions of an interface if beneficial (which it often is).

Another, subtler reason for IList<T> not extending IList is that casting to IList<T> would then return an interface with both Add(T) and Add(object) members. This would effectively defeat static type safety, because you could call Add with an object of any type.

This section covers ICollection<T>, IList<T>, and their nongeneric versions; "Dictionaries" on page 314 covers the dictionary interfaces.

There is no *consistent* rationale in the way the words *collection* and *list* are applied throughout the .NET Framework. For instance, since IList<T> is a more functional version of ICollection<T>, you might expect the class List<T> to be correspondingly more functional than the class Collection<T>. This is not the case. It's best to consider the terms *collection* and *list* as broadly synonymous, except when a specific type is involved.

ICollection<T> and ICollection

ICollection<T> is the standard interface for countable collections of objects. It provides the ability to determine the size of a collection (Count), determine whether an item exists in the collection (Contains), copy the collection into an array (ToArray), and determine whether the collection is read-only (IsReadOnly). For writable collections, you can also Add, Remove, and Clear items from the collection. And since it extends IEnumerable<T>, it can also be traversed via the foreach statement:

```
public interface ICollection<T> : IEnumerable<T>, IEnumerable
{
  int Count { get; }

  bool Contains (T item);
  void CopyTo (T[] array, int arrayIndex);
  bool IsReadOnly { get; }

  void Add(T item);
  bool Remove (T item);
  void Clear();
}
```

The nongeneric ICollection is similar in providing a countable collection but doesn't provide functionality for altering the list or checking for element membership:

```
public interface ICollection : IEnumerable
{
    int Count { get; }
    bool IsSynchronized { get; }
    object SyncRoot { get; }
    void CopyTo (Array array, int index);
}
```

The nongeneric interface also defines properties to assist with synchronization (Chapter 14)—these were dumped in the generic version because thread safety is no longer considered intrinsic to the collection.

Both interfaces are fairly straightforward to implement. If implementing a read-only ICollection<T>, the Add, Remove, and Clear methods should throw a NotSupporte dException.

These interfaces are usually implemented in conjunction with either the IList or the IDictionary interface.

IList<T> and IList

IList<T> is the standard interface for collections indexable by position. In addition to the functionality inherited from ICollection<T> and IEnumerable<T>, it provides the ability to read or write an element by position (via an indexer) and insert/ remove by position:

```
public interface IList<T> : ICollection<T>, IEnumerable<T>, IEnumerable
{
  T this [int index] { get; set; }
  int IndexOf (T item);
  void Insert (int index, T item);
  void RemoveAt (int index);
}
```

The IndexOf methods perform a linear search on the list, returning –1 if the specified item is not found.

The nongeneric version of IList has more members because it inherits less from ICollection:

```
public interface IList : ICollection, IEnumerable
{
  object this [int index] { get; set }
  bool IsFixedSize { get; }
  bool IsReadOnly  { get; }
  int  Add       (object value);
  void Clear();
  bool Contains (object value);
  int  IndexOf  (object value);
  void Insert   (int index, object value);
  void Remove   (object value);
  void RemoveAt (int index);
}
```

The Add method on the nongeneric IList interface returns an integer—this is the index of the newly added item. In contrast, the Add method on ICollection<T> has a void return type.

The general-purpose List<T> class is the quintessential implementation of both IList<T> and IList. C# arrays also implement both the generic and nongeneric

ILists (although the methods that add or remove elements are hidden via explicit interface implementation and throw a NotSupportedException if called).

An ArgumentException is thrown if you try to access a multidimensional array via IList's indexer. This is a trap when writing methods such as the following:

```
public object FirstOrNull (IList list)
{
  if (list == null || list.Count == 0) return null;
  return list[0];
}
```

This might appear bulletproof, but it will throw an exception if called with a multidimensional array. You can test for a multidimensional array at runtime with this expression (more on this in Chapter 19):

```
list.GetType().IsArray && list.GetType().GetArrayRank()>1
```

IReadOnlyList<T>

In order to interoperate with read-only Windows Runtime collections, Framework 4.5 introduced a new collection interface called IReadOnlyList<T>. This interface is useful in and of itself and can be considered a cut-down version of IList<T>, exposing just the members required for read-only operations on lists:

```
public interface IReadOnlyList<out T> : IEnumerable<T>, IEnumerable
{
  int Count { get; }
  T this[int index] { get; }
}
```

Because its type parameter is used only in output positions, it's marked as covariant. This allows a list of cats, for instance, to be treated as a read-only list of animals. In contrast, T is not marked as covariant with IList<T>, because T is used in both input and output positions.

IReadOnlyList<T> represents a read-only *view* of a list. It doesn't necessarily imply that the underlying implementation is read-only.

It would be logical for IList<T> to derive from IReadOnlyList<T>. However, Microsoft was unable to make this change because doing so would require moving members from IList<T> to IReadOnlyList<T>, which would introduce a breaking change into CLR 4.5 (consumers would need to recompile their programs to avoid runtime errors). Instead, implementers of IList<T> need to manually add IReadOnlyList<T> to their list of implemented interfaces.

IReadOnlyList<T> maps to the Windows Runtime type IVectorView<T>.

The Array Class

The Array class is the implicit base class for all single and multidimensional arrays, and it is one of the most fundamental types implementing the standard collection interfaces. The Array class provides type unification, so a common set of methods is available to all arrays, regardless of their declaration or underlying element type.

Since arrays are so fundamental, C# provides explicit syntax for their declaration and initialization, described in Chapters 2 and 3. When an array is declared using C#'s syntax, the CLR implicitly subtypes the Array class—synthesizing a *pseudotype* appropriate to the array's dimensions and element types. This pseudotype implements the typed generic collection interfaces, such as IList<string>.

The CLR also treats array types specially upon construction, assigning them a contiguous space in memory. This makes indexing into arrays highly efficient but prevents them from being resized later on.

Array implements the collection interfaces up to IList<T> in both their generic and nongeneric forms. IList<T> itself is implemented explicitly, though, to keep Array's public interface clean of methods such as Add or Remove, which throw an exception on fixed-length collections such as arrays. The Array class does actually offer a static Resize method, although this works by creating a new array and then copying over each element. As well as being inefficient, references to the array elsewhere in the program will still point to the original version. A better solution for resizable collections is to use the List<T> class (described in the following section).

An array can contain value-type or reference-type elements. Value type elements are stored in place in the array, so an array of three long integers (each 8 bytes) will occupy 24 bytes of contiguous memory. A reference type element, however, occupies only as much space in the array as a reference (4 bytes in a 32-bit environment or 8 bytes in a 64-bit environment). Figure 7-2 illustrates the effect, in memory, of the following program:

```
StringBuilder[] builders = new StringBuilder [5];
builders [0] = new StringBuilder ("builder1");
builders [1] = new StringBuilder ("builder2");
builders [2] = new StringBuilder ("builder3");

long[] numbers = new long [3];
numbers [0] = 12345;
numbers [1] = 54321;
```

Collections

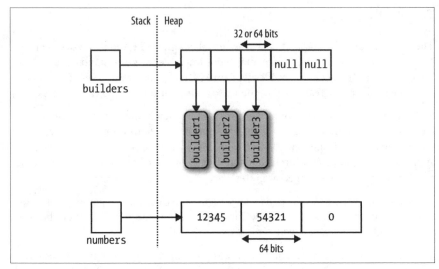

Figure 7-2. Arrays in memory

Because Array is a class, arrays are always (themselves) reference types—regardless of the array's element type. This means that the statement arrayB = arrayA results in two variables that reference the same array. Similarly, two distinct arrays will always fail an equality test—unless you use a custom equality comparer. Framework 4.0 introduced one for the purpose of comparing elements in arrays or tuples which you can access via the StructuralComparisons type:

```
object[] a1 = { "string", 123, true };
object[] a2 = { "string", 123, true };

Console.WriteLine (a1 == a2);                            // False
Console.WriteLine (a1.Equals (a2));                      // False

IStructuralEquatable se1 = a1;
Console.WriteLine (se1.Equals (a2,
  StructuralComparisons.StructuralEqualityComparer));    // True
```

Arrays can be duplicated with the Clone method: arrayB = arrayA.Clone(). However, this results in a shallow clone, meaning that only the memory represented by the array itself is copied. If the array contains value type objects, the values themselves are copied; if the array contains reference type objects, just the references are copied (resulting in two arrays whose members reference the same objects). Figure 7-3 demonstrates the effect of adding the following code to our example:

```
StringBuilder[] builders2 = builders;
StringBuilder[] shallowClone = (StringBuilder[]) builders.Clone();
```

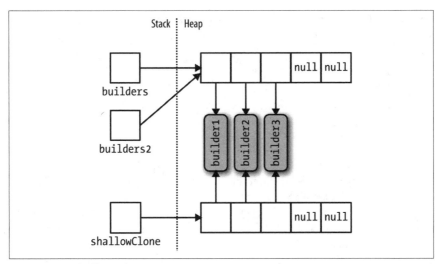

Figure 7-3. Shallow-cloning an array

To create a deep copy—where reference type subobjects are duplicated—you must loop through the array and clone each element manually. The same rules apply to other .NET collection types.

Although `Array` is designed primarily for use with 32-bit indexers, it also has limited support for 64-bit indexers (allowing an array to theoretically address up to 2^{64} elements) via several methods that accept both `Int32` and `Int64` parameters. These overloads are useless in practice because the CLR does not permit any object—including arrays—to exceed 2 GB in size (whether running on a 32- or 64-bit environment).

 Many of the methods on the `Array` class that you expect to be instance methods are in fact static methods. This is an odd design decision and means you should check for both static and instance methods when looking for a method on `Array`.

Construction and Indexing

The easiest way to create and index arrays is through C#'s language constructs:

```
int[] myArray = { 1, 2, 3 };
int first = myArray [0];
int last = myArray [myArray.Length - 1];
```

Alternatively, you can instantiate an array dynamically by calling `Array.CreateIn stance`. This allows you to specify element type and rank (number of dimensions) at runtime—as well as allowing nonzero-based arrays through specifying a lower bound. Nonzero-based arrays are not CLS (Common Language Specification)-compliant.

The GetValue and SetValue methods let you access elements in a dynamically created array (they also work on ordinary arrays):

```
// Create a string array 2 elements in length:
Array a = Array.CreateInstance (typeof(string), 2);
a.SetValue ("hi", 0);                      //  → a[0] = "hi";
a.SetValue ("there", 1);                   //  → a[1] = "there";
string s = (string) a.GetValue (0);        //  → s = a[0];

// We can also cast to a C# array as follows:
string[] cSharpArray = (string[]) a;
string s2 = cSharpArray [0];
```

Zero-indexed arrays created dynamically can be cast to a C# array of a matching or compatible type (compatible by standard array-variance rules). For example, if Apple subclasses Fruit, Apple[] can be cast to Fruit[]. This leads to the issue of why object[] was not used as the unifying array type rather the Array class. The answer is that object[] is incompatible with both multidimensional and value-type arrays (and non-zero-based arrays). An int[] array cannot be cast to object[]. Hence, we require the Array class for full type unification.

GetValue and SetValue also work on compiler-created arrays, and they are useful when writing methods that can deal with an array of any type and rank. For multidimensional arrays, they accept an *array* of indexers:

```
public object GetValue (params int[] indices)
public void   SetValue (object value, params int[] indices)
```

The following method prints the first element of any array, regardless of rank:

```
void WriteFirstValue (Array a)
{
  Console.Write (a.Rank + "-dimensional; ");

  // The indexers array will automatically initialize to all zeros, so
  // passing it into GetValue or SetValue will get/set the zero-based
  // (i.e., first) element in the array.

  int[] indexers = new int[a.Rank];
  Console.WriteLine ("First value is " +  a.GetValue (indexers));
}

void Demo()
{
  int[]  oneD = { 1, 2, 3 };
  int[,] twoD = { {5,6}, {8,9} };

  WriteFirstValue (oneD);    // 1-dimensional; first value is 1
  WriteFirstValue (twoD);    // 2-dimensional; first value is 5
}
```

For working with arrays of unknown type but known rank, generics provide an easier and more efficient solution:

```
void WriteFirstValue<T> (T[] array)
{
  Console.WriteLine (array[0]);
}
```

SetValue throws an exception if the element is of an incompatible type for the array.

When an array is instantiated, whether via language syntax or Array.CreateInstance, its elements are automatically initialized. For arrays with reference type elements, this means writing nulls; for arrays with value type elements, this means calling the value type's default constructor (effectively "zeroing" the members). The Array class also provides this functionality on demand via the Clear method:

```
public static void Clear (Array array, int index, int length);
```

This method doesn't affect the size of the array. This is in contrast to the usual use of Clear (such as in ICollection<T>.Clear), where the collection is reduced to zero elements.

Enumeration

Arrays are easily enumerated with a foreach statement:

```
int[] myArray = { 1, 2, 3};
foreach (int val in myArray)
  Console.WriteLine (val);
```

You can also enumerate using the static Array.ForEach method, defined as follows:

```
public static void ForEach<T> (T[] array, Action<T> action);
```

This uses an Action delegate, with this signature:

```
public delegate void Action<T> (T obj);
```

Here's the first example rewritten with Array.ForEach:

```
Array.ForEach (new[] { 1, 2, 3 }, Console.WriteLine);
```

Length and Rank

Array provides the following methods and properties for querying length and rank:

```
public int  GetLength     (int dimension);
public long GetLongLength (int dimension);

public int  Length     { get; }
public long LongLength { get; }

public int GetLowerBound (int dimension);
public int GetUpperBound (int dimension);

public int Rank { get; }    // Returns number of dimensions in array
```

GetLength and GetLongLength return the length for a given dimension (0 for a single-dimensional array), and Length and LongLength return the total number of elements in the array—all dimensions included.

GetLowerBound and GetUpperBound are useful with nonzero indexed arrays. GetUp perBound returns the same result as adding GetLowerBound to GetLength for any given dimension.

Searching

The Array class offers a range of methods for finding elements within a one-dimensional array:

BinarySearch *methods*
> For rapidly searching a sorted array for a particular item

IndexOf / LastIndex *methods*
> For searching unsorted arrays for a particular item

Find / FindLast / FindIndex / FindLastIndex / FindAll / Exists / TrueForAll
> For searching unsorted arrays for item(s) that satisfy a given Predicate<T>

None of the array searching methods throws an exception if the specified value is not found. Instead, if an item is not found, methods returning an integer return –1 (assuming a zero-indexed array), and methods returning a generic type return the type's default value (e.g., 0 for an int, or null for a string).

The binary search methods are fast, but they work only on sorted arrays and require that the elements be compared for *order* rather than simply *equality*. To this effect, the binary search methods can accept an IComparer or IComparer<T> object to arbitrate on ordering decisions (see the section "Plugging in Equality and Order" on page 327 later in this chapter). This must be consistent with any comparer used in originally sorting the array. If no comparer is provided, the type's default ordering algorithm will be applied, based on its implementation of IComparable / ICompara ble<T>.

The IndexOf and LastIndexOf methods perform a simple enumeration over the array, returning the position of the first (or last) element that matches the given value.

The predicate-based searching methods allow a method delegate or lambda expression to arbitrate on whether a given element is a "match." A predicate is simply a delegate accepting an object and returning true or false:

```
public delegate bool Predicate<T> (T object);
```

In the following example, we search an array of strings for a name containing the letter "a":

```
static void Main()
{
  string[] names = { "Rodney", "Jack", "Jill" };
  string match = Array.Find (names, ContainsA);
  Console.WriteLine (match);      // Jack
}
static bool ContainsA (string name) { return name.Contains ("a"); }
```

Here's the same code shortened with an anonymous method:

```
string[] names = { "Rodney", "Jack", "Jill" };
string match = Array.Find (names, delegate (string name)
  { return name.Contains ("a"); } );
```

A lambda expression shortens it further:

```
string[] names = { "Rodney", "Jack", "Jill" };
string match = Array.Find (names, n => n.Contains ("a"));      // Jack
```

FindAll returns an array of all items satisfying the predicate. In fact, it's equivalent to Enumerable.Where in the System.Linq namespace, except that FindAll returns an array of matching items rather than an IEnumerable<T> of the same.

Exists returns true if any array member satisfies the given predicate and is equivalent to Any in System.Linq.Enumerable.

TrueForAll returns true if all items satisfy the predicate, and is equivalent to All in System.Linq.Enumerable.

Sorting

Array has the following built-in sorting methods:

```
// For sorting a single array:

public static void Sort<T> (T[] array);
public static void Sort    (Array array);

// For sorting a pair of arrays:

public static void Sort<TKey,TValue> (TKey[] keys, TValue[] items);
public static void Sort              (Array keys, Array items);
```

Each of these methods is additionally overloaded to also accept:

```
int index               // Starting index at which to begin sorting
int length              // Number of elements to sort
IComparer<T> comparer    // Object making ordering decisions
Comparison<T> comparison // Delegate making ordering decisions
```

The following illustrates the simplest use of Sort:

```
int[] numbers = { 3, 2, 1 };
Array.Sort (numbers);                        // Array is now { 1, 2, 3 }
```

The methods accepting a pair of arrays work by rearranging the items of each array in tandem, basing the ordering decisions on the first array. In the next example, both the numbers and their corresponding words are sorted into numerical order:

```
int[] numbers = { 3, 2, 1 };
string[] words = { "three", "two", "one" };
Array.Sort (numbers, words);

// numbers array is now { 1, 2, 3 }
// words   array is now { "one", "two", "three" }
```

`Array.Sort` requires that the elements in the array implement `IComparable` (see the section "Order Comparison" on page 278 in Chapter 6). This means that most built-in C# types (such as integers, as in the preceding example) can be sorted. If the elements are not intrinsically comparable, or you want to override the default ordering, you must provide `Sort` with a custom `comparison` provider that reports on the relative position of two elements. There are ways to do this:

- Via a helper object that implements `IComparer` /`IComparer<T>` (see the section "Plugging in Equality and Order" on page 327 later in this chapter)

- Via a `Comparison` delegate:

```
public delegate int Comparison<T> (T x, T y);
```

The `Comparison` delegate follows the same semantics as `IComparer<T>.CompareTo`: if x comes before y, a negative integer is returned; if x comes after y, a positive integer is returned; if x and y have the same sorting position, 0 is returned.

In the following example, we sort an array of integers such that the odd numbers come first:

```
int[] numbers = { 1, 2, 3, 4, 5 };
Array.Sort (numbers, (x, y) => x % 2 == y % 2 ? 0 : x % 2 == 1 ? -1 : 1);

// numbers array is now { 1, 3, 5, 2, 4 }
```

 As an alternative to calling `Sort`, you can use LINQ's `OrderBy` and `ThenBy` operators. Unlike `Array.Sort`, the LINQ operators don't alter the original array, instead emitting the sorted result in a fresh `IEnumerable<T>` sequence.

Reversing Elements

The following `Array` methods reverse the order of all—or a portion of—elements in an array:

```
public static void Reverse (Array array);
public static void Reverse (Array array, int index, int length);
```

Copying

Array provides four methods to perform shallow copying: Clone, CopyTo, Copy and ConstrainedCopy. The former two are instance methods; the latter two are static methods.

The Clone method returns a whole new (shallow-copied) array. The CopyTo and Copy methods copy a contiguous subset of the array. Copying a multidimensional rectangular array requires you to map the multidimensional index to a linear index. For example, the middle square (position[1,1]) in a 3 × 3 array is represented with the index 4, from the calculation: 1*3 + 1. The source and destination ranges can overlap without causing a problem.

ConstrainedCopy performs an *atomic* operation: if all of the requested elements cannot be successfully copied (due to a type error, for instance), the operation is rolled back.

Array also provides a AsReadOnly method that returns a wrapper that prevents elements from being reassigned.

Converting and Resizing

Array.ConvertAll creates and returns a new array of element type TOutput, calling the supplied Converter delegate to copy over the elements. Converter is defined as follows:

```
public delegate TOutput Converter<TInput,TOutput> (TInput input)
```

The following converts an array of floats to an array of integers:

```
float[] reals = { 1.3f, 1.5f, 1.8f };
int[] wholes = Array.ConvertAll (reals, r => Convert.ToInt32 (r));

// wholes array is { 1, 2, 2 }
```

The Resize method works by creating a new array and copying over the elements, returning the new array via the reference parameter. However, any references to the original array in other objects will remain unchanged.

 The System.Linq namespace offers an additional buffet of extension methods suitable for array conversion. These methods return an IEnumerable<T>, which you can convert back to an array via Enumerable 's ToArray method.

Lists, Queues, Stacks, and Sets

The Framework provides a basic set of concrete collection classes that implement the interfaces described in this chapter. This section concentrates on the *list-like* collections (versus the *dictionary-like* collections covered in "Dictionaries" on page 314). As with the interfaces we discussed previously, you usually have a choice of generic or nongeneric versions of each type. In terms of flexibility and performance, the generic classes win, making their nongeneric counterparts redundant except for backward compatibility. This differs from the situation with collection interfaces, where the nongeneric versions are still occasionally useful.

Of the classes described in this section, the generic List class is the most commonly used.

List<T> and ArrayList

The generic List and nongeneric ArrayList classes provide a dynamically sized array of objects and are among the most commonly used of the collection classes. ArrayList implements IList, whereas List<T> implements both IList and IList<T> (and the new read-only version, IReadOnlyList<T>). Unlike with arrays, all interfaces are implemented publicly, and methods such as Add and Remove are exposed and work as you would expect.

Internally, List<T> and ArrayList work by maintaining an internal array of objects, replaced with a larger array upon reaching capacity. Appending elements is efficient (since there is usually a free slot at the end), but inserting elements can be slow (since all elements after the insertion point have to be shifted to make a free slot). As with arrays, searching is efficient if the BinarySearch method is used on a list that has been sorted, but is otherwise inefficient because each item must be individually checked.

 List<T> is up to several times faster than ArrayList if T is a value type because List<T> avoids the overhead of boxing and unboxing elements.

List<T> and ArrayList provide constructors that accept an existing collection of elements: these copy each element from the existing collection into the new List<T> or ArrayList:

```
public class List<T> : IList<T>, IReadOnlyList<T>
{
  public List ();
  public List (IEnumerable<T> collection);
  public List (int capacity);

  // Add+Insert
  public void Add         (T item);
  public void AddRange    (IEnumerable<T> collection);
  public void Insert      (int index, T item);
  public void InsertRange (int index, IEnumerable<T> collection);

  // Remove
  public bool Remove      (T item);
  public void RemoveAt    (int index);
  public void RemoveRange (int index, int count);
  public int  RemoveAll   (Predicate<T> match);

  // Indexing
  public T this [int index] { get; set; }
```

```
public List<T> GetRange (int index, int count);
public Enumerator<T> GetEnumerator();

// Exporting, copying and converting:
public T[] ToArray();
public void CopyTo (T[] array);
public void CopyTo (T[] array, int arrayIndex);
public void CopyTo (int index, T[] array, int arrayIndex, int count);
public ReadOnlyCollection<T> AsReadOnly();
public List<TOutput> ConvertAll<TOutput> (Converter <T,TOutput>
                                           converter);
// Other:
public void Reverse();               // Reverses order of elements in list.
public int Capacity { get;set; }     // Forces expansion of internal array.
public void TrimExcess();            // Trims internal array back to size.
public void Clear();                 // Removes all elements, so Count=0.
}

public delegate TOutput Converter <TInput, TOutput> (TInput input);
```

In addition to these members, List<T> provides instance versions of all of Array's searching and sorting methods.

The following code demonstrates List's properties and methods. See "The Array Class" on page 297 for examples on searching and sorting:

```
List<string> words = new List<string>();    // New string-typed list

words.Add ("melon");
words.Add ("avocado");
words.AddRange (new[] { "banana", "plum" } );
words.Insert (0, "lemon");                            // Insert at start
words.InsertRange (0, new[] { "peach", "nashi" });    // Insert at start

words.Remove ("melon");
words.RemoveAt (3);                          // Remove the 4th element
words.RemoveRange (0, 2);                     // Remove first 2 elements

// Remove all strings starting in 'n':
words.RemoveAll (s => s.StartsWith ("n"));

Console.WriteLine (words [0]);                        // first word
Console.WriteLine (words [words.Count - 1]);          // last word
foreach (string s in words) Console.WriteLine (s);    // all words
List<string> subset = words.GetRange (1, 2);          // 2nd->3rd words

string[] wordsArray = words.ToArray();    // Creates a new typed array

// Copy first two elements to the end of an existing array:
string[] existing = new string [1000];
words.CopyTo (0, existing, 998, 2);

List<string> upperCastWords = words.ConvertAll (s => s.ToUpper());
List<int> lengths = words.ConvertAll (s => s.Length);
```

The nongeneric `ArrayList` class is used mainly for backward compatibility with Framework 1.x code and requires clumsy casts—as the following example demonstrates:

```
ArrayList al = new ArrayList();
al.Add ("hello");
string first = (string) al [0];
string[] strArr = (string[]) al.ToArray (typeof (string));
```

Such casts cannot be verified by the compiler; the following compiles successfully but then fails at runtime:

```
int first = (int) al [0];    // Runtime exception
```

 An `ArrayList` is functionally similar to `List<object>`. Both are useful when you need a list of mixed-type elements that share no common base type (other than `object`). A possible advantage of choosing an `ArrayList`, in this case, would be if you need to deal with the list using reflection (Chapter 19). Reflection is easier with a nongeneric `ArrayList` than a `List<object>`.

If you import the `System.Linq` namespace, you can convert an `ArrayList` to a generic `List` by calling `Cast` and then `ToList`:

```
ArrayList al = new ArrayList();
al.AddRange (new[] { 1, 5, 9 } );
List<int> list = al.Cast<int>().ToList();
```

`Cast` and `ToList` are extension methods in the `System.Linq.Enumerable` class.

LinkedList<T>

`LinkedList<T>` is a generic doubly linked list (see Figure 7-4). A doubly linked list is a chain of nodes in which each references the node before, the node after, and the actual element. Its main benefit is that an element can always be inserted efficiently anywhere in the list, since it just involves creating a new node and updating a few references. However, finding where to insert the node in the first place can be slow, as there's no intrinsic mechanism to index directly into a linked list; each node must be traversed, and binary-chop searches are not possible.

`LinkedList<T>` implements `IEnumerable<T>` and `ICollection<T>` (and their non-generic versions), but not `IList<T>`, since access by index is not supported. List nodes are implemented via the following class:

```
public sealed class LinkedListNode<T>
{
  public LinkedList<T> List { get; }
  public LinkedListNode<T> Next { get; }
  public LinkedListNode<T> Previous { get; }
  public T Value { get; set; }
}
```

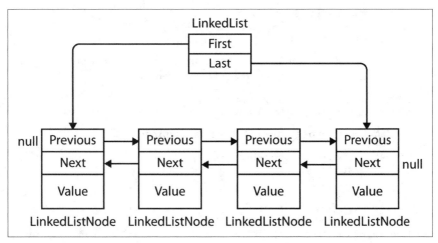

Figure 7-4. LinkedList<T>

When adding a node, you can specify its position either relative to another node or at the start/end of the list. LinkedList<T> provides the following methods for this:

```
public void AddFirst(LinkedListNode<T> node);
public LinkedListNode<T> AddFirst (T value);

public void AddLast (LinkedListNode<T> node);
public LinkedListNode<T> AddLast (T value);

public void AddAfter (LinkedListNode<T> node, LinkedListNode<T> newNode);
public LinkedListNode<T> AddAfter (LinkedListNode<T> node, T value);

public void AddBefore (LinkedListNode<T> node, LinkedListNode<T> newNode);
public LinkedListNode<T> AddBefore (LinkedListNode<T> node, T value);
```

Similar methods are provided to remove elements:

```
public void Clear();

public void RemoveFirst();
public void RemoveLast();

public bool Remove (T value);
public void Remove (LinkedListNode<T> node);
```

LinkedList<T> has internal fields to keep track of the number of elements in the list, as well as the head and tail of the list. These are exposed in the following public properties:

```
public int Count { get; }                    // Fast
public LinkedListNode<T> First { get; }      // Fast
public LinkedListNode<T> Last { get; }       // Fast
```

LinkedList<T> also supports the following searching methods (each requiring that the list be internally enumerated):

```
public bool Contains (T value);
public LinkedListNode<T> Find (T value);
public LinkedListNode<T> FindLast (T value);
```

Finally, LinkedList<T> supports copying to an array for indexed processing and obtaining an enumerator to support the foreach statement:

```
public void CopyTo (T[] array, int index);
public Enumerator<T> GetEnumerator();
```

Here's a demonstration on the use of LinkedList<string>:

```
var tune = new LinkedList<string>();
tune.AddFirst ("do");                           // do
tune.AddLast ("so");                            // do - so

tune.AddAfter (tune.First, "re");               // do - re- so
tune.AddAfter (tune.First.Next, "mi");          // do - re - mi- so
tune.AddBefore (tune.Last, "fa");               // do - re - mi - fa- so

tune.RemoveFirst();                             // re - mi - fa - so
tune.RemoveLast();                              // re - mi - fa

LinkedListNode<string> miNode = tune.Find ("mi");
tune.Remove (miNode);                           // re - fa
tune.AddFirst (miNode);                         // mi- re - fa

foreach (string s in tune) Console.WriteLine (s);
```

Queue<T> and Queue

Queue<T> and Queue are first-in, first-out (FIFO) data structures, providing methods to Enqueue (add an item to the tail of the queue) and Dequeue (retrieve and remove the item at the head of the queue). A Peek method is also provided to return the element at the head of the queue without removing it, and a Count property (useful in checking that elements are present before dequeuing).

Although queues are enumerable, they do not implement IList<T>/IList, since members cannot be accessed directly by index. A ToArray method is provided, however, for copying the elements to an array where they can be randomly accessed:

```
public class Queue<T> : IEnumerable<T>, ICollection, IEnumerable
{
  public Queue();
  public Queue (IEnumerable<T> collection);     // Copies existing elements
  public Queue (int capacity);                  // To lessen auto-resizing
  public void Clear();
  public bool Contains (T item);
  public void CopyTo (T[] array, int arrayIndex);
  public int Count { get; }
  public T Dequeue();
  public void Enqueue (T item);
  public Enumerator<T> GetEnumerator();         // To support foreach
  public T Peek();
```

```
  public T[] ToArray();
  public void TrimExcess();
}
```

The following is an example of using Queue<int>:

```
var q = new Queue<int>();
q.Enqueue (10);
q.Enqueue (20);
int[] data = q.ToArray();        // Exports to an array
Console.WriteLine (q.Count);     // "2"
Console.WriteLine (q.Peek());    // "10"
Console.WriteLine (q.Dequeue()); // "10"
Console.WriteLine (q.Dequeue()); // "20"
Console.WriteLine (q.Dequeue()); // throws an exception (queue empty)
```

Queues are implemented internally using an array that's resized as required—much like the generic List class. The queue maintains indexes that point directly to the head and tail elements; therefore, enqueuing and dequeuing are extremely quick operations (except when an internal resize is required).

Stack<T> and Stack

Stack<T> and Stack are last-in, first-out (LIFO) data structures, providing methods to Push (add an item to the top of the stack) and Pop (retrieve and remove an element from the top of the stack). A nondestructive Peek method is also provided, as is a Count property and a ToArray method for exporting the data for random access:

```
public class Stack<T> : IEnumerable<T>, ICollection, IEnumerable
{
  public Stack();
  public Stack (IEnumerable<T> collection);   // Copies existing elements
  public Stack (int capacity);                // Lessens auto-resizing
  public void Clear();
  public bool Contains (T item);
  public void CopyTo (T[] array, int arrayIndex);
  public int Count { get; }
  public Enumerator<T> GetEnumerator();       // To support foreach
  public T Peek();
  public T Pop();
  public void Push (T item);
  public T[] ToArray();
  public void TrimExcess();
}
```

The following example demonstrates Stack<int>:

```
var s = new Stack<int>();
s.Push (1);                      //              Stack = 1
s.Push (2);                      //              Stack = 1,2
s.Push (3);                      //              Stack = 1,2,3
Console.WriteLine (s.Count);     // Prints 3
Console.WriteLine (s.Peek());    // Prints 3,    Stack = 1,2,3
Console.WriteLine (s.Pop());     // Prints 3,    Stack = 1,2
```

```
Console.WriteLine (s.Pop());    // Prints 2,  Stack = 1
Console.WriteLine (s.Pop());    // Prints 1,  Stack = <empty>
Console.WriteLine (s.Pop());    // throws exception
```

Stacks are implemented internally with an array that's resized as required, as with Queue<T> and List<T>.

BitArray

A BitArray is a dynamically sized collection of compacted bool values. It is more memory-efficient than both a simple array of bool and a generic List of bool, because it uses only one bit for each value, whereas the bool type otherwise occupies one byte for each value.

BitArray's indexer reads and writes individual bits:

```
var bits = new BitArray(2);
bits[1] = true;
```

There are four bitwise operator methods (And, Or, Xor and Not). All but the last accept another BitArray:

```
bits.Xor (bits);                // Bitwise exclusive-OR bits with itself
Console.WriteLine (bits[1]);    // False
```

HashSet<T> and SortedSet<T>

HashSet<T> and SortedSet<T> are generic collections new to Framework 3.5 and 4.0, respectively. Both have the following distinguishing features:

- Their Contains methods execute quickly using a hash-based lookup.

- They do not store duplicate elements and silently ignore requests to add duplicates.

- You cannot access an element by position.

SortedSet<T> keeps elements in order, whereas HashSet<T> does not.

The commonality of these types is captured by the interface ISet<T>.

For historical reasons, HashSet<T> lives in *System.Core.dll* (whereas SortedSet<T> and ISet<T> live in *System.dll*).

HashSet<T> is implemented with a hashtable that stores just keys; SortedSet<T> is implemented with a red/black tree.

Both collections implement ICollection<T> and offer methods that you would expect, such as Contains, Add, and Remove. In addition, there's a predicate-based removal method called RemoveWhere.

The following constructs a `HashSet<char>` from an existing collection, tests for membership, and then enumerates the collection (notice the absence of duplicates):

```
var letters = new HashSet<char> ("the quick brown fox");

Console.WriteLine (letters.Contains ('t'));      // true
Console.WriteLine (letters.Contains ('j'));      // false

foreach (char c in letters) Console.Write (c);   // the quickbrownfx
```

(The reason we can pass a `string` into `HashSet<char>`'s constructor is because `string` implements `IEnumerable<char>`.)

The really interesting methods are the set operations. The following set operations are *destructive*, in that they modify the set:

```
public void UnionWith           (IEnumerable<T> other);   // Adds
public void IntersectWith       (IEnumerable<T> other);   // Removes
public void ExceptWith          (IEnumerable<T> other);   // Removes
public void SymmetricExceptWith (IEnumerable<T> other);   // Removes
```

whereas the following methods simply query the set and so are nondestructive:

```
public bool IsSubsetOf          (IEnumerable<T> other);
public bool IsProperSubsetOf    (IEnumerable<T> other);
public bool IsSupersetOf        (IEnumerable<T> other);
public bool IsProperSupersetOf  (IEnumerable<T> other);
public bool Overlaps            (IEnumerable<T> other);
public bool SetEquals           (IEnumerable<T> other);
```

`UnionWith` adds all the elements in the second set to the original set (excluding duplicates). `IntersectWith` removes the elements that are not in both sets. We can extract all the vowels from our set of characters as follows:

```
var letters = new HashSet<char> ("the quick brown fox");
letters.IntersectWith ("aeiou");
foreach (char c in letters) Console.Write (c);      // euio
```

`ExceptWith` removes the specified elements from the source set. Here, we strip all vowels from the set:

```
var letters = new HashSet<char> ("the quick brown fox");
letters.ExceptWith ("aeiou");
foreach (char c in letters) Console.Write (c);      // th qckbrwnfx
```

`SymmetricExceptWith` removes all but the elements that are unique to one set or the other:

```
var letters = new HashSet<char> ("the quick brown fox");
letters.SymmetricExceptWith ("the lazy brown fox");
foreach (char c in letters) Console.Write (c);      // quicklazy
```

Note that because `HashSet<T>` and `SortedSet<T>` implement `IEnumerable<T>`, you can use another type of set (or collection) as the argument to any of the set operation methods.

Collections

`SortedSet<T>` offers all the members of `HashSet<T>`, plus the following:

```
public virtual SortedSet<T> GetViewBetween (T lowerValue, T upperValue)
public IEnumerable<T> Reverse()
public T Min { get; }
public T Max { get; }
```

`SortedSet<T>` also accepts an optional `IComparer<T>` in its constructor (rather than an *equality comparer*).

Here's an example of loading the same letters into a `SortedSet<char>`:

```
var letters = new SortedSet<char> ("the quick brown fox");
foreach (char c in letters) Console.Write (c);    //  bcefhiknoqrtuwx
```

Following on from this, we can obtain the letters between *f* and *j* as follows:

```
foreach (char c in letters.GetViewBetween ('f', 'j'))
  Console.Write (c);                                        //  fhi
```

Dictionaries

A dictionary is a collection in which each element is a key/value pair. Dictionaries are most commonly used for lookups and sorted lists.

The Framework defines a standard protocol for dictionaries, via the interfaces `IDictionary` and `IDictionary <TKey, TValue>`, as well as a set of general-purpose dictionary classes. The classes each differ in the following regard:

- Whether or not items are stored in sorted sequence
- Whether or not items can be accessed by position (index) as well as by key
- Whether generic or nongeneric
- Whether it's fast or slow to retrieve items by key from a large dictionary

Table 7-1 summarizes each of the dictionary classes and how they differ in these respects. The performance times are in milliseconds, to perform 50,000 operations on a dictionary with integer keys and values, on a 1.5 GHz PC. (The differences in performance between generic and nongeneric counterparts using the same underlying collection structure are due to boxing, and show up only with value-type elements.)

Table 7-1. Dictionary classes

Type	Internal structure	Retrieve by index?	Memory overhead (avg. bytes per item)	Speed: random insertion	Speed: sequential insertion	Speed: retrieval by key
Unsorted						
Dictionary <K,V>	Hashtable	No	22	30	30	20
Hashtable	Hashtable	No	38	50	50	30
ListDictionary	Linked list	No	36	50,000	50,000	50,000
OrderedDictionary	Hashtable + array	Yes	59	70	70	40
Sorted						
SortedDictionary <K,V>	Red/black tree	No	20	130	100	120
SortedList <K,V>	2xArray	Yes	2	3,300	30	40
SortedList	2xArray	Yes	27	4,500	100	180

In big-O notation, retrieval time by key is:

- O(1) for Hashtable, Dictionary, and OrderedDictionary
- O(log *n*) for SortedDictionary and SortedList
- O(*n*) for ListDictionary (and nondictionary types such as List<T>)

where *n* is the number of elements in the collection.

IDictionary<TKey,TValue>

IDictionary<TKey,TValue> defines the standard protocol for all key/value-based collections. It extends ICollection<T> by adding methods and properties to access elements based on a key of arbitrary type:

```
public interface IDictionary <TKey, TValue> :
  ICollection <KeyValuePair <TKey, TValue>>, IEnumerable
{
  bool ContainsKey (TKey key);
  bool TryGetValue (TKey key, out TValue value);
  void Add        (TKey key, TValue value);
  bool Remove     (TKey key);

  TValue this [TKey key]        { get; set; } // Main indexer - by key
  ICollection <TKey> Keys       { get; }      // Returns just keys
  ICollection <TValue> Values { get; }        // Returns just values
}
```

From Framework 4.5, there's also an interface called IReadOn
lyDictionary<TKey,TValue>, which defines the read-only
subset of dictionary members. This maps to the Windows
Runtime type IMapView<K,V> and was introduced primarily
for that reason.

To add an item to a dictionary, you either call Add or use the index's set accessor—
the latter adds an item to the dictionary if the key is not already present (or updates
the item if it is present). Duplicate keys are forbidden in all dictionary implementations, so calling Add twice with the same key throws an exception.

To retrieve an item from a dictionary, use either the indexer or the TryGetValue
method. If the key doesn't exist, the indexer throws an exception, whereas TryGet
Value returns false. You can test for membership explicitly by calling Contain
sKey; however, this incurs the cost of two lookups if you then subsequently retrieve
the item.

Enumerating directly over an IDictionary<TKey,TValue> returns a sequence of
KeyValuePair structs:

```
public struct KeyValuePair <TKey, TValue>
{
  public TKey Key      { get; }
  public TValue Value { get; }
}
```

You can enumerate over just the keys or values via the dictionary's Keys/Values
properties.

We demonstrate the use of this interface with the generic Dictionary class in the
following section.

IDictionary

The nongeneric IDictionary interface is the same in principle as IDiction
ary<TKey,TValue>, apart from two important functional differences. It's important
to be aware of these differences, since IDictionary appears in legacy code (including the .NET Framework itself in places):

- Retrieving a nonexistent key via the indexer returns null (rather than throwing
  an exception).
- Contains tests for membership rather than ContainsKey.

Enumerating over a nongeneric IDictionary returns a sequence of DictionaryEn
try structs:

```
public struct DictionaryEntry
{
  public object Key    { get; set; }
  public object Value { get; set; }
}
```

Dictionary<TKey,TValue> and Hashtable

The generic `Dictionary` class is one of the most commonly used collections (along with the `List<T>` collection). It uses a hashtable data structure to store keys and values, and it is fast and efficient.

 The nongeneric version of `Dictionary<TKey,TValue>` is called `Hashtable`; there is no nongeneric class called `Dictio nary`. When we refer simply to `Dictionary`, we mean the generic `Dictionary<TKey,TValue>` class.

`Dictionary` implements both the generic and nongeneric `IDictionary` interfaces, the generic `IDictionary` being exposed publicly. `Dictionary` is, in fact, a "textbook" implementation of the generic `IDictionary`.

Here's how to use it:

```
var d = new Dictionary<string, int>();

d.Add("One", 1);
d["Two"] = 2;      // adds to dictionary because "two" not already present
d["Two"] = 22;     // updates dictionary because "two" is now present
d["Three"] = 3;

Console.WriteLine (d["Two"]);              // Prints "22"
Console.WriteLine (d.ContainsKey ("One")); // true (fast operation)
Console.WriteLine (d.ContainsValue (3));   // true (slow operation)
int val = 0;
if (!d.TryGetValue ("onE", out val))
  Console.WriteLine ("No val");            // "No val" (case sensitive)

// Three different ways to enumerate the dictionary:

foreach (KeyValuePair<string, int> kv in d)       //  One ; 1
  Console.WriteLine (kv.Key + "; " + kv.Value);    //  Two ; 22
                                                   //  Three ; 3

foreach (string s in d.Keys) Console.Write (s);   // OneTwoThree
Console.WriteLine();
foreach (int i in d.Values) Console.Write (i);    // 1223
```

Its underlying hashtable works by converting each element's key into an integer hashcode—a pseudounique value—and then applying an algorithm to convert the hashcode into a hash key. This hash key is used internally to determine which "bucket" an entry belongs to. If the bucket contains more than one value, a linear search is performed on the bucket. A good hash function does not strive to return strictly unique hashcodes (which would usually be impossible); it strives to return hashcodes that are evenly distributed across the 32-bit integer space. This avoids the scenario of ending up with a few very large (and inefficient) buckets.

A dictionary can work with keys of any type, providing it's able to determine equality between keys and obtain hashcodes. By default, equality is determined via the key's `object.Equals` method, and the pseudounique hashcode is obtained via the key's GetHashCode method. This behavior can be changed, either by overriding these methods or by providing an IEqualityComparer object when constructing the dictionary. A common application of this is to specify a case-insensitive equality comparer when using string keys:

```
var d = new Dictionary<string, int> (StringComparer.OrdinalIgnoreCase);
```

We discuss this further in "Plugging in Equality and Order" on page 327.

As with many other types of collections, the performance of a dictionary can be improved slightly by specifying the collection's expected size in the constructor, avoiding or lessening the need for internal resizing operations.

The nongeneric version is named Hashtable and is functionally similar apart from differences stemming from it exposing the nongeneric IDictionary interface discussed previously.

The downside to Dictionary and Hashtable is that the items are not sorted. Furthermore, the original order in which the items were added is not retained. As with all dictionaries, duplicate keys are not allowed.

 When the generic collections were introduced in Framework 2.0, the CLR team chose to name them according to what they represent (Dictionary, List) rather than how they are internally implemented (Hashtable, ArrayList). While this is good because it gives them the freedom to later change the implementation, it also means that the *performance contract* (often the most important criteria in choosing one kind of collection over another) is no longer captured in the name.

OrderedDictionary

An OrderedDictionary is a nongeneric dictionary that maintains elements in the same order that they were added. With an OrderedDictionary, you can access elements both by index and by key.

 An OrderedDictionary is not a *sorted* dictionary.

An OrderedDictionary is a combination of a Hashtable and an ArrayList. This means it has all the functionality of a Hashtable, plus functions such as RemoveAt, as well as an integer indexer. It also exposes Keys and Values properties that return elements in their original order.

This class was introduced in .NET 2.0, yet peculiarly, there's no generic version.

ListDictionary and HybridDictionary

ListDictionary uses a singly linked list to store the underlying data. It doesn't provide sorting, although it does preserve the original entry order of the items. ListDic

---

tionary is extremely slow with large lists. Its only real "claim to fame" is its efficiency with very small lists (fewer than 10 items).

HybridDictionary is a ListDictionary that automatically converts to a Hashtable upon reaching a certain size, to address ListDictionary's problems with performance. The idea is to get a low memory footprint when the dictionary is small, and good performance when the dictionary is large. However, given the overhead in converting from one to the other—and the fact that a Dictionary is not excessively heavy or slow in either scenario—you wouldn't suffer unreasonably by using a Dictionary to begin with.

Both classes come only in nongeneric form.

Sorted Dictionaries

The Framework provides two dictionary classes internally structured such that their content is always sorted by key:

- SortedDictionary<TKey,TValue>
- SortedList<TKey,TValue>[1]

(In this section, we will abbreviate <TKey,TValue> to <,>.)

SortedDictionary<,> uses a red/black tree: a data structure designed to perform consistently well in any insertion or retrieval scenario.

SortedList<,> is implemented internally with an ordered array pair, providing fast retrieval (via a binary-chop search) but poor insertion performance (because existing values have to be shifted to make room for a new entry).

SortedDictionary<,> is much faster than SortedList<,> at inserting elements in a random sequence (particularly with large lists). SortedList<,>, however, has an extra ability: to access items by index as well as by key. With a sorted list, you can go directly to the nth element in the sorting sequence (via the indexer on the Keys/Values properties). To do the same with a SortedDictionary<,>, you must manually enumerate over n items. (Alternatively, you could write a class that combines a sorted dictionary with a list class.)

None of the three collections allows duplicate keys (as is the case with all dictionaries).

The following example uses reflection to load all the methods defined in System.Object into a sorted list keyed by name, and then enumerates their keys and values:

Collections

---

1 There's also a functionally identical nongeneric version of this called SortedList.

```
// MethodInfo is in the System.Reflection namespace

var sorted = new SortedList <string, MethodInfo>();

foreach (MethodInfo m in typeof (object).GetMethods())
  sorted [m.Name] = m;

foreach (string name in sorted.Keys)
  Console.WriteLine (name);

foreach (MethodInfo m in sorted.Values)
  Console.WriteLine (m.Name + " returns a " + m.ReturnType);
```

Here's the result of the first enumeration:

```
Equals
GetHashCode
GetType
ReferenceEquals
ToString
```

Here's the result of the second enumeration:

```
Equals returns a System.Boolean
GetHashCode returns a System.Int32
GetType returns a System.Type
ReferenceEquals returns a System.Boolean
ToString returns a System.String
```

Notice that we populated the dictionary through its indexer. If we instead used the Add method, it would throw an exception because the object class upon which we're reflecting overloads the Equals method, and you can't add the same key twice to a dictionary. By using the indexer, the later entry overwrites the earlier entry, preventing this error.

 You can store multiple members of the same key by making each value element a list:

```
SortedList <string, List<MethodInfo>>
```

Extending our example, the following retrieves the MethodInfo whose key is "GetHashCode", just as with an ordinary dictionary:

```
Console.WriteLine (sorted ["GetHashCode"]);       // Int32 GetHashCode()
```

So far, everything we've done would also work with a SortedDictionary<,>. The following two lines, however, which retrieve the last key and value, work only with a sorted list:

```
Console.WriteLine (sorted.Keys  [sorted.Count - 1]);            // ToString
Console.WriteLine (sorted.Values[sorted.Count - 1].IsVirtual);  // True
```

Customizable Collections and Proxies

The collection classes discussed in previous sections are convenient in that they can be directly instantiated, but they don't allow you to control what happens when an item is added to or removed from the collection. With strongly typed collections in an application, you sometimes need this control—for instance:

- To fire an event when an item is added or removed
- To update properties because of the added or removed item
- To detect an "illegal" add/remove operation and throw an exception (for example, if the operation violates a business rule)

The .NET Framework provides collection classes for this exact purpose, in the `Sys tem.Collections.ObjectModel` namespace. These are essentially proxies or wrappers that implement `IList<T>` or `IDictionary<,>` by forwarding the methods through to an underlying collection. Each `Add`, `Remove`, or `Clear` operation is routed via a virtual method that acts as a "gateway" when overridden.

Customizable collection classes are commonly used for publicly exposed collections; for instance, a collection of controls exposed publicly on a `System.Win dows.Form` class.

Collection<T> and CollectionBase

The `Collection<T>` class is a customizable wrapper for `List<T>`.

As well as implementing `IList<T>` and `IList`, it defines four additional virtual methods and a protected property as follows:

```
public class Collection<T> :
  IList<T>, ICollection<T>, IEnumerable<T>, IList, ICollection, IEnumerable
{
  // ...

  protected virtual void ClearItems();
  protected virtual void InsertItem (int index, T item);
  protected virtual void RemoveItem (int index);
  protected virtual void SetItem (int index, T item);

  protected IList<T> Items { get; }
}
```

The virtual methods provide the gateway by which you can "hook in" to change or enhance the list's normal behavior. The protected `Items` property allows the implementer to directly access the "inner list"—this is used to make changes internally without the virtual methods firing.

The virtual methods need not be overridden; they can be left alone until there's a requirement to alter the list's default behavior. The following example demonstrates the typical "skeleton" use of `Collection<T>`:

```
public class Animal
{
  public string Name;
  public int Popularity;

  public Animal (string name, int popularity)
  {
    Name = name; Popularity = popularity;
  }
}

public class AnimalCollection : Collection <Animal>
{
  // AnimalCollection is already a fully functioning list of animals.
  // No extra code is required.
}

public class Zoo    // The class that will expose AnimalCollection.
{                   // This would typically have additional members.

  public readonly AnimalCollection Animals = new AnimalCollection();
}

class Program
{
  static void Main()
  {
    Zoo zoo = new Zoo();
    zoo.Animals.Add (new Animal ("Kangaroo", 10));
    zoo.Animals.Add (new Animal ("Mr Sea Lion", 20));
    foreach (Animal a in zoo.Animals) Console.WriteLine (a.Name);
  }
}
```

As it stands, AnimalCollection is no more functional than a simple List<Animal> ;
its role is to provide a base for future extension. To illustrate, we'll now add a Zoo
property to Animal so it can reference the Zoo in which it lives and override each of
the virtual methods in Collection<Animal> to maintain that property automatically:

```
public class Animal
{
  public string Name;
  public int Popularity;
  public Zoo Zoo { get; internal set; }
  public Animal(string name, int popularity)
  {
    Name = name; Popularity = popularity;
  }
}

public class AnimalCollection : Collection <Animal>
{
  Zoo zoo;
  public AnimalCollection (Zoo zoo) { this.zoo = zoo; }
```

```
    protected override void InsertItem (int index, Animal item)
    {
      base.InsertItem (index, item);
      item.Zoo = zoo;
    }
    protected override void SetItem (int index, Animal item)
    {
      base.SetItem (index, item);
      item.Zoo = zoo;
    }
    protected override void RemoveItem (int index)
    {
      this [index].Zoo = null;
      base.RemoveItem (index);
    }
    protected override void ClearItems()
    {
      foreach (Animal a in this) a.Zoo = null;
      base.ClearItems();
    }
  }

  public class Zoo
  {
    public readonly AnimalCollection Animals;
    public Zoo() { Animals = new AnimalCollection (this); }
  }
```

Collection<T> also has a constructor accepting an existing IList<T>. Unlike with other collection classes, the supplied list is *proxied* rather than *copied*, meaning that subsequent changes will be reflected in the wrapping Collection<T> (although *without* Collection<T>'s virtual methods firing). Conversely, changes made via the Collection<T> will change the underlying list.

CollectionBase

CollectionBase is the nongeneric version of Collection<T> introduced in Framework 1.0. This provides most of the same features as Collection<T> but is clumsier to use. Instead of the template methods InsertItem, RemoveItem SetItem, and ClearItem, CollectionBase has "hook" methods that double the number of methods required: OnInsert, OnInsertComplete, OnSet, OnSetComplete, OnRemove, OnRemoveComplete, OnClear, and OnClearComplete. Because CollectionBase is nongeneric, you must also implement typed methods when subclassing it—at a minimum, a typed indexer and Add method.

KeyedCollection<TKey,TItem> and DictionaryBase

KeyedCollection<TKey,TItem> subclasses Collection<TItem>. It both adds and subtracts functionality. What it adds is the ability to access items by key, much like with a dictionary. What it subtracts is the ability to proxy your own inner list.

A keyed collection has some resemblance to an OrderedDictionary in that it combines a linear list with a hashtable. However, unlike OrderedDictionary, it doesn't implement IDictionary and doesn't support the concept of a key/value *pair*. Keys are obtained instead from the items themselves: via the abstract GetKeyForItem method. This means enumerating a keyed collection is just like enumerating an ordinary list.

KeyedCollection<TKey,TItem> is best thought of as Collection<TItem> plus fast lookup by key.

Because it subclasses Collection<>, a keyed collection inherits all of Collection<>'s functionality, except for the ability to specify an existing list in construction. The additional members it defines are as follows:

```
public abstract class KeyedCollection <TKey, TItem> : Collection <TItem>

// ...

protected abstract TKey GetKeyForItem(TItem item);
protected void ChangeItemKey(TItem item, TKey newKey);

// Fast lookup by key - this is in addition to lookup by index.
public TItem this[TKey key] { get; }

protected IDictionary<TKey, TItem> Dictionary { get; }
}
```

GetKeyForItem is what the implementer overrides to obtain an item's key from the underlying object. The ChangeItemKey method must be called if the item's key property changes in order to update the internal dictionary. The Dictionary property returns the internal dictionary used to implement the lookup, which is created when the first item is added. This behavior can be changed by specifying a creation threshold in the constructor, delaying the internal dictionary from being created until the threshold is reached (in the interim, a linear search is performed if an item is requested by key). A good reason not to specify a creation threshold is that having a valid dictionary can be useful in obtaining an ICollection<> of keys, via the Dictionary's Keys property. This collection can then be passed on to a public property.

The most common use for KeyedCollection<,> is in providing a collection of items accessible both by index and by name. To demonstrate this, we'll revisit the zoo, this time implementing AnimalCollection as a KeyedCollection<string,Animal>:

```
public class Animal
{
  string name;
  public string Name
  {
    get { return name; }
    set {
      if (Zoo != null) Zoo.Animals.NotifyNameChange (this, value);
      name = value;
```

```
    }
  }
  public int Popularity;
  public Zoo Zoo { get; internal set; }

  public Animal (string name, int popularity)
  {
    Name = name; Popularity = popularity;
  }
}

public class AnimalCollection : KeyedCollection <string, Animal>
{
  Zoo zoo;
  public AnimalCollection (Zoo zoo) { this.zoo = zoo; }

  internal void NotifyNameChange (Animal a, string newName)
  {
    this.ChangeItemKey (a, newName);
  }

  protected override string GetKeyForItem (Animal item)
  {
    return item.Name;
  }

  // The following methods would be implemented as in the previous example
  protected override void InsertItem (int index, Animal item)...
  protected override void SetItem (int index, Animal item)...
  protected override void RemoveItem (int index)...
  protected override void ClearItems()...
}

public class Zoo
{
  public readonly AnimalCollection Animals;
  public Zoo() { Animals = new AnimalCollection (this); }
}

class Program
{
  static void Main()
  {
    Zoo zoo = new Zoo();
    zoo.Animals.Add (new Animal ("Kangaroo", 10));
    zoo.Animals.Add (new Animal ("Mr Sea Lion", 20));
    Console.WriteLine (zoo.Animals [0].Popularity);              // 10
    Console.WriteLine (zoo.Animals ["Mr Sea Lion"].Popularity);  // 20
    zoo.Animals ["Kangaroo"].Name = "Mr Roo";
    Console.WriteLine (zoo.Animals ["Mr Roo"].Popularity);       // 10
  }
}
```

DictionaryBase

The nongeneric version of KeyedCollection is called DictionaryBase. This legacy class takes very different in its approach: it implements IDictionary and uses clumsy hook methods like CollectionBase : OnInsert, OnInsertComplete, OnSet, OnSetComplete, OnRemove, OnRemoveComplete, OnClear, and OnClearComplete (and additionally, OnGet). The primary advantage of implementing IDictionary over taking the KeyedCollection approach is that you don't need to subclass it in order to obtain keys. But since the very purpose of DictionaryBase is to be subclassed, it's no advantage at all. The improved model in KeyedCollection is almost certainly due to the fact that it was written some years later, with the benefit of hindsight. DictionaryBase is best considered useful for backward compatibility.

ReadOnlyCollection<T>

ReadOnlyCollection<T> is a wrapper, or *proxy*, that provides a read-only view of a collection. This is useful in allowing a class to publicly expose read-only access to a collection that the class can still update internally.

A read-only collection accepts the input collection in its constructor, to which it maintains a permanent reference. It doesn't take a static copy of the input collection, so subsequent changes to the input collection are visible through the read-only wrapper.

To illustrate, suppose your class wants to provide read-only public access to a list of strings called Names:

```
public class Test
{
  public List<string> Names { get; private set; }
}
```

This does only half the job. Although other types cannot reassign the Names property, they can still call Add, Remove, or Clear on the list. The ReadOnlyCollection<T> class resolves this:

```
public class Test
{
  List<string> names;
  public ReadOnlyCollection<string> Names { get; private set; }

  public Test()
  {
    names = new List<string>();
    Names = new ReadOnlyCollection<string> (names);
  }

  public void AddInternally() { names.Add ("test"); }
}
```

Now, only members within the Test class can alter the list of names:

```
Test t = new Test();

Console.WriteLine (t.Names.Count);        // 0
t.AddInternally();
Console.WriteLine (t.Names.Count);        // 1

t.Names.Add ("test");                     // Compiler error
((IList<string>) t.Names).Add ("test");   // NotSupportedException
```

Plugging in Equality and Order

In the sections "Equality Comparison" on page 267 and "Order Comparison" on page 278 in Chapter 6, we described the standard .NET protocols that make a type equatable, hashable, and comparable. A type that implements these protocols can function correctly in a dictionary or sorted list "out of the box." More specifically:

- A type for which Equals and GetHashCode return meaningful results can be used as a key in a Dictionary or Hashtable.

- A type that implements IComparable /IComparable<T> can be used as a key in any of the *sorted* dictionaries or lists.

A type's default equating or comparison implementation typically reflects what is most "natural" for that type. Sometimes, however, the default behavior is not what you want. You might need a dictionary whose string -type key is treated case-insensitively. Or you might want a sorted list of customers, sorted by each customer's postcode. For this reason, the .NET Framework also defines a matching set of "plug-in" protocols. The plug-in protocols achieve two things:

- They allow you to switch in alternative equating or comparison behavior.

- They allow you to use a dictionary or sorted collection with a key type that's not intrinsically equatable or comparable.

The plug-in protocols consist of the following interfaces:

IEqualityComparer *and* IEqualityComparer<T>
- Performs plug-in *equality comparison and hashing*
- Recognized by Hashtable and Dictionary

IComparer *and* IComparer<T>
- Performs plug-in *order comparison*
- Recognized by the sorted dictionaries and collections; also, Array.Sort

Each interface comes in both generic and nongeneric forms. The IEqualityComparer interfaces also have a default implementation in a class called EqualityComparer.

In addition, in Framework 4.0 we got two new interfaces called IStructuralEquata
ble and IStructuralComparable that allow for the option of structural comparisons on classes and arrays.

IEqualityComparer and EqualityComparer

An equality comparer switches in nondefault equality and hashing behavior, primarily for the Dictionary and Hashtable classes.

Recall the requirements of a hashtable-based dictionary. It needs answers to two
questions for any given key:

- Is it the same as another?
- What is its integer hashcode?

An equality comparer answers these questions by implementing the IEqualityCom
parer interfaces:

```
public interface IEqualityComparer<T>
{
   bool Equals (T x, T y);
   int GetHashCode (T obj);
}

public interface IEqualityComparer      // Nongeneric version
{
   bool Equals (object x, object y);
   int GetHashCode (object obj);
}
```

To write a custom comparer, you implement one or both of these interfaces (implementing both gives maximum interoperability). As this is somewhat tedious, an
alternative is to subclass the abstract EqualityComparer class, defined as follows:

```
public abstract class EqualityComparer<T> : IEqualityComparer,
                                            IEqualityComparer<T>
{
   public abstract bool Equals (T x, T y);
   public abstract int GetHashCode (T obj);

   bool IEqualityComparer.Equals (object x, object y);
   int IEqualityComparer.GetHashCode (object obj);

   public static EqualityComparer<T> Default { get; }
}
```

EqualityComparer implements both interfaces; your job is simply to override the
two abstract methods.

The semantics for Equals and GetHashCode follow the same rules for
object.Equals and object.GetHashCode, described in Chapter 6. In the following

example, we define a `Customer` class with two fields, and then write an equality comparer that matches both the first and last names:

```
public class Customer
{
  public string LastName;
  public string FirstName;

  public Customer (string last, string first)
  {
    LastName = last;
    FirstName = first;
  }
}
public class LastFirstEqComparer : EqualityComparer <Customer>
{
  public override bool Equals (Customer x, Customer y)
    => x.LastName == y.LastName && x.FirstName == y.FirstName;

  public override int GetHashCode (Customer obj)
    => (obj.LastName + ";" + obj.FirstName).GetHashCode();
}
```

To illustrate how this works, we'll create two customers:

```
Customer c1 = new Customer ("Bloggs", "Joe");
Customer c2 = new Customer ("Bloggs", "Joe");
```

Because we've not overridden `object.Equals`, normal reference type equality semantics apply:

```
Console.WriteLine (c1 == c2);          // False
Console.WriteLine (c1.Equals (c2));    // False
```

The same default equality semantics apply when using these customers in a `Dictionary` without specifying an equality comparer:

```
var d = new Dictionary<Customer, string>();
d [c1] = "Joe";
Console.WriteLine (d.ContainsKey (c2));        // False
```

Now with the custom equality comparer:

```
var eqComparer = new LastFirstEqComparer();
var d = new Dictionary<Customer, string> (eqComparer);
d [c1] = "Joe";
Console.WriteLine (d.ContainsKey (c2));        // True
```

In this example, we would have to be careful not to change the customer's `First Name` or `LastName` while it was in use in the dictionary. Otherwise, its hashcode would change and the `Dictionary` would break.

EqualityComparer<T>.Default

Calling `EqualityComparer<T>.Default` returns a general-purpose equality comparer that can be used as an alternative to the static `object.Equals` method. The advantage is that first checks if T implements IEquatable<T> and if so, calls that implementation instead, avoiding the boxing overhead. This is particularly useful in generic methods:

```
static bool Foo<T> (T x, T y)
{
  bool same = EqualityComparer<T>.Default.Equals (x, y);
  ...
```

IComparer and Comparer

Comparers are used to switch in custom ordering logic for sorted dictionaries and collections.

Note that a comparer is useless to the unsorted dictionaries such as Dictionary and Hashtable—these require an IEqualityComparer to get hashcodes. Similarly, an equality comparer is useless for sorted dictionaries and collections.

Here are the IComparer interface definitions:

```
public interface IComparer
{
  int Compare(object x, object y);
}
public interface IComparer <in T>
{
  int Compare(T x, T y);
}
```

As with equality comparers, there's an abstract class you can subtype instead of implementing the interfaces:

```
public abstract class Comparer<T> : IComparer, IComparer<T>
{
  public static Comparer<T> Default { get; }

  public abstract int Compare (T x, T y);        // Implemented by you
  int IComparer.Compare (object x, object y);    // Implemented for you
}
```

The following example illustrates a class that describes a wish and a comparer that sorts wishes by priority:

```
class Wish
{
  public string Name;
  public int Priority;

  public Wish (string name, int priority)
  {
    Name = name;
    Priority = priority;
  }
}
```

```
class PriorityComparer : Comparer <Wish>
{
  public override int Compare (Wish x, Wish y)
  {
    if (object.Equals (x, y)) return 0;        // Fail-safe check
    return x.Priority.CompareTo (y.Priority);
  }
}
```

The object.Equals check ensures that we can never contradict the Equals method. Calling the static object.Equals method in this case is better than calling x.Equals because it still works if x is null!

Here's how our PriorityComparer is used to sort a List:

```
var wishList = new List<Wish>();
wishList.Add (new Wish ("Peace", 2));
wishList.Add (new Wish ("Wealth", 3));
wishList.Add (new Wish ("Love", 2));
wishList.Add (new Wish ("3 more wishes", 1));

wishList.Sort (new PriorityComparer());
foreach (Wish w in wishList) Console.Write (w.Name + " | ");

// OUTPUT: 3 more wishes | Love | Peace | Wealth |
```

In the next example, SurnameComparer allows you to sort surname strings in an order suitable for a phonebook listing:

```
class SurnameComparer : Comparer <string>
{
  string Normalize (string s)
  {
    s = s.Trim().ToUpper();
    if (s.StartsWith ("MC")) s = "MAC" + s.Substring (2);
    return s;
  }

  public override int Compare (string x, string y)
    => Normalize (x).CompareTo (Normalize (y));
}
```

Here's SurnameComparer in use in a sorted dictionary:

```
var dic = new SortedDictionary<string,string> (new SurnameComparer());
dic.Add ("MacPhail", "second!");
dic.Add ("MacWilliam", "third!");
dic.Add ("McDonald", "first!");

foreach (string s in dic.Values)
  Console.Write (s + " ");               // first! second! third!
```

Collections

StringComparer

StringComparer is a predefined plug-in class for equating and comparing strings, allowing you to specify language and case sensitivity. StringComparer implements both IEqualityComparer and IComparer (and their generic versions), so it can be used with any type of dictionary or sorted collection:

```
// CultureInfo is defined in System.Globalization

public abstract class StringComparer : IComparer, IComparer <string>,
                                       IEqualityComparer,
                                       IEqualityComparer <string>
{
  public abstract int Compare (string x, string y);
  public abstract bool Equals (string x, string y);
  public abstract int GetHashCode (string obj);

  public static StringComparer Create (CultureInfo culture,
                                       bool ignoreCase);
  public static StringComparer CurrentCulture { get; }
  public static StringComparer CurrentCultureIgnoreCase { get; }
  public static StringComparer InvariantCulture { get; }
  public static StringComparer InvariantCultureIgnoreCase { get; }
  public static StringComparer Ordinal { get; }
  public static StringComparer OrdinalIgnoreCase { get; }
}
```

Because StringComparer is abstract, you obtain instances via its static methods and properties. StringComparer.Ordinal mirrors the default behavior for string-equality comparison and StringComparer.CurrentCulture for order comparison.

In the following example, an ordinal case-insensitive dictionary is created, such that dict["Joe"] and dict["JOE"] mean the same thing:

```
var dict = new Dictionary<string, int> (StringComparer.OrdinalIgnoreCase);
```

In the next example, an array of names is sorted, using Australian English:

```
string[] names = { "Tom", "HARRY", "sheila" };
CultureInfo ci = new CultureInfo ("en-AU");
Array.Sort<string> (names, StringComparer.Create (ci, false));
```

The final example is a culture-aware version of the SurnameComparer we wrote in the previous section (to compare names suitable for a phonebook listing):

```
class SurnameComparer : Comparer <string>
{
  StringComparer strCmp;

  public SurnameComparer (CultureInfo ci)
  {
    // Create a case-sensitive, culture-sensitive string comparer
    strCmp = StringComparer.Create (ci, false);
  }
```

```
string Normalize (string s)
{
  s = s.Trim();
  if (s.ToUpper().StartsWith ("MC")) s = "MAC" + s.Substring (2);
  return s;
}

public override int Compare (string x, string y)
{
  // Directly call Compare on our culture-aware StringComparer
  return strCmp.Compare (Normalize (x), Normalize (y));
}
}
```

IStructuralEquatable and IStructuralComparable

As we said in the previous chapter, structs implement *structural comparison* by default: two structs are equal if all of their fields are equal. Sometimes, however, structural equality and order comparison are useful as plug-in options on other types as well—such as arrays and tuples. Framework 4.0 introduced two new interfaces to help with this:

```
public interface IStructuralEquatable
{
  bool Equals (object other, IEqualityComparer comparer);
  int GetHashCode (IEqualityComparer comparer);
}

public interface IStructuralComparable
{
  int CompareTo (object other, IComparer comparer);
}
```

The IEqualityComparer/IComparer that you pass in are applied to each individual element in the composite object. We can demonstrate this using arrays and tuples, both of which implement these interfaces. In the following example, we compare two arrays for equality, first using the default Equals method, then using IStructur alEquatable's version:

```
int[] a1 = { 1, 2, 3 };
int[] a2 = { 1, 2, 3 };
IStructuralEquatable se1 = a1;
Console.Write (a1.Equals (a2));                                    // False
Console.Write (se1.Equals (a2, EqualityComparer<int>.Default));   // True
```

Here's another example:

```
string[] a1 = "the quick brown fox".Split();
string[] a2 = "THE QUICK BROWN FOX".Split();
IStructuralEquatable se1 = a1;
bool isTrue = se1.Equals (a2, StringComparer.InvariantCultureIgnoreCase);
```

Tuples work in the same way:

```
var t1 = Tuple.Create (1, "foo");
var t2 = Tuple.Create (1, "FOO");
IStructuralEquatable se1 = t1;
bool isTrue = se1.Equals (t2, StringComparer.InvariantCultureIgnoreCase);
IStructuralComparable sc1 = t1;
int zero = sc1.CompareTo (t2, StringComparer.InvariantCultureIgnoreCase);
```

The difference with tuples, though, is that their *default* equality and order comparison implementations also apply structural comparisons:

```
var t1 = Tuple.Create (1, "FOO");
var t2 = Tuple.Create (1, "FOO");
Console.WriteLine (t1.Equals (t2));    // True
```

8

LINQ Queries

LINQ, or Language Integrated Query, is a set of language and framework features for writing structured type-safe queries over local object collections and remote data sources. LINQ was introduced in C# 3.0 and Framework 3.5.

LINQ enables you to query any collection implementing IEnumerable<T>, whether an array, list, or XML DOM, as well as remote data sources, such as tables in a SQL Server database. LINQ offers the benefits of both compile-time type checking and dynamic query composition.

This chapter describes the LINQ architecture and the fundamentals of writing queries. All core types are defined in the System.Linq and System.Linq.Expressions namespaces.

 The examples in this and the following two chapters are preloaded into an interactive querying called LINQPad. You can download LINQPad from *www.linqpad.net*.

Getting Started

The basic units of data in LINQ are *sequences* and *elements*. A sequence is any object that implements IEnumerable<T> and an element is each item in the sequence. In the following example, names is a sequence, and "Tom", "Dick", and "Harry" are elements:

```
string[] names = { "Tom", "Dick", "Harry" };
```

We call this a *local sequence* because it represents a local collection of objects in memory.

A *query operator* is a method that transforms a sequence. A typical query operator accepts an *input sequence* and emits a transformed *output sequence*. In the Enumerable class in System.Linq, there are around 40 query operators—all implemented as static extension methods. These are called *standard query operators*.

Queries that operate over local sequences are called local queries or *LINQ-to-objects* queries.

LINQ also supports sequences that can be dynamically fed from a remote data source, such as a SQL Server database. These sequences additionally implement the IQueryable<T> interface and are supported through a matching set of standard query operators in the Queryable class. We discuss this further in the section "Interpreted Queries" on page 364 later in this chapter.

A query is an expression that, when enumerated, transforms sequences with query operators. The simplest query comprises one input sequence and one operator. For instance, we can apply the Where operator on a simple array to extract those whose length is at least four characters as follows:

```
string[] names = { "Tom", "Dick", "Harry" };
IEnumerable<string> filteredNames = System.Linq.Enumerable.Where
                                     (names, n => n.Length >= 4);
foreach (string n in filteredNames)
  Console.WriteLine (n);

Dick
Harry
```

Because the standard query operators are implemented as extension methods, we can call Where directly on names—as though it were an instance method:

```
IEnumerable<string> filteredNames = names.Where (n => n.Length >= 4);
```

For this to compile, you must import the System.Linq namespace. Here's a complete example:

```
using System;
usign System.Collections.Generic;
using System.Linq;

class LinqDemo
{
  static void Main()
  {
    string[] names = { "Tom", "Dick", "Harry" };

    IEnumerable<string> filteredNames = names.Where (n => n.Length >= 4);
    foreach (string name in filteredNames) Console.WriteLine (name);
  }
}

Dick
Harry
```

We could further shorten our code by implicitly typing `filter edNames`:

```
var filteredNames = names.Where (n => n.Length >= 4);
```

This can hinder readability, however, particularly outside of an IDE, where there are no tool tips to help.

In this chapter, we avoid implicitly typing query results except when it's mandatory (as we'll see later, in the section "Projection Strategies" on page 362.), or when a query's type is irrelevant to an example.

Most query operators accept a lambda expression as an argument. The lambda expression helps guide and shape the query. In our example, the lambda expression is as follows:

```
n => n.Length >= 4
```

The input argument corresponds to an input element. In this case, the input argument n represents each name in the array and is of type `string`. The `Where` operator requires that the lambda expression return a `bool` value, which if `true`, indicates that the element should be included in the output sequence. Here's its signature:

```
public static IEnumerable<TSource> Where<TSource>
  (this IEnumerable<TSource> source, Func<TSource,bool> predicate)
```

The following query extracts all names that contain the letter "a":

```
IEnumerable<string> filteredNames = names.Where (n => n.Contains ("a"));

foreach (string name in filteredNames)
  Console.WriteLine (name);          // Harry
```

So far, we've built queries using extension methods and lambda expressions. As we'll see shortly, this strategy is highly composable in that it allows the chaining of query operators. In the book, we refer to this as *fluent syntax*.[1] C# also provides another syntax for writing queries, called *query expression* syntax. Here's our preceding query written as a query expression:

```
IEnumerable<string> filteredNames = from n in names
                                    where n.Contains ("a")
                                    select n;
```

Fluent syntax and query syntax are complementary. In the following two sections, we explore each in more detail.

Fluent Syntax

Fluent syntax is the most flexible and fundamental. In this section, we describe how to chain query operators to form more complex queries—and show why extension

---

1 The term is based on Eric Evans & Martin Fowler's work on fluent interfaces.

methods are important to this process. We also describe how to formulate lambda expressions for a query operator and introduce several new query operators.

Chaining Query Operators

In the preceding section, we showed two simple queries, each comprising a single query operator. To build more complex queries, you append additional query operators to the expression, creating a chain. To illustrate, the following query extracts all strings containing the letter "a", sorts them by length, and then converts the results to uppercase:

```
using System;
using System.Collections.Generic;
using System.Linq;

class LinqDemo
{
  static void Main()
  {
    string[] names = { "Tom", "Dick", "Harry", "Mary", "Jay" };

    IEnumerable<string> query = names
      .Where   (n => n.Contains ("a"))
      .OrderBy (n => n.Length)
      .Select  (n => n.ToUpper());

    foreach (string name in query) Console.WriteLine (name);
  }
}

JAY
MARY
HARRY
```

> The variable, n, in our example, is privately scoped to each of the lambda expressions. We can reuse the identifier n for the same reason we can reuse the identifier c in the following method:
>
> ```
> void Test()
> {
>   foreach (char c in "string1") Console.Write (c);
>   foreach (char c in "string2") Console.Write (c);
>   foreach (char c in "string3") Console.Write (c);
> }
> ```

Where, OrderBy, and Select are standard query operators that resolve to extension methods in the Enumerable class (if you import the System.Linq namespace).

We already introduced the Where operator, which emits a filtered version of the input sequence. The OrderBy operator emits a sorted version of its input sequence; the Select method emits a sequence where each input element is transformed or *projected* with a given lambda expression (n.ToUpper(), in this case). Data flows from left to right through the chain of operators, so the data is first filtered, then sorted, then projected.

 A query operator never alters the input sequence; instead, it returns a new sequence. This is consistent with the *functional programming* paradigm, from which LINQ was inspired.

Here are the signatures of each of these extension methods (with the `OrderBy` signature simplified slightly):

```
public static IEnumerable<TSource> Where<TSource>
  (this IEnumerable<TSource> source, Func<TSource,bool> predicate)

public static IEnumerable<TSource> OrderBy<TSource,TKey>
  (this IEnumerable<TSource> source, Func<TSource,TKey> keySelector)

public static IEnumerable<TResult> Select<TSource,TResult>
  (this IEnumerable<TSource> source, Func<TSource,TResult> selector)
```

When query operators are chained as in this example, the output sequence of one operator is the input sequence of the next. The complete query resembles a production line of conveyor belts, as illustrated in Figure 8-1.

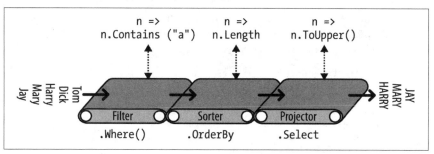

Figure 8-1. Chaining query operators

We can construct the identical query *progressively*, as follows:

```
// You must import the System.Linq namespace for this to compile:

IEnumerable<string> filtered   = names    .Where   (n => n.Contains ("a"));
IEnumerable<string> sorted     = filtered.OrderBy (n => n.Length);
IEnumerable<string> finalQuery = sorted   .Select  (n => n.ToUpper());
```

`finalQuery` is compositionally identical to the query we had constructed previously. Further, each intermediate step also comprises a valid query that we can execute:

```
foreach (string name in filtered)
  Console.Write (name + "|");        // Harry|Mary|Jay|

Console.WriteLine();
foreach (string name in sorted)
  Console.Write (name + "|");        // Jay|Mary|Harry|
```

```
Console.WriteLine();
foreach (string name in finalQuery)
  Console.Write (name + "|");        // JAY|MARY|HARRY|
```

Why extension methods are important

Instead of using extension method syntax, you can use conventional static method syntax to call the query operators. For example:

```
IEnumerable<string> filtered = Enumerable.Where (names,
                                      n => n.Contains ("a"));
IEnumerable<string> sorted = Enumerable.OrderBy (filtered, n => n.Length);
IEnumerable<string> finalQuery = Enumerable.Select (sorted,
                                      n => n.ToUpper());
```

This is, in fact, how the compiler translates extension method calls. Shunning extension methods comes at a cost, however, if you want to write a query in a single statement as we did earlier. Let's revisit the single-statement query—first in extension method syntax:

```
IEnumerable<string> query = names.Where   (n => n.Contains ("a"))
                                 .OrderBy (n => n.Length)
                                 .Select  (n => n.ToUpper());
```

Its natural linear shape reflects the left-to-right flow of data, as well as keeping lambda expressions alongside their query operators (*infix* notation). Without extension methods, the query loses its *fluency*:

```
IEnumerable<string> query =
  Enumerable.Select (
    Enumerable.OrderBy (
      Enumerable.Where (
        names, n => n.Contains ("a")
      ), n => n.Length
    ), n => n.ToUpper()
  );
```

Composing Lambda Expressions

In previous examples, we fed the following lambda expression to the Where operator:

```
n => n.Contains ("a")      // Input type=string, return type=bool.
```

 A lambda expression that takes a value and returns a bool is called a *predicate*.

The purpose of the lambda expression depends on the particular query operator. With the Where operator, it indicates whether an element should be included in the output sequence. In the case of the OrderBy operator, the lambda expression maps each element in the input sequence to its sorting key. With the Select operator, the lambda expression determines how each element in the input sequence is transformed before being fed to the output sequence.

A lambda expression in a query operator always works on individual elements in the input sequence—not the sequence as a whole.

The query operator evaluates your lambda expression upon demand—typically once per element in the input sequence. Lambda expressions allow you to feed your own logic into the query operators. This makes the query operators versatile—as well as being simple under the hood. Here's a complete implementation of `Enumerable.Where`, exception handling aside:

```
public static IEnumerable<TSource> Where<TSource>
  (this IEnumerable<TSource> source, Func<TSource,bool> predicate)
{
  foreach (TSource element in source)
    if (predicate (element))
      yield return element;
}
```

Lambda expressions and Func signatures

The standard query operators utilize generic `Func` delegates. `Func` is a family of general-purpose generic delegates in the `System` namespace, defined with the following intent:

> The type arguments in `Func` appear in the same order they do in lambda expressions.

Hence, `Func<TSource,bool>` matches a `TSource=>bool` lambda expression: one that accepts a `TSource` argument and returns a `bool` value.

Similarly, `Func<TSource,TResult>` matches a `TSource=>TResult` lambda expression.

The `Func` delegates are listed in the section "Lambda Expressions" on page 143 in Chapter 4.

Lambda expressions and element typing

The standard query operators use the following type parameter names:

Generic type letter	Meaning
TSource	Element type for the input sequence
TResult	Element type for the output sequence—if different from TSource
TKey	Element type for the *key* used in sorting, grouping, or joining

`TSource` is determined by the input sequence. `TResult` and `TKey` are typically *inferred from your lambda expression.*

For example, consider the signature of the `Select` query operator:

```
public static IEnumerable<TResult> Select<TSource,TResult>
  (this IEnumerable<TSource> source, Func<TSource,TResult> selector)
```

Func<TSource,TResult> matches a TSource=>TResult lambda expression: one that maps an *input element* to an *output element*. TSource and TResult can be different types, so the lambda expression can change the type of each element. Further, the lambda expression *determines the output sequence type*. The following query uses Select to transform string type elements to integer type elements:

```
string[] names = { "Tom", "Dick", "Harry", "Mary", "Jay" };
IEnumerable<int> query = names.Select (n => n.Length);

foreach (int length in query)
  Console.Write (length + "|");     // 3|4|5|4|3|
```

The compiler can *infer* the type of TResult from the return value of the lambda expression. In this case, n.Length returns an int value, so TResultis inferred to be of type int.

The Where query operator is simpler and requires no type inference for the output, since input and output elements are of the same type. This makes sense because the operator merely filters elements; it does not *transform* them:

```
public static IEnumerable<TSource> Where<TSource>
  (this IEnumerable<TSource> source, Func<TSource,bool> predicate)
```

Finally, consider the signature of the OrderBy operator:

```
// Slightly simplified:
public static IEnumerable<TSource> OrderBy<TSource,TKey>
  (this IEnumerable<TSource> source, Func<TSource,TKey> keySelector)
```

Func<TSource,TKey> maps an input element to a *sorting key*. TKey is inferred from your lambda expression and is separate from the input and output element types. For instance, we could choose to sort a list of names by length (int key) or alphabetically (string key):

```
string[] names = { "Tom", "Dick", "Harry", "Mary", "Jay" };
IEnumerable<string> sortedByLength, sortedAlphabetically;
sortedByLength       = names.OrderBy (n => n.Length);   // int key
sortedAlphabetically = names.OrderBy (n => n);          // string key
```

 You can call the query operators in Enumerable with traditional delegates that refer to methods instead of lambda expressions. This approach is effective in simplifying certain kinds of local queries—particularly with LINQ to XML—and is demonstrated in Chapter 10. It doesn't work with IQueryable<T>-based sequences, however (e.g., when querying a database), because the operators in Queryable require lambda expressions in order to emit expression trees. We discuss this later in the section "Interpreted Queries" on page 364.

Natural Ordering

The original ordering of elements within an input sequence is significant in LINQ. Some query operators rely on this ordering, such as Take, Skip, and Reverse.

The Take operator outputs the first x elements, discarding the rest:

```
int[] numbers    = { 10, 9, 8, 7, 6 };
IEnumerable<int> firstThree = numbers.Take (3);      // { 10, 9, 8 }
```

The Skip operator ignores the first x elements and outputs the rest:

```
IEnumerable<int> lastTwo    = numbers.Skip (3);      // { 7, 6 }
```

Reverse does exactly as it says:

```
IEnumerable<int> reversed   = numbers.Reverse();     // { 6, 7, 8, 9, 10 }
```

With local queries (LINQ-to-objects), operators such as Where and Select preserve the original ordering of the input sequence (as do all other query operators, except for those that specifically change the ordering).

Other Operators

Not all query operators return a sequence. The *element* operators extract one element from the input sequence; examples are First, Last, and ElementAt:

```
int[] numbers     = { 10, 9, 8, 7, 6 };
int firstNumber   = numbers.First();                         // 10
int lastNumber    = numbers.Last();                          // 6
int secondNumber  = numbers.ElementAt(1);                    // 9
int secondLowest  = numbers.OrderBy(n=>n).Skip(1).First();   // 7
```

The *aggregation* operators return a scalar value; usually of numeric type:

```
int count = numbers.Count();        // 5;
int min = numbers.Min();            // 6;
```

The *quantifiers* return a bool value:

```
bool hasTheNumberNine = numbers.Contains (9);          // true
bool hasMoreThanZeroElements = numbers.Any();          // true
bool hasAnOddElement = numbers.Any (n => n % 2 != 0);  // true
```

Because these operators return a single element, you don't usually call further query operators on their result unless that element itself is a collection.

Some query operators accept two input sequences. Examples are Concat, which appends one sequence to another, and Union, which does the same but with duplicates removed:

```
int[] seq1 = { 1, 2, 3 };
int[] seq2 = { 3, 4, 5 };
IEnumerable<int> concat = seq1.Concat (seq2);    // { 1, 2, 3, 3, 4, 5 }
IEnumerable<int> union  = seq1.Union (seq2);     // { 1, 2, 3, 4, 5 }
```

The joining operators also fall into this category. Chapter 9 covers all the query operators in detail.

Query Expressions

C# provides a syntactic shortcut for writing LINQ queries, called *query expressions*. Contrary to popular belief, a query expression is not a means of embedding SQL into C#. In fact, the design of query expressions was inspired primarily by *list comprehensions* from functional programming languages such as LISP and Haskell, although SQL had a cosmetic influence.

 In this book, we refer to query expression syntax simply as "query syntax."

In the preceding section, we wrote a fluent-syntax query to extract strings containing the letter "a", sorted by length and converted to uppercase. Here's the same thing in query syntax:

```
using System;
using System.Collections.Generic;
using System.Linq;

class LinqDemo
{
  static void Main()
  {
    string[] names = { "Tom", "Dick", "Harry", "Mary", "Jay" };

    IEnumerable<string> query =
      from    n in names
      where   n.Contains ("a")    // Filter elements
      orderby n.Length            // Sort elements
      select  n.ToUpper();        // Translate each element (project)

    foreach (string name in query) Console.WriteLine (name);
  }
}

JAY
MARY
HARRY
```

Query expressions always start with a `from` clause and end with either a `select` or `group` clause. The `from` clause declares a *range variable* (in this case, n), which you can think of as traversing the input sequence—rather like `foreach`. Figure 8-2 illustrates the complete syntax as a railroad diagram.

To read this diagram, start at the left and then proceed along the track as if you were a train. For instance, after the mandatory from clause, you can optionally include an orderby, where, let or join clause. After that, you can either continue with a select or group clause, or go back and include another from, orderby, where, let or join clause.

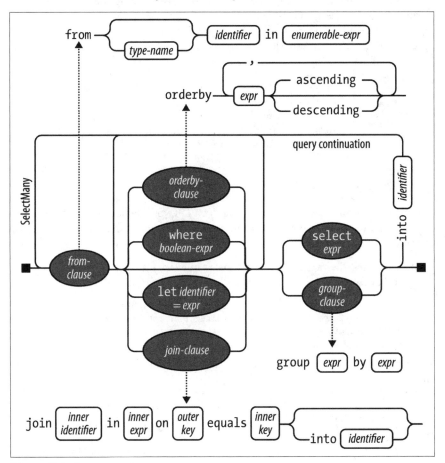

Figure 8-2. Query syntax

The compiler processes a query expression by translating it into fluent syntax. It does this in a fairly mechanical fashion—much like it translates foreach statements into calls to GetEnumerator and MoveNext. This means that anything you can write in query syntax you can also write in fluent syntax. The compiler (initially) translates our example query into the following:

```
IEnumerable<string> query = names.Where   (n => n.Contains ("a"))
                                  .OrderBy (n => n.Length)
                                  .Select  (n => n.ToUpper());
```

LINQ
Queries

The Where, OrderBy, and Select operators then resolve using the same rules that would apply if the query were written in fluent syntax. In this case, they bind to extension methods in the Enumerable class, since the System.Linq namespace is imported and names implements IEnumerable<string>. The compiler doesn't specifically favor the Enumerable class, however, when translating query expressions. You can think of the compiler as mechanically injecting the words "Where," "OrderBy," and "Select" into the statement, and then compiling it as though you'd typed the method names yourself. This offers flexibility in how they resolve. The operators in the database queries that we'll write in later sections, for instance, will bind instead to extension methods in Queryable.

If we remove the using System.Linq directive from our program, the query would not compile, since the Where, OrderBy, and Select methods would have nowhere to bind. Query expressions *cannot compile* unless you import System.Linq or another namespace with an implementation of these query methods.

Range Variables

The identifier immediately following the from keyword syntax is called the *range variable*. A range variable refers to the current element in the sequence that the operation is to be performed on.

In our examples, the range variable n appears in every clause in the query. And yet, the variable actually enumerates over a *different* sequence with each clause:

```
from    n in names          // n is our range variable
where   n.Contains ("a")    // n = directly from the array
orderby n.Length            // n = subsequent to being filtered
select  n.ToUpper()         // n = subsequent to being sorted
```

This becomes clear when we examine the compiler's mechanical translation to fluent syntax:

```
names.Where   (n => n.Contains ("a"))    // Locally scoped n
     .OrderBy (n => n.Length)            // Locally scoped n
     .Select  (n => n.ToUpper())         // Locally scoped n
```

As you can see, each instance of n is scoped privately to its own lambda expression.

Query expressions also let you introduce new range variables, via the following clauses:

- let
- into
- An additional from clause
- join

We cover these later in this chapter in the section "Composition Strategies" on page 358, and also in Chapter 9, in the sections "Projecting" on page 394 and "Joining" on page 394.

Query Syntax Versus SQL Syntax

Query expressions look superficially like SQL, yet the two are very different. A LINQ query boils down to a C# expression, and so follows standard C# rules. For example, with LINQ, you cannot use a variable before you declare it. In SQL, you can reference a table alias in the SELECT clause before defining it in a FROM clause.

A subquery in LINQ is just another C# expression and so requires no special syntax. Subqueries in SQL are subject to special rules.

With LINQ, data logically flows from left to right through the query. With SQL, the order is less well-structured with regard data flow.

A LINQ query comprises a conveyor belt, or *pipeline*, of operators that accept and emit sequences whose element order can matter. A SQL query comprises a *network* of clauses that work mostly with *unordered sets*.

Query Syntax Versus Fluent Syntax

Query and fluent syntax each have advantages.

Query syntax is simpler for queries that involve any of the following:

- A let clause for introducing a new variable alongside the range variable
- SelectMany, Join, or GroupJoin, followed by an outer range variable reference

(We describe the let clause in the later section, "Composition Strategies" on page 358; we describe SelectMany, Join, and GroupJoin in Chapter 9.)

The middle ground is queries that involve the simple use of Where, OrderBy, and Select. Either syntax works well; the choice here is largely personal.

For queries that comprise a single operator, fluent syntax is shorter and less cluttered.

Finally, there are many operators that have no keyword in query syntax. These require that you use fluent syntax—at least in part. This means any operator outside of the following:

```
Where, Select, SelectMany
OrderBy, ThenBy, OrderByDescending, ThenByDescending
GroupBy, Join, GroupJoin
```

Mixed-Syntax Queries

If a query operator has no query-syntax support, you can mix query syntax and fluent syntax. The only restriction is that each query-syntax component must be complete (i.e., start with a `from` clause and end with a `select` or `group` clause).

Assuming this array declaration:

```
string[] names = { "Tom", "Dick", "Harry", "Mary", "Jay" };
```

the following example counts the number of names containing the letter "a":

```
int matches = (from n in names where n.Contains ("a") select n).Count();
// 3
```

The next query obtains the first name in alphabetical order:

```
string first = (from n in names orderby n select n).First();   // Dick
```

The mixed-syntax approach is sometimes beneficial in more complex queries. With these simple examples, however, we could stick to fluent syntax throughout without penalty:

```
int matches = names.Where (n => n.Contains ("a")).Count();   // 3
string first = names.OrderBy (n => n).First();               // Dick
```

> There are times when mixed-syntax queries offer by far the highest "bang for the buck" in terms of function and simplicity. It's important not to unilaterally favor either query or fluent syntax; otherwise, you'll be unable to write mixed-syntax queries without feeling a sense of failure!

Where applicable, the remainder of this chapter will show key concepts in both fluent and query syntax.

Deferred Execution

An important feature of most query operators is that they execute not when constructed, but when *enumerated* (in other words, when `MoveNext` is called on its enumerator). Consider the following query:

```
var numbers = new List<int>();
numbers.Add (1);

IEnumerable<int> query = numbers.Select (n => n * 10);   // Build query

numbers.Add (2);                 // Sneak in an extra element

foreach (int n in query)
  Console.Write (n + "|");       // 10|20|
```

The extra number that we sneaked into the list *after* constructing the query is included in the result, since it's not until the `foreach` statement runs that any filtering or sorting takes place. This is called *deferred* or *lazy* execution and is the same as what happens with delegates:

```
Action a = () => Console.WriteLine ("Foo");
// We've not written anything to the Console yet. Now let's run it:
a();  // Deferred execution!
```

All standard query operators provide deferred execution, with the following exceptions:

- Operators that return a single element or scalar value, such as `First` or `Count`
- The following *conversion operators*:

  `ToArray, ToList, ToDictionary, ToLookup`

These operators cause immediate query execution because their result types have no mechanism for providing deferred execution. The `Count` method, for instance, returns a simple integer, which doesn't then get enumerated. The following query is executed immediately:

```
int matches = numbers.Where (n => n < 2).Count();    // 1
```

Deferred execution is important because it decouples query *construction* from query *execution*. This allows you to construct a query in several steps, as well as making database queries possible.

 Subqueries provide another level of indirection. Everything in a subquery is subject to deferred execution—including aggregation and conversion methods. We describe this in the section "Subqueries" on page 355 later in this chapter.

Reevaluation

Deferred execution has another consequence: a deferred execution query is reevaluated when you re-enumerate:

```
var numbers = new List<int>() { 1, 2 };

IEnumerable<int> query = numbers.Select (n => n * 10);
foreach (int n in query) Console.Write (n + "|");    // 10|20|

numbers.Clear();
foreach (int n in query) Console.Write (n + "|");    // <nothing>
```

There are a couple of reasons why reevaluation is sometimes disadvantageous:

- Sometimes you want to "freeze" or cache the results at a certain point in time.
- Some queries are computationally intensive (or rely on querying a remote database), so you don't want to unnecessarily repeat them.

You can defeat reevaluation by calling a conversion operator, such as `ToArray` or `ToList`. `ToArray` copies the output of a query to an array; `ToList` copies to a generic `List<T>`:

```
var numbers = new List<int>() { 1, 2 };

List<int> timesTen = numbers
  .Select (n => n * 10)

  .ToList();                        // Executes immediately into a List<int>

numbers.Clear();
Console.WriteLine (timesTen.Count);     // Still 2
```

Captured Variables

If your query's lambda expressions *capture* outer variables, the query will honor the value of those variables at the time the query *runs*:

```
int[] numbers = { 1, 2 };

int factor = 10;
IEnumerable<int> query = numbers.Select (n => n * factor);
factor = 20;
foreach (int n in query) Console.Write (n + "|");    // 20|40|
```

This can be a trap when building up a query within a for loop. For example, suppose we wanted to remove all vowels from a string. The following, although inefficient, gives the correct result:

```
IEnumerable<char> query = "Not what you might expect";

query = query.Where (c => c != 'a');
query = query.Where (c => c != 'e');
query = query.Where (c => c != 'i');
query = query.Where (c => c != 'o');
query = query.Where (c => c != 'u');

foreach (char c in query) Console.Write (c);  // Nt wht y mght xpct
```

Now watch what happens when we refactor this with a for loop:

```
IEnumerable<char> query = "Not what you might expect";
string vowels = "aeiou";

for (int i = 0; i < vowels.Length; i++)
  query = query.Where (c => c != vowels[i]);

foreach (char c in query) Console.Write (c);
```

An IndexOutOfRangeException is thrown upon enumerating the query, because as we saw in Chapter 4 (see "Capturing Outer Variables" on page 144), the compiler scopes the iteration variable in the for loop as if it was declared *outside* the loop. Hence each closure captures the *same* variable (i) whose value is 5 when the query is actually enumerated. To solve this, you must assign the loop variable to another variable declared *inside* the statement block:

```
for (int i = 0; i < vowels.Length; i++)
{
  char vowel = vowels[i];
  query = query.Where (c => c != vowel);
}
```

This forces a fresh local variable to be captured on each loop iteration.

From C# 5.0, another way to solve the problem is to replace the `for` loop with a `foreach` loop:

```
foreach (char vowel in vowels)
    query = query.Where (c => c != vowel);
```

This works in C# 5.0 but fails in earlier versions of C# for the reasons we described in Chapter 4.

How Deferred Execution Works

Query operators provide deferred execution by returning *decorator* sequences.

Unlike a traditional collection class, such as an array or linked list, a decorator sequence (in general) has no backing structure of its own to store elements. Instead, it wraps another sequence that you supply at runtime, to which it maintains a permanent dependency. Whenever you request data from a decorator, it in turn must request data from the wrapped input sequence.

The query operator's transformation constitutes the "decoration." If the output sequence performed no transformation, it would be a *proxy* rather than a decorator.

Calling `Where` merely constructs the decorator wrapper sequence, holding a reference to the input sequence, the lambda expression, and any other arguments supplied. The input sequence is enumerated only when the decorator is enumerated.

Figure 8-3 illustrates the composition of the following query:

```
IEnumerable<int> lessThanTen = new int[] { 5, 12, 3 }.Where (n => n < 10);
```

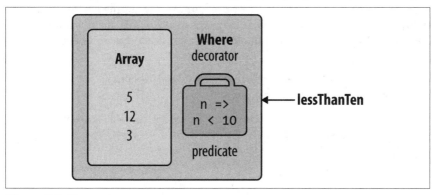

Figure 8-3. Decorator sequence

When you enumerate lessThanTen, you're, in effect, querying the array through the Where decorator.

The good news—if you ever want to write your own query operator—is that implementing a decorator sequence is easy with a C# iterator. Here's how you can write your own Select method:

```
public static IEnumerable<TResult> Select<TSource,TResult>
  (this IEnumerable<TSource> source, Func<TSource,TResult> selector)
{
  foreach (TSource element in source)
    yield return selector (element);
}
```

This method is an iterator by virtue of the yield return statement. Functionally, it's a shortcut for the following:

```
public static IEnumerable<TResult> Select<TSource,TResult>
  (this IEnumerable<TSource> source, Func<TSource,TResult> selector)
{
  return new SelectSequence (source, selector);
}
```

where SelectSequence is a (compiler-written) class whose enumerator encapsulates the logic in the iterator method.

Hence, when you call an operator such as Select or Where, you're doing nothing more than instantiating an enumerable class that decorates the input sequence.

Chaining Decorators

Chaining query operators creates a layering of decorators. Consider the following query:

```
IEnumerable<int> query = new int[] { 5, 12, 3 }.Where   (n => n < 10)
                                               .OrderBy (n => n)
                                               .Select  (n => n * 10);
```

Each query operator instantiates a new decorator that wraps the previous sequence (rather like a Russian nesting doll). The object model of this query is illustrated in Figure 8-4. Note that this object model is fully constructed prior to any enumeration.

When you enumerate query, you're querying the original array, transformed through a layering or chain of decorators.

 Adding ToList onto the end of this query would cause the preceding operators to execute right away, collapsing the whole object model into a single list.

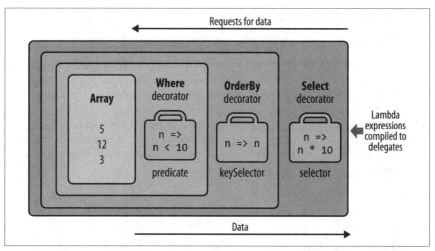

Figure 8-4. Layered decorator sequences

Figure 8-5 shows the same object composition in UML syntax. Select's decorator references the OrderBy decorator, which references Where's decorator, which references the array. A feature of deferred execution is that you build the identical object model if you compose the query progressively:

```
IEnumerable<int>
   source    = new int[] { 5, 12, 3 },
   filtered  = source   .Where   (n => n < 10),
   sorted    = filtered .OrderBy (n => n),
   query     = sorted   .Select  (n => n * 10);
```

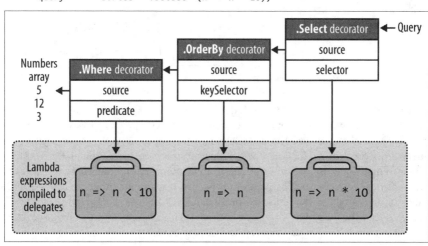

Figure 8-5. UML decorator composition

How Queries Are Executed

Here are the results of enumerating the preceding query:

```
foreach (int n in query) Console.WriteLine (n);
```

```
30
50
```

Behind the scenes, the `foreach` calls `GetEnumerator` on `Select`'s decorator (the last or outermost operator), which kicks everything off. The result is a chain of enumerators that structurally mirrors the chain of decorator sequences. Figure 8-6 illustrates the flow of execution as enumeration proceeds.

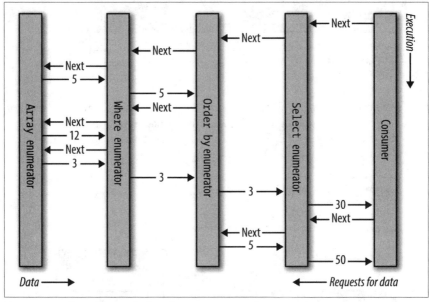

Figure 8-6. Execution of a local query

In the first section of this chapter, we depicted a query as a production line of conveyor belts. Extending this analogy, we can say a LINQ query is a lazy production line where the conveyor belts roll elements only upon *demand*. Constructing a query constructs a production line—with everything in place—but with nothing rolling. Then when the consumer requests an element (enumerates over the query), the rightmost conveyor belt activates; this in turn triggers the others to roll—as and when input sequence elements are needed. LINQ follows a demand-driven *pull* model, rather than a supply-driven *push* model. This is important—as we'll see later —in allowing LINQ to scale to querying SQL databases.

Subqueries

A subquery is a query contained within another query's lambda expression. The following example uses a subquery to sort musicians by their last name:

```
string[] musos =
  { "David Gilmour", "Roger Waters", "Rick Wright", "Nick Mason" };

IEnumerable<string> query = musos.OrderBy (m => m.Split().Last());
```

m.Split converts each string into a collection of words, upon which we then call the Last query operator. m.Split().Last is the subquery; query references the *outer query*.

Subqueries are permitted because you can put any valid C# expression on the right-hand side of a lambda. A subquery is simply another C# expression. This means that the rules for subqueries are a consequence of the rules for lambda expressions (and the behavior of query operators in general).

> The term *subquery*, in the general sense, has a broader meaning. For the purpose of describing LINQ, we use the term only for a query referenced from within the lambda expression of another query. In a query expression, a subquery amounts to a query referenced from an expression in any clause except the from clause.

A subquery is privately scoped to the enclosing expression and is able to reference parameters in the outer lambda expression (or range variables in a query expression).

m.Split().Last is a very simple subquery. The next query retrieves all strings in an array whose length matches that of the shortest string:

```
string[] names = { "Tom", "Dick", "Harry", "Mary", "Jay" };

IEnumerable<string> outerQuery = names
  .Where (n => n.Length == names.OrderBy (n2 => n2.Length)
                                .Select (n2 => n2.Length).First());
```

```
Tom, Jay
```

Here's the same thing as a query expression:

```
IEnumerable<string> outerQuery =
  from   n in names
  where  n.Length ==
          (from n2 in names orderby n2.Length select n2.Length).First()
  select n;
```

Because the outer range variable (n) is in scope for a subquery, we cannot reuse n as the subquery's range variable.

A subquery is executed whenever the enclosing lambda expression is evaluated. This means a subquery is executed upon demand, at the discretion of the outer query. You could say that execution proceeds from the *outside in*. Local queries follow this model literally; interpreted queries (e.g., database queries) follow this model *conceptually*.

The subquery executes as and when required, to feed the outer query. In our example, the subquery (the top conveyor belt in Figure 8-7) executes once for every outer loop iteration. This is illustrated in Figures 8-7 and 8-8.

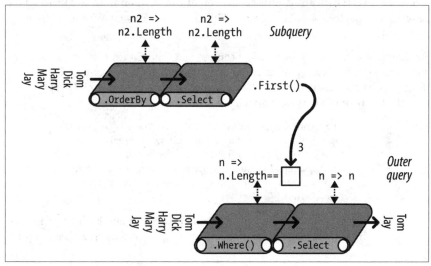

Figure 8-7. Subquery composition

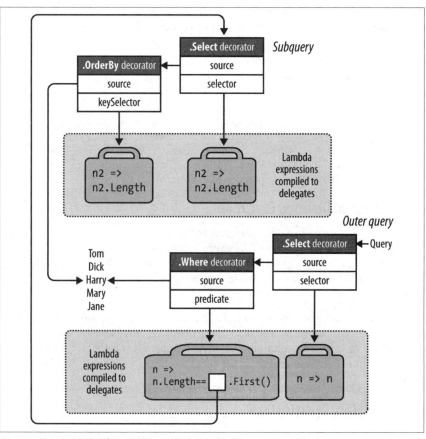

Figure 8-8. UML subquery composition

We can express our preceding subquery more succinctly as follows:

```
IEnumerable<string> query =
    from  n in names
    where n.Length == names.OrderBy (n2 => n2.Length).First().Length
    select n;
```

With the Min aggregation function, we can simplify the query further:

```
IEnumerable<string> query =
    from  n in names
    where n.Length == names.Min (n2 => n2.Length)
    select n;
```

In "Interpreted Queries" on page 364, we'll describe how remote sources such as SQL tables can be queried. Our example makes an ideal database query, since it would be processed as a unit, requiring only one round trip to the database server. This query, however, is inefficient for a local collection because the subquery is recalculated on each outer loop iteration. We can avoid this inefficiency by running the subquery separately (so that it's no longer a subquery):

```
int shortest = names.Min (n => n.Length);

IEnumerable<string> query = from    n in names
                            where   n.Length == shortest
                            select n;
```

 Factoring out subqueries in this manner is nearly always desirable when querying local collections. An exception is when the subquery is *correlated*, meaning that it references the outer range variable. We explore correlated subqueries in "Projecting" on page 394 in Chapter 9.

Subqueries and Deferred Execution

An element or aggregation operator such as First or Count in a subquery doesn't force the *outer* query into immediate execution—deferred execution still holds for the outer query. This is because subqueries are called *indirectly*—through a delegate in the case of a local query, or through an expression tree in the case of an interpreted query.

An interesting case arises when you include a subquery within a Select expression. In the case of a local query, you're actually *projecting a sequence of queries*—each itself subject to deferred execution. The effect is generally transparent, and it serves to further improve efficiency. We revisit Select subqueries in some detail in Chapter 9.

Composition Strategies

In this section, we describe three strategies for building more complex queries:

- Progressive query construction
- Using the into keyword
- Wrapping queries

All are *chaining* strategies and produce identical runtime queries.

Progressive Query Building

At the start of the chapter, we demonstrated how you could build a fluent query progressively:

```
var filtered  = names   .Where  (n => n.Contains ("a"));
var sorted    = filtered .OrderBy (n => n);
var query     = sorted  .Select (n => n.ToUpper());
```

Because each of the participating query operators returns a decorator sequence, the resultant query is the same chain or layering of decorators that you would get from

---

a single-expression query. There are a couple of potential benefits, however, to building queries progressively:

- It can make queries easier to write.

- You can add query operators *conditionally*. For example:

```
if (includeFilter) query = query.Where (...)
```

This is more efficient than:

```
query = query.Where (n => !includeFilter || <expression>)
```

because it avoids adding an extra query operator if `includeFilter` is false.

A progressive approach is often useful in query comprehensions. To illustrate, imagine we want to remove all vowels from a list of names and then present in alphabetical order those whose length is still more than two characters. In fluent syntax, we could write this query as a single expression—by projecting *before* we filter:

```
IEnumerable<string> query = names
    .Select  (n => n.Replace ("a", "").Replace ("e", "").Replace ("i", "")
                     .Replace ("o", "").Replace ("u", ""))
    .Where   (n => n.Length > 2)
    .OrderBy (n => n);

RESULT: { "Dck", "Hrry", "Mry" }
```

> Rather than calling `string`'s `Replace` method five times, we could remove vowels from a string more efficiently with a regular expression:
>
> ```
> n => Regex.Replace (n, "[aeiou]", "")
> ```
>
> `string`'s `Replace` method has the advantage, though, of also working in database queries.

Translating this directly into a query expression is troublesome because the `select` clause must come after the `where` and `orderby` clauses. And if we rearrange the query so as to project last, the result would be different:

```
IEnumerable<string> query =
    from   n in names
    where  n.Length > 2
    orderby n
    select n.Replace ("a", "").Replace ("e", "").Replace ("i", "")
             .Replace ("o", "").Replace ("u", "");

RESULT: { "Dck", "Hrry", "Jy", "Mry", "Tm" }
```

Fortunately, there are a number of ways to get the original result in query syntax. The first is by querying progressively:

```
IEnumerable<string> query =
    from   n in names
```

```
select n.Replace ("a", "").Replace ("e", "").Replace ("i", "")
        .Replace ("o", "").Replace ("u", "");

query = from n in query where n.Length > 2 orderby n select n;

RESULT: { "Dck", "Hrry", "Mry" }
```

The into Keyword

 The into keyword is interpreted in two very different ways by query expressions, depending on context. The meaning we're describing now is for signaling *query continuation* (the other is for signaling a GroupJoin).

The into keyword lets you "continue" a query after a projection and is a shortcut for progressively querying. With into, we can rewrite the preceding query as:

```
IEnumerable<string> query =
  from    n in names
  select n.Replace ("a", "").Replace ("e", "").Replace ("i", "")
          .Replace ("o", "").Replace ("u", "")
  into noVowel
    where noVowel.Length > 2 orderby noVowel select noVowel;
```

The only place you can use into is after a select or group clause. into "restarts" a query, allowing you to introduce fresh where, orderby, and select clauses.

 Although it's easiest to think of into as restarting a query from the perspective of a query expression, it's *all one query* when translated to its final fluent form. Hence, there's no intrinsic performance hit with into. Nor do you lose any points for its use!

The equivalent of into in fluent syntax is simply a longer chain of operators.

Scoping rules

All range variables are out of scope following an into keyword. The following will not compile:

```
var query =
  from n1 in names
  select n1.ToUpper()
  into n2                       // Only n2 is visible from here on.
    where n1.Contains ("x")     // Illegal: n1 is not in scope.
    select n2;
```

To see why, consider how this maps to fluent syntax:

```
var query = names
  .Select (n1 => n1.ToUpper())
  .Where  (n2 => n1.Contains ("x"));    // Error: n1 no longer in scope
```

The original name (n1) is lost by the time the Where filter runs. Where's input sequence contains only uppercase names, so it cannot filter based on n1.

Wrapping Queries

A query built progressively can be formulated into a single statement by wrapping one query around another. In general terms:

```
var tempQuery = tempQueryExpr
var finalQuery = from ... in tempQuery ...
```

can be reformulated as:

```
var finalQuery = from ... in (tempQueryExpr)
```

Wrapping is semantically identical to progressive query building or using the into keyword (without the intermediate variable). The end result in all cases is a linear chain of query operators. For example, consider the following query:

```
IEnumerable<string> query =
  from   n in names
  select n.Replace ("a", "").Replace ("e", "").Replace ("i", "")
            .Replace ("o", "").Replace ("u", "");

query = from n in query where n.Length > 2 orderby n select n;
```

Reformulated in wrapped form, it's the following:

```
IEnumerable<string> query =
  from n1 in
  (
     from   n2 in names
     select n2.Replace ("a", "").Replace ("e", "").Replace ("i", "")
               .Replace ("o", "").Replace ("u", "")
  )
  where n1.Length > 2 orderby n1 select n1;
```

When converted to fluent syntax, the result is the same linear chain of operators as in previous examples:

```
IEnumerable<string> query = names
  .Select (n => n.Replace ("a", "").Replace ("e", "").Replace ("i", "")
                  .Replace ("o", "").Replace ("u", ""))
  .Where  (n => n.Length > 2)
  .OrderBy (n => n);
```

(The compiler does not emit the final .Select (n => n) because it's redundant.)

Wrapped queries can be confusing because they resemble the *subqueries* we wrote earlier. Both have the concept of an inner and outer query. When converted to fluent syntax, however, you can see that wrapping is simply a strategy for sequentially chaining operators. The end result bears no resemblance to a subquery, which embeds an inner query within the *lambda expression* of another.

Returning to a previous analogy: when wrapping, the "inner" query amounts to the *preceding conveyor belts*. In contrast, a subquery rides above a conveyor belt and is activated upon demand through the conveyor belt's lambda worker (as illustrated in Figure 8-7).

Projection Strategies

Object Initializers

So far, all our `select` clauses have projected scalar element types. With C# object initializers, you can project into more complex types. For example, suppose, as a first step in a query, we want to strip vowels from a list of names while still retaining the original versions alongside, for the benefit of subsequent queries. We can write the following class to assist:

```
class TempProjectionItem
{
  public string Original;    // Original name
  public string Vowelless;   // Vowel-stripped name
}
```

and then project into it with object initializers:

```
string[] names = { "Tom", "Dick", "Harry", "Mary", "Jay" };

IEnumerable<TempProjectionItem> temp =
  from n in names
  select new TempProjectionItem
  {
    Original  = n,
    Vowelless = n.Replace ("a", "").Replace ("e", "").Replace ("i", "")
                 .Replace ("o", "").Replace ("u", "")
  };
```

The result is of type `IEnumerable<TempProjectionItem>`, which we can subsequently query:

```
IEnumerable<string> query = from   item in temp
                            where  item.Vowelless.Length > 2
                            select item.Original;
Dick
Harry
Mary
```

Anonymous Types

Anonymous types allow you to structure your intermediate results without writing special classes. We can eliminate the `TempProjectionItem` class in our previous example with anonymous types:

```
var intermediate = from n in names

  select new
```

```
  {
    Original = n,
    Vowelless = n.Replace ("a", "").Replace ("e", "").Replace ("i", "")
                .Replace ("o", "").Replace ("u", "")
  };

  IEnumerable<string> query = from   item in intermediate
                             where  item.Vowelless.Length > 2
                             select item.Original;
```

This gives the same result as the previous example, but without needing to write a one-off class. The compiler does the job instead, generating a temporary class with fields that match the structure of our projection. This means, however, that the intermediate query has the following type:

```
  IEnumerable <random-compiler-generated-name>
```

The only way we can declare a variable of this type is with the var keyword. In this case, var is more than just a clutter reduction device; it's a necessity.

We can write the whole query more succinctly with the into keyword:

```
var query = from n in names
  select new
  {
    Original = n,
    Vowelless = n.Replace ("a", "").Replace ("e", "").Replace ("i", "")
                .Replace ("o", "").Replace ("u", "")
  }
  into temp
  where temp.Vowelless.Length > 2
  select temp.Original;
```

Query expressions provide a shortcut for writing this kind of query: the let keyword.

The let Keyword

The let keyword introduces a new variable alongside the range variable.

With let, we can write a query extracting strings whose length, excluding vowels, exceeds two characters, as follows:

```
string[] names = { "Tom", "Dick", "Harry", "Mary", "Jay" };

IEnumerable<string> query =
  from n in names
  let vowelless = n.Replace ("a", "").Replace ("e", "").Replace ("i", "")
                  .Replace ("o", "").Replace ("u", "")
  where vowelless.Length > 2
  orderby vowelless
  select n;        // Thanks to let, n is still in scope.
```

The compiler resolves a let clause by projecting into a temporary anonymous type that contains both the range variable and the new expression variable. In other words, the compiler translates this query into the preceding example.

let accomplishes two things:

- It projects new elements alongside existing elements.
- It allows an expression to be used repeatedly in a query without being rewritten.

The let approach is particularly advantageous in this example because it allows the select clause to project either the original name (n) or its vowel-removed version (vowelless).

You can have any number of let statements, before or after a where statement (see Figure 8-2). A let statement can reference variables introduced in earlier let statements (subject to the boundaries imposed by an into clause). let *reprojects* all existing variables transparently.

A let expression need not evaluate to a scalar type: sometimes it's useful to have it evaluate to a subsequence, for instance.

Interpreted Queries

LINQ provides two parallel architectures: *local* queries for local object collections, and *interpreted* queries for remote data sources. So far, we've examined the architecture of local queries, which operate over collections implementing IEnumerable<T>. Local queries resolve to query operators in the Enumerable class (by default), which in turn resolve to chains of decorator sequences. The delegates that they accept—whether expressed in query syntax, fluent syntax, or traditional delegates—are fully local to Intermediate Language (IL) code, just like any other C# method.

By contrast, interpreted queries are *descriptive*. They operate over sequences that implement IQueryable<T>, and they resolve to the query operators in the Querya ble class, which emit *expression trees* that are interpreted at runtime.

 The query operators in Enumerable can actually work with IQueryable<T> sequences. The difficulty is that the resultant queries always execute locally on the client—this is why a second set of query operators is provided in the Queryable class.

There are two IQueryable<T> implementations in the .NET Framework:

- LINQ to SQL
- Entity Framework (EF)

These *LINQ-to-db* technologies are very similar in their LINQ support: the LINQ-to-db queries in this book will work with both LINQ to SQL and EF unless otherwise specified.

It's also possible to generate an IQueryable<T> wrapper around an ordinary enumerable collection by calling the AsQueryable method. We describe AsQueryable in the section "Building Query Expressions" on page 385 later in this chapter.

In this section, we'll use LINQ to SQL to illustrate interpreted query architecture because LINQ to SQL lets us query without having to first write an Entity Data Model. The queries that we write, however, work equally well with Entity Framework (and also many third-party products).

 IQueryable<T> is an extension of IEnumerable<T> with additional methods for constructing expression trees. Most of the time, you can ignore the details of these methods; they're called indirectly by the Framework. "Building Query Expressions" on page 385 covers IQueryable<T> in more detail.

Suppose we create a simple customer table in SQL Server and populate it with a few names using the following SQL script:

```
create table Customer
(
  ID int not null primary key,
  Name varchar(30)
)
insert Customer values (1, 'Tom')
insert Customer values (2, 'Dick')
insert Customer values (3, 'Harry')
insert Customer values (4, 'Mary')
insert Customer values (5, 'Jay')
```

With this table in place, we can write an interpreted LINQ query in C# to retrieve customers whose name contains the letter "a" as follows:

```
using System;
using System.Linq;
using System.Data.Linq;              // in System.Data.Linq.dll
using System.Data.Linq.Mapping;

[Table] public class Customer
{
  [Column(IsPrimaryKey=true)] public int ID;
  [Column]                    public string Name;
}

class Test
{
  static void Main()
  {
    DataContext dataContext = new DataContext ("connection string");
    Table<Customer> customers = dataContext.GetTable <Customer>();
```

```
IQueryable<string> query = from c in customers
  where   c.Name.Contains ("a")
  orderby c.Name.Length
  select  c.Name.ToUpper();

  foreach (string name in query) Console.WriteLine (name);
}
}
```

LINQ to SQL translates this query into the following SQL:

```
SELECT UPPER([t0].[Name]) AS [value]
FROM [Customer] AS [t0]
WHERE [t0].[Name] LIKE @p0
ORDER BY LEN([t0].[Name])
```

with the following end result:

```
JAY
MARY
HARRY
```

How Interpreted Queries Work

Let's examine how the preceding query is processed.

First, the compiler converts query syntax to fluent syntax. This is done exactly as with local queries:

```
IQueryable<string> query = customers.Where   (n => n.Name.Contains ("a"))
                                    .OrderBy (n => n.Name.Length)
                                    .Select  (n => n.Name.ToUpper());
```

Next, the compiler resolves the query operator methods. Here's where local and interpreted queries differ—interpreted queries resolve to query operators in the Queryable class instead of the Enumerable class.

To see why, we need to look at the customers variable, the source upon which the whole query builds. customers is of type Table<T>, which implements IQueryable<T> (a subtype of IEnumerable<T>). This means the compiler has a choice in resolving Where: it could call the extension method in Enumerable or the following extension method in Queryable:

```
public static IQueryable<TSource> Where<TSource> (this
  IQueryable<TSource> source, Expression <Func<TSource,bool>> predicate)
```

The compiler chooses Queryable.Where because its signature is a *more specific match*.

Queryable.Where accepts a predicate wrapped in an Expression<TDelegate> type. This instructs the compiler to translate the supplied lambda expression—in other words, n=>n.Name.Contains("a")—to an *expression tree* rather than a compiled delegate. An expression tree is an object model based on the types in System.Linq.Expressions that can be inspected at runtime (so that LINQ to SQL or EF can later translate it to a SQL statement).

Because `Queryable.Where` also returns `IQueryable<T>`, the same process follows with the `OrderBy` and `Select` operators. The end result is illustrated in Figure 8-9. In the shaded box, there is an *expression tree* describing the entire query that can be traversed at runtime.

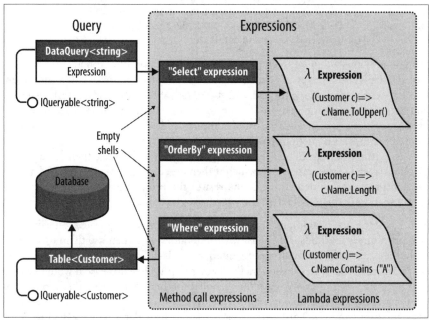

Figure 8-9. Interpreted query composition

Execution

Interpreted queries follow a deferred execution model—just like local queries. This means that the SQL statement is not generated until you start enumerating the query. Further, enumerating the same query twice results in the database being queried twice.

Under the covers, interpreted queries differ from local queries in how they execute. When you enumerate over an interpreted query, the outermost sequence runs a program that traverses the entire expression tree, processing it as a unit. In our example, LINQ to SQL translates the expression tree to a SQL statement, which it then executes, yielding the results as a sequence.

To work, LINQ to SQL needs some clues as to the schema of the database. The Table and Column attributes that we applied to the Customer class serve just this function. The section "LINQ to SQL and Entity Framework" on page 371, later in this chapter, describes these attributes in more detail. Entity Framework is similar except that it also requires an Entity Data Model (EDM)—an XML file describing the mapping between database and entities.

We said previously that a LINQ query is like a production line. When you enumerate an IQueryable conveyor belt, though, it doesn't start up the whole production line, like with a local query. Instead, just the IQueryable belt starts up, with a special enumerator that calls upon a production manager. The manager reviews the entire production line—which consists not of compiled code, but of *dummies* (method call expressions) with instructions pasted to their *foreheads* (expression trees). The manager then traverses all the expressions, in this case transcribing them to a single piece of paper (a SQL statement), which it then executes, feeding the results back to the consumer. Only one belt turns; the rest of the production line is a network of empty shells, existing just to describe what has to be done.

This has some practical implications. For instance, with local queries, you can write your own query methods (fairly easily, with iterators) and then use them to supplement the predefined set. With remote queries, this is difficult, and even undesirable. If you wrote a MyWhere extension method accepting IQueryable<T>, it would be like putting your own dummy into the production line. The production manager wouldn't know what to do with your dummy. Even if you intervened at this stage, your solution would be hard-wired to a particular provider, such as LINQ to SQL, and would not work with other IQueryable implementations. Part of the benefit of having a standard set of methods in Queryable is that they define a *standard vocabulary* for querying *any* remote collection. As soon as you try to extend the vocabulary, you're no longer interoperable.

Another consequence of this model is that an IQueryable provider may be unable to cope with some queries—even if you stick to the standard methods. LINQ to SQL and EF are both limited by the capabilities of the database server; some LINQ queries have no SQL translation. If you're familiar with SQL, you'll have a good intuition for what these are, although at times you have to experiment to see what causes a runtime error; it can be surprising what *does* work!

Combining Interpreted and Local Queries

A query can include both interpreted and local operators. A typical pattern is to have the local operators on the *outside* and the interpreted components on the *inside*; in other words, the interpreted queries feed the local queries. This pattern works well with LINQ-to-database queries.

For instance, suppose we write a custom extension method to pair up strings in a collection:

```
public static IEnumerable<string> Pair (this IEnumerable<string> source)
{
  string firstHalf = null;
  foreach (string element in source)
    if (firstHalf == null)
      firstHalf = element;
    else
    {
      yield return firstHalf + ", " + element;
      firstHalf = null;
    }
}
```

We can use this extension method in a query that mixes LINQ to SQL and local operators:

```
DataContext dataContext = new DataContext ("connection string");
Table<Customer> customers = dataContext.GetTable <Customer>();

IEnumerable<string> q = customers
  .Select (c => c.Name.ToUpper())
  .OrderBy (n => n)
  .Pair()                           // Local from this point on.
  .Select ((n, i) => "Pair " + i.ToString() + " = " + n);

foreach (string element in q) Console.WriteLine (element);

Pair 0 = HARRY, MARY
Pair 1 = TOM, DICK
```

Because customers is of a type implementing IQueryable<T>, the Select operator resolves to Queryable.Select. This returns an output sequence also of type IQuery able<T>, so the OrderBy operator similarly resolves to Queryable.OrderBy. But the next query operator, Pair, has no overload accepting IQueryable<T>—only the less specific IEnumerable<T>. So, it resolves to our local Pair method—wrapping the interpreted query in a local query. Pair also returns IEnumerable, so the Select that follows resolves to another local operator.

On the LINQ to SQL side, the resulting SQL statement is equivalent to:

```
SELECT UPPER (Name) FROM Customer ORDER BY UPPER (Name)
```

The remaining work is done locally. In effect, we end up with a local query (on the outside), whose source is an interpreted query (the inside).

AsEnumerable

Enumerable.AsEnumerable is the simplest of all query operators. Here's its complete definition:

```
public static IEnumerable<TSource> AsEnumerable<TSource>
              (this IEnumerable<TSource> source)
{
    return source;
}
```

Its purpose is to cast an `IQueryable<T>` sequence to `IEnumerable<T>`, forcing subsequent query operators to bind to `Enumerable` operators instead of `Queryable` operators. This causes the remainder of the query to execute locally.

To illustrate, suppose we had a `MedicalArticles` table in SQL Server and wanted to use LINQ to SQL or EF to retrieve all articles on influenza whose abstract contained less than 100 words. For the latter predicate, we need a regular expression:

```
Regex wordCounter = new Regex (@"\b(\w|[-'])+\b");

var query = dataContext.MedicalArticles
  .Where (article => article.Topic == "influenza" &&
                     wordCounter.Matches (article.Abstract).Count < 100);
```

The problem is that SQL Server doesn't support regular expressions, so the LINQ-to-db providers will throw an exception, complaining that the query cannot be translated to SQL. We can solve this by querying in two steps: first retrieving all articles on influenza through a LINQ to SQL query, and then filtering *locally* for abstracts of less than 100 words:

```
Regex wordCounter = new Regex (@"\b(\w|[-'])+\b");

IEnumerable<MedicalArticle> sqlQuery = dataContext.MedicalArticles
  .Where (article => article.Topic == "influenza");

IEnumerable<MedicalArticle> localQuery = sqlQuery
  .Where (article => wordCounter.Matches (article.Abstract).Count < 100);
```

Because `sqlQuery` is of type `IEnumerable<MedicalArticle>`, the second query binds to the local query operators, forcing that part of the filtering to run on the client.

With `AsEnumerable`, we can do the same in a single query:

```
Regex wordCounter = new Regex (@"\b(\w|[-'])+\b");

var query = dataContext.MedicalArticles
  .Where (article => article.Topic == "influenza")

  .AsEnumerable()
  .Where (article => wordCounter.Matches (article.Abstract).Count < 100);
```

An alternative to calling `AsEnumerable` is to call `ToArray` or `ToList`. The advantage of `AsEnumerable` is that it doesn't force immediate query execution, nor does it create any storage structure.

 Moving query processing from the database server to the client can hurt performance, especially if it means retrieving more rows. A more efficient (though more complex) way to solve our example would be to use SQL CLR integration to expose a function on the database that implemented the regular expression.

We demonstrate combined interpreted and local queries further in Chapter 10.

LINQ to SQL and Entity Framework

Throughout this and the following chapter, we use LINQ to SQL (L2S) and Entity Framework (EF) to demonstrate interpreted queries. We'll now examine the key features of these technologies.

 If you're already familiar with L2S, take an advance look at Table 8-1 (at the end of this section) for a summary of the API differences with respect to querying.

LINQ to SQL Versus Entity Framework

Both LINQ to SQL and Entity Framework are LINQ-enabled object-relational mappers. The essential difference is that EF allows for stronger decoupling between the database schema and the classes that you query. Instead of querying classes that closely represent the database schema, you query a higher-level abstraction described by an *Entity Data Model*. This offers extra flexibility but incurs a cost in both performance and simplicity.

L2S was written by the C# team and was released with Framework 3.5; EF was written by the ADO.NET team and was released later as part of Service Pack 1. L2S has since been taken over by the ADO.NET team. This has resulted in the product receiving only minor subsequent improvements, with the team concentrating more on EF.

EF has improved considerably in later versions, although each technology still has unique strengths. L2S's strengths are ease of use, simplicity, performance, and the quality of its SQL translations. EF's strength is its flexibility in creating sophisticated mappings between the database and entity classes. EF also allows for databases other than SQL Server via a *provider model* (L2S also features a provider model, but this was made internal to encourage third parties to focus on EF instead).

L2S is excellent for learning how to query databases in LINQ—because it keeps the object-relational side of things simple while you learn querying principles that also work with EF.

LINQ to SQL Entity Classes

L2S allows you to use any class to represent data, as long as you decorate it with appropriate attributes. Here's a simple example:

```
[Table]
public class Customer
{
  [Column(IsPrimaryKey=true)]
  public int ID;

  [Column]
  public string Name;
}
```

The [Table] attribute, in the `System.Data.Linq.Mapping` namespace, tells L2S that an object of this type represents a row in a database table. By default, it assumes the table name matches the class name; if this is not the case, you can specify the table name as follows:

```
[Table (Name="Customers")]
```

A class decorated with the [Table] attribute is called an *entity* in L2S. To be useful, its structure must closely—or exactly—match that of a database table, making it a low-level construct.

The [Column] attribute flags a field or property that maps to a column in a table. If the column name differs from the field or property name, you can specify the column name as follows:

```
[Column (Name="FullName")]
public string Name;
```

The IsPrimaryKey property in the [Column] attribute indicates that the column partakes in the table's primary key and is required for maintaining object identity, as well as allowing updates to be written back to the database.

Instead of defining public fields, you can define public properties in conjunction with private fields. This allows you to write validation logic into the property accessors. If you take this route, you can optionally instruct L2S to bypass your property accessors and write to the field directly when populating from the database:

```
string _name;

[Column (Storage="_name")]
public string Name { get { return _name; } set { _name = value; } }
```

Column(Storage="_name") tells L2S to write directly to the _name field (rather than the Name property) when populating the entity. L2S's use of reflection allows the field to be private—as in this example.

 You can generate entity classes automatically from a database using either Visual Studio (add a new "LINQ to SQL Classes" project item) or with the *SqlMetal* command-line tool.

Entity Framework Entity Classes

As with L2S, EF lets you use any class to represent data (although you have to implement special interfaces if you want functionality such as navigation properties).

The following entity class, for instance, represents a customer that ultimately maps to a *customer* table in the database:

```
// You'll need to reference System.Data.Entity.dll

[EdmEntityType (NamespaceName = "NutshellModel", Name = "Customer")]
public partial class Customer
```

```
{
    [EdmScalarPropertyAttribute (EntityKeyProperty=true, IsNullable=false)]
    public int ID { get; set; }

    [EdmScalarProperty (EntityKeyProperty = false, IsNullable = false)]
    public string Name { get; set; }
}
```

Unlike with L2S, however, a class such as this is not enough on its own. Remember that with EF, you're not querying the database directly—you're querying a higher-level model called the *Entity Data Model* (EDM). There needs to be some way to describe the EDM, and this is most commonly done via an XML file with an *.edmx* extension, which contains three parts:

- The *conceptual model*, which describes the EDM in isolation of the database
- The *store model*, which describes the database schema
- The *mapping*, which describes how the conceptual model maps to the store

The easiest way to create an *.edmx* file is to add an "ADO.NET Entity Data Model" project item in Visual Studio and then follow the wizard for generating entities from a database. This creates not only the *.edmx* file, but the entity classes as well.

 The entity classes in EF map to the *conceptual model*. The types that support querying and updating the conceptual model are collectively called *Object Services*.

The designer assumes that you initially want a simple 1:1 mapping between tables and entities. You can enrich this, however, by tweaking the EDM either with the designer or by editing the underlying *.edmx* file that it creates for you. Here are some of the things you can do:

- Map several tables into one entity.
- Map one table into several entities.
- Map inherited types to tables using the three standard kinds of strategies popular in the ORM world.

The three kinds of inheritance strategies are:

Table per hierarchy
A single table maps to a whole class hierarchy. The table contains a discriminator column to indicate which type each row should map to.

Table per type
A single table maps to one type, meaning that an inherited type maps to several tables. EF generates a SQL JOIN when you query an entity, to merge all its base types together.

Table per concrete type

A separate table maps to each concrete type. This means that a base type maps to several tables and EF generates a SQL UNION when you query for entities of a base type.

(In contrast, L2S supports only table per hierarchy.)

The EDM is complex: a thorough discussion can fill hundreds of pages! A good book that describes this in detail is Julia Lerman's *Programming Entity Framework*.

EF also lets you query through the EDM without LINQ—using a textual language called Entity SQL (ESQL). This can be useful for dynamically constructed queries.

DataContext and ObjectContext

Once you've defined entity classes (and an EDM in the case of EF), you can start querying. The first step is to instantiate a DataContext (L2S) or ObjectContext (EF), specifying a connection string:

```
var l2sContext = new DataContext ("database connection string");
var efContext = new ObjectContext ("entity connection string");
```

Instantiating a DataContext/ObjectContext directly is a low-level approach and is good for demonstrating how the classes work. More typically, though, you instantiate a *typed context* (a subclassed version of these classes), a process we'll describe shortly.

With L2S, you pass in the database connection string; with EF, you must pass an *entity connection string*, which incorporates the database connection string plus information on how to find the EDM. (If you've created an EDM in Visual Studio, you can find the entity connection string for your EDM in the *app.config* file.)

You can then obtain a queryable object by calling GetTable (L2S) or CreateObject Set (EF). The following example uses the Customer class that we defined earlier:

```
var context = new DataContext ("database connection string");
Table<Customer> customers = context.GetTable <Customer>();

Console.WriteLine (customers.Count());          // # of rows in table.

Customer cust = customers.Single (c => c.ID == 2);  // Retrieves Customer
                                                    // with ID of 2.
```

Here's the same thing with EF:

```
var context = new ObjectContext ("entity connection string");
context.DefaultContainerName = "NutshellEntities";
ObjectSet<Customer> customers = context.CreateObjectSet<Customer>();

Console.WriteLine (customers.Count());          // # of rows in table.
```

```
Customer cust = customers.Single (c => c.ID == 2);   // Retrieves Customer
                                                     // with ID of 2.
```

 The Single operator is ideal for retrieving a row by primary
key. Unlike First, it throws an exception if more than one element is returned.

A DataContext/ObjectContext object does two things. First, it acts as a factory for
generating objects that you can query. Second, it keeps track of any changes that you
make to your entities so that you can write them back. We can continue our previous example to update a customer with L2S as follows:

```
Customer cust = customers.OrderBy (c => c.Name).First();
cust.Name = "Updated Name";
context.SubmitChanges();
```

With EF, the only difference is that you call SaveChanges instead:

```
Customer cust = customers.OrderBy (c => c.Name).First();
cust.Name = "Updated Name";
context.SaveChanges();
```

Typed contexts

Having to call GetTable<Customer>() or CreateObjectSet<Customer>() all the
time is awkward. A better approach is to subclass DataContext/ObjectContext for a
particular database, adding properties that do this for each entity. This is called a
typed context:

```
class NutshellContext : DataContext    // For LINQ to SQL
{
    public Table<Customer> Customers => GetTable<Customer>();
    // ... and so on, for each table in the database
}
```

Here's the same thing for EF:

```
class NutshellContext : ObjectContext    // For Entity Framework
{
    public ObjectSet<Customer> Customers => CreateObjectSet<Customer>();
    // ... and so on, for each entity in the conceptual model
}
```

You can then simply do this:

```
var context = new NutshellContext ("connection string");
Console.WriteLine (context.Customers.Count());
```

If you use Visual Studio to create a "LINQ to SQL Classes" or "ADO.NET Entity
Data Model" project item, it builds a typed context for you automatically. The
designers can also do additional work such as pluralizing identifiers—in this example, it's context.Customers and not context.Customer, even though the SQL table
and entity class are both called Customer.

Disposing DataContext/ObjectContext

Although `DataContext/ObjectContext` implement `IDisposable`, you can (in general) get away without disposing instances. Disposing forces the context's connection to dispose—but this is usually unnecessary because L2S and EF close connections automatically whenever you finish retrieving results from a query.

Disposing a context can actually be problematic because of lazy evaluation. Consider the following:

```
IQueryable<Customer> GetCustomers (string prefix)
{
  using (var dc = new NutshellContext ("connection string"))
    return dc.GetTable<Customer>()
             .Where (c => c.Name.StartsWith (prefix));
}
...
foreach (Customer c in GetCustomers ("a"))
  Console.WriteLine (c.Name);
```

This will fail because the query is evaluated when we enumerate it—which is *after* disposing its `DataContext`.

There are some caveats, though, on not disposing contexts:

- It relies on the connection object releasing all unmanaged resources on the `Close` method. While this holds true with `SqlConnection`, it's theoretically possible for a third-party connection to keep resources open if you call `Close` but not `Dispose` (though this would arguably violate the contract defined by `IDbConnection.Close`).

- If you manually call `GetEnumerator` on a query (instead of using `foreach`) and then fail to either dispose the enumerator or consume the sequence, the connection will remain open. Disposing the `DataContext/ObjectContext` provides a backup in such scenarios.

- Some people feel that it's tidier to dispose contexts (and all objects that implement `IDisposable`).

If you want to explicitly dispose contexts, you must pass a `DataContext/ObjectContext` instance into methods such as `GetCustomers` to avoid the problem described.

Object tracking

A `DataContext/ObjectContext` instance keeps track of all the entities it instantiates, so it can feed the same ones back to you whenever you request the same rows in a table. In other words, a context in its lifetime will never emit two separate entities that refer to the same row in a table (where a row is identified by primary key).

You can disable this behavior in L2S by setting `ObjectTrackin gEnabled` to `false` on the `DataContext` object. In EF, you can disable change tracking on a per-type basis:

```
context.Customers.MergeOption = MergeOption.NoTracking;
```

Disabling object tracking also prevents you from submitting updates to the data.

To illustrate object tracking, suppose the customer whose name is alphabetically first also has the lowest ID. In the following example, a and b will reference the same object:

```
var context = new NutshellContext ("connection string");

Customer a = context.Customers.OrderBy (c => c.Name).First();
Customer b = context.Customers.OrderBy (c => c.ID).First();
```

This has a couple of interesting consequences. First, consider what happens when L2S or EF encounters the second query. It starts by querying the database—and obtaining a single row. It then reads the primary key of this row and performs a lookup in the context's entity cache. Seeing a match, it returns the existing object *without updating any values*. So, if another user had just updated that customer's Name in the database, the new value would be ignored. This is essential for avoiding unexpected side effects (the Customer object could be in use elsewhere) and also for managing concurrency. If you had altered properties on the Customer object and not yet called SubmitChanges/SaveChanges, you wouldn't want your properties automatically overwritten.

To get fresh information from the database, you must either instantiate a new context or call its Refresh method, passing in the entity or entities that you want refreshed.

The second consequence is that you cannot explicitly project into an entity type—to select a subset of the row's columns—without causing trouble. For example, if you want to retrieve only a customer's name, any of the following approaches is valid:

```
customers.Select (c => c.Name);
customers.Select (c => new { Name = c.Name } );
customers.Select (c => new MyCustomType { Name = c.Name } );
```

The following, however, is not:

```
customers.Select (c => new Customer { Name = c.Name } );
```

This is because the Customer entities will end up partially populated. So, the next time you perform a query that requests *all* customer columns, you get the same cached Customer objects with only the Name property populated.

In a multitier application, you cannot use a single static instance of a `DataContext` or `ObjectContext` in the middle tier to handle all requests, because contexts are not thread-safe. Instead, middle-tier methods must create a fresh context per client request. This is actually beneficial because it shifts the burden in handling simultaneous updates to the database server, which is properly equipped for the job. A database server, for instance, will apply transaction isolation-level semantics.

Associations

The entity generation tools perform another useful job. For each relationship defined in your database, they generate properties on each side that allow you to query that relationship. For example, suppose we define customer and purchase tables in a one-to-many relationship:

```
create table Customer
(
  ID int not null primary key,
  Name varchar(30) not null
)

create table Purchase
(
  ID int not null primary key,
  CustomerID int references Customer (ID),
  Description varchar(30) not null,
  Price decimal not null
)
```

With automatically generated entity classes, we can write queries such as this:

```
var context = new NutshellContext ("connection string");

// Retrieve all purchases made by the first customer (alphabetically):

Customer cust1 = context.Customers.OrderBy (c => c.Name).First();
foreach (Purchase p in cust1.Purchases)
  Console.WriteLine (p.Price);

// Retrieve the customer who made the lowest value purchase:

Purchase cheapest = context.Purchases.OrderBy (p => p.Price).First();
Customer cust2 = cheapest.Customer;
```

Further, if cust1 and cust2 happened to refer to the same customer, c1 and c2 would *refer to the same object*: cust1==cust2 would return true.

Let's examine the signature of the automatically generated Purchases property on the Customer entity. With L2S:

```
[Association (Storage="_Purchases", OtherKey="CustomerID")]
public EntitySet <Purchase> Purchases { get {...} set {...} }
```

With EF:

```
[EdmRelationshipNavigationProperty ("NutshellModel", "FK...", "Purchase")]
public EntityCollection<Purchase> Purchases { get {...} set {...} }
```

An `EntitySet` or `EntityCollection` is like a predefined query, with a built-in `Where` clause that extracts related entities. The `[Association]` attribute gives L2S the information it needs to formulate the SQL query; the `[EdmRelationshipNaviga tionProperty]` attribute tells EF where to look in the EDM for information about that relationship.

As with any other type of query, you get deferred execution. With L2S, an `Entity Set` is populated when you enumerate over it; with EF, an `EntityCollection` is populated when you explicitly call its `Load` method.

Here's the `Purchases.Customer` property, on the other side of the relationship, with L2S:

```
[Association (Storage="_Customer",ThisKey="CustomerID",IsForeignKey=true)]
public Customer Customer { get {...} set {...} }
```

Although the property is of type `Customer`, its underlying field (`_Customer`) is of type `EntityRef`. The `EntityRef` type implements deferred loading, so the related `Customer` is not retrieved from the database until you actually ask for it.

EF works in the same way, except that it doesn't populate the property simply by you accessing it: you must call `Load` on its `EntityReference` object. This means EF contexts must expose properties for both the actual parent object and its `EntityRefer ence` wrapper:

```
[EdmRelationshipNavigationProperty ("NutshellModel", "FK...", "Customer")]
public Customer Customer { get {...} set {...} }

public EntityReference<Customer> CustomerReference { get; set; }
```

 You can make EF behave like L2S and have it populate `Entity Collections` and `EntityReferences` simply by virtue of their properties being accessed as follows:

```
context.ContextOptions.DeferredLoadingEnabled = true;
```

Deferred Execution with L2S and EF

L2S and EF queries are subject to deferred execution, just like local queries. This allows you to build queries progressively. There is one aspect, however, in which L2S/EF have special deferred execution semantics, and that is when a subquery appears inside a `Select` expression:

- With local queries, you get double deferred execution, because from a functional perspective, you're selecting a sequence of *queries*. So, if you enumerate the outer result sequence, but never enumerate the inner sequences, the subquery will never execute.

- With L2S/EF, the subquery is executed at the same time as the main outer query. This avoids excessive round-tripping.

For example, the following query executes in a single round trip upon reaching the first `foreach` statement:

```
.var context = new NutshellContext ("connection string");

var query = from c in context.Customers
            select
                from p in c.Purchases
                select new { c.Name, p.Price };

foreach (var customerPurchaseResults in query)
    foreach (var namePrice in customerPurchaseResults)
        Console.WriteLine (namePrice.Name + " spent " + namePrice.Price);
```

Any `EntitySets`/`EntityCollections` that you explicitly project are fully populated in a single round trip:

```
var query = from c in context.Customers
            select new { c.Name, c.Purchases };

foreach (var row in query)
    foreach (Purchase p in row.Purchases)     // No extra round-tripping
        Console.WriteLine (row.Name + " spent " + p.Price);
```

But if we enumerate `EntitySet`/`EntityCollection` properties without first having projected, deferred execution rules apply. In the following example, L2S and EF execute another `Purchases` query on each loop iteration:

```
context.ContextOptions.DeferredLoadingEnabled = true;   // For EF only.

foreach (Customer c in context.Customers)
    foreach (Purchase p in c.Purchases)     // Another SQL round-trip
        Console.WriteLine (c.Name + " spent " + p.Price);
```

This model is advantageous when you want to *selectively* execute the inner loop, based on a test that can be performed only on the client:

```
foreach (Customer c in context.Customers)
    if (myWebService.HasBadCreditHistory (c.ID))
        foreach (Purchase p in c.Purchases)     // Another SQL round trip
            Console.WriteLine (...);
```

(In Chapter 9, we explore `Select` subqueries in more detail, in "Projecting" on page 394.)

We've seen that you can avoid round-tripping by explicitly projecting associations. L2S and EF offer other mechanisms for this, too, which we cover in the following two sections.

DataLoadOptions

The `DataLoadOptions` class is specific to L2S. It has two distinct uses:

- It lets you specify, in advance, a filter for `EntitySet` associations (`Associate With`).
- It lets you request that certain `EntitySets` be eagerly loaded, to lessen round-tripping (`LoadWith`).

Specifying a filter in advance

Let's refactor our previous example as follows:

```
foreach (Customer c in context.Customers)
  if (myWebService.HasBadCreditHistory (c.ID))
    ProcessCustomer (c);
```

We'll define `ProcessCustomer` like this:

```
void ProcessCustomer (Customer c)
{
  Console.WriteLine (c.ID + " " + c.Name);
  foreach (Purchase p in c.Purchases)
    Console.WriteLine ("  - purchased a " + p.Description);
}
```

Now suppose we want to feed `ProcessCustomer` only a *subset* of each customer's purchases; say, the high-value ones. Here's one solution:

```
foreach (Customer c in context.Customers)
  if (myWebService.HasBadCreditHistory (c.ID))
    ProcessCustomer (c.ID,
                     c.Name,
                     c.Purchases.Where (p => p.Price > 1000));
...
void ProcessCustomer (int custID, string custName,
                      IEnumerable<Purchase> purchases)
{
  Console.WriteLine (custID + " " + custName);
  foreach (Purchase p in purchases)
    Console.WriteLine ("  - purchased a " + p.Description);
}
```

This is messy. It would get messier still if `ProcessCustomer` required more `Customer` fields. A better solution is to use `DataLoadOptions`'s `AssociateWith` method:

```
DataLoadOptions options = new DataLoadOptions();
options.AssociateWith <Customer>
 (c => c.Purchases.Where (p => p.Price > 1000));
context.LoadOptions = options;
```

This instructs our `DataContext` instance always to filter a `Customer`'s `Purchases` using the given predicate. We can now use the original version of `ProcessCustomer`.

`AssociateWith` doesn't change deferred execution semantics. When a particular relationship is used, it simply instructs to implicitly add a particular filter to the equation.

Eager loading

The second use for a `DataLoadOptions` is to request that certain `EntitySets` be eagerly loaded with their parent. For instance, suppose you want to load all customers and their purchases in a single SQL round trip. The following does exactly this:

```
DataLoadOptions options = new DataLoadOptions();
options.LoadWith <Customer> (c => c.Purchases);
context.LoadOptions = options;

foreach (Customer c in context.Customers)     // One round trip:
  foreach (Purchase p in c.Purchases)
    Console.WriteLine (c.Name + " bought a " + p.Description);
```

This instructs that whenever a `Customer` is retrieved, its `Purchases` should also be retrieved at the same time. You can combine `LoadWith` with `AssociateWith`. The following instructs that whenever a customer is retrieved, its *high-value* purchases should be retrieved in the same round trip:

```
options.LoadWith <Customer> (c => c.Purchases);
options.AssociateWith <Customer>
  (c => c.Purchases.Where (p => p.Price > 1000));
```

Eager Loading in Entity Framework

You can request in EF that associations be eagerly loaded with the `Include` method. The following enumerates over each customer's purchases—while generating just one SQL query:

```
foreach (Customer c in context.Customers.Include ("Purchases"))
  foreach (Purchase p in c.Purchases)
    Console.WriteLine (p.Description);
```

`Include` can be used with arbitrary breadth and depth. For example, if each `Purchase` also had `PurchaseDetails` and `SalesPersons` navigation properties, the entire nested structure could be eagerly loaded as follows:

```
context.Customers.Include ("Purchases.PurchaseDetails")
                 .Include ("Purchases.SalesPersons")
```

Updates

L2S and EF also keep track of changes that you make to your entities and allow you to write them back to the database by calling `SubmitChanges` on the `DataContext` object, or `SaveChanges` on the `ObjectContext` object.

L2S's `Table<T>` class provides `InsertOnSubmit` and `DeleteOnSubmit` methods for inserting and deleting rows in a table; EF's `ObjectSet<T>` class provides `AddObject` and `DeleteObject` methods to do the same thing. Here's how to insert a row:

```
var context = new NutshellContext ("connection string");

Customer cust = new Customer { ID=1000, Name="Bloggs" };
context.Customers.InsertOnSubmit (cust);   // AddObject with EF
context.SubmitChanges();                    // SaveChanges with EF
```

We can later retrieve that row, update it, and then delete it:

```
var context = new NutshellContext ("connection string");

Customer cust = context.Customers.Single (c => c.ID == 1000);
cust.Name = "Bloggs2";
context.SubmitChanges();                    // Updates the customer

context.Customers.DeleteOnSubmit (cust);   // DeleteObject with EF
context.SubmitChanges();                    // Deletes the customer
```

`SubmitChanges`/`SaveChanges` gathers all the changes that were made to its entities since the context's creation (or the last save) and then executes a SQL statement to write them to the database. Any `TransactionScope` is honored; if none is present, it wraps all statements in a new transaction.

You can also add new or existing rows to an `EntitySet`/`EntityCollection` by calling `Add`. L2S and EF automatically populate the foreign keys when you do this (after calling `SubmitChanges` or `SaveChanges`):

```
Purchase p1 = new Purchase { ID=100, Description="Bike",  Price=500 };
Purchase p2 = new Purchase { ID=101, Description="Tools", Price=100 };

Customer cust = context.Customers.Single (c => c.ID == 1);

cust.Purchases.Add (p1);
cust.Purchases.Add (p2);

context.SubmitChanges();  // (or SaveChanges with EF)
```

 If you don't want the burden of allocating unique keys, you can use either an auto-incrementing field (IDENTITY in SQL Server) or a Guid for the primary key.

In this example, L2S/EF automatically writes 1 into the `CustomerID` column of each of the new purchases (L2S knows to do this because of the association attribute that we defined on the `Purchases` property; EF knows to do this because of information in the EDM):

```
[Association (Storage="_Purchases", OtherKey="CustomerID")]
public EntitySet <Purchase> Purchases { get {...} set {...} }
```

If the `Customer` and `Purchase` entities were generated by the Visual Studio designer or the *SqlMetal* command-line tool, the generated classes would include further

LINQ
Queries

code to keep the two sides of each relationship in sync. In other words, assigning the Purchase.Customer property would automatically add the new customer to the Customer.Purchases entity set—and vice versa. We can illustrate this by rewriting the preceding example as follows:

```
var context = new NutshellContext ("connection string");

Customer cust = context.Customers.Single (c => c.ID == 1);
new Purchase { ID=100, Description="Bike",  Price=500, Customer=cust };
new Purchase { ID=101, Description="Tools", Price=100, Customer=cust };

context.SubmitChanges();   // (SaveChanges with EF)
```

When you remove a row from an EntitySet/EntityCollection, its foreign key field is automatically set to null. The following disassociates our two recently added purchases from their customer:

```
var context = new NutshellContext ("connection string");

Customer cust = context.Customers.Single (c => c.ID == 1);

cust.Purchases.Remove (cust.Purchases.Single (p => p.ID == 100));
cust.Purchases.Remove (cust.Purchases.Single (p => p.ID == 101));

context.SubmitChanges();    // Submit SQL to database (SaveChanges in EF)
```

Because this tries to set each purchase's CustomerID field to null, Purchase.CustomerID must be nullable in the database; otherwise, an exception is thrown. (Further, the CustomerID field or property in the entity class must be a nullable type.)

To delete child entities entirely, remove them from the Table<T> or ObjectSet<T> instead (this means you much retrieve them first). With L2S:

```
var c = context;
c.Purchases.DeleteOnSubmit (c.Purchases.Single (p => p.ID == 100));
c.Purchases.DeleteOnSubmit (c.Purchases.Single (p => p.ID == 101));
c.SubmitChanges();          // Submit SQL to database
```

With EF:

```
var c = context;
c.Purchases.DeleteObject (c.Purchases.Single (p => p.ID == 100));
c.Purchases.DeleteObject (c.Purchases.Single (p => p.ID == 101));
c.SaveChanges();            // Submit SQL to database
```

API Differences Between L2S and EF

As we've seen, L2S and EF are similar in the aspect of querying with LINQ and performing updates. Table 8-1 summarizes the API differences.

Table 8-1. API differences between L2S and EF

Purpose	LINQ to SQL	Entity Framework
Gatekeeper class for all CRUD operations	DataContext	ObjectContext
Method to (lazily) retrieve all entities of a given type from the store	GetTable	CreateObjectSet
Type returned by the above method	Table<T>	ObjectSet<T>
Method to update the store with any additions, modifications, or deletions to entity objects	SubmitChanges	SaveChanges
Method to add a new entity to the store when the context is updated	InsertOnSubmit	AddObject
Method to delete an entity from the store when the context is updated	DeleteOnSubmit	DeleteObject
Type to represent one side of a relationship property, when that side has a multiplicity of many	EntitySet<T>	EntityCollection<T>
Type to represent one side of a relationship property, when that side has a multiplicity of one	EntityRef<T>	EntityReference<T>
Default strategy for loading relationship properties	Lazy	Explicit
Construct that enables eager loading	DataLoadOptions	.Include()

Building Query Expressions

So far in this chapter, when we've needed to dynamically compose queries, we've done so by conditionally chaining query operators. Although this is adequate in many scenarios, sometimes you need to work at a more granular level and dynamically compose the lambda expressions that feed the operators.

In this section, we'll assume the following Product class:

```
[Table] public partial class Product
{
  [Column(IsPrimaryKey=true)] public int ID;
  [Column]                    public string Description;
  [Column]                    public bool Discontinued;
  [Column]                    public DateTime LastSale;
}
```

LINQ
Queries

Delegates Versus Expression Trees

Recall that:

- Local queries, which use `Enumerable` operators, take delegates.

- Interpreted queries, which use `Queryable` operators, take expression trees.

We can see this by comparing the signature of the `Where` operator in `Enumerable` and `Queryable`:

```
public static IEnumerable<TSource> Where<TSource> (this
  IEnumerable<TSource> source, Func<TSource,bool> predicate)

public static IQueryable<TSource> Where<TSource> (this
  IQueryable<TSource> source, Expression<Func<TSource,bool>> predicate)
```

When embedded within a query, a lambda expression looks identical whether it binds to `Enumerable`'s operators or `Queryable`'s operators:

```
IEnumerable<Product> q1 = localProducts.Where (p => !p.Discontinued);
IQueryable<Product>  q2 = sqlProducts.Where   (p => !p.Discontinued);
```

When you assign a lambda expression to an intermediate variable, however, you must be explicit on whether to resolve to a delegate (i.e., `Func<>`) or an expression tree (i.e., `Expression<Func<>>`). In the following example, `predicate1` and `predicate2` are not interchangeable:

```
Func <Product, bool> predicate1 = p => !p.Discontinued;
IEnumerable<Product> q1 = localProducts.Where (predicate1);

Expression <Func <Product, bool>> predicate2 = p => !p.Discontinued;
IQueryable<Product> q2 = sqlProducts.Where (predicate2);
```

Compiling expression trees

You can convert an expression tree to a delegate by calling `Compile`. This is of particular value when writing methods that return reusable expressions. To illustrate, we'll add a static method to the `Product` class that returns a predicate evaluating to true if a product is not discontinued and has sold in the past 30 days:

```
public partial class Product
{
  public static Expression<Func<Product, bool>> IsSelling()
  {
    return p => !p.Discontinued && p.LastSale > DateTime.Now.AddDays (-30);
  }
}
```

(We've defined this in a separate partial class to avoid being overwritten by an automatic `DataContext` generator such as Visual Studio's code generator.)

The method just written can be used both in interpreted and in local queries as follows:

```
void Test()
{
  var dataContext = new NutshellContext ("connection string");
  Product[] localProducts = dataContext.Products.ToArray();

  IQueryable<Product> sqlQuery =
    dataContext.Products.Where (Product.IsSelling());

  IEnumerable<Product> localQuery =
    localProducts.Where (Product.IsSelling.Compile());
}
```

 NET does not provide an API to convert in the reverse direction, from a delegate to an expression tree. This makes expression trees more versatile.

AsQueryable

The AsQueryable operator lets you write whole *queries* that can run over either local or remote sequences:

```
IQueryable<Product> FilterSortProducts (IQueryable<Product> input)
{
  return from p in input
         where ...
         order by ...
         select p;
}

void Test()
{
  var dataContext = new NutshellContext ("connection string");
  Product[] localProducts = dataContext.Products.ToArray();

  var sqlQuery   = FilterSortProducts (dataContext.Products);
  var localQuery = FilterSortProducts (localProducts.AsQueryable());
  ...
}
```

AsQueryable wraps IQueryable<T> clothing around a local sequence so that subsequent query operators resolve to expression trees. When you later enumerate over the result, the expression trees are implicitly compiled (at a small performance cost), and the local sequence enumerates as it would ordinarily.

Expression Trees

We said previously that an implicit conversion from a lambda expression to Expression<TDelegate> causes the C# compiler to emit code that builds an expression tree. With some programming effort, you can do the same thing manually at runtime—in other words, dynamically build an expression tree from scratch. The result can be cast to an `Expression<TDelegate>` and used in LINQ-to-db queries or compiled into an ordinary delegate by calling `Compile`.

The Expression DOM

An expression tree is a miniature code DOM. Each node in the tree is represented by a type in the `System.Linq.Expressions` namespace; these types are illustrated in Figure 8-10.

 From Framework 4.0, this namespace features additional expression types and methods to support language constructs that can appear in code blocks. These are for the benefit of the DLR and not lambda expressions. In other words, code-block-style lambdas still cannot be converted to expression trees:

```
Expression<Func<Customer,bool>> invalid =
    c => { return true; }  // Code blocks not permitted
```

The base class for all nodes is the (nongeneric) `Expression` class. The generic `Expression<TDelegate>` class actually means "typed lambda expression" and might have been named `LambdaExpression<TDelegate>` if it wasn't for the clumsiness of this:

```
LambdaExpression<Func<Customer,bool>> f = ...
```

`Expression<T>`'s base type is the (nongeneric) `LambdaExpression` class. `LamdbaExpression` provides type unification for lambda expression trees: any typed `Expression<T>` can be cast to a `LambdaExpression`.

The thing that distinguishes `LambdaExpressions` from ordinary `Expressions` is that lambda expressions have *parameters*.

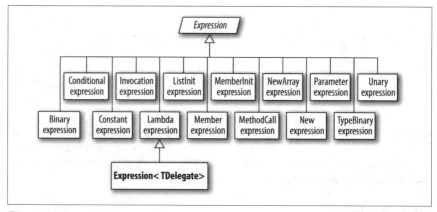

Figure 8-10. Expression types

To create an expression tree, don't instantiate node types directly; rather, call static methods provided on the `Expression` class. Here are all the methods:

Add	ElementInit	MakeMemberAccess	Or
AddChecked	Equal	MakeUnary	OrElse
And	ExclusiveOr	MemberBind	Parameter
AndAlso	Field	MemberInit	Power
ArrayIndex	GreaterThan	Modulo	Property
ArrayLength	GreaterThanOrEqual	Multiply	PropertyOrField
Bind	Invoke	MultiplyChecked	Quote
Call	Lambda	Negate	RightShift
Coalesce	LeftShift	NegateChecked	Subtract
Condition	LessThan	New	SubtractChecked
Constant	LessThanOrEqual	NewArrayBounds	TypeAs
Convert	ListBind	NewArrayInit	TypeIs
ConvertChecked	ListInit	Not	UnaryPlus
Divide	MakeBinary	NotEqual	

Figure 8-11 shows the expression tree that the following assignment creates:

```
Expression<Func<string, bool>> f = s => s.Length < 5;
```

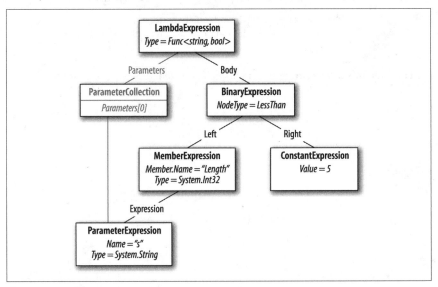

Figure 8-11. Expression tree

We can demonstrate this as follows:

```
Console.WriteLine (f.Body.NodeType);                    // LessThan
Console.WriteLine (((BinaryExpression) f.Body).Right);  // 5
```

Let's now build this expression from scratch. The principle is that you start from the bottom of the tree and work your way up. The bottommost thing in our tree is a ParameterExpression, the lambda expression parameter called "s" of type string:

```
ParameterExpression p = Expression.Parameter (typeof (string), "s");
```

The next step is to build the MemberExpression and ConstantExpression. In the former case, we need to access the Length *property* of our parameter, "s":

```
MemberExpression stringLength = Expression.Property (p, "Length");
ConstantExpression five = Expression.Constant (5);
```

Next is the LessThan comparison:

```
BinaryExpression comparison = Expression.LessThan (stringLength, five);
```

The final step is to construct the lambda expression, which links an expression Body to a collection of parameters:

```
Expression<Func<string, bool>> lambda
  = Expression.Lambda<Func<string, bool>> (comparison, p);
```

A convenient way to test our lambda is by compiling it to a delegate:

```
Func<string, bool> runnable = lambda.Compile();

Console.WriteLine (runnable ("kangaroo"));        // False
Console.WriteLine (runnable ("dog"));             // True
```

 The easiest way to figure out which expression type to use is to examine an existing lambda expression in the Visual Studio debugger.

We continue this discussion online, at *http://www.albahari.com/expressions/*.

9

LINQ Operators

This chapter describes each of the LINQ query operators. As well as serving as a reference, two of the sections, "Projecting" on page 394 and "Joining" on page 394, cover a number of conceptual areas:

- Projecting object hierarchies
- Joining with Select, SelectMany, Join, and GroupJoin
- Query expressions with multiple range variables

All of the examples in this chapter assume that a names array is defined as follows:

```
string[] names = { "Tom", "Dick", "Harry", "Mary", "Jay" };
```

Examples that query a database assume that a variable called dataContext is instantiated as follows:

```
var dataContext = new NutshellContext ("connection string...");

...

public class NutshellContext : DataContext
{
  public NutshellContext (string cxString) : base (cxString) {}

  public Table<Customer> Customers { get { return GetTable<Customer>(); } }
  public Table<Purchase> Purchases { get { return GetTable<Purchase>(); } }
}

[Table] public class Customer
{
  [Column(IsPrimaryKey=true)]  public int ID;
  [Column]                     public string Name;

  [Association (OtherKey="CustomerID")]
  public EntitySet<Purchase> Purchases = new EntitySet<Purchase>();
```

```
}

[Table] public class Purchase
{
    [Column(IsPrimaryKey=true)]   public int ID;
    [Column]                      public int? CustomerID;
    [Column]                      public string Description;
    [Column]                      public decimal Price;
    [Column]                      public DateTime Date;

    EntityRef<Customer> custRef;

    [Association (Storage="custRef",ThisKey="CustomerID",IsForeignKey=true)]
    public Customer Customer
    {
      get { return custRef.Entity; } set { custRef.Entity = value; }
    }
}
```

 All the examples in this chapter are preloaded into LINQPad, along with a sample database with a matching schema. You can download LINQPad from *http://www.linqpad.net*.

The entity classes shown are a simplified version of what LINQ to SQL tools typically produce and do not include code to update the opposing side in a relationship when their entities have been reassigned.

Here are the corresponding SQL table definitions:

```
create table Customer
(
  ID int not null primary key,
  Name varchar(30) not null
)
create table Purchase
(
  ID int not null primary key,
  CustomerID int references Customer (ID),
  Description varchar(30) not null,
  Price decimal not null
)
```

 All examples will also work with Entity Framework, except where otherwise indicated. You can build an Entity Framework ObjectContext from these tables by creating a new Entity Data Model in Visual Studio, and then dragging the tables on to the designer surface.

Overview

In this section, we provide an overview of the standard query operators.

The standard query operators fall into three categories:

- Sequence in, sequence out (sequence-to-sequence)
- Sequence in, single element or scalar value out
- Nothing in, sequence out (*generation* methods)

We first present each of the three categories and the query operators they include, and then we take up each individual query operator in detail.

Sequence→Sequence

Most query operators fall into this category—accepting one or more sequences as input and emitting a single output sequence. Figure 9-1 illustrates those operators that restructure the shape of the sequences.

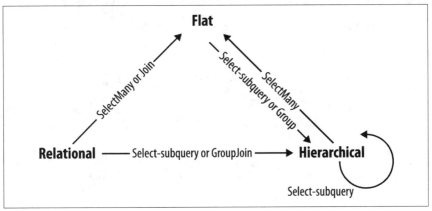

Figure 9-1. Shape-changing operators

Filtering

```
IEnumerable<TSource> → IEnumerable<TSource>
```

Returns a subset of the original elements:

```
Where, Take, TakeWhile, Skip, SkipWhile, Distinct
```

Projecting

`IEnumerable<TSource> →IEnumerable<TResult>`

Transforms each element with a lambda function. `SelectMany` flattens nested sequences; `Select` and `SelectMany` perform inner joins, left outer joins, cross joins, and non-equi joins with LINQ to SQL and EF:

    Select, SelectMany

Joining

`IEnumerable<TOuter>, IEnumerable<TInner>→ IEnumerable<TResult>`

Meshes elements of one sequence with another. `Join` and `GroupJoin` operators are designed to be efficient with local queries and support inner and left outer joins. The `Zip` operator enumerates two sequences in step, applying a function over each element pair. Rather than naming the type arguments `TOuter` and `TInner`, the `Zip` operator names them `TFirst` and `TSecond`:

`IEnumerable<TFirst>, IEnumerable<TSecond>→ IEnumerable<TResult>`

    Join, GroupJoin, Zip

Ordering

`IEnumerable<TSource> →IOrderedEnumerable<TSource>`

Returns a reordering of a sequence:

    OrderBy, ThenBy, Reverse

Grouping

`IEnumerable<TSource> →IEnumerable<IGrouping<TKey,TElement>>`

Groups a sequence into subsequences:

    GroupBy

Set operators

`IEnumerable<TSource>, IEnumerable<TSource>→ IEnumerable<TSource>`

Takes two same-typed sequences and returns their commonality, sum, or difference:

    Concat, Union, Intersect, Except

Conversion methods: Import

`IEnumerable→IEnumerable<TResult>`

    OfType, Cast

Conversion methods: Export

IEnumerable<TSource> →An array, list, dictionary, lookup, or sequence:

```
ToArray, ToList, ToDictionary, ToLookup, AsEnumerable, AsQueryable
```

Sequence→Element or Value

The following query operators accept an input sequence and emit a single element or value.

Element operators

IEnumerable<TSource> →TSource

Picks a single element from a sequence:

```
First, FirstOrDefault, Last, LastOrDefault, Single, SingleOrDefault,
ElementAt, ElementAtOrDefault, DefaultIfEmpty
```

Aggregation methods

IEnumerable<TSource> →*scalar*

Performs a computation across a sequence, returning a scalar value (typically a number):

```
Aggregate, Average, Count, LongCount, Sum, Max, Min
```

Quantifiers

IEnumerable<TSource> →*bool*

An aggregation returning true or false:

```
All, Any, Contains, SequenceEqual
```

Void→Sequence

In the third and final category are query operators that produce an output sequence from scratch.

Generation methods

void→IEnumerable<TResult>

Manufactures a simple sequence:

```
Empty, Range, Repeat
```

Filtering

`IEnumerable<TSource>→ IEnumerable<TSource>`

Method	Description	SQL equivalents
Where	Returns a subset of elements that satisfy a given condition	WHERE
Take	Returns the first count elements and discards the rest	WHERE ROW_NUMBER()... or TOP *n* subquery
Skip	Ignores the first count elements and returns the rest	WHERE ROW_NUMBER()... or NOT IN (SELECT TOP *n*...)
TakeWhile	Emits elements from the input sequence until the predicate is false	Exception thrown
SkipWhile	Ignores elements from the input sequence until the predicate is false, and then emits the rest	Exception thrown
Distinct	Returns a sequence that excludes duplicates	SELECT DISTINCT...

> The "SQL equivalents" column in the reference tables in this chapter do not necessarily correspond to what an IQueryable implementation such as LINQ to SQL will produce. Rather, it indicates what you'd typically use to do the same job if you were writing the SQL query yourself. Where there is no simple translation, the column is left blank. Where there is no translation at all, the column reads "Exception thrown".
>
> Enumerable implementation code, when shown, excludes checking for null arguments and indexing predicates.

With each of the filtering methods, you always end up with either the same number or fewer elements than you started with. You can never get more! The elements are also identical when they come out; they are not transformed in any way.

Where

Argument	Type
Source sequence	IEnumerable<TSource>
Predicate	TSource => bool or (TSource,int) => bool

Query syntax

```
where bool-expression
```

Enumerable.Where implementation

The internal implementation of `Enumerable.Where`, null checking aside, is function-ally equivalent to the following:

```
public static IEnumerable<TSource> Where<TSource>
  (this IEnumerable<TSource> source, Func <TSource, bool> predicate)
{
  foreach (TSource element in source)
    if (predicate (element))
      yield return element;
}
```

Overview

`Where` returns the elements from the input sequence that satisfy the given predicate.

For instance:

```
string[] names = { "Tom", "Dick", "Harry", "Mary", "Jay" };
IEnumerable<string> query = names.Where (name => name.EndsWith ("y"));

// Result: { "Harry", "Mary", "Jay" }
```

In query syntax:

```
IEnumerable<string> query = from n in names
                            where n.EndsWith ("y")
                            select n;
```

A where clause can appear more than once in a query and be interspersed with `let`, `orderby` and `join` clauses:

```
from n in names
where n.Length > 3
let u = n.ToUpper()
where u.EndsWith ("Y")
select u;                    // Result: { "HARRY", "MARY" }
```

Standard C# scoping rules apply to such queries. In other words, you cannot refer to a variable prior to declaring it with a range variable or a `let` clause.

Indexed filtering

`Where`'s predicate optionally accepts a second argument, of type `int`. This is fed with the position of each element within the input sequence, allowing the predicate to use this information in its filtering decision. For example, the following skips every second element:

```
IEnumerable<string> query = names.Where ((n, i) => i % 2 == 0);

// Result: { "Tom", "Harry", "Jay" }
```

An exception is thrown if you use indexed filtering in LINQ to SQL or EF.

SQL LIKE comparisons in LINQ to SQL and EF

The following methods on `string` translate to SQL's `LIKE` operator:

```
Contains, StartsWith, EndsWith
```

For instance, `c.Name.Contains ("abc")` translates to `customer.Name LIKE '%abc %'` (or more accurately, a parameterized version of this). `Contains` lets you compare only against a locally evaluated expression; to compare against another column, you must use the `SqlMethods.Like` method:

```
... where SqlMethods.Like (c.Description, "%" + c.Name + "%")
```

`SqlMethods.Like` also lets you perform more complex comparisons (e.g., `LIKE 'abc%def%'`).

< and > string comparisons in LINQ to SQL and EF

You can perform *order* comparison on strings with `string`'s `CompareTo` method; this maps to SQL's < and > operators:

```
dataContext.Purchases.Where (p => p.Description.CompareTo ("C") < 0)
```

WHERE x IN (…, …, …) in LINQ to SQL and EF

With LINQ to SQL and EF, you can apply the `Contains` operator to a local collection within a filter predicate. For instance:

```
string[] chosenOnes = { "Tom", "Jay" };

from c in dataContext.Customers
where chosenOnes.Contains (c.Name)
...
```

This maps to SQL's IN operator—in other words:

```
WHERE customer.Name IN ("Tom", "Jay")
```

If the local collection is an array of entities or nonscalar types, LINQ to SQL or EF may instead emit an `EXISTS` clause.

Take and Skip

Argument	Type
Source sequence	IEnumerable<TSource>
Number of elements to take or skip	int

`Take` emits the first *n* elements and discards the rest; `Skip` discards the first *n* elements and emits the rest. The two methods are useful together when implementing a web page allowing a user to navigate through a large set of matching records. For instance, suppose a user searches a book database for the term "mercury," and there are 100 matches. The following returns the first 20:

```
IQueryable<Book> query = dataContext.Books
  .Where   (b => b.Title.Contains ("mercury"))
  .OrderBy (b => b.Title)
  .Take (20);
```

The next query returns books 21 to 40:

```
IQueryable<Book> query = dataContext.Books
  .Where   (b => b.Title.Contains ("mercury"))
  .OrderBy (b => b.Title)
  .Skip (20).Take (20);
```

LINQ to SQL and EF translate Take and Skip to the ROW_NUMBER function in SQL Server 2005, or a TOP *n* subquery in earlier versions of SQL Server.

TakeWhile and SkipWhile

Argument	Type
Source sequence	IEnumerable<TSource>
Predicate	TSource => bool or (TSource,int) => bool

TakeWhile enumerates the input sequence, emitting each item, until the given predicate is false. It then ignores the remaining elements:

```
int[] numbers          = { 3, 5, 2, 234, 4, 1 };
var takeWhileSmall = numbers.TakeWhile (n => n < 100);   // { 3, 5, 2 }
```

SkipWhile enumerates the input sequence, ignoring each item until the given predicate is false. It then emits the remaining elements:

```
int[] numbers          = { 3, 5, 2, 234, 4, 1 };
var skipWhileSmall = numbers.SkipWhile (n => n < 100);   // { 234, 4, 1 }
```

TakeWhile and SkipWhile have no translation to SQL and throws an exception if used in a LINQ-to-db query.

Distinct

Distinct returns the input sequence, stripped of duplicates. You can optionally pass in a custom equality comparer. The following returns distinct letters in a string:

```
char[] distinctLetters = "HelloWorld".Distinct().ToArray();
string s = new string (distinctLetters);              // HeloWrd
```

We can call LINQ methods directly on a string, because string implements IEnumerable<char>.

Projecting

IEnumerable<TSource>→ IEnumerable<TResult>

Method	Description	SQL equivalents
Select	Transforms each input element with the given lambda expression	SELECT
SelectMany	Transforms each input element and then flattens and concatenates the resultant subsequences	INNER JOIN, LEFT OUTER JOIN, CROSS JOIN

 When querying a database, Select and SelectMany are the most versatile joining constructs; for local queries, Join and GroupJoin are the most *efficient* joining constructs.

Select

Argument	Type
Source sequence	IEnumerable<TSource>
Result selector	TSource => TResult or (TSource,int) => TResult

Query syntax

```
select projection-expression
```

Enumerable implementation

```
public static IEnumerable<TResult> Select<TSource,TResult>
  (this IEnumerable<TSource> source, Func<TSource,TResult> selector)
{
  foreach (TSource element in source)
    yield return selector (element);
}
```

Overview

With Select, you always get the same number of elements that you started with. Each element, however, can be transformed in any manner by the lambda function.

The following selects the names of all fonts installed on the computer (from System.Drawing):

```
IEnumerable<string> query = from f in FontFamily.Families
                            select f.Name;

foreach (string name in query) Console.WriteLine (name);
```

In this example, the `select` clause converts a `FontFamily` object to its name. Here's the lambda equivalent:

```
IEnumerable<string> query = FontFamily.Families.Select (f => f.Name);
```

Select statements are often used to project into anonymous types:

```
var query =
  from f in FontFamily.Families
  select new { f.Name, LineSpacing = f.GetLineSpacing (FontStyle.Bold) };
```

A projection with no transformation is sometimes used with query syntax, in order to satisfy the requirement that the query end in a `select` or `group` clause. The following selects fonts supporting strikeout:

```
IEnumerable<FontFamily> query =
  from f in FontFamily.Families
  where f.IsStyleAvailable (FontStyle.Strikeout)
  select f;

foreach (FontFamily ff in query) Console.WriteLine (ff.Name);
```

In such cases, the compiler omits the projection when translating to fluent syntax.

Indexed projection

The `selector` expression can optionally accept an integer argument, which acts as an indexer, providing the expression with the position of each input in the input sequence. This works only with local queries:

```
string[] names = { "Tom", "Dick", "Harry", "Mary", "Jay" };

IEnumerable<string> query = names
  .Select ((s,i) => i + "=" + s);      // { "0=Tom", "1=Dick", ... }
```

Select subqueries and object hierarchies

You can nest a subquery in a `select` clause to build an object hierarchy. The following example returns a collection describing each directory under *D:\source*, with a subcollection of files under each directory:

```
DirectoryInfo[] dirs = new DirectoryInfo (@"d:\source").GetDirectories();

var query =
  from d in dirs
  where (d.Attributes & FileAttributes.System) == 0
  select new
  {
    DirectoryName = d.FullName,
    Created = d.CreationTime,

    Files = from f in d.GetFiles()
            where (f.Attributes & FileAttributes.Hidden) == 0
            select new { FileName = f.Name, f.Length, }
  };
```

```
foreach (var dirFiles in query)
{
  Console.WriteLine ("Directory: " + dirFiles.DirectoryName);
  foreach (var file in dirFiles.Files)
    Console.WriteLine ("   " + file.FileName + " Len: " + file.Length);
}
```

The inner portion of this query can be called a *correlated subquery*. A subquery is correlated if it references an object in the outer query—in this case, it references d, the directory being enumerated.

A subquery inside a Select allows you to map one object hierarchy to another, or map a relational object model to a hierarchical object model.

With local queries, a subquery within a Select causes double-deferred execution. In our example, the files don't get filtered or projected until the inner foreach statement enumerates.

Subqueries and joins in LINQ to SQL and EF

Subquery projections work well in LINQ to SQL and EF and can be used to do the work of SQL-style joins. Here's how we retrieve each customer's name along with their high-value purchases:

```
var query =
  from c in dataContext.Customers
  select new {
              c.Name,
              Purchases = from p in dataContext.Purchases
                          where p.CustomerID == c.ID && p.Price > 1000
                          select new { p.Description, p.Price }
             };

foreach (var namePurchases in query)
{
  Console.WriteLine ("Customer: " + namePurchases.Name);
  foreach (var purchaseDetail in namePurchases.Purchases)
    Console.WriteLine ("   - $$$: " + purchaseDetail.Price);
}
```

This style of query is ideally suited to interpreted queries. The outer query and subquery are processed as a unit, avoiding unnecessary round-tripping. With local queries, however, it's inefficient because every combination of outer and inner elements must be enumerated to get the few matching combinations. A better choice for local queries is Join or GroupJoin, described in the following sections.

This query matches up objects from two disparate collections, and it can be thought of as a "Join". The difference between this and a conventional database join (or subquery) is that we're not flattening the output into a single two-dimensional result set. We're mapping the relational data to hierarchical data, rather than to flat data.

Here's the same query simplified by using the `Purchases` association property on the `Customer` entity:

```
from c in dataContext.Customers
select new
{
  c.Name,
  Purchases = from p in c.Purchases      // Purchases is EntitySet<Purchase>
              where p.Price > 1000
              select new { p.Description, p.Price }
};
```

Both queries are analogous to a left outer join in SQL in the sense that we get all customers in the outer enumeration, regardless of whether they have any purchases. To emulate an inner join—where customers without high-value purchases are excluded—we would need to add a filter condition on the purchases collection:

```
from c in dataContext.Customers
where c.Purchases.Any (p => p.Price > 1000)
select new {
            c.Name,
            Purchases = from p in c.Purchases
                        where p.Price > 1000
                        select new { p.Description, p.Price }
           };
```

This is slightly untidy, however, in that we've written the same predicate (Price > 1000) twice. We can avoid this duplication with a `let` clause:

```
from c in dataContext.Customers
let highValueP = from p in c.Purchases
                 where p.Price > 1000
                 select new { p.Description, p.Price }
where highValueP.Any()
select new { c.Name, Purchases = highValueP };
```

This style of query is flexible. By changing `Any` to `Count`, for instance, we can modify the query to retrieve only customers with at least two high-value purchases:

```
...
where highValueP.Count() >= 2
select new { c.Name, Purchases = highValueP };
```

Projecting into concrete types

Projecting into anonymous types is useful in obtaining intermediate results, but not so useful if you want to send a result set back to a client, for instance, because anonymous types can exist only as local variables within a method. An alternative is to use concrete types for projections, such as DataSets or custom business entity classes. A custom business entity is simply a class that you write with some properties, similar to a LINQ to SQL [Table] annotated class or an EF Entity, but designed to hide lower-level (database-related) details. You might exclude foreign key fields from business entity classes, for instance. Assuming we wrote custom entity classes called `CustomerEntity` and `PurchaseEntity`, here's how we could project into them:

```
IQueryable<CustomerEntity> query =
  from c in dataContext.Customers
  select new CustomerEntity
  {
    Name = c.Name,
    Purchases =
      (from p in c.Purchases
       where p.Price > 1000
       select new PurchaseEntity {
                                   Description = p.Description,
                                   Value = p.Price
                                 }
      ).ToList()
  };

// Force query execution, converting output to a more convenient List:
List<CustomerEntity> result = query.ToList();
```

Notice that so far, we've not had to use a `Join` or `SelectMany` statement. This is because we're maintaining the hierarchical shape of the data, as illustrated in Figure 9-2. With LINQ, you can often avoid the traditional SQL approach of flattening tables into a two-dimensional result set.

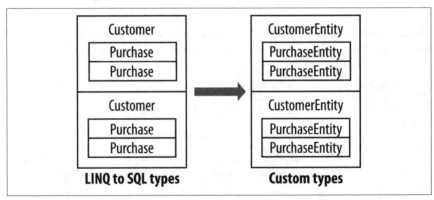

Figure 9-2. Projecting an object hierarchy

SelectMany

Argument	Type
Source sequence	`IEnumerable<TSource>`
Result selector	`TSource => IEnumerable<TResult>` or `(TSource,int) => IEnumerable<TResult>`

Query syntax

```
from identifier1 in enumerable-expression1
from identifier2 in enumerable-expression2
...
```

Enumerable implementation

```
public static IEnumerable<TResult> SelectMany<TSource,TResult>
  (IEnumerable<TSource> source,
   Func <TSource,IEnumerable<TResult>> selector)
{
  foreach (TSource element in source)
    foreach (TResult subElement in selector (element))
      yield return subElement;
}
```

Overview

`SelectMany` concatenates subsequences into a single, flat output sequence.

Recall that for each input element, `Select` yields exactly one output element. In contrast, `SelectMany` yields *0..n* output elements. The *0..n* elements come from a subsequence or child sequence that the lambda expression must emit.

`SelectMany` can be used to expand child sequences, flatten nested collections, and join two collections into a flat output sequence. Using the conveyor belt analogy, `SelectMany` funnels fresh material onto a conveyor belt. With `SelectMany`, each input element is the *trigger* for the introduction of fresh material. The fresh material is emitted by the `selector` lambda expression and must be a sequence. In other words, the lambda expression must emit a *child sequence* per input *element*. The final result is a concatenation of the child sequences emitted for each input element.

Starting with a simple example, suppose we have an array of names as follows:

```
string[] fullNames = { "Anne Williams", "John Fred Smith", "Sue Green" };
```

which we wish to convert to a single flat collection of words—in other words:

```
"Anne", "Williams", "John", "Fred", "Smith", "Sue", Green"
```

`SelectMany` is ideal for this task, because we're mapping each input element to a variable number of output elements. All we must do is come up with a `selector` expression that converts each input element to a child sequence. `string.Split` does the job nicely: it takes a string and splits it into words, emitting the result as an array:

```
string testInputElement = "Anne Williams";
string[] childSequence  = testInputElement.Split();

// childSequence is { "Anne", "Williams" };
```

So, here's our `SelectMany` query and the result:

```
IEnumerable<string> query = fullNames.SelectMany (name => name.Split());
```

```
foreach (string name in query)
  Console.Write (name + "|");   // Anne|Williams|John|Fred|Smith|Sue|Green|
```

 If you replace SelectMany with Select, you get the same
results in hierarchical form. The following emits a sequence of
string *arrays*, requiring nested foreach statements to enumerate:

```
IEnumerable<string[]> query =
  fullNames.Select (name => name.Split());
```

```
foreach (string[] stringArray in query)
  foreach (string name in stringArray)
    Console.Write (name + "|");
```

The benefit of SelectMany is that it yields a single *flat* result
sequence.

SelectMany is supported in query syntax and is invoked by having an *additional generator*—in other words, an extra from clause in the query. The from keyword has two meanings in query syntax. At the start of a query, it introduces the original range variable and input sequence. *Anywhere else* in the query, it translates to SelectMany. Here's our query in query syntax:

```
IEnumerable<string> query =
  from fullName in fullNames
  from name in fullName.Split()       // Translates to SelectMany
  select name;
```

Note that the additional generator introduces a new range variable—in this case, name. The old range variable stays in scope, however, and we can subsequently access both.

Multiple range variables

In the preceding example, both name and fullName remain in scope until the query either ends or reaches an into clause. The extended scope of these variables is *the* killer scenario for query syntax over fluent syntax.

To illustrate, we can take the preceding query and include fullName in the final projection:

```
IEnumerable<string> query =
  from fullName in fullNames
  from name in fullName.Split()
  select name + " came from " + fullName;
```

```
Anne came from Anne Williams
Williams came from Anne Williams
John came from John Fred Smith
...
```

Behind the scenes, the compiler must pull some tricks to let you access both variables. A good way to appreciate this is to try writing the same query in fluent syntax. It's tricky! It gets harder still if you insert a where or orderby clause before projecting:

```
from fullName in fullNames
from name in fullName.Split()
orderby fullName, name
select name + " came from " + fullName;
```

The problem is that SelectMany emits a flat sequence of child elements—in our case, a flat collection of words. The original "outer" element from which it came (fullName) is lost. The solution is to "carry" the outer element with each child, in a temporary anonymous type:

```
from fullName in fullNames
from x in fullName.Split().Select (name => new { name, fullName } )
orderby x.fullName, x.name
select x.name + " came from " + x.fullName;
```

The only change here is that we're wrapping each child element (name) in an anonymous type that also contains its fullName. This is similar to how a let clause is resolved. Here's the final conversion to fluent syntax:

```
IEnumerable<string> query = fullNames
  .SelectMany (fName => fName.Split()
                              .Select (name => new { name, fName } ))
  .OrderBy (x => x.fName)
  .ThenBy  (x => x.name)
  .Select  (x => x.name + " came from " + x.fName);
```

Thinking in query syntax

As we just demonstrated, there are good reasons to use query syntax if you need multiple range variables. In such cases, it helps not only to use query syntax, but also to think directly in its terms.

There are two basic patterns when writing additional generators. The first is *expanding and flattening subsequences*. To do this, you call a property or method on an existing range variable in your additional generator. We did this in the previous example:

```
from fullName in fullNames
from name in fullName.Split()
```

Here, we've expanded from enumerating full names to enumerating words. An analogous LINQ-to-db query is when you expand child association properties. The following query lists all customers along with their purchases:

```
IEnumerable<string> query = from c in dataContext.Customers
                            from p in c.Purchases
                            select c.Name + " bought a " + p.Description;

Tom bought a Bike
```

```
Tom bought a Holiday
Dick bought a Phone
Harry bought a Car
...
```

Here, we've expanded each customer into a subsequence of purchases.

The second pattern is performing a *cartesian product* or *cross join*—where every element of one sequence is matched with every element of another. To do this, introduce a generator whose `selector` expression returns a sequence unrelated to a range variable:

```
int[] numbers = { 1, 2, 3 };  string[] letters = { "a", "b" };

IEnumerable<string> query = from n in numbers
                            from l in letters
                            select n.ToString() + l;

RESULT: { "1a", "1b", "2a", "2b", "3a", "3b" }
```

This style of query is the basis of `SelectMany`-style *joins*.

Joining with SelectMany

You can use `SelectMany` to join two sequences, simply by filtering the results of a cross product. For instance, suppose we wanted to match players for a game. We could start as follows:

```
string[] players = { "Tom", "Jay", "Mary" };

IEnumerable<string> query = from name1 in players
                            from name2 in players
                            select name1 + " vs " + name2;

RESULT: { "Tom vs Tom", "Tom vs Jay", "Tom vs Mary",
          "Jay vs Tom", "Jay vs Jay", "Jay vs Mary",
          "Mary vs Tom", "Mary vs "Jay", "Mary vs Mary" }
```

The query reads: "For every player, reiterate every player, selecting player 1 versus player 2." Although we got what we asked for (a cross join), the results are not useful until we add a filter:

```
IEnumerable<string> query = from name1 in players
                            from name2 in players
                            where name1.CompareTo (name2) < 0
                            orderby name1, name2
                            select name1 + " vs " + name2;

RESULT: { "Jay vs Mary", "Jay vs Tom", "Mary vs Tom" }
```

The filter predicate constitutes the *join condition*. Our query can be called a *non-equi join*, because the join condition doesn't use an equality operator.

We'll demonstrate the remaining types of joins with LINQ to SQL (they'll also work with EF except where we explicitly use a foreign key field).

SelectMany in LINQ to SQL and EF

`SelectMany` in LINQ to SQL and EF can perform cross joins, non-equi joins, inner joins, and left outer joins. You can use `SelectMany` with both predefined associations and ad hoc relationships—just as with `Select`. The difference is that `Select Many` returns a flat rather than a hierarchical result set.

A LINQ-to-db cross join is written just as in the preceding section. The following query matches every customer to every purchase (a cross join):

```
var query = from c in dataContext.Customers
            from p in dataContext.Purchases
            select c.Name + " might have bought a " + p.Description;
```

More typically, though, you'd want to match customers to their own purchases only. You achieve this by adding a `where` clause with a joining predicate. This results in a standard SQL-style equi-join:

```
var query = from c in dataContext.Customers
            from p in dataContext.Purchases
            where c.ID == p.CustomerID
            select c.Name + " bought a " + p.Description;
```

This translates well to SQL. In the next section, we'll see how it extends to support outer joins. Reformulating such queries with LINQ's `Join` operator actually makes them *less* extensible —LINQ is opposite to SQL in this sense.

If you have association properties for relationships in your entities, you can express the same query by expanding the subcollection instead of filtering the cross product:

```
from c in dataContext.Customers
from p in c.Purchases
select new { c.Name, p.Description };
```

Entity Framework doesn't expose foreign keys in the entities, so for recognized relationships, you *must* use its association properties rather than joining manually as we did previously.

The advantage is that we've eliminated the joining predicate. We've gone from filtering a cross product to expanding and flattening. Both queries, however, will result in the same SQL.

You can add `where` clauses to such a query for additional filtering. For instance, if we wanted only customers whose names started with "T", we could filter as follows:

```
from c in dataContext.Customers
where c.Name.StartsWith ("T")
from p in c.Purchases
select new { c.Name, p.Description };
```

This LINQ-to-db query would work equally well if the where clause is moved one line down. If it is a local query, however, moving the where clause down would make it less efficient. With local queries, you should filter *before* joining.

You can introduce new tables into the mix with additional from clauses. For instance, if each purchase had purchase item child rows, you could produce a flat result set of customers with their purchases, each with their purchase detail lines as follows:

```
from c in dataContext.Customers
from p in c.Purchases
from pi in p.PurchaseItems
select new { c.Name, p.Description, pi.DetailLine };
```

Each from clause introduces a new *child* table. To include data from a *parent* table (via an association property), you don't add a from clause—you simply navigate to the property. For example, if each customer has a salesperson whose name you want to query, just do this:

```
from c in dataContext.Customers
select new { Name = c.Name, SalesPerson = c.SalesPerson.Name };
```

You don't use SelectMany in this case because there's no subcollection to flatten. Parent association properties return a single item.

Outer joins with SelectMany

We saw previously that a Select subquery yields a result analogous to a left outer join.

```
from c in dataContext.Customers
select new {
            c.Name,
            Purchases = from p in c.Purchases
                        where p.Price > 1000
                        select new { p.Description, p.Price }
          };
```

In this example, every outer element (customer) is included, regardless of whether the customer has any purchases. But suppose we rewrite this query with Select Many so we can obtain a single flat collection rather than a hierarchical result set:

```
from c in dataContext.Customers
from p in c.Purchases
where p.Price > 1000
select new { c.Name, p.Description, p.Price };
```

In the process of flattening the query, we've switched to an inner join: customers are now included only for whom one or more high-value purchases exist. To get a left outer join with a flat result set, we must apply the DefaultIfEmpty query operator on the inner sequence. This method returns a sequence with a single null element if its input sequence has no elements.

Here's such a query, price predicate aside:

```
from c in dataContext.Customers
from p in c.Purchases.DefaultIfEmpty()
select new { c.Name, p.Description, Price = (decimal?) p.Price };
```

This works perfectly with LINQ to SQL and EF, returning all customers, even if they have no purchases. But if we were to run this as a local query, it would crash, because when p is null, p.Description and p.Price throw a NullReferenceExcep tion. We can make our query robust in either scenario as follows:

```
from c in dataContext.Customers
from p in c.Purchases.DefaultIfEmpty()
select new {
            c.Name,
            Descript = p == null ? null : p.Description,
            Price = p == null ? (decimal?) null : p.Price
          };
```

Let's now reintroduce the price filter. We cannot use a where clause as we did before, because it would execute *after* DefaultIfEmpty:

```
from c in dataContext.Customers
from p in c.Purchases.DefaultIfEmpty()
where p.Price > 1000...
```

The correct solution is to splice the Where clause *before* DefaultIfEmpty with a sub-query:

```
from c in dataContext.Customers
from p in c.Purchases.Where (p => p.Price > 1000).DefaultIfEmpty()
select new {
            c.Name,
            Descript = p == null ? null : p.Description,
            Price = p == null ? (decimal?) null : p.Price
          };
```

LINQ to SQL and EF translate this to a left outer join. This is an effective pattern for writing such queries.

> If you're used to writing outer joins in SQL, you might be tempted to overlook the simpler option of a Select subquery for this style of query, in favor of the awkward but familiar SQL-centric flat approach. The hierarchical result set from a Select subquery is often better suited to outer join-style queries because there are no additional nulls to deal with.

Joining

Method	Description	SQL equivalents
Join	Applies a lookup strategy to match elements from two collections, emitting a flat result set	INNER JOIN
GroupJoin	As above, but emits a *hierarchical* result set	INNER JOIN, LEFT OUTER JOIN
Zip	Enumerates two sequences in step (like a zipper), applying a function over each element pair.	Exception thrown

Join and GroupJoin

IEnumerable<TOuter>, IEnumerable<TInner>→IEnumerable<TResult>

Join arguments

Argument	Type
Outer sequence	IEnumerable<TOuter>
Inner sequence	IEnumerable<TInner>
Outer key selector	TOuter => TKey
Inner key selector	TInner => TKey
Result selector	(TOuter,TInner) => TResult

GroupJoin arguments

Argument	Type
Outer sequence	IEnumerable<TOuter>
Inner sequence	IEnumerable<TInner>
Outer key selector	TOuter => TKey
Inner key selector	TInner => TKey
Result selector	(TOuter,**IEnumerable<TInner>**) => TResult

Query syntax

```
from outer-var in outer-enumerable
join inner-var in inner-enumerable on outer-key-expr equals inner-key-expr
  [ into identifier ]
```

Overview

`Join` and `GroupJoin` mesh two input sequences into a single output sequence. `Join` emits flat output; `GroupJoin` emits hierarchical output.

`Join` and `GroupJoin` provide an alternative strategy to `Select` and `SelectMany`. The advantage of `Join` and `GroupJoin` is that they execute efficiently over local in-memory collections, since they first load the inner sequence into a keyed lookup, avoiding the need to repeatedly enumerate over every inner element. The disadvantage is that they offer the equivalent of inner and left outer joins only; cross joins and non-equi joins must still be done with `Select`/`SelectMany`. With LINQ to SQL and Entity Framework queries, `Join` and `GroupJoin` offer no real benefits over `Select` and `SelectMany`.

Table 9-1 summarizes the differences between each of the joining strategies.

Table 9-1. Joining strategies

Strategy	Result shape	Local query efficiency	Inner joins	Left outer joins	Cross joins	Non-equi joins
`Select + SelectMany`	Flat	Bad	Yes	Yes	Yes	Yes
`Select + Select`	Nested	Bad	Yes	Yes	Yes	Yes
`Join`	Flat	Good	Yes	-	-	-
`GroupJoin`	Nested	Good	Yes	Yes	-	-
`GroupJoin + SelectMany`	Flat	Good	Yes	Yes	-	-

Join

The `Join` operator performs an inner join, emitting a flat output sequence.

 Entity Framework hides foreign key fields, so you can't manually join across natural relationships (instead, you can query across association properties, as we described in the previous two sections).

The simplest way to demonstrate `Join` is with LINQ to SQL. The following query lists all customers alongside their purchases, without using an association property:

```
IQueryable<string> query =
  from c in dataContext.Customers
  join p in dataContext.Purchases on c.ID equals p.CustomerID
  select c.Name + " bought a " + p.Description;
```

The results match what we would get from a `SelectMany`-style query:

```
Tom bought a Bike
Tom bought a Holiday
Dick bought a Phone
Harry bought a Car
```

To see the benefit of Join over SelectMany, we must convert this to a local query. We can demonstrate this by first copying all customers and purchases to arrays and then querying the arrays:

```
Customer[] customers = dataContext.Customers.ToArray();
Purchase[] purchases = dataContext.Purchases.ToArray();
var slowQuery = from c in customers
                from p in purchases where c.ID == p.CustomerID
                select c.Name + " bought a " + p.Description;

var fastQuery = from c in customers
                join p in purchases on c.ID equals p.CustomerID
                select c.Name + " bought a " + p.Description;
```

Although both queries yield the same results, the Join query is considerably faster because its implementation in Enumerable preloads the inner collection (purchases) into a keyed lookup.

The query syntax for join can be written in general terms as follows:

```
join inner-var in inner-sequence on outer-key-expr equals inner-key-expr
```

Join operators in LINQ differentiate between the *outer sequence* and *inner sequence*. Syntactically:

- The *outer sequence* is the input sequence (in this case, customers).
- The *inner sequence* is the new collection you introduce (in this case, purchases).

Join performs inner joins, meaning customers without purchases are excluded from the output. With inner joins, you can swap the inner and outer sequences in the query and still get the same results:

```
from p in purchases                              // p is now outer
join c in customers on p.CustomerID equals c.ID  // c is now inner
...
```

You can add further join clauses to the same query. If each purchase, for instance, has one or more purchase items, you could join the purchase items as follows:

```
from c in customers
join p in purchases on c.ID equals p.CustomerID      // first join
join pi in purchaseItems on p.ID equals pi.PurchaseID  // second join
...
```

purchases acts as the *inner* sequence in the first join and as the *outer* sequence in the second join. You could obtain the same results (inefficiently) using nested foreach statements as follows:

```
foreach (Customer c in customers)
  foreach (Purchase p in purchases)
    if (c.ID == p.CustomerID)
      foreach (PurchaseItem pi in purchaseItems)
```

```
        if (p.ID == pi.PurchaseID)
            Console.WriteLine (c.Name + "," + p.Price + "," + pi.Detail);
```

In query syntax, variables from earlier joins remain in scope—just as they do with SelectMany-style queries. You're also permitted to insert where and let clauses in between join clauses.

Joining on multiple keys

You can join on multiple keys with anonymous types as follows:

```
from x in sequenceX
join y in sequenceY on new { K1 = x.Prop1, K2 = x.Prop2 }
                equals new { K1 = y.Prop3, K2 = y.Prop4 }
...
```

For this to work, the two anonymous types must be structured identically. The compiler then implements each with the same internal type, making the joining keys compatible.

Joining in fluent syntax

The following query syntax join:

```
from c in customers
join p in purchases on c.ID equals p.CustomerID
select new { c.Name, p.Description, p.Price };
```

in fluent syntax is as follows:

```
customers.Join (                    // outer collection
    purchases,                      // inner collection
    c => c.ID,                      // outer key selector
    p => p.CustomerID,              // inner key selector
    (c, p) => new
        { c.Name, p.Description, p.Price }    // result selector
);
```

The result selector expression at the end creates each element in the output sequence. If you have additional clauses prior to projecting, such as orderby in this example:

```
from c in customers
join p in purchases on c.ID equals p.CustomerID
orderby p.Price
select c.Name + " bought a " + p.Description;
```

you must manufacture a temporary anonymous type in the result selector in fluent syntax. This keeps both c and p in scope following the join:

```
customers.Join (                    // outer collection
    purchases,                      // inner collection
    c => c.ID,                      // outer key selector
    p => p.CustomerID,              // inner key selector
    (c, p) => new { c, p } )        // result selector
```

```
.OrderBy (x => x.p.Price)
.Select  (x => x.c.Name + " bought a " + x.p.Description);
```

Query syntax is usually preferable when joining; it's less fiddly.

GroupJoin

GroupJoin does the same work as Join, but instead of yielding a flat result, it yields a hierarchical result, grouped by each outer element. It also allows left outer joins.

The query syntax for GroupJoin is the same as for Join but is followed by the into keyword.

Here's the most basic example:

```
IEnumerable<IEnumerable<Purchase>> query =
  from c in customers
  join p in purchases on c.ID equals p.CustomerID
  into custPurchases
  select custPurchases;   // custPurchases is a sequence
```

 An into clause translates to GroupJoin only when it appears directly after a join clause. After a select or group clause, it means *query continuation*. The two uses of the into keyword are quite different, although they have one feature in common: they both introduce a new range variable.

The result is a sequence of sequences, which we could enumerate as follows:

```
foreach (IEnumerable<Purchase> purchaseSequence in query)
  foreach (Purchase p in purchaseSequence)
    Console.WriteLine (p.Description);
```

This isn't very useful, however, because purchaseSequence has no reference to the customer. More commonly, you'd do this:

```
from c in customers
join p in purchases on c.ID equals p.CustomerID
into custPurchases
select new { CustName = c.Name, custPurchases };
```

This gives the same results as the following (inefficient) Select subquery:

```
from c in customers
select new
{
  CustName = c.Name,
  custPurchases = purchases.Where (p => c.ID == p.CustomerID)
};
```

By default, GroupJoin does the equivalent of a left outer join. To get an inner join—where customers without purchases are excluded—you need to filter on custPurchases:

```
from c in customers join p in purchases on c.ID equals p.CustomerID
into custPurchases
```

```
where custPurchases.Any()
select ...
```

Clauses after a group-join into operate on *subsequences* of inner child elements, not *individual* child elements. This means that to filter individual purchases, you'd have to call Where *before* joining:

```
from c in customers
join p in purchases.Where (p2 => p2.Price > 1000)
  on c.ID equals p.CustomerID
into custPurchases ...
```

You can construct lambda queries with GroupJoin as you would with Join.

Flat outer joins

You run into a dilemma if you want both an outer join and a flat result set. Group Join gives you the outer join; Join gives you the flat result set. The solution is to first call GroupJoin, and then DefaultIfEmpty on each child sequence, and then finally SelectMany on the result:

```
from c in customers
join p in purchases on c.ID equals p.CustomerID into custPurchases
from cp in custPurchases.DefaultIfEmpty()
select new
{
  CustName = c.Name,
  Price = cp == null ? (decimal?) null : cp.Price
};
```

DefaultIfEmpty emits a sequence with a single null value if a subsequence of purchases is empty. The second from clause translates to SelectMany. In this role, it *expands and flattens* all the purchase subsequences, concatenating them into a single sequence of purchase *elements*.

Joining with lookups

The Join and GroupJoin methods in Enumerable work in two steps. First, they load the inner sequence into a *lookup*. Second, they query the outer sequence in combination with the lookup.

A *lookup* is a sequence of groupings that can be accessed directly by key. Another way to think of it is as a dictionary of sequences—a dictionary that can accept many elements under each key (sometimes called a *multidictionary*). Lookups are read-only and defined by the following interface:

```
public interface ILookup<TKey,TElement> :
   IEnumerable<IGrouping<TKey,TElement>>, IEnumerable
{
  int Count { get; }
  bool Contains (TKey key);
  IEnumerable<TElement> this [TKey key] { get; }
}
```

The joining operators—like other sequence-emitting operators—honor deferred or lazy execution semantics. This means the lookup is not built until you begin enumerating the output sequence (and then the *entire* lookup is built right then).

You can create and query lookups manually as an alternative strategy to using the joining operators, when dealing with local collections. There are a couple of benefits in doing so:

- You can reuse the same lookup over multiple queries—as well as in ordinary imperative code.

- Querying a lookup is an excellent way of understanding how Join and Group Join work.

The ToLookup extension method creates a lookup. The following loads all purchases into a lookup—keyed by their CustomerID:

```
ILookup<int?,Purchase> purchLookup =
  purchases.ToLookup (p => p.CustomerID, p => p);
```

The first argument selects the key; the second argument selects the objects that are to be loaded as values into the lookup.

Reading a lookup is rather like reading a dictionary, except that the indexer returns a *sequence* of matching items, rather than a *single* matching item. The following enumerates all purchases made by the customer whose ID is 1:

```
foreach (Purchase p in purchLookup [1])
  Console.WriteLine (p.Description);
```

With a lookup in place, you can write SelectMany/Select queries that execute as efficiently as Join/GroupJoin queries. Join is equivalent to using SelectMany on a lookup:

```
from c in customers
from p in purchLookup [c.ID]
select new { c.Name, p.Description, p.Price };

Tom Bike 500
Tom Holiday 2000
Dick Bike 600
Dick Phone 300
...
```

Adding a call to DefaultIfEmpty makes this into an outer join:

```
from c in customers
from p in purchLookup [c.ID].DefaultIfEmpty()
  select new {
            c.Name,
            Descript = p == null ? null : p.Description,
            Price = p == null ? (decimal?) null : p.Price
          };
```

GroupJoin is equivalent to reading the lookup inside a projection:

```
from c in customers
select new {
             CustName = c.Name,
             CustPurchases = purchLookup [c.ID]
           };
```

Enumerable implementations

Here's the simplest valid implementation of Enumerable.Join, null checking aside:

```
public static IEnumerable <TResult> Join
                                  <TOuter,TInner,TKey,TResult> (
  this IEnumerable <TOuter>    outer,
  IEnumerable <TInner>         inner,
  Func <TOuter,TKey>           outerKeySelector,
  Func <TInner,TKey>           innerKeySelector,
  Func <TOuter,TInner,TResult> resultSelector)
{
  ILookup <TKey, TInner> lookup = inner.ToLookup (innerKeySelector);
  return
    from outerItem in outer
    from innerItem in lookup [outerKeySelector (outerItem)]
    select resultSelector (outerItem, innerItem);
}
```

GroupJoin's implementation is like that of Join, but simpler:

```
public static IEnumerable <TResult> GroupJoin
                                  <TOuter,TInner,TKey,TResult> (
  this IEnumerable <TOuter>    outer,
  IEnumerable <TInner>         inner,
  Func <TOuter,TKey>           outerKeySelector,
  Func <TInner,TKey>           innerKeySelector,
  Func <TOuter,IEnumerable<TInner>,TResult>  resultSelector)
{
  ILookup <TKey, TInner> lookup = inner.ToLookup (innerKeySelector);
  return
    from outerItem in outer
    select resultSelector
      (outerItem, lookup [outerKeySelector (outerItem)]);
}
```

The Zip Operator

IEnumerable<TFirst>, IEnumerable<TSecond>→ IEnumerable<TResult>

The Zip operator was added in Framework 4.0. It enumerates two sequences in step (like a zipper), returning a sequence based on applying a function over each element pair. For instance, the following:

```
int[] numbers = { 3, 5, 7 };
string[] words = { "three", "five", "seven", "ignored" };
IEnumerable<string> zip = numbers.Zip (words, (n, w) => n + "=" + w);
```

produces a sequence with the following elements:

```
3=three
5=five
7=seven
```

Extra elements in either input sequence are ignored. Zip is not supported by EF and L2S.

Ordering

IEnumerable<TSource>→ IOrderedEnumerable<TSource>

Method	Description	SQL equivalents
OrderBy, ThenBy	Sorts a sequence in ascending order	ORDER BY ...
OrderByDescending, ThenByDescending	Sorts a sequence in descending order	ORDER BY ... DESC
Reverse	Returns a sequence in reverse order	Exception thrown

Ordering operators return the same elements in a different order.

OrderBy, OrderByDescending, ThenBy, and ThenByDescending

OrderBy and OrderByDescending arguments

Argument	Type
Input sequence	IEnumerable<TSource>
Key selector	TSource => TKey

Return type = IOrderedEnumerable<TSource>

ThenBy and ThenByDescending arguments

Argument	Type
Input sequence	IOrderedEnumerable<TSource>
Key selector	TSource => TKey

Query syntax

```
orderby expression1 [descending] [, expression2 [descending] ... ]
```

Overview

OrderBy returns a sorted version of the input sequence, using the keySelector expression to make comparisons. The following query emits a sequence of names in alphabetical order:

```
IEnumerable<string> query = names.OrderBy (s => s);
```

The following sorts names by length:

```
IEnumerable<string> query = names.OrderBy (s => s.Length);

// Result: { "Jay", "Tom", "Mary", "Dick", "Harry" };
```

The relative order of elements with the same sorting key (in this case, Jay/Tom and Mary/Dick) is indeterminate—unless you append a ThenBy operator:

```
IEnumerable<string> query = names.OrderBy (s => s.Length).ThenBy (s => s);

// Result: { "Jay", "Tom", "Dick", "Mary", "Harry" };
```

ThenBy reorders only elements that had the same sorting key in the preceding sort. You can chain any number of ThenBy operators. The following sorts first by length, then by the second character, and finally by the first character:

```
names.OrderBy (s => s.Length).ThenBy (s => s[1]).ThenBy (s => s[0]);
```

The equivalent in query syntax is this:

```
from s in names
orderby s.Length, s[1], s[0]
select s;
```

 The following variation is *incorrect*—it will actually order first by s[1] and then by s.Length (or in the case of a database query, it will order *only* by s[1] and discard the former ordering):

```
from s in names
orderby s.Length
orderby s[1]
...
```

LINQ also provides OrderByDescending and ThenByDescending operators, which do the same things, emitting the results in reverse order. The following LINQ-to-db query retrieves purchases in descending order of price, with those of the same price listed alphabetically:

```
dataContext.Purchases.OrderByDescending (p => p.Price)
                     .ThenBy (p => p.Description);
```

In query syntax:

```
from p in dataContext.Purchases
orderby p.Price descending, p.Description
select p;
```

Comparers and collations

In a local query, the key selector objects themselves determine the ordering algorithm via their default IComparable implementation (see Chapter 7). You can override the sorting algorithm by passing in an IComparer object. The following performs a case-insensitive sort:

```
names.OrderBy (n => n, StringComparer.CurrentCultureIgnoreCase);
```

Passing in a comparer is not supported in query syntax, nor in any way by LINQ to SQL or EF. When querying a database, the comparison algorithm is determined by the participating column's collation. If the collation is case-sensitive, you can request a case-insensitive sort by calling ToUpper in the key selector:

```
from p in dataContext.Purchases
orderby p.Description.ToUpper()
select p;
```

IOrderedEnumerable and IOrderedQueryable

The ordering operators return special subtypes of IEnumerable<T>. Those in Enumerable return IOrderedEnumerable<TSource>; those in Queryable return IOrderedQueryable<TSource>. These subtypes allow a subsequent ThenBy operator to refine rather than replace the existing ordering.

The additional members that these subtypes define are not publicly exposed, so they present like ordinary sequences. The fact that they are different types comes into play when building queries progressively:

```
IOrderedEnumerable<string> query1 = names.OrderBy (s => s.Length);
IOrderedEnumerable<string> query2 = query1.ThenBy (s => s);
```

If we instead declare query1 of type IEnumerable<string>, the second line would not compile—ThenBy requires an input of type IOrderedEnumerable<string>. You can avoid worrying about this by implicitly typing range variables:

```
var query1 = names.OrderBy (s => s.Length);
var query2 = query1.ThenBy (s => s);
```

Implicit typing can create problems of its own, though. The following will not compile:

```
var query = names.OrderBy (s => s.Length);
query = query.Where (n => n.Length > 3);        // Compile-time error
```

The compiler infers query to be of type IOrderedEnumerable<string>, based on OrderBy's output sequence type. However, the Where on the next line returns an ordinary IEnumerable<string>, which cannot be assigned back to query. You can work around this either with explicit typing or by calling AsEnumerable() after OrderBy:

```
var query = names.OrderBy (s => s.Length).AsEnumerable();
query = query.Where (n => n.Length > 3);             // OK
```

The equivalent in interpreted queries is to call `AsQueryable`.

Grouping

`IEnumerable<TSource>→ IEnumerable<IGrouping<TKey,TElement>>`

Method	Description	SQL equivalents
GroupBy	Groups a sequence into subsequences	GROUP BY

GroupBy

Argument	Type
Input sequence	IEnumerable<TSource>
Key selector	TSource => TKey
Element selector (optional)	TSource => TElement
Comparer (optional)	IEqualityComparer<TKey>

Query syntax

```
group element-expression by key-expression
```

Overview

`GroupBy` organizes a flat input sequence into sequences of *groups*. For example, the following organizes all the files in *c:\temp* by extension:

```
string[] files = Directory.GetFiles ("c:\\temp");

IEnumerable<IGrouping<string,string>> query =
   files.GroupBy (file => Path.GetExtension (file));
```

Or if you're comfortable with implicit typing:

```
var query = files.GroupBy (file => Path.GetExtension (file));
```

Here's how to enumerate the result:

```
foreach (IGrouping<string,string> grouping in query)
{
  Console.WriteLine ("Extension: " + grouping.Key);
  foreach (string filename in grouping)
    Console.WriteLine ("   - " + filename);
}

Extension: .pdf
  -- chapter03.pdf
  -- chapter04.pdf
Extension: .doc
  -- todo.doc
  -- menu.doc
```

```
    -- Copy of menu.doc
    ...
```

`Enumerable.GroupBy` works by reading the input elements into a temporary dictionary of lists so that all elements with the same key end up in the same sublist. It then emits a sequence of *groupings*. A grouping is a sequence with a `Key` property:

```
public interface IGrouping <TKey,TElement> : IEnumerable<TElement>,
                                             IEnumerable
{
  TKey Key { get; }     // Key applies to the subsequence as a whole
}
```

By default, the elements in each grouping are untransformed input elements, unless you specify an `elementSelector` argument. The following projects each input element to uppercase:

```
files.GroupBy (file => Path.GetExtension (file), file => file.ToUpper());
```

An `elementSelector` is independent of the `keySelector`. In our case, this means that the Key on each grouping is still in its original case:

```
Extension: .pdf
    -- CHAPTER03.PDF
    -- CHAPTER04.PDF
Extension: .doc
    -- TODO.DOC
```

Note that the subcollections are not emitted in alphabetical order of key. `GroupBy` groups only; it does not *sort*; in fact, it preserves the original ordering. To sort, you must add an `OrderBy` operator:

```
files.GroupBy (file => Path.GetExtension (file), file => file.ToUpper())
    .OrderBy (grouping => grouping.Key);
```

`GroupBy` has a simple and direct translation in query syntax:

```
group element-expr by key-expr
```

Here's our example in query syntax:

```
from file in files
group file.ToUpper() by Path.GetExtension (file);
```

As with `select`, `group` "ends" a query—unless you add a query continuation clause:

```
from file in files
group file.ToUpper() by Path.GetExtension (file) into grouping
orderby grouping.Key
select grouping;
```

Query continuations are often useful in a `group` by query. The next query filters out groups that have fewer than five files in them:

```
from file in files
group file.ToUpper() by Path.GetExtension (file) into grouping
```

```
where grouping.Count() >= 5
select grouping;
```

 A where after a group by is equivalent to HAVING in SQL. It applies to each subsequence or grouping as a whole, rather than the individual elements.

Sometimes you're interested purely in the result of an aggregation on a grouping and so can abandon the subsequences:

```
string[] votes = { "Bush", "Gore", "Gore", "Bush", "Bush" };

IEnumerable<string> query = from vote in votes
                           group vote by vote into g
                           orderby g.Count() descending
                           select g.Key;

string winner = query.First();     // Bush
```

GroupBy in LINQ to SQL and EF

Grouping works in the same way when querying a database. If you have association properties set up, you'll find, however, that the need to group arises less frequently than with standard SQL. For instance, to select customers with at least two purchases, you don't need to group; the following query does the job nicely:

```
from c in dataContext.Customers
where c.Purchases.Count >= 2
select c.Name + " has made " + c.Purchases.Count + " purchases";
```

An example of when you might use grouping is to list total sales by year:

```
from p in dataContext.Purchases
group p.Price by p.Date.Year into salesByYear
select new {
            Year       = salesByYear.Key,
            TotalValue = salesByYear.Sum()
           };
```

LINQ's grouping is more powerful than SQL's "GROUP BY". For instance, it's legal to fetch all detail rows without any aggregation:

```
from p in dataContext.Purchases
group p by p.Date.Year
```

This works well in EF, but in L2S it causes excessive round-tripping. An easy workaround is to call .AsEnumerable() just before grouping, so that the grouping happens on the client. This is no less efficient, as long as you perform any filtering *before* grouping, so that you only fetch the data you need from the server.

Another departure from traditional SQL comes in there being no obligation to project the variables or expressions used in grouping or sorting.

Grouping by multiple keys

You can group by a composite key, using an anonymous type:

```
from n in names
group n by new { FirstLetter = n[0], Length = n.Length };
```

Custom equality comparers

You can pass a custom equality comparer into `GroupBy`, in a local query, to change the algorithm for key comparison. Rarely is this required, though, because changing the key selector expression is usually sufficient. For instance, the following creates a case-insensitive grouping:

```
group name by name.ToUpper()
```

Set Operators

IEnumerable<TSource>, IEnumerable<TSource>→IEnumerable<TSource>

Method	Description	SQL equivalents
Concat	Returns a concatenation of elements in each of the two sequences	UNION ALL
Union	Returns a concatenation of elements in each of the two sequences, excluding duplicates	UNION
Intersect	Returns elements present in both sequences	WHERE ... IN (...)
Except	Returns elements present in the first, but not the second sequence	EXCEPT *or* WHERE ... NOT IN (...)

Concat and Union

`Concat` returns all the elements of the first sequence, followed by all the elements of the second. `Union` does the same, but removes any duplicates:

```
int[] seq1 = { 1, 2, 3 }, seq2 = { 3, 4, 5 };

IEnumerable<int>
    concat = seq1.Concat (seq2),    // { 1, 2, 3, 3, 4, 5 }
    union  = seq1.Union  (seq2);    // { 1, 2, 3, 4, 5 }
```

Specifying the type argument explicitly is useful when the sequences are differently typed, but the elements have a common base type. For instance, with the reflection API (Chapter 19), methods and properties are represented with `MethodInfo` and `PropertyInfo` classes, which have a common base class called `MemberInfo`. We can concatenate methods and properties by stating that base class explicitly when calling `Concat`:

```
MethodInfo[] methods = typeof (string).GetMethods();
PropertyInfo[] props = typeof (string).GetProperties();
IEnumerable<MemberInfo> both = methods.Concat<MemberInfo> (props);
```

In the next example, we filter the methods before concatenating:

```
var methods = typeof (string).GetMethods().Where (m => !m.IsSpecialName);
var props = typeof (string).GetProperties();
var both = methods.Concat<MemberInfo> (props);
```

This example relies on interface type parameter variance: methods is of type IEnu
merable<MethodInfo>, which requires a covariant conversion to IEnumerable<Mem
berInfo>. It's a good illustration of how variance makes things work more as you'd
expect.

Intersect and Except

Intersect returns the elements that two sequences have in common. Except
returns the elements in the first input sequence that are *not* present in the second:

```
int[] seq1 = { 1, 2, 3 }, seq2 = { 3, 4, 5 };

IEnumerable<int>
  commonality = seq1.Intersect (seq2),    // { 3 }
  difference1 = seq1.Except    (seq2),    // { 1, 2 }
  difference2 = seq2.Except    (seq1);    // { 4, 5 }
```

Enumerable.Except works internally by loading all of the elements in the first collection into a dictionary, then removing from the dictionary all elements present in
the second sequence. The equivalent in SQL is a NOT EXISTS or NOT IN subquery:

```
SELECT number FROM numbers1Table
WHERE number NOT IN (SELECT number FROM numbers2Table)
```

Conversion Methods

LINQ deals primarily in sequences—in other words, collections of type IEnumera
ble<T>. The conversion methods convert to and from other types of collections:

Method	Description
OfType	Converts IEnumerable to IEnumerable<T>, discarding wrongly typed elements
Cast	Converts IEnumerable to IEnumerable<T>, throwing an exception if there are any wrongly typed elements
ToArray	Converts IEnumerable<T> to T[]
ToList	Converts IEnumerable<T> to List<T>
ToDictionary	Converts IEnumerable<T> to Dictionary<TKey,TValue>
ToLookup	Converts IEnumerable<T> to ILookup<TKey,TElement>
AsEnumerable	Downcasts to IEnumerable<T>
AsQueryable	Casts or converts to IQueryable<T>

OfType and Cast

OfType and Cast accept a nongeneric IEnumerable collection and emit a generic IEnumerable<T> sequence that you can subsequently query:

```
ArrayList classicList = new ArrayList();          // in System.Collections
classicList.AddRange ( new int[] { 3, 4, 5 } );
IEnumerable<int> sequence1 = classicList.Cast<int>();
```

Cast and OfType differ in their behavior when encountering an input element that's of an incompatible type. Cast throws an exception; OfType ignores the incompatible element. Continuing the preceding example:

```
DateTime offender = DateTime.Now;
classicList.Add (offender);
IEnumerable<int>
  sequence2 = classicList.OfType<int>(), // OK - ignores offending DateTime
  sequence3 = classicList.Cast<int>();   // Throws exception
```

The rules for element compatibility exactly follow those of C#'s is operator, and therefore consider only reference conversions and unboxing conversions. We can see this by examining the internal implementation of OfType:

```
public static IEnumerable<TSource> OfType <TSource> (IEnumerable source)
{
  foreach (object element in source)
    if (element is TSource)
      yield return (TSource)element;
}
```

Cast has an identical implementation, except that it omits the type compatibility test:

```
public static IEnumerable<TSource> Cast <TSource> (IEnumerable source)
{
  foreach (object element in source)
    yield return (TSource)element;
}
```

A consequence of these implementations is that you cannot use Cast to perform numeric or custom conversions (for these, you must perform a Select operation instead). In other words, Cast is not as flexible as C#'s cast operator:

```
int i = 3;
long l = i;         // Implicit numeric conversion int->long
int i2 = (int) l;   // Explicit numeric conversion long->int
```

We can demonstrate this by attempting to use OfType or Cast to convert a sequence of ints to a sequence of longs:

```
int[] integers = { 1, 2, 3 };

IEnumerable<long> test1 = integers.OfType<long>();
IEnumerable<long> test2 = integers.Cast<long>();
```

When enumerated, `test1` emits zero elements and `test2` throws an exception. Examining `OfType`'s implementation, it's fairly clear why. After substituting `TSource`, we get the following expression:

```
(element is long)
```

which returns `false` for an `int` `element`, due to the lack of an inheritance relationship.

 The reason for `test2` throwing an exception, when enumerated, is subtler. Notice in `Cast`'s implementation that `element` is of type `object`. When `TSource` is a value type, the CLR assumes this is an *unboxing conversion* and synthesizes a method that reproduces the scenario described in the section "Boxing and Unboxing" on page 98 in Chapter 3:

```
int value = 123;
object element = value;
long result = (long) element;  // exception
```

Because the `element` variable is declared of type `object`, an `object-to-long` cast is performed (an unboxing) rather than an `int-to-long` numeric conversion. Unboxing operations require an exact type match, so the `object-to-long` unbox fails when given an `int`.

As we suggested previously, the solution is to use an ordinary `Select`:

```
IEnumerable<long> castLong = integers.Select (s => (long) s);
```

`OfType` and `Cast` are also useful in downcasting elements in a generic input sequence. For instance, if you have an input sequence of type `IEnumerable<Fruit>`, `OfType<Apple>` would return just the apples. This is particularly useful in LINQ to XML (see Chapter 10).

`Cast` has query syntax support: simply precede the range variable with a type:

```
from TreeNode node in myTreeView.Nodes
...
```

ToArray, ToList, ToDictionary, and ToLookup

`ToArray` and `ToList` emit the results into an array or generic list. These operators force the immediate enumeration of the input sequence (unless indirected via a subquery or expression tree). For examples, refer to the section "Deferred Execution" on page 348 in Chapter 8.

`ToDictionary` and `ToLookup` accept the following arguments:

Argument	Type
Input sequence	IEnumerable<TSource>
Key selector	TSource => TKey
Element selector (optional)	TSource => TElement
Comparer (optional)	IEqualityComparer<TKey>

ToDictionary also forces immediate execution of a sequence, writing the results to a generic Dictionary. The keySelector expression you provide must evaluate to a unique value for each element in the input sequence; otherwise, an exception is thrown. In contrast, ToLookup allows many elements of the same key. We describe lookups in the earlier section "Joining with lookups" on page 417.

AsEnumerable and AsQueryable

AsEnumerable upcasts a sequence to IEnumerable<T>, forcing the compiler to bind subsequent query operators to methods in Enumerable, instead of Queryable. For an example, see the section "Combining Interpreted and Local Queries" on page 368 in Chapter 8.

AsQueryable downcasts a sequence to IQueryable<T> if it implements that interface. Otherwise, it instantiates an IQueryable<T> wrapper over the local query.

Element Operators

IEnumerable<TSource>→ TSource

Method	Description	SQL equivalents
First, FirstOrDefault	Returns the first element in the sequence, optionally satisfying a predicate	SELECT TOP 1 ... ORDER BY ...
Last, LastOrDefault	Returns the last element in the sequence, optionally satisfying a predicate	SELECT TOP 1 ... ORDER BY ... DESC
Single, SingleOrDefault	Equivalent to First/FirstOrDefault, but throws an exception if there is more than one match	
ElementAt, ElementAtOrDefault	Returns the element at the specified position	Exception thrown
DefaultIfEmpty	Returns a single-element sequence whose value is default(TSource) if the sequence has no elements	OUTER JOIN

Methods ending in "OrDefault" return default(TSource) rather than throwing an exception if the input sequence is empty or if no elements match the supplied predicate.

default(TSource) is null for reference type elements, false for the bool type and zero for numeric types.

First, Last, and Single

Argument	Type
Source sequence	IEnumerable<TSource>
Predicate (optional)	TSource => bool

The following example demonstrates First and Last:

```
int[] numbers   = { 1, 2, 3, 4, 5 };
int first       = numbers.First();                      // 1
int last        = numbers.Last();                       // 5
int firstEven   = numbers.First  (n => n % 2 == 0);     // 2
int lastEven    = numbers.Last   (n => n % 2 == 0);     // 4
```

The following demonstrates First versus FirstOrDefault:

```
int firstBigError  = numbers.First          (n => n > 10);  // Exception
int firstBigNumber = numbers.FirstOrDefault (n => n > 10);  // 0
```

To avoid an exception, Single requires exactly one matching element; SingleOrDe fault requires one *or zero* matching elements:

```
int onlyDivBy3 = numbers.Single (n => n % 3 == 0);  // 3
int divBy2Err  = numbers.Single (n => n % 2 == 0);  // Error: 2 & 4 match

int singleError = numbers.Single          (n => n > 10);      // Error
int noMatches   = numbers.SingleOrDefault (n => n > 10);      // 0
int divBy2Error = numbers.SingleOrDefault (n => n % 2 == 0);  // Error
```

Single is the "fussiest" in this family of element operators. FirstOrDefault and Las tOrDefault are the most tolerant.

In LINQ to SQL and EF, Single is often used to retrieve a row from a table by primary key:

```
Customer cust = dataContext.Customers.Single (c => c.ID == 3);
```

ElementAt

Argument	Type
Source sequence	IEnumerable<TSource>
Index of element to return	int

ElementAt picks the *n*th element from the sequence:

```
int[] numbers   = { 1, 2, 3, 4, 5 };
int third       = numbers.ElementAt (2);        // 3
```

```
int tenthError = numbers.ElementAt (9);          // Exception
int tenth      = numbers.ElementAtOrDefault (9);  // 0
```

Enumerable.ElementAt is written such that if the input sequence happens to implement IList<T>, it calls IList<T>'s indexer. Otherwise, it enumerates *n* times and then returns the next element. ElementAt is not supported in LINQ to SQL or EF.

DefaultIfEmpty

DefaultIfEmpty returns a sequence containing a single element whose value is default(TSource) if the input sequence has no elements. Otherwise it returns the input sequence unchanged. This is used in writing flat outer joins: see the earlier sections "Outer joins with SelectMany" on page 410 and "Flat outer joins" on page 417.

Aggregation Methods

IEnumerable<TSource>→ *scalar*

Method	Description	SQL equivalents
Count, LongCount	Returns the number of elements in the input sequence, optionally satisfying a predicate	COUNT (...)
Min, Max	Returns the smallest or largest element in the sequence	MIN (...), MAX (...)
Sum, Average	Calculates a numeric sum or average over elements in the sequence	SUM (...), AVG (...)
Aggregate	Performs a custom aggregation	Exception thrown

Count and LongCount

Argument	Type
Source sequence	IEnumerable<TSource>
Predicate (optional)	TSource => bool

Count simply enumerates over a sequence, returning the number of items:

```
int fullCount = new int[] { 5, 6, 7 }.Count();    // 3
```

The internal implementation of Enumerable.Count tests the input sequence to see whether it happens to implement ICollection<T>. If it does, it simply calls ICollection<T>.Count. Otherwise, it enumerates over every item, incrementing a counter.

You can optionally supply a predicate:

```
int digitCount = "pa55w0rd".Count (c => char.IsDigit (c));   // 3
```

LongCount does the same job as Count, but returns a 64-bit integer, allowing for sequences of greater than 2 billion elements.

Min and Max

Argument	Type
Source sequence	IEnumerable<TSource>
Result selector (optional)	TSource => TResult

Min and Max return the smallest or largest element from a sequence:

```
int[] numbers = { 28, 32, 14 };
int smallest = numbers.Min();  // 14;
int largest  = numbers.Max();  // 32;
```

If you include a selector expression, each element is first projected:

```
int smallest = numbers.Max (n => n % 10);  // 8;
```

A selector expression is mandatory if the items themselves are not intrinsically comparable—in other words, if they do not implement IComparable<T>:

```
Purchase runtimeError = dataContext.Purchases.Min ();          // Error
decimal? lowestPrice = dataContext.Purchases.Min (p => p.Price);  // OK
```

A selector expression determines not only how elements are compared, but also the final result. In the preceding example, the final result is a decimal value, not a purchase object. To get the cheapest purchase, you need a subquery:

```
Purchase cheapest = dataContext.Purchases
  .Where (p => p.Price == dataContext.Purchases.Min (p2 => p2.Price))
  .FirstOrDefault();
```

In this case, you could also formulate the query without an aggregation—using an OrderBy followed by FirstOrDefault.

Sum and Average

Argument	Type
Source sequence	IEnumerable<TSource>
Result selector (optional)	TSource => TResult

Sum and Average are aggregation operators that are used in a similar manner to Min and Max:

```
decimal[] numbers  = { 3, 4, 8 };
decimal sumTotal   = numbers.Sum();       // 15
decimal average    = numbers.Average();   // 5   (mean value)
```

The following returns the total length of each of the strings in the names array:

```
int combinedLength = names.Sum (s => s.Length);    // 19
```

Sum and Average are fairly restrictive in their typing. Their definitions are hard-wired to each of the numeric types (int, long, float, double, decimal, and their nullable versions). In contrast, Min and Max can operate directly on anything that implements IComparable<T>—such as a string, for instance.

Further, Average always returns either decimal, float or double, according to the following table:

Selector type	Result type
decimal	decimal
float	float
int, long, double	double

This means the following does not compile ("cannot convert double to int"):

```
int avg = new int[] { 3, 4 }.Average();
```

But this will compile:

```
double avg = new int[] { 3, 4 }.Average();    // 3.5
```

Average implicitly upscales the input values to avoid loss of precision. In this example, we averaged integers and got 3.5, without needing to resort to an input element cast:

```
double avg = numbers.Average (n => (double) n);
```

When querying a database, Sum and Average translate to the standard SQL aggregations. The following query returns customers whose average purchase was more than $500:

```
from c in dataContext.Customers
where c.Purchases.Average (p => p.Price) > 500
select c.Name;
```

Aggregate

Aggregate allows you to specify a custom accumulation algorithm for implementing unusual aggregations. Aggregate is not supported in LINQ to SQL or Entity Framework and is somewhat specialized in its use cases. The following demonstrates how Aggregate can do the work of Sum:

```
int[] numbers = { 2, 3, 4 };
int sum = numbers.Aggregate (0, (total, n) => total + n);    // 9
```

The first argument to Aggregate is the *seed*, from which accumulation starts. The second argument is an expression to update the accumulated value, given a fresh element. You can optionally supply a third argument to project the final result value from the accumulated value.

Most problems for which `Aggregate` has been designed can be solved as easily with a `foreach` loop—and with more familiar syntax. The advantage of using `Aggregate` is that with large or complex aggregations, you can automatically parallelize the operation with PLINQ (see Chapter 23).

Unseeded aggregations

You can omit the seed value when calling `Aggregate`, in which case the first element becomes the *implicit* seed, and aggregation proceeds from the second element. Here's the preceding example, *unseeded*:

```
int[] numbers = { 1, 2, 3 };
int sum = numbers.Aggregate ((total, n) => total + n);   // 6
```

This gives the same result as before, but we're actually doing a *different calculation*. Before, we were calculating 0+1+2+3; now we're calculating 1+2+3. We can better illustrate the difference by multiplying instead of adding:

```
int[] numbers = { 1, 2, 3 };
int x = numbers.Aggregate (0, (prod, n) => prod * n);   // 0*1*2*3 = 0
int y = numbers.Aggregate (   (prod, n) => prod * n);   //   1*2*3 = 6
```

As we'll see in Chapter 23, unseeded aggregations have the advantage of being parallelizable without requiring the use of special overloads. However, there are some traps with unseeded aggregations.

Traps with unseeded aggregations

The unseeded aggregation methods are intended for use with delegates that are *commutative* and *associative*. If used otherwise, the result is either *unintuitive* (with ordinary queries) or *nondeterministic* (in the case that you parallelize the query with PLINQ). For example, consider the following function:

```
(total, n) => total + n * n
```

This is neither commutative nor associative. (For example, 1+2*2 != 2+1*1). Let's see what happens when we use it to sum the square of the numbers 2, 3, and 4:

```
int[] numbers = { 2, 3, 4 };
int sum = numbers.Aggregate ((total, n) => total + n * n);     // 27
```

Instead of calculating:

```
2*2 + 3*3 + 4*4   // 29
```

it calculates:

```
2 + 3*3 + 4*4   // 27
```

We can fix this in a number of ways. First, we could include 0 as the first element:

```
int[] numbers = { 0, 2, 3, 4 };
```

Not only is this inelegant, but it will still give incorrect results if parallelized—because PLINQ leverages the function's assumed associativity by selecting *multiple* elements as seeds. To illustrate, if we denote our aggregation function as follows:

```
f(total, n) => total + n * n
```

then LINQ to Objects would calculate this:

```
f(f(f(0, 2),3),4)
```

whereas PLINQ may do this:

```
f(f(0,2),f(3,4))
```

with the following result:

```
First partition:     a = 0 + 2*2   (= 4)
Second partition:    b = 3 + 4*4   (= 19)
Final result:        a + b*b       (= 365)
OR EVEN:             b + a*a       (= 35)
```

There are two good solutions. The first is to turn this into a seeded aggregation—with zero as the seed. The only complication is that with PLINQ, we'd need to use a special overload in order for the query not to execute sequentially (see "Optimizing PLINQ" on page 956 in Chapter 23).

The second solution is to restructure the query such that the aggregation function is commutative and associative:

```
int sum = numbers.Select (n => n * n).Aggregate ((total, n) => total + n);
```

Of course, in such simple scenarios, you can (and should) use the Sum operator instead of Aggregate:

```
int sum = numbers.Sum (n => n * n);
```

You can actually go quite far just with Sum and Average. For instance, you can use Average to calculate a root-mean-square:

```
Math.Sqrt (numbers.Average (n => n * n))
```

and even standard deviation:

```
double mean = numbers.Average();
double sdev = Math.Sqrt (numbers.Average (n =>
                {
                    double dif = n - mean;
                    return dif * dif;
                }));
```

Both are safe, efficient and fully parallelizable. In Chapter 23, we'll give a practical example of a custom aggregation that can't be reduced to Sum or Average.

Quantifiers

`IEnumerable<TSource>`→ *bool*

Method	Description	SQL equivalents
Contains	Returns `true` if the input sequence contains the given element	WHERE ... IN (...)
Any	Returns `true` if any elements satisfy the given predicate	WHERE ... IN (...)
All	Returns `true` if all elements satisfy the given predicate	WHERE (...)
SequenceEqual	Returns `true` if the second sequence has identical elements to the input sequence	

Contains and Any

The `Contains` method accepts an argument of type `TSource`; `Any` accepts an optional *predicate*.

`Contains` returns `true` if the given element is present:

```
bool hasAThree = new int[] { 2, 3, 4 }.Contains (3);        // true;
```

`Any` returns `true` if the given expression is true for at least one element. We can rewrite the preceding query with `Any` as follows:

```
bool hasAThree = new int[] { 2, 3, 4 }.Any (n => n == 3);  // true;
```

`Any` can do everything that `Contains` can do, and more:

```
bool hasABigNumber = new int[] { 2, 3, 4 }.Any (n => n > 10);  // false;
```

Calling `Any` without a predicate returns `true` if the sequence has one or more elements. Here's another way to write the preceding query:

```
bool hasABigNumber = new int[] { 2, 3, 4 }.Where (n => n > 10).Any();
```

`Any` is particularly useful in subqueries and is used often when querying databases, for example:

```
from c in dataContext.Customers
where c.Purchases.Any (p => p.Price > 1000)
select c
```

All and SequenceEqual

`All` returns `true` if all elements satisfy a predicate. The following returns customers whose purchases are less than $100:

```
dataContext.Customers.Where (c => c.Purchases.All (p => p.Price < 100));
```

SequenceEqual compares two sequences. To return true, each sequence must have identical elements, in the identical order. You can optionally provide an equality comparer; the default is EqualityComparer<T>.Default.

Generation Methods

void→IEnumerable<TResult>

Method	Description
Empty	Creates an empty sequence
Repeat	Creates a sequence of repeating elements
Range	Creates a sequence of integers

Empty, Repeat, and Range are static (nonextension) methods that manufacture simple local sequences.

Empty

Empty manufactures an empty sequence and requires just a type argument:

```
foreach (string s in Enumerable.Empty<string>())
  Console.Write (s);                              // <nothing>
```

In conjunction with the ?? operator, Empty does the reverse of DefaultIfEmpty. For example, suppose we have a jagged array of integers, and we want to get all the integers into a single flat list. The following SelectMany query fails if any of the inner arrays is null:

```
int[][] numbers =
{
  new int[] { 1, 2, 3 },
  new int[] { 4, 5, 6 },
  null                      // this null makes the query below fail.
};

IEnumerable<int> flat = numbers.SelectMany (innerArray => innerArray);
```

Empty in conjunction with ?? fixes the problem:

```
IEnumerable<int> flat = numbers
  .SelectMany (innerArray => innerArray ?? Enumerable.Empty <int>());

foreach (int i in flat)
  Console.Write (i + " ");     // 1 2 3 4 5 6
```

Range and Repeat

Range accepts a starting index and count (both integers):

```
foreach (int i in Enumerable.Range (5, 3))
  Console.Write (i + " ");                // 5 6 7
```

Repeat accepts an element to repeat, and the number of repetitions:

```
foreach (bool x in Enumerable.Repeat (true, 3))
  Console.Write (x + " ");                      // True True True
```

10

LINQ to XML

The .NET Framework provides a number of APIs for working with XML data. From .NET Framework 3.5, the primary choice for general-purpose XML document processing is *LINQ to XML*. LINQ to XML comprises a lightweight LINQ-friendly XML document object model, plus a set of supplementary query operators.

In this chapter, we concentrate entirely on LINQ to XML. In Chapter 11, we cover the more specialized XML types and APIs, including the forward-only reader/writer, the types for working with schemas, stylesheets and XPaths, and the legacy XmlDocument-based DOM.

 The LINQ to XML DOM is extremely well designed and highly performant. Even without LINQ, the LINQ to XML DOM is valuable as a lightweight façade over the low-level XmlReader and XmlWriter classes.

All LINQ to XML types are defined in the System.Xml.Linq namespace.

Architectural Overview

This section starts with a very brief introduction to the concept of a DOM and then explains the rationale behind LINQ to XML's DOM.

What Is a DOM?

Consider the following XML file:

```
<?xml version="1.0" encoding="utf-8"?>
<customer id="123" status="archived">
  <firstname>Joe</firstname>
  <lastname>Bloggs</lastname>
</customer>
```

As with all XML files, we start with a *declaration*, and then a root *element*, whose name is customer. The customer element has two *attributes*, each with a name (id and status) and value ("123" and "archived"). Within customer, there are two child elements, firstname and lastname, each having simple text content ("Joe" and "Bloggs").

Each of these constructs—declaration, element, attribute, value, and text content—can be represented with a class. And if such classes have collection properties for storing child content, we can assemble a *tree* of objects to fully describe a document. This is called a *document object model*, or DOM.

The LINQ to XML DOM

LINQ to XML comprises two things:

- An XML DOM, which we call the *X-DOM*
- A set of about 10 supplementary query operators

As you might expect, the X-DOM consists of types such as XDocument, XElement, and XAttribute. Interestingly, the X-DOM types are not tied to LINQ—you can load, instantiate, update, and save an X-DOM without ever writing a LINQ query.

Conversely, you could use LINQ to query a DOM created of the older W3C-compliant types. However, this would be frustrating and limiting. The distinguishing feature of the X-DOM is that it's *LINQ-friendly*. This means:

- It has methods that emit useful IEnumerable sequences, upon which you can query.
- Its constructors are designed such that you can build an X-DOM tree through a LINQ projection.

X-DOM Overview

Figure 10-1 shows the core X-DOM types. The most frequently used of these types is XElement. XObject is the root of the *inheritance* hierarchy; XElement and XDocument are roots of the *containership* hierarchy.

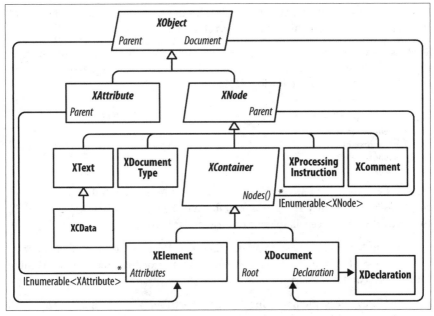

Figure 10-1. Core X-DOM types

Figure 10-2 shows the X-DOM tree created from the following code:

```
string xml = @"<customer id='123' status='archived'>
                 <firstname>Joe</firstname>
                 <lastname>Bloggs<!--nice name--></lastname>
               </customer>";

XElement customer = XElement.Parse (xml);
```

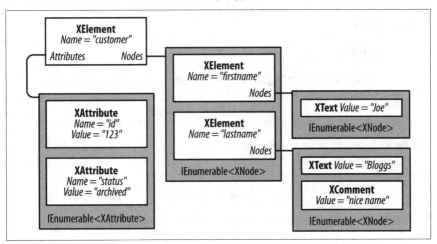

Figure 10-2. A simple X-DOM tree

XObject is the abstract base class for all XML content. It defines a link to the Parent element in the containership tree as well as an optional XDocument.

XNode is the base class for most XML content excluding attributes. The distinguishing feature of XNode is that it can sit in an ordered collection of mixed-type XNodes. For instance, consider the following XML:

```
<data>
   Hello world
   <subelement1/>
   <!--comment-->
   <subelement2/>
</data>
```

Within the parent element <data>, there's first an XText node (Hello world), then an XElement node, then an XComment node, and then a second XElement node. In contrast, an XAttribute will tolerate only other XAttributes as peers.

Although an XNode can access its parent XElement, it has no concept of *child* nodes: this is the job of its subclass XContainer. XContainer defines members for dealing with children and is the abstract base class for XElement and XDocument.

XElement introduces members for managing attributes—as well as a Name and Value. In the (fairly common) case of an element having a single XText child node, the Value property on XElement encapsulates this child's content for both get and set operations, cutting unnecessary navigation. Thanks to Value, you can mostly avoid working directly with XText nodes.

XDocument represents the root of an XML tree. More precisely, it *wraps* the root XElement, adding an XDeclaration, processing instructions, and other root-level "fluff." Unlike with the W3C DOM, its use is optional: you can load, manipulate, and save an X-DOM without ever creating an XDocument! The nonreliance on XDocument also means you can efficiently and easily move a node subtree to another X-DOM hierarchy.

Loading and Parsing

Both XElement and XDocument provide static Load and Parse methods to build an X-DOM tree from an existing source:

- Load builds an X-DOM from a file, URI, Stream, TextReader, or XmlReader.
- Parse builds an X-DOM from a string.

For example:

```
XDocument fromWeb = XDocument.Load ("http://albahari.com/sample.xml");

XElement fromFile = XElement.Load (@"e:\media\somefile.xml");

XElement config = XElement.Parse (
    @"<configuration>
```

```
  <client enabled='true'>
    <timeout>30</timeout>
  </client>
</configuration>");
```

In later sections, we describe how to traverse and update an X-DOM. As a quick preview, here's how to manipulate the config element we just populated:

```
foreach (XElement child in config.Elements())
  Console.WriteLine (child.Name);                     // client

XElement client = config.Element ("client");

bool enabled = (bool) client.Attribute ("enabled");   // Read attribute
Console.WriteLine (enabled);                           // True
client.Attribute ("enabled").SetValue (!enabled);      // Update attribute

int timeout = (int) client.Element ("timeout");        // Read element
Console.WriteLine (timeout);                            // 30
client.Element ("timeout").SetValue (timeout * 2);     // Update element

client.Add (new XElement ("retries", 3));              // Add new elememt

Console.WriteLine (config);        // Implicitly call config.ToString()
```

Here's the result of that last Console.WriteLine:

```
<configuration>
  <client enabled="false">
    <timeout>60</timeout>
    <retries>3</retries>
  </client>
</configuration>
```

XNode also provides a static ReadFrom method that instantiates and populates any type of node from an XmlReader. Unlike Load, it stops after reading one (complete) node, so you can continue to read manually from the XmlReader afterward.

You can also do the reverse and use an XmlReader or XmlWriter to read or write an XNode, via its CreateReader and CreateWriter methods.

We describe XML readers and writers and how to use them with the X-DOM in Chapter 11.

Saving and Serializing

Calling ToString on any node converts its content to an XML string—formatted with line breaks and indentation as we just saw. (You can disable the line breaks and indentation by specifying SaveOptions.DisableFormatting when calling ToString.)

XElement and XDocument also provide a Save method that writes an X-DOM to a file, Stream, TextWriter, or XmlWriter. If you specify a file, an XML declaration is automatically written. There is also a `WriteTo` method defined in the `XNode` class, which accepts just an `XmlWriter`.

We describe the handling of XML declarations when saving in more detail in the section "Documents and Declarations" on page 459 later in this chapter.

Instantiating an X-DOM

Rather than using the `Load` or `Parse` methods, you can build an X-DOM tree by manually instantiating objects and adding them to a parent via `XContainer`'s `Add` method.

To construct an `XElement` and `XAttribute`, simply provide a name and value:

```
XElement lastName = new XElement ("lastname", "Bloggs");
lastName.Add (new XComment ("nice name"));

XElement customer = new XElement ("customer");
customer.Add (new XAttribute ("id", 123));
customer.Add (new XElement ("firstname", "Joe"));
customer.Add (lastName);

Console.WriteLine (customer.ToString());
```

The result:

```
<customer id="123">
  <firstname>Joe</firstname>
  <lastname>Bloggs<!--nice name--></lastname>
</customer>
```

A value is optional when constructing an `XElement`—you can provide just the element name and add content later. Notice that when we did provide a value, a simple string sufficed—we didn't need to explicitly create and add an `XText` child node. The X-DOM does this work automatically, so you can deal simply with "values."

Functional Construction

In our preceding example, it's hard to glean the XML structure from the code. X-DOM supports another mode of instantiation, called *functional construction* (from functional programming). With functional construction, you build an entire tree in a single expression:

```
XElement customer =
  new XElement ("customer", new XAttribute ("id", 123),
    new XElement ("firstname", "joe"),
    new XElement ("lastname", "bloggs",
      new XComment ("nice name")
    )
  );
```

This has two benefits. First, the code resembles the shape of the XML. Second, it can be incorporated into the `select` clause of a LINQ query. For example, the following LINQ to SQL query projects directly into an X-DOM:

```
XElement query =
  new XElement ("customers",
    from c in dataContext.Customers
    select
      new XElement ("customer", new XAttribute ("id", c.ID),
        new XElement ("firstname", c.FirstName),
        new XElement ("lastname", c.LastName,
          new XComment ("nice name")
        )
      )
  );
```

More on this later in this chapter, in "Projecting into an X-DOM" on page 469.

Specifying Content

Functional construction is possible because the constructors for `XElement` (and `XDo cument`) are overloaded to accept a `params` object array:

```
public XElement (XName name, params object[] content)
```

The same holds true for the `Add` method in `XContainer`:

```
public void Add (params object[] content)
```

Hence, you can specify any number of child objects of any type when building or appending an X-DOM. This works because *anything* counts as legal content. To see how, we need to examine how each content object is processed internally. Here are the decisions made by `XContainer`, in order:

1. If the object is `null`, it's ignored.

2. If the object is based on `XNode` or `XStreamingElement`, it's added as is to the `Nodes` collection.

3. If the object is an `XAttribute`, it's added to the `Attributes` collection.

4. If the object is a `string`, it gets wrapped in an `XText` node and added to `Nodes`.[1]

5. If the object implements `IEnumerable`, it's enumerated, and the same rules are applied to each element.

6. Otherwise, the object is converted to a string, wrapped in an `XText` node, and then added to `Nodes`.[2]

---

[1] The X-DOM actually optimizes this step internally by storing simple text content in a string. The XTEXT node is not actually created until you call `Nodes( )` on the `XContainer`.

[2] See footnote 1.

Everything ends up in one of two buckets: Nodes or Attributes. Furthermore, any object is valid content because it can always ultimately call ToString on it and treat it as an XText node.

Before calling ToString on an arbitrary type, XContainer first tests whether it is one of the following types:

```
float, double, decimal, bool,
DateTime, DateTimeOffset, TimeSpan
```

If so, it calls an appropriate typed ToString method on the XmlConvert helper class instead of calling ToString on the object itself. This ensures that the data is round-trippable and compliant with standard XML formatting rules.

Automatic Deep Cloning

When a node or attribute is added to an element (whether via functional construction or an Add method), the node or attribute's Parent property is set to that element. A node can have only one parent element: if you add an already parented node to a second parent, the node is automatically *deep-cloned*. In the following example, each customer has a separate copy of address:

```
var address = new XElement ("address",
                new XElement ("street", "Lawley St"),
                new XElement ("town", "North Beach")
            );
var customer1 = new XElement ("customer1", address);
var customer2 = new XElement ("customer2", address);

customer1.Element ("address").Element ("street").Value = "Another St";
Console.WriteLine (
    customer2.Element ("address").Element ("street").Value);    // Lawley St
```

This automatic duplication keeps X-DOM object instantiation free of side effects—another hallmark of functional programming.

Navigating and Querying

As you might expect, the XNode and XContainer classes define methods and properties for traversing the X-DOM tree. Unlike a conventional DOM, however, these functions don't return a collection that implements IList<T>. Instead, they return either a single value or a *sequence* that implements IEnumerable<T>—upon which you are then expected to execute a LINQ query (or enumerate with a foreach). This allows for advanced queries as well as simple navigation tasks—using familiar LINQ query syntax.

Element and attribute names are case-sensitive in the X-DOM —just as they are in XML.

Child Node Navigation

Return type	Members	Works on
XNode	FirstNode { get; }	XContainer
	LastNode { get; }	XContainer
IEnumerable<XNode>	Nodes()	XContainer*
	DescendantNodes()	XContainer*
	DescendantNodesAndSelf()	XElement*
XElement	Element (XName)	XContainer
IEnumerable<XElement>	Elements()	XContainer*
	Elements (XName)	XContainer*
	Descendants()	XContainer*
	Descendants (XName)	XContainer*
	DescendantsAndSelf()	XElement*
	DescendantsAndSelf (XName)	XElement*
bool	HasElements { get; }	XElement

Functions marked with an asterisk in the third column of this and other tables also operate on *sequences* of the same type. For instance, you can call Nodes on either an XContainer or a sequence of XContainer objects. This is possible because of extension methods defined in System.Xml.Linq—the supplementary query operators we talked about in the overview.

FirstNode, LastNode, and Nodes

FirstNode and LastNode give you direct access to the first or last child node; Nodes returns all children as a sequence. All three functions consider only direct descendants. For example:

```
var bench = new XElement ("bench",
              new XElement ("toolbox",
                new XElement ("handtool", "Hammer"),
                new XElement ("handtool", "Rasp")
              ),
              new XElement ("toolbox",
                new XElement ("handtool", "Saw"),
                new XElement ("powertool", "Nailgun")
              ),
              new XComment ("Be careful with the nailgun")
            );
foreach (XNode node in bench.Nodes())
  Console.WriteLine (node.ToString (SaveOptions.DisableFormatting) + ".");
```

This is the output:

```
<toolbox><handtool>Hammer</handtool><handtool>Rasp</handtool></toolbox>.
<toolbox><handtool>Saw</handtool><powertool>Nailgun</powertool></toolbox>.
<!--Be careful with the nailgun-->.
```

Retrieving elements

The `Elements` method returns just the child nodes of type `XElement`:

```
foreach (XElement e in bench.Elements())
  Console.WriteLine (e.Name + "=" + e.Value);    // toolbox=HammerRasp
                                                 // toolbox=SawNailgun
```

The following LINQ query finds the toolbox with the nail gun:

```
IEnumerable<string> query =
  from toolbox in bench.Elements()
  where toolbox.Elements().Any (tool => tool.Value == "Nailgun")
  select toolbox.Value;

RESULT: { "SawNailgun" }
```

The next example uses a `SelectMany` query to retrieve the hand tools in all toolboxes:

```
IEnumerable<string> query =
  from toolbox in bench.Elements()
  from tool in toolbox.Elements()
  where tool.Name == "handtool"
  select tool.Value;

RESULT: { "Hammer", "Rasp", "Saw" }
```

 `Elements` itself is equivalent to a LINQ query on `Nodes`. Our preceding query could be started as follows:

```
from toolbox in bench.Nodes().OfType<XElement>()
where ...
```

`Elements` can also return just the elements of a given name. For example:

```
int x = bench.Elements ("toolbox").Count();    // 2
```

This is equivalent to:

```
int x = bench.Elements().Where (e => e.Name == "toolbox").Count();  // 2
```

`Elements` is also defined as an extension method accepting `IEnumerable<XContainer>` or, more precisely, it accepts an argument of this type:

```
IEnumerable<T> where T : XContainer
```

This allows it to work with sequences of elements, too. Using this method, we can rewrite the query that finds the hand tools in all toolboxes as follows:

```
from tool in bench.Elements ("toolbox").Elements ("handtool")
select tool.Value.ToUpper();
```

The first call to `Elements` binds to `XContainer`'s instance method; the second call to `Elements` binds to the extension method.

Retrieving a single element

The method `Element` (singular) returns the first matching element of the given name. `Element` is useful for simple navigation, as follows:

```
XElement settings = XElement.Load ("databaseSettings.xml");
string cx = settings.Element ("database").Element ("connectString").Value;
```

`Element` is equivalent to calling `Elements()` and then applying LINQ's `FirstOrDefault` query operator with a name-matching predicate. `Element` returns `null` if the requested element doesn't exist.

 `Element("xyz").Value` will throw a `NullReferenceException` if element xyz does not exist. If you'd prefer a `null` rather than an exception, cast the `XElement` to a `string` instead of querying its `Value` property. In other words:

```
string xyz = (string) settings.Element ("xyz");
```

This works because `XElement` defines an explicit `string` conversion—just for this purpose!

From C# 6, an alternative is to use the null-conditioner operator, i.e., `Element {"xyz"}?.Value`.

Retrieving descendants

`XContainer` also provides `Descendants` and `DescendantNodes` methods that return child elements or nodes plus all of their children, and so on (the entire tree). `Descendants` accepts an optional element name. Returning to our earlier example, we can use `Descendants` to find all the hand tools as follows:

```
Console.WriteLine (bench.Descendants ("handtool").Count());  // 3
```

Both parent and leaf nodes are included, as the following example demonstrates:

```
foreach (XNode node in bench.DescendantNodes())
  Console.WriteLine (node.ToString (SaveOptions.DisableFormatting));
```

```
<toolbox><handtool>Hammer</handtool><handtool>Rasp</handtool></toolbox>
<handtool>Hammer</handtool>
Hammer
<handtool>Rasp</handtool>
Rasp
<toolbox><handtool>Saw</handtool><powertool>Nailgun</powertool></toolbox>
<handtool>Saw</handtool>
Saw
<powertool>Nailgun</powertool>
Nailgun
<!--Be careful with the nailgun-->
```

The next query extracts all comments anywhere within the X-DOM that contain the word "careful":

```
IEnumerable<string> query =
  from c in bench.DescendantNodes().OfType<XComment>()
  where c.Value.Contains ("careful")
  orderby c.Value
  select c.Value;
```

Parent Navigation

All XNodes have a `Parent` property and `AncestorXXX` methods for parent navigation. A parent is always an XElement:

Return type	Members	Works on
XElement	Parent { get; }	XNode*
Enumerable<XElement>	Ancestors()	XNode*
	Ancestors (XName)	XNode*
	AncestorsAndSelf()	XElement*
	AncestorsAndSelf (XName)	XElement*

If x is an XElement, the following always prints `true`:

```
foreach (XNode child in x.Nodes())
  Console.WriteLine (child.Parent == x);
```

The same is not the case, however, if x is an XDocument. XDocument is peculiar: it can have children, but can never be anyone's parent! To access the XDocument, you instead use the `Document` property—this works on any object in the X-DOM tree.

`Ancestors` returns a sequence whose first element is `Parent` and whose next element is `Parent.Parent`, and so on, until the root element.

> You can navigate to the root element with the LINQ query `AncestorsAndSelf().Last()`.
>
> Another way to achieve the same thing is to call `Document.Root`—although this works only if an XDocument is present.

Peer Node Navigation

Return type	Members	Defined in
bool	IsBefore (XNode node)	XNode
	IsAfter (XNode node)	XNode
XNode	PreviousNode { get; }	XNode
	NextNode { get; }	XNode

Return type	Members	Defined in
IEnumerable<XNode>	NodesBeforeSelf()	XNode
	NodesAfterSelf()	XNode
IEnumerable<XElement>	ElementsBeforeSelf()	XNode
	ElementsBeforeSelf (XName name)	XNode
	ElementsAfterSelf()	XNode
	ElementsAfterSelf (XName name)	XNode

With PreviousNode and NextNode (and FirstNode/LastNode), you can traverse nodes with the feel of a linked list. This is noncoincidental: internally, nodes are stored in a linked list.

 XNode internally uses a *singly* linked list, so PreviousNode is not performant.

Attribute Navigation

Return type	Members	Defined in
bool	HasAttributes { get; }	XElement
XAttribute	Attribute (XName name)	XElement
	FirstAttribute { get; }	XElement
	LastAttribute { get; }	XElement
IEnumerable<XAttribute>	Attributes()	XElement
	Attributes (XName name)	XElement

In In addition, XAttribute defines PreviousAttribute and NextAttribute properties, as well as Parent.

The Attributes method that accepts a name returns a sequence with either zero or one element; an element cannot have duplicate attribute names in XML.

Updating an X-DOM

You can update elements and attributes in the following ways:

- Call SetValue or reassign the Value property.
- Call SetElementValue or SetAttributeValue.
- Call one of the Remove*XXX* methods.
- Call one of the Add*XXX* or Replace*XXX* methods, specifying fresh content.

You can also reassign the `Name` property on `XElement` objects.

Simple Value Updates

Members	Works on
SetValue (object value)	XElement, XAttribute
Value { get; set }	XElement, XAttribute

The `SetValue` method replaces an element or attribute's content with a simple value. Setting the `Value` property does the same, but accepts string data only. We describe both of these functions in detail later in this chapter (see the section "Working with Values" on page 456).

An effect of calling `SetValue` (or reassigning `Value`) is that it replaces all child nodes:

```
XElement settings = new XElement ("settings",
                        new XElement ("timeout", 30)
                    );
settings.SetValue ("blah");
Console.WriteLine (settings.ToString());  // <settings>blah</settings>
```

Updating Child Nodes and Attributes

Category	Members	Works on
Add	Add (params object[] content)	XContainer
	AddFirst (params object[] content)	XContainer
Remove	RemoveNodes()	XContainer
	RemoveAttributes()	XElement
	RemoveAll()	XElement
Update	ReplaceNodes (params object[] content)	XContainer
	ReplaceAttributes (params object[] content)	XElement
	ReplaceAll (params object[] content	XElement
	SetElementValue (XName name, object value)	XElement
	SetAttributeValue (XName name, object value)	XElement

The most convenient methods in this group are the last two: `SetElementValue` and `SetAttributeValue`. They serve as shortcuts for instantiating an `XElement` or `XAttribute` and then Adding it to a parent, replacing any existing element or attribute of that name:

```
XElement settings = new XElement ("settings");
settings.SetElementValue ("timeout", 30);    // Adds child node
settings.SetElementValue ("timeout", 60);    // Update it to 60
```

Add appends a child node to an element or document. `AddFirst` does the same thing, but inserts at the beginning of the collection rather than the end.

You can remove all child nodes or attributes in one hit with `RemoveNodes` or `RemoveAttributes`. `RemoveAll` is equivalent to calling both of these methods.

The Replace*XXX* methods are equivalent to Removing and then Adding. They take a snapshot of the input, so `e.ReplaceNodes(e.Nodes())` works as expected.

Updating Through the Parent

Members	Works on
AddBeforeSelf (params object[] content)	XNode
AddAfterSelf (params object[] content)	XNode
Remove()	XNode*, XAttribute*
ReplaceWith (params object[] content)	XNode

The methods `AddBeforeSelf`, `AddAfterSelf`, `Remove`, and `ReplaceWith` don't operate on the node's children. Instead, they operate on the collection in which the node itself is in. This requires that the node have a parent element—otherwise, an exception is thrown. `AddBeforeSelf` and `AddAfterSelf` are useful for inserting a node into an arbitrary position:

```
XElement items = new XElement ("items",
                    new XElement ("one"),
                    new XElement ("three")
                  );
items.FirstNode.AddAfterSelf (new XElement ("two"));
```

Here's the result:

```
<items><one /><two /><three /></items>
```

Inserting into an arbitrary position within a long sequence of elements is actually quite efficient, because nodes are stored internally in a linked list.

The `Remove` method removes the current node from its parent. `ReplaceWith` does the same—and then inserts some other content at the same position. For instance:

```
XElement items = XElement.Parse ("<items><one/><two/><three/></items>");
items.FirstNode.ReplaceWith (new XComment ("One was here"));
```

Here's the result:

```
<items><!--one was here--><two /><three /></items>
```

Removing a sequence of nodes or attributes

Thanks to extension methods in `System.Xml.Linq`, you can also call `Remove` on a *sequence* of nodes or attributes. Consider this X-DOM:

```
XElement contacts = XElement.Parse (
@"<contacts>
    <customer name='Mary'/>
    <customer name='Chris' archived='true'/>
    <supplier name='Susan'>
      <phone archived='true'>012345678<!--confidential--></phone>
    </supplier>
  </contacts>");
```

The following removes all customers:

```
contacts.Elements ("customer").Remove();
```

The next statement removes all archived contacts (so *Chris* disappears):

```
contacts.Elements().Where (e => (bool?) e.Attribute ("archived") == true)
                   .Remove();
```

If we replaced `Elements()` with `Descendants()`, all archived elements throughout the DOM would disappear, with this result:

```
<contacts>
  <customer name="Mary" />
  <supplier name="Susan" />
</contacts>
```

The next example removes all contacts that feature the comment "confidential" anywhere in their tree:

```
contacts.Elements().Where (e => e.DescendantNodes()
                                 .OfType<XComment>()
                                 .Any (c => c.Value == "confidential")
                           ).Remove();
```

This is the result:

```
<contacts>
  <customer name="Mary" />
  <customer name="Chris" archived="true" />
</contacts>
```

Contrast this with the following simpler query, which strips all comment nodes from the tree:

```
contacts.DescendantNodes().OfType<XComment>().Remove();
```

 Internally, the `Remove` methods first read all matching elements into a temporary list, and then enumerate over the temporary list to perform the deletions. This avoids errors that could otherwise result from deleting and querying at the same time.

Working with Values

`XElement` and `XAttribute` both have a `Value` property of type `string`. If an element has a single `XText` child node, `XElement`'s `Value` property acts as a convenient short-

---

cut to the content of that node. With `XAttribute`, the `Value` property is simply the attribute's value.

Despite the storage differences, the X-DOM provides a consistent set of operations for working with element and attribute values.

Setting Values

There are two ways to assign a value: call `SetValue` or assign the `Value` property. `SetValue` is more flexible because it accepts not just strings, but other simple data types, too:

```
var e = new XElement ("date", DateTime.Now);
e.SetValue (DateTime.Now.AddDays(1));
Console.Write (e.Value);            // 2007-03-02T16:39:10.734375+09:00
```

We could have instead just set the element's `Value` property, but this would mean manually converting the `DateTime` to a string. This is more complicated than calling `ToString`—it requires the use of `XmlConvert` for an XML-compliant result.

When you pass a *value* into `XElement` or `XAttribute`'s constructor, the same automatic conversion takes place for nonstring types. This ensures that `DateTimes` are correctly formatted; `true` is written in lowercase, and `double.NegativeInfinity` is written as "-INF".

Getting Values

To go the other way around and parse a `Value` back to a base type, you simply cast the `XElement` or `XAttribute` to the desired type. It sounds like it shouldn't work—but it does! For instance:

```
XElement e = new XElement ("now", DateTime.Now);
DateTime dt = (DateTime) e;

XAttribute a = new XAttribute ("resolution", 1.234);
double res = (double) a;
```

An element or attribute doesn't store `DateTimes` or numbers natively—they're always stored as text and then parsed as needed. It also doesn't "remember" the original type, so you must cast it correctly to avoid a runtime error. To make your code robust, you can put the cast in a `try`/`catch` block, catching a `FormatException`.

Explicit casts on `XElement` and `XAttribute` can parse to the following types:

- All standard numeric types
- `string`, `bool`, `DateTime`, `DateTimeOffset`, `TimeSpan`, and `Guid`
- `Nullable<>` versions of the aforementioned value types

Casting to a nullable type is useful in conjunction with the `Element` and `Attribute` methods, because if the requested name doesn't exist, the cast still works. For instance, if x has no `timeout` element, the first line generates a runtime error, and the second line does not:

```
int timeout = (int) x.Element ("timeout");      // Error
int? timeout = (int?) x.Element ("timeout");    // OK; timeout is null.
```

You can factor away the nullable type in the final result with the `??` operator. The following evaluates to `1.0` if the `resolution` attribute doesn't exist:

```
double resolution = (double?) x.Attribute ("resolution") ?? 1.0;
```

Casting to a nullable type won't get you out of trouble, though, if the element or attribute *exists* and has an empty (or improperly formatted) value. For this, you must catch a `FormatException`.

You can also use casts in LINQ queries. The following returns "John":

```
var data = XElement.Parse (
  @"<data>
      <customer id='1' name='Mary' credit='100' />
      <customer id='2' name='John' credit='150' />
      <customer id='3' name='Anne' />
   </data>");

IEnumerable<string> query = from cust in data.Elements()
                            where (int?) cust.Attribute ("credit") > 100
                            select cust.Attribute ("name").Value;
```

Casting to a nullable `int` avoids a `NullReferenceException` in the case of Anne, who has no `credit` attribute. Another solution would be to add a predicate to the `where` clause:

```
where cust.Attributes ("credit").Any() && (int) cust.Attribute...
```

The same principles apply in querying element values.

Values and Mixed Content Nodes

Given the value of `Value`, you might wonder when you'd ever need to deal directly with `XText` nodes. The answer is when you have mixed content. For example:

```
<summary>An XAttribute is <bold>not</bold> an XNode</summary>
```

A simple `Value` property is not enough to capture `summary`'s content. The `summary` element contains three children: an `XText` node followed by an `XElement`, followed by another `XText` node. Here's how to construct it:

```
XElement summary = new XElement ("summary",
                     new XText ("An XAttribute is "),
                     new XElement ("bold", "not"),
                     new XText (" an XNode")
                   );
```

Interestingly, we can still query `summary`'s `Value`—without getting an exception. Instead, we get a concatenation of each child's value:

An XAttribute is not an XNode

It's also legal to reassign summary's Value, at the cost of replacing all previous children with a single new XText node.

Automatic XText Concatenation

When you add simple content to an XElement, the X-DOM appends to the existing XText child rather than creating a new one. In the following examples, e1 and e2 end up with just one child XText element whose value is HelloWorld:

```
var e1 = new XElement ("test", "Hello"); e1.Add ("World");
var e2 = new XElement ("test", "Hello", "World");
```

If you specifically create XText nodes, however, you end up with multiple children:

```
var e = new XElement ("test", new XText ("Hello"), new XText ("World"));
Console.WriteLine (e.Value);            // HelloWorld
Console.WriteLine (e.Nodes().Count());  // 2
```

XElement doesn't concatenate the two XText nodes, so the nodes' object identities are preserved.

Documents and Declarations

XDocument

As we said previously, an XDocument wraps a root XElement and allows you to add an XDeclaration, processing instructions, a document type, and root-level comments. An XDocument is optional and can be ignored or omitted: unlike with the W3C DOM, it does not serve as glue to keep everything together.

An XDocument provides the same functional constructors as XElement. And because it's based on XContainer, it also supports the Add*XXX*, Remove*XXX*, and Replace*XXX* methods. Unlike XElement, however, an XDocument can accept only limited content:

- A single XElement object (the "root")

- A single XDeclaration object

- A single XDocumentType object (to reference a DTD)

- Any number of XProcessingInstruction objects

- Any number of XComment objects

> Of these, only the root XElement is mandatory in order to have a valid XDocument. The XDeclaration is optional—if omitted, default settings are applied during serialization.

The simplest valid XDocument has just a root element:

```
var doc = new XDocument (
            new XElement ("test", "data")
          );
```

Notice that we didn't include an XDeclaration object. The file generated by calling doc.Save would still contain an XML declaration, however, because one is generated by default.

The next example produces a simple but correct XHTML file, illustrating all the constructs that an XDocument can accept:

```
var styleInstruction = new XProcessingInstruction (
  "xml-stylesheet", "href='styles.css' type='text/css'");

var docType = new XDocumentType ("html",
  "-//W3C//DTD XHTML 1.0 Strict//EN",
  "http://www.w3.org/TR/xhtml1/DTD/xhtml1-strict.dtd", null);

XNamespace ns = "http://www.w3.org/1999/xhtml";
var root =
  new XElement (ns + "html",
    new XElement (ns + "head",
      new XElement (ns + "title", "An XHTML page")),
    new XElement (ns + "body",
      new XElement (ns + "p", "This is the content"))
  );

var doc =
  new XDocument (
    new XDeclaration ("1.0", "utf-8", "no"),
    new XComment ("Reference a stylesheet"),
    styleInstruction,
    docType,
    root);

doc.Save ("test.html");
```

The resultant *test.html* reads as follows:

```
<?xml version="1.0" encoding="utf-8" standalone="no"?>
<!--Reference a stylesheet-->
<?xml-stylesheet href='styles.css' type='text/css'?>
<!DOCTYPE html PUBLIC "-//W3C//DTD XHTML 1.0 Strict//EN"
                      "http://www.w3.org/TR/xhtml1/DTD/xhtml1-strict.dtd">
<html xmlns="http://www.w3.org/1999/xhtml">
  <head>
    <title>An XHTML page</title>
  </head>
  <body>
    <p>This is the content</p>
  </body>
</html>
```

XDocument has a `Root` property that serves as a shortcut for accessing a document's single `XElement`. The reverse link is provided by `XObject`'s `Document` property, which works for all objects in the tree:

```
Console.WriteLine (doc.Root.Name.LocalName);        // html
XElement bodyNode = doc.Root.Element (ns + "body");
Console.WriteLine (bodyNode.Document == doc);        // True
```

Recall that a document's children have no `Parent`:

```
Console.WriteLine (doc.Root.Parent == null);        // True
foreach (XNode node in doc.Nodes())
  Console.Write (node.Parent == null);              // TrueTrueTrueTrue
```

 An `XDeclaration` is not an `XNode` and does not appear in the document's `Nodes` collection—unlike comments, processing instructions, and the root element. Instead, it gets assigned to a dedicated property called `Declaration`. This is why "True" is repeated four and not five times in the last example.

XML Declarations

A standard XML file starts with a declaration such as the following:

```
<?xml version="1.0" encoding="utf-8" standalone="yes"?>
```

An XML declaration ensures that the file will be correctly parsed and understood by a reader. `XElement` and `XDocument` follow these rules in emitting XML declarations:

- Calling `Save` with a filename always writes a declaration.

- Calling `Save` with an `XmlWriter` writes a declaration unless the `XmlWriter` is instructed otherwise.

- The `ToString` method never emits an XML declaration.

 You can instruct an `XmlWriter` not to produce a declaration by setting the `OmitXmlDeclaration` and `ConformanceLevel` properties of an `XmlWriterSettings` object when constructing the `XmlWriter`. We describe this in Chapter 11.

The presence or absence of an `XDeclaration` object has no effect on whether an XML declaration gets written. The purpose of an `XDeclaration` is instead to *hint the XML serialization*—in two ways:

- What text encoding to use

- What to put in the XML declaration's `encoding` and `standalone` attributes (should a declaration be written)

XDeclaration's constructor accepts three arguments, which correspond to the attributes version, encoding, and standalone. In the following example, *test.xml* is encoded in UTF-16:

```
var doc = new XDocument (
        new XDeclaration ("1.0", "utf-16", "yes"),
        new XElement ("test", "data")
      );
doc.Save ("test.xml");
```

 Whatever you specify for the XML version is ignored by the XML writer: it always writes "1.0".

The encoding must use an IETF code such as "utf-16"—just as it would appear in the XML declaration.

Writing a declaration to a string

Suppose we want to serialize an XDocument to a string—including the XML declaration. Because ToString doesn't write a declaration, we'd have to use an XmlWriter instead:

```
var doc = new XDocument (
        new XDeclaration ("1.0", "utf-8", "yes"),
        new XElement ("test", "data")
      );
var output = new StringBuilder();
var settings = new XmlWriterSettings { Indent = true };
using (XmlWriter xw = XmlWriter.Create (output, settings))
  doc.Save (xw);
Console.WriteLine (output.ToString());
```

This is the result:

```
<?xml version="1.0" encoding="utf-16" standalone="yes"?>
<test>data</test>
```

Notice that we got UTF-16 in the output—even though we explicitly requested UTF-8 in an XDeclaration! This might look like a bug, but in fact, XmlWriter is being remarkably smart. Because we're writing to a string and not a file or stream, it's impossible to apply any encoding other than UTF-16—the format in which strings are internally stored. Hence, XmlWriter writes "utf-16"—so as not to lie.

This also explains why the ToString method doesn't emit an XML declaration. Imagine that instead of calling Save, you did the following to write an XDocument to a file:

```
File.WriteAllText ("data.xml", doc.ToString());
```

As it stands, *data.xml* would lack an XML declaration, making it incomplete but still parsable (you can infer the text encoding). But if ToString() emitted an XML declaration, *data.xml* would actually contain an *incorrect* declaration (encoding="utf-16"), which might prevent it from being read at all, because Write AllText encodes using UTF-8.

Names and Namespaces

Just as .NET types can have namespaces, so too can XML elements and attributes.

XML namespaces achieve two things. First, rather like namespaces in C#, they help avoid naming collisions. This can become an issue when you merge data from one XML file into another. Second, namespaces assign *absolute* meaning to a name. The name "nil," for instance, could mean anything. Within the *http://www.w3.org/2001/ xmlschema-instance* namespace, however, "nil" means something equivalent to null in C# and comes with specific rules on how it can be applied.

Because XML namespaces are a significant source of confusion, we'll cover the topic first in general and then move on to how they're used in LINQ to XML.

Namespaces in XML

Suppose we want to define a customer element in the namespace OReilly.Nut shell.CSharp. There are two ways to proceed. The first is to use the xmlns attribute as follows:

```
<customer xmlns="OReilly.Nutshell.CSharp"/>
```

xmlns is a special reserved attribute. When used in this manner, it performs two functions:

- It specifies a namespace for the element in question.
- It specifies a default namespace for all descendant elements.

This means that in the following example, address and postcode implicitly live in the OReilly.Nutshell.CSharp namespace:

```
<customer xmlns="OReilly.Nutshell.CSharp">
  <address>
    <postcode>02138</postcode>
  </address>
</customer>
```

If we want address and postcode to have *no* namespace, we'd have to do this:

```
<customer xmlns="OReilly.Nutshell.CSharp">
  <address xmlns="">
    <postcode>02138</postcode>        <!-- postcode now inherits empty ns -->
  </address>
</customer>
```

Prefixes

The other way to specify a namespace is with a *prefix*. A prefix is an alias that you assign to a namespace to save typing. There are two steps in using a prefix—*defining* the prefix and *using* it. You can do both together as follows:

```
<nut:customer xmlns:nut="OReilly.Nutshell.CSharp"/>
```

Two distinct things are happening here. On the right, xmlns:nut="..." defines a prefix called nut and makes it available to this element and all its descendants. On the left, nut:customer assigns the newly allocated prefix to the customer element.

A prefixed element *does not* define a default namespace for descendants. In the following XML, firstname has an empty namespace:

```
<nut:customer xmlns:nut="OReilly.Nutshell.CSharp">
  <firstname>Joe</firstname>
</customer>
```

To give firstname the OReilly.Nutshell.CSharp prefix, we must do this:

```
<nut:customer xmlns:nut="OReilly.Nutshell.CSharp">
  <nut:firstname>Joe</firstname>
</customer>
```

You can also define a prefix—or prefixes—for the convenience of your descendants, without assigning any of them to the parent element itself. The following defines two prefixes, i and z, while leaving the customer element itself with an empty namespace:

```
<customer xmlns:i="http://www.w3.org/2001/XMLSchema-instance"
          xmlns:z="http://schemas.microsoft.com/2003/10/Serialization/">
  ...
</customer>
```

If this was the root node, the whole document would have i and z at its fingertips. Prefixes are convenient when elements need to draw from a number of namespaces.

Notice that both namespaces in this example are URIs. Using URIs (that you own) is standard practice: it ensures namespace uniqueness. So, in real life, our customer element would more likely be:

```
<customer xmlns="http://oreilly.com/schemas/nutshell/csharp"/>
```

or:

```
<nut:customer xmlns:nut="http://oreilly.com/schemas/nutshell/csharp"/>
```

Attributes

You can assign namespaces to attributes too. The main difference is that it always requires a prefix. For instance:

```
<customer xmlns:nut="OReilly.Nutshell.CSharp" nut:id="123" />
```

Another difference is that an unqualified attribute always has an empty namespace: it never inherits a default namespace from a parent element.

Attributes tend not to need namespaces because their meaning is usually local to the element. An exception is with general-purpose or metadata attributes, such as the nil attribute defined by W3C:

```
<customer xmlns:xsi="http://www.w3.org/2001/XMLSchema-instance">
  <firstname>Joe</firstname>
  <lastname xsi:nil="true"/>
</customer>
```

This indicates unambiguously that lastname is nil (null in C#) and not an empty string. Because we've used the standard namespace, a general-purpose parsing utility could know with certainty our intention.

Specifying Namespaces in the X-DOM

So far in this chapter, we've used just simple strings for XElement and XAttribute names. A simple string corresponds to an XML name with an empty namespace—rather like a .NET type defined in the global namespace.

There are a couple of ways to specify an XML namespace. The first is to enclose it in braces, before the local name. For example:

```
var e = new XElement ("{http://domain.com/xmlspace}customer", "Bloggs");
Console.WriteLine (e.ToString());
```

Here's the resulting XML:

```
<customer xmlns="http://domain.com/xmlspace">Bloggs</customer>
```

The second (and more performant) approach is to use the XNamespace and XName types. Here are their definitions:

```
public sealed class XNamespace
{
  public string NamespaceName { get; }
}

public sealed class XName      // A local name with optional namespace
{
  public string LocalName { get; }
  public XNamespace Namespace { get; }   // Optional
}
```

Both types define implicit casts from string, so the following is legal:

```
XNamespace ns    = "http://domain.com/xmlspace";
XName localName = "customer";
XName fullName  = "{http://domain.com/xmlspace}customer";
```

XNamespace also overloads the + operator, allowing you to combine a namespace and name into an XName without using braces:

```
XNamespace ns = "http://domain.com/xmlspace";
XName fullName = ns + "customer";
Console.WriteLine (fullName);    // {http://domain.com/xmlspace}customer
```

All constructors and methods in the X-DOM that accept an element or attribute name actually accept an XName object rather than a string. The reason you can substitute a string—as in all our examples to date—is because of the implicit cast.

Specifying a namespace is the same whether for an element or an attribute:

```
XNamespace ns = "http://domain.com/xmlspace";
var data = new XElement (ns + "data",
                new XAttribute (ns + "id", 123)
            );
```

The X-DOM and Default Namespaces

The X-DOM ignores the concept of default namespaces until it comes time to actually output XML. This means that when you construct a child XElement, you must give it a namespace explicitly if needed: it *will not* inherit from the parent:

```
XNamespace ns = "http://domain.com/xmlspace";
var data = new XElement (ns + "data",
                new XElement (ns + "customer", "Bloggs"),
                new XElement (ns + "purchase", "Bicycle")
            );
```

The X-DOM does, however, apply default namespaces when reading and outputting XML:

```
Console.WriteLine (data.ToString());

OUTPUT:
  <data xmlns="http://domain.com/xmlspace">
    <customer>Bloggs</customer>
    <purchase>Bicycle</purchase>
  </data>

Console.WriteLine (data.Element (ns + "customer").ToString());

OUTPUT:
  <customer xmlns="http://domain.com/xmlspace">Bloggs</customer>
```

If you construct XElement children without specifying namespaces—in other words:

```
XNamespace ns = "http://domain.com/xmlspace";
var data = new XElement (ns + "data",
              new XElement ("customer", "Bloggs"),
              new XElement ("purchase", "Bicycle")
          );
Console.WriteLine (data.ToString());
```

you get this result instead:

```
<data xmlns="http://domain.com/xmlspace">
  <customer xmlns="">Bloggs</customer>
```

```
    <purchase xmlns="">Bicycle</purchase>
  </data>
```

Another trap is failing to include a namespace when navigating an X-DOM:

```
XNamespace ns = "http://domain.com/xmlspace";
var data = new XElement (ns + "data",
            new XElement (ns + "customer", "Bloggs"),
            new XElement (ns + "purchase", "Bicycle")
          );
XElement x = data.Element (ns + "customer");    // ok
XElement y = data.Element ("customer");         // null
```

If you build an X-DOM tree without specifying namespaces, you can subsequently assign every element to a single namespace as follows:

```
foreach (XElement e in data.DescendantsAndSelf())
  if (e.Name.Namespace == "")
    e.Name = ns + e.Name.LocalName;
```

Prefixes

The X-DOM treats prefixes just as it treats namespaces: purely as a serialization function. This means you can choose to completely ignore the issue of prefixes—and get by! The only reason you might want to do otherwise is for efficiency when outputting to an XML file. For example, consider this:

```
XNamespace ns1 = "http://domain.com/space1";
XNamespace ns2 = "http://domain.com/space2";

var mix = new XElement (ns1 + "data",
            new XElement (ns2 + "element", "value"),
            new XElement (ns2 + "element", "value"),
            new XElement (ns2 + "element", "value")
          );
```

By default, XElement will serialize this as follows:

```
<data xmlns="http://domain.com/space1">
  <element xmlns="http://domain.com/space2">value</element>
  <element xmlns="http://domain.com/space2">value</element>
  <element xmlns="http://domain.com/space2">value</element>
</data>
```

As you can see, there's a bit of unnecessary duplication. The solution is *not* to change the way you construct the X-DOM, but instead to hint the serializer prior to writing the XML. Do this by adding attributes defining prefixes that you want to see applied. This is typically done on the root element:

```
mix.SetAttributeValue (XNamespace.Xmlns + "ns1", ns1);
mix.SetAttributeValue (XNamespace.Xmlns + "ns2", ns2);
```

This assigns the prefix "ns1" to our XNamespace variable ns1, and "ns2" to ns2. The X-DOM automatically picks up these attributes when serializing and uses them to condense the resulting XML. Here's the result now of calling ToString on mix:

```
<ns1:data xmlns:ns1="http://domain.com/space1"
          xmlns:ns2="http://domain.com/space2">
  <ns2:element>value</ns2:element>
  <ns2:element>value</ns2:element>
  <ns2:element>value</ns2:element>
</ns1:data>
```

Prefixes don't change the way you construct, query, or update the X-DOM—for these activities, you ignore the presence of prefixes and continue to use full names. Prefixes come into play only when converting to and from XML files or streams.

Prefixes are also honored in serializing attributes. In the following example, we record a customer's date of birth and credit as "nil" using the W3C-standard attribute. The highlighted line ensures that the prefix is serialized without unnecessary namespace repetition:

```
XNamespace xsi = "http://www.w3.org/2001/XMLSchema-instance";
var nil = new XAttribute (xsi + "nil", true);

var cust = new XElement ("customers",
             new XAttribute (XNamespace.Xmlns + "xsi", xsi),
             new XElement ("customer",
               new XElement ("lastname", "Bloggs"),
               new XElement ("dob", nil),
               new XElement ("credit", nil)
             )
           );
```

This is its XML:

```
<customers xmlns:xsi="http://www.w3.org/2001/XMLSchema-instance">
  <customer>
    <lastname>Bloggs</lastname>
    <dob xsi:nil="true" />
    <credit xsi:nil="true" />
  </customer>
</customers>
```

For brevity, we predeclared the nil XAttribute so that we could use it twice in building the DOM. You're allowed to reference the same attribute twice because it's automatically duplicated as required.

Annotations

You can attach custom data to any XObject with an annotation. Annotations are intended for your own private use and are treated as black boxes by X-DOM. If you've ever used the Tag property on a Windows Forms or WPF control, you'll be familiar with the concept—the difference is that you have multiple annotations, and your annotations can be *privately scoped*. You can create an annotation that other types cannot even see—let alone overwrite.

The following methods on XObject add and remove annotations:

```
public void AddAnnotation (object annotation)
public void RemoveAnnotations<T>()      where T : class
```

The following methods retrieve annotations:

```
public T Annotation<T>()                where T : class
public IEnumerable<T> Annotations<T>() where T : class
```

Each annotation is keyed by its *type*, which must be a reference type. The following adds and then retrieves a `string` annotation:

```
XElement e = new XElement ("test");
e.AddAnnotation ("Hello");
Console.WriteLine (e.Annotation<string>());    // Hello
```

You can add multiple annotations of the same type, and then use the `Annotations` method to retrieve a *sequence* of matches.

A public type such as `string` doesn't make a great key, however, because code in other types can interfere with your annotations. A better approach is to use an internal or (nested) private class:

```
class X
{
  class CustomData { internal string Message; }    // Private nested type

  static void Test()
  {
    XElement e = new XElement ("test");
    e.AddAnnotation (new CustomData { Message = "Hello" } );
    Console.Write (e.Annotations<CustomData>().First().Message);    // Hello
  }
}
```

To remove annotations, you must also have access to the key's type:

```
e.RemoveAnnotations<CustomData>();
```

Projecting into an X-DOM

So far, we've shown how to use LINQ to get data *out* of an X-DOM. You can also use LINQ queries to project *into* an X-DOM. The source can be anything over which LINQ can query, such as:

- LINQ to SQL or Entity Framework queries
- A local collection
- Another X-DOM

Regardless of the source, the strategy is the same in using LINQ to emit an X-DOM: first write a *functional construction* expression that produces the desired X-DOM shape, and then build a LINQ query around the expression.

For instance, suppose we want to retrieve customers from a database into the following XML:

```xml
<customers>
  <customer id="1">
    <name>Sue</name>
    <buys>3</buys>
  </customer>
  ...
</customers>
```

We start by writing a functional construction expression for the X-DOM using simple literals:

```
var customers =
  new XElement ("customers",
    new XElement ("customer", new XAttribute ("id", 1),
      new XElement ("name", "Sue"),
      new XElement ("buys", 3)
    )
  );
```

We then turn this into a projection and build a LINQ query around it:

```
var customers =
  new XElement ("customers",
    from c in dataContext.Customers
    select
      new XElement ("customer", new XAttribute ("id", c.ID),
        new XElement ("name", c.Name),
        new XElement ("buys", c.Purchases.Count)
      )
  );
```

 In Entity Framework, you must call .ToList() after retrieving customers, so that the third line reads:

```
from c in objectContext.Customers.ToList()
```

Here's the result:

```xml
<customers>
  <customer id="1">
    <name>Tom</name>
    <buys>3</buys>
  </customer>
  <customer id="2">
    <name>Harry</name>
    <buys>2</buys>
  </customer>
  ...
</customers>
```

We can see how this works more clearly by constructing the same query in two steps. First:

```
IEnumerable<XElement> sqlQuery =
  from c in dataContext.Customers
  select
    new XElement ("customer", new XAttribute ("id", c.ID),
      new XElement ("name", c.Name),
      new XElement ("buys", c.Purchases.Count)
  );
```

This inner portion is a normal LINQ to SQL query that projects into custom types (from LINQ to SQL's perspective). Here's the second step:

```
var customers = new XElement ("customers", sqlQuery);
```

This constructs the root XElement. The only thing unusual is that the content, sqlQuery, is not a single XElement but an IQueryable<XElement>—which implements IEnumerable<XElement>. Remember that in the processing of XML content, collections are automatically enumerated. So, each XElement gets added as a child node.

This outer query also defines the line at which the query transitions from being a database query to a local LINQ to enumerable query. XElement's constructor doesn't know about IQueryable<>, so it forces enumeration of the database query—and execution of the SQL statement.

Eliminating Empty Elements

Suppose in the preceding example that we also wanted to include details of the customer's most recent high-value purchase. We could do this as follows:

```
var customers =
  new XElement ("customers",
    from c in dataContext.Customers
    let lastBigBuy = (from p in c.Purchases
                      where p.Price > 1000
                      orderby p.Date descending
                      select p).FirstOrDefault()
    select
      new XElement ("customer", new XAttribute ("id", c.ID),
        new XElement ("name", c.Name),
        new XElement ("buys", c.Purchases.Count),
        new XElement ("lastBigBuy",
          new XElement ("description", lastBigBuy?.Description,
          new XElement ("price", lastBigBuy?.Price ?? 0m)
        )
      )
  );
```

This emits empty elements, though, for customers with no high-value purchases. (If it was a local query rather than a database query, it would throw a NullReferenceException.) In such cases, it would be better to omit the lastBigBuy node entirely. We can achieve this by wrapping the constructor for the lastBigBuy element in a conditional operator:

```
    select
      new XElement ("customer", new XAttribute ("id", c.ID),
        new XElement ("name", c.Name),
        new XElement ("buys", c.Purchases.Count),
        lastBigBuy == null ? null :
          new XElement ("lastBigBuy",
            new XElement ("description", lastBigBuy.Description),
            new XElement ("price", lastBigBuy.Price)
```

For customers with no `lastBigBuy`, a `null` is emitted instead of an empty `XElement`. This is what we want, because `null` content is simply ignored.

Streaming a Projection

If you're projecting into an X-DOM only to `Save` it (or call `ToString` on it), you can improve memory efficiency through an `XStreamingElement`. An `XStreamingElement` is a cut-down version of `XElement` that applies *deferred loading* semantics to its child content. To use it, you simply replace the outer `XElements` with `XStreamingElements`:

```
var customers =
  new XStreamingElement ("customers",
    from c in dataContext.Customers
    select
      new XStreamingElement ("customer", new XAttribute ("id", c.ID),
        new XElement ("name", c.Name),
        new XElement ("buys", c.Purchases.Count)
      )
  );
customers.Save ("data.xml");
```

The queries passed into an `XStreamingElement`'s constructor are not enumerated until you call `Save`, `ToString`, or `WriteTo` on the element; this avoids loading the whole X-DOM into memory at once. The flipside is that the queries are reevaluated, should you re-`Save`. Also, you cannot traverse an `XStreamingElement`'s child content—it does not expose methods such as `Elements` or `Attributes`.

`XStreamingElement` is not based on `XObject`—or any other class—because it has such a limited set of members. The only members it has, besides `Save`, `ToString`, and `WriteTo`, are:

- An `Add` method, which accepts content like the constructor
- A `Name` property

`XStreamingElement` does not allow you to *read* content in a streamed fashion—for this, you must use an `XmlReader` in conjunction with the X-DOM. We describe how to do this in the section "Patterns for Using XmlReader/XmlWriter" on page 489 in Chapter 11.

Transforming an X-DOM

You can transform an X-DOM by reprojecting it. For instance, suppose we want to transform an *msbuild* XML file, used by the C# compiler and Visual Studio to describe a project, into a simple format suitable for generating a report. An msbuild file looks like this:

```
<Project DefaultTargets="Build" xmlns="http://schemas.microsoft.com/dev...>
  <PropertyGroup>
    <Platform Condition=" '$(Platform)' == '' ">AnyCPU</Platform>
    <ProductVersion>9.0.11209</ProductVersion>
    ...
  </PropertyGroup>
  <ItemGroup>
    <Compile Include="ObjectGraph.cs" />
    <Compile Include="Program.cs" />
    <Compile Include="Properties\AssemblyInfo.cs" />
    <Compile Include="Tests\Aggregation.cs" />
    <Compile Include="Tests\Advanced\RecursiveXml.cs" />
  </ItemGroup>
  <ItemGroup>
    ...
  </ItemGroup>
  ...
</Project>
```

Let's say we want to include only files, as follows:

```
<ProjectReport>
  <File>ObjectGraph.cs</File>
  <File>Program.cs</File>
  <File>Properties\AssemblyInfo.cs</File>
  <File>Tests\Aggregation.cs</File>
  <File>Tests\Advanced\RecursiveXml.cs</File>
</ProjectReport>
```

The following query performs this transformation:

```
XElement project = XElement.Load ("myProjectFile.csproj");
XNamespace ns = project.Name.Namespace;
var query =
  new XElement ("ProjectReport",
    from compileItem in
      project.Elements (ns + "ItemGroup").Elements (ns + "Compile")
    let include = compileItem.Attribute ("Include")
    where include != null
    select new XElement ("File", include.Value)
  );
```

The query first extracts all ItemGroup elements and then uses the Elements extension method to obtain a flat sequence of all their Compile subelements. Notice that we had to specify an XML namespace—everything in the original file inherits the namespace defined by the Project element—so a local element name such as Item Group won't work on its own. Then, we extracted the Include attribute value and projected its value as an element.

Advanced transformations

When querying a local collection such as an X-DOM, you're free to write custom query operators to assist with more complex queries.

Suppose in the preceding example that we instead wanted a hierarchical output, based on folders:

```
<Project>
  <File>ObjectGraph.cs</File>
  <File>Program.cs</File>
  <Folder name="Properties">
    <File>AssemblyInfo.cs</File>
  </Folder>
  <Folder name="Tests">
    <File>Aggregation.cs</File>
    <Folder name="Advanced">
      <File>RecursiveXml.cs</File>
    </Folder>
  </Folder>
</Project>
```

To produce this, we need to process path strings such as *Tests\Advanced\RecursiveXml.cs* recursively. The following method does just this: it accepts a sequence of path strings and emits an X-DOM hierarchy consistent with our desired output:

```
static IEnumerable<XElement> ExpandPaths (IEnumerable<string> paths)
{
  var brokenUp = from path in paths
                 let split = path.Split (new char[] { '\\' }, 2)
                 orderby split[0]
                 select new
                 {
                   name = split[0],
                   remainder = split.ElementAtOrDefault (1)
                 };

  IEnumerable<XElement> files = from b in brokenUp
                                where b.remainder == null
                                select new XElement ("file", b.name);

  IEnumerable<XElement> folders = from b in brokenUp
                                  where b.remainder != null
                                  group b.remainder by b.name into grp
                                  select new XElement ("folder",
                                    new XAttribute ("name", grp.Key),
                                    ExpandPaths (grp)
                                  );
  return files.Concat (folders);
}
```

The first query splits each path string at the first backslash, into a name + remainder:

```
Tests\Advanced\RecursiveXml.cs -> Tests + Advanced\RecursiveXml.cs
```

If `remainder` is null, we're dealing with a straight filename. The `files` query extracts these cases.

If `remainder` is not null, we've got a folder. The `folders` query handles these cases. Because other files can be in the same folder, it must `group` by folder name to bring them all together. For each group, it then executes the same function for the subelements.

The final result is a concatenation of `files` and `folders`. The `Concat` operator preserves order, so all the files come first, alphabetically, then all the folders, alphabetically.

With this method in place, we can complete the query in two steps. First, we extract a simple sequence of path strings:

```
IEnumerable<string> paths =
  from compileItem in
    project.Elements (ns + "ItemGroup").Elements (ns + "Compile")
  let include = compileItem.Attribute ("Include")
  where include != null
  select include.Value;
```

Then, we feed this into our `ExpandPaths` method for the final result:

```
var query = new XElement ("Project", ExpandPaths (paths));
```

11

Other XML Technologies

The System.Xml namespace comprises the following namespaces and core classes:

System.Xml.*

> XmlReader *and* XmlWriter
> High-performance, forward-only cursors for reading or writing an XML stream

> XmlDocument
> Represents an XML document in a W3C-style DOM (obsolete)

System.Xml.XLinq
> Modern LINQ-centric DOM for working with XML (see Chapter 10)

System.Xml.XmlSchema
> Infrastructure and API for (W3C) XSD schemas

System.Xml.Xsl
> Infrastructure and API (XslCompiledTransform) for performing (W3C) XSLT transformations of XML

System.Xml.Serialization
> Supports the serialization of classes to and from XML (see Chapter 17)

W3C is an abbreviation for World Wide Web Consortium, where the XML standards are defined.

XmlConvert, the static class for parsing and formatting XML strings, is covered in Chapter 6.

XmlReader

`XmlReader` is a high-performance class for reading an XML stream in a low-level, forward-only manner.

Consider the following XML file:

```
<?xml version="1.0" encoding="utf-8" standalone="yes"?>
<customer id="123" status="archived">
  <firstname>Jim</firstname>
  <lastname>Bo</lastname>
</customer>
```

To instantiate an `XmlReader`, you call the static `XmlReader.Create` method, passing in a `Stream`, a `TextReader`, or a URI string. For example:

```
using (XmlReader reader = XmlReader.Create ("customer.xml"))
  ...
```

 Because `XmlReader` lets you read from potentially slow sources (`Stream`s and URIs), it offers asynchronous versions of most of its methods so that you can easily write nonblocking code. We'll cover asynchrony in detail in Chapter 14.

To construct an `XmlReader` that reads from a string:

```
XmlReader reader = XmlReader.Create (
  new System.IO.StringReader (myString));
```

You can also pass in an `XmlReaderSettings` object to control parsing and validation options. The following three properties on `XmlReaderSettings` are particularly useful for skipping over superfluous content:

```
bool IgnoreComments                  // Skip over comment nodes?
bool IgnoreProcessingInstructions    // Skip over processing instructions?
bool IgnoreWhitespace                // Skip over whitespace?
```

In the following example, we instruct the reader not to emit whitespace nodes, which are a distraction in typical scenarios:

```
XmlReaderSettings settings = new XmlReaderSettings();
settings.IgnoreWhitespace = true;

using (XmlReader reader = XmlReader.Create ("customer.xml", settings))
  ...
```

Another useful property on `XmlReaderSettings` is `ConformanceLevel`. Its default value of `Document` instructs the reader to assume a valid XML document with a single root node. This is a problem if you want to read just an inner portion of XML containing multiple nodes:

```
<firstname>Jim</firstname>
<lastname>Bo</lastname>
```

To read this without throwing an exception, you must set `ConformanceLevel` to `Fragment`.

`XmlReaderSettings` also has a property called `CloseInput`, which indicates whether to close the underlying stream when the reader is closed (there's an analogous property on `XmlWriterSettings` called `CloseOutput`). The default value for `CloseInput` and `CloseOutput` is `false`.

Reading Nodes

The units of an XML stream are *XML nodes*. The reader traverses the stream in textual (depth-first) order. The `Depth` property of the reader returns the current depth of the cursor.

The most primitive way to read from an `XmlReader` is to call `Read`. It advances to the next node in the XML stream, rather like `MoveNext` in `IEnumerator`. The first call to `Read` positions the cursor at the first node. When `Read` returns `false`, it means the cursor has advanced *past* the last node, at which point the `XmlReader` should be closed and abandoned.

In this example, we read every node in the XML stream, outputting each node type as we go:

```
XmlReaderSettings settings = new XmlReaderSettings();
settings.IgnoreWhitespace = true;

using (XmlReader reader = XmlReader.Create ("customer.xml", settings))
  while (reader.Read())
  {
    Console.Write (new string (' ',reader.Depth*2));  // Write indentation
    Console.WriteLine (reader.NodeType);
  }
```

The output is as follows:

```
XmlDeclaration
Element
  Element
    Text
  EndElement
  Element
    Text
  EndElement
EndElement
```

 Attributes are not included in `Read`-based traversal (see the section "Reading Attributes" on page 485 later in this chapter).

`NodeType` is of type `XmlNodeType`, which is an enum with these members:

None	Comment	Document
XmlDeclaration	Entity	DocumentType
Element	EndEntity	DocumentFragment
EndElement	EntityReference	Notation
Text	ProcessingInstruction	Whitespace
Attribute	CDATA	SignificantWhitespace

Two string properties on XmlReader provide access to a node's content: Name and Value. Depending on the node type, either Name or Value (or both) is populated:

```
XmlReaderSettings settings = new XmlReaderSettings();
settings.IgnoreWhitespace = true;
settings.DtdProcessing = DtdProcessing.Parse;     // Required to read DTDs

using (XmlReader r = XmlReader.Create ("customer.xml", settings))
  while (r.Read())
  {
    Console.Write (r.NodeType.ToString().PadRight (17, '-'));
    Console.Write ("> ".PadRight (r.Depth * 3));

    switch (r.NodeType)
    {
      case XmlNodeType.Element:
      case XmlNodeType.EndElement:
        Console.WriteLine (r.Name); break;

      case XmlNodeType.Text:
      case XmlNodeType.CDATA:
      case XmlNodeType.Comment:
      case XmlNodeType.XmlDeclaration:
        Console.WriteLine (r.Value); break;

      case XmlNodeType.DocumentType:
        Console.WriteLine (r.Name + " - " + r.Value); break;

      default: break;
    }
  }
```

To demonstrate this, we'll expand our XML file to include a document type, entity, CDATA, and comment:

```
<?xml version="1.0" encoding="utf-8" ?>
<!DOCTYPE customer [ <!ENTITY tc "Top Customer"> ]>
<customer id="123" status="archived">
  <firstname>Jim</firstname>
  <lastname>Bo</lastname>
  <quote><![CDATA[C#'s operators include: < > &]]></quote>
  <notes>Jim Bo is a &tc;</notes>
  <!-- That wasn't so bad! -->
</customer>
```

An entity is like a macro; a CDATA is like a verbatim string (@"...") in C#. Here's the result:

```
XmlDeclaration---> version="1.0" encoding="utf-8"
DocumentType-----> customer -  <!ENTITY tc "Top Customer">
Element---------> customer
Element---------> firstname
Text-----------> Jim
EndElement------> firstname
Element---------> lastname
Text-----------> Bo
EndElement------> lastname
Element---------> quote
CDATA-----------> C#'s operators include: < > &
EndElement------> quote
Element---------> notes
Text-----------> Jim Bo is a Top Customer
EndElement------> notes
Comment---------> That wasn't so bad!
EndElement------> customer
```

XmlReader automatically resolves entities, so in our example, the entity reference &tc; expands into Top Customer.

Reading Elements

Often, you already know the structure of the XML document that you're reading. To help with this, XmlReader provides a range of methods that read while *presuming* a particular structure. This simplifies your code, as well as performing some validation at the same time.

 XmlReader throws an XmlException if any validation fails. XmlException has LineNumber and LinePosition properties indicating where the error occurred—logging this information is essential if the XML file is large!

ReadStartElement verifies that the current NodeType is Element, and then calls Read. If you specify a name, it verifies that it matches that of the current element.

ReadEndElement verifies that the current NodeType is EndElement, and then calls Read.

For instance, we could read this:

```
<firstname>Jim</firstname>
```

as follows:

```
reader.ReadStartElement ("firstname");
Console.WriteLine (reader.Value);
reader.Read();
reader.ReadEndElement();
```

The ReadElementContentAsString method does all of this in one hit. It reads a start element, a text node, and an end element, returning the content as a string:

```
string firstName = reader.ReadElementContentAsString ("firstname", "");
```

The second argument refers to the namespace, which is blank in this example. There are also typed versions of this method, such as ReadElementContentAsInt, which parse the result. Returning to our original XML document:

```
<?xml version="1.0" encoding="utf-8" standalone="yes"?>
<customer id="123" status="archived">
  <firstname>Jim</firstname>
  <lastname>Bo</lastname>
  <creditlimit>500.00</creditlimit>    <!-- OK, we sneaked this in! -->
</customer>
```

We could read it in as follows:

```
XmlReaderSettings settings = new XmlReaderSettings();
settings.IgnoreWhitespace = true;

using (XmlReader r = XmlReader.Create ("customer.xml", settings))
{
  r.MoveToContent();                    // Skip over the XML declaration
  r.ReadStartElement ("customer");
  string firstName    = r.ReadElementContentAsString ("firstname", "");
  string lastName     = r.ReadElementContentAsString ("lastname", "");
  decimal creditLimit = r.ReadElementContentAsDecimal ("creditlimit", "");

  r.MoveToContent();      // Skip over that pesky comment
  r.ReadEndElement();     // Read the closing customer tag
}
```

 The MoveToContent method is really useful. It skips over all the fluff: XML declarations, whitespace, comments, and processing instructions. You can also instruct the reader to do most of this automatically through the properties on XmlRea derSettings.

Optional elements

In the previous example, suppose that <lastname> was optional. The solution to this is straightforward:

```
r.ReadStartElement ("customer");
string firstName    = r. ReadElementContentAsString ("firstname", "");
string lastName     = r.Name == "lastname"
                      ? r.ReadElementContentAsString() : null;
decimal creditLimit = r.ReadElementContentAsDecimal ("creditlimit", "");
```

Random element order

The examples in this section rely on elements appearing in the XML file in a set order. If you need to cope with elements appearing in any order, the easiest solution is to read that section of the XML into an X-DOM. We describe how to do this later in the section "Patterns for Using XmlReader/XmlWriter" on page 489.

Empty elements

The way that `XmlReader` handles empty elements presents a horrible trap. Consider the following element:

```
<customerList></customerList>
```

In XML, this is equivalent to:

```
<customerList/>
```

And yet, `XmlReader` treats the two differently. In the first case, the following code works as expected:

```
reader.ReadStartElement ("customerList");
reader.ReadEndElement();
```

In the second case, `ReadEndElement` throws an exception, because there is no separate "end element" as far as `XmlReader` is concerned. The workaround is to check for an empty element as follows:

```
bool isEmpty = reader.IsEmptyElement;
reader.ReadStartElement ("customerList");
if (!isEmpty) reader.ReadEndElement();
```

In reality, this is a nuisance only when the element in question may contain child elements (such as a customer list). With elements that wrap simple text (such as firstname), you can avoid the whole issue by calling a method such as `ReadElement ContentAsString`. The `ReadElementXXX` methods handle both kinds of empty elements correctly.

Other ReadXXX methods

Table 11-1 summarizes all `ReadXXX` methods in `XmlReader`. Most of these are designed to work with elements. The sample XML fragment shown in bold is the section read by the method described.

Table 11-1. Read methods

Members	Works on NodeType	Sample XML fragment	Input parameters	Data returned
ReadContentAs*XXX*	Text	`<a>x</a>`		x
ReadString	Text	`<a>x</a>`		x
ReadElementString	Element	**`<a>x</a>`**		x
ReadElementContentAs*XXX*	Element	**`<a>x</a>`**		x
ReadInnerXml	Element	**`<a>x</a>`**		x
ReadOuterXml	Element	**`<a>x</a>`**		`<a>x</a>`
ReadStartElement	Element	**`<a>`**x</a>		
ReadEndElement	Element	<a>x**`</a>`**		

Members	Works on NodeType	Sample XML fragment	Input parameters	Data returned
ReadSubtree	Element	`<a>x</a>`		`<a>x</a>`
ReadToDescendant	Element	`<a>x<b></b></a>`	"b"	
ReadToFollowing	Element	`<a>x<b></b></a>`	"b"	
ReadToNextSibling	Element	`<a>x</a><b></b>`	"b"	
ReadAttributeValue	Attribute	See "Reading Attributes" on page 485		

The ReadContentAs*XXX* methods parse a text node into type *XXX*. Internally, the XmlConvert class performs the string-to-type conversion. The text node can be within an element or an attribute.

The ReadElementContentAs*XXX* methods are wrappers around corresponding Read ContentAs*XXX* methods. They apply to the *element* node, rather than the *text* node enclosed by the element.

 The typed Read*XXX* methods also include versions that read base 64 and BinHex formatted data into a byte array.

ReadInnerXml is typically applied to an element, and it reads and returns an element and all its descendants. When applied to an attribute, it returns the value of the attribute.

ReadOuterXml is the same as ReadInnerXml, except it includes rather than excludes the element at the cursor position.

ReadSubtree returns a proxy reader that provides a view over just the current element (and its descendants). The proxy reader must be closed before the original reader can be safely read again. At the point the proxy reader is closed, the cursor position of the original reader moves to the end of the subtree.

ReadToDescendant moves the cursor to the start of the first descendant node with the specified name/namespace.

ReadToFollowing moves the cursor to the start of the first node—regardless of depth—with the specified name/namespace.

ReadToNextSibling moves the cursor to the start of the first sibling node with the specified name/namespace.

ReadString and ReadElementString behave like ReadContentAsString and ReadE lementContentAsString, except that they throw an exception if there's more than a *single* text node within the element. In general, these methods should be avoided because they throw an exception if an element contains a comment.

Reading Attributes

XmlReader provides an indexer giving you direct (random) access to an element's attributes—by name or position. Using the indexer is equivalent to calling GetAttribute.

Given the following XML fragment:

```
<customer id="123" status="archived"/>
```

we could read its attributes as follows:

```
Console.WriteLine (reader ["id"]);            // 123
Console.WriteLine (reader ["status"]);        // archived
Console.WriteLine (reader ["bogus"] == null); // True
```

> The XmlReader must be positioned *on a start element* in order to read attributes. *After* calling ReadStartElement, the attributes are gone forever!

Although attribute order is semantically irrelevant, you can access attributes by their ordinal position. We could rewrite the preceding example as follows:

```
Console.WriteLine (reader [0]);            // 123
Console.WriteLine (reader [1]);            // archived
```

The indexer also lets you specify the attribute's namespace—if it has one.

AttributeCount returns the number of attributes for the current node.

Attribute nodes

To explicitly traverse attribute nodes, you must make a special diversion from the normal path of just calling Read. A good reason to do so is if you want to parse attribute values into other types, via the ReadContentAs*XXX* methods.

The diversion must begin from a *start element*. To make the job easier, the forward-only rule is relaxed during attribute traversal: you can jump to any attribute (forward or backward) by calling MoveToAttribute.

> MoveToElement returns you to the start element from any-place within the attribute node diversion.

Returning to our previous example:

```
<customer id="123" status="archived"/>
```

we can do this:

```
reader.MoveToAttribute ("status");
string status = reader.ReadContentAsString();

reader.MoveToAttribute ("id");
int id = reader.ReadContentAsInt();
```

`MoveToAttribute` returns `false` if the specified attribute doesn't exist.

You can also traverse each attribute in sequence by calling the `MoveToFirstAttri` bute and then the `MoveToNextAttribute` methods:

```
if (reader.MoveToFirstAttribute())
  do
  {
    Console.WriteLine (reader.Name + "=" + reader.Value);
  }
  while (reader.MoveToNextAttribute());

// OUTPUT:
id=123
status=archived
```

Namespaces and Prefixes

`XmlReader` provides two parallel systems for referring to element and attribute names:

- `Name`
- `NamespaceURI` and `LocalName`

Whenever you read an element's `Name` property or call a method that accepts a single name argument, you're using the first system. This works well if no namespaces or prefixes are present; otherwise, it acts in a crude and literal manner. Namespaces are ignored, and prefixes are included exactly as they were written. For example:

Sample fragment	Name
`<customer ...>`	customer
`<customer xmlns='blah' ...>`	customer
`<x:customer ...>`	x:customer

The following code works with the first two cases:

```
reader.ReadStartElement ("customer");
```

The following is required to handle the third case:

```
reader.ReadStartElement ("x:customer");
```

The second system works through two *namespace-aware* properties: `NamespaceURI` and `LocalName`. These properties take into account prefixes and default namespaces defined by parent elements. Prefixes are automatically expanded. This means that `NamespaceURI` always reflects the semantically correct namespace for the current element, and `LocalName` is always free of prefixes.

When you pass two name arguments into a method such as `ReadStartElement`, you're using this same system. For example, consider the following XML:

```
<customer xmlns="DefaultNamespace" xmlns:other="OtherNamespace">
  <address>
    <other:city>
      ...
```

We could read this as follows:

```
reader.ReadStartElement ("customer", "DefaultNamespace");
reader.ReadStartElement ("address", "DefaultNamespace");
reader.ReadStartElement ("city",    "OtherNamespace");
```

Abstracting away prefixes is usually exactly what you want. If necessary, you can see what prefix was used through the Prefix property and convert it into a namespace by calling LookupNamespace.

XmlWriter

XmlWriter is a forward-only writer of an XML stream. The design of XmlWriter is symmetrical to XmlReader.

As with XmlTextReader, you construct an XmlWriter by calling Create with an optional settings object. In the following example, we enable indenting to make the output more human-readable, and then write a simple XML file:

```
XmlWriterSettings settings = new XmlWriterSettings();
settings.Indent = true;

using (XmlWriter writer = XmlWriter.Create ("..\\..\\foo.xml", settings))
{
  writer.WriteStartElement ("customer");
  writer.WriteElementString ("firstname", "Jim");
  writer.WriteElementString ("lastname"," Bo");
  writer.WriteEndElement();
}
```

This produces the following document (the same as the file we read in the first example of XmlReader):

```
<?xml version="1.0" encoding="utf-8" ?>
<customer>
  <firstname>Jim</firstname>
  <lastname>Bo</lastname>
</customer>
```

XmlWriter automatically writes the declaration at the top unless you indicate otherwise in XmlWriterSettings, by setting OmitXmlDeclaration to true or Conforman ceLevel to Fragment. The latter also permits writing multiple root nodes—something that otherwise throws an exception.

The WriteValue method writes a single text node. It accepts both string and nonstring types such as bool and DateTime, internally calling XmlConvert to perform XML-compliant string conversions:

```
writer.WriteStartElement ("birthdate");
writer.WriteValue (DateTime.Now);
writer.WriteEndElement();
```

In contrast, if we call:

```
WriteElementString ("birthdate", DateTime.Now.ToString());
```

the result would be both non-XML-compliant and vulnerable to incorrect parsing.

WriteString is equivalent to calling WriteValue with a string. XmlWriter automatically escapes characters that would otherwise be illegal within an attribute or element, such as & < >, and extended Unicode characters.

Writing Attributes

You can write attributes immediately after writing a start element:

```
writer.WriteStartElement ("customer");
writer.WriteAttributeString ("id", "1");
writer.WriteAttributeString ("status", "archived");
```

To write nonstring values, call WriteStartAttribute, WriteValue, and then Write
EndAttribute.

Writing Other Node Types

XmlWriter also defines the following methods for writing other kinds of nodes:

```
WriteBase64        // for binary data
WriteBinHex        // for binary data
WriteCData
WriteComment
WriteDocType
WriteEntityRef
WriteProcessingInstruction
WriteRaw
WriteWhitespace
```

WriteRaw directly injects a string into the output stream. There is also a WriteNode method that accepts an XmlReader, echoing everything from the given XmlReader.

Namespaces and Prefixes

The overloads for the Write* methods allow you to associate an element or attribute with a namespace. Let's rewrite the contents of the XML file in our previous example. This time we will associate all the elements with the *http://oreilly.com* namespace, declaring the prefix o at the customer element:

```
writer.WriteStartElement ("o", "customer", "http://oreilly.com");
writer.WriteElementString ("o", "firstname", "http://oreilly.com", "Jim");
writer.WriteElementString ("o", "lastname", "http://oreilly.com", "Bo");
writer.WriteEndElement();
```

The output is now as follows:

```
<?xml version="1.0" encoding="utf-8" standalone="yes"?>
<o:customer xmlns:o='http://oreilly.com'>
  <o:firstname>Jim</o:firstname>
  <o:lastname>Bo</o:lastname>
</o:customer>
```

Notice how for brevity XmlWriter omits the child element's namespace declarations when they are already declared by the parent element.

Patterns for Using XmlReader/XmlWriter

Working with Hierarchical Data

Consider the following classes:

```
public class Contacts
{
  public IList<Customer> Customers = new List<Customer>();
  public IList<Supplier> Suppliers = new List<Supplier>();
}

public class Customer { public string FirstName, LastName; }
public class Supplier { public string Name;                 }
```

Suppose you want to use XmlReader and XmlWriter to serialize a Contacts object to XML as in the following:

```
<?xml version="1.0" encoding="utf-8" standalone="yes"?>
<contacts>
    <customer id="1">
        <firstname>Jay</firstname>
        <lastname>Dee</lastname>
    </customer>
    <customer>                      <!-- we'll assume id is optional -->
        <firstname>Kay</firstname>
        <lastname>Gee</lastname>
    </customer>
    <supplier>
        <name>X Technologies Ltd</name>
    </supplier>
</contacts>
```

The best approach is not to write one big method, but to encapsulate XML functionality in the Customer and Supplier types themselves by writing ReadXml and WriteXml methods on these types. The pattern in doing so is straightforward:

- ReadXml and WriteXml leave the reader/writer at the same depth when they exit.

- ReadXml reads the outer element, whereas WriteXml writes only its inner content.

Here's how we would write the Customer type:

```
public class Customer
{
  public const string XmlName = "customer";
  public int? ID;
  public string FirstName, LastName;

  public Customer () { }
  public Customer (XmlReader r) { ReadXml (r); }

  public void ReadXml (XmlReader r)
  {
    if (r.MoveToAttribute ("id")) ID = r.ReadContentAsInt();
    r.ReadStartElement();
    FirstName = r.ReadElementContentAsString ("firstname", "");
    LastName = r.ReadElementContentAsString ("lastname", "");
    r.ReadEndElement();
  }

  public void WriteXml (XmlWriter w)
  {
    if (ID.HasValue) w.WriteAttributeString ("id", "", ID.ToString());
    w.WriteElementString ("firstname", FirstName);
    w.WriteElementString ("lastname", LastName);
  }
}
```

Notice that ReadXml reads the outer start and end element nodes. If its caller did this job instead, Customer couldn't read its own attributes. The reason for not making WriteXml symmetrical in this regard is twofold:

- The caller might need to choose how the outer element is named.
- The caller might need to write extra XML attributes, such as the element's *subtype* (which could then be used to decide which class to instantiate when reading back the element).

Another benefit of following this pattern is that it makes your implementation compatible with IXmlSerializable (see Chapter 17).

The Supplier class is analogous:

```
public class Supplier
{
  public const string XmlName = "supplier";
  public string Name;

  public Supplier () { }
  public Supplier (XmlReader r) { ReadXml (r); }

  public void ReadXml (XmlReader r)
  {
    r.ReadStartElement();
    Name = r.ReadElementContentAsString ("name", "");
    r.ReadEndElement();
```

```
  }

  public void WriteXml (XmlWriter w)
  {
    w.WriteElementString ("name", Name);
  }
}
```

With the Contacts class, we must enumerate the customers element in ReadXml, checking whether each subelement is a customer or a supplier. We also have to code around the empty element trap:

```
public void ReadXml (XmlReader r)
{
  bool isEmpty = r.IsEmptyElement;       // This ensures we don't get
  r.ReadStartElement();                  // snookered by an empty
  if (isEmpty) return;                   // <contacts/> element!
  while (r.NodeType == XmlNodeType.Element)
  {
    if (r.Name == Customer.XmlName)       Customers.Add (new Customer (r));
    else if (r.Name == Supplier.XmlName) Suppliers.Add (new Supplier (r));
    else
      throw new XmlException ("Unexpected node: " + r.Name);
  }
  r.ReadEndElement();
}

public void WriteXml (XmlWriter w)
{
  foreach (Customer c in Customers)
  {
    w.WriteStartElement (Customer.XmlName);
    c.WriteXml (w);
    w.WriteEndElement();
  }
  foreach (Supplier s in Suppliers)
  {
    w.WriteStartElement (Supplier.XmlName);
    s.WriteXml (w);
    w.WriteEndElement();
  }
}
```

Mixing XmlReader/XmlWriter with an X-DOM

You can fly in an X-DOM at any point in the XML tree where XmlReader or XmlWriter becomes too cumbersome. Using the X-DOM to handle inner elements is an excellent way to combine X-DOM's ease of use with the low-memory footprint of XmlReader and XmlWriter.

Using XmlReader with XElement

To read the current element into an X-DOM, you call `XNode.ReadFrom`, passing in the `XmlReader`. Unlike `XElement.Load`, this method is not "greedy" in that it doesn't expect to see a whole document. Instead, it reads just the end of the current subtree.

For instance, suppose we have an XML logfile structured as follows:

```
<log>
  <logentry id="1">
    <date>...</date>
    <source>...</source>
    ...
  </logentry>
  ...
</log>
```

If there were a million `logentry` elements, reading the whole thing into an X-DOM would waste memory. A better solution is to traverse each `logentry` with an `XmlReader`, and then use `XElement` to process the elements individually:

```
XmlReaderSettings settings = new XmlReaderSettings();
settings.IgnoreWhitespace = true;

using (XmlReader r = XmlReader.Create ("logfile.xml", settings))
{
  r.ReadStartElement ("log");
  while (r.Name == "logentry")
  {
    XElement logEntry = (XElement) XNode.ReadFrom (r);
    int id = (int) logEntry.Attribute ("id");
    DateTime date = (DateTime) logEntry.Element ("date");
    string source = (string) logEntry.Element ("source");
    ...
  }
  r.ReadEndElement();
}
```

If you follow the pattern described in the previous section, you can slot an `XElement` into a custom type's `ReadXml` or `WriteXml` method without the caller ever knowing you've cheated! For instance, we could rewrite `Customer`'s `ReadXml` method as follows:

```
public void ReadXml (XmlReader r)
{
  XElement x = (XElement) XNode.ReadFrom (r);
  FirstName = (string) x.Element ("firstname");
  LastName = (string) x.Element ("lastname");
}
```

`XElement` collaborates with `XmlReader` to ensure that namespaces are kept intact and prefixes are properly expanded—even if defined at an outer level. So, if our XML file read like this:

```
<log xmlns="http://loggingspace">
  <logentry id="1">
    ...
```

the XElements we constructed at the logentry level would correctly inherit the outer namespace.

Using XmlWriter with XElement

You can use an XElement just to write inner elements to an XmlWriter. The following code writes a million logentry elements to an XML file using XElement—without storing the whole thing in memory:

```
using (XmlWriter w = XmlWriter.Create ("log.xml"))
{
  w.WriteStartElement ("log");
  for (int i = 0; i < 1000000; i++)
  {
    XElement e = new XElement ("logentry",
                new XAttribute ("id", i),
                new XElement ("date", DateTime.Today.AddDays (-1)),
                new XElement ("source", "test"));
    e.WriteTo (w);
  }
  w.WriteEndElement ();
}
```

Using an XElement incurs minimal execution overhead. If we amend this example to use XmlWriter throughout, there's no measurable difference in execution time.

XSD and Schema Validation

The content of a particular XML document is nearly always domain-specific, such as a Microsoft Word document, an application configuration document, or a web service. For each domain, the XML file conforms to a particular pattern. There are several standards for describing the schema of such a pattern, to standardize and automate the interpretation and validation of XML documents. The most widely accepted standard is *XSD*, short for *XML Schema Definition*. Its precursors, DTD and XDR, are also supported by System.Xml.

Consider the following XML document:

```
<?xml version="1.0"?>
<customers>
  <customer id="1" status="active">
    <firstname>Jim</firstname>
    <lastname>Bo</lastname>
  </customer>
  <customer id="1" status="archived">
    <firstname>Thomas</firstname>
    <lastname>Jefferson</lastname>
  </customer>
</customers>
```

We can write an XSD for this document as follows:

```xml
<?xml version="1.0" encoding="utf-8"?>
<xs:schema attributeFormDefault="unqualified"
           elementFormDefault="qualified"
           xmlns:xs="http://www.w3.org/2001/XMLSchema">
  <xs:element name="customers">
    <xs:complexType>
      <xs:sequence>
        <xs:element maxOccurs="unbounded" name="customer">
          <xs:complexType>
            <xs:sequence>
              <xs:element name="firstname" type="xs:string" />
              <xs:element name="lastname" type="xs:string" />
            </xs:sequence>
            <xs:attribute name="id" type="xs:int" use="required" />
            <xs:attribute name="status" type="xs:string" use="required" />
          </xs:complexType>
        </xs:element>
      </xs:sequence>
    </xs:complexType>
  </xs:element>
</xs:schema>
```

As you can see, XSD documents are themselves written in XML. Furthermore, an XSD document is describable with XSD—you can find that definition at *http://www.w3.org/2001/xmlschema.xsd*.

Performing Schema Validation

You can validate an XML file or document against one or more schemas before reading or processing it. There are a number of reasons to do so:

- You can get away with less error checking and exception handling.

- Schema validation picks up errors you might otherwise overlook.

- Error messages are detailed and informative.

To perform validation, plug a schema into an XmlReader, an XmlDocument, or an X-DOM object, and then read or load the XML as you would normally. Schema validation happens automatically as content is read, so the input stream is not read twice.

Validating with an XmlReader

Here's how to plug a schema from the file *customers.xsd* into an XmlReader:

```
XmlReaderSettings settings = new XmlReaderSettings();
settings.ValidationType = ValidationType.Schema;
settings.Schemas.Add (null, "customers.xsd");

using (XmlReader r = XmlReader.Create ("customers.xml", settings))
    ...
```

If the schema is inline, set the following flag instead of adding to Schemas:

```
settings.ValidationFlags |= XmlSchemaValidationFlags.ProcessInlineSchema;
```

You then Read as you would normally. If schema validation fails at any point, an XmlSchemaValidationException is thrown.

 Calling Read on its own validates both elements and attributes: you don't need to navigate to each individual attribute for it to be validated.

If you want *only* to validate the document, you can do this:

```
using (XmlReader r = XmlReader.Create ("customers.xml", settings))
  try { while (r.Read()) ; }
  catch (XmlSchemaValidationException ex)
  {
    ...
  }
```

XmlSchemaValidationException has properties for the error Message, LineNumber, and LinePosition. In this case, it only tells you about the first error in the document. If you want to report on all errors in the document, you instead must handle the ValidationEventHandler event:

```
XmlReaderSettings settings = new XmlReaderSettings();
settings.ValidationType = ValidationType.Schema;
settings.Schemas.Add (null, "customers.xsd");
settings.ValidationEventHandler += ValidationHandler;
using (XmlReader r = XmlReader.Create ("customers.xml", settings))
  while (r.Read()) ;
```

When you handle this event, schema errors no longer throw exceptions. Instead, they fire your event handler:

```
static void ValidationHandler (object sender, ValidationEventArgs e)
{
  Console.WriteLine ("Error: " + e.Exception.Message);
}
```

The Exception property of ValidationEventArgs contains the XmlSchemaValidationException that would have otherwise been thrown.

 The System.Xml namespace also contains a class called XmlValidatingReader. This was used to perform schema validation prior to Framework 2.0, and it is now deprecated.

Validating an X-DOM

To validate an XML file or stream while reading into an X-DOM, you create an XmlReader, plug in the schemas, and then use the reader to load the DOM:

```
XmlReaderSettings settings = new XmlReaderSettings();
settings.ValidationType = ValidationType.Schema;
settings.Schemas.Add (null, "customers.xsd");
```

```
XDocument doc;
using (XmlReader r = XmlReader.Create ("customers.xml", settings))
  try { doc = XDocument.Load (r); }
  catch (XmlSchemaValidationException ex) { ... }
```

You can also validate an XDocument or XElement that's already in memory by calling extension methods in System.Xml.Schema. These methods accept an XmlSchemaSet (a collection of schemas) and a validation event handler:

```
XDocument doc = XDocument.Load (@"customers.xml");
XmlSchemaSet set = new XmlSchemaSet ();
set.Add (null, @"customers.xsd");
StringBuilder errors = new StringBuilder ();
doc.Validate (set, (sender, args) => { errors.AppendLine
                                          (args.Exception.Message); }
             );
Console.WriteLine (errors.ToString());
```

XSLT

XSLT stands for *Extensible Stylesheet Language Transformations*. It is an XML language that describes how to transform one XML language into another. The quintessential example of such a transformation is transforming an XML document (that typically describes data) into an XHTML document (that describes a formatted document).

Consider the following XML file:

```
<customer>
  <firstname>Jim</firstname>
  <lastname>Bo</lastname>
</customer>
```

The following XSLT file describes such a transformation:

```
<?xml version="1.0" encoding="UTF-8"?>
  <xsl:stylesheet xmlns:xsl="http://www.w3.org/1999/XSL/Transform"
version="1.0">
  <xsl:template match="/">
    <html>
      <p><xsl:value-of select="//firstname"/></p>
      <p><xsl:value-of select="//lastname"/></p>
    </html>
  </xsl:template>
</xsl:stylesheet>
```

The output is as follows:

```
<html>
 <p>Jim</p>
 <p>Bo</p>
</html>
```

The `System.Xml.Xsl.XslCompiledTransform` transform class efficiently performs XSLT transforms. It renders `XmlTransform` obsolete. `XslCompiledTransform` works very simply:

```
XslCompiledTransform transform = new XslCompiledTransform();
transform.Load ("test.xslt");
transform.Transform ("input.xml", "output.xml");
```

Generally, it's more useful to use the overload of `Transform` that accepts an `XmlWriter` rather than an output file, so you can control the formatting.

12

Disposal and Garbage Collection

Some objects require explicit teardown code to release resources such as open files, locks, operating system handles, and unmanaged objects. In .NET parlance, this is called *disposal*, and it is supported through the IDisposable interface. The managed memory occupied by unused objects must also be reclaimed at some point; this function is known as *garbage collection* and is performed by the CLR.

Disposal differs from garbage collection in that disposal is usually explicitly instigated; garbage collection is totally automatic. In other words, the programmer takes care of such things as releasing file handles, locks, and operating system resources while the CLR takes care of releasing memory.

This chapter discusses both disposal and garbage collection, also describing C# finalizers and the pattern by which they can provide a backup for disposal. Lastly, we discuss the intricacies of the garbage collector and other memory management options.

IDisposable, Dispose, and Close

The .NET Framework defines a special interface for types requiring a tear-down method:

```
public interface IDisposable
{
  void Dispose();
}
```

C#'s using statement provides a syntactic shortcut for calling Dispose on objects that implement IDisposable, using a try/finally block. For example:

```
using (FileStream fs = new FileStream ("myFile.txt", FileMode.Open))
{
  // ... Write to the file ...
}
```

The compiler converts this to:

```
FileStream fs = new FileStream ("myFile.txt", FileMode.Open);
try
{
  // ... Write to the file ...
}
finally
{
  if (fs != null) ((IDisposable)fs).Dispose();
}
```

The finally block ensures that the Dispose method is called even when an exception is thrown[1] or the code exits the block early.

In simple scenarios, writing your own disposable type is just a matter of implementing IDisposable and writing the Dispose method:

```
sealed class Demo : IDisposable
{
  public void Dispose()
  {
    // Perform cleanup / tear-down.
    ...
  }
}
```

 This pattern works well in simple cases and is appropriate for sealed classes. In "Calling Dispose from a Finalizer" on page 508, we'll describe a more elaborate pattern that can provide a backup for consumers that forget to call Dispose. With unsealed types, there's a strong case for following this latter pattern from the outset—otherwise, it becomes very messy if the subtype wants to add such functionality itself.

Standard Disposal Semantics

The Framework follows a de facto set of rules in its disposal logic. These rules are not hard-wired to the Framework or C# language in any way; their purpose is to define a consistent protocol to consumers. Here they are:

1. Once disposed, an object is beyond redemption. It cannot be reactivated, and calling its methods or properties (other than Dispose) throws an ObjectDispo sedException.

2. Calling an object's Dispose method repeatedly causes no error.

---

1 In "Interrupt and Abort" in Chapter 22, we describe how aborting a thread can violate the safety of this pattern. This is rarely an issue in practice because aborting threads is widely discouraged for precisely this (and other) reasons.

3. If disposable object *x* "owns" disposable object *y*, *x*'s `Dispose` method automatically calls *y*'s `Dispose` method—unless instructed otherwise.

These rules are also helpful when writing your own types, though not mandatory. Nothing prevents you from writing an "Undispose" method, other than, perhaps, the flak you might cop from colleagues!

According to rule 3, a container object automatically disposes its child objects. A good example is a Windows container control such as a `Form` or `Panel`. The container may host many child controls, yet you don't dispose every one of them explicitly: closing or disposing the parent control or form takes care of the whole lot. Another example is when you wrap a `FileStream` in a `DeflateStream`. Disposing the `DeflateStream` also disposes the `FileStream`—unless you instructed otherwise in the constructor.

Close and Stop

Some types define a method called `Close` in addition to `Dispose`. The Framework is not completely consistent on the semantics of a `Close` method, although in nearly all cases it's either:

- Functionally identical to `Dispose`
- A functional *subset* of `Dispose`

An example of the latter is `IDbConnection`: a `Closed` connection can be re-`Opened`; a `Disposed` connection cannot. Another example is a Windows `Form` activated with `ShowDialog`: `Close` hides it; `Dispose` releases its resources.

Some classes define a `Stop` method (e.g., `Timer` or `HttpListener`). A `Stop` method may release unmanaged resources, like `Dispose`, but unlike `Dispose`, it allows for re-`Start`ing.

With WinRT, `Close` is considered identical to `Dispose`—in fact, the runtime *projects* methods called `Close` into methods called `Dispose` to make their types friendly to `using` statements.

When to Dispose

A safe rule to follow (in nearly all cases) is "if in doubt, dispose." A disposable object —if it could talk—would say the following:

> *When you've finished with me, let me know. If simply abandoned, I might cause trouble for other object instances, the application domain, the computer, the network, or the database!*

Objects wrapping an unmanaged resource handle will nearly always require disposal in order to free the handle. Examples include Windows Forms controls, file or network streams, network sockets, GDI+ pens, brushes, and bitmaps. Conversely, if a type is disposable, it will often (but not always) reference an unmanaged handle, directly or indirectly. This is because unmanaged handles provide the gateway to the "outside world" of operating system resources, network connections, database locks —the primary means by which objects can create trouble outside of themselves if improperly abandoned.

There are, however, three scenarios for *not* disposing:

- When you don't "own" the object e.g., when obtaining a *shared* object via a static field or property

- When an object's Dispose method does something that you don't want

- When an object's Dispose method is unnecessary *by design*, and disposing that object would add complexity to your program

The first category is rare. The main cases are in the System.Drawing namespace: the GDI+ objects obtained through *static fields or properties* (such as Brushes.Blue) must never be disposed because the same instance is used throughout the life of the application. Instances that you obtain through constructors, however (such as new SolidBrush), *should* be disposed, as should instances obtained through static *methods* (such as Font.FromHdc).

The second category is more common. There are some good examples in the System.IO and System.Data namespaces:

Type	Disposal function	When not to dispose
MemoryStream	Prevents further I/O	When you later need to read/write the stream
StreamReader, StreamWriter	Flushes the reader/ writer and closes the underlying stream	When you want to keep the underlying stream open (you must instead call Flush on a StreamWriter when you're done)
IDbConnection	Releases a database connection and clears the connection string	If you need to re-Open it, you should call Close instead of Dispose
DataContext (LINQ to SQL)	Prevents further use	When you might have lazily evaluated queries connected to that context

MemoryStream's Dispose method disables only the object; it doesn't perform any critical cleanup because a MemoryStream holds no unmanaged handles or other such resources.

The third category includes the following classes: WebClient, StringReader, String Writer, and BackgroundWorker (in System.ComponentModel). These types are disposable under the duress of their base class rather than through a genuine need to perform essential cleanup. If you happen to instantiate and work with such an object entirely in one method, wrapping it in a using block adds little inconvenience. But if the object is longer-lasting, keeping track of when it's no longer used so that you can dispose of it adds unnecessary complexity. In such cases, you can simply ignore object disposal.

 Ignoring disposal can sometimes incur a performance cost (see "Calling Dispose from a Finalizer" on page 508).

Opt-in Disposal

Because IDisposable makes a type tractable with C#'s using construct, there's a temptation to extend the reach of IDisposable to nonessential activities. For instance:

```
public sealed class HouseManager : IDisposable
{
  public void Dispose()
  {
    CheckTheMail();
  }
  ...
}
```

The idea is that a consumer of this class can choose to circumvent the nonessential cleanup—simply by not calling Dispose. This, however, relies on the consumer knowing what's inside HouseManager's Dispose method. It also breaks if *essential* cleanup activity is later added:

```
public void Dispose()
{
  CheckTheMail();    // Nonessential
  LockTheHouse();    // Essential
}
```

The solution to this problem is the opt-in disposal pattern:

```
public sealed class HouseManager : IDisposable
{
  public readonly bool CheckMailOnDispose;

  public HouseManager (bool checkMailOnDispose)
  {
    CheckMailOnDispose = checkMailOnDispose;
  }

  public void Dispose()
  {
    if (CheckMailOnDispose) CheckTheMail();
    LockTheHouse();
  }
  ...
}
```

The consumer can then always call `Dispose`—providing simplicity and avoiding the need for special documentation or reflection. An example of where this pattern is implemented is in the `DeflateStream` class, in `System.IO.Compression`. Here's its constructor:

```
public DeflateStream (Stream stream, CompressionMode mode, bool leaveOpen)
```

The nonessential activity is closing the inner `stream` (the first parameter) upon disposal. There are times when you want to leave the inner stream open and yet still dispose the `DeflateStream` to perform its *essential* tear-down activity (flushing buffered data).

This pattern might look simple, yet until Framework 4.5, it escaped `StreamReader` and `StreamWriter` (in the `System.IO` namespace). The result is messy: `Stream Writer` must expose another method (`Flush`) to perform essential cleanup for consumers not calling `Dispose`. (Framework 4.5 now exposes a constructor on these classes that lets you keep the stream open.) The `CryptoStream` class in `System.Security.Cryptography` suffers a similar problem and requires that you call `FlushFinalBlock` to tear it down while keeping the inner stream open.

 You could describe this as an *ownership* issue. The question for a disposable object is: do I really own the underlying resource that I'm using? Or am I just renting it from someone else who manages both the underlying resource lifetime and, by some undocumented contract, my lifetime?

Following the opt-in pattern avoids this problem by making the ownership contract documented and explicit.

Clearing Fields in Disposal

In general, you don't need to clear an object's fields in its `Dispose` method. However, it is good practice to unsubscribe from events that the object has subscribed to internally over its lifetime (see "Managed Memory Leaks" on page 516 for an example). Unsubscribing from such events avoids receiving unwanted event notifications —and avoids unintentionally keeping the object alive in the eyes of the garbage collector (GC).

 A `Dispose` method itself does not cause (managed) memory to be released—this can happen only in garbage collection.

It's also worth setting a field to indicate that the object is disposed so that you can throw an `ObjectDisposedException` if a consumer later tries to call members on the object. A good pattern is to use a publicly readable automatic property for this:

```
public bool IsDisposed { get; private set; }
```

Although technically unnecessary, it can also be good to clear an object's own event handlers (by setting them to `null`) in the `Dispose` method. This eliminates the possibility of those events firing during or after disposal.

Occasionally, an object holds high-value secrets, such as encryption keys. In these cases, it can make sense to clear such data from fields during disposal (to avoid discovery by less privileged assemblies or malware). The SymmetricAlgorithm class in System.Security.Cryptography does exactly this, by calling Array.Clear on the byte array holding the encryption key.

Automatic Garbage Collection

Regardless of whether an object requires a Dispose method for custom tear-down logic, at some point, the memory it occupies on the heap must be freed. The CLR handles this side of it entirely automatically, via an automatic GC. You never deallocate managed memory yourself. For example, consider the following method:

```
public void Test()
{
  byte[] myArray = new byte[1000];
  ...
}
```

When Test executes, an array to hold 1,000 bytes is allocated on the memory heap. The array is referenced by the variable myArray, stored on the local variable stack. When the method exits, this local variable myArray pops out of scope, meaning that nothing is left to reference the array on the memory heap. The orphaned array then becomes eligible to be reclaimed in garbage collection.

 In debug mode with optimizations disabled, the lifetime of an object referenced by a local variable extends to the end of the code block to ease debugging. Otherwise, it becomes eligible for collection at the earliest point at which it's no longer used.

Garbage collection does not happen immediately after an object is orphaned. Rather like garbage collection on the street, it happens periodically, although (unlike garbage collection on the street) not to a fixed schedule. The CLR bases its decision on when to collect upon a number of factors, such as the available memory, the amount of memory allocation, and the time since the last collection. This means that there's an indeterminate delay between an object being orphaned and being released from memory. This delay can range from nanoseconds to days.

 The GC doesn't collect all garbage with every collection. Instead, the memory manager divides objects into *generations*, and the GC collects new generations (recently allocated objects) more frequently than old generations (long-lived objects). We'll discuss this in more detail in "How the Garbage Collector Works" on page 512.

Garbage Collection and Memory Consumption

The GC tries to strike a balance between the time it spends doing garbage collection and the application's memory consumption (working set). Consequently, applications can consume more memory than they need, particularly if large temporary arrays are constructed.

You can monitor a process's memory consumption via the Windows Task Manager or Resource Monitor—or programmatically by querying a performance counter:

```
// These types are in System.Diagnostics:
string procName = Process.GetCurrentProcess().ProcessName;
using (PerformanceCounter pc = new PerformanceCounter
    ("Process", "Private Bytes", procName))
  Console.WriteLine (pc.NextValue());
```

This queries the *private working set*, which gives the best overall indication of your program's memory consumption. Specifically, it excludes memory that the CLR has internally deallocated and is willing to rescind to the operating system should another process need it.

Roots

A root is something that keeps an object alive. If an object is not directly or indirectly referenced by a root, it will be eligible for garbage collection.

A root is one of the following:

- A local variable or parameter in an executing method (or in any method in its call stack)
- A static variable
- An object on the queue that stores objects ready for finalization (see next section)

It's impossible for code to execute in a deleted object, so if there's any possibility of an (instance) method executing, its object must somehow be referenced in one of these ways.

Note that a group of objects that reference each other cyclically are considered dead without a root referee (see Figure 12-1). To put it in another way, objects that cannot be accessed by following the arrows (references) from a root object are *unreachable*—and therefore subject to collection.

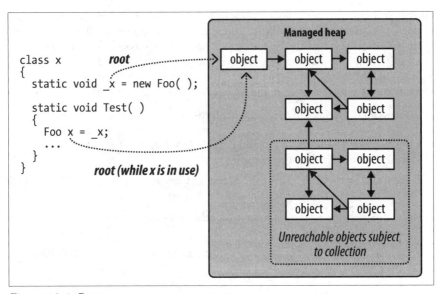

Figure 12-1. Roots

Garbage Collection and WinRT

Windows Runtime relies on COM's reference-counting mechanism to release memory instead of depending on an automatic garbage collector. Despite this, WinRT
objects that you instantiate from C# have their lifetime managed by the CLR's
garbage collector, because the CLR mediates access to the COM object through an
object that it creates behind the scenes called a *runtime callable wrapper* (Chapter 24).

Finalizers

Prior to an object being released from memory, its *finalizer* runs, if it has one. A
finalizer is declared like a constructor, but it is prefixed by the ~ symbol:

```
class Test
{
  ~Test()
  {
    // Finalizer logic...
  }
}
```

(Although similar in declaration to a constructor, finalizers cannot be declared as
public or static, cannot have parameters, and cannot call the base class.)

Finalizers are possible because garbage collection works in distinct phases. First, the
GC identifies the unused objects ripe for deletion. Those without finalizers are
deleted right away. Those with pending (unrun) finalizers are kept alive (for now)
and are put onto a special queue.

At that point, garbage collection is complete, and your program continues executing. The *finalizer thread* then kicks in and starts running in parallel to your program, picking objects off that special queue and running their finalization methods. Prior to each object's finalizer running, it's still very much alive—that queue acts as a root object. Once it's been dequeued and the finalizer executed, the object becomes orphaned and will get deleted in the next collection (for that object's *generation*).

Finalizers can be useful, but they come with some provisos:

- Finalizers slow the allocation and collection of memory (the GC needs to keep track of which finalizers have run).

- Finalizers prolong the life of the object and any *referred* objects (they must all await the next garbage truck for actual deletion).

- It's impossible to predict in what order the finalizers for a set of objects will be called.

- You have limited control over when the finalizer for an object will be called.

- If code in a finalizer blocks, other objects cannot get finalized.

- Finalizers may be circumvented altogether if an application fails to unload cleanly.

In summary, finalizers are somewhat like lawyers—although there are cases in which you really need them, in general you don't want to use them unless absolutely necessary. If you do use them, you need to be 100% sure you understand what they are doing for you.

Here are some guidelines for implementing finalizers:

- Ensure that your finalizer executes quickly.

- Never block in your finalizer (Chapter 14).

- Don't reference other finalizable objects.

- Don't throw exceptions.

 An object's finalizer can get called even if an exception is thrown during construction. For this reason, it pays not to assume that fields are correctly initialized when writing a finalizer.

Calling Dispose from a Finalizer

A popular pattern is to have the finalizer call `Dispose`. This makes sense when cleanup is not urgent and hastening it by calling `Dispose` is more of an optimization than a necessity.

Bear in mind that with this pattern, you couple memory deal-location to resource deallocation—two things with potentially divergent interests (unless the resource is itself memory). You also increase the burden on the finalization thread.

This pattern can also be used as a backup for cases when a consumer simply forgets to call Dispose. However, it's then a good idea to log the failure so that you can fix the bug.

There's a standard pattern for implementing this, as follows:

```
class Test : IDisposable
{
  public void Dispose()            // NOT virtual
  {
    Dispose (true);
    GC.SuppressFinalize (this);    // Prevent finalizer from running.
  }

  protected virtual void Dispose (bool disposing)
  {
    if (disposing)
    {
      // Call Dispose() on other objects owned by this instance.
      // You can reference other finalizable objects here.
      // ...
    }

    // Release unmanaged resources owned by (just) this object.
    // ...
  }

  ~Test()
  {
    Dispose (false);
  }
}
```

Dispose is overloaded to accept a bool disposing flag. The parameterless version is *not* declared as virtual and simply calls the enhanced version with true.

The enhanced version contains the actual disposal logic and is protected and virtual; this provides a safe point for subclasses to add their own disposal logic. The disposing flag means it's being called "properly" from the Dispose method rather than in "last-resort mode" from the finalizer. The idea is that when called with disposing set to false, this method should not, in general, reference other objects with finalizers (because such objects may themselves have been finalized and so be in an unpredictable state). This rules out quite a lot! Here are a couple of tasks it can still perform in last-resort mode when disposing is false:

- Releasing any *direct references* to operating system resources (obtained, per-haps, via a P/Invoke call to the Win32 API)

- Deleting a temporary file created on construction

To make this robust, any code capable of throwing an exception should be wrapped in a try/catch block, and the exception, ideally, logged. Any logging should be as simple and robust as possible.

Notice that we call GC.SuppressFinalize in the parameterless Dispose method—this prevents the finalizer from running when the GC later catches up with it. Technically, this is unnecessary, as Dispose methods must tolerate repeated calls. However, doing so improves performance because it allows the object (and its referenced objects) to be garbage-collected in a single cycle.

Resurrection

Suppose a finalizer modifies a living object such that it refers back to the dying object. When the next garbage collection happens (for the object's generation), the CLR will see the previously dying object as no longer orphaned—and so it will evade garbage collection. This is an advanced scenario and is called *resurrection*.

To illustrate, suppose we want to write a class that manages a temporary file. When an instance of that class is garbage-collected, we'd like the finalizer to delete the temporary file. It sounds easy:

```
public class TempFileRef
{
  public readonly string FilePath;
  public TempFileRef (string filePath) { FilePath = filePath; }

  ~TempFileRef() { File.Delete (FilePath); }
}
```

Unfortunately, this has a bug: File.Delete might throw an exception (due to a lack of permissions, perhaps, or the file being in use, or having already been deleted). Such an exception would take down the whole application (as well as preventing other finalizers from running). We could simply "swallow" the exception with an empty catch block, but then we'd never know that anything went wrong. Calling some elaborate error reporting API would also be undesirable because it would burden the finalizer thread, hindering garbage collection for other objects. We want to restrict finalization actions to those that are simple, reliable, and quick.

A better option is to record the failure to a static collection as follows:

```
public class TempFileRef
{
  static ConcurrentQueue<TempFileRef> _failedDeletions
    = new ConcurrentQueue<TempFileRef>();

  public readonly string FilePath;
  public Exception DeletionError { get; private set; }

  public TempFileRef (string filePath) { FilePath = filePath; }
```

```
~TempFileRef()
{
  try { File.Delete (FilePath); }
  catch (Exception ex)
  {
    DeletionError = ex;
    _failedDeletions.Enqueue (this);    // Resurrection
  }
}
}
```

Enqueuing the object to the static `_failedDeletions` collection gives the object another referee, ensuring that it remains alive until the object is eventually dequeued.

 `ConcurrentQueue<T>` is a thread-safe version of `Queue<T>` and is defined in `System.Collections.Concurrent` (see Chapter 23). There are a couple of reasons for using a thread-safe collection. First, the CLR reserves the right to execute finalizers on more than one thread in parallel. This means that when accessing shared state such as a static collection, we must consider the possibility of two objects being finalized at once. Second, at some point we're going to want to dequeue items from `_failedDeletions` so that we can do something about them. This also has to be done in a thread-safe fashion, because it could happen while the finalizer is concurrently enqueuing another object.

GC.ReRegisterForFinalize

A resurrected object's finalizer will not run a second time—unless you call `GC.ReRegisterForFinalize`.

In the following example, we try to delete a temporary file in a finalizer (as in the last example). But if the deletion fails, we reregister the object so as to try again in the next garbage collection:

```
public class TempFileRef
{
  public readonly string FilePath;
  int _deleteAttempt;

  public TempFileRef (string filePath) { FilePath = filePath; }

  ~TempFileRef()
  {
    try { File.Delete (FilePath); }
    catch
    {
      if (_deleteAttempt++ < 3) GC.ReRegisterForFinalize (this);
    }
  }
}
```

After the third failed attempt, our finalizer will silently give up trying to delete the file. We could enhance this by combining it with the previous example—in other words, adding it to the _failedDeletions queue after the third failure.

 Be careful to call ReRegisterForFinalize just once in the finalizer method. If you call it twice, the object will be reregistered twice and will have to undergo two more finalizations!

How the Garbage Collector Works

The standard CLR uses a generational mark-and-compact GC that performs automatic memory management for objects stored on the managed heap. The GC is considered to be a *tracing* garbage collector in that it doesn't interfere with every access to an object, but rather wakes up intermittently and traces the graph of objects stored on the managed heap to determine which objects can be considered garbage and therefore collected.

The GC initiates a garbage collection upon performing a memory allocation (via the new keyword) either after a certain threshold of memory has been allocated, or at other times to reduce the application's memory footprint. This process can also be initiated manually by calling System.GC.Collect. During a garbage collection, all threads may by frozen (more on this in the next section).

The GC begins with its root object references and walks the object graph, marking all the objects it touches as reachable. Once this process is complete, all objects that have not been marked are considered unused and are subject to garbage collection.

Unused objects without finalizers are immediately discarded; unused objects with finalizers are enqueued for processing on the finalizer thread after the GC is complete. These objects then become eligible for collection in the next GC for the object's generation (unless resurrected).

The remaining "live" objects are then shifted to the start of the heap (compacted), freeing space for more objects. This compaction serves two purposes: it avoids memory fragmentation, and it allows the GC to employ a very simple strategy when allocating new objects, which is to always allocate memory at the end of the heap. This avoids the potentially time-consuming task of maintaining a list of free memory segments.

If there is insufficient space to allocate memory for a new object after garbage collection, and the operating system is unable to grant further memory, an OutOfMemoryException is thrown.

Optimization Techniques

The GC incorporates various optimization techniques to reduce the garbage collection time.

Generational collection

The most important optimization is that the GC is generational. This takes advantage of the fact that although many objects are allocated and discarded rapidly, certain objects are long-lived and thus don't need to be traced during every collection.

Basically, the GC divides the managed heap into three generations. Objects that have just been allocated are in *Gen0*, and objects that have survived one collection cycle are in *Gen1*; all other objects are in *Gen2*. Gen0 and Gen1 are known as *ephemeral* (short-lived) generations.

The CLR keeps the Gen0 section relatively small (a maximum of 256 MB on the 64-bit workstation CLR, with a typical size of a few hundred KB to a few MB). When the Gen0 section fills up, the GC instigates a Gen0 collection—which happens relatively often. The GC applies a similar memory threshold to Gen1 (which acts as a buffer to Gen2), and so Gen1 collections are relatively quick and frequent, too. Full collections that include Gen2, however, take much longer and so happen infrequently. Figure 12-2 shows the effect of a full collection.

Garbage Collection

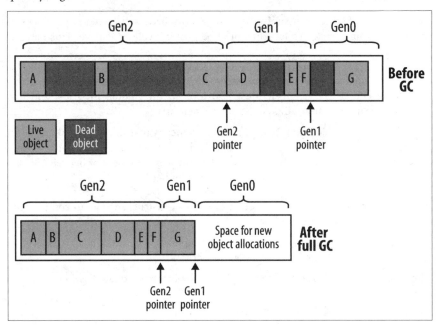

Figure 12-2. Heap generations

To give some very rough ballpark figures, a Gen0 collection might take less than 1 ms, which is not enough to be noticed in a typical application. A full collection, however, might take as long as 100 ms on a program with large object graphs. These figures depend on numerous factors and so may vary considerably—particularly in the case of Gen2, whose size is *unbounded* (unlike Gen0 and Gen1).

The upshot is that short-lived objects are very efficient in their use of the GC. The `StringBuilders` created in the following method would almost certainly be collected in a fast Gen0:

```
string Foo()
{
  var sb1 = new StringBuilder ("test");
  sb1.Append ("...");
  var sb2 = new StringBuilder ("test");
  sb2.Append (sb1.ToString());
  return sb2.ToString();
}
```

The large object heap

The GC uses a separate heap called the large object heap (LOH) for objects larger than a certain threshold (currently 85,000 bytes). This avoids excessive Gen0 collections—without the LOH, allocating a series of 16 MB objects might trigger a Gen0 collection after every allocation.

By default, the LOH is not subject to compaction, because moving large blocks of memory during garbage collection would be prohibitively expensive. This has two consequences:

- Allocations can be slower, because the GC can't always simply allocate objects at the end of the heap—it must also look in the middle for gaps, and this requires maintaining a linked list of free memory blocks.[2]

- The LOH is subject to *fragmentation*. This means that the freeing of an object can create a hole in the LOH that may be hard to fill later. For instance, a hole left by an 86,000-byte object can be filled only by an object of between 85,000 bytes and 86,000 bytes (unless adjoined by another hole).

In cases where this might cause problems, you can instruct the GC to compact the LOH in the next collection as follows:

```
GCSettings.LargeObjectHeapCompactionMode =
  GCLargeObjectHeapCompactionMode.CompactOnce;
```

The large object heap is also nongenerational: all objects are treated as Gen2.

Concurrent and background collection

The GC must freeze (block) your execution threads for periods during a collection. This includes the entire period during which a Gen0 or Gen1 collection takes place.

The GC makes a special attempt, though, at allowing threads to run during a Gen2 collection as it's undesirable to freeze an application for a potentially long period.

---

2 The same thing may occur occasionally in the generational heap due to pinning (see "The fixed Statement" on page 187 in Chapter 4).

This optimization applies to the workstation version of the CLR only, which is used on desktop versions of Windows (and on all versions of Windows with standalone applications). The rationale is that the latency from a blocking collection is less likely to be a problem for server applications that don't have a user interface.

 A mitigating factor is that the server CLR leverages all available cores to perform GCs, so an eight-core server will perform a full GC many times faster. In effect, the server GC is tuned to maximize throughput rather than minimize latency.

The workstation optimization has historically been called *concurrent collection*. From CLR 4.0, it's been revamped and renamed to *background collection*. Background collection removes a limitation whereby a concurrent collection would cease to be concurrent if the Gen0 section filled up while a Gen2 collection was running. This means that from CLR 4.0, applications that continually allocate memory will be more responsive.

GC notifications (server CLR)

The server version of the CLR can notify you just before a full GC will occur. This is intended for server farm configurations: the idea is that you divert requests to another server just before a collection. You then instigate the collection immediately and wait for it to complete before rerouting requests back to that server.

To start notification, call `GC.RegisterForFullGCNotification`. Then start up another thread (see Chapter 14) that first calls `GC.WaitForFullGCApproach`. When this method returns a `GCNotificationStatus` indicating that a collection is near, you can reroute requests to other servers and force a manual collection (see the following section). You then call `GC.WaitForFullGCComplete`: when this method returns, GC is complete, and you can again accept requests. You then repeat the whole cycle.

Forcing Garbage Collection

You can manually force a GC at any time by calling `GC.Collect`. Calling `GC.Collect` without an argument instigates a full collection. If you pass in an integer value, only generations to that value are collected, so `GC.Collect(0)` performs only a fast Gen0 collection.

In general, you get the best performance by allowing the GC to decide when to collect: forcing collection can hurt performance by unnecessarily promoting Gen0 objects to Gen1 (and Gen1 objects to Gen2). It can also upset the GC's *self-tuning* ability, whereby the GC dynamically tweaks the thresholds for each generation to maximize performance as the application executes.

There are exceptions, however. The most common case for intervention is when an application goes to sleep for a while: a good example is a Windows Service that performs a daily activity (checking for updates, perhaps). Such an application might use a `System.Timers.Timer` to initiate the activity every 24 hours. After completing the activity, no further code executes for 24 hours, which means that for this period, no memory allocations are made and so the GC has no opportunity to activate. Whatever memory the service consumed in performing its activity, it will continue to consume for the following 24 hours—even with an empty object graph! The solution is to call GC.Collect right after the daily activity completes.

To ensure the collection of objects for which collection is delayed by finalizers, you can take the additional step of calling WaitForPendingFinalizers and re-collecting:

```
GC.Collect();
GC.WaitForPendingFinalizers();
GC.Collect();
```

Often this is done in a loop: the act of running finalizers can free up more objects that themselves have finalizers.

Another case for calling GC.Collect is when you're testing a class that has a finalizer.

Tuning Garbage Collection

The static GCSettings.LatencyMode property determines how the GC balances latency with overall efficiency. Changing this from its default value of Interactive to LowLatency instructs the CLR to favor quicker (but more frequent) collections. This is useful if your application needs to respond very quickly to real-time events.

From Framework 4.6, you can also tell the GC to temporarily suspend GC by calling GC.TryStartNoGCRegion, and resume it with GC.EndNoGCRegion.

Memory Pressure

The runtime decides when to initiate collections based on a number of factors, including the total memory load on the machine. If your program allocates unmanaged memory (Chapter 25), the runtime will get an unrealistically optimistic perception of its memory usage, because the CLR knows only about managed memory. You can mitigate this by telling the CLR to *assume* a specified quantity of unmanaged memory has been allocated by calling GC.AddMemoryPressure. To undo this (when the unmanaged memory is released), call GC.RemoveMemoryPressure.

Managed Memory Leaks

In unmanaged languages such as C++, you must remember to manually deallocate memory when an object is no longer required; otherwise, a *memory leak* will result. In the managed world, this kind of error is impossible due to the CLR's automatic garbage collection system.

Nonetheless, large and complex .NET applications can exhibit a milder form of the same syndrome with the same end result: the application consumes more and more memory over its lifetime until it eventually has to be restarted. The good news is that managed memory leaks are usually easier to diagnose and prevent.

Managed memory leaks are caused by unused objects remaining alive by virtue of unused or forgotten references. A common candidate is event handlers—these hold a reference to the target object (unless the target is a static method). For instance, consider the following classes:

```
class Host
{
  public event EventHandler Click;
}

class Client
{
  Host _host;
  public Client (Host host)
  {
    _host = host;
    _host.Click += HostClicked;
  }

  void HostClicked (object sender, EventArgs e) { ... }
}
```

The following test class contains a method that instantiates 1,000 clients:

```
class Test
{
  static Host _host = new Host();

  public static void CreateClients()
  {
    Client[] clients = Enumerable.Range (0, 1000)
      .Select (i => new Client (_host))
      .ToArray();

    // Do something with clients ...
  }
}
```

You might expect that after CreateClients finishes executing, the 1,000 Client objects will become eligible for collection. Unfortunately, each client has another referee: the _host object whose Click event now references each Client instance. This may go unnoticed if the Click event doesn't fire—or if the HostClicked method doesn't do anything to attract attention.

One way to solve this is to make Client implement IDisposable, and in the Dis pose method, unhook the event handler:

```
public void Dispose() { _host.Click -= HostClicked; }
```

Consumers of Client then dispose of the instances when they're done with them:

```
Array.ForEach (clients, c => c.Dispose());
```

In "Weak References" on page 520 we'll describe another solution to this problem, which can be useful in environments which tend not to use disposable objects (an example is WPF). In fact, the WPF framework offers a class called `WeakEventManager` that leverages a pattern employing weak references.

On the topic of WPF, *data binding* is another common cause for memory leaks: the issue is described at *http://support.microsoft.com/kb/938416*.

Timers

Forgotten timers can also cause memory leaks (we discuss timers in Chapter 22). There are two distinct scenarios, depending on the kind of timer. Let's first look at the timer in the `System.Timers` namespace. In the following example, the `Foo` class (when instantiated) calls the `tmr_Elapsed` method once every second:

```
using System.Timers;

class Foo
{
  Timer _timer;

  Foo()
  {
    _timer = new System.Timers.Timer { Interval = 1000 };
    _timer.Elapsed += tmr_Elapsed;
    _timer.Start();
  }

  void tmr_Elapsed (object sender, ElapsedEventArgs e) { ... }
}
```

Unfortunately, instances of `Foo` can never be garbage-collected! The problem is the .NET Framework itself holds references to active timers so that it can fire their `Elapsed` events. Hence:

- The .NET Framework will keep `_timer` alive.

- `_timer` will keep the `Foo` instance alive, via the `tmr_Elapsed` event handler.

The solution is obvious when you realize that `Timer` implements `IDisposable`. Disposing of the timer stops it and ensures that the .NET Framework no longer references the object:

```
class Foo : IDisposable
{
  ...
  public void Dispose() { _timer.Dispose(); }
}
```

A good guideline is to implement `IDisposable` yourself if any field in your class is assigned an object that implements `IDisposable`.

The WPF and Windows Forms timers behave in exactly the same way, with respect to what's just been discussed.

The timer in the `System.Threading` namespace, however, is special. The .NET Framework doesn't hold references to active threading timers; it instead references the callback delegates directly. This means that if you forget to dispose of a threading timer, a finalizer can fire which will automatically stop and dispose the timer. For example:

```
static void Main()
{
  var tmr = new System.Threading.Timer (TimerTick, null, 1000, 1000);
  GC.Collect();
  System.Threading.Thread.Sleep (10000);    // Wait 10 seconds
}

static void TimerTick (object notUsed) { Console.WriteLine ("tick"); }
```

If this example is compiled in "release" mode (debugging disabled and optimizations enabled), the timer will be collected and finalized before it has a chance to fire even once! Again, we can fix this by disposing of the timer when we're done with it:

```
using (var tmr = new System.Threading.Timer (TimerTick, null, 1000, 1000))
{
  GC.Collect();
  System.Threading.Thread.Sleep (10000);    // Wait 10 seconds
}
```

The implicit call to `tmr.Dispose` at the end of the `using` block ensures that the `tmr` variable is "used" and so not considered dead by the GC until the end of the block. Ironically, this call to `Dispose` actually keeps the object alive *longer*!

Diagnosing Memory Leaks

The easiest way to avoid managed memory leaks is to proactively monitor memory consumption as an application is written. You can obtain the current memory consumption of a program's objects as follows (the `true` argument tells the GC to perform a collection first):

```
long memoryUsed = GC.GetTotalMemory (true);
```

If you're practicing test-driven development, one possibility is to use unit tests to assert that memory is reclaimed as expected. If such an assertion fails, you then have to examine only the changes that you've made recently.

If you already have a large application with a managed memory leak, the *windbg.exe* tool can assist in finding it. There are also friendlier graphical tools such as Microsoft's CLR Profiler, SciTech's Memory Profiler, and Red Gate's ANTS Memory Profiler.

The CLR also exposes numerous Windows WMI counters to assist with resource monitoring.

Weak References

Occasionally, it's useful to hold a reference to an object that's "invisible" to the GC in terms of keeping the object alive. This is called a *weak reference* and is implemented by the System.WeakReference class.

To use WeakReference, construct it with a target object as follows:

```
var sb = new StringBuilder ("this is a test");
var weak = new WeakReference (sb);
Console.WriteLine (weak.Target);      // This is a test
```

If a target is referenced *only* by one or more weak references, the GC will consider the target eligible for collection. When the target gets collected, the Target property of the WeakReference will be null:

```
var weak = new WeakReference (new StringBuilder ("weak"));
Console.WriteLine (weak.Target);   // weak
GC.Collect();
Console.WriteLine (weak.Target);   // (nothing)
```

To avoid the target being collected in between testing for it being null and consuming it, assign the target to a local variable:

```
var weak = new WeakReference (new StringBuilder ("weak"));
var sb = (StringBuilder) weak.Target;
if (sb != null) { /* Do something with sb */ }
```

Once a target's been assigned to a local variable, it has a strong root and so cannot be collected while that variable's in use.

The following class uses weak references to keep track of all Widget objects that have been instantiated, without preventing those objects from being collected:

```
class Widget
{
  static List<WeakReference> _allWidgets = new List<WeakReference>();

  public readonly string Name;

  public Widget (string name)
  {
    Name = name;
    _allWidgets.Add (new WeakReference (this));
  }

  public static void ListAllWidgets()
  {
    foreach (WeakReference weak in _allWidgets)
    {
      Widget w = (Widget)weak.Target;
      if (w != null) Console.WriteLine (w.Name);
```

```
      }
    }
  }
```

The only proviso with such a system is that the static list will grow over time, accumulating weak references with null targets. So you need to implement some cleanup strategy.

Weak References and Caching

One use for `WeakReference` is to cache large object graphs. This allows memory-intensive data to be cached briefly without causing excessive memory consumption:

```
_weakCache = new WeakReference (...);   // _weakCache is a field
...
var cache = _weakCache.Target;
if (cache == null) { /* Re-create cache & assign it to _weakCache */ }
```

This strategy may be only mildly effective in practice, because you have little control over when the GC fires and what generation it chooses to collect. In particular, if your cache remains in Gen0, it may be collected within microseconds (and remember that the GC doesn't collect only when memory is low—it collects regularly under normal memory conditions). So at a minimum, you should employ a two-level cache whereby you start out by holding strong references that you convert to weak references over time.

Weak References and Events

We saw earlier how events can cause managed memory leaks. The simplest solution is to either avoid subscribing in such conditions, or implement a `Dispose` method to unsubscribe. Weak references offer another solution.

Imagine a delegate that holds only weak references to its targets. Such a delegate would not keep its targets alive—unless those targets had independent referees. Of course, this wouldn't prevent a firing delegate from hitting an unreferenced target— in the time between the target being eligible for collection and the GC catching up with it. For such a solution to be effective, your code must be robust in that scenario. Assuming that is the case, a *weak delegate* class can be implemented as follows:

```
public class WeakDelegate<TDelegate> where TDelegate : class
{
  class MethodTarget
  {
    public readonly WeakReference Reference;
    public readonly MethodInfo Method;

    public MethodTarget (Delegate d)
    {
      Reference = new WeakReference (d.Target);
      Method = d.Method;
    }
  }
```

```
List<MethodTarget> _targets = new List<MethodTarget>();

public WeakDelegate()
{
  if (!typeof (TDelegate).IsSubclassOf (typeof (Delegate)))
    throw new InvalidOperationException
      ("TDelegate must be a delegate type");
}

public void Combine (TDelegate target)
{
  if (target == null) return;

  foreach (Delegate d in (target as Delegate).GetInvocationList())
    _targets.Add (new MethodTarget (d));
}

public void Remove (TDelegate target)
{
  if (target == null) return;
  foreach (Delegate d in (target as Delegate).GetInvocationList())
  {
    MethodTarget mt = _targets.Find (w =>
      Equals (d.Target, (w.Reference?.Target) &&
      Equals (d.Method.MethodHandle, w.Method.MethodHandle));

    if (mt != null) _targets.Remove (mt);
  }
}

public TDelegate Target
{
  get
  {
    var deadRefs = new List<MethodTarget>();

    foreach (MethodTarget mt in _targets.ToArray())
    {
      WeakReference wr = mt.Reference;

      // Static target || alive instance target
      if (wr == null || wr.Target != null)
      {
        var newDelegate = Delegate.CreateDelegate (
          typeof(TDelegate), wr?.Target, mt.Method);
        combinedTarget = Delegate.Combine (combinedTarget, newDelegate);
      }
      else
        _targets.Remove (mt);
    }

    return combinedTarget as TDelegate;
  }
  set
```

```
    {
      _targets.Clear();
      Combine (value);
    }
  }
}
```

This code illustrates a number of interesting points in C# and the CLR. First, note that we check that TDelegate is a delegate type in the constructor. This is because of a limitation in C#—the following type constraint is illegal because C# considers System.Delegate a special type for which constraints are not supported:

```
... where TDelegate : Delegate   // Compiler doesn't allow this
```

Instead, we must choose a class constraint and perform a runtime check in the constructor.

In the Combine and Remove methods, we perform the reference conversion from target to Delegate via the as operator rather than the more usual cast operator. This is because C# disallows the cast operator with this type parameter—because of a potential ambiguity between a *custom conversion* and a *reference conversion*.

We then call GetInvocationList because these methods might be called with multicast delegates—delegates with more than one method recipient.

In the Target property, we build up a multicast delegate that combines all the delegates referenced by weak references whose targets are alive, removing the remaining (dead) references from the list to avoid the _targets list endlessly growing. (We could improve our class by doing the same in the Combine method; yet another improvement would be to add locks for thread safety [Chapter 22]).

The following illustrates how to consume this delegate in implementing an event:

We also allow delegates without a weak reference at all; these represent delegates whose target is a static method.

```
public class Foo
{
  WeakDelegate<EventHandler> _click = new WeakDelegate<EventHandler>();

  public event EventHandler Click
  {
    add { _click.Combine (value); } remove { _click.Remove (value); }
  }

  protected virtual void OnClick (EventArgs e)
    => _click.Target?.Invoke (this, e);
}
```

13

Diagnostics and Code Contracts

When things go wrong, it's important that information is available to aid in diagnosing the problem. An IDE or debugger can assist greatly to this effect—but it is usually available only during development. Once an application ships, the application itself must gather and record diagnostic information. To meet this requirement, the .NET Framework provides a set of facilities to log diagnostic information, monitor application behavior, detect runtime errors, and integrate with debugging tools if available.

The .NET Framework also allows you to enforce *code contracts*. Introduced in Framework 4.0, code contracts allow methods to interact through a set of mutual obligations and fail *early* if those obligations are violated.

The types in this chapter are defined primarily in the `System.Diagnostics` and `Sys tem.Diagnostics.Contracts` namespaces.

Conditional Compilation

You can conditionally compile any section of code in C# with *preprocessor directives*. Preprocessor directives are special instructions to the compiler that begin with the # symbol (and, unlike other C# constructs, must appear on a line of their own). Logically, they execute before the main compilation takes place (although in practice, the compiler processes them during the lexical parsing phase). The preprocessor directives for conditional compilation are `#if`, `#else`, `#endif`, and `#elif`.

The `#if` directive instructs the compiler to ignore a section of code unless a specified *symbol* has been defined. You can define a symbol with either the `#define` directive or a compilation switch. `#define` applies to a particular *file*; a compilation switch applies to a whole *assembly*:

```
#define TESTMODE          // #define directives must be at top of file
                          // Symbol names are uppercase by convention.
using System;

class Program
{
  static void Main()
  {
#if TESTMODE
    Console.WriteLine ("in test mode!");      // OUTPUT: in test mode!
#endif
  }
}
```

If we deleted the first line, the program would compile with the Console.WriteLine statement completely eliminated from the executable, as though it was commented out.

The #else statement is analogous to C#'s else statement, and #elif is equivalent to #else followed by #if. The | |, &&, and ! operators can be used to perform *or*, *and*, and *not* operations:

```
#if TESTMODE && !PLAYMODE      // if TESTMODE and not PLAYMODE
    ...
```

Bear in mind, however, that you're not building an ordinary C# expression, and the symbols upon which you operate have absolutely no connection to *variables*—static or otherwise.

To define a symbol assembly-wide, specify the /define switch when compiling:

```
csc Program.cs /define:TESTMODE,PLAYMODE
```

Visual Studio provides an option to enter conditional compilation symbols under Project Properties.

If you've defined a symbol at the assembly level and then want to "undefine" it for a particular file, you can do so with the #undef directive.

Conditional Compilation Versus Static Variable Flags

The preceding example could instead be implemented with a simple static field:

```
static internal bool TestMode = true;

static void Main()
{
  if (TestMode) Console.WriteLine ("in test mode!");
}
```

This has the advantage of allowing runtime configuration. So, why choose conditional compilation? The reason is that conditional compilation can take you places variable flags cannot, such as:

- Conditionally including an attribute

- Changing the declared type of variable

- Switching between different namespaces or type aliases in a `using` directive—for example:

```
using TestType =
  #if V2
      MyCompany.Widgets.GadgetV2;
  #else
      MyCompany.Widgets.Gadget;
  #endif
```

You can even perform major refactoring under a conditional compilation directive so you can instantly switch between old and new versions and write libraries that can compile against multiple Framework versions, leveraging the latest Framework features where available.

Another advantage of conditional compilation is that debugging code can refer to types in assemblies that are not included in deployment.

The Conditional Attribute

The `Conditional` attribute instructs the compiler to ignore any calls to a particular class or method, if the specified symbol has not been defined.

To see how this is useful, suppose you write a method for logging status information as follows:

```
static void LogStatus (string msg)
{
  string logFilePath = ...
  System.IO.File.AppendAllText (logFilePath, msg + "\r\n");
}
```

Now imagine you wanted this to execute only if the `LOGGINGMODE` symbol is defined. The first solution is to wrap all calls to `LogStatus` around an `#if` directive:

```
#if LOGGINGMODE
LogStatus ("Message Headers: " + GetMsgHeaders());
#endif
```

This gives an ideal result, but it is tedious. The second solution is to put the `#if` directive inside the `LogStatus` method. This, however, is problematic should `LogSta tus` be called as follows:

```
LogStatus ("Message Headers: " + GetComplexMessageHeaders());
```

`GetComplexMessageHeaders` would always get called—which might incur a performance hit.

We can combine the functionality of the first solution with the convenience of the second by attaching the Conditional attribute (defined in System.Diagnostics) to the LogStatus method:

```
[Conditional ("LOGGINGMODE")]
static void LogStatus (string msg)
{
  ...
}
```

This instructs the compiler to treat calls to LogStatus as though they were wrapped in an #if LOGGINGMODE directive. If the symbol is not defined, any calls to LogSta tus get eliminated entirely in compilation—including their argument evaluation expressions. (Hence any side-effecting expressions will be bypassed.) This works even if LogStatus and the caller are in different assemblies.

 Another benefit of [Conditional] is that the conditionality check is performed when the *caller* is compiled, rather than when the *called method* is compiled. This is beneficial because it allows you to write a library containing methods such as Log Status—and build just one version of that library.

The Conditional attribute is ignored at runtime—it's purely an instruction to the compiler.

Alternatives to the Conditional attribute

The Conditional attribute is useless if you need to dynamically enable or disable functionality at runtime: instead, you must use a variable-based approach. This leaves the question of how to elegantly circumvent the evaluation of arguments when calling conditional logging methods. A functional approach solves this:

```
using System;
using System.Linq;

class Program
{
  public static bool EnableLogging;

  static void LogStatus (Func<string> message)
  {
    string logFilePath = ...
    if (EnableLogging)
      System.IO.File.AppendAllText (logFilePath, message() + "\r\n");
  }
}
```

A lambda expression lets you call this method without syntax bloat:

```
LogStatus ( () => "Message Headers: " + GetComplexMessageHeaders() );
```

If EnableLogging is false, GetComplexMessageHeaders is never evaluated.

Debug and Trace Classes

Debug and Trace are static classes that provide basic logging and assertion capabilities. The two classes are very similar; the main differentiator is their intended use. The Debug class is intended for debug builds; the Trace class is intended for both debug and release builds. To this effect:

- All methods of the Debug class are defined with [Conditional("DEBUG")].
- All methods of the Trace class are defined with [Conditional("TRACE")].

This means that all calls that you make to Debug or Trace are eliminated by the compiler unless you define DEBUG or TRACE symbols. By default, Visual Studio defines both DEBUG and TRACE symbols in a project's *debug* configuration—and just the TRACE symbol in the *release* configuration.

Both the Debug and Trace classes provide Write, WriteLine, and WriteIf methods. By default, these send messages to the debugger's output window:

```
Debug.Write     ("Data");
Debug.WriteLine (23 * 34);
int x = 5, y = 3;
Debug.WriteIf   (x > y, "x is greater than y");
```

The Trace class also provides the methods TraceInformation, TraceWarning, and TraceError. The difference in behavior between these and the Write methods depends on the active TraceListeners (we'll cover this in "TraceListener" on page 530).

Fail and Assert

The Debug and Trace classes both provide Fail and Assert methods. Fail sends the message to each TraceListener in the Debug or Trace class's Listeners collection (see the following section), which by default writes the message to the debug output as well as displaying it in a dialog:

```
Debug.Fail ("File data.txt does not exist!");
```

The dialog that appears asks you whether to ignore, abort, or retry. The latter then lets you attach a debugger, which is useful in instantly diagnosing the problem.

Assert simply calls Fail if the bool argument is false—this is called *making an assertion* and indicates a bug in the code if violated. Specifying a failure message is optional:

```
Debug.Assert (File.Exists ("data.txt"), "File data.txt does not exist!");
var result = ...
Debug.Assert (result != null);
```

The Write, Fail, and Assert methods are also overloaded to accept a string category in addition to the message, which can be useful in processing the output.

An alternative to assertion is to throw an exception if the opposite condition is true. This is a common practice when validating method arguments:

```
public void ShowMessage (string message)
{
  if (message == null) throw new ArgumentNullException ("message");
  ...
}
```

Such "assertions" are compiled unconditionally and are less flexible in that you can't control the outcome of a failed assertion via TraceListeners. And technically, they're not assertions. An assertion is something that, if violated, indicates a bug in the current method's code. Throwing an exception based on argument validation indicates a bug in the *caller's* code.

 We'll see soon how *code contracts* extend the principles of Fail and Assert, providing more power and flexibility.

TraceListener

The Debug and Trace classes each have a Listeners property, comprising a static collection of TraceListener instances. These are responsible for processing the content emitted by the Write, Fail, and Trace methods.

By default, the Listeners collection of each includes a single listener (DefaultTraceListener). The default listener has two key features:

- When connected to a debugger such as Visual Studio, messages are written to the debug output window; otherwise, message content is ignored.
- When the Fail method is called (or an assertion fails), a dialog appears asking the user whether to continue, abort, or retry (attach/debug)—regardless of whether a debugger is attached.

You can change this behavior by (optionally) removing the default listener and then adding one or more of your own. You can write trace listeners from scratch (by subclassing TraceListener) or use one of the predefined types:

- TextWriterTraceListener writes to a Stream or TextWriter or appends to a file.
- EventLogTraceListener writes to the Windows event log.
- EventProviderTraceListener writes to the Event Tracing for Windows (ETW) subsystem in Windows Vista and later.
- WebPageTraceListener writes to an ASP.NET web page.

TextWriterTraceListener is further subclassed to ConsoleTraceListener, DelimitedListTraceListener, XmlWriterTraceListener, and EventSchemaTraceListener.

None of these listeners display a dialog when Fail is called—only DefaultTraceListener has this behavior.

The following example clears Trace's default listener, then adds three listeners—one that appends to a file, one that writes to the console, and one that writes to the Windows event log:

```
// Clear the default listener:
Trace.Listeners.Clear();

// Add a writer that appends to the trace.txt file:
Trace.Listeners.Add (new TextWriterTraceListener ("trace.txt"));

// Obtain the Console's output stream, then add that as a listener:
System.IO.TextWriter tw = Console.Out;
Trace.Listeners.Add (new TextWriterTraceListener (tw));

// Set up a Windows Event log source and then create/add listener.
// CreateEventSource requires administrative elevation, so this would
// typically be done in application setup.
if (!EventLog.SourceExists ("DemoApp"))
  EventLog.CreateEventSource ("DemoApp", "Application");

Trace.Listeners.Add (new EventLogTraceListener ("DemoApp"));
```

(It's also possible to add listeners via the application configuration file; this is handy in allowing testers to configure tracing after an application has been built—go to *http://albahari.com/traceconfig* for the MSDN article.)

In the case of the Windows event log, messages that you write with the Write, Fail, or Assert method always display as "Information" messages in the Windows event viewer. Messages that you write via the TraceWarning and TraceError methods, however, show up as warnings or errors.

TraceListener also has a Filter of type TraceFilter that you can set to control whether a message gets written to that listener. To do this, you either instantiate one of the predefined subclasses (EventTypeFilter or SourceFilter), or subclass Trace Filter and override the ShouldTrace method. You could use this to filter by category, for instance.

TraceListener also defines IndentLevel and IndentSize properties for controlling indentation and the TraceOutputOptions property for writing extra data:

```
TextWriterTraceListener tl = new TextWriterTraceListener (Console.Out);
tl.TraceOutputOptions = TraceOptions.DateTime | TraceOptions.Callstack;
```

TraceOutputOptions are applied when using the Trace methods:

```
Trace.TraceWarning ("Orange alert");

DiagTest.vshost.exe Warning: 0 : Orange alert
    DateTime=2007-03-08T05:57:13.6250000Z
    Callstack=   at System.Environment.GetStackTrace(Exception e, Boolean
```

```
    needFileInfo)
        at System.Environment.get_StackTrace()      at ...
```

Flushing and Closing Listeners

Some listeners, such as TextWriterTraceListener, ultimately write to a stream that is subject to caching. This has two implications:

- A message may not appear in the output stream or file immediately.

- You must close—or at least flush—the listener before your application ends; otherwise, you lose what's in the cache (up to 4 KB, by default, if you're writing to a file).

The Trace and Debug classes provide static Close and Flush methods that call Close or Flush on all listeners (which in turn calls Close or Flush on any underlying writers and streams). Close implicitly calls Flush, closes file handles, and prevents further data from being written.

As a general rule, call Close before an application ends and call Flush anytime you want to ensure that current message data is written. This applies if you're using stream- or file-based listeners.

Trace and Debug also provide an AutoFlush property, which, if true, forces a Flush after every message.

 It's a good policy to set AutoFlush to true on Debug and Trace if you're using any file- or stream-based listeners. Otherwise, if an unhandled exception or critical error occurs, the last 4 KB of diagnostic information may be lost.

Code Contracts Overview

We mentioned previously the concept of an *assertion*, whereby you check that certain conditions are met throughout your program. If a condition fails, it indicates a bug, which is typically handled by invoking a debugger (in debug builds) or throwing an exception (in release builds).

Assertions follow the principle that if something goes wrong, it's best to fail early and close to the source of the error. This is usually better than trying to continue with invalid data—which can result in incorrect results, undesired side-effects, or an exception later on in the program (all of which are harder to diagnose).

Historically, there have been two ways to enforce assertions:

- By calling the Assert method on Debug or Trace

- By throwing exceptions (such as ArgumentNullException)

Framework 4.0 introduced a new feature called *code contracts*, which replaces both of these approaches with a unified system. That system allows you to make not only simple assertions but also more powerful *contract*-based assertions.

Code contracts derive from the principle of "Design by Contract" from the Eiffel programming language, where functions interact with each other through a system of mutual obligations and benefits. Essentially, a function specifies *preconditions* that must be met by the client (caller) and in return guarantees *postconditions* that the client can depend on when the function returns.

The types for code contracts live in the `System.Diagnostics.Contracts` namespace.

 Although the types that support code contracts are built into the .NET Framework, the binary rewriter and the static checking tools are available as a separate download at the Microsoft DevLabs site (*http://msdn.microsoft.com/devlabs*). You must install these tools before you can use code contracts in Visual Studio.

Why Use Code Contracts?

To illustrate, we'll write a method that adds an item to a list only if it's not already present—with two *preconditions* and a *postcondition*:

```
public static bool AddIfNotPresent<T> (IList<T> list, T item)
{
  Contract.Requires (list != null);           // Precondition
  Contract.Requires (!list.IsReadOnly);       // Precondition
  Contract.Ensures (list.Contains (item));    // Postcondition
  if (list.Contains(item)) return false;
  list.Add (item);
  return true;
}
```

The preconditions are defined by `Contract.Requires` and are verified when the method starts. The postcondition is defined by `Contract.Ensures` and is verified not where it appears in the code, but *when the method exits*.

Preconditions and postconditions act like assertions and, in this case, detect the following errors:

- Calling the method with a null or read-only list
- A bug in the method whereby we forgot to add the item to the list

 Preconditions and postconditions must appear at the start of the method. This is conducive to good design: if you fail to fulfill the contract in subsequently writing the method, the error will be detected.

Moreover, these conditions form a discoverable *contract* for that method. `AddIfNot Present` advertises to consumers:

- "You must call me with a non-null writable list."
- "When I return, that list will contain the item you specified."

These facts can be emitted into the assembly's XML documentation file (you can do this in Visual Studio by going to the Code Contracts tab of the Project Properties window, enabling the building of a contracts reference assembly, and checking "Emit Contracts into XML doc file"). Tools such as SandCastle can then incorporate contract details into documentation files.

Contracts also enable your program to be analyzed for correctness by static contract validation tools. If you try to call `AddIfNotPresent` with a `list` whose value might be null, for example, a static validation tool could warn you before you even run the program.

Another benefit of contracts is ease of use. In our example, it's easier to code the postcondition upfront than at both exit points. Contracts also support *object invariants*—which further reduce repetitive coding and make for more reliable enforcement.

Conditions can also be placed on interface members and abstract methods, something that is impossible with standard validation approaches. And conditions on virtual methods cannot be accidentally circumvented by subclasses.

Yet another benefit of code contracts is that contract violation behavior can be customized easily and in more ways than if you rely on calling `Debug.Assert` or throwing exceptions. And it's possible to ensure that contract violations are always recorded—even if contract violation exceptions are swallowed by exception handlers higher in the call stack.

The disadvantage of using code contracts is that the .NET implementation relies on a *binary rewriter*—a tool that mutates the assembly after compilation. This slows the build process, as well as complicating services that rely on calling the C# compiler (whether explicitly or via the `CSharpCodeProvider` class).

The enforcing of code contracts may also incur a runtime performance hit, although this is easily mitigated by scaling back contract checking in release builds.

 Another limitation of code contracts is that you can't use them to enforce security-sensitive checks, because they can be circumvented at runtime (by handling the `ContractFailed` event).

Contract Principles

Code contracts comprise *preconditions*, *postconditions*, *assertions*, and *object invariants*. These are all discoverable assertions. They differ based on when they are verified:

- *Preconditions* are verified when a function starts.

- *Postconditions* are verified before a function exits.

- *Assertions* are verified wherever they appear in the code.

- *Object invariants* are verified after every public function in a class.

Code contracts are defined entirely by calling (static) methods in the Contract class. This makes contracts *language-independent*.

Contracts can appear not only in methods, but in other functions as well, such as constructors, properties, indexers, and operators.

Compilation

Almost all methods in the Contract class are defined with the [Conditional("CON TRACTS_FULL")] attribute. This means that unless you define the CONTRACTS_FULL symbol, (most) contract code is stripped out. Visual Studio defines the CON TRACTS_FULL symbol automatically if you enable contract checking in the Code Contracts tab of the Project Properties page. (For this tab to appear, you must download and install the Contracts tools from the Microsoft DevLabs site.)

> Removing the CONTRACTS_FULL symbol might seem like an easy way to disable all contract checking. However, it doesn't apply to Requires<TException> conditions (which we'll describe in detail soon).
>
> The only way to disable contracts in code that uses Requires<TException> is to enable the CONTRACTS_FULL symbol and then get the binary rewriter to strip out contract code by choosing an enforcement level of "none."

The binary rewriter

After compiling code that contains contracts, you must call the binary rewriter tool, *ccrewrite.exe* (Visual Studio does this automatically if contract checking is enabled). The binary rewriter moves postconditions (and object invariants) into the right place, calls any conditions and object invariants in overridden methods, and replaces calls to Contract with calls to a *contracts runtime class*. Here's a (simplified) version of what our earlier example would look like after rewriting:

```
static bool AddIfNotPresent<T> (IList<T> list, T item)
{
  __ContractsRuntime.Requires (list != null);
  __ContractsRuntime.Requires (!list.IsReadOnly);
  bool result;
  if (list.Contains (item))
    result = false;
  else
  {
    list.Add (item);
    result = true;
```

```
    }
        __ContractsRuntime.Ensures (list.Contains (item));    // Postcondition
        return result;
    }
```

If you fail to call the binary rewriter, Contract won't get replaced with __Contrac
tsRuntime and the former will end up throwing exceptions.

 The __ContractsRuntime type is the default contracts runtime
class. In advanced scenarios, you can specify your own contracts runtime class via the /rw switch or Visual Studio's Code
Contracts tab in Project Properties.

Because __ContractsRuntime is shipped with the binary
rewriter (which is not a standard part of the .NET Framework), the binary rewriter actually injects the __ContractsRun
time class into your compiled assembly. You can examine its
code by disassembling any assembly that enables code contracts.

The binary rewriter also offers switches to strip away some or all contract checking:
we describe these in "Selectively Enforcing Contracts." You typically enable full contract checking in debug build configurations and a subset of contract checking in
release configurations.

Asserting versus throwing on failure

The binary rewriter also lets you choose between displaying a dialog and throwing a
ContractException upon contract failure. The former is typically used for debug
builds; the latter for release builds. To enable the latter, specify /throwonfailure
when calling the binary rewriter, or uncheck the "Assert on contract failure" checkbox in Visual Studio's Code Contracts tab in Project Properties.

We'll revisit this topic in more detail in "Dealing with Contract Failure" on page
546.

Purity

All functions that you call from arguments passed to contract methods (Requires,
Assumes, Assert, etc.) must be *pure*—that is, side-effect-free (they must not alter the
values of fields). You must signal to the binary rewriter that any functions you call
are pure by applying the [Pure] attribute:

```
[Pure]
public static bool IsValidUri (string uri) { ... }
```

This makes the following legal:

```
Contract.Requires (IsValidUri (uri));
```

The contract tools implicitly assume that all property get accessors are pure, as are
all C# operators (+, *, %, etc.) and members on selected Framework types, including
string, Contract, Type, System.IO.Path, and LINQ's query operators. It also

assumes that methods invoked via delegates marked with the [Pure] attribute are pure (the Comparison<T> and Predicate<T> attributes are marked with this attribute).

Preconditions

You can define code contract preconditions by calling Contract.Requires, Contract.Requires<TException> or Contract.EndContractBlock.

Contract.Requires

Calling Contract.Requires at the start of a function enforces a precondition:

```
static string ToProperCase (string s)
{
  Contract.Requires (!string.IsNullOrEmpty(s));
  ...
}
```

Diagnostics
and Code
Contracts

This is like making an assertion, except that the precondition forms a discoverable fact about your function that can be extracted from the compiled code and consumed by documentation or static checking tools (so that they can warn you should they see some code elsewhere in your program that tries to call ToProperCase with a null or empty string).

A further benefit of preconditions is that subclasses that override virtual methods with preconditions cannot prevent the base class method's preconditions from being checked. And preconditions defined on *interface* members will be implicitly woven into the concrete implementations (see "Contracts on Interfaces and Abstract Methods" on page 545).

 Preconditions should access only members that are at least as accessible as the function itself—this ensures that callers can make sense of the contract. If you need to read or call less accessible members, it's likely that you're validating *internal state* rather than enforcing the *calling contract*, in which case you should make an assertion instead.

You can call Contract.Requires as many times as necessary at the start of the method to enforce different conditions.

What Should You Put in Preconditions?

The guideline from the Code Contracts team is that preconditions should:

- Be possible for the client (caller) to easily validate.
- Rely only on data & functions at least as accessible as the method itself.
- Always indicate a *bug* if violated.

A consequence of the last point is that a client should never specifically "catch" a contract failure (the ContractException type, in fact, is internal to help enforce that principle). Instead, the client should call the target properly; if it fails, this indicates a bug that should be handled via your general exception backstop (which may include terminating the application). In other words, if you decide control-flow or do other things based on a precondition failure, it's not really a contract because you can continue executing if it fails.

This leads to the following advice when choosing between preconditions and throwing ordinary exceptions:

- If failure *always* indicates a bug in the client, favor a precondition.

- If failure indicates an *abnormal condition*, which *may* mean a bug in the client, throw a (catchable) exception instead.

To illustrate, suppose we're writing the Int32.Parse function. It's reasonable to assume that a null input string always indicates a bug in the caller, so we'd enforce this with a precondition:

```
public static int Parse (string s)
{
  Contract.Requires (s != null);
  ...
}
```

Next, we need to check that the string contains only digits and symbols such as + and - (in the right place). It would place an unreasonable burden on the caller to validate this, and so we'd enforce it not as a precondition, but a manual check that throws a (catchable) FormatException if violated.

To illustrate the member accessibility issue, consider the following code, which often appears in types implementing the IDisposable interface:

```
public void Foo()
{
  if (_isDisposed)  // _isDisposed is a private field
    throw new ObjectDisposedException ("...");
  ...
}
```

This check should not be made into a precondition unless we make _isDisposed accessible to the caller (by refactoring it into a publicly readable property, for instance).

Finally, consider the File.ReadAllText method. The following would be *inappropriate* use of a precondition:

```
public static string ReadAllText (string path)
{
  Contract.Requires (File.Exists (path));
  ...
}
```

The caller cannot reliably know that the file exists before calling this method (it could be deleted between making that check and calling the method). So, we'd enforce this in the old-fashioned way—by throwing a catchable `FileNotFoundException` instead.

Contract.Requires<TException>

The introduction of code contracts challenges the following deeply entrenched pattern established in the .NET Framework from version 1.0:

```
static void SetProgress (string message, int percent)  // Classic approach
{
  if (message == null)
    throw new ArgumentNullException ("message");

  if (percent < 0 || percent > 100)
    throw new ArgumentOutOfRangeException ("percent");
  ...
}

static void SetProgress (string message, int percent)  // Modern approach
{
  Contract.Requires (message != null);
  Contract.Requires (percent >= 0 && percent <= 100);
  ...
}
```

If you have a large assembly that enforces classic argument checking, writing new methods with preconditions will create an inconsistent library: some methods will throw argument exceptions whereas others will throw a `ContractException`. One solution is to update all existing methods to use contracts, but this has two problems:

- It's time-consuming.
- Callers may have come to *depend* on an exception type such as `ArgumentNullException` being thrown. (This almost certainly indicates bad design, but may be the reality nonetheless.)

The solution is to call the generic version of `Contract.Requires`. This lets you specify an exception type to throw upon failure:

```
Contract.Requires<ArgumentNullException> (message != null, "message");
Contract.Requires<ArgumentOutOfRangeException>
  (percent >= 0 && percent <= 100, "percent");
```

(The second argument gets passed to the constructor of the exception class).

This results in the same behavior as with old-fashioned argument checking, while delivering the benefits of contracts (conciseness, support for interfaces, implicit documentation, static checking, and runtime customization).

The specified exception is thrown only if you specify /thro wonfailure when rewriting the assembly (or *uncheck* the *Assert on Contract Failure* checkbox in Visual Studio). Otherwise, a dialog box appears.

It's also possible to specify a contract-checking level of *ReleaseRequires* in the binary rewriter (see "Selectively Enforcing Contracts" on page 548). Calls to the generic Contract.Requires<TException> then remain in place while all other checks are stripped away: this results in an assembly that behaves just as in the past.

Contract.EndContractBlock

The Contract.EndContractBlock method lets you get the benefit of code contracts with traditional argument-checking code—avoiding the need to refactor code written prior to Framework 4.0. All you do is call this method after performing manual argument checks:

```
static void Foo (string name)
{
  if (name == null) throw new ArgumentNullException ("name");
  Contract.EndContractBlock();
  ...
}
```

The binary rewriter then converts this code into something equivalent to:

```
static void Foo (string name)
{
  Contract.Requires<ArgumentNullException> (name != null, "name");
  ...
}
```

The code that precedes EndContractBlock must comprise simple statements of the form:

```
if <condition> throw <expression>;
```

You can mix traditional argument checking with code contract calls: simply put the latter after the former:

```
static void Foo (string name)
{
  if (name == null) throw new ArgumentNullException ("name");
  Contract.Requires (name.Length >= 2);
  ...
}
```

Calling any of the contract-enforcing methods implicitly ends the contract block.

The point is to define a region at the beginning of the method where the contract rewriter knows that every if statement is part of a contract. Calling any of the contract-enforcing methods implicitly extends the contract block, so you don't need to use EndContractBlock if you use another method such as Contract.Ensures.

Preconditions and Overridden Methods

When overriding a virtual method, you cannot add preconditions, because doing so would *change the contract* (by making it more restrictive)—breaking the principles of polymorphism.

(Technically, the designers could have allowed overridden methods to *weaken* preconditions; they decided against this because the scenarios weren't sufficiently compelling to justify adding this complexity).

 The binary rewriter ensures that a base method's preconditions are always enforced in subclasses—whether or not the overridden method calls the base method.

Postconditions

Contract.Ensures

`Contract.Ensures` enforces a postcondition: something which must be true when the method exits. We saw an example earlier:

```
static bool AddIfNotPresent<T> (IList<T> list, T item)
{
  Contract.Requires (list != null);        // Precondition
  Contract.Ensures (list.Contains (item)); // Postcondition
  if (list.Contains(item)) return false;
  list.Add (item);
  return true;
}
```

The binary rewriter moves postconditions to the exit points of the method. Postconditions are checked if you return early from a method (as in this example)—but not if you return early via an unhandled exception.

Unlike preconditions, which detect misuse by the *caller*, postconditions detect an error in the function itself (rather like assertions). Therefore, postconditions may access private state (subject to the caveat stated shortly, in "Postconditions and Overridden Methods" on page 543).

Postconditions and Thread Safety

Multithreaded scenarios (Chapter 14) challenge the usefulness of postconditions. For instance, suppose we wrote a thread-safe wrapper for a List<T> with a method as follows:

```
public class ThreadSafeList<T>
{
  List<T> _list = new List<T>();
  object _locker = new object();

  public bool AddIfNotPresent (T item)
  {
```

```
        Contract.Ensures (_list.Contains (item));
        lock (_locker)
        {
            if (_list.Contains(item)) return false;
            _list.Add (item);
            return true;
        }
    }

    public void Remove (T item)
    {
        lock (_locker)
            _list.Remove (item);
    }
}
```

The postcondition in the `AddIfNotPresent` method is checked *after* the lock is released—at which point the item may no longer exist in the list if another thread called `Remove` right then. There is currently no workaround for this problem, other than to enforce such conditions as assertions (see "Assertions and Object Invariants" on page 543) rather than postconditions.

Contract.EnsuresOnThrow<TException>

Occasionally, it's useful to ensure that a certain condition is true should a particular type of exception be thrown. The `EnsuresOnThrow` method does exactly this:

```
Contract.EnsuresOnThrow<WebException> (this.ErrorMessage != null);
```

Contract.Result<T> and Contract.ValueAtReturn<T>

Because postconditions are not evaluated until a function ends, it's reasonable to want to access the return value of a method. The `Contract.Result<T>` method does exactly that:

```
Random _random = new Random();
int GetOddRandomNumber()
{
    Contract.Ensures (Contract.Result<int>() % 2 == 1);
    return _random.Next (100) * 2 + 1;
}
```

The `Contract.ValueAtReturn<T>` method fulfills the same function—but for `ref` and `out` parameters.

Contract.OldValue<T>

`Contract.OldValue<T>` returns the original value of a method parameter. This is useful with postconditions because the latter are checked at the *end* of a function. Therefore, any expressions in postconditions that incorporate parameters will read the *modified* parameter values.

For example, the postcondition in the following method will always fail:

```
static string Middle (string s)
{
  Contract.Requires (s != null && s.Length >= 2);
  Contract.Ensures (Contract.Result<string>().Length < s.Length);
  s = s.Substring (1, s.Length - 2);
  return s.Trim();
}
```

Here's how we can correct it:

```
static string Middle (string s)
{
  Contract.Requires (s != null && s.Length >= 2);
  Contract.Ensures (Contract.Result<string>().Length <
                    Contract.OldValue (s).Length);
  s = s.Substring (1, s.Length - 2);
  return s.Trim();
}
```

Postconditions and Overridden Methods

An overridden method cannot circumvent postconditions defined by its base, but it can add new ones. The binary rewriter ensures that a base method's postconditions are always checked—even if the overridden method doesn't call the base implementation.

> For the reason just stated, postconditions on virtual methods should not access private members. Doing so will result in the binary rewriter weaving code into the subclass that will try to access private members in the base class—causing a runtime error.

Assertions and Object Invariants

In addition to preconditions and postconditions, the code contracts API lets you make assertions and define *object invariants*.

Assertions

Contract.Assert

You can make assertions anywhere in a function by calling Contract.Assert. You can optionally specify an error message if the assertion fails:

```
...
int x = 3;
...
Contract.Assert (x == 3);                  // Fail unless x is 3
Contract.Assert (x == 3, "x must be 3");
...
```

The binary rewriter doesn't move assertions around. There are two reasons for favoring Contract.Assert over Debug.Assert:

- You can leverage the more flexible failure-handling mechanisms offered by code contracts.

- Static checking tools can attempt to validate `Contract.Asserts`.

Contract.Assume

`Contract.Assume` behaves exactly like `Contract.Assert` at run-time but has slightly different implications for static checking tools. Essentially, static checking tools won't *challenge* an assumption, whereas they may challenge an assertion. This is useful in that there will always be things a static checker is unable to prove, and this may lead to it "crying wolf" over a valid assertion. Changing the assertion to an assumption keeps the static checker quiet.

Object Invariants

For a class, you can specify one or more *object invariant* methods. These methods run automatically after every *public* function in the class and allow you to assert that the object is in an internally consistent state.

Support for multiple object invariant methods was included to make object invariants work well with partial classes.

To define an object invariant method, write a parameterless void method and annotate it with the [ContractInvariantMethod] attribute. In that method, call `Contract.Invariant` to enforce each condition that should hold true:

```
class Test
{
  int _x, _y;

  [ContractInvariantMethod]
  void ObjectInvariant()
  {
    Contract.Invariant (_x >= 0);
    Contract.Invariant (_y >= _x);
  }

  public int X { get { return _x; } set { _x = value; } }
  public void Test1() { _x = -3; }
  void Test2()        { _x = -3; }
}
```

The binary rewriter translates the X property, `Test1` method and `Test2` method to something equivalent to this:

```
public void X { get { return _x; } set { _x = value; ObjectInvariant(); } }
public void Test1() { _x = -3; ObjectInvariant(); }
void Test2()        { _x = -3; }    // No change because it's private
```

Object invariants don't *prevent* an object from entering an invalid state: they merely *detect* when that condition has occurred.

Contract.Invariant is rather like Contract.Assert, except that it can appear only in a method marked with the [ContractInvariantMethod] attribute. And conversely, a contract invariant method can only contain calls to Contract.Invariant.

A subclass can introduce its own object invariant method, too, and this will be checked in addition to the base class's invariant method. The caveat, of course, is that the check will take place only after a public method is called.

Contracts on Interfaces and Abstract Methods

A powerful feature of code contracts is that you can attach conditions to interface members and abstract methods. The binary rewriter then automatically weaves these conditions into the members' concrete implementations.

A special mechanism lets specify a separate contract class for interfaces and abstract methods, so that you can write method bodies to house the contract conditions. Here's how it works:

```
[ContractClass (typeof (ContractForITest))]
interface ITest
{
  int Process (string s);
}

[ContractClassFor (typeof (ITest))]
sealed class ContractForITest : ITest
{
  int ITest.Process (string s)      // Must use explicit implementation.
  {
    Contract.Requires (s != null);
    return 0;                       // Dummy value to satisfy compiler.
  }
}
```

Notice that we had to return a value when implementing ITest.Process to satisfy the compiler. The code that returns 0 will not run, however. Instead, the binary rewriter extracts just the conditions from that method and weaves them into the real implementations of ITest.Process. This means that the contract class is never actually instantiated (and any constructors that you write will not execute).

You can assign a temporary variable within the contract block to make it easier to reference other members of the interface. For instance, if our ITest interface also defined a Message property of type string, we could write the following in ITest.Process:

```
int ITest.Process (string s)
{
  ITest test = this;
```

Diagnostics and Code Contracts

```
    Contract.Requires (s != test.Message);
    ...
}
```

This is easier than:

```
    Contract.Requires (s != ((ITest)this).Message);
```

(Simply using this.Message won't work because Message must be explicitly implemented.) The process of defining contract classes for abstract classes is exactly the
same, except that the contract class should be marked abstract instead of sealed.

Dealing with Contract Failure

The binary rewriter lets you specify what happens when a contract condition fails,
via the /throwonfailure switch (or the *Assert on Contract Failure* checkbox in Visual Studio's *Contracts* tab in *Project Properties*).

If you don't specify /throwonfailure—or check *Assert on Contract Failure*—a dialog appears upon contract failure, allowing you to abort, debug or ignore the error.

> There are a couple of nuances to be aware of:
>
> - If the CLR is hosted (i.e., in SQL Server or Exchange),
>   the host's escalation policy is triggered instead of a dialog
>   appearing.
>
> - Otherwise, if the current process can't pop up a dialog
>   box to the user, Environment.FailFast is called.

The dialog is useful in debug builds for a couple of reasons:

- It makes it easy to diagnose and debug contract failures on the spot—without
  having to re-run the program. This works regardless of whether Visual Studio
  is configured to break on first-chance exceptions. And unlike with exceptions
  in general, contract failure almost certainly means a bug in your code.

- It lets you know about contract failure—even if a caller higher up in the stack
  "swallows" exceptions as follows:

```
try
{
  // Call some method whose contract fails
}
catch { }
```

> The code above is considered an antipattern in most scenarios
> because it *masks* failures, including conditions that the author
> never anticipated.

If you specify the /throwonfailure switch and uncheck *Assert on Contract Failure* in Visual Studio—a ContractException is thrown upon failure. This is desirable for:

- Release builds—where you would let the exception bubble up the stack and be treated like any other unexpected exception (perhaps by having a top-level exception handler log the error or invite the user to report it).

- Unit-testing environments— where the process of logging errors is automated.

 ContractException cannot appear in a catch block because this type is not public. The rationale is that there's no reason that you'd want to *specifically* catch a ContractException— you'd want to catch it only as part of a general exception backstop.

The ContractFailed Event

When a contract fails the static Contract.ContractFailed event fires before any further action is taken. If you handle this event, you can query the event arguments object for details of the error. You can also call SetHandled to prevent a ContractException from being subsequently thrown (or a dialog appearing).

Handling this event is particularly useful when /throwonfailure is specified, because it lets you log *all* contract failures—even if code higher in the call stack swallows exceptions as we described just before. A great example is with automated unit testing:

```
Contract.ContractFailed += (sender, args) =>
{
  string failureMessage = args.FailureKind + ": " + args.Message;
  // Log failureMessage with unit testing framework:
  // ...
  args.SetUnwind();
};
```

This handler logs all contract failures while allowing the normal ContractException (or contract failure dialog) to run its course after the event handler has finished. Notice that we also call SetUnwind: this neutralizes the effect of any calls to SetHandled from other event subscribers. In other words, it ensures that a ContractException (or dialog) will always follow after all event handlers have run.

If you throw an exception from within this handler, any other event handlers will still execute. The exception that you threw then populates the InnerException property of the ContractException that's eventually thrown.

Exceptions Within Contract Conditions

If an exception is thrown within a contract condition itself, then that exception propagates like any other—regardless of whether /throwonfailure is specified. The following method throws a NullReferenceException if called with a null string:

```
string Test (string s)
{
  Contract.Requires (s.Length > 0);
  ...
}
```

This precondition is essentially faulty. It should instead be:

```
Contract.Requires (!string.IsNullOrEmpty (s));
```

Selectively Enforcing Contracts

The binary rewriter offers two switches that strip away some or all contract checking: /publicsurface and /level. You can control these from Visual Studio via the *Code Contracts* tab of *Project Properties*. The /publicsurface switch tells the rewriter to check contracts only on public members. The /level switch has the following options:

None (level 0)
> Strips out *all* contract verification

ReleaseRequires (level 1)
> Enables only calls to the generic version of Contract.Requires<TExcep tion>

Preconditions (level 2)
> Enables all preconditions (level 1 plus normal preconditions)

Pre and Post (level 3)
> Enables level 2 checking plus postconditions

Full (level 4)
> Enables level 3 checking plus object invariants and assertions (i.e., everything)

You typically enable full contract checking in debug build configurations.

Contracts in Release Builds

When it comes to making release builds, there are two general philosophies:

- Favor safety and enable full contract checking
- Favor performance and disable all contract checking

If you're building a library for public consumption, though, the second approach creates a problem. Imagine that you compile and distribute library L in release mode with contract checking disabled. A client then builds project C in *debug* mode that references library L. Assembly C can then call members of L incorrectly without contract violations! In this situation, you actually want to enforce the parts of L's contract that ensure correct usage of L—in other words, the *preconditions* in L's *public* members.

The simplest way to resolve this is to enable /publicsurface checking in L with a level of *Preconditions* or *ReleaseRequires*. This ensures that the essential preconditions are enforced for the benefit of consumers, while incurring the performance cost of only those preconditions.

In extreme cases, you might not want to pay even this small performance price—in which case you can take the more elaborate approach of *call-site checking*.

Call-Site Checking

Call-site checking moves precondition validation from *called* methods into *calling* methods (call sites). This solves the problem just described—by enabling consumers of library L to perform L's precondition validation themselves in debug configurations.

To enable call-site checking, you must first build a separate *contracts reference assembly*—a supplementary assembly that contains just the preconditions for the referenced assembly. To do this, you can either use the *ccrefgen* command-line tool, or proceed in Visual Studio as follows:

1. In the release configuration of the *referenced library* (L), go to the *Code Contracts* tab of *Project Properties* and disable runtime contract checking while ticking "Build a Contract Reference Assembly". This then generates a supplementary contracts reference assembly (with the suffix *.contracts.dll*).

2. In the *release* configuration of the *referencing* assemblies, disable all contract checking.

3. In the *debug* configuration of the *referencing* assemblies, tick "Call-site Requires Checking."

The third step is equivalent to calling *ccrewrite* with the /callsiterequires switch. It reads the preconditions from the contracts reference assembly and weaves them into the calling sites in the referencing assembly.

Static Contract Checking

Code contracts make *static contract checking* possible, whereby a tool analyzes contract conditions to find potential bugs in your program before it's run. For example, statically checking the following code generates a warning:

```
static void Main()
{
  string message = null;
  WriteLine (message);      // Static checking tool will generate warning
}

static void WriteLine (string s)
{
  Contract.Requires (s != null);
  Console.WriteLine (s);
}
```

You can run Microsoft's static contracts tool from the command line via *cccheck* or by enabling static contract checking in Visual Studio's project properties dialog.

For static checking to work, you may need to add preconditions and postconditions to your methods. To give a simple example, the following will generate a warning:

```
static void WriteLine (string s, bool b)
{
  if (b)
    WriteLine (s);     // Warning: requires unproven
}

static void WriteLine (string s)
{
  Contract.Requires (s != null);
  Console.WriteLine (s);
}
```

Because we're calling a method that requires the parameter to be non-null, we must prove that the argument is non-null. To do this, we can add a precondition to the first method as follows:

```
static void WriteLine (string s, bool b)
{
  Contract.Requires (s != null);
  if (b)
    WriteLine (s);    // OK
}
```

The ContractVerification Attribute

Static checking is easiest if instigated from the beginning of a project's lifecycle—otherwise you're likely to get overwhelmed with warnings.

If you do want to apply static contract checking to an existing codebase, it can help by initially applying it just to selective parts of a program—via the ContractVerifi cation attribute (in System.Diagnostics.Contracts). This attribute can be applied at the assembly, type, and member level. If you apply it at multiple levels, the more granular wins. Therefore, to enable static contract verification just for a particular class, start by disabling verification at the assembly-level as follows:

```
[assembly: ContractVerification (false)]
```

and then enable it just for the desired class:

```
[ContractVerification (true)]
class Foo { ... }
```

Baselines

Another tactic in applying static contract verification to an existing codebase is to run the static checker with the *Baseline* option checked in Visual Studio. All the warnings that are produced are then written to a specified XML file. Next time you run static verification, all the warnings in that that file are ignored—so you see only messages generated as a result of *new* code that you've written.

The SuppressMessage Attribute

You can also tell the static checker to ignore certain types of warnings via the Sup pressMessage attribute (in System.Diagnostics.CodeAnalysis):

```
[SuppressMessage ("Microsoft.Contracts", warningFamily)]
```

where *warningFamily* is one of the following values:

```
Requires Ensures Invariant NonNull DivByZero MinValueNegation
ArrayCreation ArrayLowerBound ArrayUpperBound
```

You can apply this attribute at an assembly or type level.

Debugger Integration

Sometimes it's useful for an application to interact with a debugger if one is available. During development, the debugger is usually your IDE (e.g., Visual Studio); in deployment, the debugger is more likely to be:

- DbgCLR
- One of the lower-level debugging tools, such as WinDbg, Cordbg, or Mdbg

DbgCLR is Visual Studio stripped of everything but the debugger, and it is a free download with the .NET Framework SDK. It's the easiest debugging option when an IDE is not available, although it requires that you download the whole SDK.

Attaching and Breaking

The static Debugger class in System.Diagnostics provides basic functions for interacting with a debugger—namely Break, Launch, Log, and IsAttached.

A debugger must first attach to an application in order to debug it. If you start an application from within an IDE, this happens automatically, unless you request otherwise (by choosing "Start without debugging"). Sometimes, though, it's inconvenient or impossible to start an application in debug mode within the IDE. An example is a Windows Service application or (ironically) a Visual Studio designer. One solution is to start the application normally, and then choose Debug Process in your IDE. This doesn't allow you to set breakpoints early in the program's execution, however.

The workaround is to call `Debugger.Break` from within your application. This method launches a debugger, attaches to it, and suspends execution at that point. (`Launch` does the same, but without suspending execution.) Once attached, you can log messages directly to the debugger's output window with the `Log` method. You can tell whether you're attached to a debugger with the `IsAttached` property.

Debugger Attributes

The `DebuggerStepThrough` and `DebuggerHidden` attributes provide suggestions to the debugger on how to handle single-stepping for a particular method, constructor, or class.

`DebuggerStepThrough` requests that the debugger step through a function without any user interaction. This attribute is useful in automatically generated methods and in proxy methods that forward the real work to a method somewhere else. In the latter case, the debugger will still show the proxy method in the call stack if a breakpoint is set within the "real" method—unless you also add the `DebuggerHidden` attribute. These two attributes can be combined on proxies to help the user focus on debugging the application logic rather than the plumbing:

```
[DebuggerStepThrough, DebuggerHidden]
void DoWorkProxy()
{
  // setup...
  DoWork();
  // teardown...
}

void DoWork() {...}   // Real method...
```

Processes and Process Threads

We described in the last section of Chapter 6 how to launch a new process with `Process.Start`. The `Process` class also allows you to query and interact with other processes running on the same, or another, computer. Note that the `Process` class is unavailable to Windows Store apps.

Examining Running Processes

The `Process.GetProcessXXX` methods retrieve a specific process by name or process ID, or all processes running on the current or nominated computer. This includes both managed and unmanaged processes. Each `Process` instance has a wealth of properties mapping statistics such as name, ID, priority, memory and processor utilization, window handles, and so on. The following sample enumerates all the running processes on the current computer:

```
foreach (Process p in Process.GetProcesses())
using (p)
{
  Console.WriteLine (p.ProcessName);
  Console.WriteLine ("   PID:     " + p.Id);
  Console.WriteLine ("   Memory:  " + p.WorkingSet64);
  Console.WriteLine ("   Threads: " + p.Threads.Count);
}
```

Process.GetCurrentProcess returns the current process. If you've created additional application domains, all will share the same process.

You can terminate a process by calling its Kill method.

Examining Threads in a Process

You can also enumerate over the threads of other processes, with the Pro cess.Threads property. The objects that you get, however, are not System.Thread ing.Thread objects, but rather ProcessThread objects and are intended for administrative rather than synchronization tasks. A ProcessThread object provides diagnostic information about the underlying thread and allows you to control some aspects of it, such as its priority and processor affinity:

```
public void EnumerateThreads (Process p)
{
  foreach (ProcessThread pt in p.Threads)
  {
    Console.WriteLine (pt.Id);
    Console.WriteLine ("   State:    " + pt.ThreadState);
    Console.WriteLine ("   Priority: " + pt.PriorityLevel);
    Console.WriteLine ("   Started:  " + pt.StartTime);
    Console.WriteLine ("   CPU time: " + pt.TotalProcessorTime);
  }
}
```

StackTrace and StackFrame

The StackTrace and StackFrame classes provide a read-only view of an execution call stack and are part of the standard desktop .NET Framework. You can obtain stack traces for the current thread, another thread in the same process, or an Excep tion object. Such information is useful mostly for diagnostic purposes, though it can also be used in programming (hacks). StackTrace represents a complete call stack; StackFrame represents a single method call within that stack.

If you instantiate a StackTrace object with no arguments—or with a bool argument —you get a snapshot of the current thread's call stack. The bool argument, if true, instructs StackTrace to read the assembly *.pdb* (project debug) files if they are present, giving you access to filename, line number, and column offset data. Project debug files are generated when you compile with the /debug switch. (Visual Studio compiles with this switch unless you request otherwise via *Advanced Build Settings*.)

Once you've obtained a `StackTrace`, you can examine a particular frame by calling `GetFrame`—or obtain the whole lot with `GetFrames`:

```
static void Main() { A (); }
static void A()    { B (); }
static void B()    { C (); }
static void C()
{
  StackTrace s = new StackTrace (true);

  Console.WriteLine ("Total frames:   " + s.FrameCount);
  Console.WriteLine ("Current method: " + s.GetFrame(0).GetMethod().Name);
  Console.WriteLine ("Calling method: " + s.GetFrame(1).GetMethod().Name);
  Console.WriteLine ("Entry method:   " + s.GetFrame
                                      (s.FrameCount-1).GetMethod().Name);
  Console.WriteLine ("Call Stack:");
  foreach (StackFrame f in s.GetFrames())
    Console.WriteLine (
      "  File: "   + f.GetFileName() +
      "  Line: "   + f.GetFileLineNumber() +
      "  Col: "    + f.GetFileColumnNumber() +
      "  Offset: " + f.GetILOffset() +
      "  Method: " + f.GetMethod().Name);
}
```

Here's the output:

```
Total frames:  4
Current method: C
Calling method: B
Entry method: Main
Call stack:
  File: C:\Test\Program.cs  Line: 15  Col: 4   Offset: 7  Method: C
  File: C:\Test\Program.cs  Line: 12  Col: 22  Offset: 6  Method: B
  File: C:\Test\Program.cs  Line: 11  Col: 22  Offset: 6  Method: A
  File: C:\Test\Program.cs  Line: 10  Col: 25  Offset: 6  Method: Main
```

The IL offset indicates the offset of the instruction that will execute *next* —not the instruction that's currently executing. Peculiarly, though, the line and column number (if a *.pdb* file is present) usually indicate the actual execution point.

This happens because the CLR does its best to *infer* the actual execution point when calculating the line and column from the IL offset. The compiler emits IL in such a way as to make this possible—including inserting nop (no-operation) instructions into the IL stream.

Compiling with optimizations enabled, however, disables the insertion of nop instructions, and so the stack trace may show the line and column number of the next statement to execute. Obtaining a useful stack trace is further hampered by the fact that optimization can pull other tricks, including collapsing entire methods.

A shortcut to obtaining the essential information for an entire StackTrace is to call ToString on it. Here's what the result looks like:

```
at DebugTest.Program.C() in C:\Test\Program.cs:line 16
at DebugTest.Program.B() in C:\Test\Program.cs:line 12
at DebugTest.Program.A() in C:\Test\Program.cs:line 11
at DebugTest.Program.Main() in C:\Test\Program.cs:line 10
```

To obtain the stack trace for another thread, pass the other Thread into Stack Trace's constructor. This can be a useful strategy for profiling a program, although you must suspend the thread while obtaining the stack trace. This is actually quite tricky to do without risking a deadlock—we illustrate a reliable approach in "Suspend and Resume" on page 939 in Chapter 22.

You can also get the stack trace for an Exception object (showing what led up to the exception being thrown) by passing the Exception into StackTrace's constructor.

> Exception already has a StackTrace property; however, this property returns a simple string—not a StackTrace object. A StackTrace object is far more useful in logging exceptions that occur after deployment—where no .pdb files are available —because you can log the *IL offset* in lieu of line and column numbers. With an IL offset and *ildasm*, you can pinpoint where within a method an error occurred.

Windows Event Logs

The Win32 platform provides a centralized logging mechanism, in the form of the Windows event logs.

The Debug and Trace classes we used earlier write to a Windows event log if you register an EventLogTraceListener. With the EventLog class, however, you can write directly to a Windows event log without using Trace or Debug. You can also use this class to read and monitor event data.

> Writing to the Windows event log makes sense in a Windows Service application, because if something goes wrong, you can't pop up a user interface directing the user to some special file where diagnostic information has been written. Also, because it's common practice for services to write to the Windows event log, this is the first place an administrator is likely to look if your service falls over.
>
> The EventLog class is not available to Windows Store apps.

There are three standard Windows event logs, identified by these names:

- Application
- System
- Security

The *Application* log is where most applications normally write.

Writing to the Event Log

To write to a Windows event log:

1. Choose one of the three event logs (usually *Application*).

2. Decide on a *source name* and create it if necessary.

3. Call EventLog.WriteEntry with the log name, source name, and message data.

The *source name* is an easily identifiable name for your application. You must register a source name before you use it—the CreateEventSource method performs this function. You can then call WriteEntry:

```
const string SourceName = "MyCompany.WidgetServer";

// CreateEventSource requires administrative permissions, so this would
// typically be done in application setup.
if (!EventLog.SourceExists (SourceName))
  EventLog.CreateEventSource (SourceName, "Application");

EventLog.WriteEntry (SourceName,
  "Service started; using configuration file=...",
  EventLogEntryType.Information);
```

EventLogEntryType can be Information, Warning, Error, SuccessAudit, or Failur eAudit. Each displays with a different icon in the Windows event viewer. You can also optionally specify a category and event ID (each is a number of your own choosing) and provide optional binary data.

CreateEventSource also allows you to specify a machine name: this is to write to another computer's event log, if you have sufficient permissions.

Reading the Event Log

To read an event log, instantiate the EventLog class with the name of the log you wish to access and optionally the name of another computer on which the log resides. Each log entry can then be read via the Entries collection property:

```
EventLog log = new EventLog ("Application");

Console.WriteLine ("Total entries: " + log.Entries.Count);

EventLogEntry last = log.Entries [log.Entries.Count - 1];
Console.WriteLine ("Index:   " + last.Index);
Console.WriteLine ("Source:  " + last.Source);
Console.WriteLine ("Type:    " + last.EntryType);
Console.WriteLine ("Time:    " + last.TimeWritten);
Console.WriteLine ("Message: " + last.Message);
```

You can enumerate over all logs for the current (or another) computer with the static method EventLog.GetEventLogs (this requires administrative privileges):

```
foreach (EventLog log in EventLog.GetEventLogs())
  Console.WriteLine (log.LogDisplayName);
```

This normally prints, at a minimum, *Application, Security,* and *System.*

Monitoring the Event Log

You can be alerted whenever an entry is written to a Windows event log, via the
EntryWritten event. This works for event logs on the local computer, and it fires
regardless of what application logged the event.

To enable log monitoring:

1. Instantiate an EventLog and set its EnableRaisingEvents property to true.

2. Handle the EntryWritten event.

For example:

```
static void Main()
{
  using (var log = new EventLog ("Application"))
  {
    log.EnableRaisingEvents = true;
    log.EntryWritten += DisplayEntry;
    Console.ReadLine();
  }
}

static void DisplayEntry (object sender, EntryWrittenEventArgs e)
{
  EventLogEntry entry = e.Entry;
  Console.WriteLine (entry.Message);
}
```

Performance Counters

The logging mechanisms we've discussed to date are useful for capturing information for future analysis. However, to gain insight into the current state of an application (or the system as a whole), a more real-time approach is needed. The Win32
solution to this need is the performance-monitoring infrastructure, which consists
of a set of performance counters that the system and applications expose, and the
Microsoft Management Console (MMC) snap-ins used to monitor these counters in
real time.

Performance counters are grouped into categories such as "System," "Processor,"
".NET CLR Memory," and so on. These categories are sometimes also referred to as
"performance objects" by the GUI tools. Each category groups a related set of performance counters that monitor one aspect of the system or application. Examples
of performance counters in the ".NET CLR Memory" category include "% Time in
GC," "# Bytes in All Heaps," and "Allocated bytes/sec."

Each category may optionally have one or more instances that can be monitored independently. For example, this is useful in the "% Processor Time" performance counter in the "Processor" category, which allows one to monitor CPU utilization. On a multiprocessor machine, this counter supports an instance for each CPU, allowing one to monitor the utilization of each CPU independently.

The following sections illustrate how to perform commonly needed tasks, such as determining which counters are exposed, monitoring a counter, and creating your own counters to expose application status information.

 Reading performance counters or categories may require administrator privileges on the local or target computer, depending on what is accessed.

Enumerating the Available Counters

The following example enumerates over all of the available performance counters on the computer. For those that have instances, it enumerates the counters for each instance:

```
PerformanceCounterCategory[] cats =
  PerformanceCounterCategory.GetCategories();

foreach (PerformanceCounterCategory cat in cats)
{
  Console.WriteLine ("Category: " + cat.CategoryName);

  string[] instances = cat.GetInstanceNames();
  if (instances.Length == 0)
  {
    foreach (PerformanceCounter ctr in cat.GetCounters())
      Console.WriteLine ("  Counter: " + ctr.CounterName);
  }
  else   // Dump counters with instances
  {
    foreach (string instance in instances)
    {
      Console.WriteLine ("  Instance: " + instance);
      if (cat.InstanceExists (instance))
        foreach (PerformanceCounter ctr in cat.GetCounters (instance))
          Console.WriteLine ("    Counter: " + ctr.CounterName);
    }
  }
}
```

 The result is more than 10,000 lines long! It also takes a while to execute because `PerformanceCounterCategory.Instan ceExists` has an inefficient implementation. In a real system, you'd want to retrieve the more detailed information only on demand.

The next example uses a LINQ query to retrieve just .NET performance counters, writing the result to an XML file:

```
var x =
  new XElement ("counters",
    from PerformanceCounterCategory cat in
        PerformanceCounterCategory.GetCategories()
    where cat.CategoryName.StartsWith (".NET")
    let instances = cat.GetInstanceNames()
    select new XElement ("category",
      new XAttribute ("name", cat.CategoryName),
      instances.Length == 0
      ?
        from c in cat.GetCounters()
        select new XElement ("counter",
          new XAttribute ("name", c.CounterName))
      :
        from i in instances
        select new XElement ("instance", new XAttribute ("name", i),
          !cat.InstanceExists (i)
          ?
            null
          :
            from c in cat.GetCounters (i)
            select new XElement ("counter",
              new XAttribute ("name", c.CounterName))
        )
    )
  );
x.Save ("counters.xml");
```

Reading Performance Counter Data

To retrieve the value of a performance counter, instantiate a `PerformanceCounter` object and then call the `NextValue` or `NextSample` method. `NextValue` returns a simple `float` value; `NextSample` returns a `CounterSample` object that exposes a more advanced set of properties, such as `CounterFrequency`, `TimeStamp`, `BaseValue`, and `RawValue`.

`PerformanceCounter`'s constructor takes a category name, counter name, and optional instance. So, to display the current processor utilization for all CPUs, you would do the following:

```
using (PerformanceCounter pc = new PerformanceCounter ("Processor",
                                                       "% Processor Time",
                                                       "_Total"))
  Console.WriteLine (pc.NextValue());
```

Or to display the "real" (i.e., private) memory consumption of the current process:

```
string procName = Process.GetCurrentProcess().ProcessName;
using (PerformanceCounter pc = new PerformanceCounter ("Process",
                                                       "Private Bytes",
                                                       procName))
  Console.WriteLine (pc.NextValue());
```

PerformanceCounter doesn't expose a ValueChanged event, so if you want to monitor for changes, you must poll. In the next example, we poll every 200 ms—until signaled to quit by an EventWaitHandle:

```
// need to import System.Threading as well as System.Diagnostics

static void Monitor (string category, string counter, string instance,
                     EventWaitHandle stopper)
{
  if (!PerformanceCounterCategory.Exists (category))
    throw new InvalidOperationException ("Category does not exist");

  if (!PerformanceCounterCategory.CounterExists (counter, category))
    throw new InvalidOperationException ("Counter does not exist");

  if (instance == null) instance = "";   // "" == no instance (not null!)
  if (instance != "" &&
      !PerformanceCounterCategory.InstanceExists (instance, category))
    throw new InvalidOperationException ("Instance does not exist");

  float lastValue = 0f;
  using (PerformanceCounter pc = new PerformanceCounter (category,
                                             counter, instance))
    while (!stopper.WaitOne (200, false))
    {
      float value = pc.NextValue();
      if (value != lastValue)           // Only write out the value
      {                                 // if it has changed.
        Console.WriteLine (value);
        lastValue = value;
      }
    }
}
```

Here's how we can use this method to simultaneously monitor processor and hard-disk activity:

```
static void Main()
{
  EventWaitHandle stopper = new ManualResetEvent (false);

  new Thread (() =>
    Monitor ("Processor", "% Processor Time", "_Total", stopper)
  ).Start();

  new Thread (() =>
    Monitor ("LogicalDisk", "% Idle Time", "C:", stopper)
  ).Start();

  Console.WriteLine ("Monitoring - press any key to quit");
  Console.ReadKey();
  stopper.Set();
}
```

Creating Counters and Writing Performance Data

Before writing performance counter data, you need to create a performance category and counter. You must create the performance category along with all the counters that belong to it in one step, as follows:

```
string category = "Nutshell Monitoring";

// We'll create two counters in this category:
string eatenPerMin = "Macadamias eaten so far";
string tooHard = "Macadamias deemed too hard";

if (!PerformanceCounterCategory.Exists (category))
{
  CounterCreationDataCollection cd = new CounterCreationDataCollection();

  cd.Add (new CounterCreationData (eatenPerMin,
          "Number of macadamias consumed, including shelling time",
          PerformanceCounterType.NumberOfItems32));

  cd.Add (new CounterCreationData (tooHard,
          "Number of macadamias that will not crack, despite much effort",
          PerformanceCounterType.NumberOfItems32));

  PerformanceCounterCategory.Create (category, "Test Category",
    PerformanceCounterCategoryType.SingleInstance, cd);
}
```

The new counters then show up in the Windows performance-monitoring tool when you choose Add Counters, as shown in Figure 13-1.

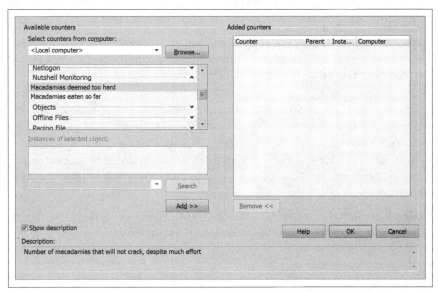

Figure 13-1. Custom performance counter

If you later want to define more counters in the same category, you must first delete the old category by calling `PerformanceCounterCategory.Delete`.

 Creating and deleting performance counters requires administrative privileges. For this reason, it's usually done as part of the application setup.

Once a counter is created, you can update its value by instantiating a `Performance Counter`, setting `ReadOnly` to `false`, and setting `RawValue`. You can also use the `Increment` and `IncrementBy` methods to update the existing value:

```
string category = "Nutshell Monitoring";
string eatenPerMin = "Macadamias eaten so far";

using (PerformanceCounter pc = new PerformanceCounter (category,
                                                      eatenPerMin, ""))
{
  pc.ReadOnly = false;
  pc.RawValue = 1000;
  pc.Increment();
  pc.IncrementBy (10);
  Console.WriteLine (pc.NextValue());     // 1011
}
```

The Stopwatch Class

The `Stopwatch` class provides a convenient mechanism for measuring execution times. `Stopwatch` uses the highest-resolution mechanism that the operating system and hardware provide, which is typically less than a microsecond. (In contrast, `Date Time.Now` and `Environment.TickCount` have a resolution of about 15ms).

To use `Stopwatch`, call `StartNew`—this instantiates a `Stopwatch` and starts it ticking. (Alternatively, you can instantiate it manually and then call `Start`.) The `Elapsed` property returns the elapsed interval as a `TimeSpan`:

```
Stopwatch s = Stopwatch.StartNew();
System.IO.File.WriteAllText ("test.txt", new string ('*', 30000000));
Console.WriteLine (s.Elapsed);           // 00:00:01.4322661
```

`Stopwatch` also exposes an `ElapsedTicks` property, which returns the number of elapsed "ticks" as a `long`. To convert from ticks to seconds, divide by `StopWatch.Fre quency`. There's also an `ElapsedMilliseconds` property, which is often the most convenient.

Calling `Stop` freezes `Elapsed` and `ElapsedTicks`. There's no background activity incurred by a "running" `Stopwatch`, so calling `Stop` is optional.

14

Concurrency and Asynchrony

Most applications need to deal with more than one thing happening at a time (*concurrency*). In this chapter, we start with the essential prerequisites, namely the basics of threading and tasks, and then describe the principles of asynchrony and C#'s asynchronous functions in detail.

In Chapter 22, we'll revisit multithreading in greater detail, and in Chapter 23, we'll cover the related topic of parallel programming.

Introduction

The most common concurrency scenarios are:

Writing a responsive user interface
In WPF, mobile, and Windows Forms applications, you must run time-consuming tasks concurrently with the code that runs your user interface to maintain responsiveness.

Allowing requests to process simultaneously
On a server, client requests can arrive concurrently and so must be handled in parallel to maintain scalability. If you use ASP.NET, WCF, or Web Services, the .NET Framework does this for you automatically. However, you still need to be aware of shared state (for instance, the effect of using static variables for caching.)

Parallel programming
Code that performs intensive calculations can execute faster on multicore/multiprocessor computers if the workload is divided between cores (Chapter 23 is dedicated to this).

Speculative execution
> On multicore machines, you can sometimes improve performance by predicting something that might need to be done, and then doing it ahead of time. LINQPad uses this technique to speed up the creation of new queries. A variation is to run a number of different algorithms in parallel that all solve the same task. Whichever one finishes first "wins"—this is effective when you can't know ahead of time which algorithm will execute fastest.

The general mechanism by which a program can simultaneously execute code is called *multithreading*. Multithreading is supported by both the CLR and operating system and is a fundamental concept in concurrency. Understanding the basics of threading, and in particular, the effects of threads on *shared state*, is therefore essential.

Threading

A *thread* is an execution path that can proceed independently of others.

Each thread runs within an operating system process, which provides an isolated environment in which a program runs. With a *single-threaded* program, just one thread runs in the process's isolated environment, and so that thread has exclusive access to it. With a *multithreaded* program, multiple threads run in a single process, sharing the same execution environment (memory, in particular). This, in part, is why multithreading is useful: one thread can fetch data in the background, for instance, while another thread displays the data as it arrives. This data is referred to as *shared state*.

Creating a Thread

In Windows Store apps, you cannot create and start threads directly; instead you must do this via tasks (see "Tasks" on page 581). Tasks add a layer of indirection that complicates learning, so the best way to start is with Console applications (or LINQPad) and create threads directly until you're comfortable with how they work.

A *client* program (Console, WPF, Windows Store, or Windows Forms) starts in a single thread that's created automatically by the operating system (the "main" thread). Here it lives out its life as a single-threaded application, unless you do otherwise by creating more threads (directly or indirectly).[1]

You can create and start a new thread by instantiating a `Thread` object and calling its `Start` method. The simplest constructor for `Thread` takes a `ThreadStart` delegate: a parameterless method indicating where execution should begin. For example:

---

1 The CLR creates other threads behind the scenes for garbage collection and finalization.

```
// NB: All samples in this chapter assume the following namespace imports:
using System;
using System.Threading;

class ThreadTest
{
  static void Main()
  {
    Thread t = new Thread (WriteY);         // Kick off a new thread
    t.Start();                              // running WriteY()

    // Simultaneously, do something on the main thread.
    for (int i = 0; i < 1000; i++) Console.Write ("x");
  }

  static void WriteY()
  {
    for (int i = 0; i < 1000; i++) Console.Write ("y");
  }
}

// Typical Output:
xxxxxxxxxxxxxxxxxxxxxyyyyyyyyyyyyyyyyyyyyyyyyyyyyyyyyyyyyyyyyy
xxxxxxxxxxxxxxxxxxxxxxxxxxxxxxxxxxxxxxxxxxxxxyyyyyyyyyyyyyyyyy
yyyyyyyyyyyyyyyyyyyyyyyyyyyyyyyyyyyxxxxxxxxxxxxxxxxxxxxxxxxxxx
xxxxxxxxxxxxxxxxxxxxxxxxxyyyyyyyyyyyyyyyyyyyyyyyyyyyyyyyyyyyyy
yyyyyyyyyyyyxxxxxxxxxxxxxxxxxxxxxxxxxxxxxxxxxxxxxxxxxxxxxxxxxx
...
```

The main thread creates a new thread t on which it runs a method that repeatedly
prints the character *y*. Simultaneously, the main thread repeatedly prints the character *x*, as shown in Figure 14-1. On a single-core computer, the operating system
must allocate "slices" of time to each thread (typically 20 ms in Windows) to simulate concurrency, resulting in repeated blocks of *x* and *y*. On a multicore or multiprocessor machine, the two threads can genuinely execute in parallel (subject to
competition by other active processes on the computer), although you still get
repeated blocks of *x* and *y* in this example because of subtleties in the mechanism by
which Console handles concurrent requests.

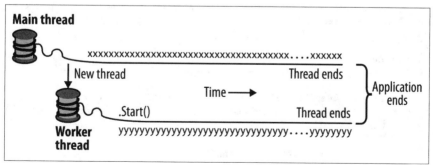

Figure 14-1. Starting a new thread

A thread is said to be *preempted* at the points where its execution is interspersed with the execution of code on another thread. The term often crops up in explaining why something has gone wrong!

Once started, a thread's `IsAlive` property returns `true`, until the point where the thread ends. A thread ends when the delegate passed to the `Thread`'s constructor finishes executing. Once ended, a thread cannot restart.

Each thread has a `Name` property that you can set for the benefit of debugging. This is particularly useful in Visual Studio, since the thread's name is displayed in the Threads Window and Debug Location toolbar. You can set a thread's name just once; attempts to change it later will throw an exception.

The static `Thread.CurrentThread` property gives you the currently executing thread:

```
Console.WriteLine (Thread.CurrentThread.Name);
```

Join and Sleep

You can wait for another thread to end by calling its `Join` method:

```
static void Main()
{
  Thread t = new Thread (Go);
  t.Start();
  t.Join();
  Console.WriteLine ("Thread t has ended!");
}

static void Go() { for (int i = 0; i < 1000; i++) Console.Write ("y"); }
```

This prints "y" 1,000 times, followed by "Thread t has ended!" immediately afterward. You can include a timeout when calling `Join`, either in milliseconds or as a `TimeSpan`. It then returns `true` if the thread ended or `false` if it timed out.

`Thread.Sleep` pauses the current thread for a specified period:

```
Thread.Sleep (TimeSpan.FromHours (1));  // Sleep for 1 hour
Thread.Sleep (500);                     // Sleep for 500 milliseconds
```

`Thread.Sleep(0)` relinquishes the thread's current time slice immediately, voluntarily handing over the CPU to other threads. `Thread.Yield()` does the same thing—except that it relinquishes only to threads running on the *same* processor.

`Sleep(0)` or `Yield` is occasionally useful in production code for advanced performance tweaks. It's also an excellent diagnostic tool for helping to uncover thread safety issues: if inserting `Thread.Yield()` anywhere in your code breaks the program, you almost certainly have a bug.

While waiting on a `Sleep` or `Join`, a thread is *blocked*.

Blocking

A thread is deemed *blocked* when its execution is paused for some reason, such as when Sleeping or waiting for another to end via Join. A blocked thread immediately *yields* its processor time slice, and from then on consumes no processor time until its blocking condition is satisfied. You can test for a thread being blocked via its ThreadState property:

```
bool blocked = (someThread.ThreadState & ThreadState.WaitSleepJoin) != 0;
```

 ThreadState is a flags enum, combining three "layers" of data in a bitwise fashion. Most values, however, are redundant, unused, or deprecated. The following extension method strips a ThreadState to one of four useful values: Unstarted, Running, WaitSleepJoin, and Stopped:

```
public static ThreadState Simplify (this ThreadState ts)
{
   return ts & (ThreadState.Unstarted |
                ThreadState.WaitSleepJoin |
                ThreadState.Stopped);
}
```

The ThreadState property is useful for diagnostic purposes, but unsuitable for synchronization because a thread's state may change in between testing ThreadState and acting on that information.

When a thread blocks or unblocks, the operating system performs a *context switch*. This incurs a small overhead, typically one or two microseconds.

I/O-bound versus compute-bound

An operation that spends most of its time *waiting* for something to happen is called *I/O-bound*—an example is downloading a web page or calling Console.ReadLine. (I/O-bound operations typically involve input or output, but this is not a hard requirement: Thread.Sleep is also deemed I/O-bound.) In contrast, an operation that spends most of its time performing CPU-intensive work is called *compute-bound*.

Blocking versus spinning

An I/O-bound operation works in one of two ways: it either waits *synchronously* on the current thread until the operation is complete (such as Console.ReadLine, Thread.Sleep, or Thread.Join), or operates *asynchronously*, firing a callback when the operation finishes some time later (more on this later).

I/O-bound operations that wait synchronously spend most of their time blocking a thread. They may also "spin" in a loop periodically:

```
while (DateTime.Now < nextStartTime)
   Thread.Sleep (100);
```

Leaving aside that there are better ways to do this (such as timers or signaling constructs), another option is that a thread may spin continuously:

```
while (DateTime.Now < nextStartTime);
```

In general, this is very wasteful on processor time: as far as the CLR and operating system are concerned, the thread is performing an important calculation and so gets allocated resources accordingly. In effect, we've turned what should be an I/O-bound operation into a compute-bound operation.

 There are a couple of nuances with regard spinning versus blocking. First, spinning *very briefly* can be effective when you expect a condition to be satisfied soon (perhaps within a few microseconds) because it avoids the overhead and latency of a context switch. The .NET Framework provides special methods and classes to assist—see "SpinLock and SpinWait" in *http://albahari.com/threading/*.

Second, blocking does not incur a *zero* cost. This is because each thread ties up around 1MB of memory for as long as it lives and causes an ongoing administrative overhead for the CLR and operating system. For this reason, blocking can be troublesome in the context of heavily I/O-bound programs that need to handle hundreds or thousands of concurrent operations. Instead, such programs need to use a callback-based approach, rescinding their thread entirely while waiting. This is (in part) the purpose of the asynchronous patterns that we'll discuss later.

Local Versus Shared State

The CLR assigns each thread its own memory stack so that local variables are kept separate. In the next example, we define a method with a local variable, then call the method simultaneously on the main thread and a newly created thread:

```
static void Main()
{
  new Thread (Go).Start();    // Call Go() on a new thread
  Go();                       // Call Go() on the main thread
}

static void Go()
{
  // Declare and use a local variable - 'cycles'
  for (int cycles = 0; cycles < 5; cycles++) Console.Write ('?');
}
```

A separate copy of the `cycles` variable is created on each thread's memory stack, and so the output is, predictably, 10 question marks.

Threads share data if they have a common reference to the same object instance:

```
class ThreadTest
{
```

```
bool _done;

static void Main()
{
  ThreadTest tt = new ThreadTest();    // Create a common instance
  new Thread (tt.Go).Start();
  tt.Go();
}

void Go()    // Note that this is an instance method
{
    if (!_done) { _done = true; Console.WriteLine ("Done"); }
}
}
```

Because both threads call Go() on the same ThreadTest instance, they share the _done field. This results in "Done" being printed once instead of twice.

Local variables captured by a lambda expression or anonymous delegate are converted by the compiler into fields, and so can also be shared:

```
class ThreadTest
{
  static void Main()
  {
    bool done = false;
    ThreadStart action = () =>
    {
        if (!done) { done = true; Console.WriteLine ("Done"); }
    };
    new Thread (action).Start();
    action();
  }
}
```

Static fields offer another way to share data between threads:

```
class ThreadTest
{
  static bool _done;    // Static fields are shared between all threads
                        // in the same application domain.
  static void Main()
  {
    new Thread (Go).Start();
    Go();
  }

  static void Go()
  {
    if (!_done) { _done = true; Console.WriteLine ("Done"); }
  }
}
```

All three examples illustrate another key concept: that of thread safety (or rather, lack of it!) The output is actually indeterminate: it's possible (though unlikely) that

"Done" could be printed twice. If, however, we swap the order of statements in the Go method, the odds of "Done" being printed twice go up dramatically:

```
static void Go()
{
  if (!_done) { Console.WriteLine ("Done"); _done = true; }
}
```

The problem is that one thread can be evaluating the if statement right as the other thread is executing the WriteLine statement—before it's had a chance to set done to true.

Our example illustrates one of many ways that *shared writable state* can introduce the kind of intermittent errors for which multithreading is notorious. We'll see next how to fix our program with locking; however it's better to avoid shared state altogether where possible. We'll see later how asynchronous programming patterns help with this.

Locking and Thread Safety

Locking and thread safety are large topics. For a full discussion, see "Exclusive Locking" on page 904 and "Locking and Thread Safety" on page 570 in Chapter 22.

We can fix the previous example by obtaining an *exclusive lock* while reading and writing to the shared field. C# provides the lock statement for just this purpose:

```
class ThreadSafe
{
  static bool _done;
  static readonly object _locker = new object();

  static void Main()
  {
    new Thread (Go).Start();
    Go();
  }

  static void Go()
  {
    lock (_locker)
    {
      if (!_done) { Console.WriteLine ("Done"); _done = true; }
    }
  }
}
```

When two threads simultaneously contend a lock (which can be upon any reference-type object, in this case, _locker), one thread waits, or blocks, until the lock becomes available. In this case, it ensures only one thread can enter its code block at a time, and "Done" will be printed just once. Code that's protected in such a manner—from indeterminacy in a multithreaded context—is called *thread-safe*.

Even the act of autoincrementing a variable is not thread-safe: the expression x++ executes on the underlying processor as distinct read-increment-write operations. So, if two threads execute x++ at once outside a lock, the variable may end up getting incremented once rather than twice (or worse, x could be *torn*, ending up with a bitwise-mixture of old and new content, under certain conditions).

Locking is not a silver bullet for thread safety—it's easy to forget to lock around accessing a field, and locking can create problems of its own (such as deadlocking).

A good example of when you might use locking is around accessing a shared in-memory cache for frequently accessed database objects in an ASP.NET application. This kind of application is simple to get right, and there's no chance of deadlocking. We give an example in "Thread Safety in Application Servers" on page 916 in Chapter 22.

Passing Data to a Thread

Sometimes you'll want to pass arguments to the thread's startup method. The easiest way to do this is with a lambda expression that calls the method with the desired arguments:

```
static void Main()
{
  Thread t = new Thread ( () => Print ("Hello from t!") );
  t.Start();
}

static void Print (string message) { Console.WriteLine (message); }
```

With this approach, you can pass in any number of arguments to the method. You can even wrap the entire implementation in a multistatement lambda:

```
new Thread (() =>
{
  Console.WriteLine ("I'm running on another thread!");
  Console.WriteLine ("This is so easy!");
}).Start();
```

Lambda expressions didn't exist prior to C# 3.0. So you might also come across an old-school technique, which is to pass an argument into Thread's Start method:

```
static void Main()
{
  Thread t = new Thread (Print);
  t.Start ("Hello from t!");
}

static void Print (object messageObj)
{
  string message = (string) messageObj;     // We need to cast here
  Console.WriteLine (message);
}
```

This works because Thread's constructor is overloaded to accept either of two delegates:

```
public delegate void ThreadStart();
public delegate void ParameterizedThreadStart (object obj);
```

The limitation of ParameterizedThreadStart is that it accepts only one argument. And because it's of type object, it usually needs to be cast.

Lambda expressions and captured variables

As we saw, a lambda expression is the most convenient and powerful way to pass data to a thread. However, you must be careful about accidentally modifying *captured variables* after starting the thread. For instance, consider the following:

```
for (int i = 0; i < 10; i++)
  new Thread (() => Console.Write (i)).Start();
```

The output is nondeterministic! Here's a typical result:

```
0223557799
```

The problem is that the i variable refers to the *same* memory location throughout the loop's lifetime. Therefore, each thread calls Console.Write on a variable whose value may change as it is running! The solution is to use a temporary variable as follows:

```
for (int i = 0; i < 10; i++)
{
  int temp = i;
  new Thread (() => Console.Write (temp)).Start();
}
```

Each of the digits 0 to 9 is then written exactly once. (The *ordering* is still undefined because threads may start at indeterminate times.)

> This is analogous to the problem we described in "Captured Variables" on page 350 in Chapter 8. The problem is just as much about C#'s rules for capturing variables in for loops as it is about multithreading.
>
> This problem also applies to foreach loops prior to C# 5.

Variable temp is now local to each loop iteration. Therefore, each thread captures a different memory location and there's no problem. We can illustrate the problem in the earlier code more simply with the following example:

```
string text = "t1";
Thread t1 = new Thread ( () => Console.WriteLine (text) );

text = "t2";
Thread t2 = new Thread ( () => Console.WriteLine (text) );

t1.Start(); t2.Start();
```

Because both lambda expressions capture the same text variable, t2 is printed twice.

Exception Handling

Any try/catch/finally blocks in effect when a thread is created are of no relevance to the thread when it starts executing. Consider the following program:

```
public static void Main()
{
  try
  {
    new Thread (Go).Start();
  }
  catch (Exception ex)
  {
    // We'll never get here!
    Console.WriteLine ("Exception!");
  }
}

static void Go() { throw null; }   // Throws a NullReferenceException
```

The try/catch statement in this example is ineffective, and the newly created thread will be encumbered with an unhandled NullReferenceException. This behavior makes sense when you consider that each thread has an independent execution path.

The remedy is to move the exception handler into the Go method:

```
public static void Main()
{
    new Thread (Go).Start();
}

static void Go()
{
  try
  {
    ...
    throw null;    // The NullReferenceException will get caught below
    ...
  }
  catch (Exception ex)
  {
    Typically log the exception, and/or signal another thread
    that we've come unstuck
    ...
  }
}
```

You need an exception handler on all thread entry methods in production applications—just as you do (usually at a higher level, in the execution stack) on your main thread. An unhandled exception causes the whole application to shut down. With an ugly dialog box!

> In writing such exception handling blocks, rarely would you *ignore* the error: typically, you'd log the details of the exception, and then perhaps display a dialog box allowing the user to automatically submit those details to your web server. You then might choose to restart the application, because it's possible that an unexpected exception might leave your program in an invalid state.

Centralized exception handling

In WPF, Windows Store, and Windows Forms applications, you can subscribe to "global" exception handling events, `Application.DispatcherUnhandledException` and `Application.ThreadException`, respectively. These fire after an unhandled exception in any part of your program that's called via the message loop (this amounts to all code that runs on the main thread while the `Application` is active). This is useful as a backstop for logging and reporting bugs (although it won't fire for unhandled exceptions on non-UI threads that you create). Handling these events prevents the program from shutting down, although you may choose to restart the application to avoid the potential corruption of state that can follow from (or that led to) the unhandled exception.

`AppDomain.CurrentDomain.UnhandledException` fires on any unhandled exception on any thread, but since CLR 2.0, the CLR forces application shutdown after your event handler completes. However, you can prevent shutdown by adding the following to your application configuration file:

```
<configuration>
  <runtime>
    <legacyUnhandledExceptionPolicy enabled="1" />
  </runtime>
</configuration>
```

This can be useful in programs that host multiple application domains (Chapter 24): if an unhandled exception occurs in a nondefault application domain, you can destroy and recreate the offending domain rather than restarting the whole application.

Foreground Versus Background Threads

By default, threads you create explicitly are *foreground threads*. Foreground threads keep the application alive for as long as any one of them is running, whereas *background threads* do not. Once all foreground threads finish, the application ends, and any background threads still running abruptly terminate.

> A thread's foreground/background status has no relation to its *priority* (allocation of execution time).

You can query or change a thread's background status using its `IsBackground` property:

```
static void Main (string[] args)
{
  Thread worker = new Thread ( () => Console.ReadLine() );
  if (args.Length > 0) worker.IsBackground = true;
  worker.Start();
}
```

If this program is called with no arguments, the worker thread assumes foreground status and will wait on the `ReadLine` statement for the user to press Enter. Meanwhile, the main thread exits, but the application keeps running because a foreground thread is still alive. On the other hand, if an argument is passed to `Main()`, the worker is assigned background status, and the program exits almost immediately as the main thread ends (terminating the `ReadLine`).

When a process terminates in this manner, any `finally` blocks in the execution stack of background threads are circumvented. If your program employs `finally` (or `using`) blocks to perform cleanup work such as deleting temporary files, you can avoid this by explicitly waiting out such background threads upon exiting an application, either by joining the thread, or with a signaling construct (see "Signaling" on page 576). In either case, you should specify a timeout so you can abandon a renegade thread should it refuse to finish; otherwise your application will fail to close without the user having to enlist help from the Task Manager.

Foreground threads don't require this treatment, but you must take care to avoid bugs that could cause the thread not to end. A common cause for applications failing to exit properly is the presence of active foreground threads.

Thread Priority

A thread's `Priority` property determines how much execution time it gets relative to other active threads in the operating system, on the following scale:

```
enum ThreadPriority { Lowest, BelowNormal, Normal, AboveNormal, Highest }
```

This becomes relevant when multiple threads are simultaneously active. Elevating a thread's priority should be done with care as it can starve other threads. If you want a thread to have higher priority than threads in *other* processes, you must also elevate the process priority using the `Process` class in `System.Diagnostics`:

```
using (Process p = Process.GetCurrentProcess())
  p.PriorityClass = ProcessPriorityClass.High;
```

This can work well for non-UI processes that do minimal work and need low latency (the ability to respond very quickly) in the work they do. With compute-hungry applications (particularly those with a user interface), elevating process priority can starve other processes, slowing down the entire computer.

Signaling

Sometimes you need a thread to wait until receiving notification(s) from other thread(s). This is called *signaling*. The simplest signaling construct is `ManualResetE vent`. Calling `WaitOne` on a `ManualResetEvent` blocks the current thread until another thread "opens" the signal by calling `Set`. In the following example, we start up a thread that waits on a `ManualResetEvent`. It remains blocked for two seconds until the main thread *signals* it:

```
var signal = new ManualResetEvent (false);

new Thread ((() =>
{
  Console.WriteLine ("Waiting for signal...");
  signal.WaitOne();
  signal.Dispose();
  Console.WriteLine ("Got signal!");
}).Start();

Thread.Sleep(2000);
signal.Set();          // "Open" the signal
```

After calling `Set`, the signal remains open; it may be closed again by calling `Reset`.

`ManualResetEvent` is one of several signaling constructs provided by the CLR; we cover all of them in detail in Chapter 22.

Threading in Rich-Client Applications

In WPF, Windows Store, and Windows Forms applications, executing long-running operations on the main thread makes the application unresponsive, because the main thread also processes the message loop which performs rendering and handles keyboard and mouse events.

A popular approach is to start up "worker" threads for time-consuming operations. The code on a worker thread runs a time-consuming operation and then updates the UI when complete. However, all rich-client applications have a threading model whereby UI elements and controls can be accessed only from the thread that created them (typically the main UI thread). Violating this causes either unpredictable behavior or an exception to be thrown.

Hence when you want to update the UI from a worker thread, you must forward the request to the UI thread (the technical term is *marshal*). The low-level way to do this is as follows (later, we'll discuss other solutions which build on these):

- In WPF, call `BeginInvoke` or `Invoke` on the element's `Dispatcher` object.

- In Windows Store apps, call `RunAsync` or `Invoke` on the `Dispatcher` object.

- In Windows Forms, call `BeginInvoke` or `Invoke` on the control.

All of these methods accept a delegate referencing the method you want to run. BeginInvoke/RunAsync work by enqueuing the delegate to the UI thread's *message queue* (the same queue that handles keyboard, mouse, and timer events). Invoke does the same thing, but then blocks until the message has been read and processed by the UI thread. Because of this, Invoke lets you get a return value back from the method. If you don't need a return value, BeginInvoke/RunAsync are preferable in that they don't block the caller and don't introduce the possibility of deadlock (see "Deadlocks" on page 910 in Chapter 22).

You can imagine that when you call Application.Run, the following pseudocode executes:

```
while (!thisApplication.Ended)
{
    wait for something to appear in message queue
    Got something: what kind of message is it?
        Keyboard/mouse message -> fire an event handler
        User BeginInvoke message -> execute delegate
        User Invoke message -> execute delegate & post result
}
```

It's this kind of loop that enables a worker thread to marshal a delegate for execution onto the UI thread.

To demonstrate, suppose that we have a WPF window that contains a text box called txtMessage, whose content we wish a worker thread to update after performing a time-consuming task (which we will simulate by calling Thread.Sleep). Here's how we'd do it:

```
partial class MyWindow : Window
{
    public MyWindow()
    {
        InitializeComponent();
        new Thread (Work).Start();
    }

    void Work()
    {
        Thread.Sleep (5000);            // Simulate time-consuming task
        UpdateMessage ("The answer");
    }

    void UpdateMessage (string message)
    {
        Action action = () => txtMessage.Text = message;
        Dispatcher.BeginInvoke (action);
    }
}
```

Running this results in a responsive window appearing immediately. Five seconds later, it updates the textbox. The code is similar for Windows Forms, except that we call the (Form's) BeginInvoke method instead:

```
void UpdateMessage (string message)
{
  Action action = () => txtMessage.Text = message;
  this.BeginInvoke (action);
}
```

Multiple UI Threads

It's possible to have multiple UI threads if they each own different windows. The main scenario is when you have an application with multiple top-level windows, often called a *Single Document Interface* (SDI) application, such as Microsoft Word. Each SDI window typically shows itself as a separate "application" on the taskbar and is mostly isolated, functionally, from other SDI windows. By giving each such window its own UI thread, each window can be made more responsive with respect to the others.

Synchronization Contexts

In the `System.ComponentModel` namespace, there's an abstract class called `Synchro nizationContext` that enables the generalization of thread marshaling.

The rich-client APIs for mobile and desktop (Windows Store, WPF, and Windows Forms) each define and instantiate `SynchronizationContext` subclasses which you can obtain via the static property `SynchronizationContext.Current` (while running on a UI thread). Capturing this property let you later "post" to UI controls from a worker thread:

```
partial class MyWindow : Window
{
  SynchronizationContext _uiSyncContext;

  public MyWindow()
  {
    InitializeComponent();
    // Capture the synchronization context for the current UI thread:
    _uiSyncContext = SynchronizationContext.Current;
    new Thread (Work).Start();
  }

  void Work()
  {
    Thread.Sleep (5000);              // Simulate time-consuming task
    UpdateMessage ("The answer");
  }

  void UpdateMessage (string message)
  {
    // Marshal the delegate to the UI thread:
    _uiSyncContext.Post (_ => txtMessage.Text = message, null);
  }
}
```

This is useful because the same technique works with all rich-client User Interface APIs (SynchronizationContext also has a ASP.NET specialization where it serves a more subtle role, ensuring that page processing events are processed sequentially following asynchronous operations, and to preserve the HttpContext.)

Calling Post is equivalent to calling BeginInvoke on a Dispatcher or Control; there's also a Send method which is equivalent to Invoke.

 Framework 2.0 introduced the BackgroundWorker class which used the SynchronizationContext class to make the job of managing worker threads in rich-client applications a little easier. BackgroundWorker has since been made redundant by the Tasks and asynchronous functions, which as we'll see, also leverage SynchronizationContext.

The Thread Pool

Whenever you start a thread, a few hundred microseconds are spent organizing such things as a fresh local variable stack. The *thread pool* cuts this overhead by having a pool of pre-created recyclable threads. Thread pooling is essential for efficient parallel programming and fine-grained concurrency; it allows short operations to run without being overwhelmed with the overhead of thread startup.

There are a few things to be wary of when using pooled threads:

- You cannot set the Name of a pooled thread, making debugging more difficult (although you can attach a description when debugging in Visual Studio's Threads window).
- Pooled threads are always *background threads*.
- Blocking pooled threads can degrade performance (see "Hygiene in the thread pool" on page 580).

You are free to change the priority of a pooled thread—it will be restored to normal when released back to the pool.

You can query if you're currently executing on a pooled thread via the property Thread.CurrentThread.IsThreadPoolThread.

Entering the thread pool

The easiest way to explicitly run something on a pooled thread is to use Task.Run (we'll cover this in more detail in the following section):

```
// Task is in System.Threading.Tasks
Task.Run (() => Console.WriteLine ("Hello from the thread pool"));
```

As tasks didn't exist prior to Framework 4.0, a common alternative is to call Thread Pool.QueueUserWorkItem:

```
ThreadPool.QueueUserWorkItem (notUsed => Console.WriteLine ("Hello"));
```

The following use the thread pool implicitly:

- WCF, Remoting, ASP.NET, and ASMX Web Services application servers
- `System.Timers.Timer` and `System.Threading.Timer`
- The parallel programming constructs that we describe in Chapter 23
- The (now redundant) `BackgroundWorker` class
- Asynchronous delegates (also now redundant)

Hygiene in the thread pool

The thread pool serves another function, which is to ensure that a temporary excess of compute-bound work does not cause CPU *oversubscription*. Oversubscription is the condition of there being more active threads than CPU cores, with the operating system having to time-slice threads. Oversubscription hurts performance because time-slicing requires expensive context switches and can invalidate the CPU caches that have become essential in delivering performance to modern processors.

The CLR avoids oversubscription in the thread pool by queuing tasks and throttling their startup. It begins by running as many concurrent tasks as there are hardware cores, and then tunes the level of concurrency via a hill-climbing algorithm, continually adjusting the workload in a particular direction. If throughput improves, it continues in the same direction (otherwise it reverses). This ensures that it always tracks the optimal performance curve—even in the face of competing process activity on the computer.

The CLR's strategy works best if two conditions are met:

- Work items are mostly short-running (<250 ms, or ideally <100 ms), so that the CLR has plenty of opportunities to measure and adjust.
- Jobs that spend most of their time blocked do not dominate the pool.

Blocking is troublesome because it gives the CLR the false idea that it's loading up the CPU. The CLR is smart enough to detect and compensate (by injecting more threads into the pool), although this can make the pool vulnerable to subsequent oversubscription. It also may introduce latency, as the CLR throttles the rate at which it injects new threads, particularly early in an application's life (more so on client operating systems where it favors lower resource consumption).

Maintaining good hygiene in the thread pool is particularly relevant when you want to fully utilize the CPU (e.g., via the parallel programming APIs in Chapter 23).

Tasks

A thread is a low-level tool for creating concurrency, and as such it has limitations. In particular:

- While it's easy to pass data into a thread that you start, there's no easy way to get a "return value" back from a thread that you Join. You have to set up some kind of shared field. And if the operation throws an exception, catching and propagating that exception is equally painful.

- You can't tell a thread to start something else when it's finished; instead you must Join it (blocking your own thread in the process).

These limitations discourage fine-grained concurrency; in other words, they make it hard to compose larger concurrent operations by combining smaller ones (something essential for the asynchronous programming that we'll look at in following sections). This in turn leads to greater reliance on manual synchronization (locking, signaling, and so on) and the problems that go with it.

The direct use of threads also has performance implications that we discussed in "The Thread Pool" on page 579. And should you need to run hundreds or thousands of concurrent I/O-bound operations, a thread-based approach consumes hundreds or thousands of MB of memory purely in thread overhead.

The Task class helps with all of these problems. Compared to a thread, a Task is higher-level abstraction—it represents a concurrent operation that may or may not be backed by a thread. Tasks are *compositional* (you can chain them together through the use of *continuations*). They can use the *thread pool* to lessen startup latency, and with a TaskCompletionSource, they can leverage a callback approach that avoids threads altogether while waiting on I/O-bound operations.

The Task types were introduced in Framework 4.0 as part of the parallel programming library. However they have since been enhanced (through the use of *awaiters*) to play equally well in more general concurrency scenarios and are backing types for C#'s asynchronous functions.

 In this section, we'll ignore the features of tasks that are aimed specifically at parallel programming and cover them instead in Chapter 23.

Starting a Task

From Framework 4.5, the easiest way to start a Task backed by a thread is with the static method Task.Run (the Task class is in the System.Threading.Tasks namespace). Simply pass in an Action delegate:

```
Task.Run (() => Console.WriteLine ("Foo"));
```

The `Task.Run` method was introduced in Framework 4.5. In Framework 4.0, you can accomplish the same thing by calling `Task.Factory.StartNew`. (The former is mostly a shortcut for the latter.)

 Tasks use pooled threads by default, which are background threads. This means that when the main thread ends, so do any tasks that you create. Hence, to run these examples from a Console application, you must block the main thread after starting the task (for instance, by `Waiting` the task or by calling `Console.ReadLine`):

```
static void Main()
{
  Task.Run (() => Console.WriteLine ("Foo"));
  Console.ReadLine();
}
```

In the book's LINQPad companion samples, `Console.Read Line` is omitted because the LINQPad process keeps background threads alive.

Calling `Task.Run` in this manner is similar to starting a thread as follows (except for the thread pooling implications that we'll discuss shortly):

```
new Thread (() => Console.WriteLine ("Foo")).Start();
```

`Task.Run` returns a `Task` object that we can use to monitor its progress, rather like a `Thread` object. (Notice, however, that we didn't call `Start` after calling `Task.Run` because this method creates "hot" tasks; you can instead use `Task`'s constructor to create "cold" tasks, although this is rarely done in practice.)

You can track a task's execution status via its `Status` property.

Wait

Calling `Wait` on a task blocks until it completes and is the equivalent of calling `Join` on a thread:

```
Task task = Task.Run (() =>
{
  Thread.Sleep (2000);
  Console.WriteLine ("Foo");
});
Console.WriteLine (task.IsCompleted);  // False
task.Wait();  // Blocks until task is complete
```

`Wait` lets you optionally specify a timeout and a cancellation token to end the wait early (see "Cancellation" on page 610).

Long-running tasks

By default, the CLR runs tasks on pooled threads, which is ideal for short-running compute-bound work. For longer-running and blocking operations (such as our preceding example), you can prevent use of a pooled thread as follows:

```
Task task = Task.Factory.StartNew (() => ...,
                        TaskCreationOptions.LongRunning);
```

Running *one* long-running task on a pooled thread won't cause trouble; it's when you run multiple long-running tasks in parallel (particularly ones that block) that performance can suffer. And in that case, there are usually better solutions than TaskCreationOptions.LongRunning:

- If the tasks are I/O-bound, TaskCompletionSource and *asynchronous functions* let you implement concurrency with callbacks (continuations) instead of threads.

- If the tasks are compute-bound, a *producer/consumer queue* lets you throttle the concurrency for those tasks, avoiding starvation for other threads and processes (see "Writing a Producer/Consumer Queue" on page 984 in Chapter 23).

Returning values

Task has a generic subclass called Task<TResult> that allows a task to emit a return value. You can obtain a Task<TResult> by calling Task.Run with a Func<TResult> delegate (or a compatible lambda expression) instead of an Action:

```
Task<int> task = Task.Run (() => { Console.WriteLine ("Foo"); return 3; });
// ...
```

You can obtain the result later by querying the Result property. If the task hasn't yet finished, accessing this property will block the current thread until the task finishes:

```
int result = task.Result;      // Blocks if not already finished
Console.WriteLine (result);    // 3
```

In the following example, we create a task that uses LINQ to count the number of prime numbers in the first three million (+2) integers:

```
Task<int> primeNumberTask = Task.Run (() =>
  Enumerable.Range (2, 3000000).Count (n =>
    Enumerable.Range (2, (int)Math.Sqrt(n)-1).All (i => n % i > 0)));

Console.WriteLine ("Task running...");
Console.WriteLine ("The answer is " + primeNumberTask.Result);
```

This writes "Task running...", and then a few seconds later, writes the answer of 216815.

Task<TResult> can be thought of as a "future," in that it encapsulates a Result that becomes available later in time.

Interestingly, when Task and Task<TResult> first debuted in an early CTP, the latter was actually called Future<TResult>.

Exceptions

Unlike with threads, tasks conveniently propagate exceptions. So, if the code in your task throws an unhandled exception (in other words, if your task *faults*), that exception is automatically rethrown to whoever calls Wait()—or accesses the Result property of a Task<TResult>:

```
// Start a Task that throws a NullReferenceException:
Task task = Task.Run (() => { throw null; });
try
{
  task.Wait();
}
catch (AggregateException aex)
{
  if (aex.InnerException is NullReferenceException)
    Console.WriteLine ("Null!");
  else
    throw;
}
```

(The CLR wraps the exception in an AggregateException in order to play well with parallel programming scenarios; we discuss this in Chapter 23.)

You can test for a faulted task without rethrowing the exception via the IsFaulted and IsCanceled properties of the Task. If both properties return false, no error occurred; if IsCanceled is true, an OperationCanceledException was thrown for that task (see "Cancellation" on page 610); if IsFaulted is true, another type of exception was thrown, and the Exception property will indicate the error.

Exceptions and autonomous tasks

With autonomous "set-and-forget" tasks (those for which you don't rendezvous via Wait() or Result or a continuation that does the same), it's good practice to explicitly exception-handle the task code to avoid silent failure, just as you would with a thread.

Unhandled exceptions on autonomous tasks are called *unobserved exceptions*, and in CLR 4.0, they would actually terminate your program (the CLR would rethrow the exception on the finalizer thread when the task dropped out of scope and was garbage collected). This was helpful in indicating that a problem had occurred that you might not have been aware of; however the timing of the error could be deceptive in that the garbage collector can lag significantly behind the offending task. Hence, when it was discovered that this behavior complicated certain patterns of asynchrony (see "Parallelism" on page 604 and "WhenAll" on page 615), it was dropped in CLR 4.5.

Ignoring exceptions is fine when an exception solely indicates a failure to obtain a result that you're no longer interested in. For example, if a user cancels a request to download a web page, we wouldn't care if turns out that the web page didn't exist.

Ignoring exceptions is problematic when an exception indicates a bug in your program, for two reasons:

- The bug may have left your program in an invalid state.

- More exceptions may occur later as a result of the bug, and failure to log the initial error can make diagnosis difficult.

You can subscribe to unobserved exceptions at a global level via the static event `Task Scheduler.UnobservedTaskException`; handling this event and logging the error can make good sense.

There are a couple of interesting nuances on what counts as unobserved:

- Tasks waited upon with a timeout will generate an unobserved exception if the faults occurs *after* the timeout interval.

- The act of checking a task's `Exception` property after it has faulted makes the exception "observed."

Continuations

A continuation says to a task, "When you've finished, continue by doing something else." A continuation is usually implemented by a callback that executes once upon completion of an operation. There are two ways to attach a continuation to a task. The first was introduced in Framework 4.5 and is particularly significant because it's used by C#'s asynchronous functions, as we'll see soon. We can demonstrate it with the prime number counting task that we wrote a short while ago in "Returning values" on page 583:

```
Task<int> primeNumberTask = Task.Run (() =>
  Enumerable.Range (2, 3000000).Count (n =>
    Enumerable.Range (2, (int)Math.Sqrt(n)-1).All (i => n % i > 0)));

var awaiter = primeNumberTask.GetAwaiter();
awaiter.OnCompleted (() =>
{
  int result = awaiter.GetResult();
  Console.WriteLine (result);       // Writes result
});
```

Calling `GetAwaiter` on the task returns an *awaiter* object whose `OnCompleted` method tells the *antecedent* task (`primeNumberTask`) to execute a delegate when it finishes (or faults). It's valid to attach a continuation to an already-completed task, in which case the continuation will be scheduled to execute right away.

 An *awaiter* is any object that exposes the two methods that we've just seen (OnCompleted and GetResult), and a Boolean property called IsCompleted. There's no interface or base class to unify all of these members (although OnCompleted is part of the interface INotifyCompletion). We'll explain the significance of the pattern in "Asynchronous Functions in C#" on page 594.

If an antecedent task faults, the exception is rethrown when the continuation code calls awaiter.GetResult(). Rather than calling GetResult, we could simply access the Result property of the antecedent. The benefit of calling GetResult is that if the antecedent faults, the exception is thrown directly without being wrapped in Aggre gateException, allowing for simpler and cleaner catch blocks.

For nongeneric tasks, GetResult() has a void return value. Its useful function is then solely to rethrow exceptions.

If a synchronization context is present, OnCompleted automatically captures it and posts the continuation to that context. This is very useful in rich-client applications, as it bounces the continuation back to the UI thread. In writing libraries, however, it's not usually desirable because the relatively expensive UI-thread-bounce should occur just once upon leaving the library, rather than between method calls. Hence you can defeat it the ConfigureAwait method:

```
var awaiter = primeNumberTask.ConfigureAwait (false).GetAwaiter();
```

If no synchronization context is present—or you use ConfigureAwait(false)—the continuation will (in general) execute on the same thread as the antecedent, avoiding unnecessary overhead.

The other way to attach a continuation is by calling the task's ContinueWith method:

```
primeNumberTask.ContinueWith (antecedent =>
{
  int result = antecedent.Result;
  Console.WriteLine (result);          // Writes 123
});
```

ContinueWith itself returns a Task, which is useful if you want to attach further continuations. However, you must deal directly with AggregateException if the task faults and write extra code to marshal the continuation in UI applications (see "Task Schedulers" on page 977 in Chapter 23). And in non-UI contexts, you must specify TaskContinuationOptions.ExecuteSynchronously if you want the continuation to execute on the same thread; otherwise it will bounce to the thread pool. ContinueWith is particularly useful in parallel programming scenarios; we cover it in detail in "Continuations" on page 585 in Chapter 23.

TaskCompletionSource

We've seen how `Task.Run` creates a task that runs a delegate on a pooled (or non-pooled) thread. Another way to create a task is with `TaskCompletionSource`.

`TaskCompletionSource` lets you create a task out of any operation that starts and finishes some time later. It works by giving you a "slave" task that you manually drive—by indicating when the operation finishes or faults. This is ideal for I/O-bound work: you get all the benefits of tasks (with their ability to propagate return values, exceptions, and continuations) without blocking a thread for the duration of the operation.

To use `TaskCompletionSource`, you simply instantiate the class. It exposes a `Task` property that returns a task upon which you can wait and attach continuations—just as with any other task. The task, however, is controlled entirely by the `TaskCompletionSource` object via the following methods:

```
public class TaskCompletionSource<TResult>
{
  public void SetResult (TResult result);
  public void SetException (Exception exception);
  public void SetCanceled();

  public bool TrySetResult (TResult result);
  public bool TrySetException (Exception exception);
  public bool TrySetCanceled();
  public bool TrysetCanceled (CancellationToken cancellationToken);
  ...
}
```

Calling any of these methods *signals* the task, putting it into a completed, faulted, or canceled state (we'll cover the latter in the section "Cancellation" on page 610). You're supposed to call one of these methods exactly once: if called again, `SetResult`, `SetException`, or `SetCanceled` will throw an exception, whereas the `Try*` methods return `false`.

The following example prints 42 after waiting for five seconds:

```
var tcs = new TaskCompletionSource<int>();

new Thread (() => { Thread.Sleep (5000); tcs.SetResult (42); })
  { IsBackground = true }
  .Start();

Task<int> task = tcs.Task;            // Our "slave" task.
Console.WriteLine (task.Result);      // 42
```

With `TaskCompletionSource`, we can write our own `Run` method:

```
Task<TResult> Run<TResult> (Func<TResult> function)
{
  var tcs = new TaskCompletionSource<TResult>();
  new Thread (() =>
  {
```

```
      try { tcs.SetResult (function()); }
      catch (Exception ex) { tcs.SetException (ex); }
    }).Start();
    return tcs.Task;
  }
  ...
  Task<int> task = Run (() => { Thread.Sleep (5000); return 42; });
```

Calling this method is equivalent to calling `Task.Factory.StartNew` with the `Task CreationOptions.LongRunning` option to request a nonpooled thread.

The real power of `TaskCompletionSource` is in creating tasks that don't tie up threads. For instance, consider a task that waits for five seconds and then returns the number 42. We can write this without a thread by using the `Timer` class, which with the help of the CLR (and in turn, the operating system) fires an event in x milliseconds (we revisit timers in Chapter 22):

```
Task<int> GetAnswerToLife()
{
  var tcs = new TaskCompletionSource<int>();
  // Create a timer that fires once in 5000 ms:
  var timer = new System.Timers.Timer (5000) { AutoReset = false };
  timer.Elapsed += delegate { timer.Dispose(); tcs.SetResult (42); };
  timer.Start();
  return tcs.Task;
}
```

Hence our method returns a task that completes five seconds later, with a result of 42. By attaching a continuation to the task, we can write its result without blocking *any* thread:

```
var awaiter = GetAnswerToLife().GetAwaiter();
awaiter.OnCompleted (() => Console.WriteLine (awaiter.GetResult()));
```

We could make this more useful and turn it into a general-purpose `Delay` method by parameterizing the delay time and getting rid of the return value. This means having it return a `Task` instead of a `Task<int>`. However, there's no nongeneric version of `TaskCompletionSource`, which means we can't directly create a nongeneric `Task`. The workaround is simple: since `Task<TResult>` derives from `Task`, we create a `TaskCompletionSource<anything>` and then implicitly convert the `Task<any thing>` that it gives you into a `Task`, like this:

```
var tcs = new TaskCompletionSource<object>();
Task task = tcs.Task;
```

Now we can write our general-purpose `Delay` method:

```
Task Delay (int milliseconds)
{
  var tcs = new TaskCompletionSource<object>();
  var timer = new System.Timers.Timer (milliseconds) { AutoReset = false };
  timer.Elapsed += delegate { timer.Dispose(); tcs.SetResult (null); };
  timer.Start();
```

```
        return tcs.Task;
    }
```

Here's how we can use it to write "42" after five seconds:

```
Delay (5000).GetAwaiter().OnCompleted (() => Console.WriteLine (42));
```

Our use of `TaskCompletionSource` without a thread means that a thread is engaged only when the continuation starts, five seconds later. We can demonstrate this by starting 10,000 of these operations at once without error or excessive resource consumption:

```
for (int i = 0; i < 10000; i++)
    Delay (5000).GetAwaiter().OnCompleted (() => Console.WriteLine (42));
```

 Timers fire their callbacks on pooled threads, so after 5 seconds, the thread pool will receive 10,000 requests to call `SetResult(null)` on a `TaskCompletionSource`. If the requests arrive faster than they can be processed, the thread pool will respond by enqueuing and then processing them at the optimum level of parallelism for the CPU. This is ideal if the thread-bound jobs are short-running, which is true in this case: the thread-bound job is merely the call to `SetResult` plus either the action of posting the continuation to the synchronization context (in a UI application) or otherwise the continuation itself (`Console.WriteLine(42)`).

Task.Delay

The `Delay` method that we just wrote is sufficiently useful that it's available as a static method on the `Task` class:

```
Task.Delay (5000).GetAwaiter().OnCompleted (() => Console.WriteLine (42));
```

or:

```
Task.Delay (5000).ContinueWith (ant => Console.WriteLine (42));
```

`Task.Delay` is the *asynchronous* equivalent of `Thread.Sleep`.

Principles of Asynchrony

In demonstrating `TaskCompletionSource`, we ended up writing *asynchronous* methods. In this section, we'll define exactly what asynchronous operations are and explain how this leads to asynchronous programming.

Synchronous Versus Asynchronous Operations

A *synchronous operation* does its work *before* returning to the caller.

An *asynchronous operation* does (most or all of) its work *after* returning to the caller.

The majority of methods that you write and call are synchronous. An example is `List<T>.Add` , or `Console.WriteLine`, or `Thread.Sleep`. Asynchronous methods are less common and initiate *concurrency* because work continues in parallel to the caller. Asynchronous methods typically return quickly (or immediately) to the caller; hence they are also called *nonblocking methods.*

Most of the asynchronous methods that we've seen so far can be described as general-purpose methods:

- `Thread.Start`
- `Task.Run`
- Methods that attach continuations to tasks

In addition, some of the methods that we discussed in "Synchronization Contexts" on page 578 (`Dispatcher.BeginInvoke`, `Control.BeginInvoke` and `Synchroniza tionContext.Post`) are asynchronous, as are the methods that we wrote in the section, "TaskCompletionSource" on page 587, including `Delay`.

What is Asynchronous Programming?

The principle of asynchronous programming is that you write long-running (or potentially long-running) functions asynchronously. This is in contrast to the conventional approach of writing long-running functions synchronously and then calling those functions from a new thread or task to introduce concurrency as required.

The difference with the asynchronous approach is that concurrency is initiated *inside* the long-running function, rather than from *outside* the function. This has two benefits:

- I/O-bound concurrency can be implemented without tying up threads (as we demonstrated in "TaskCompletionSource" on page 587), improving scalability and efficiency.
- Rich-client applications end up with less code on worker threads, simplifying thread safety.

This, in turn, leads to two distinct uses for asynchronous programming. The first is writing (typically server-side) applications that deal efficiently with a lot of concurrent I/O. The challenge here is not thread-*safety* (as there's usually minimal shared state) but thread *efficiency*; in particular, not consuming a thread per network request. Hence in this context, it's only I/O-bound operations that benefit from asynchrony.

The second use is to simplify thread-safety in rich-client applications. This is particularly relevant as a program grows in size, because to deal with complexity, we typically refactor larger methods into smaller ones, resulting in chains of methods that call one another (*call graphs*).

With a traditional *synchronous* call graph, if any operation within the graph is long-running, we must run the entire call graph on a worker thread to maintain a responsive UI. Hence, we end up with a single concurrent operation that spans many methods (*course-grained concurrency*), and this requires considering thread-safety for every method in the graph.

With an *asynchronous* call graph, we need not start a thread until it's actually needed, typically low in the graph (or not at all in the case of I/O-bound operations). All other methods can run entirely on the UI thread, with much-simplified thread-safety. This results in *fine-grained concurrency*—a sequence of small concurrent operations, in between which execution bounces to the UI thread.

To benefit from this, both I/O- and compute-bound operations need to be written asynchronously; a good rule of thumb is to include anything that might take longer than 50 ms.

(On the flipside, *excessively* fine-grained asynchrony can hurt performance, because asynchronous operations incur an overhead—see "Optimizations" on page 607.)

In this chapter, we'll focus mostly on the rich-client scenario, which is the more complex of the two. In Chapter 16, we give two examples that illustrate the I/O-bound scenario (see "Concurrency with TCP" on page 707 and "Writing an HTTP Server" on page 698).

The Windows store (and Silverlight) .NET profiles encourage asynchronous programming to the point where synchronous versions of some long-running methods are not even exposed. Instead, you get asynchronous methods that return tasks (or objects that can be converted into tasks via the AsTask extension method).

Asynchronous Programming and Continuations

Tasks are ideally suited to asynchronous programming because they support continuations which are essential for asynchrony (consider the Delay method that we wrote previously in "TaskCompletionSource" on page 587). In writing Delay, we used TaskCompletionSource, which is a standard way to implement "bottom-level" I/O-bound asynchronous methods.

For compute-bound methods, we use Task.Run to initiate thread-bound concurrency. Simply by returning the task to the caller, we create an asynchronous method. What distinguishes asynchronous programming is that we aim to do so lower in the call graph, so that in rich-client applications, higher-level methods can remain on the UI thread and access controls and shared state without thread-safety issues. To illustrate, consider the following method which computes and counts prime numbers, using all available cores (we discuss ParallelEnumerable in Chapter 23):

```
int GetPrimesCount (int start, int count)
{
  return
```

```
        ParallelEnumerable.Range (start, count).Count (n =>
          Enumerable.Range (2, (int)Math.Sqrt(n)-1).All (i => n % i > 0));
    }
```

The details of how this works are unimportant; what matters is that it can take a while to run. We can demonstrate this by writing another method to call it:

```
void DisplayPrimeCounts()
{
  for (int i = 0; i < 10; i++)
    Console.WriteLine (GetPrimesCount (i*1000000 + 2, 1000000) +
      " primes between " + (i*1000000) + " and " + ((i+1)*1000000-1));
  Console.WriteLine ("Done!");
}
```

with the following output:

```
78498 primes between 0 and 999999
70435 primes between 1000000 and 1999999
67883 primes between 2000000 and 2999999
66330 primes between 3000000 and 3999999
65367 primes between 4000000 and 4999999
64336 primes between 5000000 and 5999999
63799 primes between 6000000 and 6999999
63129 primes between 7000000 and 7999999
62712 primes between 8000000 and 8999999
62090 primes between 9000000 and 9999999
```

Now we have a *call graph*, with DisplayPrimeCounts calling GetPrimesCount. The former uses Console.WriteLine for simplicity, although in reality, it would more likely be updating UI controls in a rich-client application, as we'll demonstrate later. We can initiate course-grained concurrency for this call graph as follows:

```
Task.Run (() => DisplayPrimeCounts());
```

With a fine-grained asynchronous approach, we instead start by writing an asynchronous version of GetPrimesCount:

```
Task<int> GetPrimesCountAsync (int start, int count)
{
  return Task.Run (() =>
    ParallelEnumerable.Range (start, count).Count (n =>
      Enumerable.Range (2, (int) Math.Sqrt(n)-1).All (i => n % i > 0)));
}
```

Why Language Support Is Important

Now we must modify DisplayPrimeCounts so that it calls GetPrimesCountAsync. This is where C#'s new await and async keywords come into play, because to do so otherwise is trickier than it sounds. If we simply modify the loop as follows:

```
for (int i = 0; i < 10; i++)
{
  var awaiter = GetPrimesCountAsync (i*1000000 + 2, 1000000).GetAwaiter();
  awaiter.OnCompleted (() =>
    Console.WriteLine (awaiter.GetResult() + " primes between... "));
```

```
}
Console.WriteLine ("Done");
```

then the loop will rapidly spin through 10 iterations (the methods being nonblock-ing), and all 10 operations will execute in parallel (followed by a premature "Done").

 Executing these tasks in parallel is undesirable in this case because their internal implementations are already parallel-ized; it will only make us wait longer to see the first results (and muck up the ordering).

There is a much more common reason, however, for needing to *serialize* the execution of tasks, which is that Task B depends on the result of Task A. For example, in fetching a web page, a DNS lookup must precede the HTTP request.

To get them running sequentially, we must trigger the next loop iteration from the continuation itself. This means eliminating the for loop and resorting to a recursive call in the continuation:

```
void DisplayPrimeCounts()
{
  DisplayPrimeCountsFrom (0);
}

void DisplayPrimeCountsFrom (int i)
{
  var awaiter = GetPrimesCountAsync (i*1000000 + 2, 1000000).GetAwaiter();
  awaiter.OnCompleted (() =>
  {
    Console.WriteLine (awaiter.GetResult() + " primes between...");
    if (i++ < 10) DisplayPrimeCountsFrom (i);
    else Console.WriteLine ("Done");
  });
}
```

It gets even worse if we want to make DisplayPrimesCount *itself* asynchronous, returning a task that it signals upon completion. To accomplish this requires creat-ing a TaskCompletionSource:

```
Task DisplayPrimeCountsAsync()
{
  var machine = new PrimesStateMachine();
  machine.DisplayPrimeCountsFrom (0);
  return machine.Task;
}

class PrimesStateMachine
{
  TaskCompletionSource<object> _tcs = new TaskCompletionSource<object>();
  public Task Task { get { return _tcs.Task; } }

  public void DisplayPrimeCountsFrom (int i)
  {
    var awaiter = GetPrimesCountAsync (i*1000000+2, 1000000).GetAwaiter();
```

```
    awaiter.OnCompleted (() =>
    {
      Console.WriteLine (awaiter.GetResult());
      if (i++ < 10) DisplayPrimeCountsFrom (i);
      else { Console.WriteLine ("Done"); _tcs.SetResult (null); }
    });
  }
}
```

Fortunately, C#'s *asynchronous functions* do all of this work for us. With the `async` and `await` keywords, we need only write this:

```
async Task DisplayPrimeCountsAsync()
{
  for (int i = 0; i < 10; i++)
    Console.WriteLine (await GetPrimesCountAsync (i*1000000 + 2, 1000000) +
      " primes between " + (i*1000000) + " and " + ((i+1)*1000000-1));
  Console.WriteLine ("Done!");
}
```

Hence `async` and `await` are essential for implementing asynchrony without excessive complexity. Let's now see how these keywords work.

Another way of looking at the problem is that imperative looping constructs (`for`, `foreach` and so on), do not mix well with continuations because they rely on the *current local state* of the method ("How many more times is this loop going to run?").

While the `async` and `await` keywords offer one solution, it's sometimes possible to solve it in another way by replacing the imperative looping constructs with the *functional* equivalent (in other words, LINQ queries). This is the basis of *Reactive Framework* (Rx) and can be a good option when you want to execute query operators over the result—or combine multiple sequences. The price to pay is that to avoid blocking, Rx operates over *push*-based sequences, which can be conceptually tricky.

Asynchronous Functions in C#

C# 5.0 introduced the `async` and `await` keywords. These keywords let you write asynchronous code that has the same structure and simplicity as synchronous code and eliminates the "plumbing" of asynchronous programming.

Awaiting

The `await` keyword simplifies the attaching of continuations. Starting with a basic scenario, the compiler expands:

```
var result = await expression;
statement(s);
```

into something functionally similar to:

```
var awaiter = expression.GetAwaiter();
awaiter.OnCompleted (() =>
{
  var result = awaiter.GetResult();
  statement(s);
});
```

The compiler also emits code to short-circuit the continuation in case of synchronous completion (see "Optimizations" on page 607) and to handle various nuances that we'll pick up in later sections.

To demonstrate, let's revisit the asynchronous method that we wrote previously that computes and counts prime numbers:

```
Task<int> GetPrimesCountAsync (int start, int count)
{
  return Task.Run (() =>
    ParallelEnumerable.Range (start, count).Count (n =>
      Enumerable.Range (2, (int)Math.Sqrt(n)-1).All (i => n % i > 0)));
}
```

With the await keyword, we can call it as follows:

```
int result = await GetPrimesCountAsync (2, 1000000);
Console.WriteLine (result);
```

In order to compile, we need to add the async modifier to the containing method:

```
async void DisplayPrimesCount()
{
  int result = await GetPrimesCountAsync (2, 1000000);
  Console.WriteLine (result);
}
```

The async modifier tells the compiler to treat await as a keyword rather than an identifier should an ambiguity arise within that method (this ensures that code written prior to C# 5 that might use await as an identifier will still compile without error). The async modifier can be applied only to methods (and lambda expressions) that return void or (as we'll see later) a Task or Task<TResult>.

The async modifier is similar to the unsafe modifier in that it has no effect on a method's signature or public metadata; it affects only what happens *inside* the method. For this reason, it makes no sense to use async in an interface. However it is legal, for instance, to introduce async when overriding a non-async virtual method, as long as you keep the signature the same.

Methods with the async modifier are called *asynchronous functions*, because they themselves are typically asynchronous. To see why, let's look at how execution proceeds through an asynchronous function.

Upon encountering an await expression, execution (normally) returns to the caller —rather like with yield return in an iterator. But before returning, the runtime attaches a continuation to the awaited task, ensuring that when the task completes, execution jumps back into the method and continues where it left off. If the task faults, its exception is rethrown, otherwise its return value is assigned to the await expression. We can summarize everything we just said by looking at the logical expansion of the preceding asynchronous method:

```
void DisplayPrimesCount()
{
  var awaiter = GetPrimesCountAsync (2, 1000000).GetAwaiter();
  awaiter.OnCompleted (() =>
  {
    int result = awaiter.GetResult();
    Console.WriteLine (result);
  });
}
```

The expression upon which you await is typically a task; however any object with a GetAwaiter method that returns an *awaitable object* (implementing INotifyComple tion.OnCompleted and with an appropriately typed GetResult method and a bool IsCompleted property) will satisfy the compiler.

Notice that our await expression evaluates to an int type; this is because the expression that we awaited was a Task<int> (whose GetAwaiter().GetResult() method returns an int).

Awaiting a nongeneric task is legal and generates a void expression:

```
await Task.Delay (5000);
Console.WriteLine ("Five seconds passed!");
```

Capturing local state

The real power of await expressions is that they can appear almost anywhere in code. Specifically, an await expression can appear in place of any expression (within an asynchronous function) except for inside a lock expression, unsafe context or an executable's entry point (main method).

In the following example, we await inside a loop:

```
async void DisplayPrimeCounts()
{
  for (int i = 0; i < 10; i++)
    Console.WriteLine (await GetPrimesCountAsync (i*1000000+2, 1000000));
}
```

Upon first executing GetPrimesCount, execution returns to the caller by virtue of the await expression. When the method completes (or faults), execution resumes where it left off, with the values of local variables and loop counters preserved.

Without the await keyword, the simplest equivalent might be the example we wrote in "Why Language Support Is Important" on page 592. The compiler, however, takes the more general strategy of refactoring such methods into state machines (rather like it does with iterators).

The compiler relies on continuations (via the awaiter pattern) to resume execution after an await expression. This means that if running on the UI thread of a rich-client application, the synchronization context ensures execution resumes on the same thread. Otherwise, execution resumes on whatever thread the task finished on. The change of thread does not affect the order of execution and is of little consequence unless you're somehow relying on thread affinity, perhaps through the use of thread-local storage (see "Thread-Local Storage" on page 936 in Chapter 22). It's rather like touring a city and hailing taxis to get from one destination to another. With a synchronization context, you'll always get the same taxi; with no synchronization context, you'll usually get a different taxi each time. In either case, though, the journey is the same.

Awaiting in a UI

We can demonstrate asynchronous functions in a more practical context by writing a simple UI that remains responsive while calling a compute-bound method. Let's start with a synchronous solution:

```
class TestUI : Window
{
  Button _button = new Button { Content = "Go" };
  TextBlock _results = new TextBlock();

  public TestUI()
  {
    var panel = new StackPanel();
    panel.Children.Add (_button);
    panel.Children.Add (_results);
    Content = panel;
    _button.Click += (sender, args) => Go();
  }

  void Go()
  {
    for (int i = 1; i < 5; i++)
      _results.Text += GetPrimesCount (i * 1000000, 1000000) +
        " primes between " + (i*1000000) + " and " + ((i+1)*1000000-1) +
        Environment.NewLine;
  }

  int GetPrimesCount (int start, int count)
  {
    return ParallelEnumerable.Range (start, count).Count (n =>
      Enumerable.Range (2, (int) Math.Sqrt(n)-1).All (i => n % i > 0));
  }
}
```

Upon pressing the "Go" button, the application becomes unresponsive for the time it takes to execute the compute-bound code. There are two steps in asynchronizing this; the first is to switch to the asynchronous version of GetPrimesCount that we used in previous examples:

```
Task<int> GetPrimesCountAsync (int start, int count)
{
  return Task.Run (() =>
    ParallelEnumerable.Range (start, count).Count (n =>
      Enumerable.Range (2, (int) Math.Sqrt(n)-1).All (i => n % i > 0)));
}
```

The second step is to modify Go to call GetPrimesCountAsync:

```
async void Go()
{
  _button.IsEnabled = false;
  for (int i = 1; i < 5; i++)
    _results.Text += await GetPrimesCountAsync (i * 1000000, 1000000) +
      " primes between " + (i*1000000) + " and " + ((i+1)*1000000-1) +
      Environment.NewLine;
  _button.IsEnabled = true;
}
```

This illustrates the simplicity of programming with asynchronous functions: you program as you would synchronously but call asynchronous functions instead of blocking functions and await them. Only the code within GetPrimesCountAsync runs on a worker thread; the code in Go "leases" time on the UI thread. We could say that Go executes *pseudoconcurrently* to the message loop (in that its execution is interspersed with other events that the UI thread processes). With this pseudoconcurrency, the only point at which preemption can occur is during an await. This simplifies thread-safety: in our case, the only problem that this could cause is *reentrancy* (clicking the button again while it's running, which we avoid by disabling the button). True concurrency occurs lower in the call stack, inside code called by Task.Run. To benefit from this model, truly concurrent code avoids accessing shared state or UI controls.

To give another example, suppose that instead of calculating prime numbers, we want to download several web pages and sum their lengths. Framework 4.5 (and later) exposes numerous task-returning asynchronous methods, one of which is the WebClient class in System.Net. The DownloadDataTaskAsync method asynchronously downloads a URI to a byte array, returning a Task<byte[]>, so by awaiting it, we get a byte[]. Let's now rewrite our Go method:

```
async void Go()
{
  _button.IsEnabled = false;
  string[] urls = "www.albahari.com www.oreilly.com www.linqpad.net".Split();
  int totalLength = 0;
  try
  {
    foreach (string url in urls)
    {
      var uri = new Uri ("http://" + url);
      byte[] data = await new WebClient().DownloadDataTaskAsync (uri);
```

```
        _results.Text += "Length of " + url + " is " + data.Length +
                         Environment.NewLine;
        totalLength += data.Length;
      }
      _results.Text += "Total length: " + totalLength;
    }
    catch (WebException ex)
    {
      _results.Text += "Error: " + ex.Message;
    }
    finally { _button.IsEnabled = true; }
  }
```

Again, this mirrors how we'd write it synchronously—including the use of catch and finally blocks. Even though execution returns to the caller after the first await, the finally block does not execute until the method has logically completed (by virtue of all its code executing—or an early return or unhandled exception).

It can be helpful to consider exactly what's happening underneath. First, we need to revisit the pseudocode that runs the message loop on the UI thread:

```
Set synchronization context for this thread to WPF sync context
while (!thisApplication.Ended)
{
  wait for something to appear in message queue
  Got something: what kind of message is it?
    Keyboard/mouse message -> fire an event handler
    User BeginInvoke/Invoke message -> execute delegate
}
```

Event handlers that we attach to UI elements execute via this message loop. When our Go method runs, execution proceeds as far as the await expression and then returns to the message loop (freeing the UI to respond to further events). The compiler's expansion of await ensures that before returning, however, a continuation is set up such that execution resumes where it left off upon completion of the task. And because we awaited on a UI thread, the continuation posts to the synchronization context which executes it via the message loop, keeping our entire Go method executing pseudoconcurrently on the UI thread. True (I/O-bound) concurrency occurs within the implementation of DownloadDataTaskAsync.

Comparison to coarse-grained concurrency

Asynchronous programming was difficult prior to C# 5, not only because there was no language support, but because the .NET Framework exposed asynchronous functionality through clumsy patterns called the EAP and the APM (see "Obsolete Patterns" on page 618), rather than task-returning methods.

The popular workaround was course-grained concurrency (in fact, there was even a type called BackgroundWorker to help with that). Returning to our original *synchronous* example with GetPrimesCount, we can demonstrate course-grained asynchrony by modifying the button's event handler as follows:

```
...
_button.Click += (sender, args) =>
{
  _button.IsEnabled = false;
  Task.Run (() => Go());
};
```

(We've chosen to use Task.Run rather than BackgroundWorker because the latter would do nothing to simplify our particular example.) In either case, the end result is that our entire synchronous call graph (Go plus GetPrimesCount) runs on a worker thread. And because Go updates UI elements, we must now litter our code with Dispatcher.BeginInvoke:

```
void Go()
{
  for (int i = 1; i < 5; i++)
  {
    int result = GetPrimesCount (i * 1000000, 1000000);
    Dispatcher.BeginInvoke (new Action (() =>
      _results.Text += result + " primes between " + (i*1000000) +
      " and " + ((i+1)*1000000-1) + Environment.NewLine));
  }
  Dispatcher.BeginInvoke (new Action (() => _button.IsEnabled = true));
}
```

Unlike with the asynchronous version, the loop itself runs on a worker thread. This might seem innocuous, and yet, even in this simple case, our use of multithreading has introduced a race condition. (Can you spot it? If not, try running the program: it will almost certainly become apparent.)

Implementing cancellation and progress reporting creates more possibilities for thread-safety errors, as does any additional code in the method. For instance, suppose the upper limit for the loop is not hardcoded but comes from a method call:

```
for (int i = 1; i < GetUpperBound(); i++)
```

Now suppose GetUpperBound() reads the value from a lazily loaded configuration file, which loads from disk upon first call. All of this code now runs on your worker thread, code that's most likely not thread-safe. This is the danger of starting worker threads high in the call graph.

Writing Asynchronous Functions

With any asynchronous function, you can replace the void return type with a Task to make the method itself *usefully* asynchronous (and awaitable). No further changes are required:

```
async Task PrintAnswerToLife()    // We can return Task instead of void
{
  await Task.Delay (5000);
  int answer = 21 * 2;
  Console.WriteLine (answer);
}
```

Notice that we don't explicitly return a task in the method body. The compiler manufactures the task, which it signals upon completion of the method (or upon an unhandled exception). This makes it easy to create asynchronous call chains:

```
async Task Go()
{
  await PrintAnswerToLife();
  Console.WriteLine ("Done");
}
```

And because we've declared Go with a Task return type, Go itself is awaitable.

The compiler expands asynchronous functions that return tasks into code that leverages TaskCompletionSource to create a task that it then signals or faults.

The compiler actually calls TaskCompletionSource indirectly, via types named Async*MethodBuilder in the System.Compi lerServices namespace. These types handle edge cases such as putting the task into a canceled state upon an Operation CanceledException and implementing the nuances we describe in "Asynchrony and Synchronization Contexts" on page 606.

Nuances aside, we can expand PrintAnswerToLife into the following functional equivalent:

```
Task PrintAnswerToLife()
{
  var tcs = new TaskCompletionSource<object>();
  var awaiter = Task.Delay (5000).GetAwaiter();
  awaiter.OnCompleted (() =>
  {
    try
    {
      awaiter.GetResult();      // Rethrow any exceptions
      int answer = 21 * 2;
      Console.WriteLine (answer);
      tcs.SetResult (null);
    }
    catch (Exception ex) { tcs.SetException (ex); }
  });
  return tcs.Task;
}
```

Hence, whenever a task-returning asynchronous method finishes, execution jumps back to whoever awaited it (by virtue of a continuation).

In a rich-client scenario, execution bounces at this point back to the UI thread (if it's not already on the UI thread). Otherwise, it continues on whatever thread the continuation came back on. This means that there's no latency cost in bubbling up asynchronous call graphs, other than the first "bounce" if it was UI-thread-initiated.

Returning Task<TResult>

You can return a Task<TResult> if the method body returns TResult:

```
async Task<int> GetAnswerToLife()
{
  await Task.Delay (5000);
  int answer = 21 * 2;
  return answer;    // Method has return type Task<int> we return int
}
```

Internally, this results in the TaskCompletionSource being signaled with a value rather than null. We can demonstrate GetAnswerToLife by calling it from PrintAnswerToLife (which is turn, called from Go):

```
async Task Go()
{
  await PrintAnswerToLife();
  Console.WriteLine ("Done");
}

async Task PrintAnswerToLife()
{
  int answer = await GetAnswerToLife();
  Console.WriteLine (answer);
}

async Task<int> GetAnswerToLife()
{
  await Task.Delay (5000);
  int answer = 21 * 2;
  return answer;
}
```

In effect, we've refactored our original PrintAnswerToLife into two methods—with the same ease as if we were programming synchronously. The similarity to synchronous programming is intentional; here's the synchronous equivalent of our call graph, for which calling Go() gives the same result after blocking for five seconds:

```
void Go()
{
  PrintAnswerToLife();
  Console.WriteLine ("Done");
}

void PrintAnswerToLife()
{
  int answer = GetAnswerToLife();
  Console.WriteLine (answer);
}

int GetAnswerToLife()
{
  Thread.Sleep (5000);
  int answer = 21 * 2;
```

```
    return answer;
}
```

 This also illustrates the basic principle of how to design with asynchronous functions in C#:

1. Write your methods synchronously.

2. Replace *synchronous* method calls with *asynchronous* method calls, and `await` them.

3. Except for "top-level" methods (typically event handlers for UI controls), upgrade your asynchronous methods' return types to `Task` or `Task<TResult>` so that they're awaitable.

The compiler's ability to manufacture tasks for asynchronous functions means that for the most part, you need to explicitly instantiate a `TaskCompletionSource` only in bottom-level methods that initiate I/O-bound concurrency. (And for methods that initiate compute-bound currency, you create the task with `Task.Run`.)

Asynchronous call graph execution

To see exactly how this executes, it's helpful to rearrange our code as follows:

```
async Task Go()
{
  var task = PrintAnswerToLife();
  await task; Console.WriteLine ("Done");
}

async Task PrintAnswerToLife()
{
  var task = GetAnswerToLife();
  int answer = await task; Console.WriteLine (answer);
}

async Task<int> GetAnswerToLife()
{
  var task = Task.Delay (5000);
  await task; int answer = 21 * 2; return answer;
}
```

Go calls `PrintAnswerToLife`, which calls `GetAnswerToLife`, which calls `Delay` and then awaits. The `await` causes execution to return to `PrintAnswerToLife`, which itself awaits, returning to `Go`, which also awaits and returns to the caller. All of this happens synchronously, on the thread that called `Go`; this is the brief *synchronous* phase of execution.

Five seconds later, the continuation on `Delay` fires and execution returns to `GetAns werToLife` on a pooled thread. (If we started on a UI thread, execution now bounces to that thread). The remaining statements in `GetAnswerToLife` then run, after which the method's `Task<int>` completes with a result of 42 and executes the continuation in `PrintAnswerToLife`, which executes the remaining statements in that method. The process continues until Go's task is signaled as complete.

Execution flow matches the synchronous call graph that we showed earlier because we're following a pattern whereby we `await` every asynchronous method right after calling it. This creates a sequential flow with no parallelism or overlapping execution within the call graph. Each `await` expression creates a "gap" in execution, after which the program resumes where it left off.

Parallelism

Calling an asynchronous method without awaiting it allows the code that follows to execute in parallel. You might have noticed in earlier examples that we had a button whose event handler called `Go` as follows:

```
_button.Click += (sender, args) => Go();
```

Despite `Go` being an asynchronous method, we didn't await it, and this is indeed what facilitates the concurrency needed to maintain a responsive UI.

We can use this same principle to run two asynchronous operations in parallel:

```
var task1 = PrintAnswerToLife();
var task2 = PrintAnswerToLife();
await task1; await task2;
```

(By awaiting both operations afterward, we "end" the parallelism at that point. Later, we'll describe how the `WhenAll` task combinator helps with this pattern.)

Concurrency created in this manner occurs whether or not the operations are initiated on a UI thread, although there's a difference in how it occurs. In both cases, we get the same "true" concurrency occurring in the bottom-level operations that initiate it (such as `Task.Delay`, or code farmed to `Task.Run`). Methods above this in the call stack will be subject to true concurrency only if the operation was initiated without a synchronization context present; otherwise they will be subject to the pseudoconcurrency (and simplified thread-safety) that we talked about earlier, whereby the only places at which we can be preempted is at an `await` statement. This lets us, for instance, define a shared field, `_x`, and increment it in `GetAnswerToLife` without locking:

```
async Task<int> GetAnswerToLife()
{
  _x++;
  await Task.Delay (5000);
  return 21 * 2;
}
```

(We would, though, be unable to assume that `_x` had the same value before and after the `await`.)

Asynchronous Lambda Expressions

Just as ordinary *named* methods can be asynchronous:

```
async Task NamedMethod()
{
  await Task.Delay (1000);
  Console.WriteLine ("Foo");
}
```

so can *unnamed* methods (lambda expressions and anonymous methods), if preceded by the async keyword:

```
Func<Task> unnamed = async () =>
{
  await Task.Delay (1000);
  Console.WriteLine ("Foo");
};
```

We can call and await these in the same way:

```
await NamedMethod();
await unnamed();
```

Asynchronous lambda expressions can be used when attaching event handlers:

```
myButton.Click += async (sender, args) =>
{
  await Task.Delay (1000);
  myButton.Content = "Done";
};
```

This is more succinct than the following, which has the same effect:

```
myButton.Click += ButtonHandler;
...
async void ButtonHander (object sender, EventArgs args)
{
  await Task.Delay (1000);
  myButton.Content = "Done";
};
```

Asynchronous lambda expressions can also return Task<TResult>:

```
Func<Task<int>> unnamed = async () =>
{
  await Task.Delay (1000);
  return 123;
};
int answer = await unnamed();
```

Asynchronous Methods in WinRT

In WinRT, the equivalent of Task is IAsyncAction and the equivalent of Task<TRe
sult> is IAsyncOperation<TResult> (defined in the Windows.Foundation namespace).

You can convert from either into a Task or Task<TResult> via the AsTask extension method in the System.Runtime.WindowsRuntime.dll assembly. This assembly also defines a GetAwaiter method that operates on IAsyncAction and IAsyncOpera tion<TResult> types, which allows you to await them directly. For instance:

```
Task<StorageFile> fileTask = KnownFolders.DocumentsLibrary.CreateFileAsync
                              ("test.txt").AsTask();
```

or:

```
StorageFile file = await KnownFolders.DocumentsLibrary.CreateFileAsync
                        ("test.txt");
```

 Due to limitations in the COM type system, IAsyncOpera tion<TResult> is not based on IAsyncAction as you might expect. Instead, both inherit from a common base type called IAsyncInfo.

The AsTask method is also overloaded to accept a cancellation token (see "Cancellation" on page 610) and an IProgress<T> object (see "Progress Reporting" on page 612).

Asynchrony and Synchronization Contexts

We've already seen how the presence of a synchronization context is significant in terms of posting continuations. There are a couple of other more subtle ways in which such synchronization contexts come into play with void-returning asynchronous functions. These are not a direct result of C# compiler expansions, but a function of the Async*MethodBuilder types in the System.CompilerServices namespace that the compiler uses in expanding asynchronous functions.

Exception posting

It's common practice in rich-client applications to rely on the central exception-handling event (Application.DispatcherUnhandledException in WPF) to process unhandled exceptions thrown on the UI thread. And in ASP.NET applications, the Application_Error in *global.asax* does a similar job. Internally, they work by invoking UI events (or in ASP.NET, the pipeline of page processing methods) in their own try/catch block.

Top-level asynchronous functions complicate this. Consider the following event handler for a button click:

```
async void ButtonClick (object sender, RoutedEventArgs args)
{
  await Task.Delay(1000);
  throw new Exception ("Will this be ignored?");
}
```

When the button is clicked and the event handler runs, execution returns normally to the message loop after the await statement, and the exception that's thrown a second later cannot be caught by the catch block in the message loop.

To mitigate this problem, `AsyncVoidMethodBuilder` catches unhandled exceptions (in void-returning asynchronous functions) and posts them to the synchronization context if present, ensuring that global exception-handling events still fire.

 The compiler applies this logic only to *void*-returning asynchronous functions. So if we changed `ButtonClick` to return a `Task` instead of `void`, the unhandled exception would fault the resultant `Task`, which would then have nowhere to go (resulting in an *unobserved* exception).

An interesting nuance is that it makes no difference whether you throw before or after an `await`. So in the following example, the exception is posted to the synchronization context (if present) and never to the caller:

```
async void Foo() { throw null; await Task.Delay(1000); }
```

If no synchronization context is present, the exception will go unobserved. It might seem odd that the exception isn't thrown right back to the caller, although it's not entirely different to what happens with iterators:

```
IEnumerable<int> Foo() { throw null; yield return 123; }
```

In this example, an exception is never thrown straight back to the caller: not until the sequence is enumerated is the exception thrown.

OperationStarted and OperationCompleted

If a synchronization context is present, void-returning asynchronous functions also call its `OperationStarted` method upon entering the function and its `OperationCompleted` method when the function finishes. These methods are leveraged by ASP.NET's synchronization context to ensure sequential execution in the page-processing pipeline.

Overriding these methods is useful if writing a custom synchronization context for unit testing void-returning asynchronous methods. This is discussed on Microsoft's Parallel Programming blog at *http://blogs.msdn.com/b/pfxteam*.

Optimizations

Completing synchronously

An asynchronous function may return *before* awaiting. Consider the following method that caches the downloading of web pages:

```
static Dictionary<string,string> _cache = new Dictionary<string,string>();

async Task<string> GetWebPageAsync (string uri)
{
  string html;
  if (_cache.TryGetValue (uri, out html)) return html;
  return _cache [uri] =
```

```
    await new WebClient().DownloadStringTaskAsync (uri);
}
```

Should a URI already exist in the cache, execution returns to the caller with no awaiting having occurred, and the method returns an *already-signaled* task. This is referred to as synchronous completion.

When you await a synchronously completed task, execution does not return to the caller and bounce back via a continuation—instead, it proceeds immediately to the next statement. The compiler implements this optimization by checking the IsCom pleted property on the awaiter; in other words, whenever you await:

```
Console.WriteLine (await GetWebPageAsync ("http://oreilly.com"));
```

the compiler emits code to short-circuit the continuation in case of synchronization completion:

```
var awaiter = GetWebPageAsync().GetAwaiter();
if (awaiter.IsCompleted)
  Console.WriteLine (awaiter.GetResult());
else
  awaiter.OnCompleted (() => Console.WriteLine (awaiter.GetResult()));
```

Awaiting an asynchronous function that returns synchro-nously still incurs a small overhead—maybe 50-100 nanosec-onds on a 2015-era PC.

In contrast, bouncing to the thread pool introduces the cost of a context switch—perhaps one or two microseconds, and bouncing to a UI message loop, at least 10 times that (much longer if the UI thread is busy).

It's even legal to write asynchronous methods that *never* await, although the com-piler will generate a warning:

```
async Task<string> Foo() { return "abc"; }
```

Such methods can be useful when overriding virtual/abstract methods if your implementation doesn't happen to need asynchrony. (An example is MemoryStream's ReadAsync/WriteAsync methods—see Chapter 15.) Another way to achieve the same result is to use Task.FromResult, which returns an already-signaled task:

```
Task<string> Foo() { return Task.FromResult ("abc"); }
```

Our GetWebPageAsync method is implicitly thread-safe if called from a UI thread, in that you could invoke it several times in succession (thereby initiating multiple con-current downloads), and no locking is required to protect the cache. If the series of calls were to the same URI, though, we'd end up initiating multiple redundant downloads, all of which would eventually update the same cache entry (the last one winning). While not erroneous, it would be more efficient if subsequent calls to the same URI could instead (asynchronously) wait upon the result of the in-progress request.

There's an easy way to accomplish this—without resorting to locks or signaling constructs. Instead of a cache of strings, we create a cache of "futures" (Task<string>):

```
static Dictionary<string,Task<string>> _cache =
  new Dictionary<string,Task<string>>();

Task<string> GetWebPageAsync (string uri)
{
  Task<string> downloadTask;
  if (_cache.TryGetValue (uri, out downloadTask)) return downloadTask;
  return _cache [uri] = new WebClient().DownloadStringTaskAsync (uri);
}
```

(Notice that we don't mark the method as async, because we're directly returning the task we obtain from calling WebClient's method).

If we call GetWebPageAsync repeatedly with the same URI, we're now guaranteed to get the same Task<string> object back. (This has the additional benefit of minimizing GC load.) And if the task is complete, awaiting it is cheap, thanks to the compiler optimization that we just discussed.

We could further extend our example to make it thread-safe without the protection of a synchronization context, by locking around the entire method body:

```
lock (_cache)
{
  Task<string> downloadTask;
  if (_cache.TryGetValue (uri, out downloadTask)) return downloadTask;
  return _cache [uri] = new WebClient().DownloadStringTaskAsync (uri);
}
```

This works because we're not locking for the duration of downloading a page (which would hurt concurrency); we're locking for the small duration of checking the cache, starting a new task if necessary, and updating the cache with that task.

Avoiding excessive bouncing

For methods that are called many times in a loop, you can avoid the cost of repeatedly bouncing to a UI message loop by calling ConfigureAwait. This forces a task not to bounce continuations to the synchronization context, cutting the overhead closer to the cost of a context switch (or much less if the method that you're awaiting completes synchronously):

```
async void A() { ... await B(); ... }

async Task B()
{
  for (int i = 0; i < 1000; i++)
    await C().ConfigureAwait (false);
}

async Task C() { ... }
```

This means that for the B and C methods, we rescind the simple thread-safety model in UI apps whereby code runs on the UI thread and can be preempted only during an await statement. Method A, however, is unaffected and will remain on a UI thread if it started on one.

This optimization is particularly relevant when writing libraries: you don't need the benefit of simplified thread-safety because your code typically does not share state with the caller—and does not access UI controls. (It would also make sense, in our example, for method C to complete synchronously if it knew the operation was likely to be short-running.)

Asynchronous Patterns

Cancellation

It's often important to be able to cancel a concurrent operation after it's started, perhaps in response to a user request. A simple way to implement this is with a cancellation flag, which we could encapsulate by writing a class like this:

```
class CancellationToken
{
  public bool IsCancellationRequested { get; private set; }
  public void Cancel() { IsCancellationRequested = true; }
  public void ThrowIfCancellationRequested()
  {
    if (IsCancellationRequested)
      throw new OperationCanceledException();
  }
}
```

We could then write a cancellable asynchronous method as follows:

```
async Task Foo (CancellationToken cancellationToken)
{
  for (int i = 0; i < 10; i++)
  {
    Console.WriteLine (i);
    await Task.Delay (1000);
    cancellationToken.ThrowIfCancellationRequested();
  }
}
```

When the caller wants to cancel, it calls Cancel on the cancellation token that it passed into Foo. This sets IsCancellationRequested to true which causes Foo to fault a short time later with an OperationCanceledException (a predefined exception in the System namespace designed for this purpose).

Thread-safety aside (we should be locking around reading/writing IsCancellation Requested), this pattern is effective and the CLR provides a type called Cancella tionToken which is very similar to what we've just shown. However, it lacks a Can cel method; this method is instead exposed on another type called CancellationTo kenSource. This separation provides some security: a method which has access only to a CancellationToken object can check for but not *initiate* cancellation.

To get a cancellation token, we first instantiate a CancellationTokenSource:

```
var cancelSource = new CancellationTokenSource();
```

This exposes a Token property which returns a CancellationToken. Hence, we could call our Foo method as follows:

```
var cancelSource = new CancellationTokenSource();
Task foo = Foo (cancelSource.Token);
...
... (some time later)
cancelSource.Cancel();
```

Most asynchronous methods in the CLR support cancellation tokens, including Delay. If we modify Foo such that it passes its token into the Delay method, the task will end immediately upon request (rather than up to a second later):

```
async Task Foo (CancellationToken cancellationToken)
{
  for (int i = 0; i < 10; i++)
  {
    Console.WriteLine (i);
    await Task.Delay (1000, cancellationToken);
  }
}
```

Notice that we no longer need to call ThrowIfCancellationRequested because Task.Delay is doing that for us. Cancellation tokens propagate nicely down the call stack (just as cancellation requests cascade *up* the call stack, by virtue of being exceptions).

> Asynchronous methods in WinRT follow an inferior protocol for cancellation whereby instead of accepting a Cancella tionToken, the IAsyncInfo type exposes a Cancel method. The AsTask extension method is overloaded to accept a cancellation token, however, bridging the gap.

Synchronous methods can support cancellation, too (such as Task's Wait method). In such cases, the instruction to cancel will have to come asynchronously (e.g., from another task). For example:

```
var cancelSource = new CancellationTokenSource();
Task.Delay (5000).ContinueWith (ant => cancelSource.Cancel());
...
```

In fact, from Framework 4.5, you can specify a time interval when constructing Can cellationTokenSource to initiate cancellation after a set period of time (just as we demonstrated). It's useful for implementing timeouts, whether synchronous or asynchronous:

```
var cancelSource = new CancellationTokenSource (5000);
try { await Foo (cancelSource.Token); }
catch (OperationCanceledException ex) { Console.WriteLine ("Cancelled"); }
```

The CancellationToken struct provides a Register method which lets you register a callback delegate that will be fired upon cancellation; it returns an object that can be disposed to undo the registration.

Tasks generated by the compiler's asynchronous functions automatically enter a "Canceled" state upon an unhandled OperationCanceledException (IsCanceled returns true and IsFaulted returns false). The same goes for tasks created with Task.Run for which you pass the (same) CancellationToken to the constructor. The distinction between a faulted and a canceled task is unimportant in asynchronous scenarios, in that both throw an OperationCanceledException when awaited; it matters in advanced parallel programming scenarios (specifically conditional continuations). We pick up this topic in "Canceling Tasks" on page 971 in Chapter 23.

Progress Reporting

Sometimes you'll want an asynchronous operation to report back progress as it's running. A simple solution is to pass an Action delegate to the asynchronous method, which the method fires whenever progress changes:

```
Task Foo (Action<int> onProgressPercentChanged)
{
  return Task.Run (() =>
  {
    for (int i = 0; i < 1000; i++)
    {
      if (i % 10 == 0) onProgressPercentChanged (i / 10);
      // Do something compute-bound...
    }
  });
}
```

Here's how we could call it:

```
Action<int> progress = i => Console.WriteLine (i + " %");
await Foo (progress);
```

While this works well in a Console application, it's not ideal in rich-client scenarios because it reports progress from a worker thread, causing potential thread-safety issues for the consumer. (In effect, we've allowed a side-effect of concurrency to "leak" to the outside world, which is unfortunate as the method is otherwise isolated if called from a UI thread.)

IProgress<T> and Progress<T>

The CLR provides a pair of types to solve this problem: an interface called IProgress<T> and a class that implements this interface called Progress<T>. Their purpose, in effect, is to "wrap" a delegate, so that UI applications can report progress safely through the synchronization context.

The interface defines just one method:

```
public interface IProgress<in T>
{
  void Report (T value);
}
```

Using IProgress<T> is easy: our method hardly changes:

```
Task Foo (IProgress<int> onProgressPercentChanged)
{
  return Task.Run (() =>
  {
    for (int i = 0; i < 1000; i++)
    {
      if (i % 10 == 0) onProgressPercentChanged.Report (i / 10);
      // Do something compute-bound...
    }
  });
}
```

The Progress<T> class has a constructor that accepts a delegate of type Action<T> that it wraps:

```
var progress = new Progress<int> (i => Console.WriteLine (i + " %"));
await Foo (progress);
```

(Progress<T> also has a ProgressChanged event that you can subscribe to instead of [or in addition to] passing an action delegate to the constructor.) Upon instantiating Progress<int>, the class captures the synchronization context, if present. When Foo then calls Report, the delegate is invoked through that context.

Asynchronous methods can implement more elaborate progress reporting by replacing int with a custom type that exposes a range of properties.

 If you're familiar with Reactive Framework, you'll notice that IProgress<T> together with the task returned by the asynchronous function provide a feature set similar to IObserver<T>. The difference is that a task can expose a "final" return value *in addition* to (and differently typed to) the values emitted by IProgress<T>.

Values emitted by IProgress<T> are typically "throwaway" values (e.g., percent complete or bytes downloaded so far) whereas values pushed by IObserver<T>'s OnNext typically comprise the result itself and are the very reason for calling it.

Asynchronous methods in WinRT also offer progress reporting, although the protocol is complicated by COM's (relatively) retarded type system. Instead of accepting an IProgress<T> object, asynchronous WinRT methods that report progress

return one of the following interfaces, in place of IAsyncAction and IAsyncOpera
tion<TResult>:

```
IAsyncActionWithProgress<TProgress>
IAsyncOperationWithProgress<TResult, TProgress>
```

Interestingly, both and are based on IAsyncInfo (and not IAsyncAction and IAsyn
cOperation<TResult>).

The good news is that the AsTask extension method is also overloaded to accept
IProgress<T> for the above interfaces, so as a .NET consumer, you can ignore the
COM interfaces and do this:

```
var progress = new Progress<int> (i => Console.WriteLine (i + " %"));
CancellationToken cancelToken = ...
var task = someWinRTobject.FooAsync().AsTask (cancelToken, progress);
```

The Task-based Asynchronous Pattern (TAP)

Framework 4.5 and later exposes hundreds of task-returning asynchronous methods that you can await (mainly related to I/O). Most of these methods (at least
partly) follow a pattern called the *Task-based Asynchronous Pattern* (TAP) which is a
sensible formalization of what we have described to date. A TAP method:

- Returns a "hot" (running) Task or Task<TResult>

- Has a "Async" suffix (except for special cases such as task combinators)

- Is overloaded to accept a cancellation token and/or IProgress<T> if it supports
  cancellation and/or progress reporting

- Returns quickly to the caller (has only a small initial *synchronous phase*)

- Does not tie up a thread if I/O-bound

As we've seen, TAP methods are easy to write with C#'s asynchronous functions.

Task Combinators

A nice consequence of there being a consistent protocol for asynchronous functions
(whereby they consistently return tasks) is that it's possible to use and write *task
combinators*—functions that usefully combine tasks, without regard for what those
specific tasks do.

The CLR includes two task combinators: Task.WhenAny and Task.WhenAll. In
describing them, we'll assume the following methods are defined:

```
async Task<int> Delay1() { await Task.Delay (1000); return 1; }
async Task<int> Delay2() { await Task.Delay (2000); return 2; }
async Task<int> Delay3() { await Task.Delay (3000); return 3; }
```

WhenAny

`Task.WhenAny` returns a task that completes when any one of a set of tasks complete. The following completes in one second:

```
Task<int> winningTask = await Task.WhenAny (Delay1(), Delay2(), Delay3());
Console.WriteLine ("Done");
Console.WriteLine (winningTask.Result);    // 1
```

Because `Task.WhenAny` itself returns a task, we await it, which returns the task that finished first. Our example is entirely nonblocking—including the last line when we access the `Result` property (because `winningTask` will already have finished). Nonetheless, it's usually better to `await` the `winningTask`:

```
Console.WriteLine (await winningTask);    // 1
```

because any exceptions are then rethrown without an `AggregateException` wrapping. In fact, we can perform both `await`s in one step:

```
int answer = await await Task.WhenAny (Delay1(), Delay2(), Delay3());
```

If a non-winning task subsequently faults, the exception will go unobserved unless you subsequently await the task (or query its `Exception` property).

`WhenAny` is useful for applying timeouts or cancellation to operations that don't otherwise support it:

```
Task<string> task = SomeAsyncFunc();
Task winner = await (Task.WhenAny (task, Task.Delay(5000)));
if (winner != task) throw new TimeoutException();
string result = await task;    // Unwrap result/rethrow
```

Notice that because in this case we're calling `WhenAny` with differently typed tasks, the winner is reported as a plain `Task` (rather than a `Task<string>`).

WhenAll

`Task.WhenAll` returns a task that completes when *all* of the tasks that you pass to it complete. The following completes after three seconds (and demonstrates the *fork/join* pattern):

```
await Task.WhenAll (Delay1(), Delay2(), Delay3());
```

We could get a similar result by awaiting `task1`, `task2` and `task3` in turn rather than using `WhenAll`:

```
Task task1 = Delay1(), task2 = Delay2(), task3 = Delay3();
await task1; await task2; await task3;
```

The difference (apart from it being less efficient by virtue of requiring three awaits rather than one), is that should `task1` fault, we'll never get to await `task2`/`task3`, and any of their exceptions will go unobserved. In fact, this is why they relaxed the unobserved task exception behavior from CLR 4.5: it would be confusing if, despite an exception handling block around the entire code block above, an exception from `task2` or `task3` could crash your application sometime later when garbage collected.

In contrast, Task.WhenAll doesn't complete until all tasks have completed—even when there's a fault. And if there are multiple faults, their exceptions are combined into the task's AggregateException (this is when AggregateException actually becomes useful—should you be interested in all the exceptions, that is). Awaiting the combined task, however, throws only the first exception, so to see all the exceptions you need to do this:

```
Task task1 = Task.Run (() => { throw null; } );
Task task2 = Task.Run (() => { throw null; } );
Task all = Task.WhenAll (task1, task2);
try { await all; }
catch
{
  Console.WriteLine (all.Exception.InnerExceptions.Count);   // 2
}
```

Calling WhenAll with tasks of type Task<TResult> returns a Task<TResult[]>, giving the combined results of all the tasks. This reduces to a TResult[] when awaited:

```
Task<int> task1 = Task.Run (() => 1);
Task<int> task2 = Task.Run (() => 2);
int[] results = await Task.WhenAll (task1, task2);   // { 1, 2 }
```

To give a practical example, the following downloads URIs in parallel and sums their total length:

```
async Task<int> GetTotalSize (string[] uris)
{
  IEnumerable<Task<byte[]>> downloadTasks = uris.Select (uri =>
    new WebClient().DownloadDataTaskAsync (uri));

  byte[][] contents = await Task.WhenAll (downloadTasks);
  return contents.Sum (c => c.Length);
}
```

There's a slight inefficiency here, though, in that we're unnecessarily hanging onto the byte arrays that we download until every task is complete. It would be more efficient if we collapsed byte arrays into their lengths right after downloading them. This is where an asynchronous lambda comes in handy, because we need to feed an await expression into LINQ's Select query operator:

```
async Task<int> GetTotalSize (string[] uris)
{
  IEnumerable<Task<int>> downloadTasks = uris.Select (async uri =>
    (await new WebClient().DownloadDataTaskAsync (uri)).Length);

  int[] contentLengths = await Task.WhenAll (downloadTasks);
  return contentLengths.Sum();
}
```

Custom combinators

It can be useful to write your own task combinators. The simplest "combinator" accepts a single task, such as the following, which lets you await any task with a timeout:

```
async static Task<TResult> WithTimeout<TResult> (this Task<TResult> task,
                                                 TimeSpan timeout)
{
  Task winner = await (Task.WhenAny (task, Task.Delay (timeout)));
  if (winner != task) throw new TimeoutException();
  return await task;    // Unwrap result/rethrow
}
```

The following lets you "abandon" a task via a CancellationToken:

```
static Task<TResult> WithCancellation<TResult> (this Task<TResult> task,
                                                CancellationToken cancelToken)
{
  var tcs = new TaskCompletionSource<TResult>();
  var reg = cancelToken.Register (() => tcs.TrySetCanceled ());
  task.ContinueWith (ant =>
  {
    reg.Dispose();
    if (ant.IsCanceled)
      tcs.TrySetCanceled();
    else if (ant.IsFaulted)
      tcs.TrySetException (ant.Exception.InnerException);
    else
      tcs.TrySetResult (ant.Result);
  });
  return tcs.Task;
}
```

Task combinators can be complex to write, sometimes requiring the use of signaling constructs that we cover in Chapter 22. This is actually a good thing, because it keeps concurrency-related complexity out of your business logic and into reusable methods that can be tested in isolation.

The next combinator works like WhenAll, except that if any of the tasks fault, the resultant task faults immediately:

```
async Task<TResult[]> WhenAllOrError<TResult>
  (params Task<TResult>[] tasks)
{
  var killJoy = new TaskCompletionSource<TResult[]>();
  foreach (var task in tasks)
    task.ContinueWith (ant =>
    {
      if (ant.IsCanceled)
        killJoy.TrySetCanceled();
      else if (ant.IsFaulted)
        killJoy.TrySetException (ant.Exception.InnerException);
    });
  return await await Task.WhenAny (killJoy.Task, Task.WhenAll (tasks));
}
```

We start by creating a TaskCompletionSource whose sole job is to end the party if a task faults. Hence, we never call its SetResult method; only its TrySetCanceled and TrySetException methods. In this case, ContinueWith is more convenient than GetAwaiter().OnCompleted because we're not accessing the tasks' results and wouldn't want to bounce to a UI thread at that point.

Obsolete Patterns

The Framework employs other patterns for asynchrony which precede tasks and asynchronous functions. These are now rarely required, since task-based asynchrony has become the dominant pattern as of Framework 4.5.

Asynchronous Programming Model (APM)

The oldest pattern is called the APM ("Asynchronous Programming Model") and uses a pair of methods starting in "Begin" and "End," and an interface called IAsyncResult. To illustrate, we'll take the Stream class in System.IO, and look at its Read method. First, the synchronous version:

```
public int Read (byte[] buffer, int offset, int size);
```

You can probably predict what the *task*-based asynchronous version looks like:

```
public Task<int> ReadAsync (byte[] buffer, int offset, int size);
```

Now let's examine the APM version:

```
public IAsyncResult BeginRead (byte[] buffer, int offset, int size,
                               AsyncCallback callback, object state);
public int EndRead (IAsyncResult asyncResult);
```

Calling the Begin* method initiates the operation, returning an IAsyncResult object which acts as a token for the asynchronous operation. When the operation completes (or faults), the AsyncCallback delegate fires:

```
public delegate void AsyncCallback (IAsyncResult ar);
```

Whoever handles this delegate then calls the End* method which provides the operation's return value, as well as rethrowing an exception if the operation faulted.

The APM is not only awkward to use, but surprisingly difficult to implement correctly. The easiest way to deal with APM methods is to call the Task.Factory.FromAsync adapter method, which converts an APM method pair into a Task. Internally, it uses a TaskCompletionSource to give you a task that's signaled when an APM operation completes or faults.

The FromAsync method requires the following parameters:

- A delegate specifying a Begin*XXX* method
- A delegate specifying a End*XXX* method
- Additional arguments that will get passed to these methods

FromAsync is overloaded to accept delegate types and arguments that match nearly all the asynchronous method signatures found in the .NET Framework. For instance, assuming stream is a Stream and buffer is a byte[], we could do this:

```
Task<int> readChunk = Task<int>.Factory.FromAsync (
    stream.BeginRead, stream.EndRead, buffer, 0, 1000, null);
```

Asynchronous delegates

The CLR still supports *asynchronous delegates*, a feature whereby you can call any delegate asynchronously using APM-style BeginInvoke/EndInvoke methods:

```
Func<string> foo = () => { Thread.Sleep(1000); return "foo"; };
foo.BeginInvoke (asyncResult =>
    Console.WriteLine (foo.EndInvoke (asyncResult)), null);
```

Asynchronous delegates incur a surprising overhead—and are painfully redundant with tasks:

```
Func<string> foo = () => { Thread.Sleep(1000); return "foo"; };
Task.Run (foo).ContinueWith (ant => Console.WriteLine (ant.Result));
```

Event-Based Asynchronous Pattern (EAP)

The *Event-based Asynchronous Pattern* (EAP) was introduced in Framework 2.0 to provide a simpler alternative to the APM, particularly in UI scenarios. It was implemented in only a handful of types, however, most notably WebClient in System.Net. The EAP is just a pattern; no types are provided to assist. Essentially the pattern is this: a class offers a family of members that internally manage concurrency, similar to the following.

```
// These members are from the WebClient class:

public byte[] DownloadData (Uri address);      // Synchronous version
public void DownloadDataAsync (Uri address);
public void DownloadDataAsync (Uri address, object userToken);
public event DownloadDataCompletedEventHandler DownloadDataCompleted;

public void CancelAsync (object userState);    // Cancels an operation
public bool IsBusy { get; }                    // Indicates if still running
```

The *Async methods initiate an operation asynchronously. When the operation completes, the *Completed event fires (automatically posting to the captured synchronization context if present). This event passes back an event arguments object that contains:

- A flag indicating whether the operation was canceled (by the consumer calling CancelAsync)
- An Error object indicating an exception that was thrown (if any)
- The userToken object if supplied when calling the Async method

EAP types may also expose a progress reporting event, which fires whenever progress changes (also posted through the synchronization context):

```
public event DownloadProgressChangedEventHandler DownloadProgressChanged;
```

Implementing the EAP requires a large amount of boilerplate code, making the pattern poorly compositional.

BackgroundWorker

BackgroundWorker in System.ComponentModel is a general-purpose implementation of the EAP. It allows rich-client apps to start a worker thread and report completion and percentage-based progress without needing to explicitly capture synchronization context. For instance:

```
var worker = new BackgroundWorker { WorkerSupportsCancellation = true };
worker.DoWork += (sender, args) =>
{                                         // This runs on a worker thread
  if (args.Cancel) return;
  Thread.Sleep(1000);
  args.Result = 123;
};
worker.RunWorkerCompleted += (sender, args) =>
{                                         // Runs on UI thread
  // We can safely update UI controls here...
  if (args.Cancelled)
    Console.WriteLine ("Cancelled");
  else if (args.Error != null)
    Console.WriteLine ("Error: " + args.Error.Message);
  else
    Console.WriteLine ("Result is: " + args.Result);
};
worker.RunWorkerAsync();   // Captures sync context and starts operation
```

RunWorkerAsync starts the operation, firing the DoWork event on a pooled worker thread. It also captures the synchronization context, and when the operation completes (or faults), the RunWorkerCompleted event is invoked through that synchronization context (like a continuation).

BackgroundWorker creates course-grained concurrency, in that the DoWork event runs entirely on a worker thread. If you need to update UI controls in that event

---

handler (other than posting a percentage-complete message), you must use `Dispatcher.BeginInvoke` or similar).

We describe `BackgroundWorker` in more detail at *http://albahari.com/threading*.

15

Streams and I/O

This chapter describes the fundamental types for input and output in .NET, with emphasis on the following topics:

- The .NET stream architecture and how it provides a consistent programming interface for reading and writing across a variety of I/O types

- Classes for manipulating files and directories on disk

- Specialized streams for compression, named pipes, and memory-mapped files.

This chapter concentrates on the types in the System.IO namespace, the home of lower-level I/O functionality. The .NET Framework also provides higher-level I/O functionality in the form of SQL connections and commands, LINQ to SQL and LINQ to XML, Windows Communication Foundation, Web Services, and Remoting.

Stream Architecture

The .NET stream architecture centers on three concepts: backing stores, decorators, and adapters, as shown in Figure 15-1.

A *backing store* is the endpoint that makes input and output useful, such as a file or network connection. Precisely, it is either or both of the following:

- A source from which bytes can be sequentially read

- A destination to which bytes can be sequentially written

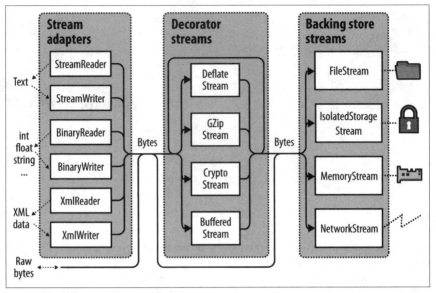

Figure 15-1. Stream architecture

A backing store is of no use, though, unless exposed to the programmer. A `Stream` is the standard .NET class for this purpose; it exposes a standard set of methods for reading, writing, and positioning. Unlike an array, where all the backing data exists in memory at once, a stream deals with data serially—either one byte at a time or in blocks of a manageable size. Hence, a stream can use little memory regardless of the size of its backing store.

Streams fall into two categories:

Backing store streams

These are hard-wired to a particular type of backing store, such as `File Stream` or `NetworkStream`

Decorator streams

These feed off another stream, transforming the data in some way, such as `DeflateStream` or `CryptoStream`

Decorator streams have the following architectural benefits:

- They liberate backing store streams from needing to implement such features as compression and encryption themselves.

- Streams don't suffer a change of interface when decorated.

- You connect decorators at runtime.

- You can chain decorators together (e.g., a compressor followed by an encryptor).

Both backing store and decorator streams deal exclusively in bytes. Although this is flexible and efficient, applications often work at higher levels such as text or XML. *Adapters* bridge this gap by wrapping a stream in a class with specialized methods typed to a particular format. For example, a text reader exposes a ReadLine method; an XML writer exposes a WriteAttributes method.

 An adapter wraps a stream, just like a decorator. Unlike a decorator, however, an adapter is not *itself* a stream; it typically hides the byte-oriented methods completely.

To summarize, backing store streams provide the raw data; decorator streams provide transparent binary transformations such as encryption; adapters offer typed methods for dealing in higher-level types such as strings and XML. Figure 15-1 illustrates their associations. To compose a chain, you simply pass one object into another's constructor.

Using Streams

The abstract Stream class is the base for all streams. It defines methods and properties for three fundamental operations: *reading*, *writing*, and *seeking*, as well as for administrative tasks such as closing, flushing, and configuring timeouts (see Table 15-1).

Table 15-1. Stream class members

Category	Members
Reading	public abstract bool CanRead { get; }
	public abstract int Read (byte[] buffer, int offset, int count)
	public virtual int ReadByte();
Writing	public abstract bool CanWrite { get; }
	public abstract void Write (byte[] buffer, int offset, int count);
	public virtual void WriteByte (byte value);
Seeking	public abstract bool CanSeek { get; }
	public abstract long Position { get; set; }
	public abstract void SetLength (long value);
	public abstract long Length { get; }
	public abstract long Seek (long offset, SeekOrigin origin);

Category	Members
Closing/flushing	`public virtual void Close();`
	`public void Dispose();`
	`public abstract void Flush();`
Timeouts	`public virtual bool CanTimeout { get; }`
	`public virtual int ReadTimeout { get; set; }`
	`public virtual int WriteTimeout { get; set; }`
Other	`public static readonly Stream Null; // "Null" stream`
	`public static Stream Synchronized (Stream stream);`

From Framework 4.5, there are also asynchronous versions of the Read and Write methods, both of which return Tasks and optionally accept a cancellation token.

In the following example, we use a file stream to read, write, and seek:

```
using System;
using System.IO;

class Program
{
  static void Main()
  {
    // Create a file called test.txt in the current directory:
    using (Stream s = new FileStream ("test.txt", FileMode.Create))
    {
      Console.WriteLine (s.CanRead);       // True
      Console.WriteLine (s.CanWrite);      // True
      Console.WriteLine (s.CanSeek);       // True

      s.WriteByte (101);
      s.WriteByte (102);
      byte[] block = { 1, 2, 3, 4, 5 };
      s.Write (block, 0, block.Length);    // Write block of 5 bytes

      Console.WriteLine (s.Length);        // 7
      Console.WriteLine (s.Position);      // 7
      s.Position = 0;                      // Move back to the start

      Console.WriteLine (s.ReadByte());    // 101
      Console.WriteLine (s.ReadByte());    // 102

      // Read from the stream back into the block array:
      Console.WriteLine (s.Read (block, 0, block.Length));   // 5

      // Assuming the last Read returned 5, we'll be at
      // the end of the file, so Read will now return 0:
      Console.WriteLine (s.Read (block, 0, block.Length));   // 0
    }
  }
}
```

Reading or writing asynchronously is simply a question of calling ReadAsync/Write
Async instead of Read/Write, and awaiting the expression. (We must also add the
async keyword to the calling method, as we described in Chapter 14.)

```
async static void AsyncDemo()
{
  using (Stream s = new FileStream ("test.txt", FileMode.Create))
  {
    byte[] block = { 1, 2, 3, 4, 5 };
    await s.WriteAsync (block, 0, block.Length);     // Write asychronously

    s.Position = 0;                                  // Move back to the start

    // Read from the stream back into the block array:
    Console.WriteLine (await s.ReadAsync (block, 0, block.Length));   // 5
  }
}
```

The asynchronous methods make it easy to write responsive and scalable applications that work with potentially slow streams (particularly network streams),
without tying up a thread.

For the sake of brevity, we'll continue to use synchronous
methods for most of the examples in this chapter; however we
recommend the asynchronous Read/Write operations as preferable in most scenarios involving network I/O.

Reading and Writing

A stream may support reading, writing, or both. If CanWrite returns false, the
stream is read-only; if CanRead returns false, the stream is write-only.

Read receives a block of data from the stream into an array. It returns the number of
bytes received, which is always either less than or equal to the count argument. If it's
less than count, it means either that the end of the stream has been reached or the
stream is giving you the data in smaller chunks (as is often the case with network
streams). In either case, the balance of bytes in the array will remain unwritten, their
previous values preserved.

With Read, you can be certain you've reached the end of the
stream only when the method returns 0. So, if you have a
1,000-byte stream, the following code may fail to read it all
into memory:

```
// Assuming s is a stream:
byte[] data = new byte [1000];
s.Read (data, 0, data.Length);
```

The Read method could read anywhere from 1 to 1,000 bytes,
leaving the balance of the stream unread.

Here's the correct way to read a 1,000-byte stream:

```
byte[] data = new byte [1000];

// bytesRead will always end up at 1000, unless the stream is
// itself smaller in length:

int bytesRead = 0;
int chunkSize = 1;
while (bytesRead < data.Length && chunkSize > 0)
  bytesRead +=
    chunkSize = s.Read (data, bytesRead, data.Length - bytesRead);
```

Fortunately, the BinaryReader type provides a simpler way to achieve the same result:

```
byte[] data = new BinaryReader (s).ReadBytes (1000);
```

If the stream is less than 1,000 bytes long, the byte array returned reflects the actual stream size. If the stream is seekable, you can read its entire contents by replacing 1000 with (int)s.Length.

We describe the BinaryReader type further in the section "Stream Adapters" on page 639, later in this chapter.

The ReadByte method is simpler: it reads just a single byte, returning –1 to indicate the end of the stream. ReadByte actually returns an int rather than a byte, as the latter cannot return –1.

The Write and WriteByte methods send data to the stream. If they are unable to send the specified bytes, an exception is thrown.

In the Read and Write methods, the offset argument refers to the index in the buffer array at which reading or writing begins, not the position within the stream.

Seeking

A stream is seekable if CanSeek returns true. With a seekable stream (such as a file stream), you can query or modify its Length (by calling SetLength) and at any time change the Position at which you're reading or writing. The Position property is relative to the beginning of the stream; the Seek method, however, allows you to move relative to the current position or the end of the stream.

Changing the Position on a FileStream typically takes a few microseconds. If you're doing this millions of times in a loop, the MemoryMappedFile class may be a better choice than a FileStream (see "Memory-Mapped Files" on page 663, later in this chapter).

With a nonseekable stream (such as an encryption stream), the only way to determine its length is to read it right through. Furthermore, if you need to reread a previous section, you must close the stream and start afresh with a new one.

Closing and Flushing

Streams must be disposed after use to release underlying resources such as file and socket handles. A simple way to guarantee this is by instantiating streams within `using` blocks. In general, streams follow standard disposal semantics:

- `Dispose` and `Close` are identical in function.
- Disposing or closing a stream repeatedly causes no error.

Closing a decorator stream closes both the decorator and its backing store stream. With a chain of decorators, closing the outermost decorator (at the head of the chain) closes the whole lot.

Some streams internally buffer data to and from the backing store to lessen round-tripping and so improve performance (file streams are a good example of this). This means data you write to a stream may not hit the backing store immediately; it can be delayed as the buffer fills up. The `Flush` method forces any internally buffered data to be written immediately. `Flush` is called automatically when a stream is closed, so you never need to do the following:

```
s.Flush(); s.Close();
```

Timeouts

A stream supports read and write timeouts if `CanTimeout` returns `true`. Network streams support timeouts; file and memory streams do not. For streams that support timeouts, the `ReadTimeout` and `WriteTimeout` properties determine the desired timeout in milliseconds, where 0 means no timeout. The `Read` and `Write` methods indicate that a timeout has occurred by throwing an exception.

Thread Safety

As a rule, streams are not thread-safe, meaning that two threads cannot concurrently read or write to the same stream without possible error. The `Stream` class offers a simple workaround via the static `Synchronized` method. This method accepts a stream of any type and returns a thread-safe wrapper. The wrapper works by obtaining an exclusive lock around each read, write, or seek, ensuring that only one thread can perform such an operation at a time. In practice, this allows multiple threads to simultaneously append data to the same stream—other kinds of activities (such as concurrent reading) require additional locking to ensure that each thread accesses the desired portion of the stream. We discuss thread safety fully in Chapter 22.

Backing Store Streams

Figure 15-2 shows the key backing store streams provided by the .NET Framework. A "null stream" is also available, via the `Stream`'s static `Null` field.

In the following sections, we describe `FileStream` and `MemoryStream`; in the final section in this chapter, we describe `IsolatedStorageStream`. In Chapter 16, we cover `NetworkStream`.

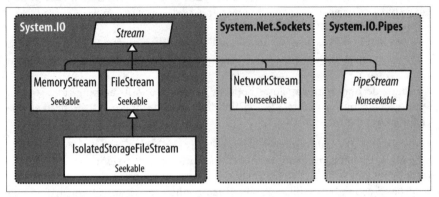

Figure 15-2. Backing store streams

FileStream

Earlier in this section, we demonstrated the basic use of a `FileStream` to read and write bytes of data. We'll now examine the special features of this class.

 `FileStream` is unavailable to Windows Store applications. Instead, use the Windows Runtime types in `Windows.Storage` (see "File I/O in Windows Runtime" on page 661).

Constructing a FileStream

The simplest way to instantiate a `FileStream` is to use one of the following static façade methods on the `File` class:

```
FileStream fs1 = File.OpenRead  ("readme.bin");             // Read-only
FileStream fs2 = File.OpenWrite (@"c:\temp\writeme.tmp");   // Write-only
FileStream fs3 = File.Create    (@"c:\temp\writeme.tmp");   // Read/write
```

`OpenWrite` and `Create` differ in behavior if the file already exists. `Create` truncates any existing content; `OpenWrite` leaves existing content intact with the stream positioned at zero. If you write fewer bytes than were previously in the file, `OpenWrite` leaves you with a mixture of old and new content.

You can also instantiate a `FileStream` directly. Its constructors provide access to every feature, allowing you to specify a filename or low-level file handle, file creation and access modes, and options for sharing, buffering, and security. The following opens an existing file for read/write access without overwriting it:

```
var fs = new FileStream ("readwrite.tmp", FileMode.Open);  // Read/write
```

More on `FileMode` shortly.

Shortcut Methods on the File Class

The following static methods read an entire file into memory in one step:

- `File.ReadAllText` (returns a string)
- `File.ReadAllLines` (returns an array of strings)
- `File.ReadAllBytes` (returns a byte array)

The following static methods write an entire file in one step:

- `File.WriteAllText`
- `File.WriteAllLines`
- `File.WriteAllBytes`
- `File.AppendAllText` (great for appending to a log file)

There's also a static method called `File.ReadLines`: this is like `ReadAllLines` except that it returns a lazily-evaluated `IEnumerable<string>`. This is more efficient because it doesn't load the entire file into memory at once. LINQ is ideal for consuming the results: the following calculates the number of lines greater than 80 characters in length:

```
int longLines = File.ReadLines ("filePath")
                    .Count (l => l.Length > 80);
```

Specifying a filename

A filename can be either absolute (e.g., *c:\temp\test.txt*) or relative to the current directory (e.g., *test.txt* or *temp\test.txt*). You can access or change the current directory via the static `Environment.CurrentDirectory` property.

 When a program starts, the current directory may or may not coincide with that of the program's executable. For this reason, you should never rely on the current directory for locating additional runtime files packaged along with your executable.

`AppDomain.CurrentDomain.BaseDirectory` returns the *application base directory*, which in normal cases is the folder containing the program's executable. To specify a filename relative to this directory, you can call `Path.Combine`:

```
string baseFolder = AppDomain.CurrentDomain.BaseDirectory;
string logoPath = Path.Combine (baseFolder, "logo.jpg");
Console.WriteLine (File.Exists (logoPath));
```

You can read and write across a network via a UNC path, such as *\\JoesPC\PicShare\pic.jpg* or *\\10.1.1.2\PicShare\pic.jpg*.

Specifying a FileMode

All of `FileStream`'s constructors that accept a filename also require a `FileMode` enum argument. Figure 15-3 shows how to choose a `FileMode`, and the choices yield results akin to calling a static method on the `File` class.

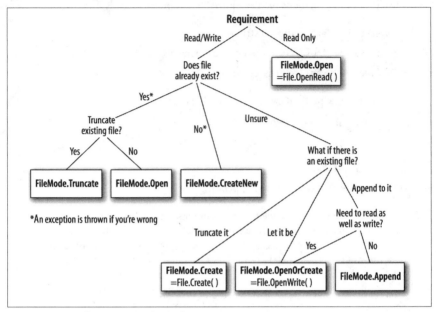

Figure 15-3. Choosing a FileMode

 `File.Create` and `FileMode.Create` will throw an exception if used on hidden files. To overwrite a hidden file, you must delete and re-create it:

```
if (File.Exists ("hidden.txt")) File.Delete ("hidden.txt");
```

Constructing a `FileStream` with just a filename and `FileMode` gives you (with just one exception) a readable writable stream. You can request a downgrade if you also supply a `FileAccess` argument:

```
[Flags]
public enum FileAccess { Read = 1, Write = 2, ReadWrite = 3 }
```

The following returns a read-only stream, equivalent to calling `File.OpenRead`:

```
using (var fs = new FileStream ("x.bin", FileMode.Open, FileAccess.Read))
  ...
```

`FileMode.Append` is the odd one out: with this mode, you get a *write-only* stream. To append with read-write support, you must instead use `FileMode.Open` or `File Mode.OpenOrCreate` and then seek the end of the stream:

```
using (var fs = new FileStream ("myFile.bin", FileMode.Open))
{
  fs.Seek (0, SeekOrigin.End);
  ...
```

Advanced FileStream features

Here are other optional arguments you can include when constructing a File
Stream:

- A FileShare enum describing how much access to grant other processes want-
  ing to dip into the same file before you've finished (None, Read [default], Read
  Write, or Write).
- The size, in bytes, of the internal buffer (default is currently 4 KB).
- A flag indicating whether to defer to the operating system for asynchronous
  I/O.
- A FileSecurity object describing what user and role permissions to assign a
  new file.
- A FileOptions flags enum for requesting operating system encryption (Encryp
  ted), automatic deletion upon closure for temporary files (DeleteOnClose),
  and optimization hints (RandomAccess and SequentialScan). There is also a
  WriteThrough flag that requests that the operating system disable write-behind
  caching; this is for transactional files or logs.

Opening a file with FileShare.ReadWrite allows other processes or users to simultaneously read and write to the same file. To avoid chaos, you can all agree to lock
specified portions of the file before reading or writing, using these methods:

```
// Defined on the FileStream class:
public virtual void Lock   (long position, long length);
public virtual void Unlock (long position, long length);
```

Lock throws an exception if part or all of the requested file section has already been
locked. This is the system used in file-based databases such as Access and FoxPro.

MemoryStream

MemoryStream uses an array as a backing store. This partly defeats the purpose of
having a stream, because the entire backing store must reside in memory at once.
MemoryStream still has uses, however; an example is when you need random access
to a nonseekable stream. If you know the source stream will be of a manageable size,
you can copy it into a MemoryStream as follows:

```
var ms = new MemoryStream();
sourceStream.CopyTo (ms);
```

You can convert a MemoryStream to a byte array by calling ToArray. The GetBuffer
method does the same job more efficiently by returning a direct reference to the

underlying storage array; unfortunately, this array is usually longer than the stream's real length.

 Closing and flushing a MemoryStream is optional. If you close a MemoryStream, you can no longer read or write to it, but you are still permitted to call ToArray to obtain the underlying data. Flush does absolutely nothing on a memory stream.

You can find further MemoryStream examples in the section "Compression Streams" on page 647 later in this chapter, and in the section "Cryptography Overview" on page 889 in Chapter 21.

PipeStream

PipeStream was introduced in Framework 3.5. It provides a simple means by which one process can communicate with another through the Windows *pipes* protocol. There are two kinds of pipe:

Anonymous pipe
Allows one-way communication between a parent and child process on the same computer

Named pipe
Allows two-way communication between arbitrary processes on the same computer—or different computers across a Windows network

A pipe is good for interprocess communication (IPC) on a single computer: it doesn't rely on a network transport, which equates to good performance and no issues with firewalls. Pipes are not supported in Windows Store applications.

 Pipes are stream-based, so one process waits to receive a series of bytes while another process sends them. An alternative is for processes to communicate via a block of shared memory— we describe how to do this later, in the section "Memory-Mapped Files" on page 663.

PipeStream is an abstract class with four concrete subtypes. Two are used for anonymous pipes and the other two for named pipes:

Anonymous pipes
AnonymousPipeServerStream and AnonymousPipeClientStream

Named pipes
NamedPipeServerStream and NamedPipeClientStream

Named pipes are simpler to use, so we'll describe them first.

A pipe is a low-level construct that allows just the sending and receiving of bytes (or *messages*, which are groups of bytes). The WCF and Remoting APIs offer higher-level messaging frameworks with the option of using an IPC channel for communication.

Named pipes

With named pipes, the parties communicate through a pipe of the same name. The protocol defines two distinct roles: the client and server. Communication happens between the client and server as follows:

- The server instantiates a NamedPipeServerStream and then calls WaitForConnection.

- The client instantiates a NamedPipeClientStream and then calls Connect (with an optional timeout).

The two parties then read and write the streams to communicate.

The following example demonstrates a server that sends a single byte (100) and then waits to receive a single byte:

```
using (var s = new NamedPipeServerStream ("pipedream"))
{
  s.WaitForConnection();
  s.WriteByte (100);
  Console.WriteLine (s.ReadByte());
}
```

Here's the corresponding client code:

```
using (var s = new NamedPipeClientStream ("pipedream"))
{
  s.Connect();
  Console.WriteLine (s.ReadByte());
  s.WriteByte (200);                  // Send the value 200 back.
}
```

Named pipe streams are bidirectional by default, so either party can read or write their stream. This means the client and server must agree on some protocol to coordinate their actions so both parties don't end up sending or receiving at once.

There also needs to be agreement on the length of each transmission. Our example was trivial in this regard, because we bounced just a single byte in each direction. To help with messages longer than one byte, pipes provide a *message* transmission mode. If this is enabled, a party calling Read can know when a message is complete by checking the IsMessageComplete property. To demonstrate, we'll start by writing a helper method that reads a whole message from a message-enabled PipeStream—in other words, reads until IsMessageComplete is true:

```
static byte[] ReadMessage (PipeStream s)
{
```

```
MemoryStream ms = new MemoryStream();
byte[] buffer = new byte [0x1000];        // Read in 4 KB blocks

do   { ms.Write (buffer, 0, s.Read (buffer, 0, buffer.Length)); }
while (!s.IsMessageComplete);

return ms.ToArray();
}
```

(To make this asynchronous, replace "s.Read" with "await s.ReadAsync".)

 You cannot determine whether a PipeStream has finished reading a message simply by waiting for Read to return 0. This is because, unlike most other stream types, pipe streams and network streams have no definite end. Instead, they temporarily "dry up" between message transmissions.

Now we can activate message transmission mode. On the server, this is done by specifying PipeTransmissionMode.Message when constructing the stream:

```
using (var s = new NamedPipeServerStream ("pipedream", PipeDirection.InOut,
                                   1, PipeTransmissionMode.Message))
{
  s.WaitForConnection();

  byte[] msg = Encoding.UTF8.GetBytes ("Hello");
  s.Write (msg, 0, msg.Length);

  Console.WriteLine (Encoding.UTF8.GetString (ReadMessage (s)));
}
```

On the client, we activate message transmission mode by setting ReadMode after calling Connect:

```
using (var s = new NamedPipeClientStream ("pipedream"))
{
  s.Connect();
  s.ReadMode = PipeTransmissionMode.Message;

  Console.WriteLine (Encoding.UTF8.GetString (ReadMessage (s)));

  byte[] msg = Encoding.UTF8.GetBytes ("Hello right back!");
  s.Write (msg, 0, msg.Length);
}
```

Anonymous pipes

An anonymous pipe provides a one-way communication stream between a parent and child process. Instead of using a system-wide name, anonymous pipes tune in through a private handle.

As with named pipes, there are distinct client and server roles. The system of communication is a little different, however, and proceeds as follows:

1. The server instantiates an AnonymousPipeServerStream, committing to a Pipe Direction of In or Out.

2. The server calls GetClientHandleAsString to obtain an identifier for the pipe, which it then passes to the client (typically as an argument when starting the child process).

3. The child process instantiates an AnonymousPipeClientStream, specifying the opposite PipeDirection.

4. The server releases the local handle that was generated in Step 2, by calling Dis poseLocalCopyOfClientHandle.

5. The parent and child processes communicate by reading/writing the stream.

Because anonymous pipes are unidirectional, a server must create two pipes for bidirectional communication. The following demonstrates a server that sends a single byte to the child process and then receives a single byte back from that process:

```
string clientExe = @"d:\PipeDemo\ClientDemo.exe";

HandleInheritability inherit = HandleInheritability.Inheritable;

using (var tx = new AnonymousPipeServerStream (PipeDirection.Out, inherit))
using (var rx = new AnonymousPipeServerStream (PipeDirection.In, inherit))
{
  string txID = tx.GetClientHandleAsString();
  string rxID = rx.GetClientHandleAsString();

  var startInfo = new ProcessStartInfo (clientExe, txID + " " + rxID);
  startInfo.UseShellExecute = false;      // Required for child process
  Process p = Process.Start (startInfo);

  tx.DisposeLocalCopyOfClientHandle();    // Release unmanaged
  rx.DisposeLocalCopyOfClientHandle();    // handle resources.

  tx.WriteByte (100);
  Console.WriteLine ("Server received: " + rx.ReadByte());

  p.WaitForExit();
}
```

Here's the corresponding client code that would be compiled to *d:\PipeDemo\Client-Demo.exe*:

```
string rxID = args[0];    // Note we're reversing the
string txID = args[1];    // receive and transmit roles.

using (var rx = new AnonymousPipeClientStream (PipeDirection.In, rxID))
using (var tx = new AnonymousPipeClientStream (PipeDirection.Out, txID))
{
  Console.WriteLine ("Client received: " + rx.ReadByte());
  tx.WriteByte (200);
}
```

As with named pipes, the client and server must coordinate their sending and receiving and agree on the length of each transmission. Anonymous pipes don't, unfortunately, support message mode, so you must implement your own protocol for message length agreement. One solution is to send, in the first 4 bytes of each transmission, an integer value defining the length of the message to follow. The Bit Converter class provides methods for converting between an integer and an array of 4 bytes.

BufferedStream

BufferedStream decorates, or wraps, another stream with buffering capability, and it is one of a number of decorator stream types in the core .NET Framework, all of which are illustrated in Figure 15-4.

Buffering improves performance by reducing round trips to the backing store. Here's how we wrap a FileStream in a 20 KB BufferedStream:

```
// Write 100K to a file:
File.WriteAllBytes ("myFile.bin", new byte [100000]);

using (FileStream fs = File.OpenRead ("myFile.bin"))
using (BufferedStream bs = new BufferedStream (fs, 20000))  //20K buffer
{
  bs.ReadByte();
  Console.WriteLine (fs.Position);          // 20000
}
```

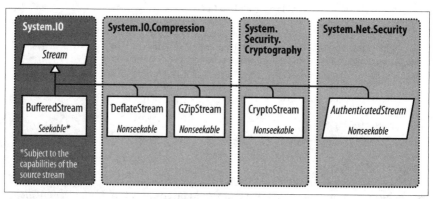

Figure 15-4. Decorator streams

In this example, the underlying stream advances 20,000 bytes after reading just 1 byte, thanks to the read-ahead buffering. We could call ReadByte another 19,999 times before the FileStream would be hit again.

Coupling a BufferedStream to a FileStream, as in this example, is of limited value because FileStream already has built-in buffering. Its only use might be in enlarging the buffer on an already constructed FileStream.

Closing a `BufferedStream` automatically closes the underlying backing store stream.

Stream Adapters

A `Stream` deals only in bytes; to read or write data types such as strings, integers, or XML elements, you must plug in an adapter. Here's what the Framework provides:

Text adapters (for string and character data)
    `TextReader, TextWriter`
    `StreamReader, StreamWriter`
    `StringReader, StringWriter`

Binary adapters (for primitive types such as `int`, `bool`, `string`, *and* `float`)
    `BinaryReader, BinaryWriter`

XML adapters (covered in Chapter 11)
    `XmlReader, XmlWriter`

The relationships between these types are illustrated in Figure 15-5.

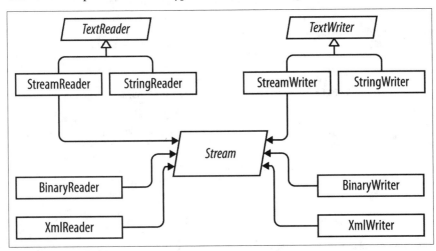

Figure 15-5. Readers and writers

Text Adapters

`TextReader` and `TextWriter` are the abstract base classes for adapters that deal exclusively with characters and strings. Each has two general-purpose implementations in the framework:

`StreamReader/StreamWriter`
    Uses a `Stream` for its raw data store, translating the stream's bytes into characters or strings

StringReader/StringWriter

Implements TextReader/TextWriter using in-memory strings

Table 15-2 lists TextReader's members by category. Peek returns the next character in the stream without advancing the position. Both Peek and the zero-argument version of Read return –1 if at the end of the stream; otherwise, they return an integer that can be cast directly to a char. The overload of Read that accepts a char[] buffer is identical in functionality to the ReadBlock method. ReadLine reads until reaching either a CR (character 13) or LF (character 10), or a CR+LF pair in sequence. It then returns a string, discarding the CR/LF characters.

Table 15-2. TextReader members

Category	Members
Reading one char	`public virtual int Peek(); // Cast the result to a char`
	`public virtual int Read(); // Cast the result to a char`
Reading many chars	`public virtual int Read (char[] buffer, int index, int count);`
	`public virtual int ReadBlock (char[] buffer, int index, int count);`
	`public virtual string ReadLine();`
	`public virtual string ReadToEnd();`
Closing	`public virtual void Close();`
	`public void Dispose(); // Same as Close`
Other	`public static readonly TextReader Null;`
	`public static TextReader Synchronized (TextReader reader);`

 The new line sequence in Windows is loosely modeled on a mechanical typewriter: a carriage return (character 13) followed by a line feed (character 10). The C# string is "\r\n" (think "ReturN"). Reverse the order and you'll get either two new lines or none!

TextWriter has analogous methods for writing, as shown in Table 15-3. The Write and WriteLine methods are additionally overloaded to accept every primitive type, plus the object type. These methods simply call the ToString method on whatever is passed in (optionally through an IFormatProvider specified either when calling the method or when constructing the TextWriter).

Table 15-3. TextWriter members

Category	Members
Writing one char	`public virtual void Write (char value);`
Writing many chars	`public virtual void Write (string value);`
	`public virtual void Write (char[] buffer, int index, int count);`
	`public virtual void Write (string format, params object[] arg);`
	`public virtual void WriteLine (string value);`
Closing and flushing	`public virtual void Close();`
	`public void Dispose(); // Same as Close`
	`public virtual void Flush();`
Formatting and encoding	`public virtual IFormatProvider FormatProvider { get; }`
	`public virtual string NewLine { get; set; }`
	`public abstract Encoding Encoding { get; }`
Other	`public static readonly TextWriter Null;`
	`public static TextWriter Synchronized (TextWriter writer);`

`WriteLine` simply appends the given text with CR+LF. You can change this via the `NewLine` property (this can be useful for interoperability with Unix file formats).

As with `Stream`, `TextReader` and `TextWriter` offer task-based asynchronous versions of their read/write methods.

StreamReader and StreamWriter

In the following example, a `StreamWriter` writes two lines of text to a file, and then a `StreamReader` reads the file back:

```
using (FileStream fs = File.Create ("test.txt"))
using (TextWriter writer = new StreamWriter (fs))
{
  writer.WriteLine ("Line1");
  writer.WriteLine ("Line2");
}

using (FileStream fs = File.OpenRead ("test.txt"))
using (TextReader reader = new StreamReader (fs))
{
  Console.WriteLine (reader.ReadLine());        // Line1
```

```
    Console.WriteLine (reader.ReadLine());        // Line2
  }
```

Because text adapters are so often coupled with files, the File class provides the static methods CreateText, AppendText, and OpenText to shortcut the process:

```
using (TextWriter writer = File.CreateText ("test.txt"))
{
  writer.WriteLine ("Line1");
  writer.WriteLine ("Line2");
}

using (TextWriter writer = File.AppendText ("test.txt"))
  writer.WriteLine ("Line3");

using (TextReader reader = File.OpenText ("test.txt"))
  while (reader.Peek() > -1)
    Console.WriteLine (reader.ReadLine());        // Line1
                                                  // Line2
                                                  // Line3
```

This also illustrates how to test for the end of a file (viz. reader.Peek()). Another option is to read until reader.ReadLine returns null.

You can also read and write other types such as integers, but because TextWriter invokes ToString on your type, you must parse a string when reading it back:

```
using (TextWriter w = File.CreateText ("data.txt"))
{
  w.WriteLine (123);           // Writes "123"
  w.WriteLine (true);          // Writes the word "true"
}

using (TextReader r = File.OpenText ("data.txt"))
{
  int myInt = int.Parse (r.ReadLine());      // myInt == 123
  bool yes = bool.Parse (r.ReadLine());      // yes == true
}
```

Character encodings

TextReader and TextWriter are by themselves just abstract classes with no connection to a stream or backing store. The StreamReader and StreamWriter types, however, are connected to an underlying byte-oriented stream, so they must convert between characters and bytes. They do so through an Encoding class from the System.Text namespace, which you choose when constructing the StreamReader or StreamWriter. If you choose none, the default UTF-8 encoding is used.

If you explicitly specify an encoding, StreamWriter will, by default, write a prefix to the start of the stream to identity the encoding. This is usually undesirable, and you can prevent it by constructing the encoding as follows:

```
var encoding = new UTF8Encoding (
  encoderShouldEmitUTF8Identifier:false,
  throwOnInvalidBytes:true);
```

The second argument tells the StreamWriter (or Stream Reader) to throw an exception if it encounters bytes that do not have a valid string translation for their encoding, which matches its default behavior if you do not specify an encoding.

The simplest of the encodings is ASCII, because each character is represented by one byte. The ASCII encoding maps the first 127 characters of the Unicode set into its single byte, covering what you see on a US-style keyboard. Most other characters, including specialized symbols and non-English characters, cannot be represented and are converted to the □ character. The default UTF-8 encoding can map all allocated Unicode characters, but it is more complex. The first 127 characters encode to a single byte, for ASCII compatibility; the remaining characters encode to a variable number of bytes (most commonly two or three). Consider this:

```
using (TextWriter w = File.CreateText ("but.txt"))   // Use default UTF-8
  w.WriteLine ("but-");                               // encoding.

using (Stream s = File.OpenRead ("but.txt"))
  for (int b; (b = s.ReadByte()) > -1;)
    Console.WriteLine (b);
```

The word "but" is followed not by a stock-standard hyphen, but by the longer em dash (—) character, U+2014. This is the one that won't get you into trouble with your book editor! Let's examine the output:

```
98      // b
117     // u
116     // t
226     // em dash byte 1      Note that the byte values
128     // em dash byte 2      are >= 128 for each part
148     // em dash byte 3      of the multibyte sequence.
13      // <CR>
10      // <LF>
```

Because the em dash is outside the first 127 characters of the Unicode set, it requires more than a single byte to encode in UTF-8 (in this case, three). UTF-8 is efficient with the Western alphabet as most popular characters consume just one byte. It also downgrades easily to ASCII simply by ignoring all bytes above 127. Its disadvantage is that seeking within a stream is troublesome, since a character's position does not correspond to its byte position in the stream. An alternative is UTF-16 (labeled just "Unicode" in the Encoding class). Here's how we write the same string with UTF-16:

```
using (Stream s = File.Create ("but.txt"))
using (TextWriter w = new StreamWriter (s, Encoding.Unicode))
  w.WriteLine ("but-");

foreach (byte b in File.ReadAllBytes ("but.txt"))
  Console.WriteLine (b);
```

The output is then:

```
255    // Byte-order mark 1
254    // Byte-order mark 2
98     // 'b' byte 1
0      // 'b' byte 2
117    // 'u' byte 1
0      // 'u' byte 2
116    // 't' byte 1
0      // 't' byte 2
20     // '--' byte 1
32     // '--' byte 2
13     // <CR> byte 1
0      // <CR> byte 2
10     // <LF> byte 1
0      // <LF> byte 2
```

Technically, UTF-16 uses either 2 or 4 bytes per character (there are close to a million Unicode characters allocated or reserved, so 2 bytes is not always enough). However, because the C# char type is itself only 16 bits wide, a UTF-16 encoding will always use exactly 2 bytes per .NET char. This makes it easy to jump to a particular character index within a stream.

UTF-16 uses a 2-byte prefix to identify whether the byte pairs are written in a "little-endian" or "big-endian" order (the least significant byte first or the most significant byte first). The default little-endian order is standard for Windows-based systems.

StringReader and StringWriter

The StringReader and StringWriter adapters don't wrap a stream at all; instead, they use a string or StringBuilder as the underlying data source. This means no byte translation is required—in fact, the classes do nothing you couldn't easily achieve with a string or StringBuilder coupled with an index variable. Their advantage, though, is that they share a base class with StreamReader/StreamWriter. For instance, suppose we have a string containing XML and want to parse it with an XmlReader. The XmlReader.Create method accepts one of the following:

- A URI
- A Stream
- A TextReader

So, how do we XML-parse our string? Because StringReader is a subclass of TextReader, we're in luck. We can instantiate and pass in a StringReader as follows:

```
XmlReader r = XmlReader.Create (new StringReader (myString));
```

Binary Adapters

BinaryReader and BinaryWriter read and write native data types: bool, byte, char, decimal, float, double, short, int, long, sbyte, ushort, uint, and ulong, as well as strings and arrays of the primitive data types.

Unlike StreamReader and StreamWriter, binary adapters store primitive data types efficiently, as they are represented in memory. So, an int uses 4 bytes; a double 8 bytes. Strings are written through a text encoding (as with StreamReader and StreamWriter) but are length-prefixed in order to make it possible to read back a series of strings without needing special delimiters.

Imagine we have a simple type, defined as follows:

```
public class Person
{
  public string Name;
  public int    Age;
  public double Height;
}
```

We can add the following methods to Person to save/load its data to/from a stream using binary adapters:

```
public void SaveData (Stream s)
{
  var w = new BinaryWriter (s);
  w.Write (Name);
  w.Write (Age);
  w.Write (Height);
  w.Flush();         // Ensure the BinaryWriter buffer is cleared.
                     // We won't dispose/close it, so more data
}                    // can be written to the stream.

public void LoadData (Stream s)
{
  var r = new BinaryReader (s);
  Name   = r.ReadString();
  Age    = r.ReadInt32();
  Height = r.ReadDouble();
}
```

BinaryReader can also read into byte arrays. The following reads the entire contents of a seekable stream:

```
byte[] data = new BinaryReader (s).ReadBytes ((int) s.Length);
```

This is more convenient than reading directly from a stream, because it doesn't require a loop to ensure that all data has been read.

Closing and Disposing Stream Adapters

You have four choices in tearing down stream adapters:

1. Close the adapter only.
2. Close the adapter, and then close the stream.
3. (For writers) Flush the adapter, and then close the stream.
4. (For readers) Close just the stream.

Close and Dispose are synonymous with adapters, just as they are with streams.

Options 1 and 2 are semantically identical, because closing an adapter automatically closes the underlying stream. Whenever you nest using statements, you're implicitly taking option 2:

```
using (FileStream fs = File.Create ("test.txt"))
using (TextWriter writer = new StreamWriter (fs))
  writer.WriteLine ("Line");
```

Because the nest disposes from the inside out, the adapter is first closed, and then the stream. Furthermore, if an exception is thrown within the adapter's constructor, the stream still closes. It's hard to go wrong with nested using statements!

Never close a stream before closing or flushing its writer—you'll amputate any data that's buffered in the adapter.

Options 3 and 4 work because adapters are in the unusual category of *optionally* disposable objects. An example of when you might choose not to dispose an adapter is when you've finished with the adapter but you want to leave the underlying stream open for subsequent use:

```
using (FileStream fs = new FileStream ("test.txt", FileMode.Create))
{
  StreamWriter writer = new StreamWriter (fs);
  writer.WriteLine ("Hello");
  writer.Flush();

  fs.Position = 0;
  Console.WriteLine (fs.ReadByte());
}
```

Here we write to a file, reposition the stream, and then read the first byte before closing the stream. If we disposed the StreamWriter, it would also close the underlying FileStream, causing the subsequent read to fail. The proviso is that we call Flush to ensure that the StreamWriter's buffer is written to the underlying stream.

Stream adapters—with their optional disposal semantics—do not implement the extended disposal pattern where the finalizer calls Dispose. This allows an abandoned adapter to evade automatic disposal when the garbage collector catches up with it.

From Framework 4.5, there's a new constructor on StreamReader/StreamWriter that instructs it to keep the stream open after disposal. Hence we can rewrite the preceding example as follows:

```
using (var fs = new FileStream ("test.txt", FileMode.Create))
{
  using (var writer = new StreamWriter (fs, new UTF8Encoding (false, true),
                                        0x400, true))
    writer.WriteLine ("Hello");

  fs.Position = 0;
  Console.WriteLine (fs.ReadByte());
  Console.WriteLine (fs.Length);
}
```

Compression Streams

Two general-purpose compression streams are provided in the System.IO.Compression namespace: DeflateStream and GZipStream. Both use a popular compression algorithm similar to that of the ZIP format. They differ in that GZipStream writes an additional protocol at the start and end—including a CRC to detect errors. GZipStream also conforms to a standard recognized by other software.

Both streams allow reading and writing, with the following provisos:

- You always *write* to the stream when compressing.
- You always *read* from the stream when decompressing.

DeflateStream and GZipStream are decorators; they compress or decompress data from another stream that you supply in construction. In the following example, we compress and decompress a series of bytes, using a FileStream as the backing store:

```
using (Stream s = File.Create ("compressed.bin"))
using (Stream ds = new DeflateStream (s, CompressionMode.Compress))
  for (byte i = 0; i < 100; i++)
    ds.WriteByte (i);

using (Stream s = File.OpenRead ("compressed.bin"))
using (Stream ds = new DeflateStream (s, CompressionMode.Decompress))
  for (byte i = 0; i < 100; i++)
    Console.WriteLine (ds.ReadByte());      // Writes 0 to 99
```

Even with the smaller of the two algorithms, the compressed file is 241 bytes long: more than double the original! Compression works poorly with "dense," nonrepetitive binary data (and worst of all with encrypted data, which lacks regularity by design). It works well with most text files; in the next example, we compress and decompress a text stream composed of 1,000 words chosen randomly from a small sentence. This also demonstrates chaining a backing store stream, a decorator stream, and an adapter (as depicted at the start of the chapter in Figure 15-1), as well as the use of asynchronous methods:

```
string[] words = "The quick brown fox jumps over the lazy dog".Split();
Random rand = new Random();

using (Stream s = File.Create ("compressed.bin"))
using (Stream ds = new DeflateStream (s, CompressionMode.Compress))
using (TextWriter w = new StreamWriter (ds))
  for (int i = 0; i < 1000; i++)
    await w.WriteAsync (words [rand.Next (words.Length)] + " ");

Console.WriteLine (new FileInfo ("compressed.bin").Length);      // 1073

using (Stream s = File.OpenRead ("compressed.bin"))
using (Stream ds = new DeflateStream (s, CompressionMode.Decompress))
using (TextReader r = new StreamReader (ds))
  Console.Write (await r.ReadToEndAsync());  // Output below:

lazy lazy the fox the quick The brown fox jumps over fox over fox The
brown brown brown over brown quick fox brown dog dog lazy fox dog brown
over fox jumps lazy lazy quick The jumps fox jumps The over jumps dog...
```

In this case, `DeflateStream` compresses efficiently to 1,073 bytes—slightly more than 1 byte per word.

Compressing in Memory

Sometimes you need to compress entirely in memory. Here's how to use a `Memory Stream` for this purpose:

```
byte[] data = new byte[1000];          // We can expect a good compression
                                       // ratio from an empty array!
var ms = new MemoryStream();
using (Stream ds = new DeflateStream (ms, CompressionMode.Compress))
  ds.Write (data, 0, data.Length);

byte[] compressed = ms.ToArray();
Console.WriteLine (compressed.Length);       // 11

// Decompress back to the data array:
ms = new MemoryStream (compressed);
using (Stream ds = new DeflateStream (ms, CompressionMode.Decompress))
  for (int i = 0; i < 1000; i += ds.Read (data, i, 1000 - i));
```

The `using` statement around the `DeflateStream` closes it in a textbook fashion, flushing any unwritten buffers in the process. This also closes the `MemoryStream` it wraps—meaning we must then call `ToArray` to extract its data.

Here's an alternative that avoids closing the `MemoryStream` and uses the asynchronous read and write methods:

```
byte[] data = new byte[1000];

MemoryStream ms = new MemoryStream();
using (Stream ds = new DeflateStream (ms, CompressionMode.Compress, true))
  await ds.WriteAsync (data, 0, data.Length);

Console.WriteLine (ms.Length);          // 113
ms.Position = 0;
using (Stream ds = new DeflateStream (ms, CompressionMode.Decompress))
  for (int i = 0; i < 1000; i += await ds.ReadAsync (data, i, 1000 - i));
```

The additional flag sent to DeflateStream's constructor tells it not to follow the usual protocol of taking the underlying stream with it in disposal. In other words, the MemoryStream is left open, allowing us to position it back to zero and reread it.

Working with ZIP Files

Support for the popular zip-file compression format was introduced in Framework 4.5, via the new ZipArchive and ZipFile classes in System.IO.Compression (in an assembly called *System.IO.Compression.FileSystem.dll*). The advantage of this format over DeflateStream and GZipStream is that it acts as a container for multiple files and is compatible with ZIP files created with Windows Explorer or other compression utilities.

ZipArchive works with streams, whereas ZipFile addresses the more common scenario of working with files. (ZipFile is a static helper class for ZipArchive).

ZipFile's CreateFromDirectory method adds all the files in a specified directory into a ZIP file:

```
ZipFile.CreateFromDirectory (@"d:\MyFolder", @"d:\compressed.zip");
```

whereas ExtractToDirectory does the opposite and extracts a ZIP file to a directory:

```
ZipFile.ExtractToDirectory (@"d:\compressed.zip", @"d:\MyFolder");
```

When compressing, you can specify whether to optimize for file size or speed, and whether to include the name of the source directory in the archive. Enabling the latter option in our example would create a subdirectory in the archive called *MyFolder* into which the compressed files would go.

ZipFile has an Open method for reading/writing individual entries. This returns a ZipArchive object (which you can also obtain by instantiating ZipArchive with a Stream object). When calling Open, you must specify a filename and indicate whether you want to Read, Create or Update the archive. You can then enumerate existing entries via the Entries property or find a particular file with GetEntry:

```
using (ZipArchive zip = ZipFile.Open (@"d:\zz.zip", ZipArchiveMode.Read))
  foreach (ZipArchiveEntry entry in zip.Entries)
    Console.WriteLine (entry.FullName + " " + entry.Length);
```

ZipArchiveEntry also has a Delete method, an ExtractToFile method (this is actually an extension method in the ZipFileExtensions class), and an Open method that returns a readable/writable Stream. You can create new entries by calling Crea teEntry (or the CreateEntryFromFile extension method) on the ZipArchive. The following creates the archive *d:\zz.zip*, to which it adds *foo.dll*, under a directory structure within the archive called *bin\X86*:

```
byte[] data = File.ReadAllBytes (@"d:\foo.dll");
using (ZipArchive zip = ZipFile.Open (@"d:\zz.zip", ZipArchiveMode.Update))
    zip.CreateEntry (@"bin\X64\foo.dll").Open().Write (data, 0, data.Length);
```

You could do the same thing entirely in memory by constructing ZipArchive with a MemoryStream.

File and Directory Operations

The System.IO namespace provides a set of types for performing "utility" file and directory operations, such as copying and moving, creating directories, and setting file attributes and permissions. For most features, you can choose between either of two classes, one offering static methods and the other instance methods:

Static classes
    File and Directory

Instance method classes (constructed with a file or directory name)
    FileInfo and DirectoryInfo

Additionally, there's a static class called Path. This does nothing to files or directories; instead, it provides string manipulation methods for filenames and directory paths. Path also assists with temporary files.

All three classes are unavailable to Windows Store applications (see "File I/O in Windows Runtime" on page 661).

The File Class

File is a static class whose methods all accept a filename. The filename can be either relative to the current directory or fully qualified with a directory. Here are its methods (all public and static):

```
bool Exists (string path);       // Returns true if the file is present

void Delete  (string path);
void Copy    (string sourceFileName, string destFileName);
void Move    (string sourceFileName, string destFileName);
void Replace (string sourceFileName, string destinationFileName,
                                      string destinationBackupFileName);

FileAttributes GetAttributes (string path);
void SetAttributes           (string path, FileAttributes fileAttributes);
```

```
void Decrypt (string path);
void Encrypt (string path);

DateTime GetCreationTime   (string path);      // UTC versions are
DateTime GetLastAccessTime (string path);      // also provided.
DateTime GetLastWriteTime  (string path);

void SetCreationTime   (string path, DateTime creationTime);
void SetLastAccessTime (string path, DateTime lastAccessTime);
void SetLastWriteTime  (string path, DateTime lastWriteTime);

FileSecurity GetAccessControl (string path);
FileSecurity GetAccessControl (string path,
                               AccessControlSections includeSections);
void SetAccessControl (string path, FileSecurity fileSecurity);
```

Move throws an exception if the destination file already exists; Replace does not. Both methods allow the file to be renamed as well as moved to another directory.

Delete throws an UnauthorizedAccessException if the file is marked read-only; you can tell this in advance by calling GetAttributes. Here are all the members of the FileAttribute enum that GetAttributes returns:

```
Archive, Compressed, Device, Directory, Encrypted,
Hidden, Normal, NotContentIndexed, Offline, ReadOnly,
ReparsePoint, SparseFile, System, Temporary
```

Members in this enum are combinable. Here's how to toggle a single file attribute without upsetting the rest:

```
string filePath = @"c:\temp\test.txt";

FileAttributes fa = File.GetAttributes (filePath);
if ((fa & FileAttributes.ReadOnly) != 0)
{
    fa ^= FileAttributes.ReadOnly;
    File.SetAttributes (filePath, fa);
}

// Now we can delete the file, for instance:
File.Delete (filePath);
```

 FileInfo offers an easier way to change a file's read-only flag:

```
new FileInfo (@"c:\temp\test.txt").IsReadOnly = false;
```

Compression and encryption attributes

The Compressed and Encrypted file attributes correspond to the compression and encryption checkboxes on a file or directory's *properties* dialog box in Windows Explorer. This type of compression and encryption is *transparent* in that the operating system does all the work behind the scenes, allowing you to read and write plain data.

You cannot use SetAttributes to change a file's Compressed or Encrypted attributes—it fails silently if you try! The workaround is simple in the latter case: you instead call the Encrypt() and Decrypt() methods in the File class. With compression, it's more complicated; one solution is to use the Windows Management Instrumentation (WMI) API in System.Management. The following method compresses a directory, returning 0 if successful (or a WMI error code if not):

```
static uint CompressFolder (string folder, bool recursive)
{
  string path = "Win32_Directory.Name='" + folder + "'";
  using (ManagementObject dir = new ManagementObject (path))
  using (ManagementBaseObject p = dir.GetMethodParameters ("CompressEx"))
  {
    p ["Recursive"] = recursive;
    using (ManagementBaseObject result = dir.InvokeMethod ("CompressEx",
                                                            p, null))
      return (uint) result.Properties ["ReturnValue"].Value;
  }
}
```

To uncompress, replace CompressEx with UncompressEx.

Transparent encryption relies on a key seeded from the logged-in user's password. The system is robust to password changes performed by the authenticated user, but if a password is reset via an administrator, data in encrypted files is unrecoverable.

 Transparent encryption and compression require special file-system support. NTFS (used most commonly on hard drives) supports these features; CDFS (on CD-ROMs) and FAT (on removable media cards) do not.

You can determine whether a volume supports compression and encryption with Win32 interop:

```
using System;
using System.IO;
using System.Text;
using System.ComponentModel;
using System.Runtime.InteropServices;

class SupportsCompressionEncryption
{
  const int SupportsCompression = 0x10;
  const int SupportsEncryption = 0x20000;

  [DllImport ("Kernel32.dll", SetLastError = true)]
  extern static bool GetVolumeInformation (string vol, StringBuilder name,
    int nameSize, out uint serialNum, out uint maxNameLen, out uint flags,
    StringBuilder fileSysName, int fileSysNameSize);

  static void Main()
  {
    uint serialNum, maxNameLen, flags;
    bool ok = GetVolumeInformation (@"C:\", null, 0, out serialNum,
```

```
                              out maxNameLen, out flags, null, 0);
  if (!ok)
    throw new Win32Exception();

  bool canCompress = (flags & SupportsCompression) != 0;
  bool canEncrypt = (flags & SupportsEncryption) != 0;
  }
}
```

File security

The `GetAccessControl` and `SetAccessControl` methods allow you to query and change the operating system permissions assigned to users and roles via a `FileSe` `curity` object (namespace `System.Security.AccessControl`). You can also pass a `FileSecurity` object to a `FileStream`'s constructor to specify permissions when creating a new file.

In this example, we list a file's existing permissions and then assign execution permission to the "Users" group:

```
using System;
using System.IO;
using System.Security.AccessControl;
using System.Security.Principal;

...

FileSecurity sec = File.GetAccessControl (@"d:\test.txt");
AuthorizationRuleCollection rules = sec.GetAccessRules (true, true,
                                          typeof (NTAccount));
foreach (FileSystemAccessRule rule in rules)
{
  Console.WriteLine (rule.AccessControlType);      // Allow or Deny
  Console.WriteLine (rule.FileSystemRights);       // e.g., FullControl
  Console.WriteLine (rule.IdentityReference.Value); // e.g., MyDomain/Joe
}

var sid = new SecurityIdentifier (WellKnownSidType.BuiltinUsersSid, null);
string usersAccount = sid.Translate (typeof (NTAccount)).ToString();

FileSystemAccessRule newRule = new FileSystemAccessRule
  (usersAccount, FileSystemRights.ExecuteFile, AccessControlType.Allow);

sec.AddAccessRule (newRule);
File.SetAccessControl (@"d:\test.txt", sec);
```

We give another example, later, in "Special Folders" on page 657.

The Directory Class

The static `Directory` class provides a set of methods analogous to those in the `File` class—for checking whether a directory exists (`Exists`), moving a directory (`Move`), deleting a directory (`Delete`), getting/setting times of creation or last access, and getting/setting security permissions. Furthermore, `Directory` exposes the following static methods:

```
string GetCurrentDirectory ();
void   SetCurrentDirectory (string path);

DirectoryInfo CreateDirectory  (string path);
DirectoryInfo GetParent        (string path);
string        GetDirectoryRoot (string path);

string[] GetLogicalDrives();

// The following methods all return full paths:

string[] GetFiles            (string path);
string[] GetDirectories      (string path);
string[] GetFileSystemEntries (string path);

IEnumerable<string> EnumerateFiles            (string path);
IEnumerable<string> EnumerateDirectories       (string path);
IEnumerable<string> EnumerateFileSystemEntries (string path);
```

 The last three methods were added in Framework 4.0. They're potentially more efficient than the `Get*` variants because they're lazily evaluated—fetching data from the file system as you enumerate the sequence. They're particularly well-suited to LINQ queries.

The `Enumerate*` and `Get*` methods are overloaded to also accept `searchPattern` (string) and `searchOption` (enum) parameters. If you specify `SearchOp` `tion.SearchAllSubDirectories`, a recursive subdirectory search is performed. The `*FileSystemEntries` methods combine the results of `*Files` with `*Directories`.

Here's how to create a directory if it doesn't already exist:

```
if (!Directory.Exists (@"d:\test"))
   Directory.CreateDirectory (@"d:\test");
```

FileInfo and DirectoryInfo

The static methods on `File` and `Directory` are convenient for executing a single file or directory operation. If you need to call a series of methods in a row, the `FileInfo` and `DirectoryInfo` classes provide an object model that makes the job easier.

`FileInfo` offers most of the `File`'s static methods in instance form—with some additional properties such as `Extension`, `Length`, `IsReadOnly`, and `Directory`—for returning a `DirectoryInfo` object. For example:

```
FileInfo fi = new FileInfo (@"c:\temp\FileInfo.txt");
Console.WriteLine (fi.Exists);        // false

using (TextWriter w = fi.CreateText())
  w.Write ("Some text");
```

```
Console.WriteLine (fi.Exists);          // false (still)
fi.Refresh();
Console.WriteLine (fi.Exists);          // true

Console.WriteLine (fi.Name);            // FileInfo.txt
Console.WriteLine (fi.FullName);        // c:\temp\FileInfo.txt
Console.WriteLine (fi.DirectoryName);   // c:\temp
Console.WriteLine (fi.Directory.Name);  // temp
Console.WriteLine (fi.Extension);       // .txt
Console.WriteLine (fi.Length);          // 9

fi.Encrypt();
fi.Attributes ^= FileAttributes.Hidden;   // (Toggle hidden flag)
fi.IsReadOnly = true;

Console.WriteLine (fi.Attributes);      // ReadOnly,Archive,Hidden,Encrypted
Console.WriteLine (fi.CreationTime);

fi.MoveTo (@"c:\temp\FileInfoX.txt");

DirectoryInfo di = fi.Directory;
Console.WriteLine (di.Name);            // temp
Console.WriteLine (di.FullName);        // c:\temp
Console.WriteLine (di.Parent.FullName); // c:\
di.CreateSubdirectory ("SubFolder");
```

Here's how to use `DirectoryInfo` to enumerate files and subdirectories:

```
DirectoryInfo di = new DirectoryInfo (@"e:\photos");

foreach (FileInfo fi in di.GetFiles ("*.jpg"))
  Console.WriteLine (fi.Name);

foreach (DirectoryInfo subDir in di.GetDirectories())
  Console.WriteLine (subDir.FullName);
```

Path

The static `Path` class defines methods and fields for working with paths and file-names. Assuming this setup code:

```
string dir  = @"c:\mydir";
string file = "myfile.txt";
string path = @"c:\mydir\myfile.txt";

Directory.SetCurrentDirectory (@"k:\demo");
```

we can demonstrate `Path`'s methods and fields with the following expressions:

Expression	Result
`Directory.GetCurrentDirectory()`	k:\demo\
`Path.IsPathRooted (file)`	False
`Path.IsPathRooted (path)`	True

Expression	Result
Path.GetPathRoot (path)	c:\
Path.GetDirectoryName (path)	c:\mydir
Path.GetFileName (path)	myfile.txt
Path.GetFullPath (file)	k:\demo\myfile.txt
Path.Combine (dir, file)	c:\mydir\myfile.txt
File extensions:	
Path.HasExtension (file)	True
Path.GetExtension (file)	.txt
Path.GetFileNameWithoutExtension (file)	myfile
Path.ChangeExtension (file, ".log")	myfile.log
Separators and characters:	
Path.AltDirectorySeparatorChar	/
Path.PathSeparator	;
Path.VolumeSeparatorChar	:
Path.GetInvalidPathChars()	chars 0 to 31 and "<>|
Path.GetInvalidFileNameChars()	chars 0 to 31 and "<>|:*?\/
Temporary files:	
Path.GetTempPath()	*<local user folder>*\Temp
Path.GetRandomFileName()	*d2dwuzjf.dnp*
Path.GetTempFileName()	*<local user folder>*\Temp*tmp14B.tmp*

Combine is particularly useful: it allows you to combine a directory and filename—or two directories—without first having to check whether a trailing backslash is present.

GetFullPath converts a path relative to the current directory to an absolute path. It accepts values such as ..\..*file.txt*.

GetRandomFileName returns a genuinely unique 8.3 character filename, without actually creating any file. GetTempFileName generates a temporary filename using an auto-incrementing counter that repeats every 65,000 files. It then creates a zero-byte file of this name in the local temporary directory.

 You must delete the file generated by GetTempFileName when you're done; otherwise, it will eventually throw an exception (after your 65,000th call to GetTempFileName). If this is a problem, you can instead Combine GetTempPath with GetRandomFileName. Just be careful not to fill up the user's hard drive!

Special Folders

One thing missing from `Path` and `Directory` is a means to locate folders such as *My Documents, Program Files, Application Data,* and so on. This is provided instead by the `GetFolderPath` method in the `System.Environment` class:

```
string myDocPath = Environment.GetFolderPath
  (Environment.SpecialFolder.MyDocuments);
```

`Environment.SpecialFolder` is an enum whose values encompass all special directories in Windows:

AdminTools	CommonVideos	Personal
ApplicationData	Cookies	PrinterShortcuts
CDBurning	Desktop	ProgramFiles
CommonAdminTools	DesktopDirectory	ProgramFilesX86
CommonApplicationData	Favorites	Programs
CommonDesktopDirectory	Fonts	Recent
CommonDocuments	History	Resources
CommonMusic	InternetCache	SendTo
CommonOemLinks	LocalApplicationData	StartMenu
CommonPictures	LocalizedResources	Startup
CommonProgramFiles	MyComputer	System
CommonProgramFilesX86	MyDocuments	SystemX86
CommonPrograms	MyMusic	Templates
CommonStartMenu	MyPictures	UserProfile
CommonStartup	MyVideos	Windows
CommonTemplates	NetworkShortcuts	

 Everything is covered here, except the .NET Framework directory, which you can obtain as follows:

```
System.Runtime.InteropServices.
RuntimeEnvironment.GetRuntimeDirectory()
```

Of particular value is `ApplicationData`: this is where you can store settings that travel with a user across a network (if roaming profiles are enabled on the network domain); and `LocalApplicationData`, which is for non-roaming data (specific to the logged-in user); and `CommonApplicationData`, which is shared by every user of the computer. Writing application data to these folders is considered preferable to using the Windows Registry. The standard protocol for storing data in these folders is to create a subdirectory with the name of your application:

```
string localAppDataPath = Path.Combine (
  Environment.GetFolderPath (Environment.SpecialFolder.ApplicationData),
  "MyCoolApplication");

if (!Directory.Exists (localAppDataPath))
  Directory.CreateDirectory (localAppDataPath);
```

 Programs that run in the most restrictive sandboxes, such as Silverlight applications, cannot access these folders. Instead, use isolated storage (see the final section in this chapter) or for Windows Store apps, use the WinRT libraries (see "File I/O in Windows Runtime" on page 661).

There's a horrible trap when using CommonApplicationData: if a user starts your program with administrative elevation and your program then creates folders and files in CommonApplicationData, that user might lack permissions to replace those files later, when run under a restricted Windows login. (A similar problem exists when switching between restricted-permission accounts.) You can work around it by creating the desired folder (with permissions assigned to everyone) as part of your setup. Alternatively, if you run the following code immediately after creating a folder under CommonApplicationData (before writing any files), it will ensure that everyone in the "users" group is given unrestricted access:

```
public void AssignUsersFullControlToFolder (string path)
{
  try
  {
    var sec = Directory.GetAccessControl (path);
    if (UsersHaveFullControl (sec)) return;

    var rule = new FileSystemAccessRule (
      GetUsersAccount().ToString(),
      FileSystemRights.FullControl,
      InheritanceFlags.ContainerInherit | InheritanceFlags.ObjectInherit,
      PropagationFlags.None,
      AccessControlType.Allow);

    sec.AddAccessRule (rule);
    Directory.SetAccessControl (path, sec);
  }
  catch (UnauthorizedAccessException)
  {
    // Folder was already created by another user
  }
}

bool UsersHaveFullControl (FileSystemSecurity sec)
{
  var usersAccount = GetUsersAccount();
  var rules = sec.GetAccessRules (true, true, typeof (NTAccount))
                 .OfType<FileSystemAccessRule>();

  return rules.Any (r =>
    r.FileSystemRights == FileSystemRights.FullControl &&
```

```
        r.AccessControlType == AccessControlType.Allow &&
        r.InheritanceFlags == (InheritanceFlags.ContainerInherit |
                                InheritanceFlags.ObjectInherit) &&
        r.IdentityReference == usersAccount);
}

NTAccount GetUsersAccount()
{
    var sid = new SecurityIdentifier (WellKnownSidType.BuiltinUsersSid, null);
    return (NTAccount)sid.Translate (typeof (NTAccount));
}
```

Another place to write configuration and log files is to the application's base directory, which you can obtain with AppDomain.CurrentDomain.BaseDirectory. This is not recommended, however, because the operating system is likely to deny your application permissions to write to this folder after initial installation (without administrative elevation).

Querying Volume Information

You can query the drives on a computer with the DriveInfo class:

```
DriveInfo c = new DriveInfo ("C");        // Query the C: drive.

long totalSize = c.TotalSize;             // Size in bytes.
long freeBytes = c.TotalFreeSpace;        // Ignores disk quotas.
long freeToMe  = c.AvailableFreeSpace;    // Takes quotas into account.

foreach (DriveInfo d in DriveInfo.GetDrives())   // All defined drives.
{
    Console.WriteLine (d.Name);            // C:\
    Console.WriteLine (d.DriveType);       // Fixed
    Console.WriteLine (d.RootDirectory);   // C:\

    if (d.IsReady)   // If the drive is not ready, the following two
                     // properties will throw exceptions:
    {
        Console.WriteLine (d.VolumeLabel);   // The Sea Drive
        Console.WriteLine (d.DriveFormat);   // NTFS
    }
}
```

The static GetDrives method returns all mapped drives, including CD-ROMs, media cards, and network connections. DriveType is an enum with the following values:

```
Unknown, NoRootDirectory, Removable, Fixed, Network, CDRom, Ram
```

Catching Filesystem Events

The FileSystemWatcher class lets you monitor a directory (and optionally, subdirectories) for activity. FileSystemWatcher has events that fire when files or subdirectories are created, modified, renamed, and deleted, as well as when their attributes change. These events fire regardless of the user or process performing the change. Here's an example:

```
static void Main() { Watch (@"c:\temp", "*.txt", true); }

static void Watch (string path, string filter, bool includeSubDirs)
{
  using (var watcher = new FileSystemWatcher (path, filter))
  {
    watcher.Created += FileCreatedChangedDeleted;
    watcher.Changed += FileCreatedChangedDeleted;
    watcher.Deleted += FileCreatedChangedDeleted;
    watcher.Renamed += FileRenamed;
    watcher.Error   += FileError;

    watcher.IncludeSubdirectories = includeSubDirs;
    watcher.EnableRaisingEvents = true;

    Console.WriteLine ("Listening for events - press <enter> to end");
    Console.ReadLine();
  }
  // Disposing the FileSystemWatcher stops further events from firing.
}

static void FileCreatedChangedDeleted (object o, FileSystemEventArgs e)
  => Console.WriteLine ("File {0} has been {1}", e.FullPath, e.ChangeType);

static void FileRenamed (object o, RenamedEventArgs e)
  => Console.WriteLine ("Renamed: {0}->{1}", e.OldFullPath, e.FullPath);

static void FileError (object o, ErrorEventArgs e)
  => Console.WriteLine ("Error: " + e.GetException().Message);
```

 Because FileSystemWatcher raises events on a separate thread, you must exception-handle the event-handling code to prevent an error from taking down the application. See "Exception Handling" on page 573 in Chapter 14 for more information.

The Error event does not inform you of filesystem errors; instead, it indicates that the FileSystemWatcher's event buffer overflowed because it was overwhelmed by Changed, Created, Deleted, or Renamed events. You can change the buffer size via the InternalBufferSize property.

IncludeSubdirectories applies recursively. So, if you create a FileSystemWatcher on C:\ with IncludeSubdirectories true, its events will fire when a file or directory changes anywhere on the hard drive.

A trap in using `FileSystemWatcher` is to open and read newly created or updated files before the file has been fully populated or updated. If you're working in conjunction with some other software that's creating files, you might need to consider some strategy to mitigate this, such as creating files with an unwatched extension and then renaming them once fully written.

File I/O in Windows Runtime

The `FileStream` and `Directory`/`File` classes are unavailable to Windows Store applications. Instead, there are WinRT types in the `Windows.Storage` namespace for this purpose, the two primary classes being `StorageFolder` and `StorageFile`.

Working with Directories

The `StorageFolder` class represents a directory. You can obtain a `StorageFolder` via its static method `GetFolderFromPathAsync`, giving it a full path to the folder. However, given that WinRT lets you access files only in certain locations, an easier approach is to obtain a `StorageFolder` via the `KnownFolders` class, which exposes a static property for each of the (potentially) permitted locations:

```
public static StorageFolder DocumentsLibrary { get; }
public static StorageFolder PicturesLibrary { get; }
public static StorageFolder MusicLibrary { get; }
public static StorageFolder VideosLibrary { get; }
```

File access is further restricted by what's declared in the package manifest. In particular, Windows Store applications can access only those files whose extensions match their declared file type associations.

In addition, `Package.Current.InstalledLocation` returns the `StorageFolder` of your current application (to which you have read-only access).

`KnownFolders` also has properties for accessing removable devices and home group folders.

`StorageFolder` has the properties you'd expect (`Name`, `Path`, `DateCreated`, `DateModified`, `Attributes`, and so on), methods to delete/rename the folder (`DeleteAsync`/`RenameAsync`), and methods to list files and subfolders (`GetFilesAsync` and `GetFoldersAsync`).

As is evident from their names, the methods are asynchronous, returning an object that you can convert into a task with the `AsTask` extension method or directly await. The following obtains a directory listing of all files in the documents folder:

```
StorageFolder docsFolder = KnownFolders.DocumentsLibrary;
IReadOnlyList<StorageFile> files = await docsFolder.GetFilesAsync();
foreach (IStorageFile file in files)
  Debug.WriteLine (file.Name);
```

The `CreateFileQueryWithOptions` method lets you filter to a specific extension:

```
StorageFolder docsFolder = KnownFolders.DocumentsLibrary;
var queryOptions = new QueryOptions (CommonFileQuery.DefaultQuery,
                                    new[] { ".txt" });
var txtFiles = await docsFolder.CreateFileQueryWithOptions (queryOptions)
                               .GetFilesAsync();
foreach (StorageFile file in txtFiles)
  Debug.WriteLine (file.Name);
```

The `QueryOptions` class exposes properties to further control the search. For example, the `FolderDepth` property requests a recursive directory listing:

```
queryOptions.FolderDepth = FolderDepth.Deep;
```

Working with Files

`StorageFile` is the primary class for working with files. You can obtain an instance from a full path (to which you have permission) with the static `StorageFile.GetFileFromPathAsync` method or from a relative path by calling `GetFileAsync` method on a `StorageFolder` (or `IStorageFolder`) object:

```
StorageFolder docsFolder = KnownFolders.DocumentsLibrary;
StorageFile file = await docsFolder.GetFileAsync ("foo.txt");
```

If the file does not exist, a `FileNotFoundException` is thrown at that point.

`StorageFile` has properties such as `Name`, `Path`, etc., and methods for working with files, such as `Move`, `Rename`, `Copy`, and `Delete` (all `Async`). The `CopyAsync` method returns a `StorageFile` corresponding to the new file. There's also a `CopyAndReplaceAsync` that accepts a target `StorageFile` object rather than a target name and folder.

`StorageFile` also exposes methods to open the file for reading/writing via .NET streams (`OpenStreamForReadAsync` and `OpenStreamForWriteAsync`). For example, the following creates and writes to a file called *test.txt* in the documents folder:

```
StorageFolder docsFolder = KnownFolders.DocumentsLibrary;

StorageFile file = await docsFolder.CreateFileAsync
  ("test.txt", CreationCollisionOption.ReplaceExisting);

using (Stream stream = await file.OpenStreamForWriteAsync())
using (StreamWriter writer = new StreamWriter (stream))
  await writer.WriteLineAsync ("This is a test");
```

 If you don't specify `CreationCollisionOption.ReplaceExisting` and the file already exists, it will automatically append a number to the filename to make it unique.

The following reads the file back:

```
StorageFolder docsFolder = KnownFolders.DocumentsLibrary;
StorageFile file = await docsFolder.GetFileAsync ("test.txt");
```

```
using (var stream = await file.OpenStreamForReadAsync ())
using (StreamReader reader = new StreamReader (stream))
  Debug.WriteLine (await reader.ReadToEndAsync());
```

Isolated Storage in Windows Store Apps

Windows Store apps also have access to private folders that are isolated from other applications and can be used to store application-specific data:

```
Windows.Storage.ApplicationData.Current.LocalFolder
Windows.Storage.ApplicationData.Current.RoamingFolder
Windows.Storage.ApplicationData.Current.TemporaryFolder
```

Each of these static properties returns a `StorageFolder` object that can be used to read/write and list files as we described previously.

Memory-Mapped Files

Memory-mapped files provide two key features:

- Efficient random access to file data
- The ability to share memory between different processes on the same computer

The types for memory-mapped files reside in the `System.IO.MemoryMappedFiles` namespace and were introduced in Framework 4.0. Internally, they work by wrapping the Win32 API for memory-mapped files and are unavailable in Windows Store apps.

Memory-Mapped Files and Random File I/O

Although an ordinary `FileStream` allows random file I/O (by setting the stream's `Position` property), it's optimized for sequential I/O. As a rough rule of thumb:

- `FileStream`s are 10 times faster than memory-mapped files for sequential I/O.
- Memory-mapped files are 10 times faster than `FileStream`s for random I/O.

Changing a `FileStream`'s `Position` can cost several microseconds—which adds up if done within a loop. A `FileStream` is also unsuitable for multithreaded access—because its position changes as it is read or written.

To create a memory-mapped file:

1. Obtain a `FileStream` as you would ordinarily.
2. Instantiate a `MemoryMappedFile`, passing in the file stream.
3. Call `CreateViewAccessor` on the memory-mapped file object.

The last step gives you a `MemoryMappedViewAccessor` object that provides methods for randomly reading and writing simple types, structures, and arrays (more on this in "Working with View Accessors" on page 665).

The following creates a one million-byte file and then uses the memory-mapped file API to read and then write a byte at position 500,000:

```
File.WriteAllBytes ("long.bin", new byte [1000000]);

using (MemoryMappedFile mmf = MemoryMappedFile.CreateFromFile ("long.bin"))
using (MemoryMappedViewAccessor accessor = mmf.CreateViewAccessor())
{
  accessor.Write (500000, (byte) 77);
  Console.WriteLine (accessor.ReadByte (500000));    // 77
}
```

You can also specify a map name and capacity when calling `CreateFromFile`. Specifying a non-null map name allows the memory block to be shared with other processes (see the following section); specifying a capacity automatically enlarges the file to that value. The following creates a 1,000-byte file:

```
using (var mmf = MemoryMappedFile.CreateFromFile
                  ("long.bin", FileMode.Create, null, 1000))
  ...
```

Memory-Mapped Files and Shared Memory

You can also use memory-mapped files as a means of sharing memory between processes on the same computer. One process creates a shared memory block by calling `MemoryMappedFile.CreateNew`, while other processes subscribe to that same memory block by calling `MemoryMappedFile.OpenExisting` with the same name. Although it's still referred to as a memory-mapped "file," it lives entirely in memory and has no disk presence.

The following creates a 500-byte shared memory-mapped file and writes the integer 12345 at position 0:

```
using (MemoryMappedFile mmFile = MemoryMappedFile.CreateNew ("Demo", 500))
using (MemoryMappedViewAccessor accessor = mmFile.CreateViewAccessor())
{
  accessor.Write (0, 12345);
  Console.ReadLine();    // Keep shared memory alive until user hits Enter.
}
```

while the following opens that same memory-mapped file and reads that integer:

```
// This can run in a separate EXE:
using (MemoryMappedFile mmFile = MemoryMappedFile.OpenExisting ("Demo"))
using (MemoryMappedViewAccessor accessor = mmFile.CreateViewAccessor())
  Console.WriteLine (accessor.ReadInt32 (0));    // 12345
```

Working with View Accessors

Calling CreateViewAccessor on a MemoryMappedFile gives you a view accessor that lets you read/write values at random positions.

The Read*/Write* methods accept numeric types, bool, and char, as well as arrays and structs that contain value-type elements or fields. Reference types—and arrays or structs that contain reference types—are prohibited because they cannot map into unmanaged memory. So if you want to write a string, you must encode it into an array of bytes:

```
byte[] data = Encoding.UTF8.GetBytes ("This is a test");
accessor.Write (0, data.Length);
accessor.WriteArray (4, data, 0, data.Length);
```

Notice that we wrote the length first. This means we know how many bytes to read back later:

```
byte[] data = new byte [accessor.ReadInt32 (0)];
accessor.ReadArray (4, data, 0, data.Length);
Console.WriteLine (Encoding.UTF8.GetString (data));   // This is a test
```

Here's an example of reading/writing a struct:

```
struct Data { public int X, Y; }
...
var data = new Data { X = 123, Y = 456 };
accessor.Write (0, ref data);
accessor.Read (0, out data);
Console.WriteLine (data.X + " " + data.Y);   // 123 456
```

The Read and Write methods are surprisingly slow. You can get much better performance by directly accessing the underlying unmanaged memory via a pointer. Following on from the previous example:

```
unsafe
{
  byte* pointer = null;
  try
  {
    accessor.SafeMemoryMappedViewHandle.AcquirePointer (ref pointer);
    int* intPointer = (int*) pointer;
    Console.WriteLine (*intPointer);            // 123
  }
  finally
  {
    if (pointer != null)
      accessor.SafeMemoryMappedViewHandle.ReleasePointer();
  }
}
```

The performance advantage of pointers is even more pronounced when working with large structures because they let you work directly with the raw data rather than using Read/Write to *copy* data between managed and unmanaged memory. We explore this further in Chapter 25.

Isolated Storage

Each .NET program has access to a local storage area unique to that program, called *isolated storage*. Isolated storage is useful when your program can't access the standard file system, and so cannot write to `ApplicationData`, `LocalApplicationData`, `CommonApplicationData`, `MyDocuments`, and so on (see "Special Folders" on page 657). This is the case with Silverlight applications and ClickOnce applications deployed with restricted "Internet" permissions.

Isolated storage has the following disadvantages:

- The API is awkward to use.
- You can read/write only via an `IsolatedStorageStream`—you cannot obtain a file or directory path and then use ordinary file I/O.
- The machines stores (equivalent to `CommonApplicationData`) won't let users with restricted OS permissions delete or overwrite files if they were created by another user (although they can modify them). This is effectively a bug.

In terms of security, isolated storage is a fence designed more to keep you in than to keep other applications out. Data in isolated storage is strongly protected against intrusion from other .NET applications running under the most restricted permission set (i.e., the "Internet" zone). In other cases, there's no hard security preventing another application from accessing your isolated storage if it really wants to. The benefit of isolated storage is that applications must go out of their way to interfere with each other—it cannot happen through carelessness or by accident.

Applications running in a sandbox typically have their quota of isolated storage limited via permissions. The default is 1 MB for Internet and Silverlight applications.

 A hosted UI-based application (e.g., Silverlight) can ask the user for permission to increase the isolated storage quota by calling the `IncreaseQuotaTo` method on an `IsolatedStorage File` object. This must be called from a user-initiated event, such as a button click. If the user agrees, the method returns `true`.

You can query the current allowance via the `Quota` property.

Isolation Types

Isolated storage can separate by both program and user. This results in three basic types of compartments:

Local user compartments
    One per user, per program, per computer

Roaming user compartments
    One per user, per program

Machine compartments

One per program, per computer (shared by all users of a program)

The data in a roaming user compartment follows the user across a network—with appropriate operating system and domain support. If this support is unavailable, it behaves like a local user compartment.

So far, we've talked about how isolated storage separates by "program." Isolated storage considers a program to be one of two things, depending on which mode you choose:

- An assembly

- An assembly running within the context of a particular application

The latter is called *domain isolation* and is more commonly used than *assembly isolation*. Domain isolation segregates according to two things: the currently executing assembly and the executable or web application that originally started it. Assembly isolation segregates only according to the currently executing assembly—so different applications calling the same assembly will share the same store.

 Assemblies and applications are identified by their strong name. If no strong name is present, the assembly's full file path or URI is used instead. This means that if you move or rename a weakly named assembly, its isolated storage is reset.

In total, then, there are six kinds of isolated storage compartments. Table 15-4 compares the isolation provided by each.

Table 15-4. Isolated storage containers

Type	Computer?	Application?	Assembly?	User?	Method to obtain store
Domain User (default)	✓	✓	✓	✓	GetUserStoreForDomain
Domain Roaming		✓	✓	✓	
Domain Machine	✓	✓	✓		GetMachineStoreForDomain
Assembly User	✓		✓	✓	GetUserStoreForAssembly
Assembly Roaming			✓	✓	
Assembly Machine	✓		✓		GetMachineStoreForAssembly

There is no such thing as domain-only isolation. If you want to share an isolated store across all assemblies within an application, there's a simple workaround, however. Just expose a public method in one of the assemblies that instantiates and returns an `IsolatedStorageFileStream` object. Any assembly can access any isolated store if given an `IsolatedStorageFile` object—isolation restrictions are imposed upon construction, not subsequent use.

Similarly, there's no such thing as machine-only isolation. If you want to share an isolated store across a variety of applications, the workaround is to write a common assembly that all applications reference and then expose a method on the common assembly that creates and returns an assembly-isolated `IsolatedStorageFileStream`. The common assembly must be strongly named for this to work.

Reading and Writing Isolated Storage

Isolated storage uses streams that work much like ordinary file streams. To obtain an isolated storage stream, you first specify the kind of isolation you want by calling one of the static methods on `IsolatedStorageFile`—as shown previously in Table 15-4. You then use it to construct an `IsolatedStorageFileStream`, along with a filename and `FileMode`:

```
// IsolatedStorage classes live in System.IO.IsolatedStorage

using (IsolatedStorageFile f =
        IsolatedStorageFile.GetMachineStoreForDomain())
using (var s = new IsolatedStorageFileStream ("hi.txt",FileMode.Create,f))
using (var writer = new StreamWriter (s))
  writer.WriteLine ("Hello, World");

// Read it back:

using (IsolatedStorageFile f =
        IsolatedStorageFile.GetMachineStoreForDomain())
using (var s = new IsolatedStorageFileStream ("hi.txt", FileMode.Open, f))
using (var reader = new StreamReader (s))
  Console.WriteLine (reader.ReadToEnd());        // Hello, world
```

 `IsolatedStorageFile` is poorly named in that it doesn't represent a file, but rather a *container* for files (basically, a directory).

A better (though more verbose) way to obtain an `IsolatedStorageFile` is to call `IsolatedStorageFile.GetStore`, passing in the right combination of `IsolatedStorageScope` flags (as shown in Figure 15-6):

```
var flags = IsolatedStorageScope.Machine
            | IsolatedStorageScope.Application
            | IsolatedStorageScope.Assembly;

using (IsolatedStorageFile f = IsolatedStorageFile.GetStore (flags,
    typeof (StrongName), typeof (StrongName)))
{
    ...
```

The advantage of doing it this way is that we can tell `GetStore` what kind of *evidence* to consider when identifying our program, rather than letting it choose automatically. Most commonly, you'll want to use the strong names of your program's assemblies (as we have done in this example) because a strong name is unique and easy to keep consistent across versions.

The danger of letting the CLR choose evidence automatically is that also considers Authenticode signatures (Chapter 18). This is usually undesirable because it means that an Authenticode-related change will trigger a change of identity. In particular, if you start out without Authenticode and then later decide to add it, the CLR will see your application as different from the perspective of isolated storage, and this can mean users losing data between versions.

IsolatedStorageScope is a flags enum whose members you must combine in exactly the right way to get a valid store. Figure 15-6 lists all the valid combinations. Note that they let you access the roaming stores (these are like local stores but with the capability to "roam" via Windows Roaming Profiles).

	Assembly	Assembly & domain
Local user	Assembly | User	Assembly | Domain | User
Roaming user	Assembly | User | Roaming	Assembly | Domain | User | Roaming
Machine	Assembly | Machine	Assembly | Domain | Machine

Figure 15-6. Valid IsolatedStorageScope combinations

Here's how to write to a store isolated by assembly and roaming user:

```
var flags = IsolatedStorageScope.Assembly
          | IsolatedStorageScope.User
          | IsolatedStorageScope.Roaming;

using (IsolatedStorageFile f = IsolatedStorageFile.GetStore (flags,
                                                         null, null))
using (var s = new IsolatedStorageFileStream ("a.txt", FileMode.Create, f))
using (var writer = new StreamWriter (s))
  writer.WriteLine ("Hello, World");
```

Store Location

Here's where .NET writes isolated storage files:

Scope	Location
Local user	[LocalApplicationData]*IsolatedStorage*
Roaming user	[ApplicationData]*IsolatedStorage*
Machine	[CommonApplicationData]*IsolatedStorage*

You can obtain the locations of each of the folders in square brackets by calling the Environment.GetFolderPath method. Here are the defaults for Windows Vista and above:

Scope	Location
Local user	\Users\<user>\AppData\Local\IsolatedStorage
Roaming user	\Users\<user>\AppData\Roaming\IsolatedStorage
Machine	\ProgramData\IsolatedStorage

For Windows XP:

Scope	Location
Local user	\Documents and Settings\<user>\Local Settings\Application Data\IsolatedStorage
Roaming user	\Documents and Settings\<user>\Application Data\IsolatedStorage
Machine	\Documents and Settings\All Users\Application Data\IsolatedStorage

These are merely the base folders; the data files themselves are buried deep in a labyrinth of subdirectories whose names derive from hashed assembly names. This is both a reason to use—and not to use—isolated storage. On the one hand, it makes isolation possible: a permission-restricted application wanting to interfere with another can be stumped by being denied a directory listing—despite having the same filesystem rights as its peers. On the other hand, it makes administration impractical from outside the application. Sometimes it's handy—or essential—to edit an XML configuration file in Notepad so that an application can start up properly. Isolated storage makes this impractical.

Enumerating Isolated Storage

An IsolatedStorageFile object also provides methods for listing files in the store:

```
using (IsolatedStorageFile f = IsolatedStorageFile.GetUserStoreForDomain())
{
  using (var s = new IsolatedStorageFileStream ("f1.x",FileMode.Create,f))
    s.WriteByte (123);

  using (var s = new IsolatedStorageFileStream ("f2.x",FileMode.Create,f))
    s.WriteByte (123);

  foreach (string s in f.GetFileNames ("*.*"))
    Console.Write (s + " ");                      // f1.x f2.x
}
```

You can also create and remove subdirectories, as well as files:

```
using (IsolatedStorageFile f = IsolatedStorageFile.GetUserStoreForDomain())
{
  f.CreateDirectory ("subfolder");

  foreach (string s in f.GetDirectoryNames ("*.*"))
    Console.WriteLine (s);                               // subfolder

  using (var s = new IsolatedStorageFileStream (@"subfolder\sub1.txt",
                                                 FileMode.Create, f))
```

```
      s.WriteByte (100);

   f.DeleteFile (@"subfolder\sub1.txt");
   f.DeleteDirectory ("subfolder");
}
```

With sufficient permissions, you can also enumerate over all isolated stores created by the current user, as well as all machine stores. This function can violate program privacy, but not user privacy. Here's an example:

```
System.Collections.IEnumerator rator =
   IsolatedStorageFile.GetEnumerator (IsolatedStorageScope.User);

while (rator.MoveNext())
{
   var isf = (IsolatedStorageFile) rator.Current;

   Console.WriteLine (isf.AssemblyIdentity);    // Strong name or URI
   Console.WriteLine (isf.CurrentSize);
   Console.WriteLine (isf.Scope);               // User + ...
}
```

The GetEnumerator method is unusual in accepting an argument (this makes its containing class foreach-unfriendly). GetEnumerator accepts one of three values:

IsolatedStorageScope.User
   Enumerates all local stores belonging to the current user

IsolatedStorageScope.User | IsolatedStorageScope.Roaming
   Enumerates all roaming stores belonging to the current user

IsolatedStorageScope.Machine
   Enumerates all machine stores on the computer

Once you have the IsolatedStorageFile object, you can list its content by calling GetFiles and GetDirectories.

16

Networking

The Framework offers a variety of classes in the `System.Net.*` namespaces for communicating via standard network protocols, such as HTTP, TCP/IP, and FTP. Here's a summary of the key components:

- A `WebClient` façade class for simple download/upload operations via HTTP or FTP
- `WebRequest` and `WebResponse` classes for low-level control over client-side HTTP or FTP operations
- `HttpClient` for consuming HTTP web APIs and RESTful services
- `HttpListener` for writing an HTTP server
- `SmtpClient` for constructing and sending mail messages via SMTP
- `Dns` for converting between domain names and addresses
- `TcpClient`, `UdpClient`, `TcpListener`, and `Socket` classes for direct access to the transport and network layers

Window Store applications can access only a subset of these types, namely `WebRequest`/`WebResponse`, and `HttpClient`. However, they can also use WinRT types for TCP and UDP communication in `Windows.Networking.Sockets`, which we demonstrate in the final section in this chapter.

The .NET types in this chapter are in the `System.Net.*` and `System.IO` namespaces.

Network Architecture

Figure 16-1 illustrates the .NET networking types and the communication layers in which they reside. Most types reside in the *transport layer* or *application layer*. The transport layer defines basic protocols for sending and receiving bytes (TCP and UDP); the application layer defines higher-level protocols designed for specific applications such as retrieving web pages (HTTP), transferring files (FTP), sending mail (SMTP), and converting between domain names and IP addresses (DNS).

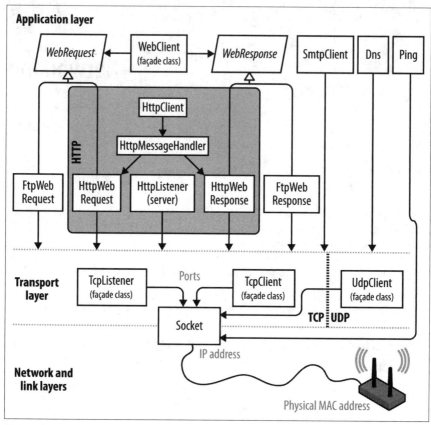

Figure 16-1. Network architecture

It's usually most convenient to program at the application layer; however, there are a couple of reasons you might want to work directly at the transport layer. One is if you need an application protocol not provided in the Framework, such as POP3 for retrieving mail. Another is if you want to invent a custom protocol for a special application such as a peer-to-peer client.

Of the application protocols, HTTP is special in its applicability to general-purpose communication. Its basic mode of operation—"Give me the web page with this URL"—adapts nicely to, "Get me the result of calling this endpoint with these arguments." (In addition to the "get" verb, there is "put," "post," and "delete," allowing for REST-based services.)

HTTP also has a rich set of features that are useful in multitier business applications and service-oriented architectures, such as protocols for authentication and encryption, message chunking, extensible headers and cookies, and the ability to have many server applications share a single port and IP address. For these reasons, HTTP is well supported in the Framework—both directly, as described in this chapter, and at a higher level, through such technologies as WCF, Web Services, and ASP.NET.

The Framework provides client-side support for FTP, the popular Internet protocol for sending and receiving files. Server-side support comes in the form of IIS or Unix-based server software.

As the preceding discussion makes clear, networking is a field that is awash in acronyms. We list the most common in Table 16-1.

Table 16-1. Network acronyms

Acronym	Expansion	Notes
DNS	Domain Name Service	Converts between domain names (e.g., ebay.com) and IP addresses (e.g., 199.54.213.2)
FTP	File Transfer Protocol	Internet-based protocol for sending and receiving files
HTTP	Hypertext Transfer Protocol	Retrieves web pages and runs web services
IIS	Internet Information Services	Microsoft's web server software
IP	Internet Protocol	Network-layer protocol below TCP and UDP
LAN	Local Area Network	Most LANs use Internet-based protocols such as TCP/IP
POP	Post Office Protocol	Retrieves Internet mail
REST	REpresentational State Transfer	A popular alternative to Web Services that leverages machine-followable links in responses and that can operate over basic HTTP
SMTP	Simple Mail Transfer Protocol	Sends Internet mail
TCP	Transmission and Control Protocol	Transport-layer Internet protocol on top of which most higher-layer services are built
UDP	Universal Datagram Protocol	Transport-layer Internet protocol used for low-overhead services such as VoIP
UNC	Universal Naming Convention	\\computer\sharename\filename
URI	Uniform Resource Identifier	Ubiquitous resource naming system (e.g., http://www.amazon.com or mailto:joe@bloggs.org)
URL	Uniform Resource Locator	Technical meaning (fading from use): subset of URI; popular meaning: synonym of URI

Addresses and Ports

For communication to work, a computer or device requires an address. The Internet uses two addressing systems:

IPv4

Currently the dominant addressing system; IPv4 addresses are 32 bits wide. When string-formatted, IPv4 addresses are written as four dot-separated decimals (e.g., 101.102.103.104). An address can be unique in the world—or unique within a particular *subnet* (such as on a corporate network).

IPv6

The newer 128-bit addressing system. Addresses are string-formatted in hexadecimal with a colon separator (e.g., [3EA0:FFFF:198A:E4A3: 4FF2:54fA:41BC:8D31]). The .NET Framework requires that you add square brackets around the address.

The `IPAddress` class in the `System.Net` namespace represents an address in either protocol. It has a constructor accepting a byte array, and a static `Parse` method accepting a correctly formatted string:

```
IPAddress a1 = new IPAddress (new byte[] { 101, 102, 103, 104 });
IPAddress a2 = IPAddress.Parse ("101.102.103.104");
Console.WriteLine (a1.Equals (a2));              // True
Console.WriteLine (a1.AddressFamily);            // InterNetwork

IPAddress a3 = IPAddress.Parse
  ("[3EA0:FFFF:198A:E4A3:4FF2:54fA:41BC:8D31]");
Console.WriteLine (a3.AddressFamily);   // InterNetworkV6
```

The TCP and UDP protocols break out each IP address into 65,535 ports, allowing a computer on a single address to run multiple applications, each on its own port. Many applications have standard port assignments; for instance, HTTP uses port 80; SMTP uses port 25.

The TCP and UDP ports from 49152 to 65535 are officially unassigned, so they are good for testing and small-scale deployments.

An IP address and port combination is represented in the .NET Framework by the `IPEndPoint` class:

```
IPAddress a = IPAddress.Parse ("101.102.103.104");
IPEndPoint ep = new IPEndPoint (a, 222);          // Port 222
Console.WriteLine (ep.ToString());                // 101.102.103.104:222
```

Firewalls block ports. In many corporate environments, only a few ports are open—typically, port 80 (for unencrypted HTTP) and port 443 (for secure HTTP).

URIs

A URI is a specially formatted string that describes a resource on the Internet or a LAN, such as a web page, file, or email address. Examples include *http:// www.ietf.org*, *ftp://myisp/doc.txt*, and *mailto:joe@bloggs.com*. The exact formatting is defined by the Internet Engineering Task Force (*http://www.ietf.org/*).

A URI can be broken up into a series of elements—typically, *scheme, authority,* and *path.* The Uri class in the System namespace performs just this division, exposing a property for each element. This is illustrated in Figure 16-2.

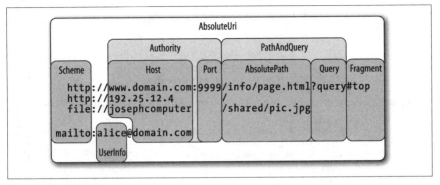

Figure 16-2. URI properties

The Uri class is useful when you need to validate the format of a URI string or to split a URI into its component parts. Otherwise, you can treat a URI simply as a string—most networking methods are overloaded to accept either a Uri object or a string.

You can construct a Uri object by passing any of the following strings into its constructor:

- A URI string, such as *http://www.ebay.com* or *file://janespc/sharedpics/dolphin.jpg*
- An absolute path to a file on your hard disk, such as *c:\myfiles\data.xls*
- A UNC path to a file on the LAN, such as *\\janespc\sharedpics\dolphin.jpg*

File and UNC paths are automatically converted to URIs: the "file:" protocol is added, and backslashes are converted to forward slashes. The Uri constructors also perform some basic cleanup on your string before creating the Uri, including converting the scheme and hostname to lowercase and removing default and blank port numbers. If you supply a URI string without the scheme, such as "*www.test.com*", a UriFormatException is thrown.

Uri has an IsLoopback property, which indicates whether the Uri references the local host (IP address 127.0.0.1), and an IsFile property, which indicates whether the Uri references a local or UNC (IsUnc) path. If IsFile returns true, the Local Path property returns a version of AbsolutePath that is friendly to the local operating system (with backslashes), on which you can call File.Open.

Instances of Uri have read-only properties. To modify an existing Uri, instantiate a UriBuilder object—this has writable properties and can be converted back via its Uri property.

Uri also provides methods for comparing and subtracting paths:

```
Uri info = new Uri ("http://www.domain.com:80/info/");
Uri page = new Uri ("http://www.domain.com/info/page.html");

Console.WriteLine (info.Host);        // www.domain.com
Console.WriteLine (info.Port);        // 80
Console.WriteLine (page.Port);        // 80  (Uri knows the default HTTP port)

Console.WriteLine (info.IsBaseOf (page));        // True
Uri relative = info.MakeRelativeUri (page);
Console.WriteLine (relative.IsAbsoluteUri);      // False
Console.WriteLine (relative.ToString());         // page.html
```

A relative Uri, such as *page.html* in this example, will throw an exception if you call almost any property or method other than IsAbsoluteUri and ToString(). You can instantiate a relative Uri directly as follows:

```
Uri u = new Uri ("page.html", UriKind.Relative);
```

 A trailing slash is significant in a URI and makes a difference as to how a server processes a request if a path component is present.

For instance, given the URI *http://www.albahari.com/nutshell/*, you can expect an HTTP web server to look in the *nutshell* subdirectory in the site's web folder and return the default document (usually *index.html*).

Without the trailing slash, the web server will instead look for a file called *nutshell* (without an extension) directly in the site's root folder—which is usually not what you want. If no such file exists, most web servers will assume the user mistyped and will return a 301 *Permanent Redirect* error, suggesting the client retries with the trailing slash. A .NET HTTP client, by default, will respond transparently to a 301 in the same way as a web browser—by retrying with the suggested URI. This means that if you omit a trailing slash when it should have been included, your request will still work—but will suffer an unnecessary extra round trip.

The Uri class also provides static helper methods such as EscapeUriString(), which converts a string to a valid URL by converting all characters with an ASCII value greater than 127 to hexadecimal representation. The CheckHostName() and CheckSchemeName() methods accept a string and check whether it is syntactically valid for the given property (although they do not attempt to determine whether a host or URI exists).

Client-Side Classes

WebRequest and WebResponse are the common base classes for managing both HTTP and FTP client-side activity, as well as the "file:" protocol. They encapsulate the "request/response" model that these protocols all share: the client makes a request and then awaits a response from a server.

WebClient is a convenient façade class that does the work of calling WebRequest and WebResponse, saving you some coding. WebClient gives you a choice of dealing in strings, byte arrays, files, or streams; WebRequest and WebResponse support just streams. Unfortunately, you cannot rely entirely on WebClient because it doesn't support some features (such as cookies).

HttpClient is another class that builds on WebRequest and WebResponse (or more specifically, HttpWebRequest and HttpWebResponse) and was introduced in Framework 4.5. Whereas WebClient acts mostly as a thin layer over the request/response classes, HttpClient adds functionality to help you work with HTTP-based web APIs, REST-based services, and custom authentication schemes.

For simply downloading/uploading a file, string or byte array, both WebClient and HttpClient are suitable. Both have asynchronous methods, although only Web Client offers progress reporting.

WinRT applications can't use WebClient at all and must use either WebRequest/ WebResponse or HttpClient (for HTTP).

 By default, the CLR throttles HTTP concurrency. If you plan to use asynchronous methods or multithreading to make more than two requests at once (whether via WebRequest, Web Client or HttpClient), you'll need to first increase the concurrency limit via the static property ServicePointMan ager.DefaultConnectionLimit. There's a good MSDN blog article on this topic at *http://tinyurl.com/44axxby*.

WebClient

Here are the steps in using WebClient:

1. Instantiate a WebClient object.
2. Assign the Proxy property.
3. Assign the Credentials property if authentication is required.
4. Call a Download*XXX* or Upload*XXX* method with the desired URI.

Its download methods are as follows:

```
public void   DownloadFile   (string address, string fileName);
public string DownloadString (string address);
public byte[] DownloadData   (string address);
public Stream OpenRead       (string address);
```

Each is overloaded to accept a `Uri` object instead of a string address. The upload methods are similar; their return values contain the response (if any) from the server:

```
public byte[] UploadFile  (string address, string fileName);
public byte[] UploadFile  (string address, string method, string fileName);
public string UploadString(string address, string data);
public string UploadString(string address, string method, string data);
public byte[] UploadData  (string address, byte[] data);
public byte[] UploadData  (string address, string method, byte[] data);
public byte[] UploadValues(string address, NameValueCollection data);
public byte[] UploadValues(string address, string method,
                                           NameValueCollection data);
public Stream OpenWrite    (string address);
public Stream OpenWrite    (string address, string method);
```

The `UploadValues` methods can be used to post values to an HTTP form, with a method argument of "POST". `WebClient` also has a `BaseAddress` property; this allows you to specify a string to be prefixed to all addresses, such as *http://www.mysite.com/data/*.

Here's how to download the code samples page for this book to a file in the current folder and then display it in the default web browser:

```
WebClient wc = new WebClient { Proxy = null };
wc.DownloadFile ("http://www.albahari.com/nutshell/code.aspx", "code.htm");
System.Diagnostics.Process.Start ("code.htm");
```

> `WebClient` implements `IDisposable` under *duress*—by virtue of deriving from `Component` (this allows it to be sited in the Visual Studio's Designer's component tray). Its `Dispose` method does nothing useful at runtime, however, so you don't need to dispose `WebClient` instances.

From Framework 4.5, `WebClient` provides *asynchronous* versions of its long-running methods (Chapter 14) that return tasks that you can await:

```
await wc.DownloadFileTaskAsync ("http://oreilly.com", "webpage.htm");
```

(The "TaskAsync" suffix disambiguates these methods from the old EAP-based asynchronous methods which use the "Async" suffix). Unfortunately, the new methods don't support the standard "TAP" pattern for cancellation and progress reporting. Instead, for cancellation, you must call the `CancelAsync` method on the `Web Client` object, and for progress reporting, handle the `DownloadProgressChanged`/`UploadProgressChanged` event. The following downloads a web page with progress reporting, canceling the download if it takes longer than five seconds:

```
var wc = new WebClient();

wc.DownloadProgressChanged += (sender, args) =>
  Console.WriteLine (args.ProgressPercentage + "% complete");

Task.Delay (5000).ContinueWith (ant => wc.CancelAsync());
```

```
await wc.DownloadFileTaskAsync ("http://oreilly.com", "webpage.htm");
```

 When a request is canceled, a WebException is thrown whose Status property is WebExceptionStatus.RequestCanceled. (For historical reasons, an OperationCanceledException is not thrown.)

The progress-related events capture and post to the active synchronization context, so their handlers can update UI controls without needing Dispatcher.BeginInvoke.

 Using the same WebClient object to perform more than one operation in sequence should be avoided if you're relying on cancellation or progress reporting, as it can result in race conditions.

WebRequest and WebResponse

WebRequest and WebResponse are more complex to use than WebClient but also more flexible. Here's how to get started:

1. Call WebRequest.Create with a URI to instantiate a web request.

2. Assign the Proxy property.

3. Assign the Credentials property if authentication is required.

To upload data:

4. Call GetRequestStream on the request object, and then write to the stream. Go to step 5 if a response is expected.

To download data:

5. Call GetResponse on the request object to instantiate a web response.

6. Call GetResponseStream on the response object, and then read the stream (a StreamReader can help!).

The following downloads and displays the code samples web page (a rewrite of the preceding example):

```
WebRequest req = WebRequest.Create
                ("http://www.albahari.com/nutshell/code.html");
req.Proxy = null;
using (WebResponse res = req.GetResponse())
using (Stream rs = res.GetResponseStream())
using (FileStream fs = File.Create ("code.html"))
  rs.CopyTo (fs);
```

Here's the asynchronous equivalent:

Networking

```
WebRequest req = WebRequest.Create
                  ("http://www.albahari.com/nutshell/code.html");
req.Proxy = null;
using (WebResponse res = await req.GetResponseAsync())
using (Stream rs = res.GetResponseStream())
using (FileStream fs = File.Create ("code.html"))
  await rs.CopyToAsync (fs);
```

The web response object has a ContentLength property, indicating the length of the response stream in bytes, as reported by the server. This value comes from the response headers and may be missing or incorrect. In particular, if an HTTP server chooses the "chunked" mode to break up a large response, the ContentLength value is usually -1. The same can apply with dynamically generated pages.

The static Create method instantiates a subclass of the WebRequest type, such as HttpWebRequest or FtpWebRequest. Its choice of subclass depends on the URI's prefix, and is shown in Table 16-2.

Table 16-2. URI prefixes and web request types

Prefix	Web request type
http: or https:	HttpWebRequest
ftp:	FtpWebRequest
file:	FileWebRequest

Casting a web request object to its concrete type (HttpWebRequest or FtpWebRequest) allows you to access its protocol-specific features.

You can also register your own prefixes by calling WebRequest.RegisterPrefix. This requires a prefix along with a factory object with a Create method that instantiates an appropriate web request object.

The "https:" protocol is for secure (encrypted) HTTP, via Secure Sockets Layer, or SSL. Both WebClient and WebRequest activate SSL transparently upon seeing this prefix (see "SSL" on page 697 under "Working with HTTP" on page 692 later in this chapter). The "file:" protocol simply forwards requests to a FileStream object. Its purpose is in meeting a consistent protocol for reading a URI, whether it be a web page, FTP site, or file path.

WebRequest has a Timeout property, in milliseconds. If a timeout occurs, a WebException is thrown with a Status property of WebExceptionStatus.Timeout. The default timeout is 100 seconds for HTTP and infinite for FTP.

You cannot recycle a WebRequest object for multiple requests—each instance is good for one job only.

HttpClient

HttpClient is new to Framework 4.5 and provides another layer on top of HttpWe
bRequest and HttpWebResponse. It was written in response to the growth of HTTP-
based web APIs and REST services, to provide a better experience than WebClient
when dealing with protocols more elaborate than simply fetching a web page.
Specifically:

- A single HttpClient instance supports concurrent requests. To get concurrency with WebClient, you need to create a fresh instance per concurrent
  request, which can get awkward when you introduce custom headers, cookies,
  and authentication schemes.

- HttpClient lets you write and plug in custom message handlers. This enables
  mocking in unit tests and the creation of custom pipelines (for logging, compression, encryption, and so on). Unit testing code that calls WebClient is a
  pain.

- HttpClient has a richer and extensible type system for headers and content.

 HttpClient is not a complete replacement for WebClient
because it doesn't support progress reporting. WebClient also
has the advantage of supporting FTP, *file://* and custom URI
schemes. It's also available in older Framework versions.

The simplest way to use HttpClient is to instantiate it and then call one of its Get*
methods, passing in a URI:

```
string html = await new HttpClient().GetStringAsync ("http://linqpad.net");
```

(There's also GetByteArrayAsync and GetStreamAsync.) All I/O-bound methods in
HttpClient are asynchronous (there are no synchronous equivalents).

Unlike with WebClient, to get the best performance with HttpClient, you *must* reuse same instance (otherwise things such as DNS resolution may be unnecessarily
repeated.) HttpClient permits concurrent operations, so the following is legal and
downloads two web pages at once:

```
var client = new HttpClient();
var task1 = client.GetStringAsync ("http://www.linqpad.net");
var task2 = client.GetStringAsync ("http://www.albahari.com");
Console.WriteLine (await task1);
Console.WriteLine (await task2);
```

HttpClient has a Timeout property and a BaseAddress property, which prefixes a
URI to every request. HttpClient is somewhat of a thin shell: most of the other
properties that you might expect to find here are defined in another classed called
HttpClientHandler. To access this class, you instantiate it and then pass the
instance into HttpClient's constructor:

```
var handler = new HttpClientHandler { UseProxy = false };
var client = new HttpClient (handler);
...
```

In this example, we told the handler to disable proxy support. There are also properties to control cookies, automatic redirection, authentication, and so on (we'll
describe these in the following sections, and in "Working with HTTP" on page 692).

GetAsync and response messages

The GetStringAsync, GetByteArrayAsync, and GetStreamAsync methods are convenient shortcuts for calling the more general GetAsync method, which returns a
response message:

```
var client = new HttpClient();
// The GetAsync method also accepts a CancellationToken.
HttpResponseMessage response = await client.GetAsync ("http://...");
response.EnsureSuccessStatusCode();
string html = await response.Content.ReadAsStringAsync();
```

HttpResponseMessage exposes properties for accessing the headers (see "Working
with HTTP" on page 692) and the HTTP StatusCode. Unlike with WebClient, an
unsuccessful status code such as 404 (not found) doesn't cause an exception to be
thrown unless you explicitly call EnsureSuccessStatusCode. Communication or
DNS errors, however, do throw exceptions (see "Exception Handling" on page 573).

HttpContent has a CopyToAsync method for writing to another stream, which is
useful in writing the output to a file:

```
using (var fileStream = File.Create ("linqpad.html"))
    await response.Content.CopyToAsync (fileStream);
```

GetAsync is one of four methods corresponding to HTTP's four verbs (the others
are PostAsync, PutAsync and DeleteAsync). We demonstrate PostAsync later in
"Uploading Form Data" on page 693.

SendAsync and request messages

The four methods just described are all shortcuts for calling SendAsync, the single
low-level method into which everything else feeds. To use this, you first construct
an HttpRequestMessage:

```
var client = new HttpClient();
var request = new HttpRequestMessage (HttpMethod.Get, "http://...");
HttpResponseMessage response = await client.SendAsync (request);
response.EnsureSuccessStatusCode();
...
```

Instantiating a HttpRequestMessage object means you can customize properties of
the request, such as the headers (see "Headers" on page 692) and the content itself,
allowing you to upload data.

Uploading data and HttpContent

After instantiating a HttpRequestMessage object, you can upload content by assigning its Content property. The type for this property is an abstract class called HttpContent. The Framework includes the following concrete subclasses for different kinds of content (you can also write your own):

- ByteArrayContent
- StringContent
- FormUrlEncodedContent (see "Uploading Form Data" on page 693)
- StreamContent

For example:

```
var client = new HttpClient (new HttpClientHandler { UseProxy = false });
var request = new HttpRequestMessage (
  HttpMethod.Post, "http://www.albahari.com/EchoPost.aspx");
request.Content = new StringContent ("This is a test");
HttpResponseMessage response = await client.SendAsync (request);
response.EnsureSuccessStatusCode();
Console.WriteLine (await response.Content.ReadAsStringAsync());
```

HttpMessageHandler

We said previously that most of the properties for customizing requests are defined not in HttpClient but in HttpClientHandler. The latter is actually a subclass of the abstract HttpMessageHandler class, defined as follows:

```
public abstract class HttpMessageHandler : IDisposable
{
  protected internal abstract Task<HttpResponseMessage> SendAsync
    (HttpRequestMessage request, CancellationToken cancellationToken);

  public void Dispose();
  protected virtual void Dispose (bool disposing);
}
```

The SendAsync method is called from HttpClient's SendAsync method.

HttpMessageHandler is simple enough to subclass easily and offers an extensibility point into HttpClient.

Unit testing and mocking

We can subclass HttpMessageHandler to create a *mocking* handler to assist with unit testing:

```
class MockHandler : HttpMessageHandler
{
  Func <HttpRequestMessage, HttpResponseMessage> _responseGenerator;

  public MockHandler
```

```
    (Func <HttpRequestMessage, HttpResponseMessage> responseGenerator)
    {
      _responseGenerator = responseGenerator;
    }

    protected override Task <HttpResponseMessage> SendAsync
      (HttpRequestMessage request, CancellationToken cancellationToken)
    {
      cancellationToken.ThrowIfCancellationRequested();
      var response = _responseGenerator (request);
      response.RequestMessage = request;
      return Task.FromResult (response);
    }
  }
```

Its constructor accepts a function that tells the mocker how to generate a response from a request. This is the most versatile approach, as the same handler can test multiple requests.

SendAsynch is synchronous by virtue of Task.FromResult. We could have maintained asynchrony by having our response generator return a Task<HttpResponse Message>, but this is pointless given that we can expect a mocking function to be short-running. Here's how to use our mocking handler:

```
var mocker = new MockHandler (request =>
  new HttpResponseMessage (HttpStatusCode.OK)
  {
    Content = new StringContent ("You asked for " + request.RequestUri)
  });

var client = new HttpClient (mocker);
var response = await client.GetAsync ("http://www.linqpad.net");
string result = await response.Content.ReadAsStringAsync();
Assert.AreEqual ("You asked for http://www.linqpad.net/", result);
```

(Assert.AreEqual is a method you'd expect to find in a unit-testing framework such as NUnit.)

Chaining handlers with DelegatingHandler

You can create a message handler that calls another (resulting in a chain of handlers) by subclassing DelegatingHandler. This can be used to implement custom authentication, compression, and encryption protocols. The following demonstrates a simple logging handler:

```
class LoggingHandler : DelegatingHandler
{
  public LoggingHandler (HttpMessageHandler nextHandler)
  {
    InnerHandler = nextHandler;
  }

  protected async override Task <HttpResponseMessage> SendAsync
    (HttpRequestMessage request, CancellationToken cancellationToken)
```

```
    {
        Console.WriteLine ("Requesting: " + request.RequestUri);
        var response = await base.SendAsync (request, cancellationToken);
        Console.WriteLine ("Got response: " + response.StatusCode);
        return response;
    }
}
```

Notice that we've maintained asynchrony in overriding SendAsync. Introducing the async modifier when overriding a task-returning method is perfectly legal—and desirable in this case.

A better solution than writing to the Console would be to have the constructor accept some kind of logging object. Better still would be to accept a couple of Action<T> delegates which tell it how to log the request and response objects.

Proxies

A *proxy server* is an intermediary through which HTTP and FTP requests can be routed. Organizations sometimes set up a proxy server as the only means by which employees can access the Internet—primarily because it simplifies security. A proxy has an address of its own and can demand authentication so that only selected users on the local area network can access the Internet.

You can instruct a WebClient or WebRequest object to route requests through a proxy server with a WebProxy object:

```
// Create a WebProxy with the proxy's IP address and port. You can
// optionally set Credentials if the proxy needs a username/password.

WebProxy p = new WebProxy ("192.178.10.49", 808);
p.Credentials = new NetworkCredential ("username", "password");
// or:
p.Credentials = new NetworkCredential ("username", "password", "domain");

WebClient wc = new WebClient();
wc.Proxy = p;
    ...

// Same procedure with a WebRequest object:
WebRequest req = WebRequest.Create ("...");
req.Proxy = p;
```

To use a proxy with HttpClient, first create an HttpClientHandler, assign its Proxy property, and then feed that into HttpClient's constructor:

```
WebProxy p = new WebProxy ("192.178.10.49", 808);
p.Credentials = new NetworkCredential ("username", "password", "domain");

var handler = new HttpClientHandler { Proxy = p };
var client = new HttpClient (handler);
    ...
```

If you know there's no proxy, it's worth setting the Proxy property to null on WebClient and WebRequest objects. Otherwise, the Framework may attempt to "auto-detect" your proxy settings, adding up to 30 seconds to your request. If you're wondering why your web requests execute slowly, this is probably it!

HttpClientHandler also has a UseProxy property that you can assign to false instead of nulling out the Proxy property to defeat auto-detection.

If you supply a domain when constructing the NetworkCredential, Windows-based authentication protocols are used. To use the currently authenticated Windows user, assign the static CredentialCache.DefaultNetworkCredentials value to the proxy's Credentials property.

As an alternative to repeatedly setting the Proxy, you can set the global default as follows:

```
WebRequest.DefaultWebProxy = myWebProxy;
```

or:

```
WebRequest.DefaultWebProxy = null;
```

Whatever you set applies for the life of the application domain (unless some other code changes it!).

Authentication

You can supply a username and password to an HTTP or FTP site by creating a NetworkCredential object and assigning it to the Credentials property of Web Client or WebRequest:

```
WebClient wc = new WebClient { Proxy = null };
wc.BaseAddress = "ftp://ftp.albahari.com";

// Authenticate, then upload and download a file to the FTP server.
// The same approach also works for HTTP and HTTPS.

string username = "nutshell";
string password = "oreilly";
wc.Credentials = new NetworkCredential (username, password);

wc.DownloadFile ("guestbook.txt", "guestbook.txt");

string data = "Hello from " + Environment.UserName + "!\r\n";
File.AppendAllText ("guestbook.txt", data);

wc.UploadFile ("guestbook.txt", "guestbook.txt");
```

HttpClient exposes the same Credentials property through HttpClientHandler:

```
var handler = new HttpClientHandler();
handler.Credentials = new NetworkCredential (username, password);
```

```
var client = new HttpClient (handler);
...
```

This works with dialog-based authentication protocols, such as Basic and Digest, and is extensible through the AuthenticationManager class. It also supports Windows NTLM and Kerberos (if you include a domain name when constructing the NetworkCredential object). If you want to use the currently authenticated Windows user, you can leave the Credentials property null and instead set UseDe faultCredentials true.

 Assigning Credentials is useless for getting through forms-based authentication. We discuss forms-based authentication separately (see "Forms Authentication" on page 696).

The authentication is ultimately handled by a WebRequest subtype (in this case, FtpWebRequest), which automatically negotiates a compatible protocol. In the case of HTTP, there can be a choice: if you examine the initial response from a Microsoft Exchange server web mail page, for instance, it might contain the following headers:

```
HTTP/1.1 401 Unauthorized
Content-Length: 83
Content-Type: text/html
Server: Microsoft-IIS/6.0
WWW-Authenticate: Negotiate
WWW-Authenticate: NTLM
WWW-Authenticate: Basic realm="exchange.somedomain.com"
X-Powered-By: ASP.NET
Date: Sat, 05 Aug 2006 12:37:23 GMT
```

The 401 code signals that authorization is required; the "WWW-Authenticate" headers indicate what authentication protocols are understood. If you configure a WebClient or WebRequest object with the correct username and password, however, this message will be hidden from you because the Framework responds automatically by choosing a compatible authentication protocol and then resubmitting the original request with an extra header. For example:

```
Authorization: Negotiate TlRMTVNTUAAABAAAt5II2gjACDArAAACAwACACgAAAAQ
ATmKAAAADO1VDRdPUksHUq9VUA==
```

This mechanism provides transparency but generates an extra round trip with each request. You can avoid the extra round trips on subsequent requests to the same URI by setting the PreAuthenticate property to true. This property is defined on the WebRequest class (and works only in the case of HttpWebRequest). WebClient doesn't support this feature at all.

CredentialCache

You can force a particular authentication protocol with a CredentialCache object. A credential cache contains one or more NetworkCredential objects, each keyed to a particular protocol and URI prefix. For example, you might want to avoid the

Basic protocol when logging into an Exchange Server, as it transmits passwords in plain text:

```
CredentialCache cache = new CredentialCache();
Uri prefix = new Uri ("http://exchange.somedomain.com");
cache.Add (prefix, "Digest",   new NetworkCredential ("joe", "passwd"));
cache.Add (prefix, "Negotiate", new NetworkCredential ("joe", "passwd"));

WebClient wc = new WebClient();
wc.Credentials = cache;
...
```

An authentication protocol is specified as a string. The valid values are as follows:

```
Basic, Digest, NTLM, Kerberos, Negotiate
```

In this particular example, WebClient will choose Negotiate, because the server didn't indicate that it supported Digest in its authentication headers. Negotiate is a Windows protocol that boils down to either Kerberos or NTLM, depending on the capabilities of the server.

The static CredentialCache.DefaultNetworkCredentials property allows you to add the currently authenticated Windows user to the credential cache without having to specify a password:

```
cache.Add (prefix, "Negotiate", CredentialCache.DefaultNetworkCredentials);
```

Authenticating via headers with HttpClient

If you're using HttpClient, another way to authenticate is to set the authentication header directly:

```
var client = new HttpClient();
client.DefaultRequestHeaders.Authorization =
  new AuthenticationHeaderValue ("Basic",
    Convert.ToBase64String (Encoding.UTF8.GetBytes ("username:password")));
...
```

This strategy also works with custom authentication systems such as OAuth. We discuss headers in more detail soon.

Exception Handling

WebRequest, WebResponse, WebClient, and their streams all throw a WebException in the case of a network or protocol error. HttpClient does the same but then wraps the WebException in an HttpRequestException. You can determine the specific error via the WebException's Status property; this returns a WebExceptionStatus enum that has the following members:

CacheEntryNotFound	RequestCanceled
ConnectFailure	RequestProhibitedByCachePolicy
ConnectionClosed	RequestProhibitedByProxy
KeepAliveFailure	SecureChannelFailure
MessageLengthLimitExceeded	SendFailure
NameResolutionFailure	ServerProtocolViolation
Pending	Success
PipelineFailure	Timeout
ProtocolError	TrustFailure
ProxyNameResolutionFailure	UnknownError
ReceiveFailure	

An invalid domain name causes a NameResolutionFailure; a dead network causes a ConnectFailure; a request exceeding WebRequest.Timeout milliseconds causes a Timeout.

Errors such as "Page not found," "Moved Permanently," and "Not Logged In" are specific to the HTTP or FTP protocols, and so are all lumped together under the ProtocolError status. With HttpClient, these errors are not thrown unless you call EnsureSuccessStatusCode on the response object. Prior to doing so, you can get the specific status code by querying the StatusCode property:

```
var client = new HttpClient();
var response = await client.GetAsync ("http://linqpad.net/foo");
HttpStatusCode responseStatus = response.StatusCode;
```

With WebClient and WebRequest/WebResponse, you must actually catch the WebException and then:

1. Cast the WebException's Response property to HttpWebResponse or FtpWebResponse.

2. Examine the response object's Status property (an HttpStatusCode or FtpStatusCode enum) and/or its StatusDescription property (string).

For example:

```
WebClient wc = new WebClient { Proxy = null };
try
{
  string s = wc.DownloadString ("http://www.albahari.com/notthere");
}
catch (WebException ex)
{
  if (ex.Status == WebExceptionStatus.NameResolutionFailure)
    Console.WriteLine ("Bad domain name");
  else if (ex.Status == WebExceptionStatus.ProtocolError)
  {
    HttpWebResponse response = (HttpWebResponse) ex.Response;
    Console.WriteLine (response.StatusDescription);     // "Not Found"
    if (response.StatusCode == HttpStatusCode.NotFound)
```

```
    Console.WriteLine ("Not there!");                    // "Not there!"
  }
  else throw;
}
```

 If you want the three-digit status code, such as 401 or 404, simply cast the HttpStatusCode or FtpStatusCode enum to an integer.

By default, you'll never get a redirection error because Web Client and WebRequest automatically follow redirection responses. You can switch off this behavior in a WebRequest object by setting AllowAutoRedirect to false.

The redirection errors are 301 (Moved Permanently), 302 (Found/Redirect), and 307 (Temporary Redirect).

If an exception is thrown because you've incorrectly used the WebClient or WebRe quest classes, it will more likely be an InvalidOperationException or Protocol ViolationException than a WebException.

Working with HTTP

This section describes HTTP-specific request and response features of WebClient, HttpWebRequest/HttpWebResponse, and the HttpClient class.

Headers

WebClient, WebRequest, and HttpClient all let you add custom HTTP headers, as well as enumerate the headers in a response. A header is simply a key/value pair containing metadata, such as the message content type or server software. Here's how to add a custom header to a request, then list all headers in a response message in a WebClient:

```
WebClient wc = new WebClient { Proxy = null };
wc.Headers.Add ("CustomHeader", "JustPlaying/1.0");
wc.DownloadString ("http://www.oreilly.com");

foreach (string name in wc.ResponseHeaders.Keys)
  Console.WriteLine (name + "=" + wc.ResponseHeaders [name]);

Age=51
X-Cache=HIT from oregano.bp
X-Cache-Lookup=HIT from oregano.bp:3128
Connection=keep-alive
Accept-Ranges=bytes
Content-Length=95433
Content-Type=text/html
...
```

HttpClient instead exposes strongly typed collections with properties for standard HTTP headers. The DefaultRequestHeaders property is for headers which apply to every request:

```
var client = new HttpClient (handler);

client.DefaultRequestHeaders.UserAgent.Add (
  new ProductInfoHeaderValue ("VisualStudio", "2015"));

client.DefaultRequestHeaders.Add ("CustomHeader", "VisualStudio/2015");
```

whereas the `Headers` property on the `HttpRequestMessage` class is for headers specific to a request.

Query Strings

A query string is simply a string appended to a URI with a question mark, used to send simple data to the server. You can specify multiple key/value pairs in a query string with the following syntax:

```
?key1=value1&key2=value2&key3=value3...
```

`WebClient` provides an easy way to add query strings through a dictionary-style property. The following searches Google for the word "WebClient" on page 679, displaying the result page in French:

```
WebClient wc = new WebClient { Proxy = null };
wc.QueryString.Add ("q", "WebClient");       // Search for "WebClient"
wc.QueryString.Add ("hl", "fr");             // Display page in French
wc.DownloadFile ("http://www.google.com/search", "results.html");
System.Diagnostics.Process.Start ("results.html");
```

To achieve the same result with `WebRequest` or with `HttpClient`, you must manually append a correctly formatted string to the request URI:

```
string requestURI = "http://www.google.com/search?q=WebClient&hl=fr";
```

If there's a possibility of your query including symbols or spaces, you can leverage `Uri`'s `EscapeDataString` method to create a legal URI:

```
string search = Uri.EscapeDataString ("(WebClient OR HttpClient)");
string language = Uri.EscapeDataString ("fr");
string requestURI = "http://www.google.com/search?q=" + search +
                    "&hl=" + language;
```

This resultant URI is:

```
http://www.google.com/search?q=(WebClient%20OR%20HttpClient)&hl=fr
```

(`EscapeDataString` is similar to `EscapeUriString` except that it also encodes characters such as & and = which would otherwise mess up the query string.)

Microsoft's Web Protection library (*http://wpl.codeplex.com*) offers another encoding/decoding solution which takes into account cross-site scripting vulnerabilities.

Uploading Form Data

`WebClient` provides `UploadValues` methods for posting data to an HTML form:

```
WebClient wc = new WebClient { Proxy = null };

var data = new System.Collections.Specialized.NameValueCollection();
data.Add ("Name", "Joe Albahari");
data.Add ("Company", "O'Reilly");

byte[] result = wc.UploadValues ("http://www.albahari.com/EchoPost.aspx",
                                 "POST", data);

Console.WriteLine (Encoding.UTF8.GetString (result));
```

The keys in the NameValueCollection, such as searchtextbox and searchMode, correspond to the names of input boxes on the HTML form.

Uploading form data is more work via WebRequest. (You'll need to take this route if you need to use features such as cookies.) Here's the procedure:

1. Set the request's ContentType to "application/x-www-form-urlencoded" and its Method to "POST".

2. Build a string containing the data to upload, encoded as follows:

   ```
   name1=value1&name2=value2&name3=value3...
   ```

3. Convert the string to a byte array, with Encoding.UTF8.GetBytes.

4. Set the web request's ContentLength property to the byte array length.

5. Call GetRequestStream on the web request and write the data array.

6. Call GetResponse to read the server's response.

Here's the previous example written with WebRequest:

```
var req = WebRequest.Create ("http://www.albahari.com/EchoPost.aspx");
req.Proxy = null;
req.Method = "POST";
req.ContentType = "application/x-www-form-urlencoded";

string reqString = "Name=Joe+Albahari&Company=O'Reilly";
byte[] reqData = Encoding.UTF8.GetBytes (reqString);
req.ContentLength = reqData.Length;

using (Stream reqStream = req.GetRequestStream())
  reqStream.Write (reqData, 0, reqData.Length);

using (WebResponse res = req.GetResponse())
using (Stream resSteam = res.GetResponseStream())
using (StreamReader sr = new StreamReader (resSteam))
  Console.WriteLine (sr.ReadToEnd());
```

With HttpClient, you instead create and populate FormUrlEncodedContent object, which you can then either pass into the PostAsync method, or assign to a request's Content property:

```
string uri = "http://www.albahari.com/EchoPost.aspx";
var client = new HttpClient();
var dict = new Dictionary<string,string>
{
    { "Name", "Joe Albahari" },
    { "Company", "O'Reilly" }
};
var values = new FormUrlEncodedContent (dict);
var response = await client.PostAsync (uri, values);
response.EnsureSuccessStatusCode();
Console.WriteLine (await response.Content.ReadAsStringAsync());
```

Cookies

A cookie is a name/value string pair that an HTTP server sends to a client in a response header. A web browser client typically remembers cookies and replays them to the server in each subsequent request (to the same address) until their expiry. A cookie allows a server to know whether it's talking to the same client it was a minute ago—or yesterday—without needing a messy query string in the URI.

By default, HttpWebRequest ignores any cookies received from the server. To accept cookies, create a CookieContainer object and assign it to the WebRequest. The cookies received in a response can then be enumerated:

```
var cc = new CookieContainer();

var request = (HttpWebRequest) WebRequest.Create ("http://www.google.com");
request.Proxy = null;
request.CookieContainer = cc;
using (var response = (HttpWebResponse) request.GetResponse())
{
  foreach (Cookie c in response.Cookies)
  {
    Console.WriteLine (" Name:   " + c.Name);
    Console.WriteLine (" Value:  " + c.Value);
    Console.WriteLine (" Path:   " + c.Path);
    Console.WriteLine (" Domain: " + c.Domain);
  }
  // Read response stream...
}

Name:   PREF
Value:  ID=6b10df1da493a9c4:TM=1179025486:LM=1179025486:S=EJCZri0aWEHlk4tt
Path:   /
Domain: .google.com
```

To do the same with HttpClient, first instantiate a HttpClientHandler:

```
var cc = new CookieContainer();
var handler = new HttpClientHandler();
handler.CookieContainer = cc;
var client = new HttpClient (handler);
...
```

The WebClient façade class does not support cookies.

To replay the received cookies in future requests, simply assign the same CookieContainer object to each new WebRequest object; or with HttpClient, keep using the same object to make requests. CookieContainer is serializable, so it can be written to disk—see Chapter 17. Alternatively, you can start with a fresh CookieContainer and then add cookies manually as follows:

```
Cookie c = new Cookie ("PREF",
                       "ID=6b10df1da493a9c4:TM=1179...",
                       "/",
                       ".google.com");
freshCookieContainer.Add (c);
```

The third and fourth arguments indicate the path and domain of the originator. A CookieContainer on the client can house cookies from many different places; WebRequest sends only those cookies whose path and domain match those of the server.

Forms Authentication

We saw in the previous section how a NetworkCredentials object can satisfy authentication systems such as Basic or NTLM (that pop up a dialog box in a web browser). Most websites requiring authentication, however, use some type of forms-based approach. Enter your username and password into text boxes that are part of an HTML form decorated in appropriate corporate graphics, press a button to post the data, and then receive a cookie upon successful authentication. The cookie allows you greater privileges in browsing pages in the website. With WebRequest or HttpClient, you can do all this programmatically, with the features discussed in the preceding two sections. This can be useful for testing, or for automation in cases where there's not a proper API.

A typical website that implements forms authentication will contain HTML like this:

```
<form action="http://www.somesite.com/login" method="post">
  <input type="text" id="user" name="username">
  <input type="password" id="pass" name="password">
  <button type="submit" id="login-btn">Log In</button>
</form>
```

Here's how to log into such a site with WebRequest/WebResponse:

```
string loginUri = "http://www.somesite.com/login";
string username = "username";   // (Your username)
string password = "password";   // (Your password)
string reqString = "username=" + username + "&password=" + password;
byte[] requestData = Encoding.UTF8.GetBytes (reqString);

CookieContainer cc = new CookieContainer();
var request = (HttpWebRequest)WebRequest.Create (loginUri);
request.Proxy = null;
request.CookieContainer = cc;
request.Method = "POST";

request.ContentType = "application/x-www-form-urlencoded";
```

```
request.ContentLength = requestData.Length;

using (Stream s = request.GetRequestStream())
  s.Write (requestData, 0, requestData.Length);

using (var response = (HttpWebResponse) request.GetResponse())
  foreach (Cookie c in response.Cookies)
    Console.WriteLine (c.Name + " = " + c.Value);

// We're now logged in. As long as we assign cc to subsequent WebRequest
// objects, we'll be treated as an authenticated user.
```

And with HttpClient:

```
string loginUri = "http://www.somesite.com/login";
string username = "username";
string password = "password";

CookieContainer cc = new CookieContainer();
var handler = new HttpClientHandler { CookieContainer = cc };

var request = new HttpRequestMessage (HttpMethod.Post, loginUri);
request.Content = new FormUrlEncodedContent (new Dictionary<string,string>
{
  { "username", username },
  { "password", password }
});

var client = new HttpClient (handler);
var response = await client.SendAsync (request);
response.EnsureSuccessStatusCode();
...
```

SSL

WebClient, HttpClient, and WebRequest all use SSL automatically when you specify an "https:" prefix. The only complication that can arise relates to bad X.509 certificates. If the server's site certificate is invalid in any way (for instance, if it's a test certificate), an exception is thrown when you attempt to communicate. To work around this, you can attach a custom certificate validator to the static ServicePoint Manager class:

```
using System.Net;
using System.Net.Security;
using System.Security.Cryptography.X509Certificates;
...
static void ConfigureSSL()
{
  ServicePointManager.ServerCertificateValidationCallback = CertChecker;
}
```

ServerCertificateValidationCallback is a delegate. If it returns true, the certificate is accepted:

```
static bool CertChecker (object sender, X509Certificate certificate,
                         X509Chain chain, SslPolicyErrors errors)
{
  // Return true if you're happy with the certificate
  ...
}
```

Writing an HTTP Server

You can write your own .NET HTTP server with the HttpListener class. The following is a simple server that listens on port 51111, waits for a single client request, and then returns a one-line reply.

```
static void Main()
{
  ListenAsync();                          // Start server
  WebClient wc = new WebClient();         // Make a client request.
  Console.WriteLine (wc.DownloadString
    ("http://localhost:51111/MyApp/Request.txt"));
}

async static void ListenAsync()
{
  HttpListener listener = new HttpListener();
  listener.Prefixes.Add ("http://localhost:51111/MyApp/");  // Listen on
  listener.Start();                                         // port 51111.

  // Await a client request:
  HttpListenerContext context = await listener.GetContextAsync();

  // Respond to the request:
  string msg = "You asked for: " + context.Request.RawUrl;
  context.Response.ContentLength64 = Encoding.UTF8.GetByteCount (msg);
  context.Response.StatusCode = (int) HttpStatusCode.OK;

  using (Stream s = context.Response.OutputStream)
  using (StreamWriter writer = new StreamWriter (s))
    await writer.WriteAsync (msg);

  listener.Stop();
}
```

```
OUTPUT: You asked for: /MyApp/Request.txt
```

HttpListener does not internally use .NET Socket objects; it instead calls the Windows HTTP Server API. This allows many applications on a computer to listen on the same IP address and port—as long as each registers different address prefixes. In our example, we registered the prefix *http://localhost/myapp*, so another application would be free to listen on the same IP and port on another prefix such as *http://localhost/anotherapp*. This is of value because opening new ports on corporate firewalls can be politically arduous.

HttpListener waits for the next client request when you call GetContext, returning an object with Request and Response properties. Each is analogous to a WebRequest and WebResponse object, but from the server's perspective. You can read and write headers and cookies, for instance, to the request and response objects, much as you would at the client end.

You can choose how fully to support features of the HTTP protocol, based on your anticipated client audience. At a bare minimum, you should set the content length and status code on each request.

Here's a very simple web page server, written *asynchronously*:

```
using System;
using System.IO;
using System.Net;
using System.Text;
using System.Threading.Tasks;

class WebServer
{
  HttpListener _listener;
  string _baseFolder;      // Your web page folder.

  public WebServer (string uriPrefix, string baseFolder)
  {
    _listener = new HttpListener();
    _listener.Prefixes.Add (uriPrefix);
    _baseFolder = baseFolder;
  }

  public async void Start()
  {
    _listener.Start();
    while (true)
      try
      {
        var context = await _listener.GetContextAsync();
        Task.Run (() => ProcessRequestAsync (context));
      }
      catch (HttpListenerException)    { break; }   // Listener stopped.
      catch (InvalidOperationException) { break; }  // Listener stopped.
  }

  public void Stop() { _listener.Stop(); }

  async void ProcessRequestAsync (HttpListenerContext context)
  {
    try
    {
      string filename = Path.GetFileName (context.Request.RawUrl);
      string path = Path.Combine (_baseFolder, filename);
      byte[] msg;
      if (!File.Exists (path))
      {
```

```
          Console.WriteLine ("Resource not found: " + path);
          context.Response.StatusCode = (int) HttpStatusCode.NotFound;
          msg = Encoding.UTF8.GetBytes ("Sorry, that page does not exist");
        }
        else
        {
          context.Response.StatusCode = (int) HttpStatusCode.OK;
          msg = File.ReadAllBytes (path);
        }
        context.Response.ContentLength64 = msg.Length;
        using (Stream s = context.Response.OutputStream)
          await s.WriteAsync (msg, 0, msg.Length);
      }
      catch (Exception ex) { Console.WriteLine ("Request error: " + ex); }
    }
  }
```

Here's a main method to set things in motion:

```
static void Main()
{
  // Listen on port 51111, serving files in d:\webroot:
  var server = new WebServer ("http://localhost:51111/", @"d:\webroot");
  try
  {
    server.Start();
    Console.WriteLine ("Server running... press Enter to stop");
    Console.ReadLine();
  }
  finally { server.Stop(); }
}
```

You can test this at the client end with any web browser; the URI in this case will be
http://localhost:51111/ plus the name of the web page.

> HttpListener will not start if other software is competing for
> the same port (unless that software also uses the Windows
> HTTP Server API). Examples of applications that might listen
> on the default port 80 include a web server or a peer-to-peer
> program such as Skype.

Our use of asynchronous functions makes this server scalable and efficient. Starting
this from a UI thread, however, would hinder scalability because for each *request*,
execution would bounce back to the UI thread after each await. Incurring such
overhead is particularly pointless given that we don't have shared state, so in a UI
scenario we'd get off the UI thread, either like this:

```
Task.Run (Start);
```

or by calling ConfigureAwait(false) after calling GetContextAsync.

Note that we used Task.Run to call ProcessRequestAsync, even though the method
was already asynchronous. This allows the caller to process another request *immediately*, rather than having to first wait out the synchronous phase of the method (up
until the first await).

Using FTP

For simple FTP upload and download operations, you can use `WebClient` as we did previously:

```
WebClient wc = new WebClient { Proxy = null };
wc.Credentials = new NetworkCredential ("nutshell", "oreilly");
wc.BaseAddress = "ftp://ftp.albahari.com";
wc.UploadString ("tempfile.txt", "hello!");
Console.WriteLine (wc.DownloadString ("tempfile.txt"));   // hello!
```

There's more to FTP, however, than just uploading and downloading files. The protocol also lists a set of commands or "methods," defined as string constants in `WebRequestMethods.Ftp`:

AppendFile	ListDirectory	Rename
DeleteFile	ListDirectoryDetails	UploadFile
DownloadFile	MakeDirectory	UploadFileWithUniqueName
GetDateTimestamp	PrintWorkingDirectory	
GetFileSize	RemoveDirectory	

To run one of these commands, you assign its string constant to the web request's `Method` property and then call `GetResponse()`. Here's how to get a directory listing:

```
var req = (FtpWebRequest) WebRequest.Create ("ftp://ftp.albahari.com");
req.Proxy = null;
req.Credentials = new NetworkCredential ("nutshell", "oreilly");
req.Method = WebRequestMethods.Ftp.ListDirectory;

using (WebResponse resp = req.GetResponse())
using (StreamReader reader = new StreamReader (resp.GetResponseStream()))
  Console.WriteLine (reader.ReadToEnd());

RESULT:
.
..
guestbook.txt
tempfile.txt
test.doc
```

In the case of getting a directory listing, we needed to read the response stream to get the result. Most other commands, however, don't require this step. For instance, to get the result of the `GetFileSize` command, just query the response's `ContentLength` property:

```
var req = (FtpWebRequest) WebRequest.Create (
                        "ftp://ftp.albahari.com/tempfile.txt");
req.Proxy = null;
req.Credentials = new NetworkCredential ("nutshell", "oreilly");

req.Method = WebRequestMethods.Ftp.GetFileSize;
```

```
using (WebResponse resp = req.GetResponse())
  Console.WriteLine (resp.ContentLength);          // 6
```

The GetDateTimestamp command works in a similar way, except that you query the response's LastModified property. This requires that you cast to FtpWebResponse:

```
...
req.Method = WebRequestMethods.Ftp.GetDateTimestamp;

using (var resp = (FtpWebResponse) req.GetResponse() )
  Console.WriteLine (resp.LastModified);
```

To use the Rename command, you must populate the request's RenameTo property with the new filename (without a directory prefix). For example, to rename a file in the *incoming* directory from *tempfile.txt* to *deleteme.txt*:

```
var req = (FtpWebRequest) WebRequest.Create (
                        "ftp://ftp.albahari.com/tempfile.txt");
req.Proxy = null;
req.Credentials = new NetworkCredential ("nutshell", "oreilly");

req.Method = WebRequestMethods.Ftp.Rename;
req.RenameTo = "deleteme.txt";

req.GetResponse().Close();          // Perform the rename
```

Here's how to delete a file:

```
var req = (FtpWebRequest) WebRequest.Create (
                        "ftp://ftp.albahari.com/deleteme.txt");
req.Proxy = null;
req.Credentials = new NetworkCredential ("nutshell", "oreilly");

req.Method = WebRequestMethods.Ftp.DeleteFile;

req.GetResponse().Close();          // Perform the deletion
```

> In all these examples, you would typically use an exception handling block to catch network and protocol errors. A typical catch block looks like this:
>
> ```
> catch (WebException ex)
> {
>   if (ex.Status == WebExceptionStatus.ProtocolError)
>   {
>     // Obtain more detail on error:
>     var response = (FtpWebResponse) ex.Response;
>     FtpStatusCode errorCode = response.StatusCode;
>     string errorMessage = response.StatusDescription;
>     ...
>   }
>   ...
> }
> ```

Using DNS

The static `Dns` class encapsulates the Domain Name Service, which converts between a raw IP address, such as 66.135.192.87, and a human-friendly domain name, such as *ebay.com*.

The `GetHostAddresses` method converts from domain name to IP address (or addresses):

```
foreach (IPAddress a in Dns.GetHostAddresses ("albahari.com"))
    Console.WriteLine (a.ToString());      // 205.210.42.167
```

The `GetHostEntry` method goes the other way around, converting from address to domain name:

```
IPHostEntry entry = Dns.GetHostEntry ("205.210.42.167");
Console.WriteLine (entry.HostName);                     // albahari.com
```

`GetHostEntry` also accepts an `IPAddress` object, so you can specify an IP address as a byte array:

```
IPAddress address = new IPAddress (new byte[] { 205, 210, 42, 167 });
IPHostEntry entry = Dns.GetHostEntry (address);
Console.WriteLine (entry.HostName);                     // albahari.com
```

Domain names are automatically resolved to IP addresses when you use a class such as `WebRequest` or `TcpClient`. If you plan to make many network requests to the same address over the life of an application, however, you can sometimes improve performance by first using `Dns` to explicitly convert the domain name into an IP address and then communicating directly with the IP address from that point on. This avoids repeated round-tripping to resolve the same domain name, and it can be of benefit when dealing at the transport layer (via `TcpClient`, `UdpClient`, or `Socket`).

The DNS class also provides awaitable task-based asynchronous methods:

```
foreach (IPAddress a in await Dns.GetHostAddressesAsync ("albahari.com"))
    Console.WriteLine (a.ToString());
```

Sending Mail with SmtpClient

The `SmtpClient` class in the `System.Net.Mail` namespace allows you to send mail messages through the ubiquitous Simple Mail Transfer Protocol. To send a simple text message, instantiate `SmtpClient`, set its `Host` property to your SMTP server address, and then call `Send`:

```
SmtpClient client = new SmtpClient();
client.Host = "mail.myisp.net";
client.Send ("from@adomain.com", "to@adomain.com", "subject", "body");
```

To frustrate spammers, most SMTP servers on the Internet will accept connections only from the ISP's subscribers, so you need the SMTP address appropriate to the current connection for this to work.

Constructing a `MailMessage` object exposes further options, including the ability to add attachments:

```
SmtpClient client = new SmtpClient();
client.Host = "mail.myisp.net";
MailMessage mm = new MailMessage();

mm.Sender  = new MailAddress ("kay@domain.com", "Kay");
mm.From    = new MailAddress ("kay@domain.com", "Kay");
mm.To.Add  (new MailAddress ("bob@domain.com", "Bob"));
mm.CC.Add  (new MailAddress ("dan@domain.com", "Dan"));
mm.Subject = "Hello!";
mm.Body = "Hi there. Here's the photo!";
mm.IsBodyHtml = false;
mm.Priority = MailPriority.High;

Attachment a = new Attachment ("photo.jpg",
                         System.Net.Mime.MediaTypeNames.Image.Jpeg);
mm.Attachments.Add (a);
client.Send (mm);
```

`SmtpClient` allows you to specify `Credentials` for servers requiring authentication, `EnableSsl` if supported, and change the TCP `Port` to a nondefault value. By changing the `DeliveryMethod` property, you can instruct the `SmtpClient` to instead use IIS to send mail messages or simply to write each message to an *.eml* file in a specified directory:

```
SmtpClient client = new SmtpClient();
client.DeliveryMethod = SmtpDeliveryMethod.SpecifiedPickupDirectory;
client.PickupDirectoryLocation = @"c:\mail";
```

Using TCP

TCP and UDP constitute the transport layer protocols on top of which most Internet—and local area network—services are built. HTTP, FTP, and SMTP use TCP; DNS uses UDP. TCP is connection-oriented and includes reliability mechanisms; UDP is connectionless, has a lower overhead, and supports broadcasting. *BitTorrent* uses UDP, as does Voice over IP.

The transport layer offers greater flexibility—and potentially improved performance—over the higher layers, but it requires that you handle such tasks as authentication and encryption yourself.

With TCP in .NET, you have a choice of either the easier-to-use `TcpClient` and `TcpListener` façade classes, or the feature-rich `Socket` class. (In fact, you can mix and match, because `TcpClient` exposes the underlying `Socket` object through the `Client` property.) The `Socket` class exposes more configuration options and allows direct access to the network layer (IP) and non-Internet-based protocols such as Novell's SPX/IPX.

(TCP and UDP communication is also possible in WinRT: see "TCP in Windows Runtime" on page 709.)

As with other protocols, TCP differentiates a client and server: the client initiates a request, while the server waits for a request. Here's the basic structure for a synchronous TCP client request:

```
using (TcpClient client = new TcpClient())
{
  client.Connect ("address", port);
  using (NetworkStream n = client.GetStream())
  {
    // Read and write to the network stream...
  }
}
```

TcpClient's Connect method blocks until a connection is established (ConnectA sync is the asynchronous equivalent). The NetworkStream then provides a means of two-way communication for both transmitting and receiving bytes of data from a server.

A simple TCP server looks like this:

```
TcpListener listener = new TcpListener (<ip address>, port);
listener.Start();

while (keepProcessingRequests)
  using (TcpClient c = listener.AcceptTcpClient())
  using (NetworkStream n = c.GetStream())
  {
    // Read and write to the network stream...
  }

listener.Stop();
```

TcpListener requires the local IP address on which to listen (a computer with two network cards, for instance, may have two addresses). You can use IPAddress.Any to tell it to listen on all (or the only) local IP addresses. AcceptTcpClient blocks until a client request is received (again, there's also an asynchronous version), at which point we call GetStream, just as on the client side.

When working at the transport layer, you need to decide on a protocol for who talks when, and for how long—rather like with a walkie-talkie. If both parties talk or listen at the same time, communication breaks down!

Let's invent a protocol where the client speaks first, saying "Hello," and then the server responds by saying "Hello right back!" Here's the code:

```
using System;
using System.IO;
using System.Net;
using System.Net.Sockets;
using System.Threading;

class TcpDemo
{
  static void Main()
```

```
    {
      new Thread (Server).Start();        // Run server method concurrently.
      Thread.Sleep (500);                 // Give server time to start.
      Client();
    }

    static void Client()
    {
      using (TcpClient client = new TcpClient ("localhost", 51111))
      using (NetworkStream n = client.GetStream())
      {
        BinaryWriter w = new BinaryWriter (n);
        w.Write ("Hello");
        w.Flush();
        Console.WriteLine (new BinaryReader (n).ReadString());
      }
    }

    static void Server()     // Handles a single client request, then exits.
    {
      TcpListener listener = new TcpListener (IPAddress.Any, 51111);
      listener.Start();
      using (TcpClient c = listener.AcceptTcpClient())
      using (NetworkStream n = c.GetStream())
      {
        string msg = new BinaryReader (n).ReadString();
        BinaryWriter w = new BinaryWriter (n);
        w.Write (msg + " right back!");
        w.Flush();                         // Must call Flush because we're not
      }                                    // disposing the writer.
      listener.Stop();
    }
  }
}

// OUTPUT: Hello right back!
```

In this example, we're using the localhost loopback to run the client and server on the same machine. We've arbitrarily chosen a port in the unallocated range (above 49152) and used a BinaryWriter and BinaryReader to encode the text messages. We've avoided closing or disposing the readers and writers in order to keep the underlying NetworkStream open until our conversation completes.

BinaryReader and BinaryWriter might seem like odd choices for reading and writing strings. However, they have a major advantage over StreamReader and Stream Writer: they prefix strings with an integer indicating the length, so a BinaryReader always knows exactly how many bytes to read. If you call StreamReader.ReadToEnd, you might block indefinitely—because a NetworkStream doesn't have an end! As long as the connection is open, the network stream can never be sure that the client isn't going to send more data.

StreamReader is in fact completely out of bounds with Net
workStream, even if you plan only to call ReadLine. This is
because StreamReader has a read-ahead buffer, which can
result in it reading more bytes than are currently available,
blocking indefinitely (or until the socket times out). Other
streams such as FileStream don't suffer this incompatibility
with StreamReader because they have a definite *end*—at which
point Read returns immediately with a value of 0.

Concurrency with TCP

TcpClient and TcpListener offer task-based asynchronous methods for scalable
concurrency. Using these is simply a question of replacing blocking method calls
with their *Async versions and awaiting the task that's returned.

In the following example, we write an asynchronous TCP server that accepts
requests of 5,000 bytes in length, reverses the bytes, and then sends them back to the
client:

```
async void RunServerAsync ()
{
  var listener = new TcpListener (IPAddress.Any, 51111);
  listener.Start ();
  try
  {
    while (true)
      Accept (await listener.AcceptTcpClientAsync ());
  }
  finally { listener.Stop(); }
}

async Task Accept (TcpClient client)
{
  await Task.Yield ();
  try
  {
    using (client)
    using (NetworkStream n = client.GetStream ())
    {
      byte[] data = new byte [5000];

      int bytesRead = 0; int chunkSize = 1;
      while (bytesRead < data.Length && chunkSize > 0)
        bytesRead += chunkSize =
          await n.ReadAsync (data, bytesRead, data.Length - bytesRead);

      Array.Reverse (data);   // Reverse the byte sequence
      await n.WriteAsync (data, 0, data.Length);
    }
  }
  catch (Exception ex) { Console.WriteLine (ex.Message); }
}
```

Such a program is scalable in that it does not block a thread for the duration of a request. So, if a thousand clients were to connect at once over a slow network connections (so that each request took several seconds from start to finish, for example), this program would not require 1,000 threads for that time (unlike with a synchronous solution). Instead, it leases threads only for the small periods of time required to execute code before and after the await expressions.

Receiving POP3 Mail with TCP

The .NET Framework provides no application-layer support for POP3, so you have to write at the TCP layer in order to receive mail from a POP3 server. Fortunately, this is a simple protocol; a POP3 conversation goes like this:

Client	Mail server	Notes
Client connects...	+OK Hello there.	Welcome message
USER joe	+OK Password required.	
PASS password	+OK Logged in.	
LIST	+OK 1 1876 2 5412 3 845 .	Lists the ID and file size of each message on the server
RETR 1	+OK 1876 octets *Content of message #1...* .	Retrieves the message with the specified ID
DELE 1	+OK Deleted.	Deletes a message from the server
QUIT	+OK Bye-bye.	

Each command and response is terminated by a new line (CR + LF), except for the multiline LIST and RETR commands, which are terminated by a single dot on a separate line. Because we can't use StreamReader with NetworkStream, we can start by writing a helper method to read a line of text in a nonbuffered fashion:

```
static string ReadLine (Stream s)
{
  List<byte> lineBuffer = new List<byte>();
  while (true)
  {
    int b = s.ReadByte();
    if (b == 10 || b < 0) break;
    if (b != 13) lineBuffer.Add ((byte)b);
  }
  return Encoding.UTF8.GetString (lineBuffer.ToArray());
}
```

We also need a helper method to send a command. Because we always expect to receive a response starting with "+OK," we can read and validate the response at the same time:

```
static void SendCommand (Stream stream, string line)
{
  byte[] data = Encoding.UTF8.GetBytes (line + "\r\n");
  stream.Write (data, 0, data.Length);
  string response = ReadLine (stream);
  if (!response.StartsWith ("+OK"))
    throw new Exception ("POP Error: " + response);
}
```

With these methods written, the job of retrieving mail is easy. We establish a TCP connection on port 110 (the default POP3 port) and then start talking to the server. In this example, we write each mail message to a randomly named file with an *.eml* extension before deleting the message off the server:

```
using (TcpClient client = new TcpClient ("mail.isp.com", 110))
using (NetworkStream n = client.GetStream())
{
  ReadLine (n);                          // Read the welcome message.
  SendCommand (n, "USER username");
  SendCommand (n, "PASS password");
  SendCommand (n, "LIST");               // Retrieve message IDs
  List<int> messageIDs = new List<int>();
  while (true)
  {
    string line = ReadLine (n);          // e.g.,  "1 1876"
    if (line == ".") break;
    messageIDs.Add (int.Parse (line.Split (' ')[0] ));   // Message ID
  }

  foreach (int id in messageIDs)         // Retrieve each message.
  {
    SendCommand (n, "RETR " + id);
    string randomFile = Guid.NewGuid().ToString() + ".eml";
    using (StreamWriter writer = File.CreateText (randomFile))
      while (true)
      {
        string line = ReadLine (n);      // Read next line of message.
        if (line == ".") break;          // Single dot = end of message.
        if (line == "..") line = ".";    // "Escape out" double dot.
        writer.WriteLine (line);         // Write to output file.
      }
    SendCommand (n, "DELE " + id);       // Delete message off server.
  }
  SendCommand (n, "QUIT");
}
```

TCP in Windows Runtime

Windows Runtime exposes TCP functionality through the Windows.Networking.Sockets namespace. As with the .NET implementation, there are two primary

classes to handle server and client roles. In WinRT, these are `StreamSocketLis`
`tener` and `StreamSocket`.

The following method starts a server on port 51111 and waits for a client to connect. It then reads a single message comprising a length-prefixed string:

```
async void Server()
{
  var listener = new StreamSocketListener();
  listener.ConnectionReceived += async (sender, args) =>
  {
    using (StreamSocket socket = args.Socket)
    {
      var reader = new DataReader (socket.InputStream);
      await reader.LoadAsync (4);
      uint length = reader.ReadUInt32();
      await reader.LoadAsync (length);
      Debug.WriteLine (reader.ReadString (length));
    }
    listener.Dispose();   // Close listener after one message.
  };
  await listener.BindServiceNameAsync ("51111");
}
```

In this example, we used a WinRT type called `DataReader` (in `Windows.Networking`)
to read from the input stream, rather than converting to a .NET `Stream` object and
using a `BinaryReader`. `DataReader` is rather like `BinaryReader` except that it supports asynchrony. The `LoadAsync` method asynchronously reads a specified number
of bytes into an internal buffer, which then allows you to call methods such as `Read`
`UInt32` or `ReadString`. The idea is that if you wanted to, say, read 1,000 integers in a
row, you'd first call `LoadAsync` with a value of `4000`, and then `ReadInt32` 1,000 times
in a loop. This avoids the overhead of calling asynchronous operations in a loop (as
each asynchronous operation incurs a small overhead).

> `DataReader`/`DataWriter` have a `ByteOrder` property to control
> whether numbers are encoding in big- or little-endian format.
> Big-endian is the default.

The `StreamSocket` object that we obtained from awaiting `AcceptAsync` has separate
input and output streams. So, to write a message back, we'd use the socket's `Output`
`Stream`. We can illustrate the use of `OutputStream` and `DataWriter` with the corresponding client code:

```
async void Client()
{
  using (var socket = new StreamSocket())
  {
    await socket.ConnectAsync (new HostName ("localhost"), "51111",
                               SocketProtectionLevel.PlainSocket);
    var writer = new DataWriter (socket.OutputStream);
    string message = "Hello!";
    uint length = (uint) Encoding.UTF8.GetByteCount (message);
    writer.WriteUInt32 (length);
```

```
      writer.WriteString (message);
      await writer.StoreAsync();
  }
}
```

We start by instantiating a `StreamSocket` directly and then call `ConnectAsync` with the host name and port. (You can pass either a DNS name or an IP address string into `HostName`'s constructor.) By specifying `SocketProtectionLevel.Ssl`, you can request SSL encryption (if configured on the server).

Again, we used a WinRT `DataWriter` rather than a .NET `BinaryWriter` and wrote the length of the string (measured in bytes rather than characters), followed by the string itself which is UTF-8 encoded. Finally, we called `StoreAsync`, which writes the buffer to the backing stream, and closed the socket.

Networking

17

Serialization

This chapter introduces serialization and deserialization, the mechanism by which objects can be represented in a flat text or binary form. Unless otherwise stated, the types in this chapter all exist in the following namespaces:

```
System.Runtime.Serialization
System.Xml.Serialization
```

Serialization Concepts

Serialization is the act of taking an in-memory object or *object graph* (set of objects that reference each other) and flattening it into a stream of bytes or XML nodes that can be stored or transmitted. *Deserialization* works in reverse, taking a data stream and reconstituting it into an in-memory object or object graph.

Serialization and deserialization are typically used to:

- Transmit objects across a network or application boundary
- Store representations of objects within a file or database

Another, less common use is to deep-clone objects. The data contract and XML serialization engines can also be used as general-purpose tools for loading and saving XML files of a known structure.

The .NET Framework supports serialization and deserialization both from the perspective of clients wanting to serialize and deserialize objects, and from the perspective of types wanting some control over how they are serialized.

Serialization Engines

There are four serialization mechanisms in the .NET Framework:

- The data contract serializer
- The binary serializer (in desktop apps)
- The (attribute-based) XML serializer (`XmlSerializer`)
- The `IXmlSerializable` interface

Of these, the first three are serialization "engines" that do most or all of the serialization work for you. The last is just a hook for doing the serialization yourself, using `XmlReader` and `XmlWriter`. `IXmlSerializable` can work in conjunction with the data contract serializer or `XmlSerializer` to handle the more complicated XML serialization tasks.

Table 17-1 compares each of the engines. More stars equate to a better score.

Table 17-1. Serialization engine comparison

Feature	Data contract serializer	Binary serializer	XmlSerializer	IXmlSerializable
Level of automation	***	*****	****	*
Type coupling	Choice	Tight	Loose	Loose
Version tolerance	*****	***	*****	*****
Preserves object references	Choice	Yes	No	Choice
Can serialize nonpublic fields	Yes	Yes	No	Yes
Suitability for interoperable messaging	*****	**	****	****
Flexibility in reading/writing XML files	**	-	****	*****
Compact output	**	****	**	**
Performance	***	****	* to ***	***

The scores for `IXmlSerializable` assume you've (hand)coded optimally using `XmlReader` and `XmlWriter`. The XML serialization engine requires that you recycle the same `XmlSerializer` object for good performance.

Why three engines?

The reason for there being three engines is partly historical. The Framework started out with two distinct goals in serialization:

- Serializing .NET object graphs with type and reference fidelity
- Interoperating with XML and SOAP messaging standards

The first was led by the requirements of Remoting; the second, by Web Services. The job of writing one serialization engine to do both was too daunting, so Microsoft wrote two engines: the binary serializer and the XML serializer.

When Windows Communication Foundation (WCF) was later written, as part of Framework 3.0, part of the goal was to unify Remoting and Web Services. This required a new serialization engine—hence, the *data contract serializer*. The data contract serializer unifies the features of the older two engines *relevant to (interoperable) messaging*. Outside of this context, however, the two older engines are still important.

The data contract serializer

The data contract serializer is the newest and the most versatile of the three serialization engines and is used by WCF. The serializer is particularly strong in two scenarios:

- When exchanging information through standards-compliant messaging protocols
- When you need good version tolerance, plus the option of preserving object references

The data contract serializer supports a *data contract* model that helps you decouple the low-level details of the types you want to serialize from the structure of the serialized data. This provides excellent version tolerance, meaning you can deserialize data that was serialized from an earlier or later version of a type. You can even deserialize types that have been renamed or moved to a different assembly.

The data contract serializer can cope with most object graphs, although it can require more assistance than the binary serializer. It can also be used as a general-purpose tool for reading/writing XML files, if you're flexible on how the XML is structured. (If you need to store data in attributes or cope with XML elements presenting in a random order, you cannot use the data contract serializer.)

The binary serializer

The binary serialization engine is easy to use, highly automatic, and well supported throughout the .NET Framework. Remoting uses binary serialization—including when communicating between two application domains in the same process (see Chapter 24).

The binary serializer is highly automated: quite often, a single attribute is all that's required to make a complex type fully serializable. The binary serializer is also faster than the data contract serializer when full type fidelity is needed. However, it tightly couples a type's internal structure to the format of the serialized data, resulting in poor version tolerance. (Prior to Framework 2.0, even adding a simple field was a version-breaking change.) The binary engine is also not really designed to produce XML, although it offers a formatter for SOAP-based messaging that provides limited interoperability with simple types.

XmlSerializer

The XML serialization engine can *only* produce XML, and it is less powerful than other engines in saving and restoring a complex object graph (it cannot restore shared object references). It's the most flexible of the three, however, in following an arbitrary XML structure. For instance, you can choose whether properties are serialized to elements or attributes and the handling of a collection's outer element. The XML engine also provides excellent version tolerance.

XmlSerializer is used by ASMX Web Services.

IXmlSerializable

Implementing IXmlSerializable means to do the serialization yourself with an XmlReader and XmlWriter. The IXmlSerializable interface is recognized both by XmlSerializer and by the data contract serializer, so it can be used selectively to handle the more complicated types. (It also can be used directly by WCF and ASMX Web Services.) We describe XmlReader and XmlWriter in detail in Chapter 11.

Formatters

The output of the data contract and binary serializers is shaped by a pluggable *formatter*. The role of a formatter is the same with both serialization engines, although they use completely different classes to do the job.

A formatter shapes the final presentation to suit a particular medium or context of serialization. In general, you can choose between XML and binary formatters. An XML formatter is designed to work within the context of an XML reader/writer, text file/stream, or SOAP messaging packet. A binary formatter is designed to work in a context where an arbitrary stream of bytes will do—typically a file/stream or proprietary messaging packet. Binary output is usually smaller than XML—sometimes radically so.

The term "binary" in the context of a formatter is unrelated to the "binary" serialization engine. Each of the two engines ships with both XML and binary formatters!

In theory, the engines are decoupled from their formatters. In practice, the design of each engine is geared toward one kind of formatter. The data contract serializer is geared toward the interoperability requirements of XML messaging. This is good for the XML formatter but means its binary formatter doesn't always achieve the gains you might hope. In contrast, the binary engine provides a relatively good binary formatter, but its XML formatter is highly limited, offering only crude SOAP interoperability.

Explicit Versus Implicit Serialization

Serialization and deserialization can be initiated in two ways.

The first is *explicitly*, by requesting that a particular object be serialized or deserialized. When you serialize or deserialize explicitly, you choose both the serialization engine and the formatter.

In contrast, *implicit* serialization is initiated by the Framework. This happens when:

- A serializer recursively serializes a child object.
- You use a feature that relies on serialization, such as WCF, Remoting, or Web Services.

WCF always uses the data contract serializer, although it can interoperate with the attributes and interfaces of the other engines.

Remoting always uses the binary serialization engine.

Web Services always uses `XmlSerializer`.

The Data Contract Serializer

Here are the basic steps in using the data contract serializer:

1. Decide whether to use the `DataContractSerializer` or the `NetDataContract Serializer`.

2. Decorate the types and members you want to serialize with `[DataContract]` and `[DataMember]` attributes, respectively.

3. Instantiate the serializer and call `WriteObject` or `ReadObject`.

If you chose the `DataContractSerializer`, you will also need to register "known types" (subtypes that can also be serialized), and decide whether to preserve object references.

You may also need to take special action to ensure that collections are properly serialized.

 Types for the data contract serializer are defined in the `Sys tem.Runtime.Serialization` namespace, in an assembly of the same name.

DataContractSerializer Versus NetDataContractSerializer

There are two data contract serializers:

`DataContractSerializer`
> Loosely couples .NET types to data contract types

`NetDataContractSerializer`
> Tightly couples .NET types to data contract types

The `DataContractSerializer` can produce interoperable standards-compliant XML such as this:

```
<Person xmlns="...">
  ...
</Person>
```

It requires, however, that you explicitly register serializable subtypes in advance so that it can map a data contract name such as "Person" to the correct .NET type. The `NetDataContractSerializer` requires no such assistance because it writes the full type and assembly names of the types it serializes, rather like the binary serialization engine:

```
<Person z:Type="SerialTest.Person" z:Assembly=
  "SerialTest, Version=1.0.0.0, Culture=neutral, PublicKeyToken=null">
  ...
</Person>
```

Such output, however, is proprietary. It also relies on the presence of a specific .NET type in a specific namespace and assembly in order to deserialize.

If you're saving an object graph to a "black box," you can choose either serializer, depending on what benefits are more important to you. If you're communicating through WCF, or reading/writing an XML file, you'll most likely want the `DataContractSerializer`.

Another difference between the two serializers is that `NetDataContractSerializer` always preserves referential equality; `DataContractSerializer` does so only upon request.

We'll go into each of these topics in more detail in the following sections.

Using the Serializers

After choosing a serializer, the next step is to attach attributes to the types and members you want to serialize. At a minimum:

- Add the `[DataContract]` attribute to each type.
- Add the `[DataMember]` attribute to each member that you want to include.

Here's an example:

```
namespace SerialTest
{
  [DataContract] public class Person
  {
    [DataMember] public string Name;
    [DataMember] public int Age;
  }
}
```

These attributes are enough to make a type *implicitly* serializable through the data contract engine.

You can then *explicitly* serialize or deserialize an object instance by instantiating a DataContractSerializer or NetDataContractSerializer and calling WriteObject or ReadObject:

```
Person p = new Person { Name = "Stacey", Age = 30 };

var ds = new DataContractSerializer (typeof (Person));

using (Stream s = File.Create ("person.xml"))
  ds.WriteObject (s, p);                          // Serialize

Person p2;
using (Stream s = File.OpenRead ("person.xml"))
  p2 = (Person) ds.ReadObject (s);                // Deserialize

Console.WriteLine (p2.Name + " " + p2.Age);       // Stacey 30
```

DataContractSerializer's constructor requires the *root object* type (the type of the object you're explicitly serializing). In contrast, NetDataContractSerializer does not:

```
var ns = new NetDataContractSerializer();

// NetDataContractSerializer is otherwise the same to use
// as DataContractSerializer.
...
```

Both types of serializer use the XML formatter by default. With an XmlWriter, you can request that the output be indented for readability:

```
Person p = new Person { Name = "Stacey", Age = 30 };
var ds = new DataContractSerializer (typeof (Person));

XmlWriterSettings settings = new XmlWriterSettings() { Indent = true };
using (XmlWriter w = XmlWriter.Create ("person.xml", settings))
  ds.WriteObject (w, p);

System.Diagnostics.Process.Start ("person.xml");
```

Here's the result:

```
<Person xmlns="http://schemas.datacontract.org/2004/07/SerialTest"
        xmlns:i="http://www.w3.org/2001/XMLSchema-instance">
  <Age>30</Age>
  <Name>Stacey</Name>
</Person>
```

The XML element name <Person> reflects the *data contract name*, which, by default, is the .NET type name. You can override this and explicitly state a data contract name as follows:

```
[DataContract (Name="Candidate")]
public class Person { ... }
```

The XML namespace reflects the *data contract namespace*, which, by default, is *http://schemas.datacontract.org/2004/07/*, plus the .NET type namespace. You can override this in a similar fashion:

```
[DataContract (Namespace="http://oreilly.com/nutshell")]
public class Person { ... }
```

 Specifying a name and namespace decouples the contract identity from the .NET type name. It ensures that, should you later refactor and change the type's name or namespace, serialization is unaffected.

You can also override names for data members:

```
[DataContract (Name="Candidate", Namespace="http://oreilly.com/nutshell")]
public class Person
{
  [DataMember (Name="FirstName")]  public string Name;
  [DataMember (Name="ClaimedAge")] public int Age;
}
```

Here's the output:

```
<?xml version="1.0" encoding="utf-8"?>
<Candidate xmlns="http://oreilly.com/nutshell"
           xmlns:i="http://www.w3.org/2001/XMLSchema-instance" >
  <ClaimedAge>30</ClaimedAge>
  <FirstName>Stacey</FirstName>
</Candidate>
```

[DataMember] supports both fields and properties—public and private. The field or property's data type can be any of the following:

- Any primitive type
- DateTime, TimeSpan, Guid, Uri, or an Enum value
- Nullable versions of the above
- byte[] (serializes in XML to base 64)
- Any "known" type decorated with DataContract

- Any IEnumerable type (see the section "Serializing Collections" on page 747 later in this chapter)

- Any type with the [Serializable] attribute or implementing ISerializable (see the section "Extending Data Contracts" on page 730 later in this chapter)

- Any type implementing IXmlSerializable

Specifying a binary formatter

You can use a binary formatter with DataContractSerializer or NetDataContract Serializer. The process is the same:

```
Person p = new Person { Name = "Stacey", Age = 30 };
var ds = new DataContractSerializer (typeof (Person));

var s = new MemoryStream();
using (XmlDictionaryWriter w = XmlDictionaryWriter.CreateBinaryWriter (s))
  ds.WriteObject (w, p);

var s2 = new MemoryStream (s.ToArray());
Person p2;
using (XmlDictionaryReader r = XmlDictionaryReader.CreateBinaryReader (s2,
                              XmlDictionaryReaderQuotas.Max))
  p2 = (Person) ds.ReadObject (r);
```

The output varies between being slightly smaller than that of the XML formatter, and radically smaller if your types contain large arrays.

Serializing Subclasses

You don't need to do anything special to handle the serializing of subclasses with the NetDataContractSerializer. The only requirement is that subclasses have the DataContract attribute. The serializer will write the fully qualified names of the actual types that it serializes as follows:

```
<Person ... z:Type="SerialTest.Person" z:Assembly=
  "SerialTest, Version=1.0.0.0, Culture=neutral, PublicKeyToken=null">
```

A DataContractSerializer, however, must be informed about all subtypes that it may have to serialize or deserialize. To illustrate, suppose we subclass Person as follows:

```
[DataContract] public class Person
{
  [DataMember] public string Name;
  [DataMember] public int Age;
}
[DataContract] public class Student : Person { }
[DataContract] public class Teacher : Person { }
```

and then write a method to clone a Person:

```
static Person DeepClone (Person p)
{
  var ds = new DataContractSerializer (typeof (Person));
  MemoryStream stream = new MemoryStream();
  ds.WriteObject (stream, p);
  stream.Position = 0;
  return (Person) ds.ReadObject (stream);
}
```

which we call as follows:

```
Person  person  = new Person  { Name = "Stacey", Age = 30 };
Student student = new Student { Name = "Stacey", Age = 30 };
Teacher teacher = new Teacher { Name = "Stacey", Age = 30 };

Person  p2 =            DeepClone (person);   // OK
Student s2 = (Student) DeepClone (student);   // SerializationException
Teacher t2 = (Teacher) DeepClone (teacher);   // SerializationException
```

DeepClone works if called with a Person but throws an exception with a Student or Teacher, because the deserializer has no way of knowing what .NET type (or assembly) a "Student" or "Teacher" should resolve to. This also helps with security, in that it prevents the deserialization of unexpected types.

The solution is to specify all permitted or "known" subtypes. You can do this either when constructing the DataContractSerializer:

```
var ds = new DataContractSerializer (typeof (Person),
  new Type[] { typeof (Student), typeof (Teacher) } );
```

or in the type itself, with the KnownType attribute:

```
[DataContract, KnownType (typeof (Student)), KnownType (typeof (Teacher))]
public class Person
...
```

Here's what a serialized Student now looks like:

```
<Person xmlns="..."
        xmlns:i="http://www.w3.org/2001/XMLSchema-instance"
        i:type="Student" >
  ...
<Person>
```

Because we specified Person as the root type, the root element still has that name. The actual subclass is described separately—in the type attribute.

The NetDataContractSerializer suffers a performance hit when serializing subtypes—with either formatter. It seems that when it encounters a subtype, it has to stop and think for a while!

Serialization performance matters on an application server that's handling many concurrent requests.

Object References

References to other objects are serialized, too. Consider the following classes:

```
[DataContract] public class Person
{
  [DataMember] public string Name;
  [DataMember] public int Age;
  [DataMember] public Address HomeAddress;
}

[DataContract] public class Address
{
  [DataMember] public string Street, Postcode;
}
```

Here's the result of serializing this to XML using the `DataContractSerializer`:

```
<Person...>
  <Age>...</Age>
  <HomeAddress>
    <Street>...</Street>
    <Postcode>...</Postcode>
  </HomeAddress>
  <Name>...</Name>
</Person>
```

The DeepClone method we wrote in the preceding section would clone HomeAddress, too—distinguishing it from a simple MemberwiseClone.

If you're using a `DataContractSerializer`, the same rules apply when subclassing `Address` as when subclassing the root type. So, if we define a `USAddress` class, for instance:

```
[DataContract]
public class USAddress : Address { }
```

and assign an instance of it to a `Person`:

```
Person p = new Person { Name = "John", Age = 30 };
p.HomeAddress = new USAddress { Street="Fawcett St", Postcode="02138" };
```

p could not be serialized. The solution is either to apply the `KnownType` attribute to `Address`:

```
[DataContract, KnownType (typeof (USAddress))]
public class Address
{
  [DataMember] public string Street, Postcode;
}
```

or to tell `DataContractSerializer` about `USAddress` in construction:

```
var ds = new DataContractSerializer (typeof (Person),
  new Type[] { typeof (USAddress) } );
```

(We don't need to tell it about `Address` because it's the declared type of the `HomeAd` dress data member.)

Preserving object references

The `NetDataContractSerializer` always preserves referential equality. The `Data` `ContractSerializer` does not, unless you specifically ask it to.

This means that if the same object is referenced in two different places, a `DataCon` `tractSerializer` ordinarily writes it twice. So, if we modify the preceding example so that `Person` also stores a work address:

```
[DataContract] public class Person
{
  ...
  [DataMember] public Address HomeAddress, WorkAddress;
}
```

and then serialize an instance as follows:

```
Person p = new Person { Name = "Stacey", Age = 30 };
p.HomeAddress = new Address { Street = "Odo St", Postcode = "6020" };
p.WorkAddress = p.HomeAddress;
```

we would see the same address details twice in the XML:

```
...
<HomeAddress>
  <Postcode>6020</Postcode>
  <Street>Odo St</Street>
</HomeAddress>
...
<WorkAddress>
  <Postcode>6020</Postcode>
  <Street>Odo St</Street>
</WorkAddress>
```

When this was later deserialized, `WorkAddress` and `HomeAddress` would be different objects. The advantage of this system is that it keeps the XML simple and standards-compliant. The disadvantages of this system include larger XML, loss of referential integrity, and the inability to cope with cyclical references.

You can request referential integrity by specifying `true` for `preserveObjectReferen` ces when constructing a `DataContractSerializer`:

```
var ds = new DataContractSerializer (typeof (Person),
                         null, 1000, false, true, null);
```

The third argument is mandatory when `preserveObjectReferences` is `true`: it indicates the maximum number of object references that the serializer should keep track of. The serializer throws an exception if this number is exceeded (this prevents a denial of service attack through a maliciously constructed stream).

Here's what the XML then looks like for a `Person` with the same home and work addresses:

```
<Person xmlns="http://schemas.datacontract.org/2004/07/SerialTest"
        xmlns:i="http://www.w3.org/2001/XMLSchema-instance"
        xmlns:z="http://schemas.microsoft.com/2003/10/Serialization/"
        z:Id="1">
  <Age>30</Age>
  <HomeAddress z:Id="2">
    <Postcode z:Id="3">6020</Postcode>
    <Street z:Id="4">Odo St</Street>
  </HomeAddress>
  <Name z:Id="5">Stacey</Name>
  <WorkAddress z:Ref="2" i:nil="true" />
</Person>
```

The cost of this is in reduced interoperability (notice the proprietary namespace of the Id and Ref attributes).

Version Tolerance

You can add and remove data members without breaking forward or backward compatibility. By default, the data contract deserializers do the following:

- Skip over data for which there is no [DataMember] in the type.
- Don't complain if any [DataMember] is missing in the serialization stream.

Rather than skipping over unrecognized data, you can instruct the deserializer to store unrecognized data members in a black box and then replay them should the type later be reserialized. This allows you to correctly round-trip data that's been serialized by a later version of your type. To activate this feature, implement IExtensibleDataObject. This interface really means "IBlackBoxProvider." It requires that you implement a single property, to get/set the black box:

```
[DataContract] public class Person : IExtensibleDataObject{
  [DataMember] public string Name;
  [DataMember] public int Age;

  ExtensionDataObject IExtensibleDataObject.ExtensionData { get; set; }
}
```

Required members

If a member is essential for a type, you can demand that it be present with IsRequired:

```
[DataMember (IsRequired=true)] public int ID;
```

If that member is not present, an exception is then thrown upon deserialization.

Member Ordering

The data contract serializers are extremely fussy about the ordering of data members. The deserializers, in fact, *skip over any members considered out of sequence.*

Members are written in the following order when serializing:

1. Base class to subclass
2. Low Order to high Order (for data members whose Order is set)
3. Alphabetical order (using *ordinal* string comparison)

So, in the preceding examples, Age comes before Name. In the following example, Name comes before Age:

```
[DataContract] public class Person
{
    [DataMember (Order=0)] public string Name;
    [DataMember (Order=1)] public int Age;
}
```

If Person has a base class, the base class's data members would all serialize first.

The main reason to specify an order is to comply with a particular XML schema. XML element order equates to data member order.

If you don't need to interoperate with anything else, the easiest approach is *not* to specify a member Order and rely purely on alphabetical ordering. A discrepancy will then never arise between serialization and deserialization as members are added and removed. The only time you'll come unstuck is if you move a member between a base class and a subclass.

Null and Empty Values

There are two ways to deal with a data member whose value is null or empty:

1. Explicitly write the null or empty value (the default).
2. Omit the data member from the serialization output.

In XML, an explicit null value looks like this:

```
<Person xmlns="..."
        xmlns:i="http://www.w3.org/2001/XMLSchema-instance">
  <Name i:nil="true" />
</Person>
```

Writing null or empty members can waste space, particularly on a type with lots of fields or properties that are usually left empty. More importantly, you may need to follow an XML schema that expects the use of optional elements (e.g., minOc curs="0") rather than nil values.

You can instruct the serializer not to emit data members for null/empty values as follows:

```
[DataContract] public class Person
{
  [DataMember (EmitDefaultValue=false)] public string Name;
  [DataMember (EmitDefaultValue=false)] public int Age;
}
```

Name is omitted if its value is null; Age is omitted if its value is 0 (the default value for the int type). If we were to make Age a nullable int, then it would be omitted if (and only if) its value was null.

The data contract deserializer, in rehydrating an object, bypasses the type's constructors and field initializers. This allows you to omit data members as described without breaking fields that are assigned nondefault values through an initializer or constructor. To illustrate, suppose we set the default Age for a Person to 30 as follows:

```
[DataMember (EmitDefaultValue=false)]
public int Age = 30;
```

Now suppose that we instantiate Person, explicitly set its Age from 30 to 0, and then serialize it. The output won't include Age, because 0 is the default value for the int type. This means that in deserialization, Age will be ignored and the field will remain at its default value—which fortunately is 0, given that field initializers and constructors were bypassed.

Data Contracts and Collections

The data contract serializers can save and repopulate any enumerable collection. For instance, suppose we define Person to have a List<> of addresses:

```
[DataContract] public class Person
{
  ...
  [DataMember] public List<Address> Addresses;
}

[DataContract] public class Address
{
  [DataMember] public string Street, Postcode;
}
```

Here's the result of serializing a Person with two addresses:

```
<Person ...>
  ...
  <Addresses>
    <Address>
      <Postcode>6020</Postcode>
      <Street>Odo St</Street>
    </Address>
```

```
  <Address>
    <Postcode>6152</Postcode>
    <Street>Comer St</Street>
  </Address>
</Addresses>
  ...
</Person>
```

Notice that the serializer doesn't encode any information about the particular *type* of collection it serialized. If the `Addresses` field was instead of type `Address[]`, the output would be identical. This allows the collection type to change between serialization and deserialization without causing an error.

Sometimes, though, you need your collection to be of a more specific type than you expose. An extreme example is with interfaces:

```
[DataMember] public IList<Address> Addresses;
```

This serializes correctly (as before), but a problem arises in deserialization. There's no way the deserializer can know which concrete type to instantiate, so it chooses the simplest option—an array. The deserializer sticks to this strategy even if you initialize the field with a different concrete type:

```
[DataMember] public IList<Address> Addresses = new List<Address>();
```

(Remember that the deserializer bypasses field initializers.) The workaround is to make the data member a private field and add a public property to access it:

```
[DataMember (Name="Addresses")] List<Address> _addresses;

public IList<Address> Addresses { get { return _addresses; } }
```

In a nontrivial application, you would probably use properties in this manner anyway. The only unusual thing here is that we've marked the private field as the data member, rather than the public property.

Subclassed Collection Elements

The serializer handles subclassed collection elements transparently. You must declare the valid subtypes just as you would if they were used anywhere else:

```
[DataContract, KnownType (typeof (USAddress))]
public class Address
{
  [DataMember] public string Street, Postcode;
}

public class USAddress : Address { }
```

Adding a `USAddress` to a `Person`'s address list then generates XML like this:

```
  ...
  <Addresses>
    <Address i:type="USAddress">
      <Postcode>02138</Postcode>
      <Street>Fawcett St</Street>
```

```
    </Address>
  </Addresses>
```

Customizing Collection and Element Names

If you subclass a collection class itself, you can customize the XML name used to describe each element by attaching a `CollectionDataContract` attribute:

```
[CollectionDataContract (ItemName="Residence")]
public class AddressList : Collection<Address> { }

[DataContract] public class Person
{
  ...
  [DataMember] public AddressList Addresses;
}
```

Here's the result:

```
  ...
    <Addresses>
      <Residence>
        <Postcode>6020</Postcode>
        <Street>Odo St</Street>
      </Residence>
      ...
```

`CollectionDataContract` also lets you specify a `Namespace` and `Name`. The latter is not used when the collection is serialized as a property of another object (such as in this example), but it is when the collection is serialized as the root object.

You can also use `CollectionDataContract` to control the serialization of dictionaries:

```
[CollectionDataContract (ItemName="Entry",
                         KeyName="Kind",
                         ValueName="Number")]
public class PhoneNumberList : Dictionary <string, string> { }

[DataContract] public class Person
{
  ...
  [DataMember] public PhoneNumberList PhoneNumbers;
}
```

Here's how this formats:

```
  ...
    <PhoneNumbers>
      <Entry>
        <Kind>Home</Kind>
        <Number>08 1234 5678</Number>
      </Entry>
      <Entry>
        <Kind>Mobile</Kind>
        <Number>040 8765 4321</Number>
```

Serialization

```
    </Entry>
  </PhoneNumbers>
```

Extending Data Contracts

This section describes how you can extend the capabilities of the data contract serializer through serialization hooks, [Serializable] and IXmlSerializable.

Serialization and Deserialization Hooks

You can request that a custom method be executed before or after serialization by flagging the method with one of the following attributes:

[OnSerializing]
> Indicates a method to be called just *before* serialization

[OnSerialized]
> Indicates a method to be called just *after* serialization

Similar attributes are supported for deserialization:

[OnDeserializing]
> Indicates a method to be called just *before* deserialization

[OnDeserialized]
> Indicates a method to be called just *after* deserialization

The custom method must have a single parameter of type StreamingContext. This parameter is required for consistency with the binary engine, and it is not used by the data contract serializer.

[OnSerializing] and [OnDeserialized] are useful in handling members that are outside the capabilities of the data contract engine, such as a collection that has an extra payload or that does not implement standard interfaces. Here's the basic approach:

```
[DataContract] public class Person
{
  public SerializationUnfriendlyType Addresses;

  [DataMember (Name="Addresses")]
  SerializationFriendlyType _serializationFriendlyAddresses;

  [OnSerializing]
  void PrepareForSerialization (StreamingContext sc)
  {
    // Copy Addresses-> _serializationFriendlyAddresses
    // ...
  }

  [OnDeserialized]
  void CompleteDeserialization (StreamingContext sc)
```

```
    {
      // Copy _serializationFriendlyAddresses-> Addresses
      // ...
    }
}
```

An [OnSerializing] method can also be used to conditionally serialize fields:

```
public DateTime DateOfBirth;

[DataMember] public bool Confidential;

[DataMember (Name="DateOfBirth", EmitDefaultValue=false)]
DateTime? _tempDateOfBirth;

[OnSerializing]
void PrepareForSerialization (StreamingContext sc)
{
  if (Confidential)
    _tempDateOfBirth = DateOfBirth;
  else
    _tempDateOfBirth = null;
}
```

Recall that the data contract deserializers bypass field initializers and constructors. An [OnDeserializing] method acts as a pseudoconstructor for deserialization, and it is useful for initializing fields excluded from serialization:

```
[DataContract] public class Test
{
  bool _editable = true;

  public Test() { _editable = true; }

  [OnDeserializing]
  void Init (StreamingContext sc)
  {
    _editable = true;
  }
}
```

If it wasn't for the Init method, _editable would be false in a deserialized instance of Test—despite the other two attempts at making it true.

Methods decorated with these four attributes can be private. If subtypes need to participate, they can define their own methods with the same attributes, and they will get executed, too.

Interoperating with [Serializable]

The data contract serializer can also serialize types marked with the binary serialization engine's attributes and interfaces. This ability is important, since support for the binary engine has been woven into much of what was written prior to Framework 3.0—including the .NET Framework itself!

The following things flag a type as being serializable for the binary engine:

- The [Serializable] attribute
- Implementing ISerializable

Binary interoperability is useful in serializing existing types as well as new types that need to support both engines. It also provides another means of extending the capability of the data contract serializer, because the binary engine's ISerializable is more flexible than the data contract attributes. Unfortunately, the data contract serializer is inefficient in how it formats data added via ISerializable.

A type wanting the best of both worlds cannot define attributes for both engines. This creates a problem for types such as string and DateTime, which for historical reasons cannot divorce the binary engine attributes. The data contract serializer works around this by filtering out these basic types and processing them specially. For all other types marked for binary serialization, the data contract serializer applies similar rules to what the binary engine would use. This means it honors attributes such as NonSerialized or calls ISerializable if implemented. It does not *thunk* to the binary engine itself—this ensures that output is formatted in the same style as if data contract attributes were used.

Types designed to be serialized with the binary engine expect object references to be preserved. You can enable this option through the DataContractSerializer (or by using the NetDa taContractSerializer).

The rules for registering known types also apply to objects and subobjects serialized through the binary interfaces.

The following example illustrates a class with a [Serializable] data member:

```
[DataContract] public class Person
{
  ...
  [DataMember] public Address MailingAddress;
}
[Serializable] public class Address
{
  public string Postcode, Street;
}
```

Here's the result of serializing it:

```
<Person ...>
  ...
  <MailingAddress>
    <Postcode>6020</Postcode>
    <Street>Odo St</Street>
  </MailingAddress>
  ...
```

Had `Address` implemented `ISerializable`, the result would be less efficiently formatted:

```
<MailingAddress>
  <Street xmlns:d3p1="http://www.w3.org/2001/XMLSchema"
    i:type="d3p1:string" xmlns="">str</Street>
  <Postcode xmlns:d3p1="http://www.w3.org/2001/XMLSchema"
    i:type="d3p1:string" xmlns="">pcode</Postcode>
</MailingAddress>
```

Interoperating with IXmlSerializable

A limitation of the data contract serializer is that it gives you little control over the structure of the XML. In a WCF application, this can actually be beneficial, in that it makes it easier for the infrastructure to comply with standard messaging protocols.

If you do need precise control over the XML, you can implement `IXmlSerializa ble` and then use `XmlReader` and `XmlWriter` to manually read and write the XML. The data contract serializer allows you to do this just on the types for which this level of control is required. We describe the `IXmlSerializable` interface further in the final section of this chapter.

The Binary Serializer

The binary serialization engine is used implicitly by Remoting. It can also be used to perform such tasks as saving and restoring objects to disk. The binary serialization is highly automated and can handle complex object graphs with minimum intervention. It's not available, however, in Windows Store apps.

There are two ways to make a type support binary serialization. The first is attribute-based; the second involves implementing `ISerializable`. Adding attributes is simpler; implementing `ISerializable` is more flexible. You typically implement `ISerializable` to:

- Dynamically control what gets serialized.
- Make your serializable type friendly to being subclassed by other parties.

Getting Started

A type can be made serializable with a single attribute:

```
[Serializable] public sealed class Person
{
  public string Name;
  public int Age;
}
```

The [Serializable] attribute instructs the serializer to include all fields in the type. This includes both private and public fields (but not properties). Every field must itself be serializable; otherwise, an exception is thrown. Primitive .NET types such as `string` and `int` support serialization (as do many other .NET types).

The `Serializable` attribute is not inherited, so subclasses are not automatically serializable unless also marked with this attribute.

With automatic properties, the binary serialization engine serializes the underlying compiler-generated field. The name of this field, unfortunately, can change when its type is recompiled, breaking compatibility with existing serialized data. The workaround is either to avoid automatic properties in [`Serializable`] types or to implement `ISerializable`.

To serialize an instance of `Person`, you instantiate a formatter and call `Serialize`. There are two formatters for use with the binary engine:

`BinaryFormatter`

This is the more efficient of the two, producing smaller output in less time. Its namespace is `System.Runtime.Serialization.Formatters.Binary`.

`SoapFormatter`

This supports basic SOAP-style messaging when used with Remoting. Its namespace is `System.Runtime.Serialization.Formatters.Soap`.

`BinaryFormatter` is contained in *mscorlib*; `SoapFormatter` is contained in *System.Runtime.Serialization.Formatters.Soap.dll*.

The `SoapFormatter` is less functional than the `BinaryFormatter`. The `SoapFormatter` doesn't support generic types or the filtering of extraneous data necessary for version tolerant serialization.

The two formatters are otherwise exactly the same to use. The following serializes a `Person` with a `BinaryFormatter`:

```
Person p = new Person() { Name = "George", Age = 25 };

IFormatter formatter = new BinaryFormatter();

using (FileStream s = File.Create ("serialized.bin"))
  formatter.Serialize (s, p);
```

All the data necessary to reconstruct the `Person` object is written to the file *serialized.bin*. The `Deserialize` method restores the object:

```
using (FileStream s = File.OpenRead ("serialized.bin"))
{
  Person p2 = (Person) formatter.Deserialize (s);
  Console.WriteLine (p2.Name + " " + p.Age);      // George 25
}
```

The deserializer bypasses all constructors when re-creating objects. Behind the scenes, it calls `FormatterServices.GetU ninitializedObject` to do this job. You can call this method yourself to implement some very grubby design patterns!

The serialized data includes full type and assembly information, so if we try to cast the result of deserialization to a matching `Person` type in a different assembly, an error would result. The deserializer fully restores object references to their original state upon deserialization. This includes collections, which are just treated as serializable objects like any other (all collection types in `System.Collections.*` are marked as serializable).

The binary engine can handle large, complex object graphs without special assistance (other than ensuring that all participating members are serializable). One thing to be wary of is that the serializer's performance degrades in proportion to the number of references in your object graph. This can become an issue in a Remoting server that has to process many concurrent requests.

Binary Serialization Attributes

[NonSerialized]

Unlike data contracts, which have an *opt-in* policy in serializing fields, the binary engine has an *opt-out* policy. Fields that you don't want serialized, such as those used for temporary calculations, or for storing file or window handles, you must mark explicitly with the `[NonSerialized]` attribute:

```
[Serializable] public sealed class Person
{
  public string Name;
  public DateTime DateOfBirth;

  // Age can be calculated, so there's no need to serialize it.
  [NonSerialized] public int Age;
}
```

This instructs the serializer to ignore the `Age` member.

Nonserialized members are always empty or `null` when deserialized—even if field initializers or constructors set them otherwise.

[OnDeserializing] and [OnDeserialized]

Deserialization bypasses all your normal constructors as well as field initializers. This is of little consequence if every field partakes in serialization, but it can be problematic if some fields are excluded via `[NonSerialized]`. We can illustrate this by adding a `bool` field called `Valid`:

```
public sealed class Person
{
  public string Name;
  public DateTime DateOfBirth;

  [NonSerialized] public int Age;
  [NonSerialized] public bool Valid = true;

  public Person() { Valid = true; }
}
```

A deserialized Person will not be Valid—despite the constructor and field initializer.

The solution is the same as with the data contract serializer: to define a special deserialization "constructor" with the [OnDeserializing] attribute. A method that you flag with this attribute gets called just prior to deserialization:

```
[OnDeserializing]
void OnDeserializing (StreamingContext context)
{
  Valid = true;
}
```

We could also write an [OnDeserialized] method to update the calculated Age field (this fires just *after* deserialization):

```
[OnDeserialized]
void OnDeserialized (StreamingContext context)
{
  TimeSpan ts = DateTime.Now - DateOfBirth;
  Age = ts.Days / 365;                          // Rough age in years
}
```

[OnSerializing] and [OnSerialized]

The binary engine also supports the [OnSerializing] and [OnSerialized] attributes. These flag a method for execution before or after serialization. To see how they can be useful, we'll define a Team class that contains a generic List of players:

```
[Serializable] public sealed class Team
{
  public string Name;
  public List<Person> Players = new List<Person>();
}
```

This class serializes and deserializes correctly with the binary formatter but not the SOAP formatter. This is because of an obscure limitation: the SOAP formatter refuses to serialize generic types! An easy solution is to convert Players to an array just prior to serialization, then convert it back to a generic List upon deserialization. To make this work, we can add another field for storing the array, mark the original Players field as [NonSerialized], and then write the conversion code in as follows:

```
[Serializable] public sealed class Team
{
  public string Name;
  Person[] _playersToSerialize;

  [NonSerialized] public List<Person> Players = new List<Person>();

  [OnSerializing]
  void OnSerializing (StreamingContext context)
  {
    _playersToSerialize = Players.ToArray();
  }

  [OnSerialized]
  void OnSerialized (StreamingContext context)
  {
    _playersToSerialize = null;    // Allow it to be freed from memory
  }

  [OnDeserialized]
  void OnDeserialized (StreamingContext context)
  {
    Players = new List<Person> (_playersToSerialize);
  }
}
```

[OptionalField] and Versioning

By default, adding a field breaks compatibility with data that's already serialized, unless you attach the [OptionalField] attribute to the new field.

To illustrate, suppose we start with a Person class that has just one field. Let's call it Version 1:

```
[Serializable] public sealed class Person        // Version 1
{
  public string Name;
}
```

Later, we realize we need a second field, so we create Version 2 as follows:

```
[Serializable] public sealed class Person        // Version 2
{
  public string Name;
  public DateTime DateOfBirth;
}
```

If two computers were exchanging Person objects via Remoting, deserialization would go wrong unless they both updated to Version 2 at *exactly the same time*. The OptionalField attribute gets around this problem:

```
[Serializable] public sealed class Person        // Version 2 Robust
{
  public string Name;
```

```
    [OptionalField (VersionAdded = 2)] public DateTime DateOfBirth;
}
```

This tells the deserializer not to panic if it sees no `DateOfBirth` in the data stream, and instead to treat the missing field as nonserialized. This means you end up with an empty `DateTime` (you can assign a different value in an `[OnDeserializing]` method).

The `VersionAdded` argument is an integer that you increment each time you augment a type's fields. This serves as documentation, and it has no effect on serialization semantics.

 If versioning robustness is important, avoid renaming and deleting fields and avoid retrospectively adding the `NonSerial``ized` attribute. Never change a field's type.

So far we've focused on the backward-compatibility problem: the deserializer failing to find an expected field in the serialization stream. But with two-way communication, a forward-compatibility problem can also arise whereby the deserializer encounters an extraneous field with no knowledge of how to process it. The binary formatter is programmed to automatically cope with this by throwing away the extraneous data; the SOAP formatter instead throws an exception! Hence, you must use the binary formatter if two-way versioning robustness is required; otherwise, manually control the serialization by implementing `ISerializable`.

Binary Serialization with ISerializable

Implementing `ISerializable` gives a type complete control over its binary serialization and deserialization.

Here's the `ISerializable` interface definition:

```
public interface ISerializable
{
    void GetObjectData (SerializationInfo info, StreamingContext context);
}
```

`GetObjectData` fires upon serialization; its job is to populate the `Serializatio``nInfo` object (a name-value dictionary) with data from all fields that you want serialized. Here's how we would write a `GetObjectData` method that serializes two fields, called `Name` and `DateOfBirth`:

```
public virtual void GetObjectData (SerializationInfo info,
                                   StreamingContext context)
{
    info.AddValue ("Name", Name);
    info.AddValue ("DateOfBirth", DateOfBirth);
}
```

In this example, we've chosen to name each item according to its corresponding field. This is not required; any name can be used, as long as the same name is used upon deserialization. The values themselves can be of any serializable type; the

Framework will recursively serialize as necessary. It's legal to store null values in the dictionary.

 It's a good idea to make the GetObjectData method virtual —unless your class is sealed. This allows subclasses to extend serialization without having to reimplement the interface.

SerializationInfo also contains properties that you can use to control the type and assembly that the instance should deserialize as. The StreamingContext parameter is a structure that contains, among other things, an enumeration value indicating to where the serialized instance is heading (disk, Remoting, etc., although this value is not always populated).

In addition to implementing ISerializable, a type controlling its own serialization needs to provide a deserialization constructor that takes the same two parameters as GetObjectData. The constructor can be declared with any accessibility and the runtime will still find it. Typically, though, you would declare it protected so that subclasses can call it.

In the following example, we implement ISerializable in the Team class. When it comes to handling the List of players, we serialize the data as an array rather than a generic list, so as to offer compatibility with the SOAP formatter:

```
[Serializable] public class Team : ISerializable
{
  public string Name;
  public List<Person> Players;

  public virtual void GetObjectData (SerializationInfo si,
                                     StreamingContext sc)
  {
    si.AddValue ("Name", Name);
    si.AddValue ("PlayerData", Players.ToArray());
  }

  public Team() {}

  protected Team (SerializationInfo si, StreamingContext sc)
  {
    Name = si.GetString ("Name");

    // Deserialize Players to an array to match our serialization:
    Person[] a = (Person[]) si.GetValue ("PlayerData", typeof (Person[]));

    // Construct a new List using this array:
    Players = new List<Person> (a);
  }
}
```

For commonly used types, the SerializationInfo class has typed "Get" methods such as GetString in order to make writing deserialization constructors easier. If you specify a name for which no data exists, an exception is thrown. This happens most often when there's a version mismatch between the code doing the serialization and deserialization. You've added an extra field, for instance, and then forgotten about the implications of deserializing an old instance. To work around this problem, you can either:

- Add exception handling around code that retrieves a data member added in a later version.

- Implement your own version numbering system. For example:

```
public string MyNewField;

public virtual void GetObjectData (SerializationInfo si,
                                   StreamingContext sc)
{
  si.AddValue ("_version", 2);
  si.AddValue ("MyNewField", MyNewField);
  ...
}

protected Team (SerializationInfo si, StreamingContext sc)
{
  int version = si.GetInt32 ("_version");
  if (version >= 2) MyNewField = si.GetString ("MyNewField");
  ...
}
```

Subclassing Serializable Classes

In the preceding examples, we sealed the classes that relied on attributes for serialization. To see why, consider the following class hierarchy:

```
[Serializable] public class Person
{
  public string Name;
  public int Age;
}

[Serializable] public sealed class Student : Person
{
  public string Course;
}
```

In this example, both Person and Student are serializable, and both classes use the default runtime serialization behavior since neither class implements ISerializable.

Now imagine that the developer of Person decides for some reason to implement ISerializable and provide a deserialization constructor to control Person serialization. The new version of Person might look like this:

```
[Serializable] public class Person : ISerializable
{
  public string Name;
```

```
  public int Age;

  public virtual void GetObjectData (SerializationInfo si,
                                     StreamingContext sc)
  {
    si.AddValue ("Name", Name);
    si.AddValue ("Age", Age);
  }

  protected Person (SerializationInfo si, StreamingContext sc)
  {
    Name = si.GetString ("Name");
    Age = si.GetInt32 ("Age");
  }

  public Person() {}
}
```

Although this works for instances of Person, this change breaks serialization of Stu dent instances. Serializing a Student instance would appear to succeed, but the Course field in the Student type isn't saved to the stream because the implementation of ISerializable.GetObjectData on Person has no knowledge of the members of the Student-derived type. Additionally, deserialization of Student instances throws an exception since the runtime is looking (unsuccessfully) for a deserialization constructor on Student.

The solution to this problem is to implement ISerializable from the outset for serializable classes that are public and nonsealed. (With internal classes, it's not so important because you can easily modify the subclasses later if required.)

If we started out by writing Person as in the preceding example, Student would then be written as follows:

```
[Serializable]
public class Student : Person
{
  public string Course;

  public override void GetObjectData (SerializationInfo si,
                                      StreamingContext sc)
  {
    base.GetObjectData (si, sc);
    si.AddValue ("Course", Course);
  }

  protected Student (SerializationInfo si, StreamingContext sc)
    : base (si, sc)
  {
    Course = si.GetString ("Course");
  }

  public Student() {}
}
```

XML Serialization

The Framework provides a dedicated XML serialization engine called `XmlSerial izer` in the `System.Xml.Serialization` namespace. It's suitable for serializing .NET types to XML files and is also used implicitly by ASMX Web Services.

As with the binary engine, there are two approaches you can take:

- Sprinkle attributes throughout your types (defined in `System.Xml.Serializa tion`).

- Implement `IXmlSerializable`.

Unlike with the binary engine, however, implementing the interface (i.e., `IXmlSeria lizable`) eschews the engine completely, leaving you to code the serialization your-self with `XmlReader` and `XmlWriter`.

Getting Started with Attribute-Based Serialization

To use `XmlSerializer`, you instantiate it and call `Serialize` or `Deserialize` with a `Stream` and object instance. To illustrate, suppose we define the following class:

```
public class Person
{
  public string Name;
  public int Age;
}
```

The following saves a `Person` to an XML file and then restores it:

```
Person p = new Person();
p.Name = "Stacey"; p.Age = 30;

XmlSerializer xs = new XmlSerializer (typeof (Person));

using (Stream s = File.Create ("person.xml"))
  xs.Serialize (s, p);

Person p2;
using (Stream s = File.OpenRead ("person.xml"))
  p2 = (Person) xs.Deserialize (s);

Console.WriteLine (p2.Name + " " + p2.Age);   // Stacey 30
```

`Serialize` and `Deserialize` can work with a `Stream`, `XmlWriter`/`XmlReader`, or `TextWriter`/`TextReader`. Here's the resultant XML:

```
<?xml version="1.0"?>
<Person xmlns:xsi="http://www.w3.org/2001/XMLSchema-instance"
        xmlns:xsd="http://www.w3.org/2001/XMLSchema">
  <Name>Stacey</Name>
  <Age>30</Age>
</Person>
```

`XmlSerializer` can serialize types without any attributes—such as our `Person` type. By default, it serializes all *public fields and properties* on a type. You can exclude members you don't want serialized with the `XmlIgnore` attribute:

```
public class Person
{
  ...
  [XmlIgnore] public DateTime DateOfBirth;
}
```

Unlike the other two engines, `XmlSerializer` does not recognize the `[OnDeserializing]` attribute and relies instead on a parameterless constructor for deserialization, throwing an exception if one is not present. (In our example, `Person` has an *implicit* parameterless constructor.) This also means field initializers execute prior to deserialization:

```
public class Person
{
  public bool Valid = true;    // Executes before deserialization
}
```

Although `XmlSerializer` can serialize almost any type, it recognizes the following types and treats them specially:

- The primitive types, `DateTime`, `TimeSpan`, `Guid`, and nullable versions
- `byte[]` (which is converted to base 64)
- An `XmlAttribute` or `XmlElement` (whose contents are injected into the stream)
- Any type implementing `IXmlSerializable`
- Any collection type

The deserializer is version tolerant: it doesn't complain if elements or attributes are missing or if superfluous data is present.

Attributes, names, and namespaces

By default, fields and properties serialize to an XML element. You can request an XML attribute be used instead as follows:

```
[XmlAttribute] public int Age;
```

You can control an element or attribute's name as follows:

```
public class Person
{
  [XmlElement ("FirstName")] public string Name;
  [XmlAttribute ("RoughAge")] public int Age;
}
```

Here's the result:

```
<Person RoughAge="30" ...>
  <FirstName>Stacey</FirstName>
</Person>
```

The default XML namespace is blank (unlike the data contract serializer, which uses the type's namespace). To specify an XML namespace, [XmlElement] and [XmlAttribute] both accept a Namespace argument. You can also assign a name and namespace to the type itself with [XmlRoot]:

```
[XmlRoot ("Candidate", Namespace = "http://mynamespace/test/")]
public class Person { ... }
```

This names the person element "Candidate" as well as assigning a namespace to this element and its children.

XML element order

XmlSerializer writes elements in the order that they're defined in the class. You can change this by specifying an Order in the XmlElement attribute:

```
public class Person
{
  [XmlElement (Order = 2)] public string Name;
  [XmlElement (Order = 1)] public int Age;
}
```

If you use Order at all, you must use it throughout.

The deserializer is not fussy about the order of elements—they can appear in any sequence and the type will properly deserialize.

Subclasses and Child Objects

Subclassing the root type

Suppose your root type has two subclasses as follows:

```
public class Person { public string Name; }

public class Student : Person { }
public class Teacher : Person { }
```

and you write a reusable method to serialize the root type:

```
public void SerializePerson (Person p, string path)
{
  XmlSerializer xs = new XmlSerializer (typeof (Person));
  using (Stream s = File.Create (path))
    xs.Serialize (s, p);
}
```

To make this method work with a Student or Teacher, you must inform XmlSerializer about the subclasses. There are two ways to do this. The first is to register each subclass with the XmlInclude attribute:

```
[XmlInclude (typeof (Student))]
[XmlInclude (typeof (Teacher))]
public class Person { public string Name; }
```

The second is to specify each of the subtypes when constructing XmlSerializer:

```
XmlSerializer xs = new XmlSerializer (typeof (Person),
                   new Type[] { typeof (Student), typeof (Teacher) } );
```

In either case, the serializer responds by recording the subtype in the type attribute (just like with the data contract serializer):

```
<Person xmlns:xsi="http://www.w3.org/2001/XMLSchema-instance"
        xsi:type="Student">
  <Name>Stacey</Name>
</Person>
```

This deserializer then knows from this attribute to instantiate a Student and not a Person.

> You can control the name that appears in the XML type attribute by applying [XmlType] to the subclass:
>
> ```
> [XmlType ("Candidate")]
> public class Student : Person { }
> ```
>
> Here's the result:
>
> ```
> <Person xmlns:xsi="..."
>         xsi:type="Candidate">
> ```

Serializing child objects

XmlSerializer automatically recurses object references such as the HomeAddress field in Person:

```
public class Person
{
  public string Name;
  public Address HomeAddress = new Address();
}

public class Address { public string Street, PostCode; }
```

To demonstrate:

```
Person p = new Person(); p.Name = "Stacey";
p.HomeAddress.Street = "Odo St";
p.HomeAddress.PostCode = "6020";
```

Here's the XML to which this serializes:

```
<Person ... >
  <Name>Stacey</Name>
  <HomeAddress>
    <Street>Odo St</Street>
    <PostCode>6020</PostCode>
  </HomeAddress>
</Person>
```

If you have two fields or properties that refer to the same object, that object is serialized twice. If you need to preserve referential equality, you must use another serialization engine.

Subclassing child objects

Suppose you need to serialize a `Person` that can reference *subclasses* of `Address` as follows:

```
public class Address { public string Street, PostCode; }
public class USAddress : Address {  }
public class AUAddress : Address {  }

public class Person
{
  public string Name;
  public Address HomeAddress = new USAddress();
}
```

There are two distinct ways to proceed, depending on how you want the XML structured. If you want the element name always to match the field or property name with the subtype recorded in a type attribute:

```
<Person ...>
  ...
  <HomeAddress xsi:type="USAddress">
    ...
  </HomeAddress>
</Person>
```

you use [XmlInclude] to register each of the subclasses with `Address` as follows:

```
[XmlInclude (typeof (AUAddress))]
[XmlInclude (typeof (USAddress))]
public class Address
{
  public string Street, PostCode;
}
```

If, on the other hand, you want the element name to reflect the name of the subtype, to the following effect:

```
<Person ...>
  ...
  <USAddress>
    ...
  </USAddress>
</Person>
```

you instead stack multiple [XmlElement] attributes onto the field or property in the parent type:

```
public class Person
{
  public string Name;
```

```
[XmlElement ("Address", typeof (Address))]
[XmlElement ("AUAddress", typeof (AUAddress))]
[XmlElement ("USAddress", typeof (USAddress))]
public Address HomeAddress = new USAddress();
}
```

Each XmlElement maps an element name to a type. If you take this approach, you don't require the [XmlInclude] attributes on the Address type (although their presence doesn't break serialization).

If you omit the element name in [XmlElement] (and specify just a type), the type's default name is used (which is influenced by [XmlType] but not [XmlRoot]).

Serializing Collections

XmlSerializer recognizes and serializes concrete collection types without intervention:

```
public class Person
{
  public string Name;
  public List<Address> Addresses = new List<Address>();
}

public class Address { public string Street, PostCode; }
```

Here's the XML to which this serializes:

```
<Person ... >
  <Name>...</Name>
  <Addresses>
    <Address>
      <Street>...</Street>
      <Postcode>...</Postcode>
    </Address>
    <Address>
      <Street>...</Street>
      <Postcode>...</Postcode>
    </Address>
    ...
  </Addresses>
</Person>
```

The [XmlArray] attribute lets you rename the *outer* element (i.e., Addresses).

The [XmlArrayItem] attribute lets you rename the *inner* elements (i.e., the Address elements).

For instance, the following class:

```
public class Person
{
  public string Name;
```

```
    [XmlArray ("PreviousAddresses")]
    [XmlArrayItem ("Location")]
    public List<Address> Addresses = new List<Address>();
}
```

serializes to this:

```
<Person ... >
  <Name>...</Name>
  <PreviousAddresses>
    <Location>
      <Street>...</Street>
      <Postcode>...</Postcode>
    </Location>
    <Location>
      <Street>...</Street>
      <Postcode>...</Postcode>
    </Location>
    ...
  </PreviousAddresses>
</Person>
```

The XmlArray and XmlArrayItem attributes also allow you to specify XML namespaces.

To serialize collections *without* the outer element, for example:

```
<Person ... >
  <Name>...</Name>
  <Address>
    <Street>...</Street>
    <Postcode>...</Postcode>
  </Address>
  <Address>
    <Street>...</Street>
    <Postcode>...</Postcode>
  </Address>
</Person>
```

instead add [XmlElement] to the collection field or property:

```
public class Person
{
  ...
  [XmlElement ("Address")]
  public List<Address> Addresses = new List<Address>();
}
```

Working with subclassed collection elements

The rules for subclassing collection elements follow naturally from the other subclassing rules. To encode subclassed elements with the type attribute, for example:

```
<Person ... >
  <Name>...</Name>
  <Addresses>
```

```
<Address xsi:type="AUAddress">
  ...
```

add [XmlInclude] attributes to the base (Address) type as we did before. This works whether or not you suppress serialization of the outer element.

If you want subclassed elements to be named according to their type, for example:

```
<Person ... >
  <Name>...</Name>
  <!-start of optional outer element->
  <AUAddress>
    <Street>...</Street>
    <Postcode>...</Postcode>
  </AUAddress>
  <USAddress>
    <Street>...</Street>
    <Postcode>...</Postcode>
  </USAddress>
  <!-end of optional outer element->
</Person>
```

you must stack multiple [XmlArrayItem] or [XmlElement] attributes onto the collection field or property.

Stack multiple [XmlArrayItem] attributes if you want to *include* the outer collection element:

```
[XmlArrayItem ("Address",   typeof (Address))]
[XmlArrayItem ("AUAddress", typeof (AUAddress))]
[XmlArrayItem ("USAddress", typeof (USAddress))]
public List<Address> Addresses = new List<Address>();
```

Stack multiple [XmlElement] attributes if you want to *exclude* the outer collection element:

```
[XmlElement ("Address",   typeof (Address))]
[XmlElement ("AUAddress", typeof (AUAddress))]
[XmlElement ("USAddress", typeof (USAddress))]
public List<Address> Addresses = new List<Address>();
```

IXmlSerializable

Although attribute-based XML serialization is flexible, it has limitations. For instance, you cannot add serialization hooks—nor can you serialize nonpublic members. It's also awkward to use if the XML might present the same element or attribute in a number of different ways.

On that last issue, you can push the boundaries somewhat by passing an XmlAttributeOverrides object into XmlSerializer's constructor. There comes a point, however, when it's easier to take an imperative approach. This is the job of IXmlSerializable:

```
public interface IXmlSerializable
{
```

```
XmlSchema GetSchema();
void ReadXml (XmlReader reader);
void WriteXml (XmlWriter writer);
}
```

Implementing this interface gives you total control over the XML that's read or written.

 A collection class that implements IXmlSerializable bypasses XmlSerializer's rules for serializing collections. This can be useful if you need to serialize a collection with a payload—in other words, additional fields or properties that would otherwise be ignored.

The rules for implementing IXmlSerializable are as follows:

- ReadXml should read the outer start element, then the content, and then the outer end element.

- WriteXml should write just the content.

For example:

```
using System;
using System.Xml;
using System.Xml.Schema;
using System.Xml.Serialization;

public class Address : IXmlSerializable
{
  public string Street, PostCode;

  public XmlSchema GetSchema() { return null; }

  public void ReadXml(XmlReader reader)
  {
    reader.ReadStartElement();
    Street   = reader.ReadElementContentAsString ("Street", "");
    PostCode = reader.ReadElementContentAsString ("PostCode", "");
    reader.ReadEndElement();
  }

  public void WriteXml (XmlWriter writer)
  {
    writer.WriteElementString ("Street", Street);
    writer.WriteElementString ("PostCode", PostCode);
  }
}
```

Serializing and deserializing an instance of Address via XmlSerializer automatically calls the WriteXml and ReadXml methods. Further, if Person was defined as follows:

```
public class Person
{
```

```
    public string Name;
    public Address HomeAddress;
}
```

IXmlSerializable would be called upon selectively to serialize the HomeAddress
field.

We describe XmlReader and XmlWriter at length in the first section of Chapter 11.
Also in Chapter 11, in "Patterns for Using XmlReader/XmlWriter" on page 489, we
provide examples of IXmlSerializable-ready classes.

18

Assemblies

An assembly is the basic unit of deployment in .NET and is also the container for all types. An assembly contains compiled types with their IL (Intermediate Language) code, runtime resources, and information to assist with versioning, security, and referencing other assemblies. An assembly also defines a boundary for type resolution and security permissioning. In general, an assembly comprises a single Windows *Portable Executable* (PE) file—with an *.exe* extension in the case of an application or a *.dll* extension in the case of a reusable library. A WinRT library has a *.winmd* extension and is similar to a *.dll*, except that it contains only metadata and no IL code.

Most of the types in this chapter come from the following namespaces:

```
System.Reflection
System.Resources
System.Globalization
```

What's in an Assembly

An assembly contains four kinds of things:

An assembly manifest
> Provides information to the .NET runtime, such as the assembly's name, version, requested permissions, and other assemblies that it references

An application manifest
> Provides information to the operating system, such as how the assembly should be deployed and whether administrative elevation is required

Compiled types
> The compiled IL code and metadata of the types defined within the assembly

Resources

Other data embedded within the assembly, such as images and localizable text

Of these, only the *assembly manifest* is mandatory, although an assembly nearly always contains compiled types (unless it's a WinRT reference assembly).

Assemblies are structured similarly whether they're executables or libraries. The main difference with an executable is that it defines an entry point.

The Assembly Manifest

The assembly manifest serves two purposes:

- It describes the assembly to the managed hosting environment.
- It acts as a directory to the modules, types, and resources in the assembly.

Assemblies are hence *self-describing*. A consumer can discover all of an assembly's data, types, and functions—without needing additional files.

 An assembly manifest is not something you add explicitly to an assembly—it's automatically embedded into an assembly as part of compilation.

Here's a summary of the functionally significant data stored in the manifest:

- The simple name of the assembly
- A version number (`AssemblyVersion`)
- A public key and signed hash of the assembly, if strongly named
- A list of referenced assemblies, including their version and public key
- A list of modules that comprise the assembly
- A list of types defined in the assembly and the module containing each type
- An optional set of security permissions requested or refused by the assembly (`SecurityPermission`)
- The culture it targets, if a satellite assembly (`AssemblyCulture`)

The manifest can also store the following informational data:

- A full title and description (`AssemblyTitle` and `AssemblyDescription`)
- Company and copyright information (`AssemblyCompany` and `AssemblyCopyright`)
- A display version (`AssemblyInformationalVersion`)
- Additional attributes for custom data

Some of this data is derived from arguments given to the compiler, such as the list of referenced assemblies or the public key with which to sign the assembly. The rest comes from assembly attributes, indicated in parentheses.

 You can view the contents of an assembly's manifest with the .NET tool *ildasm.exe*. In Chapter 19, we describe how to use reflection to do the same programmatically.

Specifying assembly attributes

You can control much of the manifest's content with assembly attributes. For example:

```
[assembly: AssemblyCopyright ("\x00a9 Corp Ltd. All rights reserved.")]
[assembly: AssemblyVersion ("2.3.2.1")]
```

These declarations are usually all defined in one file in your project. Visual Studio automatically creates a file called *AssemblyInfo.cs* in the *Properties* folder with every new C# project for this purpose, prepopulated with a default set of assembly attributes that provide a starting point for further customization.

The Application Manifest

An application manifest is an XML file that communicates information about the assembly to the operating system. An application manifest, if present, is read and processed before the .NET-managed hosting environment loads the assembly—and can influence how the operating system launches an application's process.

A .NET application manifest has a root element called assembly in the XML namespace urn:schemas-microsoft-com:asm.v1:

```
<?xml version="1.0" encoding="utf-8"?>
<assembly manifestVersion="1.0" xmlns="urn:schemas-microsoft-com:asm.v1">
  <!-- contents of manifest -->
</assembly>
```

The following manifest instructs the OS to request administrative elevation:

```
<?xml version="1.0" encoding="utf-8"?>
<assembly manifestVersion="1.0" xmlns="urn:schemas-microsoft-com:asm.v1">
  <trustInfo xmlns="urn:schemas-microsoft-com:asm.v2">
    <security>
      <requestedPrivileges>
        <requestedExecutionLevel level="requireAdministrator" />
      </requestedPrivileges>
    </security>
  </trustInfo>
</assembly>
```

We describe the consequences of requesting administrative elevation in Chapter 21.

Windows Store applications have a far more elaborate manifest, described in the *Package.appxmanifest* file. This includes a declaration of the program's capabilities, which determine permissions granted by the operating system. The easiest way to edit this file is with Visual Studio, which presents a UI when you double-click the manifest file.

Deploying a .NET application manifest

You can deploy a .NET application manifest in two ways:

- As a specially named file located in the same folder as the assembly
- Embedded within the assembly itself

As a separate file, its name must match that of the assembly's, plus *.manifest*. So, if an assembly was named *MyApp.exe*, its manifest would be named *MyApp.exe.manifest*.

To embed an application manifest file into an assembly, first build the assembly and then call the .NET mt tool as follows:

```
mt -manifest MyApp.exe.manifest -outputresource:MyApp.exe;#1
```

 The .NET tool *ildasm.exe* is blind to the presence of an embedded application manifest. Visual Studio, however, indicates whether an embedded application manifest is present if you double-click the assembly in Solution Explorer.

Modules

The contents of an assembly are actually packaged within one or more intermediate containers, called *modules*. A module corresponds to a file containing the contents of an assembly. The reason for this extra layer of containership is to allow an assembly to span multiple files—a feature that's useful when building an assembly containing code compiled in a mixture of programming languages.

Figure 18-1 shows the normal case of an assembly with a single module. Figure 18-2 shows a multifile assembly. In a multifile assembly, the "main" module always contains the manifest; additional modules can contain IL and/or resources. The manifest describes the relative location of all the other modules that make up the assembly.

Multifile assemblies have to be compiled from the command line: there's no support in Visual Studio. To do this, you invoke the csc compiler with the /t switch to create each module and then link them with the assembly linker tool, *al.exe*.

Although the need for multifile assemblies is rare, at times you need to be aware of the extra level of containership that modules impose—even when dealing just with single-module assemblies. The main scenario is with reflection (see "Reflecting Assemblies" on page 810 and "Emitting Assemblies and Types" on page 825 in Chapter 19).

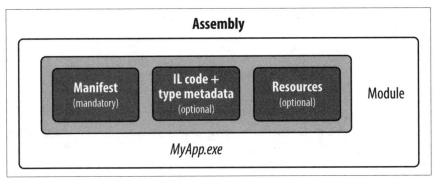

Figure 18-1. Single-file assembly

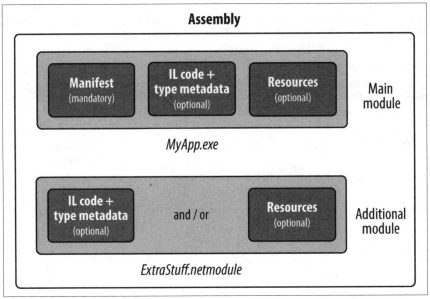

Figure 18-2. Multifile assembly

The Assembly Class

The Assembly class in System.Reflection is a gateway to accessing assembly metadata at runtime. There are a number of ways to obtain an assembly object: the simplest is via a Type's Assembly property:

```
Assembly a = typeof (Program).Assembly;
```

or, in Windows Store applications:

```
Assembly a = typeof (Program).GetTypeInfo().Assembly;
```

In desktop apps, you can also obtain an `Assembly` object by calling one of `Assembly`'s static methods:

GetExecutingAssembly
> Returns the assembly of the type that defines the currently executing function

GetCallingAssembly
> Does the same as `GetExecutingAssembly`, but for the function that called the currently executing function

GetEntryAssembly
> Returns the assembly defining the application's original entry method

Once you have an `Assembly` object, you can use its properties and methods to query the assembly's metadata and reflect upon its types. Table 18-1 shows a summary of these functions.

Table 18-1. Assembly members

Functions	Purpose	See the section...
`FullName, GetName`	Returns the fully qualified name or an `AssemblyName` object	"Assembly Names" on page 761
`CodeBase, Location`	Location of the assembly file	"Resolving and Loading Assemblies" on page 779
`Load, LoadFrom, LoadFile`	Manually loads an assembly into the current application domain	"Resolving and Loading Assemblies" on page 779
`GlobalAssemblyCache`	Indicates whether the assembly is in the GAC	"The Global Assembly Cache" on page 768
`GetSatelliteAssembly`	Locates the satellite assembly of a given culture	"Resources and Satellite Assemblies" on page 770
`GetType, GetTypes`	Returns a type, or all types, defined in the assembly	"Reflecting and Activating Types" on page 790 in Chapter 19
`EntryPoint`	Returns the application's entry method, as a `MethodInfo`	"Reflecting and Invoking Members" on page 797 in Chapter 19
`GetModules, ManifestModule`	Returns all modules, or the main module, of an assembly	"Reflecting Assemblies" on page 810 in Chapter 19
`GetCustomAttributes`	Returns the assembly's attributes	"Working with Attributes" on page 812 in Chapter 19

Strong Names and Assembly Signing

A *strongly named* assembly has a unique and untamperable identity. It works by adding two bits of metadata to the manifest:

- A *unique number* that belongs to the authors of the assembly
- A *signed hash* of the assembly, proving that the unique number holder produced the assembly

This requires a public/private key pair. The *public key* provides the unique identifying number, and the *private key* facilitates signing.

Strong-name-signing is not the same as *Authenticode*-signing. We cover Authenticode later in this chapter.

The public key is valuable in guaranteeing the uniqueness of assembly references: a strongly named assembly incorporates the public key into its identity. The signature is valuable for security—it prevents a malicious party from tampering with your assembly. Without your private key, no one can release a modified version of the assembly without the signature breaking (causing an error when loaded). Of course, someone could re-sign the assembly with a different key pair—but this would give the assembly a different identity. Any application referencing the original assembly would shun the imposter because public key tokens are written into references.

Adding a strong name to a previously "weak" named assembly changes its identity. For this reason, it pays to give production assemblies strong names from the outset.

A strongly named assembly can also be registered in the GAC.

How to Strongly Name an Assembly

To give an assembly a strong name, first generate a public/private key pair with the *sn.exe* utility:

```
sn.exe -k MyKeyPair.snk
```

This manufactures a new key pair and stores it to a file called *MyApp.snk*. If you subsequently lose this file, you will permanently lose the ability to recompile your assembly with the same identity.

You then compile with the /keyfile switch:

```
csc.exe /keyfile:MyKeyPair.snk Program.cs
```

Visual Studio assists you with both steps in the Project Properties window.

A strongly named assembly cannot reference a weakly named assembly. This is another compelling reason to strongly name all your production assemblies.

The same key pair can sign multiple assemblies—they'll still have distinct identities if their simple names differ. The choice as to how many key pair files to use within an organization depends on a number of factors. Having a separate key pair for every assembly is advantageous should you later transfer ownership of a particular application (along with its referenced assemblies), in terms of minimum disclosure. But it makes it harder for you to create a security policy that recognizes all of your assemblies. It also makes it harder to validate dynamically loaded assemblies.

 Prior to C# 2.0, the compiler did not support the /keyfile switch, and you would specify a key file with the AssemblyKey File attribute instead. This presented a security risk, because the path to the key file would remain embedded in the assembly's metadata. For instance, with *ildasm*, you can see quite easily that the path to the key file used to sign *mscorlib* in CLR 1.1 was as follows:

> F:\qfe\Tools\devdiv\EcmaPublicKey.snk

Obviously, you need access to that folder on Microsoft's .NET Framework build machine to take advantage of that information!

Delay Signing

In an organization with hundreds of developers, you might want to restrict access to the key pairs used for signing assemblies, for a couple of reasons:

- If a key pair gets leaked, your assemblies are no longer untamperable.

- A test assembly, if signed and leaked, could be maliciously propagated as the real assembly.

Withholding key pairs from developers, though, means they cannot compile and test assemblies with their correct identity. *Delay signing* is a system for working around this problem.

A delay-signed assembly is flagged with the correct public key, but not *signed* with the private key. A delay-signed assembly is equivalent to a tampered assembly and would normally be rejected by the CLR. The developer, however, instructs the CLR to bypass validation for the delay-sign assemblies on *that computer*, allowing the unsigned assemblies to run. When it comes time for final deployment, the private key holder re-signs the assembly with the real key pair.

To delay-sign, you need a file containing *just* the public key. You can extract this from a key pair by calling sn with the -p switch:

```
sn -k KeyPair.snk
sn -p KeyPair.snk PublicKeyOnly.pk
```

KeyPair.snk is kept secure and *PublicKeyOnly.pk* is freely distributed.

 You can also obtain *PublicKeyOnly.pk* from an existing signed assembly with the -e switch:

> sn -e YourLibrary.dll PublicKeyOnly.pk

You then delay-sign with *PublicKeyOnly.pk* by calling csc with the /delaysign+ switch:

```
csc /delaysign+ /keyfile: PublicKeyOnly.pk /target:library YourLibrary.cs
```

Visual Studio does the same if you tick the "Delay sign" checkbox in Project Properties.

The next step is to instruct the .NET runtime to skip assembly identity verification on the development computers running the delay-signed assemblies. This can be done on either a per-assembly or a per-public key basis, by calling the sn tool with the Vr switch:

```
sn -Vr YourLibrary.dll
```

 Visual Studio does not perform this step automatically. You must disable assembly verification manually from the command line. Otherwise, your assembly will not execute.

The final step is to fully sign the assembly prior to deployment. This is when you replace the null signature with a real signature that can be generated only with access to the private key. To do this, you call sn with the R switch:

```
sn -R YourLibrary.dll KeyPair.snk
```

You can then reinstate assembly verification on development machines as follows:

```
sn -Vu YourLibrary.dll
```

You won't need to recompile any applications that reference the delay-signed assembly, because you've changed only the assembly's signature, not its *identity*.

Assembly Names

An assembly's "identity" comprises four pieces of metadata from its manifest:

- Its simple name
- Its version ("0.0.0.0" if not present)
- Its culture ("neutral" if not a satellite)
- Its public key token ("null" if not strongly named)

The simple name comes not from any attribute, but from the name of the file to which it was originally compiled (less any extension). So, the simple name of the *System.Xml.dll* assembly is "System.Xml." Renaming a file doesn't change the assembly's simple name.

The version number comes from the AssemblyVersion attribute. It's a string divided into four parts as follows:

```
major.minor.build.revision
```

You can specify a version number as follows:

```
[assembly: AssemblyVersion ("2.5.6.7")]
```

The culture comes from the `AssemblyCulture` attribute and applies to satellite assemblies, described later in the section "Resources and Satellite Assemblies" on page 770.

The public key token comes from a key pair supplied at compile time via the `/keyfile` switch, as we saw earlier, in the section "How to Strongly Name an Assembly" on page 759.

Fully Qualified Names

A fully qualified assembly name is a string that includes all four identifying components, in this format:

```
simple-name, Version=version, Culture=culture, PublicKeyToken=public-key
```

For example, the fully qualified name of *System.Xml.dll* is:

```
"System.Xml, Version=2.0.0.0, Culture=neutral,
PublicKeyToken=b77a5c561934e089"
```

If the assembly has no `AssemblyVersion` attribute, the version appears as "0.0.0.0". If it is unsigned, its public key token appears as "null".

An `Assembly` object's `FullName` property returns its fully qualified name. The compiler always uses fully qualified names when recording assembly references in the manifest.

A fully qualified assembly name does not include a directory path to assist in locating it on disk. Locating an assembly residing in another directory is an entirely separate matter that we pick up in "Resolving and Loading Assemblies" on page 779.

The AssemblyName Class

`AssemblyName` is a class with a typed property for each of the four components of a fully qualified assembly name. `AssemblyName` has two purposes:

- It parses or builds a fully qualified assembly name.
- It stores some extra data to assist in resolving (finding) the assembly.

You can obtain an `AssemblyName` object in any of the following ways:

- Instantiate an `AssemblyName`, providing a fully qualified name.
- Call `GetName` on an existing `Assembly`.
- Call `AssemblyName.GetAssemblyName`, providing the path to an assembly file on disk (desktop apps only).

You can also instantiate an `AssemblyName` object without any arguments and then set each of its properties to build a fully qualified name. An `AssemblyName` is mutable when constructed in this manner.

Here are its essential properties and methods:

```
string      FullName    { get; }            // Fully qualified name
string      Name        { get; set; }       // Simple name
Version     Version     { get; set; }       // Assembly version
CultureInfo CultureInfo { get; set; }       // For satellite assemblies
string      CodeBase    { get; set; }       // Location

byte[]      GetPublicKey();                  // 160 bytes
void        SetPublicKey (byte[] key);
byte[]      GetPublicKeyToken();             // 8-byte version
void        SetPublicKeyToken (byte[] publicKeyToken);
```

`Version` is itself a strongly typed representation, with properties for `Major`, `Minor`, `Build`, and `Revision` numbers. `GetPublicKey` returns the full cryptographic public key; `GetPublicKeyToken` returns the last eight bytes used in establishing identity.

To use `AssemblyName` to obtain the simple name of an assembly:

```
Console.WriteLine (typeof (string).Assembly.GetName().Name);  // mscorlib
```

To get an assembly version:

```
string v = myAssembly.GetName().Version.ToString();
```

We'll examine the `CodeBase` property in the later section "Resolving and Loading Assemblies" on page 779.

Assembly Informational and File Versions

Because an integral part of an assembly name is its version, changing the `Assembly Version` attribute changes the assembly's identity. This affects compatibility with referencing assemblies, which can be undesirable when making nonbreaking updates. To address this, there are two other independent assembly-level attributes for expressing version-related information, both of which are ignored by the CLR:

`AssemblyInformationalVersion`

The version as displayed to the end user. This is visible in the Windows File Properties dialog box as "Product Version." Any string can go here, such as "5.1 Beta 2." Typically, all the assemblies in an application would be assigned the same informational version number.

`AssemblyFileVersion`

This is intended to refer to the build number for that assembly. This is visible in the Windows File Properties dialog box as "File Version." As with `AssemblyVersion`, it must contain a string consisting of up to four numbers separated by periods.

Authenticode Signing

Authenticode is a code-signing system whose purpose is to prove the identity of the publisher. Authenticode and *strong-name* signing are independent: you can sign an assembly with either or both systems.

While strong-name signing can prove that assemblies A, B, and C came from the same party (assuming the private key hasn't been leaked), it can't tell you who that party was. In order to know that the party was Joe Albahari—or Microsoft Corporation—you need Authenticode.

Authenticode is useful when downloading programs from the Internet because it provides assurance that a program came from whoever was named by the Certificate Authority and was not modified in transit. It also prevents the "Unknown Publisher" warning shown in Figure 18-3 when running a downloaded application for the first time. Authenticode signing is also a requirement when submitting apps to the Windows Store, and for assemblies in general as part of the Windows Logo program.

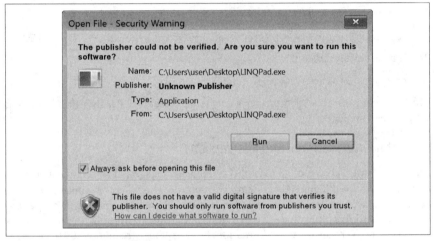

Figure 18-3. Unsigned file warning

Authenticode works with not only .NET assemblies, but also unmanaged executables and binaries such as ActiveX controls or *.msi* deployment files. Of course, Authenticode doesn't guarantee that a program is free from malware—although it does make it less likely. A person or entity has been willing to put its name (backed by a passport or company document) behind the executable or library.

 The CLR does not treat an Authenticode signature as part of an assembly's identity. However, it can read and validate Authenticode signatures on demand, as we'll see soon.

Signing with Authenticode requires that you contact a *certificate authority* (CA) with evidence of your personal identity or company's identity (articles of incorporation, etc.). Once the CA has checked your documents, it will issue an X.509 code-signing certificate that is typically valid for one to five years. This enables you to sign assemblies with the *signtool* utility. You can also make a certificate yourself with the *makecert* utility, however it will be recognized only on computers on which the certificate is explicitly installed.

The fact that (non-self-signed) certificates can work on any computer relies on public key infrastructure. Essentially, your certificate is signed with another certificate belonging to a CA. The CA is trusted because all CAs are loaded into the operating system (to see them, go to the Windows Control Panel and choose Internet Options→Content tab→Certificates button→Trusted Root Certification Authorities tab). A CA can revoke a publisher's certificate if leaked, so verifying an Authenticode signature requires periodically asking the CA for an up-to-date list of certification revocations.

Because Authenticode uses cryptographic signing, an Authenticode signature is invalid if someone subsequently tampers with the file. We discuss cryptography, hashing, and signing in Chapter 21.

How to Sign with Authenticode

Obtaining and installing a certificate

The first step is to obtain a code-signing certificate from a CA (see "Where to Get a Code-Signing Certificate" on page 766). You can then either work with the certificate as a password-protected file or load the certificate into the computer's certificate store. The benefit of doing the latter is that you can sign without needing to specify a password. This is advantageous because it avoids having a password visible in automated build scripts or batch files.

Where to Get a Code-Signing Certificate

Just a handful of code-signing CAs are preloaded into Windows as root certification authorities. These include (with prices for one-year code-signing certificates at the time of publication): Comodo ($180), Go Daddy ($200), GlobalSign ($220), Digi-Cert ($223), thawte ($299), and Semantic ($499).

There is also a reseller called Ksoftware (*http://www.ksoftware.net*), which currently offers Comodo code-signing certificates for $95 per year.

The Authenticode certificates issued by Ksoftware, Comodo, Go Daddy, and Global-Sign are advertised as less restrictive in that they will also sign non-Microsoft programs. Aside from this, the products from all vendors are functionally equivalent.

Note that a certificate for SSL cannot generally be used for Authenticode signing (despite using the same X.509 infrastructure). This is, in part, because a certificate for SSL is about proving ownership of a domain; Authenticode is about proving who you are.

To load a certificate into the computer's certificate store, go to the Windows Control Panel and select Internet Options→Content tab→Certificates button→Import. Once the import is complete, click the View button on the certificate, go to the Details tab, and copy the certificate's *thumbprint*. This is the SHA-1 hash that you'll subsequently need to identity the certificate when signing.

> If you also want to strong-name-sign your assembly (which is highly recommended), you must do so *before* Authenticode signing. This is because the CLR knows about Authenticode signing, but not vice versa. So if you strong-name-sign an assembly *after* Authenticode-signing it, the latter will see the addition of the CLR's strong name as an unauthorized modification and consider the assembly tampered.

Signing with signtool.exe

You can Authenticode-sign your programs with the *signtool* utility that comes with Visual Studio. It displays a UI if you call it with the `signwizard` flag; otherwise, you can use it in command-line style as follows:

```
signtool sign /sha1 (thumbprint) filename
```

The thumbprint is that of the certificate as shown in the computer's certificate store. (If the certificate is in a file instead, specify the filename with /f, and the password with /p.)

For example:

```
signtool sign /sha1 ff813c473dc93aaca4bac681df472b037fa220b3 LINQPad.exe
```

You can also specify a description and product URL with /d and /du:

```
... /d LINQPad /du http://www.linqpad.net
```

In most cases, you will also want to specify a *time-stamping server*.

Time stamping

After your certificate expires, you'll no longer be able to sign programs. However, programs that you signed *before* its expiry will still be valid—if you specified a *time-stamping server* with the /t switch when signing. The CA will provide you with a URI for this purpose: the following is for Comodo (or Ksoftware):

```
... /t http://timestamp.comodoca.com/authenticode
```

Verifying that a program has been signed

The easiest way to view an Authenticode signature on a file is to view the file's properties in Windows Explorer (look in the Digital Signatures tab). The *signtool* utility also provides an option for this.

Authenticode Validation

Both the operating system and the CLR may validate Authenticode signatures.

Windows validates Authenticode signatures before running programs marked as "blocked"—in practice, this means programs run for the first time after having been downloaded from the Internet. The status—or absence—of Authenticode information is then shown in the dialog box we saw in Figure 18-3.

The CLR reads and validates Authenticode signatures when you ask for assembly evidence. Here's how to do that:

```
Publisher p = someAssembly.Evidence.GetHostEvidence<Publisher>();
```

The Publisher class (in System.Security.Policy) exposes a Certificate property. If this returns a non-null value, it has been Authenticode-signed. You can then query this object for the details of the certificate.

 Prior to Framework 4.0, the CLR would read and validate Authenticode signatures when an assembly was loaded—rather than waiting until you called GetHostEvidence. This had potentially disastrous performance consequences, because Authenticode validation may round-trip to the CA to update the certificate revocation list—which can take up to 30 seconds (to fail) if there are Internet connectivity problems. For this reason, it's best to avoid Authenticode-signing .NET 3.5 or earlier assemblies if possible. (Signing *.msi* setup files, though, is fine.)

Regardless of the Framework version, if a program has a bad or unverifiable Authenticode signature, the CLR will merely make that information available via GetHostEvidence: it will never display a warning to the user or prevent the assembly from running.

Assemblies

As we said previously, an Authenticode signature has no effect on an assembly's identity or *name*.

The Global Assembly Cache

As part of the .NET Framework installation, a central repository is created on the computer for storing .NET assemblies, called the *Global Assembly Cache*, or GAC. The GAC contains a centralized copy of the .NET Framework itself, and it can also be used to centralize your own assemblies.

The main factor in choosing whether to load your assemblies into the GAC relates to versioning. For assemblies in the GAC, versioning is centralized at the machine level and controlled by the computer's administrator. For assemblies outside the GAC, versioning is handled on an application basis, so each application looks after its own dependency and update issues (typically by maintaining its own copy of each assembly that it references).

The GAC is useful in the minority of cases where machine-centralized versioning is genuinely advantageous. For example, consider a suite of interdependent plug-ins, each referencing some shared assemblies. We'll assume each plug-in is in its own directory, and for this reason, there's a possibility of there being multiple copies of a shared assembly (maybe some later than others). Further, we'll assume the hosting application will want to load each shared assembly just once for the sake of efficiency and type compatibility. The task of assembly resolution is now difficult for the hosting application, requiring careful planning and an understanding of the subtleties of assembly loading contexts. The simple solution here is to put the shared assemblies into the GAC. This ensures that the CLR always makes straightforward and consistent assembly-resolution choices.

In more typical scenarios, however, the GAC is best avoided because it adds the following complications:

- XCOPY or ClickOnce deployment is no longer possible; an administrative setup is required to install your application.

- Updating assemblies in the GAC also requires administrative privileges.

- Use of the GAC can complicate development and testing, because *fusion*, the CLR's assembly resolution mechanism, always favors GAC assemblies over local copies.

- Versioning and *side-by-side* execution require some planning, and a mistake may break other applications.

On the positive side, the GAC can improve startup time for very large assemblies, because the CLR verifies the signatures of assemblies in the GAC only once upon installation, rather than every time the assembly loads. In percentage terms, this is relevant if you've generated native images for your assemblies with the *ngen.exe* tool, choosing non-overlapping base addresses. A good article describing these issues is available online at the MSDN site, titled "To NGen or Not to NGen?"

Assemblies in the GAC are always fully trusted—even when called from an assembly running in a limited-permissions sandbox. We discuss this further in Chapter 21.

How to Install Assemblies to the GAC

To install assemblies to the GAC, the first step is to give your assembly a strong name. Then you can install it using the .NET command-line tool, `gacutil`:

```
gacutil /i MyAssembly.dll
```

If the assembly already exists in the GAC with the *same public key and version*, it's updated. You don't have to uninstall the old one first.

To uninstall an assembly (note the lack of a file extension):

```
gacutil /u MyAssembly
```

You can also specify that assemblies be installed to the GAC as part of a setup project in Visual Studio.

Calling `gacutil` with the /l switch lists all assemblies in the GAC.

Once an assembly is loaded into the GAC, applications can reference it without needing a local copy of that assembly.

If a local copy *is* present, it's *ignored in favor of the GAC image*. This means there's no way to reference or test a recompiled version of your library—until you update the GAC. This holds true as long as you preserve the assembly's version and identity.

GAC and Versioning

Changing an assembly's `AssemblyVersion` gives it a brand-new identity. To illustrate, let's say you write a *utils* assembly, version it "1.0.0.0", strongly name it, and then install it in the GAC. Then suppose later you add some new features, change the version to "1.0.0.1", recompile it, and reinstall it into the GAC. Instead of overwriting the original assembly, the GAC now holds *both* versions. This means:

- You can choose which version to reference when compiling another application that uses *utils*.

- Any application previously compiled to reference *utils* 1.0.0.0 will *continue to do so*.

This is called *side-by-side* execution. Side-by-side execution prevents the "DLL hell" that can otherwise occur when a shared assembly is unilaterally updated: applications designed for the older version might unexpectedly break.

A complication arises, though, when you want to apply bug fixes or minor updates to existing assemblies. You have two options:

- Reinstall the fixed assembly to the GAC with the same version number.
- Compile the fixed assembly with a new version number and install that to the GAC.

The difficulty with the first option is that there's no way to apply the update *selectively* to certain applications. It's all or nothing. The difficulty with the second option is that applications will not normally use the newer assembly version without being recompiled. There is a workaround—you can create a *publisher policy* allowing assembly version redirection—at the cost of increasing deployment complexity.

Side-by-side execution is good for mitigating some of the problems of shared assemblies. If you avoid the GAC altogether—instead allowing each application to maintain its own private copy of *utils*—you eliminate *all* of the problems of shared assemblies!

Resources and Satellite Assemblies

An application typically contains not only executable code, but also content such as text, images, or XML files. Such content can be represented in an assembly through a *resource*. There are two overlapping use cases for resources:

- Incorporating data that cannot go into source code, such as images
- Storing data that might need translation in a multilingual application

An assembly resource is ultimately a byte stream with a name. You can think of an assembly as containing a dictionary of byte arrays keyed by string. This can be seen in *ildasm* if we disassemble an assembly that contains a resource called *banner.jpg* and a resource called *data.xml*:

```
.mresource public banner.jpg
{
  // Offset: 0x00000F58 Length: 0x000004F6
}
.mresource public data.xml
{
  // Offset: 0x00001458 Length: 0x0000027E
}
```

In this case, *banner.jpg* and *data.xml* were included directly in the assembly—each as its own embedded resource. This is the simplest way to work.

The Framework also lets you add content through intermediate *.resources* containers. There are designed for holding content that may require translation into different languages. Localized *.resources* can be packaged as individual satellite assemblies that are automatically picked up at runtime, based on the user's operating system language.

Figure 18-4 illustrates an assembly that contains two directly embedded resources, plus a *.resources* container called *welcome.resources*, for which we've created two localized satellites.

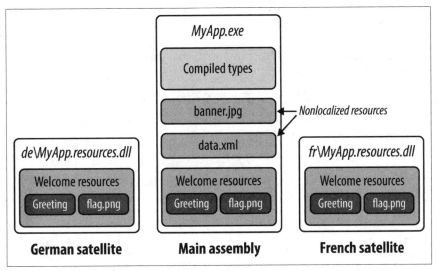

Figure 18-4. Resources

Directly Embedding Resources

 Embedding resources into assemblies is not supported in Window Store apps. Instead, add any extra files to your deployment package, and access them by reading from your application StorageFolder (Package.Current.InstalledLocation).

To directly embed a resource at the command line, use the /resource switch when compiling:

```
csc /resource:banner.jpg /resource:data.xml MyApp.cs
```

You can optionally specify that the resource be given a different name in the assembly as follows:

```
csc /resource:<file-name>,<resource-name>
```

To directly embed a resource using Visual Studio:

- Add the file to your project.
- Set its build action to "Embedded Resource."

Visual Studio always prefixes resource names with the project's default namespace, plus the names of any subfolders in which the file is contained. So, if your project's default namespace was `Westwind.Reports`, and your file was called *banner.jpg* in the folder *pictures*, the resource name would be *Westwind.Reports.pictures.banner.jpg*.

Resource names are case-sensitive. This makes project sub-folder names in Visual Studio that contain resources effectively case-sensitive.

To retrieve a resource, you call `GetManifestResourceStream` on the assembly containing the resource. This returns a stream, which you can then read as any other:

```
Assembly a = Assembly.GetEntryAssembly();

using (Stream s = a.GetManifestResourceStream ("TestProject.data.xml"))
using (XmlReader r = XmlReader.Create (s))
  ...

System.Drawing.Image image;
using (Stream s = a.GetManifestResourceStream ("TestProject.banner.jpg"))
  image = System.Drawing.Image.FromStream (s);
```

The stream returned is seekable, so you can also do this:

```
byte[] data;
using (Stream s = a.GetManifestResourceStream ("TestProject.banner.jpg"))
  data = new BinaryReader (s).ReadBytes ((int) s.Length);
```

If you've used Visual Studio to embed the resource, you must remember to include the namespace-based prefix. To help avoid error, you can specify the prefix in a separate argument, using a *type*. The type's namespace is used as the prefix:

```
using (Stream s = a.GetManifestResourceStream (typeof (X), "XmlData.xml"))
```

X can be any type with the desired namespace of your resource (typically, a type in the same project folder).

Setting a project item's build action in Visual Studio to "Resource" within a WPF application is *not* the same as setting its build action to "Embedded Resource". The former actually adds the item to a *.resources* file called *<Assembly-Name>.g.resources*, whose content you access through WPF's `Application` class, using a URI as a key.

To add to the confusion, WPF further overloads the term "resource." *Static resources* and *dynamic resources* are both unrelated to assembly resources!

`GetManifestResourceNames` returns the names of all resources in the assembly.

.resources Files

The Framework also lets you add *.resources* files are containers for potentially localizable content. A *.resources* file ends up as an embedded resource within an assembly—just like any other kind of file. The difference is that you must:

- Package your content into the *.resources* file to begin with

- Access its content through a `ResourceManager` or *pack URI*, rather than a `Get ManifestResourceStream`

.resources files are structured in binary and so are not human-editable; therefore, you must rely on tools provided by the Framework and Visual Studio to work with them. The standard approach with strings or simple data types is to use the *.resx* format, which can be converted to a *.resources* file either by Visual Studio or the `resgen` tool. The *.resx* format is also suitable for images intended for a Windows Forms or ASP.NET application.

In a WPF application, you must use Visual Studio's "Resource" build action for images or similar content needing to be referenced by URI. This applies whether localization is needed or not.

We describe how to do each of these in the following sections.

.resx Files

The Framework also lets you add A *.resx* file is a design-time format for producing *.resources* files. A *.resx* file uses XML and is structured with name/value pairs as follows:

```
<root>
  <data name="Greeting">
    <value>hello</value>
  </data>
  <data name="DefaultFontSize" type="System.Int32, mscorlib">
    <value>10</value>
  </data>
</root>
```

To create a *.resx* file in Visual Studio, add a project item of type "Resources File". The rest of the work is done automatically:

- The correct header is created.

- A designer is provided for adding strings, images, files, and other kinds of data.

- The *.resx* file is automatically converted to the *.resources* format and embedded into the assembly upon compilation.

- A class is written to help you access the data later on.

 The resource designer adds images as typed `Image` objects (*System.Drawing.dll*), rather than as byte arrays, making them unsuitable for WPF applications.

Creating a .resx file at the command line

If you're working at the command line, you must start with a *.resx* file that has a valid header. The easiest way to accomplish this is to create a simple *.resx* file programmatically. The System.Resources.ResXResourceWriter class (which, peculiarly, resides in the *System.Windows.Forms.dll* assembly) does exactly this job:

```
using (ResXResourceWriter w = new ResXResourceWriter ("welcome.resx")) { }
```

From here, you can either continue to use the ResXResourceWriter to add resources (by calling AddResource) or manually edit the *.resx* file that it wrote.

The easiest way to deal with images is to treat the files as binary data and convert them to an image upon retrieval. This is also more versatile than encoding them as a typed Image object. You can include binary data within a *.resx* file in base 64 format as follows:

```
<data name="flag.png" type="System.Byte[], mscorlib">
  <value>Qk32BAAAAAAAAHYAAAAoAAAAMAMDAwACAgIAAAAD/AA....</value>
</data>
```

or as a reference to another file that is then read by resgen:

```
<data name="flag.png"
  type="System.Resources.ResXFileRef, System.Windows.Forms">
  <value>flag.png;System.Byte[], mscorlib</value>
</data>
```

When you're done, you must convert the *.resx* file by calling resgen. The following converts *welcome.resx* into *welcome.resources*:

```
resgen welcome.resx
```

The final step is to include the *.resources* file when compiling, as follows:

```
csc /resources:welcome.resources MyApp.cs
```

Reading .resources files

 If you create a *.resx* file in Visual Studio, a class of the same name is generated automatically with properties to retrieve each of its items.

The ResourceManager class reads *.resources* files embedded within an assembly:

```
ResourceManager r = new ResourceManager ("welcome",
                                Assembly.GetExecutingAssembly());
```

(The first argument must be namespace-prefixed if the resource was compiled in Visual Studio.)

You can then access what's inside by calling GetString or GetObject with a cast:

```
string greeting = r.GetString ("Greeting");
int fontSize = (int) r.GetObject ("DefaultFontSize");
```

```
Image image = (Image) r.GetObject ("flag.png");     // (Visual Studio)
byte[] imgData = (byte[]) r.GetObject ("flag.png");  // (Command line)
```

To enumerate the contents of a *.resources* file:

```
ResourceManager r = new ResourceManager (...);
ResourceSet set = r.GetResourceSet (CultureInfo.CurrentUICulture,
                                         true, true);
foreach (System.Collections.DictionaryEntry entry in set)
  Console.WriteLine (entry.Key);
```

Creating a pack URI resource in Visual Studio

In a WPF application, XAML files need to be able to access resources by URI. For instance:

```
<Button>
  <Image Height="50" Source="flag.png"/>
</Button>
```

Or, if the resource is in another assembly:

```
<Button>
  <Image Height="50" Source="UtilsAssembly;Component/flag.png"/>
</Button>
```

(Component is a literal keyword.)

To create resources that can be loaded in this manner, you cannot use *.resx* files. Instead, you must add the files to your project and set their build action to "Resource" (not "Embedded Resource"). Visual Studio then compiles them into a *.resources* file called *<AssemblyName>.g.resources*—also the home of compiled XAML (*.baml*) files.

To load a URI-keyed resource programmatically, call Application.GetResource-Stream:

```
Uri u = new Uri ("flag.png", UriKind.Relative);
using (Stream s = Application.GetResourceStream (u).Stream)
```

Notice we used a relative URI. You can also use an absolute URI in exactly the following format (the three commas are not a typo):

```
Uri u = new Uri ("pack://application:,,,/flag.png");
```

If you'd rather specify an Assembly object, you can retrieve content instead with a ResourceManager:

```
Assembly a = Assembly.GetExecutingAssembly();
ResourceManager r = new ResourceManager (a.GetName().Name + ".g", a);
using (Stream s = r.GetStream ("flag.png"))
  ...
```

A ResourceManager also lets you enumerate the content of a *.g.resources* container within a given assembly.

Satellite Assemblies

Data embedded in *.resources* is localizable.

Resource localization is relevant when your application runs on a version of Windows built to display everything in a different language. For consistency, your application should use that same language, too.

A typical setup is as follows:

- The main assembly contains *.resources* for the default or *fallback* language.

- Separate *satellite assemblies* contain localized *.resources* translated to different languages.

When your application runs, the Framework examines the language of the current operating system (from `CultureInfo.CurrentUICulture`). Whenever you request a resource using `ResourceManager`, the Framework looks for a localized satellite assembly. If one's available—and it contains the resource key you requested—it's used in place of the main assembly's version.

This means you can enhance language support simply by adding new satellites—without changing the main assembly.

 A satellite assembly cannot contain executable code, only resources.

Satellite assemblies are deployed in subdirectories of the assembly's folder as follows:

```
programBaseFolder\MyProgram.exe
               \MyLibrary.exe
               \XX\MyProgram.resources.dll
               \XX\MyLibrary.resources.dll
```

XX refers to the two-letter language code (such as "de" for German) or a language and region code (such as "en-GB" for English in Great Britain). This naming system allows the CLR to find and load the correct satellite assembly automatically.

Building satellite assemblies

Recall our previous *.resx* example, which included the following:

```
<root>
  ...
  <data name="Greeting"
    <value>hello</value>
  </data>
</root>
```

We then retrieved the greeting at runtime as follows:

```
ResourceManager r = new ResourceManager ("welcome",
                              Assembly.GetExecutingAssembly());
Console.Write (r.GetString ("Greeting"));
```

Suppose we want this to instead write "Hallo" if running on the German version of Windows. The first step is to add another *.resx* file named *welcome.de.resx* that substitutes *hello* for *hallo*:

```
<root>
  <data name="Greeting">
    <value>hallo<value>
  </data>
</root>
```

In Visual Studio, this is all you need to do—when you rebuild, a satellite assembly called *MyApp.resources.dll* is automatically created in a subdirectory called *de*.

If you're using the command line, you call resgen to turn the *.resx* file into a *.resources* file:

```
resgen MyApp.de.resx
```

and then call al to build the satellite assembly:

```
al /culture:de /out:MyApp.resources.dll /embed:MyApp.de.resources /t:lib
```

You can specify /template:MyApp.exe to import the main assembly's strong name.

Testing satellite assemblies

To simulate running on an operating system with a different language, you must change the CurrentUICulture using the Thread class:

```
System.Threading.Thread.CurrentThread.CurrentUICulture
  = new System.Globalization.CultureInfo ("de");
```

CultureInfo.CurrentUICulture is a read-only version of the same property.

> A useful testing strategy is to ℓo¢aℓïzǝ into words that can still be read as English but do not use the standard Roman Unicode characters.

Visual Studio designer support

The designers in Visual Studio provide extended support for localizing components and visual elements. The WPF designer has its own workflow for localization; other Component-based designers use a design-time-only property to make it appear that a component or Windows Forms control has a Language property. To customize for another language, simply change the Language property and then start modifying the component. All properties of controls that are attributed as Localizable will be persisted to a *.resx* file for that language. You can switch between languages at any time just by changing the Language property.

Cultures and Subcultures

Cultures are split into cultures and subcultures. A culture represents a particular language; a subculture represents a regional variation of that language. The Framework follows the RFC1766 standard, which represents cultures and subcultures with two-letter codes. Here are the codes for English and German cultures:

```
en
de
```

Here are the codes for the Australian English and Austrian German subcultures:

```
en-AU
de-AT
```

A culture is represented in .NET with the System.Globalization.CultureInfo class. You can examine the current culture of your application as follows:

```
Console.WriteLine (System.Threading.Thread.CurrentThread.CurrentCulture);
Console.WriteLine (System.Threading.Thread.CurrentThread.CurrentUICulture);
```

Running this on a computer localized for Australia illustrates the difference between the two:

```
EN-AU
EN-US
```

CurrentCulture reflects the regional settings of the Windows control panel, whereas CurrentUICulture reflects the language of the operating system.

Regional settings include such things as time zone and the formatting of currency and dates. CurrentCulture determines the default behavior of such functions as DateTime.Parse. Regional settings can be customized to the point where they no longer resemble any particular culture.

CurrentUICulture determines the language in which the computer communicates with the user. Australia doesn't need a separate version of English for this purpose, so it just uses the US one. If I spent a couple of months working in Austria, I would go to the control panel and change my CurrentCulture to Austrian-German. However, since I can't speak German, my CurrentUICulture would remain US English.

ResourceManager, by default, uses the current thread's CurrentUICulture property to determine the correct satellite assembly to load. ResourceManager uses a fallback mechanism when loading resources. If a subculture assembly is defined, that one is used; otherwise, it falls back to the generic culture. If the generic culture is not present, it falls back to the default culture in the main assembly.

Resolving and Loading Assemblies

A typical application comprises a main executable assembly plus a set of referenced library assemblies. For example:

```
AdventureGame.exe
Terrain.dll
UIEngine.dll
```

Assembly resolution refers to the process of locating referenced assemblies. Assembly resolution happens both at compile time and at runtime. The compile-time system is simple: the compiler knows where to find referenced assemblies because it's told where to look. You (or Visual Studio) provide the full path to referenced assemblies that are not in the current directory.

Runtime resolution is more complicated. The compiler writes the strong names of referenced assemblies to the manifest—but not any hints as to where to find them. In the simple case where you put all referenced assemblies in the same folder as the main executable, there's no issue because that's (close to) the first place the CLR looks. The complexities arise:

- When you deploy referenced assemblies in other places
- When you dynamically load assemblies

 Windows Store apps are very limited in what you can do in the way of customizing assembly loading and resolution. In particular, loading an assembly from an arbitrary file location isn't supported, and there's no `AssemblyResolve` event.

Assembly and Type Resolution Rules

All types are scoped to an assembly. An assembly is like an address for a type. To give an analogy, we can refer to a person as "Joe" (type name without namespace), or "Joe Bloggs" (full type name), or "Joe Bloggs of 100 Barker Ave, WA" (assembly-qualified type name).

During compilation, we don't need to go further than a full type name for uniqueness, because you can't reference two assemblies that define the same full type name (at least not without special tricks). At runtime, though, it's possible to have many identically named types in memory. This happens within the Visual Studio designer, for instance, whenever you *rebuild* the components you're designing. The only way to distinguish such types is by their assembly; therefore, an assembly forms an essential part of a type's runtime identity. An assembly is also a type's handle to its code and metadata.

The CLR loads assemblies at the point in execution when they're first needed. This happens when you refer to one of the assembly's types. For example, suppose that

AdventureGame.exe instantiates a type called `TerrainModel.Map`. Assuming no additional configuration files, the CLR answers the following questions:

- What's the fully qualified name of the assembly that contained `TerrainModel.Map` when *AdventureGame.exe* was compiled?

- Have I already loaded into memory an assembly with this fully qualified name in the same (resolution) context?

If the answer to the second question is yes, it uses the existing copy in memory; otherwise, it goes looking for the assembly. The CLR first checks the GAC, then the *probing* paths (generally the application base directory), and as a final resort, fires the `AppDomain.AssemblyResolve` event. If none returns a match, the CLR throws an exception.

AssemblyResolve

The `AssemblyResolve` event allows you to intervene and manually load an assembly that the CLR can't find. If you handle this event, you can scatter referenced assemblies in a variety of locations and still have them load.

Within the `AssemblyResolve` event handler, you locate the assembly and load it by calling one of three static methods in the `Assembly` class: `Load`, `LoadFrom`, or `Load File`. These methods return a reference to the newly loaded assembly, which you then return to the caller:

```
static void Main()
{
  AppDomain.CurrentDomain.AssemblyResolve += FindAssembly;
  ...
}

static Assembly FindAssembly (object sender, ResolveEventArgs args)
{
  string fullyQualifiedName = args.Name;
  Assembly a = Assembly.LoadFrom (...);
  return a;
}
```

The `ResolveEventArgs` event is unusual in that it has a return type. If there are multiple handlers, the first one to return a nonnull `Assembly` wins.

Loading Assemblies

The `Load` methods in `Assembly` are useful both inside and outside an `AssemblyResolve` handler. Outside the event handler, they can load and execute assemblies not referenced at compilation. An example of when you might do this is to execute a plug-in.

Think carefully before calling Load, LoadFrom, or LoadFile: these methods permanently load an assembly into the current application domain—even if you do nothing with the resultant Assembly object. Loading an assembly has side effects: it locks the assembly files as well as affecting subsequent type resolution.

The only way to unload an assembly is to unload the whole application domain. (There's also a technique to avoid locking assemblies called *shadow copying* for assemblies in the probing path—go to *http://albahari.com/shadowcopy* for the MSDN article.)

If you just want to examine an assembly without executing any of its code, you can instead use the reflection-only context (see Chapter 19).

To load an assembly from a fully qualified name (without a location), call Assembly.Load. This instructs the CLR to find the assembly using its normal automatic resolution system. The CLR itself uses Load to find referenced assemblies.

To load an assembly from a filename, call LoadFrom or LoadFile.

To load an assembly from a URI, call LoadFrom.

To load an assembly from a byte array, call Load.

You can see what assemblies are currently loaded in memory by calling AppDomain's GetAssemblies method:

```
foreach (Assembly a in
AppDomain.CurrentDomain.GetAssemblies())
{
  Console.WriteLine (a.Location);        // File path
  Console.WriteLine (a.CodeBase);        // URI
  Console.WriteLine (a.GetName().Name);  // Simple name
}
```

Loading from a filename

LoadFrom and LoadFile can both load an assembly from a filename. They differ in two ways. First, if an assembly with the same identity has already been loaded into memory from another location, LoadFrom gives you the previous copy:

```
Assembly a1 = Assembly.LoadFrom (@"c:\temp1\lib.dll");
Assembly a2 = Assembly.LoadFrom (@"c:\temp2\lib.dll");
Console.WriteLine (a1 == a2);              // true
```

LoadFile gives you a fresh copy:

```
Assembly a1 = Assembly.LoadFile (@"c:\temp1\lib.dll");
Assembly a2 = Assembly.LoadFile (@"c:\temp2\lib.dll");
Console.WriteLine (a1 == a2);              // false
```

If you load twice from an *identical* location, however, both methods give you the previously cached copy. (In contrast, loading an assembly twice from an identical byte array gives you two distinct Assembly objects.)

 Types from two identical assemblies in memory are incompatible. This is the primary reason to avoid loading duplicate assemblies and hence a reason to favor LoadFrom over Load File.

The second difference between LoadFrom and LoadFile is that LoadFrom hints the CLR as to the location of onward references, whereas LoadFile does not. To illustrate, suppose your application in *\folder1* loads an assembly in *\folder2* called *TestLib.dll*, which references *\folder2\Another.dll*:

```
\folder1\MyApplication.exe

\folder2\TestLib.dll
\folder2\Another.dll
```

If you load *TestLib* with LoadFrom, the CLR will find and load *Another.dll*.

If you load *TestLib* with LoadFile, the CLR will be unable to find *Another.dll* and will throw an exception—unless you also handle the AssemblyResolve event.

In following sections, we demonstrate these methods in the context of some practical applications.

Statically referenced types and LoadFrom/LoadFile

When you refer to a type directly in your code, you're *statically referencing* that type. The compiler bakes a reference to that type into the assembly being compiled, as well as the name of the assembly containing the type in question (but not any information on where to find it at runtime).

For instance, suppose there's a type called Foo in an assembly called *foo.dll* and your application *bar.exe* includes the following code:

```
var foo = new Foo();
```

The *bar.exe* application statically references the Foo type in the *foo* assembly. We could instead dynamically load *foo* as follows:

```
Type t = Assembly.LoadFrom (@"d:\temp\foo.dll").GetType ("Foo");
var foo = Activator.CreateInstance (t);
```

If you mix the two approaches, you will usually end up with two copies of the assembly in memory, because the CLR considers each to be a different "resolution context."

We said previously that when resolving static references, the CLR looks first in the GAC, then in the *probing path* (normally the application base directory), and then fires the AssemblyResolve event as a last resort. Before any of this, though, it checks whether the assembly has already been loaded. However, it considers *only* assemblies that have either:

- Been loaded from a path that it would otherwise have found on its own (probing path)
- Been loaded in response to the `AssemblyResolve` event

Hence, if you've already loaded it from an unprobed path via `LoadFrom` or `LoadFile`, you'll end up with two copies of the assembly in memory (with incompatible types). To avoid this, you must be careful, when calling `LoadFrom`/`LoadFile`, to first check whether the assembly exists in the application base directory (unless you *want* to load multiple versions of an assembly).

Loading in response to the `AssemblyResolve` event is immune to this problem (whether you use `LoadFrom`, `LoadFile`—or load from a byte array as we'll see later), because the event fires only for assemblies outside the probing path.

> Whether you use `LoadFrom` or `LoadFile`, the CLR always looks first for the requested assembly in the GAC. You can bypass the GAC with `ReflectionOnlyLoadFrom` (which loads the assembly into a reflection-only context). Even loading from a byte array doesn't bypass the GAC, although it gets around the problem of locking assembly files:
>
> ```
> byte[] image = File.ReadAllBytes (assemblyPath);
> Assembly a = Assembly.Load (image);
> ```
>
> If you do this, you must handle the AppDomain's `AssemblyResolve` event in order to resolve any assemblies that the loaded assembly itself references and keep track of all loaded assemblies (see "Packing a Single-File Executable" on page 785).

Location versus CodeBase

An `Assembly`'s `Location` property usually returns its physical location in the file system (if it has one). The `CodeBase` property mirrors this in URI form except in special cases, such as if loaded from the Internet, where `CodeBase` is the Internet URI and `Location` is the temporary path to which it was downloaded. Another special case is with *shadow-copied* assemblies, where `Location` is blank and `CodeBase` is its unshadowed location. ASP.NET and the popular NUnit testing framework employ shadow copying to allow assemblies to be updated while the website or unit tests are running (for the MSDN reference, go to *http://albahari.com/shadowcopy*). LINQPad does something similar when you reference custom assemblies.

Hence relying solely on `Location` is dangerous if you're looking for an assembly's location on disk. The better approach is to check both properties. The following method returns an assembly's containing folder (or null if it cannot be determined):

```
public static string GetAssemblyFolder (Assembly a)
{
  try
```

```
    {
      if (!string.IsNullOrEmpty (a.Location))
        return Path.GetDirectoryName (a.Location);

      if (string.IsNullOrEmpty (a.CodeBase)) return null;

      var uri = new Uri (a.CodeBase);
      if (!uri.IsFile) return null;

      return Path.GetDirectoryName (uri.LocalPath);
    }
    catch (NotSupportedException)
    {
      return null;  // Dynamic assembly generated with Reflection.Emit
    }
  }
```

Note that because CodeBase returns a URI, we use the Uri class to obtain its local file path.

Deploying Assemblies Outside the Base Folder

Sometimes you might choose to deploy assemblies to locations other than the application base directory, for instance:

```
..\MyProgram\Main.exe
..\MyProgram\Libs\V1.23\GameLogic.dll
..\MyProgram\Libs\V1.23\3DEngine.dll
..\MyProgram\Terrain\Map.dll
..\Common\TimingController.dll
```

To make this work, you must assist the CLR in finding the assemblies outside the base folder. The easiest solution is to handle the AssemblyResolve event.

In the following example, we assume all additional assemblies are located in *c: \ExtraAssemblies*:

```
using System;
using System.IO;
using System.Reflection;

class Loader
{
  static void Main()
  {
    AppDomain.CurrentDomain.AssemblyResolve += FindAssembly;

    // We must switch to another class before attempting to use
    // any of the types in c:\ExtraAssemblies:
    Program.Go();
  }

  static Assembly FindAssembly (object sender, ResolveEventArgs args)
  {
    string simpleName = new AssemblyName (args.Name).Name;
```

```
    string path = @"c:\ExtraAssemblies\" + simpleName + ".dll";

    if (!File.Exists (path)) return null;      // Sanity check
    return Assembly.LoadFrom (path);           // Load it up!
  }
}

class Program
{
  internal static void Go()
  {
    // Now we can reference types defined in c:\ExtraAssemblies
  }
}
```

 It's vitally important in this example not to reference types in
c:\ExtraAssemblies directly from the Loader class (e.g., as
fields), because the CLR would then attempt to resolve the
type before hitting Main().

In this example, we could use either LoadFrom or LoadFile. In either case, the CLR
verifies that the assembly that we hand it has the exact identity it requested. This
maintains the integrity of strongly named references.

In Chapter 24, we describe another approach that can be used when creating new
application domains. This involves setting the application domain's PrivateBinPath
to include the directories containing the additional assemblies—extending the standard assembly probing locations. A limitation of this is that the additional directories must all be *below* the application base directory.

Packing a Single-File Executable

Suppose you've written an application comprising 10 assemblies: 1 main executable
file, plus 9 DLLs. Although such granularity can be great for design and debugging,
it's also good to be able to pack the whole thing into a single "click and run" executable—without demanding the user perform some setup or file extraction ritual.
You can accomplish this by including the compiled assembly DLLs in the main executable project as embedded resources, and then writing an AssemblyResolve event
handler to load their binary images on demand. Here's how it's done:

```
using System;
using System.IO;
using System.Reflection;
using System.Collections.Generic;

public class Loader
{
  static Dictionary <string, Assembly> _libs
    = new Dictionary <string, Assembly>();

  static void Main()
  {
```

```
      AppDomain.CurrentDomain.AssemblyResolve += FindAssembly;
      Program.Go();
    }

    static Assembly FindAssembly (object sender, ResolveEventArgs args)
    {
      string shortName = new AssemblyName (args.Name).Name;
      if (_libs.ContainsKey (shortName)) return _libs [shortName];

      using (Stream s = Assembly.GetExecutingAssembly().
             GetManifestResourceStream ("Libs." + shortName + ".dll"))
      {
        byte[] data = new BinaryReader (s).ReadBytes ((int) s.Length);
        Assembly a = Assembly.Load (data);
        _libs [shortName] = a;
        return a;
      }
    }
  }

  public class Program
  {
    public static void Go()
    {
      // Run main program...
    }
  }
```

Because the Loader class is defined in the main executable, the call to Assem
bly.GetExecutingAssembly will always return the main executable assembly, where
we've included the compiled DLLs as embedded resources. In this example, we prefix the name of each embedded resource assembly with "Libs.". If the Visual Studio IDE was used, you would change "Libs." to the project's default namespace (go
to Project Properties→Application). You would also need to ensure that the "Build
Action" IDE property on each of the DLL files included in the main project was set
to "Embedded Resource".

The reason for caching requested assemblies in a dictionary is to ensure that if the
CLR requests the same assembly again, we return exactly the same object. Otherwise, an assembly's types will be incompatible with those loaded previously (despite
their binary images being identical).

A variation of this would be to compress the referenced assemblies at compilation,
then decompress them in FindAssembly using a DeflateStream.

Selective Patching

Suppose in this example that we want the executable to be able to autonomously
update itself—perhaps from a network server or website. Directly patching the executable not only would be awkward and dangerous, but also the required file I/O
permissions may not be forthcoming (if installed in *Program Files*, for instance). An
excellent workaround is to download any updated libraries to isolated storage (each

---

as a separate DLL) and then modify the FindAssembly method such that it first checks for the presence of a library in its isolated storage area before loading it from a resource in the executable. This leaves the original executable untouched and avoids leaving any unpleasant residue on the user's computer. Security is not compromised if your assemblies are strongly named (assuming they were referenced in compilation), and if something goes wrong, the application can always revert to its original state—simply by deleting all files in its isolated storage.

Working with Unreferenced Assemblies

Sometimes it's useful to explicitly load .NET assemblies that may not have been referenced in compilation.

If the assembly in question is an executable and you simply want to run it, calling ExecuteAssembly on the current application domain does the job. ExecuteAssembly loads the executable using LoadFrom semantics and then calls its entry method with optional command-line arguments. For instance:

```
string dir = AppDomain.CurrentDomain.BaseDirectory;
AppDomain.CurrentDomain.ExecuteAssembly (Path.Combine (dir, "test.exe"));
```

ExecuteAssembly works synchronously, meaning the calling method is blocked until the called assembly exits. To work asynchronously, you must call ExecuteAssembly on another thread or task (see Chapter 14).

In most cases, though, the assembly you'll want to load is a library. The approach then is to call LoadFrom, and then use reflection to work with the assembly's types. For example:

```
string ourDir = AppDomain.CurrentDomain.BaseDirectory;
string plugInDir = Path.Combine (ourDir, "plugins");
Assembly a = Assembly.LoadFrom (Path.Combine (plugInDir, "widget.dll"));
Type t = a.GetType ("Namespace.TypeName");
object widget = Activator.CreateInstance (t);      // (See Chapter 19)
...
```

We used LoadFrom rather than LoadFile to ensure that any private assemblies *widget.dll* referenced in the same folder were also loaded. We then retrieved a type from the assembly by name and instantiated it.

The next step could be to use reflection to dynamically call methods and properties on widget; we describe how to do this in the following chapter. An easier—and faster—approach is to cast the object to a type that both assemblies understand. This is often an interface defined in a common assembly:

```
public interface IPluggable
{
  void ShowAboutBox();
  ...
}
```

This allows us to do this:

```
Type t = a.GetType ("Namespace.TypeName");
IPluggable widget = (IPluggable) Activator.CreateInstance (t);
widget.ShowAboutBox();
```

You can use a similar system for dynamically publishing services in a WCF or Remoting Server. The following assumes the libraries we want to expose end in "server":

```
using System.IO;
using System.Reflection;
...
string dir = AppDomain.CurrentDomain.BaseDirectory;
foreach (string assFile in Directory.GetFiles (dir, "*Server.dll"))
{
  Assembly a = Assembly.LoadFrom (assFile);
  foreach (Type t in a.GetTypes())
    if (typeof (MyBaseServerType).IsAssignableFrom (t))
    {
      // Expose type t
    }
}
```

This does make it very easy, though, for someone to add rogue assemblies, maybe even accidentally! Assuming no compile-time references, the CLR has nothing against which to check an assembly's identity. If everything that you load is signed with a known public key, the solution is to check that key explicitly. In the following example, we assume that all libraries are signed with the same key pair as the executing assembly:

```
byte[] ourPK = Assembly.GetExecutingAssembly().GetName().GetPublicKey();

foreach (string assFile in Directory.GetFiles (dir, "*Server.dll"))
{
  byte[] targetPK = AssemblyName.GetAssemblyName (assFile).GetPublicKey();
  if (Enumerable.SequenceEqual (ourPK, targetPK))
  {
    Assembly a = Assembly.LoadFrom (assFile);
    ...
```

Notice how AssemblyName allows you to check the public key *before* loading the assembly. To compare the byte arrays, we used LINQ's SequenceEqual method (System.Linq).

19

Reflection and Metadata

As we saw in the previous chapter, a C# program compiles into an assembly that includes metadata, compiled code, and resources. Inspecting the metadata and compiled code at runtime is called *reflection*.

The compiled code in an assembly contains almost all of the content of the original source code. Some information is lost, such as local variable names, comments, and preprocessor directives. However, reflection can access pretty much everything else, even making it possible to write a decompiler.

Many of the services available in .NET and exposed via C# (such as dynamic binding, serialization, data binding, and Remoting) depend on the presence of metadata. Your own programs can also take advantage of this metadata and even extend it with new information using custom attributes. The `System.Reflection` namespace houses the reflection API. It is also possible at runtime to dynamically create new metadata and executable instructions in IL (Intermediate Language) via the classes in the `System.Reflection.Emit` namespace.

The examples in this chapter assume that you import the `System` and `System.Reflection`, as well as `System.Reflection.Emit`, namespaces.

 When we use the term "dynamically" in this chapter, we mean using reflection to perform some task whose type safety is enforced only at runtime. This is similar in principle to *dynamic binding* via C#'s `dynamic` keyword, although the mechanism and functionality is different.

To compare the two, dynamic binding is much easier to use and leverages the DLR for dynamic language interoperability. Reflection is relatively clumsy to use, is concerned with the CLR only—but is more flexible in terms of what you can do with the CLR. For instance, reflection lets you obtain lists of types and members, instantiate an object whose name comes from a string, and build assemblies on the fly.

Reflecting and Activating Types

In this section, we examine how to obtain a Type, inspect its metadata, and use it to dynamically instantiate an object.

Obtaining a Type

An instance of System.Type represents the metadata for a type. Since Type is widely used, it lives in the System namespace rather than the System.Reflection namespace.

You can get an instance of a System.Type by calling GetType on any object or with C#'s typeof operator:

```
Type t1 = DateTime.Now.GetType();    // Type obtained at runtime
Type t2 = typeof (DateTime);         // Type obtained at compile time
```

You can use typeof to obtain array types and generic types as follows:

```
Type t3 = typeof (DateTime[]);       // 1-d Array type
Type t4 = typeof (DateTime[,]);      // 2-d Array type
Type t5 = typeof (Dictionary<int,int>); // Closed generic type
Type t6 = typeof (Dictionary<,>);    // Unbound generic type
```

You can also retrieve a Type by name. If you have a reference to its Assembly, call Assembly.GetType (we describe this further in the section "Reflecting Assemblies" on page 810 later in this chapter):

```
Type t = Assembly.GetExecutingAssembly().GetType ("Demos.TestProgram");
```

If you don't have an Assembly object, you can obtain a type through its *assembly qualified name* (the type's full name followed by the assembly's fully qualified name). The assembly implicitly loads as if you called Assembly.Load(string):

```
Type t = Type.GetType ("System.Int32, mscorlib, Version=2.0.0.0, " +
                       "Culture=neutral, PublicKeyToken=b77a5c561934e089");
```

Once you have a System.Type object, you can use its properties to access the type's name, assembly, base type, visibility, and so on. For example:

```
Type stringType = typeof (string);
string name     = stringType.Name;       // String
Type baseType   = stringType.BaseType;   // typeof(Object)
Assembly assem  = stringType.Assembly;   // mscorlib.dll
bool isPublic   = stringType.IsPublic;   // true
```

A System.Type instance is a window into the entire metadata for the type—and the assembly in which it's defined.

 System.Type is abstract, so the typeof operator must actually give you a subclass of Type. The subclass that the CLR uses is internal to *mscorlib* and is called RuntimeType.

TypeInfo and Windows Store applications

The Windows Store profile hides most of Type's members and exposes them on a class called TypeInfo instead, which you obtain by calling GetTypeInfo. So to get our previous example to run in a Windows Store application, you do this:

```
Type stringType = typeof(string);
string name = stringType.Name;
Type baseType = stringType.GetTypeInfo().BaseType;
Assembly assem = stringType.GetTypeInfo().Assembly;
bool isPublic = stringType.GetTypeInfo().IsPublic;
```

Many of the code listings in this chapter will require this modification in order to work in Windows Store applications. So if an example won't compile for lack of a member, add .GetTypeInfo() to the Type expression.

TypeInfo also exists in the full .NET Framework, so code that works in Windows Store apps also works in desktop apps that target Framework 4.5 or later. TypeInfo also includes additional properties and methods for reflecting over members.

Windows Store applications are restricted in what they can do with regarding reflection. Specifically, they cannot access nonpublic members of types, and they cannot use Reflection.Emit.

Obtaining array types

As we just saw, typeof and GetType work with array types. You can also obtain an array type by calling MakeArrayType on the *element* type:

```
Type simpleArrayType = typeof (int).MakeArrayType();
Console.WriteLine (simpleArrayType == typeof (int[]));      // True
```

MakeArrayType can be passed an integer argument to make multidimensional rectangular arrays:

```
Type cubeType = typeof (int).MakeArrayType (3);      // cube shaped
Console.WriteLine (cubeType == typeof (int[,,]));    // True
```

GetElementType does the reverse: it retrieves an array type's element type:

```
Type e = typeof (int[]).GetElementType();      // e == typeof (int)
```

GetArrayRank returns the number of dimensions of a rectangular array:

```
int rank = typeof (int[,,]).GetArrayRank();   // 3
```

Obtaining nested types

To retrieve nested types, call GetNestedTypes on the containing type. For example:

```
foreach (Type t in typeof (System.Environment).GetNestedTypes())
  Console.WriteLine (t.FullName);

OUTPUT: System.Environment+SpecialFolder
```

Or, in Window Store:

```
foreach (TypeInfo t in typeof (System.Environment).GetTypeInfo()
                                     .DeclaredNestedTypes)
    Debug.WriteLine (t.FullName);
```

The one caveat with nested types is that the CLR treats a nested type as having special "nested" accessibility levels. For example:

```
Type t = typeof (System.Environment.SpecialFolder);
Console.WriteLine (t.IsPublic);            // False
Console.WriteLine (t.IsNestedPublic);      // True
```

Type Names

A type has Namespace, Name, and FullName properties. In most cases, FullName is a composition of the former two:

```
Type t = typeof (System.Text.StringBuilder);

Console.WriteLine (t.Namespace);    // System.Text
Console.WriteLine (t.Name);         // StringBuilder
Console.WriteLine (t.FullName);     // System.Text.StringBuilder
```

There are two exceptions to this rule: nested types and closed generic types.

Type also has a property called AssemblyQualifiedName, which returns FullName followed by a comma and then the full name of its assembly. This is the same string that you can pass to Type.GetType, and it uniquely identifies a type within the default loading context.

Nested type names

With nested types, the containing type appears only in FullName:

```
Type t = typeof (System.Environment.SpecialFolder);

Console.WriteLine (t.Namespace);    // System
Console.WriteLine (t.Name);         // SpecialFolder
Console.WriteLine (t.FullName);     // System.Environment+SpecialFolder
```

The + symbol differentiates the containing type from a nested namespace.

Generic type names

Generic type names are suffixed with the ' symbol, followed by the number of type parameters. If the generic type is unbound, this rule applies to both Name and Full Name:

```
Type t = typeof (Dictionary<,>); // Unbound
Console.WriteLine (t.Name);      // Dictionary'2
Console.WriteLine (t.FullName);  // System.Collections.Generic.Dictionary'2
```

If the generic type is closed, however, FullName (only) acquires a substantial extra appendage. Each type parameter's full *assembly qualified name* is enumerated:

```
Console.WriteLine (typeof (Dictionary<int,string>).FullName);
```

```
// OUTPUT:
System.Collections.Generic.Dictionary'2[[System.Int32, mscorlib,
Version=2.0.0.0, Culture=neutral, PublicKeyToken=b77a5c561934e089],
[System.String, mscorlib, Version=2.0.0.0, Culture=neutral,
PublicKeyToken=b77a5c561934e089]]
```

This ensures that AssemblyQualifiedName (a combination of the type's full name and assembly name) contains enough information to fully identify both the generic type and its type parameters.

Array and pointer type names

Arrays present with the same suffix that you use in a typeof expression:

```
Console.WriteLine (typeof ( int[]  ).Name);      // Int32[]
Console.WriteLine (typeof ( int[,] ).Name);      // Int32[,]
Console.WriteLine (typeof ( int[,] ).FullName);  // System.Int32[,]
```

Pointer types are similar:

```
Console.WriteLine (typeof (byte*).Name);      // Byte*
```

ref and out parameter type names

A Type describing a ref or out parameter has an & suffix:

```
Type t = typeof (bool).GetMethod ("TryParse").GetParameters()[1]
                                             .ParameterType;
Console.WriteLine (t.Name);    // Boolean&
```

More on this later, in the section "Reflecting and Invoking Members" on page 797.

Base Types and Interfaces

Type exposes a BaseType property:

```
Type base1 = typeof (System.String).BaseType;
Type base2 = typeof (System.IO.FileStream).BaseType;

Console.WriteLine (base1.Name);    // Object
Console.WriteLine (base2.Name);    // Stream
```

The GetInterfaces method returns the interfaces that a type implements:

```
foreach (Type iType in typeof (Guid).GetInterfaces())
  Console.WriteLine (iType.Name);

IFormattable
IComparable
IComparable'1
IEquatable'1
```

Reflection provides two dynamic equivalents to C#'s static is operator:

IsInstanceOfType
  Accepts a type and instance

IsAssignableFrom
  Accepts two types

Here's an example of the first:

```
object obj  = Guid.NewGuid();
Type target = typeof (IFormattable);

bool isTrue   = obj is IFormattable;          // Static C# operator
bool alsoTrue = target.IsInstanceOfType (obj);  // Dynamic equivalent
```

IsAssignableFrom is more versatile:

```
Type target = typeof (IComparable), source = typeof (string);
Console.WriteLine (target.IsAssignableFrom (source));       // True
```

The IsSubclassOf method works on the same principle as IsAssignableFrom but excludes interfaces.

Instantiating Types

There are two ways to dynamically instantiate an object from its type:

- Call the static Activator.CreateInstance method.
- Call Invoke on a ConstructorInfo object obtained from calling GetConstruc tor on a Type (advanced scenarios).

Activator.CreateInstance accepts a Type and optional arguments that get passed to the constructor:

```
int i = (int) Activator.CreateInstance (typeof (int));

DateTime dt = (DateTime) Activator.CreateInstance (typeof (DateTime),
                                                   2000, 1, 1);
```

CreateInstance lets you specify many other options, such as the assembly from which to load the type, the target application domain, and whether to bind to a non-public constructor. A MissingMethodException is thrown if the runtime can't find a suitable constructor.

Calling Invoke on a ConstructorInfo is necessary when your argument values can't disambiguate between overloaded constructors. For example, suppose class X has two constructors: one accepting a parameter of type string, and another accepting a parameter of type StringBuilder. The target is ambiguous should you pass a null argument into Activator.CreateInstance. This is when you need to use a Con structorInfo instead:

```
// Fetch the constructor that accepts a single parameter of type string:
ConstructorInfo ci = typeof (X).GetConstructor (new[] { typeof (string) });

// Construct the object using that overload, passing in null:
object foo = ci.Invoke (new object[] { null });
```

Or, in Windows Store applications:

```
ConstructorInfo ci = typeof (X).GetTypeInfo().DeclaredConstructors
  .FirstOrDefault (c =>
     c.GetParameters().Length == 1 &&
     c.GetParameters()[0].ParameterType == typeof (string));
```

To obtain a nonpublic constructor, you need to specify BindingFlags—see "Accessing Nonpublic Members" on page 806 in the later section "Reflecting and Invoking Members" on page 797.

Dynamic instantiation adds a few microseconds onto the time taken to construct the object. This is quite a lot in relative terms because the CLR is ordinarily very fast in instantiating objects (a simple new on a small class takes in the region of tens of nanoseconds).

To dynamically instantiate arrays based on just element type, first call MakeArray Type. You can also instantiate generic types: we describe this in the following section.

To dynamically instantiate a delegate, call Delegate.CreateDelegate. The following example demonstrates instantiating both an instance delegate and a static delegate:

```
class Program
{
  delegate int IntFunc (int x);

  static int Square (int x) { return x * x; }      // Static method
  int        Cube   (int x) { return x * x * x; }  // Instance method

  static void Main()
  {
    Delegate staticD = Delegate.CreateDelegate
      (typeof (IntFunc), typeof (Program), "Square");

    Delegate instanceD = Delegate.CreateDelegate
      (typeof (IntFunc), new Program(), "Cube");

    Console.WriteLine (staticD.DynamicInvoke (3));    // 9
    Console.WriteLine (instanceD.DynamicInvoke (3));  // 27
  }
}
```

You can invoke the Delegate object that's returned by calling DynamicInvoke, as we did in this example, or by casting to the typed delegate:

```
IntFunc f = (IntFunc) staticD;
Console.WriteLine (f(3));              // 9 (but much faster!)
```

You can pass a MethodInfo into CreateDelegate instead of a method name. We describe MethodInfo shortly, in the section "Reflecting and Invoking Members" on page 797, along with the rationale for casting a dynamically created delegate back to the static delegate type.

Generic Types

A Type can represent a closed or unbound generic type. Just as at compile time, a closed generic type can be instantiated whereas an unbound type cannot:

```
Type closed = typeof (List<int>);
List<int> list = (List<int>) Activator.CreateInstance (closed);  // OK

Type unbound  = typeof (List<>);
object anError = Activator.CreateInstance (unbound);     // Runtime error
```

The MakeGenericType method converts an unbound into a closed generic type. Simply pass in the desired type arguments:

```
Type unbound = typeof (List<>);
Type closed = unbound.MakeGenericType (typeof (int));
```

The GetGenericTypeDefinition method does the opposite:

```
Type unbound2 = closed.GetGenericTypeDefinition();  // unbound == unbound2
```

The IsGenericType property returns true if a Type is generic, and the IsGenericTy peDefinition property returns true if the generic type is unbound. The following tests whether a type is a nullable value type:

```
Type nullable = typeof (bool?);
Console.WriteLine (
  nullable.IsGenericType &&
  nullable.GetGenericTypeDefinition() == typeof (Nullable<>));  // True
```

GetGenericArguments returns the type arguments for closed generic types:

```
Console.WriteLine (closed.GetGenericArguments()[0]);     // System.Int32
Console.WriteLine (nullable.GetGenericArguments()[0]);   // System.Boolean
```

For unbound generic types, GetGenericArguments returns pseudotypes that represent the placeholder types specified in the generic type definition:

```
Console.WriteLine (unbound.GetGenericArguments()[0]);     // T
```

At runtime, all generic types are either *unbound* or *closed*. They're unbound in the (relatively unusual) case of an expression such as typeof(Foo<>); otherwise, they're closed. There's no such thing as an *open* generic type at runtime: all open types are closed by the compiler. The method in the following class always prints False:

```
class Foo<T>
{
  public void Test()
  {
    Console.Write (GetType().IsGenericTypeDefinition);
  }
}
```

Reflecting and Invoking Members

The GetMembers method returns the members of a type. Consider the following class:

```
class Walnut
{
  private bool cracked;
  public void Crack() { cracked = true; }
}
```

We can reflect on its public members as follows:

```
MemberInfo[] members = typeof (Walnut).GetMembers();
foreach (MemberInfo m in members)
  Console.WriteLine (m);
```

This is the result:

```
Void Crack()
System.Type GetType()
System.String ToString()
Boolean Equals(System.Object)
Int32 GetHashCode()
Void .ctor()
```

Reflecting Members with TypeInfo

`TypeInfo` exposes a different (and somewhat simpler) protocol for reflecting over members. Using this API is optional in applications that target Framework 4.5 or later but mandatory in Windows Store apps, since there's no exact equivalent to the `GetMembers` method.

Instead of exposing methods like `GetMembers` that return arrays, `TypeInfo` exposes *properties* that return `IEnumerable<T>`, upon which you typically run LINQ queries. The broadest is `DeclaredMembers`:

```
IEnumerable<MemberInfo> members =
    typeof(Walnut).GetTypeInfo().DeclaredMembers;
```

Unlike with `GetMembers()`, the result excludes inherited members:

```
Void Crack()
Void .ctor()
Boolean cracked
```

There are also properties for returning specific kinds of members (`DeclaredProper ties`, `DeclaredMethods`, `DeclaredEvents`, and so on) and methods for returning a specific member by name (e.g., `GetDeclaredMethod`). The latter cannot be used on overloaded methods (as there's no way to specify parameter types). Instead, you run a LINQ query over `DeclaredMethods`:

```
MethodInfo method = typeof (int).GetTypeInfo().DeclaredMethods
  .FirstOrDefault (m => m.Name == "ToString" &&
                        m.GetParameters().Length == 0);
```

When called with no arguments, `GetMembers` returns all the public members for a type (and its base types). `GetMember` retrieves a specific member by name—although it still returns an array because members can be overloaded:

```
MemberInfo[] m = typeof (Walnut).GetMember ("Crack");
Console.WriteLine (m[0]);                                    // Void Crack()
```

`MemberInfo` also has a property called `MemberType` of type `MemberTypes`. This is a flags enum with these values:

All	Custom	Field	NestedType	TypeInfo
Constructor	Event	Method	Property	

When calling `GetMembers`, you can pass in a `MemberTypes` instance to restrict the kinds of members that it returns. Alternatively, you can restrict the result set by calling `GetMethods`, `GetFields`, `GetProperties`, `GetEvents`, `GetConstructors`, or `Get NestedTypes`. There are also singular versions of each of these to hone in on a specific member.

It pays to be as specific as possible when retrieving a type member, so your code doesn't break if additional members are added later. If retrieving a method by name, specifying all parameter types ensures your code will still work if the method is later overloaded (we provide examples shortly, in the section "Method Parameters" on page 804).

A MemberInfo object has a Name property and two Type properties:

DeclaringType

> Returns the Type that defines the member

ReflectedType

> Returns the Type upon which GetMembers was called

The two differ when called on a member that's defined in a base type: Declaring Type returns the base type whereas ReflectedType returns the subtype. The following example highlights this:

```
class Program
{
  static void Main()
  {
    // MethodInfo is a subclass of MemberInfo; see Figure 19-1.

    MethodInfo test = typeof (Program).GetMethod ("ToString");
    MethodInfo obj  = typeof (object) .GetMethod ("ToString");

    Console.WriteLine (test.DeclaringType);    // System.Object
    Console.WriteLine (obj.DeclaringType);     // System.Object

    Console.WriteLine (test.ReflectedType);    // Program
    Console.WriteLine (obj.ReflectedType);     // System.Object

    Console.WriteLine (test == obj);           // False
  }
}
```

Because they have different ReflectedTypes, the test and obj objects are not equal. Their difference, however, is purely a fabrication of the reflection API; our Program type has no distinct ToString method in the underlying type system. We can verify that the two MethodInfo objects refer to the same method in either of two ways:

```
Console.WriteLine (test.MethodHandle == obj.MethodHandle);    // True

Console.WriteLine (test.MetadataToken == obj.MetadataToken    // True
              && test.Module == obj.Module);
```

A MethodHandle is unique to each (genuinely distinct) method within an application domain; a MetadataToken is unique across all types and members within an assembly module.

MemberInfo also defines methods to return custom attributes (see the section "Retrieving Attributes at Runtime" on page 815 later in this chapter).

 You can obtain the MethodBase of the currently executing method by calling MethodBase.GetCurrentMethod.

Member Types

MemberInfo itself is light on members because it's an abstract base for the types shown in Figure 19-1.

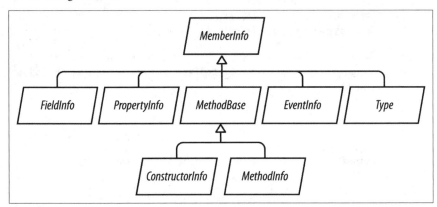

Figure 19-1. Member types

You can cast a MemberInfo to its subtype—based on its MemberType property. If you obtained a member via GetMethod, GetField, GetProperty, GetEvent, GetConstructor, or GetNestedType (or their plural versions), a cast isn't necessary. Table 19-1 summarizes what methods to use for each kind of C# construct.

Table 19-1. Retrieving member metadata

C# construct	Method to use	Name to use	Result
Method	GetMethod	(Method name)	MethodInfo
Property	GetProperty	(Property name)	PropertyInfo
Indexer	GetDefaultMembers		MemberInfo[] (containing PropertyInfo objects if compiled in C#)
Field	GetField	(Field name)	FieldInfo
Enum member	GetField	(Member name)	FieldInfo
Event	GetEvent	(Event name)	EventInfo
Constructor	GetConstructor		ConstructorInfo
Finalizer	GetMethod	"Finalize"	MethodInfo

C# construct	Method to use	Name to use	Result
Operator	GetMethod	"op_" + operator name	MethodInfo
Nested type	GetNestedType	(Type name)	Type

Each `MemberInfo` subclass has a wealth of properties and methods, exposing all aspects of the member's metadata. This includes such things as visibility, modifiers, generic type arguments, parameters, return type, and custom attributes.

Here is an example of using `GetMethod`:

```
MethodInfo m = typeof (Walnut).GetMethod ("Crack");
Console.WriteLine (m);                        // Void Crack()
Console.WriteLine (m.ReturnType);             // System.Void
```

All `*Info` instances are cached by the reflection API on first use:

```
MethodInfo method = typeof (Walnut).GetMethod ("Crack");
MemberInfo member = typeof (Walnut).GetMember ("Crack") [0];

Console.Write (method == member);        // True
```

As well as preserving object identity, caching improves the performance of what is otherwise a fairly slow API.

C# Members Versus CLR Members

The preceding table illustrates that some of C#'s functional constructs don't have a 1:1 mapping with CLR constructs. This makes sense because the CLR and reflection API were designed with all .NET languages in mind—you can use reflection even from Visual Basic.

Some C# constructs—namely indexers, enums, operators, and finalizers—are contrivances as far as the CLR is concerned. Specifically:

- A C# indexer translates to a property accepting one or more arguments, marked as the type's [DefaultMember].
- A C# enum translates to a subtype of System.Enum with a static field for each member.
- A C# operator translates to a specially named static method, starting in "op_"; for example, "op_Addition".
- A C# finalizer translates to a method that overrides Finalize.

Another complication is that properties and events actually comprise two things:

- Metadata describing the property or event (encapsulated by `PropertyInfo` or `EventInfo`)
- One or two backing methods

In a C# program, the backing methods are encapsulated within the property or event definition. But when compiled to IL, the backing methods present as ordinary methods that you can call like any other. This means `GetMethods` returns property and event backing methods alongside ordinary methods. To illustrate:

```
class Test { public int X { get { return 0; } set {} } }

void Demo()
{
  foreach (MethodInfo mi in typeof (Test).GetMethods())
    Console.Write (mi.Name + " ");
}

// OUTPUT:
get_X set_X GetType ToString Equals GetHashCode
```

You can identify these methods through the `IsSpecialName` property in `Method Info`. `IsSpecialName` returns `true` for property, indexer, and event accessors—as well as operators. It returns `false` only for conventional C# methods—and the `Finalize` method if a finalizer is defined.

Here are the backing methods that C# generates:

C# construct	Member type	Methods in IL
Property	Property	get_*XXX* and set_*XXX*
Indexer	Property	get_Item and set_Item
Event	Event	add_*XXX* and remove_*XXX*

Each backing method has its own associated `MethodInfo` object. You can access these as follows:

```
PropertyInfo pi = typeof (Console).GetProperty ("Title");
MethodInfo getter = pi.GetGetMethod();                    // get_Title
MethodInfo setter = pi.GetSetMethod();                    // set_Title
MethodInfo[] both = pi.GetAccessors();                    // Length==2
```

`GetAddMethod` and `GetRemoveMethod` perform a similar job for `EventInfo`.

To go in the reverse direction—from a `MethodInfo` to its associated `PropertyInfo` or `EventInfo`—you need to perform a query. LINQ is ideal for this job:

```
PropertyInfo p = mi.DeclaringType.GetProperties()
                   .First (x => x.GetAccessors (true).Contains (mi));
```

Generic Type Members

You can obtain member metadata for both unbound and closed generic types:

```
PropertyInfo unbound = typeof (IEnumerator<>)   .GetProperty ("Current");
PropertyInfo closed = typeof (IEnumerator<int>).GetProperty ("Current");

Console.WriteLine (unbound);    // T Current
Console.WriteLine (closed);     // Int32 Current

Console.WriteLine (unbound.PropertyType.IsGenericParameter);   // True
Console.WriteLine (closed.PropertyType.IsGenericParameter);    // False
```

The MemberInfo objects returned from unbound and closed generic types are always distinct—even for members whose signatures don't feature generic type parameters:

```
PropertyInfo unbound = typeof (List<>)   .GetProperty ("Count");
PropertyInfo closed = typeof (List<int>).GetProperty ("Count");

Console.WriteLine (unbound);    // Int32 Count
Console.WriteLine (closed);     // Int32 Count

Console.WriteLine (unbound == closed);   // False

Console.WriteLine (unbound.DeclaringType.IsGenericTypeDefinition); // True
Console.WriteLine (closed.DeclaringType.IsGenericTypeDefinition); // False
```

Members of unbound generic types cannot be *dynamically invoked*.

Dynamically Invoking a Member

Once you have a MethodInfo, PropertyInfo or FieldInfo object, you can dynamically call it or get/set its value. This is called *dynamic binding* or *late binding*, because you choose which member to invoke at runtime rather than compile time.

To illustrate, the following uses ordinary *static binding*:

```
string s = "Hello";
int length = s.Length;
```

Here's the same thing performed dynamically with reflection:

```
object s = "Hello";
PropertyInfo prop = s.GetType().GetProperty ("Length");
int length = (int) prop.GetValue (s, null);              // 5
```

GetValue and SetValue get and set the value of a PropertyInfo or FieldInfo. The first argument is the instance, which can be null for a static member. Accessing an indexer is just like accessing a property called "Item," except that you provide indexer values as the second argument when calling GetValue or SetValue.

To dynamically call a method, call Invoke on a MethodInfo, providing an array of arguments to pass to that method. If you get any of the argument types wrong, an exception is thrown at runtime. With dynamic invocation, you lose compile-time type safety but still have runtime type safety (just as with the dynamic keyword).

Method Parameters

Suppose we want to dynamically call string's Substring method. Statically, this would be done as follows:

```
Console.WriteLine ("stamp".Substring(2));                    // "amp"
```

Here's the dynamic equivalent with reflection:

```
Type type = typeof (string);
Type[] parameterTypes = { typeof (int) };
MethodInfo method = type.GetMethod ("Substring", parameterTypes);

object[] arguments = { 2 };
object returnValue = method.Invoke ("stamp", arguments);
Console.WriteLine (returnValue);                             // "amp"
```

Because the Substring method is overloaded, we had to pass an array of parameter types to GetMethod to indicate which version we wanted. Without the parameter types, GetMethod would throw an AmbiguousMatchException.

The GetParameters method, defined on MethodBase (the base class for MethodInfo and ConstructorInfo), returns parameter metadata. We can continue our previous example as follows:

```
ParameterInfo[] paramList = method.GetParameters();
foreach (ParameterInfo x in paramList)
{
  Console.WriteLine (x.Name);                // startIndex
  Console.WriteLine (x.ParameterType);       // System.Int32
}
```

Dealing with ref and out parameters

To pass ref or out parameters, call MakeByRefType on the type before obtaining the method. For instance, this code:

```
int x;
bool successfulParse = int.TryParse ("23", out x);
```

can be dynamically executed as follows:

```
object[] args = { "23", 0 };
Type[] argTypes = { typeof (string), typeof (int).MakeByRefType() };
MethodInfo tryParse = typeof (int).GetMethod ("TryParse", argTypes);
bool successfulParse = (bool) tryParse.Invoke (null, args);

Console.WriteLine (successfulParse + " " + args[1]);        // True 23
```

This same approach works for both ref and out parameter types.

Retrieving and invoking generic methods

Explicitly specifying parameter types when calling GetMethod can be essential in disambiguating overloaded methods. However, it's impossible to specify generic parameter types. For instance, consider the System.Linq.Enumerable class, which overloads the Where method as follows:

```
public static IEnumerable<TSource> Where<TSource>
  (this IEnumerable<TSource> source, Func<TSource, bool> predicate);

public static IEnumerable<TSource> Where<TSource>
  (this IEnumerable<TSource> source, Func<TSource, int, bool> predicate);
```

To retrieve a specific overload, we must retrieve all methods and then manually find the desired overload. The following query retrieves the former overload of Where:

```
from m in typeof (Enumerable).GetMethods()
where m.Name == "Where" && m.IsGenericMethod
let parameters = m.GetParameters()
where parameters.Length == 2
let genArg = m.GetGenericArguments().First()
let enumerableOfT = typeof (IEnumerable<>).MakeGenericType (genArg)
let funcOfTBool = typeof (Func<,>).MakeGenericType (genArg, typeof (bool))
where parameters[0].ParameterType == enumerableOfT
    && parameters[1].ParameterType == funcOfTBool
select m
```

Calling .Single() on this query gives the correct MethodInfo object with unbound type parameters. The next step is to close the type parameters by calling MakeGenericMethod:

```
var closedMethod = unboundMethod.MakeGenericMethod (typeof (int));
```

In this case, we've closed TSource with int, allowing us to call Enumerable.Where with a source of type IEnumerable<int>, and a predicate of type Func<int,bool>:

```
int[] source = { 3, 4, 5, 6, 7, 8 };
Func<int, bool> predicate = n => n % 2 == 1;    // Odd numbers only
```

We can now invoke the closed generic method as follows:

```
var query = (IEnumerable<int>) closedMethod.Invoke
  (null, new object[] { source, predicate });

foreach (int element in query) Console.Write (element + "|");   // 3|5|7|
```

If you're using the System.Linq.Expressions API to dynamically build expressions (Chapter 8), you don't need to go to
this trouble to specify a generic method. The Expres
sion.Call method is overloaded to let you specify the closed
type arguments of the method you wish to call:

```
int[] source = { 3, 4, 5, 6, 7, 8 };
Func<int, bool> predicate = n => n % 2 == 1;

var sourceExpr = Expression.Constant (source);
var predicateExpr = Expression.Constant (predicate);

var callExpression = Expression.Call (
  typeof (Enumerable), "Where",
  new[] { typeof (int) },  // Closed generic arg type.
  sourceExpr, predicateExpr);
```

Using Delegates for Performance

Dynamic invocations are relatively inefficient, with an overhead typically in the few-
microseconds region. If you're calling a method repeatedly in a loop, you can shift
the per-call overhead into the nanoseconds region by instead calling a dynamically
instantiated delegate that targets your dynamic method. In the following example,
we dynamically call string's Trim method a million times without significant overhead:

```
delegate string StringToString (string s);

static void Main()
{
  MethodInfo trimMethod = typeof (string).GetMethod ("Trim", new Type[0]);
  var trim = (StringToString) Delegate.CreateDelegate
                                (typeof (StringToString), trimMethod);
  for (int i = 0; i < 1000000; i++)
    trim ("test");
}
```

This is faster because the costly dynamic binding (shown in bold) happens just
once.

Accessing Nonpublic Members

All of the methods on types used to probe metadata (e.g., GetProperty, GetField,
etc.) have overloads that take a BindingFlags enum. This enum serves as a metadata filter and allows you to change the default selection criteria. The most common
use for this is to retrieve nonpublic members (this works only in desktop apps).

For instance, consider the following class:

```
class Walnut
{
  private bool cracked;
  public void Crack() { cracked = true; }
```

```
  public override string ToString() { return cracked.ToString(); }
}
```

We can *uncrack* the walnut as follows:

```
Type t = typeof (Walnut);
Walnut w = new Walnut();
w.Crack();
FieldInfo f = t.GetField ("cracked", BindingFlags.NonPublic |
                                     BindingFlags.Instance);
f.SetValue (w, false);
Console.WriteLine (w);          // False
```

Using reflection to access nonpublic members is powerful, but it is also dangerous, since you can bypass encapsulation, creating an unmanageable dependency on the internal implementation of a type.

The BindingFlags enum

BindingFlags is intended to be bitwise-combined. In order to get any matches at all, you need to start with one of the following four combinations:

```
BindingFlags.Public    | BindingFlags.Instance
BindingFlags.Public    | BindingFlags.Static
BindingFlags.NonPublic | BindingFlags.Instance
BindingFlags.NonPublic | BindingFlags.Static
```

NonPublic includes internal, protected, protected internal, and private.

The following example retrieves all the public static members of type object:

```
BindingFlags publicStatic = BindingFlags.Public | BindingFlags.Static;
MemberInfo[] members = typeof (object).GetMembers (publicStatic);
```

The following example retrieves all the nonpublic members of type object, both static and instance:

```
BindingFlags nonPublicBinding =
    BindingFlags.NonPublic | BindingFlags.Static | BindingFlags.Instance;

MemberInfo[] members = typeof (object).GetMembers (nonPublicBinding);
```

The DeclaredOnly flag excludes functions inherited from base types, unless they are overridden.

> The DeclaredOnly flag is somewhat confusing in that it *restricts* the result set (whereas all the other binding flags *expand* the result set).

Generic Methods

Generic methods cannot be invoked directly; the following throws an exception:

```
class Program
{
  public static T Echo<T> (T x) { return x; }
```

```
static void Main()
{
  MethodInfo echo = typeof (Program).GetMethod ("Echo");
  Console.WriteLine (echo.IsGenericMethodDefinition);     // True
  echo.Invoke (null, new object[] { 123 } );              // Exception
}
}
```

An extra step is required, which is to call MakeGenericMethod on the MethodInfo, specifying concrete generic type arguments. This returns another MethodInfo, which you can then invoke as follows:

```
MethodInfo echo = typeof (Program).GetMethod ("Echo");
MethodInfo intEcho = echo.MakeGenericMethod (typeof (int));
Console.WriteLine (intEcho.IsGenericMethodDefinition);    // False
Console.WriteLine (intEcho.Invoke (null, new object[] { 3 } ));   // 3
```

Anonymously Calling Members of a Generic Interface

Reflection is useful when you need to invoke a member of a generic interface and you don't know the type parameters until runtime. In theory, the need for this arises rarely if types are perfectly designed; of course, types are not always perfectly designed.

For instance, suppose we want to write a more powerful version of ToString that could expand the result of LINQ queries. We could start out as follows:

```
public static string ToStringEx <T> (IEnumerable<T> sequence)
{
  ...
}
```

This is already quite limiting. What if sequence contained *nested* collections that we also want to enumerate? We'd have to overload the method to cope:

```
public static string ToStringEx <T> (IEnumerable<IEnumerable<T>> sequence)
```

And then what if sequence contained groupings, or *projections* of nested sequences? The static solution of method overloading becomes impractical—we need an approach that can scale to handle an arbitrary object graph, such as the following:

```
public static string ToStringEx (object value)
{
  if (value == null) return "<null>";
  StringBuilder sb = new StringBuilder();

  if (value is List<>)                                           // Error
    sb.Append ("List of " + ((List<>) value).Count + " items");  // Error

  if (value is IGrouping<,>)                                     // Error
    sb.Append ("Group with key=" + ((IGrouping<,>) value).Key);  // Error

  // Enumerate collection elements if this is a collection,
  // recursively calling ToStringEx()
```

```
// ...
    return sb.ToString();
}
```

Unfortunately, this won't compile: you cannot invoke members of an *unbound* generic type such as `List<>` or `IGrouping<>`. In the case of `List<>`, we can solve the problem by using the nongeneric `IList` interface instead:

```
if (value is IList)
    sb.AppendLine ("A list with " + ((IList) value).Count + " items");
```

> We can do this because the designers of `List<>` had the foresight to implement `IList` classic (as well as `IList` *generic*). The same principle is worthy of consideration when writing your own generic types: having a nongeneric interface or base class upon which consumers can fall back can be extremely valuable.

The solution is not as simple for `IGrouping<,>`. Here's how the interface is defined:

```
public interface IGrouping <TKey,TElement> : IEnumerable <TElement>,
                                             IEnumerable
{
    TKey Key { get; }
}
```

There's no nongeneric type we can use to access the `Key` property, so here we must use reflection. The solution is not to invoke members of an unbound generic type (which is impossible), but to invoke members of a *closed* generic type, whose type arguments we establish at runtime.

> In the following chapter, we solve this more simply with C#'s `dynamic` keyword. A good indication for dynamic binding is when you would otherwise have to perform *type gymnastics*— as we are doing right now.

The first step is to determine whether `value` implements `IGrouping<>`, and if so, obtain its closed generic interface. We can do this most easily with a LINQ query. Then we retrieve and invoke the `Key` property:

```
public static string ToStringEx (object value)
{
    if (value == null) return "<null>";
    if (value.GetType().IsPrimitive) return value.ToString();

    StringBuilder sb = new StringBuilder();

    if (value is IList)
        sb.Append ("List of " + ((IList)value).Count + " items: ");

    Type closedIGrouping = value.GetType().GetInterfaces()
        .Where (t => t.IsGenericType &&
                     t.GetGenericTypeDefinition() == typeof (IGrouping<,>))
```

```
      .FirstOrDefault();

  if (closedIGrouping != null)    // Call the Key property on IGrouping<,>
  {
    PropertyInfo pi = closedIGrouping.GetProperty ("Key");
    object key = pi.GetValue (value, null);
    sb.Append ("Group with key=" + key + ": ");
  }

  if (value is IEnumerable)
    foreach (object element in ((IEnumerable)value))
      sb.Append (ToStringEx (element) + " ");

  if (sb.Length == 0) sb.Append (value.ToString());

  return "\r\n" + sb.ToString();
}
```

This approach is robust: it works whether IGrouping<,> is implemented implicitly
or explicitly. The following demonstrates this method:

```
Console.WriteLine (ToStringEx (new List<int> { 5, 6, 7 } ));
Console.WriteLine (ToStringEx ("xyyzzz".GroupBy (c => c) ));

List of 3 items: 5 6 7

Group with key=x: x
Group with key=y: y y
Group with key=z: z z z
```

Reflecting Assemblies

You can dynamically reflect an assembly by calling GetType or GetTypes on an
Assembly object. The following retrieves from the current assembly, the type called
TestProgram in the Demos namespace:

```
Type t = Assembly.GetExecutingAssembly().GetType ("Demos.TestProgram");
```

In a Windows Store app, you can obtain an assembly from an existing type:

```
typeof (Foo).GetTypeInfo().Assembly.GetType ("Demos.TestProgram");
```

The next example lists all the types in the assembly *mylib.dll* in *e:\demo*:

```
Assembly a = Assembly.LoadFrom (@"e:\demo\mylib.dll");

foreach (Type t in a.GetTypes())
  Console.WriteLine (t);
```

Or, in a Windows Store app:

```
Assembly a = typeof (Foo).GetTypeInfo().Assembly;

foreach (Type t in a.ExportedTypes)
  Console.WriteLine (t);
```

`GetTypes` and `ExportedTypes` return only top-level and not nested types.

Loading an Assembly into a Reflection-Only Context

In the preceding example, we loaded an assembly into the current application domain in order to list its types. This can have undesirable side effects, such as executing static constructors or upsetting subsequent type resolution. The solution, if you just need to inspect type information (and not instantiate or invoke types), is to load the assembly into a *reflection-only* context (desktop apps only):

```
Assembly a = Assembly.ReflectionOnlyLoadFrom (@"e:\demo\mylib.dll");
Console.WriteLine (a.ReflectionOnly);    // True

foreach (Type t in a.GetTypes())
  Console.WriteLine (t);
```

This is the starting point for writing a class browser.

There are three methods for loading an assembly into the reflection-only context:

- `ReflectionOnlyLoad (byte[])`
- `ReflectionOnlyLoad (string)`
- `ReflectionOnlyLoadFrom (string)`

Even in a reflection-only context, it is not possible to load multiple versions of *mscorlib.dll*. A workaround is to use Microsoft's CCI libraries (*http://cciast.codeplex.com*) or Mono.Cecil (*http://www.mono-project.com/Cecil*).

Modules

Calling `GetTypes` on a multimodule assembly returns all types in all modules. As a result, you can ignore the existence of modules and treat an assembly as a type's container. There is one case, though, where modules are relevant—and that's when dealing with metadata tokens.

A metadata token is an integer that uniquely refers to a type, member, string, or resource within the scope of a module. IL uses metadata tokens, so if you're parsing IL, you'll need to be able to resolve them. The methods for doing this are defined in the `Module` type and are called `ResolveType`, `ResolveMember`, `ResolveString`, and `ResolveSignature`. We revisit this in the final section of this chapter, on writing a disassembler.

You can obtain a list of all the modules in an assembly by calling `GetModules`. You can also access an assembly's main module directly—via its `ManifestModule` property.

Working with Attributes

The CLR allows additional metadata to be attached to types, members, and assemblies through attributes. This is the mechanism by which many CLR functions such as serialization and security are directed, making attributes an indivisible part of an application.

A key characteristic of attributes is that you can write your own, and then use them just as you would any other attribute to "decorate" a code element with additional information. This additional information is compiled into the underlying assembly and can be retrieved at runtime using reflection to build services that work declaratively, such as automated unit testing.

Attribute Basics

There are three kinds of attributes:

- Bit-mapped attributes
- Custom attributes
- Pseudocustom attributes

Of these, only *custom attributes* are extensible.

 The term "attribute" by itself can refer to any of the three, although in the C# world, it most often refers to custom attributes or pseudocustom attributes.

Bit-mapped attributes (our terminology) map to dedicated bits in a type's metadata. Most of C#'s modifier keywords, such as `public`, `abstract`, and `sealed`, compile to bit-mapped attributes. These attributes are very efficient because they consume minimal space in the metadata (usually just one bit), and the CLR can locate them with little or no indirection. The reflection API exposes them via dedicated properties on `Type` (and other `MemberInfo` subclasses), such as `IsPublic`, `IsAbstract`, and `IsSealed`. The `Attributes` property returns a flags enum that describes most of them in one hit:

```
static void Main()
{
  TypeAttributes ta = typeof (Console).Attributes;
  MethodAttributes ma = MethodInfo.GetCurrentMethod().Attributes;
  Console.WriteLine (ta + "\r\n" + ma);
}
```

Here's the result:

```
AutoLayout, AnsiClass, Class, Public, Abstract, Sealed, BeforeFieldInit
PrivateScope, Private, Static, HideBySig
```

In contrast, *custom attributes* compile to a blob that hangs off the type's main metadata table. All custom attributes are represented by a subclass of `System.Attribute` and, unlike bit-mapped attributes, are extensible. The blob in the metadata identifies the attribute class and also stores the values of any positional or named argument that was specified when the attribute was applied. Custom attributes that you define yourself are architecturally identical to those defined in the .NET Framework.

Chapter 4 describes how to attach custom attributes to a type or member in C#. Here, we attach the predefined Obsolete attribute to the Foo class:

```
[Obsolete] public class Foo {...}
```

This instructs the compiler to incorporate an instance of ObsoleteAttribute into the metadata for Foo, which can then be reflected at runtime by calling GetCustomAttributes on a Type or MemberInfo object.

Pseudocustom attributes look and feel just like standard custom attributes. They are represented by a subclass of System.Attribute and are attached in the standard manner:

```
[Serializable] public class Foo {...}
```

The difference is that the compiler or CLR internally optimizes pseudocustom attributes by converting them to bit-mapped attributes. Examples include [Serializable] (Chapter 17), StructLayout, In, and Out (Chapter 25). Reflection exposes pseudocustom attributes through dedicated properties such as IsSerializable; and in many cases, they are also returned as System.Attribute objects when you call GetCustomAttributes (SerializableAttribute included). This means you can (almost) ignore the difference between pseudo- and non-pseudocustom attributes (a notable exception is when using Reflection.Emit to generate types dynamically at runtime; see "Emitting Assemblies and Types" on page 825 later in this chapter).

The AttributeUsage Attribute

AttributeUsage is an attribute applied to attribute classes. It tells the compiler how the target attribute should be used:

```
public sealed class AttributeUsageAttribute : Attribute
{
  public AttributeUsageAttribute (AttributeTargets validOn);

  public bool AllowMultiple     { get; set; }
  public bool Inherited         { get; set; }
  public AttributeTargets ValidOn { get; }
}
```

AllowMultiple controls whether the attribute being defined can be applied more than once to the same target; Inherited controls whether an attribute applied to a base class also applies to derived classes (or in the case of methods, whether an attribute applied to a virtual method also applies to overriding methods). ValidOn determines the set of targets (classes, interfaces, properties, methods, parameters, etc.) to which the attribute can be attached. It accepts any combination of values from the `AttributeTargets` enum, which has the following members:

All	Delegate	GenericParameter	Parameter
Assembly	Enum	Interface	Property
Class	Event	Method	ReturnValue
Constructor	Field	Module	Struct

To illustrate, here's how the authors of the .NET Framework have applied `Attribu teUsage` to the `Serializable` attribute:

```
[AttributeUsage (AttributeTargets.Delegate |
                 AttributeTargets.Enum     |
                 AttributeTargets.Struct   |
                 AttributeTargets.Class,    Inherited = false)
]
public sealed class SerializableAttribute : Attribute { }
```

This is, in fact, almost the complete definition of the `Serializable` attribute. Writing an attribute class that has no properties or special constructors is this simple.

Defining Your Own Attribute

Here's how you write your own attribute:

1. Derive a class from `System.Attribute` or a descendent of `System.Attribute`. By convention, the class name should end with the word "Attribute," although this isn't required.

2. Apply the `AttributeUsage` attribute, described in the preceding section.

   If the attribute requires no properties or arguments in its constructor, the job is done.

3. Write one or more public constructors. The parameters to the constructor define the positional parameters of the attribute and will become mandatory when using the attribute.

4. Declare a public field or property for each named parameter you wish to support. Named parameters are optional when using the attribute.

Attribute properties and constructor parameters must be of
the following types:

- A sealed primitive type: in other words, bool, byte, char,
double, float, int, long, short, or string
- The Type type
- An enum type
- A one-dimensional array of any of these

When an attribute is applied, it must also be possible for the
compiler to statically evaluate each of the properties or constructor arguments.

The following class defines an attribute for assisting an automated unit-testing system. It indicates that a method should be tested, the number of test repetitions, and
a message in case of failure:

```
[AttributeUsage (AttributeTargets.Method)]
public sealed class TestAttribute : Attribute
{
  public int     Repetitions;
  public string  FailureMessage;

  public TestAttribute () : this (1)     { }
  public TestAttribute (int repetitions) { Repetitions = repetitions; }
}
```

Here's a Foo class with methods decorated in various ways with the Test attribute:

```
class Foo
{
  [Test]
  public void Method1() { ... }

  [Test(20)]
  public void Method2() { ... }

  [Test(20, FailureMessage="Debugging Time!")]
  public void Method3() { ... }
}
```

Retrieving Attributes at Runtime

There are two standard ways to retrieve attributes at runtime:

- Call GetCustomAttributes on any Type or MemberInfo object.
- Call Attribute.GetCustomAttribute or Attribute.GetCustomAttributes.

These latter two methods are overloaded to accept any reflection object that corresponds to a valid attribute target (Type, Assembly, Module, MemberInfo, or Parame
terInfo).

From Framework 4.0, you can also call `GetCustomAttri`
`butesData()` on a type or member to obtain attribute information. The difference between this and `GetCustomAttri`
`butes()` is that the former tells you *how* the attribute was
instantiated: it reports the constructor overload that was used,
and the value of each constructor argument and named
parameter. This is useful when you want to emit code or IL to
reconstruct the attribute to the same state (see "Emitting Type
Members" on page 828 later in this chapter).

Here's how we can enumerate each method in the preceding `Foo` class that has a
`TestAttribute`:

```
foreach (MethodInfo mi in typeof (Foo).GetMethods())
{
  TestAttribute att = (TestAttribute) Attribute.GetCustomAttribute
    (mi, typeof (TestAttribute));

  if (att != null)
    Console.WriteLine ("Method {0} will be tested; reps={1}; msg={2}",
                        mi.Name, att.Repetitions, att.FailureMessage);
}
```

Or, in a Windows Store app:

```
foreach (MethodInfo mi in typeof (Foo).GetTypeInfo().DeclaredMethods)
  ...
```

Here's the output:

```
Method Method1 will be tested; reps=1; msg=
Method Method2 will be tested; reps=20; msg=
Method Method3 will be tested; reps=20; msg=Debugging Time!
```

To complete the illustration on how we could use this to write a unit-testing system,
here's the same example expanded so that it actually calls the methods decorated
with the `Test` attribute:

```
foreach (MethodInfo mi in typeof (Foo).GetMethods())
{
  TestAttribute att = (TestAttribute) Attribute.GetCustomAttribute
    (mi, typeof (TestAttribute));

  if (att != null)
    for (int i = 0; i < att.Repetitions; i++)
      try
      {
        mi.Invoke (new Foo(), null);    // Call method with no arguments
      }
      catch (Exception ex)       // Wrap exception in att.FailureMessage
      {
        throw new Exception ("Error: " + att.FailureMessage, ex);
      }
}
```

Returning to attribute reflection, here's an example that lists the attributes present on a specific type:

```
[Serializable, Obsolete]
class Test
{
  static void Main()
  {
    object[] atts = Attribute.GetCustomAttributes (typeof (Test));
    foreach (object att in atts) Console.WriteLine (att);
  }
}
```

Output:

```
System.ObsoleteAttribute
System.SerializableAttribute
```

Retrieving Attributes in the Reflection-Only Context

Calling GetCustomAttributes on a member loaded in the reflection-only context is prohibited because it would require instantiating arbitrarily typed attributes (remember that object instantiation isn't allowed in the reflection-only context). To work around this, there's a special type called CustomAttributeData for reflecting over such attributes. Here's an example of how it's used:

```
IList<CustomAttributeData> atts = CustomAttributeData.GetCustomAttributes
                                  (myReflectionOnlyType);
foreach (CustomAttributeData att in atts)
{
  Console.Write (att.GetType());              // Attribute type

  Console.WriteLine (" " + att.Constructor);   // ConstructorInfo object

  foreach (CustomAttributeTypedArgument arg in att.ConstructorArguments)
    Console.WriteLine ("   " +arg.ArgumentType + "=" + arg.Value);

  foreach (CustomAttributeNamedArgument arg in att.NamedArguments)
    Console.WriteLine ("   " + arg.MemberInfo.Name + "=" + arg.TypedValue);
}
```

In many cases, the attribute types will be in a different assembly from the one you're reflecting. One way to cope with this is to handle the ReflectionOnlyAssemblyRe solve event on the current application domain:

```
ResolveEventHandler handler = (object sender, ResolveEventArgs args)
                => Assembly.ReflectionOnlyLoad (args.Name);

AppDomain.CurrentDomain.ReflectionOnlyAssemblyResolve += handler;

// Reflect over attributes...

AppDomain.CurrentDomain.ReflectionOnlyAssemblyResolve -= handler;
```

Dynamic Code Generation

The `System.Reflection.Emit` namespace contains classes for creating metadata and IL at runtime. Generating code dynamically is useful for certain kinds of programming tasks. An example is the regular expressions API, which emits performant types tuned to specific regular expressions. Other uses of `Reflection.Emit` in the Framework include dynamically generating transparent proxies for Remoting and generating types that perform specific XSLT transforms with minimum runtime overhead. LINQPad uses `Reflection.Emit` to dynamically generate typed `DataContext` classes.

Reflection.Emit is not supported in the Windows Store profile.

Generating IL with DynamicMethod

The `DynamicMethod` class is a lightweight tool in the `System.Reflection.Emit` namespace for generating methods on the fly. Unlike `TypeBuilder`, it doesn't require that you first set up a dynamic assembly, module, and type in which to contain the method. This makes it suitable for simple tasks—as well as serving as a good introduction to `Reflection.Emit`.

 A `DynamicMethod` and the associated IL are garbage-collected when no longer referenced. This means you can repeatedly generate dynamic methods without filling up memory. (To do the same with dynamic *assemblies*, you must apply the `Assem blyBuilderAccess.RunAndCollect` flag when creating the assembly.)

Here is a simple use of `DynamicMethod` to create a method that writes `Hello world` to the console:

```
public class Test
{
  static void Main()
  {
    var dynMeth = new DynamicMethod ("Foo", null, null, typeof (Test));
    ILGenerator gen = dynMeth.GetILGenerator();
    gen.EmitWriteLine ("Hello world");
    gen.Emit (OpCodes.Ret);
    dynMeth.Invoke (null, null);                    // Hello world
  }
}
```

`OpCodes` has a static read-only field for every IL opcode. Most of the functionality is exposed through various opcodes, although `ILGenerator` also has specialized methods for generating labels and local variables and for exception handling. A method always ends in `Opcodes.Ret`, which means "return," or some kind of branching/throwing instruction. The `EmitWriteLine` method on `ILGenerator` is a shortcut for `Emit`ting a number of lower-level opcodes. We could have replaced the call to `Emit WriteLine` with this, and we would have gotten the same result:

```
MethodInfo writeLineStr = typeof (Console).GetMethod ("WriteLine",
                          new Type[] { typeof (string) });
gen.Emit (OpCodes.Ldstr, "Hello world");    // Load a string
gen.Emit (OpCodes.Call, writeLineStr);      // Call a method
```

Note that we passed typeof(Test) into DynamicMethod's constructor. This gives the
dynamic method access to the nonpublic methods of that type, allowing us to do
this:

```
public class Test
{
  static void Main()
  {
    var dynMeth = new DynamicMethod ("Foo", null, null, typeof (Test));
    ILGenerator gen = dynMeth.GetILGenerator();

    MethodInfo privateMethod = typeof(Test).GetMethod ("HelloWorld",
      BindingFlags.Static | BindingFlags.NonPublic);

    gen.Emit (OpCodes.Call, privateMethod);    // Call HelloWorld
    gen.Emit (OpCodes.Ret);

    dynMeth.Invoke (null, null);               // Hello world
  }

  static void HelloWorld()        // private method, yet we can call it
  {
    Console.WriteLine ("Hello world");
  }
}
```

Understanding IL requires a considerable investment of time. Rather than understand all the opcodes, it's much easier to compile a C# program then to examine,
copy, and tweak the IL. LINQPad displays the IL for any method or code snippet
that you type, and assembly viewing tools such as *ildasm* or .NET Reflector are useful for examining existing assemblies.

The Evaluation Stack

Central to IL is the concept of the *evaluation stack*. To call a method with arguments, you first push ("load") the arguments onto the evaluation stack and then call
the method. The method then pops the arguments it needs from the evaluation
stack. We demonstrated this previously, in calling Console.WriteLine. Here's a similar example with an integer:

```
var dynMeth = new DynamicMethod ("Foo", null, null, typeof(void));
ILGenerator gen = dynMeth.GetILGenerator();
MethodInfo writeLineInt = typeof (Console).GetMethod ("WriteLine",
                          new Type[] { typeof (int) });

// The Ldc* op-codes load numeric literals of various types and sizes.

gen.Emit (OpCodes.Ldc_I4, 123);        // Push a 4-byte integer onto stack
gen.Emit (OpCodes.Call, writeLineInt);
```

```
gen.Emit (OpCodes.Ret);
dynMeth.Invoke (null, null);              // 123
```

To add two numbers together, you first load each number onto the evaluation stack, and then call Add. The Add opcode pops two values from the evaluation stack and pushes the result back on. The following adds 2 and 2, and then writes the result using the writeLine method obtained previously:

```
gen.Emit (OpCodes.Ldc_I4, 2);            // Push a 4-byte integer, value=2
gen.Emit (OpCodes.Ldc_I4, 2);            // Push a 4-byte integer, value=2
gen.Emit (OpCodes.Add);                  // Add the result together
gen.Emit (OpCodes.Call, writeLineInt);
```

To calculate 10 / 2 + 1, you can do either this:

```
gen.Emit (OpCodes.Ldc_I4, 10);
gen.Emit (OpCodes.Ldc_I4, 2);
gen.Emit (OpCodes.Div);
gen.Emit (OpCodes.Ldc_I4, 1);
gen.Emit (OpCodes.Add);
gen.Emit (OpCodes.Call, writeLineInt);
```

or this:

```
gen.Emit (OpCodes.Ldc_I4, 1);
gen.Emit (OpCodes.Ldc_I4, 10);
gen.Emit (OpCodes.Ldc_I4, 2);
gen.Emit (OpCodes.Div);
gen.Emit (OpCodes.Add);
gen.Emit (OpCodes.Call, writeLineInt);
```

Passing Arguments to a Dynamic Method

You can load an argument passed into a dynamic method onto the stack with the Ldarg and Ldarg_*XXX* opcodes. To return a value, leave exactly one value on the stack upon finishing. For this to work, you must specify the return type and argument types when calling DynamicMethod's constructor. The following creates a dynamic method that returns the sum of two integers:

```
DynamicMethod dynMeth = new DynamicMethod ("Foo",
    typeof (int),                         // Return type = int
    new[] { typeof (int), typeof (int) }, // Parameter types = int, int
    typeof (void));

ILGenerator gen = dynMeth.GetILGenerator();

gen.Emit (OpCodes.Ldarg_0);    // Push first arg onto eval stack
gen.Emit (OpCodes.Ldarg_1);    // Push second arg onto eval stack
gen.Emit (OpCodes.Add);        // Add them together (result on stack)
gen.Emit (OpCodes.Ret);        // Return with stack having 1 value

int result = (int) dynMeth.Invoke (null, new object[] { 3, 4 } );    // 7
```

When you exit, the evaluation stack must have exactly 0 or 1 item (depending on whether your method returns a value). If you violate this, the CLR will refuse to execute your method. You can remove an item from the stack without processing it with `OpCodes.Pop`.

Rather than calling `Invoke`, it can be more convenient to work with a dynamic method as a typed delegate. The `CreateDelegate` method achieves just this. To illustrate, suppose we define a delegate called `BinaryFunction`:

```
delegate int BinaryFunction (int n1, int n2);
```

We could then replace the last line of our preceding example with this:

```
BinaryFunction f = (BinaryFunction) dynMeth.CreateDelegate
                                    (typeof (BinaryFunction));
int result = f (3, 4);       // 7
```

A delegate also eliminates the overhead of dynamic method invocation—saving a few microseconds per call.

We demonstrate how to pass by reference later in the section "Emitting Type Members" on page 828.

Generating Local Variables

You can declare a local variable by calling `DeclareLocal` on an `ILGenerator`. This returns a `LocalBuilder` object, which can be used in conjunction with opcodes such as `Ldloc` (load a local variable) or `Stloc` (store a local variable). `Ldloc` pushes the evaluation stack; `Stloc` pops it. For example, consider the following C# code:

```
int x = 6;
int y = 7;
x *= y;
Console.WriteLine (x);
```

The following generates the preceding code dynamically:

```
var dynMeth = new DynamicMethod ("Test", null, null, typeof (void));
ILGenerator gen = dynMeth.GetILGenerator();

LocalBuilder localX = gen.DeclareLocal (typeof (int));   // Declare x
LocalBuilder localY = gen.DeclareLocal (typeof (int));   // Declare y

gen.Emit (OpCodes.Ldc_I4, 6);       // Push literal 6 onto eval stack
gen.Emit (OpCodes.Stloc, localX);   // Store in localX
gen.Emit (OpCodes.Ldc_I4, 7);       // Push literal 7 onto eval stack
gen.Emit (OpCodes.Stloc, localY);   // Store in localY

gen.Emit (OpCodes.Ldloc, localX);   // Push localX onto eval stack
gen.Emit (OpCodes.Ldloc, localY);   // Push localY onto eval stack
gen.Emit (OpCodes.Mul);             // Multiply values together
gen.Emit (OpCodes.Stloc, localX);   // Store the result to localX
```

```
gen.EmitWriteLine (localX);              // Write the value of localX
gen.Emit (OpCodes.Ret);

dynMeth.Invoke (null, null);             // 42
```

 Redgate's .NET Reflector is great for examining dynamic methods for errors: if you decompile to C#, it's usually quite obvious where you've gone wrong! We explain how to save dynamic emissions to disk in "Emitting Assemblies and Types" on page 825. Another useful tool is Microsoft's IL visualizer for Visual Studio (*http://albahari.com/ilvisualizer*).

Branching

In IL, there are no `while`, `do`, and `for` loops; it's all done with labels and the equivalent of `goto` and conditional `goto` statements. These are the branching opcodes, such as `Br` (branch unconditionally), `Brtrue` (branch if the value on the evaluation stack is `true`), and `Blt` (branch if the first value is less than the second value).

To set a branch target, first call `DefineLabel` (this returns a `Label` object), and then call `MarkLabel` at the place where you want to anchor the label. For example, consider the following C# code:

```
int x = 5;
while (x <= 10) Console.WriteLine (x++);
```

We can emit this as follows:

```
ILGenerator gen = ...

Label startLoop = gen.DefineLabel();              // Declare labels
Label endLoop = gen.DefineLabel();

LocalBuilder x = gen.DeclareLocal (typeof (int));  // int x
gen.Emit (OpCodes.Ldc_I4, 5);                      //
gen.Emit (OpCodes.Stloc, x);                       // x = 5
gen.MarkLabel (startLoop);
  gen.Emit (OpCodes.Ldc_I4, 10);                   // Load 10 onto eval stack
  gen.Emit (OpCodes.Ldloc, x);                     // Load x onto eval stack

  gen.Emit (OpCodes.Blt, endLoop);                 // if (x > 10) goto endLoop

  gen.EmitWriteLine (x);                           // Console.WriteLine (x)

  gen.Emit (OpCodes.Ldloc, x);                     // Load x onto eval stack
  gen.Emit (OpCodes.Ldc_I4, 1);                    // Load 1 onto the stack
  gen.Emit (OpCodes.Add);                          // Add them together
  gen.Emit (OpCodes.Stloc, x);                     // Save result back to x

  gen.Emit (OpCodes.Br, startLoop);                // return to start of loop
gen.MarkLabel (endLoop);

gen.Emit (OpCodes.Ret);
```

Instantiating Objects and Calling Instance Methods

The IL equivalent of new is the Newobj opcode. This takes a constructor and loads the constructed object onto the evaluation stack. For instance, the following constructs a StringBuilder:

```
var dynMeth = new DynamicMethod ("Test", null, null, typeof (void));
ILGenerator gen = dynMeth.GetILGenerator();

ConstructorInfo ci = typeof (StringBuilder).GetConstructor (new Type[0]);
gen.Emit (OpCodes.Newobj, ci);
```

Once an object is on the evaluation stack, you can call its instance methods using the Call or Callvirt opcode. Extending this example, we'll query the String Builder's MaxCapacity property by calling the property's get accessor and then write out the result:

```
gen.Emit (OpCodes.Callvirt, typeof (StringBuilder)
                         .GetProperty ("MaxCapacity").GetGetMethod());

gen.Emit (OpCodes.Call, typeof (Console).GetMethod ("WriteLine",
                         new[] { typeof (int) } ));
gen.Emit (OpCodes.Ret);
dynMeth.Invoke (null, null);        // 2147483647
```

To emulate C# calling semantics:

- Use Call to invoke static methods and value type instance methods.
- Use Callvirt to invoke reference type instance methods (whether or not they're declared virtual).

In our example, we used Callvirt on the StringBuilder instance—even though MaxProperty is not virtual. This doesn't cause an error: it simply performs a nonvirtual call instead. Always invoking reference type instance methods with Callvirt avoids risking the opposite condition: invoking a virtual method with Call. (The risk is real. The author of the target method may later *change* its declaration.) Call virt also has the benefit of checking that the receiver is non-null.

 Invoking a virtual method with Call bypasses virtual calling semantics and calls that method directly. This is rarely desirable and, in effect, violates type safety.

In the following example, we construct a StringBuilder passing in two arguments, append ", world!" to the StringBuilder, and then call ToString on it:

```
// We will call:   new StringBuilder ("Hello", 1000)

ConstructorInfo ci = typeof (StringBuilder).GetConstructor (
                     new[] { typeof (string), typeof (int) } );

gen.Emit (OpCodes.Ldstr, "Hello");   // Load a string onto the eval stack
gen.Emit (OpCodes.Ldc_I4, 1000);     // Load an int onto the eval stack
```

```
gen.Emit (OpCodes.Newobj, ci);          // Construct the StringBuilder

Type[] strT = { typeof (string) };
gen.Emit (OpCodes.Ldstr, ", world!");
gen.Emit (OpCodes.Call, typeof (StringBuilder).GetMethod ("Append", strT));
gen.Emit (OpCodes.Callvirt, typeof (object).GetMethod ("ToString"));
gen.Emit (OpCodes.Call, typeof (Console).GetMethod ("WriteLine", strT));
gen.Emit (OpCodes.Ret);
dynMeth.Invoke (null, null);            // Hello, world!
```

For fun, we called `GetMethod` on `typeof(object)` and then used `Callvirt` to perform a virtual method call on `ToString`. We could have gotten the same result by
calling `ToString` on the `StringBuilder` type itself:

```
gen.Emit (OpCodes.Callvirt, typeof (StringBuilder).GetMethod ("ToString",
                                                    new Type[0] ));
```

(The empty type array is required in calling `GetMethod` because `StringBuilder`
overloads `ToString` with another signature.)

> Had we called `object`'s `ToString` method nonvirtually:
>
> ```
> gen.Emit (OpCodes.Call,
>         typeof (object).GetMethod ("ToString"));
> ```
>
> the result would have been "System.Text.StringBuilder." In
> other words, we would have circumvented `StringBuilder`'s
> `ToString` override and called `object`'s version directly.

Exception Handling

`ILGenerator` provides dedicated methods for exception handling. The translation
for the following C# code:

```
try                                { throw new NotSupportedException(); }
catch (NotSupportedException ex)   { Console.WriteLine (ex.Message);    }
finally                            { Console.WriteLine ("Finally");     }
```

is this:

```
MethodInfo getMessageProp = typeof (NotSupportedException)
                    .GetProperty ("Message").GetGetMethod();

MethodInfo writeLineString = typeof (Console).GetMethod ("WriteLine",
                                        new[] { typeof (object) } );
gen.BeginExceptionBlock();
  ConstructorInfo ci = typeof (NotSupportedException).GetConstructor (
                                                    new Type[0] );
  gen.Emit (OpCodes.Newobj, ci);
  gen.Emit (OpCodes.Throw);
gen.BeginCatchBlock (typeof (NotSupportedException));
  gen.Emit (OpCodes.Callvirt, getMessageProp);
  gen.Emit (OpCodes.Call, writeLineString);
gen.BeginFinallyBlock();
  gen.EmitWriteLine ("Finally");
gen.EndExceptionBlock();
```

Just as in C#, you can include multiple `catch` blocks. To rethrow the same exception, emit the `Rethrow` opcode.

 `ILGenerator` provides a helper method called `ThrowExcep tion`. This contains a bug, however, preventing it from being used with a `DynamicMethod`. It works only with a `Method Builder` (see the next section).

Emitting Assemblies and Types

Although `DynamicMethod` is convenient, it can generate only methods. If you need to emit any other construct—or a complete type—you need to use the full "heavyweight" API. This means dynamically building an assembly and module. The assembly need not have a disk presence, however; it can live entirely in memory.

Let's assume we want to dynamically build a type. Since a type must live in a module within an assembly, we must first create the assembly and module before we can create the type. This is the job of the `AssemblyBuilder` and `ModuleBuilder` types:

```
AppDomain appDomain = AppDomain.CurrentDomain;

AssemblyName aname = new AssemblyName ("MyDynamicAssembly");

AssemblyBuilder assemBuilder =
  appDomain.DefineDynamicAssembly (aname, AssemblyBuilderAccess.Run);

ModuleBuilder modBuilder = assemBuilder.DefineDynamicModule ("DynModule");
```

 You can't add a type to an existing assembly, because an assembly is immutable once created.

Dynamic assemblies are not garbage collected and remain in memory until the application domain ends, unless you specify `AssemblyBuilderAccess.RunAndCollect` when defining the assembly. Various restrictions apply to collectible assemblies (see *http://albahari.com/dynamiccollect*).

Once we have a module where the type can live, we can use `TypeBuilder` to create the type. The following defines a class called `Widget`:

```
TypeBuilder tb = modBuilder.DefineType ("Widget", TypeAttributes.Public);
```

The `TypeAttributes` flags enum supports the CLR type modifiers you see when disassembling a type with *ildasm*. As well as member visibility flags, this includes type modifiers such as `Abstract` and `Sealed`—and `Interface` for defining a .NET interface. It also includes `Serializable`, which is equivalent to applying the [`Serializa ble`] attribute in C#, and `Explicit`, which is equivalent to applying [`StructLay out(LayoutKind.Explicit)`]. We describe how to apply other kinds of attributes later in this chapter, in the section "Attaching Attributes" on page 834.

The `DefineType` method also accepts an optional base type:

- To define a struct, specify a base type of `System.Value Type`.
- To define a delegate, specify a base type of `System.Multi castDelegate`.
- To implement an interface, use the constructor that accepts an array of interface types.
- To define an interface, specify `TypeAttributes.Inter face | TypeAttributes.Abstract`.

Defining a delegate type requires a number of extra steps. In his weblog at *http://blogs.msdn.com/joelpob/*, Joel Pobar demonstrates how this is done in his article titled "Creating delegate types via Reflection.Emit."

We can now create members within the type:

```
MethodBuilder methBuilder = tb.DefineMethod ("SayHello",
                                              MethodAttributes.Public,
                                              null, null);
ILGenerator gen = methBuilder.GetILGenerator();
gen.EmitWriteLine ("Hello world");
gen.Emit (OpCodes.Ret);
```

We're now ready to create the type, which finalizes its definition:

```
Type t = tb.CreateType();
```

Once the type is created, we use ordinary reflection to inspect and perform dynamic binding:

```
object o = Activator.CreateInstance (t);
t.GetMethod ("SayHello").Invoke (o, null);        // Hello world
```

Saving Emitted Assemblies

The `Save` method on `AssemblyBuilder` writes a dynamically generated assembly to a specified filename. For this to work, though, you must do two things:

- Specify an `AssemblyBuilderAccess` of `Save` or `RunAndSave` when constructing the `AssemblyBuilder`.
- Specify a filename when constructing the `ModuleBuilder` (this should match the assembly filename unless you want to create a multimodule assembly).

You can also optionally set properties of the `AssemblyName` object, such as `Version` or `KeyPair` (for signing).

For example:

```
AppDomain domain = AppDomain.CurrentDomain;

AssemblyName aname = new AssemblyName ("MyEmissions");
aname.Version = new Version (2, 13, 0, 1);

AssemblyBuilder assemBuilder = domain.DefineDynamicAssembly (
  aname, AssemblyBuilderAccess.RunAndSave);

ModuleBuilder modBuilder = assemBuilder.DefineDynamicModule (
  "MainModule", "MyEmissions.dll");

// Create types as we did previously...
// ...

assemBuilder.Save ("MyEmissions.dll");
```

This writes the assembly to the application's base directory. To save to a different location, you must provide the alternative directory when constructing `Assembly Builder`:

```
AssemblyBuilder assemBuilder = domain.DefineDynamicAssembly (
  aname, AssemblyBuilderAccess.RunAndSave, @"d:\assemblies" );
```

A dynamic assembly, once written to a file, becomes an ordinary assembly just like any other. A program could statically reference the assembly we just built and do this:

```
Widget w = new Widget();
w.SayHello();
```

The Reflection.Emit Object Model

Figure 19-2 illustrates the essential types in `System.Reflection.Emit`. Each type describes a CLR construct and is based on a counterpart in the `System.Reflection` namespace. This allows you to use emitted constructs in place of normal constructs when building a type. For example, we previously called `Console.WriteLine` as follows:

```
MethodInfo writeLine = typeof(Console).GetMethod ("WriteLine",
                                    new Type[] { typeof (string) });
gen.Emit (OpCodes.Call, writeLine);
```

We could just as easily call a dynamically generated method by calling `gen.Emit` with a `MethodBuilder` instead of a `MethodInfo`. This is essential—otherwise, you couldn't write one dynamic method that called another in the same type.

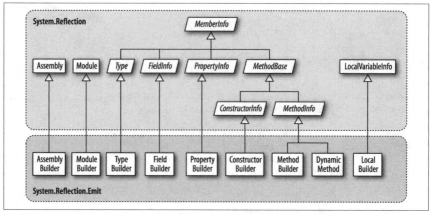

Figure 19-2. System.Reflection.Emit

Recall that you must call `CreateType` on a `TypeBuilder` when you've finished populating it. Calling `CreateType` seals the `TypeBuilder` and all its members—so nothing more can be added or changed—and gives you back a real `Type` that you can instantiate.

Before you call `CreateType`, the `TypeBuilder` and its members are in an "uncreated" state. There are significant restrictions on what you can do with uncreated constructs. In particular, you cannot call any of the members that return `MemberInfo` objects, such as `GetMembers`, `GetMethod`, or `GetProperty`—these all throw an exception. If you want to refer to members of an uncreated type, you must use the original emissions:

```
TypeBuilder tb = ...

MethodBuilder method1 = tb.DefineMethod ("Method1", ...);
MethodBuilder method2 = tb.DefineMethod ("Method2", ...);

ILGenerator gen1 = method1.GetILGenerator();

// Suppose we want method1 to call method2:

gen1.Emit (OpCodes.Call, method2);                   // Right
gen1.Emit (OpCodes.Call, tb.GetMethod ("Method2"));  // Wrong
```

After calling `CreateType`, you can reflect on and activate not only the `Type` returned, but also the original `TypeBuilder` object. The `TypeBuilder`, in fact, morphs into a proxy for the real `Type`. We'll see why this feature is important later in this chapter in the section "Awkward Emission Targets" on page 836.

Emitting Type Members

All the examples in this section assume a `TypeBuilder`, tb, has been instantiated as follows:

```
AppDomain domain = AppDomain.CurrentDomain;
AssemblyName aname = new AssemblyName ("MyEmissions");

AssemblyBuilder assemBuilder = domain.DefineDynamicAssembly (
  aname, AssemblyBuilderAccess.RunAndSave);

ModuleBuilder modBuilder = assemBuilder.DefineDynamicModule (
  "MainModule", "MyEmissions.dll");

TypeBuilder tb = modBuilder.DefineType ("Widget", TypeAttributes.Public);
```

Emitting Methods

You can specify a return type and parameter types when calling DefineMethod, in the same manner as when instantiating a DynamicMethod. For instance, the following method:

```
public static double SquareRoot (double value)
{
  return Math.Sqrt (value);
}
```

can be generated like this:

```
MethodBuilder mb = tb.DefineMethod ("SquareRoot",
  MethodAttributes.Static | MethodAttributes.Public,
  CallingConventions.Standard,
  typeof (double),                  // Return type
  new[] { typeof (double) } );      // Parameter types

mb.DefineParameter (1, ParameterAttributes.None, "value");  // Assign name

ILGenerator gen = mb.GetILGenerator();
gen.Emit (OpCodes.Ldarg_0);                                  // Load 1st arg
gen.Emit (OpCodes.Call, typeof(Math).GetMethod ("Sqrt"));
gen.Emit (OpCodes.Ret);

Type realType = tb.CreateType();
double x = (double) tb.GetMethod ("SquareRoot").Invoke (null,
                                          new object[] { 10.0 });
Console.WriteLine (x);    // 3.16227766016838
```

Calling DefineParameter is optional and is typically done to assign the parameter a name. The number 1 refers to the first parameter (0 refers to the return value). If you call DefineParameter, the parameter is implicitly named __p1, __p2, and so on. Assigning names makes sense if you will write the assembly to disk; it makes your methods friendly to consumers.

> DefineParameter returns a ParameterBuilder object upon which you can call SetCustomAttribute to attach attributes (see "Attaching Attributes" on page 834 later in this chapter).

To emit pass-by-reference parameters, such as in the following C# method:

```
public static void SquareRoot (ref double value)
{
  value = Math.Sqrt (value);
}
```

call MakeByRefType on the parameter type(s):

```
MethodBuilder mb = tb.DefineMethod ("SquareRoot",
  MethodAttributes.Static | MethodAttributes.Public,
  CallingConventions.Standard,
  null,
  new Type[] { typeof (double).MakeByRefType() } );

mb.DefineParameter (1, ParameterAttributes.None, "value");

ILGenerator gen = mb.GetILGenerator();
gen.Emit (OpCodes.Ldarg_0);
gen.Emit (OpCodes.Ldarg_0);
gen.Emit (OpCodes.Ldind_R8);
gen.Emit (OpCodes.Call, typeof (Math).GetMethod ("Sqrt"));
gen.Emit (OpCodes.Stind_R8);
gen.Emit (OpCodes.Ret);

Type realType = tb.CreateType();
object[] args = { 10.0 };
tb.GetMethod ("SquareRoot").Invoke (null, args);
Console.WriteLine (args[0]);                    // 3.16227766016838
```

The opcodes here were copied from a disassembled C# method. Notice the difference in semantics for accessing parameters passed by reference: Ldind and Stind mean "load indirectly" and "store indirectly," respectively. The R8 suffix means an 8-byte floating-point number.

The process for emitting out parameters is identical, except that you call Define Parameter as follows:

```
mb.DefineParameter (1, ParameterAttributes.Out, "value");
```

Generating instance methods

To generate an instance method, specify MethodAttributes.Instance when calling DefineMethod:

```
MethodBuilder mb = tb.DefineMethod ("SquareRoot",
  MethodAttributes.Instance | MethodAttributes.Public
  ...
```

With instance methods, argument zero is implicitly this; the remaining arguments start at 1. So, Ldarg_0 loads this onto the evaluation stack; Ldarg_1 loads the first real method argument.

Overriding methods

Overriding a virtual method in a base class is easy: simply define a method with an identical name, signature and return type, specifying `MethodAttributes.Virtual` when calling `DefineMethod`. The same applies when implementing interface methods.

`TypeBuilder` also exposes a method called `DefineMethodOverride` that overrides a method with a different name. This makes sense only with explicit interface implementation; in other scenarios, use `DefineMethod`.

HideBySig

If you're subclassing another type, it's nearly always worth specifying `MethodAttributes.HideBySig` when defining methods. `HideBySig` ensures that C#-style method hiding semantics are applied, which is that a base method is hidden only if a subtype defines a method with an identical *signature*. Without `HideBySig`, method hiding considers only the *name*, so `Foo(string)` in the subtype will hide `Foo()` in the base type, which is generally undesirable.

Emitting Fields and Properties

To create a field, you call `DefineField` on a `TypeBuilder`, telling it the desired field name, type, and visibility. The following creates a private integer field called "length":

```
FieldBuilder field = tb.DefineField ("length", typeof (int),
                               FieldAttributes.Private);
```

Creating a property or indexer requires a few more steps. First, call `DefineProperty` on a `TypeBuilder`, telling it the name and type of the property:

```
PropertyBuilder prop = tb.DefineProperty (
                "Text",                     // Name of property
                PropertyAttributes.None,
                typeof (string),            // Property type
                new Type[0]                 // Indexer types
          );
```

(If you're writing an indexer, the final argument is an array of indexer types.) Note that we haven't specified the property visibility: this is done individually on the accessor methods.

The next step is to write the get and set methods. By convention, their names are prefixed with "get_" or "set_". You then attach them to the property by calling Set GetMethod and SetSetMethod on the `PropertyBuilder`.

To give a complete example, we'll take the following field and property declaration:

```
string _text;
public string Text
{
  get           { return _text; }
```

```
      internal set { _text = value; }
  }
```

and generate it dynamically:

```
FieldBuilder field = tb.DefineField ("_text", typeof (string),
                                     FieldAttributes.Private);
PropertyBuilder prop = tb.DefineProperty (
                        "Text",                    // Name of property
                        PropertyAttributes.None,
                        typeof (string),           // Property type
                        new Type[0]);              // Indexer types

MethodBuilder getter = tb.DefineMethod (
  "get_Text",                                      // Method name
  MethodAttributes.Public | MethodAttributes.SpecialName,
  typeof (string),                                 // Return type
  new Type[0]);                                    // Parameter types

ILGenerator getGen = getter.GetILGenerator();
getGen.Emit (OpCodes.Ldarg_0);         // Load "this" onto eval stack
getGen.Emit (OpCodes.Ldfld, field);    // Load field value onto eval stack
getGen.Emit (OpCodes.Ret);             // Return

MethodBuilder setter = tb.DefineMethod (
  "set_Text",
  MethodAttributes.Assembly | MethodAttributes.SpecialName,
  null,                                            // Return type
  new Type[] { typeof (string) } );                // Parameter types

ILGenerator setGen = setter.GetILGenerator();
setGen.Emit (OpCodes.Ldarg_0);         // Load "this" onto eval stack
setGen.Emit (OpCodes.Ldarg_1);         // Load 2nd arg, i.e., value
setGen.Emit (OpCodes.Stfld, field);    // Store value into field
setGen.Emit (OpCodes.Ret);             // return

prop.SetGetMethod (getter);            // Link the get method and property
prop.SetSetMethod (setter);            // Link the set method and property
```

We can test the property as follows:

```
Type t = tb.CreateType();
object o = Activator.CreateInstance (t);
t.GetProperty ("Text").SetValue (o, "Good emissions!", new object[0]);
string text = (string) t.GetProperty ("Text").GetValue (o, null);

Console.WriteLine (text);              // Good emissions!
```

Notice that in defining the accessor MethodAttributes, we included SpecialName.
This instructs compilers to disallow direct binding to these methods when statically
referencing the assembly. It also ensures that the accessors are handled appropriately by reflection tools and Visual Studio's IntelliSense.

You can emit events in a similar manner, by calling DefineE
vent on a TypeBuilder. You then write explicit event accessor
methods and attach them to the EventBuilder by calling
SetAddOnMethod and SetRemoveOnMethod.

Emitting Constructors

You can define your own constructors by calling DefineConstructor on a type
builder. You're not obliged to do so—a default parameterless constructor is provided
automatically if you don't. The default constructor calls the base class constructor if
subtyping, just like in C#. Defining one or more constructors displaces this default
constructor.

If you need to initialize fields, the constructor's a good spot. In fact, it's the only
spot: C#'s field initializers don't have special CLR support—they are simply a syntactic shortcut for assigning values to fields in the constructor.

So, to reproduce this:

```
class Widget
{
  int _capacity = 4000;
}
```

you would define a constructor as follows:

```
FieldBuilder field = tb.DefineField ("_capacity", typeof (int),
                                     FieldAttributes.Private);
ConstructorBuilder c = tb.DefineConstructor (
  MethodAttributes.Public,
  CallingConventions.Standard,
  new Type[0]);                    // Constructor parameters

ILGenerator gen = c.GetILGenerator();

gen.Emit (OpCodes.Ldarg_0);           // Load "this" onto eval stack
gen.Emit (OpCodes.Ldc_I4, 4000);      // Load 4000 onto eval stack
gen.Emit (OpCodes.Stfld, field);      // Store it to our field
gen.Emit (OpCodes.Ret);
```

Calling base constructors

If subclassing another type, the constructor we just wrote would *circumvent the base
class constructor*. This is unlike C#, where the base class constructor is always called,
whether directly or indirectly. For instance, given the following code:

```
class A    { public A() { Console.Write ("A"); } }
class B : A { public B() {} }
```

the compiler, in effect, will translate the second line into this:

```
class B : A { public B() : base() {} }
```

This is not the case when generating IL: you must explicitly call the base constructor if you want it to execute (which nearly always, you do). Assuming the base class is called A, here's how to do it:

```
gen.Emit (OpCodes.Ldarg_0);
ConstructorInfo baseConstr = typeof (A).GetConstructor (new Type[0]);
gen.Emit (OpCodes.Call, baseConstr);
```

Calling constructors with arguments is just the same as with methods.

Attaching Attributes

You can attach custom attributes to a dynamic construct by calling SetCustomAttri bute with a CustomAttributeBuilder. For example, suppose we want to attach the following attribute declaration to a field or property:

```
[XmlElement ("FirstName", Namespace="http://test/", Order=3)]
```

This relies on the XmlElementAttribute constructor that accepts a single string. To use CustomAttributeBuilder, we must retrieve this constructor, as well as the two additional properties we wish to set (Namespace and Order):

```
Type attType = typeof (XmlElementAttribute);

ConstructorInfo attConstructor = attType.GetConstructor (
  new Type[] { typeof (string) } );

var att = new CustomAttributeBuilder (
  attConstructor,                         // Constructor
  new object[] { "FirstName" },           // Constructor arguments
  new PropertyInfo[]
  {
    attType.GetProperty ("Namespace"),    // Properties
    attType.GetProperty ("Order")
  },
  new object[] { "http://test/", 3 }      // Property values
);

myFieldBuilder.SetCustomAttribute (att);
// or propBuilder.SetCustomAttribute (att);
// or typeBuilder.SetCustomAttribute (att);  etc
```

Emitting Generic Methods and Types

All the examples in this section assume that modBuilder has been instantiated as follows:

```
AppDomain domain = AppDomain.CurrentDomain;
AssemblyName aname = new AssemblyName ("MyEmissions");

AssemblyBuilder assemBuilder = domain.DefineDynamicAssembly (
  aname, AssemblyBuilderAccess.RunAndSave);
```

```
ModuleBuilder modBuilder = assemBuilder.DefineDynamicModule (
  "MainModule", "MyEmissions.dll");
```

Defining Generic Methods

To emit a generic method:

1. Call `DefineGenericParameters` on a `MethodBuilder` to obtain an array of `GenericTypeParameterBuilder` objects.
2. Call `SetSignature` on a `MethodBuilder` using these generic type parameters.
3. Optionally, name the parameters as you would otherwise.

For example, the following generic method:

```
public static T Echo<T> (T value)
{
  return value;
}
```

can be emitted like this:

```
TypeBuilder tb = modBuilder.DefineType ("Widget", TypeAttributes.Public);

MethodBuilder mb = tb.DefineMethod ("Echo", MethodAttributes.Public |
                                            MethodAttributes.Static);
GenericTypeParameterBuilder[] genericParams
  = mb.DefineGenericParameters ("T");

mb.SetSignature (genericParams[0],      // Return type
                 null, null,
                 genericParams,         // Parameter types
                 null, null);

mb.DefineParameter (1, ParameterAttributes.None, "value");   // Optional

ILGenerator gen = mb.GetILGenerator();
gen.Emit (OpCodes.Ldarg_0);
gen.Emit (OpCodes.Ret);
```

The `DefineGenericParameters` method accepts any number of string arguments—these correspond to the desired generic type names. In this example, we needed just one generic type called T. `GenericTypeParameterBuilder` is based on `System.Type`, so it can be used in place of a `TypeBuilder` when emitting opcodes.

`GenericTypeParameterBuilder` also lets you specify a base type constraint:

```
genericParams[0].SetBaseTypeConstraint (typeof (Foo));
```

and interface constraints:

```
genericParams[0].SetInterfaceConstraints (typeof (IComparable));
```

To replicate this:

```
public static T Echo<T> (T value) where T : IComparable<T>
```

you would write:

```
genericParams[0].SetInterfaceConstraints (
  typeof (IComparable<>).MakeGenericType (genericParams[0]) );
```

For other kinds of constraints, call SetGenericParameterAttributes. This accepts a member of the GenericParameterAttributes enum, which includes the following values:

```
DefaultConstructorConstraint
NotNullableValueTypeConstraint
ReferenceTypeConstraint
Covariant
Contravariant
```

The last two are equivalent to applying the out and in modifiers to the type parameters.

Defining Generic Types

You can define generic types in a similar fashion. The difference is that you call DefineGenericParameters on the TypeBuilder rather than the MethodBuilder. So, to reproduce this:

```
public class Widget<T>
{
  public T Value;
}
```

you would do the following:

```
TypeBuilder tb = modBuilder.DefineType ("Widget", TypeAttributes.Public);

GenericTypeParameterBuilder[] genericParams
  = tb.DefineGenericParameters ("T");

tb.DefineField ("Value", genericParams[0], FieldAttributes.Public);
```

Generic constraints can be added just as with a method.

Awkward Emission Targets

All the examples in this section assume that a modBuilder has been instantiated as in previous sections.

Uncreated Closed Generics

Suppose you want to emit a method that uses a closed generic type:

```
public class Widget
{
  public static void Test() { var list = new List<int>(); }
}
```

The process is fairly straightforward:

```
TypeBuilder tb = modBuilder.DefineType ("Widget", TypeAttributes.Public);

MethodBuilder mb = tb.DefineMethod ("Test", MethodAttributes.Public |
                                            MethodAttributes.Static);
ILGenerator gen = mb.GetILGenerator();

Type variableType = typeof (List<int>);

ConstructorInfo ci = variableType.GetConstructor (new Type[0]);

LocalBuilder listVar = gen.DeclareLocal (variableType);
gen.Emit (OpCodes.Newobj, ci);
gen.Emit (OpCodes.Stloc, listVar);
gen.Emit (OpCodes.Ret);
```

Now suppose that instead of a list of integers, we want a list of widgets:

```
public class Widget
{
  public static void Test() { var list = new List<Widget>(); }
}
```

In theory, this is a simple modification; all we do is replace this line:

```
Type variableType = typeof (List<int>);
```

with this:

```
Type variableType = typeof (List<>).MakeGenericType (tb);
```

Unfortunately, this causes a NotSupportedException to be thrown when we then call GetConstructor. The problem is that you cannot call GetConstructor on a generic type closed with an uncreated type builder. The same goes for GetField and GetMethod.

The solution is unintuitive. TypeBuilder provides three static methods as follows:

```
public static ConstructorInfo GetConstructor (Type, ConstructorInfo);
public static FieldInfo       GetField       (Type, FieldInfo);
public static MethodInfo      GetMethod      (Type, MethodInfo);
```

Although it doesn't appear so, these methods exist specifically to obtain members of generic types closed with uncreated type builders! The first parameter is the closed generic type; the second parameter is the member you want on the *unbound* generic type. Here's the corrected version of our example:

```
MethodBuilder mb = tb.DefineMethod ("Test", MethodAttributes.Public |
                                            MethodAttributes.Static);
ILGenerator gen = mb.GetILGenerator();

Type variableType = typeof (List<>).MakeGenericType (tb);

ConstructorInfo unbound = typeof (List<>).GetConstructor (new Type[0]);
ConstructorInfo ci = TypeBuilder.GetConstructor (variableType, unbound);

LocalBuilder listVar = gen.DeclareLocal (variableType);
gen.Emit (OpCodes.Newobj, ci);
```

```
gen.Emit (OpCodes.Stloc, listVar);
gen.Emit (OpCodes.Ret);
```

Circular Dependencies

Suppose you want to build two types that reference each other. For instance:

```
class A { public B Bee; }
class B { public A Aye; }
```

You can generate this dynamically as follows:

```
var publicAtt = FieldAttributes.Public;

TypeBuilder aBuilder = modBuilder.DefineType ("A");
TypeBuilder bBuilder = modBuilder.DefineType ("B");

FieldBuilder bee = aBuilder.DefineField ("Bee", bBuilder, publicAtt);
FieldBuilder aye = bBuilder.DefineField ("Aye", aBuilder, publicAtt);

Type realA = aBuilder.CreateType();
Type realB = bBuilder.CreateType();
```

Notice that we didn't call CreateType on aBuilder or bBuilder until we populated both objects. The principle is: first hook everything up, and then call CreateType on each type builder.

Interestingly, the realA type is valid but *dysfunctional* until you call CreateType on bBuilder. (If you started using aBuilder prior to this, an exception would be thrown when you tried to access field Bee.)

You might wonder how bBuilder knows to "fix up" realA after creating realB. The answer is that it doesn't: realA can fix *itself* the next time it's used. This is possible because after calling CreateType, a TypeBuilder morphs into a proxy for the real runtime type. So, realA, with its references to bBuilder, can easily obtain the metadata it needs for the upgrade.

This system works when the type builder demands simple information of the unconstructed type—information that can be *predetermined*—such as type, member, and object references. In creating realA, the type builder doesn't need to know, for instance, how many bytes realB will eventually occupy in memory. This is just as well, because realB has not yet been created! But now imagine that realB was a struct. The final size of realB is now critical information in creating realA.

If the relationship is noncyclical—for instance:

```
struct A { public B Bee; }
struct B {                 }
```

you can solve this by first creating struct B, and then struct A. But consider this:

```
struct A { public B Bee; }
struct B { public A Aye; }
```

We won't try to emit this because it's nonsensical to have two structs contain each other (C# generates a compile-time error if you try). But the following variation is both legal and useful:

```
public struct S<T> { ... }    // S can be empty and this demo will work.

class A { S<B> Bee; }
class B { S<A> Aye; }
```

In creating A, a `TypeBuilder` now needs to know the memory footprint of B, and vice versa. To illustrate, we'll assume that struct S is defined statically. Here's the code to emit classes A and B:

```
var pub = FieldAttributes.Public;

TypeBuilder aBuilder = modBuilder.DefineType ("A");
TypeBuilder bBuilder = modBuilder.DefineType ("B");

aBuilder.DefineField ("Bee", typeof(S<>).MakeGenericType (bBuilder), pub);
bBuilder.DefineField ("Aye", typeof(S<>).MakeGenericType (aBuilder), pub);

Type realA = aBuilder.CreateType();    // Error: cannot load type B
Type realB = bBuilder.CreateType();
```

`CreateType` now throws a `TypeLoadException` no matter in which order you go:

- Call `aBuilder.CreateType` first and it says "cannot load type B".
- Call `bBuilder.CreateType` first and it says "cannot load type A"!

You'll run into this problem if you emit typed LINQ to SQL `DataContexts` dynamically. The generic `EntityRef` type is a struct, equivalent to S in our examples. The circular reference happens when two tables in the database link to each other through reciprocal parent/child relationships.

To solve this, you must allow the type builder to create `realB` partway through creating `realA`. This is done by handling the `TypeResolve` event on the current application domain just before calling `CreateType`. So, in our example, we replace the last two lines with this:

```
TypeBuilder[] uncreatedTypes = { aBuilder, bBuilder };

ResolveEventHandler handler = delegate (object o, ResolveEventArgs args)
{
  var type = uncreatedTypes.FirstOrDefault (t => t.FullName == args.Name);
  return type == null ? null : type.CreateType().Assembly;
};

AppDomain.CurrentDomain.TypeResolve += handler;

Type realA = aBuilder.CreateType();
Type realB = bBuilder.CreateType();
```

```
AppDomain.CurrentDomain.TypeResolve -= handler;
```

The TypeResolve event fires during the call to aBuilder.CreateType, at the point when it needs you to call CreateType on bBuilder.

Handling the TypeResolve event as in this example is also necessary when defining a nested type, when the nested and parent types refer to each other.

Parsing IL

You can obtain information about the content of an existing method by calling Get MethodBody on a MethodBase object. This returns a MethodBody object that has properties for inspecting a method's local variables, exception handling clauses, stack size—as well as the raw IL. Rather like the reverse of Reflection.Emit!

Inspecting a method's raw IL can be useful in profiling code. A simple use would be to determine which methods in an assembly have changed, when an assembly is updated.

To illustrate parsing IL, we'll write an application that disassembles IL in the style of *ildasm*. This could be used as the starting point for a code analysis tool or a higher-level language disassembler.

Remember that in the reflection API, all of C#'s functional constructs are either represented by a MethodBase subtype or (in the case of properties, events, and indexers) have Method Base objects attached to them.

Writing a Disassembler

You can download the source code for this at *http://www.alba hari.com/nutshell/*.

Here is a sample of the output our disassembler will produce:

```
IL_00EB:  ldfld      Disassembler._pos
IL_00F0:  ldloc.2
IL_00F1:  add
IL_00F2:  ldelema    System.Byte
IL_00F7:  ldstr      "Hello world"
IL_00FC:  call       System.Byte.ToString
IL_0101:  ldstr      " "
IL_0106:  call       System.String.Concat
```

To obtain this output, we must parse the binary tokens that make up the IL. The first step is to call the GetILAsByteArray method on MethodBody to obtain the IL as a byte array. In order to make the rest of the job easier, we will write this into a class as follows:

```
public class Disassembler
{
  public static string Disassemble (MethodBase method)
    => new Disassembler (method).Dis();

  StringBuilder _output;     // The result to which we'll keep appending
  Module _module;            // This will come in handy later
  byte[] _il;                // The raw byte code
  int _pos;                  // The position we're up to in the byte code

  Disassembler (MethodBase method)
  {
    _module = method.DeclaringType.Module;
    _il = method.GetMethodBody().GetILAsByteArray();
  }

  string Dis()
  {
    _output = new StringBuilder();
    while (_pos < _il.Length) DisassembleNextInstruction();
    return _output.ToString();
  }
}
```

The static `Disassemble` method will be the only public member of this class. All other members will be private to the disassembly process. The `Dis` method contains the "main" loop where we process each instruction.

With this skeleton in place, all that remains is to write `DisassembleNextInstruction`. But before doing so, it will help to load all the opcodes into a static dictionary so we can access them by their 8- or 16-bit value. The easiest way to accomplish this is to use reflection to retrieve all the static fields whose type is `OpCode` in the `OpCodes` class:

```
static Dictionary<short,OpCode> _opcodes = new Dictionary<short,OpCode>();

static Disassembler()
{
  Dictionary<short, OpCode> opcodes = new Dictionary<short, OpCode>();
    foreach (FieldInfo fi in typeof (OpCodes).GetFields
                           (BindingFlags.Public | BindingFlags.Static))
      if (typeof (OpCode).IsAssignableFrom (fi.FieldType))
      {
        OpCode code = (OpCode) fi.GetValue (null);   // Get field's value
        if (code.OpCodeType != OpCodeType.Nternal)
          _opcodes.Add (code.Value, code);
      }
}
```

We've written it in a static constructor so that it executes just once.

Now we can write `DisassembleNextInstruction`. Each IL instruction consists of a 1- or 2-byte opcode, followed by an operand of zero, 1, 2, 4, or 8 bytes. (An excep-

tion is inline switch opcodes, which are followed by a variable number of operands).
So, we read the opcode, then the operand and then write out the result:

```
void DisassembleNextInstruction()
{
  int opStart = _pos;

  OpCode code = ReadOpCode();
  string operand = ReadOperand (code);

  _output.AppendFormat ("IL_{0:X4}:  {1,-12} {2}",
                        opStart, code.Name, operand);
  _output.AppendLine();
}
```

To read an opcode, we advance one byte and see whether we have a valid instruction. If not, we advance another byte and look for a 2-byte instruction:

```
OpCode ReadOpCode()
{
  byte byteCode = _il [_pos++];
  if (_opcodes.ContainsKey (byteCode)) return _opcodes [byteCode];

  if (_pos == _il.Length)  throw new Exception ("Unexpected end of IL");

  short shortCode = (short) (byteCode * 256 + _il [_pos++]);

  if (!_opcodes.ContainsKey (shortCode))
    throw new Exception ("Cannot find opcode " + shortCode);

  return _opcodes [shortCode];
}
```

To read an operand, we first must establish its length. We can do this based on the
operand type. Because most are 4 bytes long, we can filter out the exceptions fairly
easily in a conditional clause.

The next step is to call FormatOperand, which will attempt to format the operand:

```
string ReadOperand (OpCode c)
{
  int operandLength =
    c.OperandType == OperandType.InlineNone
      ? 0 :
    c.OperandType == OperandType.ShortInlineBrTarget ||
    c.OperandType == OperandType.ShortInlineI ||
    c.OperandType == OperandType.ShortInlineVar
      ? 1 :
    c.OperandType == OperandType.InlineVar
      ? 2 :
    c.OperandType == OperandType.InlineI8 ||
    c.OperandType == OperandType.InlineR
      ? 8 :
    c.OperandType == OperandType.InlineSwitch
      ? 4 * (BitConverter.ToInt32 (_il, _pos) + 1) :
      4;  // All others are 4 bytes
```

```
    if (_pos + operandLength > _il.Length)
      throw new Exception ("Unexpected end of IL");

    string result = FormatOperand (c, operandLength);
    if (result == null)
    {                           // Write out operand bytes in hex
      result = "";
      for (int i = 0; i < operandLength; i++)
        result += _il [_pos + i].ToString ("X2") + " ";
    }
    _pos += operandLength;
    return result;
  }
```

If the result of calling FormatOperand is null, it means the operand needs no special formatting, so we simply write it out in hexadecimal. We could test the disassembler at this point by writing a FormatOperand method that always returns null.
Here's what the output would look like:

```
IL_00A8:  ldfld      98 00 00 04
IL_00AD:  ldloc.2
IL_00AE:  add
IL_00AF:  ldelema    64 00 00 01
IL_00B4:  ldstr      26 04 00 70
IL_00B9:  call       B6 00 00 0A
IL_00BE:  ldstr      11 01 00 70
IL_00C3:  call       91 00 00 0A
    ...
```

Although the opcodes are correct, the operands are not much use. Instead of hexadecimal numbers, we want member names and strings. The FormatOperand
method, once written, will address this—identifying the special cases that benefit
from such formatting. These comprise most 4-byte operands and the short branch
instructions:

```
string FormatOperand (OpCode c, int operandLength)
{
  if (operandLength == 0) return "";

  if (operandLength == 4)
    return Get4ByteOperand (c);
  else if (c.OperandType == OperandType.ShortInlineBrTarget)
    return GetShortRelativeTarget();
  else if (c.OperandType == OperandType.InlineSwitch)
    return GetSwitchTarget (operandLength);
  else
    return null;
}
```

There are three kinds of 4-byte operands that we treat specially. The first is references to members or types—with these, we extract the member or type name by
calling the defining module's ResolveMember method. The second case is strings—
these are stored in the assembly module's metadata and can be retrieved by calling

ResolveString. The final case is branch targets, where the operand refers to a byte offset in the IL. We format these by working out the absolute address *after* the current instruction (+ 4 bytes):

```
string Get4ByteOperand (OpCode c)
{
  int intOp = BitConverter.ToInt32 (_il, _pos);

  switch (c.OperandType)
  {
    case OperandType.InlineTok:
    case OperandType.InlineMethod:
    case OperandType.InlineField:
    case OperandType.InlineType:
      MemberInfo mi;
      try   { mi = _module.ResolveMember (intOp); }
      catch { return null; }
      if (mi == null) return null;

      if (mi.ReflectedType != null)
        return mi.ReflectedType.FullName + "." + mi.Name;
      else if (mi is Type)
        return ((Type)mi).FullName;
      else
        return mi.Name;

    case OperandType.InlineString:
      string s = _module.ResolveString (intOp);
      if (s != null) s = "'" + s + "'";
      return s;

    case OperandType.InlineBrTarget:
      return "IL_" + (_pos + intOp + 4).ToString ("X4");

    default:
      return null;
  }
}
```

 The point where we call ResolveMember is a good window for a code analysis tool that reports on method dependencies.

For any other 4-byte opcode, we return null (this will cause ReadOperand to format the operand as hex digits).

The final kinds of operand that need special attention are short branch targets and inline switches. A short branch target describes the destination offset as a single signed byte, as at the end of the current instruction (i.e., + 1 byte). A switch target is followed by a variable number of 4-byte branch destinations:

```
string GetShortRelativeTarget()
{
  int absoluteTarget = _pos + (sbyte) _il [_pos] + 1;
  return "IL_" + absoluteTarget.ToString ("X4");
```

```
}

string GetSwitchTarget (int operandLength)
{
  int targetCount = BitConverter.ToInt32 (_il, _pos);
  string [] targets = new string [targetCount];
  for (int i = 0; i < targetCount; i++)
  {
    int ilTarget = BitConverter.ToInt32 (_il, _pos + (i + 1) * 4);
    targets [i] = "IL_" + (_pos + ilTarget + operandLength).ToString ("X4");
  }
  return "(" + string.Join (", ", targets) + ")";
}
```

This completes the disassembler. We can test it by disassembling one of its own methods:

```
MethodInfo mi = typeof (Disassembler).GetMethod (
  "ReadOperand", BindingFlags.Instance | BindingFlags.NonPublic);

Console.WriteLine (Disassembler.Disassemble (mi));
```

20

Dynamic Programming

In Chapter 4, we explained how dynamic binding works in the C# language. In this chapter, we look briefly at the DLR and then explore the following dynamic programming patterns:

- Numeric type unification

- Dynamic member overload resolution

- Custom binding (implementing dynamic objects)

- Dynamic language interoperability

In Chapter 25, we'll describe how dynamic can improve COM interoperability.

The types in this chapter live in the System.Dynamic namespace, except for Call Site<>, which lives in System.Runtime.CompilerServices.

The Dynamic Language Runtime

C# relies on the *dynamic language runtime* (DLR) to perform dynamic binding.

Contrary to its name, the DLR is not a dynamic version of the CLR. Rather, it's a library that sits atop the CLR—just like any other library such as *System.Xml.dll*. Its primary role is to provide runtime services to *unify* dynamic programming—in both statically and dynamically typed languages. Hence languages such as C#, VB, IronPython, and IronRuby all use the same protocol for calling functions dynamically. This allows them to share libraries and call code written in other languages.

The DLR also makes it relatively easy to write new dynamic languages in .NET. Instead of having to emit IL, dynamic language authors work at the level of *expression trees* (the same expression trees in System.Linq.Expressions that we talked about in Chapter 8).

The DLR further ensures that all consumers get the benefit of *call-site caching*, an optimization whereby the DLR avoids unnecessarily repeating the potentially expensive member resolution decisions made during dynamic binding.

 Framework 4.0 was the first Framework version to ship with the DLR. Prior to that, the DLR existed as a separate download on Codeplex. That site still contains some additional useful resources for language developers.

What Are Call Sites?

When the compiler encounters a dynamic expression, it has no idea who will evaluate that expression at runtime. For instance, consider the following method:

```
public dynamic Foo (dynamic x, dynamic y)
{
  return x / y;   // Dynamic expression
}
```

The x and y variables could be any CLR object, a COM object, or even an object hosted in a dynamic language. The compiler cannot, therefore, take its usual static approach of emitting a call to a known method of a known type. Instead, the compiler emits code that eventually results in an expression tree that describes the operation, managed by a *call site* that the DLR will bind at runtime. The call site essentially acts as an intermediary between caller and callee.

A call site is represented by the CallSite<> class in *System.Core.dll*. We can see this by disassembling the preceding method—the result is something like this:

```
static CallSite<Func<CallSite,object,object,object>> divideSite;

[return: Dynamic]
public object Foo ([Dynamic] object x, [Dynamic] object y)
{
  if (divideSite == null)
    divideSite =
      CallSite<Func<CallSite,object,object,object>>.Create (
        Microsoft.CSharp.RuntimeBinder.Binder.BinaryOperation (
          CSharpBinderFlags.None,
          ExpressionType.Divide,
          /* Remaining arguments omitted for brevity */ ));

  return divideSite.Target (divideSite, x, y);
}
```

As you can see, the call site is cached in a static field to avoid the cost of re-creating it on each call. The DLR further caches the result of the binding phase and the actual method targets. (There may be multiple targets depending on the types of x and y.)

The actual dynamic call then happens by calling the site's `Target` (a delegate), passing in the x and y operands.

Notice that the `Binder` class is specific to C#. Every language with support for dynamic binding provides a language-specific binder to help the DLR interpret expressions in a manner specific to that language, so as not to surprise the programmer. For instance, if we called `Foo` with integer values of 5 and 2, the C# binder would ensure that we got back 2. In contrast, a VB.NET binder would give us 2.5.

Numeric Type Unification

We saw in Chapter 4 how `dynamic` lets us write a single method that works across all numeric types:

```
static dynamic Mean (dynamic x, dynamic y) => (x + y) / 2;

static void Main()
{
  int x = 3, y = 5;
  Console.WriteLine (Mean (x, y));
}
```

 It's a humorous reflection on C# that the keywords `static` and `dynamic` can appear adjacently! The same applies to the keywords `internal` and `extern`.

However, this (unnecessarily) sacrifices static type safety. The following compiles without error, but then fails at runtime:

```
string s = Mean (3, 5);   // Runtime error!
```

We can fix this by introducing a generic type parameter, and then casting to `dynamic` within the calculation itself:

```
static T Mean<T> (T x, T y)
{
  dynamic result = ((dynamic) x + y) / 2;
  return (T) result;
}
```

Notice that we *explicitly* cast the result back to T. If we omitted this cast, we'd be relying on an implicit cast, which might at first appear to work correctly. The implicit cast would fail at runtime, though, upon calling the method with an 8- or 16-bit integral type. To understand why, consider what happens with ordinary static typing when you sum two 8-bit numbers together:

```
byte b = 3;
Console.WriteLine ((b + b).GetType().Name);  // Int32
```

We get an `Int32`—because the compiler "promotes" 8- or 16-bit numbers to `Int32` prior to performing arithmetic operations. For consistency, the C# binder tells the DLR to do exactly the same thing, and we end up with an `Int32` that requires an explicit cast to the smaller numeric type. Of course, this could create the possibility of overflow if we were, say, summing rather than averaging the values.

Dynamic binding incurs a small performance hit—even with call-site caching. You can mitigate this by adding statically typed overloads that cover just the most commonly used types. For example, if subsequent performance profiling showed that calling Mean with doubles was a bottleneck, you could add the following overload:

```
static double Mean (double x, double y) => (x + y) / 2;
```

The compiler will favor that overload when Mean is called with arguments that are known at compile time to be of type double.

Dynamic Member Overload Resolution

Calling a statically known method with dynamically typed arguments defers member overload resolution from compile time to runtime. This is useful in simplifying certain programming tasks—such as simplifying the *Visitor* design pattern. It's also useful in working around limitations imposed by C#'s static typing.

Simplifying the Visitor Pattern

In essence, the Visitor pattern allows you to "add" a method to a class hierarchy without altering existing classes. Although useful, this pattern in its static incarnation is subtle and unintuitive compared to most other design patterns. It also requires that visited classes be made "Visitor-friendly" by exposing an Accept method, which can be impossible if the classes are not under your control.

With dynamic binding, you can achieve the same goal more easily—and without needing to modify existing classes. To illustrate, consider the following class hierarchy:

```
class Person
{
  public string FirstName { get; set; }
  public string LastName  { get; set; }

  // The Friends collection may contain Customers & Employees:
  public readonly IList<Person> Friends = new Collection<Person> ();
}

class Customer : Person { public decimal CreditLimit { get; set; } }
class Employee : Person { public decimal Salary      { get; set; } }
```

Suppose we want to write a method that programmatically exports a Person's details to an XML XElement. The most obvious solution is to write a virtual method called ToXElement() in the Person class that returns an XElement populated with a Person's properties. We would then override it in Customer and Employee classes such that the XElement was also populated with CreditLimit and Salary. This pattern can be problematic, however, for two reasons:

- You might not own the `Person`, `Customer`, and `Employee` classes, making it impossible to add methods to them. (And extension methods wouldn't give polymorphic behavior.)
- The `Person`, `Customer`, and `Employee` classes might already be quite big. A frequent antipattern is the "god object," where a class such as `Person` attracts so much functionality that it becomes a nightmare to maintain. A good antidote is to avoid adding functions to `Person` that don't need to access `Person`'s private state. A `ToXElement` method might be an excellent candidate.

With dynamic member overload resolution, we can write the `ToXElement` functionality in a separate class, without resorting to ugly switches based on type:

```
class ToXElementPersonVisitor
{
  public XElement DynamicVisit (Person p) => Visit ((dynamic)p);

  XElement Visit (Person p)
  {
    return new XElement ("Person",
      new XAttribute ("Type", p.GetType().Name),
      new XElement ("FirstName", p.FirstName),
      new XElement ("LastName", p.LastName),
      p.Friends.Select (f => DynamicVisit (f))
    );
  }

  XElement Visit (Customer c)   // Specialized logic for customers
  {
    XElement xe = Visit ((Person)c);   // Call "base" method
    xe.Add (new XElement ("CreditLimit", c.CreditLimit));
    return xe;
  }

  XElement Visit (Employee e)   // Specialized logic for employees
  {
    XElement xe = Visit ((Person)e);   // Call "base" method
    xe.Add (new XElement ("Salary", e.Salary));
    return xe;
  }
}
```

The `DynamicVisit` method performs a dynamic dispatch—calling the most specific version of `Visit` as determined at runtime. Notice the line in boldface, where we call `DynamicVisit` on each person in the `Friends` collection. This ensures that if a friend is a `Customer` or `Employee`, the correct overload is called.

We can demonstrate this class as follows:

```
var cust = new Customer
{
  FirstName = "Joe", LastName = "Bloggs", CreditLimit = 123
};
```

```
cust.Friends.Add (
  new Employee { FirstName = "Sue", LastName = "Brown", Salary = 50000 }
);

Console.WriteLine (new ToXElementPersonVisitor().DynamicVisit (cust));
```

Here's the result:

```
<Person Type="Customer">
  <FirstName>Joe</FirstName>
  <LastName>Bloggs</LastName>
  <Person Type="Employee">
    <FirstName>Sue</FirstName>
    <LastName>Brown</LastName>
    <Salary>50000</Salary>
  </Person>
  <CreditLimit>123</CreditLimit>
</Person>
```

Variations

If you plan more than one visitor class, a useful variation is to define an abstract
base class for visitors:

```
abstract class PersonVisitor<T>
{
  public T DynamicVisit (Person p) { return Visit ((dynamic)p); }

  protected abstract T Visit (Person p);
  protected virtual T Visit (Customer c) { return Visit ((Person) c); }
  protected virtual T Visit (Employee e) { return Visit ((Person) e); }
}
```

Subclasses then don't need to define their own DynamicVisit method: all they do is
override the versions of Visit whose behavior they want to specialize. This also has
the advantages of centralizing the methods that encompass the Person hierarchy,
and allowing implementers to call base methods more naturally:

```
class ToXElementPersonVisitor : PersonVisitor<XElement>
{
  protected override XElement Visit (Person p)
  {
    return new XElement ("Person",
      new XAttribute ("Type", p.GetType().Name),
      new XElement ("FirstName", p.FirstName),
      new XElement ("LastName", p.LastName),
      p.Friends.Select (f => DynamicVisit (f))
    );
  }

  protected override XElement Visit (Customer c)
  {
    XElement xe = base.Visit (c);
    xe.Add (new XElement ("CreditLimit", c.CreditLimit));
    return xe;
```

```
    }

    protected override XElement Visit (Employee e)
    {
      XElement xe = base.Visit (e);
      xe.Add (new XElement ("Salary", e.Salary));
      return xe;
    }
}
```

You can even then subclass ToXElementPersonVisitor itself.

Multiple Dispatch

C# and the CLR have always supported a limited form of dynamism in the form of
virtual method calls. This differs from C#'s dynamic binding in that for virtual
method calls, the compiler must commit to a particular virtual member at compile
time—based on the name and signature of a member you called. This means that:

- The calling expression must be fully understood by the compiler (e.g., it must
  decide at compile time whether a target member is a field or property).

- Overload resolution must be completed entirely by the compiler, based on the
  compile-time argument types.

A consequence of that last point is that the ability to perform virtual method calls is
known as *single dispatch*. To see why, consider the following method call (where
Walk is a virtual method):

```
animal.Walk (owner);
```

The runtime decision of whether to invoke a dog's Walk method or a cat's Walk
method depends only on the type of the *receiver*, animal (hence "single"). If many
overloads of Walk accept different kinds of owner, an overload will be selected at
compile time without regard to the actual runtime type of the owner object. In other
words, only the runtime type of the *receiver* can vary which method gets called.

In contrast, a dynamic call defers overload resolution until runtime:

```
animal.Walk ((dynamic) owner);
```

The final choice of which Walk method to call now depends on the types of both
animal and owner—this is called *multiple dispatch* since the runtime types of arguments, in addition to the receiver type, contribute to the determination of which
Walk method to call.

Anonymously Calling Members of a Generic Type

The strictness of C#'s static typing is a two-edged sword. On the one hand, it enforces a degree of correctness at compile time. On the other hand, it occasionally
makes certain kinds of code difficult or impossible to express, at which point you

have to resort to reflection. In these situations, dynamic binding is a cleaner and faster alternative to reflection.

An example is when you need to work with an object of type G<T> where T is unknown. We can illustrate this by defining the following class:

```
public class Foo<T> { public T Value; }
```

Suppose we then write a method as follows:

```
static void Write (object obj)
{
  if (obj is Foo<>)                          // Illegal
    Console.WriteLine ((Foo<>) obj).Value);  // Illegal
}
```

This method won't compile: you can't invoke members of *unbound* generic types.

Dynamic binding offers two means by which we can work around this. The first is to access the Value member dynamically as follows:

```
static void Write (dynamic obj)
{
  try { Console.WriteLine (obj.Value); }
  catch (Microsoft.CSharp.RuntimeBinder.RuntimeBinderException) {...}
}
```

This has the (potential) advantage of working with any object that defines a Value field or property. However, there are a couple of problems. First, catching an exception in this manner is somewhat messy and inefficient (and there's no way to ask the DLR in advance, "Will this operation succeed?"). Second, this approach wouldn't work if Foo was an interface (say, IFoo<T>), and either of the following conditions was true:

- Value was implemented explicitly.

- The type that implemented IFoo<T> was inaccessible (more on this soon).

A better solution is to write an overloaded helper method called GetFooValue and to call it using *dynamic member overload resolution*:

```
static void Write (dynamic obj)
{
  object result = GetFooValue (obj);
  if (result != null) Console.WriteLine (result);
}

static T GetFooValue<T> (Foo<T> foo) { return foo.Value; }
static object GetFooValue (object foo) { return null; }
```

Notice that we overloaded GetFooValue to accept an object parameter, which acts as a fallback for any type. At runtime, the C# dynamic binder will pick the best overload when calling GetFooValue with a dynamic argument. If the object in question is not based on Foo<T>, it will choose the object-parameter overload instead of throwing an exception.

 An alternative is to write just the first GetFooValue overload, and then catch the RuntimeBinderException. The advantage is that it distinguishes the case of foo.Value being null. The disadvantage is that it incurs the performance overhead of throwing and catching an exception.

In Chapter 19, we solved the same problem with an interface using reflection—with a lot more effort (see "Anonymously Calling Members of a Generic Interface" on page 808). The example we used was to design a more powerful version of ToString() that could understand objects such as IEnumerable and IGrouping<,>. Here's the same example solved more elegantly with dynamic binding:

```
static string GetGroupKey<TKey,TElement> (IGrouping<TKey,TElement> group)
{
  return "Group with key=" + group.Key + ": ";
}

static string GetGroupKey (object source) { return null; }

public static string ToStringEx (object value)
{
  if (value == null) return "<null>";
  if (value is string) return (string) value;
  if (value.GetType().IsPrimitive) return value.ToString();

  StringBuilder sb = new StringBuilder();

  string groupKey = GetGroupKey ((dynamic)value);    // Dynamic dispatch
  if (groupKey != null) sb.Append (groupKey);

  if (value is IEnumerable)
    foreach (object element in ((IEnumerable)value))
      sb.Append (ToStringEx (element) + " ");

  if (sb.Length == 0) sb.Append (value.ToString());

  return "\r\n" + sb.ToString();
}
```

In action:

```
Console.WriteLine (ToStringEx ("xyyzzz".GroupBy (c => c) ));

Group with key=x: x
Group with key=y: y y
Group with key=z: z z z
```

Notice that we used dynamic *member overload resolution* to solve this problem. If we did the following instead:

```
dynamic d = value;
try { groupKey = d.Value); }
catch (Microsoft.CSharp.RuntimeBinder.RuntimeBinderException) {...}
```

it would fail, because LINQ's GroupBy operator returns a type implementing IGroup
ing<,> which itself is internal, and therefore inaccessible:

```
internal class Grouping : IGrouping<TKey,TElement>, ...
{
  public TKey Key;
  ...
}
```

Even though the Key property is declared public, its containing class caps it at
internal, making it accessible only via the IGrouping<,> interface. And as we
explained in Chapter 4, there's no way to tell the DLR to bind to that interface when
invoking the Value member dynamically.

Implementing Dynamic Objects

An object can provide its binding semantics by implementing IDynamicMetaObject
Provider—or more easily by subclassing DynamicObject, which provides a default
implementation of this interface. We demonstrated this briefly in Chapter 4, with
the following example:

```
static void Main()
{
  dynamic d = new Duck();
  d.Quack();              // Quack method was called
  d.Waddle();             // Waddle method was called
}

public class Duck : DynamicObject
{
  public override bool TryInvokeMember (
    InvokeMemberBinder binder, object[] args, out object result)
  {
    Console.WriteLine (binder.Name + " method was called");
    result = null;
    return true;
  }
}
```

DynamicObject

In the preceding example, we overrode TryInvokeMember, which allows the consumer to invoke a method on the dynamic object—such as a Quack or Waddle.
DynamicObject exposes other virtual methods that enable consumers to use other
programming constructs as well. The following correspond to constructs that have
representations in C#:

Method	Programming construct
TryInvokeMember	Method
TryGetMember, TrySetMember	Property or field
TryGetIndex, TrySetIndex	Indexer
TryUnaryOperation	Unary operator such as !
TryBinaryOperation	Binary operator such as ==
TryConvert	Conversion (cast) to another type
TryInvoke	Invocation on the object itself—e.g., d("foo")

These methods should return true if successful. If they return false, then the DLR will fall back to the language binder, looking for a matching member on the DynamicObject (subclass) itself. If this fails, then a RuntimeBinderException is thrown.

We can illustrate TryGetMember and TrySetMember with a class that lets us dynamically access an attribute in an XElement (System.Xml.Linq):

```
static class XExtensions
{
  public static dynamic DynamicAttributes (this XElement e)
    => new XWrapper (e);

  class XWrapper : DynamicObject
  {
    XElement _element;
    public XWrapper (XElement e) { _element = e; }

    public override bool TryGetMember (GetMemberBinder binder,
                                       out object result)
    {
      result = _element.Attribute (binder.Name).Value;
      return true;
    }

    public override bool TrySetMember (SetMemberBinder binder,
                                       object value)
    {
      _element.SetAttributeValue (binder.Name, value);
      return true;
    }
  }
}
```

Here's how to use it:

```
XElement x = XElement.Parse (@"<Label Text=""Hello"" Id=""5""/>");
dynamic da = x.DynamicAttributes();
Console.WriteLine (da.Id);         // 5
da.Text = "Foo";
Console.WriteLine (x.ToString());  // <Label Text="Foo" Id="5" />
```

The following does a similar thing for System.Data.IDataRecord, making it easier to use data readers:

```
public class DynamicReader : DynamicObject
{
  readonly IDataRecord _dataRecord;
  public DynamicReader (IDataRecord dr) { _dataRecord = dr; }

  public override bool TryGetMember (GetMemberBinder binder,
                                      out object result)
  {
    result = _dataRecord [binder.Name];
    return true;
  }
}
...
using (IDataReader reader = someDbCommand.ExecuteReader())
{
  dynamic dr = new DynamicReader (reader);
  while (reader.Read())
  {
    int id = dr.ID;
    string firstName = dr.FirstName;
    DateTime dob = dr.DateOfBirth;
    ...
  }
}
```

The following demonstrates TryBinaryOperation and TryInvoke:

```
static void Main()
{
  dynamic d = new Duck();
  Console.WriteLine (d + d);          // foo
  Console.WriteLine (d (78, 'x'));    // 123
}

public class Duck : DynamicObject
{
  public override bool TryBinaryOperation (BinaryOperationBinder binder,
                                            object arg, out object result)
  {
    Console.WriteLine (binder.Operation);   // Add
    result = "foo";
    return true;
  }

  public override bool TryInvoke (InvokeBinder binder,
                                  object[] args, out object result)
  {
    Console.WriteLine (args[0]);   // 78
    result = 123;
    return true;
  }
}
```

DynamicObject also exposes some virtual methods for the benefit of dynamic languages. In particular, overriding GetDynamicMemberNames allows you to return a list of all member names that your dynamic object provides.

> Another reason to implement GetDynamicMemberNames is that Visual Studio's debugger makes use of this method to display a view of a dynamic object.

ExpandoObject

Another simple application of DynamicObject would be to write a dynamic class that stored and retrieved objects in a dictionary, keyed by string. However, this functionality is already provided via the ExpandoObject class:

```
dynamic x = new ExpandoObject();
x.FavoriteColor = ConsoleColor.Green;
x.FavoriteNumber = 7;
Console.WriteLine (x.FavoriteColor);    // Green
Console.WriteLine (x.FavoriteNumber);   // 7
```

ExpandoObject implements IDictionary<string,object>—so we can continue our example and do this:

```
var dict = (IDictionary<string,object>) x;
Console.WriteLine (dict ["FavoriteColor"]);   // Green
Console.WriteLine (dict ["FavoriteNumber"]);  // 7
Console.WriteLine (dict.Count);               // 2
```

Interoperating with Dynamic Languages

Although C# supports dynamic binding via the dynamic keyword, it doesn't go as far as allowing you to execute an expression described in a string at runtime:

```
string expr = "2 * 3";
// We can't "execute" expr
```

> This is because the code to translate a string into an expression tree requires a lexical and semantic parser. These features are built into the C# compiler and are not available as a runtime service. At runtime, C# merely provides a *binder*—which tells the DLR how to interpret an already-built expression tree.

True dynamic languages such as IronPython and IronRuby do allow you to execute an arbitrary string, and this is useful in tasks such as scripting, dynamic configuration, and implementing dynamic rules engines. So although you may write most of your application in C#, it can be useful to call out to a dynamic language for such tasks. In addition, you might want to leverage an API that is written in a dynamic language where no equivalent functionality is available in a .NET library.

In the following example, we use IronPython to evaluate an expression created at runtime from within C#. This script could be used to write a calculator:

To run this code, download IronPython (search the Internet for *IronPython*), and then reference the *IronPython*, *Microsoft.Scripting*, and *Microsoft.Scripting.Core* assemblies from your C# application.

```csharp
using System;
using IronPython.Hosting;
using Microsoft.Scripting;
using Microsoft.Scripting.Hosting;

class Calculator
{
  static void Main()
  {
    int result = (int) Calculate ("2 * 3");
    Console.WriteLine (result);              // 6
  }

  static object Calculate (string expression)
  {
    ScriptEngine engine = Python.CreateEngine();
    return engine.Execute (expression);
  }
}
```

Because we're passing a string into Python, the expression will be evaluated according to Python's rules and not C#'s. It also means we can use Python's language features, such as lists:

```csharp
var list = (IEnumerable) Calculate ("[1, 2, 3] + [4, 5]");
foreach (int n in list) Console.Write (n);  // 12345
```

Passing State Between C# and a Script

To pass variables from C# to Python, a few more steps are required. The following example illustrates those steps and could be the basis of a rules engine:

```csharp
// The following string could come from a file or database:
string auditRule = "taxPaidLastYear / taxPaidThisYear > 2";

ScriptEngine engine = Python.CreateEngine ();

ScriptScope scope = engine.CreateScope ();
scope.SetVariable ("taxPaidLastYear", 20000m);
scope.SetVariable ("taxPaidThisYear", 8000m);

ScriptSource source = engine.CreateScriptSourceFromString (
                  auditRule, SourceCodeKind.Expression);

bool auditRequired = (bool) source.Execute (scope);
Console.WriteLine (auditRequired);   // True
```

You can also get variables back by calling GetVariable:

```
string code = "result = input * 3";

ScriptEngine engine = Python.CreateEngine();

ScriptScope scope = engine.CreateScope();
scope.SetVariable ("input", 2);

ScriptSource source = engine.CreateScriptSourceFromString (code,
                                   SourceCodeKind.SingleStatement);
source.Execute (scope);
Console.WriteLine (engine.GetVariable (scope, "result"));    // 6
```

Notice that we specified SourceCodeKind.SingleStatement in the second example (rather than Expression) to tell the engine that we want to execute a statement.

Types are automatically marshaled between the .NET and Python worlds. You can even access members of .NET objects from the scripting side:

```
string code = @"sb.Append (""World"")";

ScriptEngine engine = Python.CreateEngine ();

ScriptScope scope = engine.CreateScope ();
var sb = new StringBuilder ("Hello");
scope.SetVariable ("sb", sb);

ScriptSource source = engine.CreateScriptSourceFromString (
                        code, SourceCodeKind.SingleStatement);
source.Execute (scope);
Console.WriteLine (sb.ToString());    // HelloWorld
```

21

Security

In this chapter, we discuss the two main components of .NET security:

- Permissions
- Cryptography

Permissions, in .NET, provide a layer of security independent of that imposed by the operating system. Their job is twofold:

Sandboxing
Limiting the kinds of operations that partially trusted .NET assemblies can perform

Authorization
Limiting *who* can do what

The cryptography support in .NET allows you to store or exchange high-value data, prevent eavesdropping, detect message tampering, generate one-way hashes for storing passwords, and create digital signatures.

The types covered in this chapter are defined in the following namespaces:

```
System.Security;
System.Security.Permissions;
System.Security.Principal;
System.Security.Cryptography;
```

Permissions

The Framework uses permissions for both sandboxing and authorization. A *permission* acts as a gate that conditionally prevents code from executing. Sandboxing uses *code access* permissions; authorization uses *identity* and *role* permissions.

Although both follow a similar model, they feel quite different to use. Part of the reason for this is that they typically put you on a different side of the fence: with code access security, you're usually the *untrusted* party; with identity and role security, you're usually the *untrusting* party. Code access security is most often forced upon you by the CLR or a hosting environment such as ASP.NET or Internet Explorer, whereas authorization is usually something you implement to prevent unprivileged callers from accessing your program.

As an application developer, you'll need to understand code access security (CAS) in order to write assemblies that will run in a limited permissions environment. If you're writing and selling a component library, it's easy to overlook the possibility that your customers will call your library from a *sandboxed* environment such as a SQL Server CLR host.

Another reason to understand CAS is if you want to create your own hosting environment that sandboxes other assemblies. For example, you might write an application that allows third parties to write plug-in components. Running those plug-ins in an application domain with limited permissions reduces the chance of a plug-in destabilizing your application or compromising its security.

The main scenario for identity and role security is when writing middle-tier or web application servers. You typically decide on a set of roles, and then for each method that you expose, you demand that callers are members of a particular role.

CodeAccessPermission and PrincipalPermission

There are essentially two kinds of permissions:

CodeAccessPermission
> The abstract base class for all code access security (CAS) permissions, such as FileIOPermission, ReflectionPermission, or PrintingPermission

PrincipalPermission
> Describes an identity and/or role (e.g., "Mary" or "Human Resources")

The term *permission* is somewhat misleading in the case of CodeAccessPermission, because it suggests something has been granted. This is not necessarily the case. A CodeAccessPermission object describes a *privileged operation*.

For instance, a FileIOPermission object describes the privilege of being able to Read, Write, or Append to a particular set of files or directories. Such an object can be used in a variety of ways:

- To verify that you and all your callers have the rights to perform these actions (Demand)

- To verify that your immediate caller has the rights to perform these actions (LinkDemand)

- To temporarily escape a sandbox and Assert your assembly-given rights to perform these actions, regardless of callers' privileges

 You'll also see the following security actions in the CLR: Deny, RequestMinimum, RequestOptional, RequestRefuse, and PermitOnly. However, these (along with link demands) have been deprecated or discouraged since Framework 4.0, in favor of the new *transparency* model.

PrincipalPermission is much simpler. Its only security method is Demand, which checks that the specified user or role is valid given the current execution thread.

IPermission

Both CodeAccessPermission and PrincipalPermission implement the IPermission interface:

```
public interface IPermission
{
  void Demand();
  IPermission Intersect (IPermission target);
  IPermission Union (IPermission target);
  bool IsSubsetOf (IPermission target);
  IPermission Copy();
}
```

The crucial method here is Demand. It performs a spot-check to see whether the permission or privileged operation is currently permitted, and it throws a SecurityException if not. If you're the *untrusting* party, *you* will be Demanding. If you're the *untrusted* party, code that you *call* will be Demanding.

For example, to ensure that only Mary can run management reports, you could write this:

```
new PrincipalPermission ("Mary", null).Demand();
// ... run management reports
```

In contrast, suppose your assembly was sandboxed such that file I/O was prohibited, so the following line threw a SecurityException:

```
using (FileStream fs = new FileStream ("test.txt", FileMode.Create))
  ...
```

The Demand, in this case, is made by code that you call—in other words, FileStream's constructor:

```
...
new FileIOPermission (...).Demand();
```

A code access security Demand checks right up the call stack in order to ensure that the requested operation is allowed for every party in the calling chain (within the current application domain). Effectively, it's asking, "Is this application domain entitled to this permission?"

With code access security, an interesting case arises with assemblies that run in the GAC, which are considered *fully trusted*. If such an assembly runs in a sandbox, any Demands that it makes are still subject to the sandbox's permission set. Fully trusted assemblies can, however, temporarily *escape* the sandbox by calling Assert on a CodeAccessPermission object. After doing so, Demands for the permissions that were asserted always succeed. An Assert ends either when the current method finishes or when you call CodeAccessPermis sion.RevertAssert.

The Intersect and Union methods combine two same-typed permission objects into one. The purpose of Intersect is to create a "smaller" permission object, whereas the purpose of Union is to create a "larger" permission object.

With code access permissions, a "larger" permission object is *more* restrictive when Demanded, because a greater number of permissions must be met.

With principle permissions, a "larger" permission object is *less* restrictive when Demanded, because only *one* of the principles or identities is enough to satisfy the demand.

IsSubsetOf returns true if the given target contains at least its permissions:

```
PrincipalPermission jay = new PrincipalPermission ("Jay", null);
PrincipalPermission sue = new PrincipalPermission ("Sue", null);

PrincipalPermission jayOrSue = (PrincipalPermission) jay.Union (sue);
Console.WriteLine (jay.IsSubsetOf (jayOrSue));   // True
```

In this example, calling Intersect on jay and sue would generate an empty permission, because they don't overlap.

PermissionSet

A PermissionSet represents a collection of differently typed IPermission objects. The following creates a permission set with three code access permissions, and then Demands all of them in one hit:

```
PermissionSet ps = new PermissionSet (PermissionState.None);

ps.AddPermission (new UIPermission (PermissionState.Unrestricted));
ps.AddPermission (new SecurityPermission (
                      SecurityPermissionFlag.UnmanagedCode));
ps.AddPermission (new FileIOPermission (
                      FileIOPermissionAccess.Read, @"c:\docs"));
ps.Demand();
```

PermissionSet's constructor accepts a `PermissionState` enum, which indicates whether the set should be considered "unrestricted." An unrestricted permission set is treated as though it contained every possible permission (even though its collection is empty). Assemblies that execute with unrestricted code access security are said to be *fully trusted*.

`AddPermission` applies `Union`-like semantics in that it creates a "larger" set. Calling `AddPermission` on an unrestricted permission set has no effect (as it already has, logically, all possible permissions).

You can `Union` and `Intersect` permission sets just as you can with `IPermission` objects.

Declarative Versus Imperative Security

So far, we manually instantiated permission objects and called `Demand` on them. This is *imperative security*. You can achieve the same result by adding attributes to a method, constructor, class, struct, or assembly—this is *declarative security*. Although imperative security is more flexible, declarative security has three advantages:

- It can mean less coding.
- It allows the CLR to determine in advance what permissions your assembly requires.
- It can improve performance.

For example:

```
[PrincipalPermission (SecurityAction.Demand, Name="Mary")]
public ReportData GetReports()
{
    ...
}

[UIPermission(SecurityAction.Demand, Window=UIPermissionWindow.AllWindows)]
public Form FindForm()
{
    ...
}
```

This works because every permission type has a sister attribute type in the .NET Framework. `PrincipalPermission` has a `PrincipalPermissionAttribute` sister. The first argument of the attribute's constructor is always a `SecurityAction`, which indicates what security method to call once the permission object is constructed (usually `Demand`). The remaining named parameters mirror the properties on the corresponding permission object.

Code Access Security (CAS)

The CodeAccessPermission types that are enforced throughout the .NET Framework are listed by category in Tables 21-1 through 21-6. Collectively, these are intended to cover all the means by which a program can do mischief!

Table 21-1. Core permissions

Type	Enables
SecurityPermission	Advanced operations, such as calling unmanaged code
ReflectionPermission	Use of reflection
EnvironmentPermission	Reading/writing command-line environment settings
RegistryPermission	Reading or writing to the Windows Registry

SecurityPermission accepts a SecurityPermissionFlag argument. This is an enum that allows any combination of the following:

```
AllFlags                ControlThread
Assertion               Execution
BindingRedirects        Infrastructure
ControlAppDomain        NoFlags
ControlDomainPolicy     RemotingConfiguration
ControlEvidence         SerializationFormatter
ControlPolicy           SkipVerification
ControlPrincipal        UnmanagedCode
```

The most significant member of this enum is Execution, without which code will not run. The other members should be granted only in full-trust scenarios, because they enable a grantee to compromise or escape a sandbox. ControlAppDomain allows the creation of new application domains (see Chapter 24); UnmanagedCode allows you to call native methods (see Chapter 25).

ReflectionPermission accepts a ReflectionPermissionFlag enum, which includes the members MemberAccess and RestrictedMemberAccess. If you're sandboxing assemblies, the latter is safer to grant while permitting reflection scenarios required by APIs such as LINQ to SQL.

Table 21-2. I/O and data permissions

Type	Enables
FileIOPermission	Reading/writing files and directories
FileDialogPermission	Reading/writing to a file chosen through an Open or Save dialog box
IsolatedStorageFilePermission	Reading/writing to own isolated storage
ConfigurationPermission	Reading of application configuration files

Type	Enables
SqlClientPermission, OleDbPermission, OdbcPermission	Communicating with a database server using the SqlClient, OleDb, or Odbc class
DistributedTransactionPermission	Participation in distributed transactions

FileDialogPermission controls access to the OpenFileDialog and SaveFileDia
log classes. These classes are defined in Microsoft.Win32 (for use in WPF applications) and in System.Windows.Forms (for use in Windows Forms applications). For
this to work, UIPermission is also required. FileIOPermission is not also required,
however, if you access the chosen file by calling OpenFile on the OpenFileDialog or
SaveFileDialog object.

Table 21-3. Networking permissions

Type	Enables
DnsPermission	DNS lookup
WebPermission	WebRequest-based network access
SocketPermission	Socket-based network access
SmtpPermission	Sending mail through the SMTP libraries
NetworkInformationPermission	Use of classes such as Ping and NetworkInterface

Table 21-4. Encryption permissions

Type	Enables
DataProtectionPermission	Use of the Windows data protection methods
KeyContainerPermission	Public key encryption and signing
StorePermission	Access to X.509 certificate stores

Table 21-5. UI permissions

Type	Enables
UIPermission	Creating windows and interacting with the clipboard
WebBrowserPermission	Use of the WebBrowser control
MediaPermission	Image, audio, and video support in WPF
PrintingPermission	Accessing a printer

Table 21-6. Diagnostics permissions

Type	Enables
EventLogPermission	Reading or writing to the Windows event log
PerformanceCounterPermission	Use of Windows performance counters

Demands for these permission types are enforced within the .NET Framework. There are also some permission classes for which the intention is that Demands are enforced in your own code. The most important of these are concerned with establishing identity of the calling assembly, and are listed in Table 21-7. The caveat is that (as with all CAS permissions) a Demand always succeeds if the application domain is running in full trust (see the following section).

Table 21-7. Identity permissions

Type	Enforces
GacIdentityPermission	The assembly is loaded into the GAC
StrongNameIdentityPermission	The calling assembly has a particular strong name
PublisherIdentityPermission	The calling assembly is Authenticode-signed with a particular certificate

How Code Access Security Is Applied

When you run a .NET executable from the Windows shell or command prompt, it runs with unrestricted permissions. This is called *full trust*.

If you execute an assembly via another hosting environment—such as a SQL Server CLR integration host, ASP.NET, ClickOnce, or a custom host—the host decides what permissions to give your assembly. If it restricts permissions in any way, this is called *partial trust* or *sandboxing*.

More accurately, a host does not restrict permissions to your *assembly*. Rather, it creates an application domain with restricted permissions and then loads your assembly into that sandboxed domain. This means that any other assemblies that load into that domain (such as assemblies that you reference) run in that same sandbox with the same permission set. There are two exceptions, however:

- Assemblies registered in the GAC (including the .NET Framework)
- Assemblies that a host has nominated to fully trust

Assemblies in those two categories are considered *fully trusted* and can escape the sandbox by Asserting any permission they want. They can also call methods marked as [SecurityCritical] in other fully trusted assemblies, run unverifiable (`unsafe`) code, and call methods that enforce link demands, and those link demands will always succeed.

So when we say that a *partially trusted* assembly calls a *fully trusted* assembly, we mean that an assembly running in a sandboxed application domain calls a GAC assembly—or an assembly nominated by the host for full trust.

Testing for Full Trust

You can test whether you have unrestricted permissions as follows:

```
new PermissionSet (PermissionState.Unrestricted).Demand();
```

This throws an exception if your application domain is sandboxed. However, it might be that your assembly is, in fact, fully trusted and so can `Assert` its way out of the sandbox. You can test for this by querying the `IsFullyTrusted` property on the `Assembly` in question.

Allowing Partially Trusted Callers

Allowing an assembly to accept partially trusted callers creates the possibility of an elevation of privilege attack and is therefore disallowed by the CLR unless you request otherwise. To see why this is so, let's look first at an elevation of privilege attack.

Elevation of Privilege

Let's suppose the CLR didn't enforce the rule just described and you wrote a library intended to be used in full-trust scenarios. One of your properties was as follows:

```
public string ConnectionString
    => File.ReadAllText (_basePath + "cxString.txt");
```

Now, assume that the user who deploys your library decides (rightly or wrongly) to load your assembly into the GAC. That user then runs a totally unrelated application hosted in ClickOnce or ASP.NET, inside a restrictive sandbox. The sandboxed application now loads your fully trusted assembly—and tries to call the `Connection String` property. Fortunately, it throws a `SecurityException` because `File.Read AllText` will demand a `FileIOPermission`, which the caller won't have (remember that a `Demand` checks right up the calling stack). But now consider the following method:

```
public unsafe void Poke (int offset, int data)
{
    int* target = (int*) _origin + offset;
    *target = data;
    ...
}
```

Without an implicit `Demand`, the sandboxed assembly can call this method—and use it to inflict damage. This is an *elevation of privilege* attack.

The problem in this case is that you never intended for your library to be called by partially trusted assemblies. Fortunately, the CLR helps you by preventing this situation by default.

APTCA and [SecurityTransparent]

To help avoid elevation of privilege attacks, the CLR does not allow partially trusted assemblies to call fully trusted assemblies by default.[1]

To allow such calls, you must do one of two things to the fully trusted assembly:

- Apply the [AllowPartiallyTrustedCallers] attribute (called APTCA for short).

- Apply the [SecurityTransparent] attribute.

Applying these attributes means that you must think about the possibility of being the *untrusting* party (rather than the *untrusted* party).

Prior to CLR 4.0, only the APTCA attribute was supported. And all that it did was to enable partially trusted callers. From CLR 4.0, the APTCA also has the effect of implicitly marking all the methods (and functions) in your assembly as *security transparent*. We'll explain this in detail in the next section; for now, we can summarize it by saying that security transparent methods can't do any of the following (whether running in full or partial trust):

- Run unverifiable (unsafe) code.

- Run native code via P/Invoke or COM.

- Assert permissions to elevate their security level.

- Satisfy a link demand.

- Call methods in the .NET Framework marked as [SecurityCritical]. Essentially, these comprise methods that do one of the preceding four things without appropriate safeguards or security checks.

 The rationale is that an assembly that doesn't do any of these things cannot, in general, be susceptible to an elevation of privilege attack.

The [SecurityTransparent] attribute applies a stronger version of the same rules. The difference is that with APTCA, you can nominate selected methods in your assembly as nontransparent, whereas with [SecurityTransparent], all methods must be transparent.

---

1 Before CLR 4.0, partially trusted assemblies could not even call other partially trusted assemblies if the target was strongly named (unless you applied the APTCA). This restriction didn't really aid security and so was dropped in CLR 4.0.

If your assembly can work with [SecurityTransparent], your job is done as a library author. You can ignore the nuances of the transparency model and skip ahead to "Operating System Security" on page 885!

Before we look at how to nominate selected methods as nontransparent, let's first look at when you'd apply these attributes.

The first (and more obvious) scenario is if you plan to write a fully trusted assembly that will run in a partially trusted domain. We walk through an example in "Sandboxing Another Assembly" on page 881.

The second (and less obvious) scenario is writing a library without knowledge of how it will be deployed. For instance, suppose you write an object relational mapper and sell it over the Internet. Customers have three options in how they call your library:

1. From a fully trusted environment

2. From a sandboxed domain

3. From a sandboxed domain, but with your assembly fully trusted (e.g., by loading it into the GAC)

It's easy to overlook the third option—and this is where the transparency model helps.

The Transparency Model

To follow this, you'll need to have read the previous section and understand the scenarios for applying APTCA and [SecurityTransparent].

The security transparency model makes it easier to secure assemblies that might be fully trusted and then called from partially trusted code.

By way of analogy, let's imagine that being a partially trusted assembly is like being convicted of a crime and being sent to prison. In prison, you discover that there are a set of privileges (permissions) that you can earn for good behavior. These permissions entitle you to perform activities such as watching TV or playing basketball. There are some activities, however, that you can never perform—such as getting the keys to the TV room (or the prison gates)—because such activities (methods) would undermine the whole security system. These methods are called *security-critical*.

If writing a fully trusted library, you would want to protect those security-critical methods. One way to do so is to Demand that callers be fully trusted. This was the approach prior to CLR 4.0:

```
[PermissionSet (SecurityAction.Demand, Unrestricted = true)]
public Key GetTVRoomKey() { ... }
```

This creates two problems. First, Demands are slow because they must check right up the call stack; this matters because *security-critical* methods are sometimes *performance-critical*. A Demand can become particularly wasteful if a security-critical method is called in a loop—perhaps from another fully trusted assembly in the Framework. The CLR 2.0 workaround with such methods was to instead enforce *link demands*, which check only the immediate caller. But this also comes at a price. To maintain security, methods that call link-demanded methods must themselves perform demands or link demands—or be audited to ensure that they don't allow anything potentially harmful if called from a less trusted party. Such an audit becomes burdensome when call graphs are complicated.

The second problem is that it's easy to forget to perform a demand or link demand on security-critical methods (again, complex call graphs exacerbate this). It would be nice if the CLR could somehow help out and enforce that security-critical functions are not unintentionally exposed to inmates.

The transparency model does exactly that.

 The introduction of the transparency model is totally unrelated to the removal of CAS *policy* (see sidebar, "Security Policy in CLR 2.0" on page 881).

How the Transparency Model Works

In the transparency model, security-critical methods are marked with the [SecurityCritical] attribute:

```
[SecurityCritical]
public Key GetTVRoomKey() { ... }
```

All "dangerous" methods (containing code that the CLR considers could breach security and allow an inmate to escape) must be marked with [SecurityCritical] or [SecuritySafeCritical]. This comprises:

- Unverifiable (unsafe) methods
- Methods that call unmanaged code via P/Invoke or COM interop
- Methods that Assert permissions or call link-demanding methods
- Methods that *call* [SecurityCritical] methods
- Methods that *override* virtual [SecurityCritical] methods

[SecurityCritical] means "this method could allow a partially trusted caller to escape a sandbox".

[SecuritySafeCritical] means "this method does security-critical things—but with appropriate safeguards and so is safe for partially trusted callers."

Methods in partially trusted assemblies can never call security critical methods in fully trusted assemblies. [SecurityCritical] methods can be called only by:

- Other [SecurityCritical] methods
- Methods marked as [SecuritySafeCritical]

Security-safe critical methods act as gatekeepers for security-critical methods (see Figure 21-1), and can be called by any method in any assembly (fully or partially trusted, subject to permission-based CAS demands). To illustrate, suppose that as an inmate you want to watch television. The WatchTV method that you'll call will need to call GetTVRoomKey, which means that WatchTV must be *security-safe-critical*:

```
[SecuritySafeCritical]
public void WatchTV()
{
    new TVPermission().Demand();
    using (Key key = GetTVRoomKey())
        PrisonGuard.OpenDoor (key);
}
```

Notice that we Demand a TVPermission to ensure that the caller actually has TV-watching rights, and we carefully dispose of the key we create. We are wrapping a *security-critical* method, making it *safe* to be called by anyone.

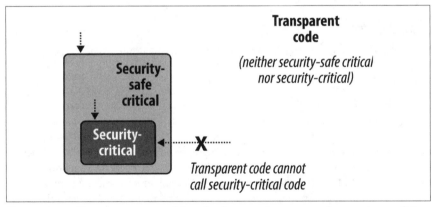

Figure 21-1. Transparency model; only the area in gray needs security auditing

 Some methods partake in the activities considered "danger-ous" by the CLR but are not actually dangerous. You can mark these methods directly with [SecuritySafeCritical] instead of [SecurityCritical]. An example is the Array.Copy method: it has an unmanaged implementation for efficiency and yet cannot be abused by partially trusted callers.

The UnsafeXXX Pattern

There's a potential inefficiency in our TV-watching example in that if a prison guard wants to watch TV via the WatchTV method, he must (unnecessarily) satisfy a TVPer mission demand. As a remedy, the CLR team recommends a pattern whereby you define two versions of the method. The first is security-critical and is prefixed by the word *Unsafe*:

```
[SecurityCritical]
public void UnsafeWatchTV()
{
    using (Key key = GetTVRoomKey())
        PrisonGuard.OpenDoor(key);
}
```

The second is security-safe-critical, and calls the first after satisfying a full stack-walking demand:

```
[SecuritySafeCritical]
public void WatchTV()
{
    new TVPermission().Demand();
    UnsafeWatchTV();
}
```

Transparent code

Under the transparency model, all methods fall into one of three categories:

- *Security-critical*
- *Security-safe-critical*
- Neither (in which case, they're called *transparent*)

Transparent methods are so called because you can ignore them when it comes to auditing code for elevation of privilege attacks. All you need to focus on are the [SecuritySafeCritical] methods (the gatekeepers), which typically comprise just a small fraction of an assembly's methods. If an assembly comprises entirely transparent methods, the entire assembly can be marked with the [SecurityTransparent] attribute:

```
[assembly: SecurityTransparent]
```

We then say that the *assembly itself* is transparent. Transparent assemblies don't need auditing for elevation of privilege attacks and implicitly allow partially trusted callers—you don't need to apply APTCA.

Setting the transparency default for an assembly

To summarize what we said previously, there are two ways to specify transparency at the assembly level:

- Apply the APTCA. All methods are then implicitly transparent except those you mark otherwise.

- Apply the [SecurityTransparent] assembly attribute. All methods are then implicitly transparent, without exception.

The third option is to do nothing. This still opts you *into* the transparency rules, but with every method implicitly [SecurityCritical] (apart from any virtual [Securi tySafeCritical] methods that you override, which will remain safe-critical). The effect is that you can call any method you like (assuming you're fully trusted), but transparent methods in other assemblies won't be able to call you.

How to Write APTCA Libraries with Transparency

To follow the transparency model, first identify the potentially "dangerous" methods in your assembly (as described in the previous section). Unit tests will pick these up, because the CLR will refuse to run such methods—even in a fully trusted environment. (The .NET Framework also ships with a tool called *SecAnnotate.exe* to help with this.) Then mark each such method with:

- [SecurityCritical], if the method might be harmful if called from a less trusted assembly

- [SecuritySafeCritical], if the method performs appropriate checks/safeguards and can be safely called from a less trusted assembly

To illustrate, consider the following method, which calls a security-critical method in the .NET Framework:

```
public static void LoadLibraries()
{
  GC.AddMemoryPressure (1000000);   // Security critical
  ...
}
```

This method could be abused by being called repeatedly from less trusted callers. We could apply the [SecurityCritical] attribute, but then the method would be callable only from other trusted parties via critical or safe-critical methods. A better solution is to fix the method so that it's secure and then apply the [SecuritySafe Critical] attribute:

```
static bool _loaded;

[SecuritySafeCritical]
public static void LoadLibraries()
{
  if (_loaded) return;
  _loaded = true;
  GC.AddMemoryPressure (1000000);
  ...
}
```

(This has the benefit of making it safer for trusted callers, too.)

Securing unsafe methods

Next, suppose we have an unsafe method that is potentially harmful if called by a less trusted assembly. We simply decorate it with [SecurityCritical]:

```
[SecurityCritical]
public unsafe void Poke (int offset, int data)
{
  int* target = (int*) _origin + offset;
  *target = data;
  ...
}
```

 If you write unsafe code in a transparent method, the CLR will throw a VerificationException ("Operation could destabilize the runtime") before executing the method.

We then secure the upstream methods, marking them with [SecurityCritical] or [SecuritySafeCritical] as appropriate.

Next, consider the following unsafe method, which filters a bitmap. This is intrinsically harmless, so we can mark it SecuritySafeCritical:

```
[SecuritySafeCritical]
unsafe void BlueFilter (int[,] bitmap)
{
  int length = bitmap.Length;
  fixed (int* b = bitmap)
  {
    int* p = b;
    for (int i = 0; i < length; i++)
      *p++ &= 0xFF;
  }
}
```

Conversely, you might write a function that doesn't perform anything "dangerous" as far as the CLR is concerned but poses a security risk nonetheless. You can decorate these, too, with [SecurityCritical]:

```
public string Password
{
  [SecurityCritical] get { return _password; }
}
```

P/Invokes and [SuppressUnmanagedSecurity]

Finally, consider the following unmanaged method, which returns a window handle from a Point (System.Drawing):

```
[DllImport ("user32.dll")]
public static extern IntPtr WindowFromPoint (Point point);
```

Remember that you can call unmanaged code only from [SecurityCritical] and [SecuritySafeCritical] methods.

 You could say that all extern methods are implicitly [Securi tyCritical], although there is a subtle difference: applying [SecurityCritical] explicitly to an extern method has the subtle effect of advancing the security check from runtime to JIT time. To illustrate, consider the following method:

```
static void Foo (bool exec)
{
  if (exec) WindowFromPoint (...)
}
```

If called with false, this will be subject to a security check only if WindowFromPoint is marked explicitly with [Security Critical].

Because we've made the method public, other fully trusted assemblies can call Win dowFromPoint directly from [SecurityCritical] methods. For partially trusted callers, we expose the following secure version, which eliminates the danger, by Demanding UI permission and returning a managed class instead of an IntPtr:

```
[UIPermission (SecurityAction.Demand, Unrestricted = true)]
[SecuritySafeCritical]
public static System.Windows.Forms.Control ControlFromPoint (Point point)
{
  IntPtr winPtr = WindowFromPoint (point);
  if (winPtr == IntPtr.Zero) return null;
  return System.Windows.Forms.Form.FromChildHandle (winPtr);
}
```

Just one problem remains: the CLR performs an implicit Demand for unmanaged permission whenever you P/Invoke. And because a Demand checks right up the call stack, the WindowFromPoint method will fail if the caller's caller is partially trusted. There are two ways around this. The first is to *assert* permission for unmanaged code in the first line of the ControlFromPoint method:

```
new SecurityPermission (SecurityPermissionFlag.UnmanagedCode).Assert();
```

Asserting our assembly-given unmanaged right here will ensure that the subsequent implicit Demand in WindowFromPoint will succeed. Of course, this assertion would fail if the assembly itself wasn't fully trusted (by virtue of being loaded into the GAC or being nominated as fully trusted by the host). We'll cover assertions in more detail in "Sandboxing Another Assembly" on page 881.

The second (and more performant) solution is to apply the [SuppressUnmanagedCo deSecurity] attribute to the unmanaged method:

```
[DllImport ("user32.dll"), SuppressUnmanagedCodeSecurity]
public static extern IntPtr WindowFromPoint (Point point);
```

This tells the CLR to skip the expensive stack-walking unmanaged Demand (an opti-mization that could be particularly valuable if WindowFromPoint was called from other trusted classes or assemblies). We can then dump the unmanaged permission assertion in `ControlFromPoint`.

 Because you're following the transparency model, applying this attribute to an `extern` method doesn't create the same security risk as in CLR 2.0. This is because you're still protected by the fact that P/Invokes are implicitly security-critical, and so can be called only by other critical or safe-critical methods.

Transparency in Full-Trust Scenarios

In a fully trusted environment, you might want to write critical code and yet avoid the burden of security attributes and method auditing. The easiest way to achieve this is not to attach any assembly security attributes—in which case all your methods are implicitly [`SecurityCritical`].

This works well as long as *all* partaking assemblies do the same thing—or if the transparency-enabled assemblies are at the *bottom* of the call graph. In other words, you can still call transparent methods in third-party libraries (and in the .NET Framework).

To go in the reverse direction is troublesome; however, this trouble typically guides you to a better solution. Suppose you're writing assembly T, which is partly or wholly transparent, and you want to call assembly X, which is unattributed (and therefore fully critical). You have three options:

- Go fully critical yourself. If your domain will always be fully trusted, you don't need to support partially trusted callers. Making that lack of support *explicit* makes sense.

- Write [`SecuritySafeCritical`] wrappers around methods in X. This then highlights the security vulnerability points (although this can be burdensome).

- Ask the author of X to consider transparency. If X does nothing critical, this will be as simple as applying [`SecurityTransparent`] to X. If X does perform critical functions, the process of following the transparency model will force the author of X to at least identify (if not address) X's vulnerability points.

Sandboxing Another Assembly

Suppose you write an application that allows consumers to install third-party plugins. Most likely you'd want to prevent plug-ins from leveraging your privileges as a trusted application, so as not to destabilize your application—or the end user's computer. The best way to achieve this is to run each plug-in in its own sandboxed application domain.

For this example, we'll assume a plug-in is packaged as a .NET assembly called *plugin.exe* and that activating it is simply a matter of starting the executable. (In Chapter 24, we describe how to load a library into an application domain and interact with it in a more sophisticated way.)

Here's the complete code, for the *host* program:

```
using System;
using System.IO;
using System.Net;
using System.Reflection;
using System.Security;
using System.Security.Policy;
using System.Security.Permissions;

class Program
{
  static void Main()
  {
    string pluginFolder = Path.Combine (
      AppDomain.CurrentDomain.BaseDirectory, "plugins");

    string plugInPath = Path.Combine (pluginFolder, "plugin.exe");

    PermissionSet ps = new PermissionSet (PermissionState.None);

    ps.AddPermission
      (new SecurityPermission (SecurityPermissionFlag.Execution));

    ps.AddPermission
      (new FileIOPermission (FileIOPermissionAccess.PathDiscovery |
                             FileIOPermissionAccess.Read, plugInPath));

    ps.AddPermission (new UIPermission (PermissionState.Unrestricted));

    AppDomainSetup setup = AppDomain.CurrentDomain.SetupInformation;
    AppDomain sandbox = AppDomain.CreateDomain ("sbox", null, setup, ps);
    sandbox.ExecuteAssembly (plugInPath);
    AppDomain.Unload (sandbox);
  }
}
```

 You can optionally pass an array of StrongName objects into the CreateDomain method, indicating assemblies to fully trust. We'll give an example in the following section.

First, we create a limited permission set to describe the privileges we want to give to the sandbox. This must include at least execution rights and permission for the plug-in to read its own assembly; otherwise, it won't start. In this case, we also give unrestricted UI permissions. Then we construct a new application domain, specifying our custom permission set, which will be awarded to all assemblies loaded into that domain. We then execute the plug-in assembly in the new domain, and unload the domain when the plug-in finishes executing.

> In this example, we load the plug-in assemblies from a subdirectory called *plugins*. Putting plug-ins in the same directory as the fully trusted host creates the potential for an elevation of privilege attack, whereby the fully trusted domain implicitly loads and runs code in a plug-in assembly in order to resolve a type. An example of how this could happen is if the plug-in throws a custom exception whose type is defined in its own assembly. When the exception bubbles up to the host, the host will implicitly load the plug-in assembly if it can find it— in an attempt to deserialize the exception. Putting the plug-ins in a separate folder prevents such a load from succeeding.

Asserting Permissions

Permission assertions are useful when writing methods that can be called from a partially trusted assembly. They allow fully trusted assemblies to temporarily escape the sandbox in order to perform actions that would otherwise be prohibited by downstream `Demands`.

> Assertions in the world of CAS have nothing to do with diagnostic or contract-based assertions. Calling `Debug.Assert`, in fact, is more akin to `Demand`ing a permission than `Assert`ing a permission. In particular, asserting a permission has *side-effects* if the assertion succeeds, whereas `Debug.Assert` does not.

Recall that we previously wrote an application that ran third-party plug-ins in a restricted permission set. Suppose we want to extend this by providing a library of safe methods for plug-ins to call. For instance, we might prohibit plug-ins from accessing a database directly and yet still allow them to perform certain queries through methods in a library that we provide. Or we might want to expose a method for writing to a log file—without giving them any file-based permission.

The first step in doing this is to create a separate assembly for this (e.g., *utilities*) and add the `AllowPartiallyTrustedCallers` attribute. Then we can expose a method as follows:

```
public static void WriteLog (string msg)
{
  // Write to log
  ...
}
```

The difficulty here is that writing to a file requires `FileIOPermission`. Even though our *utilities* assembly will be fully trusted, the caller won't be, and so any file-based `Demands` will fail. The solution is to first `Assert` the permission:

```
public class Utils
{
  string _logsFolder = ...;

  [SecuritySafeCritical]
  public static void WriteLog (string msg)
  {
    FileIOPermission f = new FileIOPermission (PermissionState.None);
    f.AddPathList (FileIOPermissionAccess.AllAccess, _logsFolder);
    f.Assert();

    // Write to log
    ...
  }
}
```

 Because we're asserting a permission, we must mark the
method as [SecurityCritical] or [SecuritySafeCritical]
(unless we're targeting an earlier version of the Framework).
In this case, the method is safe for partially trusted callers, so
we choose SecuritySafeCritical. This, of course, means
that we can't mark the assembly as a whole with [Security
Transparent]; we must use APTCA instead.

Remember that Demand performs a spot-check and throws an exception if the permission is not satisfied. It then walks the stack, checking that all callers also have
that permission (within the current AppDomain). An assertion checks only that the
current assembly has the necessary permissions, and if successful, makes a mark on
the stack, indicating that from now on, the caller's rights should be ignored and only
the current assembly's rights should be considered with respect to those permissions. An Assert ends when the method finishes or when you call CodeAccessPer
mission.RevertAssert.

To complete our example, the remaining step is to create a sandboxed application
domain that fully trusts the *utilities* assembly. Then we can instantiate a StrongName
object that describes the assembly, and pass it into AppDomain's CreateDomain
method:

```
static void Main()
{
  string pluginFolder = Path.Combine (
    AppDomain.CurrentDomain.BaseDirectory, "plugins");

  string plugInPath = Path.Combine (pluginFolder, "plugin.exe");

  PermissionSet ps = new PermissionSet (PermissionState.None);

  // Add desired permissions to ps as we did before
  // ...

  Assembly utilAssembly = typeof (Utils).Assembly;
  StrongName utils = utilAssembly.Evidence.GetHostEvidence<StrongName>();
```

```
    AppDomainSetup setup = AppDomain.CurrentDomain.SetupInformation;
    AppDomain sandbox = AppDomain.CreateDomain ("sbox", null, setup, ps,
                                                utils);
    sandbox.ExecuteAssembly (plugInPath);
    AppDomain.Unload (sandbox);
}
```

For this to work, the *utilities* assembly must be strong-name signed.

 Prior to Framework 4.0, you couldn't obtain a `StrongName` by calling `GetHostEvidence` as we did. The solution was to instead do this:

```
AssemblyName name = utilAssembly.GetName();
StrongName utils = new StrongName (
    new StrongNamePublicKeyBlob (name.GetPublicKey()),
    name.Name,
    name.Version);
```

The old-fashioned approach is still useful when you don't want to load the assembly into the host's domain. This is because you can obtain an `AssemblyName` without needing an `Assembly` or `Type` object:

```
AssemblyName name = AssemblyName.GetAssemblyName
                        (@"d:\utils.dll");
```

Operating System Security

The operating system can further restrict what an application can do, based on the user's login privileges. In Windows, there are two types of accounts:

- An administrative account that imposes no restrictions in accessing the local computer
- A limited permissions account that restricts administrative functions and visibility of other users' data

A feature called User Account Control (UAC) introduced in Windows Vista means that administrators receive two tokens or "hats" when logging in: an administrative hat and an ordinary user hat. By default, programs run wearing the ordinary user hat—with restricted permissions—unless the program requests *administrative elevation*. The user must then approve the request in the dialog box that's presented.

For application developers, UAC means that *by default*, your application will run with restricted user privileges. This means you must either:

- Write your application such that it can run without administrative privileges
- Demand administrative elevation in the application manifest

The first option is safer and more convenient to the user. Designing your program to run without administrative privileges is easy in most cases: the restrictions are much less draconian than those of a typical *code access security* sandbox.

You can find out whether you're running under an administrative account with the following method:

```
[DllImport ("shell32.dll", EntryPoint = "#680")]
static extern bool IsUserAnAdmin();
```

With UAC enabled, this returns `true` only if the current process has administrative elevation.

Running in a Standard User Account

Here are the key things that you *cannot* do in a standard Windows user account:

- Write to the following directories:
  - The operating system folder (typically *Windows*) and subdirectories
  - The program files folder (*Program Files*) and subdirectories
  - The root of the operating system drive (e.g., *C:*)
- Write to the HKEY_LOCAL_MACHINE branch of the Registry
- Read performance monitoring (WMI) data

Additionally, as an ordinary user (or even as an administrator), you may be refused access to files or resources that belong to other users. Windows uses a system of Access Control Lists (ACLs) to protect such resources—you can query and assert your own rights in the ACLs via types in `System.Security.AccessControl`. ACLs can also be applied to cross-process wait handles, described in Chapter 22.

If you're refused access to anything as a result of operating system security, an `Unau thorizedAccessException` is thrown. This is different from the `SecurityExcep tion` thrown when a .NET permission demand fails.

The .NET code access permission classes are mostly independent of ACLs. This means you can successfully `Demand` a `FileIOPermission`—but still get an `UnauthorizedAccessEx ception` due to ACL restrictions when trying to access the file.

In most cases, you can deal with standard user restrictions as follows:

- Write files to their recommended locations.
- Avoid using the Registry for information that can be stored in files (aside of the HKEY_CURRENT_USER hive, which you will have read/write access to).
- Register ActiveX or COM components during setup.

The recommended location for user documents is `SpecialFolder.MyDocuments`:

```
string docsFolder = Environment.GetFolderPath
                    (Environment.SpecialFolder.MyDocuments);

string path = Path.Combine (docsFolder, "test.txt");
```

The recommended location for configuration files that a user might need to modify outside of your application is SpecialFolder.ApplicationData (current user only) or SpecialFolder.CommonApplicationData (all users). You typically create subdirectories within these folders based on your organization and product name.

A good place to put data that need only be accessed within your application is isolated storage.

Perhaps the most inconvenient aspect of running in a standard user account is that a program doesn't have write access to its files, making it difficult to implement an automatic update system. One option is to deploy with ClickOnce: this allows updates to be applied without administrative elevation, but places significant restrictions on the setup procedure (e.g., you cannot register ActiveX controls). Applications deployed with ClickOnce may also be sandboxed with code access security, depending on their mode of delivery. We described another, more sophisticated solution in Chapter 18, in the section "Packing a Single-File Executable" on page 785.

Administrative Elevation and Virtualization

In Chapter 18, we described how to deploy an application manifest. With an application manifest, you can request that Windows prompt the user for administrative elevation whenever running your program:

```
<?xml version="1.0" encoding="utf-8"?>
<assembly manifestVersion="1.0" xmlns="urn:schemas-microsoft-com:asm.v1">
  <trustInfo xmlns="urn:schemas-microsoft-com:asm.v2">
    <security>
      <requestedPrivileges>
        <requestedExecutionLevel level="requireAdministrator" />
      </requestedPrivileges>
    </security>
  </trustInfo>
</assembly>
```

If you replace requireAdministrator with asInvoker, it instructs Windows that administrative elevation is *not* required. The effect is almost the same as not having an application manifest at all—except that *virtualization* is disabled. Virtualization is a temporary measure introduced with Windows Vista to help old applications run correctly without administrative privileges. The absence of an application manifest with a requestedExecutionLevel element activates this backward-compatibility feature.

Virtualization comes into play when an application writes to the *Program Files* or *Windows* directory, or the HKEY_LOCAL_MACHINE area of the Registry. Instead of throwing an exception, changes are redirected to a separate location on the hard disk where they can't impact the original data. This prevents the application from interfering with the operating system—or other well-behaved applications.

Identity and Role Security

Identity and role-based security is useful when writing a middle tier server or an ASP.NET application, where you're potentially dealing with many users. It allows you to restrict functionality according to the authenticated user's name or role. An *identity* describes a username; a *role* describes a group. A *principal* is an object that describes an identity and/or a role. Hence, a `PrincipalPermission` class enforces identity and/or role security.

In a typical application server, you demand a `PrincipalPermission` on all methods exposed to the client for which you want to enforce security. For example, the following requires that the caller be a member of the "finance" role:

```
[PrincipalPermission (SecurityAction.Demand, Role = "finance")]
public decimal GetGrossTurnover (int year)
{
  ...
}
```

To enforce that only a particular user can call a method, you can specify a `Name` instead:

```
[PrincipalPermission (SecurityAction.Demand, Name = "sally")]
```

(Of course, the necessity to hardcode names makes this hard to manage.) To allow a combination of identities or roles, you have to use imperative security instead. This means instantiating `PrincipalPermission` objects, calling `Union` to combine them, and then calling `Demand` on the end result.

Assigning Users and Roles

Before a `PrincipalPermission` demand can succeed, you must attach an `IPrincipal` object to the current thread.

You can instruct that the current Windows user be used as an identity in either of two ways, depending on whether you want to impact the whole application domain or just the current thread:

```
AppDomain.CurrentDomain.SetPrincipalPolicy (PrincipalPolicy.
                                            WindowsPrincipal);
// or:
Thread.CurrentPrincipal = new WindowsPrincipal (WindowsIdentity.
                                                GetCurrent());
```

If you're using WCF or ASP.NET, their infrastructures can help with impersonating the client's identity. You can also do this yourself with the `GenericPrincipal` and `GenericIdentity` classes. The following creates a user called "Jack" and assigns him three roles:

```
GenericIdentity id = new GenericIdentity ("Jack");
GenericPrincipal p = new GenericPrincipal
  (id, new string[] { "accounts", "finance", "management" } );
```

For this to take effect, you'd assign it to the current thread as follows:

```
Thread.CurrentPrincipal = p;
```

A principal is thread-based because an application server typically processes many client requests concurrently—each on its own thread. As each request may come from a different client, it needs a different principal.

You can subclass GenericIdentity and GenericPrincipal—or implement the IIdentity and IPrincipal interfaces directly in your own types. Here's how the interfaces are defined:

```
public interface IIdentity
{
  string Name { get; }
  string AuthenticationType { get; }
  bool IsAuthenticated { get; }
}

public interface IPrincipal
{
  IIdentity Identity { get; }
  bool IsInRole (string role);
}
```

The key method is IsInRole. Notice that there's no method returning a list of roles, so you're obliged only to rule on whether a particular role is valid for that principal. This can be the basis for more elaborate authorization systems.

Cryptography Overview

Table 21-8 summarizes the cryptography options in .NET. In the remaining sections, we explore each of these.

Table 21-8. Encryption and hashing options in .NET

Option	Keys to manage	Speed	Strength	Notes
File.Encrypt	0	Fast	Depends on user's password	Protects files transparently with filesystem support. A key is derived implicitly from the logged-in user's credentials.
Windows Data Protection	0	Fast	Depends on user's password	Encrypts and decrypts byte arrays using an implicitly derived key.
Hashing	0	Fast	High	One-way (irreversible) transformation. Used for storing passwords, comparing files, and checking for data corruption.
Symmetric encryption	1	Fast	High	For general-purpose encryption/decryption. The same key encrypts and decrypts. Can be used to secure messages in transit.

Option	Keys to manage	Speed	Strength	Notes
Public key encryption	2	Slow	High	Encryption and decryption use different keys. Used for exchanging a symmetric key in message transmission and for digitally signing files.

The Framework also provides more specialized support for creating and validating XML-based signatures in `System.Security.Cryptography.Xml` and types for working with digital certificates in `System.Security.Cryptography.X509Certificates`.

Windows Data Protection

In the section "File and Directory Operations" on page 650 in Chapter 15, we described how you could use `File.Encrypt` to request that the operating system transparently encrypt a file:

```
File.WriteAllText ("myfile.txt", "");
File.Encrypt ("myfile.txt");
File.AppendAllText ("myfile.txt", "sensitive data");
```

The encryption in this case uses a key derived from the logged-in user's password. You can use this same implicitly derived key to encrypt a byte array with the Windows Data Protection API. The Data Protection API is exposed through the `Protec tedData` class—a simple type with two static methods:

```
public static byte[] Protect (byte[] userData, byte[] optionalEntropy,
                              DataProtectionScope scope);

public static byte[] Unprotect (byte[] encryptedData, byte[] optionalEntropy,
                                DataProtectionScope scope);
```

 Most types in `System.Security.Cryptography` live in *mscorlib.dll* and *System.dll*. `ProtectedData` is an exception: it lives in *System.Security.dll*.

Whatever you include in `optionalEntropy` is added to the key, thereby increasing its security. The `DataProtectionScope` enum argument allows two options: `Curren tUser` or `LocalMachine`. With `CurrentUser`, a key is derived from the logged-in user's credentials; with `LocalMachine`, a machine-wide key is used, common to all users. A `LocalMachine` key provides less protection but works under a Windows Service or a program needing to operate under a variety of accounts.

Here's a simple encryption and decryption demo:

```
byte[] original = {1, 2, 3, 4, 5};
DataProtectionScope scope = DataProtectionScope.CurrentUser;

byte[] encrypted = ProtectedData.Protect (original, null, scope);
byte[] decrypted = ProtectedData.Unprotect (encrypted, null, scope);
// decrypted is now {1, 2, 3, 4, 5}
```

Windows Data Protection provides moderate security against an attacker with full access to the computer, depending on the strength of the user's password. With LocalMachine scope, it's effective only against those with restricted physical and electronic access.

Hashing

Hashing provides one-way encryption. This is ideal for storing passwords in a database, as you might never need (or want) to see a decrypted version. To authenticate, simply hash what the user types in and compare it to what's stored in the database.

A hash code is always a small fixed size regardless of the source data length. This makes it good for comparing files or detecting errors in a data stream (rather like a checksum). A single-bit change anywhere in the source data results in a significantly different hash code.

To hash, you call ComputeHash on one of the HashAlgorithm subclasses such as SHA256 or MD5:

```
byte[] hash;
using (Stream fs = File.OpenRead ("checkme.doc"))
  hash = MD5.Create().ComputeHash (fs);        // hash is 16 bytes long
```

The ComputeHash method also accepts a byte array, which is convenient for hashing passwords:

```
byte[] data = System.Text.Encoding.UTF8.GetBytes ("stRhong%pword");
byte[] hash = SHA256.Create().ComputeHash (data);
```

The GetBytes method on an Encoding object converts a string to a byte array; the GetString method converts it back. An Encoding object cannot, however, convert an encrypted or hashed byte array to a string, because scrambled data usually violates text encoding rules. Instead, use Con vert.ToBase64String and Convert.FromBase64String: these convert between any byte array and a legal (and XML-friendly) string.

MD5 and SHA256 are two of the HashAlgorithm subtypes provided by the .NET Framework. Here are all the major algorithms, in ascending order of security (and hash length, in bytes):

MD5(16) → SHA1(20) → SHA256(32) → SHA384(48) → SHA512(64)

The shorter the algorithm, the faster it executes. MD5 is more than 20 times faster than SHA512 and is well suited to calculating file checksums. You can hash hundreds of megabytes per second with MD5 and then store its result in a Guid. (A Guid happens to be exactly 16 bytes long, and as a value type it is more tractable than a byte array; you can meaningfully compare Guids with the simple equality operator, for instance.) However, shorter hashes increase the possibility of *collision* (two distinct files yielding the same hash).

Use *at least* SHA256 when hashing passwords or other security-sensitive data. MD5 and SHA1 are considered insecure for this purpose and are suitable to protect only against accidental corruption, not deliberate tampering.

SHA384 is no faster than SHA512, so if you want more security than SHA256, you may as well use SHA512.

The longer SHA algorithms are suitable for password hashing, but they require that you enforce a strong password policy to mitigate a *dictionary attack*—a strategy whereby an attacker builds a password lookup table by hashing every word in a dictionary. You can provide additional protection against this by "stretching" your password hashes—repeatedly rehashing to obtain more computationally intensive byte sequences. If you rehash 100 times, a dictionary attack that might otherwise take 1 month would take 8 years. The Rfc2898DeriveBytes and PasswordDerive Bytes classes perform exactly this kind of stretching.

Another technique to avoid dictionary attacks is to incorporate "salt"—a long series of bytes that you initially obtain via a random number generator and then combine with each password before hashing. This frustrates hackers in two ways: hashes take longer to compute, and they may not have access to the salt bytes.

The Framework also provides a 160-bit RIPEMD hashing algorithm, slightly above SHA1 in security. It suffers an inefficient .NET implementation, though, making it slower to execute than even SHA512.

Symmetric Encryption

Symmetric encryption uses the same key for encryption as for decryption. The Framework provides four symmetric algorithms, of which Rijndael is the premium (pronounced "Rhine Dahl" or "Rain Doll"). Rijndael is both fast and secure and has two implementations:

- The Rijndael class, which was available since Framework 1.0
- The Aes class, which was introduced in Framework 3.5

The two are almost identical, except that Aes does not let you weaken the cipher by changing the block size. Aes is recommended by the CLR's security team.

Rijndael and Aes allow symmetric keys of length 16, 24, or 32 bytes: all are currently considered secure. Here's how to encrypt a series of bytes as they're written to a file, using a 16-byte key:

```
byte[] key = {145,12,32,245,98,132,98,214,6,77,131,44,221,3,9,50};
byte[] iv  = {15,122,132,5,93,198,44,31,9,39,241,49,250,188,80,7};

byte[] data = { 1, 2, 3, 4, 5 };   // This is what we're encrypting.
```

```
using (SymmetricAlgorithm algorithm = Aes.Create())
using (ICryptoTransform encryptor = algorithm.CreateEncryptor (key, iv))
using (Stream f = File.Create ("encrypted.bin"))
using (Stream c = new CryptoStream (f, encryptor, CryptoStreamMode.Write))
  c.Write (data, 0, data.Length);
```

The following code decrypts the file:

```
byte[] key = {145,12,32,245,98,132,98,214,6,77,131,44,221,3,9,50};
byte[] iv  = {15,122,132,5,93,198,44,31,9,39,241,49,250,188,80,7};

byte[] decrypted = new byte[5];

using (SymmetricAlgorithm algorithm = Aes.Create())
using (ICryptoTransform decryptor = algorithm.CreateDecryptor (key, iv))
using (Stream f = File.OpenRead ("encrypted.bin"))
using (Stream c = new CryptoStream (f, decryptor, CryptoStreamMode.Read))
  for (int b; (b = c.ReadByte()) > -1;)
    Console.Write (b + " ");                        // 1 2 3 4 5
```

In this example, we made up a key of 16 randomly chosen bytes. If the wrong key was used in decryption, CryptoStream would throw a CryptographicException. Catching this exception is the only way to test whether a key is correct.

As well as a key, we made up an IV, or *Initialization Vector*. This 16-byte sequence forms part of the cipher—much like the key—but is not considered *secret*. If transmitting an encrypted message, you would send the IV in plain text (perhaps in a message header) and then *change it with every message*. This would render each encrypted message unrecognizable from any previous one—even if their unencrypted versions were similar or identical.

If you don't need—or want—the protection of an IV, you can defeat it by using the same 16-byte value for both the key and the IV. Sending multiple messages with the same IV, though, weakens the cipher and might even make it possible to crack.

The cryptography work is divided among the classes. Aes is the mathematician; it applies the cipher algorithm, along with its encryptor and decryptor transforms. CryptoStream is the plumber; it takes care of stream plumbing. You can replace Aes with a different symmetric algorithm, yet still use CryptoStream.

CryptoStream is *bidirectional*, meaning you can read or write to the stream depending on whether you choose CryptoStreamMode.Read or CryptoStreamMode.Write. Both encryptors and decryptors are read- *and* write-savvy, yielding four combinations—the choice can have you staring at a blank screen for a while! It can be helpful to model reading as "pulling" and writing as "pushing." If in doubt, start with Write for encryption and Read for decryption; this is often the most natural.

To generate a random key or IV, use RandomNumberGenerator in System.Cryptogra phy. The numbers it produces are genuinely unpredictable, or *cryptographically strong* (the System.Random class does not offer the same guarantee). Here's an example:

```
byte[] key = new byte [16];
byte[] iv  = new byte [16];
RandomNumberGenerator rand = RandomNumberGenerator.Create();
rand.GetBytes (key);
rand.GetBytes (iv);
```

If you don't specify a key and IV, cryptographically strong random values are generated automatically. You can query these through the Aes object's Key and IV properties.

Encrypting in Memory

With a MemoryStream, you can encrypt and decrypt entirely in memory. Here are helper methods that do just this, with byte arrays:

```
public static byte[] Encrypt (byte[] data, byte[] key, byte[] iv)
{
  using (Aes algorithm = Aes.Create())
  using (ICryptoTransform encryptor = algorithm.CreateEncryptor (key, iv))
    return Crypt (data, encryptor);
}

public static byte[] Decrypt (byte[] data, byte[] key, byte[] iv)
{
  using (Aes algorithm = Aes.Create())
  using (ICryptoTransform decryptor = algorithm.CreateDecryptor (key, iv))
    return Crypt (data, decryptor);
}

static byte[] Crypt (byte[] data, ICryptoTransform cryptor)
{
  MemoryStream m = new MemoryStream();
  using (Stream c = new CryptoStream (m, cryptor, CryptoStreamMode.Write))
    c.Write (data, 0, data.Length);
  return m.ToArray();
}
```

Here, CryptoStreamMode.Write works best for both encryption and decryption, since in both cases we're "pushing" into a fresh memory stream.

Here are overloads that accept and return strings:

```
public static string Encrypt (string data, byte[] key, byte[] iv)
{
  return Convert.ToBase64String (
    Encrypt (Encoding.UTF8.GetBytes (data), key, iv));
}

public static string Decrypt (string data, byte[] key, byte[] iv)
{
  return Encoding.UTF8.GetString (
    Decrypt (Convert.FromBase64String (data), key, iv));
}
```

The following demonstrates their use:

```
byte[] kiv = new byte[16];
RandomNumberGenerator.Create().GetBytes (kiv);

string encrypted = Encrypt ("Yeah!", kiv, kiv);
Console.WriteLine (encrypted);           // R1/5gYvcxyR2vzPjnT7yaQ==

string decrypted = Decrypt (encrypted, kiv, kiv);
Console.WriteLine (decrypted);           // Yeah!
```

Chaining Encryption Streams

CryptoStream is a decorator, meaning it can be chained with other streams. In the following example, we write compressed encrypted text to a file and then read it back:

```
// Use default key/iv for demo.
using (Aes algorithm = Aes.Create())
{
  using (ICryptoTransform encryptor = algorithm.CreateEncryptor())
  using (Stream f = File.Create ("serious.bin"))
  using (Stream c = new CryptoStream (f,encryptor,CryptoStreamMode.Write))
  using (Stream d = new DeflateStream (c, CompressionMode.Compress))
  using (StreamWriter w = new StreamWriter (d))
    await w.WriteLineAsync ("Small and secure!");

  using (ICryptoTransform decryptor = algorithm.CreateDecryptor())
  using (Stream f = File.OpenRead ("serious.bin"))
  using (Stream c = new CryptoStream (f, decryptor, CryptoStreamMode.Read))
  using (Stream d = new DeflateStream (c, CompressionMode.Decompress))
  using (StreamReader r = new StreamReader (d))
    Console.WriteLine (await r.ReadLineAsync());     // Small and secure!
}
```

(As a final touch, we make our program asynchronous by calling WriteLineAsync and ReadLineAsync, and awaiting the result.)

In this example, all one-letter variables form part of a chain. The mathematicians—algorithm, encryptor, and decyptor—are there to assist CryptoStream in the cipher work. The diagram in Figure 21-2 shows this.

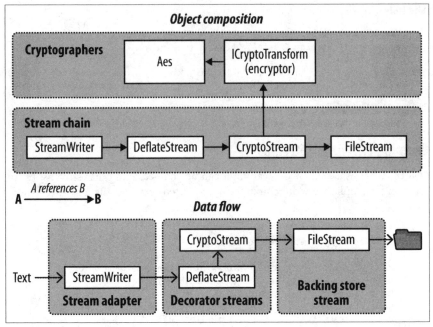

Figure 21-2. Chaining encryption and compression streams

Chaining streams in this manner demands little memory, regardless of the ultimate stream sizes.

As an alternative to nesting multiple `using` statements, you can construct a chain as follows:

```
using (ICryptoTransform encryptor = algorithm.CreateEncryptor())
using
  (StreamWriter w = new StreamWriter (
    new DeflateStream (
      new CryptoStream (
        File.Create ("serious.bin"),
        encryptor,
        CryptoStreamMode.Write
      ),
      CompressionMode.Compress)
    )
  )
```

This is less robust than the previous approach, however, because should an exception be thrown in an object's constructor (e.g., `DeflateStream`), any objects already instantiated (e.g., `FileStream`) would not be disposed.

Disposing Encryption Objects

Disposing a `CryptoStream` ensures that its internal cache of data is flushed to the underlying stream. Internal caching is necessary for encryption algorithms because they process data in blocks, rather than one byte at a time.

`CryptoStream` is unusual in that its `Flush` method does nothing. To flush a stream (without disposing it) you must call `FlushFinalBlock`. In contrast to `Flush`, `Flush FinalBlock` can be called only once, and then no further data can be written.

In our examples, we also disposed the mathematicians—the `Aes` algorithm and `ICryptoTransform` objects (`encryptor` and `decryptor`). Disposal is actually optional with the Rijndael transforms, because their implementations are purely managed. Disposal still serves a useful role, however: it wipes the symmetric key and related data from memory, preventing subsequent discovery by other software running on the computer (we're talking malware). You can't rely on the garbage collector for this job because it merely flags sections of memory as available; it doesn't write zeros over every byte.

The easiest way to dispose an `Aes` object outside of a `using` statement is to call `Clear`. Its `Dispose` method is hidden via explicit implementation (to signal its unusual disposal semantics).

Key Management

It is inadvisable to hardcode encryption keys because popular tools exist to decompile assemblies with little expertise. A better option is to manufacture a random key for each installation, storing it securely with Windows Data Protection (or encrypt the entire message with Windows Data Protection). If you're encrypting a message stream, public key encryption provides the best option still.

Public Key Encryption and Signing

Public key cryptography is *asymmetric*, meaning that encryption and decryption use different keys.

Unlike symmetric encryption, where any arbitrary series of bytes of appropriate length can serve as a key, asymmetric cryptography requires specially crafted key pairs. A key pair contains a *public key* and *private key* component that work together as follows:

- The public key encrypts messages.
- The private key decrypts messages.

The party "crafting" a key pair keeps the private key secret while distributing the public key freely. A special feature of this type of cryptography is that you cannot calculate a private key from a public key. So, if the private key is lost, encrypted data cannot be recovered; conversely, if a private key is leaked, the encryption system becomes useless.

A public key handshake allows two computers to communicate securely over a public network, with no prior contact and no existing shared secret. To see how this works, suppose computer *Origin* wants to send a confidential message to computer *Target*:

1. *Target* generates a public/private key pair and then sends its public key to *Origin*.

2. *Origin* encrypts the confidential message using *Target*'s public key and then sends it to *Target*.

3. *Target* decrypts the confidential message using its private key.

An eavesdropper will see the following:

- *Target*'s public key
- The secret message, encrypted with *Target*'s public key

But without *Target*'s private key, the message cannot be decrypted.

 This doesn't guard against a man-in-the-middle attack: in other words, *Origin* cannot know that *Target* isn't some malicious party. In order to authenticate the recipient, the originator needs to already know the recipient's public key or be able to validate its key through a *digital site certificate*.

The secret message sent from *Origin* to *Target* typically contains a fresh key for subsequent *symmetric* encryption. This allows public key encryption to be abandoned for the remainder of the session, in favor of a symmetric algorithm capable of handling larger messages. This protocol is particularly secure if a fresh public/private key pair is generated for each session, as no keys then need to be stored on either computer.

 The public key encryption algorithms rely on the message being smaller than the key. This makes them suitable for encrypting only small amounts of data, such as a key for subsequent symmetric encryption. If you try to encrypt a message much larger than half the key size, the provider will throw an exception.

The RSA Class

The .NET Framework provides a number of asymmetric algorithms, of which RSA is the most popular. Here's how to encrypt and decrypt with RSA:

```
byte[] data = { 1, 2, 3, 4, 5 };   // This is what we're encrypting.

using (var rsa = new RSACryptoServiceProvider())
```

```
{
  byte[] encrypted = rsa.Encrypt (data, true);
  byte[] decrypted = rsa.Decrypt (encrypted, true);
}
```

Because we didn't specify a public or private key, the cryptographic provider auto-matically generated a key pair, using the default length of 1,024 bits; you can request longer keys in increments of eight bytes, through the constructor. For security-critical applications, it's prudent to request 2,048 bits:

```
var rsa = new RSACryptoServiceProvider (2048);
```

Generating a key pair is computationally intensive—taking perhaps 100 ms. For this reason, the RSA implementation delays this until a key is actually needed, such as when calling Encrypt. This gives you the chance to load in an existing key—or key pair, should it exist.

The methods ImportCspBlob and ExportCspBlob load and save keys in byte array format. FromXmlString and ToXmlString do the same job in a string format, the string containing an XML fragment. A bool flag lets you indicate whether to include the private key when saving. Here's how to manufacture a key pair and save it to disk:

```
using (var rsa = new RSACryptoServiceProvider())
{
  File.WriteAllText ("PublicKeyOnly.xml", rsa.ToXmlString (false));
  File.WriteAllText ("PublicPrivate.xml", rsa.ToXmlString (true));
}
```

Since we didn't provide existing keys, ToXmlString forced the manufacture of a fresh key pair (on the first call). In the next example, we read back these keys and use them to encrypt and decrypt a message:

```
byte[] data = Encoding.UTF8.GetBytes ("Message to encrypt");

string publicKeyOnly = File.ReadAllText ("PublicKeyOnly.xml");
string publicPrivate = File.ReadAllText ("PublicPrivate.xml");

byte[] encrypted, decrypted;

using (var rsaPublicOnly = new RSACryptoServiceProvider())
{
  rsaPublicOnly.FromXmlString (publicKeyOnly);
  encrypted = rsaPublicOnly.Encrypt (data, true);

  // The next line would throw an exception because you need the private
  // key in order to decrypt:
  // decrypted = rsaPublicOnly.Decrypt (encrypted, true);
}

using (var rsaPublicPrivate = new RSACryptoServiceProvider())
{
  // With the private key we can successfully decrypt:
  rsaPublicPrivate.FromXmlString (publicPrivate);
```

```
    decrypted = rsaPublicPrivate.Decrypt (encrypted, true);
}
```

Digital Signing

Public key algorithms can also be used to digitally sign messages or documents. A
signature is like a hash, except that its production requires a private key and so cannot be forged. The public key is used to verify the signature. Here's an example:

```
byte[] data = Encoding.UTF8.GetBytes ("Message to sign");
byte[] publicKey;
byte[] signature;
object hasher = SHA1.Create();          // Our chosen hashing algorithm.

// Generate a new key pair, then sign the data with it:
using (var publicPrivate = new RSACryptoServiceProvider())
{
  signature = publicPrivate.SignData (data, hasher);
  publicKey = publicPrivate.ExportCspBlob (false);     // get public key
}

// Create a fresh RSA using just the public key, then test the signature.
using (var publicOnly = new RSACryptoServiceProvider())
{
  publicOnly.ImportCspBlob (publicKey);
  Console.Write (publicOnly.VerifyData (data, hasher, signature)); // True

  // Let's now tamper with the data, and recheck the signature:
  data[0] = 0;
  Console.Write (publicOnly.VerifyData (data, hasher, signature)); // False

  // The following throws an exception as we're lacking a private key:
  signature = publicOnly.SignData (data, hasher);
}
```

Signing works by first hashing the data and then applying the asymmetric algorithm
to the resultant hash. Because hashes are of a small fixed size, large documents can
be signed relatively quickly (public key encryption is much more CPU-intensive
than hashing). If you want, you can do the hashing yourself and then call SignHash
instead of SignData:

```
using (var rsa = new RSACryptoServiceProvider())
{
  byte[] hash = SHA1.Create().ComputeHash (data);
  signature = rsa.SignHash (hash, CryptoConfig.MapNameToOID ("SHA1"));
  ...
}
```

SignHash still needs to know what hash algorithm you used; CryptoConfig.MapNa
meToOID provides this information in the correct format from a friendly name such
as "SHA1".

`RSACryptoServiceProvider` produces signatures whose size matches that of the key. Currently, no mainstream algorithm produces secure signatures significantly smaller than 128 bytes (suitable for product activation codes, for instance).

 For signing to be effective, the recipient must know, and trust, the sender's public key. This can happen via prior communication, preconfiguration, or a site certificate. A site certificate is an electronic record of the originator's public key and name—itself signed by an independent trusted authority. The namespace `System.Security.Cryptography.X509Certificates` defines the types for working with certificates.

22

Advanced Threading

We started Chapter 14 with the basics of threading as a precursor to tasks and asynchrony. Specifically, we showed how to start/configure a thread and covered essential concepts such as thread pooling, blocking, spinning, and synchronization contexts. We also introduced locking and thread safety, and demonstrated the simplest signaling construct, `ManualResetEvent`.

This chapter resumes where we left off on the topic of threading. In the first three sections, we flesh out synchronization, locking, and thread safety in greater detail. We then cover:

- Nonexclusive locking (`Semaphore` and reader/writer locks)

- All of the signaling constructs (`AutoResetEvent`, `ManualResetEvent`, `Countdow nEvent`, and `Barrier`)

- Lazy initialization (`Lazy<T>` and `LazyInitializer`)

- Thread-local storage (`ThreadStaticAttribute`, `ThreadLocal<T>`, and `GetData/ SetData`)

- Preemptive threading methods (`Interrupt`, `Abort`, `Suspend`, and `Resume`)

- Timers

Threading is such a vast topic that we've put additional material online to complete the picture. Visit *http://albahari.com/threading/* for a discussion on the following, more arcane, topics:

- `Monitor.Wait` and `Monitor.Pulse` for specialized signaling scenarios

- Nonblocking synchronization techniques for micro-optimization (`Inter locked`, memory barriers, `volatile`)

- `SpinLock` and `SpinWait` for high-concurrency scenarios

Synchronization Overview

Synchronization is the act of coordinating concurrent actions for a predictable outcome. Synchronization is particularly important when multiple threads access the same data; it's surprisingly easy to run aground in this area.

The simplest and most useful synchronization tools are arguably the continuations and task combinators we described in Chapter 14. By formulating concurrent programs into asynchronous operations strung together with continuations and combinators, you lessen the need for locking and signaling. However, there are still times when the lower-level constructs come into play.

The synchronization constructs can be divided into three categories:

Exclusive locking
> Exclusive locking constructs allow just one thread to perform some activity or execute a section of code at a time. Their primary purpose is to let threads access shared writing state without interfering with one other. The exclusive locking constructs are lock, Mutex, and SpinLock.

Nonexclusive locking
> Nonexclusive locking lets you *limit* concurrency. The nonexclusive locking constructs are Semaphore(Slim) and ReaderWriterLock(Slim).

Signaling
> These allow a thread to block until receiving one or more notifications from other thread(s). The signaling constructs include ManualResetE vent(Slim), AutoResetEvent, CountdownEvent, and Barrier. The former three are referred to as *event wait handles*.

It's also possible (and tricky) to perform certain concurrent operations on shared state without locking, through the use of *nonblocking synchronization constructs*. These are Thread.MemoryBarrier, Thread.VolatileRead, Thread.VolatileWrite, the volatile keyword, and the Interlocked class. We cover this topic online, along with Monitor's Wait/Pulse methods, which can be used to write custom signaling logic—see *http://albahari.com/threading/*.

Exclusive Locking

There are three exclusive locking constructs: the lock statement, Mutex, and Spin Lock. The lock construct is the most convenient and widely used, whereas the other two target niche scenarios:

- Mutex lets you span multiple processes (computer-wide locks).

- SpinLock implements a micro-optimization that can lessen context switches in high-concurrency scenarios (see *http://albahari.com/threading/*).

The lock Statement

To illustrate the need for locking, consider the following class:

```
class ThreadUnsafe
{
  static int _val1 = 1, _val2 = 1;

  static void Go()
  {
    if (_val2 != 0) Console.WriteLine (_val1 / _val2);
    _val2 = 0;
  }
}
```

This class is not thread-safe: if Go was called by two threads simultaneously, it would be possible to get a division-by-zero error, because _val2 could be set to zero in one thread right as the other thread was in between executing the if statement and Con sole.WriteLine. Here's how lock fixes the problem:

```
class ThreadSafe
{
  static readonly object _locker = new object();
  static int _val1 = 1, _val2 = 1;

  static void Go()
  {
    lock (_locker)
    {
      if (_val2 != 0) Console.WriteLine (_val1 / _val2);
      _val2 = 0;
    }
  }
}
```

Only one thread can lock the synchronizing object (in this case, _locker) at a time, and any contending threads are blocked until the lock is released. If more than one thread contends the lock, they are queued on a "ready queue" and granted the lock on a first-come, first-served basis.[1] Exclusive locks are sometimes said to enforce *serialized* access to whatever's protected by the lock, because one thread's access cannot overlap with that of another. In this case, we're protecting the logic inside the Go method, as well as the fields _val1 and _val2.

Monitor.Enter and Monitor.Exit

C#'s lock statement is in fact a syntactic shortcut for a call to the methods Moni tor.Enter and Monitor.Exit, with a try/finally block. Here's (a simplified version of) what's actually happening within the Go method of the preceding example:

---

1 Nuances in the behavior of Windows and the CLR mean that the fairness of the queue can sometimes be violated.

```
Monitor.Enter (_locker);
try
{
  if (_val2 != 0) Console.WriteLine (_val1 / _val2);
  _val2 = 0;
}
finally { Monitor.Exit (_locker); }
```

Calling Monitor.Exit without first calling Monitor.Enter on the same object throws an exception.

The lockTaken overloads

The code that we just demonstrated is exactly what the C# 1.0, 2.0, and 3.0 compilers produce in translating a lock statement.

There's a subtle vulnerability in this code, however. Consider the (unlikely) event of an exception being thrown between the call to Monitor.Enter and the try block (due, perhaps, to Abort being called on that thread—or an OutOfMemoryException being thrown). In such a scenario, the lock may or may not be taken. If the lock *is* taken, it won't be released—because we'll never enter the try/finally block. This will result in a leaked lock. To avoid this danger, CLR 4.0's designers added the following overload to Monitor.Enter:

```
public static void Enter (object obj, ref bool lockTaken);
```

lockTaken is false after this method if (and only if) the Enter method throws an exception and the lock was not taken.

Here's the more robust pattern of use (which is exactly how C# 4.0 and later translate a lock statement):

```
bool lockTaken = false;
try
{
  Monitor.Enter (_locker, ref lockTaken);
  // Do your stuff...
}
finally { if (lockTaken) Monitor.Exit (_locker); }
```

TryEnter

Monitor also provides a TryEnter method that allows a timeout to be specified, either in milliseconds or as a TimeSpan. The method then returns true if a lock was obtained, or false if no lock was obtained because the method timed out. TryEnter can also be called with no argument, which "tests" the lock, timing out immediately if the lock can't be obtained right away. As with the Enter method, TryEnter is overloaded in CLR 4.0 to accept a lockTaken argument.

Choosing the Synchronization Object

Any object visible to each of the partaking threads can be used as a synchronizing object, subject to one hard rule: it must be a reference type. The synchronizing object is typically private (because this helps to encapsulate the locking logic) and is typically an instance or static field. The synchronizing object can double as the object it's protecting, as the _list field does in the following example:

```
class ThreadSafe
{
  List <string> _list = new List <string>();

  void Test()
  {
    lock (_list)
    {
      _list.Add ("Item 1");
      ...
```

A field dedicated for the purpose of locking (such as _locker, in the example prior) allows precise control over the scope and granularity of the lock. The containing object (this)—or even its type—can also be used as a synchronization object:

```
lock (this) { ... }
```

or:

```
lock (typeof (Widget)) { ... }    // For protecting access to statics
```

The disadvantage of locking in this way is that you're not encapsulating the locking logic, so it becomes harder to prevent deadlocking and excessive blocking. A lock on a type may also seep through application domain boundaries (within the same process—see Chapter 24).

You can also lock on local variables captured by lambda expressions or anonymous methods.

> Locking doesn't restrict access to the synchronizing object itself in any way. In other words, x.ToString() will not block because another thread has called lock(x); both threads must call lock(x) in order for blocking to occur.

When to Lock

As a basic rule, you need to lock around accessing *any writable shared field*. Even in the simplest case—an assignment operation on a single field—you must consider synchronization. In the following class, neither the Increment nor the Assign method is thread-safe:

```
class ThreadUnsafe
{
  static int _x;
  static void Increment() { _x++; }
```

```
    static void Assign()     { _x = 123; }
}
```

Here are thread-safe versions of `Increment` and `Assign`:

```
static readonly object _locker = new object();
static int _x;

static void Increment() { lock (_locker) _x++; }
static void Assign()     { lock (_locker) _x = 123; }
```

Without locks, two problems can arise:

- Operations such as incrementing a variable (or even reading/writing a variable, under certain conditions) are not atomic.

- The compiler, CLR and processor are entitled to reorder instructions and cache variables in CPU registers to improve performance—as long as such optimizations don't change the behavior of a *single*-threaded program (or a multi-threaded program that uses locks).

Locking mitigates the second problem because it creates a *memory barrier* before and after the lock. A memory barrier is a "fence" around which the effects or reordering and caching cannot cross.

 This applies not just to locks, but to all synchronization constructs. So if your use of a *signaling* construct, for instance, ensures that just one thread reads/writes a variable at a time, you don't need to lock. Hence, the following code is thread-safe without locking around x:

```
var signal = new ManualResetEvent (false);
int x = 0;
new Thread (() => { x++; signal.Set(); }).Start();
signal.WaitOne();
Console.WriteLine (x);    // 1 (always)
```

In "Nonblocking Synchronization" at *http://albahari.com/threading*, we explain how this need arises and how the memory barriers and the `Interlocked` class can provide alternatives to locking in these situations.

Locking and Atomicity

If a group of variables are always read and written within the same lock, you can say the variables are read and written *atomically*. Let's suppose fields x and y are always read and assigned within a `lock` on object `locker`:

```
lock (locker) { if (x != 0) y /= x; }
```

One can say x and y are accessed atomically, because the code block cannot be divided or preempted by the actions of another thread in such a way that it will change x or y and *invalidate its outcome*. You'll never get a division-by-zero error, providing x and y are always accessed within this same exclusive lock.

The atomicity provided by a lock is violated if an exception is thrown within a lock block. For example, consider the following:

```
decimal _savingsBalance, _checkBalance;

void Transfer (decimal amount)
{
  lock (_locker)
  {
    _savingsBalance += amount;
    _checkBalance -= amount + GetBankFee();
  }
}
```

If an exception was thrown by GetBankFee(), the bank would lose money. In this case, we could avoid the problem by calling GetBankFee earlier. A solution for more complex cases is to implement "rollback" logic within a catch or finally block.

Instruction atomicity is a different, although analogous concept: an instruction is atomic if it executes indivisibly on the underlying processor.

Nested Locking

A thread can repeatedly lock the same object in a nested (*reentrant*) fashion:

```
lock (locker)
  lock (locker)
    lock (locker)
    {
        // Do something...
    }
```

or:

```
Monitor.Enter (locker); Monitor.Enter (locker);  Monitor.Enter (locker);
// Do something...
Monitor.Exit (locker);  Monitor.Exit (locker);   Monitor.Exit (locker);
```

In these scenarios, the object is unlocked only when the outermost lock statement has exited—or a matching number of Monitor.Exit statements have executed.

Nested locking is useful when one method calls another from within a lock:

```
static readonly object _locker = new object();

static void Main()
{
  lock (_locker)
  {
     AnotherMethod();
     // We still have the lock - because locks are reentrant.
  }
}

static void AnotherMethod()
```

```
{
    lock (_locker) { Console.WriteLine ("Another method"); }
}
```

A thread can block on only the first (outermost) lock.

Deadlocks

A deadlock happens when two threads each wait for a resource held by the other, so neither can proceed. The easiest way to illustrate this is with two locks:

```
object locker1 = new object();
object locker2 = new object();

new Thread (() => {
                    lock (locker1)
                    {
                      Thread.Sleep (1000);
                      lock (locker2);          // Deadlock
                    }
                  }).Start();
lock (locker2)
{
  Thread.Sleep (1000);
  lock (locker1);                              // Deadlock
}
```

More elaborate deadlocking chains can be created with three or more threads.

 The CLR, in a standard hosting environment, is not like SQL Server and does not automatically detect and resolve deadlocks by terminating one of the offenders. A threading deadlock causes participating threads to block indefinitely, unless you've specified a locking timeout. (Under the SQL CLR integration host, however, deadlocks *are* automatically detected and a [catchable] exception is thrown on one of the threads.)

Deadlocking is one of the hardest problems in multithreading—especially when there are many interrelated objects. Fundamentally, the hard problem is that you can't be sure what locks your *caller* has taken out.

So, you might lock private field a within your class x, unaware that your caller (or caller's caller) has already locked field b within class y. Meanwhile, another thread is doing the reverse—creating a deadlock. Ironically, the problem is exacerbated by (good) object-oriented design patterns, because such patterns create call chains that are not determined until runtime.

The popular advice, "Lock objects in a consistent order to avoid deadlocks," although helpful in our initial example, is hard to apply to the scenario just described. A better strategy is to be wary of locking around calls to methods in objects that may have references back to your own object. Also, consider whether you really need to lock around calls to methods in other classes (often you do—as we'll see in "Thread Safety" on page 629—but sometimes there are other options).

Relying more on higher-level synchronization options such as task continuations/ combinators, data parallelism, and immutable types (later in this chapter) can lessen the need for locking.

Here is an alternative way to perceive the problem: when you call out to other code while holding a lock, the encapsulation of that lock subtly *leaks*. This is not a fault in the CLR or .NET Framework, but a fundamental limitation of locking in general. The problems of locking are being addressed in various research projects, including *Software Transactional Memory*.

Another deadlocking scenario arises when calling `Dispatcher.Invoke` (in a WPF application) or `Control.Invoke` (in a Windows Forms application) while in possession of a lock. If the UI happens to be running another method that's waiting on the same lock, a deadlock will happen right there. This can often be fixed simply by calling `BeginInvoke` instead of `Invoke` (or relying on asynchronous functions which do this implicitly when a synchronization context is present). Alternatively, you can release your lock before calling `Invoke`, although this won't work if your *caller* took out the lock.

Performance

Locking is fast: you can expect to acquire and release a lock in less than 50 nanoseconds on a 2015-era computer if the lock is uncontended. If it is contended, the consequential context switch moves the overhead closer to the microsecond region, although it may be longer before the thread is actually rescheduled.

Mutex

A `Mutex` is like a C# `lock`, but it can work across multiple processes. In other words, `Mutex` can be *computer-wide* as well as *application-wide*. Acquiring and releasing an uncontended `Mutex` takes around a microsecond—about 20 times slower than a `lock`.

With a `Mutex` class, you call the `WaitOne` method to lock and `ReleaseMutex` to unlock. Just as with the `lock` statement, a `Mutex` can be released only from the same thread that obtained it.

If you forget to call `ReleaseMutex` and simply call `Close` or `Dispose`, an `AbandonedMutexException` will be thrown upon anyone else waiting upon that mutex.

A common use for a cross-process `Mutex` is to ensure that only one instance of a program can run at a time. Here's how it's done:

```
class OneAtATimePlease
{
  static void Main()
  {
    // Naming a Mutex makes it available computer-wide. Use a name that's
```

```
// unique to your company and application (e.g., include your URL).

using (var mutex = new Mutex (true, "oreilly.com OneAtATimeDemo"))
{
  // Wait a few seconds if contended, in case another instance
  // of the program is still in the process of shutting down.

  if (!mutex.WaitOne (TimeSpan.FromSeconds (3), false))
  {
    Console.WriteLine ("Another instance of the app is running. Bye!");
    return;
  }
  try { RunProgram(); }
  finally { mutex.ReleaseMutex (); }
}
}

static void RunProgram()
{
  Console.WriteLine ("Running. Press Enter to exit");
  Console.ReadLine();
}
}
```

 If running under Terminal Services, a computer-wide `Mutex` is ordinarily visible only to applications in the same terminal server session. To make it visible to all terminal server sessions, prefix its name with *Global*.

Locking and Thread Safety

A program or method is thread-safe if it can work correctly in any multithreading scenario. Thread safety is achieved primarily with locking and by reducing the possibilities for thread interaction.

General-purpose types are rarely thread-safe in their entirety, for the following reasons:

- The development burden in full thread safety can be significant, particularly if a type has many fields (each field is a potential for interaction in an arbitrarily multithreaded context).

- Thread safety can entail a performance cost (payable, in part, whether or not the type is actually used by multiple threads).

- A thread-safe type does not necessarily make the program using it thread-safe, and often the work involved in the latter makes the former redundant.

Thread safety is thus usually implemented just where it needs to be, in order to handle a specific multithreading scenario.

There are, however, a few ways to "cheat" and have large and complex classes run safely in a multithreaded environment. One is to sacrifice granularity by wrapping large sections of code—even access to an entire object—within a single exclusive lock, enforcing serialized access at a high level. This tactic is, in fact, essential if you want to use thread-unsafe third-party code (or most Framework types, for that matter) in a multithreaded context. The trick is simply to use the same exclusive lock to protect access to all properties, methods, and fields on the thread-unsafe object. The solution works well if the object's methods all execute quickly (otherwise, there will be a lot of blocking).

 Primitive types aside, few .NET Framework types, when instantiated, are thread-safe for anything more than concurrent read-only access. The onus is on the developer to superimpose thread safety, typically with exclusive locks. (The collections in System.Collections.Concurrent that we cover in Chapter 23 are an exception.)

Another way to cheat is to minimize thread interaction by minimizing shared data. This is an excellent approach and is used implicitly in "stateless" middle-tier application and web page servers. Since multiple client requests can arrive simultaneously, the server methods they call must be thread-safe. A stateless design (popular for reasons of scalability) intrinsically limits the possibility of interaction, since classes do not persist data between requests. Thread interaction is then limited just to the static fields one may choose to create, for such purposes as caching commonly used data in memory and in providing infrastructure services such as authentication and auditing.

Yet another solution (in rich-client applications) is to run code that accesses shared state on the UI thread. As we saw in Chapter 14, asynchronous functions make this easy.

The final approach in implementing thread safety is to use an automatic locking regime. The .NET Framework does exactly this, if you subclass ContextBoundObject and apply the Synchronization attribute to the class. Whenever a method or property on such an object is then called, an object-wide lock is automatically taken for the whole execution of the method or property. Although this reduces the thread-safety burden, it creates problems of its own: deadlocks that would not otherwise occur, impoverished concurrency, and unintended reentrancy. For these reasons, manual locking is generally a better option—at least until a less simplistic automatic locking regime becomes available.

Thread Safety and .NET Framework Types

Locking can be used to convert thread-unsafe code into thread-safe code. A good application of this is the .NET Framework: nearly all of its nonprimitive types are not thread-safe (for anything more than read-only access) when instantiated, and yet they can be used in multithreaded code if all access to any given object is protected via a lock. Here's an example, where two threads simultaneously add an item to the same List collection, then enumerate the list:

```
class ThreadSafe
{
  static List <string> _list = new List <string>();

  static void Main()
  {
    new Thread (AddItem).Start();
    new Thread (AddItem).Start();
  }

  static void AddItem()
  {
    lock (_list) _list.Add ("Item " + _list.Count);

    string[] items;
    lock (_list) items = _list.ToArray();
    foreach (string s in items) Console.WriteLine (s);
  }
}
```

In this case, we're locking on the _list object itself. If we had two interrelated lists, we would have to choose a common object upon which to lock (we could nominate one of the lists, or better: use an independent field).

Enumerating .NET collections is also thread-unsafe in the sense that an exception is thrown if the list is modified during enumeration. Rather than locking for the duration of enumeration, in this example, we first copy the items to an array. This avoids holding the lock excessively if what we're doing during enumeration is potentially time-consuming. (Another solution is to use a reader/writer lock; see "Reader/Writer Locks" on page 919.)

Locking around thread-safe objects

Sometimes you also need to lock around accessing thread-safe objects. To illustrate, imagine that the Framework's List class was, indeed, thread-safe, and we want to add an item to a list:

```
if (!_list.Contains (newItem)) _list.Add (newItem);
```

Whether or not the list was thread-safe, this statement is certainly not! The whole if statement would have to be wrapped in a lock in order to prevent preemption in between testing for containership and adding the new item. This same lock would then need to be used everywhere we modified that list. For instance, the following statement would also need to be wrapped in the identical lock:

```
_list.Clear();
```

to ensure that it did not preempt the former statement. In other words, we would have to lock exactly as with our thread-unsafe collection classes (making the List class's hypothetical thread safety redundant).

Locking around accessing a collection can cause excessive blocking in highly concurrent environments. To this end, Framework 4.0 provides a thread-safe queue, stack, and dictionary, which we discuss in Chapter 23.

Static members

Wrapping access to an object around a custom lock works only if all concurrent threads are aware of—and use—the lock. This may not be the case if the object is widely scoped. The worst case is with static members in a public type. For instance, imagine if the static property on the `DateTime` struct, `DateTime.Now`, was not thread-safe, and that two concurrent calls could result in garbled output or an exception. The only way to remedy this with external locking might be to lock the type itself—`lock(typeof(DateTime))`—before calling `DateTime.Now`. This would work only if all programmers agreed to do this (which is unlikely). Furthermore, locking a type creates problems of its own.

For this reason, static members on the `DateTime` struct have been carefully programmed to be thread-safe. This is a common pattern throughout the .NET Framework: *static members are thread-safe; instance members are not*. Following this pattern also makes sense when writing types for public consumption, so as not to create impossible thread-safety conundrums. In other words, by making static methods thread-safe, you're programming so as not to *preclude* thread safety for consumers of that type.

**Advanced
Threading**

Thread safety in static methods is something that you must explicitly code: it doesn't happen automatically by virtue of the method being static!

Read-only thread safety

Making types thread-safe for concurrent read-only access (where possible) is advantageous because it means that consumers can avoid excessive locking. Many of the .NET Framework types follow this principle: collections, for instance, are thread-safe for concurrent readers.

Following this principle yourself is simple: if you document a type as being thread-safe for concurrent read-only access, don't write to fields within methods that a consumer would expect to be read-only (or lock around doing so). For instance, in implementing a `ToArray()` method in a collection, you might start by compacting the collection's internal structure. However, this would make it thread-unsafe for consumers that expected this to be read-only.

Read-only thread safety is one of the reasons that enumerators are separate from "enumerables": two threads can simultaneously enumerate over a collection because each gets a separate enumerator object.

In the absence of documentation, it pays to be cautious in assuming whether a method is read-only in nature. A good example is the Random class: when you call Random.Next(), its internal implementation requires that it update private seed values. Therefore, you must either lock around using the Ran dom class or maintain a separate instance per thread.

Thread Safety in Application Servers

Application servers need to be multithreaded to handle simultaneous client requests. WCF, ASP.NET, and Web Services applications are implicitly multithreaded; the same holds true for Remoting server applications that use a network channel such as TCP or HTTP. This means that when writing code on the server side, you must consider thread safety if there's any possibility of interaction among the threads processing client requests. Fortunately, such a possibility is rare; a typical server class is either stateless (no fields) or has an activation model that creates a separate object instance for each client or each request. Interaction usually arises only through static fields, sometimes used for caching in memory parts of a database to improve performance.

For example, suppose you have a RetrieveUser method that queries a database:

```
// User is a custom class with fields for user data
internal User RetrieveUser (int id) { ... }
```

If this method was called frequently, you could improve performance by caching the results in a static Dictionary. Here's a solution that takes thread safety into account:

```
static class UserCache
{
  static Dictionary <int, User> _users = new Dictionary <int, User>();

  internal static User GetUser (int id)
  {
    User u = null;

    lock (_users)
      if (_users.TryGetValue (id, out u))
        return u;

    u = RetrieveUser (id);          // Method to retrieve from database;
    lock (_users) _users [id] = u;
    return u;
  }
}
```

We must, at a minimum, lock around reading and updating the dictionary to ensure thread safety. In this example, we choose a practical compromise between simplicity and performance in locking. Our design actually creates a very small potential for inefficiency: if two threads simultaneously called this method with the same previously unretrieved id, the RetrieveUser method would be called twice—and the dictionary would be updated unnecessarily. Locking once across the whole method would prevent this, but would create a worse inefficiency: the entire cache would be locked up for the duration of calling `RetrieveUser`, during which time other threads would be blocked in retrieving *any* user.

Immutable Objects

An immutable object is one whose state cannot be altered—externally or internally. The fields in an immutable object are typically declared read-only and are fully initialized during construction.

Immutability is a hallmark of functional programming—where instead of *mutating* an object, you create a new object with different properties. LINQ follows this paradigm. Immutability is also valuable in multithreading in that it avoids the problem of shared writable state—by eliminating (or minimizing) the writable.

One pattern is to use immutable objects to encapsulate a group of related fields to minimize lock durations. To take a very simple example, suppose we had two fields as follows:

```
int _percentComplete;
string _statusMessage;
```

and we wanted to read/write them atomically. Rather than locking around these fields, we could define the following immutable class:

```
class ProgressStatus    // Represents progress of some activity
{
  public readonly int PercentComplete;
  public readonly string StatusMessage;

  // This class might have many more fields...

  public ProgressStatus (int percentComplete, string statusMessage)
  {
    PercentComplete = percentComplete;
    StatusMessage = statusMessage;
  }
}
```

Then we could define a single field of that type, along with a locking object:

```
readonly object _statusLocker = new object();
ProgressStatus _status;
```

We can now read/write values of that type without holding a lock for more than a single assignment:

```
var status = new ProgressStatus (50, "Working on it");
// Imagine we were assigning many more fields...
// ...
lock (_statusLocker) _status = status;    // Very brief lock
```

To read the object, we first obtain a copy of the object reference (within a lock). Then we can read its values without needing to hold on to the lock:

```
ProgressStatus status;
lock (_statusLocker) status = _status;    // Again, a brief lock
int pc = status.PercentComplete;
string msg = status.StatusMessage;
...
```

Nonexclusive Locking

Semaphore

A semaphore is like a nightclub: it has a certain capacity, enforced by a bouncer. Once it's full, no more people can enter, and a queue builds up outside. Then, for each person that leaves, one person enters. The constructor requires a minimum of two arguments: the number of places currently available in the nightclub and the club's total capacity.

A semaphore with a capacity of one is similar to a `Mutex` or `lock`, except that the semaphore has no "owner"—it's *thread-agnostic*. Any thread can call `Release` on a `Semaphore`, whereas with `Mutex` and `lock`, only the thread that obtained the lock can release it.

 There are two functionally similar versions of this class: `Semaphore` and `SemaphoreSlim`. The latter was introduced in Framework 4.0 and has been optimized to meet the low-latency demands of parallel programming. It's also useful in traditional multithreading because it lets you specify a cancellation token when waiting (see "Cancellation" on page 610 in Chapter 14 and it exposes a `WaitAsync` method for asynchronous programming. It cannot, however, be used for interprocess signaling.

`Semaphore` incurs about 1 microsecond in calling `WaitOne` and `Release`; `SemaphoreSlim` incurs about one-tenth of that.

Semaphores can be useful in limiting concurrency—preventing too many threads from executing a particular piece of code at once. In the following example, five threads try to enter a nightclub that allows only three threads in at once:

```
class TheClub      // No door lists!
{
  static SemaphoreSlim _sem = new SemaphoreSlim (3);    // Capacity of 3

  static void Main()
  {
    for (int i = 1; i <= 5; i++) new Thread (Enter).Start (i);
  }

  static void Enter (object id)
  {
    Console.WriteLine (id + " wants to enter");
    _sem.Wait();
```

```
    Console.WriteLine (id + " is in!");        // Only three threads
    Thread.Sleep (1000 * (int) id);            // can be here at
    Console.WriteLine (id + " is leaving");    // a time.
    _sem.Release();
  }
}
```

```
1 wants to enter
1 is in!
2 wants to enter
2 is in!
3 wants to enter
3 is in!
4 wants to enter
5 wants to enter
1 is leaving
4 is in!
2 is leaving
5 is in!
```

A Semaphore, if named, can span processes in the same way as a Mutex.

Reader/Writer Locks

Quite often, instances of a type are thread-safe for concurrent read operations, but not for concurrent updates (nor for a concurrent read and update). This can also be true with resources such as a file. Although protecting instances of such types with a simple exclusive lock for all modes of access usually does the trick, it can unreasonably restrict concurrency if there are many readers and just occasional updates. An example of where this could occur is in a business application server, where commonly used data is cached for fast retrieval in static fields. The ReaderWriterLock Slim class is designed to provide maximum-availability locking in just this scenario.

 ReaderWriterLockSlim was introduced in Framework 3.5 and is a replacement for the older "fat" ReaderWriterLock class. The latter is similar in functionality, but it is several times slower and has an inherent design fault in its mechanism for handling lock upgrades.

When compared to an ordinary lock (Monitor.Enter/Exit), ReaderWriterLockSlim is still twice as slow, though. The trade-off is less contention (when there's a lot of reading and minimal writing.)

With both classes, there are two basic kinds of lock—a read lock and a write lock:

- A write lock is universally exclusive.
- A read lock is compatible with other read locks.

So, a thread holding a write lock blocks all other threads trying to obtain a read *or* write lock (and vice versa). But if no thread holds a write lock, any number of threads may concurrently obtain a read lock.

ReaderWriterLockSlim defines the following methods for obtaining and releasing read/write locks:

```
public void EnterReadLock();
public void ExitReadLock();
public void EnterWriteLock();
public void ExitWriteLock();
```

Additionally, there are "Try" versions of all Enter*XXX* methods that accept timeout arguments in the style of Monitor.TryEnter (timeouts can occur quite easily if the resource is heavily contended). ReaderWriterLock provides similar methods, named Acquire*XXX* and Release*XXX*. These throw an ApplicationException if a timeout occurs, rather than returning false.

The following program demonstrates ReaderWriterLockSlim. Three threads continually enumerate a list, while two further threads append a random number to the list every second. A read lock protects the list readers, and a write lock protects the list writers:

```
class SlimDemo
{
  static ReaderWriterLockSlim _rw = new ReaderWriterLockSlim();
  static List<int> _items = new List<int>();
  static Random _rand = new Random();

  static void Main()
  {
    new Thread (Read).Start();
    new Thread (Read).Start();
    new Thread (Read).Start();

    new Thread (Write).Start ("A");
    new Thread (Write).Start ("B");
  }

  static void Read()
  {
    while (true)
    {
      _rw.EnterReadLock();
      foreach (int i in _items) Thread.Sleep (10);
      _rw.ExitReadLock();
    }
  }

  static void Write (object threadID)
  {
    while (true)
    {
      int newNumber = GetRandNum (100);
      _rw.EnterWriteLock();
      _items.Add (newNumber);
      _rw.ExitWriteLock();
      Console.WriteLine ("Thread " + threadID + " added " + newNumber);
```

```
      Thread.Sleep (100);
    }
  }

  static int GetRandNum (int max) { lock (_rand) return _rand.Next(max); }
}
```

In production code, you'd typically add try/finally blocks to ensure that locks were released if an exception was thrown.

Here's the result:

```
Thread B added 61
Thread A added 83
Thread B added 55
Thread A added 33
...
```

ReaderWriterLockSlim allows more concurrent Read activity than a simple lock. We can illustrate this by inserting the following line in the Write method, at the start of the while loop:

```
Console.WriteLine (_rw.CurrentReadCount + " concurrent readers");
```

This nearly always prints "3 concurrent readers" (the Read methods spend most of their time inside the foreach loops). As well as CurrentReadCount, ReaderWriter LockSlim provides the following properties for monitoring locks:

```
public bool IsReadLockHeld            { get; }
public bool IsUpgradeableReadLockHeld { get; }
public bool IsWriteLockHeld           { get; }

public int  WaitingReadCount          { get; }
public int  WaitingUpgradeCount       { get; }
public int  WaitingWriteCount         { get; }

public int  RecursiveReadCount        { get; }
public int  RecursiveUpgradeCount     { get; }
public int  RecursiveWriteCount       { get; }
```

Upgradeable locks

Sometimes it's useful to swap a read lock for a write lock in a single atomic operation. For instance, suppose you want to add an item to a list only if the item wasn't already present. Ideally, you'd want to minimize the time spent holding the (exclusive) write lock, so you might proceed as follows:

1. Obtain a read lock.

2. Test if the item is already present in the list, and if so, release the lock and return.

3. Release the read lock.

4. Obtain a write lock.

5. Add the item.

The problem is that another thread could sneak in and modify the list (e.g., adding the same item) between steps 3 and 4. ReaderWriterLockSlim addresses this through a third kind of lock called an *upgradeable lock*. An upgradeable lock is like a read lock except that it can later be promoted to a write lock in an atomic operation. Here's how you use it:

1. Call EnterUpgradeableReadLock.

2. Perform read-based activities (e.g., test whether the item is already present in the list).

3. Call EnterWriteLock (this converts the upgradeable lock to a write lock).

4. Perform write-based activities (e.g., add the item to the list).

5. Call ExitWriteLock (this converts the write lock back to an upgradeable lock).

6. Perform any other read-based activities.

7. Call ExitUpgradeableReadLock.

From the caller's perspective, it's rather like nested or recursive locking. Functionally, though, in step 3, ReaderWriterLockSlim releases your read lock and obtains a fresh write lock, atomically.

There's another important difference between upgradeable locks and read locks. Although an upgradeable lock can coexist with any number of *read* locks, only one upgradeable lock can itself be taken out at a time. This prevents conversion deadlocks by *serializing* competing conversions—just as update locks do in SQL Server:

SQL Server	ReaderWriterLockSlim
Share lock	Read lock
Exclusive lock	Write lock
Update lock	Upgradeable lock

We can demonstrate an upgradeable lock by changing the Write method in the preceding example such that it adds a number to list only if not already present:

```
while (true)
{
  int newNumber = GetRandNum (100);
  _rw.EnterUpgradeableReadLock();
  if (!_items.Contains (newNumber))
  {
    _rw.EnterWriteLock();
    _items.Add (newNumber);
    _rw.ExitWriteLock();
    Console.WriteLine ("Thread " + threadID + " added " + newNumber);
```

```
    }
    _rw.ExitUpgradeableReadLock();
    Thread.Sleep (100);
}
```

 ReaderWriterLock can also do lock conversions—but unreliably because it doesn't support the concept of upgradeable locks. This is why the designers of ReaderWriterLockSlim had to start afresh with a new class.

Lock recursion

Ordinarily, nested or recursive locking is prohibited with ReaderWriterLockSlim. Hence, the following throws an exception:

```
var rw = new ReaderWriterLockSlim();
rw.EnterReadLock();
rw.EnterReadLock();
rw.ExitReadLock();
rw.ExitReadLock();
```

It runs without error, however, if you construct ReaderWriterLockSlim as follows:

```
var rw = new ReaderWriterLockSlim (LockRecursionPolicy.SupportsRecursion);
```

This ensures that recursive locking can happen only if you plan for it. Recursive locking can create undesired complexity because it's possible to acquire more than one kind of lock:

```
rw.EnterWriteLock();
rw.EnterReadLock();
Console.WriteLine (rw.IsReadLockHeld);     // True
Console.WriteLine (rw.IsWriteLockHeld);    // True
rw.ExitReadLock();
rw.ExitWriteLock();
```

The basic rule is that once you've acquired a lock, subsequent recursive locks can be less, but not greater, on the following scale:

- Read Lock→Upgradeable Lock→Write Lock

A request to promote an upgradeable lock to a write lock, however, is always legal.

Signaling with Event Wait Handles

The simplest kind of signaling constructs are called *event wait handles* (unrelated to C# events). Event wait handles come in three flavors: AutoResetEvent, ManualRese
tEvent(Slim), and CountdownEvent. The former two are based on the common
EventWaitHandle class, where they derive all their functionality.

AutoResetEvent

An AutoResetEvent is like a ticket turnstile: inserting a ticket lets exactly one person through. The "auto" in the class's name refers to the fact that an open turnstile automatically closes or "resets" after someone steps through. A thread waits, or blocks, at the turnstile by calling WaitOne (wait at this "one" turnstile until it opens), and a ticket is inserted by calling the Set method. If a number of threads call WaitOne, a queue[2] builds up behind the turnstile. A ticket can come from any thread; in other words, any (unblocked) thread with access to the AutoResetEvent object can call Set on it to release one blocked thread.

You can create an AutoResetEvent in two ways. The first is via its constructor:

```
var auto = new AutoResetEvent (false);
```

(Passing true into the constructor is equivalent to immediately calling Set upon it.) The second way to create an AutoResetEvent is as follows:

```
var auto = new EventWaitHandle (false, EventResetMode.AutoReset);
```

In the following example, a thread is started whose job is simply to wait until signaled by another thread (see Figure 22-1):

```
class BasicWaitHandle
{
  static EventWaitHandle _waitHandle = new AutoResetEvent (false);

  static void Main()
  {
    new Thread (Waiter).Start();
    Thread.Sleep (1000);                  // Pause for a second...
    _waitHandle.Set();                    // Wake up the Waiter.
  }

  static void Waiter()
  {
    Console.WriteLine ("Waiting...");
    _waitHandle.WaitOne();                // Wait for notification
    Console.WriteLine ("Notified");
  }
}

// Output:
Waiting... (pause) Notified.
```

---

2 As with locks, the fairness of the queue can sometimes be violated due to nuances in the operating system.

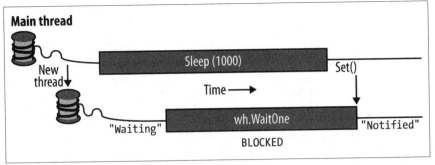

Main thread

New thread

Sleep (1000)

Set()

Time ⟶

wh.WaitOne

"Waiting"

"Notified"

BLOCKED

Figure 22-1. Signaling with an EventWaitHandle

If Set is called when no thread is waiting, the handle stays open for as long as it takes until some thread calls WaitOne. This behavior helps avoid a race between a thread heading for the turnstile, and a thread inserting a ticket ("Oops, inserted the ticket a microsecond too soon; now you'll have to wait indefinitely!"). However, calling Set repeatedly on a turnstile at which no one is waiting doesn't allow a whole party through when they arrive: only the next single person is let through and the extra tickets are "wasted."

Calling Reset on an AutoResetEvent closes the turnstile (should it be open) without waiting or blocking.

WaitOne accepts an optional timeout parameter, returning false if the wait ended because of a timeout rather than obtaining the signal.

> Calling WaitOne with a timeout of 0 tests whether a wait handle is "open," without blocking the caller. Bear in mind, though, that doing this resets the AutoResetEvent if it's open.

Disposing Wait Handles

Once you've finished with a wait handle, you can call its Close method to release the operating system resource. Alternatively, you can simply drop all references to the wait handle and allow the garbage collector to do the job for you sometime later (wait handles implement the disposal pattern whereby the finalizer calls Close). This is one of the few scenarios where relying on this backup is (arguably) acceptable, because wait handles have a light OS burden.

Wait handles are released automatically when an application domain unloads.

Two-way signaling

Let's say we want the main thread to signal a worker thread three times in a row. If the main thread simply calls Set on a wait handle several times in rapid succession, the second or third signal may get lost, since the worker may take time to process each signal.

The solution is for the main thread to wait until the worker's ready before signaling it. This can be done with another AutoResetEvent, as follows:

```
class TwoWaySignaling
{
  static EventWaitHandle _ready = new AutoResetEvent (false);
  static EventWaitHandle _go = new AutoResetEvent (false);
  static readonly object _locker = new object();
  static string _message;

  static void Main()
  {
    new Thread (Work).Start();

    _ready.WaitOne();                    // First wait until worker is ready
    lock (_locker) _message = "ooo";
    _go.Set();                           // Tell worker to go

    _ready.WaitOne();
    lock (_locker) _message = "ahhh";    // Give the worker another message
    _go.Set();

    _ready.WaitOne();
    lock (_locker) _message = null;      // Signal the worker to exit
    _go.Set();
  }

  static void Work()
  {
    while (true)
    {
      _ready.Set();                              // Indicate that we're ready
      _go.WaitOne();                             // Wait to be kicked off...
      lock (_locker)
      {
        if (_message == null) return;            // Gracefully exit
        Console.WriteLine (_message);
      }
    }
  }
}

// Output:
ooo
ahhh
```

Figure 22-2 shows this process visually.

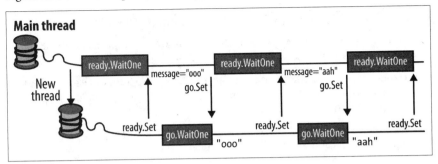

Figure 22-2. Two-way signaling

Here, we're using a null message to indicate that the worker should end. With threads that run indefinitely, it's important to have an exit strategy!

ManualResetEvent

As we described in Chapter 14, a `ManualResetEvent` functions like a simple gate. Calling `Set` opens the gate, allowing *any* number of threads calling `WaitOne` to be let through. Calling `Reset` closes the gate. Threads that call `WaitOne` on a closed gate will block; when the gate is next opened, they will be released all at once. Apart from these differences, a `ManualResetEvent` functions like an `AutoResetEvent`.

As with `AutoResetEvent`, you can construct a `ManualResetEvent` in two ways:

```
var manual1 = new ManualResetEvent (false);
var manual2 = new EventWaitHandle (false, EventResetMode.ManualReset);
```

 From Framework 4.0, there's another version of `ManualResetE vent` called `ManualResetEventSlim`. The latter is optimized for short waiting times—with the ability to opt into spinning for a set number of iterations. It also has a more efficient managed implementation and allows a `Wait` to be canceled via a `CancellationToken`. It cannot, however, be used for interprocess signaling. `ManualResetEventSlim` doesn't subclass `Wai tHandle`; however, it exposes a `WaitHandle` property that returns a `WaitHandle`-based object when called (with the performance profile of a traditional wait handle).

A `ManualResetEvent` is useful in allowing one thread to unblock many other threads. The reverse scenario is covered by `CountdownEvent`.

CountdownEvent

`CountdownEvent` lets you wait on more than one thread. The class was introduced in Framework 4.0 and has an efficient fully managed implementation. To use the class, instantiate it with the number of threads or "counts" that you want to wait on:

```
var countdown = new CountdownEvent (3);   // Initialize with "count" of 3.
```

Calling `Signal` decrements the "count"; calling `Wait` blocks until the count goes down to zero. For example:

```
static CountdownEvent _countdown = new CountdownEvent (3);

static void Main()
{
  new Thread (SaySomething).Start ("I am thread 1");
  new Thread (SaySomething).Start ("I am thread 2");
  new Thread (SaySomething).Start ("I am thread 3");
  _countdown.Wait();    // Blocks until Signal has been called 3 times
  Console.WriteLine ("All threads have finished speaking!");
}

static void SaySomething (object thing)
{
  Thread.Sleep (1000);
  Console.WriteLine (thing);
  _countdown.Signal();
}
```

> Problems for which `CountdownEvent` is effective can sometimes be solved more easily using the *structured parallelism* constructs that we describe in Chapter 23 (PLINQ and the `Parallel` class).

You can re-increment a CountdownEvent's count by calling AddCount. However, if it has already reached zero, this throws an exception: you can't "unsignal" a Countdow nEvent by calling AddCount. To avoid the possibility of an exception being thrown, you can instead call TryAddCount, which returns false if the countdown is zero.

To unsignal a countdown event, call Reset: this both unsignals the construct and resets its count to the original value.

Like ManualResetEventSlim, CountdownEvent exposes a WaitHandle property for scenarios where some other class or method expects an object based on WaitHandle.

Creating a Cross-Process EventWaitHandle

EventWaitHandle's constructor allows a "named" EventWaitHandle to be created, capable of operating across multiple processes. The name is simply a string, and it can be any value that doesn't unintentionally conflict with someone else's! If the name is already in use on the computer, you get a reference to the same underlying EventWaitHandle; otherwise, the operating system creates a new one. Here's an example:

```
EventWaitHandle wh = new EventWaitHandle (false, EventResetMode.AutoReset,
                                          "MyCompany.MyApp.SomeName");
```

If two applications each ran this code, they would be able to signal each other: the wait handle would work across all threads in both processes.

Wait Handles and Continuations

Rather than waiting on a wait handle (and blocking your thread), you can attach a "continuation" to it by calling ThreadPool.RegisterWaitForSingleObject. This method accepts a delegate that is executed when a wait handle is signaled:

```
static ManualResetEvent _starter = new ManualResetEvent (false);

public static void Main()
{
  RegisteredWaitHandle reg = ThreadPool.RegisterWaitForSingleObject
    (_starter, Go, "Some Data", -1, true);
  Thread.Sleep (5000);
  Console.WriteLine ("Signaling worker...");
  _starter.Set();
  Console.ReadLine();
  reg.Unregister (_starter);     // Clean up when we're done.
}

public static void Go (object data, bool timedOut)
{
  Console.WriteLine ("Started - " + data);
  // Perform task...
}

// Output:
```

```
(5 second delay)
Signaling worker...
Started - Some Data
```

When the wait handle is signaled (or a timeout elapses), the delegate runs on a pooled thread. You are then supposed to call Unregister to release the unmanaged handle to the callback.

In addition to the wait handle and delegate, RegisterWaitForSingleObject accepts a "black box" object that it passes to your delegate method (rather like Parameteri zedThreadStart), as well as a timeout in milliseconds (−1 meaning no timeout) and a boolean flag indicating whether the request is one-off rather than recurring.

Converting Wait Handles to Tasks

Using ThreadPool.RegisterWaitForSingleObject is awkward in practice, because you'll usually want to call Unregister from the callback itself—before the registration token is available. Thus, it makes sense to write an extension method such as the following, which converts a wait handle into a Task that you can await:

```
public static Task<bool> ToTask (this WaitHandle waitHandle,
                                 int timeout = -1)
{
  var tcs = new TaskCompletionSource<bool>();
  RegisteredWaitHandle token = null;
  var tokenReady = new ManualResetEventSlim();
  token = ThreadPool.RegisterWaitForSingleObject (
    waitHandle,
    (state, timedOut) =>
    {
      tokenReady.Wait();
      tokenReady.Dispose();
      token.Unregister (waitHandle);
      tcs.SetResult (!timedOut);
    },
    null,
    timeout,
    true);
  tokenReady.Set();
  return tcs.Task;
}
```

This lets us attach a continuation to a wait handle as follows:

```
myWaitHandle.ToTask().ContinueWith (...)
```

or await it:

```
await myWaitHandle.ToTask();
```

with an optional timeout:

```
if (!await (myWaitHandle.ToTask (5000)))
  Console.WriteLine ("Timed out");
```

Notice that in implementing `ToTask`, we used another wait handle (a `ManualResetE ventSlim`) to avoid a race condition whereby the callback runs before the registration token is assigned to the `token` variable.

WaitAny, WaitAll, and SignalAndWait

In addition to the `Set`, `WaitOne`, and `Reset` methods, there are static methods on the `WaitHandle` class to crack more complex synchronization nuts. The `WaitAny`, `WaitAll`, and `SignalAndWait` methods perform signaling and waiting operations on multiple handles. The wait handles can be of differing types (including `Mutex` and `Semphore`, since these also derive from the abstract `WaitHandle` class). `ManualResetEventSlim` and `CountdownEvent` can also partake in these methods via their `WaitHandle` properties.

 WaitAll and SignalAndWait have a weird connection to the legacy COM architecture: these methods require that the caller be in a multithreaded apartment, the model least suitable for interoperability. The main thread of a WPF or Windows Forms application, for example, is unable to interact with the clipboard in this mode. We'll discuss alternatives shortly.

`WaitHandle.WaitAny` waits for any one of an array of wait handles; `WaitHandle.WaitAll` waits on all of the given handles, atomically. This means that if you wait on two `AutoResetEvents`:

- `WaitAny` will never end up "latching" both events.
- `WaitAll` will never end up "latching" only one event.

`SignalAndWait` calls `Set` on one `WaitHandle` and then calls `WaitOne` on another `WaitHandle`. After signaling the first handle, it will jump to the head of the queue in waiting on the second handle; this helps it succeed (although the operation is not truly atomic). You can think of this method as "swapping" one signal for another and use it on a pair of `EventWaitHandles` to set up two threads to rendezvous or "meet" at the same point in time. Either `AutoResetEvent` or `ManualResetEvent` will do the trick. The first thread executes the following:

```
WaitHandle.SignalAndWait (wh1, wh2);
```

whereas the second thread does the opposite:

```
WaitHandle.SignalAndWait (wh2, wh1);
```

Alternatives to WaitAll and SignalAndWait

`WaitAll` and `SignalAndWait` won't run in a single-threaded apartment. Fortunately, there are alternatives. In the case of `SignalAndWait`, it's rare that you need its queue-jumping semantics: in our rendezvous example, for instance, it would be valid simply to call `Set` on the first wait handle and then `WaitOne` on the other, if wait handles were used solely for that rendezvous. In the following section, we'll explore yet another option for implementing a thread rendezvous.

In the case of WaitAny and WaitAll, if you don't need atomicity, you can use the code we wrote in the previous section to convert the wait handles to tasks and then use Task.WhenAny and Task.WhenAll (Chapter 14).

If you need atomicity, you can take the lowest-level approach to signaling and write the logic yourself with Monitor's Wait and Pulse methods. We describe Wait and Pulse in detail in *http://albahari.com/threading/*.

The Barrier Class

The Barrier class implements a *thread execution barrier*, allowing many threads to rendezvous at a point in time. The class is very fast and efficient, and is built upon Wait, Pulse, and spinlocks.

To use this class:

1. Instantiate it, specifying how many threads should partake in the rendezvous (you can change this later by calling AddParticipants/RemoveParticipants).

2. Have each thread call SignalAndWait when it wants to rendezvous.

Instantiating Barrier with a value of 3 causes SignalAndWait to block until that method has been called three times. It then starts over: calling SignalAndWait again blocks until called another three times. This keeps each thread "in step" with every other thread.

In the following example, each of three threads writes the numbers 0 through 4, while keeping in step with the other threads:

```
static Barrier _barrier = new Barrier (3);

static void Main()
{
  new Thread (Speak).Start();
  new Thread (Speak).Start();
  new Thread (Speak).Start();
}

static void Speak()
{
  for (int i = 0; i < 5; i++)
  {
    Console.Write (i + " ");
    _barrier.SignalAndWait();
  }
}

OUTPUT:  0 0 0 1 1 1 2 2 2 3 3 3 4 4 4
```

A really useful feature of Barrier is that you can also specify a *post-phase action* when constructing it. This is a delegate that runs after SignalAndWait has been called *n* times, but *before* the threads are unblocked (as shown in the shaded area in Figure 22-3). In our example, if we instantiate our barrier as follows:

```
static Barrier _barrier = new Barrier (3, barrier => Console.WriteLine());
```

then the output is:

```
0 0 0
1 1 1
2 2 2
3 3 3
4 4 4
```

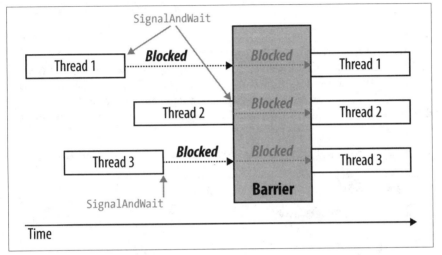

Figure 22-3. Barrier

A post-phase action can be useful for coalescing data from each of the worker threads. It doesn't have to worry about preemption, because all workers are blocked while it does its thing.

Lazy Initialization

A frequent problem in threading is how to lazily initialize a shared field in a thread-safe fashion. The need arises when you have a field of a type that's expensive to construct:

```
class Foo
{
  public readonly Expensive Expensive = new Expensive();
  ...
}
class Expensive {  /* Suppose this is expensive to construct */  }
```

The problem with this code is that instantiating Foo incurs the performance cost of instantiating Expensive—whether or not the Expensive field is ever accessed. The obvious answer is to construct the instance *on demand*:

```
class Foo
{
  Expensive _expensive;
  public Expensive Expensive         // Lazily instantiate Expensive
  {
    get
    {
      if (_expensive == null) _expensive = new Expensive();
      return _expensive;
    }
  }
  ...
}
```

The question then arises, is this thread-safe? Aside from the fact that we're accessing _expensive outside a lock without a memory barrier, consider what would happen if two threads accessed this property at once. They could both satisfy the if statement's predicate and each thread end up with a *different* instance of Expensive. As this may lead to subtle errors, we would say, in general, that this code is not thread-safe.

The solution to the problem is to lock around checking and initializing the object:

```
Expensive _expensive;
readonly object _expenseLock = new object();

public Expensive Expensive
{
  get
  {
    lock (_expenseLock)
    {
      if (_expensive == null) _expensive = new Expensive();
      return _expensive;
    }
  }
}
```

Lazy<T>

From Framework 4.0, the Lazy<T> class is available to help with lazy initialization. If instantiated with an argument of true, it implements the thread-safe initialization pattern just described.

 Lazy<T> actually implements a micro-optimized version of this pattern, called *double-checked locking*. Double-checked locking performs an additional volatile read to avoid the cost of obtaining a lock if the object is already initialized.

To use Lazy<T>, instantiate the class with a value factory delegate that tells it how to initialize a new value, and the argument true. Then access its value via the Value property:

```
Lazy<Expensive> _expensive = new Lazy<Expensive>
  (() => new Expensive(), true);

public Expensive Expensive { get { return _expensive.Value; } }
```

If you pass false into Lazy<T>'s constructor, it implements the thread-unsafe lazy initialization pattern that we described at the start of this section—this makes sense when you want to use Lazy<T> in a single-threaded context.

LazyInitializer

LazyInitializer is a static class that works exactly like Lazy<T> except:

- Its functionality is exposed through a static method that operates directly on a field in your own type. This avoids a level of indirection, improving performance in cases where you need extreme optimization.
- It offers another mode of initialization in which multiple threads can race to initialize.

To use LazyInitializer, call EnsureInitialized before accessing the field, passing a reference to the field and the factory delegate:

```
Expensive _expensive;
public Expensive Expensive
{
  get          // Implement double-checked locking
  {
    LazyInitializer.EnsureInitialized (ref _expensive,
                                       () => new Expensive());
    return _expensive;
  }
}
```

You can also pass in another argument to request that competing threads *race* to initialize. This sounds similar to our original thread-unsafe example, except that the first thread to finish always wins—and so you end up with only one instance. The advantage of this technique is that it's even faster (on multicores) than double-checked locking—because it can be implemented entirely without locks using advanced techniques that we describe in "Nonblocking Synchronization" and "Lazy Initialization" at *http://albahari.com/threading/*. This is an extreme (and rarely needed) optimization that comes at a cost:

- It's slower when more threads race to initialize than you have cores.
- It potentially wastes CPU resources performing redundant initialization.
- The initialization logic must be thread-safe (in this case, it would be thread-unsafe if Expensive's constructor wrote to static fields, for instance).

- If the initializer instantiates an object requiring disposal, the "wasted" object won't get disposed without additional logic.

Thread-Local Storage

Much of this chapter has focused on synchronization constructs and the issues arising from having threads concurrently access the same data. Sometimes, however, you want to keep data isolated, ensuring that each thread has a separate copy. Local variables achieve exactly this, but they are useful only with transient data.

The solution is *thread-local storage*. You might be hard-pressed to think of a requirement: data you'd want to keep isolated to a thread tends to be transient by nature. Its main application is for storing "out-of-band" data—that which supports the execution path's infrastructure, such as messaging, transaction, and security tokens. Passing such data around in method parameters is extremely clumsy and alienates all but your own methods; storing such information in ordinary static fields means sharing it among all threads.

Thread-local storage can also be useful in optimizing parallel code. It allows each thread to exclusively access its own version of a thread-unsafe object without needing locks—and without needing to reconstruct that object between method calls.

However, it doesn't mix well with asynchronous code, because continuations may execute on a different thread to the antecedent.

There are three ways to implement thread-local storage.

[ThreadStatic]

The easiest approach to thread-local storage is to mark a static field with the `Thread Static` attribute:

```
[ThreadStatic] static int _x;
```

Each thread then sees a separate copy of _x.

Unfortunately, [ThreadStatic] doesn't work with instance fields (it simply does nothing); nor does it play well with field initializers—they execute only *once* on the thread that's running when the static constructor executes. If you need to work with instance fields—or start with a nondefault value—ThreadLocal<T> provides a better option.

ThreadLocal<T>

ThreadLocal<T> is new to Framework 4.0. It provides thread-local storage for both static and instance fields—and allows you to specify default values.

Here's how to create a ThreadLocal<int> with a default value of 3 for each thread:

```
static ThreadLocal<int> _x = new ThreadLocal<int> (() => 3);
```

You then use _x's Value property to get or set its thread-local value. A bonus of using ThreadLocal is that values are lazily evaluated: the factory function evaluates on the first call (for each thread).

ThreadLocal<T> and instance fields

ThreadLocal<T> is also useful with instance fields and captured local variables. For example, consider the problem of generating random numbers in a multithreaded environment. The Random class is not thread-safe, so we have to either lock around using Random (limiting concurrency) or generate a separate Random object for each thread. ThreadLocal<T> makes the latter easy:

```
var localRandom = new ThreadLocal<Random>(() => new Random());
Console.WriteLine (localRandom.Value.Next());
```

Our factory function for creating the Random object is a bit simplistic, though, in that Random's parameterless constructor relies on the system clock for a random number seed. This may be the same for two Random objects created within ~10 ms of each other. Here's one way to fix it:

```
var localRandom = new ThreadLocal<Random>
  ( () => new Random (Guid.NewGuid().GetHashCode()) );
```

We use this in the following chapter (see the parallel spellchecking example in "PLINQ").

GetData and SetData

The third approach is to use two methods in the Thread class: GetData and SetData. These store data in thread-specific "slots." Thread.GetData reads from a thread's isolated data store; Thread.SetData writes to it. Both methods require a LocalDataStoreSlot object to identify the slot. The same slot can be used across all threads and they'll still get separate values. Here's an example:

```
class Test
{
  // The same LocalDataStoreSlot object can be used across all threads.
  LocalDataStoreSlot _secSlot = Thread.GetNamedDataSlot ("securityLevel");

  // This property has a separate value on each thread.
  int SecurityLevel
  {
    get
    {
      object data = Thread.GetData (_secSlot);
      return data == null ? 0 : (int) data;     // null == uninitialized
    }
    set { Thread.SetData (_secSlot, value); }
```

```
    }
    ...
```

In this instance, we called `Thread.GetNamedDataSlot`, which creates a named slot—this allows sharing of that slot across the application. Alternatively, you can control a slot's scope yourself with an unnamed slot, obtained by calling `Thread.Allocate DataSlot`:

```
class Test
{
  LocalDataStoreSlot _secSlot = Thread.AllocateDataSlot();
    ...
```

`Thread.FreeNamedDataSlot` will release a named data slot across all threads, but only once all references to that `LocalDataStoreSlot` have dropped out of scope and have been garbage-collected. This ensures that threads don't get data slots pulled out from under their feet, as long as they keep a reference to the appropriate `LocalDa taStoreSlot` object while the slot is needed.

Interrupt and Abort

The `Interrupt` and `Abort` methods act preemptively on another thread. `Interrupt` has no valid use-case, whereas `Abort` is occasionally useful.

`Interrupt` forcibly releases a blocked thread, throwing a `ThreadInterruptedExcep tion` on the thread. If the thread is not blocked, execution continues until it next blocks, and then a `ThreadInterruptedException` is thrown. `Interrupt` is useless because there is no scenario that can't be better solved with signaling constructs and cancellation tokens (or the `Abort` method). It's also inherently dangerous because you can never really be sure where, in the code, a thread will be forcibly unblocked (it could within the internals of the .NET Framework, for instance).

`Abort` attempts to forcibly end another thread, throwing a `ThreadAbortException` on the thread right where it's executing (unmanaged code excepted). `ThreadAbor tException` is unusual in that while it can be caught, the exception is rethrown at the end of the `catch` block (in an attempt to terminate the thread for good) unless you call `Thread.ResetAbort` within the `catch` block. (In the interim, the thread has a `ThreadState` of `AbortRequested`.)

 An unhandled `ThreadAbortException` is one of only two types of exception that does not cause application shutdown (the other is `AppDomainUnloadException`).

To preserve the integrity of the application domain, any `finally` blocks are honored and static constructors are never aborted part-way through. Despite this, `Abort` is unsuitable for general-purpose cancellation because it's still possible for an aborted thread to cause trouble and pollute the application domain (or even the process). For example, suppose that a type's instance constructor obtains an unmanaged resource (e.g., a file handle), which it releases in its `Dispose` method. If a thread is aborted before the constructor completes, the partially constructed object cannot be disposed, and the unmanaged handle will leak. (The finalizer, if present, will still run, but not until the GC catches up with it.) This vulnerability applies to basic .NET Framework types, including FileStream, making Abort unsuitable in most scenarios. For an extended discussion on why aborting .NET Framework code is not safe, see the topic "Aborting Threads" at *http://www.albahari.com/threading/*.

When there's no alternative to using Abort, you can mitigate most of the potential damage by running the thread in another application domain and recreating the domain after aborting the thread (this is what LINQPad does when you cancel a query). We discuss application domains in Chapter 24.

 It's valid and safe to call Abort on your own thread because you know exactly where you are. This is occasionally useful when you want an exception to get rethrown after each catch block—ASP.NET does exactly this when you call Redirect.

Suspend and Resume

Suspend and Resume freeze and unfreeze another thread. A frozen thread acts as though it's blocked, although suspension is considered distinct from blocking (as reported by its ThreadState). Just as with Interrupt, Suspend/Resume lack valid use-cases and are potentially dangerous: if you suspend a thread while it holds a lock, no other thread can obtain that lock (including your own), making your program vulnerable to deadlocking. For this reason, Suspend and Resume were deprecated in Framework 2.0.

Suspending a thread is mandatory, however, if you want to obtain stack trace on another thread. This is sometimes useful for diagnostic purposes, and can be done as follows:

```
StackTrace stackTrace;    // in System.Diagnostics
targetThread.Suspend();
try { stackTrace = new StackTrace (targetThread, true); }
finally { targetThread.Resume(); }
```

Unfortunately, this is vulnerable to deadlocking, because obtaining a stack trace itself obtains locks through its use of reflection. You can work around this by having another thread call Resume if it's still suspended after, say, 200 ms (at that time, one can assume a deadlock has occurred). Of course, this will invalidate the stack trace, but this is infinitely better than deadlocking the application:

```
StackTrace stackTrace = null;
var ready = new ManualResetEventSlim();

new Thread (() =>
{
  // Backstop to release thread in case of deadlock:
  ready.Set();
  Thread.Sleep (200);
  try { targetThread.Resume(); } catch { }
```

```
    }).Start();

    ready.Wait();
    targetThread.Suspend();
    try { stackTrace = new StackTrace (targetThread, true); }
    catch { /* Deadlock */ }
    finally
    {
      try { targetThread.Resume(); }
      catch { stackTrace = null;  /* Deadlock */  }
    }
```

Timers

If you need to execute some method repeatedly at regular intervals, the easiest way
is with a *timer*. Timers are convenient and efficient in their use of memory and
resources—compared with techniques such as the following:

```
new Thread (delegate() {
                        while (enabled)
                        {
                          DoSomeAction();
                          Thread.Sleep (TimeSpan.FromHours (24));
                        }
                      }).Start();
```

Not only does this permanently tie up a thread resource, but without additional
coding, DoSomeAction will happen at a later time each day. Timers solve these prob‐
lems.

The .NET Framework provides four timers. Two of these are general-purpose mul‐
tithreaded timers:

- System.Threading.Timer
- System.Timers.Timer

The other two are special-purpose single-threaded timers:

- System.Windows.Forms.Timer (Windows Forms timer)
- System.Windows.Threading.DispatcherTimer (WPF timer)

The multithreaded timers are more powerful, accurate, and flexible; the single-
threaded timers are safer and more convenient for running simple tasks that update
Windows Forms controls or WPF elements.

Multithreaded Timers

System.Threading.Timer is the simplest multithreaded timer: it has just a con‐
structor and two methods (a delight for minimalists, as well as book authors!). In

the following example, a timer calls the Tick method, which writes "tick..." after five seconds have elapsed, and then every second after that until the user presses Enter:

```
using System;
using System.Threading;

class Program
{
  static void Main()
  {
    // First interval = 5000ms; subsequent intervals = 1000ms
    Timer tmr = new Timer (Tick, "tick...", 5000, 1000);
    Console.ReadLine();
    tmr.Dispose();        // This both stops the timer and cleans up.
  }

  static void Tick (object data)
  {
    // This runs on a pooled thread
    Console.WriteLine (data);         // Writes "tick..."
  }
}
```

 See "Timers" on page 518 in Chapter 12 for a discussion on disposing multithreaded timers.

You can change a timer's interval later by calling its Change method. If you want a timer to fire just once, specify Timeout.Infinite in the constructor's last argument.

The .NET Framework provides another timer class of the same name in the System.Timers namespace. This simply wraps the System.Threading.Timer, providing additional convenience while using the identical underlying engine. Here's a summary of its added features:

- An IComponent implementation, allowing it to be sited in the Visual Studio's Designer's component tray
- An Interval property instead of a Change method
- An Elapsed *event* instead of a callback delegate
- An Enabled property to start and stop the timer (its default value being false)
- Start and Stop methods in case you're confused by Enabled
- An AutoReset flag for indicating a recurring event (default value is true)
- A SynchronizingObject property with Invoke and BeginInvoke methods for safely calling methods on WPF elements and Windows Forms controls

Here's an example:

```
using System;
using System.Timers;    // Timers namespace rather than Threading

class SystemTimer
{
  static void Main()
  {
    Timer tmr = new Timer();      // Doesn't require any args
    tmr.Interval = 500;
    tmr.Elapsed += tmr_Elapsed;   // Uses an event instead of a delegate
    tmr.Start();                  // Start the timer
    Console.ReadLine();
    tmr.Stop();                   // Stop the timer
    Console.ReadLine();
    tmr.Start();                  // Restart the timer
    Console.ReadLine();
    tmr.Dispose();                // Permanently stop the timer
  }

  static void tmr_Elapsed (object sender, EventArgs e)
  {
    Console.WriteLine ("Tick");
  }
}
```

Multithreaded timers use the thread pool to allow a few threads to serve many timers. This means that the callback method or Elapsed event may fire on a different thread each time it is called. Furthermore, the Elapsed event always fires (approximately) on time—regardless of whether the previous Elapsed event finished executing. Hence, callbacks or event handlers must be thread-safe.

The precision of multithreaded timers depends on the operating system, and is typically in the 10–20 ms region. If you need greater precision, you can use native interop and call the Windows multimedia timer. This has precision down to 1 ms and it is defined in *winmm.dll*. First call timeBeginPeriod to inform the operating system that you need high timing precision, and then call timeSetEvent to start a multimedia timer.

When you're done, call timeKillEvent to stop the timer and timeEndPeriod to inform the OS that you no longer need high timing precision. Chapter 25 demonstrates calling external methods with P/Invoke. You can find complete examples on the Internet that use the multimedia timer by searching for the keywords *dllimport winmm.dll timesetevent*.

Single-Threaded Timers

The .NET Framework provides timers designed to eliminate thread-safety issues for WPF and Windows Forms applications:

- `System.Windows.Threading.DispatcherTimer` (WPF)
- `System.Windows.Forms.Timer` (Windows Forms)

 The single-threaded timers are not designed to work outside their respective environments. If you use a Windows Forms timer in a Windows Service application, for instance, the `Timer` event won't fire!

Both are like `System.Timers.Timer` in the members that they expose—`Interval`, `Start`, and `Stop` (and `Tick`, which is equivalent to `Elapsed`)—and are used in a similar manner. However, they differ in how they work internally. Instead of firing timer events on pooled threads, they post the events to the WPF or Windows Forms message loop. This means that the `Tick` event always fires on the same thread that originally created the timer—which, in a normal application, is the same thread used to manage all user interface elements and controls. This has a number of benefits:

- You can forget about thread safety.
- A fresh `Tick` will never fire until the previous `Tick` has finished processing.
- You can update user interface elements and controls directly from `Tick` event handling code, without calling `Control.BeginInvoke` or `Dispatcher.BeginInvoke`.

Thus, a program employing these timers is not really multithreaded: you end up with the same kind of pseudoconcurrency that we described in Chapter 14 with asynchronous functions that execute on a UI thread. One thread serves all timers— as well as the processing UI events. Which means that the `Tick` event handler must execute quickly, otherwise the user interface becomes unresponsive.

This makes the WPF and Windows Forms timers suitable for small jobs, typically updating some aspect of the UI (e.g., a clock or countdown display).

In terms of precision, the single-threaded timers are similar to the multithreaded timers (tens of milliseconds), although they are typically less *accurate* because they can be delayed while other user interface requests (or other timer events) are processed.

23

Parallel Programming

In this chapter, we cover the multithreading APIs and constructs aimed at leveraging multicore processors:

- Parallel LINQ or *PLINQ*
- The `Parallel` class
- The *task parallelism* constructs
- The *concurrent collections*

These were added in Framework 4.0 and are collectively known (loosely) as PFX (Parallel Framework). The `Parallel` class together with the task parallelism constructs is called the *Task Parallel Library*, or TPL.

You'll need to be comfortable with the fundamentals in Chapter 14 before reading this chapter—particularly locking, thread safety, and the `Task` class.

Why PFX?

Over the past 10 years, CPU manufacturers have shifted from single- to multicore processors. This is problematic for us as programmers because single-threaded code does not automatically run faster as a result of those extra cores.

Leveraging multiple cores is easy for most server applications, where each thread can independently handle a separate client request, but is harder on the desktop—because it typically requires that you take your computationally intensive code and do the following:

1. *Partition* it into small chunks.

2. Execute those chunks in parallel via multithreading.

3. *Collate* the results as they become available, in a thread-safe and performant manner.

Although you can do all of this with the classic multithreading constructs, it's awkward—particularly the steps of partitioning and collating. A further problem is that the usual strategy of locking for thread safety causes a lot of contention when many threads work on the same data at once.

The PFX libraries have been designed specifically to help in these scenarios.

 Programming to leverage multicores or multiple processors is called *parallel programming*. This is a subset of the broader concept of multithreading.

PFX Concepts

There are two strategies for partitioning work among threads: *data parallelism* and *task parallelism*.

When a set of tasks must be performed on many data values, we can parallelize by having each thread perform the (same) set of tasks on a subset of values. This is called *data parallelism* because we are partitioning the *data* between threads. In contrast, with *task parallelism*, we partition the *tasks*; in other words, we have each thread perform a different task.

In general, data parallelism is easier and scales better to highly parallel hardware, because it reduces or eliminates shared data (thereby reducing contention and thread-safety issues). Also, data parallelism leverages the fact that there are often more data values than discrete tasks, increasing the parallelism potential.

Data parallelism is also conducive to *structured parallelism*, which means that parallel work units start and finish in the same place in your program. In contrast, task parallelism tends to be unstructured, meaning that parallel work units may start and finish in places scattered across your program. Structured parallelism is simpler and less error-prone and allows you to farm the difficult job of partitioning and thread coordination (and even result collation) out to libraries.

PFX Components

PFX comprises two layers of functionality, as shown in Figure 23-1. The higher layer consists of two *structured data parallelism* APIs: PLINQ and the Parallel class. The lower layer contains the task parallelism classes—plus a set of additional constructs to help with parallel programming activities.

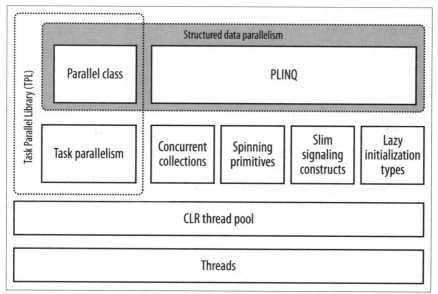

Figure 23-1. PFX components

PLINQ offers the richest functionality: it automates all the steps of parallelization—including partitioning the work into tasks, executing those tasks on threads, and collating the results into a single output sequence. It's called *declarative*—because you simply declare that you want to parallelize your work (which you structure as a LINQ query) and let the Framework take care of the implementation details. In contrast, the other approaches are *imperative*, in that you need to explicitly write code to partition or collate. In the case of the `Parallel` class, you must collate results yourself; with the task parallelism constructs, you must partition the work yourself, too:

	Partitions work	Collates results
PLINQ	Yes	Yes
The `Parallel` class	Yes	No
PFX's task parallelism	No	No

The concurrent collections and spinning primitives help you with lower-level parallel programming activities. These are important because PFX has been designed to work not only with today's hardware, but also with future generations of processors with far more cores. If you want to move a pile of chopped wood, and you have 32 workers to do the job, the biggest challenge is moving the wood without the workers getting in each other's way. It's the same with dividing an algorithm among 32 cores: if ordinary locks are used to protect common resources, the resultant blocking may mean that only a fraction of those cores are ever actually busy at once. The concurrent collections are tuned specifically for highly concurrent access, with the focus on minimizing or eliminating blocking. PLINQ and the `Parallel` class themselves rely on the concurrent collections and on spinning primitives for efficient management of work.

Other Uses for PFX

The parallel programming constructs are useful not only for leveraging multicores, but in other scenarios:

- The concurrent collections are sometimes appropriate when you want a thread-safe queue, stack, or dictionary.

- `BlockingCollection` provides an easy means to implement producer/consumer structures, and is a good way to *limit* concurrency.

- Tasks are the basis of asynchronous programming, as we saw in Chapter 14.

When to Use PFX

The primary use case for PFX is *parallel programming*: leveraging multicore processors to speed up computationally intensive code.

A challenge in leveraging multicores is Amdahl's law, which states that the maximum performance improvement from parallelization is governed by the portion of the code that must execute sequentially. For instance, if only two-thirds of an algorithm's execution time is parallelizable, you can never exceed a threefold performance gain—even with an infinite number of cores.

So, before proceeding, it's worth verifying that the bottleneck is in parallelizable code. It's also worth considering whether your code *needs* to be computationally intensive—optimization is often the easiest and most effective approach. There's a trade-off, though, in that some optimization techniques can make it harder to parallelize code.

The easiest gains come with what's called *embarrassingly parallel* problems—where a job can be divided easily into tasks that execute efficiently on their own (structured parallelism is very well suited to such problems). Examples include many image processing tasks, ray tracing, and brute force approaches in mathematics or cryptography. An example of a nonembarrassingly parallel problem is implementing an optimized version of the quicksort algorithm—a good result takes some thought and may require unstructured parallelism.

PLINQ

PLINQ automatically parallelizes local LINQ queries. PLINQ has the advantage of being easy to use in that it offloads the burden of both work partitioning and result collation to the Framework.

To use PLINQ, simply call AsParallel() on the input sequence and then continue the LINQ query as usual. The following query calculates the prime numbers between 3 and 100,000—making full use of all cores on the target machine:

```
// Calculate prime numbers using a simple (unoptimized) algorithm.

IEnumerable<int> numbers = Enumerable.Range (3, 100000-3);

var parallelQuery =
  from n in numbers.AsParallel()
  where Enumerable.Range (2, (int) Math.Sqrt (n)).All (i => n % i > 0)
  select n;

int[] primes = parallelQuery.ToArray();
```

AsParallel is an extension method in System.Linq.ParallelEnumerable. It wraps the input in a sequence based on ParallelQuery<TSource>, which causes the LINQ query operators that you subsequently call to bind to an alternate set of extension methods defined in ParallelEnumerable. These provide parallel implementations of each of the standard query operators. Essentially, they work by partitioning the input sequence into chunks that execute on different threads, collating the results back into a single output sequence for consumption (see Figure 23-2).

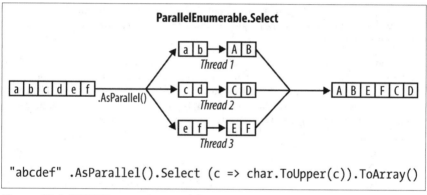

Figure 23-2. PLINQ execution model

Calling AsSequential() unwraps a ParallelQuery sequence so that subsequent query operators bind to the standard query operators and execute sequentially. This is necessary before calling methods that have side effects or are not thread-safe.

For query operators that accept two input sequences (Join, GroupJoin, Concat, Union, Intersect, Except, and Zip), you must apply AsParallel() to both input sequences (otherwise, an exception is thrown). You don't, however, need to keep applying AsParallel to a query as it progresses, because PLINQ's query operators output another ParallelQuery sequence. In fact, calling AsParallel again introduces inefficiency in that it forces merging and repartitioning of the query:

```
mySequence.AsParallel()          // Wraps sequence in ParallelQuery<int>
          .Where (n => n > 100)  // Outputs another ParallelQuery<int>
          .AsParallel()          // Unnecessary - and inefficient!
          .Select (n => n * n)
```

Not all query operators can be effectively parallelized. For those that cannot (see "PLINQ Limitations" on page 952), PLINQ implements the operator sequentially instead. PLINQ may also operate sequentially if it suspects that the overhead of parallelization will actually slow a particular query.

PLINQ is only for local collections: it doesn't work with LINQ to SQL or Entity Framework because in those cases, the LINQ translates into SQL which then executes on a database server. However, you *can* use PLINQ to perform additional local querying on the result sets obtained from database queries.

 If a PLINQ query throws an exception, it's rethrown as an AggregateException whose InnerExceptions property contains the real exception (or exceptions). See "Working with AggregateException" on page 978 for more details.

Why Isn't AsParallel the Default?

Given that AsParallel transparently parallelizes LINQ queries, the question arises, "Why didn't Microsoft simply parallelize the standard query operators and make PLINQ the default?"

There are a number of reasons for the *opt-in* approach. First, for PLINQ to be useful, there has to be a reasonable amount of computationally intensive work for it to farm out to worker threads. Most LINQ to Objects queries execute very quickly, and not only would parallelization be unnecessary, but the overhead of partitioning, collating, and coordinating the extra threads may actually slow things down.

Additionally:

- The output of a PLINQ query (by default) may differ from a LINQ query with respect to element ordering (see "PLINQ and Ordering" on page 951).

- PLINQ wraps exceptions in an AggregateException (to handle the possibility of multiple exceptions being thrown).

- PLINQ will give unreliable results if the query invokes thread-unsafe methods.

Finally, PLINQ offers quite a few hooks for tuning and tweaking. Burdening the standard LINQ to Objects API with such nuances would add distraction.

Parallel Execution Ballistics

Like ordinary LINQ queries, PLINQ queries are lazily evaluated. This means that execution is triggered only when you begin consuming the results—typically via a foreach loop (although it may also be via a conversion operator such as ToArray or an operator that returns a single element or value).

As you enumerate the results, though, execution proceeds somewhat differently from that of an ordinary sequential query. A sequential query is powered entirely by the consumer in a "pull" fashion: each element from the input sequence is fetched exactly when required by the consumer. A parallel query ordinarily uses independent threads to fetch elements from the input sequence slightly *ahead* of when they're needed by the consumer (rather like a teleprompter for newsreaders, or an antiskip buffer in CD players). It then processes the elements in parallel through the query chain, holding the results in a small buffer so that they're ready for the consumer on demand. If the consumer pauses or breaks out of the enumeration early, the query processor also pauses or stops so as not to waste CPU time or memory.

 You can tweak PLINQ's buffering behavior by calling WithMergeOptions after AsParallel. The default value of AutoBuffered generally gives the best overall results. NotBuffered disables the buffer and is useful if you want to see results as soon as possible; FullyBuffered caches the entire result set before presenting it to the consumer (the OrderBy and Reverse operators naturally work this way, as do the element, aggregation, and conversion operators).

PLINQ and Ordering

A side effect of parallelizing the query operators is that when the results are collated, it's not necessarily in the same order that they were submitted (see Figure 23-2). In other words, LINQ's normal order-preservation guarantee for sequences no longer holds.

If you need order preservation, you can force it by calling AsOrdered() after AsParallel():

```
myCollection.AsParallel().AsOrdered()...
```

Calling AsOrdered incurs a performance hit with large numbers of elements because PLINQ must keep track of each element's original position.

You can negate the effect of AsOrdered later in a query by calling AsUnordered: this introduces a "random shuffle point" that allows the query to execute more efficiently from that point on. So if you wanted to preserve input-sequence ordering for just the first two query operators, you'd do this:

```
inputSequence.AsParallel().AsOrdered()
  .QueryOperator1()
  .QueryOperator2()
  .AsUnordered()        // From here on, ordering doesn't matter
  .QueryOperator3()
  ...
```

AsOrdered is not the default because for most queries, the original input ordering doesn't matter. In other words, if AsOrdered was the default, you'd have to apply AsUnordered to the majority of your parallel queries to get the best performance, which would be burdensome.

PLINQ Limitations

There are currently some practical limitations on what PLINQ can parallelize. These limitations may loosen with subsequent service packs and Framework versions.

The following query operators prevent a query from being parallelized, unless the source elements are in their original indexing position:

- The indexed versions of Select, SelectMany, and ElementAt

Most query operators change the indexing position of elements (including those that remove elements, such as Where). This means that if you want to use the preceding operators, they'll usually need to be at the start of the query.

The following query operators are parallelizable but use an expensive partitioning strategy that can sometimes be slower than sequential processing:

- Join, GroupBy, GroupJoin, Distinct, Union, Intersect, and Except

The Aggregate operator's *seeded* overloads in their standard incarnations are not parallelizable—PLINQ provides special overloads to deal with this (see "Optimizing PLINQ" on page 956).

All other operators are parallelizable, although use of these operators doesn't guarantee that your query will be parallelized. PLINQ may run your query sequentially if it suspects that the overhead of parallelization will slow down that particular query. You can override this behavior and force parallelism by calling the following after AsParallel():

```
.WithExecutionMode (ParallelExecutionMode.ForceParallelism)
```

Example: Parallel Spellchecker

Suppose we want to write a spellchecker that runs quickly with very large documents by leveraging all available cores. By formulating our algorithm into a LINQ query, we can very easily parallelize it.

The first step is to download a dictionary of English words into a HashSet for efficient lookup:

```
if (!File.Exists ("WordLookup.txt"))    // Contains about 150,000 words
  new WebClient().DownloadFile (
    "http://www.albahari.com/ispell/allwords.txt", "WordLookup.txt");

var wordLookup = new HashSet<string> (
  File.ReadAllLines ("WordLookup.txt"),
  StringComparer.InvariantCultureIgnoreCase);
```

We'll then use our word lookup to create a test "document" comprising an array of a million random words. After building the array, we'll introduce a couple of spelling mistakes:

```
var random = new Random();
string[] wordList = wordLookup.ToArray();

string[] wordsToTest = Enumerable.Range (0, 1000000)
  .Select (i => wordList [random.Next (0, wordList.Length)])
  .ToArray();

wordsToTest [12345] = "woozsh";     // Introduce a couple
wordsToTest [23456] = "wubsie";     // of spelling mistakes.
```

Now we can perform our parallel spellcheck by testing wordsToTest against wor
dLookup. PLINQ makes this very easy:

```
var query = wordsToTest
  .AsParallel()
  .Select  ((word, index) => new IndexedWord { Word=word, Index=index })
  .Where   (iword => !wordLookup.Contains (iword.Word))
  .OrderBy (iword => iword.Index);

foreach (var mistake in query)
  Console.WriteLine (mistake.Word + " - index = " + mistake.Index);

// OUTPUT:
// woozsh - index = 12345
// wubsie - index = 23456
```

IndexedWord is a custom struct that we define as follows:

```
struct IndexedWord { public string Word; public int Index; }
```

The wordLookup.Contains method in the predicate gives the query some "meat"
and makes it worth parallelizing.

> We could simplify the query slightly by using an anonymous
> type instead of the IndexedWord struct. However, this would
> degrade performance because anonymous types (being classes
> and therefore reference types) incur the cost of heap-based
> allocation and subsequent garbage collection.
>
> The difference might not be enough to matter with sequential
> queries, but with parallel queries, favoring stack-based alloca-
> tion can be quite advantageous. This is because stack-based
> allocation is highly parallelizable (as each thread has its own
> stack), whereas all threads must compete for the same heap—
> managed by a single memory manager and garbage collector.

Using ThreadLocal<T>

Let's extend our example by parallelizing the creation of the random test-word list
itself. We structured this as a LINQ query, so it should be easy. Here's the sequential
version:

```
string[] wordsToTest = Enumerable.Range (0, 1000000)
  .Select (i => wordList [random.Next (0, wordList.Length)])
  .ToArray();
```

Unfortunately, the call to `random.Next` is not thread-safe, so it's not as simple as inserting `AsParallel()` into the query. A potential solution is to write a function that locks around `random.Next`; however, this would limit concurrency. The better option is to use `ThreadLocal<Random>` (see "Thread-Local Storage" on page 936 in the preceding chapter) to create a separate `Random` object for each thread. We can then parallelize the query as follows:

```
var localRandom = new ThreadLocal<Random>
  ( () => new Random (Guid.NewGuid().GetHashCode()) );

string[] wordsToTest = Enumerable.Range (0, 1000000).AsParallel()
  .Select (i => wordList [localRandom.Value.Next (0, wordList.Length)])
  .ToArray();
```

In our factory function for instantiating a `Random` object, we pass in a `Guid`'s hash-code to ensure that if two `Random` objects are created within a short period of time, they'll yield different random number sequences.

When to Use PLINQ

It's tempting to search your existing applications for LINQ queries and experiment with parallelizing them. This is usually unproductive, because most problems for which LINQ is obviously the best solution tend to execute very quickly and so don't benefit from parallelization. A better approach is to find a CPU-intensive bottleneck and then consider, "Can this be expressed as a LINQ query?" (A welcome side effect of such restructuring is that LINQ typically makes code smaller and more readable.)

PLINQ is well suited to embarrassingly parallel problems. It can be a poor choice for imaging, however, because collating millions of pixels into an output sequence creates a bottleneck. Instead, it's better to write pixels directly to an array or unmanaged memory block and use the `Parallel` class or task parallelism to manage the multithreading. (It is possible, however, to defeat result collation using `ForAll`—we discuss this in "Optimizing PLINQ." Doing so makes sense if the image processing algorithm naturally lends itself to LINQ.)

Functional Purity

Because PLINQ runs your query on parallel threads, you must be careful not to perform thread-unsafe operations. In particular, writing to variables is *side-effecting* and therefore thread-unsafe:

```
// The following query multiplies each element by its position.
// Given an input of Enumerable.Range(0,999), it should output squares.
int i = 0;
var query = from n in Enumerable.Range(0,999).AsParallel() select n * i++;
```

We could make incrementing `i` thread-safe by using locks, but the problem would still remain that `i` won't necessarily correspond to the position of the input element. And adding `AsOrdered` to the query wouldn't fix the latter problem, because `AsOr`

---

dered ensures only that the elements are output in an order consistent with them having been processed sequentially—it doesn't actually *process* them sequentially.

Instead, this query should be rewritten to use the indexed version of `Select`:

```
var query = Enumerable.Range(0,999).AsParallel().Select ((n, i) => n * i);
```

For best performance, any methods called from query operators should be thread-safe by virtue of not writing to fields or properties (non-side-effecting, or *functionally pure*). If they're thread-safe by virtue of *locking*, the query's parallelism potential will be limited—by the duration of the lock divided by the total time spent in that function.

Setting the Degree of Parallelism

By default, PLINQ chooses an optimum degree of parallelism for the processor in use. You can override it by calling `WithDegreeOfParallelism` after `AsParallel`:

```
...AsParallel().WithDegreeOfPallelism(4)...
```

An example of when you might increase the parallelism beyond the core count is with I/O-bound work (downloading many web pages at once, for instance). Since Framework 4.5, however, task combinators and asynchronous functions provide a similarly easy and more *efficient* solution (see "Task Combinators" on page 614 in Chapter 14. Unlike with `Tasks`, PLINQ cannot perform I/O-bound work without blocking threads (and *pooled* threads, to make matters worse).

Changing the degree of parallelism

You can call `WithDegreeOfParallelism` only once within a PLINQ query. If you need to call it again, you must force merging and repartitioning of the query by calling `AsParallel()` again within the query:

```
"The Quick Brown Fox"
  .AsParallel().WithDegreeOfParallelism (2)
  .Where (c => !char.IsWhiteSpace (c))
  .AsParallel().WithDegreeOfParallelism (3)    // Forces Merge + Partition
  .Select (c => char.ToUpper (c))
```

Cancellation

Canceling a PLINQ query whose results you're consuming in a `foreach` loop is easy: simply break out of the `foreach` and the query will be automatically canceled as the enumerator is implicitly disposed.

For a query that terminates with a conversion, element, or aggregation operator, you can cancel it from another thread via a *cancellation token* (see "Cancellation" on page 610 in Chapter 14). To insert a token, call `WithCancellation` after calling `AsParallel`, passing in the `Token` property of a `CancellationTokenSource` object. Another thread can then call `Cancel` on the token source, which throws an `Opera tionCanceledException` on the query's consumer:

```
IEnumerable<int> million = Enumerable.Range (3, 1000000);

var cancelSource = new CancellationTokenSource();

var primeNumberQuery =
  from n in million.AsParallel().WithCancellation (cancelSource.Token)
  where Enumerable.Range (2, (int) Math.Sqrt (n)).All (i => n % i > 0)
  select n;

new Thread (() => {
                    Thread.Sleep (100);      // Cancel query after
                    cancelSource.Cancel();   // 100 milliseconds.
                  }
            ).Start();
try
{
  // Start query running:
  int[] primes = primeNumberQuery.ToArray();
  // We'll never get here because the other thread will cancel us.
}
catch (OperationCanceledException)
{
  Console.WriteLine ("Query canceled");
}
```

PLINQ doesn't preemptively abort threads because of the danger of doing so (see "Interrupt and Abort" on page 938 in Chapter 22). Instead, upon cancellation, it waits for each worker thread to finish with its current element before ending the query. This means that any external methods that the query calls will run to completion.

Optimizing PLINQ

Output-side optimization

One of PLINQ's advantages is that it conveniently collates the results from parallelized work into a single output sequence. Sometimes, though, all that you end up doing with that sequence is running some function once over each element:

```
foreach (int n in parallelQuery)
  DoSomething (n);
```

If this is the case—and you don't care about the order in which the elements are processed—you can improve efficiency with PLINQ's ForAll method.

The ForAll method runs a delegate over every output element of a ParallelQuery. It hooks right into PLINQ's internals, bypassing the steps of collating and enumerating the results. To give a trivial example:

```
"abcdef".AsParallel().Select (c => char.ToUpper(c)).ForAll (Console.Write);
```

Figure 23-3 shows the process.

Collating and enumerating results is not a massively expensive operation, so the ForAll optimization yields the greatest gains when there are large numbers of quickly executing input elements.

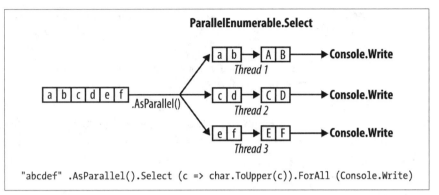

Figure 23-3. PLINQ ForAll

Input-side optimization

PLINQ has three partitioning strategies for assigning input elements to threads:

Strategy	Element allocation	Relative performance
Chunk partitioning	Dynamic	Average
Range partitioning	Static	Poor to excellent
Hash partitioning	Static	Poor

For query operators that require comparing elements (GroupBy, Join, GroupJoin, Intersect, Except, Union, and Distinct), you have no choice: PLINQ always uses *hash partitioning*. Hash partitioning is relatively inefficient in that it must precalculate the hashcode of every element (so that elements with identical hashcodes can be processed on the same thread). If you find this too slow, your only option is to call AsSequential to disable parallelization.

For all other query operators, you have a choice as to whether to use range or chunk partitioning. By default:

- If the input sequence is *indexable* (if it's an array or implements IList<T>), PLINQ chooses *range partitioning*.
- Otherwise, PLINQ chooses *chunk partitioning*.

In a nutshell, range partitioning is faster with long sequences for which every element takes a similar amount of CPU time to process. Otherwise, chunk partitioning is usually faster.

To force *range partitioning*:

- If the query starts with `Enumerable.Range`, replace that method with `ParalleLEnumerable.Range`.

- Otherwise, simply call `ToList` or `ToArray` on the input sequence (obviously, this incurs a performance cost in itself, which you should take into account).

 `ParallelEnumerable.Range` is not simply a shortcut for calling `Enumerable.Range(...).AsParallel()`. It changes the performance of the query by activating range partitioning.

To force *chunk partitioning*, wrap the input sequence in a call to `Partitioner.Create` (in `System.Collection.Concurrent`) as follows:

```
int[] numbers = { 3, 4, 5, 6, 7, 8, 9 };
var parallelQuery =
  Partitioner.Create (numbers, true).AsParallel()
  .Where (...)
```

The second argument to `Partitioner.Create` indicates that you want to *load-balance* the query, which is another way of saying that you want chunk partitioning.

Chunk partitioning works by having each worker thread periodically grab small "chunks" of elements from the input sequence to process (see Figure 23-4). PLINQ starts by allocating very small chunks (one or two elements at a time), then increases the chunk size as the query progresses: this ensures that small sequences are effectively parallelized and large sequences don't cause excessive round-tripping. If a worker happens to get "easy" elements (that process quickly), it will end up getting more chunks. This system keeps every thread equally busy (and the cores "balanced"); the only downside is that fetching elements from the shared input sequence requires synchronization (typically an exclusive lock)—and this can result in some overhead and contention.

Range partitioning bypasses the normal input-side enumeration and preallocates an equal number of elements to each worker, avoiding contention on the input sequence. But if some threads happen to get easy elements and finish early, they sit idle while the remaining threads continue working. Our earlier prime number calculator might perform poorly with range partitioning. An example of when range partitioning would do well is in calculating the sum of the square roots of the first 10 million integers:

```
ParallelEnumerable.Range (1, 10000000).Sum (i => Math.Sqrt (i))
```

`ParallelEnumerable.Range` returns a `ParallelQuery<T>`, so you don't need to subsequently call `AsParallel`.

Range partitioning doesn't necessarily allocate element ranges in *contiguous* blocks—it might instead choose a "striping" strategy. For instance, if there are two workers, one worker might process odd-numbered elements while the other processes even-numbered elements. The TakeWhile operator is almost certain to trigger a striping strategy to avoid unnecessarily processing elements later in the sequence.

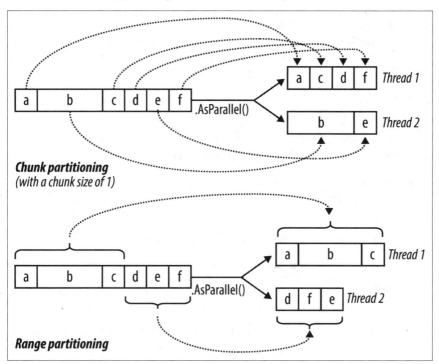

Figure 23-4. Chunk versus range partitioning

Optimizing custom aggregations

PLINQ parallelizes the Sum, Average, Min, and Max operators efficiently without additional intervention. The Aggregate operator, though, presents special challenges for PLINQ. As described in Chapter 9, Aggregate performs custom aggregations. For example, the following sums a sequence of numbers, mimicking the Sum operator:

```
int[] numbers = { 1, 2, 3 };
int sum = numbers.Aggregate (0, (total, n) => total + n);   // 6
```

We also saw in Chapter 9 that for *unseeded* aggregations, the supplied delegate must be associative and commutative. PLINQ will give incorrect results if this rule is violated, because it draws *multiple seeds* from the input sequence in order to aggregate several partitions of the sequence simultaneously.

Explicitly seeded aggregations might seem like a safe option with PLINQ, but unfortunately these ordinarily execute sequentially because of the reliance on a single seed. To mitigate this, PLINQ provides another overload of `Aggregate` that lets you specify multiple seeds—or rather, a *seed factory function*. For each thread, it executes this function to generate a separate seed, which becomes a *thread-local* accumulator into which it locally aggregates elements.

You must also supply a function to indicate how to combine the local and main accumulators. Finally, this `Aggregate` overload (somewhat gratuitously) expects a delegate to perform any final transformation on the result (you can achieve this as easily by running some function on the result yourself afterward). So, here are the four delegates, in the order they are passed:

`seedFactory`
　　Returns a new local accumulator

`updateAccumulatorFunc`
　　Aggregates an element into a local accumulator

`combineAccumulatorFunc`
　　Combines a local accumulator with the main accumulator

`resultSelector`
　　Applies any final transformation on the end result

 In simple scenarios, you can specify a *seed value* instead of a seed factory. This tactic fails when the seed is a reference type that you wish to mutate, because the same instance will then be shared by each thread.

To give a very simple example, the following sums the values in a `numbers` array:

```
numbers.AsParallel().Aggregate (
  () => 0,                                   // seedFactory
  (localTotal, n) => localTotal + n,         // updateAccumulatorFunc
  (mainTot, localTot) => mainTot + localTot, // combineAccumulatorFunc
  finalResult => finalResult)                // resultSelector
```

This example is contrived in that we could get the same answer just as efficiently using simpler approaches (such as an unseeded aggregate, or better, the `Sum` operator). To give a more realistic example, suppose we wanted to calculate the frequency of each letter in the English alphabet in a given string. A simple sequential solution might look like this:

```
string text = "Let's suppose this is a really long string";
var letterFrequencies = new int[26];
foreach (char c in text)
{
  int index = char.ToUpper (c) - 'A';
  if (index >= 0 && index <= 26) letterFrequencies [index]++;
};
```

An example of when the input text might be very long is in gene sequencing. The "alphabet" would then consist of the letters *a*, *c*, *g*, and *t*.

To parallelize this, we could replace the `foreach` statement with a call to `Parallel.ForEach` (as we'll cover in the following section), but this will leave us to deal with concurrency issues on the shared array. And locking around accessing that array would all but kill the potential for parallelization.

`Aggregate` offers a tidy solution. The accumulator, in this case, is an array just like the `letterFrequencies` array in our preceding example. Here's a sequential version using `Aggregate`:

```
int[] result =
  text.Aggregate (
    new int[26],              // Create the "accumulator"
    (letterFrequencies, c) => // Aggregate a letter into the accumulator
    {
      int index = char.ToUpper (c) - 'A';
      if (index >= 0 && index <= 26) letterFrequencies [index]++;
      return letterFrequencies;
    });
```

And now the parallel version, using PLINQ's special overload:

```
int[] result =
  text.AsParallel().Aggregate (
    () => new int[26],             // Create a new local accumulator

    (localFrequencies, c) =>       // Aggregate into the local accumulator
    {
      int index = char.ToUpper (c) - 'A';
      if (index >= 0 && index <= 26) localFrequencies [index]++;
      return localFrequencies;
    },
                                   // Aggregate local->main accumulator
    (mainFreq, localFreq) =>
      mainFreq.Zip (localFreq, (f1, f2) => f1 + f2).ToArray(),

    finalResult => finalResult     // Perform any final transformation
  );                               // on the end result.
```

Notice that the local accumulation function *mutates* the `localFrequencies` array. This ability to perform this optimization is important—and is legitimate because `localFrequencies` is local to each thread.

The Parallel Class

PFX provides a basic form of structured parallelism via three static methods in the `Parallel` class:

`Parallel.Invoke`
     Executes an array of delegates in parallel

```
Parallel.For
```
Performs the parallel equivalent of a C# `for` loop

```
Parallel.ForEach
```
Performs the parallel equivalent of a C# `foreach` loop

All three methods block until all work is complete. As with PLINQ, after an unhandled exception, remaining workers are stopped after their current iteration, and the exception (or exceptions) are thrown back to the caller—wrapped in an `Aggrega teException` (see "Working with AggregateException" on page 978).

Parallel.Invoke

`Parallel.Invoke` executes an array of `Action` delegates in parallel and then waits for them to complete. The simplest version of the method is defined as follows:

```
public static void Invoke (params Action[] actions);
```

Just as with PLINQ, the `Parallel.*` methods are optimized for compute-bound and not I/O-bound work. However, downloading two web pages at once provides a simple way to demonstrate `Parallel.Invoke`:

```
Parallel.Invoke (
  () => new WebClient().DownloadFile ("http://www.linqpad.net", "lp.html"),
  () => new WebClient().DownloadFile ("http://www.jaoo.dk", "jaoo.html"));
```

On the surface, this seems like a convenient shortcut for creating and waiting on two thread-bound `Task` objects. But there's an important difference: `Paral lel.Invoke` still works efficiently if you pass in an array of a million delegates. This is because it *partitions* large numbers of elements into batches which it assigns to a handful of underlying `Task`s—rather than creating a separate `Task` for each delegate.

As with all of `Parallel`'s methods, you're on your own when it comes to collating the results. This means you need to keep thread safety in mind. The following, for instance, is thread-unsafe:

```
var data = new List<string>();
Parallel.Invoke (
  () => data.Add (new WebClient().DownloadString ("http://www.foo.com")),
  () => data.Add (new WebClient().DownloadString ("http://www.far.com")));
```

Locking around adding to the list would resolve this, although locking would create a bottleneck if you had a much larger array of quickly executing delegates. A better solution is to use the thread-safe collections that we'll cover in later sections—`Con currentBag` would be ideal in this case.

`Parallel.Invoke` is also overloaded to accept a `ParallelOptions` object:

```
public static void Invoke (ParallelOptions options,
                           params Action[] actions);
```

With `ParallelOptions`, you can insert a cancellation token, limit the maximum concurrency, and specify a custom task scheduler. A cancellation token is relevant when you're executing (roughly) more tasks than you have cores: upon cancellation, any unstarted delegates will be abandoned. Any already-executing delegates will, however, continue to completion. See "Cancellation" on page 610 for an example of how to use cancellation tokens.

Parallel.For and Parallel.ForEach

`Parallel.For` and `Parallel.ForEach` perform the equivalent of a C# `for` and `foreach` loop, but with each iteration executing in parallel instead of sequentially. Here are their (simplest) signatures:

```
public static ParallelLoopResult For (
    int fromInclusive, int toExclusive, Action<int> body)

public static ParallelLoopResult ForEach<TSource> (
    IEnumerable<TSource> source, Action<TSource> body)
```

The following sequential `for` loop:

```
for (int i = 0; i < 100; i++)
    Foo (i);
```

is parallelized like this:

```
Parallel.For (0, 100, i => Foo (i));
```

or more simply:

```
Parallel.For (0, 100, Foo);
```

And the following sequential `foreach`:

```
foreach (char c in "Hello, world")
    Foo (c);
```

is parallelized like this:

```
Parallel.ForEach ("Hello, world", Foo);
```

To give a practical example, if we import the `System.Security.Cryptography` namespace, we can generate six public/private key-pair strings in parallel as follows:

```
var keyPairs = new string[6];

Parallel.For (0, keyPairs.Length,
              i => keyPairs[i] = RSA.Create().ToXmlString (true));
```

As with `Parallel.Invoke`, we can feed `Parallel.For` and `Parallel.ForEach` a large number of work items and they'll be efficiently partitioned onto a few tasks.

> The latter query could also be done with PLINQ:
>
> ```
> string[] keyPairs =
>     ParallelEnumerable.Range (0, 6)
>     .Select (i => RSA.Create().ToXmlString (true))
>     .ToArray();
> ```

Outer versus inner loops

`Parallel.For` and `Parallel.ForEach` usually work best on outer rather than inner loops. This is because with the former, you're offering larger chunks of work to parallelize, diluting the management overhead. Parallelizing both inner and outer loops is usually unnecessary. In the following example, we'd typically need more than 100 cores to benefit from the inner parallelization:

```
Parallel.For (0, 100, i =>
{
  Parallel.For (0, 50, j => Foo (i, j));   // Sequential would be better
});                                        // for the inner loop.
```

Indexed Parallel.ForEach

Sometimes it's useful to know the loop iteration index. With a sequential `foreach`, it's easy:

```
int i = 0;
foreach (char c in "Hello, world")
  Console.WriteLine (c.ToString() + i++);
```

Incrementing a shared variable, however, is not thread-safe in a parallel context. You must instead use the following version of `ForEach`:

```
public static ParallelLoopResult ForEach<TSource> (
  IEnumerable<TSource> source, Action<TSource,ParallelLoopState,long> body)
```

We'll ignore `ParallelLoopState` (which we'll cover in the following section). For now, we're interested in `Action`'s third type parameter of type `long`, which indicates the loop index:

```
Parallel.ForEach ("Hello, world", (c, state, i) =>
{
   Console.WriteLine (c.ToString() + i);
});
```

To put this into a practical context, we'll revisit the spellchecker that we wrote with PLINQ. The following code loads up a dictionary along with an array of a million words to test:

```
if (!File.Exists ("WordLookup.txt"))    // Contains about 150,000 words
  new WebClient().DownloadFile (
    "http://www.albahari.com/ispell/allwords.txt", "WordLookup.txt");

var wordLookup = new HashSet<string> (
  File.ReadAllLines ("WordLookup.txt"),
  StringComparer.InvariantCultureIgnoreCase);

var random = new Random();
string[] wordList = wordLookup.ToArray();

string[] wordsToTest = Enumerable.Range (0, 1000000)
  .Select (i => wordList [random.Next (0, wordList.Length)])
  .ToArray();
```

```
wordsToTest [12345] = "woozsh";      // Introduce a couple
wordsToTest [23456] = "wubsie";      // of spelling mistakes.
```

We can perform the spellcheck on our `wordsToTest` array using the indexed version of `Parallel.ForEach` as follows:

```
var misspellings = new ConcurrentBag<Tuple<int,string>>();

Parallel.ForEach (wordsToTest, (word, state, i) =>
{
  if (!wordLookup.Contains (word))
    misspellings.Add (Tuple.Create ((int) i, word));
});
```

Notice that we had to collate the results into a thread-safe collection: having to do this is the disadvantage when compared to using PLINQ. The advantage over PLINQ is that we avoid the cost of applying an indexed `Select` query operator—which is less efficient than an indexed `ForEach`.

ParallelLoopState: Breaking early out of loops

Because the loop body in a parallel `For` or `ForEach` is a delegate, you can't exit the loop early with a `break` statement. Instead, you must call `Break` or `Stop` on a `ParallelLoopState` object:

```
public class ParallelLoopState
{
  public void Break();
  public void Stop();

  public bool IsExceptional { get; }
  public bool IsStopped { get; }
  public long? LowestBreakIteration { get; }
  public bool ShouldExitCurrentIteration { get; }
}
```

Obtaining a `ParallelLoopState` is easy: all versions of `For` and `ForEach` are overloaded to accept loop bodies of type `Action<TSource,ParallelLoopState>`. So, to parallelize this:

```
foreach (char c in "Hello, world")
  if (c == ',')
    break;
  else
    Console.Write (c);
```

do this:

```
Parallel.ForEach ("Hello, world", (c, loopState) =>
{
  if (c == ',')
    loopState.Break();
  else
    Console.Write (c);
```

```
});
```

// OUTPUT: Hlloe

You can see from the output that loop bodies may complete in a random order. Aside from this difference, calling `Break` yields *at least* the same elements as executing the loop sequentially: this example will always output *at least* the letters *H, e, l, l,* and *o* in some order. In contrast, calling `Stop` instead of `Break` forces all threads to finish right after their current iteration. In our example, calling `Stop` could give us a subset of the letters *H, e, l, l,* and *o* if another thread was lagging behind. Calling `Stop` is useful when you've found something that you're looking for—or when something has gone wrong and you won't be looking at the results.

> The `Parallel.For` and `Parallel.ForEach` methods return a `ParallelLoopResult` object that exposes properties called `IsCompleted` and `LowestBreakIteration`. These tell you whether the loop ran to completion, and if not, at what cycle the loop was broken.
>
> If `LowestBreakIteration` returns `null`, it means that you called `Stop` (rather than `Break`) on the loop.

If your loop body is long, you might want other threads to break partway through the method body in case of an early `Break` or `Stop`. You can do this by polling the `ShouldExitCurrentIteration` property at various places in your code; this property becomes true immediately after a `Stop`—or soon after a `Break`.

> `ShouldExitCurrentIteration` also becomes true after a cancellation request—or if an exception is thrown in the loop.

`IsExceptional` lets you know whether an exception has occurred on another thread. Any unhandled exception will cause the loop to stop after each thread's current iteration: to avoid this, you must explicitly handle exceptions in your code.

Optimization with local values

`Parallel.For` and `Parallel.ForEach` each offer a set of overloads that feature a generic type argument called `TLocal`. These overloads are designed to help you optimize the collation of data with iteration-intensive loops. The simplest is this:

```
public static ParallelLoopResult For <TLocal> (
  int fromInclusive,
  int toExclusive,
  Func <TLocal> localInit,
  Func <int, ParallelLoopState, TLocal, TLocal> body,
  Action <TLocal> localFinally);
```

These methods are rarely needed in practice because their target scenarios are covered mostly by PLINQ (which is fortunate because these overloads are somewhat intimidating!).

Essentially, the problem is this: suppose we want to sum the square roots of the numbers 1 through 10,000,000. Calculating 10 million square roots is easily parallelizable, but summing their values is troublesome because we must lock around updating the total:

```
object locker = new object();
double total = 0;
Parallel.For (1, 10000000,
               i => { lock (locker) total += Math.Sqrt (i); });
```

The gain from parallelization is more than offset by the cost of obtaining 10 million locks—plus the resultant blocking.

The reality, though, is that we don't actually *need* 10 million locks. Imagine a team of volunteers picking up a large volume of litter. If all workers shared a single trash can, the travel and contention would make the process extremely inefficient. The obvious solution is for each worker to have a private or "local" trash can, which is occasionally emptied into the main bin.

The TLocal versions of For and ForEach work in exactly this way. The volunteers are internal worker threads, and the *local value* represents a local trash can. In order for Parallel to do this job, you must feed it two additional delegates that indicate:

1. How to initialize a new local value
2. How to combine a local aggregation with the master value

Additionally, instead of the body delegate returning void, it should return the new aggregate for the local value. Here's our example refactored:

```
object locker = new object();
double grandTotal = 0;

Parallel.For (1, 10000000,

  () => 0.0,                        // Initialize the local value.

  (i, state, localTotal) =>         // Body delegate. Notice that it
     localTotal + Math.Sqrt (i),    // returns the new local total.

  localTotal =>                               // Add the local value
     { lock (locker) grandTotal += localTotal; }   // to the master value.
);
```

We must still lock, but only around aggregating the local value to the grand total. This makes the process dramatically more efficient.

As stated earlier, PLINQ is often a good fit in these scenarios. Our example could be parallelized with PLINQ simply like this:

```
ParallelEnumerable.Range (1, 10000000)
                 .Sum (i => Math.Sqrt (i))
```

(Notice that we used `ParallelEnumerable` to force *range partitioning*: this improves performance in this case because all numbers will take equally long to process.)

In more complex scenarios, you might use LINQ's `Aggregate` operator instead of `Sum`. If you supplied a local seed factory, the situation would be somewhat analogous to providing a local value function with `Parallel.For`.

Task Parallelism

Task parallelism is the lowest-level approach to parallelization with PFX. The classes for working at this level are defined in the `System.Threading.Tasks` namespace and comprise the following:

Class	Purpose
`Task`	For managing a unit for work
`Task<TResult>`	For managing a unit for work with a return value
`TaskFactory`	For creating tasks
`TaskFactory<TResult>`	For creating tasks and continuations with the same return type
`TaskScheduler`	For managing the scheduling of tasks
`TaskCompletionSource`	For manually controlling a task's workflow

We covered the basics of tasks in Chapter 14; in this section we'll look at advanced features of tasks that are aimed at parallel programming. Specifically:

- Tuning a task's scheduling
- Establish a parent/child relationship when one task is started from another
- Advanced use of continuations
- `TaskFactory`

The Task Parallel Library lets you create hundreds (or even thousands) of tasks with minimal overhead. But if you want to create millions of tasks, you'll need to partition those tasks into larger work units to maintain efficiency. The `Parallel` class and PLINQ do this automatically.

Visual Studio provides a window for monitoring tasks (Debug→Window→Parallel Tasks). This is equivalent to the Threads window, but for tasks. The Parallel Stacks window also has a special mode for tasks.

Creating and Starting Tasks

As described in Chapter 14, `Task.Run` creates and starts a `Task` or `Task<TResult>`. This method is actually a shortcut for calling `Task.Factory.StartNew`, which allows greater flexibility through additional overloads.

Specifying a state object

`Task.Factory.StartNew` lets you specify a *state* object which is passed to the target. The target method's signature must then comprise a single object-type parameter:

```
static void Main()
{
  var task = Task.Factory.StartNew (Greet, "Hello");
  task.Wait();  // Wait for task to complete.
}

static void Greet (object state) { Console.Write (state); }    // Hello
```

This avoids the cost of the closure required for executing a lambda expression that calls `Greet`. This is a micro-optimization and is rarely necessary in practice, so we can put the *state* object to better use, which is to assign a meaningful name to the task. We can then use the `AsyncState` property to query its name:

```
static void Main()
{
  var task = Task.Factory.StartNew (state => Greet ("Hello"), "Greeting");
  Console.WriteLine (task.AsyncState);   // Greeting
  task.Wait();
}

static void Greet (string message) { Console.Write (message); }
```

Visual Studio displays each task's `AsyncState` in the Parallel Tasks window, so having a meaningful name here can ease debugging considerably.

TaskCreationOptions

You can tune a task's execution by specifying a `TaskCreationOptions` enum when calling `StartNew` (or instantiating a `Task`). `TaskCreationOptions` is a flags enum with the following (combinable) values:

`LongRunning, PreferFairness, AttachedToParent`

`LongRunning` suggests to the scheduler to dedicate a thread to the task, and as we described in Chapter 14, this is beneficial for I/O-bound tasks and for long-running tasks that might otherwise force short-running tasks to wait an unreasonable amount of time before being scheduled.

PreferFairness tells the scheduler to try to ensure that tasks are scheduled in the order they were started. It may ordinarily do otherwise, because it internally optimizes the scheduling of tasks using local work-stealing queues—an optimization that allows the creation of *child* tasks without incurring the contention overhead that would otherwise arise with a single work queue. A child task is created by specifying AttachedToParent.

Child tasks

When one task starts another, you can optionally establish a parent-child relationship:

```
Task parent = Task.Factory.StartNew (() =>
{
  Console.WriteLine ("I am a parent");

  Task.Factory.StartNew (() =>          // Detached task
  {
    Console.WriteLine ("I am detached");
  });

  Task.Factory.StartNew (() =>          // Child task
  {
    Console.WriteLine ("I am a child");
  }, TaskCreationOptions.AttachedToParent);
});
```

A child task is special in that when you wait for the *parent* task to complete, it waits for any children as well. At which point any child exceptions bubble up:

```
TaskCreationOptions atp = TaskCreationOptions.AttachedToParent;
var parent = Task.Factory.StartNew (() =>
{
  Task.Factory.StartNew (() =>   // Child
  {
    Task.Factory.StartNew (() => { throw null; }, atp);   // Grandchild
  }, atp);
});

// The following call throws a NullReferenceException (wrapped
// in nested AggregateExceptions):
parent.Wait();
```

This can be particularly useful when a child task is a continuation, as we'll see shortly.

Waiting on Multiple Tasks

We saw in Chapter 14 that you can wait on a single task either by calling its Wait method or accessing its Result property (if it's a Task<TResult>). You can also wait on multiple tasks at once—via the static methods `Task.WaitAll` (waits for all the specified tasks to finish) and `Task.WaitAny` (waits for just one task to finish).

`WaitAll` is similar to waiting out each task in turn, but is more efficient in that it requires (at most) just one context switch. Also, if one or more of the tasks throw an unhandled exception, `WaitAll` still waits out every task—and then rethrows an `AggregateException` that accumulates the exceptions from each faulted task (this is where `AggregateException` is genuinely useful). It's equivalent to doing this:

```
// Assume t1, t2 and t3 are tasks:
var exceptions = new List<Exception>();
try { t1.Wait(); } catch (AggregateException ex) { exceptions.Add (ex); }
try { t2.Wait(); } catch (AggregateException ex) { exceptions.Add (ex); }
try { t3.Wait(); } catch (AggregateException ex) { exceptions.Add (ex); }
if (exceptions.Count > 0) throw new AggregateException (exceptions);
```

Calling `WaitAny` is equivalent to waiting on a `ManualResetEventSlim` that's signaled by each task as it finishes.

As well as a timeout, you can also pass in a *cancellation token* to the `Wait` methods: this lets you cancel the wait—*not the task itself.*

Canceling Tasks

You can optionally pass in a cancellation token when starting a task. Then, if cancellation occurs via that token, the task itself enters the "Canceled" state:

```
var cts = new CancellationTokenSource();
CancellationToken token = cts.Token;
cts.CancelAfter (500);

Task task = Task.Factory.StartNew (() =>
{
  Thread.Sleep (1000);
  token.ThrowIfCancellationRequested();  // Check for cancellation request
}, token);

try { task.Wait(); }
catch (AggregateException ex)
{
  Console.WriteLine (ex.InnerException is TaskCanceledException);  // True
  Console.WriteLine (task.IsCanceled);                            // True
  Console.WriteLine (task.Status);                                // Canceled
}
```

`TaskCanceledException` is a subclass of `OperationCanceledException`. If you want to explicitly throw an `OperationCanceledException` (rather than calling `token.ThrowIfCancellationRequested`), you must pass the cancellation token into `OperationCanceledException`'s constructor. If you fail to do this, the task won't end up with a `TaskStatus.Canceled` status and won't trigger `OnlyOnCanceled` continuations.

If the task is canceled before it has started, it won't get scheduled—an OperationCan
celedException will instead be thrown on the task immediately.

Because cancellation tokens are recognized by other APIs, you can pass them into
other constructs and cancellations will propagate seamlessly:

```
var cancelSource = new CancellationTokenSource();
CancellationToken token = cancelSource.Token;

Task task = Task.Factory.StartNew (() =>
{
  // Pass our cancellation token into a PLINQ query:
  var query = someSequence.AsParallel().WithCancellation (token)...
  ... enumerate query ...
});
```

Calling Cancel on cancelSource in this example will cancel the PLINQ query,
which will throw an OperationCanceledException on the task body, which will
then cancel the task.

 The cancellation tokens that you can pass into methods such
as Wait and CancelAndWait allow you to cancel the *wait* operation and not the task itself.

Continuations

The ContinueWith method executes a delegate right after a task ends:

```
Task task1 = Task.Factory.StartNew (() => Console.Write ("antecedant.."));
Task task2 = task1.ContinueWith (ant => Console.Write ("..continuation"));
```

As soon as task1 (the *antecedent*) completes, fails, or is canceled, task2 (the *continuation*) starts. (If task1 had completed before the second line of code ran, task2
would be scheduled to execute right away.) The ant argument passed to the continuation's lambda expression is a reference to the antecedent task. ContinueWith itself
returns a task, making it easy to add further continuations.

By default, antecedent and continuation tasks may execute on different threads. You
can force them to execute on the same thread by specifying TaskContinuationOp
tions.ExecuteSynchronously when calling ContinueWith: this can improve performance in very fine-grained continuations by lessening indirection.

Continuations and Task<TResult>

Just like ordinary tasks, continuations can be of type Task<TResult> and return
data. In the following example, we calculate Math.Sqrt(8*2) using a series of
chained tasks and then write out the result:

```
Task.Factory.StartNew<int> (() => 8)
  .ContinueWith (ant => ant.Result * 2)
  .ContinueWith (ant => Math.Sqrt (ant.Result))
  .ContinueWith (ant => Console.WriteLine (ant.Result));    // 4
```

Our example is somewhat contrived for simplicity; in real life, these lambda expressions would call computationally intensive functions.

Continuations and exceptions

A continuation can know whether an antecedent faulted by querying the antecedent task's Exception property—or simply by invoking Result / Wait and catching the resultant AggregateException. If an antecedent faults and the continuation does neither, the exception is considered *unobserved* and the static TaskScheduler.UnobservedTaskException event fires when the task is later garbage collected.

A safe pattern is to rethrow antecedent exceptions. As long as the continuation is Waited upon, the exception will be propagated and rethrown to the Waiter:

```
Task continuation = Task.Factory.StartNew     (() => { throw null; })
                                  .ContinueWith (ant =>
    {
      ant.Wait();
      // Continue processing...
    });

continuation.Wait();     // Exception is now thrown back to caller.
```

Another way to deal with exceptions is to specify different continuations for exceptional versus nonexceptional outcomes. This is done with TaskContinuationOptions:

```
Task task1 = Task.Factory.StartNew (() => { throw null; });

Task error = task1.ContinueWith (ant => Console.Write (ant.Exception),
                                 TaskContinuationOptions.OnlyOnFaulted);

Task ok = task1.ContinueWith (ant => Console.Write ("Success!"),
                              TaskContinuationOptions.NotOnFaulted);
```

This pattern is particularly useful in conjunction with child tasks, as we'll see very soon.

The following extension method "swallows" a task's unhandled exceptions:

```
public static void IgnoreExceptions (this Task task)
{
  task.ContinueWith (t => { var ignore = t.Exception; },
    TaskContinuationOptions.OnlyOnFaulted);
}
```

(This could be improved by adding code to log the exception.) Here's how it would be used:

```
Task.Factory.StartNew (() => { throw null; }).IgnoreExceptions();
```

Continuations and child tasks

A powerful feature of continuations is that they kick off only when all child tasks have completed (see Figure 23-5). At that point, any exceptions thrown by the children are marshaled to the continuation.

In the following example, we start three child tasks, each throwing a `NullReferen ceException`. We then catch all of them in one fell swoop via a continuation on the parent:

```
TaskCreationOptions atp = TaskCreationOptions.AttachedToParent;
Task.Factory.StartNew (() =>
{
  Task.Factory.StartNew (() => { throw null; }, atp);
  Task.Factory.StartNew (() => { throw null; }, atp);
  Task.Factory.StartNew (() => { throw null; }, atp);
})
.ContinueWith (p => Console.WriteLine (p.Exception),
               TaskContinuationOptions.OnlyOnFaulted);
```

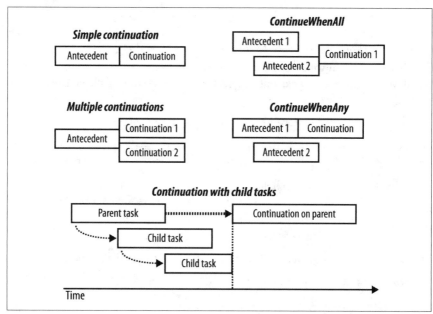

Figure 23-5. Continuations

Conditional continuations

By default, a continuation is scheduled *unconditionally*—whether the antecedent completes, throws an exception, or is canceled. You can alter this behavior via a set of (combinable) flags included within the TaskContinuationOptions enum. The three core flags that control conditional continuation are:

```
NotOnRanToCompletion = 0x10000,
NotOnFaulted = 0x20000,
NotOnCanceled = 0x40000,
```

These flags are subtractive in the sense that the more you apply, the less likely the continuation is to execute. For convenience, there are also the following precombined values:

```
OnlyOnRanToCompletion = NotOnFaulted | NotOnCanceled,
OnlyOnFaulted = NotOnRanToCompletion | NotOnCanceled,
OnlyOnCanceled = NotOnRanToCompletion | NotOnFaulted
```

(Combining all the Not* flags [NotOnRanToCompletion, NotOnFaulted, NotOnCan celed] is nonsensical, as it would result in the continuation always being canceled.)

"RanToCompletion" means the antecedent succeeded—without cancellation or unhandled exceptions.

"Faulted" means an unhandled exception was thrown on the antecedent.

"Canceled" means one of two things:

- The antecedent was canceled via its cancellation token. In other words, an Oper ationCanceledException was thrown on the antecedent—whose Cancella tionToken property matched that passed to the antecedent when it was started.

- The antecedent was implicitly canceled because *it* didn't satisfy a conditional continuation predicate.

It's essential to grasp that when a continuation doesn't execute by virtue of these flags, the continuation is not forgotten or abandoned—it's *canceled*. This means that any continuations on the continuation itself *will then run*—unless you predicate them with NotOnCanceled. For example, consider this:

```
Task t1 = Task.Factory.StartNew (...);

Task fault = t1.ContinueWith (ant => Console.WriteLine ("fault"),
                              TaskContinuationOptions.OnlyOnFaulted);

Task t3 = fault.ContinueWith (ant => Console.WriteLine ("t3"));
```

As it stands, t3 will always get scheduled—even if t1 doesn't throw an exception (see Figure 23-6). This is because if t1 succeeds, the fault task will be *canceled*, and with no continuation restrictions placed on t3, t3 will then execute unconditionally.

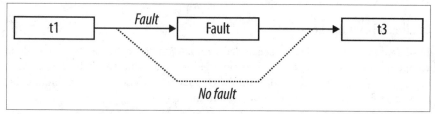

Figure 23-6. Conditional continuations

If we want t3 to execute only if fault actually runs, we must instead do this:

```
Task t3 = fault.ContinueWith (ant => Console.WriteLine ("t3"),
                          TaskContinuationOptions.NotOnCanceled);
```

(Alternatively, we could specify OnlyOnRanToCompletion; the difference is that t3 would not then execute if an exception was thrown within fault.)

Continuations with multiple antecedents

You can schedule continuation to execute based on the completion of multiple antecedents with the ContinueWhenAll and ContinueWhenAny methods in the TaskFactory class. These methods have become redundant, however, with the introduction of the task combinators that we discussed in Chapter 14 (WhenAll and WhenAny). Specifically, given the following tasks:

```
var task1 = Task.Run (() => Console.Write ("X"));
var task2 = Task.Run (() => Console.Write ("Y"));
```

we can schedule a continuation to execute when both complete as follows:

```
var continuation = Task.Factory.ContinueWhenAll (
  new[] { task1, task2 }, tasks => Console.WriteLine ("Done"));
```

Here's the same result with the WhenAll task combinator:

```
var continuation = Task.WhenAll (task1, task2)
                        .ContinueWith (ant => Console.WriteLine ("Done"));
```

Multiple continuations on a single antecedent

Calling ContinueWith more than once on the same task creates multiple continuations on a single antecedent. When the antecedent finishes, all continuations will start together (unless you specify TaskContinuationOptions.ExecuteSynchronously, in which case the continuations will execute sequentially).

The following waits for one second and then writes either "XY" or "YX":

```
var t = Task.Factory.StartNew (() => Thread.Sleep (1000));
t.ContinueWith (ant => Console.Write ("X"));
t.ContinueWith (ant => Console.Write ("Y"));
```

Task Schedulers

A *task scheduler* allocates tasks to threads and is represented by the abstract Task Scheduler class. The Framework provides two concrete implementations: the *default scheduler* that works in tandem with the CLR thread pool, and the *synchronization context scheduler*. The latter is designed (primarily) to help you with the threading model of WPF and Windows Forms, which requires that UI elements and controls are accessed only from the thread that created them (see "Threading in Rich-Client Applications" on page 576 in Chapter 14). By capturing it, we can tell a task or a continuation to execute on this context:

```
// Suppose we are on a UI thread in a Windows Forms / WPF application:
_uiScheduler = TaskScheduler.FromCurrentSynchronizationContext();
```

Assuming Foo is a compute-bound method that returns a string and lblResult is a WPF or Windows Forms label, we could then safely update the label after the operation completes as follows:

```
Task.Run (() => Foo())
    .ContinueWith (ant => lblResult.Content = ant.Result, _uiScheduler);
```

Of course, C#'s asynchronous functions would more commonly be used for this kind of thing.

It's also possible to write our own task scheduler (by subclassing TaskScheduler), although this is something you'd do only in very specialized scenarios. For custom scheduling, you'd more commonly use TaskCompletionSource.

TaskFactory

When you call Task.Factory, you're calling a static property on Task that returns a default TaskFactory object. The purpose of a task factory is to create tasks—specifically, three kinds of tasks:

- "Ordinary" tasks (via StartNew)
- Continuations with multiple antecedents (via ContinueWhenAll and Continue WhenAny)
- Tasks that wrap methods that follow the defunct APM (via FromAsync; see "Obsolete Patterns" on page 618 in Chapter 14).

Another way to create tasks is to instantiate Task and call Start. However this only lets you create "ordinary" tasks, not continuations.

Creating your own task factories

TaskFactory is not an *abstract* factory: you can actually instantiate the class, and this is useful when you want to repeatedly create tasks using the same (nonstandard) values for TaskCreationOptions, TaskContinuationOptions, or TaskSchedu ler. For example, if we wanted to repeatedly create long-running *parented* tasks, we could create a custom factory as follows:

```
var factory = new TaskFactory (
  TaskCreationOptions.LongRunning | TaskCreationOptions.AttachedToParent,
  TaskContinuationOptions.None);
```

Creating tasks is then simply a matter of calling StartNew on the factory:

```
Task task1 = factory.StartNew (Method1);
Task task2 = factory.StartNew (Method2);
...
```

The custom continuation options are applied when calling ContinueWhenAll and ContinueWhenAny.

Working with AggregateException

As we've seen, PLINQ, the Parallel class, and Tasks automatically marshal exceptions to the consumer. To see why this is essential, consider the following LINQ query, which throws a DivideByZeroException on the first iteration:

```
try
{
  var query = from i in Enumerable.Range (0, 1000000)
              select 100 / i;
  ...
}
catch (DivideByZeroException)
{
  ...
}
```

If we asked PLINQ to parallelize this query and it ignored the handling of exceptions, a DivideByZeroException would probably be thrown on a *separate thread*, bypassing our catch block and causing the application to die.

Hence, exceptions are automatically caught and rethrown to the caller. But unfortunately, it's not quite as simple as catching a DivideByZeroException. Because these libraries leverage many threads, it's actually possible for two or more exceptions to be thrown simultaneously. To ensure that all exceptions are reported, exceptions are therefore wrapped in an AggregateException container, which exposes an InnerExceptions property containing each of the caught exception(s):

```
try
{
  var query = from i in ParallelEnumerable.Range (0, 1000000)
              select 100 / i;
  // Enumerate query
  ...
}
catch (AggregateException aex)
{
  foreach (Exception ex in aex.InnerExceptions)
```

```
    Console.WriteLine (ex.Message);
}
```

 Both PLINQ and the Parallel class end the query or loop execution upon encountering the first exception—by not processing any further elements or loop bodies. More exceptions might be thrown, however, before the current cycle is complete. The first exception in AggregateException is visible in the InnerException property.

Flatten and Handle

The AggregateException class provides a couple of methods to simplify exception handling: Flatten and Handle.

Flatten

AggregateExceptions will quite often contain other AggregateExceptions. An example of when this might happen is if a child task throws an exception. You can eliminate any level of nesting to simplify handling by calling Flatten. This method returns a new AggregateException with a simple flat list of inner exceptions:

```
catch (AggregateException aex)
{
  foreach (Exception ex in aex.Flatten().InnerExceptions)
    myLogWriter.LogException (ex);
}
```

Handle

Sometimes it's useful to catch only specific exception types and have other types rethrown. The Handle method on AggregateException provides a shortcut for doing this. It accepts an exception predicate which it runs over every inner exception:

```
public void Handle (Func<Exception, bool> predicate)
```

If the predicate returns true, it considers that exception "handled." After the delegate has run over every exception, the following happens:

- If all exceptions were "handled" (the delegate returned true), the exception is not rethrown.

- If there were any exceptions for which the delegate returned false ("unhandled"), a new AggregateException is built up containing those exceptions and is rethrown.

For instance, the following ends up rethrowing another AggregateException that contains a single NullReferenceException:

```
var parent = Task.Factory.StartNew (() =>
{
  // We'll throw 3 exceptions at once using 3 child tasks:

  int[] numbers = { 0 };

  var childFactory = new TaskFactory
    (TaskCreationOptions.AttachedToParent, TaskContinuationOptions.None);

  childFactory.StartNew (() => 5 / numbers[0]);    // Division by zero
  childFactory.StartNew (() => numbers [1]);       // Index out of range
  childFactory.StartNew (() => { throw null; });   // Null reference
});

try { parent.Wait(); }
catch (AggregateException aex)
{
  aex.Flatten().Handle (ex =>    // Note that we still need to call Flatten
  {
    if (ex is DivideByZeroException)
    {
      Console.WriteLine ("Divide by zero");
      return true;                          // This exception is "handled"
    }
    if (ex is IndexOutOfRangeException)
    {
      Console.WriteLine ("Index out of range");
      return true;                          // This exception is "handled"
    }
    return false;    // All other exceptions will get rethrown
  });
}
```

Concurrent Collections

Framework 4.0 added a set of new collections in the System.Collections.Concur
rent namespace. All of these are fully thread-safe:

Concurrent collection	Nonconcurrent equivalent
ConcurrentStack<T>	Stack<T>
ConcurrentQueue<T>	Queue<T>
ConcurrentBag<T>	(none)
ConcurrentDictionary<TKey,TValue>	Dictionary<TKey,TValue>

The concurrent collections are optimized for high-concurrency scenarios; however
they can also be useful whenever need a thread-safe collection (as an alternative to
locking around an ordinary collection). However, there are some caveats:

- The conventional collections outperform the concurrent collections in all but highly concurrent scenarios.

- A thread-safe collection doesn't guarantee that the code using it will be thread-safe (see "Thread Safety" on page 629 in the preceding chapter).

- If you enumerate over a concurrent collection while another thread is modifying it, no exception is thrown—instead, you get a mixture of old and new content.

- There's no concurrent version of List<T>.

- The concurrent stack, queue, and bag classes are implemented internally with linked lists. This makes them less memory-efficient than the nonconcurrent Stack and Queue classes, but better for concurrent access because linked lists are conducive to lock-free or low-lock implementations. (This is because inserting a node into a linked list requires updating just a couple of references, while inserting an element into a List<T>-like structure may require moving thousands of existing elements.)

In other words, these collections are not merely shortcuts for using an ordinary collection with a lock. To demonstrate, if we execute the following code on a *single* thread:

```
var d = new ConcurrentDictionary<int,int>();
for (int i = 0; i < 1000000; i++) d[i] = 123;
```

it runs three times more slowly than this:

```
var d = new Dictionary<int,int>();
for (int i = 0; i < 1000000; i++) lock (d) d[i] = 123;
```

(*Reading* from a ConcurrentDictionary, however, is fast because reads are lock-free.)

The concurrent collections also differ from conventional collections in that they expose special methods to perform atomic test-and-act operations, such as TryPop. Most of these methods are unified via the IProducerConsumerCollection<T> interface.

IProducerConsumerCollection<T>

A producer/consumer collection is one for which the two primary use cases are:

- Adding an element ("producing")
- Retrieving an element while removing it ("consuming")

The classic examples are stacks and queues. Producer/consumer collections are significant in parallel programming because they're conducive to efficient lock-free implementations.

The `IProducerConsumerCollection<T>` interface represents a thread-safe producer/consumer collection. The following classes implement this interface:

```
ConcurrentStack<T>
ConcurrentQueue<T>
ConcurrentBag<T>
```

`IProducerConsumerCollection<T>` extends `ICollection`, adding the following methods:

```
void CopyTo (T[] array, int index);
T[] ToArray();
bool TryAdd (T item);
bool TryTake (out T item);
```

The `TryAdd` and `TryTake` methods test whether an add/remove operation can be performed, and if so, they perform the add/remove. The testing and acting are performed atomically, eliminating the need to lock as you would around a conventional collection:

```
int result;
lock (myStack) if (myStack.Count > 0) result = myStack.Pop();
```

`TryTake` returns `false` if the collection is empty. `TryAdd` always succeeds and returns `true` in the three implementations provided. If you wrote your own concurrent collection that prohibited duplicates, however, you'd make `TryAdd` return `false` if the element already existed (an example would be if you wrote a concurrent *set*).

The particular element that `TryTake` removes is defined by the subclass:

- With a stack, `TryTake` removes the most recently added element.
- With a queue, `TryTake` removes the least recently added element.
- With a bag, `TryTake` removes whatever element it can remove most efficiently.

The three concrete classes mostly implement the `TryTake` and `TryAdd` methods explicitly, exposing the same functionality through more specifically named public methods such as `TryDequeue` and `TryPop`.

ConcurrentBag<T>

`ConcurrentBag<T>` stores an *unordered* collection of objects (with duplicates permitted). `ConcurrentBag<T>` is suitable in situations when you *don't care* which element you get when calling `Take` or `TryTake`.

The benefit of `ConcurrentBag<T>` over a concurrent queue or stack is that a bag's `Add` method suffers almost *no* contention when called by many threads at once. In contrast, calling `Add` in parallel on a queue or stack incurs *some* contention (although a lot less than locking around a *nonconcurrent* collection). Calling `Take` on a concurrent bag is also very efficient—as long as each thread doesn't take more elements than it `Added`.

Inside a concurrent bag, each thread gets its own private linked list. Elements are added to the private list that belongs to the thread calling Add, eliminating contention. When you enumerate over the bag, the enumerator travels through each thread's private list, yielding each of its elements in turn.

When you call Take, the bag first looks at the current thread's private list. If there's at least one element,[1] it can complete the task easily and without contention. But if the list is empty, it must "steal" an element from another thread's private list and incur the potential for contention.

So, to be precise, calling Take gives you the element added most recently on that thread; if there are no elements on that thread, it gives you the element added most recently on another thread, chosen at random.

Concurrent bags are ideal when the parallel operation on your collection mostly comprises Adding elements—or when the Adds and Takes are balanced on a thread. We saw an example of the former previously, when using Parallel.ForEach to implement a parallel spellchecker:

```
var misspellings = new ConcurrentBag<Tuple<int,string>>();

Parallel.ForEach (wordsToTest, (word, state, i) =>
{
  if (!wordLookup.Contains (word))
    misspellings.Add (Tuple.Create ((int) i, word));
});
```

A concurrent bag would be a poor choice for a producer/consumer queue, because elements are added and removed by *different* threads.

BlockingCollection<T>

If you call TryTake on any of the producer/consumer collections we discussed in the previous section:

```
ConcurrentStack<T>
ConcurrentQueue<T>
ConcurrentBag<T>
```

and the collection is empty, the method returns false. Sometimes it would be more useful in this scenario to *wait* until an element is available.

Rather than overloading the TryTake methods with this functionality (which would have caused a blowout of members after allowing for cancellation tokens and timeouts), PFX's designers encapsulated this functionality into a wrapper class called BlockingCollection<T>. A blocking collection wraps any collection that imple-

Parallel
Programming

---

1 Due to an implementation detail, there actually needs to be at least two elements to avoid contention entirely.

ments `IProducerConsumerCollection<T>` and lets you `Take` an element from the wrapped collection—blocking if no element is available.

A blocking collection also lets you limit the total size of the collection, blocking the *producer* if that size is exceeded. A collection limited in this manner is called a *bounded blocking collection*.

To use `BlockingCollection<T>`:

1. Instantiate the class, optionally specifying the `IProducerConsumerCollection<T>` to wrap and the maximum size (bound) of the collection.

2. Call `Add` or `TryAdd` to add elements to the underlying collection.

3. Call `Take` or `TryTake` to remove (consume) elements from the underlying collection.

If you call the constructor without passing in a collection, the class will automatically instantiate a `ConcurrentQueue<T>`. The producing and consuming methods let you specify cancellation tokens and timeouts. `Add` and `TryAdd` may block if the collection size is bounded; `Take` and `TryTake` block while the collection is empty.

Another way to consume elements is to call `GetConsumingEnumerable`. This returns a (potentially) infinite sequence that yields elements as they become available. You can force the sequence to end by calling `CompleteAdding`: this method also prevents further elements from being enqueued.

`BlockingCollection` also provides static methods called `AddToAny` and `TakeFromAny`, which let you add or take an element while specifying several blocking collections. The action is then honored by the first collection able to service the request.

Writing a Producer/Consumer Queue

A producer/consumer queue is a useful structure, both in parallel programming and general concurrency scenarios. Here's how it works:

- A queue is set up to describe work items—or data upon which work is performed.

- When a task needs executing, it's enqueued, and the caller gets on with other things.

- One or more worker threads plug away in the background, picking off and executing queued items.

A producer/consumer queue gives you precise control over how many worker threads execute at once, which is useful not only in limiting CPU consumption, but other resources as well. If the tasks perform intensive disk I/O, for instance, you can limit concurrency to avoid starving the operating system and other applications. You can also dynamically add and remove workers throughout the queue's life. The

CLR's thread pool itself is a kind of producer/consumer queue, optimized for short-running compute-bound jobs.

A producer/consumer queue typically holds items of data upon which (the same) task is performed. For example, the items of data may be filenames, and the task might be to encrypt those files. By making the item a delegate, however, you can write a more general-purpose producer/consumer queue where each item can do anything.

At *http://albahari.com/threading*, we show how to write a producer/consumer queue from scratch using an `AutoResetEvent` (and later, using `Monitor`'s `Wait` and `Pulse`). From Framework 4.0, though, writing a producer/consumer from scratch is unnecessary because most of the functionality is provided by `BlockingCollection<T>`. Here's how we leverage it:

```
public class PCQueue : IDisposable
{
  BlockingCollection<Action> _taskQ = new BlockingCollection<Action>();

  public PCQueue (int workerCount)
  {
    // Create and start a separate Task for each consumer:
    for (int i = 0; i < workerCount; i++)
      Task.Factory.StartNew (Consume);
  }

  public void Enqueue (Action action) { _taskQ.Add (action); }

  void Consume()
  {
    // This sequence that we're enumerating will block when no elements
    // are available and will end when CompleteAdding is called.

    foreach (Action action in _taskQ.GetConsumingEnumerable())
      action();      // Perform task.
  }

  public void Dispose() { _taskQ.CompleteAdding(); }
}
```

Because we didn't pass anything into `BlockingCollection`'s constructor, it instantiated a concurrent queue automatically. Had we passed in a `ConcurrentStack`, we'd have ended up with a producer/consumer stack.

Leveraging Tasks

The producer/consumer that we just wrote is inflexible in that we can't track work items after they've been enqueued. It would be nice if we could:

- Know when a work item has completed (and `await` it)
- Cancel a work item

- Deal elegantly with any exceptions thrown by a work item

An ideal solution would be to have the Enqueue method return some object giving us the functionality just described. The good news is that a class already exists to do exactly this—the Task class, which we can generate either with a TaskCompletion Source, or by instantiating directly (creating an unstarted or *cold* task):

```
public class PCQueue : IDisposable
{
  BlockingCollection<Task> _taskQ = new BlockingCollection<Task>();

  public PCQueue (int workerCount)
  {
    // Create and start a separate Task for each consumer:
    for (int i = 0; i < workerCount; i++)
      Task.Factory.StartNew (Consume);
  }

  public Task Enqueue (Action action, CancellationToken cancelToken
                                    = default (CancellationToken))
  {
    var task = new Task (action, cancelToken);
    _taskQ.Add (task);
    return task;
  }

  public Task<TResult> Enqueue<TResult> (Func<TResult> func,
            CancellationToken cancelToken = default (CancellationToken))
  {
    var task = new Task<TResult> (func, cancelToken);
    _taskQ.Add (task);
    return task;
  }

  void Consume()
  {
    foreach (var task in _taskQ.GetConsumingEnumerable())
      try
      {
          if (!task.IsCanceled) task.RunSynchronously();
      }
      catch (InvalidOperationException) { }  // Race condition
  }

  public void Dispose() { _taskQ.CompleteAdding(); }
}
```

In Enqueue, we enqueue and return to the caller a task that we create but don't start.

In Consume, we run the task synchronously on the consumer's thread. We catch an InvalidOperationException to handle the unlikely event that the task is canceled in between checking whether it's canceled and running it.

Here's how we can use this class:

```
var pcQ = new PCQueue (2);      // Maximum concurrency of 2
string result = await pcQ.Enqueue (() => "That was easy!");
...
```

Hence we have all the benefits of tasks—with exception propagation, return values and cancellation—while taking complete control over scheduling.

24

Application Domains

An *application domain* is the runtime unit of isolation in which a .NET program runs. It provides a managed memory boundary, a container for loaded assemblies, and application configuration settings, as well as delineating a communication boundary for distributed applications.

Each .NET process usually hosts just one application domain: the default domain, created automatically by the CLR when the process starts. It's also possible—and sometimes useful—to create additional application domains within the same process. This provides isolation while avoiding the overhead and communication complications that arise with having separate processes. It's useful in scenarios such as load testing and application patching, and in implementing robust error-recovery mechanisms.

 This chapter is irrelevant to Windows Store and CoreCLR apps, which have access to only a single application domain.

Application Domain Architecture

Figure 24-1 illustrates the application domain architectures for single-domain, multidomain, and typical distributed client/server applications. In most cases, the processes housing the application domains are created implicitly by the operating system—when the user double-clicks your .NET executable file or starts a Windows service. However, an application domain can also be hosted in other processes such as IIS or in SQL Server through CLR integration.

In the case of a simple executable, the process ends when the default application domain finishes executing. With hosts such as IIS or SQL Server, however, the process controls the lifetime, creating and destroying .NET application domains as it sees fit.

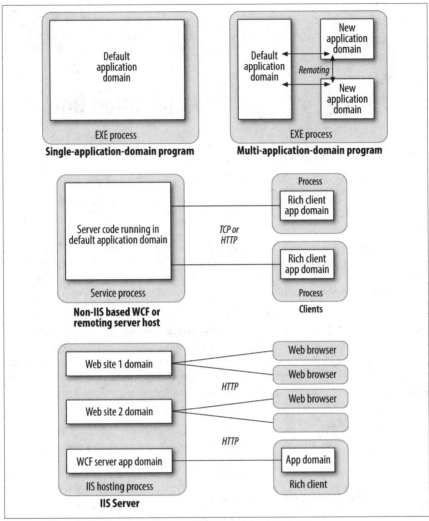

Figure 24-1. Application domain architecture

Creating and Destroying Application Domains

You can create and destroy additional application domains in a process by calling the static methods `AppDomain.CreateDomain` and `AppDomain.Unload`. In the following example, *test.exe* is executed in an isolated application domain, which is then unloaded:

```
static void Main()
{
  AppDomain newDomain = AppDomain.CreateDomain ("New Domain");
  newDomain.ExecuteAssembly ("test.exe");
```

```
AppDomain.Unload (newDomain);
}
```

Note that when the default application domain (the one created by the CLR at startup) is unloaded, all other application domains automatically unload, and the application closes. A domain can "know" whether it's the default domain via the AppDomain property IsDefaultDomain.

The AppDomainSetup class allows options to be specified for a new domain. The following properties are the most useful:

```
public string ApplicationName { get; set; }       // "Friendly" name
public string ApplicationBase { get; set; }        // Base folder

public string ConfigurationFile { get; set; }
public string LicenseFile       { get; set; }

// To assist with automatic assembly resolution:
public string PrivateBinPath      { get; set; }
public string PrivateBinPathProbe { get; set; }
```

The ApplicationBase property controls the application domain base directory, used as the root for automatic assembly probing. In the default application domain, this is the main executable's folder. In a new domain that you create, it can be anywhere you like:

```
AppDomainSetup setup = new AppDomainSetup();
setup.ApplicationBase = @"c:\MyBaseFolder";
AppDomain newDomain = AppDomain.CreateDomain ("New Domain", null, setup);
```

It's also possible to subscribe a new domain to assembly resolution events defined in the instigator's domain:

```
static void Main()
{
  AppDomain newDomain = AppDomain.CreateDomain ("test");
  newDomain.AssemblyResolve += new ResolveEventHandler (FindAssem);
  ...
}

static Assembly FindAssem (object sender, ResolveEventArgs args)
{
  ...
}
```

This is acceptable, provided that the event handler is a static method defined in a type available to both domains. The CLR is then able to execute the event handler in the correct domain. In this example, FindAssem would execute from within newDomain, even though it was subscribed from the default domain.

The PrivateBinPath property is a semicolon-separated list of subdirectories below the base directory that the CLR should automatically search for assemblies. (As with the application base folder, this can only be set prior to the application domain starting.) Take, for example, a directory structure where a program has, in its base folder, a single executable (and perhaps a configuration file) and all the referenced assemblies in subfolders as follows:

```
c:\MyBaseFolder\            -- Startup executable
            \bin
            \bin\v1.23      -- Latest assembly DLLs
            \bin\plugins    -- More DLLs
```

Here's how an application domain would be set up to use this folder structure:

```
AppDomainSetup setup  = new AppDomainSetup();
setup.ApplicationBase = @"c:\MyBaseFolder";
setup.PrivateBinPath  = @"bin\v1.23;bin\plugins";
AppDomain d = AppDomain.CreateDomain ("New Domain", null, setup);
d.ExecuteAssembly (@"c:\MyBaseFolder\Startup.exe");
```

Note that `PrivateBinPath` is always relative to, and below, the application base folder. Specifying absolute paths is illegal. `AppDomain` also provides a `PrivateBin PathProbe` property, which, if set to anything other than a blank string, excludes the base directory itself from being part of the assembly search path. (The reason `Priva teBinPathProbe` is a string rather than a `bool` type relates to COM compatibility.)

Just before any nondefault application domain unloads, the `DomainUnload` event fires. You can use this event for tear-down logic: the unloading of the domain (and the application as a whole, if necessary) is delayed until the execution of all `Domai nUnload` event handlers completes.

Just before the application itself closes, the `ProcessExit` event fires on all loaded application domains (including the default domain). Unlike with the `DomainUnload` event, `ProcessExit` event handlers are timed: the default CLR host gives event handlers two seconds per domain, and three seconds in total, before terminating their threads.

Using Multiple Application Domains

Multiple application domains have the following key uses:

- Providing process-like isolation with minimum overhead
- Allowing assembly files to be unloaded without restarting the process

When additional application domains are created within the same process, the CLR provides each with a level of isolation akin to that of running in separate processes. This means that each domain has separate memory, and objects in one domain cannot interfere with those in another. Furthermore, static members of the same class have independent values in each domain. ASP.NET uses exactly this approach to allow many sites to run in a shared process without affecting one another.

With ASP.NET, the application domains are created by the infrastructure—without your intervention. There are times, however, when you can benefit from explicitly creating multiple domains inside a single process. Suppose you've written a custom authentication system, and as part of unit testing, you want to stress-test the server code by simulating 20 clients logging in at once. You have three options in simulating 20 concurrent logins:

- Start 20 separate processes by calling `Process.Start` 20 times.
- Start 20 threads in the same process and domain.
- Start 20 threads in the same process—each in its own application domain.

The first option is clumsy and resource-intensive. It's also hard to communicate with each of the separate processes, should you want to give them more specific instructions on what to do.

The second option relies on the client-side code being thread-safe, which is unlikely —especially if static variables are used to store the current authentication state. And adding a lock around the client-side code would prevent the parallel execution that we need to stress-test the server.

The third option is ideal. It keeps each thread isolated—with independent state—and yet within easy reach of the hosting program.

Another reason to create a separate application domain is to allow assemblies to be unloaded without ending the process. This stems from the fact that there's no way to unload an assembly other than closing the application domain that loaded it. This is a problem if it was loaded in the default domain, because closing this domain means closing the application. An assembly's file is locked while loaded and so cannot be patched or replaced. Loading assemblies in a separate application domain that can be torn down gets around this problem—and helps to reduce the memory footprint of an application that occasionally needs to load large assemblies.

The LoaderOptimization Attribute

By default, assemblies that load into an explicitly created application domain are reprocessed by the JIT compiler. This includes:

- Assemblies that have already been JIT-compiled in the caller's domain
- Assemblies for which a native image has been generated with the *ngen.exe* tool
- All of the .NET Framework assemblies (except for *mscorlib*)

This can be a major performance hit, particularly if you repeatedly create and unload application domains that reference large .NET Framework assemblies. A workaround is to attach the following attribute to your program's main entry method:

```
[LoaderOptimization (LoaderOptimization.MultiDomainHost)]
```

This instructs the CLR to load GAC assemblies *domain-neutral*, so native images are honored and JIT images shared across application domains. This is usually ideal, because the GAC includes all .NET Framework assemblies (and possibly some invariant parts of your application).

You can go a stage further by specifying LoaderOptimization.MultiDomain: this instructs *all* assemblies to be loaded domain-neutral (excluding those loaded outside the normal assembly resolution mechanism). This is undesirable, however, if you want assemblies to unload with their domain. A domain-neutral assembly is shared between all domains and so does not unload until the parent process ends.

Using DoCallBack

Let's revisit the most basic multidomain scenario:

```
static void Main()
{
  AppDomain newDomain = AppDomain.CreateDomain ("New Domain");
  newDomain.ExecuteAssembly ("test.exe");
  AppDomain.Unload (newDomain);
}
```

Calling ExecuteAssembly on a separate domain is convenient but offers little opportunity to interact with the domain. It also requires that the target assembly is an executable, and it commits the caller to a single entry point. The only way to incorporate flexibility is to resort to an approach such as passing a string of arguments to the executable.

A more powerful approach is to use AppDomain's DoCallBack method. This executes on another application domain, a method on a given type. The type's assembly is automatically loaded into the domain (the CLR will know where it lives if the current domain can reference it). In the following example, a method in the currently executing class is run in a new domain:

```
class Program
{
  static void Main()
  {
    AppDomain newDomain = AppDomain.CreateDomain ("New Domain");
    newDomain.DoCallBack (new CrossAppDomainDelegate (SayHello));
    AppDomain.Unload (newDomain);
  }

  static void SayHello()
  {
    Console.WriteLine ("Hi from " + AppDomain.CurrentDomain.FriendlyName);
  }
}
```

The example works because the delegate is referencing a static method, meaning it points to a type rather than an instance. This makes the delegate "domain-agnostic" or agile. It can run in any domain, and in the same way, as there's nothing tying it to the original domain. It's also possible to use DoCallBack with a delegate referencing an instance method. However, the CLR will attempt to apply Remoting semantics (described later), which in this case happens to be the opposite of what we want.

Monitoring Application Domains

From Framework 4.0, you can monitor the memory and CPU consumption of a specific application domain. For this to work, you must first enable application domain monitoring as follows:

```
AppDomain.MonitoringIsEnabled = true;
```

This enables monitoring for all domains in the current process. Once enabled, you can't subsequently disable it—setting this property to false throws an exception.

 Another way to enable to enable domain monitoring is via the application configuration file. Add the following element:

```
<configuration>
  <runtime>
    <appDomainResourceMonitoring enabled="true"/>
  </runtime>
</configuration>
```

This enables monitoring for all application domains.

You can then query an `AppDomain`'s CPU and memory usage via the following three instance properties:

```
MonitoringTotalProcessorTime
MonitoringTotalAllocatedMemorySize
MonitoringSurvivedMemorySize
```

The first two properties return the *total* CPU consumption and managed memory allocated by that domain since it was started. (These figures can only grow and never shrink). The third property returns the actual managed memory consumption of the domain at the time of the last garbage collection.

You can access these properties from the same or another domain.

Domains and Threads

When you call a method in another application domain, execution blocks until the method finishes executing—just as though you called a method in your own domain. Although this behavior is usually desirable, there are times when you need to run a method concurrently. You can do that with multithreading.

We talked previously about using multiple application domains to simulate 20 concurrent client logins in order to test an authentication system. By having each client log in on a separate application domain, each would be isolated and unable to interfere with another client via static class members. To implement this example, we need to call a "Login" method on 20 concurrent threads, each in its own application domain:

```
class Program
{
  static void Main()
  {
    // Create 20 domains and 20 threads.
    AppDomain[] domains = new AppDomain [20];
    Thread[] threads = new Thread [20];

    for (int i = 0; i < 20; i++)
    {
      domains [i] = AppDomain.CreateDomain ("Client Login " + i);
      threads [i] = new Thread (LoginOtherDomain);
    }

    // Start all the threads, passing to each thread its app domain.
    for (int i = 0; i < 20; i++) threads [i].Start (domains [i]);

    // Wait for the threads to finish
    for (int i = 0; i < 20; i++) threads [i].Join();

    // Unload the app domains
    for (int i = 0; i < 20; i++) AppDomain.Unload (domains [i]);
    Console.ReadLine();
  }

  // Parameterized thread start - taking the domain on which to run.
  static void LoginOtherDomain (object domain)
  {
    ((AppDomain) domain).DoCallBack (Login);
  }

  static void Login()
  {
    Client.Login ("Joe", "");
    Console.WriteLine ("Logged in as: " + Client.CurrentUser + " on " +
      AppDomain.CurrentDomain.FriendlyName);
  }
}

class Client
{
  // Here's a static field that would interfere with other client logins
  // if running in the same app domain.
  public static string CurrentUser = "";

  public static void Login (string name, string password)
  {
    if (CurrentUser.Length == 0)      // If we're not already logged in...
    {
      // Sleep to simulate authentication...
      Thread.Sleep (500);
      CurrentUser = name;             // Record that we're authenticated.
    }
  }
}
```

```
// Output:
Logged in as: Joe on Client Login 0
Logged in as: Joe on Client Login 1
Logged in as: Joe on Client Login 4
Logged in as: Joe on Client Login 2
Logged in as: Joe on Client Login 3
Logged in as: Joe on Client Login 5
Logged in as: Joe on Client Login 6
...
```

See Chapter 22 for more information on multithreading.

Sharing Data Between Domains

Sharing Data via Slots

Application domains can use named slots to share data, as in the following example:

```
class Program
{
  static void Main()
  {
    AppDomain newDomain = AppDomain.CreateDomain ("New Domain");

    // Write to a named slot called "Message" - any string key will do.
    newDomain.SetData ("Message", "guess what...");

    newDomain.DoCallBack (SayMessage);
    AppDomain.Unload (newDomain);
  }

  static void SayMessage()
  {
    // Read from the "Message" data slot
    Console.WriteLine (AppDomain.CurrentDomain.GetData ("Message"));
  }
}

// Output:
guess what...
```

A slot is created automatically the first time it's used. The data being communicated (in this example, "guess what ...") must either be *serializable* (see Chapter 17) or be based on MarshalByRefObject. If the data is serializable (such as the string in our example), it's copied to the other application domain. If it implements Marshal ByRefObject, Remoting semantics are applied.

Intra-Process Remoting

The most flexible way to communicate with another application domain is to instantiate objects *in the other domain* via a proxy. This is called *Remoting*.

The class being "Remoted" must inherit from `MarshalByRefObject`. The client then calls a `CreateInstanceXXX` method on the remote domain's `AppDomain` class to remotely instantiate the object.

The following instantiates the type `Foo` in another application domain and then calls its `SayHello` method:

```
class Program
{
  static void Main()
  {
    AppDomain newDomain = AppDomain.CreateDomain ("New Domain");

    Foo foo = (Foo) newDomain.CreateInstanceAndUnwrap (
                    typeof (Foo).Assembly.FullName,
                    typeof (Foo).FullName);

    Console.WriteLine (foo.SayHello());
    AppDomain.Unload (newDomain);
    Console.ReadLine();
  }
}

public class Foo : MarshalByRefObject
{
  public string SayHello()
    => "Hello from " + AppDomain.CurrentDomain.FriendlyName;

  // This ensures the object lasts for as long as the client wants it
  public override object InitializeLifetimeService() => null;
}
```

When the `foo` object is created on the other application domain (called the "remote" domain), we don't get back a direct reference to the object, because the application domains are isolated. Instead, we get back a transparent proxy; transparent because it *appears* as though it was a direct reference to the remote object. When we subsequently call the `SayHello` method on `foo`, a message is constructed behind the scenes, which is forwarded to the "remote" application domain where it is then executed on the real `foo`. Rather like saying "hello" on a telephone: you're talking not to a real person but to a piece of plastic that acts as a transparent proxy for a person. Any return value is turned into a message and sent back to the caller.

Before Windows Communication Foundation was released in .NET Framework 3.0, Remoting was one of the two principal technologies for writing distributed applications (Web Services being the other). In a distributed Remoting application, you explicitly set up an HTTP or TCP/IP communication channel at each end, allowing communication to cross process and network boundaries.

Although WCF is superior to Remoting for distributed applications, Remoting still has a niche in inter-domain communication within a process. Its advantage in this scenario is that it requires no configuration—the communication channel is automatically created (a fast in-memory channel), and no type registration is required. You simply start using it.

The methods on `Foo` can return more `MarshalByRefObject` instances, in which case more transparent proxies are generated when those methods are called. Methods on `Foo` can also accept `MarshalByRefObject` instances as arguments—in which Remoting happens in reverse. The caller will hold the "remote" object, while the callee will have a proxy.

As well as marshaling objects by reference, application domains can exchange scalar values, or any *serializable* object. A type is serializable if it either has the `Serializable` attribute or implements `ISerializable`. Then, when crossing the application domain boundary, a complete copy of the object is returned, rather than a proxy. In other words, the object is marshaled by *value* rather than reference.

Remoting within the same process is client-activated, meaning that the CLR doesn't attempt to share or reuse remotely created objects with the same or other clients. In other words, if the client creates two `Foo` objects, two objects will be created in the remote domain, and two proxies in the client domain. This provides the most natural object semantics; however, it means that the remote domain is dependent on the client's garbage collector: the `foo` object in the remote domain is released from memory only when the client's garbage collector decides that the `foo` (proxy) is no longer in use. If the client domain crashes, it may never get released. To protect against this scenario, the CLR provides a lease-based mechanism for managing the lifetime of remotely created objects. The default behavior is for remotely created objects to self-destruct after five minutes of nonuse.

Because in this example the client runs in the default application domain, the client doesn't have the luxury of crashing. Once it ends, so does the whole process! Hence, it makes sense to disable the five-minute lifetime lease. This is the purpose of overriding `InitializeLifetimeService`—by returning a null lease, remotely created objects are destroyed only when garbage-collected by the client.

Isolating Types and Assemblies

In the preceding example, we remotely instantiated an object of type `Foo` as follows:

```
Foo foo = (Foo) newDomain.CreateInstanceAndUnwrap (
                    typeof (Foo).Assembly.FullName,
                    typeof (Foo).FullName);
```

Here's the method's signature:

```
public object CreateInstanceAndUnwrap (string assemblyName,
                                            string typeName)
```

Because this method accepts an assembly and type *name* rather than a `Type` object, you can remotely instantiate an object without loading its type locally. This is useful when you want to avoid loading the type's assembly into the caller's application domain.

 AppDomain also provides a method called `CreateIn stanceFromAndUnwrap`. The difference is:

- `CreateInstanceAndUnwrap` accepts a *fully qualified assembly name* (see Chapter 18).
- `CreateInstanceFromAndUnwrap` accepts a *path or file-name*.

To illustrate, suppose we were writing a text editor that allows the user to load and unload third-party plug-ins. We demonstrated this in Chapter 21 in the section "Sandboxing Another Assembly" on page 881, from the perspective of security. When it came to actually executing the plug-in, however, all we did was call `Execu teAssembly`. With Remoting, we can interact with plug-ins in a richer fashion.

The first step is to write a common library that both the host and the plug-ins will reference. This library will define an interface describing what plug-ins can do. Here's a simple example:

```
namespace Plugin.Common
{
  public interface ITextPlugin
  {
    string TransformText (string input);
  }
}
```

Next, we need to write a simple plug-in. We'll assume the following is compiled to *AllCapitals.dll*:

```
namespace Plugin.Extensions
{
  public class AllCapitals : MarshalByRefObject, Plugin.Common.ITextPlugin
  {
    public string TransformText (string input) => input.ToUpper();
  }
}
```

Here's how to write a host that loads *AllCapitals.dll* into a separate application domain, calls `TransformText` using Remoting, and then unloads the application domain:

```
using System;
using System.Reflection;
using Plugin.Common;

class Program
{
  static void Main()
  {
    AppDomain domain = AppDomain.CreateDomain ("Plugin Domain");

    ITextPlugin plugin = (ITextPlugin) domain.CreateInstanceFromAndUnwrap
      ("AllCapitals.dll", "Plugin.Extensions.AllCapitals");

    // Call the TransformText method using Remoting:
    Console.WriteLine (plugin.TransformText ("hello"));   // "HELLO"

    AppDomain.Unload (domain);

    // The AllCapitals.dll file is now completely unloaded and could
    // be moved or deleted.
  }
}
```

Because this program interacts with the plug-in solely through the common interface, `ITextPlugin`, the types in `AllCapitals` are never loaded into the caller's application domain. This maintains the integrity of the caller's domain and ensures that no locks are held on the plug-in assembly files after their domain is unloaded.

Type discovery

In our preceding example, a real application would need some means of discovering plug-in type names, such as `Plugin.Extensions.AllCapitals`.

You can achieve this by writing a discovery class in the *common* assembly that uses reflection as follows:

```
public class Discoverer : MarshalByRefObject
{
  public string[] GetPluginTypeNames (string assemblyPath)
  {
    List<string> typeNames = new List<string>();
    Assembly a = Assembly.LoadFrom (assemblyPath);
    foreach (Type t in a.GetTypes())
```

Application
Domains

```
      if (t.IsPublic
        && t.IsMarshalByRef
        && typeof (ITextPlugin).IsAssignableFrom (t))
    {
      typeNames.Add (t.FullName);
    }
    return typeNames.ToArray();
  }
}
```

The catch is that `Assembly.LoadFrom` loads the assembly into the current application domain. Therefore, you must call this method *in the plug-in domain*:

```
class Program
{
  static void Main()
  {
    AppDomain domain = AppDomain.CreateDomain ("Plugin Domain");

    Discoverer d = (Discoverer) domain.CreateInstanceAndUnwrap (
      typeof (Discoverer).Assembly.FullName,
      typeof (Discoverer).FullName);

    string[] plugInTypeNames = d.GetPluginTypeNames ("AllCapitals.dll");

    foreach (string s in plugInTypeNames)
      Console.WriteLine (s);                    // Plugin.Extensions.AllCapitals

    ...
```

In the *System.AddIn.Contract* assembly is an API that develops these concepts into a complete framework for program extensibility. It addresses such issues as isolation, versioning, discovery, and activation. For a good source of online information, search for "CLR Add-In Team Blog" on *http://blogs.msdn.com*.

25

Interoperability

This chapter describes how to integrate with native (unmanaged) DLLs and COM components. Unless otherwise stated, the types mentioned in this chapter exist in either the System or the System.Runtime.InteropServices namespace.

Calling into Native DLLs

P/Invoke, short for *Platform Invocation Services*, allows you to access functions, structs, and callbacks in unmanaged DLLs. For example, consider the MessageBox function, defined in the Windows DLL *user32.dll* as follows:

```
int MessageBox (HWND hWnd, LPCTSTR lpText, LPCTSTR lpCaption, UINT uType);
```

You can call this function directly by declaring a static method of the same name, applying the extern keyword, and adding the DllImport attribute:

```
using System;
using System.Runtime.InteropServices;

class MsgBoxTest
{
  [DllImport("user32.dll")]
  static extern int MessageBox (IntPtr hWnd, string text, string caption,
                                int type);
  public static void Main()
  {
    MessageBox (IntPtr.Zero,
                "Please do not press this again.", "Attention", 0);
  }
}
```

The MessageBox classes in the System.Windows and System.Windows.Forms namespaces themselves call similar unmanaged methods.

The CLR includes a marshaler that knows how to convert parameters and return values between .NET types and unmanaged types. In this example, the int parameters translate directly to 4-byte integers that the function expects, and the string parameters are converted into null-terminated arrays of 2-byte Unicode characters. `IntPtr` is a struct designed to encapsulate an unmanaged handle and is 32 bits wide on 32-bit platforms and 64 bits wide on 64-bit platforms.

Type Marshaling

Marshaling Common Types

On the unmanaged side, there can be more than one way to represent a given data type. A string, for instance, can contain single-byte ANSI characters or double-byte Unicode characters and can be length-prefixed, null-terminated, or of fixed length. With the `MarshalAs` attribute, you can tell the CLR marshaler the variation in use so it can provide the correct translation. Here's an example:

```
[DllImport("...")]
static extern int Foo ( [MarshalAs (UnmanagedType.LPStr)] string s );
```

The `UnmanagedType` enumeration includes all the Win32 and COM types that the marshaler understands. In this case, the marshaler was told to translate to `LPStr`, which is a null-terminated single-byte ANSI string.

On the .NET side, you also have some choice as to what data type to use. Unmanaged handles, for instance, can map to `IntPtr`, `int`, `uint`, `long`, or `ulong`.

Most unmanaged handles encapsulate an address or pointer, and so must be mapped to `IntPtr` for compatibility with both 32- and 64-bit operating systems. A typical example is HWND.

Quite often with Win32 functions, you come across an integer parameter that accepts a set of constants, defined in a C++ header file such as *WinUser.h*. Rather than defining these as simple C# constants, you can define them within an enum instead. Using an enum can make for tidier code as well as increase static type safety. We provide an example in the later section "Shared Memory" on page 1008.

When installing Microsoft Visual Studio, be sure to install the C++ header files—even if you choose nothing else in the C++ category. This is where all the native Win32 constants are defined. You can then locate all header files by searching for *.h in the Visual Studio program directory.

Receiving strings from unmanaged code back to .NET requires that some memory management take place. The marshaler performs this work automatically if you declare the external method with a `StringBuilder` rather than a `string`, as follows:

```
using System;
using System.Text;
using System.Runtime.InteropServices;

class Test
```

```
{
    [DllImport("kernel32.dll")]
    static extern int GetWindowsDirectory (StringBuilder sb, int maxChars);

    static void Main()
    {
        StringBuilder s = new StringBuilder (256);
        GetWindowsDirectory (s, 256);
        Console.WriteLine (s);
    }
}
```

 If you are unsure how to call a particular Win32 method, you will usually find an example online if you search for the method name and *DllImport*. The site *http://www.pinvoke.net* is a wiki that aims to document all Win32 signatures.

Marshaling Classes and Structs

Sometimes you need to pass a struct to an unmanaged method. For example, Get SystemTime in the Win32 API is defined as follows:

```
void GetSystemTime (LPSYSTEMTIME lpSystemTime);
```

LPSYSTEMTIME conforms to this C struct:

```
typedef struct _SYSTEMTIME {
    WORD wYear;
    WORD wMonth;
    WORD wDayOfWeek;
    WORD wDay;
    WORD wHour;
    WORD wMinute;
    WORD wSecond;
    WORD wMilliseconds;
} SYSTEMTIME, *PSYSTEMTIME;
```

In order to call GetSystemTime, we must define a .NET class or struct that matches this C struct:

```
using System;
using System.Runtime.InteropServices;

[StructLayout(LayoutKind.Sequential)]
class SystemTime
{
    public ushort Year;
    public ushort Month;
    public ushort DayOfWeek;
    public ushort Day;
    public ushort Hour;
    public ushort Minute;
    public ushort Second;
    public ushort Milliseconds;
}
```

The StructLayout attribute instructs the marshaler how to map each field to its unmanaged counterpart. LayoutKind.Sequential means that we want the fields aligned sequentially on *pack-size* boundaries (we'll see what this means shortly), just as they would be in a C struct. The field names here are irrelevant; it's the ordering of fields that's important.

Now we can call GetSystemTime:

```
[DllImport("kernel32.dll")]
static extern void GetSystemTime (SystemTime t);

static void Main()
{
  SystemTime t = new SystemTime();
  GetSystemTime (t);
  Console.WriteLine (t.Year);
}
```

In both C and C#, fields in an object are located at *n* number of bytes from the address of that object. The difference is that in a C# program, the CLR finds this offset by looking it up using the field token; C field names are compiled directly into offsets. For instance, in C, wDay is just a token to represent whatever is at the address of a SystemTime instance plus 24 bytes.

For access speed, each field is placed at an offset that is a multiple of the field's size. That multiplier, however, is restricted to a maximum of *x* bytes, where *x* is the *pack size*. In the current implementation, the default pack size is 8 bytes, so a struct comprising a sbyte followed by an (8-byte) long occupies 16 bytes, and the 7 bytes following the sbyte are wasted. You can lessen or eliminate this wastage by specifying a *pack size* via the Pack property of the StructLayout attribute: this makes the fields align to offsets that are multiples of the specified pack size. So with a pack size of 1, the struct just described would occupy just 9 bytes. You can specify pack sizes of 1, 2, 4, 8, or 16 bytes.

The StructLayout attribute also lets you specify explicit field offsets (see "Simulating a C Union" on page 1007).

In and Out Marshaling

In the previous example, we implemented SystemTime as a class. We could have instead chosen a struct—providing GetSystemTime was declared with a ref or out parameter:

```
[DllImport("kernel32.dll")]
static extern void GetSystemTime (out SystemTime t);
```

In most cases, C#'s directional parameter semantics work the same with external methods. Pass-by-value parameters are copied in, C# ref parameters are copied in/out, and C# out parameters are copied out. However, there are some exceptions for types that have special conversions. For instance, array classes and the String Builder class require copying when coming out of a function, so they are in/out. It is occasionally useful to override this behavior with the In and Out attributes. For example, if an array should be read-only, the in modifier indicates to only copy the array going into the function and not coming out of it:

```
static extern void Foo ( [In] int[] array);
```

Callbacks from Unmanaged Code

The P/Invoke layer does its best to present a natural programming model on both sides of the boundary, mapping between relevant constructs where possible. Since C# can not only call out to C functions but also can be called back from the C functions (via function pointers), the P/Invoke layer maps unmanaged function pointers into the nearest equivalent in C#, which is delegates.

As an example, you can enumerate all top-level window handles with this method in *User32.dll*:

```
BOOL EnumWindows (WNDENUMPROC lpEnumFunc, LPARAM lParam);
```

WNDENUMPROC is a callback that gets fired with the handle of each window in sequence (or until the callback returns false). Here is its definition:

```
BOOL CALLBACK EnumWindowsProc (HWND hwnd, LPARAM lParam);
```

To use this, we declare a delegate with a matching signature and then pass a delegate instance to the external method:

```
using System;
using System.Runtime.InteropServices;

class CallbackFun
{
  delegate bool EnumWindowsCallback (IntPtr hWnd, IntPtr lParam);

  [DllImport("user32.dll")]
  static extern int EnumWindows (EnumWindowsCallback hWnd, IntPtr lParam);

  static bool PrintWindow (IntPtr hWnd, IntPtr lParam)
  {
    Console.WriteLine (hWnd.ToInt64());
    return true;
  }

  static void Main() => EnumWindows (PrintWindow, IntPtr.Zero);
}
```

Simulating a C Union

Each field in a struct is given enough room to store its data. Consider a struct containing one int and one char. The int is likely to start at an offset of 0 and is guaranteed at least 4 bytes. So, the char would start at an offset of at least 4. If, for some reason, the char started at an offset of 2, you'd change the value of the int if you assigned a value to the char. Sounds like mayhem, doesn't it? Strangely enough, the C language supports a variation on a struct called a *union* that does exactly this. You can simulate this in C# using LayoutKind.Explicit and the FieldOffset attribute.

It might be hard to think of a case in which this would be useful. However, suppose you want to play a note on an external synthesizer. The Windows Multimedia API provides a function for doing just this via the MIDI protocol:

```
[DllImport ("winmm.dll")]
public static extern uint midiOutShortMsg (IntPtr handle, uint message);
```

The second argument, message, describes what note to play. The problem is in constructing this 32-bit unsigned integer: it's divided internally into bytes, representing a MIDI channel, note, and velocity at which to strike. One solution is to shift and mask via the bitwise <<, >>, &, and | operators to convert these bytes to and from the 32-bit "packed" message. Far simpler, though, is to define a struct with explicit layout:

```
[StructLayout (LayoutKind.Explicit)]
public struct NoteMessage
{
  [FieldOffset(0)] public uint PackedMsg;    // 4 bytes long

  [FieldOffset(0)] public byte Channel;      // FieldOffset also at 0
  [FieldOffset(1)] public byte Note;
  [FieldOffset(2)] public byte Velocity;
}
```

The Channel, Note, and Velocity fields deliberately overlap with the 32-bit packed message. This allows you to read and write using either. No calculations are required to keep other fields in sync:

```
NoteMessage n = new NoteMessage();
Console.WriteLine (n.PackedMsg);    // 0

n.Channel = 10;
n.Note = 100;
n.Velocity = 50;
Console.WriteLine (n.PackedMsg);    // 3302410

n.PackedMsg = 3328010;
Console.WriteLine (n.Note);         // 200
```

Shared Memory

Memory-mapped files, or *shared memory*, is a feature in Windows that allows multiple processes on the same computer to share data, without the overhead of Remoting or WCF. Shared memory is extremely fast and, unlike pipes, offers *random* access to the shared data. We saw in Chapter 15 how you can use the MemoryMapped File class to access memory-mapped files; bypassing this and calling the Win32 methods directly is a good way to demonstrate P/Invoke.

The Win32 `CreateFileMapping` function allocates shared memory. You tell it how many bytes you need and the name with which to identify the share. Another application can then subscribe to this memory by calling `OpenFileMapping` with same name. Both methods return a *handle*, which you can convert to a pointer by calling `MapViewOfFile`.

Here's a class that encapsulates access to shared memory:

```
using System;
using System.Runtime.InteropServices;
using System.ComponentModel;

public sealed class SharedMem : IDisposable
{
  // Here we're using enums because they're safer than constants

  enum FileProtection : uint      // constants from winnt.h
  {
    ReadOnly = 2,
    ReadWrite = 4
  }

  enum FileRights : uint           // constants from WinBASE.h
  {
    Read = 4,
    Write = 2,
    ReadWrite = Read + Write
  }

  static readonly IntPtr NoFileHandle = new IntPtr (-1);

  [DllImport ("kernel32.dll", SetLastError = true)]
  static extern IntPtr CreateFileMapping (IntPtr hFile,
                                          int lpAttributes,
                                          FileProtection flProtect,
                                          uint dwMaximumSizeHigh,
                                          uint dwMaximumSizeLow,
                                          string lpName);

  [DllImport ("kernel32.dll", SetLastError=true)]
  static extern IntPtr OpenFileMapping (FileRights dwDesiredAccess,
                                        bool bInheritHandle,
                                        string lpName);

  [DllImport ("kernel32.dll", SetLastError = true)]
  static extern IntPtr MapViewOfFile (IntPtr hFileMappingObject,
                                      FileRights dwDesiredAccess,
                                      uint dwFileOffsetHigh,
                                      uint dwFileOffsetLow,
                                      uint dwNumberOfBytesToMap);

  [DllImport ("Kernel32.dll", SetLastError = true)]
  static extern bool UnmapViewOfFile (IntPtr map);
```

```
[DllImport ("kernel32.dll", SetLastError = true)]
static extern int CloseHandle (IntPtr hObject);

IntPtr fileHandle, fileMap;

public IntPtr Root { get { return fileMap; } }

public SharedMem (string name, bool existing, uint sizeInBytes)
{
  if (existing)
    fileHandle = OpenFileMapping (FileRights.ReadWrite, false, name);
  else
    fileHandle = CreateFileMapping (NoFileHandle, 0,
                                    FileProtection.ReadWrite,
                                    0, sizeInBytes, name);
  if (fileHandle == IntPtr.Zero)
    throw new Win32Exception();

  // Obtain a read/write map for the entire file
  fileMap = MapViewOfFile (fileHandle, FileRights.ReadWrite, 0, 0, 0);

  if (fileMap == IntPtr.Zero)
    throw new Win32Exception();
}

public void Dispose()
{
  if (fileMap != IntPtr.Zero) UnmapViewOfFile (fileMap);
  if (fileHandle != IntPtr.Zero) CloseHandle (fileHandle);
  fileMap = fileHandle = IntPtr.Zero;
}
}
```

In this example, we set SetLastError=true on the DllImport methods that use the
SetLastError protocol for emitting error codes. This ensures that the Win32Excep
tion is populated with details of the error when that exception is thrown. (It also
allows you to query the error explicitly by calling Marshal.GetLastWin32Error.)

In order to demonstrate this class, we need to run two applications. The first one
creates the shared memory, as follows:

```
using (SharedMem sm = new SharedMem ("MyShare", false, 1000))
{
  IntPtr root = sm.Root;
  // I have shared memory!

  Console.ReadLine();          // Here's where we start a second app...
}
```

The second application subscribes to the shared memory by constructing a Share
dMem object of the same name, with the existing argument true:

```
using (SharedMem sm = new SharedMem ("MyShare", true, 1000))
{
  IntPtr root = sm.Root;
```

```
    // I have the same shared memory!
    // ...
  }
```

The net result is that each program has an `IntPtr`—a pointer to the same unmanaged memory. The two applications now need somehow to read and write to memory via this common pointer. One approach is to write a serializable class that encapsulates all the shared data, then serialize (and deserialize) the data to the unmanaged memory using an `UnmanagedMemoryStream`. This is inefficient, however, if there's a lot of data. Imagine if the shared memory class had a megabyte worth of data, and just one integer needed to be updated. A better approach is to define the shared data construct as a struct, and then map it directly into shared memory. We discuss this in the following section.

Mapping a Struct to Unmanaged Memory

A struct with a `StructLayout` of `Sequential` or `Explicit` can be mapped directly into unmanaged memory. Consider the following struct:

```
[StructLayout (LayoutKind.Sequential)]
unsafe struct MySharedData
{
  public int Value;
  public char Letter;
  public fixed float Numbers [50];
}
```

The `fixed` directive allows us to define fixed-length value-type arrays inline, and it is what takes us into the `unsafe` realm. Space in this struct is allocated inline for 50 floating-point numbers. Unlike with standard C# arrays, `Numbers` is not a *reference* to an array—it *is* the array. If we run the following:

```
static unsafe void Main() => Console.WriteLine (sizeof (MySharedData));
```

the result is 208: 50 4-byte floats, plus the 4 bytes for the `Value` integer, plus 2 bytes for the `Letter` character. The total, 206, is rounded to 208 due to the `floats` being aligned on 4-byte boundaries (4 bytes being the size of a `float`).

We can demonstrate `MySharedData` in an `unsafe` context, most simply, with stack-allocated memory:

```
MySharedData d;
MySharedData* data = &d;        // Get the address of d

data->Value = 123;
data->Letter = 'X';
data->Numbers[10] = 1.45f;
```

or:

```
// Allocate the array on the stack:
MySharedData* data = stackalloc MySharedData[1];
```

```
data->Value = 123;
data->Letter = 'X';
data->Numbers[10] = 1.45f;
```

Of course, we're not demonstrating anything that couldn't otherwise be achieved in a managed context. Suppose, however, that we want to store an instance of MyShar edData on the *unmanaged heap*, outside the realm of the CLR's garbage collector. This is where pointers become really useful:

```
MySharedData* data = (MySharedData*)
  Marshal.AllocHGlobal (sizeof (MySharedData)).ToPointer();

data->Value = 123;
data->Letter = 'X';
data->Numbers[10] = 1.45f;
```

Marshal.AllocHGlobal allocates memory on the unmanaged heap. Here's how to later free the same memory:

```
Marshal.FreeHGlobal (new IntPtr (data));
```

(The result of forgetting to free the memory is a good old-fashioned memory leak.)

In keeping with its name, we'll now use MySharedData in conjunction with the SharedMem class we wrote in the preceding section. The following program allocates a block of shared memory and then maps the MySharedData struct into that memory:

```
static unsafe void Main()
{
  using (SharedMem sm = new SharedMem ("MyShare", false, 1000))
  {
    void* root = sm.Root.ToPointer();
    MySharedData* data = (MySharedData*) root;

    data->Value = 123;
    data->Letter = 'X';
    data->Numbers[10] = 1.45f;
    Console.WriteLine ("Written to shared memory");

    Console.ReadLine();

    Console.WriteLine ("Value is " + data->Value);
    Console.WriteLine ("Letter is " + data->Letter);
    Console.WriteLine ("11th Number is " + data->Numbers[10]);
    Console.ReadLine();
  }
}
```

You can use the built-in `MemoryMappedFile` class instead of `SharedMem` as follows:

```
using (MemoryMappedFile mmFile =
        MemoryMappedFile.CreateNew ("MyShare", 1000))
using (MemoryMappedViewAccessor accessor =
        mmFile.CreateViewAccessor())
{
  byte* pointer = null;
  accessor.SafeMemoryMappedViewHandle.AcquirePointer
   (ref pointer);
  void* root = pointer;
  ...
}
```

Here's a second program that attaches to the same shared memory, reading the values written by the first program. (It must be run while the first program is waiting on the `ReadLine` statement, since the shared memory object is disposed upon leaving its `using` statement.)

```
static unsafe void Main()
{
  using (SharedMem sm = new SharedMem ("MyShare", true, 1000))
  {
    void* root = sm.Root.ToPointer();
    MySharedData* data = (MySharedData*) root;

    Console.WriteLine ("Value is " + data->Value);
    Console.WriteLine ("Letter is " + data->Letter);
    Console.WriteLine ("11th Number is " + data->Numbers[10]);

    // Our turn to update values in shared memory!
    data->Value++;
    data->Letter = '!';
    data->Numbers[10] = 987.5f;
    Console.WriteLine ("Updated shared memory");
    Console.ReadLine();
  }
}
```

The output from each of these programs is as follows:

```
// First program:

Written to shared memory
Value is 124
Letter is !
11th Number is 987.5

// Second program:

Value is 123
Letter is X
11th Number is 1.45
Updated shared memory
```

Don't be put off by the pointers: C++ programmers use them throughout whole applications and are able to get everything working. At least most of the time! This sort of usage is fairly simple by comparison.

As it happens, our example is unsafe—quite literally—for another reason. We've not considered the thread-safety (or more precisely, process-safety) issues that arise with two programs accessing the same memory at once. To use this in a production application, we'd need to add the `volatile` keyword to the `Value` and `Letter` fields in the `MySharedData` struct to prevent fields from being cached in CPU registers. Furthermore, as our interaction with the fields grew beyond the trivial, we would most likely need to protect their access via a cross-process `Mutex`, just as we would use `lock` statements to protect access to fields in a multithreaded program. We discussed thread safety in detail in Chapter 22.

fixed and fixed {...}

One limitation of mapping structs directly into memory is that the struct can contain only unmanaged types. If you need to share string data, for instance, you must use a fixed character array instead. This means manual conversion to and from the `string` type. Here's how to do it:

```
[StructLayout (LayoutKind.Sequential)]
unsafe struct MySharedData
{
  ...
  // Allocate space for 200 chars (i.e., 400 bytes).
  const int MessageSize = 200;
  fixed char message [MessageSize];

  // One would most likely put this code into a helper class:
  public string Message
  {
    get { fixed (char* cp = message) return new string (cp); }
    set
    {
      fixed (char* cp = message)
      {
        int i = 0;
        for (; i < value.Length && i < MessageSize - 1; i++)
          cp [i] = value [i];

        // Add the null terminator
        cp [i] = '\0';
      }
    }
  }
}
```

 There's no such thing as a reference to a fixed array; instead, you get a pointer. When you index into a fixed array, you're actually performing pointer arithmetic!

With the first use of the `fixed` keyword, we allocate space, inline, for 200 characters in the struct. The same keyword (somewhat confusingly) has a different meaning when used later in the property definition. It tells the CLR to *pin* an object, so that should it decide to perform a garbage collection inside the `fixed` block, it doesn't move the underlying struct about on the memory heap (since its contents are being iterated via direct memory pointers). Looking at our program, you might wonder how `MySharedData` could ever shift in memory, given that it lives not on the heap, but in the unmanaged world, where the garbage collector has no jurisdiction. The compiler doesn't know this, however, and is concerned that we *might* use `MyShared Data` in a managed context, so it insists that we add the `fixed` keyword to make our `unsafe` code safe in managed contexts. And the compiler does have a point—here's all it would take to put `MySharedData` on the heap:

```
object obj = new MySharedData();
```

This results in a boxed `MySharedData`—on the heap and eligible for transit during garbage collection.

This example illustrates how a string can be represented in a struct mapped to unmanaged memory. For more complex types, you also have the option of using existing serialization code. The one proviso is that the serialized data must never exceed, in length, its allocation of space in the struct; otherwise, the result is an unintended union with subsequent fields.

COM Interoperability

The .NET runtime has had special support for COM since its first version, enabling COM objects to be used from .NET and vice versa. This support was enhanced significantly in C# 4.0, with improvements to both usability and deployment.

The Purpose of COM

COM is an acronym for Component Object Model, a binary standard for APIs released by Microsoft in 1993. The motivation for inventing COM was to enable components to communicate with each other in a language-independent and version-tolerant manner. Before COM, the approach in Windows was to publish Dynamic Link Libraries (DLLs) that declared structures and functions using the C programming language. Not only is this approach language-specific, but it's also brittle. The specification of a type in such a library is inseparable from its implementation: even updating a structure with a new field means breaking its specification.

The beauty of COM was to separate the specification of a type from its underlying implementation through a construct known as a *COM interface*. COM also allowed for the calling of methods on stateful *objects*—rather than being limited to simple procedure calls.

In a way, the .NET programming model is an evolution of the principles of COM programming: the .NET platform also facilitates cross-language development and allows binary components to evolve without breaking applications that depend on them.

The Basics of the COM Type System

The COM type system revolves around interfaces. A COM interface is rather like a .NET interface, but it's more prevalent because a COM type exposes its functionality *only* through an interface. In the .NET world, for instance, we could declare a type simply as follows:

```
public class Foo
{
  public string Test() => "Hello, world";
}
```

Consumers of that type can use Foo directly. And if we later changed the *implementation* of Test(), calling assemblies would not require recompilation. In this respect, .NET separates interface from implementation—without requiring interfaces. We could even add an overload without breaking callers:

```
public string Test (string s) => "Hello, world " + s;
```

In the COM world, Foo exposes its functionality through an interface to achieve this same decoupling. So, in Foo's type library, an interface such as this would exist:

```
public interface IFoo { string Test(); }
```

(We've illustrated this by showing a C# interface—not a COM interface. The principle, however, is the same—although the plumbing is different.)

Callers would then interact with IFoo rather than Foo.

When it comes to adding the overloaded version of Test, life is more complicated with COM than with .NET. First, we would avoid modifying the IFoo interface—because this would break binary compatibility with the previous version (one of the principles of COM is that interfaces, once published, are *immutable*). Second, COM doesn't allow method overloading. The solution is to instead have Foo implement a *second interface*:

```
public interface IFoo2 { string Test (string s); }
```

(Again, we've transliterated this into a .NET interface for familiarity.)

Supporting multiple interfaces is of key importance in making COM libraries versionable.

IUnknown and IDispatch

All COM interfaces are identified with a GUID.

The root interface in COM is `IUnknown`—all COM objects must implement it. This interface has three methods:

- `AddRef`
- `Release`
- `QueryInterface`

`AddRef` and `Release` are for lifetime management, since COM uses reference counting rather than automatic garbage collection (COM was designed to work with unmanaged code, where automatic garbage collection isn't feasible). The `QueryInterface` method returns an object reference that supports that interface, if it can do so.

To enable dynamic programming (e.g., scripting and Automation), a COM object may also implement `IDispatch`. This enables dynamic languages such as VBScript to call COM objects in a late-bound manner—rather like `dynamic` in C# (although only for simple invocations).

Calling a COM Component from C#

The CLR's built-in support for COM means that you don't work directly with `IUnknown` and `IDispatch`. Instead, you work with CLR objects, and the runtime marshals your calls to the COM world via runtime-callable wrappers (RCWs). The runtime also handles lifetime management by calling `AddRef` and `Release` (when the .NET object is finalized) and takes care of the primitive type conversions between the two worlds. Type conversion ensures that each side sees, for example, the integer and string types in their familiar forms.

Additionally, there needs to be some way to access RCWs in a statically typed fashion. This is the job of *COM interop types*. COM interop types are automatically generated proxy types that expose a .NET member for each COM member. The type library importer tool (*tlbimp.exe*) generates COM interop types from the command line, based on a COM library that you choose, and compiles them into a *COM interop assembly*.

 If a COM component implements multiple interfaces, the *tlbimp.exe* tool generates a single type that contains a union of members from all interfaces.

You can create a COM interop assembly in Visual Studio by going to the Add Reference dialog box and choosing a library from the COM tab. For example, if you have Microsoft Excel 2007 installed, adding a reference to the Microsoft Excel 12.0 Office Library allows you to interoperate with Excel's COM classes. Here's the C# code to create and show a workbook and then populate a cell in that workbook:

```
using System;
using Excel = Microsoft.Office.Interop.Excel;
```

```
class Program
{
  static void Main()
  {
    var excel = new Excel.Application();
    excel.Visible = true;
    Excel.Workbook workBook = excel.Workbooks.Add();
    excel.Cells [1, 1].Font.FontStyle = "Bold";
    excel.Cells [1, 1].Value2 = "Hello World";
    workBook.SaveAs (@"d:\temp.xlsx");
  }
}
```

The `Excel.Application` class is a COM interop type whose runtime type is an RCW. When we access the `Workbooks` and `Cells` properties, we get back more interop types.

This code is fairly simple, thanks to a number of COM-specific enhancements that were introduced in C# 4.0. Without these enhancements, our `Main` method looks like this instead:

```
var missing = System.Reflection.Missing.Value;

var excel = new Excel.Application();
excel.Visible = true;
Excel.Workbook workBook = excel.Workbooks.Add (missing);
var range = (Excel.Range) excel.Cells [1, 1];
range.Font.FontStyle = "Bold";
range.Value2 = "Hello world";

workBook.SaveAs (@"d:\temp.xlsx", missing, missing, missing, missing,
    missing, Excel.XlSaveAsAccessMode.xlNoChange, missing, missing,
    missing, missing, missing);
```

We'll look now at what those language enhancements are, and how they help with COM programming.

Optional Parameters and Named Arguments

Because COM APIs don't support function overloading, it's very common to have functions with numerous parameters, many of which are optional. For instance, here's how you might call an Excel workbook's `Save` method:

```
var missing = System.Reflection.Missing.Value;

workBook.SaveAs (@"d:\temp.xlsx", missing, missing, missing, missing,
    missing, Excel.XlSaveAsAccessMode.xlNoChange, missing, missing,
    missing, missing, missing);
```

The good news is that the C#'s support for optional parameters is COM-aware, so we can just do this:

```
workBook.SaveAs (@"d:\temp.xlsx");
```

(As we stated in Chapter 3, optional parameters are "expanded" by the compiler into the full verbose form.)

Named arguments allow you to specify additional arguments, regardless of their position:

```
workBook.SaveAs (@"c:\test.xlsx", Password:"foo");
```

Implicit ref Parameters

Some COM APIs (Microsoft Word, in particular) expose functions that declare *every* parameter as pass-by-reference—whether or not the function modifies the parameter value. This is because of the perceived performance gain from not copying argument values (the *real* performance gain is negligible).

Historically, calling such methods from C# has been clumsy because you must specify the ref keyword with every argument, and this prevents the use of optional parameters. For instance, to open a Word document, we used to have to do this:

```
object filename = "foo.doc";
object notUsed1 = Missing.Value;
object notUsed2 = Missing.Value;
object notUsed3 = Missing.Value;
...
Open (ref filename, ref notUsed1, ref notUsed2, ref notUsed3, ...);
```

Since C# 4.0, however, you can omit the ref modifier on COM function calls, allowing the use of optional parameters:

```
word.Open ("foo.doc");
```

The caveat is that you will get neither a compile-time nor a runtime error if the COM method you're calling actually does mutate an argument value.

Indexers

The ability to omit the ref modifier has another benefit: it makes COM indexers with ref parameters accessible via ordinary C# indexer syntax. This would otherwise be forbidden because ref/out parameters are not supported with C# indexers (the somewhat clumsy workaround in older versions of C# was to call the backing methods such as get_*XXX* and set_*XXX*; this workaround is still legal for backward compatibility).

Interop with indexers was further enhanced in C# 4.0 such that you can call COM properties that accept arguments. In the following example, Foo is a property that accepts an integer argument:

```
myComObject.Foo [123] = "Hello";
```

Writing such properties yourself in C# is still prohibited: a type can expose an indexer only on itself (the "default" indexer). Therefore, if you wanted to write code in C# that would make the preceding statement legal, Foo would need to return another type that exposed a (default) indexer.

Dynamic Binding

There are two ways that dynamic binding can help when calling COM components. The first is if you want to access a COM component without a COM interop type. To do this, call `Type.GetTypeFromProgID` with the COM component name to obtain a COM instance, and then use dynamic binding to call members from then on. Of course, there's no IntelliSense, and compile-time checks are impossible:

```
Type excelAppType = Type.GetTypeFromProgID ("Excel.Application", true);
dynamic excel = Activator.CreateInstance (excelAppType);
excel.Visible = true;
dynamic wb = excel.Workbooks.Add();
excel.Cells [1, 1].Value2 = "foo";
```

(The same thing can be achieved, much more clumsily, with reflection instead of dynamic binding.)

 A variation of this theme is calling a COM component that supports *only* IDispatch. Such components are quite rare, however.

Dynamic binding can also be useful (to a lesser extent) in dealing with the COM variant type. For reasons due more to poor design that necessity, COM API functions are often peppered with this type, which is roughly equivalent to object in .NET. If you enable "Embed Interop Types" in your project (more on this soon), the runtime will map variant to dynamic, instead of mapping variant to object, avoiding the need for casts. For instance, you could legally do this:

```
excel.Cells [1, 1].Font.FontStyle = "Bold";
```

instead of:

```
var range = (Excel.Range) excel.Cells [1, 1];
range.Font.FontStyle = "Bold";
```

The disadvantage of working in this way is that you lose auto-completion, so you must know that a property called Font happens to exist. For this reason, it's usually easier to *dynamically* assign the result to its known interop type:

```
Excel.Range range = excel.Cells [1, 1];
range.Font.FontStyle = "Bold";
```

As you can see, this saves only five characters over the old-fashioned approach!

The mapping of variant to dynamic is the default from Visual Studio 2010 onwards, and is a function of enabling Embed Interop Types on a reference.

Embedding Interop Types

We said previously that C# ordinarily calls COM components via interop types that are generated by calling the *tlbimp.exe* tool (directly, or via Visual Studio).

Historically, your only option was to *reference* interop assemblies just as you would with any other assembly. This could be troublesome because interop assemblies can get quite large with complex COM components. A tiny add-in for Microsoft Word, for instance, requires an interop assembly that is orders of magnitude larger than itself.

From C# 4.0, rather than *referencing* an interop assembly, you have the option of *linking* to it. When you do this, the compiler analyzes the assembly to work out precisely the types and members that your application actually uses. It then embeds definitions for those types and members directly in your application. This means that you don't have to worry about bloat, because only the COM interfaces that you actually use are included in your application.

Interop linking is the default in Visual Studio 2010 and later for COM references. If you want to *disable* it, select the reference in the Solution Explorer, and then go to its properties and set Embed Interop Types to False.

To enable interop linking from the command-line compiler, call `csc` with `/link` instead of `/reference` (or `/L` instead of `/R`).

Type Equivalence

CLR 4.0 and later support *type equivalence* for linked interop types. That means that if two assemblies each link to an interop type, those types will be considered equivalent if they wrap the same COM type. This holds true even if the interop assemblies to which they linked were generated independently.

Type equivalence relies on the `TypeIdentifierAttribute` attribute in the `System.Runtime.InteropServices` namespace. The compiler automatically applies this attribute when you link to interop assemblies. COM types are then considered equivalent if they have the same GUID.

Type equivalence does away with the need for *primary interop assemblies*.

Primary Interop Assemblies

Until C# 4.0, there was no interop linking and no option of type equivalence. This created a problem in that if two developers each ran the *tlbimp.exe* tool on the same COM component, they'd end up with incompatible interop assemblies, hindering interoperability. The workaround was for the author of each COM library to release an official version of the interop assembly, called the *primary interop assembly* (PIA). PIAs are still prevalent, mainly because of the wealth of legacy code.

PIAs are a poor solution for the following reasons:

PIAs were not always used
    Since everyone could run the type library importer tool, they often did so, rather than using the official version. In some cases, there was no choice as the authors of the COM library didn't actually publish a PIA.

PIAs require registration

PIAs require registration in the GAC. This burden falls on developers writing simple add-ins for a COM component.

PIAs bloat deployment

PIAs exemplify the problem of interop assembly bloat that we described earlier. In particular, the Microsoft Office team chose not to deploy their PIAs with their product.

Exposing C# Objects to COM

It's also possible to write classes in C# that can be consumed in the COM world. The CLR makes this possible through a proxy called a COM-callable wrapper (CCW). A CCW marshals types between the two worlds (as with an RCW) and implements IUnknown (and optionally IDispatch) as required by the COM protocol. A CCW is lifetime-controlled from the COM side via reference counting (rather than through the CLR's garbage collector).

You can expose any public class to COM. The one requirement is to define an assembly attribute that assigns a GUID to identify the COM type library:

```
[assembly: Guid ("...")]      // A unique GUID for the COM type library
```

By default, all public types will be visible to COM consumers. You can make specific types invisible, however, by applying the [ComVisible(false)] attribute. If you want all types invisible by default, apply [ComVisible(false)] to the assembly, and then [ComVisible(true)] to the types you wish to expose.

The final step is to call the *tlbexp.exe* tool:

```
tlbexp.exe myLibrary.dll
```

This generates a COM type library (*.tlb*) file which you can then register and consume in COM applications. COM interfaces to match the COM-visible classes are generated automatically.

26

Regular Expressions

The regular expressions language identifies character patterns. The .NET types supporting regular expressions are based on Perl 5 regular expressions and support both search and search/replace functionality.

Regular expressions are used for tasks such as:

- Validating text input such as passwords and phone numbers (ASP.NET provides the RegularExpressionValidator control just for this purpose)
- Parsing textual data into more structured forms (e.g., extracting data from an HTML page for storage in a database)
- Replacing patterns of text in a document (e.g., whole words only)

This chapter is split into both conceptual sections teaching the basics of regular expressions in .NET and reference sections describing the regular expressions language.

All regular expression types are defined in System.Text.RegularExpressions.

 For more on regular expressions, *http://regular-expressions.info* is a good online reference with lots of examples, and *Mastering Regular Expressions* by Jeffrey E. F. Friedl, is invaluable for the serious.

The samples in this chapter are all preloaded into LINQPad. There is also an interactive utility available called Expresso (*http://www.ultrapico.com*), which assists in building and visualizing regular expressions and comes with its own expression library.

Regular Expression Basics

One of the most common regular expression operators is a *quantifier*. ? is a quantifier that matches the preceding item 0 or 1 time. In other words, ? means *optional*. An item is either a single character or a complex structure of characters in square brackets. For example, the regular expression "colou?r" matches color and colour, but not colouur:

```
Console.WriteLine (Regex.Match ("color",   @"colou?r").Success); // True
Console.WriteLine (Regex.Match ("colour",  @"colou?r").Success); // True
Console.WriteLine (Regex.Match ("colouur", @"colou?r").Success); // False
```

Regex.Match searches within a larger string. The object that it returns has properties for the Index and Length of the match, as well as the actual Value matched:

```
Match m = Regex.Match ("any colour you like", @"colou?r");
```

```
Console.WriteLine (m.Success);     // True
Console.WriteLine (m.Index);       // 4
Console.WriteLine (m.Length);      // 6
Console.WriteLine (m.Value);       // colour
Console.WriteLine (m.ToString());  // colour
```

You can think of Regex.Match as a more powerful version of the string's IndexOf method. The difference is that it searches for a *pattern* rather than a literal string.

The IsMatch method is a shortcut for calling Match and then testing the Success property.

The regular expressions engine works from left to right by default, so only the leftmost match is returned. You can use the NextMatch method to return more matches:

```
Match m1 = Regex.Match ("One color? There are two colours in my head!",
                        @"colou?rs?");
Match m2 = m1.NextMatch();
Console.WriteLine (m1);       // color
Console.WriteLine (m2);       // colours
```

The Matches method returns all matches in an array. We can rewrite the preceding example as follows:

```
foreach (Match m in Regex.Matches
         ("One color? There are two colours in my head!", @"colou?rs?"))
  Console.WriteLine (m);
```

Another common regular expressions operator is the *alternator*, expressed with a vertical bar, |. An alternator expresses alternatives. The following matches "Jen", "Jenny", and "Jennifer":

```
Console.WriteLine (Regex.IsMatch ("Jenny", "Jen(ny|nifer)?")); // True
```

The brackets around an alternator separate the alternatives from the rest of the expression.

From Framework 4.5, you can specify a timeout when matching regular expressions. If a match operation takes longer than the specified TimeSpan, a RegexMatchTimeoutException is thrown. This can be useful if your program processes arbitrary regular expressions (for instance, in an advanced search dialog box) because it prevents malformed regular expressions from infinitely spinning.

Compiled Regular Expressions

In some of the preceding examples, we called a static RegEx method repeatedly with the same pattern. An alternative approach in these cases is to instantiate a Regex object with the pattern and RegexOptions.Compiled and then call instance methods:

```
Regex r = new Regex (@"sausages?" , RegexOptions.Compiled);
Console.WriteLine (r.Match ("sausage"));   // sausage
Console.WriteLine (r.Match ("sausages"));  // sausages
```

RegexOptions.Compiled instructs the RegEx instance to use lightweight code generation (DynamicMethod in Reflection.Emit) to dynamically build and compile code tailored to that particular regular expression. This results in faster matching at the expense of an initial compilation cost.

A Regex instance is immutable.

The regular expressions engine is fast. Even without compilation, a simple match typically takes less than a microsecond.

RegexOptions

The RegexOptions flags enum lets you tweak matching behavior. A common use for RegexOptions is to perform a case-insensitive search:

```
Console.WriteLine (Regex.Match ("a", "A", RegexOptions.IgnoreCase)); // a
```

This applies the current culture's rules for case equivalence. The CultureInvariant flag lets you request the invariant culture instead:

```
Console.WriteLine (Regex.Match ("a", "A", RegexOptions.IgnoreCase
                                | RegexOptions.CultureInvariant));
```

Most of the RegexOptions flags can also be activated within a regular expression itself, using a single-letter code as follows:

```
Console.WriteLine (Regex.Match ("a", @"(?i)A"));                    // a
```

You can turn options on and off throughout an expression as follows:

```
Console.WriteLine (Regex.Match ("AAAa", @"(?i)a(?-i)a"));           // Aa
```

Another useful option is `IgnorePatternWhitespace` or `(?x)`. This allows you to insert whitespace to make a regular expression more readable—without the whitespace being taken literally.

Table 26-1 lists all `RegExOptions` values along with their single-letter codes.

Table 26-1. Regular expression options

Enum value	Regular expressions code	Description
None		
IgnoreCase	i	Ignores case (by default, regular expressions are case-sensitive)
Multiline	m	Changes ^ and $ so that they match the start/end of a line instead of start/end of the string
ExplicitCapture	n	Captures only explicitly named or explicitly numbered groups (see "Groups" on page 1032)
Compiled		Forces compilation to IL (see "Compiled Regular Expressions" on page 1025)
Singleline	s	Makes . match every character (instead of matching every character except \n)
IgnorePatternWhitespace	x	Eliminates unescaped whitespace from the pattern
RightToLeft	r	Searches from right to left; can't be specified midstream
ECMAScript		Forces ECMA compliance (by default, the implementation is not ECMA-compliant)
CultureInvariant		Turns off culture-specific behavior for string comparisons

Character Escapes

Regular expressions have the following metacharacters, which have a special rather than literal meaning:

- \ * + ? | { [( ) ^ $. #

To use a metacharacter literally, you must prefix the character with a backslash. In the following example, we escape the ? character to match the string "what?":

```
Console.WriteLine (Regex.Match ("what?", @"what\?")); // what? (correct)
Console.WriteLine (Regex.Match ("what?", @"what?"));  // what  (incorrect)
```

 If the character is inside a *set* (square brackets), this rule does not apply, and the metacharacters are interpreted literally. We will discuss sets in the following section.

The Regex's `Escape` and `Unescape` methods convert a string containing regular expression metacharacters by replacing them with escaped equivalents, and vice versa. For example:

```
Console.WriteLine (Regex.Escape   (@"?"));   // \?
Console.WriteLine (Regex.Unescape (@"\?"));   // ?>
```

All the regular expression strings in this chapter we express with the C# @ literal. This is to bypass C#'s escape mechanism, which also uses the backslash. Without the @, a literal backslash would require four backslashes:

```
Console.WriteLine (Regex.Match ("\\", "\\\\"));   // \
```

Unless you include the `(?x)` option, spaces are treated literally in regular expressions:

```
Console.Write (Regex.IsMatch ("hello world", @"hello world"));   // True
```

Character Sets

Character sets act as wildcards for a particular set of characters.

Expression	Meaning	Inverse ("not")
`[abcdef]`	Matches a single character in the list	`[^abcdef]`
`[a-f]`	Matches a single character in a *range*	`[^a-f]`
`\d`	Matches a decimal digit Same as `[0-9]`	`\D`
`\w`	Matches a *word* character (by default, varies according to `CultureInfo.CurrentCulture`; for example, in English, same as `[a-zA-Z_0-9]`)	`\W`
`\s`	Matches a whitespace character Same as `[\n\r\t\f\v ]`	`\S`
`\p{category}`	Matches a character in a specified *category*	`\P`
`.`	(Default mode) Matches any character except `\n`	`\n`
`.`	(SingleLine mode) Matches any character	`\n`

To match exactly one of a set of characters, put the character set in square brackets:

```
Console.Write (Regex.Matches ("That is that.", "[Tt]hat").Count);   // 2
```

To match any character *except* those in a set, put the set in square brackets with a ^ symbol before the first character:

```
Console.Write (Regex.Match ("quiz qwerty", "q[^aeiou]").Index);   // 5
```

You can specify a range of characters with a hyphen. The following regular expression matches a chess move:

```
Console.Write (Regex.Match ("b1-c4", @"[a-h]\d-[a-h]\d").Success);   // True
```

\d indicates a digit character, so \d will match any digit. \D matches any nondigit character.

\w indicates a word character, which includes letters, numbers, and the underscore. \W matches any nonword character. These work as expected for non-English letters, too, such as Cyrillic.

. matches any character except \n (but allows \r).

\p matches a character in a specified category, such as {Lu} for uppercase letter or {P} for punctuation (we list the categories in the reference section later in the chapter):

```
Console.Write (Regex.IsMatch ("Yes, please", @"\p{P}"));    // True
```

We will find more uses for \d, \w, and . when we combine them with *quantifiers*.

Quantifiers

Quantifiers match an item a specified number of times.

Quantifier	Meaning
*	Zero or more matches
+	One or more matches
?	Zero or one match
{*n*}	Exactly *n* matches
{*n*,}	At least *n* matches
{*n*,*m*}	Between *n* and *m* matches

The * quantifier matches the preceding character or group zero or more times. The following matches *cv.doc*, along with any numbered versions of the same file (e.g., *cv2.doc*, *cv15.doc*):

```
Console.Write (Regex.Match ("cv15.doc", @"cv\d*\.doc").Success); // True
```

Notice that we have to escape out the period in the file extension with a backslash.

The following allows anything between *cv* and *.doc* and is equivalent to dir cv*.doc:

```
Console.Write (Regex.Match ("cvjoint.doc", @"cv.*\.doc").Success); // True
```

The + quantifier matches the preceding character or group one or more times. For example:

```
Console.Write (Regex.Matches ("slow! yeah slooow!", "slo+w").Count); // 2
```

The {} quantifier matches a specified number (or range) of repetitions. The following matches a blood pressure reading:

```
Regex bp = new Regex (@"\d{2,3}/\d{2,3}");
Console.WriteLine (bp.Match ("It used to be 160/110"));  // 160/110
Console.WriteLine (bp.Match ("Now it's only 115/75"));   // 115/75
```

Greedy Versus Lazy Quantifiers

By default, quantifiers are *greedy*, as opposed to *lazy*. A greedy quantifier repeats as *many* times as it can before advancing. A lazy quantifier repeats as *few* times as it can before advancing. You can make any quantifier lazy by suffixing it with the ? symbol. To illustrate the difference, consider the following HTML fragment:

```
string html = "<i>By default</i> quantifiers are <i>greedy</i> creatures";
```

Suppose we want to extract the two phrases in italics. If we execute the following:

```
foreach (Match m in Regex.Matches (html, @"<i>.*</i>"))
  Console.WriteLine (m);
```

the result is not two matches, but a *single* match, as follows:

```
<i>By default</i> quantifiers are <i>greedy</i>
```

The problem is that our * quantifier greedily repeats as many times as it can before matching </i>. So, it passes right by the first </i>, stopping only at the final </i> (the *last point* at which the rest of the expression can still match).

If we make the quantifier lazy:

```
foreach (Match m in Regex.Matches (html, @"<i>.*?</i>"))
  Console.WriteLine (m);
```

the * bails out at the *first* point at which the rest of the expression can match. Here's the result:

```
<i>By default</i>
<i>greedy</i>
```

Zero-Width Assertions

The regular expressions language lets you place conditions on what should occur *before* or *after* a match, through *lookbehind*, *lookahead*, *anchors*, and *word boundaries*. These are called *zero-width* assertions because they don't increase the width (or length) of the match itself.

Lookahead and Lookbehind

The (?=*expr*) construct checks whether the text that follows matches *expr*, without including expr in the result. This is called *positive lookahead*. In the following example, we look for a number followed by the word "miles":

```
Console.WriteLine (Regex.Match ("say 25 miles more", @"\d+\s(?=miles)"));
```

OUTPUT: 25

Notice the word "miles" was not returned in the result, even though it was required to *satisfy* the match.

After a successful *lookahead*, matching continues as though the sneak preview never took place. So, if we append .* to our expression as follows:

```
Console.WriteLine (Regex.Match ("say 25 miles more", @"\d+\s(?=miles).*"));
```

the result is 25 miles more.

Lookahead can be useful in enforcing rules for a strong password. Suppose a password has to be at least six characters and contain at least one digit. With a lookup, we could achieve this as follows:

```
string password = "...";
bool ok = Regex.IsMatch (password, @"(?=.*\d).{6,}");
```

This first performs a *lookahead* to ensure that a digit occurs somewhere in the string. If satisfied, it returns to its position before the sneak preview began and matches six or more characters. (In the section "Cookbook Regular Expressions" on page 1035, later in this chapter, we include a more substantial password validation example.)

The opposite is the *negative lookahead* construct, (?!*expr*). This requires that the match *not* be followed by *expr*. The following expression matches "good"—unless "however" or "but" appears later in the string:

```
string regex = "(?i)good(?!.*(however|but))";
Console.WriteLine (Regex.IsMatch ("Good work! But...", regex));  // False
Console.WriteLine (Regex.IsMatch ("Good work! Thanks!", regex));  // True
```

The (?<=*expr*) construct denotes *positive lookbehind* and requires that a match be *preceded* by a specified expression. The opposite construct, (?<!*expr*), denotes *negative lookbehind* and requires that a match *not be preceded* by a specified expression. For example, the following matches "good"—unless "however" appears *earlier* in the string:

```
string regex = "(?i)(?<!however.*)good";
Console.WriteLine (Regex.IsMatch ("However good, we...", regex)); // False
Console.WriteLine (Regex.IsMatch ("Very good, thanks!", regex)); // True
```

We could improve these examples by adding *word boundary assertions*, which we will introduce shortly.

Anchors

The anchors ^ and $ match a particular *position*. By default:

^

  Matches the *start* of the string

$

  Matches the *end* of the string

---

^ has two context-dependent meanings: an *anchor* and a *character class negator*.

$ has two context-dependent meanings: an *anchor* and a *replacement group denoter*.

For example:

```
Console.WriteLine (Regex.Match ("Not now", "^[Nn]o"));    // No
Console.WriteLine (Regex.Match ("f = 0.2F", "[Ff]$"));    // F
```

If you specify `RegexOptions.Multiline` or include `(?m)` in the expression:

- ^ matches the start of the string or *line* (directly after a \n).
- $ matches the end of the string or *line* (directly before a \n).

There's a catch to using $ in multiline mode: a new line in Windows is nearly always denoted with \r\n rather than just \n. This means that for $ to be useful, you must usually match the \r as well, with a *positive lookahead*:

```
(?=\r?$)
```

The *positive lookahead* ensures that \r doesn't become part of the result. The following matches lines that end in ".txt":

```
string fileNames = "a.txt" + "\r\n" + "b.doc" + "\r\n" + "c.txt";
string r = @".+\.txt(?=\r?$)";
foreach (Match m in Regex.Matches (fileNames, r, RegexOptions.Multiline))
  Console.Write (m + " ");
```

```
OUTPUT: a.txt c.txt
```

The following matches all empty lines in string s:

```
MatchCollection emptyLines = Regex.Matches (s, "^(?=\r?$)",
                                            RegexOptions.Multiline);
```

The following matches all lines that are either empty or contain only whitespace:

```
MatchCollection blankLines = Regex.Matches (s, "^[ \t]*(?=\r?$)",
                                            RegexOptions.Multiline);
```

Since an anchor matches a position rather than a character, specifying an anchor on its own matches an empty string:

```
Console.WriteLine (Regex.Match ("x", "$").Length);   // 0
```

Word Boundaries

The word boundary assertion \b matches where word characters (\w) adjoin either:

- Nonword characters (\W)
- The beginning/end of the string (^ and $)

\b is often used to match whole words. For example:

```
foreach (Match m in Regex.Matches ("Wedding in Sarajevo", @"\b\w+\b"))
  Console.WriteLine (m);
```

Wedding
in
Sarajevo

The following statements highlight the effect of a word boundary:

```
int one = Regex.Matches ("Wedding in Sarajevo", @"\bin\b").Count; // 1
int two = Regex.Matches ("Wedding in Sarajevo", @"in").Count;     // 2
```

The next query uses *positive lookahead* to return words followed by "(sic)":

```
string text = "Don't loose (sic) your cool";
Console.Write (Regex.Match (text, @"\b\w+\b\s(?=\(sic\))")); // loose
```

Groups

Sometimes it's useful to separate a regular expression into a series of subexpressions, or *groups*. For instance, consider the following regular expression that represents a US phone number such as 206-465-1918:

\d{3}-\d{3}-\d{4}

Suppose we wish to separate this into two groups: area code and local number. We can achieve this by using parentheses to *capture* each group:

(\d{3})-(\d{3}-\d{4})

We then retrieve the groups programmatically as follows:

```
Match m = Regex.Match ("206-465-1918", @"(\d{3})-(\d{3}-\d{4})");

Console.WriteLine (m.Groups[1]);   // 206
Console.WriteLine (m.Groups[2]);   // 465-1918
```

The zeroth group represents the entire match. In other words, it has the same value as the match's Value:

```
Console.WriteLine (m.Groups[0]);   // 206-465-1918
Console.WriteLine (m);             // 206-465-1918
```

Groups are part of the regular expressions language itself. This means you can refer to a group within a regular expression. The \n syntax lets you index the group by group number 'n within the expression. For example, the expression (\w)ee\1 matches deed and peep. In the following example, we find all words in a string starting and ending in the same letter:

```
foreach (Match m in Regex.Matches ("pop pope peep", @"\b(\w)\w+\1\b"))
  Console.Write (m + " ");  // pop peep
```

The brackets around the \w instruct the regular expressions engine to store the sub-match in a group (in this case, a single letter) so it can be used later. We refer to that group later using \1, meaning the first group in the expression.

Named Groups

In a long or complex expression, it can be easier to work with groups by *name* rather than index. Here's a rewrite of the previous example, using a group that we name 'letter':

```
string regEx =
  @"\b"              + // word boundary
  @"(?'letter'\w)"   + // match first letter, and name it 'letter'
  @"\w+"             + // match middle letters
  @"\k'letter'"      + // match last letter, denoted by 'letter'
  @"\b";               // word boundary

foreach (Match m in Regex.Matches ("bob pope peep", regEx))
  Console.Write (m + " ");  // bob peep
```

To name a captured group:

```
(?'group-name'group-expr)  or  (?<group-name>group-expr)
```

To refer to a group:

```
\k'group-name'  or  \k<group-name>
```

The following example matches a simple (nonnested) XML/HTML element by looking for start and end nodes with a matching name:

```
string regFind =
  @"<(?'tag'\w+?).*>" + // match first tag, and name it 'tag'
  @"(?'text'.*?)"     + // match text content, name it 'text'
  @"</\k'tag'>";        // match last tag, denoted by 'tag'

Match m = Regex.Match ("<h1>hello</h1>", regFind);
Console.WriteLine (m.Groups ["tag"]);    // h1
Console.WriteLine (m.Groups ["text"]);   // hello
```

Allowing for all possible variations in XML structure, such as nested elements, is more complex. The .NET regular expressions engine has a sophisticated extension called "matched balanced constructs" that can assist with nested tags—information on this is available on the Internet and in *Mastering Regular Expressions* by Jeffrey E. F. Friedl.

Replacing and Splitting Text

The RegEx.Replace method works like string.Replace, except that it uses a regular expression.

The following replaces "cat" with "dog". Unlike with string.Replace, "catapult" won't change into "dogapult" because we match on word boundaries:

```
string find = @"\bcat\b";
string replace = "dog";
Console.WriteLine (Regex.Replace ("catapult the cat", find, replace));

OUTPUT: catapult the dog
```

The replacement string can reference the original match with the $0 substitution construct. The following example wraps numbers within a string in angle brackets:

```
string text = "10 plus 20 makes 30";
Console.WriteLine (Regex.Replace (text, @"\d+", @"<$0>"));

OUTPUT: <10> plus <20> makes <30>
```

You can access any captured groups with $1, $2, $3, and so on, or ${name} for a named group. To illustrate how this can be useful, consider the regular expression in the previous section that matched a simple XML element. By rearranging the groups, we can form a replacement expression that moves the element's content into an XML attribute:

```
string regFind =
  @"<(?'tag'\w+?).*>" +   // match first tag, and name it 'tag'
  @"(?'text'.*?)"    +   // match text content, name it 'text'
  @"</\k'tag'>";          // match last tag, denoted by 'tag'

string regReplace =
  @"<${tag}"      +  // <tag
  @"value="""     +  // value="
  @"${text}"      +  // text
  @"""/>";        //  "/>

Console.Write (Regex.Replace ("<msg>hello</msg>", regFind, regReplace));
```

Here's the result:

```
<msg value="hello"/>
```

MatchEvaluator Delegate

Replace has an overload that takes a MatchEvaluator delegate, which is invoked per match. This allows you to delegate the content of the replacement string to C# code when the regular expressions language isn't expressive enough. For example:

```
Console.WriteLine (Regex.Replace ("5 is less than 10", @"\d+",
                   m => (int.Parse (m.Value) * 10).ToString()) );

OUTPUT: 50 is less than 100
```

In the cookbook, we show how to use a MatchEvaluator to escape Unicode characters appropriately for HTML.

Splitting Text

The static Regex.Split method is a more powerful version of the string.Split method, with a regular expression denoting the separator pattern. In this example, we split a string, where any digit counts as a separator:

```
foreach (string s in Regex.Split ("a5b7c", @"\d"))
  Console.Write (s + " ");      // a b c
```

The result, here, doesn't include the separators themselves. You can include the separators, however, by wrapping the expression in a *positive lookahead*. The following splits a camel-case string into separate words:

```
foreach (string s in Regex.Split ("oneTwoThree", @"(?=[A-Z])"))
  Console.Write (s + " ");    // one Two Three
```

Cookbook Regular Expressions

Recipes

Matching US Social Security number/phone number

```
string ssNum = @"\d{3}-\d{2}-\d{4}";

Console.WriteLine (Regex.IsMatch ("123-45-6789", ssNum));     // True

string phone = @"(?x)
  ( \d{3}[-\s] | \(\d{3}\)\s? )
    \d{3}[-\s]?
    \d{4}";

Console.WriteLine (Regex.IsMatch ("123-456-7890",  phone));   // True
Console.WriteLine (Regex.IsMatch ("(123) 456-7890", phone));  // True
```

Extracting "name = value" pairs (one per line)

Note that this starts with the *multiline* directive (?m):

```
string r = @"(?m)^\s*(?'name'\w+)\s*=\s*(?'value'.*)\s*(?=\r?$)";

string text =
  @"id = 3
    secure = true
    timeout = 30";

foreach (Match m in Regex.Matches (text, r))
  Console.WriteLine (m.Groups["name"] + " is " + m.Groups["value"]);
id is 3 secure is true timeout is 30
```

Strong password validation

The following checks whether a password has at least six characters and whether it contains a digit, symbol, or punctuation mark:

```
string r = @"(?x)^(?=.* ( \d | \p{P} | \p{S} )).{6,}";

Console.WriteLine (Regex.IsMatch ("abc12", r));    // False
Console.WriteLine (Regex.IsMatch ("abcdef", r));   // False
Console.WriteLine (Regex.IsMatch ("ab88yz", r));   // True
```

Lines of at least 80 characters

```
string r = @"(?m)^.{80,}(?=\r?$)";

string fifty = new string ('x', 50);
string eighty = new string ('x', 80);

string text = eighty + "\r\n" + fifty + "\r\n" + eighty;

Console.WriteLine (Regex.Matches (text, r).Count);    // 2
```

Parsing dates/times (N/N/N H:M:S AM/PM)

This expression handles a variety of numeric date formats—and works whether the year comes first or last. The (?x) directive improves readability by allowing white-space; the (?i) switches off case sensitivity (for the optional AM/PM designator). You can then access each component of the match through the Groups collection:

```
string r = @"(?x)(?i)
(\d{1,4}) [./-]
(\d{1,2}) [./-]
(\d{1,4}) [\sT]
(\d+):(\d+):(\d+) \s? (A\.?M\.?|P\.?M\.?)?";

string text = "01/02/2008 5:20:50 PM";

foreach (Group g in Regex.Match (text, r).Groups)
  Console.WriteLine (g.Value + " ");
01/02/2008 5:20:50 PM 01 02 2008 5 20 50 PM
```

(Of course, this doesn't verify that the date/time is correct.)

Matching Roman numerals

```
string r =
  @"(?i)\bm*"            +
  @"(d?c{0,3}|c[dm])"    +
  @"(l?x{0,3}|x[lc])"    +
  @"(v?i{0,3}|i[vx])"    +
  @"\b";

Console.WriteLine (Regex.IsMatch ("MCMLXXXIV", r));    // True
```

Removing repeated words

Here, we capture a named grouped called dupe:

```
string r = @"(?'dupe'\w+)\W\k'dupe'";

string text = "In the the beginning...";
Console.WriteLine (Regex.Replace (text, r, "${dupe}"));

In the beginning
```

Word count

```
string r = @"\b(\w|[-'])+\b";

string text = "It's all mumbo-jumbo to me";
Console.WriteLine (Regex.Matches (text, r).Count);    // 5
```

Matching a Guid

```
string r =
  @"(?i)\b"                +
  @"[0-9a-fA-F]{8}\-"      +
  @"[0-9a-fA-F]{4}\-"      +
  @"[0-9a-fA-F]{4}\-"      +
  @"[0-9a-fA-F]{4}\-"      +
  @"[0-9a-fA-F]{12}"       +
  @"\b";

string text = "Its key is {3F2504E0-4F89-11D3-9A0C-0305E82C3301}.";
Console.WriteLine (Regex.Match (text, r).Index);                    // 12
```

Parsing an XML/HTML tag

Regex is useful for parsing HTML fragments—particularly when the document may be imperfectly formed:

```
string r =
  @"<(?'tag'\w+?).*>"  + // match first tag, and name it 'tag'
  @"(?'text'.*?)"      + // match text content, name it 'textd'
  @"</\k'tag'>";         // match last tag, denoted by 'tag'

string text = "<h1>hello</h1>";

Match m = Regex.Match (text, r);

Console.WriteLine (m.Groups ["tag"]);       // h1
Console.WriteLine (m.Groups ["text"]);      // hello
```

Splitting a camel-cased word

This requires a *positive lookahead* to include the uppercase separators:

```
string r = @"(?=[A-Z])";

foreach (string s in Regex.Split ("oneTwoThree", r))
  Console.Write (s + " ");    // one Two Three
```

Obtaining a legal filename

```
string input = "My \"good\" <recipes>.txt";

char[] invalidChars = System.IO.Path.GetInvalidPathChars();
string invalidString = Regex.Escape (new string (invalidChars));

string valid = Regex.Replace (input, "[" + invalidString + "]", "");
```

```
Console.WriteLine (valid);

My good recipes.txt
```

Escaping Unicode characters for HTML

```
string htmlFragment = "© 2007";

string result = Regex.Replace (htmlFragment, @"[\u0080-\uFFFF]",
                m => @"&#" + ((int)m.Value[0]).ToString() + ";");

Console.WriteLine (result);        // &#169; 2007
```

Unescaping characters in an HTTP query string

```
string sample = "C%23 rocks";

string result = Regex.Replace (
    sample,
    @"%[0-9a-f][0-9a-f]",
    m => ((char) Convert.ToByte (m.Value.Substring (1), 16)).ToString(),
    RegexOptions.IgnoreCase
);

Console.WriteLine (result);    // C# rocks
```

Parsing Google search terms from a web stats log

This should be used in conjunction with the previous example to unescape characters in the query string:

```
string sample =
  "http://google.com/search?hl=en&q=greedy+quantifiers+regex&btnG=Search";

Match m = Regex.Match (sample, @"(?<=google\..+search\?.*q=).+?(?=(&|$))");

string[] keywords = m.Value.Split (
  new[] { '+' }, StringSplitOptions.RemoveEmptyEntries);

foreach (string keyword in keywords)
  Console.Write (keyword + " ");        // greedy quantifiers regex
```

Regular Expressions Language Reference

Tables 26-2 through 26-12 summarize the regular expressions grammar and syntax supported in the .NET implementation.

Table 26-2. Character escapes

Escape code sequence	Meaning	Hexadecimal equivalent
\a	Bell	\u0007
\b	Backspace	\u0008
\t	Tab	\u0009
\r	Carriage return	\u000A
\v	Vertical tab	\u000B
\f	Form feed	\u000C
\n	Newline	\u000D
\e	Escape	\u001B
\nnn	ASCII character nnn as octal (e.g., \n052)	
\xnn	ASCII character nn as hex (e.g., \x3F)	
\cl	ASCII control character l (e.g., \cG for Ctrl-G)	
\unnnn	Unicode character nnnn as hex (e.g., \u07DE)	
\symbol	A nonescaped symbol	

Special case: within a regular expression, \b means word boundary, except in a [ ] set, in which \b means the backspace character.

Table 26-3. Character sets

Expression	Meaning	Inverse ("not")
[abcdef]	Matches a single character in the list	[^abcdef]
[a-f]	Matches a single character in a *range*	[^a-f]
\d	Matches a decimal digit Same as [0-9]	\D
\w	Matches a *word* character (by default, varies according to CultureInfo.CurrentCulture; for example, in English, same as [a-zA-Z_0-9])	\W
\s	Matches a whitespace character Same as [\n\r\t\f\v]	\S
\p{category}	Matches a character in a specified *category* (see Table 26-6)	\P
.	(Default mode) Matches any character except \n	\n
.	(SingleLine mode) Matches any character	\n

Table 26-4. Character categories

Quantifier	Meaning
\p{L}	Letters
\p{Lu}	Uppercase letters
\p{Ll}	Lowercase letters
\p{N}	Numbers
\p{P}	Punctuation
\p{M}	Diacritic marks
\p{S}	Symbols
\p{Z}	Separators
\p{C}	Control characters

Table 26-5. Quantifiers

Quantifier	Meaning
*	Zero or more matches
+	One or more matches
?	Zero or one match
{*n*}	Exactly *n* matches
{*n*,}	At least *n* matches
{*n*,*m*}	Between *n* and *m* matches

The ? suffix can be applied to any of the quantifiers to make them *lazy* rather than *greedy*.

Table 26-6. Substitutions

Expression	Meaning
$0	Substitutes the matched text
$*group-number*	Substitutes an indexed *group-number* within the matched text
${*group-name*}	Substitutes a text *group-name* within the matched text

Substitutions are specified only within a replacement pattern.

Table 26-7. Zero-width assertions

Expression	Meaning
^	Start of string (or line in *multiline* mode)
$	End of string (or line in *multiline* mode)
\A	Start of string (ignores *multiline* mode)
\z	End of string (ignores *multiline* mode)
\Z	End of line or string
\G	Where search started
\b	On a word boundary
\B	Not on a word boundary
(?=*expr*)	Continue matching only if expression *expr* matches on right (*positive lookahead*)
(?!*expr*)	Continue matching only if expression *expr* doesn't match on right (*negative lookahead*)
(?<=*expr*)	Continue matching only if expression *expr* matches on left (*positive lookbehind*)
(?<!*expr*)	Continue matching only if expression *expr* doesn't match on left (*negative lookbehind*)
(?>*expr*)	Subexpression *expr* is matched once and not backtracked

Table 26-8. Grouping constructs

Syntax	Meaning
(*expr*)	Capture matched expression *expr* into indexed group
(?*number*)	Capture matched substring into a specified group *number*
(?'*name*')	Capture matched substring into group *name*
(?'*name1-name2*')	Undefine *name2*, and store interval and current group into *name1*; if *name2* is undefined, matching backtracks; *name1* is optional
(?:*expr*)	Noncapturing group

Table 26-9. Back references

Parameter syntax	Meaning
index	Reference a previously captured group by *index*
\k<*name*>	Reference a previously captured group by *name*

Table 26-10. Alternation

Expression syntax	Meaning
|	Logical *or*
(?(*expr*)*yes*|*no*)	Matches *yes* if expression matches; otherwise, matches *no* (*no* is optional)
(?(*name*)*yes*|*no*)	Matches *yes* if named group has a match; otherwise, matches *no* (*no* is optional)

Table 26-11. Miscellaneous constructs

Expression syntax	Meaning
(?#*comment*)	Inline comment
#*comment*	Comment to end of line (works only in `IgnorePatternWhitespace` mode)

Table 26-12. Regular expression options

Option	Meaning
(?i)	Case-insensitive match ("ignore" case)
(?m)	Multiline mode; changes ^ and $ so that they match beginning and end of any line
(?n)	Captures only explicitly named or numbered groups
(?c)	Compiles to IL
(?s)	Single-line mode; changes meaning of "." so that it matches every character
(?x)	Eliminates unescaped whitespace from the pattern
(?r)	Searches from right to left; can't be specified midstream

27

The Roslyn Compiler

C# 6.0 has a brand-new compiler, written entirely in C#. The new compiler is modular, so you can utilize its functionality in many ways besides compiling source code to an executable or library. Known as "Roslyn", the new compiler makes it easier to write static code analysis and refactoring tools, editors with syntax highlighting and code completion, and Visual Studio plugins that understand C# code.

The Roslyn libraries can be downloaded from NuGet, and there are packages for both C# and VB. As both languages share some architecture, there are common dependencies. The NuGet package ID for the C# compiler libraries is `Micro soft.CodeAnalysis.CSharp`.

The source code for Roslyn is publicly available under the Apache 2 open source license. This opens up further possibilities, including morphing C# into a custom or domain-specific language. The source code is available on GitHub, at *https://github.com/dotnet/roslyn*.

The GitHub site also hosts documentation, examples, and walkthroughs that demonstrate code analysis and refactoring.

 .NET Framework 4.6 does not ship with the Roslyn assemblies, and its version of *csc.exe* invokes the old C# 5 compiler. Installing Visual Studio 2015 remaps *csc.exe* to the C# 6 (Roslyn) compiler.

Without Visual Studio 2015, you can still *programmatically* invoke the compiler (and its services) if you download and reference the Roslyn assemblies. But the *csc.exe* tool that ships with the .NET Framework will remain pointed at C# 5 until you install Visual Studio 2015.

The assemblies that comprise the C# compiler library are as follows:

```
Microsoft.CodeAnalysis.dll
Microsoft.CodeAnalysis.CSharp.dll
System.Collections.Immutable.dll
System.Reflection.Metadata.dll
```

The former assembly is also used by the VB compiler and contains common base types for trees, symbols, compilations, and so on.

 All code listings in this chapter are available as interactive samples in LINQPad 5. Go to LINQPad's Samples tab at the bottom left, click "Download more samples," and choose "C# 6.0 in a Nutshell."

Roslyn Architecture

The Roslyn architecture separates compilation into three phases:

1. Parsing code into syntax trees (the *syntactic* layer)

2. Binding identifiers to symbols (the *semantic* layer)

3. Emitting IL

In the first phase, a *parser* reads C# code and outputs *syntax trees*. A syntax tree is a DOM (Document Object Model) that describes source code in tree structure.

The second phase is where C#'s *static binding* takes place. Assembly references are read, and the compiler figures out, for instance, that "Console" refers to System.Con sole in *mscorlib.dll*. Overload resolution and type inference are a part of this, too.

The third phase produces the output assembly. If you plan to use Roslyn for code analysis or refactoring, you won't use this functionality.

Visual Studio's editor uses the output of the syntactic layer to color keywords, strings, comments, and disabled code (in blue, red, green, and gray, respectively), whereas it uses the output of the semantic layer to color resolved type names (in turquoise).

Workspaces

In this chapter, we describe the compiler and the features it exposes. It's worth keeping in mind that there's an additional "layer" above the compiler called *workspaces*. It's also available on NuGet; the package ID is Microsoft.CodeAnaly sis.CSharp.Workspaces.

The workspaces layer understands Visual Studio solutions, projects, and documents, and includes additional services, such as code refactoring, not strictly related to the compilation processes.

The workspaces layer is open source, and by looking at the source code, it's possible to learn more about the compilation layer.

Syntax Trees

A syntax tree is a DOM for source code. The syntax tree API is completely separate from the `System.Linq.Expressions` API we discussed in "Expression Trees" on page 387 in Chapter 8, although the two have conceptual similarities. Both APIs can represent C# expressions in a DOM; however, a Roslyn syntax tree has the following unique features:

- It can represent the entire C# language, not just expressions.
- It can include comments, whitespace, and other "trivia," and can round-trip with full fidelity back to the original source code.
- It comes with a `ParseText` method that parses source code into a syntax tree.

Conversely, the `System.Linq.Expressions` API has the following unique features:

- It's built into the .NET Framework, and the C# compiler itself is programmed to emit `System.Linq.Expression` types when it encounters a lambda expression with an assignment conversion to `Expression<T>`.
- It has a fast and lightweight `Compile` method that emits a delegate. In contrast, the semantic layer that compiles Roslyn syntax trees offers only the heavyweight option of compiling a complete program into an assembly.

Something that both APIs have in common is that syntax trees are immutable, so none of its elements can be altered once created. This means that applications such as Visual Studio and LINQPad must create a new syntax tree each time you press a key in the editor in order to update syntax highlighting and autocompletion services. This is less expensive than it sounds because the new syntax tree is able to reuse most of the elements of the old (see "Transforming a Syntax Tree" on page 1056). And knowing that an object cannot change makes the API simpler to work with. It also allows for easier and faster parallelization, since multithreaded code can safely access all parts of a syntax tree without locks.

SyntaxTree Structure

A `SyntaxTree` comprises three main elements:

Nodes
> (Abstract `SyntaxNode` class.) Represents C# constructs such as expressions, statements, and method declarations. Nodes always have at least one child, so a node can never be a leaf in the tree. Nodes can have both nodes and tokens as children.

Tokens
> (`SyntaxToken` struct.) Represents the identifiers, keywords, operators, and punctuation that make up your source code. The only kind of children that

tokens can have is optional leading and trailing trivia. A token's parent is always a node.

Trivia

(`SyntaxTrivia` struct.) Trivia is for whitespace, comments, preprocessor directives, and code that's inactive due to conditional compilation. Trivia is always associated with the token that's immediately to its left or right and is exposed via that token's `TrailingTrivia` and `LeadingTrivia` properties, respectively.

Figure 27-1 shows the structure of the following code, with nodes in black, tokens in gray, and trivia in white:

```
Console.WriteLine ("Hello");
```

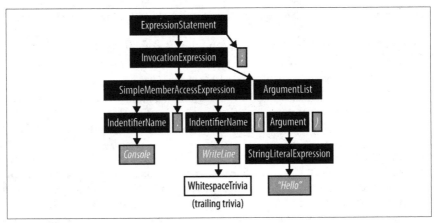

Figure 27-1. Syntax trees

`SyntaxNode` is abstract and has a C#-specific subclass for each kind of syntactic element, such as `VariableDeclarationSyntax` or `TryStatementSyntax`.

`SyntaxToken` / `SyntaxTrivia` are structs, and so a single type represents every kind of token / trivia. To distinguish different kinds of token or trivia, you must use the `RawKind` property or `Kind` extension method (which we'll explain in the following section).

The best way to explore a syntax tree is with a visualizer. Visual Studio has a downloadable visualizer for use with its debugger, and LINQPad has one built in. LINQPad displays the visualizer automatically for the code in the text editor when you click the Tree button in the output window. You can also ask LINQPad to display a visualizer for a syntax tree that you've created programmatically by calling `DumpSyntaxTree` on the tree (or `DumpSyntaxNode` on a node).

Understanding Node Types

The subclasses of `SyntaxNode` have been designed to reflect the result of syntactical parsing and are blind to semantic type/symbol information obtained from binding that occurs later. For example, consider the result of parsing the following code:

```
using System;

class Foo : SomeBaseClass
{
    void Test() { Console.WriteLine(); }
}
```

You might expect `Console.WriteLine` to be represented by a class called `MethodCallExpressionSyntax`, but no such class exists. Instead, it's represented by an `InvocationExpressionSyntax`, under which there's a `SimpleMemberAccessExpression`. This is because the parser is ignorant of types, so it cannot know that `Console` is a type and `WriteLine` is a method. There are many other possibilities: `Console` could be a property of `SomeBaseClass`, or `WriteLine` could be an event, field, or property of a delegate type. All we can know from the syntax is that we're performing a member access (*identifier.identifier*), followed by some kind of *invocation* with zero arguments.

Common properties and methods

Nodes, tokens, and trivia have a number of important common properties and methods:

`SyntaxTree` *property*
> Returns the syntax tree to which the object belongs.

`Span` *property*
> Returns the object's position in source code (see "Finding a child by its offset" on page 1052).

`Kind` *extension method*
> Returns a `SyntaxKind` enum that classifies the node, token, or trivia into one of several hundred values (e.g., `IntKeyword`, `CommaToken`, and `WhitespaceTrivia`). The same `SyntaxKind` enum covers nodes, tokens, and trivia.

ToString *method*

Returns the text (source code) for the node, token, or trivia. For tokens, the Text property is equivalent.

GetDiagnostics *method*

Returns errors or warnings generated during parsing.

IsEquivalentTo *method*

Returns true if the object is identical to another node, token, or trivia instance. Whitespace differences are significant (to ignore whitespace, call NormalizeWhitespace before comparing).

> Nodes and tokens also have a FullSpan property and ToFull String method. These take into account trivia, whereas Span and ToString do not.

The Kind extension method is a shortcut for casting the RawKind property, which is of type int, to Microsoft.CodeAnalysis.CSharp.SyntaxKind. The reason for not simply having a Kind property of type SyntaxKind is that the token and trivia types are also used in VB syntax trees, which have a different enum type for SyntaxKind.

Obtaining a Syntax Tree

The static ParseText method on CSharpSyntaxTree parses C# code into a Syntax Tree:

```
SyntaxTree tree = CSharpSyntaxTree.ParseText (@"class Test
{
  static void Main() => Console.WriteLine (""Hello"");
}");

Console.WriteLine (tree.ToString());

tree.DumpSyntaxTree();     // Displays Syntax Tree Visualizer in LINQPad
```

To run this in a Visual Studio project, install the Microsoft.CodeAnalysis.CSharp NuGet package, and import the following namespaces:

```
using Microsoft.CodeAnalysis;
using Microsoft.CodeAnalysis.CSharp;
```

You can optionally pass in a CSharpParseOptions object to specify a C# language version, preprocessor symbols, and a DocumentationMode to indicate whether XML comments should be parsed (see "Structured trivia" on page 1055). There's also an option to specify a SourceCodeKind. Choosing Interactive or Script instructs the parser to accept a single expression or statement(s) instead of requiring an entire program, although doing so currently throws a NotSupportedException.

Another way to obtain a syntax tree is to call `CSharpSyntaxTree.Create`, passing in an object graph of nodes and tokens. We describe how to create these objects in "Transforming a Syntax Tree" on page 1056.

After parsing a tree, you can obtain errors and warnings by calling `GetDiagnostics`. (You can also call this method on a specific node or token.)

If the parse resulted in unexpected errors, the tree's structure may not be as you expect. For this reason, it's worth calling `GetDiagnostics` before proceeding further.

A nice feature is that a tree with errors will round-trip back to the original text (with the same errors). In such cases, the parser does its best to provide a syntax tree that's useful to the semantic layer, creating "phantom nodes" if necessary. This allows tools such as code completion to work with incomplete code. (You can determine if a node is phantom by checking the `IsMissing` property.)

Calling `GetDiagnostics` on the syntax tree we created in the last section indicates no errors, despite having called `Console.WriteLine` without importing the `System` namespace. This is a good example of syntactic versus semantic parsing: our program is syntactically correct, and our error will not manifest until we create a compilation, add assembly references, and query the *semantic model*, where binding takes place.

Traversing and Searching a Tree

A `SyntaxTree` acts as a wrapper for the tree structure. It has a reference to a single root node, which you obtain by calling `GetRoot`:

```
var tree = CSharpSyntaxTree.ParseText (@"class Test
{
```

```
    static void Main() => Console.WriteLine ("""Hello""");
}");

SyntaxNode root = tree.GetRoot();
```

The root node of a C# program is a `CompilationUnitSyntax`:

```
Console.WriteLine (root.GetType().Name);    // CompilationUnitSyntax
```

Traversing children

`SyntaxNode` exposes LINQ-friendly methods to traverse its child nodes and tokens. The simplest are:

```
IEnumerable<SyntaxNode> ChildNodes()
IEnumerable<SyntaxToken> ChildTokens()
```

Following on from our previous example, our root node has a single child node of type `ClassDeclarationSyntax`:

```
var cds = (ClassDeclarationSyntax) root.ChildNodes().Single();
```

We can enumerate the members of `cds` via either its `ChildNodes` method or the `Mem`bers property of `ClassDeclarationSyntax`:

```
foreach (MemberDeclarationSyntax member in cds.Members)
    Console.WriteLine (member.ToString());
```

with the following result:

```
static void Main() => Console.WriteLine ("""Hello""");
```

There are also `Descendant*` methods which descend recursively into children. We can enumerate the tokens that make up our program as follows:

```
foreach (var token in root.DescendantTokens())
    Console.WriteLine ($"{token.Kind(),-30} {token.Text}");
```

Here's the result:

```
ClassKeyword                  class
IdentifierToken               Test
OpenBraceToken                {
StaticKeyword                 static
VoidKeyword                   void
IdentifierToken               Main
OpenParenToken                (
CloseParenToken               )
EqualsGreaterThanToken        =>
IdentifierToken               Console
DotToken                      .
IdentifierToken               WriteLine
OpenParenToken                (
StringLiteralToken            "Hello"
CloseParenToken               )
SemicolonToken                ;
```

```
CloseBraceToken              }
EndOfFileToken
```

Notice that there's no whitespace in the result. Replacing `token.Text` with `token.ToFullString()` would give us whitespace (and any other trivia).

The following uses the `DescendantNodes` method to locate the syntax node for our method declaration:

```
var ourMethod = root.DescendantNodes()
                    .First (m => m.Kind() == SyntaxKind.MethodDeclaration);
```

or alternatively:

```
var ourMethod = root.DescendantNodes()
                    .OfType<MethodDeclarationSyntax>()
                    .Single();
```

With the latter example, `ourMethod` is of type `MethodDeclarationSyntax`, which exposes useful properties specific to method declarations. For instance, if our example contained more than one method definition, and we wanted to find just the method whose name is "Main", we could do this:

```
var mainMethod = root.DescendantNodes()
                     .OfType<MethodDeclarationSyntax>()
                     .Single (m => m.Identifier.Text == "Main");
```

`Identifier` is a property on `MethodDeclarationSyntax` that returns the token corresponding to the method's identifier (i.e., its name). We could get the same result with more effort, as follows:

```
root.DescendantNodes().First (m =>
  m.Kind() == SyntaxKind.MethodDeclaration &&
  m.ChildTokens().Any (t =>
    t.Kind() == SyntaxKind.IdentifierToken && t.Text == "Main"));
```

`SyntaxNode` also has `GetFirstToken` and `GetLastToken` methods which are equivalent to calling `DescendantTokens().First()` and `DescendantTokens().Last()`.

> `GetLastToken()` is faster than `DescendantTokens().Last()` because it returns a direct link rather than enumerating through all descendants.

As nodes can contain both child nodes and tokens whose relative order is significant, there are also methods to enumerate both together:

```
ChildSyntaxList ChildNodesAndTokens()
IEnumerable<SyntaxNodeOrToken> DescendantNodesAndTokens()
IEnumerable<SyntaxNodeOrToken> DescendantNodesAndTokensAndSelf()
```

(`ChildSyntaxList` implements `IEnumerable<SyntaxNodeOrToken>` while also exposing a `Count` property and an indexer to access an element by position.)

You can traverse trivia directly from a node with the `GetLeadingTrivia`, `GetTrailingTrivia`, and `DescendantTrivia` methods. More commonly, though, you'd access trivia through the token to which it's attached, via the token's `LeadingTrivia` and `TrailingTrivia` properties. Or to convert to text, you'd use the `ToFullString` method, which includes trivia in the result.

Traversing parents

Nodes and tokens have a `Parent` property of type `SyntaxNode`.

For `SyntaxTrivia`, the "parent" is its token, accessible via the `Token` property.

Nodes also have methods which ascend back up the tree, which are prefixed with "Ancestor".

Finding a child by its offset

All nodes, tokens, and trivia have a `Span` property of type `TextSpan` to indicate starting and ending offsets in the source code. Nodes and tokens also have a `FullSpan` property which includes leading and trailing trivia (whereas `Span` does not). A node's `Span` does, however, include child nodes and tokens.

Working with TextSpan

The `TextSpan` struct has `Start`, `Length`, and `End` integer properties, which indicate character offsets in the source code. It also has methods such as `Overlap`, `Overlaps With`, `Intersection`, and `IntersectsWith`. The difference between overlapping and intersecting is a matter of one character: two spans *overlap* if one starts before the other ends (<), whereas they *intersect* if they merely touch (<=).

The `SyntaxTree` class exposes a `GetLineSpan` method which converts a `TextSpan` into a line and character offset. This method ignores the effects of any `#line` directives present in the source code. There's also a `GetMappedLineSpan` method which takes these directives into account.

You can find a descendant object by position with the `FindNode`, `FindToken`, and `FindTrivia` methods on `SyntaxNode`. These methods return the descendant object with the smallest span that fully contains the span that you specify. There's also a `ChildThatContainsPosition` method which searches both descendant nodes and tokens.

Should a search result in two nodes with an identical span (typically a child and grandchild), the `FindNode` method will return the outer (parent) node. You can change this behavior by passing `true` to the optional argument `getInnermostNode ForTie`.

The `Find*` methods also have an optional `findInsideTrivia` bool parameter. If true, this also searches for nodes or tokens within *structured trivia* (see "Trivia" on page 1053).

CSharpSyntaxWalker

Another way to traverse a tree is by subclassing CSharpSyntaxWalker, overriding one or more of its hundreds of virtual methods. This following class counts the number of if statements:

```
class IfCounter : CSharpSyntaxWalker
{
  public int IfCount { get; private set; }

  public override void VisitIfStatement (IfStatementSyntax node)
  {
    IfCount++;
    // Call the base method if you want to descend into children.
    base.VisitIfStatement (node);
  }
}
```

Here's how to invoke it:

```
var ifCounter = new IfCounter ();
ifCounter.Visit (root);
Console.WriteLine ($"I found {ifCounter.IfCount} if statements");
```

The result is equivalent to:

```
root.DescendantNodes().OfType<IfStatementSyntax>().Count()
```

Writing a syntax walker can be easier than using the Descendant* methods in more complex cases when you need to override multiple methods (in part, because C# has no F#-like pattern matching ability).

By default, CSharpSyntaxWalker visits just nodes. To visit tokens or trivia, you must call the base constructor with a SyntaxWalkerDepth, indicating the desired depth (node→token→trivia). Then you can override VisitToken and VisitTrivia:

```
class WhiteWalker : CSharpSyntaxWalker    // Counts space characters
{
  public int SpaceCount { get; private set; }

  public WhiteWalker() : base (SyntaxWalkerDepth.Trivia) { }

  public override void VisitTrivia (SyntaxTrivia trivia)
  {
    SpaceCount += trivia.ToString().Count (char.IsWhiteSpace);
    base.VisitTrivia (trivia);
  }
}
```

If you remove WhiteWalker's call to the base constructor, VisitTrivia will not fire.

Trivia

Trivia is for code that, after parsing, the compiler can almost entirely ignore in terms of producing an output assembly. This comprises whitespace, comments,

XML documentation, preprocessor directives, and code that's inactive by virtue of conditional compilation.

The mandatory whitespace in your code is also considered trivia. Although essential for parsing, it's not needed once the syntax tree has been produced (at least by the compiler). Trivia is still important for round-tripping back to the original source code.

Trivia belongs to the token to which it's adjacent. By convention, the parser puts whitespace and comments that follow a token, up to the end of the line, into the token's trailing trivia. Anything after that, it treats as leading trivia for the next token. (There are exceptions for the very start/end of the file.) If you're creating tokens programmatically (see "Transforming a Syntax Tree" on page 1056), you can put the whitespace in either place (or not at all, if you're not going to convert back to source code):

```
var tree = CSharpSyntaxTree.ParseText (@"class Program
{
    static /*comment*/ void Main() {}
}");

SyntaxNode root = tree.GetRoot();

// Find the static keyword token:
var method = root.DescendantTokens().Single (t =>
    t.Kind() == SyntaxKind.StaticKeyword);

// Print out the trivia around the static keyword token:
foreach (SyntaxTrivia t in method.LeadingTrivia)
    Console.WriteLine (new { Kind = "Leading " + t.Kind(), t.Span.Length });

foreach (SyntaxTrivia t in method.TrailingTrivia)
    Console.WriteLine (new { Kind = "Trailing " + t.Kind(), t.Span.Length });
```

Here's the output:

```
{ Kind = Leading WhitespaceTrivia, Length = 1 }
{ Kind = Trailing WhitespaceTrivia, Length = 1 }
{ Kind = Trailing MultiLineCommentTrivia, Length = 11 }
{ Kind = Trailing WhitespaceTrivia, Length = 1 }
```

Preprocessor directives

It might seem odd that preprocessor directives are considered trivia, given that some directives (in particular, conditional compilation directives) have a nontrivial effect on the output.

The reason is that preprocessor directives are processed semantically by the parser itself, i.e., it's the parser's job to do the preprocessing. After which, there's nothing left that the compiler need explicitly consider (except for #pragma). To illustrate, let's examine how the parser handles conditional compilation directives:

```
#define FOO

#if FOO
    Console.WriteLine ("FOO is defined");
#else
    Console.WriteLine ("FOO is not defined");
#endif
```

Upon reading the #if FOO directive, the parser knows that FOO is defined, and so the line that follows is parsed normally (as nodes and tokens), whereas the line of code following the #else directive is parsed into DisabledTextTrivia.

 When calling CSharpSyntaxTree.Parse, you can supply additional preprocessor symbols by constructing and passing in a CSharpParseOptions instance.

Hence, with conditional compilation, it is precisely the text that can be ignored that ends up in trivia (i.e., the inactive code and the preprocessor directives themselves).

The #line directive is handled similarly, in that the parser reads and interprets the directive. The information that it harvests is used when you call GetMappedLine Span on the syntax tree.

The #region directive is semantically empty: the only role of the parser is to check that #region directives are matched with #endregion directives. The #error and #warning directives are also processed by the parser, which generates errors and warnings that you can see by calling GetDiagnostics on the tree or node.

It can be still useful to examine the content of preprocessor directives for purposes other than producing the output assembly (syntax highlighting, for instance). This is made easier through *structured trivia*.

Structured trivia

There are two kinds of trivia:

Unstructured trivia
    Comments, whitespace, and code that's inactive due to conditional compilation

Structured trivia
    Preprocessor directives and XML documentation

Unstructured trivia is treated purely as text, whereas structured trivia also has its content parsed into a miniature syntax tree.

The HasStructure property on SyntaxTrivia indicates whether structured trivia is present, and the GetStructure method returns the root node for the miniature syntax tree:

```
var tree = CSharpSyntaxTree.ParseText (@"#define FOO");

// In LINQPad:
tree.DumpSyntaxTree();  // LINQPad displays structured trivia in Visualizer

SyntaxNode root = tree.GetRoot();

var trivia = root.DescendantTrivia().First();
Console.WriteLine (trivia.HasStructure);            // True
Console.WriteLine (trivia.GetStructure().Kind());   // DefineDirectiveTrivia
```

In the case of preprocessor directives, you can navigate directly to the structured trivia by calling GetFirstDirective on a SyntaxNode. There's also a ContainsDirectives property to indicate whether preprocessor trivia is present:

```
var tree = CSharpSyntaxTree.ParseText (@"#define FOO");
SyntaxNode root = tree.GetRoot();

Console.WriteLine (root.ContainsDirectives);       // True

// directive is the root node of the structured trivia:
var directive = root.GetFirstDirective();
Console.WriteLine (directive.Kind());              // DefineDirectiveTrivia
Console.WriteLine (directive.ToString());          // #define FOO

// If there were more directives, we could get to them as follows:
Console.WriteLine (directive.GetNextDirective());  // (null)
```

Once we've got a trivia node, we can cast it to a specific type and query its properties, just as we would with any other node:

```
var hashDefine = (DefineDirectiveTriviaSyntax) root.GetFirstDirective();
Console.WriteLine (hashDefine.Name.Text);    // FOO
```

 All nodes, tokens, and trivia have the IsPartOfStructuredTrivia property to indicate whether the object in question is part of a structured trivia tree (i.e., descends from a trivia object).

Transforming a Syntax Tree

You can "modify" nodes, tokens, and trivia via a set of methods with the following prefixes (most of which are extension methods):

```
Add*
Insert*
Remove*
Replace*
With*
Without*
```

Because syntax trees are immutable, all of these methods return a new object with the desired modifications, leaving the original untouched.

Handling changes to the source code

If you're writing a C# editor, for instance, you'll need to update a syntax tree based on changes to the source code. The SyntaxTree class has a WithChangedText method which does exactly this: it partially reparses the source code based on modifications that you describe with a SourceText instance (in Microsoft.CodeAnalysis.Text).

To create a SourceText, use its static From method, giving it the complete source code. You can then use this to create a syntax tree:

```
SourceText sourceText = SourceText.From ("class Program {}");
var tree = CSharpSyntaxTree.ParseText (sourceText);
```

Alternatively, you can obtain the SourceText for an existing tree by calling GetText.

You can now "update" sourceText by calling Replace or WithChanges. For example, we could replace the first five characters ("class") with "struct," as follows:

```
var newSource = sourceText.Replace (0, 5, "struct");
```

Finally, we can call WithChangedText on the tree to update it:

```
var newTree = tree.WithChangedText (newSource);
Console.WriteLine (newTree.ToString());        // struct Program {}
```

Creating new nodes, tokens, and trivia with SyntaxFactory

The static methods on SyntaxFactory programmatically create nodes, tokens, and trivia, which you can use to "transform" existing syntax trees or to create new trees from scratch.

The hardest part of doing this is figuring out exactly what kind of nodes and tokens to create. The solution is to first parse a sample of the code you want, examining the result in a syntax visualizer. For instance, suppose we want to create a syntax node for the following:

```
using System.Text;
```

We can visualize the syntax tree for this in LINQPad as follows:

```
CSharpSyntaxTree.ParseText ("using System.Text;").DumpSyntaxTree();
```

(We can parse "using System.Text;" without error because it's valid as a complete program, albeit a functionally empty one. For most other code snippets, you'll need to wrap the snippet in a method and/or type definition so that it will parse.)

The result has the following structure, of which we are interested in the second node (i.e., UsingDirective and its descendants):

```
Kind                             Token Text
===============================  ==========
CompilationUnit (node)
  UsingDirective (node)
    UsingKeyword (token)         using
```

```
      WhitespaceTrivia (trailing)
    QualifiedName (node)
      IdentifierName (node)
        IdentifierToken (token)      System
      DotToken (token)                .
      IdentifierName (node)
        IdentifierToken (token)      Text
    SemiColonToken (token)            ;
  EndOfFileToken (token)
```

Starting from the inside, we have two `IdentifierName` nodes, whose parent is a `QualifiedName`. We can create that as follows:

```
QualifiedNameSyntax qualifiedName = SyntaxFactory.QualifiedName (
  SyntaxFactory.IdentifierName ("System"),
  SyntaxFactory.IdentifierName ("Text"));
```

We used the overload of `QualifiedName` that accepts two identifiers. This overload inserts the dot token for us automatically.

We now need to wrap this in a `UsingDirective`:

```
UsingDirectiveSyntax usingDirective =
  SyntaxFactory.UsingDirective (qualifiedName);
```

Because we didn't specify tokens for the "using" keyword or the trailing semicolon, tokens for each were created and added automatically. However, the automatically created tokens don't include whitespace. This wouldn't prevent compilation, but converting the tree to a string would result in syntactically incorrect code:

```
Console.WriteLine (usingDirective.ToFullString());   // usingSystem.Text;
```

We can fix by calling `NormalizeWhitespace` on the node (or one of its ancestors); doing so automatically adds whitespace trivia (for both syntactic correctness and readability). Or for more control, we could add whitespace explicitly:

```
usingDirective = usingDirective.WithUsingKeyword (
  usingDirective.UsingKeyword.WithTrailingTrivia (
    SyntaxFactory.Whitespace (" ")));

Console.WriteLine (usingDirective.ToFullString());   // using System.Text;
```

For brevity, we "harvested" the node's existing `UsingKeyword`, to which we added trailing trivia. We could have created an equivalent token with more effort by calling `SyntaxFactory.Token(SyntaxKind.UsingKeyword)`.

The final step is to add our `UsingDirective` node to an existing or new syntax tree (or more precisely, the root node of a tree). To do the former, we cast the existing tree's root to a `CompilationUnitSyntax` and call the `AddUsings` method. We can then create a new tree from the transformed compilation unit:

```
var existingTree = CSharpSyntaxTree.ParseText ("class Program {}");
var existingUnit = (CompilationUnitSyntax) existingTree.GetRoot();

var unitWithUsing = existingUnit.AddUsings (usingDirective);
```

```
var treeWithUsing = CSharpSyntaxTree.Create (
  unitWithUsing.NormalizeWhitespace());
```

 Remember that all parts of a syntax tree are immutable. Calling AddUsings returns a new node, leaving the original
untouched. Ignoring the return value is an easy mistake to
make!

We called NormalizeWhitespace on our compilation unit so that calling ToString
on the tree will yield syntactically correct and readable code. Alternatively, we could
have added explicit new-line trivia to usingDirective as follows:

```
.WithTrailingTrivia (SyntaxFactory.EndOfLine("\r\n\r\n"))
```

Creating a compilation unit and syntax tree from scratch is a similar process. The
easiest approach is to start with an empty compilation unit and call AddUsings on
the unit as we did before:

```
var unit = SyntaxFactory.CompilationUnit().AddUsings (usingDirective);
```

We can add type definitions to our compilation unit by creating them in a similar
fashion, and then calling AddMembers:

```
// Create a simple empty class definition:
unit = unit.AddMembers (SyntaxFactory.ClassDeclaration ("Program"));
```

The final step is to create the tree:

```
var tree = CSharpSyntaxTree.Create (unit.NormalizeWhitespace());
Console.WriteLine (tree.ToString());

// Output:
using System.Text;
class Program{}
```

CSharpSyntaxRewriter

For more complex syntax tree transformations, you can subclass CSharpSyntaxRe
writer.

CSharpSyntaxRewriter is similar to the CSharpSyntaxWalker class that we looked
at previously (see "SyntaxSyntaxWalker"), except that each Visit* method accepts
and returns a syntax node. By returning something other than was passed in, you
can "rewrite" the syntax tree.

For instance, the following rewriter changes method declaration names to uppercase:

```
class MyRewriter : CSharpSyntaxRewriter
{
  public override SyntaxNode VisitMethodDeclaration
    (MethodDeclarationSyntax node)
  {
    // "Replace" the method's identifier with an uppercase version:
```

```
      return node.WithIdentifier (
        SyntaxFactory.Identifier (
          node.Identifier.LeadingTrivia,          // Preserve old trivia
          node.Identifier.Text.ToUpperInvariant(),
          node.Identifier.TrailingTrivia));       // Preserve old trivia
    }
  }
```

Here's how to use it:

```
var tree = CSharpSyntaxTree.ParseText (@"class Program
{
  static void Main() { Test(); }
  static void Test() {          }
}");

var rewriter = new MyRewriter();
var newRoot = rewriter.Visit (tree.GetRoot());
Console.WriteLine (newRoot.ToFullString());

// Output:
class Program
{
  static void MAIN() { Test(); }
  static void TEST() {          }
}
```

Notice that our call to Test() in the main method did not get renamed, because we visited just member *declarations* and ignored *invocations*. To reliably rename invocations, however, we must be able to determine whether calls to Main() or Test() refer to the Program type, and not some other type. To do this, a syntax tree is not enough on its own; we also need a *semantic model*.

Compilations and Semantic Models

A compilation comprises syntax trees, references, and compilation options. It serves two purposes:

- Allows compilation to a library or executable (the *emit* phase)
- Exposes a *semantic model* that provides symbol information (obtained from *binding*)

The semantic model is essential in implementing features such as symbol renaming or offering code completion listings in an editor.

Creating a Compilation

Whether you're interested in querying the semantic model or performing a full compilation, the first step is to create a CSharpCompilation, passing in the (simple) name of the assembly you wish to create:

```
var compilation = CSharpCompilation.Create ("test");
```

An assembly's simple name is important even if you don't plan to emit an assembly, because it forms part of the identity of the types inside the compilation.

By default, it assumes that you want to create a library. You can specify a different kind of output (windows executable, console executable, etc.) as follows:

```
compilation = compilation.WithOptions (
    new CSharpCompilationOptions (OutputKind.ConsoleApplication));
```

The `CSharpCompilationOptions` class has more than a dozen optional constructor parameters that correspond to the command-line options of the *csc.exe* tool. So if you enable compiler optimizations and give your assembly a strong name for instance, you would do this:

```
compilation = compilation.WithOptions (
    new CSharpCompilationOptions (OutputKind.ConsoleApplication,
      cryptoKeyFile:"myKeyFile.snk",
      optimizationLevel:OptimizationLevel.Release));
```

Next, we'll add syntax trees. Each syntax tree corresponds to a "file" to be included in the compilation:

```
var tree = CSharpSyntaxTree.ParseText (@"class Program
{
    static void Main() => System.Console.WriteLine (""Hello"");
}");

compilation = compilation.AddSyntaxTrees (tree);
```

Finally, we need to add references. The simplest program will require a single reference to *mscorlib.dll*, which we can add as follows:

```
compilation = compilation.AddReferences (
    MetadataReference.CreateFromFile (typeof (int).Assembly.Location));
```

The call to `MetadataReference.CreateFromFile` reads the content of an assembly into memory, but not using ordinary reflection. Instead, it uses a high-performance portable assembly reader (available on NuGet) called *System.Reflection.Metadata*. The reader is side-effect free and does not load the assembly into the current application domain.

> The `PortableExecutableReference` that you get back from `MetadataReference.CreateFromFile` can have a significant memory footprint, so be careful about holding onto references that you don't need. Also, if you find yourself repeatedly creating references to the same assembly, a cache is worth considering (one that holds weak references is ideal).

You can do everything in a single step by calling the overload of `CSharpCompilation.Create` that takes syntax trees, references, and options. Or you can do it fluently in a single expression, too:

```
var compilation = CSharpCompilation.Create ("...")
    .WithOptions (...)
```

```
.AddSyntaxTrees (...)
.AddReferences (...);
```

Diagnostics

A compilation may generate errors and warnings, even if the syntax trees are error-free. Examples include forgetting to import a namespace, a typo when referring to a type or member name, and type parameter inference failing. You can get the errors and warnings by calling `GetDiagnostics` on the compilation object. Any syntax errors will be included, too.

Emitting an Assembly

Creating an output assembly is simply a matter of calling `Emit`:

```
EmitResult result = compilation.Emit (@"c:\temp\test.exe");
Console.WriteLine (result.Success);
```

If `result.Success` is false, `EmitResult` also has a `Diagnostics` property to indicate the errors that occurred during emission (this also includes diagnostics from the previous stages). If `Emit` fails due to a file I/O error, it will throw an exception rather than generate error codes.

The `Emit` method also lets you specify a *.pdb* file path (for debug information) and an XML documentation file path.

Querying the Semantic Model

Calling `GetSemanticModel` on a compilation returns the *semantic model* for a syntax tree:

```
var tree = CSharpSyntaxTree.ParseText (@"class Program
{
  static void Main() => System.Console.WriteLine (123);
}");

var compilation = CSharpCompilation.Create ("test")
  .AddReferences (
      MetadataReference.CreateFromFile (typeof(int).Assembly.Location))
  .AddSyntaxTrees (tree);

SemanticModel model = compilation.GetSemanticModel (tree);
```

(The reason for needing to specify a tree is that a compilation can contain multiple trees.)

You might expect a semantic model to be similar to syntax tree, but with more properties and methods and a more detailed structure. This is not the case, and there is no overarching DOM associated with the semantic model. Instead, you're given set of methods to call to obtain semantic information about a particular position or node in the syntax tree.

This means that you can't "explore" a semantic model like you would a syntax tree, and using it is rather like playing 20 Questions: the challenge is figuring out the right questions to ask. There are nearly 50 methods and extension methods; in this section, we'll cover some of the most commonly used methods, in particular, those that demonstrate the principles of using the semantic model.

Following on from our previous example, we could ask for symbol information on the "WriteLine" identifier as follows:

```
var writeLineNode = tree.GetRoot().DescendantTokens().Single (
    t => t.Text == "WriteLine").Parent;

SymbolInfo symbolInfo = model.GetSymbolInfo (writeLineNode);
Console.WriteLine (symbolInfo.Symbol);   // System.Console.WriteLine(int)
```

SymbolInfo is a wrapper for symbols, whose nuances we'll discuss shortly. We'll start first with symbols.

Symbols

In the syntax tree, names such as "System", "Console", and "WriteLine" are parsed as *identifiers* (IdentifierNameSyntax node). Identifiers have little meaning, and the syntactic parser does no work on "understanding" them other than to distinguish them from contextual keywords.

The semantic model is able to transform identifiers into *symbols*, which have type information (the output of the *binding* phase).

All symbols implement the ISymbol interface, although there are more specific interfaces for each kind of symbol. In our example, "System", "Console", and "Write-Line" map to symbols of the following types:

```
"System"      INamespaceSymbol
"Console"     INamedTypeSymbol
"WriteLine"   IMethodSymbol
```

Some symbol types, such as IMethodSymbol have a conceptual analog in the System.Reflection namespace (MethodInfo, in this case); whereas some other symbol types, such as INamespaceSymbol, do not. This is because the Roslyn type system exists for the benefit of the compiler, whereas the Reflection type system exists for the benefit of the CLR (after the source code has melted away).

Nonetheless, working with ISymbol types is similar in many ways to using the Reflection API we described in Chapter 19. Extending our previous example:

```
ISymbol symbol = model.GetSymbolInfo (writeLineNode).Symbol;

Console.WriteLine (symbol.Name);                   // WriteLine
Console.WriteLine (symbol.Kind);                   // Method
Console.WriteLine (symbol.IsStatic);               // True
Console.WriteLine (symbol.ContainingType.Name);    // Console
```

```
var method = (IMethodSymbol) symbol;
Console.WriteLine (method.ReturnType.ToString()); // void
```

The output of the last line illustrates a subtle difference with Reflection. Notice that "void" is in lowercase, which is C# nomenclature (Reflection is language-agnostic). Similarly, calling `ToString()` on the `INamedTypeSymbol` for `System.Int32` returns "int". Here's something else you can't do with Reflection:

```
Console.WriteLine (symbol.Language);                // C#
```

 With the syntax trees API, the classes for syntax nodes differ for C# and VB (although they share an abstract `SyntaxNode` base type). This makes sense because the languages have a different lexical structure. In contrast, `ISymbol` and its derived interfaces are shared between C# and VB. However, their internal concrete implementations *are* specific to each language, and the output from their methods and properties reflects language-specific differences.

We can also ask the symbol where it came from:

```
var location = symbol.Locations.First();
Console.WriteLine (location.Kind);                          // MetadataFile
Console.WriteLine (location.MetadataModule
                   == compilation.References.Single()  // True
```

If the symbol was defined in our own source code (i.e., a syntax tree), the `Source Tree` property will return that tree, and `SourceSpan` will return its location in the tree:

```
Console.WriteLine (location.SourceTree == null);   // True
Console.WriteLine (location.SourceSpan);           // [0..0]
```

A partial type may have multiple definitions, in which case it will have multiple `Locations`.

The following query returns all the overloads of `WriteLine`:

```
symbol.ContainingType.GetMembers ("WriteLine").OfType<IMethodSymbol>()
```

You can also call `ToDisplayParts` on a symbol. This returns a collection of "parts" that make up the full name; in our case, `System.Console.WriteLine(int)` is comprised of four symbols interspersed with punctuation.

SymbolInfo

If you're writing code completion for an editor, you'll need to obtain symbols for code that's incomplete or incorrect. For instance, consider the following incomplete code:

```
System.Console.Writeline(
```

Because the `WriteLine` method is overloaded, it's impossible to match to a single `ISymbol`. Instead, we want to present options to the user. To deal with this, the semantic model's `GetSymbolInfo` method returns an `ISymbolInfo` struct which has the following properties:

```
ISymbol Symbol
ImmutableArray<ISymbol> CandidateSymbols
CandidateReason CandidateReason
```

If there's an error or ambiguity, the `Symbol` property returns null, and `CandidateSym` `bols` returns a collection comprising the best matches. The `CandidateReason` property returns an enum telling you what went wrong.

 To obtain error and warning information for a section of code, you can also call `GetDiagnostics` on a semantic model, specifying a `TextSpan`. Calling `GetDiagnostics` with no argument is equivalent to calling the same method on the `CSharpCompi` `lation` object.

Symbol accessibility

`ISymbol` has a `DeclaredAccessibility` property that indicates whether the symbol is public, protected, internal, and so on. However, this isn't sufficient to determine whether a given symbol is accessible at a particular position in your source code. Local variables, for instance, have a lexically limited scope, and a protected class member is accessible from source code positions within its type or a derived type. To help with this, `SemanticModel` has an `IsAccessible` method:

```
bool canAccess = model.IsAccessible (42, someSymbol);
```

This returns `true` if `someSymbol` can be accessed at offset 42 in the source code.

Declared symbols

If you call `GetSymbolInfo` on a type or member declaration, you'll get no symbols back. For instance, suppose we want the symbol for our `Main` method:

```
var mainMethod = tree.GetRoot().DescendantTokens().Single (
  t => t.Text == "Main").Parent;

SymbolInfo symbolInfo = model.GetSymbolInfo (mainMethod);
Console.WriteLine (symbolInfo.Symbol == null);          // True
Console.WriteLine (symbolInfo.CandidateSymbols.Length); // 0
```

 This applies not just to type/member declarations, but any node where you're *introducing* a new symbol rather than *consuming* an existing symbol.

To obtain the symbol, we must instead call `GetDeclaredSymbol`:

```
ISymbol symbol = model.GetDeclaredSymbol (mainMethod);
```

Unlike `GetSymbolInfo`, `GetDeclaredSymbol` either succeeds or it doesn't. (If it fails, it will because it can't find a valid declaration node.)

To give another example, suppose our `Main` method is as follows:

```
static void Main()
{
  int xyz = 123;
}
```

We can determine the type of `xyz` as follows:

```
SyntaxNode variableDecl = tree.GetRoot().DescendantTokens().Single (
  t => t.Text == "xyz").Parent;

var local = (ILocalSymbol) model.GetDeclaredSymbol (variableDecl);
Console.WriteLine (local.Type.ToString());              // int
Console.WriteLine (local.Type.BaseType.ToString());     // System.ValueType
```

TypeInfo

Sometimes you need type information about an expression or literal for which there's no explicit symbol. Consider the following:

```
var now = System.DateTime.Now;
System.Console.WriteLine (now - now);
```

To determine the type of `now - now`, we call `GetTypeInfo` on the semantic model:

```
SyntaxNode binaryExpr = tree.GetRoot().DescendantTokens().Single (
  t => t.Text == "-").Parent;

TypeInfo typeInfo = model.GetTypeInfo (binaryExpr);
```

`TypeInfo` has two properties, `Type` and `ConvertedType`. The latter indicates the type after any implicit conversions:

```
Console.WriteLine (typeInfo.Type);              // System.TimeSpan
Console.WriteLine (typeInfo.ConvertedType);     // object
```

Because `Console.WriteLine` is overloaded to accept an `object` but not a `TimeSpan`, an implicit conversion to object took place, which manifested in `typeInfo.ConvertedType`.

Looking up symbols

A powerful feature of the semantic model is the ability to ask for all symbols in scope at a particular point in the source code. The result is the basis for IntelliSense listings, when the user requests a list of available symbols.

To obtain the listing, simply call `LookupSymbols`, with the desired source code offset. To give a complete example:

```
var tree = CSharpSyntaxTree.ParseText (@"class Program
{
  static void Main()
  {
    int x = 123, y = 234;
```

```
    }
}");

CSharpCompilation compilation = CSharpCompilation.Create ("test")
  .AddReferences (
    MetadataReference.CreateFromFile (typeof(int).Assembly.Location))
  .AddSyntaxTrees (tree);

SemanticModel model = compilation.GetSemanticModel (tree);

// Look for available symbols at start of 6th line:
int index = tree.GetText().Lines[5].Start;

foreach (ISymbol symbol in model.LookupSymbols (index))
  Console.WriteLine (symbol.ToString());
```

Here's the result:

```
y
x
Program.Main()
object.ToString()
object.Equals(object)
object.Equals(object, object)
object.ReferenceEquals(object, object)
object.GetHashCode()
object.GetType()
object.~Object()
object.MemberwiseClone()
Program
Microsoft
System
Windows
```

(If we imported the System namespace, we'd see hundreds more symbols for types in that namespace.)

Example: Renaming a Symbol

To illustrate the features we've covered, we'll write a method to rename a symbol, which is robust to the most common use-cases. In particular:

- The symbol can be a type, member, local variable, range, or loop variable.

- You can specify the symbol from either its use or declaration.

- (In the case of a class or struct), it will rename the static & instance constructors.

- (In the case of a class), it will rename the finalizer (destructor).

For brevity, we'll omit some checks, such as ensuring that the new name is not already in use and that the symbol isn't an edge-case for which the rename will fail. Our method will consider just a single syntax tree and so will have the following signature:

```
public SyntaxTree RenameSymbol (SemanticModel model, SyntaxToken token,
                                string newName)
```

One obvious way to implement this is to subclass CSharpSyntaxRewriter. However, a more elegant and flexible approach is to have RenameSymbol call a lower-level method that returns the text spans to be renamed:

```
public IEnumerable<TextSpan> GetRenameSpans (SemanticModel model,
                                             SyntaxToken token)
```

This allows an editor to call GetRenameSpans directly and apply just the changes (within an Undo transaction), avoiding the loss of editor state that might otherwise result in replacing the entire text.

This makes RenameSymbol a relatively simple wrapper around GetRenameSpans. We can use SourceText's WithChanges method to apply a sequence of text changes:

```
public SyntaxTree RenameSymbol (SemanticModel model, SyntaxToken token,
                                string newName)
{
    IEnumerable<TextSpan> renameSpans = GetRenameSpans (model, token);

    SourceText newSourceText = model.SyntaxTree.GetText().WithChanges (
        renameSpans.Select (span => new TextChange (span, newName))
            .OrderBy (tc => tc));

    return model.SyntaxTree.WithChangedText (newSourceText);
}
```

WithChanges throws an exception unless the changes are in order; this is why we called OrderBy on the latter.

Now we must write GetRenameSpans. The first step is to find the symbol corresponding to the token we want to rename. The token may be part of either a declaration or usage, so we'll first call GetSymbolInfo, and if the result is null, call GetDeclaredSymbol:

```
public IEnumerable<TextSpan> GetRenameSpans (SemanticModel model,
                                             SyntaxToken token)
{
    var node = token.Parent;

    ISymbol symbol = model.GetSymbolInfo (node).Symbol
                  ?? model.GetDeclaredSymbol (node);

    if (symbol == null) return null;   // No symbol to rename.
```

Next, we need to find the symbol definitions. We can get this from the symbol's Locations property. (Our consideration of multiple locations makes us robust to the scenario of partial classes and methods, although for the former to be useful, we would need to expand the example to work with multiple syntax trees.)

```
var definitions =
    from location in symbol.Locations
```

```
    where location.SourceTree == node.SyntaxTree
  select location.SourceSpan;
```

Now we need to find usages of the symbol. For this, we start by looking for descendant tokens whose name matches the symbol's name, as this is a fast way to weed out most tokens. Then we can call `GetSymbolInfo` on the token's parent node and see whether it matches the symbol we want to rename:

```
var usages =
  from t in model.SyntaxTree.GetRoot().DescendantTokens()
  where t.Text == symbol.Name
  let s = model.GetSymbolInfo (t.Parent).Symbol
  where s == symbol
  select t.Span;
```

Binding-related operations, such as asking for symbol information, have a tendency to be slower than operations that consider just text or syntax trees. This is because the process of binding may require searching for types in assemblies, applying type inference rules, and checking for extensions methods.

If the symbol is something other than a named type (local variable, range variable, etc.), our job is done and we can return the definitions plus usages:

```
if (symbol.Kind != SymbolKind.NamedType)
  return definitions.Concat (usages);
```

If the symbol is a named type, we need to rename its constructors and destructor, if present. To do so, we enumerate the descendant nodes, looking for type declarations whose name matches the one we want to rename. Then we get its *declared* symbol, and if it matches the one we're renaming, we locate its constructor and destructor methods, returning the spans of their identifiers if present:

```
var structors =
  from type in model.SyntaxTree.GetRoot().DescendantNodes()
                             .OfType<TypeDeclarationSyntax>()
  where type.Identifier.Text == symbol.Name
  let declaredSymbol = model.GetDeclaredSymbol (type)
  where declaredSymbol == symbol
  from method in type.Members
  let constructor = method as ConstructorDeclarationSyntax
  let destructor = method as DestructorDeclarationSyntax
  where constructor != null || destructor != null
  let identifier = constructor?.Identifier ?? destructor.Identifier
  select identifier.Span;

  return definitions.Concat (usages).Concat (structors);
}
```

Here's the complete listing, along with an example of how to use it:

```
void Demo()
{
  var tree = CSharpSyntaxTree.ParseText (@"class Program
```

```
  {
    static Program() {}
    public Program() {}

    static void Main()
    {
      Program p = new Program();
      p.Foo();
    }

    static void Foo() => Bar();
    static void Bar() => Foo();
  }
  ");

    var compilation = CSharpCompilation.Create ("test")
      .AddReferences (
        MetadataReference.CreateFromFile (typeof(int).Assembly.Location))
      .AddSyntaxTrees (tree);

    var model = compilation.GetSemanticModel (tree);

    var tokens = tree.GetRoot().DescendantTokens();

    // Rename the Program class to Program2:
    SyntaxToken program = tokens.First (t => t.Text == "Program");
    Console.WriteLine (RenameSymbol (model, program, "Program2").ToString());

    // Rename the Foo method to Foo2:
    SyntaxToken foo = tokens.Last (t => t.Text == "Foo");
    Console.WriteLine (RenameSymbol (model, foo, "Foo2").ToString());

    // Rename the p local variable to p2:
    SyntaxToken p = tokens.Last (t => t.Text == "p");
    Console.WriteLine (RenameSymbol (model, p, "p2").ToString());
  }

  public SyntaxTree RenameSymbol (SemanticModel model, SyntaxToken token,
                                  string newName)
  {
    IEnumerable<TextSpan> renameSpans =
      GetRenameSpans (model, token).OrderBy (s => s);

    SourceText newSourceText = model.SyntaxTree.GetText().WithChanges (
      renameSpans.Select (s => new TextChange (s, newName)));

    return model.SyntaxTree.WithChangedText (newSourceText);
  }

  public IEnumerable<TextSpan> GetRenameSpans (SemanticModel model,
                                               SyntaxToken token)
  {
    var node = token.Parent;

    ISymbol symbol =
```

```
        model.GetSymbolInfo (node).Symbol ??
        model.GetDeclaredSymbol (node);

    if (symbol == null) return null;    // No symbol to rename.

    var definitions =
        from location in symbol.Locations
        where location.SourceTree == node.SyntaxTree
        select location.SourceSpan;

    var usages =
        from t in model.SyntaxTree.GetRoot().DescendantTokens ()
        where t.Text == symbol.Name
        let s = model.GetSymbolInfo (t.Parent).Symbol
        where s == symbol
        select t.Span;

    if (symbol.Kind != SymbolKind.NamedType)
        return definitions.Concat (usages);

    var structors =
        from type in model.SyntaxTree.GetRoot().DescendantNodes()
                                      .OfType<TypeDeclarationSyntax>()
        where type.Identifier.Text == symbol.Name
        let declaredSymbol = model.GetDeclaredSymbol (type)
        where declaredSymbol == symbol
        from method in type.Members
        let constructor = method as ConstructorDeclarationSyntax
        let destructor = method as DestructorDeclarationSyntax
        where constructor != null || destructor != null
        let identifier = constructor?.Identifier ?? destructor.Identifier
        select identifier.Span;

    return definitions.Concat (usages).Concat (structors);
}
```

Index

AssemblyName class, 762-763
AssemblyQualifiedName property, Type, 792
AssemblyResolve event, 780-780
AsSequential method, 949
Assert method, Contract, 543-544
Assert method, Debug and Trace, 529-530
assertions
    code contracts for, 532, 534, 543-544
    Debug and Trace classes for, 529-530
assignment, 43-44
assignment expressions, 51
Association attribute, 379
associations, L2S or EF, 378-379
Assume method, Contract, 544
AsTask method, 606
asterisk (*)
    * dereference operator, 187
    * multiplication operator, 29
    * in pointer type names, 793
    * in regular expressions, 1026, 1028
async keyword, 592-605, 627
asynchronous delegates, 619
asynchronous functions, 594-605
    exception posting, 606-607
    optimizations, 607-610
    WinRT methods for, 605
asynchronous programming, 589-621
    APM (asynchronous programming model), 618-619
    BackgroundWorker class, 620-621
    call graphs, 591, 603-604
    cancellation pattern, 610-612
    compared to concurrency, 590
    compared to synchronous program-ming, 599-600
    continuations with, 591-592
    EAP (event-based asynchronous pat-tern), 619-620
    fine-grained concurrency with, 591
    lambda expressions, 605
    parallelism with, 604
    progress reporting pattern, 612-614
    TAP (task-based asynchronous pat-tern), 614
    task combinators, 614-618
asynchronous programming model (APM), 618-619
asynchrony

HttpClient methods using, 683
    stream reading and writing, 627
    WebClient methods using, 680
    WebResponse methods using, 681
at sign (@)
    @ preceding identifiers, 15
    @ preceding verbatim string literals, 36, 37
Atan method, 259
atomicity, with locking, 908
Attribute method, XElement, 453
attributes, 183-185, 191-192, 812-813
    caller info attributes, 185-186
    categories of, 812-813
    classes for, 183
    conditional compilation, 527-528
    debugging, 529
    defining, 814-815
    for dynamic constructs, 834
    for LINQ to SQL entity classes, 371
    multiple, specifying, 185
    parameters for, 184
    reflecting, 815-817
    target of, 184
    usage of, determining, 813
Attributes method, XElement, 453
AttributeUsage attribute, 813
authentication
    HTTP forms, 696-697
    network, 688-690
AuthenticationManager class, 689
authenticode signing, for assemblies, 764-768
authorization (see identity and role authorization)
automatic properties, 81
AutoResetEvent class, 924-927
Average operator, LINQ, 433-434
await keyword, 592-605, 627
awaiter objects, 585

B

background collection, 514
background threads, 574-575
BackgroundWorker class, 502, 620-621
backing store streams, 623-625, 629-638
backslash (\)
    \ preceding escape sequences, 35

DescendantNodes method, XContainer, 451

Descendants method, XContainer, 451

DescendantTokens method, SyntaxNode, 1050

deserialization, 713
  (see also serialization)

destructors (see finalizers)

diagnostics, 525
  (see also code contracts; debugging)
  execution call stack, examining, 553-555
  monitoring memory usage, 506
  performance counters, 557-562
  processes, examining, 552
  stopwatch for execution times, 562
  threads, examining, 553
  Windows event logs for, 555-557

diagrams, UML notation for, xiii

dictionaries, 314-320
  Dictionary class, 317-318
  Hashtable class, 317-318
  HybridDictionary class, 318
  IDictionary interfaces, 315-316
  ListDictionary class, 318
  OrderedDictionary class, 318
  SortedDictionary class, 319-320
  SortedList class, 319-320

dictionary attack, 892

Dictionary class, 315, 317-318, 328

DictionaryBase class, 326

digital signing, 900-901

directives, preprocessor, 190-192

directories
  Directory class, 653
  DirectoryInfo class, 654-655
  drive information, 659
  filesystem events, catching, 659-661
  special folders, 657-659
  StorageFolder class, 661-662

Directory class, 653

DirectoryInfo class, 654-655

disposal, 499
  (see also garbage collection)
  calling Dispose from finalizer, 508-510
  interface for, 499-500
  semantics for, 500-501
  unsubscribing from events in, 504-505
  when not to use, 502

when to use, 501-503

Dispose method, IDisposable, 64, 152, 499-505, 508-510

Dispose method, Stream, 626, 629

Dispose method, TextReader, 640

Dispose method, TextWriter, 640

Distinct operator, LINQ, 399

DistributedTransactionPermission class, 869

DLL (Dynamic Link Library)
  native, callbacks from, 1007
  native, calling into, 1003-1004
  native, interoperability with, 1003-1007
  native, type marshaling with, 1004-1007

.dll files, 4, 13, 753

DllImport attribute, 1003

DLR (Dynamic Language Runtime), 847-849

DNS (Domain Name Service), 675, 703-704

Dns class, 674, 703-704

DnsPermission class, 869

do-while loops, 61

doc compiler switch, 193

DoCallBack method, AppDomain, 994-995

DocumenationMode property, CSharpParseOPtions, 1048

document object model (see DOM)

documentation comments, 193-196

dollar sign ($)
  $ preceding interpolated strings, 37
  $ in regular expressions, 1026, 1030

DOM (document object model), 441-442
  (see also X-DOM)
  syntax trees using (see syntax trees)

domain isolation, 667-668

Domain Name Service (see DNS)

domain names
  conversions with IP addresses, 703

domains, application (see application domains)

double type, 26, 31-33

downcasting, 90-91

drive information, 659

DriveInfo class, 659

dynamic binding, 175-183, 789, 803

MethodBase class, 804
MethodBuilder class, 829-831
MethodHandle class, 799
MethodInfo class, 799
methods, 2, 12-13, 74-76
    (see also class members; constructors)
    anonymous, 147
    constructors, 76-77
    dynamic, generating, 818-819
    dynamic, passing arguments to, 820
    emitting, 829-831
    expression-bodied methods, 75
    extension methods, 171-174
    finalizers, 86
    generic, 116-117
    modifiers for, 75
    overloading, 75, 96
    overriding, 92, 541, 543
    parameters and arguments for (see
      parameters and arguments)
    partial, 87
    plug-in methods, 128
    signature for, 75
    treating as values (see delegates)
Microsoft .NET Framework (see .NET
    Framework)
Microsoft Message Queuing (see MSMQ)
Microsoft Visual Studio (see Visual Studio
    2015)
Microsoft.CodeAnalysis.CSharp.dll
    assembly, 1044, 1049
Microsoft.CodeAnalysis.dll assembly,
    1044
Millisecond property, DateTime and
    DateTimeOffset, 232
Milliseconds property, TimeSpan, 227
Min method, Math, 259
Min method, SortedSet, 314
Min operator, LINQ, 343, 433
minus sign (-)
    - removing delegate instances, 129
    - subtraction operator, 29, 227, 232
    -- decrement operator, 29
    -0 negative zero, 31
    -= even accessor, 136, 141
    -= removing delegate instances, 129
    -> pointer-to-member operator, 187,
      188
    -∞ negative infinity, 31

Minute property, DateTime and DateTi-
    meOffset, 232
Minutes property, TimeSpan, 227
ModuleBuilder class, 825
modules, in assemblies, 756
Monitor class, 905-906
MonitoringIsEnabled property, AppDo-
    main, 995
Month property, DateTime and DateTi-
    meOffset, 232
Move method, File, 650-651
MoveNext method, IEnumerator, 286
MoveToAttribute method, XmlReader,
    485
MoveToContent method, XmlReader, 482
MoveToFirstAttribute method,
    XmlReader, 486
MoveToNextAttribute method,
    XmlReader, 486
mscorlib.dll assembly, 199, 201, 811
MSMQ (Microsoft Message Queuing),
    210
mt tool, 756
multicast delegates, 129-130
multicore processers (see parallel pro-
    gramming)
multidimensional arrays, 39-40
Multiline option, RegexOptions, 1026
multiple dispatch, 853
multithreading (see threads)
Mutex class, 911-912

N

N format string, 247
naked type constraint, 120
Name property, Type, 792
named arguments, 49-50
named attribute parameters, 184
named groups, regular expressions, 1033
named pipes, 634-636
NamedPipeClientStream class, 635
NamedPipeServerStream class, 635
nameof operator, 88
names (see identifiers)
namespace keyword, 65
Namespace property, Type, 792
namespaces, 13, 65-71
    alias qualifiers, 70-71

unmanaged memory, 516
UnmanagedType enum, 1004
unsafe code, 187
unsafe keyword, 187
UnsafeXXX pattern, 876
upcasting, 90
upgradeable locks, 921-923
UploadValues method, WebClient, 693
URI (Uniform Resource Identifier), 675, 676-678
    prefixes, registering, 682
    prefixes, Web request types for, 682
Uri class, 677-678
URL (Uniform Resource Locator), 675
User Account Control (see UAC)
user identities and roles, 888-889
user-interface-based applications, 206-209
UserDomainName property, Environment, 282
UserInteractive property, Environment, 282
UserName property, Environment, 282
ushort type, 26, 31
using directive (importing a namespace), 13, 66, 68
using statement (implicit disposal), 64, 152
using static directive, 66
UtcDateTime property, DateTimeOffset, 231
UtcNow property, DateTime, 232
UtcNow property, DateTimeOffset, 232
UTF-8 encoding, 224, 642-643
UTF-16 encoding, 224-226, 643-644
UTF-32 encoding, 224

V

value equality, 268-269
Value method, XAttribute and XElement, 454
Value property, XAttribute and XElement, 456
value types, 21-22, 24, 39
ValueAtReturn method, Contract, 542
Values method, IDictionary, 315
var keyword, 41, 50, 180
variables, 17, 42-44
    captured variables, 572

default values, 44
definite assignment, 43-44
    implicitly typed, 50
    in classes or structs (see fields)
    local, scope of, 57
    outer variables, capturing, 144-146, 147
    storage, 42-43
verbatim string literals, 36, 37
Version property, Environment, 282
vertical bar (|)
    | bitwise OR operator, 30
    | conditional or operator, 34, 165
    | in regular expressions, 1026
    || conditional OR operator, 34
    || conditional or operator, 526
vertical tab, escape sequence for, 35
view accessors, for memory-mapped files, 664-665
virtual function members, 91
virtual keyword, 106
virtualization, enabling and disabling, 887
Visitor pattern, 850-853
Visual Studio 2015
    compiler output used by, 1044
    workspaces used by, 1044
Visual Studio 2015, editions of, xii
void expressions, 51
void* pointer, 189
volume information (see drive information)

W

wait handles (see event wait handles)
Wait method, CountdownEvent, 928
Wait method, Task, 582
WaitAll method, WaitHandle, 931-932
WaitAny method, WaitHandle, 931-932
WaitForFullGCApproach method, GC, 515
WaitForFullGCComplete method, GC, 515
WaitForPendingFinalizers method, GC, 516
WaitHandle class, 931-932
WaitOne method, AutoResetEvent, 925
WaitOne method, ManualResetEvent, 927
WaitOne method, Mutex, 911

X

About the Authors

Joseph Albahari is the author of *C# 5.0 in a Nutshell*, *C# 6.0 Pocket Reference*, and *LINQ Pocket Reference*. He also wrote LINQPad—the popular code scratchpad and LINQ querying utility.

Ben Albahari is cofounder of Auditionist, a casting website for actors in the UK. He was a Program Manager at Microsoft for five years, where he worked on several projects, including the .NET Compact Framework and ADO.NET.

He was the cofounder of Genamics, a provider of tools for C# and J++ programmers, as well as software for DNA and protein sequence analysis. He is a coauthor of *C# Essentials*, the first C# book from O'Reilly, and of previous editions of *C# in a Nutshell*.

Colophon

The animal on the cover of *C# 6.0 in a Nutshell* is a numidian crane. The numidian crane (*Antropoides virgo*) is also called the demoiselle crane because of its grace and symmetry. This species of crane is native to Europe and Asia and migrates to India, Pakistan, and northeast Africa in the winter.

Though numidian cranes are the smallest cranes, they defend their territories as aggressively as other crane species, using their loud voices to warn others of trespassing. If necessary, they will fight. Numidian cranes nest in uplands rather than wetlands and will even live in the desert if there is water within 200 to 500 meters. They sometimes make nests out of pebbles in which to lay their eggs, though more often they will lay eggs directly on the ground, protected only by vegetation.

Numidian cranes are considered a symbol of good luck in some countries and are sometimes even protected by law.

Many of the animals on O'Reilly covers are endangered; all of them are important to the world. To learn more about how you can help, go to *animals.oreilly.com*.

The cover image is an original engraving from the 19th century. The cover fonts are URW Typewriter and Guardian Sans. The text font is Adobe Minion Pro; the heading font is Adobe Myriad Condensed; and the code font is Dalton Maag's Ubuntu Mono.

Have it your way.

Get even more for your money.

Join the O'Reilly Community, and register the O'Reilly books you own. It's free, and you'll get:

- $4.99 ebook upgrade offer
- 40% upgrade offer on O'Reilly print books
- Membership discounts on books and events
- Free lifetime updates to ebooks and videos
- Multiple ebook formats, DRM FREE
- Participation in the O'Reilly community
- Newsletters
- Account management
- 100% Satisfaction Guarantee

Signing up is easy:

1. Go to: oreilly.com/go/register
2. Create an O'Reilly login.
3. Provide your address.
4. Register your books.

Note: English-language books only

To order books online:
oreilly.com/store

For questions about products or an order:
orders@oreilly.com

To sign up to get topic-specific email announcements and/or news about upcoming books, conferences, special offers, and new technologies:
elists@oreilly.com

For technical questions about book content:
booktech@oreilly.com

To submit new book proposals to our editors:
proposals@oreilly.com

O'Reilly books are available in multiple DRM-free ebook formats. For more information:
oreilly.com/ebooks